The Blackwell Encyclopedia of Sociology

Volume VI

LE–M

Edited by

George Ritzer

Blackwell
Publishing

© 2007 by Blackwell Publishing Ltd

BLACKWELL PUBLISHING
350 Main Street, Malden, MA 02148-5020, USA
9600 Garsington Road, Oxford OX4 2DQ, UK
550 Swanston Street, Carlton, Victoria 3053, Australia

The right of George Ritzer to be identified as the Author of the Editorial Material in this Work has been asserted in accordance with the UK Copyright, Designs, and Patents Act 1988.

First published 2007 by Blackwell Publishing Ltd

1   2007

Library of Congress Cataloging-in-Publication Data

Blackwell encyclopedia of sociology, the / edited by George Ritzer.
   p. cm.
Includes bibliographical references and index.
ISBN 1-4051-2433-4 (hardback : alk. paper) 1. Sociology—Encyclopedias. I. Ritzer, George.

HM425.B53 2007
301.03—dc22

                                                    2006004167

ISBN-13: 978-1-4051-2433-1 (hardback : alk. paper)

A catalogue record for this title is available from the British Library.

Set in 9.5/11pt Ehrhardt
by Spi Publisher Services, Pondicherry, India
Printed in Singapore
by COS Printers Pte Ltd

The publisher's policy is to use permanent paper from mills that operate a sustainable forestry policy, and which has been manufactured from pulp processed using acid-free and elementary chlorine-free practices. Furthermore, the publisher ensures that the text paper and cover board used have met acceptable environmental accreditation standards.

For further information on
Blackwell Publishing, visit our website:
www.blackwellpublishing.com

Contents

legal profession

Mathieu Deflem

The legal profession refers to all the occupational roles purposely oriented towards the administration and maintenance of the legal system. Encompassing lawyers, judges, counselors, and experts of legal education and scholarship, the legal profession has been the subject of considerable reflection in the sociology of law. This sociological interest parallels the enormous attention devoted to the legal profession in various strands of sociolegal studies, including also other social sciences besides sociology as well as legal scholarship, which in turn is the result of the successful monopolization of the execution of legal functions and the resulting social standing and closure of the legal profession. The fact that the legal profession is among the most researched aspects of the institution of law is thus a direct function of the professionalization of the legal role itself. Yet, although most scholarly research on the legal profession comes from within legal scholarship and from law-and-society perspectives that are firmly nestled in legal education, there also exists a distinctively sociological tradition that examines societal aspects of the legal profession from the viewpoint of a multitude of theoretical orientations.

The aspiration to maintain occupational autonomy is one of the legal profession's most critical and sociologically challenging characteristics. This professional independence is a concrete expression of the autonomy of law as a whole. Rooted in Montesquieu's famous doctrine of the separation of powers, the ideal of legal autonomy finds primary expression in the establishment of an independent judiciary. Further manifestations of the autonomy of law are provided in the workings of the courts and, most importantly, the professionalization of the legal occupation. The autonomy of legal practice is primarily reflected in legal education and legal practice, as the legal profession has been successful in controlling admission to and the organization of law schools and legal work.

Theoretical differences exist on how the place and role of the legal profession are to be conceived from a sociological viewpoint. Most studies in the sociology of the professions are indebted to the focus on the professionalization of legal work in modern societies that was first systematically addressed by Weber and which was subsequently taken up by Parsons with respect to the role of the professions in the legal system's integrative function.

Weber defined law intimately in relation to the legal profession by specifying law as a normative order that is externally guaranteed by a specialized staff, including police, prosecutors, and judges. Under conditions of modern societies, Weber maintained that law rationalized in a formal sense on the basis of procedures that are applied equally to all. Legal professionals take on a special role in this context because they are involved in the adjudication of law on the basis of acquired legal expertise. The institutionalization of expertise in matters of law secures the specialized status of the legal professional on the basis of the state formally granting such monopoly.

In modern sociology, Parsons gave special consideration to the legal profession's role in securing integration through the legal system. This conception harmonizes with the functionalist attention towards law as a mechanism of social control and also betrays the broader Parsonian attention to the role of the professions in modern societies. The successful acquisition of expertise in a particular occupational role is the profession's most outstanding characteristic. The legal professional is primarily someone who is learned in the law and who can provide specialized services on the basis of this expertise. The legal professional thus mediates between the polity as legislator, on the one hand, and the public as clients of the law, on the other.

In more recent decades, sociological perspectives have offered more varied, sometimes radically alternative viewpoints on the role and status of the legal profession and its autonomy. Theoretical perspectives have been introduced that transcend the functionalist obsession with integration to contemplate the law's role in terms of power and inequality. Most distinctly focusing on the legal profession have been representatives of the so-called Critical Legal Studies movement who have pondered the behavior of judges and lawyers irrespective of, and often contrary to, law's self-proclaimed ideals of justice and equity. Arguing that legal reasoning is affected by dozens of personal biases depending on the legal professionals' sociostructural backgrounds, these perspectives have in their most radical form critiqued the very basis of the legal professional's aspiration to autonomy and expert neutrality.

While not necessarily overly critical in orientation, most recent sociological studies of the legal profession have pointed towards greater diversity in the legal profession than a simple model of professionalization can account for. Sociologists have specifically contemplated the more complex behavior of the legal profession once it has been successfully monopolized, when it also seeks to influence the state and its legislative potential. Among the more enduring sociological puzzles, also, is the increasing diversity of the legal profession since the latter half of the twentieth century. Unlike the cohesive group of old, legal professionals nowadays comprise a wide variety of practitioners, educated in a multitude of legal programs, and are more broadly representative of contemporary society with respect to gender, age, and ethnicity. The increasing diversity of the legal profession, however, has not always been accompanied by increasing equality, as many disparities have been observed to persist, such as earnings gaps among male and female lawyers and differences in cultural and economic capital between solo practitioners and employees in large law firms. The high degree of stratification in the legal profession may thus have brought about a lack of professional unity.

SEE ALSO: Law, Civil; Law, Criminal; Law, Sociology of; Occupations; Parsons, Talcott; Professions; Weber, Max; Work, Sociology of

REFERENCES AND SUGGESTED READINGS

Abel, R. L. & Lewis, P. S. C. (Eds.) (1995) *Lawyers in Society*. University of California Press, Berkeley.
Halliday, T. C. (1987) *Beyond Monopoly: Lawyers, State Crises, and Professional Empowerment*. University of Chicago Press, Chicago.
Hoy, J. van (Ed.) (2001) *Legal Professions: Work, Structure and Organization*. Elsevier, Oxford.
Sandefur, R. L. (2001) Work and Honor in the Law: Prestige and the Division of Lawyers' Labor. *American Sociological Review* 66: 382–403.
Shamir, R. (1995) *Managing Legal Uncertainty: Elite Lawyers in the New Deal*. Duke University Press, Durham, NC.
Weber, M. (1978 [1922]) *Economy and Society*. University of California Press, Berkeley.

legitimacy

Lisa Troyer

Legitimacy is defined as a state of appropriateness ascribed to an actor, object, system, structure, process, or action resulting from its integration with institutionalized norms, values, and beliefs. It is a topic of longstanding interest across the spectrum of sociological phenomena and levels of analysis. Legitimacy is a multilevel concept, as implied by the term "actor," which may refer to individuals, groups, organizations, nation-states, and world systems. It appears as a core concept in diverse areas of sociological inquiry including (but not limited to) social psychology, stratification, deviance, collective action, organizations, political systems, law, and science.

At its core, legitimacy involves a sense of appropriateness that is accorded to an entity. That is, a legitimate entity is one that we view as suited to its social environment and, as a result, deserving of support by other entities in the environment. The sense that an entity is suited to its environment arises from its perceived consistency with the institutionalized norms, values, and beliefs in which the entity is embedded. The institutionalized character of norms, values, and beliefs is a critical element of legitimacy. Institutionalized criteria are beyond the discretion of single actors. Because no single actor is perceived as dictating the norms, values, and beliefs that guide a social system (although they are socially constructed), they represent superordinate standards, uncontaminated by individual motives and preferences. Their superordinate status lends institutionalized norms, values, and beliefs a taken-for-grantedness and the sense that, irrespective of privately held views, they will be upheld by others in the social system. Consequently, an entity that is perceived as integrated with institutionalized norms, values, and beliefs is one that we believe is appropriate and thus deserving of support. That support may take the form of social approval, the investment of social capital, or material/financial rewards.

Theoretical treatments of legitimacy emphasize the importance of collective support. This is a common thread across classic sociological theory, hearkening back to the work of Marx, Mead, and Weber. It is interesting that while Marx proposed that class consciousness – a sense of shared ideology – is critical to the elimination of inequality, Della Fave (1980) argued that the shared ideology of *equity* legitimates stratification. An equity ideology, represented in the generalized other (i.e., the perception of the shared norms, values, and beliefs to which society prescribes that is held by individual actors), affects individuals' self-evaluations and, thereby, their sense of deservingness of rewards. These self-evaluations, in turn, serve as the basis for rationalizing an unequal distribution of resources in society, engendering a sense of appropriateness regarding inequality. As a result, social inequality gains legitimacy and is perpetuated.

Weber's highly influential work on authority systems likewise emphasized the importance of the perception of collective support in generating legitimacy. He proposed that legitimate authority systems are those in which authority reflects rule-based action, where the rules are collectively upheld (as opposed to action directed at maximizing one's personal outcomes and exercised at personal discretion). Thus, Weber highlights the importance of validity – the perception that others support and will act in accord with the rules governing a system – in legitimating an authority system. Subsequent theorists explicitly distinguished validity from propriety (i.e., privately held beliefs about the appropriateness or desirability of an entity), and demonstrated that validity generates legitimacy, independent of propriety. Insights on the importance of validity to legitimacy have been applied not only to authority systems, but also

to status structures, patterns of distributive justice, and identity processes.

Also, across time and different treatments of the concept, legitimacy is consistently viewed as a source of stability in social systems. As Weber noted, legitimate authority persists and provides an important foundation for bureaucracy, itself a persistent organizational form. Scholars of organizations and world systems have pointed to the isomorphic tendencies of legitimate structures and processes to diffuse across social systems. Group processes researchers have also suggested that legitimacy produces resilience in status structures and distributive justice processes, even when those structures and processes disadvantage the majority of actors in the system. Stability is a function of the ongoing ability of actors within the system to mobilize resources to perpetuate a legitimate system.

As this discussion has suggested, sociological theories involving legitimacy have drawn heavily on Weber's classic work. His insights on the legitimacy of particular organizational structures and processes (e.g., legal-rational authority and bureaucracy) begged the question of how these particular forms gained legitimacy. Meyer and Rowan (1977) addressed this question with an influential essay on the process through which social structures and processes become aligned with the collectively supported (i.e., institutionalized) norms, values, and beliefs that are socially constructed and transmitted through the environment. Recently, sociologists have turned their attention to the process of alignment itself. How do the structures and processes of social entities become aligned with collectively supported norms, values, and beliefs?

Three strategies have emerged to address this question. First from the new institutional perspective in sociology, theorists have argued that alignment with institutionalized norms, values, and beliefs (and hence, legitimacy) results from certain environmental pressures (e.g., Powell & DiMaggio 1991). These factors lead social systems to adopt structures and processes that embody institutionalized norms, beliefs, and values. The pressures arise from normative and coercive processes that reward conforming systems with legitimacy and punish deviant ones with its withdrawal. Alternatively, in the absence of coercive and normative pressures, when the norms, values, and beliefs that would dictate the desirable form are uncertain, systems are likely to mimic the form of other already successful systems.

Second, a related argument from the population ecology perspective (e.g., Hannan & Freeman 1992) proposes that the environment determines which organizational forms survive, and which languish. Within this perspective, the form (i.e., structures and processes) a system assumes at its outset is relatively stable and resistant to change. To the extent that institutionalized norms, values, and beliefs characterizing the environment are embodied in the system from the start, its legitimacy increases and, therefore, so do its odds of surviving. This is because legitimacy is critical to securing other key resources needed for survival. As this implies, the environment, rather than the strategic behavior of actors, determines the legitimacy of a system.

A third perspective on how entities align themselves with institutionalized norms, values, and beliefs to secure legitimacy is also emerging (e.g., Friedland & Alford 1991). This perspective incorporates both a strategic view of social actors and elements of social constructionism. It recognizes the diversity of sets of shared norms, values, and beliefs that characterize social environments and are closely tied to established social institutions, like the economy, political systems, and the family. These sets of norms, values, and beliefs, referred to as "institutionalized logics," may vary depending on the institutions with which they are associated. For example, a norm of equality may comprise a logic related to democracy; a norm of equity may be part of an institutionalized logic corresponding to a capitalist economic system; a norm of need-based resource distribution may be a component of the institutionalized logic governing the family. Moreover, all of these institutions (with competing logics) may coexist in the same broader social system. Emerging theory drawing on these ideas suggests that legitimacy arises when an entity is able to mobilize support for the logic it embodies through appeals to the relevant social institutions supporting that logic. Thus from this perspective, legitimation is a process through which actors successfully construct the validity of the norms, values, and beliefs characterizing their own systems through appeals to particular institutions within the broader social system.

As these developments indicate, theory related to the sources and consequences of legitimacy is growing in part through integration and diffusion across perspectives and topics, as well as competing arguments on the mechanisms of legitimacy. New institutional theory, which has catalyzed many of the contemporary developments in the study of legitimacy, emerged in the context of the sociology of organizations, but has become increasingly influential in such diverse areas as political sociology, group processes, sociology of culture, and sociology of law. At the same time, Weber's classic statements on validity and authority remain influential. Furthermore, on the one hand, social constructionist accounts have gained renewed attention with attempts such as those described above to explain strategic efforts of actors to secure legitimacy. On the other hand, recognition of inertial forces beyond the control of actors also retains significance in explaining the dynamics of legitimacy.

In contrast to the vast research on the sources and consequences of legitimacy, however, there has been less emphasis on delegitimation. Theory and research on unstable political systems are valuable examples of the importance of investigating such processes. Given the importance of validity and institutionalized norms, values, and beliefs to legitimacy, it is not surprising that this line of theorizing points to conditions that increase the salience of conflict over shared norms, values, and beliefs as a catalyst for undermining the validation of political systems. Once invalidated, legitimacy crumbles, and established political regimes are vulnerable to replacement. Researchers investigating political change have posited that political actors are carriers of endorsement or disapproval across social groups, and once disapproval becomes salient across a critical mass of groups, then legitimacy is jeopardized (e.g., Habermas 1975). Extensions of these ideas may hold promise for the theories of delegitimation, and thus social change as it characterizes other structures and systems, e.g., organizational change, economic change, changes in legal systems, changes in status and distribution systems.

Despite the long history of research related to legitimacy, it has been hindered by methodological difficulties. Researchers have had difficulty operationalizing legitimacy independent of the variables to which it is theoretically related (e.g., validity, stability, commonality, mobilization of support). For example, within organizations research, the legitimacy of an organizational structure or process is often operationalized in terms of its prevalence, the extent to which organizational actors believe that other actors endorse it, and/or the success of organizations in extracting resources from their environments. Similarly, political sociologists have also conflated legitimacy with endorsement and the stability of political systems. Within microsociological traditions, the conflation of legitimacy with its causes and consequences is less common. Instead, researchers in these traditions, like Berger et al. (1998), tend to treat legitimacy as an unmeasured theoretical construct, and focus on its constituent processes and outcomes, e.g., the relation between validity, resource mobilization, and stability. This strategy has the advantage of retaining the logical integrity of theories involving legitimacy, while still testing the social processes and outcomes that legitimacy is assumed to engender.

In summary, legitimacy continues to represent an important theoretical concept for sociology. Yet, there are a number of challenges to be addressed, such as articulating the relative effects of strategic behavior versus inertial forces in legitimacy processes, developing and testing theories of illegitimacy, and refining the operationalization of legitimacy. Because of the centrality of this concept to the understanding of social life at different levels of analysis and across different topics, legitimacy is likely to continue to play a key role in sociological theory. Indeed, Comte's vision of sociology as a science that can explain both the social order and social dynamics may be realized through theories of legitimacy that are able to specify both the legitimation processes that give rise to stability, and the delegitimation processes that give rise to social change.

SEE ALSO: Dependency and World-Systems Theories; Expectation States Theory; Institutional Theory, New; Organization Theory; Political Sociology; Social Psychology; Weber, Max

REFERENCES AND SUGGESTED READINGS

Berger, J., Ridgeway, C., Fisek, M. H., & Norman, R. Z. (1998) The Legitimation and Delegitimation of Power and Prestige Orders. *American Sociological Review* 63: 379–405.
Berger, P. L. & Luckmann, T. (1966) *The Social Construction of Reality: A Treatise in the Sociology of Knowledge*. Doubleday, New York.
Della Fave, L. R. (1980) The Meek Shall Not Inherit the Earth: Self-Evaluation and the Legitimacy of Stratification. *American Sociological Review* 45: 955–71.
Friedland, R. & Alford, R. R. (1991) Bringing Society Back In: Symbols, Practices, and Institutional, Contradictions. In: Powell, W. W. & DiMaggio, P. J. (Eds.), *The New Institutionalism in Organizational Analysis*. University of Chicago Press, Chicago.
Habermas, J. (1975) *Legitimation Crisis*. Beacon Press, Boston.
Hannan, M. T. & Freeman, J. (1992) *Dynamics of Organizational Populations: Density, Legitimation, and Competition*. Oxford University Press, New York.
Johnson, C. (Ed.) (2004) *Research in the Sociology of Organizations: Legitimacy Processes in Organizations*, Vol. 22. Elsevier JAI, Oxford.
Meyer, J. W. & Rowan, B. (1977) Institutionalized Organizations: Formal Structure as Myth and Ceremony. *American Journal of Sociology* 83: 340–63.
Powell, W. W. & DiMaggio, P. J. (Eds.) (1991) *The New Institutionalism in Organizational Analysis*. University of Chicago Press, Chicago.
Stryker, R. (1994) Rules, Resources, and Legitimacy Processes: Some Implications for Social Conflict, Order, and Change. *American Journal of Sociology* 99: 847–910.
Walker, H. A., Rogers, L., & Zelditch, M., Jr. (2003) Acts, Persons, Positions, and Institutions: Legitimating Multiple Objects and Compliance with Authority. In: Chew, S. C. & Knottnerus, J. D. (Eds.), *Structure, Culture, and History: Recent Issues in Social Theory*. Littlefield Press, Lanham, MD.
Weber, M. (1968 [1918]) *Economy and Society*. Ed. G. Roth & C. Wittich. University of California Press, Berkeley.
Zelditch, M., Jr. (2001) Theories of Legitimacy. In: Jost, J. & Major, B. (Eds.), *The Psychology of Legitimacy: Emerging Perspectives on Ideology, Justice, and Intergroup Relations*. Cambridge University Press, Cambridge, pp. 33–53.

leisure

Sheila Scraton

Leisure is a notoriously difficult concept to define. The study of leisure has early origins stretching back to the 1920s and Veblen's *The Theory of the Leisure Class* (1925). However, it was in the 1960s and 1970s that the foundations of leisure studies as an academic area were laid. Early writers such as Dumazedier in *Towards a Society of Leisure* (1967) defined leisure as activity that is set apart from other obligations such as work and family and provides individuals with the opportunity for relaxation, the broadening of knowledge, and social participation. Dumazedier's definition highlights the notion that leisure involves pleasure and freedom of choice and that this sets it apart from paid work and everyday commitments. Leisure could be seen as *compensation*, a means of escape from the routines of daily labor, or as *residual time*, time left over when other commitments have taken place.

The definition of leisure as in opposition to work and other obligations has been very significant within the sociology of leisure. In the UK, Parker (1971) was a major contribution that explored in greater detail this relationship between work and leisure and argued that leisure is an important aspect of social life that demands rigorous sociological analysis alongside the more conventional areas of work, family, education, youth, and so on. He argued that it was with industrialization that leisure became viewed as a separate sphere of life as work became more clearly demarcated in terms of time and space. Therefore, leisure cannot be understood in isolation from work. Parker identified three aspects of the work–leisure relationship: extension, opposition, and neutrality. He viewed the *extension* pattern as showing little demarcation between work and leisure activities, giving the examples of social workers, teachers, and doctors as typical of those that experience work and leisure in this way. *Opposition*, as the name suggests, relies on an intentional dissimilarity between work and leisure and Parker highlighted people with tough physical jobs such as miners or oil-rig workers as typical within this category. His third pattern of *neutrality* is defined by an "average" demarcation of spheres. Workers whose jobs are neither fulfilling nor oppressive and who tend to be passive and uninvolved in both their work and leisure activities are defined by this pattern.

There were several criticisms of Parker's early typology of the work–leisure relationship that highlighted the limitations of this analysis for those outside of the paid workforce. The unemployed, the retired, students, and women working in the home as carers and undertaking domestic work were all identified as outside this work–leisure model as paid work is not central in their lives. However, the recognition of the importance of situating leisure within a social context, not as a separate, totally autonomous sphere of individual free choice, was an important contribution to the developing sociology of leisure. As leisure became analyzed within a social context, emerging definitions reflected the different emphases of competing theoretical perspectives within leisure studies.

THEORIZING LEISURE

A feature of leisure studies throughout the 1970s and 1980s was the development of competing paradigms which sought to understand and explain leisure from different sociological perspectives. In the UK the three major traditions in leisure studies developed from pluralism, critical Marxism, and feminism, whereas in North America a more social psychological approach underpinned much of the leisure research and writing.

Roberts (1978) argued that a pluralist model of society provides the most coherent approach to understanding contemporary leisure in the 1970s. His contributions to the field of leisure studies have remained consistent within this paradigm. This "conventional wisdom" suggests that there is a plurality of tastes and interests generated by different circumstances. Both commercial and public providers of leisure supply experiences from which individuals seek to fashion their varying lifestyles. Leisure is both a "freedom from" and a "freedom to" and is primarily concerned with relatively self-determined behavior. The pluralist model does not assume that leisure is free from all influences but argues that age, gender, socioeconomic status, and other "variables" operate in a multitude of configurations (Roberts 1999).

In contrast to the pluralist model, Marxist theorists sought to understand leisure as an integral part of the structure of capitalist society. Clarke and Critcher (1985) argued that leisure's domination by the market and the state, the persistence of leisure inequalities, and the drift to post-industrialism all demonstrate how leisure is part of capitalist society. Capitalism shapes leisure through hegemonic processes of both constraint and coercion. Their work provided a powerful critique of the "conventional wisdom" of leisure studies and emphasized the importance of history and the significance of *social* processes such as work, the family, the life cycle, and the market. Leisure is about people's choices but these choices are made within structures of constraint. Leisure needs to be understood within the dialectical relationships of structure and agency, control and choice, continuity and change. A neo-Marxist approach to understanding leisure draws on the "sociological imagination" of C. Wright Mills, grasping the relationship between history and biography. Leisure as "freedom" and "constraint" is seen as socially constructed around time and space, institutional forms, and social identities. This approach to explaining and understanding leisure was derived from cultural studies and views leisure as potentially an arena for cultural contestation between dominant and subordinate groups in society.

Further criticisms of the "conventional wisdom" of leisure studies came from the developing feminist perspectives within sociology during the 1980s. Feminists began by identifying the male-dominated approach that had characterized much of sociology, including the study of leisure. Leisure understood as free time or freedom of choice was identified as being problematic and irrelevant to many women's lives. Women's lives were recognized as not being neatly compartmentalized into periods of work and periods of leisure, as most women have domestic work responsibilities as well as paid work and often childcare or other caring responsibilities. For many women, family leisure is a time when they are supporting others' free time, such as transporting children to activities, preparing meals for entertaining friends, or planning and organizing family holidays. Thus their

leisure often involves a *relative freedom* rather than clearly demarcated time. Feminist work identified the need to examine leisure in the context of women's lives as a whole and not as a separate sphere divorced from all other areas of their lives. Consequently, the existing definitions and theories of leisure were viewed as androcentric, having meaning only in relation to men. Research by Green et al. (1990) provided the world's largest study of women's leisure. Based in Sheffield, UK, between 1984 and 1987, the research focused on the cultural significance of leisure in women's lives and leisure as a potential site for conflict and inequality. They found that the concept *leisure* is extraordinarily resistant to being confined to a single, neat, definitional category. For the women in their study, leisure was a highly personal and subjective mix of experiences and was linked to, and a part of, other areas of life.

Research in the 1980s, which shifted the focus to women and leisure, also recognized that gender relations were crucially a part of leisure experiences and leisure institutions. This work identified that women occupy a subordinate position within a patriarchal society. Thus, their material position, as well as constructions of femininity and masculinity, have a determining effect on women's lives, including their leisure lives. The research and theoretical understandings of women's leisure highlighted issues relating to sexuality, respectability, and social control which paralleled work more broadly in feminist sociology. Women's leisure was shown to be constrained by constructions of femininity and gender-appropriate behavior and controlled, both directly and indirectly, by men, either individually or collectively. Although much of the work during this period focused on structural constraints of gender, there was some acknowledgment of the interlinking of gender relations with those of class and race.

Both the feminist and neo-Marxist analyses throughout the 1980s in the UK shared a predominantly materialist or structuralist approach to the sociology of leisure. In North America, however, the approach to understanding leisure has been more individualistic and located within a social psychology or social interactionist paradigm. Within these approaches the emphasis is on how leisure is *experienced* by individuals. Rather than concentrating on constraints, the focus shifts to how individuals use leisure to create roles and identities. Leisure can thus provide an important space for individuals as a *freedom to be*, self-determining and fulfilling. The work of the North American social psychologist Csikszentmihalyi has been utilized within this approach to understanding leisure; in particular the concept of *flow* has been applied. This notion of flow is associated with what Csikszentmihalyi argues is *optimal experience*, when highly skilled individuals are stretched to their limit and become totally absorbed in their activity. It is through leisure activities that many people seek to achieve this optimal experience. Focusing on leisure as experience directs attention toward motivations and satisfactions and emphasizes inner feelings and experiences rather than external contexts and constraints.

Since the 1990s, sociological approaches to understanding leisure have drawn on postmodern developments in social theory. Rojek (1993, 1995, 2000) has been the most prolific writer who has criticized the former traditions of leisure theory, which he characterizes as social formalism, the influence of critical Marxism, and cultural studies and feminism. In his writings he not only debates and challenges the paradigmatic traditions within leisure studies but also develops and engages with postmodernist perspectives on leisure. Rojek has developed theoretical debates within sociology and sought to understand and interpret postmodern cultures and their relevance for leisure and leisure studies. In doing this he has presented a challenge to the existing theories, which he argues offer universal accounts that rely on dualisms and fail to adequately theorize culture, difference, and agency. Rojek argues for a phenomenology of leisure, with experience at the center of analysis. Within postmodernity, the weakening and destabilizing of former structures and the blurring of social divisions such as class, race, and gender have led to leisure and leisure lifestyles gaining increasing significance in the construction of individual and social identities. The development of new technologies and the shifts in cultural practice to hyperreality, a loss of authenticity, a dissolution of cultural boundaries, depthlessness and superficiality, fragmentation, parody and pastiche, are all seen to find expression within postmodern leisure.

No longer are leisure places and experiences seen to be fixed as travel and tourism become virtual, theme parks, such as Disneyland, challenge the distinctions between real, imitation, and fiction, and leisure becomes more individualized with pleasure, risk, and excitement center stage. The connections between leisure lifestyles and consumption are of increasing significance, with leisure playing an important role in the reflexive project of identity construction and definition.

Although postmodernism and postmodernity have impacted on the ways in which leisure is understood and theorized, there remain many theorists who argue that such a shift is by no means total or complete. Although many accept that uncertainty, fragmentation, hyperreality, and superficiality are evident in our cultural world and leisure reflects these cultural shifts, others have argued for theoretical positions that recognize and analyze cultural differences and the complexities of multiple social identities whilst adhering to a theoretical stance that continues to consider broader structural relations of power and the persistence of material inequalities in many people's lives (Wearing 1998; Aitchison 2003).

RESEARCHING LEISURE

Information about people's leisure has been, and continues to be, routinely collected via large participation surveys such as the General Household Survey in the UK, which is conducted annually and gathers information from a nationally representative sample of households. Questions in the survey that are related to leisure provide knowledge of participation rates for different sections of the population, including the number and type of people taking part in sporting activities, visits to the countryside, and visits to museums and other leisure-related provision. Since the academic study of leisure began, information such as this has been used to evidence trends in participation over time and identify which groups in society are under- or over-represented in various activities. Other large-scale surveys provide information on consumer spending on leisure, and together, large-scale national surveys help identify the main leisure activities for different populations. Roberts (1999) identifies that the big three leisure activities are eating and drinking, tourism and holidays, and home entertainment, including the television and other audiovisual media. He argues that out-of-home food and drink are leading leisure items, and that participation in these activities and spending on them exceed the figures for sport participation and spectating, cinema attendance, or participation in other leisure forms. Tourism and holidays rate very highly in terms of expenditure, with people increasingly taking more holidays and traveling further. The media are a significant aspect of people's leisure and it is home entertainment that is a major leisure activity for many people.

Large-scale national surveys together with time budget studies and expenditure surveys have been used since the 1970s to categorize and measure the "facts" of leisure and, in turn, to influence and direct policy initiatives. This tradition of positive empiricist research underpinned the "conventional wisdom" of leisure studies as quantitative data provided knowledge about leisure participation. Empirical research utilizing quantitative data also contributed to knowledge about leisure through the life course as participation rates at different ages were identified. However, an influential piece of early work on leisure through the life course, *Leisure and the Life Cycle*, was conducted in 1975 by Rhona and Robert Rapoport. They used extended interviews in families to explore the balance of leisure, family, and work in people's lives and identified how individuals have different preoccupations throughout their lives, identifying four main stages within the family life cycle. Although there have been many criticisms of the Rapoports' approach to understanding leisure and the family, methodologically their research moved away from a rigid quantitative approach to one that sought to delve more deeply into meaning and identity.

As the questions in leisure studies turned from the *functions* of leisure to a concern to explore and identify structural inequalities, both in and through leisure opportunities and experiences, so the means of conducting such research have shifted. Increasingly, researchers have turned to in-depth, qualitative, and interactive

methods to explore the realities, meanings, and experiences of leisure. There has been a move to recognize the significance of subjective knowledge, which is largely absent or marginalized from quantitative large-scale studies. Feminist researchers in particular have argued for the importance of small-scale, qualitative, or interactive approaches that can give voice to the personal, experiential, and emotional aspects of leisure. This shift to more micro, individualized accounts of leisure, away from more macro institutional concerns, mirrors the theoretical shifts over the past few decades in the sociology of leisure. However, although there are now far more studies that use interviews, life histories, and a qualitative approach, there is still a reliance on large data sets of survey material to inform policy. Leisure research remains closely applied to policy and practice in many cases.

CURRENT RESEARCH AND FUTURE DIRECTIONS

Leisure contexts and activities are extremely broad and include sport, physical activity, tourism, media, the arts, countryside recreation, and new technologies, amongst others. Leisure continues to provide an important site through which sociological questions can be explored. Work–leisure–family balance remains crucial to achieving quality of life and is of increasing significance as paid work intensifies, becomes more flexible, and working life becomes extended. The place of leisure in achieving work–life balance remains an important sociological question, as do questions relating to retirement, "serious leisure," and volunteerism. However, the early emphasis on the work–leisure relationship is being replaced, at least to a certain extent, by questions relating to the depth and spread of consumer culture.

The growth of consumption and commercial provision, together with the theoretical concerns of postmodernism and poststructuralism, have shifted the focus of some leisure scholars away from former concerns around material inequalities to questions of representation, embodiment, and identities. Drawing on social and cultural geography, research has begun to explore the consumption of spaces and places within a leisure context. Whilst this remains underdeveloped, there is already exciting work around areas such as gay and lesbian city space, cultural tourism, and shopping.

Gender relations have been central to the study of leisure since the 1980s, including work focusing on androcentric definitions of leisure, the different meanings and motivations for women participating in leisure, leisure spaces, women's oppression in and through leisure, and, more recently, leisure as an important site for agency, negotiation, and transformation. Increasingly, research on gender is recognizing the importance of acknowledging and understanding difference and diversity between women. Studies on the experiences of different women across ethnicity, age, sexuality, and class have extended our qualitative understandings of women's leisure. Further work will be important in exploring the intersectionality of gender, race, ethnicity, sexuality, and class in the leisure lives of diverse groups of people. There remains limited work on masculinities and leisure and much of the current research is within the context of sport. There needs to be more research into shifting gender relations, new masculinities, and men's changing relationships within work, the family, and leisure.

A major gap in the literature within leisure studies is work that centers on race and ethnicity. Although there is some critical engagement with race, racism, and sport, this needs to be extended and developed into other areas of leisure. An exploration of the concept of whiteness is beginning within sport and leisure studies, although as yet this remains underdeveloped.

Leisure research is a broad and multidisciplinary arena. The theoretical shifts within the sociology of leisure are reflected in the changing focus of research away from questions of leisure choice and material and structural inequalities to more rigorous analyses of leisure forms and practices as sites for cultural production, empowerment, social inclusion, and social transformation.

SEE ALSO: Culture; Gender, Sport and; Leisure, Aging and; Leisure Class; Leisure, Popular Culture and; Media; Media and Sport; Popular Culture; Sport; Sport as Work; Work, Sociology of

REFERENCES AND SUGGESTED READINGS

Aitchison, C. C. (2003) *Gender and Leisure*. Routledge, London.

Blackshaw, T. (2003) *Leisure Life*. Routledge, London.

Clarke, J. & Critcher, C. (1985) *The Devil Makes Work: Leisure in Capitalist Britain*. Macmillan, London.

Deem, R. (1986) *All Work and No Play: The Sociology of Women and Leisure*. Routledge & Kegan Paul, London.

Featherstone, M. (1991) *Consumer Culture and Postmodernism*. Sage, London.

Green, E., Hebron, S., & Woodward, D. (1990) *Women's Leisure, What Leisure?* Macmillan, Basingstoke.

Henderson, K. A., Bialeschki, D., Shaw, S. M., & Freysinger, V. J. (1996) *A Leisure of One's Own: A Feminist Perspective on Women's Leisure*. Venture Publishing, College Park, PA.

Kelly, J. R. (1987) *Freedom to Be: A New Sociology of Leisure*. Macmillan, New York.

Parker, S. (1971) *The Future of Work and Leisure*. MacGibbon & Kee, London.

Parker, S. (1983) *Leisure and Work*. Allen & Unwin, London.

Roberts, K. (1978) *Contemporary Society and the Growth of Leisure*. Longman, London.

Roberts, K. (1999) *Leisure in Contemporary Society*. CABI Publishing, Wallingford.

Rojek, C. (1993) *Ways of Escape: Modern Transformations in Leisure and Travel*. Macmillan, London.

Rojek, C. (1995) *Decentring Leisure: Rethinking Leisure*. Macmillan, London.

Rojek, C. (2000) *Leisure and Culture*. Palgrave, Basingstoke.

Scraton, S. (1994) The Changing World of Women and Leisure: Feminism, Post-Feminism, and Leisure. *Leisure Studies* 13: 249–61.

Stebbins, R. A. (1998) *After Work: The Search for the Optimal Leisure Lifestyle*. Temeron Books, Calgary.

Wearing, B. (1998) *Feminism and Leisure Theory*. Sage, London.

leisure, aging and

Jon Hendricks

Leisure and well-being are closely entwined throughout life. Whether defined as free time or volitional activity, the significance of leisure is that it provides opportunities wherein the quest for meaning is self-absorbing and yields subjectively salutary results. Given changes in the character of work, certainty of careers, timing of retirement, and improvements in health, it is reasonable to assert that leisure will occupy an important place in the aging process.

Rather than consider free time, leisure, and aging as domains separate from the rest of life, adopting a life course perspective may provide greater insight. Leisure is grounded in societal conditions as well as the subjective and individualized world of participants. Leisure does not stand free of broader societal-based values, gendered distinctions, life course issues, family stage, work, retirement, or other sociodemographic or marketplace influences. Yet leisure is symbolically significant to individuals, helping to create meaning and sense of self. Leisure structures time, space, and social relationships. If normative prescriptions or reinforcements from other realms become unclear for any reason, leisure interests may assume greater prominence. As far as individuals are concerned, leisure facilitates self-enhancement, expression, and identity formation through intrinsic rewards, opportunities to exercise agency, and relationships rooted in the social worlds of leisure participation. Leisure serves as a context, a frame within which actors can author their own development – creating and collaborating interpretation by taking part (Hendricks & Cutler 2003; Stebbins 2004).

During the course of adulthood, leisure is fashioned by family life cycle, work roles, career stage, and demographic, socioeconomic, and other master-status characteristics such as gender or ethnicity. Though leisure interest may evolve over time, its symbolic relevance in terms of identity, integration, and bonding may remain constant. During retirement leisure likely reflects role substitution, the search for meaningful modes of engagement, and is a mechanism to maintain vigor, interests, and relations.

Among adults, an average of 40 hours a week may be devoted to leisure (Becker 2002). TV watching can account for up to 28 hours a week, but travel, reading, socializing, gardening, and other discretionary activities occupy from 1.5 hours to nearly 9 hours weekly. According to the *Statistical Abstract of the United States: 2001*, during the previous year 48 percent of adults had partaken of an arts event and half had dined out or entertained

friends or family at home as a form of leisure. Available evidence suggests European elderly follow comparable patterns.

Physical activity, vigorous hobbies, exercise, and sports are somewhat more common among people age 65–74 and older than among their younger adult counterparts. Estimates are that a third to 40 percent of older men, compared to one-quarter or less of younger adult males, engage in medium to high levels of leisure-time physical activity (Barnes & Schoenborn 2003). Gendered patterns are historically grounded, with women marginally less physically active, but the age-related slope is comparable. As the federal government's *Older Americans 2000* pointed out, approximately a third of persons aged 65 or older may be leading what can be described as inactive lifestyles. There is a direct relationship between education, income, and socioeconomic status and levels of physical activity. Despite the lore, attendance at sporting events is not overwhelmingly popular, with less than half of adults attending in the last year. For example, only about 16 percent of US adults have been to a baseball game in the past year (Becker 2002).

Such statistics do not tell the whole story, nor do they reflect variation in time devoted to particular forms of leisure depending on age, gender, socioeconomic status, and other socially relevant factors. Neither do they include volitional educational involvements or volunteerism as forms of leisure. In analyses of time spent in leisure pursuits, both education and volunteering occupy up to 10 percent of available leisure time. According to a 2003 report from the American Association of Retired Persons, volunteerism is an important source of satisfaction, sociability, and self-validation and therefore retained by larger proportions of older people than previously thought. There is yet another aspect of leisure that must be broached. Certain types of deviance may constitute leisure for those who are engaged in them and there may be "good" and "bad" categories of leisure, with the latter often overlooked (Rojek 2000).

Education level, income, health status, gender, and ethnicity, plus a host of other compositional characteristics reflecting period and cohort effects, as well as age, shape traditional forms of leisure. As these change, leisure patterns and activities will be affected. In many respects, leisure is a microcosm where such issues as gender and ethnicity play out. Participation patterns, spaces and places, enjoyment, and even definitions relate to gendered and ethnic concerns as an aspect of broader social and cultural relations and perceptions of aging.

Before drawing inferences about age-related shifts in leisure involvements the prospect of selective optimization must be considered. It is possible that as they age, people seek to get the most out of their involvements in ways that maximize subjectively meaningful returns on investments. Older persons may choose to cut back on certain forms of engagement or interaction while expanding others. A case in point can be seen in the example of volunteerism: less meaningful engagements diminish, while time and energy spent in selected others is sustained (Hendricks & Cutler 2004). The same is likely true of leisure: peripheral pursuits fall by the wayside in favor of those with more meaningful returns.

The symbolic import of leisure lies in its association with various facets of well-being. There is ample evidence that leisure lifestyles protect against physical and health declines or cognitive impairment, and provide forums for conservation of social integration, interpersonal bonding, morale, life-satisfaction, and subjective sense of control (Guinn 1999; Musick et al. 1999; Schooler & Mulatu 2001; Silverstein & Parker 2002). Above all, leisure is an expressive domain wherein personal meaning is created and continued and the effects accrue in many aspects of the aging experience.

The money involved in the leisure market provides some indication of leisure's appeal. From early in the twentieth century the commercialization of leisure has grown and is evidence of returns derived from speaking to demands for leisure lifestyles. Estimates are that at the dawn of the twenty-first century personal expenditures for entertainment, leisure, and other discretionary diversions were in the range of $568 billion to $1 trillion annually – in excess of 10 percent of total household expenditures. That does not include the $21 billion devoted to parks and recreation by local, state, and federal governments or a number of other categories, but these figures do indicate the dimensions of the leisure marketplace (Becker 2002).

SEE ALSO: Age Identity; Consumption of Sport; Identity Theory; Leisure; Leisure Class; Leisure, Popular Culture; Sport and Culture

REFERENCES AND SUGGESTED READINGS

Barnes, P. & Schoenborn, C. (2003) *Physical Activity Among Adults: United States. Advance Data from Vital and Health Statistics; No. 333.* National Center for Health Statistics, Hyattsville, MD.

Becker, P. C. (2002) *A Statistical Portrait of the United States: Social Conditions and Trends.* Bernan Press, Lanham, MD.

Guinn, B. (1999) Leisure Behavior Motivation and the Life Satisfaction of Retired Persons. *Activities, Adaptation and Aging* 23: 13–20.

Hendricks, J. & Cutler, S. J. (2003) Leisure in Life-Course Perspective. In: Settersen, R. A. (Ed.), *Invitation to the Life Course: Toward New Understandings of Later Life.* Baywood, Amityville, NY, pp. 107–34.

Hendricks, J. & Cutler, S. J. (2004) Volunteerism and Socioemotional Selectivity in Later Life. *Journal of Gerontology* 59B: S251–7.

Musick, M., Herzog, A., & House, J. (1999) Volunteering and Mortality Among Older Adults: Findings from a National Sample. *Journal of Gerontology: Social Sciences* 54B: S173–80.

Rojek, C. (2000) *Leisure and Culture.* St. Martin's Press, New York.

Schooler, C. & Mulatu, M. (2001) The Reciprocal Effects of Leisure Time Activities and Intellectual Functioning in Older People: A Longitudinal Analysis. *Psychology and Aging* 16: 466–82.

Silverstein, M. & Parker, M. (2002) Leisure Activities and Quality of Life Among the Oldest Old in Sweden. *Research on Aging* 24: 528–47.

Stebbins, R. A. (2004) *Between Work and Leisure.* Transaction Publishers, New Brunswick, NJ.

leisure class

Matthias Zick Varul

The concept of the leisure class was introduced by Thorstein Veblen in his *Theory of the Leisure Class* (1899). Leisure classes here consist of those people who, due to their social position, can afford to abstain from productive work and live on other people's labor. They confine themselves to non-industrial occupations like "government, warfare, religious observances, and sports." Their income is sourced from exploitation of industrial classes that are sub-dued by the leisure class's superior "pecuniary prowess." In order to assert their position they have to be *visibly* idle. Their leisure practices do not only demonstrate momentary inactivity, but often display skills that serve as evidence of past abstention from work – higher learning and accomplishment in gentlemanly sports, for example, count as evidence for habitual non-pro-ductivity. Positional claims are further asserted by wasteful "conspicuous consumption" of high-status goods and by vicarious leisure of family members, guests, minions, and footmen. Conspicuous consumption of high-priced goods is a form of "vicarious leisure" in which other people's labor time is taken up for the produc-tion of goods of ostensibly no practical use. Leisure class fashion, too, expresses contempt for productive activity (e.g., by deliberately lim-iting the movements of the wearer).

Apart from obstructing industrial progress by the wasteful use of social resources, Veblen sees the main effect of the modern leisure class in the exertion of a cultural dominance, setting socially accepted standards of taste. Aspiring classes emulate leisure class patterns of behavior and especially consumption, while the emulated lei-sure class in turn is constantly developing its "pecuniary canons of taste" in order to spoil the emulative efforts. The leisure class thus func-tions as a consumerist avant-garde. This claim has been criticized as highly overstated and ignoring reverse emulation of popular culture by the upper classes (Bourdieu 1979).

While historically the leisure class was formed by a ruling aristocracy, industrial capit-alism is ruled by businessmen who share leisure class values of pecuniary prowess but are no leisure class themselves; to the contrary, Veblen asserts that they work long and hard. Veblen thus anticipates a common argument against his theory (Rojek 2000): the rich of today normally continue investing most of their time in busi-ness life, forming a rather "harried leisure class" (Linder 1970). Veblen, however, sees the abstention from household labor in the upper-class wife and the pretension of leisure in the upper-middle-class wife as compensating vicarious leisure acting out the husband's lei-sure entitlement.

The term leisure class is rarely used in recent sociology, but it still is informative in approaching contemporary social phenomena. The group fitting Veblen's description best are "celebrities" who can be said, at least in terms of connubiality and commensality, to form a con-temporary leisure *class*. Their artistic, medial, or sportive activities are, in the public perception, set apart from the social process of production. Like the Veblenian leisure class, celebrities act as commodity culture innovators and serve as role models whose consumption, style, and behavior are emulated. The difference of course is that here leisure itself and the readiness of a wider audience to aspire and emulate has become the basis of the high income, which for Veblen's leisure class was what their leisure expressed. Their leisure behavior, in turn, does not simply *dictate* social taste but also has to anticipate changes in public preferences. In Veblenian terms, celebrities as directly or indirectly financed by their audiences act out vicarious leisure for the onlooking society. Given the very mixed social background of the members of this new leisure class, "trickle-up" effects here are at least as important as "trickle-down" effects.

Another contemporary "leisure class" is the unemployed. Here leisure is involuntary and problematic. While voluntary leisure in the Veblenian case is a means to assert social recog-nition, socially unlegitimized forced leisure has the reverse effect on social and self-esteem. The social expectation here is that of a quasi-work orientation toward reemployment.

Elements of leisure class behavior have been generalized in a move from leisure class to *lei-sure society* (Seabrook 1988), but they are also spatially and/or temporarily compartmentalized and contained within a work society. Within the lifecycle, old age has been discussed as a "new leisure class" (Michelon 1954). Unlike with the unemployed, leisure in old age is usually legiti-mated by reference to contributions in a long working life. Old age leisure is "deserved" or "earned," but it is also seen as problematic, requiring reinterpretations of leisure as mean-ingful or even an education for leisure.

Within the year cycle, tourism has been characterized as requiring "a new theory of the leisure class" (MacCannell 1976). While lacking the defining characteristics of a class, tourists do appear as a leisure class vis-à-vis the local population of tourist destinations. With one of the roots of modern tourism being the middle-class emulation of the aristocratic Grand Tour, it can be argued that tourism is in part a remainder of trickled-down leisure class patterns. However, like old-age retirement, tourism refers both negatively and positively to work. It is defined as the opposite of work and the closest most people come to a leisure class existence – but it also refers back to work as paid out of income and functioning as recreation for work.

SEE ALSO: Celebrity and Celetoid; Celebrity Culture; Conspicuous Consumption; Consumption; Consumption, Fashion and; Consumption, Mass Consumption, and Consumer Culture; Consumption, Tourism and; Leisure; Leisure, Aging and; Unemployment; Veblen, Thorstein

REFERENCES AND SUGGESTED READINGS

Bourdieu, P. (1979) *La Distinction*. Minuit, Paris.
Cross, G. (1993) *Time and Money*. Routledge, London.
Gileard, C. & Higgs, P. (2000) *Cultures of Ageing*. Pearson, London.
Jahoda, M. et al. (1972) *Marienthal*. Tavistock, London.
Linder, S. (1970) *The Harried Leisure Class*. Columbia University Press, New York.
Mac Cannell, D. (1976) *The Tourist: A New Theory of the Leisure Class*. Schocken, New York.
Michelon, L. C. (1954) The New Leisure Class. *American Journal of Sociology* 59(4): 371–8.
Rojek, C. (2000) Leisure and the Rich Today: Veblen's Thesis After a Century. *Leisure Studies* 19: 1–15.
Seabrook, J. (1988) *The Leisure Society*. Blackwell, Oxford.
Urry, J. (1990) *The Tourist Gaze*. Sage, London.
Veblen, T. (1899) *The Theory of the Leisure Class*. Macmillan, New York.

leisure, popular culture and

Robert A. Stebbins

Mukerji and Schudson (1991: 3) define popular culture as a widely shared set of beliefs and practices that people use to organize certain objects, these objects also being part of that culture. This intentionally general definition (formulated to avoid terminological haggling) encompasses folk beliefs, practices, and objects generated in political and commercial centers. It also includes the handful of elite cultural forms that have, by curious quirk of fate, managed to become popular.

Popular culture includes, in broadest scope, any cultural item that has achieved popularity, or that has developed a mass public. Given this definition, one might be tempted to say that leisure and popular culture are close to being identical, if not, in fact, identical. Yet numerous popular artifacts and practices exist that are decidedly not leisurely, among them petrol, toothpaste, queuing, and paying income tax. Meanwhile, some activities people do for leisure are hardly popular, including collecting rare paintings, climbing Mount Everest, raising snakes, and playing string quartets. The limited interest in bungee jumping and sadomasochistic pornography shows that even hedonic leisure occasionally fails to win mass appeal. And, finally, some popular culture is disagreeable enough for many people to be anything but leisure for them. That happens when, for example, they are unable to escape obnoxious advertising or the repulsive habits of others (e.g., smoking, for many non-smokers; boom box music, for the unappreciative; outlandish dress and bodily decoration, for those not given to in-group fashion).

THE LEISURE FRAMEWORK

Leisure is uncoerced activity undertaken during free time. Uncoerced activity is something people evidently want to do and, at a personally satisfying level using their own abilities and resources, succeed in doing. Further, as Kaplan (1960: 22–5) noted, leisure is the antithesis of work and encompasses a range of activity running from inconsequence and insignificance to weightiness and importance.

This observation about the range of leisure activity suggests that leisure is by no means cut entirely from the same cloth, a condition that any exploration of the relationship between leisure and popular culture should never lose sight of. For instance, as will become evident, the vast majority of popular leisure activities can be qualified as casual rather than serious leisure. Nonetheless, we look first at serious leisure.

SERIOUS LEISURE

Serious leisure is systematic pursuit of an amateur, hobbyist, or volunteer activity that participants find so substantial, interesting, and fulfilling that, in the typical case, they launch themselves on a (leisure) career centered on acquiring and expressing its special skills, knowledge, and experience (Stebbins 1992: 3). The term was coined years ago (Stebbins 1982) following the way in which the people Stebbins had been interviewing and observing since the early 1970s defined the importance of these three kinds of activity in their everyday lives. The adjective "serious" (a word his respondents often used) embodies such qualities as earnestness, sincerity, importance, and carefulness, rather than gravity, solemnity, joylessness, distress, and anxiety. Although the second set of terms occasionally describes serious leisure events, the terms are uncharacteristic of them and fail to nullify, or, in many cases, even dilute, the overall deep fulfillment gained by the participants. The idea of "career" in this definition follows sociological tradition, where careers are seen as available in all substantial, complex roles, including those in leisure. Finally, serious leisure, as will be made clear shortly, is distinct from casual leisure.

Amateurs are found in art, science, sport, and entertainment, where they are invariably linked in a variety of ways with professional counterparts. The two can be distinguished descriptively, in that the activity in question constitutes a livelihood for professionals but not amateurs. Furthermore, professionals work full-time at the activity whereas amateurs pursue it part-time. Hobbyists lack this professional alter ego, suggesting that, historically, all amateurs were hobbyists before their fields professionalized. Both types are drawn to their leisure pursuits significantly more by self-interest than by altruism, whereas volunteers engage in activities requiring a more or less equal blend of these two motives. That is, volunteering is uncoerced help offered either formally or informally with no or, at most, token pay and done for the benefit of both other people and the volunteer (Stebbins 2001a: ch. 4).

Hobbyists are classified according to five categories: collectors, makers and tinkerers, activity participants (in non-competitive, rule-based pursuits such as fishing and barbershop singing), players of sports and games (in competitive, rule-based activities with no professional counterparts like long-distance running and competitive swimming), and enthusiasts of the liberal arts hobbies. The rules guiding non-competitive, rule-based pursuits are, for the most part, either subcultural (informal) or regulatory (formal). Thus, seasoned hikers in Canada's Rocky Mountains know they should, for example, stay on established trails, pack out all garbage, be prepared for changes in weather, and make noise to scare off bears. Liberal arts hobbyists are enamored of the systematic acquisition of knowledge for its own sake. Many accomplish this by reading voraciously in, for example, a field of art, sport, cuisine, language, culture, history, science, philosophy, politics, or literature (Stebbins 1994).

Serious leisure is further defined by a set of distinctive qualities, qualities uniformly found among its amateurs, hobbyists, and volunteers (Stebbins 1992: 6–8). One is the occasional need to *persevere* at the core activity to continue experiencing there the same level of fulfillment. Another is the opportunity to follow a *career* (in a leisure role) in the endeavor, a career shaped by its own special contingencies, turning points, and stages of achievement and involvement. Third, serious leisure is further distinguished by the requirement that its enthusiasts make significant *personal effort* based on specially acquired knowledge, training, or skill and, indeed at times, all three.

The fourth quality is the numerous *durable benefits* or tangible, salutary outcomes such activity has for its participants. They include self-fulfillment, self-enrichment, self-expression, regeneration or renewal of self, feelings of accomplishment, enhancement of self-image, social interaction and sense of belonging, and lasting physical products of the activity (e.g., a painting, scientific paper, piece of furniture). A further benefit – self-gratification, or pure fun, which is by far the most evanescent benefit in this list – is also enjoyed by casual leisure participants. The possibility of realizing such benefits becomes a powerful goal in serious leisure.

Fifth, serious leisure is distinguished by a *unique ethos* that emerges in association with each expression of it. At the core of this ethos is the special social world that begins to take shape when enthusiasts in a particular field pursue substantial shared interests over many years. According to Unruh (1980), every social world has its characteristic groups, events, routines, practices, and organizations. Diffuse and amorphous, it is held together, to an important degree, by semiformal, or mediated, communication. The sixth quality – *distinctive identity* – springs from the fact of the other five distinctive qualities. Participants in serious leisure tend to identify strongly with their chosen pursuits.

Relatively few people – by the author's admittedly impressionistic estimate, no more than 20 percent of the adult population in the typical western society – take up a form of serious leisure. Its requirements of effort, commitment, perseverance, deferred gratification, and so on are too overwhelming and offputting for most people in the modern age. Casual leisure is easier to partake of, and therefore much more susceptible to becoming popular.

CASUAL LEISURE

Casual leisure is immediately intrinsically rewarding, relatively short-lived pleasurable activity requiring little or no special training to enjoy it. It is fundamentally hedonic, engaged in for the significant level of pure enjoyment, or pleasure, found there. Stebbins coined the term in the same conceptual statement about serious leisure (Stebbins 1982), his object at the time being to further define serious leisure by showing what it is not. So continuing in that vein, he noted that casual leisure is considerably less substantial and offers no career of the sort found in serious leisure. Yet, subsequently, it became evident that casual leisure needed a conceptual statement of its own (see Stebbins 1997, 2001b).

Eight types of casual leisure have so far been identified, seven of which are also common items of western popular culture. They include *play* (e.g., dabbling at the guitar); *relaxation* (e.g., napping, strolling, people watching); *passive entertainment* (e.g., watching commercial TV, reading trade books, listening to popular music); *active entertainment* (e.g., playing popular games of chance, card games, party games); *sociable conversation* (e.g., held over coffee, drinks); and *sensory stimulation* (e.g., sightseeing, dining at restaurants, drinking at pubs/bars). The seventh type – *pleasurable aerobic activity* (Stebbins 2004b) – finds its most popular expression in personal exercise aerobics, as pursued collectively in formal classes or individually following a television program or videotaped routine as a guide. *Casual volunteering* (a parallel to career volunteering) has yet to generate a popular form, and may never do so.

Furthermore, it is likely that people go in for the different types of casual leisure in combinations of two and three at least as often as they do them separately. For instance, every type can be relaxing, producing in this fashion play–relaxation, passive entertainment–relaxation, and so on. Various combinations of play and sensory stimulation are also possible, as in experimenting with drug use, sexual activity, and thrill seeking in movement. Additionally, sociable conversation accompanies some sessions of sensory stimulation (e.g., drug use, curiosity seeking, display of beauty) as well as some sessions of relaxation and active and passive entertainment, although such conversation normally tends to be rather truncated in the latter two.

Notwithstanding its hedonic nature, casual leisure is by no means wholly frivolous, given that some clear costs and benefits accrue from pursuing it. Moreover, unlike the evanescent hedonism of casual leisure itself, these costs and benefits are enduring. The benefits include serendipitous creativity and discovery in play, regeneration from earlier intense activity, and development and maintenance of interpersonal relationships (Stebbins 2001b). Some of its costs root in excessive casual leisure or lack of variety as manifested in boredom or lack of time for leisure activities that contribute to self through acquisition of skills, knowledge, and experience (i.e., serious leisure). Moreover, casual leisure is alone unlikely to produce a distinctive leisure identity.

Some casual leisure is deviant, even if most of the time the community tolerates such activity (Stebbins 1996b: 3–4; Rojek 1999). Tolerable deviance undertaken for pleasure – as casual leisure – encompasses a range of deviant sexual activities including cross-dressing, homosexuality, watching sex (e.g., striptease, pornographic films), and swinging and group sex. Heavy drinking and gambling, but not their more seriously regarded cousins alcoholism and compulsive gambling, are also tolerably deviant and hence forms of casual leisure, as are the use of cannabis and the illicit, pleasurable use of certain prescription drugs. Social nudism has also been analyzed according to the tolerable deviance perspective (see Stebbins 1996b: chs. 3–7, 9). Yet the very definition of these forms as deviant prevents them from being conceived of as popular culture, while pointing to yet another area where leisure and popular culture cannot be considered identical phenomena.

POPULAR CULTURE: CONSUMPTION/ PRODUCTION

Discussion so far suggests that much of casual leisure can be further understood as *consumption* of particular kinds of popular culture. Indeed, the relationship between leisure and popular culture is much more complicated than acknowledged to this point, in that some people also pursue certain forms of serious leisure (and, we shall see, remunerative work) precisely because they want to *produce* such culture. Table 1 describes this new, more complicated relationship, as expressed along two dimensions: work/leisure and consumption/production.

Both modern common sense and conventional academic wisdom tend to treat work and leisure as though they were two separate worlds, which, however, sometimes fails to jibe with the facts (Stebbins 2004a). Cell 1 of Table 1 directly confronts this misconception by introducing the idea of "occupational devotion." Occupational devotion is a strong, positive attachment to a form of self-enhancing work. Here, where there is high sense of achievement and intense attraction to the core activity (set of tasks), the line between such work and leisure is virtually erased (Stebbins 2004a: 2–6). "Occupational devotees" express this devotion through their "devotee work." In terms of the present discussion, popular culture workers meeting the criteria of occupational devotion can be said to be both consumers and producers of their popular culture. Examples include pop music stars who find deep fulfillment while simultaneously making and listening to their music, and commercial painters, writers, and filmmakers who, as they produce their works, enjoy the same kind of aesthetic experience.

The professional work considered in cell 2 is, to be sure, devotee work, but emphasis in this cell is on how popular culture is produced rather than on how it is consumed. Here the reigning conceptual separation of work and leisure is both evident and legitimate. As for cell 3, it needs no additional explanation beyond what was said about casual leisure in the preceding section.

Cell 4 in Table 1 shows that some serious leisure is, in fact, significantly related to popular culture, albeit through production rather than consumption of such culture. Amateur sport and entertainment are two main arenas where this occurs, as seen, for example, in entertainment magic (Stebbins 1993), stand-up comedy (Stebbins 1990), collegiate football (Gibson et al. 2002), and mass media-covered marathon running (Wilson 1995). Popular displays of hobbyist activities include model railroad exhibitions, barbershop shows (Stebbins 1996a), quilt fairs (King 2001), and the manifold competitions in sport that attract large numbers of spectators (e.g., alpine skiing, speed skating, auto racing, bicycle racing). One

Table 1 Relationship of leisure and popular culture.

Popular culture	*Consumption of popular culture*	*Production of popular culture*
As work	(1) Devotee work in sport and entertainment	(2) Professional work (full- and part-time) in sport and entertainment
As leisure	(3) Casual leisure (7 types)	(4) Amateur sport and entertainment, hobbies (displayable forms)

important condition that any serious leisure activity must meet if it is to be consumed as popular culture is its capacity for public display. The liberal arts hobbies as well as some of the collecting hobbies and some of the sports and games (e.g., bridge, chess, marathon running, mountain climbing) lack this capacity and hence cannot, at least in their present form, enter the realm of popular culture.

Volunteering occupies an indeterminate position in all this. Of the three types of serious leisure, it quite possibly draws the largest number of participants (no quantitative comparative data are available). It is also much talked about these days for its key role in creating and maintaining civil society and for its capacity to fill the gap left by business and government through their ongoing failure to deliver needed community services. Yet, apart from volunteering to help organize and run certain popular sports and arts events (e.g., Olympic Games, major arts festivals) – classifiable as an indirect contribution to producing these events – volunteering would appear to be yet another area where leisure and popular culture must be regarded as separate phenomena.

SEE ALSO: Consumption, Fashion and; Culture Industries; Culture, Production of; Deviance; Film; Health Lifestyles; Infotainment; Leisure; Leisure, Aging and; Lifestyle; Lifestyle Consumption; Music; Music and Media; Popular Culture; Popular Culture Forms; Pornography and Erotica; Sport, Amateur

REFERENCES AND SUGGESTED READINGS

Gibson, H., Willming, C., & Holdnak, A. (2002) "We're Gators ... Not Just Gator Fans": Serious Leisure and University of Florida Football. *Journal of Leisure Research* 34: 397–425.

Kaplan, M. (1960) *Leisure in America*. Wiley, New York.

King, F. L. (2001) Social Dynamics of Quilting. *World Leisure Journal* 43: 26–9.

Mukerji, C. & Schudson, M. (1991) Introduction: Rethinking Popular Culture. In: Mukerji, C. & Schudson, M. (Eds.), *Rethinking Popular Culture: Contemporary Perspectives in Cultural Studies*. University of California Press, Berkeley, pp. 1–62.

Rojek, C. (1999) Deviant Leisure: The Dark Side of Free-Time Activity. In: Jackson, E. L. & Burton, T. L. (Eds.), *Leisure Studies: Prospects for the Twenty-First Century*. Venture, State College, PA, pp. 81–96.

Stebbins, R. A. (1982) Serious Leisure: A Conceptual Statement. *Pacific Sociological Review* 25: 251–72.

Stebbins, R. A. (1990) *The Laugh-Makers: Stand-Up Comedy as Art, Business, and Lifestyle*. McGill-Queen's University Press, Montreal and Kingston.

Stebbins, R. A. (1992) *Amateurs, Professionals, and Serious Leisure*. McGill-Queen's University Press, Montreal and Kingston.

Stebbins, R. A. (1993) *Career, Culture, and Social Psychology in a Variety Art: The Magician*. Krieger, Malabar.

Stebbins, R. A. (1994) The Liberal Arts Hobbies: A Neglected Subtype of Serious Leisure. *Loisir et Société/Society and Leisure* 16: 173–86.

Stebbins, R. A. (1996a) *The Barbershop Singer: Inside the Social World of a Musical Hobby*. University of Toronto Press, Toronto.

Stebbins, R. A. (1996b) *Tolerable Differences: Living with Deviance*, 2nd edn. McGraw-Hill Ryerson, Toronto.

Stebbins, R. A. (1997) Casual Leisure: A Conceptual Statement. *Leisure Studies* 16: 17–25.

Stebbins, R. A. (2001a) *New Directions in the Theory and Research of Serious Leisure*. Mellen Studies in Sociology, Vol. 28. Edwin Mellen, Lewiston.

Stebbins, R. A. (2001b) The Costs and Benefits of Hedonism: Some Consequences of Taking Casual Leisure Seriously. *Leisure Studies* 20: 305–9.

Stebbins, R. A. (2004a) *Between Work and Leisure: The Common Ground of Two Separate Worlds*. Transaction, New Brunswick.

Stebbins, R. A. (2004b) Pleasurable Aerobic Activity: A Type of Casual Leisure with Salubrious Implications. *World Leisure Journal* 46(4): 55–8.

Unruh, D. (1980) The Nature of Social Worlds. *Pacific Sociological Review* 23: 271–96.

Wilson, K. (1995) Olympians or Lemmings? The Postmodernist Fun Run. *Leisure Studies* 14: 174–85.

Lemert, Edwin M. (1912–96)

Robert A. Stebbins

Edwin M. Lemert was born in Cincinnati, Ohio. He received his BA in sociology from Miami University (1934) and his doctorate from Ohio State University (1939), specializing in sociology and anthropology. He taught briefly at Kent State and Western Michigan Universities. In 1943 he moved to the University of California at Los Angeles, and in 1953 to the University of California at Davis, from which, in 1980, he retired as Professor Emeritus. After formal retirement Lemert worked almost daily in his university office, writing scholarly material until his death in 1996.

Lemert is widely recognized for his pioneering work on labeling theory in the study of deviant behavior, which he called societal reaction theory. He preferred this title because the social or community reaction to deviance in its midst formed a central feature of his perspective. His classic statement of this approach appeared in *Social Pathology: A Systematic Approach to the Theory of Sociopathic Behavior* (1951). His other prominent books were *Social Action and Legal Change* (1970); *Instead of Court: Diversion in Juvenile Justice* (1971); and *Human Deviance, Social Problems, and Social Control* (1972). The latter comprised a collection of his most significant papers to that time. It showcased his extraordinary breadth of interests, running from alcoholism through mental disorder to folklore, speech defects, and check forgery.

Lemert's theory of sociopathic behavior, set out in *Social Pathology*, rests on three central processes. The first is *differentiation*, which refers to the fact that people differ, sometimes deviate, from average characteristics of the population in which they are found and in which they interact with other people. The second process is the *societal reaction* toward the deviance observed, a reaction that includes expressive feelings as well as action directed toward its control. The third process is *individuation*, or the manifestation of the causes of deviance in individuals, which includes how they come to terms with the deviance. This latter process has become the core of modern labeling theory. More particularly, individuation is best understood by looking at the course of events and processes associated with *primary deviation* (deviant behavior that is normalized by the person) and *secondary deviation* (behavior enacted in response to problems caused by the societal reaction). The two types of deviation and their interrelationship foreshadowed the concept of deviant career, formally introduced 12 years later by Becker (1963). Lemert was

also the first to examine the role of stigma in the life of deviants – a precondition of secondary deviation and one later explored in detail by Goffman (1963).

SEE ALSO: Crime; Deviance; Deviance, Theories of; Deviant Careers; Goffman, Erving; Labeling; Labeling Theory; Social Control

REFERENCES AND SUGGESTED READINGS

Becker, H. S. (1963) *Outsiders*. Free Press, New York.
Goffman, E. (1963) *Stigma: Notes on the Management of Spoiled Identity*. Prentice-Hall, Englewood Cliffs, NJ.
Lemert, E. M. (2000) *Crime and Deviance: Essays and Innovations of Edwin M. Lemert*. Ed. C. C. Lemert & M. Winter. Rowman & Littlefield, Chicago.

lesbian feminism

Eve Shapiro

Lesbian feminism is a political and philosophical strand of feminism that emerged in the US, Canada, and Britain in the 1970s. It holds as central tenets that heterosexuality is the seat of patriarchal power; lesbianism is a political choice and not an essential identity; and lesbians occupy a unique and empowered position vis-à-vis sexism and patriarchy because they do not rely on men for emotional, financial, or sexual attention and support. Lesbian feminist ideas, writings, and activism informed and guided both feminist and lesbian movements throughout the 1970s and into the 1980s, and have continued to shape academic theorizing and political organizing to this day. As lesbian feminism evolved, several ideological variations emerged including cultural feminism and separatist feminism.

THE WOMAN-IDENTIFIED WOMAN

As Echols (1989) examined in *Daring To Be Bad*, lesbian feminism developed out of radical feminism in reaction to sexism within gay liberation movements and homophobia within feminist movements of the 1960s. Sparked by Betty Friedan's 1970 characterization of lesbians as the "lavender menace" and an impediment to the National Organization for Women's mission and to the credibility of the feminist movement, lesbians began to theorize and advocate inclusion and recognition from feminist movements. Out of the ensuing debates, groups like the New York-based "Radicalesbians," originally known as "Lavender Menace," and the Washington, DC-based "Furies" formed. These early lesbian feminist groups quickly articulated a lesbian-centered critique of society, sexism, and feminism.

In "The Woman Identified Woman" (1970), the first political statement of the lesbian feminist movement, the Radicalesbians laid out an argument about the construction of sexual identity categories like lesbian and their links to heteronormativity and patriarchy. Radicalesbians argued that "lesbian" as an identity was not just a sexual object choice, but rather a chosen identity that was comprised of a continuum of "women-identified women." Defining lesbian feminism as central to feminism, "The Woman Identified Woman" and other early writings established sexuality as a key vector of oppression and integrated these critiques into broader feminist political ideology and burgeoning feminist academic theorizing. One common lesbian feminist slogan of the time, attributed to Ti-Grace Atkinson and drawn from Jill Johnston's (1973) theorizing in *Lesbian Nation*, was "feminism is the theory and lesbianism is the practice." The implication of this statement was that feminist theorizing demanded a woman-centered focus and that this woman-identified approach was what constituted a "lesbian." Also implied is the notion that identifying as a lesbian was at the least a political choice, if not a political responsibility, for feminists. Contrary to other feminist ideological approaches that ignored sexuality, silenced lesbians, and argued that lesbian inclusion threatened the viability of the whole movement, lesbian feminism positioned lesbians at the center of a feminist liberation movement.

THE LESBIAN CONTINUUM

Approaching lesbian as a political identity required a radical redefinition of lesbian. In "Compulsory Heterosexuality and Lesbian Existence," one of the most important texts of lesbian feminist theorizing, Adrienne Rich (1980) theorized the connections between heterosexuality and patriarchy, argued for the reclamation of an erased lesbian history across cultures and times, and discussed in detail the concept of the "lesbian continuum." What Rich articulated, and what lesbian feminism organized around, was the idea that because sexuality was a socially constructed tool of patriarchy, all women had the power to reclaim the term lesbian in an effort to resist patriarchal dominance. Expanding lesbian beyond a self-identified marker of sexuality to include women who identified themselves sexually, spiritually, emotionally, *or* politically with other women, Rich argued that there was a lesbian continuum that opened up space for *all* women to be lesbians. Lesbian feminist ideology held that this was the cornerstone of dismantling patriarchy and gaining gender equity.

Elaborating her argument, Rich positioned the erasure of lesbian history as the erasure of a history of resistance to male domination and compulsory heterosexuality, and argued this erasure was necessary for the maintenance of patriarchal power. Other writers further theorized and supported the broadening of "lesbian" in their own work. Lillian Faderman's book *Surpassing the Love of Men: Romantic Friendship and Love Between Women from the Renaissance to the Present* (1991) was a critical text in reclaiming a lost history of women-identified women. Building on Rich's argument that woman identification had been erased in an effort to subordinate women, Faderman argued the long history of lesbian existence, supported by evidence of both emotional and physical intimacy between women across cultures and time periods.

Ideologically, the "lesbian continuum" fostered a belief for many white lesbian feminists that a shared woman identification united all women regardless of race, class, nation, or sexuality. In other words, gender became the primary axis of both oppression and resistance. Extension of this argument can be seen in many academic and movement texts. For example, writer and theologian Mary Daly has argued over the past 25 years for a woman-centric analytical approach, and theoretical traditions like standpoint epistemology draw on a belief in a shared "women's standpoint."

Alongside theoretical developments, lesbian feminist ideology promoted critiques of existing institutions and alternative women-centered institutions. Two related but distinct branches emerged within lesbian feminism in the 1970s. One branch often referred to as cultural feminism focused on developing and fostering woman-centered institutions. The other – lesbian separatism – took this a step further and argued for a complete withdrawal from men and male-dominated institutions.

CULTURAL FEMINISM

Out of critiques of patriarchal society and calls for a woman-identified life, lesbian feminists began advocating for and developing woman-identified counterinstitutions. They founded feminist bookstores in most cities, and publishing houses and presses like Naiad Press and Spinsters Ink, auto-shops, health collectives, and other institutions. In addition, lesbian feminist communities developed alternative cultural products like goddess-focused spiritualities, music labels like Olivia, and a genre of women's music with lesbian feminist artists like Ferron and Cris Williamson, Tret Fure, and Holly Near. Extending a critique of masculinist language lesbian feminism developed alternative language like womyn, wimmin, and wombmoon, and invented non-patrinomial naming traditions, renaming themselves with woman-focused names like Dykewomon. Lesbian feminist activists developed new repertoires including zaps, which were symbolic protests aimed at cultural/ideological change as much as at political reform. Like radical feminism, lesbian feminists argued for a refocusing on women's sexuality independent from heterosexual intercourse and/or the male gaze. Part of being a woman-identified woman meant rejecting dominant beauty and fashion norms as patriarchal, and adopting an androgynous,

makeup-free appearance. This style, characterized by flannel, jeans, sandals, and short hair, was often referred to as "the uniform" and was the dominant lesbian feminist aesthetic through the 1970s and 1980s.

This new ideological focus on gendered beauty standards and sexuality led to a critique of both the existing butch/femme lesbian culture and the emerging sex radical lesbian communities. Lesbian feminism characterized butch/femme culture as an oppressive mimicry of sexist and misogynist heterosexual gender relations. Similarly, the increasingly visible sex radical community, which included an emergent women's sadomasochism community and sex worker community, was characterized as replicating, enacting, and perpetuating violence against women. These debates, referred to as the lesbian sex wars, came to a head at the 1982 "The Scholar and the Feminist IX: Towards a Politics of Sexuality," where lesbian feminists battled each other throughout the conference over the meaning and politics of sexuality (Vance 1984).

Radical feminists both in feminist communities and in academic theorizing critiqued lesbian feminist cultural development as escapism and dubbed this "cultural feminism" counterproductive to struggles for political change. Based on field studies of 14 lesbian feminist communities Taylor and Whittier (1992) challenged this depiction and argued that the development of women's culture within lesbian feminism was critical in sustaining feminist activism during the increasing conservatism of the 1980s and 1990s. Exploring the lesbian feminist focus on personal and cultural change as well as political change, Taylor and Whittier conclude that "cultural feminism," or, as they prefer, lesbian feminist community, signaled the development of new social movement forms and tactics. The cultural products, institutions, and norms that emerged in the 1970s within lesbian feminist communities sustained and enabled these movements and movement organizations over the past 30 years.

LESBIAN SEPARATISM

Charlotte Bunch, a writer and member of the "Furies," a lesbian feminist collective of writers and activists, argued in 1972 that lesbianism is not just a political choice, but that women *must* be both lesbian and feminist to fight patriarchy and end sexism. The Furies was a short-lived Washington, DC collective (1971–2) that was profoundly influential and included writers like Charlotte Bunch and Rita Mae Brown, and activists like Ginny Berson, who went on to found Olivia Records. Unlike cultural lesbian feminist groups, however, separatist groups believed that lesbians needed to remove themselves from male-dominated society in order to effect significant social change. Like cultural feminism, separatism advocated the creation of alternative woman-oriented institutions, but went further to argue that lesbians needed to separate themselves from both men *and* heterosexual women. Many separatists argued that heterosexual women were "sleeping with the enemy" and therefore were part of the problem, not the solution. This separatist ideology encouraged the creation of women-only spaces like the Michigan Women's Music Festival as well as more permanent women's communities in rural areas. Women's communes and communities were founded across the United States, Australia, and England and many, like Womanshare in Oregon and Camp Sister-Spirit in rural Mississippi, continue to exist today.

SCHOLARSHIP

Two bodies of research have emerged in relation to lesbian feminism. Sociological research about lesbian feminist movements, culture, and communities has developed in the fields of gender studies, sexuality studies, and social movements. Additionally, for many academics lesbian feminist ideologies and beliefs were incorporated into their work, and lesbian feminist commitments guided research topics and approaches.

Many scholars like Adrienne Rich, Gayle Rubin, Charlotte Bunch, and Lillian Faderman merged academic theorizing and lesbian feminist ideology in the late 1970s and early 1980s, allowing one to inform the other. Lesbian feminist gendered critiques and theorizing around heterosexuality, patriarchy, and feminism were a catalyst for and informed theoretical developments in nascent gender and sexuality

studies. Simultaneously, the woman identification associated with lesbian feminism encouraged research on and by women and about women's lives across disciplines including history, literary studies, and the social sciences. For women of color academics like Barbara Smith and Audre Lorde, the lack of theorizing around race in both academic and activist communities led to a simultaneous and interconnected critique that was central in sparking further research and writing by women of color within lesbian feminist movements, and in the incorporation of race in lesbian feminist analysis and scholarship.

Alongside scholarship informed by lesbian feminist movements was the emergence of research about lesbian feminist movements. Contrary to earlier research on "deviant" sexuality which took an individualist and pathological approach, many sociologists began in the 1980s and 1990s to examine lesbian communities in general, and lesbian feminism more specifically, through cultural studies, gender studies, and social movements lenses. Two of the first texts to reexamine lesbian feminist movements were Taylor and Rupp (1993) and Nancy Whittier's *Feminist Generations* (1995). These studies examined the role of political ideology and collective identity within lesbian feminist communities and argued that lesbian identity needed to be examined as socially constructed within the context of social and political communities. Taylor and Rupp challenged the dismissal of culture and cultural products and argued that culture was not only central to the success and sustenance of lesbian feminist movements, but that it also plays an important role in social movements more broadly. Based on an in-depth case study of lesbian feminist communities in Columbus, Ohio, Whittier found that the meaning of feminism and the collective identity among lesbian feminists changed over time for participants. Arlene Stein (1997) extended this analysis and argued that lesbian feminism was a product of the Cold War and 1960s liberation movements. Lesbian feminism, in turn, produced new discourses about lesbian identity, feminism, and community. These new lesbian feminist discourses, according to Stein, have played crucial roles in shaping contemporary feminist and lesbian movements. Scholars like Suzanne Staggenborg have furthered these analyses and approached lesbian feminism from a social movements perspective.

CRITIQUES

There have been three main critiques of lesbian feminist movements and theorizing since the 1970s. Perhaps the most significant critique emerged alongside lesbian feminism in the 1970s from women of color and poor women. Lesbian feminist ideology relies on an essential shared womanhood that transcends other differences and situates gender as the primary vector of oppression in society. For women of color and poor women who experienced gender, class, and race as interconnected identities and oppressions, this ideology erased and invalidated their experiences. In *This Bridge Called My Back* (Anzaldúa & Moraga 1981), women of color spoke about exclusion within lesbian feminist communities and advocated for new, integrative activist and academic approaches. More recently, notions of essential womanhood (and exclusion based on this) have also been challenged by transgender communities. Transgender women continue to argue for a place within lesbian feminist and separatist spaces like Michigan Women's Music Festival, most of which maintain "woman-born-woman" policies.

Alongside critiques of essentialist arguments at the root of lesbian feminist ideology, sex radical communities have continued to challenge the rigid sexual politics within lesbian feminist communities. This rift between "pro-sex" and "anti-sex" feminists has remained volatile and has been played out in academic circles as well as in lesbian feminist communities through boycotts and protests of sex-positive writers and activists like Patrick (formerly Pat) Califia, and legislative battles over anti-pornography legislation spearheaded by Andrea Dworkin and Catherine MacKinnon.

Finally, the emergence of queer theory in the 1990s has challenged lesbian feminist theoretical and analytical approaches to gender, sexuality, and inequality. The focus in queer theory on decentering identity and focusing on sexual power broadly instead of on patriarchy or heterosexism has led to a dismissal of much of lesbian feminist research and critique of lesbian feminist ideology as outdated. As many feminists have argued, however, identity politics have been and continue to be central to lesbian and feminist organizing and community building. Despite these criticisms, lesbian feminism continues to influence contemporary feminist and lesbian movements and many of the institutions founded in the 1970s and 1980s by lesbian feminist communities continue to thrive.

SEE ALSO: Cultural Feminism; Feminism; Feminism, First, Second, and Third Waves; Feminist Activism in Latin America; Gay and Lesbian Movement; Lesbianism; Radical Feminism; Sexualities and Culture Wars; Social Movements; Women's Movements

REFERENCES AND SUGGESTED READINGS

Douglas, C. A. (1990) *Love and Politics: Radical Feminist and Lesbian Theories*. Ism Press, San Francisco.

Echols, A. (1989) *Daring To Be Bad: Radical Feminism in America, 1967–1975*. University of Minnesota Press, Minneapolis.

Faderman, L. (1991) *Odd Girls and Twilight Lovers: A History of Lesbian Life in Twentieth-Century America*. Columbia University Press, New York.

Frye, M. (1992) Willful Virgin; or, Do You Have to Be a Lesbian to be a Feminist? In: *Willful Virgin: Essays in Feminism, 1976–1992*. The Crossing Press, New York, pp. 124–37.

Johnston, J. (1973) *Lesbian Nation: The Feminist Solution*. Simon & Schuster, New York.

Krieger, S. (1983) *The Mirror Dance*. Temple University Press, Philadelphia.

Lorde, A. (1984) *Sister, Outsider: Essays and Speeches*. The Crossing Press, New York.

Moraga, C. & Anzaldúa, G. (Eds.) (1981) *This Bridge Called My Back: Writings by Radical Women of Color*. Kitchen Table Press, New York.

Rich, A. (1980) Compulsory Heterosexuality and Lesbian Existence. *Signs: Journal of Women in Culture and Society* 5(4): 631–60.

Smith, D. (1987) Women's Perspective as a Radical Critique of Sociology. In: Harding, S. (Ed.), *Feminism and Methodology: Social Science Issues*. Indiana University Press, Bloomington, pp. 17–26.

Staggenborg, S., Eder, D., & Sudderth, L. (1995) The National Women's Music Festival: Collective Identity and Diversity in a Lesbian-Feminist

Community. *Journal of Contemporary Ethnography* 23(4): 485–515.

Stein, A. (1997) *Sex and Sensibility: Stories of a Lesbian Generation.* University of California Press, Berkeley.

Taylor, V. & Rupp, L. J. (1993) Women's Culture and Lesbian Feminist Activism: A Reconsideration of Cultural Feminism. *Signs* (Autumn).

Taylor, V. & Whittier, N. (1992) Collective Identity in Social Movement Communities: Lesbian Feminist Mobilization. In: Morris, A. & Mueller, C. (Eds.), *Frontiers in Social Movement Theory.* Yale University Press, New Haven, pp. 104–29.

Vance, C. (Ed.) (1984) *Pleasure and Danger: Exploring Female Sexuality.* Routledge, New York.

Walters, S. D. (1996) From Here to Queer: Radical Feminism, Postmodernism, and the Lesbian Menace (Or, Why Can't a Woman be More Like a Fag?). *Signs* 21(4): 830–69.

lesbian and gay families

Brian Heaphy

In the narrowest sense, the term "lesbian and gay family" refers to lesbian and gay individuals or same-sex couples and their children. The term is sometimes used to refer to same-sex partnerships or cohabiting relationships. In the broadest sense, the term can denote social networks that include lesbian or gay individuals and/or couples where some or all of the members self-define as "family." These latter arrangements have also been described as "surrogate," "friendship," or "chosen" families.

Lesbian and gay families have become high-profile social and political issues since the 1980s. They touch on a broad range of sociological themes to do with family life and social change, family diversity, and alternative family practices. The topics of lesbian and gay families and families of choice have played an important part in debates on the demise of traditional conceptions of family, the legitimacy of new family forms, and contemporary reconfigurations of family obligations, responsibilities, and care. Existing sociological work on the topics includes theorizing and research into the historical, social, and political forces that have facilitated the emergence of lesbian and gay families and families of choice; theoretical discussions of their social and political significance; and studies of the meanings, structures, and social practices associated with them at local levels.

Prior to the 1960s, homosexual relationships were subject to legal and social sanctions in societies and were culturally invisible. European and North American research on lesbian and gay families in the pre-1960s era suggests that they are best conceptualized as "surrogate" family forms, made up of adults who provided mutual comfort and support in the face of hostile social environments. During the 1960s and 1970s, the politics of sexual liberation opened up distinctive possibilities for the formation of lesbian and gay identities that challenged heterosexist ideologies. Research suggests that while surrogate families continued to be important for some lesbians and gay men, other arrangements began to emerge, including self-consciously alternative family forms. While surrogate and alternative arrangements provided emotional and practical supports to their adult members, the latter more frequently included children from previous heterosexual relationships, and were more likely to be influenced by feminist and other political critiques of the role of the family in the reproduction of gendered and sexual inequalities.

Several theorists have argued that the emergence of AIDS in the 1980s and political responses to it were key factors in shaping the current emphasis in lesbian and gay politics on family issues in Europe and North America. Initially, Moral Right responses to AIDS reinforced the historical construction of lesbians and gay men as a threat to the family. In the United Kingdom, for example, legislation was introduced in the late 1980s (commonly known as Section 28) that explicitly sought to ban the promotion by local authorities of homosexuality "as a pretended family relationship." Such interventions, however, had the reverse effect of mobilizing a lesbian and gay family-oriented politics. Some theorists have further argued that community-based caring responses to AIDS were ultimately to underscore the importance of family-type relationships for lesbians and gay men. This view has been criticized on the basis that it undermines the existence of non-heterosexual caring relationships that pre-existed AIDS.

It is more generally accepted that lesbian and gay community responses to AIDS facilitated the institution building and increased cultural and political confidence that were essential in making possible greater social tolerance, if not acceptance, of lesbian and gay families. This increased confidence has also been argued to be crucial in opening up a new family vision amongst lesbians and gay men. This, some argue, is clearly visible in the sharp rise in lesbian and gay individuals and couples who are choosing to become parents *as* lesbians and gay men. It is also evident in the ways in which lesbian and gay politics has become organized around family issues such as the rights to parent, adopt, and marry. It is further evident in ways in which lesbians and gay men are nowadays likely to include accepting members of family of origin in their chosen families.

While lesbian and gay families have long been of interest to scholars of sexualities, they have more recently come to the attention of sociologists of family life. This new interest is partly due to the current concern with family diversity and changing patterns of relating. Lesbian and gay families are now being explored for the insights they provide into the challenges and possibilities presented by detraditionalized family life. From this perspective, these family forms are studied for how they are structured and operate outside institutionalized norms and supports that have traditionally shaped "the" family. Because of the lack of gender-based differences in same-sex relationships, lesbian and gay families are also examined for the possibilities of organizing family without clearly defined gendered roles. A number of theorists have argued that because of the lack of gendered assumptions, lesbian and gay families are more likely to adopt a friendship model for relating, and operate according to an egalitarian ideal. Empirical studies that have set out to explore the meanings, structure, and practices of lesbian and gay families and families of choice suggest a complex picture.

Existing research indicates various traditions of the usage of the family terminology in non-heterosexual cultures, and the complex and fluid meanings that family has for individuals. North American research has indicated that parental terminology of "mother" and "father" has been used by younger lesbians and gay men

to refer to older, non-heterosexual friends and mentors in historically and contextually specific ways. The terms "brothers" and "sisters" have long been used by some lesbians and gay men to denote the affective and/or political significance of non-heterosexual friendship. The refrain of "we are family" has also been used in lesbian and gay political life to refer to the affective-political bonds that are perceived to underpin non-heterosexual communities. Despite these traditions, the research indicates that while many lesbians and gay men embrace the terminology of family to talk about partners and friends, others see it as only applicable to relationships based on caring for children. Others still view the terminology of the family with hostility, and are critical of the normalizing potential of its employment in relation to lesbian and gay life.

Studies indicate some considerable diversity in how lesbian and gay families are structured and constituted. However, lesbians and gay men generally appear to distinguish between the families they grew up with and the relationships they "choose" as adults. Family, when used to describe the latter, can include partners, ex-partners, children where they exist, friends, and certain members of family of origin. The inclusion of "given" kin is not automatic, and is usually dependent on the quality of the commitment and emotional bond. The research does suggest, however, that lesbians and gay men are increasingly likely to maintain committed relationships with at least some members of their family of origin. This is especially the case amongst lesbians and gay parents who wish to develop generational links between their children and the families/parents they grew up with.

A number of studies have explored the place, roles, and experience of children in lesbian and gay families. Until recently, such studies tended to be concerned with the implications of growing up in these family forms. Most of this research suggests that this experience is unlikely to have any discernible long-term impact on children's sense of well-being, social connectedness, or family or personal security. Because of the changing historical circumstances in which lesbians and gay men have become parents, most existing studies are of lesbian and gay families with children who were conceived through a parent's previous heterosexual relationship. Recent studies have, however, begun to focus on the experience of families with children, where same-sex couples, individuals, or friends have chosen to take advantage of recent opportunities to become parents through self- or assisted insemination, surrogacy, adoption, and fostering. Many of these studies have moved beyond the focus on children's experience to also explore the blurring of the boundaries between biological and social parenting and the negotiated nature of same-sex parenting.

The theme of negotiation has also emerged as an important one in research that has studied how lesbian and gay couples challenge or reproduce the norms and values traditionally associated with family life. Studies indicate that same-sex couples value core beliefs about emotional commitment and mutual care and support. However, they can also structure and "do" their relationships in ways that are self-consciously opposed to assumptions and norms in heterosexual couple life. One fairly consistent finding concerns the extent to which lesbian and gay couples tend to be more reflexive and democratic than their heterosexual counterparts. This appears especially to be the case in relation to the organization and negotiation of domestic duties. Studies suggest that because same-sex couples cannot assume domestic or partnership roles based on gender, there is more scope for the negotiation of couple practices. A number of studies have argued that this is indicative of an egalitarian ideal that is common amongst same-sex partners. This, in turn, has been argued to be rooted in the friendship ethos that underpins same-sex relationships, and is seen to open up creative possibilities for mutually satisfying relationships. Same-sex couple negotiations and creativity have also been studied in relation to the negotiability of monogamy as a marker for couple commitment. While monogamy tends to be assumed in heterosexual couples, same-sex couples tend to negotiate whether the relationship will be monogamous or not. Same-sex couples often have explicit ground rules to guide the operation of non-monogamous sexual relationships and to protect the primacy of the couple's emotional commitment. Sexual exclusivity is not, however, viewed as necessary or desirable for couple commitments or stability.

Friendship families have been regarded as the most creative form of lesbian and gay relationships and research has explored these as sources of emotional, economic, and social support. Most studies confirm the significance of these for emotional sustenance and various forms of material and social support. Some studies do suggest, however, that friendship families mostly provide a context for care in relation to "everyday" problems, and tend not to be relied upon in terms of long-term physical care. While research has documented the crucial role of friendship families in caring for people with AIDS in the 1980s and 1990s, and some small qualitative studies suggest they are important sources of practical support in times of other health crises, it appears that the friendship ethos underpinning these families can inform a strong sense of what constitutes appropriate levels of physical care. The friendship ethos, it is argued, emphasizes reciprocity and co-independence. This implies that an expectation of long-term physical care from friends can be viewed as inappropriate and undesirable. Long-term couple partners, on the other hand, are most often identified in research as the first choice as providers of care should it be needed. Some studies indicate that ex-partners can also have agreements to provide mutual care. A number of studies have, however, pointed out the difficulties partners and ex-partners can face in juggling work and other commitments with long-term caring commitments. This is especially the case where the caring role is not supported or recognized as legitimate by state agencies or employers.

The issue of care in lesbian and gay families raises a number of topics that could be fruitfully explored in future research, such as: the resilience or otherwise of lesbian and gay families as sources for care and support across the life course; the significance of children, friendship, and chosen families for supporting lesbians and gay men in later life; and the range of social and political factors that limit and enable the possibilities that lesbian and gay families have been said in theory to offer. Theory and research could also explore the implications for lesbian and gay families of their marginalization and/or normalization in different national, geographical, and social contexts, and the ways in which the challenges they face are common or otherwise to other "new" family forms.

SEE ALSO: AIDS, Sociology of; Cohabitation; Family Diversity; Gay and Lesbian Movement; Homosexuality; Intimacy; Same Sex Marriage/ Civil Unions

REFERENCES AND SUGGESTED READINGS

Ali, T. (1996) *We Are Family: Testimonies of Lesbian and Gay Parents.* Cassell, London and New York.

Dunne, G. (1997) *Lesbian Lifestyles.* Macmillan, London.

Heaphy, B., Donovan, C., & Weeks, J. (1998) "That's Like My Life": Researching Stories of Non-Heterosexual Relationships. *Sexualities* 1: 435–70.

Hicks, S. & Christensen, E. H. (1998) *Lesbian and Gay Fostering and Adoption: Extraordinary yet Ordinary.* Jessica Kingsley, London.

Lewin, E. (1993) *Lesbian Mothers: Accounts of Gender in American Culture.* Cornell University Press, Ithaca, NY.

Nardi, P. (1999) *Gay Men's Friendships: Invincible Communities.* Chicago University Press, Chicago.

Tasker, F. L. & Golombok, S. (1997) *Growing Up in a Lesbian Family.* Guilford Press, New York.

Weeks, J., Heaphy, B., & Donovan, C. (2001) *Same-Sex Intimacies: Families of Choice and Other Life Experiments.* Routledge, London.

Weston, K. (1991) *Families We Choose: Lesbians, Gays, Kinship.* Columbia University Press, New York.

lesbianism

Tamsin Wilton

Although it is generally accepted that "lesbianism" refers to sexual contact between women, this is by no means an adequate definition. Indeed, it is not possible to provide such a definition. The complexities of the political economy of sexuality mean that the word is subject to continual contestation among many diverse interest groups, to the extent that there is not even agreement that sexual contact – or even desire – is necessarily definitional.

Lesbianism is equally subject to theoretical contestation, in particular between essentialists and constructionists. It is, therefore, something of an exemplary topic for demonstrating the political and theoretical processes at work within the social sciences more broadly, as well as being the commonly accepted descriptor for a group of women marginalized and subject to varying degrees of stigma and sanction because they prefer other women as their sexual partners.

There are two main strands of debate concerning the nature of lesbianism, the theoretical and the political. Both have their origins in the social processes which gave rise to the concept of lesbianism in the first place, so it is helpful to begin with a brief historical overview.

Etymologically, the word "lesbian" is of late nineteenth-century origin and refers to the island of Lesvos/Lesbos in the Greek archipelago where, in the classical period, the poet Sappho lived. Revered in her own time – Plato referred to her as "the tenth Muse" – examples of her poetry which have survived include fervent expressions of her passionate feelings for women. Love between women, therefore, became popularly known as Lesbian or Sapphic love, in the same allusive way that love between men was referred to as "Greek love."

The early sexologists employed "lesbianism" to mean "female homosexuality." This linguistic shift from using "Lesbian" as an adjective, a term which was allusive and euphemistic, to using "lesbianism" as a noun with pretensions to scientific accuracy exemplifies the theoretical and political shift toward the construct of homosexuality *as an innate condition.* It is this shift which Michel Foucault identified, in the first volume of *The History of Sexuality*, as marking the transition from ecclesiastical-juridical to medical constructions of sexuality. "The nineteenth-century homosexual," he concludes, "became a personage, a past, a case history, and a childhood, in addition to being a type of life, a life-form and a morphology, with an indiscreet anatomy and possibly a mysterious physiology" (1979: 43).

Lesbianism was initially approached by social scientists, in the 1950s and 1960s, as one of many forms of deviant behavior, and lesbians and gay men in most of the industrialized English-speaking West were studied in the context of a necessarily secretive underground subculture. As such, they tended to be presented as exemplary of Goffman's theories of stigma, and of primary and secondary deviance.

In Britain, this situation slowly changed following the 1957 publication of the Wolfenden Report, recommending the decriminalization of homosexuality. In 1968 the first key paper to offer an early social constructionist approach to sexuality, "The Homosexual Role," was published by British sociologist Mary McIntosh. McIntosh found biomedical claims for essentialism to be weak, and concluded that to ask whether homosexuality is innate or acquired is to ask the wrong question. She went on to argue that "the conception of homosexuality as a condition is, in itself, an object of study" (1981 [1968]: 31). It is arguable that her paper laid the foundations not only for the social constructionist model of sexuality but also for what later became known as queer theory, since her conclusion implies the need to problematize the taken-for-grantedness of heterosexuality.

Once the social constructionist standpoint is accepted, then, rather than ask questions such as "what is the incidence of lesbianism in the female population?" or "how have different cultures responded to their lesbian members?" we have to ask, "in whose interests is it to reproduce the idea of lesbianism, and what social and political functions does it perform?" This has meant that the social constructionist position has been of particular utility to feminist theorists, for whom the social control of female sexuality has been a key concern.

The essentialist/constructionist debates, between those who regarded same-sex behaviors as willfully chosen and those who believed they were symptomatic of an innate condition, became closely associated with two key opposing strands in lesbian and gay civil rights activism. Thus, within both essentialism and constructionism, there exist positively and negatively valued accounts of lesbianism. Within the essentialist position may be found medical scientists seeking an etiology, a definitive symptomatology, and (at least by implication) a cure, alongside lesbian and gay liberationists whose claims for human and civil rights are based on the notion that it is unethical to discriminate against a minority group on the basis of something over which they have no control.

Within the constructionist position there is radically polarized political disagreement between those for whom lesbian behaviors represent a threat to the social order and must be eradicated, and those who claim that it is an empowering and positive choice for women seeking to escape the emotional and political consequences of patriarchy.

Social constructionism has tended to be far less rigorously founded in empirical research than has essentialism, largely because it developed as a theoretical offshoot of poststructuralism and postmodernism. However, it is evidence-based, insofar as it draws upon historical texts and anthropological evidence, and McIntosh's paper is exemplary of this.

Of key importance to the sociology of sexuality in general, and of lesbianism in particular, has been the recognition that the relationship between sexual behaviors, desires, and identities is complex and may be contradictory. Here, most of the evidence comes from research done with gay men, including Laud Humphries's *Tearoom Trade* (1974), a ground-breaking study of men who have casual sex with other men, and later research carried out in the interests of HIV/AIDS prevention by groups such as Project Sigma. This body of research demonstrates that a heterosexual identity does not necessarily preclude same-sex activity, nor does a gay identity prevent men from engaging in heterosex.

Researchers have been less interested in lesbian identities and sexual behaviors, partly because sex between women carries very little risk of HIV transmission. There is also the complicating factor of lesbian feminism and, in particular, a radical lesbian feminist politics of the erotic. The renaissance of the women's movement in the 1960s and 1970s had profound consequences for lesbian theory and practice, two elements of which are of particular interest to sociologists. The first is the desexualization of lesbianism by a small group of revolutionary lesbian feminists – together with the vigorous contestation of that position by self-defined "sex-radical" lesbians such as Pat (later Patrick) Califia, Joan Nestle, and Dorothy Allison – and the second is the observation that a number of women did, indeed, make a conscious political choice to become lesbians. Some eventually returned to heterosexuality and others identified as celibate lesbian feminists. Others, however, entered into sexually active partnerships, thus changing their "sexual orientation" by an act of will, something which biomedical theories are unable to take account of.

Later research into lesbian lives and experiences demonstrates that many women "come out" as lesbian relatively late in life, after a significant period of heterosexual activity. Such findings do not, of course, automatically overturn essentialist claims, since the policing of female sexuality makes it likely that women who are "innately" lesbian might be effectively socialized into heternormativity by, for example, strong social pressures to marry and have children, and may thus not "discover" their "true nature" until something happens to make them question their assumptions. In addition, female sexuality is discursively constructed as emotional rather than pleasure-driven, and the hegemonic discourse of heterosexual sex represents men as sexually inept and women as difficult to arouse. This suggests that a woman who gains little pleasure from heterosexual activity is likely to regard this as normal, and this, too, may delay recognition of innate lesbianism.

However, detailed qualitative research using semi-structured interviews and focus groups has found that women may enter into lesbian relationships and take on a lesbian identity after many years of *successful* heterosexual relationships. Whilst some women report sexual and/or emotional unhappiness in their earlier heterosexual relationships, others report that they found heterosexuality to be physically and emotionally satisfying but that they prefer, for a variety of reasons, lesbian relationships. This body of research is relatively new, but seems likely to provide data which will make it increasingly difficult to maintain essentialist claims for female sexuality.

The development of feminist social science in the 1980s and 1990s incorporated research that paid attention to lesbian lives. Areas of interest were largely driven by the need to justify civil rights claims and to resist a particularly homophobic era in political life, represented in the UK by the government of Margaret Thatcher and in the US by the Christian Right and Reaganism. Researchers therefore looked at lesbian parenting, kinship and family formation, and the impact of homophobia on well-being. Such research played a significant part in, for example, the family courts, where it was increasingly accepted that lesbianism should not automatically result in women losing custody of their children.

The more theoretical research agenda included a specifically lesbian strand of critical and "high" theory. Lesbian academics began to produce theory from a position self-consciously marginal to the mainstream of what was (and largely continues to be) an unreflexively heteronormative social science. In the United States, lesbian-authored accounts of lesbian lives, experiences, and identities were often produced by women working outside formal academic institutions. In Britain, on the other hand, most lesbians undertaking such research did so within universities. Annabel Faraday's 1981 paper "Liberating Lesbian Research" critiqued the androcentricity of existing research, and set the tone for the next decade of British lesbian sociology. Lesbian psychologists Celia Kitzinger and Sue Wilkinson provoked an extremely defensive response when they challenged heterosexual feminist scholars to problematize their sexualities and reflect on the impact which their heterosexuality had on their feminist praxis. The resulting collection, *Heterosexuality: A Feminism and Psychology Reader* (1993), remains the only published work by heterosexual feminists critiquing their own sexuality. Shortly afterwards, Diane Richardson published *Theorizing Heterosexuality* (1996), a collection of papers by both lesbian and non-lesbian sociologists, and the "new" lesbian sociology was established.

Lesbian social science grew out of feminist theory, so it is not surprising that it followed a similar developmental trajectory. From early papers such as Faraday's, which wrote lesbians into existing research, developed work such as Tamsin Wilton's *Lesbian Studies: Setting an Agenda* (1995), which explored the intellectual and disciplinary lacunae resulting from lesbian invisibility in the academy, working from the assumption that "lesbian" was a theoretical position which might productively be adopted by any scholar, regardless of sexual preference. In her enormously influential book *Gender Trouble* (1999), Judith Butler drew upon the artifice of the drag queen to demonstrate that gender, and the sexual stereotypes with which it is associated, is performative rather than natural. *Gender Trouble* is generally regarded as the

Ur-text of queer theory, a theoretical position which problematizes all genders and all sexualities rather than simply non-normative variants.

With the (important) exception of Michel Foucault, the key queer theorists – Butler, Eve Sedgewick, Elizabeth Grosz, and others – have been lesbians who identify as feminist theorists. Since queer theory is primarily concerned with the gendering of sexualities (and vice versa), this is perhaps not surprising. Queer theory takes a social constructionist position as given. However, outside the rarefied atmosphere of universities, essentialist explanations for sexuality continue to dominate popular understandings of the subject.

The debate between essentialism and constructionism is more than merely academic. To this day, lesbianism is regarded by many as immoral or criminal, and punishment for engaging in lesbian behaviors – particularly, but not exclusively, in Islamic theocracies – may be severe. Imprisonment is not uncommon, and the death penalty is still enforced in several countries. In this context it is not surprising that activists have traditionally drawn upon essentialism, insisting that it is both irrational and unjust to penalize individuals for being who they are. It was for precisely such reasons that the early sexologists argued that lesbianism and male homosexuality were innate. English writer John Addington Symonds, summing up these debates for a British audience, argued that: "To deal with [homosexuals] according to your [legal] code is no less monstrous than if you were to punish the colour-blind, or the deaf and dumb, or albinoes, or crooked-back cripples" (1984 [1928]: 180). There is a mainstream in lesbian and gay political activism which adopts this position. Many lesbian feminists, however, take the opposite position and have argued that lesbianism represents the best kind of intimate relationship available to a woman, allowing her effectively to sidestep the psychological, cultural, and material restrictions imposed on women under male supremacy. From this political perspective, lesbianism is a choice open to all women, and it is rare to find an essentialist lesbian feminist.

One notable exception to this argument is offered by Monique Wittig who, in her 1981 paper "One Is Not Born a Woman," argues that lesbians are not women at all, since the word "woman" refers to membership of a class which stands in a specific relation to the class "man." Wittig's position might be thought of as a "strong" version of social constructionism, since she exempts lesbians from the social construct "woman" by reason of their lack of fit with the cultural and material processes which are implied by that construct.

The two extremes, essentialism and social constructionism, demarcate the political contestations which have continued to develop around "lesbianism" and which are, inevitably, key components in the ongoing social and cultural construction of female sexuality, whether lesbian or not.

The essentialist position, from which "lesbianism" is a condition of the same kind as – for example – autism, depends upon biomedical science for its evidence. Its research methods include twin studies, measurement of body parts, and microscopic analysis of brain tissue taken from cadavers. All such studies are predicated upon the assumption that for an individual to feel sexual desire and love for members of her own sex constitutes an error of gender. Thus, scientists working within the essentialist paradigm aim to identify masculine elements in the physiology of the "lesbian body." Genitals, inner-ear structure, fingerprints, relative finger length, the interstitial nucleii of a part of the brain known as the anterior hypothalamus, and secondary sex characteristics such as nipples and body hair have all been claimed by different researchers as demonstrating "wrong sex" characteristics in individuals identified (albeit sometimes after death) as lesbian or gay.

Feminists have criticized biomedical research for its traditional strong bias toward andronormativity. That is, the physiology of the male body is accepted as the ideal or typical physiology of humankind whilst that of the female body is either ignored or regarded as an extraordinary case. It is therefore not surprising to find that lesbians have been far less often the subjects of biomedical research into "homosexuality" than have men.

Another problem is that biomedicine is the product of the industrial nations of the West, and unreflexively reproduces as a generalizable norm the gender roles regarded as proper in those nations. Those gender roles themselves are intimately implicated in the social construction of heteronormativity, inasmuch as the behavior of women and of men is assumed to be largely shaped by their presumptive role in the reproduction of the species. Within the heteronormative paradigm, female sexuality is constructed as reproductively driven, in contrast to that of men, which is assumed to be pleasure-driven and instrumental. Female sexual desire, therefore, becomes something of an oxymoron, and lesbian sex, which cannot be reproductive, is not only unfeminine or masculine, it is not "really" sex at all.

The heteronormative construct of lesbian sex as non-sex, identified by lesbian theorists Diane Richardson and Anna-Marie Smith, and of female sexuality as trivial other than when associated with the reproductive imperative, compounds the existing tendency of biomedicine to ignore women altogether.

Many have suggested that it is only by ignoring lesbianism that biomedical researchers can continue to make claims for homosexuality as an innate or acquired condition, since women's sexual lives are both more complex and more fluid than are men's. As Edward Stein notes in his book *The Mismeasure of Desire* (1999), "If women's sexual desires were put at the centre of our theorizing about the origins of sexual orientation, the case for multiple origins would be readily apparent."

There are two major obstacles to conducting social scientific research into "lesbianism." The first is that the stigma which attaches to lesbianism makes this a hidden and "hard-to-reach" group of people, and that researchers have great difficulty in accessing lesbian research participants other than that small group of women confident and assertive enough to be publicly "out."

The second is that "lesbianism" is, in many ways, a term of little use to researchers. It is all but impossible to define the term in a way which allows for adequately rigorous research – as becomes evident from a critical scrutiny of most biomedical research into "lesbianism."

From a social scientific perspective, essentialist claims appear somewhat naïve, since they depend on ignoring the social and historical contingency of human sexuality. It is not even possible to claim that, always and everywhere, there have been women who demonstrate a strong sexual preference for members of their own sex. Historical documentation does exist for the existence of women whose sexual and emotional preference for other women led them to take the risk of "passing" as men and living as such with female partners. Such documentation largely takes the form of court records relating to the trial of women whose deception was uncovered. Emma Donoghue provides evidence going back to the seventeenth century in Europe, and there is some evidence that some precolonial indigenous cultures in the African, American, and Indian subcontinents had developed accepted roles for women who wanted to take on a male role in life, including "marriages" with other women. However, historical evidence about women's lives is far less detailed and robust than is the case for men's, and it is often difficult to know how useful contemporary notions of lesbianism are when interpreting historical or anthropological data.

The gendered power relations of patriarchally structured societies impact strongly upon female sexuality and upon the evidence available to historians and social scientists. It is generally the case that women's sexuality is policed by, and in the interests of, men. Patriarchal institutions, including the established religions, medicine, and the law, have also tended to exert particularly rigorous control over women's sexual and emotional lives, whilst the economic and social power of men and the relegation of women to the domestic and private sphere means that women have very little autonomy. Whilst the industrialized nations of the developed world have recently undergone a certain degree of transformation of gender relations in response to the demands of feminist political campaigns, such changes are historically recent and far from universal.

It is, therefore, very difficult to assess the likelihood of women entering into sexual relationships with each other, or even engaging in fleeting sexual contact with each other, at different historical periods or in different cultures. Whereas the historical records contain substantial evidence of sexual contact between men, this is not the case for women. Given that the material, political, and cultural circumstances required for women to achieve any degree of autonomy have been relatively rare until the twentieth century, and given that the policing of women's sexuality has been both geopolitically widespread and ideologically driven, it seems unlikely that many of the world's women have been able to develop much of a sense of themselves as sexual beings at all, much less experience and act on desire for each other.

It is, therefore, not possible to claim that something called "lesbianism" exists as any kind of universal human experience, or that it represents – as some evolutionary psychologists have claimed – a naturally existing variation with identifiable evolutionary benefits. Human sexuality is so culturally and historically specific that any universalizing claims must be treated with suspicion, and it seems likely that social constructionist accounts of both gender and sexuality will continue to dominate lesbian sociology and the sociology of lesbianism.

SEE ALSO: Essentialism and Constructionism; Female Masculinity; Femininities/Masculinities; Gay and Lesbian Movement; Homophobia and Heterosexism; Homosexuality; Lesbian Feminism; Queer Theory; Stigma

REFERENCES AND SUGGESTED READINGS

Butler, J. (1999) *Gender Trouble*. Routledge, London.
De Lauretis, T. (1994) *The Practice of Love: Lesbian Sexuality and Perverse Desire*. Indiana University Press, Bloomington.
Doan, L. (Ed.) (1994) *The Lesbian Postmodern*. Columbia University Press, New York.
Faderman, L. (1981) *Surpassing the Love of Men*. Women's Press, London.
Foucault, M. (1979) *History of Sexuality*. Vol. 1: *An Introduction*. Penguin, Harmondsworth.
Freedman, E., Gelpi, B., Johnson, S., & Weston, K. (Eds.) (1982) *The Lesbian Issue: Essays from SIGNS*. University of Chicago Press, Chicago.
Kennedy, E. & Davis, M. (1993) *Boots of Leather, Slippers of Gold: The History of a Lesbian Community*. Routledge, New York.
McIntosh, M. (1981 [1968]) The Homosexual Role. In: Plummer, K. (Ed.), *The Making of the Modern Homosexual*. Hutchinson, London.
Stein, E. (1999) *The Mismeasure of Desire: The Science, Theory, and Ethics of Sexual Orientation*. Oxford University Press, Oxford.
Symonds, J. A. (1984 [1928]) *Sexual Inversion*. Bell, New York.
Wilton, T. (1995) *Lesbian Studies: Setting an Agenda*. Routledge, London.

Levittown

Jessica W. Pardee

As the single largest housing development ever undertaken in US history, Levittown is the standard model for American suburban housing. Using assembly-line production techniques, Abraham Levitt and sons revolutionized the housing industry. While the Levitts built housing across the nation prior to World War II, Levittown, NY took mass production to a new level. Built on 4,000 acres of potato fields, the site included 17,400 single-family homes, as well as several swimming pools, baseball diamonds, playgrounds, and green spaces. Additionally, the Levitts were able to produce houses for almost $1,000 less than their competitors, while securing a $1,500 profit on each home. It is this transformation of the housing production process that makes Levittown so sociologically important.

One of the key mechanisms the Levitts employed to promote production was an absolute Taylorization of the home-building process. By identifying specific, detailed tasks, the construction labor was divided and reduced to 26 individual steps. To keep prices low, each step was then subcontracted, with all materials and equipment provided by Levitt. This allowed Levitt absolute control of the entire process, as well as the employment of non-union labor. Likewise, Levitt personally oversaw construction along with company-employed site managers to assure construction was of an acceptable standard.

Financially, the Levitt and Sons construction company and its subsidiaries were organized vertically, with all materials bought and sold through companies owned by the Levitts. The result was the consolidation of all profits, from lumber to unit sales, within the family. In total, this system resulted in extreme efficiency, a consolidation of profit flows to the Levitts, and an outsourcing system that demanded contractor services be on time and under budget. Quantified in houses, the system produced approximately 26 houses each day, at costs lower than those of competitors and at a higher profit to Levitt and Sons.

Across the country there are three Levittowns: Levittown, NY, Levittown, PA, and Levittown, NJ. Hebert Gans studied Levittown, NJ, later renamed Willingboro by the residents, between 1958 and 1962. In *The Levittowners*, Gans (1967) explores the social and democratic systems emerging in the new suburban community. As a participant observer and community resident, Gans focused his research on the emergence of a new community, the quality of suburban life, the effect of that life on resident behavior, and the quality of politics and decision-making. In contrast to suburban myths, Gans found the Levittowners to be a reasonably heterogeneous group, whose community developed out of contentions between residents, not a homogeneous view of how a suburban community should be.

Decades later, researchers Baxandall and Ewen returned to the New York Levittown to examine what the 1940s community looks like now. In *Picture Windows* (2000), they find a stark contrast to the homogeneous spatial design and ethnic demographic of the original residential development. Modern Levittown reflects a diverse environment of home designs – the result of additions and remodeling, racial and ethnic diversification of the once whites-only development, and inclusion of multigenerational and single-mother families with boarders. Thus, 50 years later, Levittown, NY reflects much of the diversity that is predominant in most inner cities.

SEE ALSO: City Planning/Urban Design; Metropolis; New Urbanism; Suburbs; Urbanization

REFERENCES AND SUGGESTED READINGS

Baxandall, R. & Ewen, E. (2000) *Picture Windows: How the Suburbs Happened*. Basic Books, New York.
Duany, A., Plater-Zyberk, E., & Speck, J. (2000) *Suburban Nation: The Rise of Sprawl and the Decline of the American Dream*. North Point Press, New York.
Gans, H. J. (1967) *The Levittowners: Ways of Life and Politics in a New Suburban Community*. Pantheon, New York.
Jackson, K. T. (1985) *Crabgrass Frontier: The Suburbanization of the United States*. Oxford University Press, New York.

Lewin, Kurt (1890–1947)

Reef Youngreen

Kurt Lewin is recognized by many as the founder of modern social psychology because of his foundational contributions in making connections between psychology, sociology, anthropology, and economics. By adapting and applying the gestalt perspective to personality theory and social dynamics and translating these ideas into social experience involving people, Lewin's field theory powerfully translated these ideas to new domains.

Born in 1890 in Molgino, Prussia into a middle-class Jewish family in which he was one of four sons, Lewin and his family moved to Berlin when he was 15. At 19 and showing an interest in studying medicine, he attended the University of Freiberg. Shortly thereafter, he transferred to the University of Munich to study biology. During his time in Munich, Lewin became interested and involved in the socialist movement, aiming to combat anti-Semitism and help improve women's social positions. It was here that he and similar others organized and taught adult education programs for working-class people. His later studies at the University of Berlin fostered his interest in the philosophy of science and exposed him to gestalt psychology, both of which are premises on which much of Lewin's legacy is grounded.

Lewin completed his doctoral work at the outset of World War I in 1914 and was awarded his degree in 1916 while serving in the German army. After joining the Psychological Institute of the University of Berlin in 1921 and becoming a popular lecturer in both philosophy and psychology, he was invited to spend six months as a visiting professor at Stanford University in 1930. The political situation in Germany at this time was deteriorating for many, particularly

Jews. As a result, Lewin and his wife and daughter relocated to the US in 1933, and in 1940 Lewin became an American citizen. He began his work in the US at the Cornell School of Home Economics. In 1935, the first year in which an English collection of Lewin's work was published (*A Dynamic Theory of Personality*), Lewin moved to the University of Iowa. For nearly a decade in the Midwestern US, he perpetuated his interests in group processes and involved himself in applied research initiatives linked to the war (e.g., troop morale, warfare psychology). His commitment to applying research techniques and findings to social problems led to the development of the MIT Research Center for Group Dynamics. Concurrently, Lewin's model of action research – research oriented to solving social problems – resulted in a number of significant studies on religious and racial prejudice for the Commission of Community Interrelations for the American Jewish Congress in New York. It is from this and similar work with other community group leaders that Lewin's "T" groups emerged. Receiving funding from the Office of Naval Research in 1947, he and a few of his contemporaries established the National Training Laboratories (NTL) in Bethel, Maine. Unfortunately, Lewin was never able to personally realize the important outcomes of the NTL because he died suddenly of a heart attack on February 11, 1947.

Perhaps one of Lewin's most recognized contributions to social psychology is his field theory, a system of ideas that highlights his gestalt psychology influences. A gestalt may be thought of as a coherent whole possessing its own laws as constructs of individual minds rather than an objective reality. From Lewin's perspective, behavior motivations were determined not by individual drives, but by all of the elements of a situation. In observing individual behaviors and group dynamics, one must give precedence to the field. In *Field Theory in Social Science: Selected Theoretical Papers*, Lewin defined the field as "the totality of coexisting facts which are conceived of as mutually interdependent." From field theory, Lewin constructed a symbolic representation of behavior expressed as $B = f(P, E)$, or behavior is a function of the person and the environment. The entire psychological field comprises the *lifespace*, or all of the

physical locations, social identities and associated roles, and psychological realities available to an individual. To understand the meanings and motivations associated with behaviors, Lewin believed that the researcher must understand the lifespaces within which people acted. Importantly, Lewin's belief that analyzing a situation required the focus on the situation's entirety – differentiated from the component parts of the situation – illustrates the prominence he granted to the gestalt view.

Lewin's ideas about why members of a group come together do not invoke familiar or common reasons (e.g., homophily). Instead, Lewin reasons that groups form in a psychological sense not necessarily because of members' similarity, but because group formation depends on individuals' realizations that their own fate depends on the fate of the entire group. To support this contention, Lewin cited the common struggle of Jews in the late 1930s as an example of this feeling of interdependent fate. Brown (1988) cites experimental support for this idea that groups require even the most basic form of interdependence. Lewin also argued for the importance of task interdependence in group formation. Fate interdependence is a weaker form of interdependence than task interdependence. The overlap of the group members' goals forms a more solid foundation on which a more powerful group dynamic may be built.

Lewin, along with other research colleagues, is credited with the development of "T" groups (an abbreviation for "basic skills training" groups). These groups, the foundation of the encounter groups of the 1960s, emerged as Lewin and his colleagues realized that the leadership and group dynamics training sessions they conducted for the Connecticut State Interracial Commission in 1964 were most effective when a tension is created between immediate experiences of group members and trainers' theoretical models. Inputs from each perspective enhanced the experiences of the other, resulting in marked increases in expected group vitality and creativity. This innovation in training practice became the basis of funding to establish the NTL.

Lewin's emphasis on the necessity of feedback to produce optimal outcomes, as illustrated by the dialectical nature of "T" groups, is also the foundation of action research, or research for social management or social engineering. He came to believe that for many sorts of experimental research, it was necessary to have a very intimate relationship between skilled social practitioners with an interest in research and skilled researchers who understood the necessity of social action (Lippitt 1947).

Lewin's action research consists of a series of spiraling steps, each step consisting of planning, action, and collecting data about the results of the action. The first step in action research is to examine an idea very carefully, from all available perspectives. This step usually requires collecting more information than is already present. From this step emerges a plan of how to reach an objective and a choice about what the first step in the plan entails. At this point, the plan to reach the goal has likely already modified the original idea. The next step consists of ongoing circles of plans, executions, and a collection of data indicating the outcome of the initial execution. Evaluations of the data representing the outcomes of initial action inform the plans for the next step or may require a modification of the entire plan. The experiential learning associated with this plan of research is specifically oriented to problem solving in both social and organizational settings. As such, Lewin's action research spiral has been adopted by organizations as a method for self-improvement. There is a danger in interpreting action research as a simple procedure for addressing and overcoming social problems. Action research is not a method, but rather a progression of commitments to observe and frame through action a set of principles for social inquiry (McTaggart 1996). Because of its association with radical political activism, action research suffered a decline in popularity. More recently, action research has found favor among community-based movements as a participatory mechanism for inciting change. As a method to improve educational experiences, the tools of action research have experienced a renaissance.

Another of Lewin's established areas of inquiry concerned the relationship between leadership types and group structure. Lewin believed that democracy was among the most difficult group structures to develop and maintain. Successful democracies result from a knowledge of and abidance by the laws of human nature in the group setting. Each new generation under a democratic structure has to learn these rules, which is one of the reasons democracy is difficult to develop and maintain. Lewin believed that democracy, unlike autocracy, could not be imposed on people. Lewin and Ronald Lippitt, one of Lewin's contemporaries, examined democratic, autocratic, and *laissez-faire* leadership models and found democratic groups embodied more originality, group-mindedness, and friendliness than other models. These researchers examined groups of children under both democratic and autocratic structures and found the friendly, open, cooperative group under a democratic structure quickly diminished with the imposition of an autocratic structure. Further, the change in children's behaviors from under an autocracy to a democracy took much longer than from democracy to autocracy. Lewin and Lippitt concluded that behavior under each of the leadership models was not entirely the result of individual differences, but rather an outcome of group structure.

Lewin's legacy in social psychological and personality research is evidenced by the quantity and array of research based on his foundational ideas. According to the Social Science Citation Index, Lewin's research was cited by published research over 150 times in 2004, 57 years after his death. The research citing his work is found in an array of publications including the *Journal of Personality and Social Psychology*, the *Journal of Retailing*, and *Theory into Practice*. The title of the final journal listed above captures the undercurrent of Lewin's life work: the integration of theory and practice. This emphasis is captured in Lewin's most notable quotation: "There is nothing so practical as good theory."

SEE ALSO: Action Research; Democracy and Organizations; Experimental Methods; Psychological Social Psychology; Social Psychology

REFERENCES AND SUGGESTED READINGS

Brown, R. (1988) *Group Processes: Dynamics Within and Between Groups*. Blackwell, Oxford.

Gold, M. (Ed.) (1999) *The Complete Social Scientist: A Kurt Lewin Reader*. United Book Press, American Psychological Association, Washington, DC.

Lewin, K. (1948) *Resolving Social Conflicts: Selected Papers on Group Dynamics*. Ed. G. W. Lewin. Harper & Row, New York.

Lippitt, R. (1947) Kurt Lewin, 1890–1947. Adventures in the Exploration of Interdependence. *Sociometry* 10(1): 87–97.

McTaggart, R. (1996) Issues for Participatory Action Researchers. In: Zuber-Skerritt, O. (Ed.), *New Directions in Action Research*. Falmer, London.

Yalom, I. D. (1995) *The Theory and Practice of Group Psychotherapy*, 4th edn. Basic Books, New York.

liberal feminism

Kristina Wolff

Liberal feminism is one of the earliest forms of feminism, stating that women's secondary status in society is based on unequal opportunities and segregation from men. Emerging out of the abolitionist and women's movement in the US, this body of feminism focuses on eliminating gender inequality. The basic beliefs are grounded in liberalist philosophical traditions, as well as French and British feminist theory. Society consists of individuals who are equals and therefore all people must have equal rights. There is a clear division between the role of the state (public) and individual freedom (private). Liberal feminists create change by working within existing social structures and changing people's attitudes.

The anti-slavery movement emerged in the early 1800s. These groups engaged in public forums and speeches, boycotted churches and businesses that supported slavery, lobbied for changes in laws, and practiced other forms of non-violent activism. These tactics reemerged during the modern black Civil Rights Movement starting in the mid-to-late 1950s. Many of the early founders of the suffrage movement or first wave of feminism were strong abolitionists and began organizing for women's rights while members of these anti-slavery organizations. Many activists such as Angelina and Sarah Grimke spoke publicly about the need for equal education and an end to women's servitude. The first public call for women's right to vote was made when Lucretia Mott and Elizabeth Cady Stanton were refused recognition as delegates to the 1840 World Anti-Slavery Convention. After this event, Mott, Stanton, and Mary Ann McClintock began organizing for women's right to vote.

In 1848 during the Seneca Falls Convention, the *Declaration of Sentiments* was presented by Stanton. This statement mirrored the writing of Thomas Jefferson, calling for voting rights for women, which would enable them to work to eliminate sexist laws, thereby seeking an end to the second-class status of women. During this time, women were legally the property of their fathers or husbands and had few rights of their own. After the Civil War, many abolitionists focused on voting rights for blacks, and women were expected to help with this effort and abandon their fight for the women's vote. This was a catalyst for Susan B. Anthony to leave the Equal Rights Association and form the National Woman's Suffrage Association with Elizabeth Cady Stanton. The new focus, along with other activists such as Alice Paul, was on the creation of a constitutional amendment for women's right to vote along with actively working on other issues such as changing inheritance and divorce laws and women's economic inequality. The 19th amendment to the US Constitution granting women the right to vote was finally ratified in 1920.

The theoretical foundation for these early feminists was a combination of their religious beliefs and the writings of John Locke, John Stuart Mill and Harriet Taylor Mill, Mary Wollstonecraft and later, Jane Addams and Harriet Martineau. Main themes in their work focused on personal independence, economic and educational opportunity, and equality for all humans. Societal change happens through individual efforts and working within existing social structures. Through the efforts of suffragists, women also won greater access to education as well as improved individual rights and autonomy. After women won the right to vote, the movement lost some momentum, but work on issues of equal rights and the end of gender inequality continued through the efforts of women like Addams, Paul, and Emma Goldman.

The 1950s saw a renewed cultural push for men and women to fulfill traditional gender roles. During this time, the modern black Civil Rights Movement was beginning to increase in scope and momentum. By the early 1960s, numerous groups – including anti-war activists and women as well as gays and lesbians – were also pushing for social reforms. In 1963 Betty Friedan published *The Feminine Mystique*. In her text, Friedan details the lives of the average American suburban housewife; she described women as being "dissatisfied" with their lives, each one "yearning" for something more. Ultimately, she concluded that women across America were suffering from "the problem that had no name." This phrase soon came to represent the contemporary Women's Liberation Movement which gave rise to modern liberal feminism. Once again, women marched in the streets, gave speeches, lobbied politicians, and worked for reform in the areas of education, employment, health care, and politics, as well as for the end of inequality based on gender.

Sexism was viewed as improper behavior by men and women, who were conditioned by society's "bad" ideas about gender roles. Social change would come from working within the system to eliminate structural barriers and change cultural expectations of women's roles as wives and mothers, as well as to establish equality between genders so women would have the same opportunities as men. The National Organization for Women (NOW) was formed by Friedan and others in October 1966. During their first national convention in 1967, they adopted a "Bill of Rights" which demanded such things as maternity leave, government-sponsored childcare centers, equal opportunities for education and job training, reproductive rights, and the establishment of the Equal Rights Amendment to eliminate discrimination based on sex. Motivated by the phrase "the personal is political," women organized across the nation, fighting for equal rights and access to traditionally male-only organizations, jobs, and educational institutions, and for change in the image of women in the media. One result of these actions was the establishment of a women's studies curriculum and departments in colleges and universities, as well as the recognition of feminist sociologists and the formal development of feminist sociology. By adopting an assimilationist approach, liberal feminism appealed to a wide array of people, as it is complementary to American ideals of individualism and success through hard work and determination.

Not surprisingly, early areas of research by feminist scholars center on the institutions of marriage, motherhood, and family, as well as work, education, and reproductive rights. Included in this scholarship is the development of feminist theories and methodologies. Research focusing on marriage and family not only illustrates the experiences of women as wives and mothers, but also challenges the expectations of gender roles. In the 1970s, women still lost their autonomy upon marriage. They were legally the property of their husband, they could not have credit without their husband's permission, many were denied jobs or admission to college due to their gender, and the dominant cultural belief was that all women would marry and therefore did not need to have a job or advanced education. Feminists successfully lobbied against these legal limitations imposed on women and also challenged the belief that the nuclear family was the "natural" family structure, thus bringing to question women and men's roles as wives and husbands as well as mothers and fathers.

By placing women at the center of analysis, sociologists have expanded understandings of marriage and family, illustrating the central role these play in perpetuating ideologies of gender roles and expectations in society. Often, the traditional nuclear family structure has been used to support the division of labor in society, where women are expected to be at home in order to care for children; therefore, men are forced to work outside of the home to support the family, thus limiting options and choices for both men and women; for example, few companies offer parental leave to men to care for their newborn child. Feminists also challenge this division due to the unequal balance of work placed on women who must care for children, operate the household, and provide support for husbands (including help to advance their careers). Additionally, for women who work for pay outside of the home, as housework is unpaid labor, researchers have found that their responsibilities at home rarely change. Husbands seldom increase their role in the household to assist women working outside of it, so when a woman returns home from her job, she has to continue to work in the household to keep it functioning. Hochschild (Hochschild & Machung 1989) labeled this phenomenon the "second shift." A liberal feminist solution to this situation is to call for changes in family law, such as providing more support through parental leave policies as well as to educate men and women about restructuring their relationship to be more balanced and equal. Additionally, liberal feminists have called for increased support for childcare, welfare reform, and laws to challenge these traditional concepts of family, as well as extend support to single parents and lower-income families.

In addition to the family structure being viewed as a means to keep women in a subordinate position in society, research on the social worlds of work and education has also demonstrated how women's secondary status has benefited men. In the 1960s, women experienced few choices in education and employment. Jobs were advertised in newspapers according to race and gender and were largely limited to lower-skilled positions. Women were expected to go into pink-collar occupations such as nursing, teaching, secretarial positions, or as maids. These positions paid low wages and offered little to no opportunities for advancement. After it became illegal to hire according to race or gender characteristics, high school counselors, teachers, and parents continued to encourage women to enter these fields, rather than pursue careers in business, mathematics, or any of the sciences.

Through socializing women to continue working in pink-collar professions, men have less competition in areas of employment as well as entry into colleges and universities. By encouraging men to enter into areas of employment that provide higher pay and benefits than the low-paying occupations women are directed into, society's gender roles are reinforced and a large gap is permanently created between the earning potential of women and men, thus further limiting women's options and opportunities.

As women gained greater access to education and began to enter into traditional male jobs, the image of the "superwoman" or "supermom" emerged in the 1980s. These women were depicted as having successful careers and marriages and happily fulfilled their primary role as mothers. This glorified image of women balancing all of these roles represented a cultural shift

in accepting women's broader entry into the working world, but it also reifies traditional gender roles women are expected to adhere to as wives and mothers. While great advances have been made in areas of education and employment, women continue to earn approximately 72 cents per every dollar a man makes, with few actually gaining positions of stature such as CEOs of large corporations or presidents of universities. The number of women holding elected office proportionately remains quite low in comparison to men.

One of the foundational tenets of liberal feminism is also its most controversial. This is the belief that all women have the right to privacy, which includes complete control over their bodies. This ideology becomes complicated when discussing issues related to sexuality, health care, and reproduction, largely because of women's biological role in procreation. Historically, conceptions of marriage have been based on people's desire to procreate, to create a family. It is only within modern history that western (specifically, US) culture has embraced the belief that marriage is based on love and fulfilling relationships. One of the main areas of focus for change with the rise of the Women's Liberation Movement was increased autonomy for women to make their own medical decisions, particularly concerning their choices connected to birth control, which includes the right to have a safe abortion. This right was gained with the 1973 US Supreme Court decision in *Roe* v. *Wade* and *Dole* v. *Bolton*. Women were granted the legal right to have access to safe abortions, but the role of the state in terms of providing funding or the actual service has been highly contestable, as is the right to abortion itself. This issue remains central to women's activism and scholarship.

Since the *Roe* decision, laws have been adopted that limit women's access to abortion, including parental notification laws for minors, time periods established between when a women seeks an abortion and can receive one, and the elimination of all federal funding for this service. One of the consequences of this has been a decrease in available reproductive health care services for all women. Often, arguments against providing services connected to birth control and abortion follow conservative ideologies reinforcing traditional gender roles for women as mothers, with the expectation that all women want to have children and that they have made a choice to become pregnant. These beliefs have been challenged by liberal feminists and researchers who have documented women's lack of reproductive options, including their ability to choose whether or not to conceive a child. Certainly, while liberal feminism strongly advocates a pro-choice ideology and therefore supports abortion, there is much debate surrounding this issue.

One of the main critiques of liberal feminism is the amount of attention that has been paid to women's right to an abortion and who exactly benefits from this right. Historically, women of color and poor women have had very different experiences to those portrayed in liberal feminism. The US has a long history of forced pregnancy of slaves and medical experimentation and forced sterilization of African American, Puerto Rican, and Native American women. These women have been legally required to and/or pressured to have abortions and hysterectomies and to utilize long-term birth control such as Norplant, which has dangerous side-effects. Many of these women have also been lower income, which provides another barrier to adequate health care. While liberal feminists and scholars present their efforts as representing all women, it has had great difficulty uniting a wide range of women. When discussing the racism and classism of liberal feminism, Angela Davis (1981: 202) writes: "rarely have the movement's leaders popularized the genuine concerns of working-class women." Liberal feminism has responded to these critiques. Larger national groups – including NOW and NARAL – have widened their efforts at working for reproductive health care options, but abortion remains the primary focus within this work.

From the beginning of the women's movement, there has been strong criticism as to the elite nature of liberal feminism. The vast majority of positions of power and authority have been held by white women with privilege. This is evident in Friedan's work, which called for women to get out of the trappings of housework but ignored the issue of who their maids were: they were usually black women who had to work to support their families. Additionally, the family is viewed as an essential part of their lives, not a burden but the foundation for strength, happiness, and community. Women activists (particularly black women from the abolitionist movement) have contributed greatly to the elimination of gender inequality, but also have largely remained invisible due to their race/ethnicity and/or class status. This is evident in Sojourner Truth's outburst during one of the early conventions, when she shouted "Ain't I a Woman?" and demanded recognition for her contributions and desire for equality based on race and gender. Her words may be famous, but they made little impact in terms of changing the role of blacks in the movement. Truth, Ida B. Wells, Anna Julia Cooper, and contemporary activists and scholars such as Ella Baker, Frances Beale, and Shirley Chisholm remain on the margins of history despite their contributions to feminism.

Liberal feminism has also been criticized for its lack of systematic analysis of the social structures that maintain gender inequality. There is no critique of existing social systems because it seeks entry into these institutions rather than changing them. This caused many fissures within the Women's Liberation Movement. Radical feminism was formed with the belief that social systems and structures need to change in order to eliminate oppression of women overall. Socialist and Marxist feminism emerged from radical feminism, focusing on capitalism as the main source of women's oppression. Other feminisms soon followed which expanded analysis into an array of areas, including analyzing what gender actually is, issues related to sexuality and age, and a host of other topics. Black Feminist Thought and Women of Color feminism emerged through the creation of their own organizations, which moved beyond focusing on a single issue as the cause of inequality, to examining oppression and domination through intersectional lenses. This moved feminism and feminist thought into broader realms, into questioning and challenging systems of oppression and domination throughout the US.

As with any social movement and body of scholarship, liberal feminism has evolved as society and culture has changed. Many of the basic goals of individual rights and freedoms, as well as an end to gender inequality, remain central to liberal feminism. Liberal feminists successfully brought the issue of equal rights into mainstream America and created significant legal and cultural changes that improved the lives of women and men in the nation. Many of the tactics they created or adopted from the black Civil Rights Movement have been utilized by other movements and organizations, including other women's groups around the world.

SEE ALSO: Addams, Jane; Black Feminist Thought; Cultural Feminism; Martineau, Harriet; Radical Feminism; Social Movements; Women's Empowerment; Women's Movements

REFERENCES AND SUGGESTED READINGS

Bernard, J. (1982) *The Future of Marriage*. Yale University Press, New Haven.
Davis, A. (1981) *Women, Race and Class*. Vintage Books, New York.
DeVault, M. (1994) *Feeding the Family: The Social Organization of Caring as Gendered Work*. University of Chicago Press, Chicago.
Eisenstein, Z. (1981) *The Radical Future of Liberal Feminism*. Longman, New York.
Evans, S. (1979) *Personal Politics: The Roots of Women's Liberation in the Civil Rights Movement and the New Left*. Vintage Books, New York.
Firestone, S. (1993) *The Dialectic of Sex: The Case for Feminist Revolution*. Farrar Straus Giroux, New York.
Friedan, B. (1963) *The Feminine Mystique*. W. W. Norton, New York.
Hochschild, A. & Machung, A. (1989) *The Second Shift: Working Parents and the Revolution at Home*. Viking Press, New York.
hooks, bell (2000) *Feminist Theory: From Margin to Center*. South End Press, Cambridge, MA.
Kensinger, L. (1997) (In)quest of Liberal Feminism. *Hypatia* 12(4): 178.
Millett, K. (2000) *Sexual Politics*. University of Illinois Press, Urbana.
Morgan, R. (1970) *Sisterhood is Powerful: An Anthology of Writings from the Women's Liberation Movement*. Vintage, New York.
Rossi, A. (1988) *The Feminist Papers from Adams to De Beauvoir*. Northeastern University Press, Boston.
Schneir, M. (1994) *Feminism: The Essential Historical Writings, World War Two to the Present*. Vintage, New York.
Thorne, B. & Yalom, M. (1992) *Rethinking the Family: Some Feminist Questions*. Northeastern University Press, Boston.
Wollstonecraft, M. & Brody, M. (1993) *A Vindication of the Rights of Women*. Penguin, New York.

liberalism

Andrew Gamble

Liberalism is the leading ideology of the modern era. The term first began to be used to denote the supporters of liberty and the opponents of arbitrary authority in Spain during the Napoleonic Wars. During the nineteenth century it came to signify adherence to the principles of individualism, liberty, limited government, progress, and equality. As such it has always been an extremely broad doctrine, espoused by thinkers as diverse as John Stuart Mill, Constant, Bentham, Tocqueville, Hobhouse, and Hayek. Many of its key ideas can be traced to earlier thinkers such as Locke, Kant, and the French and Scottish Enlightenments. At its core is a particular conception of society and human nature, based on beliefs in the moral primacy of the individual as the starting point for thinking about politics and society; the equal moral worth of every individual, regardless of class, nation, gender, or race; and the possibility of improving social conditions and reforming political institutions. Individuals are conceived as the bearers of rights which exist independently of government and for which government is brought into existence in order to protect. The legitimacy of any system of government depends therefore on how well it protects the liberty of its citizens.

Liberalism was decisively shaped by the American and French Revolutions. These two major political events marked the beginning of the modern era and the age of ideologies because they involved a decisive break with the old order and a vision of the new, the overthrow of established political authority, and the assertion of new principles of government – life, liberty, and the pursuit of happiness in the American version, and liberty, equality, and fraternity in the French. Both these revolutions proclaimed in different ways that sovereignty should be popular sovereignty, that government should be based on the will of the people, and that for this purpose all members of a political community should be regarded as equal and able to participate in their self-government. These ideals were much contradicted in practice; in America the rights of man which formed the basis of the new Constitution were not extended to slaves or women, while in France the attempt to construct representative institutions gave way to terror and dictatorship. But despite their failings the political revolutions in France and America did produce a decisive rupture in the system of monarchical absolutism, giving birth to a new kind of political imagination and political possibility.

The political revolutions were also part of much broader social and economic changes involving the rise of new technologies, new forms of organization, and new forms of knowledge, which together shaped the conception of modernity. Liberalism came to stand for progress and opposition to all forms of obscurantism, tradition, privilege, and prejudice, and therefore became identified with capitalism, rationalism, science, secularism, and more generally with modernity and the rise of the modern state. Although liberals held many different views on aspects of the new society that was emerging, they tended to be optimistic rather than pessimistic about the prospects for human progress because of their faith in reason, which came from the Enlightenment, their universalism, and their confidence in rational, scientific methods to discover the causes of things and propose improvements.

As a political doctrine liberalism emphasizes the framework of institutions and laws through which the liberty of citizens can be protected from arbitrary government. The aim is to establish a government of laws rather than of men. A well-designed constitution ensures a balance of power between the different arms of government – executive, legislature, and judiciary – so that no one arm of government can dominate. Liberals have generally sought to disperse power and to limit government, and to set obstacles to any return to tyranny and dictatorship. They have been ambivalent about democracy, divided over whether it is a new form of

unlimited government which threatens liberty and the rule of law, or whether it is the best means to promote representation, accountability, and self-government.

As an economic doctrine liberalism developed a distinctive strand of political economy, committed to free trade, sound money, and laissez-faire. These ideas were important in breaking down obstacles to the spread of markets and capitalism and promoting flows of capital, goods, and people around the world, based on the argument that if government stands back and allows the natural energies of the people full rein, countries will become stronger and richer. Governments are necessary evils, but still evils, so have to be limited in their powers as much as possible. Liberals, however, have always accepted that some powers must be exercised by the state, even if this is only the minimal state providing external defense, internal order, and the rule of law as the basis for a market order. A central tension within liberal political economy and within liberalism more generally is the proper relation between liberty and coercion. All liberals want to minimize coercion as much as possible; the question is always how much and for what purposes. In contrast, libertarians reject all coercive authority as an infringement on liberty, and therefore reject the state itself, so moving outside the bounds of liberalism.

As a cultural doctrine liberalism has been associated with tolerance, diversity rationality, and neutrality towards other beliefs. Individuals should be free to live as they choose and define the good in their own way without intervention or direction from the state or the community, so long as their choices do not harm others. Application of this principle has allowed a substantial enlargement of the realm of personal freedom, and the shrinking of intervention by the state in areas such as sexual behavior. But some critics of liberalism have argued that this self-image of liberalism is a sham because liberalism is a highly moral doctrine and as intolerant as any other moral doctrine of claims which challenge its core beliefs, such as the idea of neutrality itself or the claim that education should be secular, inculcating the values of a common citizenship.

Liberalism has developed many different strands and has undergone substantial change as the tensions inherent in its core ideas have been explored. There have been important intellectual traditions such as classical liberalism, utilitarianism, new liberalism, and neoliberalism, as well as many distinct national traditions of liberalism, such as those in Germany, Britain, Italy, and the US. Ideological disagreement among liberals themselves over the role of the state and the role of reason have divided the liberal tradition into "true" and "false" liberalism, or "skeptical" and "rational" liberalism. The divide is over whether there are strict limits to the potential of human reason to reorganize the world and what these limits are. The skeptics believe human reason can only be used to discover the constraints within which human life must be lived, while the rationalists believe human reason can and should be used to overcome those constraints.

This argument about the limits of reason is closely associated with ideas about the limits of government, and the potential of government for utilizing rational knowledge to transform society for the better. The lure of scientific knowledge and the apparently limitless possibilities it opened for understanding both physical nature and human nature seemed to provide societies with the tools for limitless improvement. The skeptics argued that progress could only be maintained if the powers of the state were kept strictly limited, so as to maximize the energy, knowledge, and enterprise of the myriad of individual actors. Rationalists, such as the utilitarians, believed public policy should be so conducted as to ensure the greatest happiness of the greatest number.

This divide also became expressed as a divide between the state and the market, and the question of how far the market needed to be protected from the depredations of the state. In the early phases of liberalism the emphasis was upon removing restrictions to enterprise and trade, challenging traditions and customs, and embracing change and new knowledge to change society. Once liberalism in the shape of liberal political economy became the orthodoxy, however, the widening of the gap between rich and poor and the relentless nature of a competitive commercial society created powerful conservative and socialist counter-movements against liberalism. Many liberals became convinced that

the achievement of their ideals required more positive action by the state to create the conditions under which all individuals could develop the capacity to exercise freedom. Such attitudes were characteristic of "new liberalism" in the late nineteenth and early twentieth centuries and moved the goal of liberalism from being about liberty to being about human flourishing and self-realization. This required the state to intervene to remedy disadvantage and to equip all its citizens with the opportunities and resources for self-realization. A long and expanding list of interventions by the state became sanctioned.

This conflict within liberalism was later formalized by Isaiah Berlin as the contrast between negative liberty and positive liberty. A liberalism that is concerned primarily with negative liberty leaves individuals free to do whatever they like so long as they do not harm others and accepts that individuals will always disagree about what constitutes a good life. A liberalism that is concerned more with positive liberty targets those conditions such as disease, ignorance, and poverty which prevent many individuals from realizing their potential for self-development. Both sets of liberals set great store on liberty as the supreme value, but disagree strongly as to how it is best secured. New liberals gravitated towards social democracy in Europe and programs like the New Deal in the US, while laissez-faire liberals after a long period of retreat in the face of collectivism finally reemerged strongly in the second half of the twentieth century in the guise of neoliberalism.

In the 1930s it became fashionable to believe that liberalism was an outmoded doctrine, no longer suited to an industrial society which was increasingly organized, managerial, and collectivist in its consciousness and ethos. The rise of collectivist ideologies and totalitarian regimes made many liberals believe that some form of collectivist organization of society and the state had become necessary for the survival of industrial society. The strong revival of liberalism after 1945 in the west was largely unexpected. It was accompanied by the development of the idea of a liberal democracy, based on constitutional safeguards for representative and limited government, a free market economy, and an active state to promote the well-being of its citizens. In the first few decades after 1945 liberalism became quite strongly associated with interventionist economic and social policies programs inspired by two English liberals, J. M. Keynes and W. H. Beveridge, as well as with permissive social policies on a range of issues from abortion and homosexuality to divorce and capital punishment. One consequence of this was that the term liberal in the US became permanently linked to a left-liberal agenda, and the revival of laissez-faire liberalism or classical liberalism in the 1970s was associated more with conservatism than with liberalism, even though it was dubbed neoliberalism by its opponents.

The collapse of the Soviet Union brought an end to the most serious twentieth-century political and ideological challenge to liberalism, and suggested to some that all the most important ideological conflicts were now within liberalism rather than between liberalism and other ideologies, and that liberalism had now established itself as the quintessential doctrine of modernity. Others regarded the triumph of liberalism as largely a mirage, reflecting the remarkable degree of dominance established by the US at the end of the twentieth century rather than any broad acceptance of liberal ideas throughout the world. Many liberals continued to be ambivalent about democracy and about the role of the state in promoting the conditions for a liberal society, while others argued that liberalism had to develop further if it was to live up to its founding principles. The restless and iconoclastic character of liberalism – with its emphasis upon the individual and upon reason – continue to define it, even if some of the conclusions that liberals draw from these principles remain diametrically opposed.

SEE ALSO: Conservatism; Democracy; Individualism; Mill, John Stuart; Neoliberalism

REFERENCES AND SUGGESTED READINGS

Arblaster, A. (1984) *The Rise and Decline of Western Liberalism*. Blackwell, Oxford.
Bellamy, R. (1992) *Liberalism and Modern Society*. Polity Press, Cambridge.
Gray, J. (1995) *Liberalism*. Open University Press, Milton Keynes.
Hall, J. S. (1988) *Liberalism, Politics and the Market*. University of North Carolina Press, Chapel Hill.
Mill, J. S. (1982) *On Liberty*. Penguin, London.

Liebow, Elliot (1925–94)

Levon Chorbajian

Elliot Liebow was born in Washington, DC. He served in World War II and received his high school equivalency diploma while in the Marine Corps. After the war, Liebow received his bachelor's degree in English literature from George Washington University. He studied ancient history at the University of Maryland and received his PhD in anthropology from Catholic University. Liebow was employed by the National Institute of Mental Health (NIMH) for 25 years and rose to the position of chief of the Center for the Study of Work and Mental Health. In his last years of retirement from NIMH, Liebow held the endowed chair as Patrick Cardinal O'Boyle professor at the National Catholic School of Social Work at Catholic University.

Liebow's reputation is heavily based on the publication of a single book, *Tally's Corner: A Study of Negro Streetcorner Men* (1967). It had been his doctoral dissertation. The book has sold in excess of 800,000 copies, and it continues to be in print. Liebow was the son of Eastern European Jewish immigrants and had grown up in a poor African American neighborhood in Washington. This experience proved to be an asset for Liebow in establishing rapport with the subjects of *Tally's Corner*. In the early 1960s Liebow spent 18 months in the company of two dozen poor African American men who regularly congregated at a particular neighborhood street corner in the District. He spent hundreds of hours with these men and accompanied them to hospitals, parties, workplaces, and courtrooms. Liebow's interpretation of the world of these men became *Tally's Corner*. The book's popularity is partly accounted for by the coincidence of its publication with urban uprisings, the rise of the Civil Rights and Black

Power movements, and the federal anti-poverty programs of the late 1960s, all of which generated an interest in urban African American communities.

Liebow's second book was published two and a half decades after *Tally's Corner*, shortly before his death. *Tell Them Who I Am: The Lives of Homeless Women* (1993) evolved out of Liebow's volunteer work in public and private homeless shelters for women in the Washington area. As in *Tally's Corner*, Liebow was interested in how people at the lower rungs of the class structure establish identity and maintain dignity in the face of great odds.

Liebow made important contributions to the breadth and diversity of sociology as a discipline. *Tally's Corner* helped to resurrect ethnography as a method at a time when Parsonian structural functionalism was still sociology's dominant theoretical paradigm and survey research its reigning methodology. Among Liebow's many awards are two from the Society for the Study of Social Problems, the C. Wright Mills Award for *Tally's Corner* and the Lee Founders Award for career achievement in sociology.

SEE ALSO: Deindustrialization; Ethnography; Ghetto; Homelessness; Inequality and the City; Observation, Participant and Non-Participant; Poverty; Race; Race (Racism); Urban Poverty

REFERENCES AND SUGGESTED READINGS

Liebow, E. (1967) *Tally's Corner: A Study of Negro Streetcorner Men*. Little, Brown, Boston.
Liebow, E. (1993) *Tell Them Who I Am: The Lives of Homeless Women*. Free Press, New York.

life chances and resources

Wout Ultee

Around the mid-1980s in the field of societal stratification, the research program of "Class, Status, and Power" had evolved into the more powerful program of "Life Chances and Resources." At that time, theoretical and empirical efforts undertaken by sociologists in various countries of the world began to converge.

An early formulation and application of the new program was given by Lenski in 1966. This study did not so much apply concepts like class, status, and power to describe concrete societies as it presented propositions to answer questions that went beyond earlier interrogations. As Lenski put it, he had taken the liberty of reformulating the once paramount question in the field of stratification about the number and nature of strata in various human societies into the question of causes and consequences of distributive processes, or more attractively, the question of who gets what and why. Lenski's theory in answer to this problem aimed to synthesize existing theories, and the book elucidating and testing his ideas carried the catchy title *Power and Privilege*. Perhaps a less categorical title, like "Resources and Advantages," would have expressed better the most general statement of the program Lenski unfolded: the members of societies who command the most resources for that reason lead a privileged existence and have the best chances in life.

Lenski's two prime derivations from the perhaps obvious proposition that power makes for privilege were the technology hypothesis and the ideology hypothesis. Whereas the idea that resources make for advantages is pitched at the individual level, these two hypotheses referred to developments within societies and differences between them. The technology hypothesis held that if a society has a higher level of technological development, stratification within this society is stronger. Culling data from monographs by anthropologists, historians, and sociologists on phenomena such as hunting skills, ownership of gardens and fields, wealth according to tax records, number of wives, size of houses, differences in diet, and the ease with which various people in a society lived, it appeared that this thesis held up remarkably well in the early stages of technological evolution, but failed with the shift from agriculture to industry.

Lenski attributed this refutation not to flaws in the auxiliary assumption that advances in technology amount to the invention of new resources, but to the other auxiliary assumption that forms of power tend to be pyramidal.

Technological progress, Lenski now proposed, does not always make for an accumulation of new and old economic resources. Industrial societies use so many different vocational skills that education becomes an economic resource independent of the ownership of factories and machines. Also, because industrial societies no longer restrict the right to vote for political offices to the wealthy but have introduced universal suffrage, the balance of political power becomes more equal. Lenski's second derivation therefore invoked the ideologies of ruling industrial societies: to the extent that these societies are governed by parties seeking redistribution from the rich to the poor, the impact of class upon the life of their inhabitants is mitigated. The testing of this ideology hypothesis was presented as a matter for future research.

The first reviews of Lenski's book centered on the matter of whether the synthesis of existing theories was a happy one. In later research, the "multilayered" nature of Lenski's theory was noticed. If power makes for privilege, then the introduction of universal suffrage in industrial societies levels the distribution of political resources, and to the extent that redistributive parties ascend to government and award the inhabitants of a country social rights, differences between a society's members in income decrease too. This was measured by using official statistics on the income shares of the upper quintile or decile (Hewitt 1977). Some time later, hypotheses concerning the effects of government by left-wing parties on father–son mobility were tested (Heath 1981).

Whereas the program of class, status, and power focused on three aggregate phenomena within a society, the program of life chances and resources took its starting point from individual resources. Sometimes resources similar to the aggregate power phenomena were postulated. An example is Runciman (1989), who held that there are three kinds of power in every society, succinctly called means of production, means of persuasion, and means of coercion. Earlier, Collins (1975) added to the proposition that forms of property like slaves, landholding, and industrial capital are upheld by the means of violence of the state, the idea being that the means of mental production and of emotional production are resources too. Bourdieu (1984), leaning on Marx, used the term capital and distinguished three forms, but in the end came up with social resources as a new type: people differ in the extent they command economic, cultural, and social capital.

The counterpart of resources (or assets) is handicaps (or liabilities). By focusing on these, questions of age, ethnicity, and gender may be brought into the program of life chances and resources. To answer the question of why males in most human societies dominate females, Collins (1975) pointed out that women on the average are less tall and muscular than men, with women being physically vulnerable too by bearing and caring for children. As other handicaps for females accounting for male dominance, Collins listed property and ideology. Collins attempted to deal with the dynamics of age stratification by indicating resources of young persons and of adults.

Several subprograms of the program on life chances and resources concentrate on one type of capital. One investigates the thesis that in advanced agrarian societies the shift from weapon-bearing and army-commanding feudal lords to the monopolization of the means of violence by an absolute ruler raised the criteria of civilized conduct by which the old feudal lords sought to distinguish themselves from other, particularly ascending, strata. This subprogram was initiated by Elias in 1939 and had been dormant before a German reprint appeared in 1969 and an English translation in 1978. It was carried forward by De Swaan (1988) with respect to the elimination by industrial states of the negative externalities of vagrancy, contagious diseases, illiteracy, and infirmities in old age. Another subprogram is that of social capital (Lin 2001). It sings to the tune of "I get by with a little help from my friends." The results, however, seem to amount to the line "Going to try with a little help from my friends." According to some studies, people who find a job through a friend rather than through answering an advertisement wind up in a worse job. However, it was shown that if the status of the helping friend was higher, the job found was higher too.

The Elias hypothesis refers to situations in which the declining returns of one resource (weapons) in agrarian societies are offset to some extent by a greater importance of another resource (good manners). Bourdieu (1984) presented several hypotheses about how the properted classes in industrial societies try to maintain their position at the top of the social scale by compensatory strategies. An example is the statement that upon the introduction of wealth taxes and inheritance taxes, parents invest more in the education of their children. The conversion of resources may be taken as another topic for a subprogram of the program of life chances and resources.

The notion that classes, status groups, and parties are phenomena of the power relationships within a society almost naturally directed attention to political stability and change. In contrast, the notion of various kinds of individual resources steers us toward the question of how scarce consumption goods are distributed within a society, and the question of whether, apart from economic resources, political and symbolic resources also make life easier and more fulfilling. Thus, in a review of the results in the field of stratification in Great Britain between 1946 and 1976, Goldthorpe and Bevan (1977) went beyond pure description and set themselves the aim of integration. It was to be attained by taking classes, status groups, and parties as phenomena of the power relationships within a society and introducing the notion of advantage as complementary to that of power. After stating that power brings advantage, Goldthorpe and Bevan pointed out that the idea of advantage may fulfill a role in the field of societal stratification at the "distributional" level, analogous to that of power at the "relational" level. When detailing life chances, they pointed toward class differentials in infant as well as in adult mortality, class differences in the use of health services (which in Britain at that time were available to all and at very low cost or entirely free), and class differentials in access to different types and levels of education and in educational attainment.

The word life chances had been used by Weber in an almost casual way. Which concrete phenomena, treated as instances of advantages in research monographs, may be taken as part of the program of life chances and resources? Wright (1979) focused on income in the US and found that, when taking class, education, and occupational status as resources for individual income, class has a significant impact on income independent of occupational status, and that, net of education, the impact of class on

income is greater than that of status on income. Income returns to education differed within classes too, with the smallest returns for workers, and the largest for employers. This sums up Wright's answer to the question of whether not only more economic resources but also more symbolic resources lead to a more privileged life, as indicated by income.

Earlier, the embourgeoisement thesis held that affluent workers would lose their distinct position in the class structure. Findings for Britain in the early 1960s (Goldthorpe et al. 1968) spoke largely against it: the Labour Party continued to be regarded as the party for the working class, support for labor unions was still strong, and the orientation of affluent workers toward their job, rather than becoming a source of intrinsic satisfaction, remained instrumental. Also, as regards leisure, manual couples were more likely to spend spare time with kin and neighbors, and white-collar couples with colleagues and others. However, members of the manual and the non-manual classes did not differ much in the aspirations they held with respect to the education of their children.

Bourdieu (1984) took the next big step in this line of research on other chances in life than income. His most concrete and interesting question perhaps may be phrased as: with jobs becoming physically less exhausting, do people come to cultivate their aesthetic capacities? Bourdieu empirically investigated such matters as the food people eat, the furniture that fills their houses, the sports they practice, and, as far as aesthetic matters go, the paintings and music they esteem beautiful, as well as the films they have seen. He also established the relation between these phenomena and the occupation of persons. By way of factor analysis of surveys undertaken in France around 1970, Bourdieu sought to establish the existence of a multidimensional social space. This did not simply consist of dots for closely related occupations and leisure activities, but comprised in various statistical exercises several axes, particularly for the volume of capital commanded and the composition of that capital. Here Bourdieu came to three categories: people who command neither economic nor cultural capital, people who command primarily economic capital, such as persons with leading positions in industry and finance, and people who primarily command cultural capital, such as secondary school teachers and lawyers. Apparently, the number of persons in a society with both economic and cultural capital turned out to be very limited. In discussing his findings, Bourdieu counted not only diplomas but also the command of high culture, supposedly part of the implicit curriculum of schools, as cultural capital. The differences in leisure activities between the three groups were assumed to go beyond those necessitated by income differences. They would indicate a leisure preference in line with the nature of people's jobs, and a tendency for the persons with certain occupations to distinguish themselves from persons with other occupations.

Weber had maintained that status groups claim a particular lifestyle, but shied away from circumscribing those styles. He simply noted that status groups are indicated by who marries whom and who shares meals with whom. Elias (1978 [1939]) studied one aspect of the lifestyle turning people into a status group, the criteria for civilized conduct in agrarian societies by which their top groups keep the lower strata of society at a distance. According to Bourdieu, Weber's thesis that status groups have distinctive lifestyles was not simply about life styles but about distinction. Arguing along the lines set out by Bourdieu, lifestyles may also be taken as combinations of life chances. Questions about the lifestyle within the working classes of industrial societies began to draw more attention after World War II. It then turned out that in industrial societies with private ownership of the means of production, mass unemployment did not always occur, and wages did not sink to the subsistence level. With the rising standard of living of the working classes, questions about how income was being spent became a topic of empirical research. Also, with the shortening of the number of hours worked each day, the contraction of the working week from six to five days, and the introduction of paid vacation weeks, questions on leisure became important. However, the idea of a hierarchy of human needs, with subsistence at its lower levels, rest and recreation a bit higher, and the appreciation of beauty on top, and other things somewhere in between, has remained until now implicit in the program of life chances and resources.

The program of class, status, and power had been plagued by the difficulty that parties and status groups are always more than mere aggregates, whereas classes are not always groups. By shifting from aggregate phenomena like classes, status groups, and parties to various individual resources, the program of life chances and resources did away with this difficulty. Ultee also offered a fresh start with respect to the conditions under which persons who have similar market positions (such as manual workers) form groups, in this case political parties and labor unions pressing their interests. The idea of false consciousness prominent in theories taking class as the fundamental dimension of stratification in all times and at all places was dropped. It now was posited that collective action was but one strategy open to the members of a society's lower strata, and individual mobility another (Boudon 1973). It was held too that rational actors face the dilemma of collective action. After all, if only a few persons participate in a class organization, the movement will not attain its goals, and if a lot of people participate, a person may withdraw since without that one person the goals will in any case be reached. The economist Olson (1965) pointed out this dilemma, first studied as the prisoner's dilemma, and the sociologist Oberschall (1973) indicated that the dilemma of collective action may be overcome not only in small groups, as Olson stated, but also in homogeneous large groups concentrated in particular localities.

Of late, a shift is taking place within the field of social stratification as regards the "outside" theories being applied. Blau and Duncan (1967) estimated statistical models of status attainment processes in the US in the mid-twentieth century, and sought to provide evidence that a general functionalist theory obtained: attainment would be governed less and less by principles of ascription such as race and social background, and more and more by principles of achievement such as education and work experience. It is easy to interpret their finding of a shift from ascription to achievement within the framework of individual resources: the effect of parental characteristics for a person's level of education and job status declined, and the return to education in terms of job status increased. Indeed, stock markets discovered that the profits of a company are not always served by making the children of founders directors, and states lowered the financial costs of schooling for children of parents who are not well-to-do.

Sociologists like Elias and Bourdieu, however, have been pointing toward the effects of competition between persons if the inequalities between them in some resources decrease. These effects may be characterized as spiralling processes: criteria for civilized conduct become more strict; if income does not distinguish as it used to do between classes, the way people spend their money and time becomes important. If primary school becomes compulsory in industrial societies, for parents who already send their children to primary school, secondary education becomes important for their children. And if the age of compulsory schooling is raised to, say, 16 years, higher education is the means to keep ahead. Blau and Duncan's results hint at spiralling processes too: a person's education influenced not only a person's first job directly, but also a person's present job, and, net of education, a higher first job made for a higher present job.

Spiralling processes differ from the equilibrium processes on competitive markets studied by neoclassical economics. However, formal models for rational persons making sequences of decisions rather than one-shot choices (Boudon 1973; Mare 1981) might have more on offer, as well as theories on market behavior in a social environment (Becker & Murphy 2000). It should be pointed out too that Goldthorpe (2000), when explaining persistent class inequalities in education attainment, tries to do away with the general assumption of rational choice theories that people go for the highest. Instead they would avoid a situation for their children that is worse than their own one, being satisfied with that situation or a better one.

SEE ALSO: Class, Status, and Power; Distinction; Stratification and Inequality, Theories of; Stratification: Technology and Ideology

REFERENCES AND SUGGESTED READINGS

Becker, G. S. & Murphy, K. M. (2000) *Social Economics: Market Behaviour in a Social Environment.* Belknap Press, Cambridge, MA.
Blau, P. M. & Duncan, O. D. (1967) *The American Occupational Structure.* Wiley, New York.
Boudon, R. (1973) *Education, Opportunity, and Social Inequality.* Wiley, New York.
Bourdieu, P. (1984) *Distinction: A Social Critique of the Judgment of Taste.* Harvard University Press, Cambridge, MA.
Collins, R. (1975) *Conflict Sociology.* Academic Press, New York.
De Swaan, A. (1988) *In Care of the State.* Polity Press, Cambridge.
Elias, N. (1978 [1939]) *The Civilizing Process.* Blackwell, Oxford.
Goldthorpe, J. H. (2000) *On Sociology.* Oxford University Press, Oxford.
Goldthorpe, J. H. & Bevan, P. (1977) The Study of Social Stratification in Great Britain: 1946–1976. *Social Science Information* 16: 279–334.
Goldthorpe, J. H., Lockwood, D., Bechhofer, F., & Platt, J. (1968) *The Affluent Worker in the Class Structure.* Cambridge University Press, Cambridge.
Heath, A. (1981) *Social Mobility.* Fontana, Glasgow.
Hewitt, C. (1977) The Effect of Political Democracy and Social Democracy on Equality in Industrial Societies: A Cross-National Comparison. *American Sociological Review* 42: 450–64.
Lenski, G. (1966) *Power and Privilege.* McGraw-Hill, New York.
Lin, N. (2001) *Social Capital: A Theory of Social Structure and Action.* Cambridge University Press, Cambridge.
Mare, R. D. (1981) Change and Stability in Educational Stratification. *American Sociological Review* 46: 72–87.
Oberschall, A. (1973) *Social Conflict and Social Movements.* Prentice-Hall, Englewood Cliffs, NJ.
Olson, M. (1965) *The Logic of Collective Action.* Harvard University Press, Cambridge, MA.
Runciman, W. G. (1989) *A Treatise on Social Theory*, Vol. 2: *Substantive Social Theory.* Cambridge University Press, Cambridge.
Wright, E. O. (1979) *Class Structure and Income Determination.* Academic Press, New York.

life course

Jens Zinn

The term life course refers to the idea that the course of one's life is not just determined by a natural process of aging but is mainly shaped by social institutions and sociocultural values as well as by decisions and unexpected events. Thus the life course consists of life stages (e.g., childhood, youth, adulthood), status passages or transitions (e.g., from youth to adulthood, from student to professional), and life events (e.g., marriage, job loss, illness). Formal institutions such as the law and the welfare state ascribe rights and duties by age and formal status, and when, for example, to start a family and how to divide labor within the household are also structured by sociocultural norms and habits.

The term life course increasingly supplants the earlier concept of the life cycle, which implies a connection to early developmental concepts in psychology. These concepts state that life is structured by a specific order of events where one built on the previous event, and that they represent a "natural" order.

The modern notion of the life course differs from concepts in small "primitive" societies as described in ethnographic research, where transitions are understood as determined by natural processes (such as first menses to indicate that girls can be married) or "rites of passage" (Gennep 1981 [1909]).

The modern notion of the life course also differs from its ancestors. During the Middle Ages in Western Europe, the understanding of life was captured in religious and magical thinking. Life seemed to be determined mainly by external powers, such as God or fate. The different stages of life were understood as an expression of an externally given order. The course of one's life could always be interrupted by unforeseeable events and often ended prematurely by death. With modernization, ongoing sociocultural and sociostructural changes shift the meaning of the life course (Kohli 1986).

The institutionalization of education and a social security system as well as the formal regulation of rights and duties by age create a new framework and understanding of the life course as something to be shaped individually. Models of normative expectations about how men and women should shape their life were institutionalized, and societal institutions orient themselves to such models of a "normal" life. Additionally, the increase in medical knowledge and standards of hygiene supports a significant change in mortality, which was moved to and concentrated on old age. A predictable life

course became a normal experience for an increasing part of the population.

Life course research is interested in specific sociostructural patterns as well as the individual's sense-making of his or her life. Sometimes the whole life is examined, but many studies focus on specific transitions, for example from youth to adulthood, from single to husband or wife and to father or mother, from unemployed to employed, or from a lower to a higher position.

How people manage their life systematically differs by sociostructural indicators such as gender, ethnicity, health/disability, or generation. It is expected, for example, that women marry younger than men and that they bear children before 30, while it is accepted that men father children in older age as well. It is also accepted that younger women marry older men, but the reverse is perceived as unusual or even deviant. Such norms are reflected in different life plans and expectations regarding the future, for example that women often expect to have a career break in order to have children whereas men often assume that children will not significantly influence their occupational career.

Early research on the life course was often influenced by sociopsychological approaches combining contextual factors (such as historical change or illness) with individual coping strategies. For example, the early study by Glen Elder, *Children of the Great Depression* (1974), showed how families mediated the individual's management of the hardships of economic slowdown. Another classic study by Barney Glaser and Anselm Strauss (1968) on status passages during the life course showed how people cope with dying. Another stream in the tradition of sociostructural analysis focuses on formal factors influencing the life course (e.g., class, educational attainment, gender, marital status, age).

In newer research the orthodoxy of sociostructural determination of individuals' sense-making of social positioning and the life course was questioned by the thesis of growing individualization, which would weaken the individual's embeddedness in traditional institutions. Growing individualization would set free new generations from traditional bonds and would open an increasing space of new opportunities and decisions, for example for youth (Furlong & Cartmel 1997). More critical examinations show that although the semantics of life course decisions have changed, the idea of growing self-responsibility does not go along with a significant change in vertical social mobility or increasing individual control of life (Vickerstaff 2006).

The life course encompasses an objective course of life and the individual's sense-making of his or her life. This is mainly analyzed by a combination of quantitative and qualitative methods that investigate the sense-making of transitions, action orientations, and coping strategies. Additionally, two streams of research have developed which concentrate on specific aspects of the life course. At the center of biographical research is the individual's sense-making of his or her life. Sociostructural researchers, on the other hand, focus on the life course patterns that are expressed in durations of working and employment status or marital status or divorce, and which factors could be linked to such patterns. While the biographical approach mainly works with qualitative methods and narrative interviewing techniques to explain current activities by the cumulated sense-making of one's former life (Rosenthal 2004), the sociostructural approach uses event history modeling (Blossfeld & Rohwer 2002) or optimal pattern matching techniques (Abbott & Tsay 2000) to examine and compare life course patterns and events.

SEE ALSO: Aging and the Life Course, Theories of; Biography; Crime, Life Course Theory of; Individualism; Life Course and Family; Life Course Perspective; Life History; Rite of Passage

REFERENCES AND SUGGESTED READINGS

Abbott, A. & Tsay, A. (2000) Sequence Analysis and Optimal Matching Methods in Sociology: Review and Prospect. *Sociological Methods Research* 29: 3–33.

Blossfeld, H.-P. & Rohwer, G. (2002) *Techniques of Event History Modelling*. Lawrence Erlbaum, Mahwah, NJ.

Elder, G. H. (1974) *Children of the Great Depression: Social Change in Life Experience*. University of Chicago Press, Chicago.

Furlong, A. & Cartmel, F. (1997) *Young People and Social Change*. Open University Press, Buckingham.

Gennep, A. von (1981 [1909]) *Les Rites de passage*. Picard, Paris.

Glaser, B. G. & Strauss, A. L. (1968) *Time for Dying*. Aldine, Chicago.

Kohli, M. (1986) Social Organization and Subjective Construction of the Life Course In: Sørensen, A. B., Weinert, F. E., & Sherrod, L. R. (Eds.), *Human Development and the Life Course: Multidisciplinary Perspectives*. Lawrence Erlbaum, Hillsdale, NJ, pp. 271–92.

Rosenthal, G. (2004) Biographical Research. In: Seale, C., Gobo, G., Gubrium, J. F., & Silverman, D. (Eds.), *Qualitative Research Practice*. Sage, Thousand Oaks, CA, pp. 48–64.

Vickerstaff, S. (2006) Risk, the Life Course, Youth, and Old Age. In: Taylor-Gooby, P. & Zinn, J. O. (Eds.), *Risk in Social Sciences*. Oxford University Press, Oxford.

life course and family

Chris Phillipson

The concept of the life course refers to the social processes shaping individuals' journey through life, in particular their interaction with major institutions associated with the family, work, education, and leisure. The life course perspective distinguishes between *trajectories* on the one side and *transitions* on the other. The former refer to the sequence of roles experienced over the life span; the latter to the changes consequent upon events such as divorce, children leaving home, and the birth of grandchildren.

Life course approaches emphasize the way in which individual trajectories and transitions are linked to the lives of significant others, with the interdependency of generations being one such example. The idea of families having "interlocking trajectories" was first explored in the work of the American sociologist Glenn Elder, most notably in his *Children of the Great Depression* (1974). This study illustrated how delays in the parents' timing of work and family careers as a result of the economic depression of the 1930s affected the subsequent timing of their children's own life transitions. Another example of the "linked-lives" phenomenon has been illustrated in research on grandparenting that examines situations where grandparents take responsibility for raising grandchildren. Silverstein et al. (2003) view this as an example of "mutual interdependency" within the family, with grandparents adopting new parental roles and parents excused from the main responsibilities associated with parenting. In this way, the researchers suggest, the family can be seen as a group of interlocking individuals who continually adapt both to their own needs and to those of others within the family system.

The idea of *time* is a central element in the concept of the life course. Hareven (1982) identifies three different levels of "time" running through the life course of any individual: familial, individual, and historical. *Family time* refers to the timing of events such as marriage which involve the individual moving into new family-based roles such as spouse or parent. *Individual time* is closely linked with family time, given the links between individual transitions and collective family-based transitions. *Historical time* refers to more general institutional changes in society, including demographic, economic, and socio-legal. Hareven argues that an understanding of the synchronization of these different levels of time is essential to the investigation of the relationship between individual lives and wider processes of social change.

The life course is itself now stretched over a longer period of time, given substantial improvements in life expectancy in most western countries. Associated with this have been significant changes in family life over the past century. For example, current cohorts of older people experience a far longer period of "post-parental" life than was the case with earlier cohorts. In 1900, women were likely to be in their mid-fifties/sixties when their last child married. Consequently, given lower life expectancy at this time, many women could expect to be widowed before their last child left home. With increased life expectancy, smaller family size associated with low fertility rates, and closer spacing of children, the average couple can now expect to live for 25 years or more after their last child has moved out. However, this postparental phase may still be associated with extensive care responsibilities associated with grandparenting and other types of informal care.

The life course approach has been highly influential in research on the family life of older people, with the idea of linked lives

demonstrating how expectations about giving and receiving support are part of a continuing interaction among parents, children, and other kin over their lives as they move through time (Hareven 2001). Although the growth of individualism may have loosened kinship ties to a degree (Beck & Beck-Gernsheim 2004), relationships between generations continue to be important in the family life of older people (Phillipson et al. 2001). The work of Attias-Donfut and Wolff (2000) in France has highlighted the role of the "pivot" (middle-age) generation in providing economic support to young people on the threshold of adulthood, as well as providing flexible forms of care for the older generation as need arises. Generations have also been shown to provide emotional support for one another at different points of the life course. Research in the US has tracked feelings of emotional closeness and support across generations and found that emotional closeness stayed stable over a period of nearly two decades, with the maintenance of strong levels of affectual solidarity across generations, with adult children both providing and receiving help from mothers and fathers.

Life course research has also underlined the variability of expectations and patterns of support, with patterns of generational assistance shaped by values and experiences that evolve throughout life. Hareven and Adams (1996) demonstrate this point from research in the US examining how the premigration history of different ethnic groups influences expectations of support in later life. They demonstrate how older cohorts tend to emphasize support from family members; younger cohorts, in contrast, tend to stress help from social and welfare programs. They further note the way in which the earlier life course experiences of each cohort, as shaped by historical events, also affect the availability of economic and educational resources and support networks.

Given greater longevity, multi-generational ties have assumed much greater importance for securing well-being and support for individuals over the life course. At the same time, the diversity of family ties must also be acknowledged. Generational relationships remain important in anchoring people at different points of the life course; however, not everyone is involved to the same degree in such relationships. The role of family relationships within the life course is likely to undergo further modification with the experiences of new cohorts influenced by wider social and historical change. The key point to acknowledge here is the dynamic process involved with different age groups both influencing the shape of the life course, while themselves being affected by changes operating at an institutional level. Families with their connecting intergenerational bonds will remain at the center of this process, and are themselves likely to contribute to what will be a major area of social change in the years ahead.

SEE ALSO: Aging and the Life Course, Theories of; Family Diversity; Grandparenthood; Life Course; Life Course Perspective

REFERENCES AND SUGGESTED READINGS

Attias-Donfut, C. & Wolff, F.-C. (2000) Complimentarity Between Private and Public Transfers. In: Arber, S. & Attias-Donfut, C. (Eds.), *The Myth of Generational Conflict*. Routledge, London, pp. 47–68.

Beck, U. & Beck-Gernsheim, E. (2004) Families in a Runaway World. In: Scott, J., Treas, J., & Richards, M. (Eds.), *The Blackwell Companion to the Sociology of Families*. Blackwell, Oxford, pp. 499–514.

Elder, G. H., Jr. (1974) *Children of the Great Depression*. University of Chicago Press, Chicago.

Elder, G. H., Jr. (1983) The Life Course and Aging: Challenges, Lessons and New Directions. In: Settersten, R. (Ed.), *Invitation to the Life Course*. Baywood Publishing, New York, pp. 49–71.

Hareven, T. K. (1982) *Family Time and Industrial Time*. Cambridge University Press, Cambridge.

Hareven, T. K. (2001) Historical Perspectives on Aging and Family Relations. In: Binstock, R. H. & George, L. K. (Eds.), *Handbook of Aging and the Social Sciences*. Academic Press, San Diego, pp. 141–59.

Hareven, T. K. & Adams, K. (1996) The Generation in the Middle: Cohort Comparisons in Assistance to Aging Parents in an American Community. In: Hareven, T. K. (Ed.), *Aging and Generational Relations Over the Life Course: A Historical and Life Course Perspective*. Walter de Gruyter, Berlin, pp. 272–93.

Phillipson, C., Bernard, M., Phillips, J., & Ogg, J. (2001) *The Family and Community Life of Older People*. Routledge, London.

Silverstein, M., Giarrusso, R., & Bengston, V. L. (2003) Grandparents and Grandchildren in Family Systems: A Social-Developmental Perspective. In: Bengston, V. L. & Lowenstein, A. (Eds.), *Global Aging and Challenges to Families*. Aldine de Gruyter, New York, pp. 75–102.

life course perspective

Glen H. Elder, Jr.

Developments after World War II called for new ways of thinking about lives, society, and their relationship. The social discontinuities of economic depression, a world war, and prosperity raised questions about the course these adults followed into the middle years. The changing age composition of society also gave more visibility to the adult life course. Problems of old age directed inquiry to earlier trajectories and to the processes by which lives are influenced by a changing society. In combination, these developments placed lives in context and focused attention on their social pathways. From this background the life course perspective was conceived as both a concept and a theoretical orientation for the study of individual lives and age cohorts.

ELEMENTARY DISTINCTIONS

As a concept, the life course refers to an age-graded sequence of events and social roles that is embedded in social structures and history. These structures vary from family relations at the micro level to age-graded educational organizations and state policies at the macro level. The life course also represents a theoretical orientation, a type of theory that guides research in terms of problem identification and formulation, rationales of design, variable selection, and explanatory analysis.

The life course evolves over an extended period of time, as in a trajectory of marriage or work; and it also takes form within a short time span, as a transition between statuses, such as leaving school and entering a full-time job. Social transitions of this kind vary in timing, whether relatively early or late, and are always embedded in trajectories which give them a distinctive form and meaning. Indeed, life trajectories in specific domains (such as work) link states, the duration of each state, and transitions between states across successive years. For example, each work trajectory is patterned by a sequence of jobs of varying duration and transitions between jobs, along with occasional episodes of unemployment. A single work transition may entail little or no change or produce a turning point – a redirection of the life course through changes in situation, meaning, and/or behavior. Marriage and stable employment have served as transitions out of crime and as turning points for young men who grew up in poverty.

Each concept – trajectory, transition, and turning point – applies to levels of the life course, from macro to micro: (1) institutionalized pathways may be defined on the macro level by social policies of the state or firm; (2) within these pathways, the individual works out his or her life course through choices and lines of action; and (3) the individual's own course of development and aging, which may be expressed in terms of self-confidence or intellectual competence. These multiple levels are illustrated by an examination of worklife. A "career line" refers to pathways that are defined by the aggregated work histories of employees. They are structured by industry sectors and the labor market. An individual's worklife varies by the career requirements of the marketplace and firm. It also may vary by the worker's family life, an integral dimension of his or her life course. On the developmental level, both negative and positive changes in work have psychological consequences, as in feelings of self-efficacy. Each level of the life course represents a field of study, though contemporary work is more likely to extend across levels.

The life course is frequently used interchangeably with other concepts, such as life span, life history, and life cycle. These concepts have an important application in studies of the life course, but they are not synonymous with its meaning. For example, life span, as in life span psychology or sociology, describes the temporal scope of inquiry and specialization that includes a substantial portion of life, especially one that links behavior in two or more life stages. The temporal frame moves well beyond age-specific studies of childhood or adolescence. Life history, on the other hand, generally refers to the chronology of events and activities across the life course (e.g., residence, household composition, marriage and childbearing). It is frequently assembled from retrospective life calendars, which record the year and month at which a transition occurs in each domain. This life record depicts an unfolding life course in ways uniquely suited to event history analyses. Lastly, the life cycle has been used to describe a sequence of social roles or events, especially the reproductive process from one generation to the next. All populations have a reproductive life cycle, but only some of the people bear children.

PARADIGMATIC PRINCIPLES OF LIFE COURSE THEORY

Over many decades, the life span was carved up into life stages which became distinct fields of study. Now we recognize that developmental and aging processes can only be understood by taking a long-term perspective. This whole life course perspective reflects the cumulation of research that documents the relevance of early learning and experience for later life. Behaviors at mid-life are influenced not only by current circumstances or by anticipation of the future, but also by the experiences of childhood. Also relevant are the developmental trajectories and the biomarkers of pre-disease pathways that extend back to the early years. Long-term studies are increasingly documenting the relationship between patterns of late-life adaptation and the formative years of life course development. By studying lives over substantial periods of time, we can also observe the potential interplay of social change with individual development. Accordingly, the principle of life span development states that: *human development and aging are lifelong processes.*

Pioneering longitudinal studies in California became lifelong enterprises without an initial vision of the life course. Larger studies have recently adopted this perspective, such as the national longitudinal studies of birth cohorts in Great Britain, marked by birth dates of 1946, 1958, 1970, and 2000. They are all scheduled to be followed into the later years of life. Studies across the life course are demonstrating that life outcomes can be modified even for those who experienced adversity in childhood. They are also changing our understanding of poverty, work, and achievement across the life course while identifying pathways of resilience and increasing vulnerability.

Individual lives are not merely shaped by social institutions or the larger environment. They are also constructed through the choices and plans people make. In the severely limited world of the inner city, families struggle with poverty and crime, but many parents manage their children's lives effectively by entering them in youth organizations and activities, including the local church. John Clausen (1993) has made the case for planful competence as a component of human agency. Adolescents who possess self-confidence, an intellectual investment, and dependability – the elements of planful competence – can more effectively prepare themselves for the future. The principle of human agency states that: *individuals construct their own life course through the choices and actions they take within the opportunities and constraints of history and social circumstance.*

Making decisions or choices plays an important role in the timing and timetables of life. Some people come to marriage early in life, while others do so much later on. These differences in timing have consequences, since early marriage may come before education is completed and late marriage severely restricts the pool of available mates. Mortimer (2003) finds that very early transitions to adulthood, such as leaving home at a very young age, have detrimental effects on mental health. Since life experiences often cumulate over time, low income and limited wealth are likely to have more potent effects on emotional and physical health in later life. Unequal groups become more unequal across the years. With these points in mind, the principle of timing states that: *the developmental antecedents and consequences of life transitions, events, and behavioral patterns vary according to their timing in a person's life.*

Both timing and individual choices occur in specific historical times and places, as expressed in the principle of time and place: *the life course of individuals is embedded in and shaped by the historical times and places they experience over their lifetime.* Consider the Chinese Cultural Revolution, which lasted from 1966 to 1976.

Thousands of urban Chinese youth had their lives drastically altered by this revolution through Mao's decision to "send them down" to the countryside, separating them from their families and communities, exposing them to hard manual labor, and limiting their education. These young people postponed marital decisions in the hope of returning to their coastal city. In this manner, the sent-down cohort was set apart from adjacent birth cohorts and those of similar age who were not sent down.

The same historical event or change may vary in substance and meaning across different places, regions, or nations. In World War II, the post-war era brought great prosperity to Americans as they returned from the war, but Germans faced widespread great poverty and hunger at the same time. With retrospective life history methods, Mayer (1988) found that German men who were born between 1915 and 1925 were almost universally involved in the armed forces. These men lost as much as nine years of their occupational careers in the war and many of the survivors could not find employment afterward. The younger cohort of 1931 also suffered widespread hardship in the war which could not be countered by the economic boom of the 1950s.

In the Great Depression, children were influenced by their father's income loss and by their mother's employment. This observation is expressed by the principle of linked lives: *lives are lived interdependently and sociohistorical influences are expressed through this network of shared relationships.* A more contemporary example comes from the US rural crisis of the 1980s and 1990s when economic indicators such as housing starts and retail sales declined by 40 percent or more. Economic hardship adversely affected the nurturance of parents because it increased their depressed feelings. At the same time, hardship made joint activities and shared responsibilities more important. These experiences had developmental value in the lives of rural youth.

In combination, these principles foster awareness of larger historical forces and the timing of events. They enhance the recognition that lives cannot be understood when they are not connected to relationships with significant others. Most importantly, when they inform inquiry they promote a holistic understanding of lives over time and across changing contexts. The ideas underlying these principles have emerged over recent decades. The first principle on human development and aging as lifelong processes represents a definitional premise of the theoretical orientation's scope – the temporal span of study extends from birth to death. The other principles first appeared in a Cooley-Mead award lecture by Glen Elder (1994) that surveyed studies of the life course and some key premises. Within the time frame of life histories, the principle of human agency depicts the individual as an active force in constructing his or her life course through choices and action. The multiple meanings of age brought temporality and timing to life course thinking, especially during the 1960s – the meanings of social age and historical time. The principle of linked lives refers to the interdependence of lives and has its origins in role theoretical accounts of life histories that date back to *The Polish Peasant* (Thomas & Znaniecki 1918–20). The fifth principle on historical time and place derives much of its richness from the emergence of social history.

THE EMERGENCE OF LIFE COURSE THEORY

Research traditions and concepts relevant to the life course began to coalesce in a theoretical orientation during the 1960s and 1970s. One of the crystallizing forces came from the pioneering longitudinal studies that followed children through the Great Depression and into adulthood – e.g., the Oakland and Berkeley Growth Studies, and the Guidance Study at the University of California, Berkeley. With study members in adulthood, the investigators had to move beyond child-based, growth-oriented accounts of development. They faced three major challenges: (1) to formulate concepts of development and aging that apply across the life course; (2) to develop ways of thinking about how lives are organized and change over time; and (3) to relate lives to an ever-changing society.

The first challenge required the formulation of life span concepts of development and aging in both sociology and developmental psychology. For sociologists, life transitions and turning points entail changes in relationships, social identity, and self-evaluation. Concepts of interpersonal and correlated constraints offer insights concerning the dynamics of behavioral continuity. Within birth cohorts, differentiating and cumulating experiences across the life course tend to generate complementary processes, greater heterogeneity or inequality between individuals over time, through the cumulation of advantages and disadvantages, and enhanced behavioral continuity within individuals. In psychology, the distinctive principles of life span development feature the relative plasticity and agency of the organism, the multidirectionality of life span development, and the lifelong interaction of person and social context.

The other challenges were prompted by the relative neglect of context in studies of the person and life span development. These studies did not take role sequences into account in concepts of careers and the life cycle, or age grading. However, a view of life patterns as role sequences dates back to the nineteenth century. Changes in social roles marked changes in social stages across the life cycle, as from marriage to parenthood. W. I. Thomas was an early proponent of this life cycle perspective. With Florian Znaniecki, he used life-record data to study the emigration of Polish peasants to European and American cities around the turn of the century (1918–20). Over the years, life cycle theory has focused on stages of parenthood and the generations. By doing so, it has brought some measure of context to lives by stressing their interdependence and providing a way of thinking about socialization. Within the life cycle of each generation, unexpected and involuntary events occur. Thus, a 30-year-old woman becomes a grandmother when her adolescent daughter has a first child. Family members lose their status as grandchildren when their grandparents die. Changing connections to family members are a defining feature of life cycle processes.

But the life cycle's emphasis on reproduction and parenting severely limited its application. It did not apply to the never married or to the multiply divorced in a world in which marriage and parenting have become uncoupled to a large extent. And its focus on one career, that of reproduction, ignored the contemporary realities of multiple roles (e.g., work and family). Equally important, the life cycle, as a role concept, was not sensitive to temporality, apart from the notion of order. It does not specify the duration of time-in-role or the timing of life transitions, distinctions that are now an essential part of an age-graded view of the life course. A sequence of parental roles, for example, could occur in a woman's twenties or thirties. Likewise social role categories, such as generational membership, failed to locate people in historical time with precision. Membership in a kinship generation may span 30 years.

Until the 1960s, the relationship perspective of the life cycle offered a popular way of thinking about the patterning of lives and their interdependence, despite the aforementioned limitations. However, these limitations soon led to a convergence with newly developing understandings of age in a sociological perspective on the life course. This perspective drew upon the key virtues of each tradition, the distinction of linked lives in the life cycle approach and of the relation between age and time that provided an age-graded model of the life course embedded in a specific historical context. More than before, human development and aging were viewed now as interacting with a changing life course and its historical context.

These new understandings of age are based on three advances: greater knowledge of the sociocultural meanings of age across the life span, more awareness of the variability among people of the same age in the pace and sequencing of life transitions (e.g., people of the same age do not move across their lives in concert), and the historical meanings of age-defined cohorts by birth year or entry into society. Age distinctions may be expressed in terms of social and normative expectations about the timing of life transitions. These expectations can be thought of as timetables – as appropriate times for entering primary school and leaving school, for marriage and the attainment of a managerial role. The existence of such expectations and informal sanctions, as well as peer pressures, makes the appropriate timing of certain transitions especially consequential, such as marriage in a traditional society. Among people born in the same year, some will come to marriage relatively early, or on time, or relatively late, and some will never marry. Such differences in timing may reflect specific historical circumstances, such as hard times in an economic depression or rapid economic growth. Birth year locates people in specific age cohorts and thus according to particular social changes.

The three dimensions of the life course as a theoretical orientation (e.g., life span concepts, social relationships and the life cycle, and age-based concepts) came together in a study of California children who were born in the 1920s, grew up in the Great Depression, and then entered service roles in World War II (Elder 1999 [1974]). The central question concerned the effects of the Great Depression on the lives and development of two birth cohorts, the Oakland children who were born in 1920–1, and the Berkeley children, with birth years of 1928–9. The Depression's effects centered on variation in economic loss for both cohorts. Two deprivational groups within the middle and working classes of 1929 were identified by income loss (1929–33) relative to the decline in cost of living (about 25 percent over this period). Deprived families were defined by a loss of more than 35 percent of their 1929 income, a figure that applies well to both age cohorts. At first an intergenerational approach seemed appropriate and adequate for addressing the above question, with emphasis on the process by which Depression hardship made a difference among children by changing family processes and socialization. But the profound change in life experiences from the 1920s into the late 1930s raised questions that could not be investigated by this perspective. For example, the effect of change depended on many circumstances, including the children's exposure to the change at different ages, as well as the differential age of parents when the economy collapsed. Birth years at opposite ends of the 1920s identified birth cohorts that experienced family income losses at different life stages. Family responses to such losses became a set of linkages between the economic collapse of the 1930s and the developmental experience of children. Dynamic notions of the family economy and its multiple actors became a way of relating the economic crisis to the lives of each cohort of children.

To understand the consequences of growing up in the Great Depression, we drew upon knowledge of life paths to adulthood, such as education, marriage, worklife advancement, and military duty. A number of young people might escape hardship through early work and military service, whereas others might do so through higher education and marriage. However, some outcomes seemed to have more to do with their timing than with their mere occurrence, such as marriage. Hardship favored early marriage by diminishing the chances of higher education and by making life in the parental home less appealing. Moreover, developmental theory suggests that the early work experience of adolescents would prompt early thinking about work and the timing of their entry into adult work roles. These and other issues made theoretical distinctions concerning the age-graded life course especially relevant to the study.

Most adults from hard-pressed families managed to rise above this disadvantage as they moved into adulthood. This resilience had much to do with entry into college and the military, along with the support of a partner, family, and friends. However, notable adverse effects of the Great Depression appear among the younger Berkeley males. They experienced the Depression crisis when they were more dependent on family nurturance and hence more vulnerable to family instability, emotional strain, and family conflict. Girls of the same age were more protected by the support of their mothers. Compared to age mates and the older Oakland cohort, the Berkeley boys were less likely to be hopeful, self-directed, and confident about their future than were youth who were spared such hardship. However, between adolescence and mid-life, postgraduate education, a supportive wife, and the developmental benefits of military service enabled many deprived Berkeley men to achieve notable gains in self-confidence and social competence. Recovery and resilience are common themes in the lives of Depression children from the two birth cohorts.

By the end of the twentieth century, across the discipline of sociology and the social sciences, the life course had become a general theoretical framework for the study of lives, human development, and aging. Symptomatic of this development is the publication of a handbook on the life course (Mortimer & Shanahan 2003), as well as the dramatic growth of longitudinal studies and the emergence of new methods for the collection and analysis of life history data.

SEE ALSO: Aging and the Life Course, Theories of; Aging, Longitudinal Studies; Aging, Sociology of; Crime, Life Course Theory of; Healthy Life Expectancy; Life Course; Life Course and Family; Socialization; Status Attainment; Transition from School to Work

REFERENCES AND SUGGESTED READINGS

Clausen, J. (1993) *American Lives: Looking Back at the Children of the Great Depression*. Free Press, New York.

Elder, G. H., Jr. (1975) Age Differentiation and the Life Course. *Annual Review of Sociology* 1: 165–90.

Elder, G. H., Jr. (1994) Time, Human Agency, and Change: Perspectives on the Life Course. *Social Psychology Quarterly* 57(1): 4–15.

Elder, G. H., Jr. (1998) The Life Course and Human Development. In: Lerner, R. M. (Ed.), *Handbook of Child Psychology*. Vol. 1: *Theoretical Models of Human Development*. Wiley, New York, pp. 939–91.

Elder, G. H., Jr. (1999 [1974]) *Children of the Great Depression: Social Change in Life Experience*, 25th anniversary edition. Westview Press, Boulder, CO.

Laub, J. H. & Sampson, R. J. (2003) *Shared Beginnings, Divergent Lives*. Harvard University Press, Cambridge, MA.

Mayer, K. U. (1988) German Survivors of World War II: The Impact on the Life Course of the Collective Experience of Birth Cohorts. In: Riley, M. W. (Ed., in association with B. J. Huber & B. B. Hess), *Social Change and the Life Course*. Vol. 1: *Social Structures and Human Lives*. Sage, Beverly Hills, CA, pp. 229–46.

Mortimer, J. T. (2003) *Working and Growing Up in America*. Harvard University Press, Cambridge, MA.

Mortimer, J. T. & Shanahan, M. J. (Eds.) (2003) *Handbook of the Life Course*. Kluwer/Plenum, New York.

Neugarten, B. L. (Ed.) (1996) *The Meanings of Age: Selected Papers of Bernice L. Neugarten*. Foreword by D. A. Neugarten. University of Chicago Press, Chicago.

Riley, M. W., Johnson, M. E., & Foner, A. (1972) *Aging and Society: A Sociology of Age Stratification*. Russell Sage Foundation, New York.

Thomas, W. I. & Znaniecki, F. (1918–20) *The Polish Peasant in Europe and America*. Badger, Chicago.

life environmentalism

Hiroyuki Torigoe and Yukiko Kada

Life environmentalism is a model that aims to resolve environmental problems from a perspective that considers conserving the community life and practices of the people who inhabit the affected area. The life environmentalism model was developed in the 1980s by Japanese environmental sociologists who were concerned with the environmental destruction wrought by industrialization. At the time, the field of environmental policy was divided into two schools of thought embracing mutually opposed ideas about the best approach to environmental policy. The first, which we call "nature environmentalism," advocated the preservation (or restoration) of the pristine natural environment, following the ideals of the natural conservation movement and ecological theory. The other, which we call "modern technicism," emphasized the development of modern technology to rehabilitate the affected environment. This was the position typically embraced by government officials who had civil engineering credentials and the power to allocate the public budget.

However, when sociologists made in-depth field research, it was discovered that the local people, as well as some government agents and nature conservationists who worked closely with the local people, were drawing on local knowledge to resolve local issues. Life environmentalism thus developed as a theory that utilizes local knowledge (and associated practices) to resolve environmental problems, recognizing that local communities depend upon the local/natural environment and have therefore developed practices that sustain it. These three points are illustrated using the case study of Lake Biwa, the largest lake in Japan.

Carried to their extreme, the principles of natural environmentalism aim to exclude humans from living close to and exploiting forests, lakes, and rivers as much as possible. It therefore strongly supports schemes such as the National Parks in the United States. The Lake Biwa conservation movement was strongly supported by people who live in large cities and tend to embrace the principles of nature environmentalism, which thus provided the basic framework for criticizing government policies. However, this approach could not generate effective measures, as more than 1 million people live around Lake Biwa, and it was practically impossible to relocate them.

Modern technicism, in contrast, advocated reclaiming land from the lake to build a sewage treatment plant to improve the water quality and to use concrete on the sides and bottoms of the feeding rivers and streams to prevent flooding. Needless to say, these proposed measures were staunchly opposed by the proponents of the nature environmentalist model. Both approaches, ecology and modern technology, are important for environmental conservation. However, it is clear that applying the principles of nature environmentalism was unrealistic while modern technicism would contribute to further destruction of the natural environment.

One case study focuses on one village, which is located next to a river that feeds into Lake Biwa. Until the 1950s, the people of this village took their drinking water from a stream running through the village. Children played in the water and adults washed their dishes and vegetables, and chilled watermelons, in the stream. The stream had symbolic importance as well; the people sent ceremonial grass ships downstream, to help the souls of their ancestors on their journey. The fish that were caught in the stream were an important part of the village's diet. In order to maintain the cleanliness of the drinking water, there were strict community rules, which, for example, forbade dumping waste into the river. In the late 1950s a modern waterworks was built in the village, a symbol of modernization. As a consequence, the wastewater ran into the river and the water quality declined. To address this declining water quality, a sewage system was eventually introduced but this did little to rectify the situation. However, even after the introduction of a waterworks and sewage system, people remained loyal to the flowing river.

The government proposed concreting the sides and bottom of the river for flood control in the 1970s. The locals were reluctant to oppose the government, not wanting to anger the local administration, which they viewed as a benefactor; but their desire to maintain their customary relationship with the running water was so strong that they eventually voiced their opposition to the proposal. After discussion in the community, the village people decided to leave the bottom of the river as (its natural) sand and opted for permeable masonry retaining walls that would allow the river water to continue to soak into the banks. This compromise ensured that the environment remained attractive for the village people's favorite aquatic insects, like fireflies, and that fish continued to live and animate the river.

The modern technicism model maintained that building stone or concrete riverbanks would prevent flooding and associated disasters, but the local people, based on their direct experience, did not believe it. Thus even after the river reconstruction, the people continue to take social responsibility for flood prevention: for example, they patrol the river during heavy rains and when the need arises, the people in the community work together to make temporary river banks with sandbags. With these processes local people have maintained their own self-government.

The underlying principle of life environmentalism is that people live in and use the environment; humans will tamper with nature and thus the environment will not be "purely natural." We must accept this as the way it is. At the same time, the life environmentalism model supports the idea of using local knowledge and local practices to both sustain the natural environment and ensure local stewardship of the environment.

Life environmentalism utilizes modern technology but also values nature. In other words, it employs "hard" technology like civil engineering construction technology, but is not determined by it, being guided always by the "soft" knowledge of everyday life experiences like community social capital of stewardship. Life environmentalism is especially appropriate in areas like the Asian regions, where population density is high, but the basic ideas of enhancing the social capital of local people will be appropriate in other areas like Africa and Latin America.

SEE ALSO: Ecological Problems; Ecological View of History; Ecology; Environment, Sociology of the; Ethnography; Knowledge; Life History; Lifeworld; Reflexivity; Social Change, Southeast Asia; Tradition; Values; Yanagita, Kunio

REFERENCES AND SUGGESTED READINGS

Kada, Y. (1995) *Seikatu Sekai no Kankyougaku* (*Environmental Studies of Everyday Life*). Nousan Gyoson Bunka Kyoukai, Tokyo.

Torigoe, H. (1989) Environmental Problems and Everyday Life. *Kwansei Gakuin University Annual Studies* 38. Nishinomiya, Japan.

Torigoe, H. (1997) Toward an Environmental Paradigm with a Priority on Social Life. In: *Environmental Awareness in Developing Countries*. Institute of Developing Economies, Tokyo, pp. 284–9. homepage3.nifty.com/torigoesan/.

life history

M. Carolyn Clark

Life history is somewhat of a stealth term – on the outside it looks harmlessly simple, but inside it is cloaked with ambiguity and its meaning is both slippery and elusive. The simple part derives from its point of origin: a researcher interviews a particular individual and elicits a richly detailed account of her or his life. It is in how that account is understood, and what is done with it, that the uncertainty and messiness begin. Nothing is straightforward. The life history interview, while privileging the informant in that that person decides what to share about his or her life and how to structure the telling, is nonetheless a co-construction between the researcher and the informant, both of whom are situated within a discursive context that shapes the definition of story as well as its telling. The product of the research, the life history itself, is the interpretive work of the researcher. That person has framed the research from the beginning around particular interests, which may or may not be significant to the informant; working from the narrative generated by the informant, it is the researcher who through the life history makes knowledge claims about the larger issue under study.

Cole and Knowles (2001) define life history as "illuminating the intersection of human experience and social context" and it is that intersection that makes all the difference. People live within particular social, cultural, and historical contexts and their life stories are shaped and defined by those contexts in complex ways. A life history, then, is a means by which we can see how that person makes sense of their experience within those contexts, as well as what impact social structures have on a person's life. Measor and Sikes (1992) think of it as biography read through a sociological lens. Unlike biography, however, life history explores the lives of ordinary rather than famous people. Tierney (1998), invoking Walt Whitman, argues life history makes it possible to say "No one is alien to me" without erasing the differences that will always continue to exist between people.

Life history can be considered an umbrella term for various genres of personal research, including such things as biography, autobiography, autoethnography, and oral history, or it can be identified as a genre in and of itself. These categories, however, are somewhat contested and they tend to blur into one another, but the common ground is that all explore personal experience. Life history has its roots in anthropology and sociology in the early 1900s, peaked in the 1930s and 1940s, then fell out of favor in the social sciences because of its lack of representativeness and its high level of subjectivity. With the interpretive turn in the 1960s, and with the growing influence of postmodern theory, those weaknesses came to be viewed as strengths, and life history again became popular in sociology and anthropology, as well as in psychology, history, education, gender and cultural studies, and linguistics (Goodson & Sikes 2001).

In life history interviews informants choose how to craft their account, selecting some events, omitting others, in order to accomplish something (e.g., create a particular identity, establish causality, or develop thematic coherence across the life span), which is to say that the stories themselves have work to do. Likewise from the perspective of the researcher the life history itself exists to accomplish something. Peacock and Holland (1988) suggest two broad conceptualizations of the purpose of life history: as portal and as process. When understood as a portal, the life history is used to illuminate a reality that stands outside the story and which the life history presumably mirrors. This could generate objective data about the person's life,

for example, in order to understand a particular historical period, or subjective data, where the focus is on the inner life of a person, whereby the researcher could understand how, for example, a particular culture shapes self-understanding. Life history conceptualized as process has a very different focus. Attention here is addressed to the narrative itself; the generated text and its interpretation is central. Geertz (1983) argues it is impossible to really understand what it's like to be a member of another culture; what is possible is to understand the symbolic and discursive categories of that culture. He likens this to how a reader understands a poem or makes sense of a proverb: it is a complex act of interpretation that is only possible by collecting a great deal of data (the notion of thick description which Geertz adopted from Gilbert Ryle) and contextualizing it. The analytic tools focus on language and other symbol systems, as well as on overarching themes.

Given the highly personal, even intimate, nature of life history research, a number of methodological and ethical issues are embedded and intertwined within it that are more salient here than in other types of qualitative research. The underlying questions being addressed are how informants make sense of their lives and how they narrate that understanding. But there is also an autobiographical dimension to this work, as there is in all research: we choose topics of personal interest to us, and those interests also shape the interpretations we render. In studying the lives of others it is particularly important that we are aware of how our life story intersects with theirs, how our personal and professional interests are being served through this work, and how our multiple positionings shape our thinking; and these personal factors need to be made visible in the life history itself. Plummer (2001) stresses that to understand any life story we must know how both the researcher and the informant are positioned, the nature of their relationship (he thinks of this in terms of the level of involvement by the researcher: stranger, acquaintance, friend, lover), and how all are positioned in the broader social context. The central responsibility of the researcher is to the informant, and that relationship must be marked by empathy, sensitivity, and respect. Cole and Knowles (2001) speak of this as a highly principled process. It is essential that the researcher work collaboratively with the informant at all stages of the process – never an easy thing to achieve, in part because both parties have different interests in engaging in this work and because unequal power relationships are challenging to overcome – but Chase (1995) argues persuasively that the researcher must do everything to enable the informant to take responsibility for the narrative if the outcome is truly to be an intersubjective construction of meaning.

Measor and Sikes (1992) lay out many of the thornier ethical issues implicit in life history research: the careful building of trust and rapport with the informant in order to elicit intimate information can have elements of voyeurism; the ambiguity of a project in which we seek intimate information of others to serve our own professional and disciplinary purposes is difficult to balance with what the informant needs or wants from participation in the study; and being aware of and sensitive to the impact on the informant of the telling of the life story itself, as well as the potential impact that reading what we write about them might have. There is also the concern that the published report not serve to other the informant. As is true with all ethical issues, there are no ready answers to these dilemmas. Plummer (2001) suggests five principles to guide researchers in dealing with these and other ethical dilemmas: respect for persons and their differences; an ethic of care; the promotion of equity and fairness in working with informants; an increase in autonomy and free choice for participants; and a commitment to minimize harm. In a postmodern era such universals may be at variance with the fragmented and ambiguous realities of life, but the need remains to honor our relationship with our informants and to continually seek their good, making judgments about that good that are highly situated, often ambivalent, but done in good faith.

What do we have when we write a life history? We certainly cannot claim that we have the life itself; no life can be captured and reduced to text. In addressing this question Denzin (1989) begins with Derrida's "metaphysics of presence": people live meaningful lives and these meanings are real and present to them, yet there is no way to access the inner life of another because it always must be done through language which itself is unstable and fluid. Denzin concludes that both the lives as told and the life histories as written are literary productions – they are, in fact, fiction: "As we write about lives, we bring the world of others into our texts. We create differences, oppositions, and presences which allow us to maintain the illusion that we have captured the 'real' experiences of 'real' people. In fact, we create the persons we write about, just as they create themselves when they engage in storytelling practices" (p. 82). This notion of our work as fiction is an important caveat for life history research. All meaning is fluid and shifting. In the telling of a story, in the transcription of that telling, in the analysis of that text, and in the reading of that text by others, meaning shifts and reforms, morphing constantly. As Riessman (1993) notes, "all texts stand on moving ground." It is essential that we recognize that what we write is fiction and that our truth claims are limited, but it is also important to know that these fictions are meant to serve larger ends, the illumination of the human condition.

Postmodernism presents other challenges to life history research. The self is also contested; no longer unitary and stable, it is now understood as nonunitary, fragmented, and unstable, which has profound implications, both in representing a life and in interpreting it. All knowledge claims must be tentative, open to multiple interpretations and reinterpretations. Tierney (1999) identifies five concerns that these issues raise: textual authority, which requires that the author be understood as the co-creator of the work; fragmentation, the multiple identities of researcher, informant, and reader that need to be made visible in the text; representation, the creation of an evocative and flexible narrative; purpose, that these are multiple and situated within the needs of the researcher, the informant, and the audience; and judgment, the need for new standards of quality for postmodern texts. Tierney's concerns themselves constitute quality standards. In addition to those, Cole and Knowles (2001) propose a principled methodological process, the use of accessible language, authenticity and internal consistency within the text, aesthetic form of the life history itself, and the theoretical and transformative potential inherent in doing this research.

The future of life history is filled with both challenge and promise. Life history has enormous emancipatory potential as a tool for exposing and confronting social structures that oppress and silence, but it will be important to do so without reifying power inequities and without providing insights that could be used by the powerful as tools to enforce their dominance over others. The direction of this research also needs to change, from studying down to studying up, that is to say by examining and illuminating the workings of power by those who wield it. The challenges involved in doing all of this are significant, but the benefits to be gained make the attempt more than worth the effort.

SEE ALSO: Autoethnography; Biography; Narrative

REFERENCES AND SUGGESTED READINGS

Chase, S. E. (1995) Taking Narrative Seriously. In: Josselson, R. & Lieblich, A. (Eds.), *Interpreting Experience: The Narrative Study of Lives*, Vol. 3. Sage, Thousand Oaks, CA.

Cole, A. L. & Knowles, J. G. (2001) *Lives in Context: The Art of Life History Research*. Alta Mira Press, Walnut Creek, CA.

Denzin, N. K. (1989) *Interpretive Biography*. Qualitative Research Methods Series, Vol. 17. Sage, Thousand Oaks, CA.

Geertz, C. (1983) *Local Knowledge: Further Essays in Interpretive Anthropology*. Basic Books, New York.

Goodson, I. & Sikes, P. (2001) *Life History Research in Educational Settings: Learning from Lives*. Open University Press, Buckingham.

Linde, C. (1993) *Life Stories: The Creation of Coherence*. Oxford University Press, New York.

Measor, L. & Sikes, P. (1992) Visiting Lives: Ethics and Methodology in Life History. In: Goodson, I. (Ed.), *Studying Teachers' Lives*. Teachers College Press, New York, pp. 209–33.

Peacock, J. & Holland, D. (1988) The Narrated Self: Life Stories and Self Construction. Symposium on Self Narrative. American Anthropological Association Meeting, Phoenix.

Plummer, K. (2001). *Documents of Life 2*. Sage, London.

Riessman, C. K. (1993) *Narrative Analysis*. Qualitative Research Methods Series, No. 30. Sage, Thousand Oaks, CA.

Tierney, W. G. (1998) Life History's History: Subjects Foretold. *Qualitative Inquiry* 4(1): 49–70.

Tierney, W. G. (1999) Guest Editor's Introduction: Writing Life's History. Special Issue, *Qualitative Inquiry* 5(3): 307–12.

lifestyle

Tally Katz-Gerro

Lifestyle involves the typical features of everyday life of an individual or a group. These features pertain to interests, opinions, behaviors, and behavioral orientations. For example, lifestyle relates to choice and allocation of leisure time; preferences in clothes and food; tastes in music, reading, art, and television programs; and choice of consumer goods and services.

At the individual level, lifestyle denotes self-expression, personal taste, and identity (Featherstone 1991). At the group level, the concept refers to shared preferences and tastes that are reflected primarily in consumption patterns and in the possession of goods (Weber 1946). Lifestyles give members of a group a sense of solidarity, and mirror the differentiation between groups in society. The distinctive lifestyles of specific groups may be hierarchically ordered to different degrees, depending on the extent to which a clear system of prestige exists that attaches value to lifestyles (Weber 1946; Sobel 1981). Arguably, it is the range and diversity of different lifestyles practiced in a given society that is of most interest, rather than the profile and makeup of a specific lifestyle. A comprehensive lifestyle analysis will emphasize the way in which arrays of lifestyles evolve over time, the degree to which different lifestyles (associated with class, race, sexuality, etc.) are legitimized, and the way lifestyles are linked to changes in social and economic structures (Zablocki & Kanter 1976).

Max Weber (1946) provided the major sociological definition of the concept, which emphasizes lifestyle as a means of social differentiation that could be used to acquire or to maintain a certain social status. Individuals and groups adopt lifestyles to express and sustain their identity at a particular time and place. In the Weberian framework, lifestyle is the expression of status groups that can be differentiated from class. Weber defines classes as groupings that are economically determined, while status groups are communities that are determined by a specific social estimation of honor. Status honor is normally expressed by a specific style of life, in as much as the consumption patterns of a status group involve the prestige or honor that is attached to those patterns. Because a status group expects that its members share a particular lifestyle, this becomes the descriptive manifestation through which affiliation, hence status, can be perceived.

Veblen (1970 [1899]) applied this framework in his study of what he termed "the new leisure class" at the turn of the twentieth century in the United States. Veblen portrayed a lifestyle that emphasizes conspicuous consumption as a strategy that individuals employ to display status. Although the possession of wealth becomes the primary evidence for successful activity, and hence the dominant basis of esteem, the translation of wealth into appropriate observable symbols is imperative. This is accomplished through the display of conspicuous leisure and conspicuous consumption.

Building on Weber's work, a body of research has developed which adopted the view that lifestyle is a major form of social stratification that can be used to characterize contemporary society. Although lifestyle segmentation reflects structural inequalities within society, lifestyle is to be distinguished from social class. The concept of class usually refers to dimensions such as education, occupation, and income in as much as they specify one's position and resources in the market. At the same time, the concept of lifestyle usually refers to dimensions such as cultural preferences and tastes, which facilitate symbolic communication of status as an order distinct from that of economic standing. Lifestyles are constructed by symbolic boundaries that mark differences between groups. Symbolic boundaries are expressed through distinctive consumption patterns that tend to be associated, in a particular social context, with shared symbolic codes that bear specific meanings.

The significant relationship between classes and status groups and its expression in material and cultural lifestyle further reverberates in Pierre Bourdieu's (1984) two-dimensional approach to stratification. Bourdieu distinguishes between economic and cultural capital. Class fractions, defined by similar positions with respect to education, income, and occupation, are united by a habitus or by cultural dispositions that are derived from similar life experiences. The habitus determines taste, which is the material and symbolic capacity to appropriate cultural objects and practices. Tastes constitute lifestyle, which is a unitary set of distinctive preferences that classify the classifiers, the upper class. A lifestyle that is associated with the upper classes is naturalized as good and noble and serves distinction. Therefore, lifestyles serve as an effective exclusionary resource and serve to reproduce existing social inequalities as long as they vary systematically with social position.

Bourdieu emphasizes that it is not only the amount of goods and services consumed that is typical of a group, it is also the characteristic mix of goods and services. Lifestyle elements, in terms of specific cultural preferences, can be studied one at a time or as stylistic unities. Stylistic unity is an internal cultural consistency in the elements comprising a lifestyle and in symbolic properties of those elements. It rests on shared perceptions that lifestyle elements are patterned in a manner that makes some sort of aesthetic or other sense. Depending on social, historical, and cultural context, stylistic unity becomes more or less elusive and difficult to identify. Stylistic unity can range from a tight system of expectations for particular tastes and preferences, all adhering to a clear set of cultural imperatives, to a system of blurred, eclectic components, loosely connected by symbolic meanings. For example, a body of research has been trying to identify snobbish unity or omnivorous unity in cultural preferences of elites in contemporary western societies (Peterson & Kern 1996).

Research on the determinants of lifestyle differentiation has predominantly concentrated on those factors that Weber (class), Veblen (income), and Bourdieu (education, parental background) emphasized in their theoretical accounts of the contours of lifestyles. Indeed, a significant body of research has shown that tastes and consumption patterns are influenced by individuals' education, financial resources, occupational characteristics, parental education, and parental lifestyle. In addition, other factors have been shown to matter, such as gender, age, and race. At the same time, there is evidence that in contemporary society lifestyle is becoming more volatile and less hierarchical so that the correlation with social divisions is no longer conclusive (Featherstone 1991). This is explained by social conditions that are becoming increasingly fragmented, partly because of the proliferation of information and cultural repertoires. Since collective affiliations are multiple, fragmented, and often conflicted, the lifestyles associated with these affiliations are more fluid, unsettled, and cross-cutting.

Research on the consequences of lifestyle has looked at its effect on individuals' life chances. This line of work attempts to establish the extent to which the deployment of tastes in everyday life helps to reproduce social class boundaries. Such research has shown how cultural preferences influence individuals' educational aspirations, school grades, and educational attainment; their occupational attainment; and their marital selection (DiMaggio 1994).

SEE ALSO: Conspicuous Consumption; Consumption, Mass Consumption, and Consumer Culture; Cultural Capital; Distinction; Health Lifestyles; Lifestyle Consumption; Status; Taste, Sociology of

REFERENCES AND SUGGESTED READINGS

Bourdieu, P. (1984) *Distinction: A Social Critique on the Judgment of Taste.* Harvard University Press, Cambridge, MA.

DiMaggio, P. (1994) Social Stratification, Life-Style, and Social Cognition. In: Grusky, D. B. (Ed.), *Social Stratification in Sociological Perspective.* Westview Press, Boulder, CO, pp. 458–65.

Featherstone, M. (1991) *Consumer Culture and Postmodernism.* Sage, London.

Peterson, R. A. & Kern, R. M. (1996) Changing Highbrow Taste: From Snob to Omnivore. *American Sociological Review* 61: 900–7.

Sobel, M. E. (1981) *Lifestyle and Social Structure: Concepts, Definitions, Analyses.* Academic Press, New York.

Veblen, T. (1970 [1899]) *The Theory of the Leisure Class.* Unwin, London.

Weber, M. (1946) Class, Status, Party. In: *Max Weber: Essays in Sociology.* Oxford University Press, New York, pp. 180–95.

Zablocki, B. D. & Kanter, R. M. (1976) The Differentiation of Life-Styles. *Annual Review of Sociology* 2: 269–98.

lifestyle consumption

Sam Binkley

Lifestyles are symbolically embellished ways of living. Sociologically, they serve two important functions: they classify or categorize the practitioner within a broader social matrix, and in so doing offer practitioners a unique sense of self and identity. Thus, lifestyles combine material and symbolic processes: they are practical ways of providing for basic needs and requirements such as food, clothing, and shelter, but also aesthetic and symbolic expressions of one's sense of self and of one's membership among certain social groups. As such, lifestyles occur at the intersection of individual agency and social structure. They project a unity that is both subjectively meaningful to practitioners themselves, and objectively legible to those defining the social context in which they are performed. For these reasons, lifestyle has sustained as a key sociological concept, capable of bridging the divide between macro-level concerns with large scale social structures and social groupings, and micro-level concerns with the subjective dimensions of agency, meaning, and identity.

The study of lifestyle also has a more current relevance. Lifestyles have attracted the interest of many contemporary sociologists for their usefulness in the analysis of processes of social change, and particularly for the perspective they offer on the unique social and cultural conditions characteristic of late capitalist or postmodern societies. Indeed, as Chaney (1996) and others have argued, the very concept of lifestyle is an inextricably historical category of analysis, bound up with social instabilities linked to patterns of modern social change. These changes include the decline of social classes (organized around production) and the emergence of personal identities (based on consumption); the rise of urban centers and the increase of social anonymity in big cities; the increasing influence of mass culture and the "bourgeoisification" of the proletariat; the increasing saturation of culture with visual technologies of communication; and the ever more pervasive commodification of everyday life. In this regard, sociological uses of the concept of lifestyle can be divided into two general areas: (1) studies of social differentiation and stratification through the use of symbols, and (2) studies of the constitution of personal identity in the context of dynamic social change.

LIFESTYLE AS STATUS EMULATION

A sociological interest in lifestyle assumes, as do many sociological narratives, a fundamental rupture between traditional and modern societies: traditional orders of social hierarchy rooted in ascribed status give way to more flexible and mobile status systems defined by achieved status, opening the way for the advancement and upward mobility of a range of social groups previously excluded from the elite strata. With the increasing mobility of social groups brought on by the extension of a money economy unfettered by the controls of the old feudal order, more people gain access to goods and luxuries through the expanding open market, increasingly available to the swelling ranks of the emerging mercantile class, or bourgeoisie. With the gradual crowding out of small, close-knit communities characterized by face-to-face interactions by the bustling traffic and anonymous crowds of the cities, social identity becomes uprooted, less constrained by longstanding tradition, more available for manipulation and affect.

Lifestyles, then, appear under these conditions as means of conferring legitimacy on one's location on a social ladder, not through the holding of resources, titles, or offices in the mode of the old aristocracy, but through the affect of specific ways of living meant to display one's wealth and cultivation – a circumstance that leaves ascendant or would-be ascendant groups open to charges of abuse, fraudulence, and falsification. With the demise of a social universe defined by a metaphysically sanctioned hierarchy, the profane, secular world of everyday practices and things emerges as a field of symbolic contest and status competition. This predicament is exacerbated by the influx of a newly monied middle class, or *nouveau riche*: possessors of economic capital who lack the legitimacy and status conferred by the established order. These newly ascendant classes seek to locate themselves through sometimes verbose and clumsy acts of emulation. They parrot, however clumsily, the styles of the older aristocratic classes in a pattern of distinction that expresses a lifestyle in the full sociological sense – an effort to classify oneself through habits of living which are at once material and symbolic.

Most notable here are the contributions of Alexis deTocqueville, whose studies of American society in the early nineteenth century reveal the strained efforts of the American gentry and their emulators to distinguish themselves through ostentatious practices of living in a society where formal hierarchies have been effectively leveled (Tocqueville 1969). Similarly, Thorstein Veblen, writing against the opulence of the Gilded Age and the materialistic excesses of the *fin-de-siècle* industrialists, outlined a genealogy of modern leisure, tracing contemporary modes of conspicuous consumption to their barbaric origins in the symbolism of social power (Veblen 1924). His view of leisure or style of life as competitive display is reflected in much mid-century American sociology, as illustrated in Lloyd Warner's studies of trickle-down status imitation in an American suburb, Robert and Helen Lynd's studies of "Middletown," an American town under the grip of the new consumer culture of the 1930s, and in Vance Packard's popular critique of postwar American consumption patterns, *The Status Seekers*.

CULTURE AND STRATIFICATION

Underscoring much sociological interest in lifestyle as a form of stratification mediated by symbols is a desire to supplement the objective categories of economic class with the subjective outlooks and meanings possessed by actual social actors themselves – a theme first introduced with Weber's (1946) analysis of the types of social power. Weber made the distinction between elite groups stratified by the varying criteria of class, status, and party, with status emerging as a claim to social esteem determined by a "social estimation of honor." Status groups, for Weber, posed an alternative grouping of social power based not on the possession of capital and valued property alone, but on recognizable characteristics shared by a community which assume the quality of honorific value.

The stratification of social groups, Weber argued, was not reducible to competition for scarce (economic) resources, but extended to struggles for (symbolic) recognition and honor between competing groups, manifested in the mundane dimensions of consumption and everyday life. This distinction would prove significant in the analysis of the cultural forms and processes of social change that would begin to take root in the latter part of the twentieth century.

Weber's influence is apparent in the sociology of Bourdieu, perhaps the most influential contemporary voice in the sociology of lifestyle, and an author who took to task the challenge of a truly cultural approach to stratification. The value of Bourdieu's sociology comes with his insistence on avoiding economic reductionism by linking the symbolic productions of everyday lifestyles to practical efforts of groups and individuals to distinguish themselves within a stratified system of cultural preferences. His expansive study of the French class system, *Distinction* (1984), documents the efforts of middle-class and working-class people to effectively classify themselves on a stratified cultural scale through the exercise of taste in clothing, art, music, and food. The expression of taste represents, for Bourdieu, a practical intervention in a classificatory scheme wherein certain tastes naturally accrue to the higher or to the lower end of an economic scale. Like Veblen, Weber, and Tocqueville, Bourdieu sees the social world as a highly conflictual arena in which lifestyle plays as a set of tactics employed by various groups to secure honorific distinction denied by others, yet unlike these figures Bourdieu pays careful attention to ways in which these strategies are enacted in unreflective, mundane choices, naturalized within the taken-for-granted disposition – or habitus – of members of these groups. In marked contrast to economic models, which conceive of actors as intentional and rational, Bourdieu's theory of the habitus considers the lifestyles of actors as a site of creative classification in the practical moments of everyday life.

Importantly for Bourdieu's sociology, the habitus's of various social groups conform to their own distinct logics, which are themselves established in a dialectical tension between dominant and subordinate classes. These two dispositions meet in what Bourdieu terms a game of "refusal and counter-refusal." The aesthetic dispositions that structure the middle-class habitus, for example, express a distain for the brutishness, obviousness, and directness contained in working-class arts, sports, foods, fashion, and films, expressing instead a preference for the indirect, thoughtful, and cultivated. At the same time, members of the working class dismiss the loftiness and rumination implicit in middle-class refinement and cultivation, preferring the straightforward, the practical, the direct, and the immediate. These logics illustrate the contrasting dispositions of these groups in which a "taste of the necessary" expressed by the subordinate groups is distinguished from an "aesthetic distanciation" expressed by dominant groups.

DETERMINISM AND AGENCY

Other sociological uses of lifestyle as an alternative category of stratification to those offered in more economic accounts developed specifically from dialogues within the Marxist tradition. An old maxim of Marxist thought, "base determines superstructure," provides a deterministic explanation of the cultural and aesthetic realms, to which Bourdieu's theory of the habitus is in part a reaction. The stamp of this determinism is evident in several branches of Marxism, most notably in the work of Frankfurt School theorists Adorno and Horkheimer, who in *The Dialectic of Enlightenment* (1982) examined mid-century forms of popular or "mass culture" as instruments of ideological control. Lifestyle practitioners are, from this perspective, cultural dopes, passive objects of control and manipulation.

But for other twentieth-century Marxists more engaged with the problem of culture (a roster that includes Italian communist Antonio Gramsci, the British historians E. P. Thompson and Eric Hobsbawm, French structuralists Roland Barthes and Louis Althusser, and later members of the British Birmingham School of Cultural Studies), investigations of the everyday lives of subaltern groups countered the parochialism and determinism of the base–superstructure model by uncovering a terrain of symbolic struggle in which opposition originated, not in the categories of economic class, but in the mundane categories of everyday lifestyle. A version of this thesis was advanced by Richard Hoggart in his influential *Uses of Literacy* (1957), which depicts the "feminization" of the British working class through a process of Americanization, or its saturation in the affects of consumer lifestyles. Hoggart's work informed the writings of leading figures of the Birmingham tradition (Stuart Hall, Dick Hebdige), who variously proposed studies of the lifestyles of subordinate groups (usually male, working-class youth cultures) as explorations of the everyday symbolic realms wherein counter-hegemonic struggles were fought out on the level of style. Notable in this tradition is Hebdige's *Subculture* (1979), a study of London punks, which set the agenda for the emerging field of cultural studies – an interdisciplinary field broadly concerned with lifestyle as a subversive practice.

MODERNITY AND LIFESTYLE

A sociology of lifestyle that stretches from Veblen to Bourdieu has, in many varied ways, related the practice of lifestyle to the conditions of social democratization. Therein, lifestyle is read in terms of strategies employed by opportunistic social groups in their effort to confirm social identities in the absence of more stable, traditionally grounded status criteria. Yet, in place of these stable traditional structures, these approaches tend to assume that there exists an equally stable symbolic matrix wherein the symbolism of lifestyle practices can be universally registered and accepted. To assume, for example, that the *nouveau riche* emulate their aristocratic superiors is to assume the existence of a stable and universally accepted framework for reading lifestyles as symbolic interventions in a fixed status hierarchy. What this line of analysis does not take into account is the ambiguity and instability inherent within these codes at every stage of modern development, and particularly the eroded state of such codes under the accelerated conditions of contemporary culture. The various effects identified with postmodern culture (saturation of culture with visual representations, the commodification of all social meanings, the breakup of traditional class groupings, the increasing mobility and globalization of

communities, the malleability of personal identities) have rendered status emulation through lifestyle an outmoded concept. In this regard, an analysis of lifestyle as a symbolic practice in the contemporary context demands an accounting of the conditions of ambivalence and ambiguity that define the daily conditions of personal and social life in the contemporary context.

A sociology of lifestyle as a response to conditions of ambiguity can be traced to Simmel's (1971) analysis of urban life in his landmark essay "The Metropolis and Mental Life." Here, Simmel contextualizes lifestyle as a developing subjective response to the changes and pressures foisted upon ordinary people by the accelerated social and cultural conditions of modern social life, where a collision of codes and symbols, an uprooting of communities, and the increasing mobility of classes and groups undermines the semiotic frameworks wherein lifestyles might have served the function of social classification.

Though Simmel discussed the crowded and disjointed conditions of urban life at the turn of the century, his observations resonate with recent sociological inquiries into the breakup of the symbolic codes underpinning status differentials in late capitalist societies. Harvey (1989) has described a shift from Fordist (production based) to post-Fordist (consumption and culture based) economies, in which a process of cultural acceleration and saturation has resulted in a time-space compression. In line with this argument is Lash and Urry's (1987) case that organized capitalism has effectively given way to new patterns of investment and growth, which have uprooted the old social groupings of class upon which lifestyles depended. New emphasis on product differentiation and market segmentation has eclipsed class solidarities and pushed lifestyles to the fore, yet at the same time it has undercut the indexical function of lifestyles as indicators of membership in larger social groups. In the new, information and service oriented capitalism, where the exchange of knowledge and the manipulation of symbols has risen to replace the manufacture of commodities (and the class fractions that follow), lifestyles have become, not indexical, but reflexive: lifestyles do not refer to real social memberships but are self-referential, referring only to the fashioning practices of the individuals who bear or enact them. Indeed, adaptations of

Bourdieu's thesis on the cultural dispositions of the middle classes have pointed to important schisms within this class between the old and new fractions, more adept to the cultural and semiotic conditions of consumer capitalism. Mike Featherstone, drawing on Bourdieu, has described the rise of a class of "new cultural intermediaries," mediators of the realms of production and consumption, skilled workers at the shaping, not of things, but of meanings.

IDENTITY AND THE SELF

While sociologists generally agree on a trend toward individualization and the aestheticization of identity, less agreement is shared on the ultimate personal and social implications of this trend. Typically dour notes are sounded by the likes of Daniel Bell (1976), who has described the disjuncture between cultural and economic spheres, resulting in a hedonistic embrace of lifestyle by the minions of the middle class, and Christopher Lasch (1978), who has criticized the "culture of narcissism" that developed from the counterculture of the 1960s. For these authors, lifestyle, unmoored from concrete social structures, is drained of political meaning and moral focus.

But this model of the new lifestyle practitioner as limp and lacking in resolve is countered by postmodernists who find vibrancy and new political potentials in the fragmentation, diversity, and multiplicity made possible by the mobility of lifestyle. Often cited in this respect is the work of Walter Benjamin, who recounted the stance of the *flâneur* as one who negotiates the discordant, disorderly world of the modern marketplace, savoring the possibilities for self-presentation and aesthetic self-styling that are presented by the crowds of anonymous spectators populating the bustling centers of the urban metropolis (Benjamin 1973). In this light, sociologists of consumer culture have recovered the emancipatory dimensions of lifestyle, asserted the implicitly imaginary dimensions of shopping and other forms of consumption as vehicles of an imaginary hedonism, with powerful potentials for rethinking personal identity as a lifestyle practice (Shields 1992).

However, others have pointed to the anxiety and instability underlying this process. For

Giddens (1991), the "reflexive modernity" thesis provides a general model understanding lifestyle in terms of the existential predicament of the modern individual: amid the patterns of rapid and seemingly haphazard social change that characterize modern historical trajectories, the reassurance and sense of what Giddens terms "ontological security" once furnished by traditional moralities are replaced with a highly individualized lifestyle identities. Against the backdrop of the uncertainties and ambiguities that characterize secular modernity, individuals are compelled to make choices and to realize themselves in these choices. "We have no choice but to choose," Giddens writes.

SEE ALSO: Bourdieu, Pierre; Commodities, Commodity Fetishism, and Commodification; Consumption, Fashion and; Consumption, Mass Consumption, and Consumer Culture; Lifestyle; Postmodern Consumption; Simmel, Georg; Status; Taste, Sociology of

REFERENCES AND SUGGESTED READINGS

Adorno, T. & Horkheimer, M. (1982) *Dialectic of Enlightenment.* Trans. J. Cumming. Continuum, New York.

Bell, D. (1976) *The Cultural Contradictions of Capitalism.* Basic Books, New York.

Benjamin, W. (1973) *Charles Baudelaire: A Lyric Poet in the Era of High Capitalism.* New Left Books, London.

Bourdieu, P. (1984) *Distinction: A Social Critique of the Judgment of Taste.* Trans. R. Nice. Harvard University Press, Cambridge, MA.

Chaney, D. (1996) *Lifestyles.* Routledge, New York.

Giddens, A. (1991) *Modernity and Self-Identity: Self and Society in the Late Modern Age.* Stanford University Press, Stanford.

Harvey, D. (1989) *The Condition of Postmodernity: An Enquiry into the Origins of Cultural Change.* Blackwell, Oxford.

Hebdige, D. (1979) *Subculture, The Meaning of Style.* Methuen, London.

Lash, S. & Urry, J. (1987) *The End of Organized Capitalism.* Polity Press, Cambridge.

Lasch, C. (1978) *The Culture of Narcissism: American Life in an Age of Diminishing Expectations.* Norton, New York.

Shields, R. (1992) *Lifestyle Shopping: The Subject of Consumption.* Routledge, New York.

Simmel, G. (1971) *On Individuality and Social Forms: Selected Writings.* Trans. D. N. Levine. University of Chicago Press, Chicago.

Slater, D. (1996) *Consumer Culture and Modernity.* Polity Press, Cambridge.

Sobel, M. (1981) *Lifestyle and Social Structure: Concepts, Definitions, Analyses.* Academic Press, New York.

Tocqueville, A. (1969) In What Spirit the Americans Cultivate the Arts. In: *Democracy in America.* Ed. J. P. Mayer. Trans. G. Lawrence. Harper & Row, New York, pp. 465–8.

Veblen, T. (1924) *Theory of the Leisure Class.* Viking Press, New York.

Weber, M. (1946) Class, Party, Status. In: Gerth, H. H. & Wright Mills, C. (Eds.), *From Max Weber.* Oxford University Press, New York, pp. 180–95.

lifeworld

Warren Fincher

Lifeworld refers to the commonsense interpretive frames and logics by which individuals prereflectively conceptually organize their perceptions of everyday life. The concept of the lifeworld is central to two theoretical traditions – phenomenology and the critical theory tradition as articulated by Habermas – but the lifeworld is also an important concept in the sociological investigations into the construction of knowledge and the social body.

Edmund Husserl, a nineteenth-century German philosopher, theorizes the importance of the lifeworld in how individuals come to understand the world around them. The primary focus of his work theorized the nature of logical thought, particularly the origins of knowledge. Husserl developed a philosophy of what he later termed the lifeworld. Two positions were prominent within the philosophical debates of the late nineteenth century. The first stressed formal systems of logic and methods of knowledge construction. The second tradition stressed the importance of lived experiences in the development of an intuitive reflection and subsequent construction. Husserl's early work attempted to bridge these two traditions. In doing so, he argued that the logic involved when thinking does not simply utilize ideal forms, but must incorporate the context of what is specifically being thought about. Thought, for Husserl, is an interplay between pure logic and the store of knowledge accumulated from lived experiences. By examining the relationship between a phenomenon as it occurs and how individuals subsequently conceptualize and make sense of that experience, Husserl attempts to find those logical frames that transcend the ongoing stream of experiences.

In elaborating on this work, Husserl recognizes that knowledge transcends the boundaries of individual perception and reflection, and he finds the need to theorize the role of others in the construction of meaning. In attending to these issues, Husserl employs the concept of the lifeworld, which for him comes to mean that set of knowledge that is shared intersubjectively. This intersubjective knowledge is about common experiences, but emerges from the common logical forms that people hold. In Husserl's lifeworld we find perhaps the most presocial iteration of the lifeworld, as Husserl links the concept to the idea that all people have a "natural attitude" or innate set of logics that predates learned modes of inquiry and that individuals all hold as a common feature of their cognitive processes.

The concept of the lifeworld enters into sociological inquiry through the work of Alfred Schütz, who incorporated the works of Husserl, Weber, and Bergson to develop his own contributions to the fledgling phenomenology of the early twentieth century. Because Schütz was particularly interested in how people both construct their own senses of reality and also must cope with others' senses of reality, his work elaborates on the intersubjective functions of the lifeworld that Husserl develops by examining the lifeworld as a product of both collective life and also individual experiences. As such, the lifeworld is external to the individual, predating his or her birth and serving to place constraints on the constructions of reality that people create, but the lifeworld is also an individualized part of our ability to make sense of the world, as it is the product of our individual ongoing experience of daily life.

Schütz enumerates a number of key characteristics of the lifeworld. Among these, it is important to note that the lifeworld requires "wide-awakeness" from individuals in that they must maintain a level of consciousness of the world around them in order to live life.

The construction and management of meaning is an active event, although not perceived to be thought, but rather taken-for-granted knowledge. Much of how we employ the lifeworld in making sense of the world around us is through typification, specifically what Schütz calls "first-order" typification that rests on the stock of knowledge found in the lifeworld, as opposed to second-order typification, which utilizes complex information beyond the scope of the lifeworld. Another important characteristic for Schütz's lifeworld is that people accept it as reality without question, until something compels them to think otherwise. When problems do occur, people then turn to various more overt logical processes to reinstate normalcy. Given this, Schütz's legacy can be seen to include the later work of Harold Garfinkel and the ethnomethodological tradition.

The philosopher Merleau-Ponty also utilized Husserl's work on the lifeworld and applied the concept to the body. The body serves as the link between phenomena and the social organization of those phenomena, and the lifeworld serves to bridge the communication between the physical world, the individual's body, and others. The lifeworld, according to Merleau-Ponty, also incorporates knowledge about the body, as evidenced by the "phantom limb syndrome" in which the individual continues to perceive a limb that no longer exists.

The next notable development in the theory of the lifeworld occurs in the work of Habermas, perhaps the most widely known scholar of the critical theory tradition. Habermas utilizes "lifeworld" to mean two related concepts. First, building on Husserl and Schütz, Habermas refers to lifeworld as the set of background assumptions and convictions that people hold. However, what sets apart Habermas's work on the lifeworld from previous theories is his focus on the function of the lifeworld in modern societies. As such, Habermas also uses the term lifeworld to denote a particular kind of integration that arises from the sharing of background assumptions among people. Because of this interest in integration, Habermas moves away from a strictly phenomenological use of lifeworld that Husserl and Schütz demonstrated.

Habermas maintains an interest in the communicative processes surrounding social integration. A key dynamic in social integration, for Habermas, is the interplay between the lifeworld and the system, two different perspectives found in modern societies. From the perspective of the lifeworld, one sees the self embedded within the social world, but from the perspective of the system, one sees the world necessarily through a macrosocial lens, distanced and seemingly only indirectly involved through mechanisms of market exchange and the dissemination of organizational power. The form of integration that the system and the lifeworld each proffers is dissimilar and analogously extends Husserl's distinction between formalized knowledge and the lived experiences of everyday life. The system is that set of formal mechanisms in a society's superstructure that functions to maintain consequences of social action. The lifeworld, on the other hand, is the perspective from the standpoint of the actors, not the structure. The lifeworld serves to transmit interpretive patterns among individuals, which facilitates key functions in modern society. The lifeworld facilitates the construction of both individual personalities and group identities. It socializes members of society toward communicative processes and the ability to manage interpersonal actions. And through its transmission, it allows for the preservation and selective modification of the stock of background knowledge common to the community's lifeworld.

Habermas is concerned with the "colonization of the lifeworld," a pathological phenomenon which occurs when the instrumental rationality common to the operations in the system is utilized in the private sphere in lieu of communicative rationality. Socialization becomes reoriented around values appropriate to the marketplace, but not ones that have been consensually negotiated through the discourses endemic to a healthy lifeworld. The processes of identify formation and value education that are key functions of the lifeworld are then organized around bureaucratic and economic values. In order to guard against the colonization of the lifeworld, Habermas advocates that societies foster a greater reliance on open communicative action that freely engages the value structures of economic and political spheres. However, this conceptualization of communicative action in the lifeworld as intrinsically harmonious has been repeatedly criticized as too idealistic and not representative of the pathologies that exist in lifeworld discourse, such as patriarchal dynamics, regardless of colonization by instrumental rationality.

The current work involving the lifeworld spans the diversity of contexts that utilize this term. Conversation analysis is one subfield in which the lifeworld remains a salient concept, both as a subject of study and a methodological issue. How people make sense of talk is a key point of inquiry for scholars working in this area, which attends not to how symbols are given meaning but rather how meaning is conveyed in the form that talk takes. As a methodological issue, conversation analysts must confront the problem that they must utilize their own lifeworlds in order to interpret the collaboration of their subjects. In making assessments about how participants carry on interaction through talk, the lifeworld lens of the researcher may be divergent from the lifeworld being preserved and modified within the participants' interaction. As well, ethnomethodological studies are interested in the sense-making mechanisms people employ to maintain seamless interactions with others.

The lifeworld remains a useful conceptual tool in other areas of investigation, particularly in the extension of Habermas's work. Studies continue to focus on the lifeworld of women, people of color, urban settings, etc. Much of this work takes Fraser's (1997) critique of Habermas's ideal speech community as a point of departure. Many of the studies that use the lifeworld concept also maintain a focus on the institutional or organizational context. Elizabeth Gill's work on the role of the lifeworld in managing death analyzes the hospice setting for the negotiation of lifeworld and system perspectives, and focuses on the role of the hospice worker in negotiating the interactions between the medical staff and the family. And recent work has also directed attention to the role of the lifeworld in a setting marked with broad-scale social change, particularly with social change related to international development and adaptations to working in large-scale organizations.

SEE ALSO: Conversation Analysis; Critical Theory/Frankfurt School; Ethnomethodology; Intersubjectivity; Phenomenology; Public Sphere; Schütz, Alfred

REFERENCES AND SUGGESTED READINGS

Fraser, N. (1997) Rethinking the Public Sphere: A Contribution to the Critique of Actually Existing Democracy. In: Calhoun, C. (Ed.), *Habermas and the Public Sphere*. MIT Press, Cambridge.

Habermas, J. (1987) *The Theory of Communicative Rationality*, Vol. 2. Trans. T. McCarthy. Beacon Press, Boston.

Husserl, E. (1995 [1950]) *Cartesian Meditation: An Introduction to Phenomenology*. Trans. D. Cairns. Kluwer Academic Publishers, Boston.

Husserl, E. (1999 [1905]) *Idea of Phenomenology*. Trans. L. Hardy. Kluwer Academic Publishers, Boston.

Maynard, D. W. (2003) *Bad News, Good News: Conversational Order in Everyday Talk and Clinical Setting*. University of Chicago Press, Chicago.

Merleau-Ponty, M. (2002) *Phenomenology of Perception*. Trans. C. Smith. Routledge, New York.

Schütz, A. (1967) *Phenomenology of the Social World*. Trans. G. Walsh & F. Lehnert. Northwestern University Press, Evanston.

literacy/illiteracy

George Farkas

Traditionally, literacy has meant the ability to read and write. As the cognitive skill requirements of work and daily life have increased, the definition has expanded. In the National Literacy Act of 1991, the US Congress defined literacy as "an individual's ability to read, write, and speak in English and compute and solve problems at levels of proficiency necessary to function on the job and in society, to achieve one's goals, and to develop one's knowledge and potential." Consistent with this, the National Assessments of Adult Literacy, conducted by the National Center for Education Statistics, have measured literacy along three dimensions: prose literacy, document literacy, and quantitative literacy. Each was measured on a scale defined by the skills needed to succeed at daily and work tasks ordered from simple to complex.

Over time and across nations, higher literacy rates have been associated with higher levels of economic development. This is a well-documented pattern, which has been most thoroughly analyzed by economists under the topic of "investment and returns to human capital" (for a review of these studies, see Hanushek & Welch 2005). Indeed, increasing the spread of literacy is one of the key strategies advocated by the World Bank in its efforts to reduce poverty worldwide (Bruns et al. 2003).

Further, at any one place and time, an individual's level of literacy has been associated with her or his place within the social class structure. Typically, the higher the parents' social class status, the more years of schooling are given to their children. Thus, education is the most common mechanism by which parental social class status is transmitted to children. Schooling is also the most common mechanism for upward mobility. Both of these patterns have become stronger as economic development has proceeded, and the cognitive skills demanded of workers have increased.

An increasing number of studies have examined years of schooling completed and individual placement within the social class structure, and found that these are strongly related within all modern societies. Indeed, researchers have now developed research and testing instruments that have been used to systematically collect similar data across a wide variety of nations (Porter & Gamoran 2002), and have discovered very similar relationships between schooling and socioeconomic attainment within all nations. Further, studies have shown that the institutional arrangements for the delivery of schooling bear strong similarities across nations (Baker & LeTendre 2005).

For the US, these patterns are illustrated by the over-time trend in the illiteracy rate – defined as the percent of individuals who can neither read nor write. Among whites, this rate declined from 20 percent in 1870 to below 1 percent in 1979. As a consequence of slavery, the illiteracy rate among African Americans in 1870 was 80 percent. By 1979 it had declined to 1.6 percent. However, as noted above, more than the bare minimum of reading and writing skills is required to succeed in twenty-first century labor markets. Thus, gaps in more advanced literacy skills, between, on the one hand, lower-income, African American, and Hispanic students, and, on the other, middle and higher-income or white and Asian students, have emerged as

among the US's greatest concerns. This has led to empirical studies on the determinants and consequences of these achievement gaps, and to the consideration of a variety of policies and programs designed to reduce them.

The importance of this focus on differentials in cognitive skill across class and race/ethnicity groups is emphasized by a variety of studies that show that, at the beginning of the twenty-first century, such skill has increasingly become *the* social stratifying variable in American society. These studies have yielded the following findings. First, the years of schooling an individual completes is the primary determinant of her or his placement within the social class system, and also the primary mechanism by which parents transfer their social class status to their children. Second, during the period 1980–2000, as the economy became more knowledge-based and globalized, and as union strength declined, the economic returns to schooling and cognitive skill increased dramatically. That is, adjusted for inflation, the earnings of workers with no more than a high school education were stagnant, while the earnings differential between college-educated and high school-educated workers increased dramatically. Third, and also during this time period, the black–white test score gap, which had narrowed between 1960 and 1980, stopped closing and remained unchanged. Fourth, the earnings differential between African American and white workers was shown to be largely explained by the cognitive skills differential between these groups.

What explains individual and group differentials in literacy, as measured by tests of cognitive skill and self-reports of educational attainment (number of years of schooling completed)? Both qualitative and quantitative studies point to parent–child interaction and children's oral language development during the preschool period as crucial for the creation of differentials in school readiness that strongly predict performance in early elementary school. Thus, the child's early literacy skill – oral vocabulary, grammatical usage, letter knowledge, and phonemic awareness (the ability to hear and manipulate the separate sounds in spoken language) – are among the principal predictors of success in first grade reading. Since scores on these variables tend to be lower for children from lower social class, African American, and

Latino backgrounds, lower preschool literacy among these students predicts lower first grade reading attainment.

How do middle-class children come to have more extensive vocabularies and standard speech patterns than lower-class children? The phenomenon in question has been publicly discussed at least since the story of Eliza Doolittle in *My Fair Lady*, whose distinctively working-class vocabulary and dialect are remade by Professor Higgins. During the 1960s, 1970s, and 1980s, sociologist Basil Bernstein and anthropologist Shirley Brice Heath reported on the more restricted speech code within lower-class families, and the more elaborated code within middle-class families, and argued that the latter better prepares middle-class children for school success. More recently, developmental psychologists Betty Hart and Todd Risley (1995, 1999) had graduate students audiotape, one evening each month, the speech utterances occurring between parents and children as the children aged from 12 to 36 months of age. They found that the middle-class parents addressed many more words to their children than did the lower-class parents, and also used many more different vocabulary words in these conversations than did the lower-class parents. Hart and Risley report that by 36 months, the children were full participants in their family's conversational culture. Not surprisingly, just like their parents, the middle-class children knew and used far more different words than the lower-class children. Other researchers have corroborated and extended these findings. Thus, preschool oral language literacy translates directly into elementary school reading literacy.

School readiness and acquisition also have a behavioral dimension. Perhaps most damaging to their success in school is the immaturity that many low-income children bring to first grade. They often come to school unready to sit still, pay attention to the teacher and the lesson, and do their own work. Parental assistance with homework, and monitoring of the child's school success, is often absent. By comparison, middle-class parents often make raising, instructing, and assuring the school success of their children one of their principal daily activities, a pattern that Lareau (2003) refers to as "concerted cultivation." As a result of differential cognitive and behavioral school readiness,

differential parental involvement in the school performance of their children, and resulting differential early school success, lower-income and middle-income children typically show very different achievement trajectories as they progress through the school grades.

The divergence of these trajectories is not surprising. Children who are engaged and successful at school typically receive positive feedback from teachers, and enjoy schoolwork, which causes them to maintain or even increase their efforts. They are typically placed in higher level "ability groups," where other students are engaged and motivated and more material is covered at a faster pace. They are assigned and complete more homework, and do more reading in their free time. On the other hand, children who are less engaged and successful in early elementary school typically receive less positive feedback from teachers, and get less pleasure from schoolwork, which causes them to become disengaged. They are often placed in lower-level "ability groups," where the other students are also less engaged, and more elementary material is covered at a slower pace. They are assigned little or no homework, and do little reading in their free time. When differential patterns such as these begin in early elementary school, and continue through later elementary, middle, and high school, the "low" and "high" trajectory groups emerge at the end of 12th grade with very different literacy levels as measured by academic skills and motivations.

Nor does the process of differential literacy development end at this point. Lower-performing children have a higher rate of school dropout, and those who graduate from high school often go straight into the labor market. There they may encounter employers who consider their literacy and mathematics skills to be inadequate for the requirements of the jobs available. By contrast, higher-performing students typically undertake four more years of academic skill development in college, often followed by graduate-level or professional training. Then, when these individuals enter the labor market, they take jobs which themselves have a strong component of continued learning and literacy development. The result is a society composed of adults who, at least when we compare the top and bottom of the occupational hierarchy, are strongly differentiated on the basis of their cognitive skills, which are in turn correlated with their earnings.

These effects have been magnified by the strong upward trend in female employment during the second half of the twentieth century, and the accompanying increase in female representation in highly paid, knowledge-based professional employment. At the same time, income inequality across worker education and skill levels has been increasing. With assortative mating by educational level at a high level, there has been significant growth in families where both parents hold highly paid jobs requiring advanced cognitive skills. Meanwhile, at the lower educational levels, wages are stagnant, and many children are raised in single-parent households. Children raised in families having these very different levels of cognitive, social, and monetary resources, typically in neighborhoods and schools segregated by income and race, can expect very different cognitive development trajectories. Thus, in US society today, social class and race/ethnicity are correlated with literacy, broadly defined as reading, writing, and mathematics skills. This correlation is a primary cause of continuing social inequality.

SEE ALSO: Educational Attainment; Educational Inequality; Educational and Occupational Attainment; Globalization, Education and; Schooling and Economic Success; Status Attainment; Stratification: Functional and Conflict Theories; Stratification and Inequality, Theories of; Urban Education

REFERENCES AND SUGGESTED READINGS

Baker, D. & LeTendre, G. (2005) *National Differences, Global Similarities: World Culture and the Future of Schooling*. Stanford University Press, Stanford.

Bruns, B., Mingat, A., & Rakotomalala, R. (2003) *Achieving Universal Primary Education by 2015: A Chance for Every Child*. World Bank, Washington, DC.

Chubb, J. & Loveless, T. (Eds.) (2002) *Bridging the Achievement Gap*. Brookings Institution, Washington, DC.

Farkas, G. (1996) *Human Capital or Cultural Capital? Ethnicity and Poverty Groups in an Urban School District*. Aldine de Gruyter, New York.

Farkas, G. (2003) Cognitive Skills and Noncognitive Traits and Behaviors in Stratification Processes. *Annual Review of Sociology* 29: 541–62.

Farkas, G. (2004) The Black–White Test Score Gap. *Contexts* 3: 12–19.

Hanushek, E. & Welch, F. (Eds.) (2005) *Handbook of the Economics of Education*. North Holland, Amsterdam.

Hart, B. & Risley, T. (1995) *Meaningful Differences in the Everyday Experience of Young American Children*. Paul Brookes Publishing, Baltimore.

Hart, B. & Risley, T. (1999) *The Social World of Children Learning to Talk*. Paul Brookes Publishing, Baltimore.

Holzer, H (1996) *What Employers Want: Job Prospects for Less-Educated Workers*. Russell Sage Foundation, New York.

Jencks, C. & Phillips, M. (Eds.) (1998) *The Black–White Test Score Gap*. Brookings Institution, Washington, DC.

Lareau, A. (2003) *Unequal Childhoods: Class, Race, and Family Life*. University of California Press, Berkeley.

Murnane, R. & Levy, F. (1996) *Teaching the New Basic Skills*. Free Press, New York.

Neuman, S. & Dickinson, D. (Eds.) (2002) *Handbook of Early Literacy Research*. Guilford Press, New York.

Porter, A. & Gamoran, A. (Eds.) (2002) *Methodological Advances in Cross-National Survey of Educational Achievement*. National Academy Press, Washington, DC.

Raudenbush, S. & Kasim, R. (1998) Cognitive Skill and Economic Inequality: Findings from the National Adult Literacy Survey. *Harvard Educational Review* 68: 33–79.

US Department of Education (1993) *Adult Literacy in America: A First Look at the Findings of the National Adult Literacy Survey*. National Center for Education Statistics 1993–275, Washington, DC.

local residents' movements

Koichi Hasegawa

Local residents' movements expanded greatly in Japan after the mid-1950s. Their names – such as "students' movements" and "women's movements" – designate types of participants. The term "residents" indicates the local inclusiveness of the movement: anyone who lives in the area, if they are interested in a local issue, can participate. No other qualification is required. People of any age beyond high school, including senior citizens, male or female, people of any political affiliation or ideology, are welcome to participate. The boundary of the local area depends on the issues. In many cases it corresponds closely to a geographical area like a local school district, city, town, or village. But when pollution comes from a large-scale project like the bullet train or an airport, the movement can even extend beyond prefectural boundaries.

In the Japanese context, local residents' movements are completely distinct from existing labor union movements and political movements led by political parties, such as the "progressive party," the Japan Socialist Party (now the Social Democratic Party), or the Japan Communist Party. Major characteristics of local residents' movements include being (1) single issue or issue limited, (2) spontaneous, (3) non-partisan, and (4) stressing democratic values like participation, self-autonomy, freedom, and transparency. In this meaning the term "self-limited radicalism," used by Cohen (1985) to described new social movements, is also appropriate to local residents' movements.

The size of residents' movement membership, from several people to 10,000 and more, depends on the issues. Typically, the issues are of two types: (1) a protection type – opposing or stopping some harmful plan or facilities; and (2) an achievement type – improving local amenities or living conditions, such as requests to build public libraries or public parks. The organizing form or management style of the movement organization can vary from a self-generated loose network to a formal organizational structure with articles of incorporation, representatives, and an annual budget.

The concept of citizens' movements resembles that of residents' movements. These two terms are commonly used without distinction, almost interchangeably. However, there are subtle nuances of difference between the terms "local residents" and "citizens." Local residents are people with loyalties bound to particular local communities. Citizens, however, in the context of Japanese social movements, are thought of as autonomous individuals pursuing generalized civic goals. Contrasting local residents' movements with citizens' movements from this perspective reveals important differences in their

character and organizing principles. In general, residents' movements are commonly organized around existing local groups such as neighborhood associations, and are strongly characterized by their focus on issues of concern to a specific local area. Typically, their membership is largely composed of the people who reside in this limited range. In contrast, citizens' movements are thought to consist of autonomous individual citizens brought together by shared ideals and objectives. They are strongly characterized by their focus on much broader issues: issues of concern to entire prefectures, the whole nation, and sometimes to the world or all of humanity (e.g., the peace movement and women's movement).

The social status of participants in local residents' movements can vary greatly, but the primary actors are often people who find it relatively easy to devote time to the movement. Such people include those involved in agriculture or fishing (during the slack season), the self-employed, public sector employees (i.e., public officials and teachers), women, and the elderly. In contrast, the people involved in citizens' movements are typically professionals and the better educated who have access to information resources. For instance, if a group to protect the natural environment of "Mt. X" was organized by people living in the immediate vicinity of the mountain, this group would be a local residents' movement; its central objective would be to protect the interests of the local people. In contrast, instead of or beyond local residents, if the group was created by the general citizenry of surrounding urban areas, lovers of nature, and specialists such as scientists, teachers, and lawyers, it would be a citizens' movement; its activities would be much more idealistic, driven by a commitment to universal values rather than direct interests.

The well-known farmers' protest during the Meiji era in the 1890s and 1900s against pollution from the Ashio copper mine provides a classic example of an early form of local residents' movement. But in that era, the prewar Great Japan Imperial Constitution substantially limited civil liberties such as freedom of speech and assembly. These restrictions made local residents' movements infrequent, sporadic, and highly localized. Only after 1955, with democratization and liberalization in place, did pollution from the rapid development of heavy industry lead to local residents' movements across the entire nation.

The increasing rates of air, water, and soil pollution by industrial waste – exemplified by the "four major cases" of Minamata mercury poisoning, Niigata mercury poisoning, Ouch-ouch cadmium poisoning, and Yikkaichi asthma, all of which appeared in the 1950s and were publicly denied by the companies and the authorities – stimulated action and protest by local residents' groups across the country. During this period, local residents' movements usually sought relief and improvement after the pollution had occurred. In these movements farmers and fishers concerned about the destruction of their means of livelihood made appeals, petitions, and demands supported by protest actions.

In the mid-1960s, residents' movements changed their strategy from reactive to proactive. They fought to prevent the construction of planned large-scale industrial development projects before they could cause pollution. The first major successful case of this type in Japan was the 1964 movement against the construction of petrochemical complexes in Numazu, Mishima, and Shimizu in Shizuoka prefecture. The organizing processes, strategies, and tactics of these movements became a model for subsequent movements. The participants in these movements came from across the whole social strata. The 1964 example provides a good illustration: in a relatively short period of time, housewives joined with teachers, researchers, and other professionals, plus a broad spectrum of local residents including laborers, farmers, and fishermen, standing shoulder to shoulder to defend their local environment.

It is worth noting that these movements were not simply responses to the actions of individual corporations (although individual corporations were often the immediate focus of protest, criticism, and litigation). Rather, they were reactions against government policies. This period of high economic growth was marked by the introduction and (attempted) implementation of several nationwide development plans. The First Comprehensive National Development Plan (1962) aimed to develop and disperse industrial activity across the nation, in part by designating and funding new industrial cities. The Second Comprehensive National Development Plan (1969) attempted to stimulate development across the nation through the construction of enormous industrial complexes and interconnecting transport networks of bullet train lines and high-speed freeways.

By this time, awareness of the four major pollution cases, the pollution problems evident in other industrial areas, and the widely reported success of protest movements against industrial complexes in Numazu and elsewhere had spread to the general public. Under these circumstances, the actual and impending pollution from the large-scale development plans stimulated the further growth of local residents' movements all over Japan. Powerful residents' movements stopped plans for new large-scale petrochemical complexes in the Second Comprehensive National Development Plan in such areas as Tomakomai City in Hokkaido, Rokkasho Village in Aomori (Funabashi et al. 1998), and the Shibushi Bay area in Kagoshima. The opposition was so fierce that in the aftermath of the 1973 oil crisis, as governments around the world reassessed their energy supply options and associated economic policies, the Japanese government abandoned its plans altogether for further petrochemical industrial complexes.

The political effectiveness of residents exercising their right to protest received great attention from the media and general public. The Japanese public embraced protesting as a tool for resisting government policies that valued economic growth above all else and lacked any mechanisms for effectively regulating pollution or preventing environmental destruction.

From the mid-1960s these movements broadened and became more active in demanding improvements to the living environment. Urban dwellers who had developed a citizens' conscientiousness began to organize in defense of the environment, to create new communities, and to revitalize towns. In the process, the foci and forms of the local residents' movements became much more diverse, and the differences with citizens' movements became far more ambiguous. Especially in and around large metropolitan areas such as Tokyo, Osaka, and Nagoya, the provision of social infrastructure had not kept up with the population explosion of the high economic growth years. Failures in water supply, sewage, road construction, employment and educational opportunities, public health, and maintaining parks and other public facilities brought about a nationwide boom in local residents' movements, especially between the late 1960s and mid-1970s.

From the mid-1970s the model of local residents' movements spread to South Korea, Taiwan, and other East Asian countries, where it helped inspire anti-pollution movements.

SEE ALSO: Benefit and Victimized Zones; Daily Life Pollution; Environmental Movements; High-Speed Transportation Pollution; New Social Movement Theory; Social Structure of Victims

REFERENCES AND SUGGESTED READINGS

Broadbent, J. (1998) *Environmental Politics in Japan: Networks of Power and Protest*. Cambridge University Press, Cambridge.

Cohen, J. L. (1985) Strategy or Identity: New Theoretical Paradigms and Contemporary Social Movements. *Social Research* 52(4): 663–716.

Funabashi, H., Hasegawa, K., Hatanaka, S., & Katsuta, H. (1985) *Shinkansen Kogai: Kosoku Bunmei no Shakai Mondai* (Bullet Train Pollution: Social Problems of a High Speed Civilization). Yuhikaku, Tokyo.

Funabashi, H., Hasegawa, K., & Iijima, N. (Eds.) (1998) *Kyodai Chiiki Kaihatsu no Koso to Kiketsu: Mutsu Ogawara Kaihatsu to Kakunenryo Saikuru shisetsu* (Vision Versus Results in a Large-Scale Industrial Development Project in the Mutsu-Ogawara District: A Sociological Study of Social Change and Confict in Rokkasho Village). University of Tokyo Press, Tokyo.

Hasegawa, K. (2004) *Constructing Civil Society in Japan: Voices of Environmental Movements*. Trans Pacific Press, Melbourne.

log-linear models

Janet C. Rice

Log-linear modeling is a data analysis technique used to explore relationships among categorical variables. Log-linear models express the logarithms of the expected cell frequencies from a multiway contingency table as a linear combination of the variables and their interactions. The simplest models yield a test equivalent to the chi square test of independence, but the technique allows exploration of relationships among more than two variables. Since log-linear models are additive with respect to the logarithm of the cell frequencies, they easily generate estimates of odds ratios.

Although statisticians such as Pearson and Yule addressed the association between two categorical variables early in the twentieth century, development of techniques similar to the analysis of variance and linear regression for continuous outcome variables was slow. Birch (1963) proposed the log-linear model. Goodman and others made log-linear modeling popular in the 1960s and 1970s (Goodman 1970; Bishop et al. 1975). Goodman and his colleagues made a computer program available in the 1970s.

A log-linear model assuming that two cross-classified categorical variables, A and B, are associated is denoted AB and has the form

$$\ln(e_{ij}) = 1 + l_i^A + l_j^B + l_{ij}^{AB}$$

where $i = 1$ to I indicates the level of variable A, $j = 1$ to J indicates the level of variable B, e_{ij} is the expected frequency for the ijth cell of the table, and the ls are parameters to be estimated. A model that assumes the two variables are independent is denoted A,B. If an interaction term is included in a model, the main effects that are involved in it are necessarily included in the model.

Parameters are most often estimated using the method of maximum likelihood. Grizzle et al. (1969) developed a weighted least squares approach that they applied to repeated measures data. Exact methods for small samples are also now available.

There are two major types of log-linear models, logit and symmetric. Logit models assign the role of predictor to some variables and the role of outcome to others. Symmetric models place all variables on an equal footing.

Logit models are members of the general linear model. They are analogous to linear and logistic regression models. In fact, for a single binary outcome and a set of categorical predictors, log-linear models yield the same results as logistic regression models. Outcomes can also be polytomous, and the models can contain more than one outcome variable.

All logit models must include the most complex interaction among the predictors and the most complex interaction among the outcomes as controlling terms. Additional components must involve relationships between predictors and outcomes.

Symmetric models allow researchers to address problems that fall outside the context of the general linear model. Researchers have applied them to problems in many disciplines including sociology, psychometrics, and epidemiology. Since there are fewer mandatory controlling terms in symmetric models, the number of models that can be considered is larger than in the logit case.

One of the earliest applications of symmetric models was in the area of social mobility. Data are in the form of a square table relating the status of one generation to that of the next. The cells on the main diagonal represent no change in status. Interaction terms in these models often require a large number of parameters. The variables are often ordinal. Modeling strategies attempt to reduce the number of needed parameters. An example of a simplifying hypothesis is that the relationship between one or more of the variables and the logarithm of the frequencies is linear.

Assessment of rater agreement also generates a square table. Observations that fall on the main diagonal represent agreement. The log-linear model allows the inclusion of covariates and the comparison of more than two raters.

Another type of symmetric model concerns the identification of latent classes. Latent class models assume that all associations among the manifest variables can be explained by their association with the unobserved latent variable(s). If X is a latent variable and A and B are manifest variables, the model is AX,BX. Clogg developed a program to fit latent class models.

Latent class models also allow tests of the hypothesis that a set of categorical items form a Guttman scale (Clogg & Sawyer 1981). These models are used in developmental research and studies of progression of drug use.

Epidemiologists use capture-recapture models to estimate the size of a population by drawing two or more samples from it. The variables are presence or absence in each sample. An important feature of data from capture-recapture studies is that the cell observed frequency indicating that an observation is absent in all samples must be estimated by the model. This technique was used to estimate the extent of undercount in the census.

Future developments in log-linear modeling are likely to be in the areas of correlated data and random effects modeling. Problems in genetics will stimulate development of techniques for many dimensions.

SEE ALSO: Correlation; General Linear Model; Multivariate Analysis; Regression and Regression Analysis; Reliability; Statistics

REFERENCES AND SUGGESTED READINGS

Agresti, A. (2002) *Categorical Data Analysis*, 2nd edn. Wiley, New York.

Birch, M. (1963) Maximum Likelihood in Three-Way Tables. *Journal of the Royal Statistical Society, Ser. B* 25: 220–33.

Bishop, Y., Fienberg, S., & Holland, P. (1975) *Discrete Multivariate Analysis: Theory and Practice*. MIT Press, Cambridge, MA.

Clogg, C. & Sawyer, D. (1981) A Comparison of Alternative Models for Analyzing the Scalability of Response Patterns. In: Leinhardt, S. (Ed.), *Sociological Methodology*. Jossey-Bass, San Francisco.

Goodman, L. (1970) The Multivariate Analysis of Qualitative Data: Interactions Among Multiple Classifications. *Journal of the American Statistical Association* 65: 226–56.

Grizzle, J., Starmer, C., & Koch, G. (1969) Analysis of Categorical Data by Linear Models. *Biometrics* 25: 489–504.

logocentrism

Warren Fincher

Coined by Jacques Derrida in his *Of Grammatology*, logocentrism refers to the tendency in western civilization to privilege the linguistic signifier (a spoken or written word) over the signified (the thing to which the word refers). The importance of the term resides in Derrida's critique of the philosophical tendency in western civilization to be logocentric. Derrida asserts that western discourses generally tend to impose hierarchies of power by defining certain concepts against necessarily subordinated alternatives. Extending this critique to logocentrism, Derrida notes the tendency in western philosophy and semiotics to value the signifier as opposed to the thing it signifies in what he calls a "metaphysics of presence."

In *Of Grammatology*, Derrida systematically problematizes much of Ferdinand de Saussure's work in semiotics. On many points, Derrida employs Saussure's work as a point of departure. For example, Saussure maintains that the signified does not inherently indicate the nature of the signifier – for example, there is nothing about the nature of a table that requires it to be called such – but rather that signifiers create a linguistic system of signs that reference each other. Likewise, Derrida agrees that linguistic systems encode certain value systems. However, Derrida rejects the dyadic model of signs that Saussure develops, wherein Saussure focuses attention on the relationship between the signifier and signified; the relationship is arbitrary but nonetheless provides insight into the form of the linguistic system. Derrida rejects the distinction between signified and signifier, between some external and objective object and its linguistic sign. Rather, he sees the two interpenetrating. Also, Derrida rejects Saussure's tenet that the relationship between signifier and signified, while arbitrary, is also static. Derrida recognizes that a gap exists between the idea and the thing it references and, through this gap, play occurs. To focus on the signifier as clearly and always indicative of the same signified object is to allow the sign more preeminence than is due and falsely implicates a centrality of the signifier over the signified.

In "Plato's Pharmacy," Derrida examines Plato's *Phaedrus*, in which Plato denounces writing as a lesser form to oration, claiming that writing is a derivative of the spoken word. This praises the spoken word as the closest manifestation to the mental experience of an idea, and writing as secondary to that. In making this argument, Plato values the presence of the speaker in oration – and its proximity to the mental experience of thought – and rebukes the absence of the author in the written form. The value system found in this "phonocentrism" may also be found more generally in the western tradition of privileging the signifier – at the moment of being read, the text is present – over the signified, which is not present. Hence, because logocentric thought reifies a division of the signifier from the signified and because logocentric philosophical orientations specifically value the present, logocentrism embodies a "metaphysics of presence."

Current sociological work in logocentrism is scant and remains mostly within the forum of philosophical debates over the nature of language. Clive Stroud-Drinkwater's (2001) defense of logocentrism critiques Derrida's approach to deconstruction, concluding that it rests on incorrect generalization of metaphysics and otherwise follows the tenets of classical logic. Beyond debates over semiotics, the concept of logocentrism has been applied to the sociology of science (Fox 2003). The idealized setting of the laboratory is contrasted with the arena of practical application. A "scientific logocentrism" emerges from the privileging of data produced from the ideal conditions of the lab and subsequently framed as a representation of reality. Deviations from that representation when applied to practical settings are then discounted as invalid because of the uncontrolled elements of the setting. The laboratory is given centrality as the articulation of a scientific reality, even though the conditions that give rise to that reality are not found in nature.

SEE ALSO: Deconstruction; Derrida, Jacques; Poststructuralism; Saussure, Ferdinand de; Semiotics

REFERENCES AND SUGGESTED READINGS

Derrida, J. (1967) *Of Grammatology*. Trans. G. C. Spivak. Johns Hopkins University Press, Baltimore.

Derrida, J. (1980) Structure, Sign, and Play in the Discourse of the Human Sciences. In: *Writing and Difference*. Trans. A. Bass. University of Chicago Press, Chicago, pp. 278–94.

Derrida, J. (1981) Plato's Pharmacy. In: *Dissemination*. Trans. B. Johnson. University of Chicago Press, Chicago, pp. 63–171.

Fox, N. J. (2003) Practice-Based Evidence: Towards Collaborative and Transgressive Research. *Sociology* 37(1): 81–102.

Stroud-Drinkwater, C. (2001) Defending Logocentrism. *Philosophy and Literature* 25: 75–86.

Lombroso, Cesare (1835–1909)

Frank P. Williams III and Marilyn D. McShane

Cesare Lombroso is considered one of the fathers of positivist criminology. His work on the traits and characteristics of offenders typifies the scientific analysis of the individual criminal in an attempt to determine the causes of crime. Although there is little support for his assumptions today, his work is valued not only as a precursor to criminal anthropology but also as an early demonstration of the use of scientific measures in theory building.

Lombroso, born in Verona, Italy, received a medical degree in 1858 and a surgical specialty in 1859. He married in 1869 and had two daughters, Paola and Gina. He served as a physician in the Italian army and also worked with the mentally ill in several hospitals. Fascinated by comparative anatomy, he hoped to establish some relationship between the form and features of individuals and their behavioral tendencies.

There is evidence of two major influences in Lombroso's work. First, he was affected by German materialism of the time that valued objective scientism over naturalistic philosophy. Second, his writings exhibit an appreciation of evolution, particularly the writings of Charles Darwin on biological evolution and of Herbert Spencer and others who proposed theories of social evolution.

True to positivist methods, Lombroso conducted painstakingly careful research, documenting the facial and body measurements of hundreds of criminals and non-criminals, using populations of soldiers, prisoners, the insane, persons with epilepsy (a disease which was misunderstood at the time), and the general population. He attempted to explain physical and mental differences as anomalies indicating a primitive or subhuman nature he referred to as atavism. He rejected the classical concept of free will and argued that criminals were cast their fate by their degenerative features. To him, criminals were evolutionary throwbacks whose defective traits were evident in the shape of their skull and bone structure, certain physical quirks, and tendencies toward slang, tattoos, and vice. All of these characteristics and features were said to be symptoms of a criminal personality, which for Lombroso was a more innate, biological concept than the way the term personality is used today.

Lombroso classified offenders into two primary groups: born criminals or hardened recidivists, and occasional criminals. The first group, which exhibited most of the traits mentioned above, is the one he emphasized and for which he is best known. The latter group occupied much of his writings because they were exceptions to his "born criminal" theory. This group was composed of three categories. First, Lombroso identified pseudocriminals who were not necessarily atavistic, but more victims of circumstance – such as a person who commits a crime in self-defense. His second type of occasional criminal was the criminaloid, who he claimed had only a touch of degeneracy. Finally, there was the habitual offender who was also not degenerate or atavistic but caught up in a pattern of bad associations and continued contact with born criminals.

His theory of the born criminal, particularly in its biological aspects, was severely criticized. In response, Lombroso incorporated the criticisms into his theory and, at the time of his death, had added social, economic, and political causes of crime. He also had increased the number of criminal types to encompass other biological features, such as an epileptoid. However, to the very end he maintained that biological factors were the dominant causes of crime.

Later in life, Lombroso worked closely with his daughter Gina and other young scholars with whom he published several articles and books. At the University of Turin he was professor of legal medicine and public hygiene, professor of psychiatry and clinical psychiatry, and professor of criminal anthropology.

Lombroso was also one of the first criminologists to study and write about the female offender. His efforts in this area demonstrate his consideration of a wider range of factors in criminality, including gender, age, poverty, and occupation. In his book *The Female Offender*, he decided that women were far more ferocious than men.

The essence of Lombroso's work was carried on by a student, Enrico Ferri, and a fellow criminologist, Raffaele Garofalo, who assisted him in establishing the *Archives of Psychiatry and Criminal Anthropology*. Both also went on to achieve acclaim in the area of criminology, although they moved away from Lombroso's emphasis on physical traits.

Criticisms of Lombroso's work center primarily on the generalizations he made about crime proneness based on ethnic characteristics. For example, he spoke of the Gypsies as a criminal race: "They are vain, like all delinquents, but they have no fear of shame. Everything they earn they spend for drink and ornaments ... They are given to orgies, love noise, and make a great outcry in the markets. They murder in cold blood in order to rob, and were formerly suspected of cannibalism. The women are very clever at stealing, and teach it to their children."

Nonetheless, some of his arguments are still popular today, such as the role of alcohol in crime, and the existence of a criminal personality. We also credit the theoretical work of the "Italian Triumvirate," Lombroso, Garofalo, and Ferri, for laying the foundation for the study of criminal offenders, particularly in their emphasis on the use of scientific methodology for the classification and prediction of behavior.

SEE ALSO: Crime; Criminology; Evolution; Positivism

REFERENCES AND SUGGESTED READINGS

Ferracuti, S. (1996) Cesare Lombroso (1835–1909). *Journal of Forensic Psychiatry* 7: 130–49.
Lombroso, C. (1876) *L'Uomo Delinquente* (*The Criminal Man*). Hoepli, Milan.
Lombroso, C. (1918 [1899]) *Le Crime, Causes et Remèdes* (*Crime: Its Causes and Remedies*). Trans. H. P. Norton. Little, Brown, Boston.
Lombroso-Ferrero, G. (1972 [1911]) *Criminal Man: According to the Classification of Cesare Lombroso.* Patterson Smith, Montclair, NJ.
Wolfgang, M. (1973) Cesare Lombroso. In: Mannheim, H. (Ed.), *Pioneers in Criminology*, 2nd edn. Patterson Smith, Montclair, NJ, pp. 232–91.

lone-parent families

Karen Rowlingson

The growth of lone parenthood is a trend common to many advanced industrial countries. In 1990 Britain had one of the highest rates of lone parenthood in Europe (with 19 percent of families with children being lone-parent families) along with Sweden (19 percent), Norway (19 percent), and Denmark (18 percent). The European countries with some of the lowest levels included Greece (5 percent), Ireland (9 percent), Italy (7 percent), Portugal (6 percent), and Spain (5 percent). This division suggests some combination of North/South, rich/poor, Protestant/Catholic factors at work. Countries that are generally rich, Protestant, and North European have much higher rates of lone parenthood than those that are mainly poor, Southern, and Catholic, though Britain cuts across this division as it has comparatively high rates of poverty but is Northern and Protestant. Culture and religion therefore seem important factors when seeking to explain variations in rates of lone parenthood. If we look outside of Europe but remain within the developed world, Japan had a very low rate of lone parenthood (4 percent) in the early 1990s, Australia had a slightly lower rate than Britain (15 percent), and the US had by far the highest rate (25 percent).

The percentage of births outside marriage also varies substantially by country. This figure cannot be taken as a direct indicator of lone parenthood as these births are often to cohabiting parents, but there does appear to be some correlation, as the highest rates of births outside marriage were in Denmark, Norway, and Sweden in the early 1990s. The lowest rates were in Greece and Italy. The United Kingdom and the US fell somewhere in between these two extremes. Divorce rates are also associated with lone parenthood. The highest rates in the early 1990s were in Denmark, the UK, and Sweden, with the lowest rates in Greece, Ireland, Italy, Portugal, and Spain. The US had by far the highest rate.

Another interesting point of comparison is the family marital status of lone parents within each country. For example, the proportion of lone parents who are never married varied dramatically, from more than half in Norway and Sweden to about a third in the US and UK. Never-married lone parents were virtually nonexistent in Greece, Portugal, and Japan in the early 1990s.

WELFARE REGIMES

Some researchers have tried to categorize countries into groups in terms of how women and lone parents fare, especially in relation to employment and social policies. This general approach of categorizing "welfare regimes" is most heavily associated with Esping-Andersen, who categorized welfare regimes in terms of the policy logics that revolved around a paid worker's dependence or independence from the labor market.

Another way of classifying countries is in terms of whether they focus on lone parents as mothers (the "caregiving" model) or workers (the "parent/worker" model). The Netherlands is a prime example of the former, where sufficient support is given to lone parents to remain in the home to look after their children. The state therefore provides support for women as mothers. Lone parents are able to establish autonomous households without suffering poverty and deprivation and they can do so without having to engage with the labor market. Sweden, however, is an example of the parent/worker model. Lone parents here are also able to establish autonomous households without suffering poverty and deprivation, but they tend to do so through engaging with the labor market. The state provides support in terms of childcare, wages are relatively generous, and there are reasonable benefit payments to those out of work.

The ability of lone parents to establish autonomous households without suffering poverty and deprivation might be seen as a benchmark with which to measure gender (and class) equality in different countries. We have seen that there are different ways of doing this: we can support lone parents to stay at home and care for their children (by having generous benefits) or we can support lone parents to take up paid work (by having affordable childcare and keeping wage rates high). Perhaps there is also a middle way in terms of supporting lone parents to combine roles by means of packaging their income – some income from part-time work, some from benefits, some from maintenance. This is more the approach taken in the UK, where in-work benefits such as Working Tax Credit (formerly Family Credit) enable lone parents to put together such a package. But in the UK, wage and benefit levels have generally been too low to avoid poverty for all but a minority of lone parents.

EFFECTS OF SOCIAL SECURITY POLICY

It is common for those on the political right to argue that lone parenthood has risen because women have access to relatively high rates of benefit. There is some evidence that appears to support this view; Greece and Portugal, for example, have low levels of social security support for lone parents and also low levels of lone parenthood. At the other end of the spectrum, Norway, Denmark, and Australia have higher levels of both social assistance and lone parenthood. But we must be careful not to draw conclusions about causation from these associations. It is possible that the high rates of benefit in some countries were the *result* of a growth in lone parenthood (due to a growing lobby group and increasing recognition of the need for higher benefits) rather than the *cause* of the growth. Also, the US provides an important exception to any correlation between levels of lone parenthood and levels of benefit. As we have seen, the US has the highest level of lone parenthood in the western world, but its level of social assistance is among the lowest (lower even than that available in Ireland and Spain).

So it seems that there is only a weak association between high rates of benefits for lone parents and high rates of lone parenthood.

Social security policy may have only weak effects on the *rate* of lone parenthood, but it may nevertheless affect the *employment partici-pation* rates of lone parents. Here again, how-ever, the evidence is inconclusive. For example, Sweden had the largest proportion of lone par-ents in paid work in the early 1990s, but the benefit replacement rate was also the highest. This means that Swedish lone parents, com-pared with lone parents in other countries, would not be much better off financially in work than on benefit. We might therefore expect them to have low employment rates, but they do not. This therefore contradicts a narrow rational economic model of behavior that assumes people weigh up the financial costs and benefits of a particular course of action and then act accordingly. France and Germany, on the other hand, had relatively high propor-tions of lone parents in work along with rela-tively low benefit replacement rates (thus supporting the rational economic model). Den-mark and France had similar proportions of lone parents in the labor force, but Denmark was relatively generous to lone parents on benefit whereas France was relatively mean.

EMPLOYMENT PATTERNS AND POLICIES

As we have seen, there is also a great deal of variation in the employment patterns of lone parents across different countries. In the early 1990s the Netherlands, the UK, and Ireland had the lowest rates of full-time paid work for lone parents: fewer than one in five lone parents in these countries had a paid job. The highest rates were found in Portugal, France, Japan, Italy, Sweden, and Denmark, where over half of all lone parents worked full-time. Overall, how-ever, lone mothers in all countries apart from the UK are either more likely to be working full-time than all mothers or the level of full-time employment is about the same. And generally, lone mothers are less likely to work part-time than all mothers are. So what explains these variations in employment rates?

Some of the variation in lone mothers' employment rates across different countries mirrors variation in the employment rates of mothers in couples. This supports a gendered approach to lone parenthood and also questions the appropriateness of singling out lone mothers as a group. If the experience of lone mothers is just an extreme version of that for all mothers, then perhaps policies should be aimed at improving the opportunities of all mothers rather than just focusing on lone mothers in particular. Or perhaps policies could be aimed at those (both women and men) with poorer educational and employment prospects.

Most advanced industrial countries are increasingly encouraging (if not compelling) lone parents to enter the labor market. But the ways in which they do this vary. Some, like the US, aim to achieve this largely by restricting access to benefits. Others, like the UK, attempt to "make work pay" principally through in-work benefits. And others, like Norway, pro-vide cheap childcare. These policies have been most successful where they fit with lone par-ents' own aspirations about employment. In the Netherlands, for example, a new policy to encourage lone parents into employment has largely failed because lone parents themselves, their employment advisers, and society more generally did not think it appropriate to push lone parents (back) into the labor market. Social and cultural norms about mothers as carers or workers have a major impact on employment patterns.

Many countries are now emphasizing paid work rather than care as the route to autonomy for lone parents. But paid work is no guarantee against poverty, as is evident in Japan and the US. The success of some countries, like Swe-den, in combining high employment rates with low poverty rates is due to a number of factors, such as:

- Lone parents working full-time rather than part-time.
- Childcare provision paid for by the state.
- Long parental leave schemes.
- Paid leave to be with sick children.
- Strong social transfers (benefit payments) for those out of work.
- State advanced maintenance schemes.

We cannot therefore simply move lone parents into paid work and expect poverty to be eradicated. Other policies, such as those relating to childcare and employment rights, also need to be put in place.

The strategy of moving lone parents into paid work places little value on the unpaid work in the home that most lone parents spend much of their time doing. Much of this unpaid work revolves around caring for children. In the past, "mothering" work was valued in as much as it attracted considerable status for women. Many states reinforced this by exempting lone parents on benefit from seeking work, as were the partners of unemployed men. From one point of view, such an approach is a positive one towards women as it enables them to carry out the "mothering" work that they wish to do. From another point of view, it reinforces patriarchal assumptions that women's role is in the home. Not only does it lack any expectation that women might want to get paid work, it also fails to provide them with any support, advice, or training should they decide they do wish to get paid jobs. Men gain access to the wages from paid work and women remain dependent either on men (if they are in couples) or on the state (if they are lone parents).

The move towards encouraging lone parents to take paid work can therefore be seen from either of these perspectives. It can be seen as lowering the status of the unpaid "mothering" work that women do or it could be seen as challenging women's confinement to the domestic sphere.

DIFFERENCE, DIVERSITY, AND IDENTITY

Lone-parent families have received a great deal of attention from the media, politicians, policy-makers, and academics. But should we focus on them as a particular group? This depends on the answer to two further questions. First, are lone parents a homogeneous group with distinctive characteristics that unite them? Second, are lone parents sufficiently distinct from other parents or other groups to warrant separate consideration?

The answer to the first question is that lone parents do have some distinctive characteristics which unite them as a particular group. They have challenged prevailing norms of the two-parent family, based on the idea of a breadwinning man and a housewife. The lone parent, to some extent, takes on both these roles and since the vast majority of lone parents are women they are also united by their gender. However, it is also widely assumed that lone parents are united in poverty, but although poverty is widespread among lone parents, it is not universal. Some lone parents are much better off than others and the social class background of lone parents can make a considerable difference to the experience of living in a lone-parent family.

Another source of difference between lone parents is how they became lone parents (and this is often linked to economic difference, too). Younger women who have babies while single are generally from very poor backgrounds, while women who separate from husbands sometimes come from better-off backgrounds and experience lone parenthood in different ways. Yet another source of difference is ethnicity. Most lone parents in western countries are white, but some ethnic minorities are over-represented in lone-parent families (such as Afro-Caribbean women in the UK and African American women in the US) and some are under-represented (such as Asian women).

There are many other potential sources of difference between lone-parent families. Some lone parents are sick or disabled and others have sick or disabled children. Sexuality and culture also vary among lone parents and all these factors can affect the experience of lone parenthood as well as the identity of the lone parent. Perhaps a lesbian lone mother will feel she has more in common with a lesbian mother in a couple than with a heterosexual lone mother?

This brings us to the second question about whether some lone parents have more in common with other parents, or other groups, than they do with other lone parents. For example, a young never-married lone mother living in poor housing may feel she has (and may actually have) more in common with the married mother living next door than she does to a divorced lone mother living in a large house in an affluent area. Of course, all lone parents face similar issues when it comes to raising children without a partner, but even in couples, one parent (usually the mother) tends to take on more of the parental responsibility and associated work than the other partner. So perhaps the difference between lone mothers and mothers in couples is not so great.

A final reason why lone parenthood should not be seen as a monolithic state is that it is not, usually, for life. Couple families turn into lone-parent families, which then turn again into couple families and so on. So to make very large distinctions between lone-parent families on the one hand and couple families on the other must be questioned. In the UK, research has found that half of all lone parents leave lone parenthood within 6 years of becoming a lone parent.

FUTURE DIRECTIONS

As already mentioned, issues around difference, diversity, and identity are complex and fluid. More research needs to be carried out to explore the homogeneity or heterogeneity of lone parenthood both on an objective level (e.g., comparing levels of income, work, disability, etc. with other groups) and on a more subjective level in terms of identity.

It is also important to consider the role of other actors rather than simply focus on the lone parent. Concern about non-resident parents has mostly revolved around issues of financial support for children, but the role of fathers more generally in relation to care work is a very important issue. And children's perspectives on family life are starting to receive more attention – deservedly so. The role of grandparents, steprelatives, broader family, and friends also needs to be considered.

Families change over time and more research needs to be carried out on the dynamics of family life. There is already some quantitative longitudinal work in this area, but very little qualitative longitudinal work. Qualitative panel studies are unusual and raise various methodological issues, but these should be explored to provide an important and currently largely lacking perspective on lone parenthood.

Finally, there is an urgent need for more up-to-date, comparative data on lone parenthood. Much of the data referred to in this entry relates to the early 1990s and yet it is highly likely that the picture has changed since then. Such research will need to consider carefully different definitions of lone parenthood in different countries so that meaningful comparisons can be made.

SEE ALSO: Child Custody and Child Support; Children and Divorce; Family Diversity; Family Poverty; Family Structure and Child Outcomes; Family Structure and Poverty; Non-Resident Parents

REFERENCES AND SUGGESTED READINGS

Bradshaw, J., Kennedy, S., Kilkey, M., Hutton, S., Cordon, A., Eardley, T., Holmes, H., & Neale, J. (1996) *The Employment of Lone Parents: A Comparison of Policy in 20 Countries*. HMSO, London.

Coleman, D. & Chandola, T. (1999) Britain's Place in Europe's Population. In: McRae, S. (Ed.), *Changing Britain: Families and Households in the 1990s*. Oxford University Press, Oxford, pp. 37–46.

Duncan, S. & Edwards, R. (Eds.) (1997) *Single Mothers in an International Context: Mothers or Workers?* UCL Press, London.

Esping-Andersen, G. (1990) *The Three Worlds of Welfare Capitalism*. Polity Press, Cambridge.

Garfinkel, I. & McLanahan, S. (1986) *Single Mothers and Their Children: A New American Dilemma*. Urban Institute Press, Washington, DC.

Gauthier, A. (1996) *The State and the Family: A Comparative Analysis of Family Policies in Industrialized Countries*. Clarendon Press, Oxford.

Kamerman, S. & Kahn, A. (Eds.) (1978) *Family Policy: Government and Family in 14 Countries*. Columbia University Press, New York.

Kamerman, S. & Kahn, A. (Eds.) (1997) *Family Change and Family Policies in Great Britain, Canada, New Zealand and the United States*. Clarendon Press, Oxford.

Lewis, J. & Hobson, B. (1997) Introduction. In: Lewis, J. (Ed.), *Lone Mothers in European Welfare Regimes*. Jessica Kingsley Publishers, London, pp. 1–20.

Orloff, A. (1993) Gender and the Social Rights of Citizenship. *American Sociological Review* 58: 303–28.

Rowlingson, K. & McKay, S. (2002) *Lone Parent Families: Gender, Class and State*. Pearson Education, Harlow.

Sainsbury, D. (1996) *Gender Equality and Welfare States*. Cambridge University Press, Cambridge.

Whiteford, P. & Bradshaw, J. (1994) Benefits and Incentives for Lone Parents: A Comparative Analysis. *International Social Security Review* 47: 69–89.

longevity, social aspects (the oldest old)

Miriam Bernard

Longevity is defined as the maximum life span attainable by the species and is measured by the age of the oldest living individual. Although there is evidence that people have lived well into late old age for many hundreds of years, a Frenchwoman, Madame Jeanne Calment, made history when she died at the age of 122 in August 1997. Other definitions of longevity refer to it as "uncommonly long duration of life," but what was once uncommon is now increasingly common. Today the World Health Organization calculates that there are approximately 600 million people aged 60 and over around the world. By 2025 this total is expected to double and, by 2050, there will be 2 billion people of this age. Historically, these changes are very recent and are a product of the twentieth century. As a result, many countries are now experiencing "rectangularization" as declining fertility and mortality (notably infant mortality) rates change their population structures from a pyramidal shape (many children at the bottom and fewer old people at the top) to a more even distribution across age groups. By the middle of the twenty-first century, demographers predict that there will be more people aged 60 years and older than children under the age of 15 years.

Although commentators agree that maximum life span has probably not extended a great deal over the centuries, what has improved markedly is life expectancy for both women and men. The rapidity of these changes can be illustrated with reference to Britain where, in 1901, life expectation at birth was only 48 years for men and 51.6 years for women. What is remarkable is that these figures had not altered since medieval times. Now however, women can expect to live to about 80 years of age and men to about 76 years of age. Despite continuing improvements in life expectancy, the gap between the sexes is closing as lifestyle factors, which researchers believe to account for about 70 percent of a person's chances of achieving longevity, begin to have an impact.

A further important feature illustrative of increased longevity is the aging of the older population itself as higher and higher proportions of people survive to age 60 and beyond. Worldwide, the fastest growing group is the "oldest old," variously defined as those aged 80 or 85 years or more. Perhaps the clearest indication of this trend is the rapid increase in the numbers of people surviving to the age of 100 years, particularly in developed countries. In 2000, the United Nations estimated that there were 180,000 centenarians around the world. By 2050, this number is projected to be 3.2 million: an eighteenfold increase. Moreover, in many countries, old age in general, and extreme old age in particular, is predominantly a female experience. In 1999 in Britain, there were 8,000 centenarians of whom 7,000 (87.5 percent) were women and 1,000 (12.5 percent) were men. Of the 50,000 centenarians in the United States, 85 percent are women and 15 percent are men. This has been termed the "feminization of later life" (Arber & Ginn 1991) and is often further reflected in other social aspects such as marital status and living arrangements. Widowhood, solo living, and reduced financial circumstances are now expectations for many older women, especially the "oldest old," while changing family forms contingent upon changing work patterns, changing attitudes to sexuality, growing numbers of minority ethnic older people, rising divorce rates, and, for some, remarriage will lead to even greater diversity of family and social situations across the life course and into old age.

Increased longevity presents us with many profound challenges. Among the persistent social issues facing all societies are how our oldest and most vulnerable members will be accommodated, given care, and supported; how we might finance old age; and how family and social networks may change. Contrary to popular opinion, the body of research evidence shows that older people have never been abandoned wholesale by their families. Rather, family and family support – albeit in different forms – will continue to remain crucial in our lives. Alongside this, prospects for many of improved health and well-being together with the blurring of the boundaries between education, work, leisure, and retirement may well open up new social opportunities and help challenge some of the age-old taboos and agist attitudes. This will include the possibility of developing different lifestyles and leisure activities in old age; having greater choice about where, how, and with whom one lives; continuing participation and involvement in local communities and in political and national life; and prospects for more rewarding and mutually beneficial intergenerational relationships.

Rapid though these changes have been in westernized nations, it is important to recognize that aging is now happening at a much faster rate in the developing world than in the developed world. For example, France's older population doubled from 7 percent to 14 percent over a period of 115 years, while the World Health Organization (2004) predicts that it will take China just 27 years to achieve the same increase. Today, 60 percent of people aged 60 and over live in the developing world, a figure that is expected to rise to 75 percent by 2025 and 85 percent by 2050. Moreover, it must be remembered that the rapidity of population aging in many developing countries is expected to outpace social and economic development, with the result that adjusting to these trends is likely to prove even more challenging than it has been to countries who became rich while they grew old.

These dramatic changes to our populations are neither temporary nor a statistical artifact: they are permanent and progressive. As the late Margot Jefferys (1988) eloquently argued, they should be seen as a triumph for public health and a cause for celebration, rather than a reason to further problematize and pathologize old people and old age.

SEE ALSO: Age Prejudice and Discrimination; Aging, Demography of; Aging and Health Policy; Aging and the Life Course, Theories of; Aging, Mental Health, and Well-Being; Aging and Social Policy; Aging and Social Support; Health Lifestyles; Healthy Life Expectancy; Leisure, Aging and; Social Support

REFERENCES AND SUGGESTED READINGS

Arber, S. & Ginn, J. (1991) *Gender and Later Life*. Sage, London.
International Longevity Center (2004) *Longevity Genes: Hunting for the Secrets of the Super Centenarians*. International Longevity Center, New York.
Jefferys, M. (1988) An Ageing Britain: What is its Future? In: Gearing, B., Johnson, M., & Heller, T. (Eds.), *Mental Health Problems in Old Age: A Reader*. Wiley, London.
Perls, T., Silver, M., & Lauerman, J. (1999) *Living to 100: Lessons in Living to Your Maximum Potential at Any Age*. Basic Books, New York.
World Health Organization (1998) *World Atlas on Ageing*. WHO Center for Health Development, Kobe.
World Health Organization (2004) *Ageing and Health: A Health Promotion Approach for Developing Countries*. WHO, Copenhagen.

looking-glass self

Jennifer Dunn

The looking-glass self is the most well-known dimension of Charles Horton Cooley's early, seminal conceptualization of what he called the social self. Cooley used the image of a mirror as a metaphor for the way in which people's self-concepts are influenced by their imputations of how they are perceived by others. Cooley distinguished three "principal elements" of the looking-glass self: "the imagination of our appearance to the other person; the imagination of his [*sic*] judgment of that appearance; and some sort of self-feeling, such as pride or mortification." Much of the time, Cooley thought, our experience of self is an emotional response to the supposed evaluations of others, especially significant others. Children learn the meaning of "I" and "me" and "mine" through the appropriation of objects they desire and claim as their own, in contrast to the things they cannot control. Importantly, among the objects they seek to control and appropriate as their own are their parents and others in the primary group. As infants and toddlers discover they can influence others by their actions, they simultaneously discover and realize reflections of themselves in these others.

Cooley based his self-theory on observations of his own children, confirming his initial hypotheses with a systematic study of his third child from shortly after birth to the thirty-third month, in order to determine how the word "I" is learned and its meaning. Children begin appropriative processes with attempts to control the things closest to them, including their own bodies, and then move outward to the people in their vicinity, even as infants "exerting [their] social power" to attract attention. They lay claim to their parents in much the same way they assert as their own their noses and their rattles. In order to learn the meaning of personal pronouns, which refer to different objects when used by different people, children must imagine themselves from the perspective of others. After coming to understand what others mean when they refer to themselves, that is, that "I" refers to self-feeling, children "sympathize" with these others and this empathetic process gives meaning to their own incipient self-feelings. "I" is social because when it is used it is always addressed to an audience (for Cooley, usually the child's mother), and its use thus indicates children's newly acquired ability to take the role of their audience. Once they begin to do this, they can also perform different selves for different audiences. Indeed, Cooley argued that even young children are capable of manipulating their audiences, care more about the opinions of some people than others, and selectively "own" those with whom they are the closest and over whom they have the most influence (e.g., "my mama"). Adults are not that much different; their imaginations are merely more complex and specific and their manipulations of others more subtle.

The self, then, emerges in interaction, becomes meaningful only in contrast to that which is not of self (society), and is, therefore, inextricable from society. Cooley described the looking-glass self in his first major work, *Human Nature and the Social Order*, published in 1902. His analysis of self was influenced by his early reading of idealist and transcendentalist literature, including Thoreau, Goethe, and Emerson, as well as the pragmatism of Dewey, also at Ann Arbor at the time. The social self draws upon the work of the psychologist and philosopher William James and the social psychologist James Mark Baldwin and was articulated within the populist, progressive intellectual milieu

of the Midwestern scholarship of Cooley's era and the sheltered academic environs of the University of Michigan, which granted him the leeway to develop his reflective notion of self based on his observations of his own children and introspection. As Cooley was also a painfully shy and reclusive man who wrote in his journals of his obsession with gaining the approbation of others, his theorization of a self that depends on a reflexive, emotion-laden response to imagined evaluations is distinctly autobiographical. Cooley's methodological approach follows directly from his conception of the self: human action must be understood in terms of the subjective meanings actors impute to situations. In his conjoining of the social self with society as the communicative imaginations of multiple selves, his looking-glass self is a culturally and historically specific product of his social location and his conceptual and political idealism.

Cooley's looking-glass self was elaborated by George Herbert Mead in the latter's development of the notion of taking the role of the other, especially the generalized other, as the mechanism through which a unified self emerges in interaction. Cooley also influenced Goffman's dramaturgical analysis of the self as a situated performance. There is a significant body of research on what is now commonly referred to as "reflected self appraisal" and its role in the development of self-concepts, and with those of Mead and Goffman, Cooley's ideas about the self have become a constitutive and foundational core of theories of self in sociological social psychology and symbolic interactionism, and because of his emphasis on the emotional aspects of identity, have influenced the sociology of emotions. Cooley has been critiqued: Mead thought his work was too "mentalistic" and others have suggested that the looking-glass self, if accurate, suggests an oversocialized human, passive and overly dependent on the opinions of others. Cooley himself answered both of these concerns, claiming in the introduction to *Social Organization* in 1907 that imagination was not all of society, but only his particular focus. His discussion of the looking-glass self, moreover, is only one dimension of the social self-conceptualization, in which he points not only to the importance of reflection, but also to the ways in which humans selectively and actively interpret and appropriate these reflections.

SEE ALSO: Cooley, Charles Horton; Generalized Other; Goffman, Erving; Identity: Social Psychological Aspects; Mead, George Herbert; Primary Groups; Self; Significant Others

REFERENCES AND SUGGESTED READINGS

Cooley, C. H. (1930) *Sociological Theory and Social Research*. Henry Holt, New York.

Cooley, C. H. (1998 [1902]) The Social Self: The Meaning of "I." In: Schubert, H. J. (Ed.), *Charles Horton Cooley: On Self and Social Organization.* University of Chicago Press, Chicago, pp. 155–75.

Franks, D. D. & Gecas, V. (1992) Autonomy and Conformity in Cooley's Self-Theory: The Looking-Glass Self and Beyond. *Symbolic Interaction* 15(1): 49–68.

Gutman, R. (1958) Cooley: A Perspective. *American Sociological Review* 23(3): 251–6.

Jandy, E. C. (1942) *Charles Horton Cooley: His Life and Social Theory*. Dryden Press, New York.

Mead, G. H. (1930) Cooley's Contribution to American Social Thought. *American Journal of Sociology* 35(5): 693–706.

love and commitment

Irene Hanson Frieze

Love is one of the most basic human emotions. Many have written about love experiences, both in popular writing and in more scholarly publications, especially as they apply to romantic relationships. As these writings indicate, there are many ways of thinking about love. Some of the types of love identified by researchers are reviewed below. Research about how people fall in love and why they choose one person over another to date or to marry also provides information about love. Much of the research on love and partner choice focuses on dating and the initial stages of relationships.

Love and feelings about the partner are only one of many determinants of commitment to that partner. Factors predicting commitment are also reviewed below. Much of the research on relationship commitment examines marital partners.

DEFINITIONS OF LOVE

One of the first modern scientific analyses of types of love was proposed by Lee (1977). Different types of love were derived from a concept analysis of fictional writing in Europe and the US since ancient Roman times. The forms of love that were identified were given names that related them to ancient Greek conceptions of love.

The first type of love identified was called *Eros*. Eros is an erotic, passionate love. The physical appearance of the beloved is an important part of eros. Eros love can be love at first sight. Having feelings of eros toward someone is a very enjoyable feeling. But eros love can also end suddenly, leaving the person wondering what they saw in their former beloved. Others may wonder what the attraction is toward the beloved, since the relationship does not appear to have a rational basis.

Another form of passionate (and apparently irrational) love is called *Mania*. While eros love is a positive, happy state, mania love is the dark side of passionate love. Mania involves obsession with the beloved person. Constant thoughts of the beloved can involve high levels of jealousy and upset about what the beloved is feeling about oneself. This type of love may be associated with stalking of the beloved.

Storge is a friendship-based love. Storge is a quiet, affectionate love that develops gradually over time. Even if the love relationship ends, the strong friendship associated with storge often means one continues to be friends with the former beloved. Highly related to relationship satisfaction, this type of love can lack strong feelings of passion.

Agape is an altruistic love. Agape love is associated with the desire to give to the beloved without asking anything in return.

Pragma love is a practical love that involves loving something about the person, such as being a good parent, being respected in the community, or being wealthy. This type of love is associated with arranged marriages.

Ludus love is not typically classified as "love" in western society today, although these feelings were found by Lee to be labeled as love in some cultures. Ludus is love for the moment. It is assumed that ludus love feelings will not last long. They may be only for an evening. Ludus is associated with flirtation and the desire to seduce someone for a sexual encounter. Ludus feelings are associated with low relationship satisfaction, shorter relationships, and not feeling "love" for the partner.

Love styles are assessed at one point in time. One's feelings can change over time. Thus, a relationship that starts out with primarily eros feelings could develop into a storge or agape type of love feeling. Love styles are also specific to the relationship. One can have eros feelings for one partner and mania feelings for another partner.

Another way of classifying love is to divide it into two basic types: passionate love and companionate love. The passionate love would include Lee's Eros and Mania. Passionate love is also called limerence. Passionate love is of much interest to psychologists since it appears to be irrational. Characteristics of passionate love include strong feelings of sexual arousal. There is also fantasy and idealization of the beloved. This type of love comes on suddenly. It is sometimes defined as a "state of intense longing for union with another." When one is feeling passionate love for another, being together brings fulfillment and ecstasy, while separation brings anxiety and despair. This type of love often does not last long, especially if reality is allowed to interfere with the fantasies one has of the beloved.

Several theories have been proposed to explain the origins of passionate love. The first of these was suggested by the psychiatrist Karl Jung and his colleague Esther Harding, who spoke of unconscious attraction as the basis of passionate love. Jung felt that people have both a conscious part and an unconscious part of their personality. Generally, one's unconscious self is of the other gender than the conscious self. A goal of Jungian therapy is to integrate the unconscious aspect of the personality into conscious awareness. Within this framework it was proposed that when one feels a sudden, passionate attraction toward someone, one is really falling in love with an unconscious aspect of the self that has the opposite gender to the conscious self. This unconscious, opposite-gender self is often derived from one's opposite-sex parent. For some reason, perhaps a resemblance to the opposite-sex parent, there is a sense of knowing the beloved person and of strong attraction. Fantasy is used to maintain the image that the beloved person has the same characteristics as the unconscious self. This theory is not directly testable, but informal observations of people attracted to those who resemble their other-sex parent provide some support for it. Passionate love does not appear to have a rational basis.

John Money, known primarily for his work with children with abnormal genitals, suggested a theory of pair bonding, a concept very similar to passionate love. Money (1980) feels that passionate, somewhat irrational feelings of love are analogous to an imprinting process that is set off by the physical appearance of the loved one. Although Money does not specify what the biological basis of pair bonding is, one possibility is that this is related to pheromones. Fantasy about the beloved is used to explain to the person why the strong attraction exists. High levels of passion are maintained for about two to three years (long enough for a pregnancy to occur). Once a woman becomes pregnant, her pheromones change and the basis of the pair bonding may be lost (explaining why so many passionate relationships end during pregnancy). After the pregnancy, if the relationship continues to exist, it must be maintained by parent–child bonds in both partners.

Another theory of love proposed by Berscheid and Walster (1969) is based on social psychological research on attribution theory. This theory builds on Zillman's work on motivation and the finding that arousal from sexual feelings, fear, physical exercise, or aggression all lead to similar forms of physiological arousal in the body. People use cues in the environment to label this physiological arousal, and if cues are ambiguous, people can mislabel the source of their arousal. Arousal from one source can be transferred to another source. Thus, when men are angry, they rate pictures of attractive women more positively than they do if not previously angered. Berscheid and Walster apply these ideas to human passionate love. Their theory argues that when one is aroused (by any source), if an appropriate love object is present, the physiological arousal may be (mis)labeled as passionate love. This theory has been extensively empirically tested and data from many studies do show support for the idea that physiological arousal can increase feelings of attraction or love of a desirable partner. When one encounters an unattractive individual under a state of physiological arousal, the reaction is more likely to be anger.

Companionate love is similar to Lee's concept of storge. This type of love is affection or deep friendship felt for those with whom our lives are deeply intertwined. Companionate love tends to develop gradually and strengthens over time (at least in theory). This type of love generally occurs among those with similar backgrounds and shared interests. It appears to be based on mutual reinforcement.

DETERMINANTS OF PARTNER CHOICE

Another way of analyzing love is to study how people select their marital or dating partners. Many studies have attempted to do this, using a variety of methodologies. Conclusions depend on the methodology used. Studies that simply ask people about what they are looking for in a partner do not yield valid findings, since it appears that people either do not know what they seek or they are unwilling to say. When asked, people often report wanting "boy scout" traits. They say they want a partner who is loyal, dependable, and honest. But these traits do not appear to explain why people select the partners that they do. When people are asked to rate how important various traits are in making partner choices, although people do continue to rate traits such as loyalty high, it is also possible to see differences in the ratings of men and women. Such studies show that men value the appearance of their partner more than women. Women rate the earning ability of their partners higher than men do. Ratings are different for short-term partners, as compared to what one wants in a marriage or long-term partner.

Another technique for studying partner choice is to analyze personal ads where people seek a partner. Since the first of them in the 1970s, these studies have consistently shown that

men seek an attractive partner, more than women do, although both sexes care about the appearance of their partner. Women mention their own appearance in their ads more than men, while men are more likely than women to mention their financial situation, or the fact that they seek a committed relationship. Men tend to respond to more ads than women, and there is less correspondence between men's own self-described characteristics and the characteristics of the women whose ads they respond to. Women tend to be more selective, responding only to ads of selected men.

Other studies analyze the people who do marry to see what variables appear to predict partner choice and breakup. When existing couples are examined, it is very difficult to show that any measure of personality compatibility consistently matters across groups of couples. In studies using photos of real couples, when the level of attractiveness of the man and the woman are similar, the couples matched on attractiveness are more stable and satisfied in relationship.

Overall, data suggest that although men value the attractiveness of their partners more than women, physical appearance is important to both sexes. People have many positive beliefs about attractive individuals, and have negative associations with unattractive individuals. The greater importance of partner appearance for men than women is seen in heterosexual as well as homosexual couples.

COMMITMENT TO A RELATIONSHIP

As noted above, many of the types of love, especially passionate love, tend to be unstable and can end very quickly. Thus, commitment to a partner involves quite different dimensions than feelings of (passionate) love. One component of commitment is the positivity of feelings about the partner and the relationship. Generally, relationship satisfaction is higher for companionate love or storge relationships than for passionate love, especially mania. Several theories of commitment are discussed below. Many of these theories focus on marriages.

Rusbult has proposed that commitment is related to relationship satisfaction, as well as to the level of investment in the relationship and to the availability of alternative attractive relationships. This model has received some empirical support. Investment is generally operationalized as the amount of time spent in developing the relationship and resources such as a shared social network and children that have become associated with the relationship. Rusbult further suggests that when a person is more committed to the relationship, they are more willing to accommodate to the partner's requests, sacrifice for the partner, feel a sense of interdependence, avoid seeking alternative relationships, and have positive beliefs about the relationship.

Levinger provides another perspective on relationship commitment. He suggests that commitment is a function of the level of positive as compared to negative feelings about the relationship and the level of barriers or restraining forces that prevent breakup of the relationship. If there are strong social pressures to maintain a marriage, for example, people would be more committed to their spouses than if divorce is relatively easy. The level of attraction to the relationship is dependent on the rewards associated with the relationship compared to the costs of being with the partner. Once people make a public commitment to their relationship, through announcing an engagement or a marriage, the external barriers to breaking up the relationship increase. Barriers are relatively low today in the US as compared to earlier historical periods and to other societies in the world.

Johnson has argued that there are three different types of commitment to a relationship. First is the personal commitment or desire to continue the relationship. This is similar to what others have labeled as relationship satisfaction or attraction to the partner. A second type of commitment is the feeling of moral obligation to remain with the partner. Such moral feelings can relate to religious beliefs about the permanence of marriage. They can also come from believing that one has to remain with the marital partner for the sake of the children. Some people may feel that breaking up a relationship is a form of failure. Such feelings may also take on the characteristic of remaining in a relationship because of feelings of obligation. In addition to these factors within the person, Johnson also considers that social pressure exerted for people to remain in relationships functions as a third predictor of relationship commitment.

Another body of research looks at personality factors in the individual, known as attachment styles, as they relate to commitment. There are three basic forms of attachment: secure, avoidant, and anxious. These are believed to develop during infancy and come from the types of interactions that occur between the infant and his or her major caretakers. Securely attached infants become upset when the caretaker is absent, but are happy when the caretaker is present, and feel free to explore their environment. Avoidant infants do not appear to be upset about the caretaker being absent and show little positive affect in the presence of the caretaker. Anxious infants appear to be overly clinging when their caretakers are present and become quite upset when they are absent. Such behaviors are believed to continue into adulthood and become manifested in romantic relationships. Work by Shaver and others has indicated that those with secure attachments are more committed to their romantic partners and feel more satisfaction about these relationships. Their relationships tend to last longer than for other groups. Those with an avoidant pattern are less committed to their romantic partners and report less relationship satisfaction. The anxious adults often form relationships very quickly, but they do not appear to have long-term commitments. Qualitative data suggest that they may be experiencing mania types of love.

SEE ALSO: Attraction; Attribution Theory; Divorce; Emotion; Cultural Aspects, Emotion, Social Psychological Aspects; Intimacy; Intimate Union Formation and Dissolution; Marital Quality; Social Psychology; Stalking

REFERENCES AND SUGGESTED READINGS

Adams, J. J. & Jones, W. H. (Eds.) (1999) *Handbook of Interpersonal Commitment and Relationship Stability*. Kluwer, New York.

Berscheid, E. & Walster, E. (1969) *Interpersonal Attraction*. Addison-Wesley, Reading, MA.

Lee, J. (1977) *Colors of Love: An Exploration of the Ways of Loving*. New Press, Don Mills, Ontario.

Money, J. (1980) *Love and Love Sickness: The Science of Sex, Gender Difference, and Pair-Bonding*. John Hopkins University Press, Baltimore.

Luhmann, Niklas (1927–98)

Ralf Rogowski

Niklas Luhmann saw it as his task to revolutionize the sociological theory of society. His theory of social systems claims nothing less than to offer sociology a new "universal theory for the discipline" (Luhmann 1995). One of the major concerns guiding his approximately 700 publications was to counter the trends, as he perceived them, of abandoning general sociological theory, confining sociological theory to exegeses of the classics, and dispersion of sociological research and thinking into subdisciplines. In countering these trends he devoted his energy to introducing a new general sociological theory that is able to provide an adequate understanding of the real challenges to modern society. He called his alternative approach autopoietic social systems theory. It borrows insights from general sciences, in particular general systems theory, epistemological constructivism, mathematical logic, and the theory of communication.

Luhmann's approach developed in three stages. In his early work he formed his ideas in discussion with the systems-theoretical approach as expounded by Talcott Parsons, whom he encountered in the 1960s during a 1-year study visit at Harvard University. He criticized Parsons for operating with a one-dimensional concept of functionalism that is preoccupied with system maintenance and proposed to replace causal relationships between structure and function with a notion of functional equivalence of structural solutions adopted by social systems. He elaborated this approach in numerous studies, including pathbreaking analyses of formal organizations and administrations. In the second phase Luhmann advanced his theoretical base by integrating the theory of autopoiesis into the study of social systems. The major publication of this period was his *Social Systems* (1995, German original 1984). The theoretical focus shifted from concerns with functions and structure to an analysis of self-reproduction of elements. The structure and the unity of a developed social system are seen as directly linked to operationally closed self-reproductive processes. In his late work Luhmann used autopoietic systems theory to create a general theory of the modern society and its major function systems. He presented this theory in 9 voluminous monographs (Luhmann 2002), including 2 general studies of society (*Soziale Systeme* of 1984 and *Gesellschaft der Gesellschaft* of 1997) and 7 studies of its major function systems covering the economy, science, law, art, politics, religion, and education, of which 4 were published between 1989 and 1995 and 3 posthumously.

Five theoretical aspects can be highlighted in characterizing Luhmann's theoretical approach. First, Luhmann combines the concepts function, differentiation, and evolution in order to analyze the development and dynamics of modern society. Luhmann distinguishes between three levels of analysis of autopoietic systems: general systems theory, the theory of social systems (as opposed to psychic systems, organisms, and machines), and the level of concrete analysis of social systems. Similar to Parsons, Luhmann considers the development of social systems as a process of differentiation and evolution. However, in Luhmann's concept the Parsonian ordering of society with just four primary subsystems is replaced by a polycentric view of society. Modern society replaces vertical stratification with horizontal functional differentiation as primary mode of social organization and thereby loses its center.

In Luhmann's theory of modern society there exists neither a fixed number of functionally differentiated social systems nor a firm ranking of functions. For analytical purposes Luhmann distinguishes between society and function systems. He considers society as a first order social system, whereas function systems like the economic and the legal system are viewed as second order social systems or societal subsystems. Society as a first order social system differs from second order social systems insofar as it has no other social system as an environment; society's environment consists only of natural and psychic systems (human beings).

In Luhmann's theory, functions are not derived from a fixed set of pattern variables (like in Parsons's approach), but are ultimately defined by the social systems themselves. Functions are represented by binary codes specific to each functional subsystem of society. Binary codes are achievements of evolution and necessary requirements of a function system in order to define the boundary and to select its elements. In applying the binary code, the functional subsystems can distinguish between societal communications that belong to the system or the environment of the system. Examples of binary codes are true/false in the case of the science system, legal/illegal in the case of the legal system, and payment/non-payment in the case of the economic system. However, these codes do not guide the behavior of the participants directly. They require programs (like methods, statutes, or invoices) that translate them into behavioral directives.

The second feature of Luhmann's theory concerns his understanding of elements and structures as key components of a system. The system derives its complexity from its elements and their innumerable relations. In abstract terms, system complexity is defined as the relationship between the set of all possible relations between elements (contingency) and the selectivity achieved by the self-constituted structure of a system. This definition combines selectivity, contingency, and self constitution of the system through specific selections.

Autopoietic systems theory develops a new understanding of structure and its relation to elements. Luhmann insists that it is not sufficient to define structure as relations of elements. In the general autopoietic conception of systems, structures result from the fact that only certain relations of elements are selected and held constant over time. Structure is thus defined as limitation of possible combinations of elements within the system. The function of structures is not to translate environmental needs into the system, but to secure the autonomy of the system's self-reproduction, which is conceived as an operationally closed process. Structures of the system emerge both from self-reproduction of the elements and from selection of relationships. The system acquires properties in the evolutionary process that cannot be explained by the properties of its elements. The system instrumentalizes the self-reproduction of the elements for its own self-reproduction, upon which in turn the self-reproduction of the elements becomes dependent. The structure of the system evolves in this process as a product of both the self-reproduction of the elements and the system itself.

A third characteristic of Luhmann's approach refers to the processes of communication, self-reference, and autopoiesis that constitute social systems. Probably the most radical departure from the Parsonian theory of the social system and, indeed, from conventional sociology, is Luhmann's assumption that the ultimate, non-decomposable elements of an autopoietic social system are communications and not human beings. For Luhmann, human beings constitute part of the environment of the social system and he views the individuality of human beings and their consciousness as separate, highly complex psychic systems. Furthermore, in Luhmann's theory, communications replace actions or interactions as the main elements of a social system. Communication consists of three components: information, utterance, and understanding. Each component is described as a selection, and communication is accordingly characterized as the coordination of three selections. The important feature of communications is that they are related in self-referential processes. Thus, without linkage to other communications, no communication can happen.

Luhmann's theory of communication incorporates logical and mathematical approaches. In this respect it has recently been elaborated by Baecker (2005) into a general systems theory of communication. Baecker, in accordance with Luhmann, emphasizes that communications as such cannot be observed but require specific forms in which they can appear. This is crucial for a social system because survival depends on its ability to observe and describe itself, which is a precondition for self-reference and autopoiesis. This requirement to become observable both for external observers and for self-observation is the main reason why, according to Luhmann and Baecker, a communication system generally ascribes itself as an action system.

Luhmann has demonstrated such ascription in his analysis of the emergence of structures in interaction systems. Structures reduce uncertainty and create trust relations (Luhmann 1979, 1993). In face-to-face interactions the mutuality of expectations binds the actors through double contingency and thus becomes a self-referential circle. Luhmann merges the theory of self-reference and double contingency and thereby arrives at a concept of action and interaction without subject.

Interaction conceived as a self-referential circle is unstable and can cease to exist from one moment to the next. In order to survive it needs the system which treats the self-referential circle as a basic element of its self-reproduction. Self-reference of the system means, in this respect, that the system produces and delimits the operative unity of its elements through the operation of its elements. It is precisely this process that Luhmann calls the autopoietic process, which lends its own unity to the system (Luhmann 1995: ch. 1).

Pre-autopoietic systems theory defined systems as open systems which are characterized by their exchange relations with the environment. Autopoietic systems theory conceives systems instead as closed systems which reproduce themselves not by variation of structure but by constant recombination of their elements. Recursive closure of the system, with respect to its elements, guarantees self-reproduction or autopoiesis. Luhmann constructs a theory of an operationally closed social system which is not dependent on other social systems or its environment for its core activity (i.e., autopoiesis). Only if autopoiesis is guaranteed can the system be open and relate to the innumerable events and conditions in its environment.

Fourth, a particularly pertinent problem for a theory of autopoietic social systems is the conceptualization of the relationship of the system with its environment and with itself. A social system can logically develop three kinds of relationships. It can relate to society, it can relate to another social system or societal subsystem, and it can relate to itself. Luhmann (1990a) calls the relationship to society *function*, to another social system *performance*, and to itself *reflexion*.

In debates within systems theory a number of concepts are used for the analysis of intersystemic relationships. Originally, Parsons adopted the notion of interpenetration as the main concept in studying exchange relations between systems. However, Luhmann uses this concept only in a limited sense and reserves interpenetration for an analysis of the relationship of social systems and psychic systems. In Luhmann's theory the central concept that explains relations between social systems is structural coupling. Luhmann adopted this concept from general systems theory and biological theory of living systems. Prominent examples of mechanisms of structural coupling are for Luhmann the semantic concepts of constitution, contract, and property. The constitution couples the political and the legal system, contract and property couple the economic and the legal system. Coupled systems increase the chances of structural variation of systems. However, they cannot determine structural changes. Structural coupling might lead to reciprocal irritation or perturbation of the coupled systems, to which each system can only respond with internal means that are limited by the autopoietic needs of the system.

A further concept of intersystemic linkage has been proposed by Teubner (1993). His notion of interference tries to capture the special nature of communication, which is always at the same time general societal and special communications in the functional system. The elements of functional systems consist of the same substance as in society at large. Indeed, the same communication is linked to the communication process or circle of society and of the functional system. Teubner calls this societal context of communication the "life world context."

A particular case of intersystemic relations constitute efforts of one system to regulate affairs in another system. In an autopoietic social world, systems can only observe each other, and cannot regulate each other's self-reproduction. Any regulatory effort has to be compatible with the autopoietic requirements of the regulated system. External regulation of self-reproduction can ultimately only be successful if it corresponds with self-regulation.

A fifth feature of Luhmann's theory relates to the fact that society becomes global as an "unavoidable consequence of functional differentiation" ("The World Society as a Social System," in Luhmann 1990b). The concept of the world society that dominates Luhmann's late work was already conceptually developed in his early work. Function systems that have a high degree of autonomy "detonate" societal boundaries. Most advanced in this respect are the economy, technology, and science. In particular science is said to have adopted universal intersubjectivity as its own structuring principle and criterion of performance. In contrast law and politics remain backward by clinging to territorial boundaries.

The globalization of function systems results from their very nature as systems of communications. It is difficult to prevent communications from flowing across territorial boundaries. It is this that makes it almost impossible to isolate function systems from world processes. All function systems are exposed to the pressure of globalization that results from worldwide communications. Furthermore, worldwide communications produce new structures at the world level. In a systems-theoretical perspective the world society can be conceived as a system characterized by specific emergent properties. New structures that transcend "inter-nationalism" occur in the form of world law, world politics, and world religions (Stichweh 2001).

Luhmann reveals nevertheless a certain pessimism in predicting the future of the world society. It is increasingly becoming itself the source for manifold regional, economic, cultural, climatic, and ecological differences that create new conditions for the function systems (on ecological communication, see Luhmann 1989; on the role of the mass media, Luhmann 2000; on modernity in general, Luhmann 1998). In particular the legal system is confronted in the world society with specific challenges. Its performances for other social systems change, in the first place due to the changing role of the political system that is no longer organized by a state at the global level.

For Luhmann, the role of law and politics as risk bearers of societal evolution decreases in the world society (Luhmann 2004: ch. 12). However, this does not mean that law is withering away, but that we can expect a change of the legal form. In one respect Luhmann is optimistic. As the result of an increase in cognitive expectations, the economy, science, and technology have begun to orientate themselves towards the future rather than the past. This cognitive transformation is gradually becoming true for all function systems and also for the world society at large.

SEE ALSO: Autopoiesis; Evolution; Function; Functionalism/Neofunctionalism; Parsons, Talcott; Reflexivity; Social System; Society; Structural Functional Theory; System Theories; Theory Construction

REFERENCES AND SUGGESTED READINGS

Baecker, D. (2005) *Form und Formen der Kommunikation*. Suhrkamp, Frankfurt am Main.
Luhmann, N. (1979) *Trust and Power*. Wiley, Chichester.
Luhmann, N. (1985) *A Sociological Theory of Law*. Routledge, London.
Luhmann, N. (1989) *Ecological Communication*. University of Chicago Press, Chicago.
Luhmann, N. (1990a) *Political Theory in the Welfare State*. Aldine de Gruyter, New York.
Luhmann, N. (1990b) *Essays on Self Reference*. Columbia University Press, New York.
Luhmann, N. (1993) *Risk: A Sociological Theory*. Aldine de Gruyter, New York.
Luhmann, N. (1995) *Social Systems*. Stanford University Press, Stanford.
Luhmann, N. (1998) *Observations on Modernity*. Stanford University Press, Stanford.
Luhmann, N. (2000) *The Reality of the Mass Media*. Stanford University Press, Stanford.
Luhmann, N. (2002) *Theorie der Gesellschaft*, 9 vols. Suhrkamp, Frankfurt am Main.
Luhmann, N. (2004) *Law as a Social System*. Oxford University Press, Oxford.
Stichweh, R. (2001) *Die Weltgesellschaft. Soziologische Analysen*. Suhrkamp, Frankfurt am Main.
Teubner, G. (1993) *Law as an Autopoietic System*. Blackwell, Oxford.

Lukács, Georg (1885–1971)

Stanley Aronowitz

Born in Budapest of a prominent banking family, Georg Lukács was among the most influential, if not always the most beloved, Marxist philosophers and social theorists of the twentieth century. His book of essays *History and Class Consciousness* (1971: *HCC*) ranks as a major contribution to Marxism, albeit of a distinctly unorthodox kind. And, adopting some of Weber's key concepts, especially the notion of the ideal type, he made huge contributions to the sociology of literature. An outstanding scholar of Kant, Hegel, and Marx, as well as the nineteenth- and twentieth-century realist novels of Balzac, Scott, Dickens, Mann, and Solzhenitsyn, he was, at the same time, one of the twentieth century's outstanding public intellectuals. He served as a minister of culture and education in two different Hungarian communist governments – that of the short-lived revolutionary regime of 1919 and the reform government of Imre Nagy in 1956. He was a leading figure in German and Hungarian intellectual life after the publication of his first book, *Soul and Form* (1974) when he was 26 years old, and his widely read *Theory of the Novel* (1973), which earned him a European-wide reputation in the years prior to World War I.

In 1912 Lukács became a member of Max Weber's Sunday Circle in Heidelberg. The circle included the historian Karl Polanyi and, important for Lukács's future development, Georg Simmel, whose influence can be seen in the famous chapter in *HCC*, "Reification and the Consciousness of the Proletariat." Simmel first introduced the concept of reification in his magnum opus, *The Philosophy of Money* (1978), a book he described as follows: "The attempt is made to construct a new storey beneath historical materialism such that the explanatory value of the incorporation of economic life into the causes of intellectual culture is preserved, while the economic forms themselves are recognized as the result of more profound valuations and currents of psychological or even metaphysical preconditions" (p. 56). While adopting a Marxist rather than Simmel's Kantian framework, Lukács retained Simmel's fundamental idea of the ineluctable link between culture and the economy. This innovation was to remain a benchmark of Lukács's explication of historical materialism for almost a half century.

Every essay in *HCC* was written from Vienna in the context of Lukács's work as a leader of the illegal Hungarian Communist Party. Many readers of *HCC*, which was reissued in German in 1967 and appeared in English 4 years later, are inevitably drawn to two essays: "What is Orthodox Marxism?" in which Lukács defends the materialist dialectic, especially the concept of the totality and its corollary, the relation of the subject and object as constitutive of the totality; and the magesterial "Reification and the Consciousness of the Proletariat" – actually an elaboration of the same themes, with particular emphases on the underpinning of the

subject/object split in everyday life, and the objective basis of this split in the universalization of the commodity-form in capitalist society. Lukács's conception of reification, derived from his reading of the section in chapter 1 of Marx's *Capital* on the fetishism of commodities, and mediated by Simmel, is that in the capitalist system, dominated by commodity production, and exchange, relations between people take on the appearance of relations between things. That is, subjectivity is subsumed under reified objects and becomes opaque to itself. Read in the context of the debates over political organization rather than exclusively a work of sociological reflection, Lukács provides a "scientific" and philosophical basis for Lenin's claim that revolutionary class consciousness cannot arise directly from the workers' struggle. For Lukács, that struggle is always conditioned by (1) rationalization in which every aspect of human activity can be calculated and classified into "specialized systems"; (2) "the fragmentation of human production necessarily entails fragmentation of the subject" (Lukács 1971: 142); (3) by the division of labor, as well as by (4) the hierarchies produced by the occupational structure of the labor market.

Consciousness, therefore, is not lodged in perception or individual understanding, but instead is determined by the logic of capital. Taken in isolation, the Reification chapter might be interpreted as an argument for either voluntarism (the doctrine according to which even adverse objective circumstances can be overcome by revolutionary will) or fatalism (the idea that the capitalist crisis will, under its own weight, lead to the system's self-destruction).

In "Toward a Methodology of Political Organization" (Lukács 1971: 295–342), the last chapter of *HCC*, which combines philosophy with social theory, Lukács sees the root of contemporary conceptions of the subject/object split in Kantian ethics. He addresses Kant, not only because Kant's three *Critiques* dominated German and French philosophy for almost a century after Hegel's death in 1831, but also because Kantian ideas had penetrated some of the leading figures of international socialism, notably Eduard Bernstein (German), Max Adler (the leader of Austrian Social Democracy), and some Russians as well. In his view, unless a sound philosophical basis is established for the objective possibility of revolutionary class consciousness, efforts to make changes are likely to founder on the twin fallacies of objectivism (the inevitability of revolution) and voluntarism (the idea that human agency can overcome under almost all circumstances the limitations of social and political conditions). The task, according to Lukács, is to provide a structural basis for explaining the reproduction of bourgeois consciousness within the proletariat in the wake of crises and war, and for the objective possibility of class consciousness.

Condemning what he calls the "contemplative attitude" towards social reality, in which the "thing-in itself" is not available to consciousness, he argues that praxis (political practice that is informed by reflection) – by linking form and content – can overcome the Kantian view that objective reality is, in principle, unknowable. However, he argues: "In so far as the principle of praxis is the prescription for changing reality, it must be tailored to the concrete material substratum of action if it is to impinge upon it to any effect" (Lukács 1971: 125–6). Here, Lukács advances a bold definition: "organization is at once the form of mediation between theory and practice" (p. 299) and, more generally, "the concrete mediation between man and history – this is the decisive characteristic of the organization now being born" (p. 318). In these passages he stresses the fallacies of the inherent hierarchy present in many workers' parties which overestimate the importance of the individual, that is the leader and his activity, and the "fatalistic" complementary passivity and subordination of the masses. Both tendencies lead to bureaucratization of the party and thwart the development of a movement that promotes the "real active participation" of members in every event, in the full scope of party life.

The idea of organization as the "concrete mediation between man and history" is closely linked to the problems of fragmentation and rationalization raised in the "Reification" essay. Every struggle is necessarily partial. According to Lukács, the party is in the first place the mediation between these struggles and the fight against capital. Second, the party indicates the principles for a better life that are inherent in these struggles and why this aspiration is frustrated by the priorities of various embodiments of the ruling class: employer, landlord,

developer, and government official. Third, the party exposes the role of the state in these struggles and raises the questions: Whose side is the state on? What are the necessary tasks regarding legislation? What are the costs of legal solutions versus direct action?

HCC was roundly condemned by the leaders of the Communist International and some of Lukács's comrades in the Hungarian party. In order to stay in the party's good graces he was forced to repudiate the book, although he wrote a spirited defense three years later called *Tailism and the Dialectic*, which remained unpublished during his lifetime. Later, as a result of his losing struggle for leadership of the exiled Hungarian Communist Party, Lukács took up residence in Moscow in 1930, where he worked in the Marx-Lenin Institute until 1945, when he returned to Hungary to take an academic appointment in Budapest University. During this period most of his work was devoted to literary theory and literary history. Among his many books, *The Historical Novel* (1983), *Studies in European Realism* (1972), and *The Young Hegel* (1975) may be considered his major works of this period. His writings on literature argued for a canon of nineteenth- and twentieth-century European novels consisting of works that adopted the standpoint of "critical realism" regardless of their own subjective political position.

Returning to Hungary, Lukács resumed his literary studies, producing a major book on Goethe (Lukács 1965), revising *The Young Hegel*, and writing *The Destruction of Reason* (1977), a blistering attack against existentialism and phenomenology. In this controversial work Lukács identifies Heidegger, Husserl, and Jaspers, among other modern thinkers, as reactionaries whose philosophy articulates with the irrationality that marked fascism and other tendencies of the modern Right. In the context of the Cold War and the simultaneous rehabilitation of Heidegger in western philosophical and literary circles, Lukács's refusal to separate philosophy from politics was, at the time, dismissed as a shrill Stalinist rant. Despite occasional evidence of Stalinist rhetoric, the analysis and conclusions of the work bear a striking resemblance to Bourdieu's (1996) condemnations where, like Lukács, he links the philosopher's works to his politics.

Lukács briefly reentered politics when he supported the 1956 popular Hungarian uprising against the Rakosi communist regime and became the education minister under the reform administration of Imre Nagy, soon to be overturned by Soviet tanks. He was taken into custody by Soviet armed forces and exiled, this time to Romania, but soon was permitted to return to Hungary where he resumed his teaching and writing. His last major project was an unfinished 8-volume Ontology of Social Being, which may be considered a vast recapitulation of many of the themes he developed throughout his career. He died at age 86.

SEE ALSO: Culture, Economy and; Hegel, G. W. F.; Marx, Karl; Marxism and Sociology; Polanyi, Karl; Simmel, Georg; Weber, Max

REFERENCES AND SUGGESTED READINGS

Bourdieu, P. (1996 [1979]) *The Political Ontology of Martin Heidegger*. Stanford University Press, Palo Alto.

Lukács, G. (1965) *Goethe and His Age*. Grossett & Dunlap, New York.

Lukács, G. (1971 [1923]) *History and Class Consciousness*. MIT Press, Cambridge, MA.

Lukács, G. (1972 [1950]) *Studies in European Realism*. Merlin Press, London.

Lukács, G. (1972) *Tactics and Ethics*. Harper Torchbooks, New York.

Lukács, G. (1973 [1916]) *Theory of the Novel*. MIT Press, Cambridge, MA.

Lukács, G. (1974) *In Defense of History and Class Consciousness*. MIT Press, Cambridge, MA.

Lukács, G. (1974 [1911]) *Soul and Form*. MIT Press, Cambridge, MA.

Lukács, G. (1974) *Writer and Critic*. Merlin Press, London.

Lukács, G. (1975) *Lenin*. New Left Books, London.

Lukács, G. (1975) *The Young Hegel*. Merlin Press, London.

Lukács, G. (1977 [1954]) *The Destruction of Reason*. Merlin Press, London.

Lukács, G. (1983 [1962]) *The Historical Novel*. Merlin Press, London.

Lukács, G. (2001) *Dialectic*. Verso, London.

Marx, K. (1976) *Capital*, Vol. 1. Penguin, London.

Simmel, G. ([1978 [1907]) *Philosophy of Money*. Routledge & Kegan Paul, London.

lust balance

Cas Wouters

The concept of the lust balance refers to the social organization and accompanying social codes (ideals and practices) regarding the relationship between the longing for sexual gratification and the longing for enduring relational intimacy. It thus draws attention to the balance between emotive charges in the desires for sex and love, and to changes in this lust balance. For although the two types of longing for sexual gratification and for an intimate relationship are clearly interconnected, these connections change in both the biographies of individuals and the histories of peoples. Nor is the interconnectedness unproblematic. Today, some people (mostly men) even view the two longings as contradictory. Moreover, the attempt to find a satisfying balance between the longing for sex and the longing for love may be complicated by many other longings; for instance, by the longing for children or by the longing to raise one's social power and rank. Therefore, the "balance" in the relationship between sex and love is a polymorphous and multidimensional tension balance. Yet it offers a wider theoretical framework that opens the possibility to integrate many different threads of long-term developments, as is demonstrated by Wouters (2004), in a study pioneering lust balance as a central concept.

Other studies of the connections and the tensions between sex and love are rare, and historical studies of this area are even harder to find. Besides the problem of distinguishing between changes in the lust balance as a dominant ideal and as a practice, there is an additional complication: studies of sexuality usually do not pay much attention, if any, to the kind of relationship in which it occurs; and studies of loving relationships usually do not take a systematic interest in sex. Both kinds of research are even reported as attracting different kinds of respondents.

However, it is well-documented (common) knowledge that the nineteenth century's main stream of social change went in the direction of a romanticization and idealization of love, which implied a lust-dominated sexuality for men and a complementary (romantic) love or relationship-dominated sexuality for women. Statements such as "the more spiritual love of a woman will refine and temper the more sensual love of a man" typify a Victorian ideal of love that was as passionate as it was exalted and desexualized (Stearns 1994), with a rather depersonalized sexuality as a drawback and outlet for the man's "raging hormones" and "wild" sensuality behind the scenes of social life. This ideal of love as feeling mirrored the Victorian attempt "to control the place of sex in marriage ... by urging the desexualization of love and the desensualization of sex" (Seidman 1991: 7). It also implied that sexual intercourse was increasingly defined as *his* "right" and *her* "marital duty."

The Victorian ideal of a highly elevated marital happiness was an ideal of the bourgeoisie. The rise of commercial groups and their world of business helps in particular to explain this idealization and also why "ladies first" became a characteristic of all the commercializing nation-states: deference to superiors was no longer the main ruling principle in nineteenth-century manners because business demanded, not deference, but trust and respect. In contrast to the aristocracy, the social existence of the bourgeoisie heavily depended upon contracts, which in turn depended upon a reputation for being financially solvent and morally solid. Moral solidity included the sexual sphere, and it seemed inconceivable how any bourgeois man could possibly create the solid impression of being able to live up to his contracts if he could not even keep his wife under control and his family in order. Therefore, in comparison with the aristocracy, the bourgeois control of the dangers of sexuality rested more strongly on the wife's obedience to her husband, and on (other kinds of) external social control such as chaperonage.

From the 1890s onwards, the processes of the desexualization of love and the desensualization of sex seemed to go into reverse gear: there occurred instead a sexualization of love and an eroticization of sex. Throughout the twentieth century – with accelerations in the 1920s, 1960s, and 1970s – the Victorian examples of how to integrate the longing for sexual gratification and the longing for relational intimacy faded, but it

was not before the spurt of informalization in the 1960s and 1970s that they disappeared. At that time, old "marriage manuals" became suspect or hopelessly obsolete, mainly because they hardly acknowledged the sensual love and carnal desires of women, if they acknowledged them at all.

Only since the sexual revolution have women themselves actively taken part in public discussions about their carnal desires and the achievement of a more satisfactory lust balance. From then on, increasingly large groups of people have been experimenting between the extremes of desexualized love (sexual longing subordinated to the continuation of a relationship) and depersonalized sexual contact, provoking new and more varied answers to what might be called the lust balance question: when or within what kinds of relationship(s) are (what kinds of) eroticism and sexuality allowed *and* desired?

This question is first raised in puberty or adolescence when bodily and erotic impulses and emotions that were banned from interaction from early childhood onwards (except in cases of incest) are again explored and experimented with. The original need for bodily contact of small children and their subsequent frank and spontaneous explorations seem to be stopped and become restricted when and where adults begin to experience them as sexual. Sexuality *and* corporality are thus separated from other forms of contact. In puberty and adolescence, the taboo on touching and bodily contact has to be gradually dismantled, which for most people is a process of trial and error. In the twentieth century, especially since the 1960s, a similar process of trial and error has been going on collectively.

Around the turn of the twentieth century, young people started to "date," that is, to go out together, both with and without a chaperone. From then on, in most western countries, changes in courting regimes and in the related relationships between children and parents, and women and men, have triggered many similar questions and discussions. The question concerning in what places young women and men could acceptably meet (private dances, clubs, skating rinks) and where not (a bachelor's apartment) more or less faded when acceptability came to include the street. Discussions about the necessity to be (properly) introduced ended with the acceptance of people simply introducing themselves. Questions regarding appropriate ways of meeting changed from focusing on how to ward off unwelcome advances to a broader focus including questions such as how to invite and respond to welcome advances. Increasingly open access to the opposite sex and easier, more comradely contacts between the sexes coincided with discussions and lamentations about the decline of courtesy towards women and the decline of poetry or romance in courting relationships, about the practice of kissing thoughtlessly and promiscuously, about girls as daredevils for whom running risks is a trump and ideal, about the public display of nudity and sex appeal in clothing, and about the trend to disclose the "secrets" or "facts of life," a trend in which women were thought to lose their innocence and purity.

A major difference between European countries and the US emerged in the early 1920s with the rise of a dating regime in the US. From the 1920s onward, advice on dating, necking and petting, the "line," the stag line, cutting in, and getting stuck appears in American manners books only. This dating regime signified the escape of young people from under parental wings and the formation of a relatively autonomous courting regime of their own, leading to a head start in the emancipation of sexuality and to the rise of the first western youth culture – an international innovation restricted to the US in contrast to the second youth culture, that of the 1960s, which was a western international one. This emancipation of young people in the US also implied an emancipation of young women; it made young women less dependent upon their parents and chaperones. But in regard to their relationship to young men, the dating regime kept women rather dependent upon men and their "treats." Just as the competitive attitude was institutionalized in the dating regime and expressed in the words "dating and rating," the uneven balance of power between the sexes was institutionalized in an attitude that linked "petting and paying." The younger generation had a common interest in breaking the taboo of the older generation, the no-sex-at-all taboo, thus creating for themselves a lust balance with

more sex. In the process of defining what sex, and on what conditions, boys and young men were clearly dominant.

In part, dating, necking, and petting became a competitive "quest of thrill" (Waller 1937), pushing all participants towards further exploration of the path of lust. Yet sexual exploration was to remain without sexual consummation. In that sense, the youth culture dating code was oriented toward sex *and* love (marriage), maintaining the adult code of abstinence of sex before and outside marriage. The responsibility for sufficiently restrained sexual emotion management was put in the hands of women. This double standard demanded that women developed increasing subtlety in the art of being both naughty and nice, of steering between yielding and rigidity, prudery and coquetry: a highly controlled indulgence of sexual impulses and emotions.

In the 1920s, liberation from the regime of older generations in the US was not followed by a feminist movement attacking the uneven balance of power between the sexes. Thus, male dominance was formalized in the dating system and subsequently more or less fossilized as part of American culture. This may help to explain why the female emancipation movements that followed the international youth culture and its sexual revolution met with tougher resistance in the US than in many European countries.

In Europe, until the sexual revolution, the emancipation of the younger generations and their sexuality was relatively limited. It consisted of the development of a type of courtship relationship that was to some extent similar to "going steady," a kind of "trial" relationship that could transform into an "engagement to be engaged." In both, some sexual experimenting came to be increasingly accepted. After World War II, young people in the US and in Europe started to "go steady" and to go steady was to play marriage. The powerful longing of women for more equal and trusting relationships allowing for a lust balance with more sex, more playful sex, and more equal play and pleasure seems to have been a major driving force of these changes.

In the 1960s, as the international western youth culture and its sexual revolution surfaced and was soon followed by a strong wave of female emancipation, sex-for-the-sake-of-sex came to be discussed in all western countries. As a result, the *whole* lust balance appeared on the public agenda. Moreover, both sexes came to participate in public discussions of lust-balance questions. Now, much stronger than in the first (US) youth culture, changes in lust-balance definitions and practices resulted from changes in the balance of power between both the generations *and* the sexes.

The accepted code regarding the pace of getting closer and expressing further interest accelerated from a three-times meeting before suggesting a "spot of dinner," via a three-times meeting before kissing and a three-date "score," to the instant intimacy of a one-night stand. Masturbation was mentioned positively. These changes coincided with rising tensions between the two types of longing. Topics and practices such as premarital sex, sexual variations, unmarried cohabitation, fornication, extramarital affairs, jealousy, homosexuality, pornography, teenage sex, abortion, exchange of partners, pedophilia, incest, and so on – all part of a wider process of informalization – implied repeated uprooting confrontations with the traditional lust balance. Since the 1980s the choir of voices expressing ideals of a lust balance with more sex lost fervor, while those defending a more traditional lust balance and attacking "excessive permissiveness" became somewhat louder again. On the whole, however, these repeated confrontations accompanied and reinforced the trend towards a collective emancipation of sexuality, that is, a collective diminution in the fear of sexuality and its expression within increasingly less rigidly curtailed relationships. Sexual impulses and emotions were allowed (once again) into the center of the personality – consciousness – and thus taken into account, whether acted upon or not. And the process of female emancipation was expressed in increasing acknowledgment of the principles of mutual attraction as well as mutual consent in courting. Surveying the twentieth-century development, women have come to feel like having sex more often, to allow more sexual incentives more easily, and they have learned to discuss these matters more freely, whereas men have been learning to connect relational satisfaction and sexual gratification.

Discussions of issues like sexual harassment, pornography, rape in marriage, and date rape can be understood as a common search for ways of becoming intimate and of keeping at a distance that are acceptable to both women and men. Precisely because of the sensitivity and caution needed to proceed in such a way, erotic and sexual consciousness and tensions have expanded and intensified, stimulating a further sexualization of love and eroticization of sex. This quest for an exciting and satisfying lust balance, avoiding the extremes of emotional wildness and emotional numbness, has also stimulated the emotional tug-of-war to a higher tension-level. That is so if only because the increased demands on emotion management will have intensified both the fantasies and the longing for (romantic) relationships characterized by greater intimacy, as well as the longing for easier (sexual) relationships in which the pressure of these demands is absent or negligible, as in one-night stands. This ambivalence, together with an increasingly more conscious (reflexive) and calculating (flexible) emotion management as a source of power, respect, and self-respect, is characteristic of the processes of decreasing segregation and increasing integration of the classes and the sexes. And as long as such integration processes continue, these ambivalent emotions may be expected to accumulate and intensify, including both longings that make up the lust balance.

SEE ALSO: Civilizing Process; Elias, Norbert; Intimacy; Love and Commitment; Sexuality Research: History; Women, Sexuality and

REFERENCES AND SUGGESTED READINGS

Elias, N. (2000) *The Civilizing Process: Sociogenetic and Psychogenetic Investigations.* Blackwell, Oxford.

Seidman, S. (1991) *Romantic Longings: Love in America, 1830–1980.* Routledge, New York.

Stearns, P. N. (1994) *American Cool: Constructing a Twentieth Century Emotional Style.* New York University Press, New York.

Stearns, P. N. (1994) *Battle Ground of Desire: The Struggle for Self-Control in Modern America.* New York University Press, New York.

Vance, C. S. (Ed.) (1984) *Pleasure and Danger: Exploring Female Sexuality*. Routledge & Kegan Paul, Boston.

Waller, W. (1937) The Rating and Dating Complex. *American Sociological Review* 2: 727–34.

Wouters, C. (2004) *Sex and Manners: Female Emancipation in the West 1890–2000*. Sage, London.

Luxemburg, Rosa (1871–1919)

Kevin B. Anderson

Rosa Luxemburg, one of the greatest theorists in the Marxian tradition, was part of the generation after Marx. She was also a political leader, a common situation in the Marxist movement of the early twentieth century. Others who held such positions were the more reformist Karl Kautsky and Eduard Bernstein in Germany, as well as the more radical-minded Russians V. I. Lenin and Leon Trotsky. However, Luxemburg was the only woman to attain such a position in this period. Her most sustained teaching position was at the German Social Democratic Party's Central Party School in Berlin, where she taught political economy and social history from 1907 to 1914.

Born into a middle-class Jewish family in Russian-ruled Poland, Luxemburg joined the socialist movement as a teenager. After coming to the attention of the Tsarist police, she left to attend the University of Zurich, where she wrote a dissertation entitled *The Industrial Development of Poland* (1898). Luxemburg lived most of her adult life in Germany, where she and her longtime companion (until 1907) Leo Jogiches led the underground Social Democracy of the Kingdom of Poland and Lithuania, which formed part of the larger Russian Social Democratic Party. This put her in continuous contact with Russian Marxists, but unlike most other political exiles from the Russian Empire, she took an active part in the political and intellectual life of Western Europe. She became a prominent leader of the German Social Democratic Party, until 1914 the world's most important Marxist

organization. During World War I, Luxemburg was jailed by the German government for her outspoken opposition to war and militarism. She now became a leading figure in the internationalist (later communist) wing of social democracy, together with the German socialist Karl Liebknecht, and the then still lesser-known Russians Lenin and Trotsky. Unlike most of the reformist socialists, the internationalists opposed the war. Freed from prison during the November 1918 uprising that brought down the Prussian monarchy, Luxemburg helped to found the German Communist Party and endorsed the notion of direct democracy through workers' councils, termed "soviets" in revolutionary Russia. In January 1919, she and Liebknecht were kidnapped and beaten to death by proto-fascist officers. This occurred during the repression of a socialist uprising in Berlin that she had helped to lead, a repression that was supported by reformist social democrats. The murder of Luxemburg and Liebknecht hardened the break between social democrats and communists. However, the publication in 1922 of Luxemburg's critique of the Russian Revolution, in which she attacked the establishment of a single-party state as inherently undemocratic, showed that she was no orthodox communist. While Lenin had called for the publication of her collected works, under Stalin, her writings were suppressed and discussion of them discouraged. During the 1920s, however, unorthodox Marxists, most notably Georg Lukács, expressed great admiration for Luxemburg. After 1933, the Nazis destroyed the writings of this Polish Jewish Marxist, whose anti-war stance was a prime example of what they called the "stab in the back" that had led to Germany's defeat in World War I.

Published while she was still in her twenties, Luxemburg's *Social Reform or Revolution?* (1899) earned her wide recognition as a theorist. In this work, she responded to Bernstein's elaboration of a gradualist, evolutionary road to socialism, which had been termed "revisionist" by his Marxist critics. In her critique of this prominent figure, whom none other than Friedrich Engels had named as his literary executor, Luxemburg argued that where Bernstein saw increased stability, there were in fact deepening social contradictions. She gave considerable attention to the danger of world war, which she theorized as an outgrowth of the battle among capitalist states for global hegemony. In this sense, Luxemburg was something of an exception within a generation where even left-wing critics tended to view the future as one of peace and progress.

A second strand of her theoretical work fell in the area of political economy, the subject of her lectures to worker activists at the party school. Luxemburg made original contributions to the theory of imperialism, in writings that included sympathetic accounts of pre-capitalist social forms in a variety of non-western societies. In her most important theoretical work, *The Accumulation of Capital* (1913), she argued that the rise of modern western capitalism was intimately tied to the exploitation of Africa, Asia, and Latin America. Moreover, Luxemburg held that the system's continued survival also depended on maintaining an imperialist system. In this book, she also critiqued some of the assumptions in volume 2 of *Capital*, which led to a series of attacks, most notably one by the Russian theorist Nikolai Bukharin in the 1920s. In *The Accumulation of Capital*, Luxemburg discussed how modern imperialism had destroyed premodern economic and social institutions in China, Algeria, India, and South Africa. She also detailed the tremendous human cost of this process, whether in the Orissa famine in British-ruled India or the mass deaths during the French conquest of Algeria. However, unlike Lenin, Luxemburg did not lend her support to anti-imperialist nationalist movements in the colonies. Instead, she viewed all forms of nationalism, including the struggle of her native Poland to reestablish its independence, as inherently reactionary and illusory in an era of imperialism and capitalist centralization. Luxemburg's *Accumulation* stands today as a classic analysis of imperialism, alongside J. A. Hobson's *Imperialism* (1902) and Lenin's *Imperialism: The Highest Stage of Capitalism* (1916). She pursued similar themes in the unfinished and posthumously published *Introduction to Political Economy*. This work is notable for its exploration of communal social forms across a wide variety of pre-capitalist societies, from the ancient Germans and the Inca Empire to nineteenth-century India, East Africa, and Russia. Luxemburg viewed each of these

societies as similarly structured by communal property. While far from uncritical of these communal social forms, she pointed to their relative egalitarianism, their flexibility, and their longevity. As the twentieth century began, international capital and imperialism were dealing the final blows to these ancient and once widespread forms of human social organization. Other Luxemburg texts in this vein, such as "Slavery," written during the same period but hidden away until the 1990s in the archives of the former Soviet Union, show that her studies of pre-capitalist social formations took account of the latest German scholarship on the Greco-Roman world, from Theodor Mommsen to Max Weber. Her last major work in political economy was *The Accumulation of Capital – An Anti-Critique*, an answer to her Marxist critics, also published posthumously.

In a third and closely related strand of her theoretical work, Luxemburg theorized war and militarism. Although she had argued for the centrality of militarism to modern capitalist society as early as *Social Reform or Revolution?*, the outbreak of World War I gave added impetus to these efforts. From her prison cell, as part of an attempt to lead socialist opposition to the war, she penned a major theoretical critique of modern militarism, *The Crisis of Social Democracy* (better known as *The Junius Pamphlet*), which was smuggled out and published under the pseudonym Junius in 1916. Luxemburg held that the war, which she termed a retrogression to barbarism, was an outgrowth of capital's quest for surplus value. She also connected the brutality of this war in the heart of Europe to the barbaric violence visited upon Africa and Asia by western imperialist powers in the decades preceding it. Finally, on the basis of the war, she questioned the notion that capitalism was inherently progressive. She wrote that another world war would lead not to socialism but to barbarism.

A fourth strand of Luxemburg's theorizing, not recognized as such until after her death, was a concept of revolution that differed from both reformist social democracy and Leninism. In the best known of these texts, *The Russian Revolution* (1918), also written from a German prison cell and published posthumously, Luxemburg indicated her overall support for the Russian Revolution, especially its break with the logic of war and imperialism and its early attempt to establish soviet democracy. However, she strongly criticized Lenin and Trotsky for having established a single-party state and defended the need for democracy after the revolution. In an earlier article, published in 1904, she had responded to Lenin on the vanguard party. A third major text critical of Lenin, the "Credo" (1911), also hidden away in the Soviet archives until the 1990s, continued her earlier critique of Lenin as an organizational "ultra-centralist," while making an even sharper one of other Russian Marxists, including Georgi Plekhanov and Trotsky.

A fifth strand of Luxemburg's work centered on the role of spontaneity in working-class movements and social revolutions. The distinctiveness of her concept of spontaneity was not widely recognized until after her death, when it began to be linked to her critiques of Lenin. In her 1906 pamphlet, *The Mass Strike, the Political Party, and the Trade Unions*, Luxemburg argued that truly revolutionary upheavals contained an important element of spontaneity. They were characterized by a radicalization from below that went beyond the perspectives of established political and trade union organizations that ostensibly represented the masses. This pamphlet focused on the experiences of the Russian Revolution of 1905–6. In it and in a later work, *Theory and Practice* (1910), she held that this upheaval in technologically backward Russia and Poland was not a repeat of the liberal revolutions of the nineteenth century, but the harbinger of a period of socialist upheaval that would draw in Western Europe as well.

A sixth strand within Luxemburg's life and work concerned gender. While many studies of Luxemburg have denied any relationship to feminism because she did not write or speak very often on women's issues, some of the recent ones have explored this question anew. Luxemburg firmly supported women's suffrage and also wrote that the participation of women might shake up the routinization of the socialist movement. Elsewhere, she singled out women's special oppression under slavery and imperialism. In addition to these occasional writings on women, Luxemburg's close friendship with Clara Zetkin, the longtime leader of the international socialist women's movement, enabled her to influence it from behind the scenes.

It has also been noted that her gender made her place within the leadership of German social democracy a very contested one. While male leaders like Kautsky resorted to openly sexist innuendo against Luxemburg in their private correspondence, the party as a whole seemed nonetheless to support this Polish Jewish woman as one of its key leaders.

Luxemburg's work on political economy, war, and imperialism, all of it recognized within her own lifetime, as well as the interest stirred up later on by her critiques of Lenin over democracy and revolution, her theory of spontaneity, and the gendered dimensions of her life and work, have led to the continued discussion of Luxemburg, especially among those critical of both globalized capitalism and authoritarian forms of socialism.

SEE ALSO: Anarchism; Capitalism; Class Consciousness; Colonialism (Neocolonialism); Communism; Economy (Sociological Approach); Gender, Social Movements and; Global Economy; Marxism and Sociology; Political Economy; Revolutions; Revolutions, Sociology of; Socialism; War

REFERENCES AND SUGGESTED READINGS

Arendt, H. (1968) *Men in Dark Times*. Harper, Brace, and World, New York.

Bronner, S. (Ed.) (1978) *The Letters of Rosa Luxemburg*. Westview Press, Boulder, CO.

Dunayevskaya, R. (1991) *Rosa Luxemburg, Women's Liberation, and Marx's Philosophy of Revolution*. Introduction by A. Rich. University of Illinois Press, Urbana.

Ettinger, E. (1986) *Rosa Luxemburg: A Life*. Beacon Press, Boston.

Frölich, P. (1972 [1939]) *Rosa Luxemburg: Her Life and Work*. Trans. J. Hoornweg. Monthly Review Press, New York.

Haug, F. (1992) *Beyond Female Masochism*. Verso, London.

Howard, D. (Ed.) (1971) *Selected Political Writings of Rosa Luxemburg*. Monthly Review Press, New York.

Hudis, P. & Anderson, K. B. (Eds.) (2004) *The Rosa Luxemburg Reader*. Monthly Review Press, New York.

Laschitza, A. (1996) *Im Lebensrausch, trotz alledem. Rosa Luxemburg, Eine Biographie*. Aufbau Verlag, Berlin.

Le Blanc, P. (Ed.) (1999) *Rosa Luxemburg: Reflections and Writings*. Humanity Books, Amherst, NY.

Looker, R. (Ed.) (1974) *Rosa Luxemburg: Selected Political Writings*. Grove, New York.

Luxemburg, R. (2003 [1913]) *The Accumulation of Capital: A Contribution to the Economic Explanation of Imperialism*. Trans. A. Schwarzchild. Routledge, New York.

Luxemburg, R. (n.d.) *Introduction to Political Economy*. Parts translated in Hudis & Anderson (2004) and Waters (1970).

Luxemburg, R. & Bukharin, N. (1972) *Imperialism and the Accumulation of Capital*. Ed. K. J. Tarbuck. Monthly Review Press, New York.

Nettl, J. P. (1966) *Rosa Luxemburg*, 2 vols. Oxford University Press, London.

Nye, A. (1994) *Philosophia: The Thought of Rosa Luxemburg, Simone Weil, and Hannah Arendt*. Routledge, New York.

Waters, M.-A. (Ed.) (1970) *Rosa Luxemburg Speaks*. Pathfinder, New York.

M

McDonaldization

Todd Stillman

McDonaldization is the process by which principles of the fast-food restaurant are coming to dominate more and more spheres of US society and the rest of the world. Coined by the sociologist George Ritzer, the term invokes the famous fast-food chain founded by Ray Kroc in 1955 as a metaphor for a widespread change in the delivery of goods and services toward more instrumentally efficient means of distribution. In a series of books and articles, Ritzer describes the competitive advantages of the McDonald's service system and catalogs the many ways in which it has shaped the expanding consumer marketplace.

McDonaldization can be understood as a specific instance of the process of rationalization: the development of instrumentally efficient means to achieve a given end. Weber first described the process of rationalization in reference to the development of administrative bureaucracies in modern Europe. Bureaucracies attain a high degree of efficiency by being organized into functionally differentiated, hierarchical systems based on written rules. After World War II the same principles of efficiency began to be applied on a widespread basis to sectors outside the bureaucracy (and factory), most notably in the fast-food restaurant and other spaces of consumption. Streamlining meant that newly minted consumers had more access to a greater variety of goods than ever before. It also meant that they could expect more consistency, lower costs, and in some cases a higher level of quality from their purchases.

The McDonald's service system can be thought of as a paradigm of contemporary rationalization. Ritzer derives five principles of McDonaldization from Weber's writings on rationalization. These are efficiency, calculability, predictability, control through the substitution of non-human for human technology, and the irrationality of rationality.

Efficiency refers to the optimal means for achieving a given end. Efficiency is often achieved by the functional differentiation of tasks and the development of discrete routines that are engineered to save time and labor. Calculability places an emphasis on the quantifiable aspects of a product or process. Calculability is achieved by an emphasis on the quantity of units sold, the speed at which units can be produced, the size of portions, or relatively low cost. Control is exerted to a high degree over workers in a McDonaldized system. Workers are trained to relate to customers using scripts, rather than their own words. They are also trained to prepare orders following scripted routines. Codified routines make it easy to train new employees and keep labor costs low. They have also contributed to a firm's ability to supply a standardized product over time and across many outlets. Predictability means that the settings, procedure, and production in a McDonaldized system are much the same from one time or place to another.

Control may be exercised through the substitution of non-human for human technology, with workers being replaced by machines. Machines save both labor and time spent on production. Kroc himself sold five-spindle milkshake mixers before he founded McDonald's. Automation is also used to prompt workers to perform their specified routines, typically using a system of timers and blinking lights to orchestrate when a particular procedure will be performed. Control may also be exercised over customers to save labor and time. The enlistment of customers as active participants, from the process of preparing their own beverages at the beginning of the dining experience through to the process of bussing their own tables at the end of it, contributes to the overall efficiency of the operation.

The irrationality of rationality refers to the negative consequences of McDonaldized systems. The crux of the matter might be termed the "subjectivity of efficiency." Operators and their efficiency engineers weigh the costs and benefits of each step in the delivery process with an eye on profitability. As a result, irrationalities that do not affect the profits of a firm accrue. For example, McDonaldization has adverse effects on the environment because of the amount of disposable material it generates as a matter of course. It has had a negative effect on public health as the emphasis on quantity over quality has been identified as a contributor to a marked increase in obesity among Americans.

Ritzer has particularly pointed criticism of the alienation consumers experience in McDonaldized settings. He suggests that McDonaldized systems do a disservice to consumers by forcing them to submit to the dehumanizing controls of a rationalized environment. Operators are at pains to make their rational system more attractive settings for consumers by using themes and spectacles, but they remain a systematic threat to genuine human sociality and diminish the possibility of deriving meaning from consumer activities.

The principles of McDonaldization have diffused primarily in two ways: first, through the competitive expansion of the franchise (now 30,000 outlets worldwide); second, by the emulative actions of competitors. Simplified products, low labor costs, and no-frills service are elements of a dominant paradigm that has spread to many sectors of the economy. Others have described the McDonaldization of non-commercial institutions, including higher education, the church, and the justice system.

Ritzer is critical of the homogenizing effects of McDonaldization on consumer culture. He worries that the success of McDonaldization has contributed to the decline of local and regional forms of consumer culture by subjecting less efficient forms of production and service delivery to intensive competition.

The theory of McDonaldization has been subject to a variety of critiques. In a volume edited by Barry Smart (1999) contributors question the effects of McDonaldization, asking whether customers are truly alienated by what they consume. The moral objection of groups such as vegetarians is evidence of resistance to the paradigm of McDonaldization. They also question the scope of McDonaldization. It is suggested that McDonaldization is an issue only for a relatively wealthy fraction of the world's population. Finally, counter-examples point to the limits of McDonaldization: for example, the diversity found in art markets suggests that streamlining is not incommensurate with creative and personal products.

The McDonaldization of Society (Ritzer 2004) is a model for how to produce socially relevant sociological theory. The concept of McDonaldization captures in an evocative way the pervasive effects of rationalization on consumption and beyond. It has contributed both to the debates over the consequences of consumerism and to the effects of globalization on cultural diversity.

SEE ALSO: Consumption; Disneyization; Globalization; Grobalization; Rationalization

REFERENCES AND SUGGESTED READINGS

Ritzer, G. (1998) *The McDonaldization Thesis*. Sage, London.
Ritzer, G. (Ed.) (2002) *McDonaldization: The Reader*. Pine Forge Press, Thousand Oaks, CA.
Ritzer, G. (2004) *The McDonaldization of Society: Revised New Century Edition*. Pine Forge Press, Thousand Oaks, CA.
Ritzer, G. (2005) *Enchanting a Disenchanted World: Revolutionizing the Means of Consumption*, 2nd edn. Pine Forge Press, Thousand Oaks, CA.
Smart, B. (Ed.) (1999) *Resisting McDonaldization*. Sage, London.

McLuhan, Marshall (1911–80)

Gary Genosko

Herbert Marshall McLuhan was born in Edmonton, Alberta, Canada in 1911. He spent his formative years up to his undergraduate and master's level studies in English literature at the University of Manitoba (1929–34) in the prairie city of Winnipeg. McLuhan earned his doctorate in English literature from Cambridge in 1942, writing a dissertation on Thomas Nashe. He taught briefly at the University of Wisconsin (1936–7) and for a longer stint at the University of St. Louis (1937–44) before returning to Canada to teach at Assumption College in Windsor, Ontario (1944–6). He joined St. Michael's College in the University of Toronto in 1946 and spent his entire career there, with the exception of one year as the Schweitzer Chair in the Humanities at Fordham University in New York (1967–8). He died at home in Toronto on New Year's Eve, 1980.

McLuhan's first book, *The Mechanical Bride* (1951), is his most sociological. It appeared during a decade rich in international examples of cultural studies, including, in France, Roland Barthes's *Mythologies* (1957); in the UK, Richard Hoggart's *The Uses of Literacy* (1957); and in the US, Reuel Denny's *The Astonished Muse* (1957). All of these books critically analyze the consequences of the emergence of a massified popular culture. Eventually, McLuhan turned his back on the critical insights of his first book into how media aid political mythology, eschewing what he considered moralizing for a poetic approach and a more flexible, less committed taking of position. McLuhan abandoned any promise of a critical sociological perspective at the outset of his career; henceforth, description would precede evaluation, satire took the place of social semiotics, and exploration superseded explanation. McLuhan forged a remarkable collection of rhetorical devices (tropes and aperçus, puns and probes) for discovering the active and largely invisible technological environments that shape human experience.

McLuhan's galactic reconfiguration of history in *The Gutenberg Galaxy* (1962) around how media alter the human sensorium was built on tropes of primitivism and technologically driven change. In McLuhan's periodization, technology is determinative for the social and this is a recipe for a kind of passivity. Instead of opposing, one copes, reacts, or contemplates, discovers but never modifies.

The pre-Gutenbergian world of traditional, pre-literate, oral and aural, intimate sociality gave way to typographic culture of the printed book with its linearity, uniformity, and status as a commodity (showing the way toward industrialization and massification). Eye displaced ear. Sound became vision. The general thesis that vision has been denigrated owes much to McLuhan. His innovation was to recode visual media like television as a tactile image machine and ultimately as a synthesthetically tactual experience. But the expansion and explosion Johannes Gutenberg detonated with his press (hotter than the existing hotness of phonetic writing) was met by the implosion of electric (and eventually electronic) media of communication in a new global village of simultaneity, non-linearity, and integrated cosmic consciousness. Television usurps the book. Electronic media recreate the conditions of pre-literate sociality. Cool, low-definition, and involving audio-tactility returns after a hot, high-definition, mechanical and well-defined interlude. McLuhan found social evidence in the 1960s and 1970s of this neotribalism in youth counterculture, happenings, television, liberal politicians, and the nascent computer culture. His descriptions were often incorrectly conflated with his personal promotion of countercultural values.

McLuhan's galaxies fit neatly into the rather grand phaseal models of history that have been proffered by Marxist historians (waning of use-value and the generalization of exchange-value) and postmodern theorists (rise of simulacra, reification, semiurgy). Such models have a certain vagueness about them. This quality makes them graftable onto numerous social issues such as intergenerational strife (mature individualism versus youthful collectivism), development and modernization (non-western underdevelopment is valorized as implosive, cool, and contemporary). The definition of phases (civilizations, empires) in terms of media of communication was adopted by McLuhan from his fellow countryman Harold Adams Innis, while shifting his emphasis from its implications for social structure onto sensory organization.

Understanding Media (1964) is perhaps McLuhan's best-known book. It contains mature versions of his key conceptual binarisms: the hot (radio and book) and cool (television) distinction is applied awkwardly to various media on the basis of how much material needs to be brought to them by receivers; and the shift from explosion (mechanical, fragmenting) to implosion (inward, integrating, space and time annihilating, speedy) is a metaphysical principle christened as reversibility or flip from one system to another at a saturation point. This "overheating" explains galactic shifts. Implosion was particularly influential in postmodern theory, yet in a nihilistic version, especially in the work of Jean Baudrillard. McLuhan is considered a pre-postmodernist. His meditations on automation and speed are consonant with the theses on the dromocratic revolution advanced by Paul Virilio.

The extensions of man thesis is fully elaborated toward a global embrace as the central nervous system is outered into the network of a world rapidly becoming wired. This Catholic humanist promise of salvation is McLuhan's technocratic media theology. It is built upon Greek myth (Narcissus) translated into technological extensions of the body (autoamputations) that in turn intensify (irritate) functions and actions. Humans are servomechanisms of these extensions, a relation to which McLuhan gave a sexual coloration. In order to bear this new intensity, perception is protectively numbed. The consequence of the outering of the central nervous system is not suicide but insight into the existential predicament of post-individual shared experience in the electric age in which "we wear all mankind as our skin."

McLuhan's famous buzzphrase "the medium is the message" reorients the study of media and communication toward the interplay of form (figure) and content (ground), but not symmetrically. Medium takes precedence over overt content (aboutness, programming) because for McLuhan content is either another medium (the content of writing is speech) or provided by the user. The implications of this shift are profound. Media massage or condition perception and produce new sense ratios. In this way media introduce new patterns into sociation. Socially, the medium is the message. Technically, media forms rise to prominence under the conditions of the information age in which speed and simultaneity of communication configure a kind of total, gestalt awareness and allegedly break down social barriers and blur identities. McLuhan's idea of a "global village" is based on the sharing of information

in dynamic interrelationships in a radically decentralized and dedifferentiated social process. Unfortunately, a focus on media characteristics does not reach into the political and economic forces shaping communication technologies; neither does it lend itself to detailed content analyses favored by social scientists.

McLuhan's formalism suggests an affinity with Georg Simmel's sociology of forms, based on dynamic relations between categories of form and content emphasizing the relative isolation of a grammar of pure forms from material and historical contents. Formal sociology is plagued by the conceptual difficulties created by the form/content distinction.

McLuhan's anti-dialectical and playfully Joycean style, with a minimum of explicit direction given for parsing hierarchies of value among heterogeneous fragments, has the feel of sociological fiction. Fictive social criticism deploys a variety of devices to slyly evoke social relations and problems. It is marked both by the inability to imagine production and by the precedence of the imaginary over the economic and semiotic over the evidential. The prime example is Georges Perec's novel *Things* illed wish of abundance in leisure society. Similarly, McLuhan imagined post-Gutenbergian salvation as a techno–Pentecost of post-semiotic and perfect global communication.

The fictive effect of McLuhan's writings owes much to his method. His "mosaic" method first announced in *The Gutenberg Galaxy* featured interacting and mutually transforming fragments. McLuhan juxtaposed texts and images in a series of kaleidoscopic print assemblages in conjunction with graphic designers. His book objects produced with Quentin Fiore and Jerome Agel – *The Medium is the Massage* (1967) and *War and Peace in the Global Village* (1968) – as well as the Harley Parker realizations of *Through the Vanishing Point* (1968) and *Counterblast* (1969), among a host of similar "non-books," underlined that their form communicated about consumer society in the manner of consumer society, but with the onus for critical anchoring placed firmly on the shoulders of readers.

The refractory quality of McLuhan's ideas and literary productions throughout the decades of the 1950s, 1960s, and 1970s made them difficult to integrate into the disciplinary categories of academic institutions. His formidable public presence as media star, which peaked in 1967, and valorization in diverse professional and cultural communities outside of the academy, generated intractable problems around the authentic sources of his legitimation. This strained relations at McLuhan's home university and called into question institutional support for his famous coach house where he directed the Center for Culture and Technology from 1963 until his death.

From the period of *Understanding Media* onwards, McLuhan sought to respond to critics of his work by refining his method. The posthumous publication of *Laws of Media* (1988), brought to press by his son Eric, presents a fourfold classification of questions that may be posed of any artifact. Although formulated in reponse to criticisms that his work lacked scientificity, it is not evident that these questions hold the possibility of scientific knowledge. The tetradic model is a stable heuristic device that gives systematic expression to McLuhan's investigations of the paradoxical effects of media technologies. It is a study of effects rather than a search for causes. Four fundamental questions are posed about innovative media: Which faculties or senses do they Enhance? Which abilities or practices do they displace or Obsolesce? Which previously sidelined capacities or practices do they regain or Retrieve? At which critical points do they flip or Reverse into their opposites? Unlike logicial or semiotic squares, McLuhan's tetrads are unencumbered by internal constraints and are thus best seen as tools for generating interpretations whose evaluation remains subject to further rhetorical justifications. McLuhan's tetrads are being tried out in diverse arenas such as the critical discourse on geographical information systems and in management theory.

Currently, McLuhan's work fits best within cultural sociology and has been taken up by cybercultural theorists and promoters of information technologies for its uncanny ability to anticipate contemporary technocultural developments.

SEE ALSO: Barthes, Roland; Cultural Studies; Media; Media and Consumer Culture; Simmel, Georg

REFERENCES AND SUGGESTED READINGS

Federman, M. & de Kerckhove, D. (2003) *McLuhan for Managers: New Tools for New Thinking*. Viking Canada, Toronto.

Genosko, G. (1999) *McLuhan and Baudrillard: The Masters of Implosion*. Routledge, London.

Kroker, A. (1984) *Technology and the Canadian Mind: Innis/Grant/McLuhan*. New World Perspectives, Montreal.

McLuhan, M. (1951) *The Mechanical Bride: Folklore of Industrial Man*. Beacon Press, Boston.

McLuhan, M. (1962) *The Gutenberg Galaxy*. University of Toronto Press, Toronto.

McLuhan, M. (1964) *Understanding Media: The Extensions of Man*. McGraw-Hill, New York.

McLuhan, M. (1969) *Counterblast*. Designed by H. Parker. McClelland & Stewart, Toronto.

McLuhan, M. (1987) *The Letters of Marshall McLuhan*. Ed. M. Molinaro et al. University of Toronto Press, Toronto.

McLuhan, M. & Fiore, Q., with Agel, J. (1967) *The Medium is the Massage*. Random House, New York.

McLuhan, M. & Fiore, Q., with Agel, J. (1968) *War and Peace in the Global Village*. Bantam, New York.

McLuhan, M. & McLuhan, E. (1988) *Laws of Media: The New Science*. University of Toronto Press, Toronto.

McLuhan, M. & Parker, H. (1968) *Through the Vanishing Point: Space in Poetry and Painting*. Harper & Row, New York.

Perec, G. (1965) *Les Choses* (*Things*). Julliard, Paris.

Sui, D. Z. & Goodchild, M. F. (2005) A Tetradic Analysis of GIS and Society Using McLuhan's Law of the Media. In: Genosko, G. (Ed.), *Marshall McLuhan: Critical Evaluations in Cultural Theory*, Vol. 3. Routledge, London, pp. 173–92.

Theall, D. (2001) *The Virtual Marshall McLuhan*. McGill-Queen's University Press, Kingston and Montreal.

madness

Raymond M. Weinstein

Madness is a layman's term for what psychiatrists and medical professionals call mental illness or psychiatric disorder. A mad person is characterized by psychopathology of one kind or another: a disordered mind, irrational or unintelligible behavior, extreme mood swings, disturbed emotions, bouts of anxiety, or a dysfunctional personality. Madness and mental illness are terms that are both distinct from "insanity," which is a legal concept. If a mentally disturbed individual comes before a court of law, the concern is whether he or she is insane (i.e., knew right from wrong, poses a danger to self or others, and/or is responsible for his or her actions).

Madness has been recognized throughout history in every known society. Primitive cultures turn to witch doctors or shamans to apply magic, herbal mixtures, or folk medicine to rid deranged persons of evil spirits or bizarre behavior. In ancient Israel it was widely believed that mental or emotional disturbances were caused by supernatural forces or an angry God as a punishment for sin or failure to follow the commandments. The Old Testament contains numerous references to kings and commoners smitten with some form of madness. The Jewish prophets were thought to be psychologically abnormal because they acted in strange ways, departed markedly from the norm in appearance, and foretold of future events that few understood. The Greeks replaced concepts of the supernatural with a secular view, insisting that afflictions of the mind were no different than diseases of the body. They saw mental as well as physical illness as due to natural causes, an imbalance in bodily humors. Hippocrates frequently wrote that an excess of black bile resulted in irrational thinking and behavior. The Romans made further contributions to psychiatry, especially contemporary practice. They put forth the idea that strong emotions could lead to bodily ailments, the basis of today's theory of psychosomatic illness. The Romans also embraced the notion of humane treatment for the mentally ill and codified into law the principle of insanity as a mitigation of responsibility for a criminal act.

The Middle Ages witnessed the end of the progressive ideas of the Greeks and Romans. With the overriding influence of the Catholic Church there was a return to the belief that supernatural forces, the Devil and witches, were causing troubled mental states in people. Many disturbed persons exhibited delusions and hallucinations of a religious nature and exorcism was commonly practiced by clerics. This Christian connection between the Devil and madness lasted for well over a thousand years. In late medieval Europe, mentally deranged people were burned at the stake, put aboard "ships of fools" for deposit on a distant shore, and placed in custodial centers for religious cures. During the Renaissance, with the rise of monarchies and state responsibility for the poor and disabled, there was a growing tendency to house mad men and women in special institutions. By the eighteenth century there was the Great Confinement, a network of asylums and hospitals all across Western Europe. Unable to work or to participate in community life, those deemed mad or insane were locked away from society, crowded into unheated cells and chained to walls or beds. At century's end, the abuses and sufferings of the mentally ill led to public outrage and a period of reform. A program of "moral treatment" was begun – institutional care based on kindness, sympathy, guidance, work, and recreation – the reeducation of patients to behave normally. In the early nineteenth century this humane pattern of care spread to the New World. Change occurred again in the mid-nineteenth century on both sides of the Atlantic. There was the decline of moral treatment and the emergence of the "medical model," the perspective that stresses mental illness is caused by biological factors and is incurable.

The twentieth century is noted for the ascendancy of a variety of different concepts and treatments in psychiatry. The idea of community involvement to prevent mental illness was bandied about in the first and second decades. In the 1920s the theories of Sigmund Freud on childhood psychosexual development and the unconscious mind profoundly affected psychiatric thinking and practice. The 1930s saw the introduction of electroconvulsive therapy, insulin treatment, and lobotomies. In the 1940s the war years uncovered a new disorder, "battle fatigue," while the post-war period, with the creation of the National Institute of Mental Health in the US, saw the beginning of the federal government's commitment to helping the mentally ill. In 1950s America the populations of state hospitals, growing for over a century, peaked and began a long period of decline. By the 1960s a "psychiatric revolution" was underway. Freud's psychoanalytic method – expensive, time consuming, and ineffective for curing seriously disturbed patients – lost favor. A new medical model emerged, with an emphasis on recently developed psychoactive drugs to maintain patients both in and out of the hospital. Deinstitutionalization was public policy and became a social movement, complete with ideology and political action. Federally funded community mental health centers were established to treat former patients and those not previously hospitalized. At the end of the twentieth century the trend in institutionalization reversed again. Many former mental patients were returned to an expanding state hospital system, as they could not be treated effectively in the community, were rejected by their families, or ended up on the streets of every major city, homeless and often in need of medical attention.

The second half of the twentieth century was marked with intense debate as to what madness is and whether hospital treatment is appropriate. Psychiatrists generally assume the presence of an abnormal condition in the individual which is manifested in specific symptomatology, but Thomas Szasz broke ranks and led the anti-psychiatry movement in the 1960s by arguing that mental illness is a myth, nothing more than "problems of living." Sociologists, on the other hand, tend to view mental illness as a label attached to persons who engage in certain types of deviant activities. Thomas Scheff, chief among them, argued that the symptoms and disturbed behavior typical of the mentally ill are more the conformity to a set of role expectations, products of situations, than the result of some personal predisposition or specific psychopathology. Walter Gove, however, severely criticized the labeling approach to mental illness advanced by his colleagues. From a psychiatric point of view hospitalization is thought of positively, as a site to both treat patients and shield them from the environment that is causing or contributing to their madness. The sociological position, articulated best by Erving Goffman, casts the mental hospital in a negative light, as a "total institution" that stigmatizes the patient and reinforces the very behavior it is supposed to correct.

The coming of the twenty-first century has not seen the end of the centuries-old controversies surrounding madness in people and its consequences for society. The causes of mental illness are still largely unknown. Whether disorders of the mind are due to organic, genetic, and biological factors or the result of developmental and environmental influences is part of the larger longstanding battle between "nature" and "nurture" among medical and social scientists. Psychiatrists have revised their *Diagnostic and Statistical Manual of Mental Disorders* many times, changing the definitions and categorizations of symptoms and diseases. Advocacy groups for the mentally ill and their families demand greater public funding for treatment programs, parity in insurance coverage with medical disorders, the right of hospitalized patients to refuse treatment, greater tolerance for former patients in the community, and expanded services for relatives. Politicians focus on the potential cost savings of halfway houses and the privatization of mental health care, while patient advocates argue for society to be motivated more by a humane concern for the mentally ill and protection of their legal rights than per capita treatment expenditures. Public opinion polls suggest that community residents favor the transfer of patients from large institutional settings to smaller neighborhood facilities, but when hypothetical situations become backyard reality they often vigorously oppose any mad person from living next door to them or across the street.

Today's problematic mental health system, changing treatment priorities, and controversial public policies may be different in substance, but are not so variant in form from the ancient and medieval debates over the nature of madness and what to do with those so afflicted.

SEE ALSO: Aging, Mental Health, and Well-Being; Dangerousness; Deinstitutionalization; Freud, Sigmund; Goffman, Erving; Labeling Theory; Mental Disorder; Psychoanalysis; Stigma; Stressful Life Events

REFERENCES AND SUGGESTED READINGS

Alexander, F. G. & Selesnick, S. T. (1964) *The History of Psychiatry: An Evaluation of Psychiatric*

Thought and Practice from Prehistoric Times to the Present. Harper & Row, New York.

Cockerham, W. C. (2005) *Sociology of Mental Disorder*. Prentice-Hall, Upper Saddle River, NJ.

Goffman, E. (1961) *Asylums: Essays on the Social Situation of Mental Patients and Other Inmates*. Doubleday Anchor, New York.

Gove, W. R. (1970) Societal Reaction as an Explanation of Mental Illness: An Evaluation. *American Sociological Review* 35: 873–84.

Rosen, G. (1968) *Madness in Society: Chapters in the Historical Sociology of Mental Illness*. Harper & Row, New York.

Scheff, T. J. (1966) *Being Mentally Ill: A Sociological Theory*. Aldine, Chicago.

Szasz, T. S. (1961) *The Myth of Mental Illness: Foundations of a Theory of Personal Conduct*. Harper & Row, New York.

magic

Tomasino Pinna

Magic is complex and difficult to define. Generally, it refers to ritual activity – usually without institutional supports – the execution of which, through words and actions considered powerful, intends to automatically induce changes of various types. There are good (white magic) or bad (black magic) aims relating to various human and natural events (health, sex life, reproductive activity, climatic events, knowledge of the future, social relationships, etc.) according to the desires of those who use it (magicians or their clients) and those who believe (magic also presupposes a system of beliefs, apart from rituals), so that the practitioner is able to bend to his or her will the powers on which the various aspects of reality depend.

The concept of magic arose and developed in western civilization and has served to define, polemically, internal mythical-ritual expressions (as do most marginalized practices) considered in opposition to religion, science, and reason. This concept was then extended and applied to people other than those of the West, assuming the value of a category which both defines and devalues cultural alterity (religions of higher ancient civilizations – Egypt, Vedic India, etc. – of primitive or colonized peoples).

The expression *mageía*, from which "magic" derives, has its origin in the name of Persian priests, *mágoi*, who belonged to the Zoroastrian priesthood (Herodotus). Thus, it originally defined an official and prestigious role. But in classical Greek and Roman culture, and later in Christianity and western culture in general, there was a radical change in the meaning of this expression, which acquired a negative and controversial character.

Greek civilization called *mágoi* marginal people. They were surrounded by scorn and considered charlatans. The expression *mágos* was used to define the foreigner, the *bárbaros*. The *magus* had the same value in Latin culture, and *magia* was viewed with distrust and as an instrument which threatened the normal order of individual, family, and social life. Magic was evaluated and repressed as a crime beginning with the Law of the Twelve Tables until the Codex of Theodosius and Justinian. Enemies were accused of magic: pagan intellectuals accused Christians of magic and later Christians accused pagans of the same.

It is often ancient and overthrown religions that are accused by the victorious religion of magic and superstition (an idea closely related to that of magic). This happened in the case of the victory of Christianity over the ancient polytheism of the Roman Empire. Christianity added a demonic character to the concept of magic, thus reducing the ancient divinities to the level of demons. This also had far-reaching consequences in the long run, such as in the witch hunts of the modern period (fifteenth to seventeenth centuries) where the devil became the cornerstone of the ideology of the witch, and even the most simple act of popular magic was considered as inspired by the devil. In the same way, magic and superstition were associated by European colonizers, in a Christian-centered view, with the myths and rituals of the peoples conquered in various continents. Within complex and industrialized societies the practices and beliefs of subordinate social classes, popular religions, and rural communities have been placed by those who hold the reins of cultural and religious power within the devaluing category of magic.

Nevertheless, apart from magic as an expression belonging to dominant groups, there exists also a learned tradition. This is the case of the *magia naturalis* (natural magic) of Humanism (with precedents in the field of occult medieval sciences, and even earlier within Neoplatonism). This is understood as esoteric knowledge of the elect few, able to penetrate into the secret mechanism of the world in order to act upon it and change it. There one finds Neoplatonic formulations and conceptions of the universe as a complex organism of empathy and consonance, in which man by his intelligence is able to intervene to foresee the future and to change it, dominating it with his knowledge and the actions inspired by it: the reality of man and Nature. Magic appears here to be a type of knowledge of the laws of the universe, as a science not yet divulged. In this sense, the Renaissance *magia naturalis* of Giambattista Della Porta, Marsilio Ficino, Pico della Mirandola, Paracelso, Tommaso Campanella, Giordano Bruno, and Cornelio Agrippa (seen as esoteric knowledge) scorned and condemned ceremonial as base, vile magic and demonic magic. In this case – in which we see a reevaluation of magic – we can also notice how there still exists the characteristic anti-magic controversy of the West. The conception of New Science was founded on the acquisition of knowledge based on experiment and – as opposed to the secrecy of knowledge – hoped for the spread of data for the benefit of everyone and refused every kind of magic, including natural magic. The Enlightenment and later positivism considered magic on a par with an irrational and unjustifiable superstition and the fruit of ignorance (Rossi 2004; de Martino 1976). On this basis, the concept of magic – as the fruit of a controversial history – is characterized as the negative half of a binomial whose opposite expression is religion, science, and rationality. Above all, this western category was applied to other civilizations (e.g., primitive peoples) who had not experienced Western alternatives.

Today, the use of magic is widespread: the fruit of urban uneasiness which looks for the short-cut of a magical miracle via unconventional operators, but also as the mystifying ability of power (Burdeau et al. 1989). The concept of magic has been the object of many studies, giving life to different interpretive theories, which consider magic from different points of view: as science in embryo, as an inferior religion, as a social function, and as a universal structure.

Anthropological evolutionism, whose major representatives are Tylor (1832–1917) and Frazer (1854–1941), studied magic according to an intellectualistic perspective, as a mode of knowledge, of organization, and of the manipulation of reality. It is considered to be a deceptive cognitive system, typical of the more primitive stages of evolution and still present, as a survival and the result of ignorance, among the lower social strata of civilized Europe, ethnocentrically assumed to be the evolutionary apex and parameter with which to measure the level of other civilizations. Frazer claims that in the evolution of humanity it is possible to identify three principal stages: magic, religion, and science. He places magic in the first and most primitive stage, when it is thought possible to intervene directly in nature through words, deeds, and signs. When one becomes aware of the ineffectiveness of magical actions and the inability to influence nature at will, then one believes it is governed by potent forces, on which man also depends, and towards which one takes an attitude of propitiation and conciliation which is manifested in prayer and sacrifice. Thus, religion is born. Science, the last stage of evolution, allows us to act directly on nature through a correct knowledge of its laws, without the intervention of superior beings. Frazer argues that magic is based on two fundamental principles: (1) the law of similarity, which produces homeopathic magic, according to which similar produces similar, and it is believed possible to produce any effect by simply imitating it (damage or kill an enemy by destroying an image of him; make it rain by pouring water; making pustules drop off by rubbing them while a falling star crosses the sky; seeding a field by a fertile woman in order to fertilize the vegetation, etc.); (2) the law of contact, on which contagious magic is based, founded on the idea that things which were once in contact will always be so, and so it is possible to influence a person even at a distance, by acting on the object with which he had been in contact (his nails or his hair, his clothes, his footprints; one can heal a wound by acting on the arrow which caused it, greasing the weapon, or, in Melanesia, putting it among fresh leaves to cure the inflammation, etc.).

According to Frazer, the magic system is substantially the same, in principle and in practice, at all times and in all places (among the ignorant and superstitious classes of modern Europe, in ancient Egypt, and among aboriginal Australians . . .), as he tries to demonstrate with a rich illustrative list which refers to indiscriminate and decontextualized comparativism. Frazer distinguishes clearly between magic and religion, and assimilates magic to science, as both are based on cognitive principles of an associative nature. Except that magic, unlike science, applies these principles, which are correct, in the wrong way, believing that things which seem alike are the same and that things which were once in contact continue to be so forever. Thus, he defines magic as "the bastard sister of science."

Frazer created, for the study of magic, a truly pioneering point of reference: many theories, even current ones, identify it as a reference or continue some of his points of view, correcting a certain evolutionistic rigidity (e.g., the neo-intellectualism of Robin Horton and John Skorupski, who emphasize the points of contact between magical thought and scientific thought), or disputing Frazer's statement, as in the symbolist approaches of John H. M. Beattie, Victor Turner, Stanley Jeyaraja Tambiah, and Clifford Geertz, who consider magic not as a cognitive instrument to be evaluted in terms of truth/falsity of a scientific type, but as a symbolic system which expresses, also at a subconscious level, collective values, social conflicts, and existential problems (Cunningham 1999).

Freud's psychoanalytic theory is influenced by evolutionism. Assimilating individual evolution (ontogenesis) and evolution of the species (phylogenesis), magic – which mixes ideal connections and real connections to satisfy the desires which derive from the pleasure principle – would constitute the first stage of the thought of human evolution, corresponding to the narcissistic phase and of omnipotence of thought of individual evolution. Religion corresponds to the stage of attachment to parents. Science would be the stage of maturity and of adapting to reality. The magic rituality of the neurotic, as a form of narcissistic regression, is for Freud assimilated to the primitive man's and child's magic forms and to those of folklore

and of occultism. He does not distinguish ritual as an individual pathology (which isolates) from ritual as a cultural fact (which socializes) (de Martino 1976).

Differing from the evolutionistic approach, Wilhelm Schmidt considers magic not as an initial moment of human evolution, but as a later and degenerative moment in comparison with an original monotheism of humanity. Research, the result of religious aims, attempts to give a scientific foundation to biblical stories, and is based on data shown as erroneous by Raffaele Pettazzoni.

Beginning with Rudolf Otto (*The Idea of the Holy*, 1917) and in general within the phenomenological current (Gerardus van der Leeuw, Mircea Eliade), magic has been considered as being connected to religion, since both represent an existential experience of the relationship with the Holy (which Otto calls "numinous," *mysterium fascinans et tremendum*). But magic is also defined as the "vestibule of religion" because it is considered as a primordial moment of the highest forms of religious life.

A notable change with regard to evolutionism is to be found in the functionalist theory of Malinowski. For him, magic, religion, and science do not represent in any way a progressive sequence. They coexist in the same social environment and each provides its own specific contribution (function) toward satisfying individual and social needs. Malinowski abandons the intellectual approach to magic as a logical error of evolutionism. Magic, for him, does not belong to the realm of science, but to that of religion, even though there are differences between them. Magic is used to solve concrete, specific problems. Religion, which is much more complex, is used to give answers to general problems and to those of meaning. However, both intervene beyond the point in which man can control reality, and have their origins in moments of anxiety and emotional tension, which are in that way confronted. Malinowski cites the ideas of Lévy-Bruhl, who contrasts the rational and scientific worldview of the modern West to the mentality of primitive peoples, which he considers as prelogical. Lévy-Bruhl thinks that primitives live within a magical dimension indifferent to the principles of identity and of non-contradiction. They are seen as obeying a law of mystical participation, which puts in contact the different orders of reality (which for us are distinct) and creates continuous interferences between the visible world and invisible powers, between sleeping and being awake, between the dead and the living. Malinowski, on the other hand, studying the natives of the Trobriand Islands, observed that they knew well how to use the tools of reason and could distinguish between technology and magic. Magic never intervenes when results are certain, but only to deal with anxiety deriving from situations that do not seem to be fully controllable. Magic, in specific contexts, is needed to reestablish psychological and social equilibrium disturbed by the uncertainty of outcome in different areas of human life (love, farming, fishing, etc.).

Durkheim and above all Marcel Mauss stress the character of magic as a social phenomenon. The magician and his magic are expressions of the social environment; they are born and they stand on social consensus, as do religion and the clergy. Like religion, magic is a system of beliefs and practices relative to the sacred (as opposed to the profane). Through its private, individual, secret, and mysterious character, and through its tendency toward the concrete and utilitarian (which links magic to science and technology), Mauss argued, medicine, metallurgy, pharmacology, botany, and astronomy would have arisen. Magic is distinguished from religion. Religion has a public character, tends toward the abstract and metaphysical, and, in Durkheim's opinion, creates a moral community, called "church," among those who belong to it. In contrast, there does not exist a magic church (even though the frontiers between the two realms of magic and religion are often imprecise).

A very close connection between social structure and magic was found by Radcliffe-Brown (who also suggested giving up the unhelpful dichotomy between religion and magic, and subsuming both under the category of ritual) and by Evans-Pritchard. The latter identifies in the Azande of the Sudan a coherent system of mystical thought, which supplements empirical thought. Witchcraft explains misfortunes, while magic provides the means to defend oneself from it or to remedy any damage caused by attacks by witches, which are discovered through oracular techniques. Oracles and magic are two different ways of overcoming witchcraft. This magic system works as an instrument of control of behavior and as a safeguard of social and normative equilibrium.

An analysis of the relationship between magic, society, and economy was undertaken by Weber. Examining the origins and developments of religion, he describes the earliest religious forms as essentially magic and characterized by coercive rituals and by material purposes. Later, religion takes on ethical values and provides a sense of individual and social life (even though magical elements remain in most religions). The overcoming of magic, or disenchantment with the world, which happens particularly through ascetic Protestantism, leads to the rationalization and moralization of religious practices and beliefs, and constitutes, with theological accentuation of the intra-worldliness of the professions, an essential instrument for the birth of modern capitalistic economy and for the development of technology (magic being an obstacle to the rationalized organization of economic activity).

Similar ideas (the influence of ideological dimensions on the economic) are present in the work of Keith Thomas, according to whom the decline of magic that took place in England in the seventeenth century with the success of Protestantism, favored by technical progress and by improvement in the material conditions of life, was due also to decisive factors of an ideological type: to a change of mentality and attitude of confidence in the progress of science, which produced an intellectual atmosphere in which the use of magic was considerably reduced and lost its credibility. Thomas's work paints a picture of the beliefs and popular magic practices of divination and witchcraft, in the sixteenth and seventeenth centuries, with great attention to the relationships with the social environment in which they operated.

Jeanne Favret Saada undertook research into the contemporary French rural world, studying it in the region of Bocage from the point of view of witchcraft. He analyzed the functional mechanisms used to give symbolic form to misfortune and aggression within the community. According to Lévi-Stauss's theory, magic (assimilated to myth and rite) and science represent two different strategies for approaching reality, directed toward its knowledge and its order. Magic is based on perception and intuition in accordance with the criteria of global and integral determinism. Nevertheless, magic thought (or "savage thought") is not to be considered as science in embryo, but as a different form of knowledge, in itself complete. Durkeim and Mauss had already stressed the cognitive functions of magical thought, conceiving magic as a primitive form of classification. According to Lévi-Strauss it was, instead, a form not only belonging to primitive people, but universal and permanent in human intellect, and is an expression of its unconscious structure – savage thought is also present in modern domesticated man.

The Italian historian of religions Ernesto de Martino dedicated several works to the study of magic, from numerous points of view. He believed that magic was primitive man's first attempt to move away from his natural condition and to become a "presence" (*presenza*), a cultural subject able to transcend nature. He studied magic also as an expression of subordinate Euromediterranean cultures and in particular of southern Italy, where conditions of misery favor the rise of magic (this interest led the way for other academics, including his follower Clara Gallini, who wrote about the evil-eye in Sardinian traditions, in which she points out the close connection between the system of production and magical ideology). It also represents a traditional device for facing critical situations (an illness, an unreciprocated love, an uncertain future, social oppression, death, etc.) which cannot be realistically solved. The negative emergency is submitted to procedures of "de-historification" (*destorificazione*) which mythically shape the crisis and mythically produce its solution. It is believed that magic rites, by repeating the myth, resolve in the same way the historically given crisis. Above all, beyond real effectivness (de Martino, like Lévi-Strauss, Mauss, and others, dwelt on the reality and symbolic effectivness of magic rites), it exercises the function of social reintegration by saving the individual from the risk of remaining entrapped in the traumatizing event without being able to act or to choose according to the codes of her social group. De Martino holds that magic is not different from religion except for the narrowness of values transmitted. Magic is to religion as the abacus is to the calculating machine:

they both serve the same purpose, but they differ in complexity. There occur continuous syncretic crossings, such that Angelo Brelich even hoped for the abolition of the expression "magic," to leave only that of "religion," noting the need to be fully aware of the conventionality of its use.

Against every liquidating attitude of a positivistic strain, magico-religious symbolism has its internal logic and exercises positive functions. The need to understand the magic world requires that we do not surrender the hegemonic choices of the West (reason and history) and its integral humanism. Magic alterity must be understood, but without irrationally falling within its coils (as critics of Jung allege, for example), and this brings de Martino to that methodological solution which, far from absolute ethnocentrism and absolute relativism, represents an original middle position, called critical ethnocentrism.

SEE ALSO: Ethnocentrism; Malinowski, Bronislaw K.; Myth; Popular Religiosity; Primitive Religion; Religion; Rite/Ritual

REFERENCES AND SUGGESTED READINGS

Bourdieu, P. (1971) Genèse et structure du champ religieux. *Revue Française de Sociologie* 12: 295–334.

Brelich, A. (1976) Tre note (Three comments). In: Xella, P. (Ed.), *Magia* (Magic). Bulzoni, Rome, pp. 103–10.

Burdeau, G., Lipp, W., Mongardini, C., Pross, H., Wassner, R., & Zingerle, A. (1989) *Il magico e il Moderno* (Magic and Modernity). Angeli, Milan.

Cardini, F. (1979) *Magia, stregoneria, superstizioni nell'Occidente medievale* (Magic, Witchcraft, Superstitions in the Medieval West). La Nuova Italia, Florence.

Cunningham, G. (1999) *Religion and Magic: Approaches and Theories.* Edinburgh University Press, Edinburgh.

De Martino, E. (1976 [1962]) *Magia e civiltà* (Magic and Civilization). Garzanti, Milan.

De Martino, E. (1999 [1948]) *Le Monde magique.* Sanofi-Synthélabo, Paris.

De Martino, E. (2001 [1959]) *Sud e magia* (South and Magic). Feltrinelli, Milan.

Garosi, R. (1976) Indagine sulla formazione del concetto di magia nella cultura romana (Essay on Making the Concept of Magic in Roman Culture).

In: Xella, P. (Ed.), *Magia* (Magic). Bulzoni, Rome, pp. 13–93.

Graf, F. (1994) *La Magie dans l'antiquité gréco-romaine*. Société d'édition de Belles Lettres, Paris.

Kieckefer, R. (1989) *Magic in the Middle Age*. Cambridge University Press, Cambridge.

Levack, B. (1995) *The Witch-Hunt in Early Modern Europe*. Longman, London.

Malinowski, B. (1982) *Magic, Science and Religion and Other Essays*. Souvenir Press, London.

Rossi, P. (2004) *Francesco Bacone. Dalla magia alla scienza* (Francis Bacon: From Magic to Science). Il Mulino, Bologna.

Tambiah, S. J. (1985) *Culture, Thought and Social Action*. Harvard University Press, Cambridge, MA, pp. 17–86.

majorities

Shirley A. Jackson

Majorities is a term that refers to the dominant group in a society, and can be defined as members of a group who hold power in a society and have access to resources. They need not be the numerical majority. They differ from minorities in that minorities do not hold power, be it economic, political, or social. Additionally, majorities develop the laws which define the rights of majority and minority group members. South Africa during the apartheid era is an excellent example of majorities (the Dutch), who were much smaller in number, oppressing the numerical majority. Historically, men prevented women from voting or from being able to handle their legal affairs. Women still receive less pay than their male counterparts for the same job.

Majorities can also refer to the group whose members share both physical and cultural similarities different from those of minority groups. Majorities may oppress their subordinates, minorities, by stereotyping them, holding prejudiced beliefs, or engaging in acts of discrimination. Majorities may hold privileged positions in society due in large part to their group membership. It should be noted, however, that with all groups, not all majorities may benefit equally from their dominant group membership.

In the US, studies on race relations often refer to majorities by dominant group – white Anglo Saxons (WASPS) or Caucasians. Majorities is not as frequently utilized as minorities as a term in race relations. The use of the term majorities in the social sciences has returned due in large part to an interest in whiteness studies, an area which points to the need to discuss the existence of whiteness as a variable in the same way that non-white races and ethnic groups have been represented in the literature. These studies also maintain that while minorities experience a sense of "oneness," this type of identification, while not always asserted in large part by the majority group, still exists.

Race is defined as a social construction that groups people according to their inherited physical or biological traits. While race is considered a social construction because we give it meaning, it holds very real consequences for those who may be considered inferior or superior based on their group identification or the group into which others categorize them. Although there is no such thing as a pure race, a superior race, a smarter sex, or an inferior sex, society may continue to act as if they exist. Thus, some groups, even contrary to evidence presented, may consider individuals as belonging to a superior or inferior group and associate certain positive or negative behaviors with members of those groups.

Ethnicity is often erroneously referred to as race. More correctly, ethnicity refers to one's cultural characteristics. It includes language, food, music, dress, surnames, and family structure. Ethnicity may be seen as something that is externally shared, in that it is not biological or does not contribute to one's physical or phenotypical characteristics.

According to some theorists, responses to group differences such as gender, age, race, ethnicity, or class are learned. Society teaches its members to consider some attributes more desirable than others. In addition, alleged differences based on intelligence and mental attributes are presumed of members based on their group membership. The degree to which individuals learn how to think of themselves also influences how they think of and treat those who are different. Prejudice is an attitude or belief whereby one holds a prejudgment based on one's group membership. While a prejudice can be either positive or negative, it is usually negative when lodged against members of groups other than one's own. Because majorities have the power to determine what qualities are positive or negative, they can assert negative prejudices that are harmful when aimed at minorities. It is because of the propensity towards discrimination that prejudices can be harmful. Discrimination is an action of usually unfair treatment. Majorities, once again, are in a position to discriminate against those who are minorities by withholding such benefits as equal employment opportunities, equal pay, or fair access to management positions.

The functionalist perspective does not consider the disparate treatment of minorities by majorities to be functional for society. Rather, functionalists assert that what is functional for one group is not always functional for the other. As such, minorities may find themselves the victims of ethnocentrism and stereotypes. These are dysfunctional for minorities, as they impact their life chances and ability to gain equal standing with those who are more powerful. For example, women who attempt to gain parity with men may find themselves the victims of sexism, receiving threats of or actual physical violence in the workplace. Members of a racial or religious minority may find themselves the victims of hate crimes. These acts are especially dysfunctional for those who are the targets, but may form the basis of group loyalty or group consciousness among those who are the perpetrators.

The conflict perspective approach to majority and minority relations attributes the power of majorities and the disfranchisement of minorities to the perceived lesser abilities of the latter. While not all members of the majority have power, their group membership, nonetheless, provides them with opportunities not afforded to minority group members. They assert that the dominant group's power gives them the ability to shape how society's members feel about themselves and others. The conflict perspective also asserts that the competition for scarce resources between minorities and majorities results in discrepancies of wealth, power, and prestige. Lacking these, minorities find themselves holding an unequal status. They do not have the ability to challenge the majority, and thus may find themselves the subject of continued domination, hostility, and oppression.

Relations between majorities and minorities have long been of special interest to sociologists studying both longstanding and emerging conflicts between men and women, and varied racial, ethnic, and immigrant populations. There appears to be no end to these conflicts in the foreseeable future, which makes certain their continued significance for social scientists.

SEE ALSO: Ethnicity; Prejudice; Race; Race (Racism); Stereotyping and Stereotypes; Whiteness

REFERENCES AND SUGGESTED READINGS

Bierstedt, R. (1948) The Sociology of Majorities. *American Sociological Review* 13(6): 700–10.

Chapman, J. & Wertheimer, A. (Eds.) (1990) *Majorities and Minorities*. New York University Press, New York.

Frankenberg, R. (1997) *Displacing Whiteness: Essays in Social and Cultural Criticism*. Duke University Press, Durham, NC.

Nakayama, T. & Martin, J. (Eds.) (1999) *Whiteness: The Communication of Social Identity*. Sage, Thousand Oaks, CA.

Pettigrew, T. (1982) *Prejudice*. Harvard University Press, Cambridge, MA.

Wirth, L. (1945) The Problem of Minority Groups. In: Linton, R. (Ed.), *The Science of Man in the World Crisis*. Columbia University Press, New York.

male rape

Philip N. S. Rumney

The phrase male rape denotes serious sexual assaults in which the victim is male. Male rape is defined in many legal codes as nonconsensual sexual intercourse, including acts of anal and oral sex, usually with another male, though it is also sometimes defined so as to include nonconsensual intercourse with a woman. There is evidence of the specific recognition of male rape within legal codes dating back to the eighteenth century. The historical evidence on the incidence of male sexual victimization is limited, though there are some records of male sexual coercion in Europe and elsewhere since the time of the Roman Empire (Jones 2000).

Male rape has long been recognized as a problem that has existed within the prison system, as well as other institutions. There is a significant body of literature on rape within prisons, primarily from research conducted within the US. This work indicates that rape in some institutions is not uncommon and that prison authorities have often failed to address the problem properly. This literature also illustrates the difficulties of measuring the prevalence of sexual coercion. For example, it has been noted that the notion of consent within prisons is "extremely slippery" because "prisons and jails are inherently coercive environments" (Human Rights Watch 2001).

In the last two decades researchers have begun to examine the prevalence and impact of male rape and sexual assault outside of institutional settings. What this research shows is that men of all ages and backgrounds can become victims, though both homosexuality and incarceration appear to be particular risk factors associated with victimization. Coxell et al. (1999) found that men with a prior history of consensual sexual contact with another male were six times more likely to be a victim of rape or sexual assault than a male with no such previous experience (Mezey & King 2000). Qualitative research has also given us an understanding of the dynamics and impact of male rape on its victims (Myers 1989; Scarce 1997), and there is a small amount of evidence on the perpetrators of male rape and sexual assault (Groth & Burgess 1980).

The consequences of male rape have given rise to several questionable claims within the literature. It has been repeatedly suggested, for example, that male rape may involve more violence and resultant trauma than rape involving female victims. The literature, however, provides only limited support for this claim (McLean 2004; Rumney & Morgan-Taylor 2004). In addition, it has also been suggested that male and female victims experience "sexual assault differently" (Novotny 2003). There is no support for this claim when the full range of emotional and psychological reactions is considered (Mezey & King 2000; Rumney & Morgan-Taylor 2004).

While research on male rape and sexual assault has improved our understanding of its prevalence and dynamics, there continue to be areas where there is a need for further work. There is limited information on the prevalence of male rape and sexual assault, with only two epidemiological studies examining the subject (Coxell et al. 1999). In addition, there is currently little qualitative evidence on the experiences of male victims within the criminal justice process or among those who access health services. The limited evidence available suggests a lack of understanding of male rape among some criminal justice professionals (Rumney & Morgan-Taylor 2004). Better understanding is required of the needs of male victims in the context of health services, as victims often access these services in order to address concerns regarding sexually transmitted diseases or to receive treatment for assault-related injuries. Finally, there is a lack of evidence on the dynamics of male rape and sexual assault within homosexual relationships. Given that homosexuality is a particular risk factor in male rape, a better understanding of sexual coercion and violence within such relationships is pressing.

SEE ALSO: Homosexuality; Law, Criminal; Prisons; Rape/Sexual Assault as Crime; Sex and Crime; Sexual Violence and Rape; Violent Crime

REFERENCES AND SUGGESTED READINGS

Coxell, A. et al. (1999) Lifetime Prevalence, Characteristics and Associated Problems of Non-Consensual Sex in Men: Cross-Sectional Survey. *British Medical Journal* 318: 846.

Groth, A. N. & Burgess, A. W. (1980) Male Rape Offenders and Victims. *American Journal of Psychiatry* 137: 806.

Human Rights Watch (2001) *No Escape: Male Rape in US Prisons.* Human Rights Watch, New York.

Jones, I. H. (2000) Cultural and Historical Aspects of Male Sexual Assault. In: Mezey, G. C. & King, M. B. (Eds.), *Male Victims of Sexual Assault*, 2nd edn. Oxford University Press, Oxford.

McLean, I. A. (2004) Forensic Medical Aspects of Male-on-Male Rape and Sexual Assault in Greater Manchester. *Medicine, Science and the Law* 44: 1.

Mezey, G. C. & King, M. B. (Eds.) (2000) *Male Victims of Sexual Assault*, 2nd edn. Oxford University Press, Oxford.

Myers, M. F. (1989) Men Sexually Assaulted as Adults and Sexually Abused as Boys. *Archives of Sexual Behavior* 18: 203.

Novotny, P. (2003) Rape Victims in the (Gender) Neutral Zone: The Assimilation of Resistance? *Seattle Journal for Social Justice* 1: 743.

Rumney, P. & Morgan-Taylor, M. (2004) The Construction of Sexual Consent in Male Rape and Sexual Assault. In: Reynolds, P. & Cowling, M. (Eds.), *Making Sense of Sexual Consent*. Ashgate, Aldershot.

Scarce, M. (1997) *Male on Male Rape: The Hidden Toll of Stigma and Shame*. Insight Books, New York.

Malinowski, Bronislaw K. (1884–1942)

Bernd Weiler

Bronislaw K. Malinowski and Alfred R. Radcliffe-Brown are generally regarded as the "founding fathers" of British social anthropology. Born in Cracow, then part of the Austrian province of Galicia, Malinowski studied natural sciences, mathematics, and later psychology and philosophy at the Jagiellonian University where his father had been an eminent professor of Slavonic philology and folklore. In his formative years the main intellectual influence on Malinowski, apart from his father's linguistic and ethnographic interests, appears to have been a combination of the philosophical current of "second positivism" – in his doctoral dissertation Malinowski analyzed the idea of "the economy of thought" in the epistemological works of Mach and Avenarius – and the neoromantic movement of Polish cultural modernism (Ellen et al. 1990; Young 2004: 3–127). After graduating in 1908, Malinowski went to Leipzig, where he studied with Wundt, the founder of the so-called *Völkerpsychologie*, and with the economic historian Bücher. In 1910 he moved to England, enrolled at the London School of Economics (LSE), and immersed himself in anthropology. Apart from his teachers at LSE (Seligman and Westermarck), Malinowski developed his ideas in critical response to and through ecletic use of the

works of Frazer, Rivers, Durkheim, and Freud, among others. During World War I, despite being an enemy alien in Australia, Malinowski was allowed to carry out fieldwork in the Trobriand Islands, located northeast of New Guinea. The results of this research were published in the book *Argonauts of the Western Pacific* (1922), which contained a detailed analysis of the intertribal exchange system known as *Kula* and which established Malinowski's international fame as an anthropologist. His ethnography of the Trobriand Islands was later complemented by *The Sexual Life of Savages in North-Western Melanesia* (1929) and *Coral Gardens and Their Magic* (1935). Upon his return to England he became a reader and in 1927 a full professor of anthropology at LSE, also playing a major role in the International Institute of African Languages and Cultures. A charismatic personality and highly gifted in promoting and popularizing the cause of anthropology, Malinowski recruited a remarkable international body of talented young scientists for his famous seminars at LSE (e.g., Firth, Evans-Pritchard, Mair, Richards, Fortes, Nadel, Hofstra, Powdermaker, Kuper), many of whom went on to hold important posts in and outside the British Commonwealth. Malinowski spent the last years of his life at Yale University, where he died in 1942.

Despite the "scandal" caused by the posthumous publication of his field diaries (which in some parts revealed a racist and abusive attitude toward the "natives") and despite the criticism that he mistook the Trobriander for *anthropos* himself, Malinowski still ranks as a pioneer of anthropological fieldwork who contributed decisively to the replacement of the older method of extensive ethnographic surveying with the modern method of intensive participant observation. Emphasizing the goal of grasping "the native's point of view" Malinowski, not least because of his considerable literary gifts, was able to convince the reader of his expertise as an empathetic "I-witness" (Geertz 1988: 73–101) and to paint a captivating yet realistic picture of "native" life. In his ethnographic accounts he sought to bridge the chasm between the "civilized" and the "primitive" by showing that the latter did not lack the rationality and scientific attitude of the former. Furthermore, he drew attention not only to the orderliness of "primitive culture," but also to the fact that the "primitive," like the "civilized," sometimes manipulated and deviated from the norms and rules of his or her community.

Within the realm of theory Malinowski, together with Radcliffe-Brown, is generally credited for having led the "synchronic and nomothetic revolution" in anthropology. Malinowski's functionalism, the doctrine most often associated with him, implied a rejection of social evolutionism and diffusionism, the two most influential theories in anthropology around 1900. Arguing forcefully, especially in his analysis of myth, that the past was not an independent force but always manipulated by and in the present, Malinowski emphasized the irretrievability of the past for anthropological studies and, concomitantly, the futility of the evolutionist's search for origins and historical stages. Criticizing the diffusionist concept of culture as an ever-changing hodgepodge of disparate elements, Malinowski stressed the integrity, inertia, and organic wholeness of culture. Anthropology's prime goal, as conceived by Malinowski, was to search for the fundamental laws governing human conduct. By arguing that culture was essentially "functional" and an instrument for the satisfaction of basic individual needs (e.g., nutrition, reproduction, safety), Malinowski sought to prove the underlying unity in cultural diversity. Some critics of Malinowski's theoretical work, especially of the naïvety, ambiguity, tautology, and the psycho-physiological reductionism of his functional analysis, have argued that it was to anthropology's benefit that in many of his writings Malinowski, like his Trobriander, did not adhere to the rules that he aimed to establish for his discipline.

SEE ALSO: Anthropology, Cultural and Social: Early History; Biosociological Theories; Culture; Function; Functionalism/Neofunctionalism

REFERENCES AND SUGGESTED READINGS

Ellen, R. et al. (Ed.) (1990) *Malinowski Between Two Worlds: The Polish Roots of an Anthropological Tradition.* Cambridge University Press, Cambridge.
Firth, R. (Ed.) (1963) *Man and Culture: An Evaluation of the Work of Bronislaw Malinowski,* 4th edn. Routledge & Kegan Paul, London.
Geertz, C. (1988) *Works and Lives: The Anthropologist as Author.* Stanford University Press, Stanford.
Gellner, E. (1998) *Language and Solitude: Wittgenstein, Malinowski and the Habsburg Dilemma.* Cambridge University Press, Cambridge.
Kuper, A. (1989) *Anthropology and Anthropologists: The Modern British School.* Routledge, New York.
Malinowski, B. (1944) *A Scientific Theory of Culture, and Other Essays.* University of North Carolina Press, Chapel Hill.
Malinowski, B. (1976 [1944]) *Freedom and Civilization.* Greenwood Press, Westport.
Malinowski, B. (1989 [1926]) *Crime and Custom in Savage Society.* Rowman & Allanheld, Totowa, NJ.
Malinowski, B. (1989 [1967]) *A Diary in the Strictest Sense of the Term.* Athlone Press, London.
Malinowski, B. (1992 [1948]) *Magic, Science and Religion, and Others Essays.* Waveland Press, Prospect Heights, IL.
Malinowski, B. (2002) *Collected Works,* 10 vols. Routledge, London.
Stocking, G. W. (Ed.) (1984) *History of Anthropology,* Vol. 2: *Functionalism Historicized: Essays on British Social Anthropology.* University of Wisconsin Press, Madison.
Stocking, G. W. (1996) *After Tylor: British Social Anthropology, 1888–1951.* Athlone Press, London.
Thornton, R. J. & Skalník, P. (Ed.) (1993) *The Early Writings of Bronislaw Malinowski.* Cambridge University Press, Cambridge.
Young, M. W. (2004) *Malinowski: Odyssey of an Anthropologist, 1884–1920.* Yale University Press, New Haven.

Malthus, Thomas Robert (1766–1834)

John R. Weeks

Thomas Robert Malthus is unquestionably the most influential writer in history on the topic of population. This was generally unintentional on his part because he was trained in Jesus College at Cambridge University in England with the early ambition of becoming a clergyman, and he was ordained into the Church of England. After graduation from Cambridge he divided his time between his duties as curate in a small parish church in Albury, south of London near his family's home, and Cambridge, where he had been elected a fellow, and it was during this period that he wrote the first edition of the book that has immortalized him: *Essay on the Principle of Population as it affects the future improvement of society; With remarks on the speculations of Mr. Godwin, M. Condorcet, and other writers.* Malthus (who went by Robert, which is why his first and middle names are usually provided) was by nature a shy man and he had a perceptible speech impediment (which limited the scope of his ambitions in the Church of England), and he published the book anonymously in 1798. However, the book's success forced him to acknowledge authorship, and he subsequently revised and expanded the book through several published editions.

Malthus must be understood in the context of his time. He was the second son of a gentleman farmer with a strong intellectual bent. His father was personal friends with Jean-Jacques Rousseau and David Hume, two of the more important Enlightenment writers. The eighteenth-century Enlightenment was a time when the goodness of the common person was championed. The idea that the rights of individuals superseded the demands of a monarchy inspired the American and French revolutions and was generally very optimistic and utopian, characterized by a great deal of enthusiasm for life and a belief in the perfectibility of humans. In France, these ideas were well expressed by Marie Jean Antoine Nicolas de Caritat, marquis de Condorcet, a member of the French aristocracy who forsook a military career to pursue a life devoted to mathematics and philosophy. Condorcet's optimism was based on his belief that technological progress has no limits. He saw prosperity and population growth increasing hand in hand, and he felt that if the limits to growth were ever reached, the final solution would be birth control, which was rudimentary at the time, but still reasonably effective if a couple was highly motivated.

Similar ideas were being expressed in England by William Godwin, whose *Enquiry Concerning Political Justice and Its Influences on Morals and Happiness* appeared in its first edition in 1793, revealing his ideas that scientific progress would enable the food supply to grow far beyond the levels of his day, and that such prosperity would not lead to overpopulation

because people would deliberately limit their sexual expression and procreation. Furthermore, he believed that most of the problems of the poor were due not to overpopulation but to the inequities of the social institutions, especially greed and accumulation of property.

As Malthus read and contemplated the works of Godwin, Condorcet, and others who shared the utopian view of the perfectibility of human society, he wanted to be able to embrace such an openly optimistic philosophy of life, yet he felt that intellectually he had to reject it. In doing so, he unleashed a controversy about population growth and its consequences that is still with us. He introduced his 1798 essay by commenting that: "I have read some of the speculations on the perfectibility of man and society, with great pleasure. I have been warmed and delighted with the enchanting picture which they hold forth. I ardently wish for such happy improvements. But I see great, and, to my understanding, unconquerable difficulties in the way to them" (Malthus 1965 [1798]: 7).

These "difficulties," of course, are the problems posed by his now famous principle of population. He derived his theory as follows:

I think I may fairly make two postulata. First, that food is necessary to the existence of man. Secondly, that the passion between the sexes is necessary, and will remain nearly in its present state. ... Assuming then, my postulata as granted, I say, that the power of population is indefinitely greater than the power in the earth to produce subsistence for man. Population, when unchecked, increases in a geometrical ratio. Subsistence increases only in an arithmetical ratio. ... By the law of our nature which makes food necessary to the life of man, the effects of these two unequal powers must be kept equal. This implies a strong and constantly operating check on population from the difficulty of subsistence. This difficulty must fall somewhere; and must necessarily be severely felt by a large portion of mankind. ... Consequently, if the premises are just, the argument is conclusive against the perfectibility of the mass of mankind. (Malthus 1965 [1798]: 11)

Malthus believed that human beings, like plants and non-rational animals, are "impelled" to increase the population of the species by what he called a powerful "instinct," the urge to reproduce. Further, if there were no checks on population growth, human beings would multiply to an "incalculable" number, filling "millions of worlds in a few thousand years" (Malthus 1971 [1872]). This does not happen, however, because of the checks to growth. According to Malthus, the ultimate check to growth is lack of food (or, more generally, the "means of subsistence"). In turn, the means of subsistence are limited by the amount of land available, the "arts" or technology that could be applied to the land, and "social organization" or land ownership patterns. A cornerstone of his argument is that populations tend to grow more rapidly than does the food supply since population has the potential for growing geometrically, whereas he believed that food production could be increased only arithmetically, by adding one acre at a time. He argued, then, that in the natural order, population growth will outstrip the food supply, and the lack of food will ultimately put a stop to the increase of people.

Malthus was aware that starvation rarely operates directly to kill people, since there were "positive checks" that killed them before they actually died of starvation. The positive checks were primarily those measures "whether of a moral or physical nature, which tend prematurely to weaken and destroy the human frame" (Malthus 1971 [1872]: 12), which today we would call the causes of mortality.

Malthus also recognized that there are preventive checks that limit population growth. In theory, the preventive checks would include all possible means of birth control, including abstinence, contraception, and abortion. However, to Malthus the only acceptable means of preventing a birth was to exercise what he called "moral restraint"; that is, to postpone marriage, remaining chaste in the meantime, until a man feels "secure that, should he have a large family, his utmost exertions can save them from rags and squalid poverty, and their consequent degradation in the community" (1971 [1872]: 13). Any other means of birth control, including contraception (either before or within marriage), abortion, infanticide, or any "improper means," was viewed as a vice that would "lower, in a marked manner, the dignity of human nature." Moral restraint was a very important point with Malthus, because he believed that if people were allowed to

prevent births by "improper means" (that is, prostitution, contraception, abortion, or sterilization), then they would expend their energies in ways that are, so to speak, not economically productive.

To Malthus, material success is a consequence of human ability to plan rationally – to be educated about future consequences of current behavior – and he was a man who practiced what he preached. He planned his family rationally, waiting to marry and have children until he was 39, at about the same time that he obtained a secure job in 1805 as a Professor of History and Political Economy at East India College in Haileybury, England (north of London). He and his wife, 11 years his junior, had three children.

An important part of the Malthusian perspective – which Karl Marx attacked vociferously – was his belief that a natural consequence of population growth was poverty. This is the logical end result of his arguments that people have a natural urge to reproduce, and that the increase in the supply of food cannot keep up with population growth. Malthus believed that the urge to reproduce always forces population pressure to precede the demand for labor. Thus, "overpopulation" (as measured by the level of unemployment) would force wages down to the point where people could not afford to marry and raise a family. At such low wages, with a surplus of labor and the need for each person to work harder just to earn a subsistence wage, cultivators could employ more labor, put more acres into production, and thus increase the means of subsistence. Malthus believed that this cycle of increased food resources leading to population growth leading to too many people for available resources leading then back to poverty was part of a natural law of population. Each increase in the food supply only meant that eventually more people could live in poverty.

Borrowing from John Locke, Malthus argued that "the endeavor to avoid pain rather than the pursuit of pleasure is the great stimulus to action in life" (1965 [1798]: 359). Pleasure will not stimulate activity until its absence is defined as being painful. Malthus suggested that the well-educated, rational person would perceive in advance the pain of having hungry children or being in debt and would postpone marriage and sexual intercourse until he was sure that he could avoid that pain. If that motivation existed and the preventive check was operating, then the miserable consequences of population growth could be avoided. Malthus objected to the use of birth control not so much on religious grounds as on more philosophical grounds: "To remove the difficulty in this way, will, surely in the opinion of most men, be to destroy that virtue, and purity of manners, which the advocates of equality, and of the perfectibility of man, profess to be the end and object of their views" (1965 [1798]: 154). The underlying concept was later adapted by Sigmund Freud in his discussion of sublimation. Sexual intercourse without the fear of pregnancy, Malthus believed, would destroy a man's work ethic.

Malthus was opposed to the English Poor Laws (welfare benefits for the poor), because he felt they would actually serve to perpetuate misery. They permitted poor people to be supported by others and thus not feel that great pain, the avoidance of which might lead to birth prevention. Malthus argued that if every man had to provide for his own children, he would be more prudent about getting married and raising a family. In his own time, the number of people on welfare had been increasing and English parliamentarians were trying to decide what to do about the problem. Although the Poor Laws were not abolished, they were reformed largely because Malthus had given legitimacy to public criticism of the entire concept of welfare payments. Marx was adamantly opposed to this idea, because his view, like Godwin's, was that poverty resulted from social injustice, not overpopulation. If capitalists (including large landowners) did not exploit the workers, then more people working ought to generate more economic productivity which would raise the standard of living, not lower it. The historical evidence does not, in fact, support Malthus's view of the Poor Laws. Those English counties with more generous welfare benefits did not have a higher birth rate than those with less generous benefits.

The crucial part of Malthus's ratio of population growth to food increase was that food (including both plants and non-human animals) would not grow exponentially. Yet when Charles Darwin acknowledged that his *Origin of the Species* was inspired by Malthus's essay,

it was because Darwin realized that all plants and animals, not just humans, had the capacity to grow exponentially. "Darwin described his own theory as 'the doctrine of Malthus applied with manifold force to the whole animal and vegetable kingdoms; for in this case there can be no artificial increase of food, and no prudential restraint from marriage.' Thus plants and animals, even more than men, would increase geometrically if unchecked" (Himmelfarb 1984: 128). The balance between humans and the resources that sustain human life was not the only battle going on in nature. Darwin understood that every living thing was competing for resources and that the result was a slow process of evolutionary change as each species worked to ensure its own survival.

Criticisms of Malthus do not, however, diminish the importance of his work. Although his writing often has a moralistic rather than a scientific tone, he laid out a very clear argument for why resources may not be sustainable in the face of continued population growth. He laid the groundwork for Darwin's theory of evolution, and offered a very modern-sounding view of the world in which humans must balance their numbers against the natural resources available on the planet.

SEE ALSO: Demographic Transition Theory; Demography; Marx, Karl; Population and Development; Population and the Environment

REFERENCES AND SUGGESTED READINGS

Godwin, W. (1946 [1793]) *Enquiry Concerning Political Justice and Its Influences on Morals and Happiness*. University of Toronto Press, Toronto.

Himmelfarb, G. (1984) *The Idea of Poverty: England in the Early Industrial Age*. Alfred A. Knopf, New York.

Malthus, T. R. (1965 [1798]) *An Essay on Population*. Augustus Kelley, New York.

Malthus, T. R. (1971 [1872]) *An Essay on the the Principle of Population*, 7th edn. Reeves & Turner, London.

Nickerson, J. (1975) *Homage to Malthus*. National University Publications, Port Washington, NY.

Petersen, W. (1979) *Malthus*. Harvard University Press, Cambridge, MA.

managed care

Teresa L. Scheid

Managed care refers to processes or techniques used by, or on behalf of, purchasers of health care that seek to control or influence the quality, accessibility, utilization, and costs of health care. Managed care emerged in the United States in the 1960s as a response to rising health care costs, and consists of different types of organizational practices to make health care more efficient and effective. Most other industrial countries have also responded to rising health care costs by managing care. Managed care emphasizes cost containment, performance assessment, and measurable outcomes and subjects the treatment actions of health care providers to external review. Treatment decisions are evaluated in light of measurable client-level outcomes; consequently, managed care has resulted in a greater emphasis on accountability. The issue is whether accountability is accessed in terms of cost savings (efficiency) or enhanced care (effectiveness). In the United States, managed care often involves a greater concern with cost savings than with enhanced quality or access.

There are numerous ways in which health care is managed, the most common being utilization review or pre-certification (where services must be authorized before a client can receive them), purchaser contracts with groups of health care providers (such as health maintenance organizations or preferred provider organizations), and capitation (where a set amount is paid for a client for specified services). Many of these forms of managed care are used in conjunction with one another. By 1995, three-fourths of American workers received some form of managed care through their private insurance plans, and with recent reforms to Medicaid and Medicare most Americans receive managed health care in one form or another.

Because of the diversity in approaches to managed care, as well as wide variation in the types of organizations which provide managed care, we do not know very much about the overall impact of managed care on health care.

While economists have focused on economic evaluations of the efficiency of managed care (i.e., reduced costs), sociologists have concentrated on the forces promoting managed care and how managed care has changed the traditional system of care.

Donald Light (1997) has argued that managed care is a revolutionary shift from a provider-driven (health care professionals and providers) to a buyer-driven system of care. Provider-driven health care was based on a professional model where, by virtue of their professional expertise, health care providers had control over treatment decisions. The buyer-based system of care is characterized by a distrust of professional authority and external monitoring of health care providers in order to enhance accountability. Scott et al. (2000) have provided an extensive analysis of the decline of professional dominance and the growth in a managerial/market-based institutional logic in the San Francisco Bay area. With managed care there is an increased emphasis on standardization of clinical practices and reliance upon evidence-based medicine. Because treatment is reimbursed when there is a valid medical diagnosis for which an efficacious treatment exists, managed care has resulted in a restricted view of care in terms of the medical model of care, which excludes many forms of support needed by individuals with chronic conditions. There is also an increased reliance on medications as the primary form of medical care.

Sociologists have examined managed care constraints on professional autonomy and conflict with bureaucratic control systems. Most of the existent research focuses on physicians. Sociologists have found that decisions about clinical care continue to rely upon medical expertise, and while physicians do conform to principles of cost containment, they maintain high levels of autonomy. That is, professional logics of care have incorporated the logic of cost containment. This may not be the case where health care providers lack the power of physicians, such as in the provision of mental health care (Scheid 2004). There needs to be more research on how managed care has affected the work of different groups of health care providers as well as patients. There is a large body of literature outside sociology that examines the ethical dilemmas providers experience when faced with conflicting demands for cost containment and patient care. Since managed care so often operates at the organizational rather than the individual level, we need to develop better models of organizational ethics and link studies of health care to sociological theories of organizational behavior.

Unfortunately, assessments of managed care have largely been conducted by health services researchers and there has been a narrow focus on efficiency. Efficiency has been defined in the health policy literature in terms of lower costs and the use of fewer resources (Sullivan 2000). The quality of care involves assessment of the effectiveness of that care (Flood 1994; Campbell et al. 2000). However, a good bit of the existent research uses efficiency to assess the effectiveness (quality) of care. For example, managed care has reduced the length of inpatient hospital stays, which certainly saves money; it is less clear if quality of care is enhanced by shortened stays. Sociologists need to take a more active role in evaluations of managed care practices and how managed care has affected the type and quality of care patients receive. Sociologists also need to focus on ways in which managed care has changed access to health care for different populations. Managed care has the potential to widen access by distributing health care more equitably; it may also restrict access by limiting care to those with acute health care problems and hence neglecting the long-term needs of patients with chronic problems. In terms of mental health, there is some evidence that managed care has in fact resulted in a democratization of care where everyone gets a similar level of services and those with chronic needs do not get the services they require (Mechanic & McAlpine 1999). We also do not know very much about the differential experience of minority groups within managed care (both as health care providers and patients). Sociologists studying health disparities rarely include organizational variables in their analysis. Consequently, we know little about how mechanisms to manage care may in fact widen access by allowing for a more equitable rationing of care, or which mechanisms ration care such as to enhance inequalities in care.

SEE ALSO: Chronic Illness and Disability; Health Care Delivery Systems; Health Locus of Control; Health Maintenance Organization

REFERENCES AND SUGGESTED READINGS

Campbell, S. M., Roland, M. O., & Buetow, S. A. (2000) Defining Quality of Care. *Social Science and Medicine* 51: 1611–25.

Flood, A. B. (1994) The Impact of Organizational and Managerial Factors on the Quality of Care in Health Care Organizations. *Medical Care Review* 38: 396–427.

Light, D. (1997) The Rhetorics and Realities of Community Health Care: The Limits of Countervailing Powers to Meet the Health Needs of the Twenty-First Century. *Journal of Health Politics, Policy, and Law* 22: 105–45.

Mechanic, D. & McAlpine, D. (1999) Mission Unfilled: Potholes on the Road to Mental Health Parity. *Health Affairs* 18: 7–21.

Scheid, T. (2004) *Tie a Knot and Hang On: Providing Mental Health Care in a Turbulent Environment*. Aldine de Gruyter, New York.

Scott, W. R., Ruef, M., Mendel, P., & Caroneer, C. A. (2000) *Institutional Change and Organizational Transformation of the Healthcare Field*. University of Chicago Press, Chicago.

Sullivan, K. (2000) On the Efficiency of Managed Care Plans. *Health Affairs* 19: 139–48.

management

Stewart Clegg and Chris Carter

On the eve of World War I, scientific management became the first big management fad, a source of innumerable new truths about work and its organization, all of which were oriented to the efficiency of the individual human body. At the same time a revolution in manufacturing also occurred when Henry Ford introduced the assembly line, modeled on the Chicago slaughterhouses (see Upton Sinclair's 1906 ethnographic novel, *The Jungle*). In the abattoirs each job was separated into a series of simple repetitive actions as the bodies moved down the line to be progressively dismembered; in Ford the car was built on the same principles that the hog was butchered.

While management saw it as important to know how much time each element requires to be accomplished, other aspects of time study techniques were not appropriate for assembly line manufacturing. Individual incentives were not appropriate because every operator was tied to the speed of the line. What remained from the Taylor system was the elemental decomposition of jobs. Jobs were small, repetitive, and routine. In fact, routine became such a problem among Ford's workers that, in the first year of full assembly line operation, the company experienced about 900 percent turnover (Williams et al. 1992). The annual turnover rate settled at around 400 percent and daily absenteeism ran between 10 and 20 percent. It was for this reason that on January 5, 1914, the Ford Motor Company announced the $5, 8-hour day for all production workers, irrespective of pieces produced (which was determined by the speed of the line, anyway, not individual effort). To ensure only deserving workers received the money, in 1914 Ford established the Sociological Department to administer the program and to investigate the home lives of workers (Marcus & Segal 1989: 236–8). It was a remarkable example of the institutionalization of a socially disciplinary apparatus in the front ranks of the emerging industrial economy of modernity and of an ultimately failed attempt to institute meta-routines governing societal politics. The $5 day was designed to include only those who were "'worthy' and who would not debauch the additional money." The rules governing eligibility were demonstrating that, if one were a man, one lived a clean, sober, industrious, and thrifty life, while women had to be "deserving" and have some relatives solely dependent upon them. Investigators from the Sociological Department visited workers' homes and suggested ways to achieve the company's standards for "better morals," sanitary living conditions, and "habits of thrift and saving." Employees who lapsed were removed from the system and given a chance to redeem themselves. Long-term failure to meet Ford Motor Company standards resulted in dismissal from the company.

Of course, there was a degree of racism at work here as well, paralleling Ford's well-documented anti-Semitism (Lee 1980): after the Civil War, black people had been leaving the sharecropper society of the Deep South in droves, fleeing a culture rooted in slavery. After hitting Highway 61, they headed for the burgeoning factories of the North, in Chicago and Detroit, in the latter of which Ford began hiring African Americans in large numbers in 1915, paying them the same wages as his white employees. The material basis of the jazz age for the many black people who headed North was working in the factories and assembly plants. By 1923, Ford employed 5,000 Detroit-area black men, far more than other plants.

As Fordist modernity became characteristic of modernity in general, in workshops large and small, the state took over the functions that private capital had hitherto assumed. Small employers or those new to business could not develop their own sociological departments, but the state, as an ideal total moralist, supplemented the work of surveillance over those in whom the churches and associated temperance movements had not succeeded in instilling a governmental soul. Power shifted its focus from the individual to the collective. We should understand these innovations as extensions of a panoptical complex. They lacked the specificity of Taylor's targeting of the body and were more oriented to what Foucault (1977) referred to as biopower, power oriented to the collective body politic. In accord with Gramsci (1971) we can see these new managerial techniques of Taylorism and Fordism seeking to suppress "the 'animality' of man, training him," as Turner (1984: 100) suggests, "for the regular disciplines of factory life," in an anatomical politics. Even as the state supplemented "the private initiatives of the industrialist" in framing the political morality of work (in an era before random drug testing of employees had become widespread), newer, more specifically targeted practices were being shaped in opposition to Taylor's political economy of the body, private initiatives by industrialists, and the state's regulatory biopower.

EMERGENCE OF THE SOUL IN THE MACHINE

Not everyone contributing to the imagination of futures at work in management theorizing shared the same dreams. There were signs that what for some augured a dream of efficiency for others foreshadowed a nightmare of isolated sociability, alienated being, and wasted humanity. Additionally, it became increasingly evident that it was an insufficient level of reform and innovation to be merely mechanically efficient in terms of the relation between the body and the immediate environment. Such reform, while necessary, could not be relied upon to create the desired results because the free will of the workers interceded.

Taylor's system of scientific management might have achieved efficiency, but at the cost of eroding civility. Mass production and large scale were made possible through efficiency in the division of labor, but this division had removed the social bonds that constrained individuals and now pitted them ruthlessly and relentlessly against each other in a highly competitive individualism. What was required, thought Mary Parker Follett (1918), was a reinstitution of civility, society, and fellowship in and through work and its organization if the corrosive effects of possessive individualism on the moral character of the American employee were to be halted. People needed to think not just of themselves and the individual benefit to be gained through competition at work, but how they fitted into an overall pattern of functions, responsibilities, and authoritative entitlements to command and to obey. Her views of Taylor's influence were evident in her assertion that individuality is represented best in the capacity for union between people, rather than in their non-relation, which she defined as evil. In her view the potentialities of the individual remain potentialities until they are released by group life. Only through the group can men and women discover their true nature, and gain their true freedom. On this basis, she opposed the modern legal conception of the corporation as an individual fiction. She thought that corporations had the capability for "real personality" only when their members were able to interknit themselves into genuine relations, as a human group. Out of this vital union comes creative power. Or, more poetically, "We find the individual through the group, we use him always as the true individual – the undivided one – who, living link of living group, is yet never embedded in the meshes but is forever

free for every new possibility of a forever unfolding life" (Follett 1918: 295).

World War I was a fillip for the adoption of Taylorism, as jobs were deskilled for the influx of female workers as men fought in Europe. World War II saw the emergence of a trenchant critique of scientific management. Against excessive individuation Mayo (1975) pitted collaboration, his version of community. Individualism has served the nation well, he says, but only in one dimension, that of organizing for material efficiency. What it has not been able to do, even in wartime conditions, is "ensure spontaneity of cooperation" or "teamwork" (p. 9), that is, social efficiency based in the skills of individuals to cooperate with others. The ability to display a capacity for receiving "communication from others" and responding to the "attitudes and ideas of others in such a fashion as to promote congenial participation in a common task" (p. 12) has been lost because scientific management has destroyed it, creating anomie and shattering community, through "the skill required of a machine-hand [having] drifted downwards; he has become more of a machine tender and less of a mechanic." All the organizing energy has been focused on developing technical skills in a more and more divided manner, while "no equivalent effort to develop social or collaborative skill has yet appeared to compensate or balance the technical development" (p. 13).

Mayo's theoretical background guided the selection of issues he was familiar with and the marginalization of the issues that did not match the theory he chose to promote. When Mayo (1933) looked at the findings from the Hawthorne Laboratory investigations he thought the results showed that employees had a strong need for shared cooperation and communication. Merely by asking for their cooperation in the test, Mayo believed the investigators had stimulated a new attitude among the employees. The assemblers considered themselves to be part of an important group whose help and advice were being sought by the company. He believed that if consultation between labor and management were instituted it would give workers a sense of belonging to a team. Here we can see the transformation produced in the modes of surveillance. A new strategy of government of the body/soul in the factory was to be based on the construction of a sentiment of freedom (and responsibility) without any apparent surveillance (Mayo 1975: 75).

These studies changed the landscape of management from Taylor's engineering approach to the political economy of the body to a social sciences approach that focused on the interior life, the mental states, the consciousness and unconsciousness, which Follett termed the "soul" of the employees: "Coercive power is the curse of the universe; coactive power, the enrichment and advancement of every human soul" (Follett 1924: xii). Worker productivity would henceforth be interpreted predominantly in terms of patterns of culture, motivation, leadership, and human relations (Maslow 1978). The locus of expert power shifted from the engineering expert, designing the job, selecting and training the right worker, and rewarding performance, to the manager, responsible for leading, motivating, communicating, and counseling the individual employee as well as designing the social milieu in which work takes place. Human relations came to the fore, as did a concern with leadership and authority.

HUMAN RELATIONS, LEADERSHIP, AND AUTHORITY

Mayo developed what became known as the Human Relations School. The emphasis of this approach was on informal work group relations, the importance of these for sustaining the formal system, and the necessity of the formal system meshing with the informal system. In the informal system special attention was to be paid to the satisfaction of individual human needs, focusing on what motivates different people, in order to try and maximize their motivation and satisfaction. Mayo thought the manager had to be a social clinician, fostering the social skills of those with whom she or he worked. Workers who argued with their managers and supervisors were expressing deep-seated neuroses lodged in their childhood history.

Chester Barnard (1938) joined forces with Mayo when he cited him to the effect that "authority depends upon a cooperative personal attitude of individuals on the one hand; and the system of communication in the organization on the other" (p. 175). What managers should communicate are strong moral values, which it was management's duty to provide, said Barnard. Good management requires emotional work, and it is the task of the managerial elite to configure others as servants of responsible authority through guiding them, emotionally, thought Barnard, and Mayo (1975) seemed to agree with this diagnosis.

For Barnard, authority relations were not a given, but had to be worked at by managers. Authority only exists insofar as people are willing to accept it. The pervasiveness of authority can be expanded by gradually enlarging the "zone of indifference" within which compliance with orders will be perceived in neutral terms without any questioning of authority by employees. Managers should seek to extend the borders of this zone through material incentives, but more especially through providing others with status, prestige, and personal power. Communications, especially in the informal organization (which Mayo had "discovered" in his interpretation of the Hawthorne experiments), are absolutely central to decision-making. Management's responsibility is to harness informal groupings and get them working for the organization, not against it. Everyone should know what the channels of communication are and should have access to formal channels of communications that should be as short and direct as possible. All of these new technologies of power should not replace the scientific management of work and organization design, but should supplement it, be added to it as new forms of persuasion. Where individuals worked with common values rather than common orders, they would work much more effectively.

In one of the most sophisticated accounts, Selznick (1957) explicitly divides the soul from the body. The organization is a corporate body, a tool or instrument rationally designed to direct human energies to a fixed goal, an expendable and limited apparatus. However, the body has a soul, something largely natural, living, and unplanned, a distinctive identity, something which Selznick identifies as an "institution." Organizational tools evolve into something infused with value and meaning, becoming soulful institutions. Or they will, if they are managed properly and there is specificity about how to achieve such proper management. Management is the job of the elites. "Maintenance of social values depends on the autonomy of elites" (p. 8). These autonomous elites must produce that commitment and identification, that great soulful boundless leap, which makes the bodies of the employees more than a mere tool. The elites must make the individual components of the tool identify with and feel committed to the elites and their purposes. They will do this both by stimulating soulful feelings and controlling them "to produce the desired balance of forces" (p. 100).

MODERN MANAGEMENT THEORIES

In the post-war era the informal organization of Mayo and his associates became fused with the stress on authority and leadership of Barnard and Selznick, and with Taylor's formal organization through the metaphor of the social system. Within this metaphor the epitome of modern rational management knowledge became the program institutionalized as contingency theory. Contingency theory developed a political edge when Child (1972) published his influential article on "strategic choice," in which he drew deeply on debates that Silverman (1970) had sparked in Britain among organization sociologists, drawing on influential sources such as Berger and Luckmann (1967) to rekindle an interpretive account of organizations. Silverman (1970) counterposed an "action frame of reference" to the open systems contingency perspective that was by now dominant in organization analysis. His key point was that organizations were neither natural nor rational systems per se, but were socially constructed phenomena. Silverman was an important, but outside Britain, largely neglected early institutional theorist (Clegg 1994). The key point that Child and Silverman were making was that organizations were a result of choices, particularly by those whom Selznick (1957) had referred to as the "dominant coalition" (see Colignon 1997).

Institutional theory quickly lost its focus on power after Meyer and Rowan (1977) and DiMaggio and Powell (1983) initiated its renaissance by asking why there are so few types of organizations. Organizations, they suggested,

are not as they are for efficiency reasons (as contingency functionalist theorists had argued), but for reasons of social construction. Hence, it is the cultural stock of knowledge rather than functional necessity that determines how and why organizations are as they are. Strangely, given Weber's preeminent role as both a cultural theorist (Clegg 1995) and analyst of power and domination (Clegg 1975), these latter terms seemed somewhat underdone in the new institutionalism. As Mizruchi and Fein (1999) suggested, research programs applying DiMaggio and Powell concentrated on mimetic isomorphism while downplaying the coercive and normative. The European Aix School (Maurice et al. 1980), who had arrived at similar conclusions to those of the North American institutional scholars, conducted comparative cross-national research in which they compared the organization structures of different countries, seeing the differences not only in terms of contingency factors but also as a "societal effect" (Sorge 1991): different relations of power were differently valued in different countries (Whitley 1994). The reason that different institutional structures were valued differently in different countries was because different national elites had formed around different constellations of values and interests, giving rise to quite distinct patterns of elite formation, recruitment, and reproduction. One such elite, of course, coalesces around those who produce management theories.

WHAT DO MANAGEMENT THEORIES DO?

As management theory became increasingly institutionalized, especially in business schools, it began to develop the traits that we would expect of any institutionalized body of knowledge. Rival camps with competing claims to territory emerged. Definitions of the field became contested. What was regarded as holy writ differed within each citation cartel, centered on different fulcra, whether journals, theories, or theorists. We can make a distinction between those objects theories construct through their concepts, methods, and models and the "naturally" occurring phenomena that these reflect. The latter would exist irrespective of their theorization or non-theorization as practices – what people do. Theory inhabits its own specialist realm and has its own terms. There is always a gap between theory and the practice it reflects on, which will be an effect of the social constructions, conventions, and grammars of analysis within which translation between them is made. Translations from practice to theory that achieve systematicity and institutionalization can become objects of analysis in their own right, creating their own truths. Theories of management are just these sorts of translations. The important question, however, is not so much to identify what it is that they construct as *true* (on this one should, properly, be agnostic rather than faithful), but to inquire what are the *functions* of the truths that they posit? What is important is to analyze the machinery of truth production. Truth claims that are granted and respected perform an essential function in ordering membership and normalcy in the social contexts in which they pertain, such as business schools and other organizations. They specify the conditions of existence for possibilities and impossibilities; they legitimate relations of domination and subordination. In this sense, what is (taken to be) true is a social fact, as Durkheim (1983: 67) puts it. Haugaard (1997: 69) suggests that those who benefit from extant machineries of truth production will be least keen to see its mechanisms exposed. Truth is typically taken to be that knowledge indubitably standing as provisional after exposure to robust skeptical procedures of conjecture and refutation (Popper 1965). Thus, the essence of science is to be protected from power at all costs. The most current accounts of management clearly serve dominant power interests and relations in ways that are only too self-evidently reminiscent of the earlier concerns with the mind and soul.

CURRENT FADS

The last 25 years have witnessed an explosion of management initiatives. Replete with their careful styling and image intensity such initiatives are now widely characterized as management fashions. Examples of management fashion over the last decade or so include Total Quality Management, Downsizing, Business Process Re-Engineering, Enterprise Resource Planning, Knowledge Management, and Shareholder Value. These initiatives do not emerge from a vacuum. The genesis of the bulk of these ideas, as writers such as Abrahamson have pointed out, rests with the "management ideas industry." A loose but very powerful actor-network of large accounting firms, management consultancies, management gurus, information technology firms, self-styled world-class companies, and business schools drives the creation of new management fashion. Tightly coupled to the managers they seek as clients, management fashions are carefully market tested to gauge managerial anxiety. The resulting fashion, by anticipating and offering solutions to managerial problems, succeeds in capturing the corporate zeitgeist. If the management ideas industry captures the supply side of the industry, it is management who are the consumers. The literature is split between those that imply that managers following fashion are to be looked down upon (Abrahamson 1997; Scarbrough & Swan 2001), to others for whom adorning one's organization with the latest fashion possesses more positive connotations (Czarniawska & Sevón 2006).

In current approaches the ordinary knowledge of ordinary people is regarded as a neglected resource that managers must access, use, and make routine. They will do this through the simple strategies of building social capital (brought into focus primarily through the work of Putnam 1993, 1995) and through the use of those coactive power strategies that Mary Parker Follett had recommended for building such capital all those years ago. Once social capital has been identified, then new routines can be constructed. Social capital takes care of the coactivity while knowledge management will structure the new routines. It is tempting to see the former as a continuation of the concern with the moral economy and the latter as a simple extension of scientific management – to incorporate the mind as well as the body and soul of the employee. We explore this proposition in what follows.

Social capital is defined as "the sum of actual and potential resources embedded within, available through, and derived from the network of relationships possessed by an individual or social unit" (Nahapiet & Ghoshal 1998). Firms are "understood as a social community specializing in the speed and efficiency in the creation and transfer of knowledge" (Kogut & Zander 1996). Organizations, designed to bring people together for task completion, supervision, and coordination, result in frequent and dense levels of social contacts, creating coactive power in Follett's terms. Social capital, as Follett realized, makes it possible for ends to be achieved that, in its absence, could otherwise only be achieved at additional cost.

The social capital concept privileges the worker as a "knowledge worker" with embrained rather than embodied knowledge (Blackler 1995). Such employees are potentially mobile and can go to another employer; thus, they must be kept loyal by avoidance of coercion (which, much as the use of tight contracts, destroys trust) and by use of soft power (on power and trust relations, see Fox 1974). Trust and control can be viewed as structures of interrelated situated practices that influence the development of different forms of expert power in particular organizational contexts. In this view, trust and control relations are generative mechanisms that play a role in the production, reproduction, and transformation of expert power. Trust is based on predictability of behavior, where some type of control or self-control mechanism influences such predictability.

Trust and control are closely associated (Maguire et al. 2001; Reed 2001). Many organizations attempt to "manage" trust as a means of control (Knights et al. 2001). Maguire et al. (2001) have suggested several ways in which this happens, including actively manipulating the employee using rewards, acquiring information about the employee and thus rendering him or her more predictable and hence controllable, and active manipulation of the goodwill of the employee by increasing his or her identification with the organization. The rhetoric of "trust" often sits uncomfortably in the context of all the routines constituting a "low trust" workplace of design of technologies and of work by standardized procedures. Contemporary labor process studies carried out or reviewed by Thompson and Ackroyd (1995, 1999) and Thompson and Warhurst (1998) suggest that we need to untangle the managerial rhetoric and intention from the realities of the situation.

Knowledge management is another new idea with deep roots that go back to Taylor and scientific management. Two aspects of knowledge management are relevant here. First, there is the treatment of knowledge as a commodity, through the mechanization and objectification of knowledge creation, diffusion, and storage. Treated this way it increases management's sense of control. Second, there is soft domination of the knowledge worker by identification-based control The highest degree of trust is when the person completely identifies with the organization, in which case their self-image is aligned with managerially determined objectives (Alvesson & Willmott 2002). What knowledge management seeks to do is to draw from the tacit knowledge of individuals and the social capital of the group to construct new and improved routines. The thrust of scientific management and the many subsequent clones spawned from its political economy, such as knowledge management, was that routines produce increased efficiency where the correspondence between relations of knowledge is closed, where the worker does exactly what the scientific manager prescribes. Taylor and his heirs sought to make workers functionaries of knowledge relations defined externally to the "being there" of the workers. Yet, paradoxically, as the Hawthorne studies first revealed, efficiency is determined by the extent to which individual knowledge and expertise is accessed and utilized (Grant 1996a).

In knowledge management efficiency is based on common knowledge as a prerequisite to the communication of direction and routine. Translating specialist information depends on the sophistication and level of common knowledge. Second, the frequency and variability of task performance changes the efficiency of knowledge integration (Nelson & Winter 1982). The efficiency of comprehending and responding appropriately among employees involved in tasks is a function of frequency of task performance. Third, organizational structure that reduces the extent and intensity of communication to achieve integration assists efficiency and to do this the employee has to be integrated into the enterprise as an obedient rather than resistant subject. Knowledge management grows out of the cross-pollination of scientific management and human relations theory to make obedient subjects creative.

Knowledge management is an instrument producing new routines that result from acquiring and distilling knowledge of tacit experiences and action that is embedded in social and institutional practice (Brown & Duguid 1991). Individual public performances draw on private parts of the self – the soul in Follett's terms – in interactions (Nelson & Winter 1982). Thus, as recent theory has it, "the primary role of the firm is in integrating specialist knowledge resident in individuals into goods and services" (Grant 1996b). Knowledge management institutes what Garrick and Clegg (2000) referred to as an "organizational gothic" at the heart of organizational life, a capacity to suck the vitality from the individual body and soul in order to enhance the vitality of the corporate body for increased efficiency and reduced costs, through greater coactive power. The secret is in extracting creativity from the individual through the use of coactive power and instilling it into the body corporate, where the body corporate retains its vitality by sucking out the vitality of those members that compose it. The allusion to Dracula is intended; the practice seems as gothic as any Hammer horror movie.

Individuals share uniquely held knowledge on the basis of what is held in common among them. Common knowledge refers to the "common cognitive ground" among employees that facilitates knowledge transfer through promoting dialogue and communication (what Nonaka and Takeuchi (1995) term redundancy). Redundancy creates an intentional overlap of information held by employees that facilitates transferring and integrating explicit and tacit knowledge. Knowledge about elements not directly related to immediate operational requirements that arises from images in tacit knowledge can be shared through redundant information about business activities, management responsibilities, the company, products, and services. Competitive, individuated, relations of power make this knowledge difficult to surface. Coercive power leads to zero-sum games, win/lose scenarios, power/resistance, and resource dependency, which creates power effects more akin to rape than seduction, as Stokes and Clegg (2002) argue. The rape and seduction analogy suggests that seduction would seek to elicit expert knowing representing a rich and anchored context, whereas rape absconds with the partial acquisition of knowledge without context, and thus, lacking situated meaning, promotes only a wrenching of something unwillingly given. That is why the projects of knowledge management and social capital are seeking to become aligned. First, use coactive power to seduce knowledge that can become the basis for the new routines. Then, when the new routines are established they take on a coercive power of their own, as individuals can be held accountable to them.

CONCLUSION

In some respects, early management theorists were situated too close to its practice to reflect overly on its theory. These early texts were embedded, precisely, in the strategies for making sense of management that the pioneers forged and the managerial techniques they advocated. The political and moral economy of the body, and the emergence of a concern with the soul of the employee, did not enter greatly into subsequent accounts. Management became ever more abstracted and sophisticated in its use of metaphors drawn from contingency and system theory, yet it still struggled with the obdurate *matériel* of the human subject at its base. Overwhelmingly, its tendency has been to rationalize and routinize this obduracy through designing systems that reduce the capacity for human inventiveness, creativity, and innovation of those within the systems designed, as Ritzer's (2005) work on McDonaldization suggests. It is through this prism that we should see the latest trends in management thinking, such as knowledge management. While the actors in the system are occasionally noted, their creativity is more often demoted, incorporated, or excluded. As Fairtlough (2006) has noted, tellingly, this is hardly the most effective way of getting many things done.

SEE ALSO: Industrial Relations; Knowledge Management; Labor Process; Management Consultants; Management Discourse; Management Education; Management Fashion; Management History; Management Improvisation; Management Innovation; Management Networks; Management Theory; Management, Workers' Participation in; Top Management Teams

2718 *management*

REFERENCES AND SUGGESTED READINGS

Abrahamson, E. (1997) The Emergence and Prevalence of Employee Management Rhetorics: The Effects of Long Waves, Labor Unions, and Turnover, 1875 to 1992. *Academy of Management Journal* 40(3): 491–533.

Alvesson, M. & Willmott, H. (2002) On the Idea of Emancipation in Management and Organization Studies. *Academy of Management Review* 17(3): 432–64.

Barnard, C. I. (1938) *Functions of the Executive.* Harvard University Press, Cambridge, MA.

Berger, P. L. & Luckmann, T. (1967) *The Social Construction of Reality: A Treatise in the Sociology of Knowledge.* Penguin, London.

Blackler, F. (1995) Knowledge, Knowledge Work and Organizations: An Overview and Interpretation. *Organization Studies* 16(6): 1021–46.

Brown, J. S. & Duguid, P. (1991) Organizational Learning and Communities of Practice: Toward a Unified View of Working, Learning and Innovation. *Organization Science* 2: 40–57.

Child, J. (1972) Organizational Structures, Environment and Performance: The Role of Strategic Choice. *Sociology* 6: 2–22.

Clegg, S. R. (1975) *Power, Rule and Domination: A Critical and Empirical Understanding of Power in Sociological Theory and Organizational Life.* Routledge, London.

Clegg, S. R. (1994) Power and Institutionalism in the Theory of Organizations. In: Parker, M. & Hassard, J. (Eds.), *Towards a New Theory of Organizations.* Routledge, London, pp. 24–52.

Clegg, S. R. (1995) Of Values and Occasional Irony: Max Weber in the Context of the Sociology of Organizations. In: Bachrach, S. B., Gagliardi, P., & Munde, B. (Eds.), *Research in the Sociology of Organizations: Studies of Organizations in the European Tradition.* JAI Press, Greenwich, CT, pp. 1–46.

Colignon, R. (1997) *Power Plays: Critical Events in the Institutionalization of the Tennessee Valley Authority.* State University of New York Press, Albany.

Czarniawska, B. & Sevón, G. (Eds.) (2006) *Global Ideas.* Liber, Oslo.

DiMaggio, P. J. & Powell, W. W. (1983) The Iron Cage Revisited: Institutional Isomorphism and Collective Rationality in Organization Fields. *American Sociological Review* 45(2): 726–43.

Durkheim, E. (1983) *Pragmatism and Sociology.* Cambridge University Press, Cambridge.

Fairtlough, G. (2005) *The Three Ways of Getting Things Done: Hierarchy, Heterarchy and Responsible Autonomy in Organizations.* Triarchy, Greenways, Dorset.

Follett, M. P. (1918) *The New State: Group Organization, the Solution for Popular Government.* Longman, Green, New York.

Follett, M. P. (1924) *Creative Experience.* Longman, Green, New York.

Foucault, M. (1977) *Discipline and Punish: The Birth of the Prison.* Allen Lane, London.

Fox, A. (1974) *Beyond Contract: Work, Power and Trust Relations.* Faber, London.

Garrick, J. & Clegg, S. R. (2000) Organizational Gothic: Transfusing Vitality and Transforming the Corporate Body Through Work-Based Learning. In: Symes, C. & McIntyre, J. (Eds.), *Working Knowledge: The New Vocationalism and Higher Education.* Society for Research into Higher Education and Open University Press, Buckingham, pp. 153–71.

Gramsci, A. (1971) *From the Prison Notebooks.* Lawrence & Wishart, London.

Grant, R. M. (1996a) Prospering in Dynamically Competitive Environments: Organizational Capability as Knowledge Integration. *Organizational Science* 7(4): 375–87.

Grant, R. M. (1996b) Toward a Knowledge-Based Theory of the Firm. *Strategic Management Journal* 17: 109–22.

Haugaard, M. (1997) *The Constitution of Power.* Manchester University Press, Manchester.

Knights, D., Noble, F., Vurdubakis, T., & Willmott, H. (2001) Chasing Shadows: Control, Virtuality and the Production of Trust. *Organization Science* 22(2): 311–36.

Kogut, B. & Zander, U. (1996) What Do Firms Do? Coordination, Identity and Learning. *Organization Science* 7: 502–18.

Lee, A. (1980) *Henry Ford and the Jews.* Stein & Day, New York.

Maguire, S., Phillips, N., & Hardy, C. (2001) When Silence = Death, Keep Talking: Trust, Control and the Discursive Construction of Identity in the Canadian HIV/AIDS Treatment Domain. *Organization Studies* 22(2): 285–310.

Marcus, A. & Segal, H. P. (1989) *Technology in America.* Harcourt Brace Johanovitch, New York.

Maslow, A. H. (1978) A Theory of Human Motivation. In: Vroom, V. H. & Deci, E. L. (Eds.), *Management and Motivation.* Penguin, London, pp. 27–41.

Maurice, M., Sorge, A., & Warner, M. (1980) Societal Differences in Organizing Manufacturing Units: A Comparison of France, West Germany and Great Britain. *Organization Studies* 1: 59–86.

Mayo, E. (1933) *The Human Problems of an Industrial Civilization.* Harvard University Press, Cambridge, MA.

Mayo, E. (1975) *The Social Problems of an Industrial Civilization*. Routledge & Kegan Paul, London.

Meyer, J. W. & Rowan, B. (1977) Institutionalized Organizations: Formal Structure as Myth and Ceremony. *American Journal of Sociology* 83: 340–63.

Mizruchi, M. S. & Fein, C. (1999) The Social Construction of Organizational Knowledge: A Study of the Uses of Coercive, Mimetic, and Normative Isomorphism. *Administrative Science Quarterly* 44: 653–83.

Nahapiet, J. & Ghoshal, S. (1998) Social Capital, Intellectual Capital and the Organization Advantage. *Academy of Management Review* 23(2): 2–26.

Nelson, R. R. & Winter, S. G. (1982) *An Evolutionary Theory of Economic Change*. Harvard University Press, Belknap Press, Cambridge, MA.

Nonaka, I. & Takeuchi, H. (1995) *The Knowledge Creating Company*. Oxford University Press, Oxford.

Popper, K. R. (1965) *Conjectures and Refutations: The Growth of Scientific Knowledge*. Basic Books, New York.

Putnam, R. D. (1993) The Prosperous Community: Social Capital and Public Life. *American Prospect* 13: 35–42.

Putnam, R. D. (1995) Bowling Alone: America's Declining Social Capital. *Journal of Democracy* 6: 65–78.

Reed, M. J. (2001) Organization, Trust and Control: A Realist Analysis. *Organization Studies* 22(2): 201–28.

Ritzer, G. (2005) *The McDonaldization of Society*, 2nd edn. Pine Forge Press, Thousand Oaks, CA.

Scarbrough, H. & Swan, J. (2001) Explaining the Diffusion of Knowledge Management: The Role of Fashion. *British Journal of Management* 12: 3–12.

Selznick, P. (1957) *Leadership in Administration: A Sociological Interpretation*. Harper & Row, Evanston, IL.

Silverman, D. (1970) *The Theory of Organization*. Heinemann, London.

Sorge, A. (1991) Fit and the Societal Effect: Interpreting Cross-National Comparisons of Technology, Organization and Human Resources. *Organization Studies* 12: 161–90.

Stokes, J. & Clegg, S. R. (2002) Once Upon a Time in a Bureaucracy. *Organization* 9(2): 225–448.

Thompson, P. & Ackroyd, S. (1995) All Quiet on the Workplace Front? A Critique of Recent Trends in British Industrial Sociology. *Sociology* 59(4): 615–33.

Thompson, P. & Ackroyd, S. (1999) *Organizational Misbehaviour*. Sage, London.

Thompson, P. & Warhurst, C. (Eds.) (1998) *Workplaces of the Future*. Macmillan, London.

Turner, B. S. (1984) *The Body and Social Theory*. Blackwell, Oxford.

Whitley, R. (1994) The Internationalization of Firms and Markets: Its Significance and Institutional Structuring. *Organization* 1: 101–24.

Williams, K., Haslam, C., & Williams, J. (1992) Ford Versus "Fordism": The Beginning of Mass Production? *Work, Employment and Society* 6: 517–55.

management consultants

Robin Fincham

Interest in management consultants, in popular management media and academic study, has expanded enormously in the past decade, reflecting the growth of consultancy and increasing numbers of managers who experience working with consultants. The emergence of consulting as a growth industry has links with many modern conditions. Trends like the service economy, increasing "marketization" of sectors, and the development of new organizational and corporate structures have created huge demand for the expertise of "outsider" groups like consultants.

But as well as the economic significance of consulting, a range of cultural and symbolic factors has meant the management consultant has become a figure of special interest or even fascination. Consultants have been linked with sociological themes of "insidious power" that define modern corporate life. They are pictured as hidden persuaders and as possessing unaccountable influence (O'Shea & Madigan 1997; Pinault 2000). Consultants are also associated with the celebrity managers and "gurus" who shape current managerial thought and management "fashion" (Sahlin-Andersson & Engwall 2002a).

Producing a clear definition of management consultants is not easy. Traditional professions tend to be defined in terms of the expert knowledge they possess. Identifying the body of knowledge effectively solves most problems of definition – we know who is a member of the profession (those who have acquired that knowledge) and what the professional does (dispenses knowledge to clients and customers).

However, management consultants have no such accepted expertise. That is not to say they have no useful knowledge. But the activity of "consulting" is not characterized by the kind of well-defined, abstract knowledge that Abbott, for example, suggested lies at the heart of professional occupations.

Neither is consulting a discrete occupation or set of activities – it is a cluster of many occupations. A purist definition of management consulting might confine itself to that of the "advice giver," in the sense that to "consult" an outside expert means seeking advice about a particular managerial problem. Early models of consulting developed a view of the consultant as "professional helper" (Schein 1969; Argyris 1970). However, the modern consultant supplies much more than merely business "advice." Consultants offer a vast range of services in specialist areas like finance and information systems, as well as in core management areas such as strategy and decision-making.

Many of these problems of definition reflect the links between management consultancy and patterns of *change*. While typical professional occupations are defined by a degree of stability and continuity in their knowledge base, consultancy is characterized by the exact opposite. The continually changing nature of consultancy more or less defies attempts to define its boundaries and some unique set of tasks. No sooner does one settle on some notion of what constitutes consultancy than a raft of new activities, ideas, and techniques emerge that transform our view. Indeed, much of the current interest in management consulting is bound up with the significance of "change" in organizations and the manner in which consultants trade on this. Traditionally, the managerial task was often defined in terms of the uncertainties lying at the heart of management. Yet in recent times uncertainty, insecurity, and change have become the driving concepts of organizational life. Change at the level required in many organizations has meant increased dependence on outside expertise, while "change management" has become almost a specialist skill delegated to the outside expert.

The origins of management consulting can be traced to the "efficiency movements" in the US and subsequently Britain and Europe. These followed the early impact of F. W. Taylor

and the more studied and "theorized" approach to management he introduced. (Taylor, who pioneered so much else in management studies, can also be seen as the father of management consulting.) For many years consultancy developed not exactly as a cottage industry, but certainly relatively slowly through sectoral mergers and organic growth. New activities of strategy consulting and organizational development were added to industrial engineering, and a group of founding firms grew in size, employing often several hundreds of professional staff and steadily expanding overseas.

However, the 1980s brought a sharp discontinuity in this pattern. The global accounting firms, such as PriceWaterhouse Cooper, Ernst & Young, and Deloitte, moved into management consulting while much larger-scale activities such as systems implementation and change programs fed the new growth, and firms operated on an increasingly international scale. Now management consulting has to be seen as part of a powerful and dynamic business services industry that includes the global accounting and law firms and the IT/systems giants. In 1980, consulting revenues worldwide stood at around $3 billion, which grew to as much as $60 billion by 1999, reflecting the "double-digit growth" the industry was famous for in these years. Explosive growth has stuttered since the millennium, in common with other business services, but has steadied and was estimated at just under $125 billion in 2004 (Kennedy Information 2004).

In light of the above, Kipping (2002) argues that changes in the management consulting industry fit a series of "waves" of development. In each wave, new forms of competitive advantage emerge, while the preeminent consulting firms are those which capture the new areas of business. Thus, in the first scientific management wave, shopfloor efficiency and industrial engineering represented the central client interest. This gave way to a strategy and organization phase that focused on core decision-making issues, and in which famous firms like McKinsey, Booz Allen, and the Boston Group emerged. Finally, in the current phase, IT networks and enterprise-wide planning are the global standards of best practice, and huge systems firms like IBM and Capgemini have begun to dominate the consulting field.

This historical framework makes an important theoretical distinction: the shape of the consulting industry reflects its relationship to and dependence on the central problems and institutions of management, while the dynamics of the client–consultant relationship are the driving force behind change in global consulting.

In terms of approaches to the topic, a large consulting literature goes back certainly as far as the 1950s. Mostly concerned with defining effective consultant techniques, and often authored by consultants themselves, this has been seen as heavily prescriptive and lacking any independent view of consulting (Clark & Salaman 1995). More recently, an alternative literature has emerged with links to the wider field of critical studies of management knowledge. Rather than accept the functionalist assumption that clients must be receiving a valuable service (otherwise why would they pay huge fees to consultants, and why would the industry have grown so fast?), a number of more critical sociological themes have been explored. These have problematized the construction of management knowledge and how consultancy itself is achieved and legitimized.

Early seminal studies emphasized the uncertainties and ambiguity surrounding the consulting "service" and the room this gives the consultant to manage impressions. For example, Clark (1995) coupled this basic observation with a dramaturgical metaphor. The consultant was seen as a kind of performer who defines social reality for the client-as-audience; given the ambiguities of the consultant role, there is "scope to construct a reality which persuades clients that they have purchased a valuable and high quality service" (p. 18). Similarly, Starbuck (1992) argued that, because clients are unable to judge the quality of the advice or solution, they rely on "symbols of expertise" such as the consultant's reputation and use of impressive techniques. And Alvesson (1993) likewise stressed the ambiguous nature of knowledge-intensive work and consultancies as "systems of persuasion."

In this vein, the symbolic nature of consultancy work and, in particular, the *rhetorical* aspects of its discourse have also been explored. The persuasive nature of the ideas employed and solutions proposed are seen as meeting managerial needs for reassurance in an uncertain world. Themes of rationality and control, threats of failure allied with promises of success, and the achievement of transcendent managerial goals have all been detected in consultant discourse (e.g., Bloomfield & Danieli 1995; Kieser 1997; Jackson 1999).

However, the critical perspective is not without its own tensions, and others have argued that the emphasis on consultants' persuasive powers almost assumes them to be omnipotent, and managers dupes. Sturdy (1997), for example, has emphasized instead the interactive nature of the client–consultant relation and consultancy itself as an "insecure business." Also Fincham (1999) has suggested the client–consultant relation is a type of contingent market relation that depends on the corporate power and knowledge base of the client organization and consultancy.

A second broad theme of the critical approach involves the role of consultants in the dissemination of "fashionable" management ideas. In a sense, management consultants are a secondary element in this literature – the formation of new knowledge itself is the focus – but among the various agents of management fashion consultants are key figures. Notably, Abrahamson has stressed the role of "fashion setters" who "attempt to convince fashion followers that a management technique is both rational and at the forefront of managerial progress" (1996: 267). In this crowded marketplace, fashion setters compete in their efforts to convince managers and increase the potential of particular ideas to become mass fashions. Sahlin-Andersson and Engwall (2002a) have also stressed new forms of transient knowledge as increasingly dominant forces in corporate life. In the model these researchers develop, the "carriers" of knowledge are the intermediaries who specialize in ideas generation (consultants, gurus, journalists, academics) as well as high-profile managers. Any internal barriers in this "self-sustaining and self-enforcing system" (p. 7) blur into a central "field" of practice within which management knowledge is constructed and expanded.

In terms of methodological issues and future research directions, because the critical study of management consultants is not much more than a decade old, advances in methods and what remains to be done stand out fairly clearly. Early studies tended to be either modest empirically (e.g., limited interviews with consultants, or attendance at consultant "events") or they analyzed consultant ideas and rhetoric from documentary material (bestselling guru books were a favorite source). The reliance on relatively "easy" empirical sources reflected the difficulty of researching the client–consultant relationship and sensitivities about granting access to ongoing projects. In this sense, the current challenge for research is to focus on "live" relationships, as well as following through some of the themes mentioned above – defining the substantive nature of "consultant knowledge" and encapsulating the contingent and varied nature of consultancy work.

SEE ALSO: Change Management; Management; Management Education; Management Fashion; Management Theory; Professions, Organized

REFERENCES AND SUGGESTED READINGS

Abrahamson, E. (1996) Management Fashion. *Academy of Management Review* 21(1): 254–85.

Abrahamson, E. & Fairchild, G. (1999) Management Fashion: Lifecycles, Triggers, and Collective Learning Processes. *Administrative Science Quarterly* 44: 708–40.

Alvesson, M. (1993) Organizations as Rhetoric: Knowledge-Intensive Firms and the Struggle with Ambiguity. *Journal of Management Studies* 30(6): 997–1015.

Argyris, C. (1970) *Intervention Theory and Method.* Addison-Wesley, Reading, MA.

Bloomfield, B. & Danieli, A. (1995) The Role of Management Consultants in the Development of Information Technology: The Indissoluble Nature of Socio-Political and Technical Skills. *Journal of Management Studies* 32(1): 23–46.

Clark, T. (1995) *Management Consultants.* Open University Press, Buckingham.

Clark, T. & Fincham, R. (Eds.) (2002) *Critical Consulting: New Perspectives on the Management Advice Industry.* Blackwell, Oxford.

Clark, T. & Salaman, G. (1995) The Use of Metaphor in the Client–Consultant Relationship: A Study of Management Consultants. In: Oswick, C. & Grant, D. (Eds.), *Organization Development: Metaphorical Explorations.* Pitman, London, pp. 154–74.

Fincham, R. (1999) The Consultant–Client Relationship: Critical Perspectives on the Management of Organizational Change. *Journal of Management Studies* 36(3): 335–52.

Jackson, B. (1999) The Goose That Laid the Golden Egg? A Rhetorical Critique of Stephen Covey and the Effectiveness Movement. *Journal of Management Studies* 36(3): 353–78.

Kennedy Information (2004) The Global Consulting Marketplace 2004–2006. Online. www.kennedyinfo.com/mc/mcindex.html.

Kieser, A. (1997) Rhetoric and Myth in Management Fashion. *Organization* 4(1): 49–73.

Kipping, M. (2002) Trapped in Their Wave: The Evolution of Management Consultancies. In: Clark, T. & Fincham, R. (Eds.), *Critical Consulting: New Perspectives on the Management Advice Industry.* Blackwell, Oxford, pp. 28–49.

O'Shea, J. & Madigan, C. (1997) *Dangerous Company: The Consulting Powerhouses and the Businesses They Save and Ruin.* Nicholas Brealy, London.

Pinault, L. (2000) *Consulting Demons: Inside the Unscrupulous World of Global Corporate Consulting.* Harper Business, New York.

Sahlin-Andersson, K. & Engwall, L. (2002a) Carriers, Flows, and Sources of Management Knowledge. In: Sahlin-Andersson, K. & Engwall, L. (Eds.), *The Expansion of Management Knowledge.* Stanford University Press, Stanford, pp. 3–32.

Sahlin-Andersson, K. & Engwall, L. (Eds.) (2002b) *The Expansion of Management Knowledge.* Stanford University Press, Stanford.

Schein, E. H. (1969) *Process Consultation: Its Role in Organization Development.* Addison-Wesley, Reading, MA.

Starbuck, W. H. (1992) Learning by Knowledge-Intensive Firms. *Journal of Management Studies* 29(4): 713–40.

Sturdy, A. (1997) The Consultancy Process: An Insecure Business. *Journal of Management Studies* 34(3): 389–413.

management discourse

Carl Rhodes

Management discourse commonly refers to the institutionalized ways that the management and organization of work are understood through language. The term discourse suggests that the culturally embedded linguistic patterns that people use to speak and write about management influence the possibilities for management action and decision-making. Here words are not seen as being in opposition to action or practice, but rather it is through language that meaning is constructed and that the possibilities of practice emerge from that meaning. Studies of discourse examine how management knowledge develops in relation to the way that it is instantiated through particular uses of language in practice, and the way that such uses of language are informed by socially available and/or dominant ways of understanding.

While the explicit focus on management discourse emerged in the management and organization studies literature from the early 1990s, earlier attention to it can be traced back to ethnomethodological studies in the 1970s (e.g., Clegg 1975; Silverman & Jones 1976). Such studies sought to establish the relationship between the "language games" in organizations and the material conditions that were produced by the practices of management. The more recent growth of interest in management discourse can be attributed to two developments. The first is the economic and political changes associated with neoliberalism in the way that management is understood and practiced. The second is a more general shift in the social sciences through what is widely referred to as the "linguistic turn."

The growth in popularity of discourse emerged in response to social, political, and economic changes since the 1980s. In particular, the turn toward neoliberal forms of governance that privilege the market as the main means of regulating economic affairs is said to have had a broad influence on management toward an entrepreneurial and post-bureaucratic model. It has been argued that the forms of language used to talk about management have changed so as to privilege particular meanings, practices, and identities that are said to support contemporary capitalism. Management discourse is interested in understanding these changes. Key aspects of this discourse are said to be a focus on normative control, entrepreneurship, and the alignment of the interests of labor and capital as they are embodied in particular management practices such as human resource management, strategy, organizational culture management, and leadership. As Deetz (1992) suggests, management discourse turns attention to the manner in which

particular ways of understanding the world become naturalized such that their politics remains largely invisible. On this basis, management discourse is not just interested in what people say about management, but is focused on how those things that are said relate to the dominant ways of understanding and doing management.

With respect to the "linguistic turn," an increasing number of researchers and theorists have examined how language is related to historically and socially contextualized ways of understanding the world and how this is in turn related to the situated existence of individual people (Deetz 2003). This broad shift in methodological and theoretical focus brought issues of language and discourse more to the center stage of the study of society in general, and the study of management in particular. While this included direct extensions of the earlier ethnomethodological work (e.g., Boden 1994), discourse now takes on a broader set of interests focused not just on talk that goes on in organizations, but on the way that organizations are socially constructed through discourse (Grant et al. 2004).

It is noteworthy that the methods and theories associated with the term management discourse are very broad and potentially incommensurable. Differences in focus can range from studies of conversation, dialogue, narrative, stories, rhetoric, and tropes and can employ methodologies such as conversation analysis, speech act theory, interaction analysis, pragmatics, sociolinguistics, social semiotics, critical discourse analysis, critical theory, and deconstructionism (Grant et al. 2004). Despite this breadth, the most common threads that unite the differences in management and organizational discourse are a concern with power and identity; power in the sense that discourse creates regularities in organizational practice that create inequities, and identity in the sense that it is created and negotiated in relation to discourse (Iedema 2003). Each of these is reviewed below.

Given that management discourse is socially contextualized, it is possible to identify dominant discourses as they relate to particular historical periods. Barley and Kunda (1992) have identified five major discourses that have emerged and become widely diffused since the late nineteenth century. These are industrial betterment (1870–1900), scientific management (1900–23), welfare capitalism and human relations (1923–55), systems rationalism (1955–80), and organizational culture (1980–present). A key focus of studies in management discourse is on the most recent of these discourses as it relates to practices such as business process reengineering, organizational culture, and quality management. Commonly this is done as a means of developing a critique of management discourse as being beholden to contemporary market capitalism such that broader issues such as social responsibility, justice, and ethics are marginalized. This focus on management discourse problematizes the way that power is related to management as the established patterns of discourse are argued to influence what can and cannot be said about management and thus exert control about what is both included and excluded from managerial agendas. What is also highlighted, however, is that although particular discourses might be more dominant than others, in any organization there are a multiplicity of discourses at play and which vie for authority. Further, the practice of management can involve resistance to dominant discourses.

An important aspect of the growth of interest in contemporary management discourse is the way that it relates to the construction of what Gee et al. (1996) call a *new work order* – an ideal work culture characterized by collaboration, communication, trust, and openness as manifested in "visionary leadership" and "core values." Such discourse attempts to construct a life world for people at work that influences more and more aspects of their lives (Casey 1995). In such organizations, managerial control can be coupled with a discourse associated with teamwork, quality consciousness, flexibility, quality circles, and learning organizations, in order to bring together the aspirations of individual employees and the commercial objectives of corporations (Chan 2000). In such discourse, the archetypes for the late modern organizations run by such managers are ones where loyalty, favoritism, informality, and non-legality are emphasized over hierarchical compliance; technical training is replaced by loyalty, style, and organizational fit; fixed salaries are replaced by performance pay; and rules are replaced by discretionary behavior (Gephardt 1996).

The study of management discourse has also been concerned with the way that contemporary forms of organizational governance relate to the identity of workers. In this sense, discourse relates not just to talk about management, but also to the possibilities of what it means to be a particular type of person at work – be it a manager or worker. In this sense, discourse is taken to be the main way that people create their social reality at work and is studied in terms of how it frames their identity – it is both the expression and construction of what management and organization means (Mumby & Clair 1997). As du Gay (1994) points out, the range of management discourses that have held sway through the twentieth century – such as scientific management, human relations, and quality of working life – constructs the category of person known as the *manager* differently. In contemporary management discourse, du Gay (1996) argues that management privileges "enterprising selves" who should derive personal satisfaction and self-fulfillment from work while undertaking activities that support organizationally sanctioned goals such as profitability and competitiveness. In such a way, management discourse conflates the notions of being a better worker with that of being a better person.

The focus in management discourse of relating the identity of the worker to the achievement of organizational goals has also been associated with the idea of corporate culture. It has been that corporate culture programs see people at work being pressured to incorporate managerial discourses into narratives of self-identity (Alvesson & Willmott 2002: 622). In this sense identity is seen as an organizational and economic resource that can be manipulated in order to achieve organizationally sanctioned goals. Management discourse not only suggests what managers should do, but also contains exemplars of what types of people are most valued at work. Discourse thus enacts control by privileging and rewarding particular identity positions against which the conduct of real people can be judged (ten Bos & Rhodes 2003). By attending to these dominant identity positions, researchers can identify the identity pressures that people at work are subject to through discourse as well as examining the extent to which people capitulate to them or are resistant to them.

Although approaches to studying management discourse are broad and can differ from one another significantly, a key contribution has been a detailed consideration of the relationship between management practice and the organization of language. Given that, in managerial work, any form of "action" largely involves language and communication, this has enabled organization theory to understand and theorize the relations between discourse and management with a particular focus on power and identity.

SEE ALSO: Conversation Analysis; Culture, Organizations and; Discourse; Management; Management Fashion; Management Theory; Neoliberalism; Organization Theory

REFERENCES AND SUGGESTED READINGS

Alvesson, M. & Willmott, H. (2002) Identity Regulation as Organizational Control: Producing the Appropriate Individual. *Journal of Management Studies* 39(5): 619–44.

Barley, S. R. & Kunda, G. (1992) Design and Devotion: Surges of Rational and Normative Ideologies of Control in Managerial Discourse. *Administrative Science Quarterly* 37: 363–99.

Boden, D. (1994) *Organizations in Action: The Business of Talk.* Polity Press, Cambridge.

Casey, C. (1995) *Work, Self, and Society: After Industrialism.* Sage, London.

Chan, A. (2000) *Critically Constituting Organization.* John Benjamins, Amsterdam.

Clegg, S. R. (1975) *Power, Rule, and Domination: A Critical and Empirical Understanding of Power in Sociological Theory.* Routledge & Kegan Paul, London.

Deetz, S. (1992) *Democracy in the Age of Corporate Colonization: Developments in Communication and the Politics of Everyday Life.* SUNY Press, Albany.

Deetz, S. (2003) Reclaiming the Legacy of the Linguistic Turn. *Organization* 10(3): 421–9.

du Gay, P. (1994) Making Up Managers: Bureaucracy, Enterprise, and the Liberal Art of Separation. *British Journal of Sociology* 45(4): 655–74.

du Gay, P. (1996) *Consumption and Identity at Work.* Sage, London.

Gee, J. P., Hull, G., & Langshear, C. (1996) *The New Work Order: Behind the Language of the New Capitalism.* Allen & Unwin, St. Leonards.

Gephardt, R. P., Jr. (1996) Management, Social Issues, and the Postmodern Era. In: Boje, D. M., Gephardt, R. P., Jr., & Thatchenkery, T. J. (Eds.), *Postmodern Management and Organization Theory.* Sage, Thousand Oaks, CA.

Grant, D., Hardy, C., Oswick, C., & Putnam, L. (2004) Organizational Discourse: Exploring the Field. In: Grant, D., Hardy, C., Oswick, C., & Putnam, L. (Eds.), *The Sage Handbook of Organizational Discourse.* Sage, London, pp. 1–36.

Iedema, R. (2003) *Discourses of Post-Bureaucratic Organization.* Benjamins, Amsterdam.

Mumby, D. K. & Clair, R. (1997) Organizational Discourse. In: Van Dijk, T. A. (Ed.), *Discourse as Structure and Process*, Vol. 2. Sage, London.

Silverman, D. & Jones, J. (1976) *Organizational Work: The Language of Grading and the Grading of Language.* London: Collier Macmillan.

ten Bos, R. & Rhodes, C. (2003) The Game of Exemplarity: Subjectivity, Work, and the Impossible Politics of Purity. *Scandinavian Journal of Management* 19: 403–23.

management education

Andrew Sturdy

Something like 25 percent of US university students currently major in business or management, and in the UK, 30 percent of undergraduates study some management. Elsewhere, business and management education is expanding its scope. A Chinese government minister is said to have recently called for a million MBA (Master of Business Administration) graduates to help fuel the national economy. Such penetration and expansion in higher education systems and other educational domains have prompted considerable comment and sociological research activity. The latter has often come from outside sociology departments, in schools of management and education, for example. While a number of concerns reflect more general educational issues such as pedagogy, vocationalism, and the social role of the university or academy, key areas of attention and debate are focused around core sociological issues: globalization, commodification, and professionalization.

Typically, management education is associated with the activities of business and management schools, mostly within universities, and the hallmark qualification of the MBA and related executive education. Here, a whole range of topics is taught, mostly linked to management functions (e.g., personnel/human resource management; finance and accounting; marketing, strategy; production and operations), and often with their own relevant core disciplines (e.g., psychology, math, economics, engineering, and sociology). However, it is important to point out not only the management education of university students majoring in other subjects, but also the activities of other educational institutions, including semi-professional associations and schools, where management is a comparatively recent subject on the formal curriculum. In addition, the mass media serves as a conduit for management being "self-taught," especially through books written by so-called management gurus. Indeed, arguably, the latter are more influential than formal education, certainly in promoting particular approaches to managing people and organizations. Peters and Waterman's *In Search of Excellence*, for example, sold millions of copies worldwide.

Considerable attention has been given to the history, development, and geographical spread of management education, notably through the work of Robert Locke. As management emerged as a separate activity, elite, and ideology, it was initially aligned with engineering/scientific management (and accounting/finance) and then, following the Hawthorne studies, with a more "sociological" approach, human relations, as large organizations with extensive supervisory hierarchies emerged in the US. The latter development in particular is associated with the expansion of the early US business schools (e.g., Wharton and Harvard, both formed pre-World War I), although most expansion followed World War II. These schools were to fuel and symbolically represent an emerging cadre of formally educated managers and consultants, although numerically, most education was carried out in various colleges or trade schools and existing (e.g., accounting) and emerging (e.g., personnel) professional associations.

Formal management education in business schools remained largely concentrated in the US for some time, although US-based practices (e.g., the assembly line) were promoted in other ways. For example, the post-war economic growth of Germany and Japan occurred in the absence of comparable educational approaches and qualifications. However, this period, often in parallel with the Marshall Aid program and more general influence of US-based multinationals, saw the establishment of some US-style business schools in Western Europe (e.g., INSEAD in France and Manchester and London Business Schools in the UK). While educational institutions remained, and continue to be, largely distinctive, university-based management education and the MBA have both grown enormously outside the US in the last 20 years. In the UK, for example, there are over 100 business schools. Some of these, along with US and Australian schools especially, have actively recruited overseas students, especially from fast-growing Asian economies, where they have also set up or partnered campuses and qualifications. This development continues, accelerated by distance learning and, in particular, "e-learning," although increasingly, it is only a minority of mostly US institutions whose MBA carries significant prestige.

This geographical expansion of management education and its particular approach/content have been subjected to sociological critique over Americanization or neo-imperialism, if not globalization. Here, arguments vary between seeing the spread of the MBA and business schools as marking a standardization of management education or that cultural and institutional systems are more or less resilient to such developments, despite superficial appearances of increasing commonality. The latter position might point to examples of how management ideas, techniques, and educational media have been adapted to existing cultural practices and institutional conditions such as prevailing value systems or economic structures. At the same time, the nature of that standard as offering a largely positivist, managerialist, masculinist, and ethnocentric view of work and organizations has been critiqued from opposing positions.

The expansion of management education and its demand combined with a more neoliberal and managerial approach to education and its funding has also led to liberal and humanist critiques over the commodification of knowledge and qualifications. Here, at the extreme, education is seen as no longer for its own sake, or even to develop useful skills, but as an income generator for student and university alike. The MBA has become probably the most widely recognized, if not always valued, qualification which can readily transcend national and sector boundaries. Although not restricted to management, this has seen the reconstitution of students into consumers, with shifts in student–teacher relations and mixed outcomes for those involved and excluded. For example, although assessment of students clearly exposes the lie of "sovereign" consumer power, reliance on fee income means that staff teaching evaluations and the provision of executive facilities combined with the maintenance of the institutional "brand" and league table positions become "educational" imperatives. This shift has also seen the increasing involvement of corporations in management education, not as sponsors of students or research but as producers, outsourcers, and consumers. In particular, some companies are setting up their own "corporate universities" while others are commissioning tailor-made MBAs.

Such developments connect with longstanding debates over management education as an ideological or professional project and thence to issues of power/privilege, control, and exclusion. This is, of course, intimately connected to various perspectives on management knowledge. There are three main views. Firstly, management knowledge is a universally applicable and testable science where there is a "one best way" of managing which varies with circumstances or change, such as increasing complexity or organizational size. Secondly, management emerged as a way of appropriating workplace control from labor, most evidently through scientific management, in order to secure profit – managers as agents of capital. Management knowledge and education then continue to develop in order to counter the associated resistance to control. Thus, they serve an ideological purpose in justifying and explaining how work is managed and the fact that it is done so by a particular elite group. This relates to the third, institutional, view put forward by Shenav, who argues that it was neither efficiency nor control imperatives *alone* that account for the rise of management, but the activities of engineers, "a new class of salaried technocrats – wishing to carve out their own domain within industrial organizations" (1999: 9). This

observation points to the start of attempts to professionalize management and its functional specialisms through education which continues today.

As in other and sometimes related and competing fields such as accounting, a core element of professionalization is the establishment of a body of technical knowledge which is deemed as necessary and to which access is limited through the regulatory practices of an independent association such as examination. This is evident in the early activities of engineers to establish management as a scientific endeavor and to form various professional bodies. Likewise, human relations and subsequently, industrial psychology formed the basis of the "science" of people management and spawned associations such as the Institute of Personnel Management (now the Chartered Institute of Personnel and Development) in the UK. However, a core tension necessarily lies between the role and identities of managers as experts or employees/agents – cosmopolitans or locals. Overall, the power of employers has prevented the kind of professionalization which occurred in earlier eras in law and medicine, for example. Alongside this is the academic status of the knowledge and the role of universities and business schools. In the 1950s, for instance, the Ford and Carnegie Reports in the US called for business schools to become less like trade schools and more academic. This helped fuel the subsequent growth of mostly positivistic management research and journals, symbols of academic respectability, and a gradual, if still incomplete, acceptance of management within university departments. For example, it is only comparatively recently that the traditional academic institutions of Oxford and Cambridge universities in the UK have established mainstream business schools, although aspects of management have been part of engineering curricula for some time.

While it is probably only a minority of university management departments that aspire to an academic research-based identity or are resourced to do so, recent debates focus on the extent to which this may be under threat. There are a number of developments, in the West at least, which relate to the more enduring themes of the purpose and beneficiaries of education, universities, and management education. Firstly and following on from consumerist trends, there are calls from students, managerial commentators, employers, and government agencies for a more applied, practical, integrative, and less analytical, (sub)disciplinary and critical approach, what has come to be known as "mode 2" knowledge. The assumption here is that management education should simply provide techniques for managers to manage (i.e., management training), perhaps at the expense of more liberal and pluralistic concerns with reflection and inclusivity. However, some see the issue in terms of currently popular approaches to knowledge and learning as embedded in practice rather than in the classroom (e.g., Mintzberg's recent book, *Managers Not MBAs*).

Indeed, more generally, knowledge and learning have become partially displaced from formal educational spaces and seen as central to governmental and corporate policy for improved competitiveness – the knowledge economy and learning organizations, for example. Moreover, given rhetorical claims made about the relative pace of organizational and social change, such knowledge is regarded as being in flux. In the context of management, emphasis is placed on increasingly dominant discourses of leadership, entrepreneurship, innovation, and continuous learning as opposed to learning a core and relatively stable body of knowledge, conceptual frameworks, and models. Indeed, and further challenging the traditional professional project of rendering knowledge specialist, abstract, and exclusive/excluding, management discourse is permeating different realms of people's "private" lives such as personal health and relationships. This does not so much democratize management, in terms of access to positions of privilege, as normalize it as a largely rationalist and instrumental orientation to the world. Such insights emerge from another, contrasting, and less audible source of critique of contemporary management education, that of "critical management studies," which draws on diverse critical social theories such as Marxism, feminism, postmodernism, postcolonialism, and queer theory. Together, although largely marginal(ized) from mainstream research, this points to the centrality of power, inequality, and exclusion within the practice and pedagogy of management education, its institutions and effects.

Management education research is not, of course, an exclusively sociological domain. In terms of everyday educational practice, it remains dominated by largely depoliticized (social) psychological concerns with learning. Both here and in more sociological studies, emphasis remains close to home, on the university, business school, and related institutions. Other educational spaces are largely lost within technicist concerns over training effectiveness or broader non-management-specific educational issues. While institutional approaches sometimes point to a variety of (e.g., national) structures and locations of management education and its elites, there is considerable scope for extending research to other domains and actors, not least because of the broad reach of management discourse and formal education. Here, traditional sociological concerns with school education and social structure might be reexplored as well as relatively new fields such as educational media corporations and industries. Finally, most management education research is written from the perspectives of western management academics. This might be usefully complemented by the voices of other (e.g., educational) sociologists and those from different geographical spaces and management traditions.

SEE ALSO: Democracy and Organizations; Education and Economy; Labor Process; Management; Management Consultants; Management Discourse; Management History

REFERENCES AND SUGGESTED READINGS

Engwall, L. & Zamagni, V. (Eds.) (1998) *Management Education in Historical Perspective*. Manchester University Press, Manchester.

French, R. & Grey, C. (1996) *Rethinking Management Education*. Sage, London.

Locke, R. (1984) *Management and Higher Education Since 1940*. Cambridge University Press, Cambridge.

Pollard, S. (1965) *The Genesis of Modern Management*. Penguin, Harmondsworth.

Shenav, Y. (1999) *Manufacturing Rationality*. Oxford University Press, Oxford.

Whitley, R., Thomas, A., & Marceau, J. (1981) *MBAs: The Making of a New Elite?* Tavistock, London.

management fashion

Chris Carter and Stewart Clegg

One of the striking features of the organizational world in the last 30 years has been the rise and fall of a dazzling array of management initiatives. Typically originating in the US, such ideas have spread across the industrialized world (Czarniawska & Sevon 1996). The raft of initiatives includes Total Quality Management (TQM), Business Process Re-Engineering (BPR), Culture Change, the Learning Organization, Knowledge Management (KM), Shareholder Value (SHV), and Enterprise Resource Planning (ERP). Of course, at least since the advent of Taylorism there have been management initiatives that have been widely appropriated. A key difference between earlier diffusions and now is the emergence of a powerful actor-network that actively packages and commodifies management initiatives as products based on a 3–5 year life cycle.

Wilson (1992) noted the emergence of a phenomenon he termed "programmed change initiatives," which were management change initiatives that styled themselves as being portable across sectors and nations. In a sense it was a return to Taylorist notions of the "One Best Way," as such initiatives were deemed by their promoters as constituting superior modes of organizing. Similarly, Pascale demonstrated there has been an exponential take-off in management initiatives from the 1980s onwards and more recent analyses have highlighted that this has continued unabated (Kieser 1997; Swan & Scarbrough 2001). This has given rise to a body of literature that seeks to understand such initiatives as management fashions, defined as "a relatively transitory collective belief, disseminated by management knowledge entrepreneurs, that a management technique leads to rational management progress" (Abrahamson & Eisenman, 2001).

Much of the literature on fashion owes a heavy debt to new institutional theory, the difference being that in most cases the fashions prove ephemeral rather than enduring. The key theorist of management fashion from a new institutional perspective is Abrahamson, who has penned a number of pathbreaking articles (Abrahamson 1991, 1996; Abrahamson & Fairchild 1999). His chief contribution has been to theorize the management ideas industry and its role in producing fashion. His central argument is that a loose coalition of "world-class companies," management gurus, business schools, large consultancies, and IT firms constitutes the supply-side of an industry that produces and commodifies fashions. Taken together, this amounts to an actor-network that has successfully packaged and commoditized managerial initiatives. These models of "best practice" have been disseminated throughout the organizational world. We argue that this has been profoundly important in terms of creating blueprints of what organizations "should" look like. Collectively, the key players of the management ideas industry have helped produce management fashions.

Little is left to chance by this industry, with ideas being carefully market researched to find whether they resonant with managerial anxieties of the zeitgeist. A management fashion – new ideas or in some cases old ideas that have been rediscovered – contains both an aesthetic and a technical dimension. The aesthetic dimension makes a robust argument in an "attempt to convince fashion followers that a management technique is both rational and at the forefront of managerial progress" (Abrahamson 1996). The new technique will be backed up by war stories that confirm its effectiveness and statistics demonstrating its worth to the organization. The careful image-intensive styling and well-crafted success stories and plausible philosophical rationale for the adoption of such a technique constitute a rhetoric-intensive manifesto of action for organizations. The technical dimension of a fashion includes a number of tools and techniques that can be used to perform a particular initiative. For TQM this included brainstorming, process mapping techniques, cause and effect diagrams, and so forth. The overarching characteristic of an initiative is that it is imperative for the success and indeed survival of the organization. A management fashion often exhibits considerable ambiguity. This lack of clarity makes it more portable across a range of different organizational contexts. For instance, for some organizations Total Quality Management came to be about developmental cultural change, while for others it was about stringent statistical checks on a range of processes.

Abrahamson argues that a fashion is likely to exhibit a bell-shaped demand curve. Such management initiatives have typically followed the life cycle of a fashion, moving from being "haute couture" and the preserve of exclusive pioneers through to being "pret a porter" (Mazza & Alvarez 2000) where the initiative has achieved mass-market penetration before gradually disappearing. Abrahamson & Rosenkopf (1993) analyze "bandwagon effects," which are diffusion processes whereby an adopter takes on an innovation simply because of the sheer number of adoptions that have already taken place. In a further development of fashion theory, Abrahamson & Fairchild (1999) propose an "evolutionary theory of institutions," focused on the population level, which puts forward stages of variation, selection, and retention, or alternatively, rejection. Bandwagon effects can create self-reinforcing loops in that legitimating effects are due to the *number* of adopters.

Abrahamsonesque-style research identifies management fashion by conducting bibliometric analyses of trade journals and the like. The number of articles on an initiative is taken as a proxy for the supposed popularity of a management fashion. This research has an undoubted capacity to illuminate broad trends as to which management ideas are in vogue at any given time through their citation or non-citation. Such an approach is, however, limited, especially through its inveterate capacity to suppress an account of the *actual means* through which managers actually consume such ideas. As Jackson (2001: 14) notes: "It is clear that a direct link cannot be made between the number of citations of a particular program and its take-up by organizations and managers."

The lack of analysis of the means through which managers consume fashion is a gap in the current literature. Much of the current research into management fashion is negative in its coverage, taking an ascetic view that fashion is trivial. Crzaniawska (2006) notes "fashion has been portrayed as an irrational deviation from rational management behavior, as indicated by the frequent repetition of the alliteration 'fads and fashions'." If being at the vanguard of fashion is regarded positively in the world of fashion proper, what justifies a negative view of managers following fashion? This is a point that Czarniawska & Sevon (2006) have made, arguing for a more positive interpretation of fashion: "Fashion is one of the ways of introducing order and uniformity into what might seem like an overwhelming variety of possibilities. In this sense, fashion helps to come to grips with the present." Czarniawska suggests the concept of translation as an alternative to the dominant models of diffusion. This conceptualization emphasizes the mutually constitutive relationship between the "fashion" and the organization (i.e., the fashion may well change aspects of the organization, but in turn the organization changes the fashion).

Management is first and foremost a discourse. It is one that is, as ten Bos (2000) argues, oriented to the ideal that modern rationality can achieve the utopia that figures in management's fallacies. Managerialist fashions have become commonplace in recent years. Given the powerful industry that has emerged to create and disseminate such ideas, this is likely to continue in the future. It is also likely that the management fashions will, in addition to the private sector, increasingly become a part of the government and NGO world. As an academic agenda, it is noteworthy that little use has been made of the rich resources of cultural studies to understand management fashion. Some management academics have called for a more interventionist approach through direct engagement in the management fashion-making process.

Fashions are instances of "blackboxed" (Latour 1987) knowledge which, while usually American in origin, are footloose and sufficiently ambiguous that they can traverse sectors and nations. As part of their pressure for capital accumulation, actors within the management ideas industry are constantly seeking the next initiative that will sell well. The search for discontinuous innovation – necessary to maintain the portfolio of new products for a market that quickly tires of the same old recipes – involves careful market research into managerial anxieties and organizational issues. Thought leaders scan the management journals for ideas and potential gurus that can be translated into profitable business. Successful fashion innovators possess sufficient *habitus* to be able to construct managerial initiatives that capture the corporate zeitgeist.

SEE ALSO: Institutional Theory, New; Knowledge Management; Management; Management Consultants; Management History; Management Improvisation; Management Innovation; Management Theory

REFERENCES AND SUGGESTED READINGS

Abrahamson, E. (1991) Managerial Fads and Fashions: The Diffusion and Rejection of Innovations. *Academy of Management Review* 16(3): 586–612.

Abrahamson, E. (1996) Management Fashion. *Academy of Management Review* 21: 254–85.

Abrahamson, E. & Eisenman, M. (2001) Why Management Scholars Must Intervene Strategically in the Management Knowledge Market. *Human Relations* 54(1): 67–75.

Abrahamson, E. & Fairchild, G. (1999) Management Fashion: Lifecycles, Triggers, and Collective Learning Processes. *Administrative Science Quarterly* 44: 708–40.

Abrahamson, E. & Fairchild, G. (2000) Who Launches Management Fashions? Gurus, Journalists, Technicians or Scholars? In: Schoonhoven, C. B. & Romanelli, E. (Eds.), *The Entrepreneurship Dynamic in Industry Evolution*. Stanford University Press, Stanford.

Abrahamson, E. & Rosenkopf, L. (1993) Institutional and Competitive Bandwagons. *Academy of Management Review* 18: 487–517.

Crzarniawska, B. (2006) Fashion in Organizing. In: Czarniawska, B. & Sevon, G. (Eds.), *Global Ideas*. Copenhagen Business School Press, Copehagen, pp. 129–46.

Czarniawska, B. & Sevon, G. (Eds.) (1996) *Translating Organizational Change*. Du Gruyter, Berlin.

Czarniawska, B. & Sevon, G. (Eds.) (2006) *Global Ideas*. Copenhagen Business School Press, Copehagen.

Jackson, B. (2001) *Management Gurus and Management Fashions*. Routledge, London.

Kieser, A. (1997) Rhetoric and Myth in Management Fashion. *Organization* 4: 49–74.

Latour, B. (1987) *Science in Action: How to Follow Scientists and Engineers Through Society*. Harvard University Press, Cambridge, MA.

Mazza, C. & Alvarez, J. (2000) Haute Couture and Pret a Porter: The Popular Press and the Diffusion of Management Prectices. *Organization Studies* 21: 567–88.

Swan, J. & Scarbrough, H. (2001) Explaining the Diffusion of Knowledge Management: The Role of Fashion. *British Journal of Management* 12: 3–12.

ten Bos, R. (2000) *Fashion and Utopia in Management Thinking*. John Benjamins, Amsterdam.

Wilson, D. C. (1992) *A Strategy of Change*. London, Routledge.

management history

Charles Booth

Management history is a scholarly endeavor which concerns itself with the investigation of the development of management thought and of managerial practice. It therefore sits in sympathetic (in principle) but uneasy (in reality) relationship with contiguous and overlapping fields such as business history, economic history, accounting history, the history of economics, and marketing history, among others. There is no satisfactory or broadly accepted statement of these fields' domain boundaries, and any treatment is necessarily idiosyncratic.

In contrast to related fields in business and economic history (and so on), management history is relatively sparsely served by scholarly associations and publication outlets. The Academy of Management established a Division of Management History in 1971 (later and currently the Management History Division), but this remains one of the smallest groupings in that institution. No domain-specific journals existed until 1994, with the establishment of the *Journal of Management History* (*JMH*). This was merged with *Management Decision* in 2001 and became a subsection of that journal – itself not at all historical in orientation – with the title "Focus on Management History." However, prospects for the field seem to be improving in this respect, with the demerger and relaunching of *JMH* currently planned, and a new journal, *Management and Organizational History*, scheduled for first publication in 2006.

Within the field, it has become commonplace to identify six different approaches to management history, some of which are in practice complementary. All offer strengths and weaknesses which are probably self-explanatory. These approaches are: (1) a stages approach, whereby the historian focuses on a particular historical era to investigate the evolution of management thought and practice within a specific temporal frame; (2) a schools approach, in which different historical approaches to management and managing are grouped and differentiated from one another, and their evolution traced; (3) an institutional approach, which analyzes the emergence and development of particular economic institutions (some commentators would see this as the specific domain of business history, however); (4) a biographical approach, which focuses on the contribution of individuals to the development of management thought and practice; (5) a revolutionary approach, in which researchers identify and investigate innovative ruptures and discontinuities in management practices; and (6) an evolutionary approach, which seeks instead to trace continuities and developments unfolding over time.

Unsurprisingly, the field has struggled to establish itself and prosper within the broader management research and teaching discipline. In part this has been due to the relentlessly universalist and presentist nature of a discipline which has been characterized as lacking a memory and a sense of its own history, or indeed of its own geography. Advantages claimed for a historical perspective in this context include a developed appreciation of current organizational practices, behaviors, and structures as culturally, spatially, and temporally specific. This appreciation, in principle, mitigates against the acceptance and perpetuation of deterministic theories of human and organizational behavior (and so on), as well as that of teleological accounts of theoretical and empirical "progress" in knowledge production.

Management history has, however, been characterized as suffering from methodological problems which may also have contributed to its relative stagnation as a scholarly field. While not particularly attracting the criticism of inveterate empiricism leveled at business history, management history has not noticeably engaged to any extent (unlike the so-called "new accounting history," for example) with recent developments in historiography or in the philosophy of social science. Secondly, with its emphasis on the development of American (and to a lesser extent British) management thought and practice, management history shares with the discipline

of management studies itself an Anglocentric focus and attitude. Thirdly, possibly as a reaction to implied critiques of irrelevance by the mainstream, the field has in practice moved to reorient itself within a presentist metanarrative. When the Management History Division reviewed its domain statement in 2000, for example, much greater emphasis was placed on the pragmatic application of historical lessons for current theory and practice. Arguably, this move offered up to critics of the field a negation of the very advantages that a historical perspective was said to bring.

Ironically, the greatest legacy of a historical approach to management scholarship is arguably one in which management historians are no longer particularly involved. Harvard Business School, established in 1908, placed an early emphasis on economic and business history in its taught programs, and scholars associated with Harvard were instrumental in the establishment of various scholarly associations and publications in the US business history field, broadly conceived. The development of the historical case study, at Harvard and elsewhere, placed historical exemplars at the heart of business and management pedagogy. The continuing success of this pedagogical technology is attested to by its rapid extension into almost every area of the management curriculum, and the development of case publication into a multimillion-dollar industry. However, although case studies remain a definitive educational technology within the management discipline, they are no longer particularly associated with a historical orientation toward management education and research, or with historical scholarship.

Management history faces different possible futures. The worst potential case is the sclerotic stagnation of the field, accompanied by continuing marginalization within the management and organization studies academy. More positively, the emergence of new publication outlets offers new possibilities for invigorating management history scholarship. The development of the new accounting history in the early 1990s, with its theoretical and methodological realignments, offers a possible exemplar. Closer connection to perspectives in organization studies which explore organizational processes through longitudinal perspectives, as well as to potentially sympathetic developments in business history such as an emerging focus on culture, offer fruitful areas for development. The emergence of a potential "historical turn" in organization studies, remarked on by some commentators, provides further opportunities for reinvigoration of the field.

SEE ALSO: Culture, Organizations and; Management; Management Discourse; Management Education; Management Theory; Organization Theory

REFERENCES AND SUGGESTED READINGS

Brech, E. F. L. (2002) *The Evolution of Modern Management*, 5 vols. Thoemmes Press, Bristol.

Clark, P. & Rowlinson, M. (2004) The Treatment of History in Organization Studies: Towards an "Historic Turn"? *Business History* 46: 331–52.

Kieser, A. (1994) Why Organization Theory Needs Historical Analyses – and How This Should Be Performed. *Organization Science* 5: 608–20.

Pugh, D. S. (Series Ed.) (1995–2003) *History of Management Thought*, 17 vols. Ashgate, Aldershot.

Thomson, A. (2001) The Case for Management History. *Accounting, Business, and Financial History* 11: 99–115.

Van Fleet, D. D. & Wren, D. A. (2005) Teaching History in Business Schools: 1982–2003. *Academy of Management Learning and Education* 4: 44–56.

Witzel, M. (2001) *Biographical Dictionary of Management*, 2 vols. Thoemmes Press, Bristol.

Wren, D. A. (2005) *The History of Management Thought*, 5th edn. Wiley, Hoboken, NJ.

management improvisation

Miguel Pina e Cunha

Management improvisation can be defined as the conception of action as it unfolds in an organizational context, drawing on the available material, cognitive, affective, and social resources. It is an individual practice which takes place in light of concrete circumstances. People improvise to solve practical problems which emerge as a result of specific and unplanned circumstances. In this sense, improvisation can be neither managed nor controlled. To improvise or not to improvise is an individual prerogative, resulting from the interaction between the person and his or her circumstances. That is why organizations are not able to manage or to control improvisation. All they can do is to nurture or facilitate it.

Improvisation was a neglected concept until the 1990s, when it started to attract the regular attention of a group of scholars. The reasons for the initial neglect and the recent surge of interest can be attributed to the dominant management paradigms. Under the classical mechanistic approach, organizations were viewed as objects of planning and stable design. They were expected to work in a systematic and predictable manner. In this representation of the organizational world, there was no space for improvisation. Improvising in a machine-like organization is not only unnecessary but also dangerous: improvising individuals could damage the smooth functioning of the organization. In such a context, improvisation can be taken as a demonstration of a planning failure. The description of business environments as hypercompetitive, high speed, and fast changing, however, stimulated scholarly attention for processes that could lead to survival and advantage in markets that required more than mechanical routines and a focus on efficiency.

It was in this context of fast change and unpredictability that the interest in improvisation flourished. Several seminal texts prepared the ground for the study of the theme, but widespread attention resulted mainly from the almost simultaneous edition of a 1998 special issue of *Organization Science* on organizational improvisation, of Hatch's (1999) paper on the jazz metaphor, Crossan et al.'s (1996) exploration of how planning meets improvisation, Brown and Eisenhardt's (1998) discussion of improvisation in semi-structured organizations, and last but not least, Weick's work on the role of improvisation in the process of organizing (e.g., Weick 1993, 1998; Weick & Sutcliffe 2001). Karl E. Weick can be regarded as the author who most consistently fertilized the soil for the 1990s momentum. He discussed the aesthetics of imperfection in orchestras and organizations, pointed out the need to find a space for improvisation in mindful organizing, used jazz as a mindset for organizing, and explored the role of minimal structuring as a source of both freedom and coordination/control. These efforts subsequently led to works of synthesis such as those of Cunha et al. (1999), who reviewed the literature on improvisation, and Kamoche et al. (2001), who compiled some of the central articles on the topic.

From a marginal and minor field, improvisation evolved to become a regular presence in the organizational vocabulary. Theories of practice, such as those developed by Giddens (1986), Bourdieu (1990), and Certeau (1988), have helped to reinforce the interest and legitimacy of improvisation not only as a topic of research but also as a framework for explaining social experience. Mentions of improvisation have appeared in discussions of a variety of topics such as planning, dynamic capabilities, strategizing, learning, and so forth. The evolution of research on the topic reflects this renewed and consequential interest. Theoretical explorations of the concept and its relevance, often at a metaphorical level and relating it with theater and jazz music, came to be complemented with empirical work in such processes as new product development, cross-cultural virtual teams, medical teams, and crisis management, for example. This combination between the theoretical understanding of improvisation and its relationship with the arts and the development of empirical work possibly reflects the three major approaches to improvisation: (1) as an intriguing metaphor for organizing; (2) as a possibility for managing the unexpected and the exceptional; and (3) as a normal, everyday organizational practice. The first approach underpins the research exploring the jazz and theatrical metaphors. The second is found in papers dealing with improvisation as a complement or a substitute of planning, namely under crisis situations. The third appears in the research dealing with contexts where traditional planning is useless or undesirable (e.g., high speed) or where, due to historical and sociocultural reasons, people reveal an attraction for improvisational practice – something which seems to happen, for example, in the southern Latin European nations (Aram & Walochik 1996; Cunha 2005).

From the definition, one can easily devise the major dimensions of organizational improvisation. Improvisation has to do mainly with:

(1) impromptu action in an organizational context and (2) bricolage, or the ability to draw on the available material, cognitive, affective, and social resources in order to solve the problem at hand.

Regarding the first dimension, impromptu action, people improvise because they have no routine to tackle a certain issue and because action is required, not optional. In some circumstances, even when faced with a sudden problem, people may decide not to react. This absence of action may suit the situation but does not correspond to improvisation. There is no improvisation without action. If someone decides not to act in the face of a given problem, he or she is not improvising. Hence the description of improvisation as impromptu action. It is in this sense that, in improvisation, planning and execution converge in time (Moorman & Miner 1998). People build their plan of action while going along, in face of practical problems, not in anticipation to imagined opportunities or threats. This effort of tackling problems does not occur, however, in a void. Improvisers rely on a minimal structure comprised of such elements as goals, deadlines, and responsibilities. These elements provide the means for coordinating action without constraining it.

Due to its inseparability from the context where it originates, improvisation must be viewed as situated practice. This situatedness poses a series of relevant methodological as well as practical questions. The latter have to do with the impossibility of prescribing how people can improvise to cope with a given issue. Practice is inseparable from the context, which means that it is not reducible to a set of general and situation-free principles and that it must instead be built by people embedded in a given situation.

Bricolage constitutes the second major dimension of improvisation. Due to the urgency of action in improvisational contexts, people need to act with the resources they have, not with those that would best fit their needs. Bricolage refers to the capacity to make do with the available materials. Confronted with the need to solve problems, people may have to use the available materials instead of triggering a process of resource allocation. Bricolage is facilitated by the ingenious use of intimately known materials. It is a key dimension of improvisation because impromptu action requires people to act fast, not to engage in a search for the best resources.

Bricoleurs use material, cognitive, affective, and social resources:

- They improvise with the material resources they have. A soft drink may be used to increase the stickiness of a *passerelle* during a fashion show.
- They use their present cognitive resources, including knowledge and memory. Cognitive styles, such as being an innovator instead of an adaptor, may facilitate creative uses of resources. Cognition involved in improvisation is also related to tacit knowledge and intuition: due to the practical, often non-codified knowledge involved in improvisation, intuition is often presented as a defining aspect of improvisation.
- They use their affective resources. Bricolage and improvisation may produce feelings of competence and flow, thus enhancing the meaning of the work to those executing it. If goals are clear, feedback is immediate, and the level of challenge matches individual skills, people will deeply engage in improvisational action, with psychologically rewarding results. Other emotional processes are involved in the improvisational process. When people internalize the importance of the goals and deadlines making the minimal structure, these may not only be a contextual factor but also a source of emotional involvement with the task, facilitating the propensity to improvise by means of an intense emotional link with the job at hand.
- Finally, bricoleurs draw on the existing social resources. They rely on those people with whom they already have some kind of relationship, regardless of these interlocutors' skills to the task. Baker et al.'s (2003) research with entrepreneurs shows how these businesspeople were constrained by their existing social networks. In fact, they made use of their networks with purposes different from those initially expected – for example, recruiting students to managerial positions to which they were not suited, because they knew them.

Analysis of the improvisational process at the organizational level would stress the relevance of other dimensions, such as organizational culture and control, power, and routines. These aspects are unequivocally important but they will not be addressed here, because they have more to do with the context where improvisation occurs than with improvisation itself.

Due to its practical, situated, and ephemeral nature, improvisation is not easy to study. It cannot be fully captured by inviting people to fill in a questionnaire asking them how much they have improvised or have relied on well-defined plans or routines. It should not be approached ex post facto, because people will possibly engage in a process of retrospective justification, reducing surprises and giving an appearance of predictability to a process which may not have been as predictable. Hence, methodologically, improvisation confronts researchers with some pertinent issues: how can we study a process involving action rather than attitudes or cognitive evaluation; a process which is ephemeral and unpredictable? How can researchers study something they do not know where and when to look for in advance? Improvisation, therefore, confronts scholars with the limitations of traditional research methods in dealing with dynamic processes rather than with discrete variables. Despite the difficulties raised by the topic, researchers are using several methods and techniques, including observational methods, ethnographic approaches, grounded theorizing, interviewing, critical incidents, case studies, and the traditional quantitative surveys. Initial attempts to uncover the improvisational process in organizations have mainly adopted qualitative, non-obtrusive research methods. Whether this preference is due to the nature of the subject itself, or whether it results from the stage of research on improvisation (leading to a preference for theory building rather than for theory testing) is something that only time will tell.

Being in its infancy as a scientific topic, the future of improvisation research is wide open. It may be further approached at the individual, group, and organizational levels. At the micro level, improvisation may be studied from a psychological perspective. Researchers may ask what individual characteristics (e.g., self-efficacy, locus of control) facilitate the willingness to improvise. Or they may compare groups of people in terms of their predisposition and proficiency in improvising (e.g., is improvisation more likely in experts or novices?). At the group level, team dynamics and demography may be influential. The same may be valid for leader behavior. Leaders favoring action orientation and autonomy may induce in members of their teams a pro-improvisation bias. At the organizational level, organizational strategy, structure, and culture may be relevant influences. Not much is known about the influence of the organizational context on the practice of organizational improvisation. In bureaucratic organizations, one may hypothesize that people will rely on the hierarchy rather than on improvisation as a guide for action. It is admissible, however, that due precisely to the limitations imposed by the organization's structure, employees will act in an improvised fashion in order to counter structural inertia.

Despite the prevalence of the image of organizational change as resulting from planned efforts managed by top management, some authors are suggesting that organizations may change as the result of the accumulation of minor changes introduced throughout the organization by people lacking the option of strategic choice (Orlikowski 1996; Lanzara 1998). This line of research suggests that improvisation should be addressed both as an individual practice and as a systemic property of organizations. This double perspective suggests that, rather than being a negligible aspect of organizational life, improvisation can be equally relevant for individuals and their organizations.

SEE ALSO: Complexity and Emergence; Management Innovation; Management Theory; Organization Theory; Organizational Contingencies

REFERENCES AND SUGGESTED READINGS

Aram, J. D. & Walochik, K. (1996) Improvisation and the Spanish Manager. *International Studies of Management and Organization* 26: 73–89.

Baker, T., Miner, A. S., & Eesley, D. T. (2003) Improvising Firms: Bricolage, Account Giving, and Improvisational Competencies in the Founding Process. *Research Policy* 32: 255–76.

Bourdieu, P. (1990) *The Logic of Practice*. Stanford University Press, Stanford.

Brown, S. L. & Eisenhardt, K. M. (1998) *Competing on the Edge: Strategy as Structured Chaos*. Harvard Business School Press, Boston.

Certeau, M. de (1988) *The Practice of Everyday Life*. University of California Press, Berkeley.

Crossan, M. M., White, R. E., Lane, H., & Klus, L. (1996) The Improvising Organization: Where Planning Meets Opportunity. *Organizational Dynamics* 24(4): 20–35.

Cunha, M. P. (2005) Adapting or Adopting? The Tension Between Local and International Mindsets in Portuguese Management. *Journal of World Business*.

Cunha, M. P., Cunha, J. V., & Kamoche, K. (1999) Organizational Improvisation: What, When, How, and Why. *International Journal of Management Reviews* 1: 299–341.

Giddens, A. (1986) *The Constitution of Society: An Outline of the Theory of Structuration*. University of California Press, Berkeley.

Hatch, M. J. (1999) Exploring the Empty Spaces of Organizing: How Improvisational Jazz Helps Redescribe Organizational Structure. *Organization Studies* 20: 75–100.

Kamoche, K., Cunha, M. P., & Cunha, J. V. (Eds.) (2001) *Organizational Improvisation*. Routledge, London.

Lanzara, G. F. (1998) Self-Destructive Processes in Institution Building and Some Modest Countervailing Mechanisms. *European Journal of Political Research* 33: 1–39.

Moorman, C. & Miner, A. (1998) The Convergence Between Planning and Execution: Improvisation in New Product Development. *Journal of Marketing* 62: 1–20.

Orlikowski, W. J. (1996) Improvising Organizational Transformation Over Time: A Situated Change Perspective. *Information Systems Research* 7(1): 63–92.

Weick, K. E. (1993) The Collapse of Sensemaking in Organizations: The Mann Gulch Disaster. *Administrative Science Quarterly* 38: 628–52.

Weick, K. E. (1998) Improvisation as a Mindset for Organizational Analysis. *Organization Science* 9: 543–55.

Weick, K. E. & Sutcliffe, K. M. (2001) *Managing the Unexpected*. Jossey Bass, San Francisco.

management innovation

Peter Clark

Innovation refers to the processes of replacing past lifestyles, products, services, knowledge, and forms of managing by a variation which is different. The difference ranges from small and incremental to radical and discontinuous. Typically, innovations have been equated with entities and artifacts which can be readily seen and touched. These innovations, however, are embodiments of vast investments in forms of knowledge and ways of organizing (Clark 2003). The role of management in the innovation process and of how the organization of management affects the pace and directions of innovation remained largely unexplored until about 50 years ago. Forms of managing and organizing are innovations which are so taken for granted that their significance might be overlooked. Organizations, especially large-scale corporations, are the pivotal arena within which invention and innovation are orchestrated. The earlier focus upon artifacts has shifted to the examination of the roles that management do and can play in orchestrating innovation.

The analysis of management innovation is noted for its bold attempts at synthesis and for increasing critiques of the pro-innovation bias (Clark 2003). Consequently, the reader is assailed by seductive narratives of how all managers can orchestrate innovations. However, published data routinely list failures in the public and private sectors. Equally, there has been a misleading focus upon the ease of transferring innovations which have been successful in one geographical context (e.g., Silicon Valley, US) to other nations. The many successful examples, especially of the transfer of services like fast food, exemplify extraordinary managerial achievements even when the consumable outcome is regarded as unwelcome. Typically, the transfer of innovations between nations results in hybrids (Clark 2003). Thus American football emerged in the 1870s from the playing of indigenous winter ball games and from the importing of two British sports: running and handling the ball (rugby) and kicking the ball (soccer). In a similar way, recent Japanese innovations have resulted in many hybrids following their transfer (Abo 1994). The core problem for management innovations is in improving our understanding of what is possible and how those possibilities can be actualized in specific contexts.

In the 1960s there was a modernist focus upon creating universal theories with a strong "can do" tendency. Consequently, important contextual details were minimized and then stripped out. Then, with the rise of Japanese innovation-led exports into America and Western Europe, there has been a strong growth of interest in how the domestic context might shape the degrees of freedom for management innovation. Even so, the strongest tendency is the creation of pro-innovation recipes. This should be resisted.

THE PRO-INNOVATION BIAS

There are very few published studies of failure, yet two-thirds or more of all attempts at innovation fail (Clark 2003). The pro-innovation bias is a discourse saying that innovations should be adopted as quickly as possible in the format recommended by their suppliers because innovations are essentially efficient (Rogers 1995 [1962]; Clark 2003). The adoption process often seems to contain easily recognized stages in a linear sequence. It is presumed that adoption will be successful and will improve the effectiveness of the firm. The pro-innovation bias is so pervasive that even articles prefaced by its recognition are guilty of its promotion. It may be noted that in diffusion studies the analysis is micro level and ignores the multiplicity of levels in the embedding context. Therefore it is essential to recognize the political processes of innovation with their contested, confrontational features. The political context of network innovations has been conflated, eviscerated, and suppressed. Opposition to innovations is ordinary and extensively implicates management. The counterpoint to the pro-innovation bias is that much if not most innovation occurs through alterations to the population of organizations through the exit of surviving firms and entrance of new firms. The inertial capacities of the existing capabilities of surviving firms are powerful constraints through time (DiMaggio & Powell 1991). Unpacking the politicality of organizations and their contexts represents an important way of advancing understanding. The suppliers distributing the innovation are not politically neutral and nor is the user passively awaiting implementation.

CORE RESEARCH PROGRAMS

For management there are three major areas of innovation: innovation design, commercialization and diffusion, and the use and consumption of innovations. These form an iterative interactive sequence and their overall connections require the construction of a complex knowledge chain. Innovation design refers to the processes of conceiving and producing prototypes. This is the moment when the future market is most distant and least certain. Many firms lack the capacity to undertake the next cycle of innovation design because fast design and prototyping have to be articulated with a robust understanding of the consumer as user.

Management innovation was a largely unexamined, secret process until three seminal publications: Burns and Stalker (1995 [1961]) on management organization; Chandler (1962) on the emergence of the multidivisional form in large multiproduct American firms; and Rogers (1995 [1962]) on the diffusion of innovations. Each of these highlighted organizational innovations as being distinct from material artifacts. They demonstrated that the managing of the innovation process is a complex struggle in which human agency wrestles with preexisting flows and processes.

Burns and Stalker (1995 [1961]) began with the problem of whether a world center for the electronics market could be established in Scotland from its wartime experiences with electronics produced under government contracts. They researched a small sample of private British firms working in contexts of varying rates of innovation, from low to high. Remarkably, they found that the roles of management and their organization of the firm varied systematically along the high–low continuum. When the rates of technical and market change are low, the firm should adopt a mechanistic management system. This requires a high functional specialization, the codification of responsibilities, precise definitions of roles, and hierarchical authority. Knowledge and control will be centralized. Prestige will arise from understanding internal politics rather than external situations. In contrast, when the rate of change is high, the management system should be organic. Control, authority, and communication are in the form of networks containing highly committed role occupants who translate external events in order to develop flexible responses. Knowledge is highly diffused yet has to be articulated and orchestrated through networks. The mechanistic/organic distinction in types of management system soon became widely known. The findings were contingent (rested upon) the rate of external change. Readers and commentators tended to race to the center of their lengthy book to extract the findings. Consequently, few readers read the second half of the book. There, the authors suggest that organic management systems could only be introduced under certain necessary conditions. These were conditions absent in Scotland. This necessary contextual feature was gradually ignored. Moreover, some commentators wrongly presumed that the switch between management systems was quick and easy: the pro-innovation bias.

Chandler (1962) undertook in-depth archival studies of four large, successful American firms to discover how their management systems altered, if at all, when the corporate strategy shifted from regional markets and single products into world markets with multiple products. The research revealed a tortuous struggle involving experiments and debates about ways of managing the apex of the firm. Each of the firms had started from a regional, single-product market. They had each adopted centralized top management. As the firms' activities grew in complexity, so the centralized control was overwhelmed. Some executives sought to experiment with various alternatives. This was an episodic and emergent process in which organizational innovations and success were interwoven. Gradually, over a period of two decades, a specific solution was identified: the multidivisional form. Successful firms with multiple, unrelated products entering new geographical markets outside America tended to create specialized divisions and to use the top board only as an investment bank. Chandler then demonstrated that this tendency could be found in a large survey of American firms. We have to presume that American managements were very active in watching how other firms recognized and resolved the generic problems of management innovation (DiMaggio & Powell 1991). The problem of growth from local into international markets transfixed the attention of American management along with a growing community of consultants and researchers. The universal relevance of Chandler's analysis is increasingly debated, but there is no dispute about his majestic contribution to the problematizing of management innovation.

Rogers (1995 [1962]) provided an exemplary account and framework synthesized from earlier research on diffusion and marketing to identify which processes and contextual factors affect the rates of adoption and rejection of innovations. This led into differentiating between early and late adopters. Those who opposed innovation were laggards and Luddites. The models covered the period from the commercialization of innovations to their purchase or rejection. Initially, the models did not explore what the users did with the innovations. The models promoted the center over the periphery and expressed a broadcast–receiver view of the supplier–user relationship. Rogers adopted the two-step theory of communication which presumed that individuals were influenced by their peers and by certain features of the innovation. The first step should consist of the massive supply of documentary information infused with features designed to enroll the purchasers. This is mainly textual information and explicit advertising. The formal media are used to target the specific users. Second, the target community is analyzed by change agents who locate those members who are highly regarded and likely to be early adopters of the innovation. The change agents then engage directly with those targets to reinforce their decision and to persuade them to engage in trial adoptions. The exemplar for this is the role of change agents in promoting new drugs to the medical profession. Rogers suggests that the center should design their innovations to enroll the perceptions of the potential innovators. Five dimensions of perception are highlighted: offering relative advantage to the adopter, being compatible in values, minimizing complexity, dividing the adoption process into stages, and showing results that can be used to communicate performance. These five features indicate that the suppliers should black box the innovation to transform any fuzziness into perceived certainties and confidence about adoption.

These three research programs provide key cognitive and practical pillars. Their influence is evident today and continues to unfold.

EVOLUTIONARY PERSPECTIVES AND EFFICIENCY CRITERIA

Evolutionary perspectives take a non-teleological approach to describing and analyzing managements' founding of firms and then their transformation or exit. Aldrich (1999) suggests that organizations are evolving as their managements struggle to resolve the three choices of producing variations, developing a retention system, and confronting the forces of selection in the external context. Variations are represented by the multidivisional form or organic management systems. New variations may arise from design, accidentally or as an unintended consequence of unintended human actions. It has been said that the British involvement with Formula One motor racing was a historical accident arising from the availability of wartime airfields as early low-cost tracks conjoined to the desire of tobacco firms to advertise on British commercial television. The unintended is also illustrated by American football. Variations exist in a selection context and that context might be unfavorable, in which case the variation disappears. Americans discarded soccer, yet this became the world's number one male winter sport. These examples illustrate the context of struggle for management innovation. Variations that survive require institutionalization within some kind of retention system. McDonald's has developed a massive retention system, an internal university, to retain and develop knowing about meat, potatoes, and apples, as well as ways of incentivizing the franchisees.

There is huge debate over whether selected variations are efficient or are simply the outcomes of multidimensional lock-ins that, once taken, then establish specific national trajectories. Is the multidivisional form an efficient universal solution, or simply an example of a genre of management innovation that arises in America? DiMaggio and Powell (1991) contend that selected variations are not necessarily efficient. If so, that might explain why certain forms of organizational innovation persist even when the competitiveness of a firm or nation is undermined. This is an uncomfortable conclusion for most economists. DiMaggio and Powell suggest that the evolution of innovations through a sector or nation may simply be a case of tendencies toward copying on the basis of excitement and status rather than performativity. Evolutionary perspectives highlight the long-term tendencies toward the destruction of formerly established practices. This suggests that the introduction of management innovations must be accompanied by the careful and focused removal of practices that hinder the new forms of organizing. Contemporary managements have gradually learned how to use greenfield sites to remove unwanted practices. This may involve transferring activities around the world.

The claim that management faces long-term waves or cycles anchored in new generic innovations such as information technology is controversial. It has been argued that there are long waves of 50 or so years equally split between the swarming of a new generic innovation, its maturity, and then replacement. If these exist, then the implications for managements would be far reaching. Their strategies and processes would have to be aligned with the state of the wave. Equally, the policies of the state would be affected. So far long-wave theory has tended to use strict calendrical units (e.g., 56-year cycles), but contemporary theories of temporality suggest that we should measure the wave by the events of process time.

The place of innovation in their sectoral life course models is important and complex. Managements tend to watch other firms in the same sector and to shape their knowledge and practices into sectoral genres of innovation. In a seminal study, Abernathy (1978) examined the archives on innovation for the Ford Motor Company and discovered that the most radical innovation occurred close to the founding of the sector. The design of the automobile gradually shifted from a high rate of radical innovation into more incremental innovation after two decades. The design of the factories followed this process. So, by the 1960s, innovation was incremental. Abernathy extrapolated this tendency into the distant future. By then Ford had established a very sophisticated combination of divisional organization (Chandler 1962) with mechanistic management systems (Burns & Stalker 1961). Abernathy's interpretation was similar to that of those who claimed that all cars would become alike and only a few enormous automobile firms would survive. However, the late 1960s was a period of increasingly radical

innovation in the design of the automobile and its means of assembly. There was a discontinuity. The increasing rate of technical and market change was coupled with the entrance of Japanese firms. According to academic theories, existing firms should be combining the switch to radical innovations with the creative removal of non-performative practices. However, existing structures and processes tend to be very sticky. The experience of the automobile industry over the past four decades illustrates the requirement for firms to develop a repertoire of mechanistic and organic management systems which can be activated contingently according to circumstance. In practice, managements have partly resolved this problem by a combination of tightly regulated outsourcing of their supply chain and of switching production around the world at greenfield sites. This has been enabled by the evolution of information technologies.

INFORMATION TECHNOLOGY AND ACTOR NETWORKS

Management innovation involves many non-human elements (Bijker et al. 1987) Climatic variations exemplify elements not designed by humans. Buildings, raw materials, equipment, and software are socially constructed technology systems. The swimming pool robot cleaner is inscribed with the designer's capacities to automate the collection and disposal of debris at times set by the user. These displace humans and are the social made durable.

Management innovation requires knowledge and knowing of how non-humans engage in action. Actor-network theory claims that extensive and depthful research has significantly clarified what can be done by management. Information technology and the electronic embrace provide a useful site to explain the theory. Computing has evolved through architectural (e.g., search engines) and incremental innovations (e.g., websites) from mathematical machines in the nineteenth century via Holerith card processors into the instantaneous, open-link systems of today. Management can assemble far more data than it is possible to categorize and interpret. This all exemplifies social activities translated into non-human artifacts.

The artifacts are inscribed with particular human assumptions during their design. Tracing these inscriptions and following the biographies of artifacts shows that the networks of management now depend and partly shape extensive heterogeneous actor networks. However, the design intentions of the originators may be differentltly interpreted by the users. The users domesticate and appropriate artifacts. Artifacts possess a wider band of interpretive flexibility than is presumed. Software designed in the US and Germany for monitoring and managing the resources used by the enterprise may be used quite differently by the users in universities from retailers. Moreover, there are likely to be important, rather hidden, national predispositions. Particular software solutions have to operate as boundary objects.

Actor-network theory suggests that innovations can be managed by establishing centers that become obligatory points of passage at which the decision processes are orchestrated (Clark 2003). For example, since the early 1990s Formula One automobile racing and its advertising-laden television broadcasting has largely been controlled by a very small number of key actors who control a large, global configuration. Explaining their position and possible eclipse introduces the four-step model: PIEM. To start, problematize (P) a situation by suggesting a particular solution. Then engage in enrolling (I) with potential collaborators, including non-human elements like engines, tires, racing circuits, finance capital, and television screen. Next enroll (E) the key elements into a particular center that excludes rivals. Finally, continuously mobilize (M) the political support (e.g., legal protection) to promote survival. PIEM is supported by a lot of excellent case studies which are remarkably enjoyable and stimulating (e.g., Bijker et al. 1987). Yet, we must inquire about the conditions under which particular examples were undertaken and became successful. Could a luxury yacht industry be located in any nation?

NATIONAL SYSTEMS OF INNOVATION

The national context was very largely neglected until the success of Japanese innovations became apparent in the 1980s. The role of the nation has an influence. In a brilliant analysis of national systems of innovation, Storper and Salais (1997) provide a suggestive framework. Their approach suggests that only some sectors are likely to prosper in particular national contexts. Each nation is likely to possess a typical variety. UK management succeeds with petrochemicals, pharmaceuticals, food, drink, and tobacco but fails with automobiles, white goods, and furniture.

There are many examples, especially with network technologies, that the nation of origin contains key enabling features absent in other contexts. America has been a key originator of organizational innovations, yet their importation by other nations has been very patchy. Japanese automobile firms and electrical firms are often able to transfer their management practices to other national contexts. When non-Japanese firms attempt to import Japanese innovations, they often fail or most frequently create hybrids (Abo 1994; Clark 2003). The growth of international supply chains indicates that within firms from many different nations there is a remarkable understanding and experience of the transfer of innovations. It seems likely that our academic understanding of the processes of successful cross-cultural transfer requires much more analytic attention to how the differences between contexts interact.

HYBRIDS AND DOMESTICATION

Management innovation involves dynamic configurations whose survival is contingent upon glocal selection contexts. Most innovations, organizational and material, are imported into an organization by particular sets of managers to resolve a problem. This importation process is highly demanding on managerial services. It is therefore highly likely that the imported innovation will be unbundled and its elements domesticated to the local situation. Therefore hybrids are highly likely. The problem is for management to articulate robust design strategies and to continually evolve the corporate languages that frame activity nets. Management innovation requires robust repertoires.

SEE ALSO: Actor-Network Theory; Consumption, Landscapes of; Hybridity; Knowledge;

Management; Management Improvisation; Management Theory; Micro–Macro Links; Organization Theory; Technological Innovation

REFERENCES AND SUGGESTED READINGS

Abernathy, W. J. (1978) *The Productivity Dilemma: Roadblock to Innovation in the Automobile Firm.* Johns Hopkins University Press, Baltimore.

Abo, T. (Ed.) (1994) *Hybrid Factory: The Japanese System in the United States.* Oxford University Press, Oxford.

Aldrich, H. (1999) *Organizations Evolving.* Sage, London.

Bijker, W. W., Hughes, T. P., & Pinch, T. (1987) *The Social Construction of Technology.* MIT Press, Cambridge, MA.

Burns, T. & Stalker, G. M. (1995 [1961]) *Management of Innovation.* Tavistock, London.

Chandler, A. D. (1962) *Strategy and Structure.* MIT Press, Cambridge, MA.

Clark, P. A. (2003) *Organizational Innovations.* Sage, London.

DiMaggio, P. J. & Powell, W. W. (1991) *The New Institutionalism in Organization Theory.* University of Chicago Press, Chicago.

Rogers, E. M. (1995 [1962]) *Diffusion of Innovations*, 3rd edn. Free Press, New York.

Storper, M. & Salais, R. (1997) *World of Production: The Action Frameworks of the Economy.* Harvard University Press, Cambridge, MA.

management networks

Tyrone S. Pitsis

A network is a broad concept whose definition is generally a function of its disciplinary context. The interest in contemporary networks research and theory has had broad interdisciplinary appeal. Network theory and research has been conducted in sociology, communications, psychology, economics, biology and medicine, and organizational behavior. It has been applied to a broad range of natural and synthetic systems such as sociopolitical systems, neural networks, disease epidemiology, terrorism and anti-terrorism, and transport. More recently, the term "network" has been popularized and most associated with information technology and the Internet and taken to mean the connection of people and organizations through computer-mediated communications technologies aimed at enabling and facilitating efficient and effective communications and transactions between them. Generally, however, the conception of networks is not far removed from its sociological roots, and a search through most sociological works will show that a network has a number of defining features. First, a network requires a group or system of individual people and/or agencies. Second, a network requires these groups or systems to be interconnected in some way. Third, the network must share common goals, interests, or values. Finally, there is an assumption that the individual and/or agencies maintain at least some level of autonomy.

There is a broad range of methodologies that can be used to study networks from a social scientific perspective. These can include traditional surveys, in-depth interviews, quasi-experiments, ethnographic research, network analysis, and network mapping. The growth of computer-mediated communications and information technologies has also made the study of networks more innovative and more widespread. Some of the key attributes studied in networks from a sociological perspective are the strength of network ties and the relationship between actors involved in the network, and the nature of the nodal points in a network. These can include what are commonly termed "brokers" and also "hubs." Brokers act as the nodal point or portal between members in a network who, for one reason or another, are unable to exchange information (Burt 1992). Hubs reflect more the power of one or more individuals in a network. Other areas of interest are distance, centrality, reciprocity, transitivity, density, and power.

Early interest in networks in sociology can be seen in the work on "tight-knit networks" developed by Elizabeth Bott (1957), who sought to understand the intricate system of social relationships within which people were involved in their everyday family life. For Bott, tight-knit networks were important because they provide social support while also acting to mobilize social control. As such, a network has a profound effect on controlling and influencing social behavior within those networked relationships. Later, Granovetter (1973, 1978,

1985) developed the notion of strong ties and loose ties. Strong ties reflect Bott's notion of tight-knit networks and typically refer to a network of family and close friends bound together through trust-based relationships which are of mutual benefit to all actors involved. Weak ties, however, are more superficial than strong or tight-knit networks because they involve less emotional investment for actors. Consequently, many had theorized that weak ties are subject to higher levels of uncertainty, abuse, and exit than strong ties.

Certainly, sociological and social psychological research has shown that strong networks, such as those found in strong family and community ties, have been linked to greater psychological adjustment, better coping skills in traumatic or stressful conditions, and lower levels of deviance and criminal behavior (see, e.g., Baron et al. 2000). However Granovetter (1973, 1985) highlighted the "strength of weak ties" and, since Granovetter, weak ties have also been shown to be just as critical as strong ties to sustainable growth and development of communities. In weak ties certain individuals emerge who act as brokers of knowledge and relationships. Such individuals typically, but not always, have strong ties with the two parties exchanging information or resources, thus the two parties exchanging any information or resources do not need to be tightly knit. The argument is that people in "loosely coupled" or "weak" networks are provided with the opportunity to form strong networks with people or agencies they might not be able to otherwise access. Such weak tie networks have been very important in explaining how people of lower socioeconomic status can access and leverage from new opportunities opened to them. As such there is a strong argument for government policies that foster weak tie relationships in a range of social policy areas such as employment, mental health, indigenous health, and regional and rural business development. For example, in the US, UK, and Australia there are ongoing debates about implementing and funding youth mentoring programs to assist young people from disadvantaged backgrounds in accessing knowledge, resources, and opportunities through mentorship by business leaders. Such policies encourage collaboration between business and the youth of any given community, thus providing people with opportunities.

While network theory and research might provide a greater understanding of how individuals might benefit from their networked relationships, both tight and weak, at a broader sociological level there is a growing body of research to suggest that the nature of network relationships can have a profound effect upon entire communities. Businesses increasingly adopt more efficient and cost-effective operating strategies, such as new technologies, wide-ranging downsizing programs, and outsourcing of non-core operations. Simultaneously, they seek to reduce regulatory control and the cost of production by moving part or all of their business operations offshore. Such business practices have had substantial effects the world over, the results of which can be seen in many communities that have traditionally depended on that key industry for survival. In the UK, the US, and Australia, for example, there have been a number of communities previously dependent on highly specialized industry such as coal mining, steel manufacture, forestry, farming, and so on, where these industries had become a socially embedded part of the community. In such a situation, the strength of ties between the industry and the community was tight indeed. In such networks, when a critical component separates itself from the network, there are some harsh outcomes for the community, such as significant levels of unemployment and an increase in poverty, along with their associated effects, including crime, alcoholism, and so on. However, recent research suggests that in communities typified by weak ties, that is, where one industry is not so embedded within that community, its members and agencies can maintain loose relationships with several other businesses within and outside that community, such that when the dominant industry relocates or shuts down, these communities fare much better on almost all socioeconomic measures of success. Economically then, weak ties suggest that communities that are less insular fare better than ones that are tightly knit.

Another area in which the sociology of networks is making a major contribution is in organization and management theory. Organizational and management scholars conceptualize the modern organizational environment as one defined by high levels of uncertainty, ambiguity, and risk. Many argue that current hierarchical and rigid structural organizational forms lack the flexibility to adequately survive under such conditions. As such a number of new organizational forms have emerged to help provide the flexibility, adaptability, and capabilities to survive. Alliances, for example, are a collection of organizations, usually two or more, who join together to complement or enhance one another's capabilities with the aim of delivering a service and/or product. More recently there has been a growing body of work on project-based organizations (Clegg & Courpasson 2004; Pitsis et al. 2003), which involves the design of a separate entity made up of a complex arrangement of networked relationships of client organization, partner organizations, internal and external stakeholders, including the community and customers, and a supply chain. As with Bott's control over "tight-knit networks," the project-based organization works to coordinate and control behavior and social relations not through strict control and surveillance but through what Foucault terms "governmentality." In this sense, governmentality refers to the active and consensual subjugation of all actors involved in the project-based network for the good of the project (Clegg et al. 2002). Such a concept has strong connotations of Granovetter's (2002) notions of social embeddedness in networks.

According to Granovetter (2002), the power of social relations embedded within networks should not be underestimated in coordinating, mobilizing, and motivating members of a network to act in ways that sustain and protect these social relations. Using project-based arrangements, organizations, both public and private, build such social embeddedness within networks via new organizational forms such as alliances.

SEE ALSO: Actor-Network Theory; Alliances; Economy, Networks and; Exchange Network Theory; Management Theory; Organization Theory; Scientific Networks and Invisible Colleges; Social Movements, Networks and; Social Network Analysis; Weak Ties (Strength of)

REFERENCES AND SUGGESTED READINGS

Baron, S., Field, J., & Schuller, T. (2000) *Social Capital: Critical Perspectives*. Oxford University Press, Oxford.

Bott, E. (1957) *Family and Social Network*. Tavistock, London.

Burt, S. (1992) *Structural Holes*. Harvard University Press, Cambridge, MA.

Clegg, S. R. & Courpasson, D. (2004) Political Hybrids: Tocquevillean Views on Project Organizations. *Journal of Management Studies* 41(4): 525–47.

Clegg, S. R., Pitsis, T., Rura-Polley, T., & Marosszeky, M. (2002) Governmentality Matters: Designing an Alliance Culture of Inter-Organizational Collaboration for Managing Projects. *Organization Studies* 23(3): 317–37.

Granovetter, M. (1973) The Strength of Weak Ties. *American Journal of Sociology* 78(May): 1360–80.

Granovetter, M. (1978) Threshold Models of Collective Behavior. *American Journal of Sociology* 83 (May): 1420–43.

Granovetter, M. (1985) Economic Action and Social Structure: The Problem of Embeddedness. *American Journal of Sociology* 91 (November): 481–510.

Granovetter, M. (2002) A Theoretical Agenda for Economic Sociology. In: Guillen, M., Collins, R., England, P., & Meyer, M. (Eds.), *The New Economic Sociology: Developments in an Emerging Field*. Russell Sage Foundation, New York.

Pitsis, T. S., Clegg, S. R., Marosszeky, M., & Rura-Polley, T. (2003) Constructing the Olympic Dream: A Future Perfect Strategy of Project Management. *Organization Science* 14(5): 574–90.

management theory

Jean-François Chanlat

From the beginning of the nineteenth century until today, the industrialized world has witnessed unparalleled socioeconomic development. At the same time, the phenomenon of historical capitalism has been the object of numerous publications. Writers as diverse as classical and neoclassical economists, Marx, and foundational thinkers in sociology were all obsessed by the socioeconomic dynamic related to this movement. In sociology an attempt to explain the emergence of capitalism was the central core of Weber's intellectual work. If, according to Weber, capitalism is singularized by private firms in a market economy, another important characteristic is the appearance of management thinking and of a new social agent: the manager.

As shown by historians of business such as Alfred Chandler, the social figure of the manager emerged at the end of the nineteenth century when business firms grew inexorably in size in the US. Since then, management thinking has undergone great development. Management is a social field in Bourdieu's sense, in which different actors play a role in its construction and transformation. Theories of management are both the products of society (mainly people and social forces in a historical context) and its producers. The sociology of management has to take into account this theoretical elaboration in order to understand the principal discourses which contribute and shape both organizational forms and managerial practices.

Management is defined as a social process and a social figure. As a social process, it is defined by the process through which an organization is effective and efficient. Whereas effectiveness is related to the attainment of goals, efficiency is related to the optimization of resources in the pursuit of organizational goals. The resulting effectiveness–efficiency dilemma underpins much management thought, as the difference is not neutral on the construction of managerial practices. Management is not restricted to the social processes of achieving effectiveness and efficiency; it also describes the social group in charge of this process: executives and managers. Theories of management are instances of speculative or scientific ideas about organizational efficiency and effectiveness. Every theory has dealt with key issues for attaining these goals: organizing, controlling, motivating, planning, and leading.

Historically, management thinking has three main contributors: practitioners, consultants, and academics. The first group is the most numerous. It includes all managers, whatever their status and functions. The second includes all the people who give advice to managers. The third includes all the management researchers and professors working in universities or higher education institutes. When we look at management as an intellectual enterprise, we can easily see that at the beginning of the last century the most popular and influential theories came from practitioners and consultants. After World War II the work of academics became increasingly influential, though there have been recent concerns about the extent to which the academic literature is read by academics rather than practitioners. While the theories of the first two groups are mostly normative and prescriptive, the theories of the third group are mostly analytical and comprehensive.

We can also notice that even if there is substantial production in other parts of the world (notably in Europe and Asia), the majority of the theories produced today come from North American practitioners, consultants, and academics, and their diffusion is ensured by all kind of media, notably those specializing in economics and management matters. Such theories are deeply embedded into the social and cultural fabric from which they emerge.

While some business historians trace managerial practices to past centuries, it is at the turning point of the twentieth century that we see the first attempts to systematize managerial thinking and the intensive use of the word itself in English. Theories of management have proved to be both numerous and very diverse. This variety is due in part to the type of producer (practitioner, consultant, academic), the disciplines mobilized (engineering, economics, management, sociology, psychology, anthropology, political sciences, etc.), the mental representation of what constitutes an organization (machine, living organism, social system, psychic and cognitive products, cultural set, etc.), the region, the country of production, and the social-historical context (social issues, social movements, and social tensions).

We can periodize management thought as follows: (1) 1880–1945: the founding and classical thinkers; (2) 1945–75: the Cold War and the establishment of American hegemony in management thinking; (3) 1975–2000: a socioeconomic slow-down, the historical victory of the western capitalist experience, and the hegemony of managerialism.

In the last quarter of the nineteenth century management thinking witnessed the first attempt to systematize efficiency at work. The central figure of this movement was Frederick Winslow Taylor. His career was not without controversy (e.g., towards the end of his life he was questioned and censured by a Congress committee). Taylorism can be seen as a political economy of the workshop. It revolutionized production in the US and it proved popular in Europe, where it was largely adopted in France, Germany, and the UK. In the Soviet Union Lenin famously quipped that Taylorism was "a system to ameliorate the production and the material level of the Soviet people." While Taylorism may now seem to belong to the past, some writers have pointed out that its principles are an enduring part of the way in which society is organized. For instance, Ritzer (2002) has drawn parallels between Taylorism and the work organization of McDonald's restaurants, while others have insisted on new forms characterized as neo–Taylorism, based on the use of technologies of information and a Taylorist division of work (e.g., as in a call center). Taylorism was not wholly original, but it did crystallize many influential ideas of the time. In particular, it was ineluctably scientist in its orientation. This presupposed that science was the main factor underpinning progress. Translated into the social domain these principles were a means of finding the "One best way" to efficiency, which in turn produced social harmony in the form of relatively high wages combined with high levels of productivity. For these reasons, reformers and revolutionaries alike saw Taylorism as emblematic of progressive thinking.

Contemporaneously to Taylor, the French engineer Henri Fayol was concerned with issues of management and organization. As a successful director of a French mining company, Fayol represents the rise of the manager described by Chandler (1977). Whereas Taylor's analysis is concerned with his reflections from the workshop, Fayol placed emphasis on the firm as a whole. He presented 14 principles that aimed to improve organization efficiency and deliver organizational success. Fayol's ideas were less popular among his compatriots than those of Taylor. At the same time, Fayol was largely unknown outside of the Francophone world. It was not until 1949 that his ideas were translated into English and started to become popular in the English-speaking world. His main principles were adopted by the planning, organizing, leading, and controlling framework which has become a common part of American

management theory. Not surprisingly, Fayol's ideas bear the imprint of his own social roots. His managerial experience was in a historical context characterized by many social conflicts and the growing influence of the socialist movement, which led his management philosophy to a form of paternalism that was sensitive to the social dimensions of the time.

Henry Ford's influence extended beyond the creation of a production system to change society as a whole. Ford's creation of the assembly line has led many to suggest that he was more innovative than Taylor. Others regard the difference between them as more a question of nuance than of substance. According to some scholars Fordism was an application of the Taylor system to mass production. Compared to Fordism, Taylorism can absorb new technologies and adapt itself to new organizational realities. The new production system had a tremendous effect on output. The doubling of workers' salaries to the famous 5 dollars a day aimed to reduce the very high turnover rate. Ford had adopted one of Taylor's principles: "Men will not do an extraordinary day's work for an ordinary day's pay."

Fordism created a modern plant populated by thousands of workers. The assembly line created the unqualified worker: it was now possible for factories to employ an unskilled immigrant workforce. Unintended consequences of Fordism included the development of worker consciousness, increased social conflict, and the development of large trade unions. In response, the Ford company further developed its operations and methods offices and also developed industrial relations specialists. Henry Ford's thinking bore the imprint of American culture, which emphasized that the US was a land of opportunities where everybody had the capacity to be successful so long as they worked hard and that production served the great majority of the people.

Mary Parker Follett was a well-known management thinker in the early twentieth century. After her death in 1933 her ideas disappeared from popular management thought, but there has recently been a reawakening of interest in her main articles. A political scientist by training, Follett was concerned with issues of state and democracy. She was interested in managerial experiments which she regarded as acts of creation. She understood that management needed to be congruent with the organizational culture and social system. Her law of situation emphasized organizational contingencies long before the advent of contingency theory per se. Her vision of organizations and management is a democratic one. The assumption was that cooperation and participation would help a business to be run more successfully. If her work was widely ignored following her death, it is perhaps attributable to her questionning of the philosophical foundations of business firms. Her theory asserts that the role of organization is to contribute to life itself. From this point of view, she can be regarded as an advocate of sustainable development long before the term became popularized.

Bureaucracy is a master concept within the classical canon of management thinking. According to Weber, bureaucratic thinking is an illustration of the process of rationalization of the modern human experience. Historically, the success of the bureaucratic theory stems from its efficiency. In Germany, for example, the bureaucratic model was taught at schools of commerce at the beginning of the twentieth century. Contrary to many popular discourses which represent bureaucracy as the stuff of organizational nightmare, bureaucracy was and remains an efficient means of organizing. In some areas (common goods) it can be more effective and efficient than market coordination.

The famous Hawthorne experiment marked the dawn of the human relations movement. Elton Mayo and his co-researchers developed an explicit link between work performance and group dynamics. Highlighting the importance of social recognition by an organization and privileging an individual approach towards employees, Mayo provided the stimulus for further human behavior research into organizational settings.The promise of human relations was to provide a solution to social conflicts, which appealed to industrialists. Paradoxically, Mayo's thinking was critical of democracy, which he regarded as unrealistic and decivilizing. Mayo also viewed the industrial revolution as a cause of decivilization by the way in which it destroyed social bonds and produced alienation at work. Mayo saw the development of a managerial elite as a way to save western civilization. Trained in different techniques (e.g., listening,

counseling), these managers could respond to worker malaise, defend a rational conception of life against the emotions, and reduce the influence of trade unions. His work opened the way for human ressources management and a psychological treatment of social problems.

Chester Barnard, the last great classical thinker, was a business manager who in 1938 wrote a hugely influential book which is considered as an important link between the classic theories and post-World War II currents of thoughts. His contribution was to build a theory of management which placed cooperation at the center of organizations. Influenced by Follett and the human relations movement, he developed a conception of authority founded on the idea that the legitimacy of managerial agency is clearly linked to personal approval.

All the contributions discussed above belong to a period of great change and social crisis (social tensions both in plants and society, World War I, the Russian Revolution). The 1929 Crash was seen by many as an illustration of capitalist contradictions and the limits of laissez-faire theory in economics. All the management theories developed in this period were created to provide answers to these social changes and crisis. Macrosocial responses varied internationally: democratic responses (e.g., the US New Deal, Keynesian policies in Scandinavian countries, the Popular Front in France) coincided with Fascism in Italy and Nazism in Germany. Peaking with the terrible experience of World War II, these historical events deeply influenced the evolution of management theory in the decades that followed.

The period from the end of World War II to the mid-1970s was characterized by extraordinary economic growth in the western world, decolonization, and a deep international division between two blocs: the West and the East. One has to understand the evolution of management thinking in this period in this sociohistorical context. The influence of American management thinking was dominant everywhere, especially in the western world. The Marshall Plan nourished Europe not only financially but also intellectually: many European missions went to the US to learn the secret of managerial success and efficiency. The rebuilding and modernizing process in the non-communist world was viewed as the main defense against the influence of the

Soviet bloc. The Cold War shaped the whole sociopolitical agenda. In other words, the export of the American model included importing American management thinking into many parts of the world, notably Europe.

Within the field of management thinking itself the theories already developed constituted a ready reckoner for educated managers. The post-World War II period was to be a theater of new ideas. One of the major developments came from life sciences, especially the development of the general theory of systems. From the closed vision of organization shared by both Taylorism and theorists of bureaucracy, the field of management theory welcomed system approaches and led to many theoretical currents, among them the socio-technical system approaches developed by the London Tavistock Institute and by Scandinavian scholars which linked technology and organization; and contingency theory (developed both in the UK and US), which stressed the importance of the relationship between an organization and its own environment. The success of a business firm or an organization became closely linked to the coherence of the internal system with its environment. Unlike Taylor's vision, such reflections concluded that there was no one "best way" to organize. Applying the equifinality principle, supported by the general theory of systems, they did not conceptualize organization adaptation to their environment as following a unique organizational form.

In psychology and economics, Carnegie Mellon researchers critiqued the lack of realism in the universalistic abstractions of neoclassical economics and proposed another version of rationality: bounded rationality. Based on cognitive psychology and studies of concrete decision-making, this conception strengthened the idea that decisions are also an embedded process. These authors were at the foundation of not only the new administrative sciences in which cognition played a central role, but also a new model of American business schools, founded on research. Management and managerial practices became objects of science, just as any other social practices. The administrative sciences would be at the core of management knowledge's scientization process.

Other developments came from sociology and psychosociology. In relationship with Weber's work, some American sociologists made case studies to describe the dynamics of bureaucracies. They discovered what they called the dysfunctions or vicious circle produced by such a dynamic. Inspired by this and by the ideas of bounded rationality, a French sociologist, Michel Crozier, described the bureaucratic vicious circle: the will to reduce uncertainty and arbitrarily push an organization so that it would be governed by impersonal rules. However, in this will to power he saw the impossibility of abolishing uncertainty as the impetus that created arbitrary behavior, which pushed the worker to seek more rules for regulation, and so on. Crozier not only described the bureaucratic system, but also developed the foundations of the actors' strategic analysis which became one of the chief conceptual instruments of the French-speaking school of sociology of organizations. His work and that of his main collaborators have been very influential in management education programs and some public and private administrative spheres.

The developing field of organizational behavior gradually replaced human relations at the end of the 1960s. The new field was pushed by critiques of managerial teaching that emerged in the 1950s that integrated all the new developments coming from industrial psychology, group dynamics, socioanalysis, sociometry, social psychology, and the sociology of work and organizations. They were to be at the base of theories of work satisfaction, work motivation, leadership, and group dynamics, and became very influential in many workplaces, notably in personnel management.

As we can see, this period is important in the reformulation of management thinking. First, there is a new scientization of management discourse, especially in American academic work, which had a great influence in many business schools all around the world. Second, many of these ideas were incorporated into management theories and management education systems. Third, American management thinking became the reference for many countries of the western bloc despite strong criticisms of American imperialism. The period was associated with a demographic explosion and increased socioeconomic growth, which saw collective and individual enrichment, a decline in economic inequalities, monetary stability, the development of mass education, and the building of a more or less elaborated welfare state in all the industrialized countries. These remarkable results were clearly an element to contain Soviet influence and communist threat.

From the second half of the 1970s crucial decisions were made and events occurred that resulted in economic slow-down and set a new socioeconomic agenda (e.g., President Nixon's decision to change the international monetary sytem; the Vietnam war; the reconstruction of Europe and Japan; the rise in petroleum prices; the challenge to Keynesian orthodoxy in econonmics by the Chicago monetary school; the emergence American conservative think-tanks). The political victories of Margaret Thatcher and Ronald Reagan provided a strong political boost for a conservative political agenda. Tax cuts, privatization, and reduced public expenditure became the new mantra in the US and the UK, gradually spreading to much of the developed world. Growing competition from Asia and Japan forced a rethink of organization and management practices. Financial markets now had more influence: Anglo-American political elites sought to develop a society of stock owners. This ambition was encouraged in 1989 by the fall of the Berlin Wall, a symbol of the historic victory of western democracies and their market economies.

The new economic model pushed for more workforce flexibility, state withdrawal from many areas in favor of marketization, a reduction of business and individual taxes, and an openess of national markets to competition – a globalization process in which every society had to be involved. Social scientists discovered that we are involved not only in a risk society, but also in a less protected social universe. Management thinking played a key role in this process. Thus, while previous ideas were produced in a relatively stable universe of increasing wealth, the ideas of the last two decades emerged in a different context. Key elements of the new social situation greatly influenced the managerial thinking of this period.

First, the reconstruction of Europe and growing competition from Asian countries (mainly Japan) led to reflection on business systems and the effects of different "national cultures": it seemed that the American model was not the only way to produce efficiency and wealth.

Different combinations were possible between state, market, and civil society at a macro level, and managerial practices dealing with national or regional cultures at the level of the firm. Organizational systems are often different from country to country. If theories of management are embedded in space (a culture and a society) and time (history), we cannot have a unique model based on a universalistic abstract approach. There were perhaps more contingencies than just those that related strictly to business – there were also cultural and historic contingencies.

Second, international competition and competitiveness helped to develop strategic management thinking. Strategy theories flourish because of the turbulence caused by changes in the environment. Market openness, international commercial agreements, currency floats, industry deregulation, and privatization all helped to build new demand for strategic management. Some thinking focused on strategic differentiation (product, market, price policy and cost leadership, construction of entry and mobility barriers) and strategic planning, which emphasized the role of planners; others emphasized strategic design by studying strengths, weaknesses, opportunitiess, and threats. Still others developed an interest in strategic positioning, strongly influenced by Michael Porter's economic vision. Another popular strategy approach involves the use of scenario planning, which tries to establish environmental scanning of social dynamics and economic, technological, and political issues to build preemptive and appropriate business answers. Unlike traditional planning, scenario planning does not have a linear conception of time. It integrates uncertainty, chance, and complexity in order to challenge custom. The "emergence" strategy perspective is based on ideas which emphasize the real processes of making strategic decisions in a context. It shows strategy as a process of social construction deeply embedded in everyday organizational life.

Third, in the western world, this period was also characterized by great innovation and diffusion of communication and information technologies. The creation of networks of all kinds – notably the Internet – reconfigured international, regional, national, and local socioeconomic links, in some cases reshaping organizational forms. Management theories incorporated these impulses in forging the words e-management, e-commerce, and virtual organizations.

Fourth, workforce mobilization greatly preoccupied management thinkers. During the 1970s many negative reactions (absenteism, high turnover, reduced quality, alienation, and industrial conflict) were observed in workforces aspiring to more individual respect. Several strategies were proposed to deal with new working-class attitudes, such as industrial democracy perspectives in the Scandinavian countries, Germany, and Austria. Negotiation between the state, unions, and employers' federations was institutionalized and in Germany and Austria co-management (or co-determination) was imposed on firms with 2,000 employees or more in an illustration of the social democratic compromise. A second strategy was to take a legal approach. In France, laws sought to organize social dialogue in the firm and give legal rights to worker expression in the workplace.This approach was clearly within the centralizing traditions of France, emerging from discussions organized by politicians with worker and employer representatives. There were also micro-strategies at the firm or plant level. Some of these harked back to the socio-technical approach, stressing semi-autonomous work groups. These strategies were very popular in Scandinavian countries and received a certain recognition in other contexts. The movement for the quality of working life emerged from this approach, strongly shaping Swedish politics around work, in particular. These ideas were close to those of Follett. Another approach used the notion of culture. In effect, in front of the Japanese challenge, America tried to react by bringing corporate and organizational culture into debate. If Japanese economic success was because its culture was founded on solidarity and group cohesion, then American companies had to find their own culture to cope with the competition. A culture of excellence was the response. In the US these ideas (mainly produced by consultants with academic business school linkages) gave legitimacy to sociological and anthropological studies in some management spheres. Organizational culture became central to management theories and became a new topic for organizational behavior courses. In its quest for excellence, "quality" became a watchword inspired by the Japanese techniques of production, themselves largely influenced by the American William Deming.

The feminization of the labor market and the rise of women managers led to great stress on women in organizations and the different management styles that they deployed. Existing mainstream management theories were seen as gender productions. The social inequalities observed between men and women in organizational settings inspired managerial practices designed to diminish them (affirmative action, salary equity, parity, mentorship, etc.), notably in Scandinavia, the UK, and the US. This movement was also related to a broader one concerning the situation of social minorities generally; in the US, the position of African Americans, Latinos, and Native Americans; more generally, visible minorities, a trend from which the idea of managing diversity emerged.

As well as collective strategies to tackle the difficulties arising from social mobilization and workforce diversity, there were also some more individual strategies. Numerous strands of psychology concerning individual satisfaction and motivation were mobilized in these individualistic strategies. They were also encouraged by the growing culture of narcissism and intimacy in the western world and elsewhere, sustained by socioeconomically dominant discourses on the role of individuals in the fabrication of social life. Annual competencies, employee evaluations, discourses on employability, salary individualization, stress management programs, and personal counseling and coaching become responses to these individualistic needs as a way of treating social issues.

None of these ideas were completely new, but the victory of capitalism and the market gave an important role to the private business firm and to managerial categories of thinking. In the last two decades, management as a system of thinking has become *the* intellectual frame that shapes the popular and political imagination, as well as ordinary people's minds. *Manage* and *management* are words now used everywhere. Categories for thought come more and more from managerial spheres. The key words – client, product, quality, reengineering, efficiency, effectiveness – come from market enterprises and are increasingly pervasive in many other organizational types: public administration, non-profit organizations, churches, schools, universities, cooperatives, cultural organizations – even politics, Weber's last redoubt against routinization.

The beginning of the twenty-first century has shown the limits of some firms' behaviors. The explosion of the Internet financial bubble, numerous corporate scandals, and the rise of the corporate social responsibility movement have all questionned some basic assumptions of dominant managerial theories. Other issues, such as global warming, ecological threat, the growth of social inequalities, and the negative effects of globalization, have created a diversity of social movements and pushed many people to rethink their management conceptions.

At the same time, the internationalization of the economy and organizations has also provoked reflection on managing according to one's own culture. The appropriateness of the managerial techniques of the western world in general and the US in particular is discussed in different regions of the world. The issue of social cohesion is debated in a context of great migratory movements and gender and ethnicity issues in which people seek to move as freely as capital. Finally, the boom in communication and information technologies led to deep questioning about appropriate organizational models and e-management. How will all these trends affect the evolution of management theories in this new century? According to many observers, we are going to see three great turns: ethics, culture, and socioeconomics.

Given numerous corporate scandals and inequities, the movement toward ethics and ethical guidelines is going to feed more and more management thinking. All the discussions about corporate governance are related to this issue. More generally, the success of managerial thought associated with poor socioeconomic performance raises many questions about management educational systems and corporate governance. Ethics are also going to be fed by the issue of sustainability. In light of scientific data, many governments and pressure groups have set a new agenda. The creation of social notation agencies, the signing of international agreements, and the diffusion of the sustainable adjective among political institutions, business firms discourse, and society as a whole are illustrations of a growing awareness of societal values. In a world which may face an environmental and social crisis, management theories have to develop new ideas and practices. Such issues are going to change elements of strategy, accounting, production, marketing, human resources, and research and development.

The second turn is socioeconomic. If the dominant values of managerial agency have to be based on acute environmental and social sensitiveness, they are going to change some managerial practices about the workforce, technology, clients, suppliers, stockholders, and communities. The issues of equity, training, wealth sharing, quality, and innovation are going to influence managerial agency more deeply to develop a new agenda of more qualitative economics, in which growth will be associated with social effects and stockholders replaced by stakeholders.

The third turn is cultural. With internationalization and regionalization processes, not only business firms but also administrations, governments, and non-profit organizations are discovering the peculiarities of some of their behaviors and social logics. These intercultural experiences are producing intercultural management thinking. Based largely on anthropology, ethnology, and history, this shows that we cannot manage with the same methods in different settings. Culture as a symbolic universe is framing the management system of meaning. In so doing, culture is key to understanding work and managerial practices in particular social contexts. Theories of management will increasingly have to discuss cultural embeddedness and the limits of universalistic approaches – even as these seek to remake the world that they address. As management theories are at the heart of our capitalist and managerial society, those who produce them (practitioners, consultants, theoreticians) have a great responsibility. According to many scientists, time is running short. We must build not only on more relevant managerial practices, but also on the human wisdom rooted in historical experience.

SEE ALSO: Bureaucracy and Public Sector Governmentality; Hawthorne Effect; Human Resource Management; Knowledge Management; Management Discourse; Management Education; Management History; Organization Theory; Organizations and the Theory of the Firm; Strategic Management (Organizations)

REFERENCES AND SUGGESTED READINGS

Chandler, A. (1977) *The Visible Hand*. Harvard University Press, Cambridge, MA.

Chanlat, J.-F. (1994). Francophone Organizational Analysis (1950–1990): An Overview. *Organization Studies* 15(1): 47–80.

Clegg, S., Pitsis, T., & Kornberger, M. (2005) *Managing and Organizations: An Introduction to Theory and Practice*. Sage, London.

Collins, D. (2000) *Management Fads and Buzzwords: Critical-Practical Perspectives*. Routledge, London.

D'Iribarne, P. (1993) *La Logique de l'honneur*. Seuil, Paris.

Djelic, M.-L. (2001) *Exporting the American Model: The Postwar Transformation of European Business*. Oxford University Press, Oxford.

Drucker, P. (1998) *Peter Drucker on the Profession of Management*. Harvard Business School Press, Cambridge, MA.

Guillén, M. (1994) *Models of Management*. University of Chicago Press, Chicago.

Hatchuel, A., David, A., & Laufer, R. (2000) *Les Nouvelles fondations des sciences de gestion*. Vuibert, Paris.

Hofstede, G. (2001 [1980]) *Cultures' Consequences: International Differences in Work-Related Values*. Sage, London.

Kanigel, R. (2005) *The One Best Way: Frederick Winslow Taylor and the Enigma of Efficiency*. MIT Press, Cambridge, MA.

Lécuyer, B. & Bouilloud, J.-P. (1994) *L'Invention de la gestion*. L'Harmattan, Paris.

Mintzberg, H. (2004) *Managers not MBA*. Harper, New York.

Morgan, G. (1986) *Images of Organization*. Sage, London.

Ritzer, G. (2002) *McDonaldization: The Reader*. Pine Forge Press, New York.

Wren, D. A. (2005) *History of Management Thought*. John Wiley & Sons, New York.

management, workers' participation in

George Strauss

Workers' participation in management (WPM), also known as organizational democracy, is a broad concept which covers a wide variety of institutional arrangements. Definitions abound, many ideologically loaded. At the minimum it is a process which allows employees to exert some influence over their work and the conditions under which they work.

Over the years WPM has been advocated on a variety of grounds (Dachler & Wilpert 1978; Heller et al. 1998). One is *political*: left wingers see it as a means of power-sharing, specifically of strengthening working-class power at the expense of capitalist management (Couch & Pizzorno 1978). A second is *managerial*. Widespread participation, it is argued, results in better decisions. Workers are more likely to carry out decisions they made themselves. Moreover, WPM improves communications, reduces the need for supervision, and overall motivates workers to work harder and more efficiently. The final arguments are *humanistic* or *psychological*. The claim is that by contributing to personal growth and satisfying non-pecuniary needs (including those for autonomy, creativity, achievement, and social approval) WPM reduces alienation and enhances human dignity.

Power equalization arguments were common in the 1960s and 1970s, especially in Europe and among leftist student groups. With the decline of the left, these are made less commonly now, especially since experience has shown that while participation may have many advantages, it is unlikely to transform society. Managerial and humanistic arguments, by contrast, were most common in the US, particularly in the 1980s. For a while, WPM was almost a fad (Marchington et al. 1993). In Britain, on the other hand, it was widely seen as linked to the highly controversial "human resources" movement.

In practice, WPM comes in many forms. Some are informal. Kinds of formal participation may be classified according to a number of dimensions. One is the level at which participation occurs (e.g., the work group, department, plant, or company). Another classification is by degree of control workers exert: whether management merely listens to employees but retains final say, or whether there is joint control and both sides must agree before a decision is reached (as in collective bargaining), or whether the workers themselves have final say (as in true producers' cooperatives). Still another dimension relates to topics regarding which participation occurs (e.g., wages, production methods, or investment decisions). A final dimension is ownership: do workers own all, some, or none of the company?

Most of the research has focused on three major types of WPM: direct participation, representative participation, and worker ownership and control.

Direct participation takes two forms, sometimes called offline (or "problem solving") and online (or semi-autonomous work) teams. Quality circles (popular in the US during the 1970–1980s) are typical of offline groups (Applebaum & Batt 1994). They consist of a small group of workers from the same work area who meet together voluntarily on a regular basis, often with a specially trained chair. They often deal not just with quality, but also such problems as work flow, productivity, safety, and employee welfare generally. Total Quality Management (TQM) and Six Sigma groups are related programs.

Offline groups typically make recommendations to management. Online teams actually make decisions. Online participation occurs when an entire work group (or work team) is given wide autonomy to make decisions as to how it does its work and how it relates to other departments and management. The concept of work teams developed out of research conducted by the Tavistock Institute in Britain on "sociotechnical systems" (Trist & Bamforth 1951) and later introduced extensively in Scandinavia. In time the practice spread to Japan and the US. Some of the most extensive use of autonomous work teams has occurred at NUMMI, the joint General Motors-Toyota Fremont, California auto plant (Adler 1992), and at Saturn (Rubenstein & Kochan 2001).

Both online and offline teams spread rapidly in the US during the 1990s. Both forms have been fairly intensively studied, with the main measures of success being productivity and satisfaction. A major finding of the research is direct participation is unlikely to prosper or even survive unless it is accompanied by other appropriate human-resources policies and conditions (Ichniowski et al. 2000). Among these are employment security, management and supervisory support (WPM may threaten supervisors' power, status, and even their jobs), work group cohesion, cooperative labor–management relations, and financial rewards for increased productivity. Cultural factors may also be important.

Unfortunately, many instances of direct participation are short lived. Management engages in "pseudo-participation" and gives workers little real autonomy, worker suggestions are not implemented, teams meet less often, and gradually the program atrophies. But in other situations direct participation (regardless of what it is called) has had significant payoffs for all concerned and the entire process has been routinized. Surveys suggest that in the US, at least, manufacturing workers on average enjoyed more autonomy by the mid-1990s than they did a quarter century earlier (Osterman 1994).

Representative participation takes many forms. Aside from unions, the best known and most studied are works councils, which exist in many European countries, with those in Germany receiving particular attention (Rogers & Streeck 1995). Quantitative research in this area has been difficult due to fuzziness in variables; nevertheless, German works councils have been credited with much of the responsibility for Germany's overall good union–management relations. One explanation is that adversarial zero-sum gain negotiations on topics such as wages have been conducted by unions at the national level, while reserving for works councils issues more susceptible to cooperation such as discipline, training, and work schedules. Yet even in Germany works councils differ in effectiveness. In some situations they are powerless, in part because of worker uninterest. Efforts have been made to explain why works councils have been more successful in Germany than in, say, France or Spain. The answer seems to be related to history and culture.

The final major category is workers' ownership and control (WOC). Ownership without control (as is the case with most US Employee Stock Ownership Plans) typically involves little participation. Effective control without ownership is difficult. Examples of situations with ownership and considerable control include Israeli kibbutzim, pre-1985 Yugoslav industry, numerous small producers' cooperatives in many countries, professional partnerships among doctors, lawyers, and accountants, and Mondragon, a Spanish conglomerate with over

30,000 employees (Whyte & Whyte 1988). All have been studied.

Research suggests that WOC is most likely to succeed in small firms in which most jobs are the same or can be performed by all members, little capital is required, member motivation is at least partly ideological, the product market favors high-quality over low-cost products, and most employees enjoy full and equal voting rights (thus professional partnerships are imperfect examples of WOC because secretaries have no vote).

WOC is beset with problems (Uvalic 1991). If economically successful, WOC firms grow too large. In large firms management of necessity becomes a specialized function performed only by a few. Under these circumstances, rotation of top management jobs among members rarely works. Further, member discipline may be divisive. Arrangements for new members to buy in or for retiring members to sell their shares are difficult. As a consequence of these problems most cases of WOC eventually become transformed into traditional hierarchical companies, or they fail altogether.

To conclude, scholarly interest in WPM peaked around 1990. Much of it was motivated by belief that WPM would be a magic cure for industrial problems. But as WPM's limitations emerged, scholarly interest rapidly declined. Nevertheless, the evidence suggests that under appropriate, fairly limited circumstances WPM can enhance both employee job satisfaction and organizational efficiency (Heller et al. 1998: ch. 8).

SEE ALSO: Democracy and Organizations; Human Resource Management; Industrial Relations; Labor–Management Relations; Labor Movement; Labor Process; Teamwork; Work, Sociology of

REFERENCES AND SUGGESTED READINGS

Adler, P. (1992) The "Learning Bureaucracy": The New United Motor Manufacturing, Inc. In: Staw, B. & Cummings, L. L. (Eds.), *Research in Organizational Behavior* 15: 111–94.

Applebaum, E. & Batt, R. (1994) *The New American Workplace: Transforming Work Systems in the United States.* ILR Press, Ithaca, NY.

Couch, C. & Pizzorno, A. (1978) *The Resurgence of Class Conflict in Western Europe Since 1968.* Holmes & Meir, New York.

Dachler, P. and Wilpert, B. (1978) Conceptual Dimensions and Boundaries of Participation in Organizations: A Critical Evaluation. *Administrative Science Quarterly* 23(1): 1–39.

Heller, F., Pusic, E., Strauss, G., & Wilpert, B. (1998) *Organizational Participation: Myth and Reality.* Oxford University Press, Oxford.

Ichniowski, C., Levine, D., Olson, C., & Strauss, G. (2000) *The American Workplace: Skills, Compensation, and Employee Involvement.* Cambridge University Press, Cambridge.

Marchington, M., Wilkinson, A., Ackers, P., & Goodman, J. (1993) The Influence of Managerial Relations on Waves of Employee Involvement. *British Journal of Industrial Relations* 32: 553–76.

Osterman, P. (1994) How Common is Workplace Transformation and Who Adopts It? *Industrial and Labor Relations Review* 47: 173–88.

Rogers, J. & Streeck, W. (Eds.) (1995) *Works Councils.* University of Chicago Press, Chicago.

Rubenstein, S. & Kochan, T. (2001) *Learning from Saturn: Possibilities for Corporate Governance and Employee Relations.* ILR Press, Ithaca, NY.

Trist, E. & Bamforth, K. W. (1951) Some Social and Psychological Consequences of the Long-Wall Method of Coal-Getting. *Human Relations* 3: 38.

Uvalic, M. (1991) *The PEPPER Report: Promotion of Employee Participation in Profits and Enterprise Results.* Brussels: Commission of the European Community.

Whyte, W. F. & Whyte, K. K. (1988) *Making Mondragon: The Growth and Dynamics of the Worker Cooperative Complex.* ILR Press, Ithaca, NY.

manifest destiny

Peter Chua

Manifest destiny refers to a belief and a sustained racial and imperialist project that the Christian God ordained United States settlers and land speculators to occupy the entire North American continent and claim territorial, political, and economic sovereignty over its people and resources. Articulations of this belief and project were prevalent yet widely contested in the nineteenth century; they persist into the twenty-first century.

Many white settlers with Northwestern European heritage believed that it was their dutiful mission to remake the "New World" in their image and spread confidently US-styled liberty and democracy. This remarkably masculinist mission as the "Great Redeemer" provided for the western expansion across the lands of North American indigenous people (such as the Seminoles, Cherokees, Siouxs, Comanches, Pawnees, Apaches, Poncas, Arapahos, and Cheyennes) into Mexico and toward the Pacific frontier, bringing industrial and national prosperity. Accordingly, this manifest destiny belief conveys the idea that expansion and possession were ordained by God, fulfilled by Christian settlers, and not established by rifles, soldiers, and atrocities.

While influential newspaper editor John O'Sullivan coined this term in 1839, Horsman's *Race and Manifest Destiny* (1981) reminds us that the white supremacist narrative of manifest destiny had already justified earlier acts related to expansionism and explorations of US colonial settlements. Significant to US history and contemporary life, it is a nationalist ideology that combines distinct forms of racial and religious thoughts to produce particular state, economic, and cultural forms of genocide, assimilation, and other racial projects.

Manifest destiny is not discussed only in relation to continental expansion. It is also associated with US colonialism, military interventions, and economic imperialism in Mexico and Latin American countries. Moreover, it served as a major reason why the US sought to enter the Chinese market, coerced Japan to open its doors to US commerce and "friendship," purchased Alaska from Russia, and forcibly acquired northern Mexico, Hawaii, Cuba, the Philippines, Puerto Rico, and other territories in the Caribbean and the Pacific. After World War II, the US continued to view as its ordained mission the promotion of US-styled democracy and ways of life as it fought wars and occasionally provided peacekeepers in Korea, Vietnam, and other countries in Central America, Northern Africa, and the Middle East.

Sociological inquiries examine closely two major impacts of the manifest destiny belief and related narratives of "white men's burden" and their "civilizing mission." First, they predominantly explore conflicts over land tenure.

Neo-Marxist sociology focuses on the class struggles and property conflicts entrenched in the earlier US economy. These economic, political, and racialized struggles transformed an early nineteenth-century semi-slavery and semi-feudal society into a global capitalist superpower after 1945. World historians and historical sociologists examine the social processes by which white settlers (such as in South Africa and the US), explorers, and soldiers annexed land, acquired property rights, and dispossessed indigenous and other non-white communities. They delve into the cultural and economic relationships among frontier violence, shifts in rural land ownership, and subsequent growth of industrial capitalism. Theoretically, they provide new ways to understand power, imperialism, gendered nationalism, states and legal sovereignty, and colonial and postcolonial wars.

The second series of sociological inquiries follows from the first. Racial and ethnic studies and the sociology of racism explore the racialized making of economic, cultural, gender, and sexual subordination and the related demographic changes in racial composition as another direct impact of the manifest destiny belief and the conflicts over land and resources. This belief and set of conflicts shifted political and economic power among racial groups and altered racialized residential patterns (such as through extermination, forced removals, and relocation), territorial sovereignty, and everyday ways of life. These studies also delve into the new expressions of racial and cultural superiority proliferated as white settlers moved westward. These studies highlight earlier stereotypical accounts such as the "disappearing Indians," "dirty Mexicans," and "little brown brothers" (to refer to Filipinos). This is in contrast to a variety of racialized narratives of white settlers and immigrants that highlight their rugged individualism and persistence in overcoming the seemingly natural brutality and savagery of the frontier.

Newer inquiries focus on recent continuation and transformation of the manifest destiny narrative as associated with new racial projects, imperialist conquest, and institutional articulations of empire, exceptionalism, and ethnic nationalism. These newer studies place greater analytical importance on culture, religion, and human agency than before. Analytically, they explore new patronizing relations (for instance, between the US and Iraq during the 2000s) as well as the associated moral sense of political, economic, cultural, and religious superiority (for instance, during the US–Vietnam War). Cultural analyses of these new projects and articulations highlight the nuanced relationships among particular Christian ideological repertories, nationalist identities (of individuals, groups, and countries), state policies, and the practices of "occasional" interventions. Particularly noteworthy are the debates regarding cultural and gendered expressions of ethnoreligious identities and nationalist atrocities involving land and forced displacement of racial/ethnic groups. Researchers are scrutinizing elite forms of art and popular cultural forms in everyday life to understand how they reflect, mediate, generate, and resist new nationalist articulations in identities and practices of manifest destiny.

SEE ALSO: Colonialism (Neocolonialism); Indigenous Peoples; Migration, Ethnic Conflicts, and Racism; Nation-State and Nationalism; Race; Race (Racism); Whiteness

REFERENCES AND SUGGESTED READINGS

Coles, R. L. (2002) Manifest Destiny Adapted for 1990s War Discourse: Mission and Destiny. *Sociology and Religion* 63: 403–26.

Filler, L. & Guttmann, A. (Eds.) (1962) *The Removal of the Cherokee Nation: Manifest Destiny or National Dishonor?* Heath, Boston.

Horsman, R. (1981) *Race and Manifest Destiny: The Origins of American Racial Anglo-Saxonism*, rpt edn. Harvard University Press, Cambridge, MA.

Kelly, J. D. (2003) US Power, After 9/11 and Before It: If Not an Empire, Then What? *Public Culture* 15: 347–69.

Lockard, C. A. (1994) Meeting Yesterday Head-On: The Vietnam War in Vietnamese, American, and World History. *Journal of World History* 5: 227–70.

San Buenaventura, S. (1998) The Colors of Manifest Destiny: Filipinos and the American Other(s). *Amerasia Journal* 24: 1–26.

Venegas, Y. (2004) The Erotics of Racialization: Gender and Sexuality in the Making of California. *Frontiers* 25: 63–89.

Wade, P. (2001) Racial Identity and Nationalism: A Theoretical View from Latin America. *Ethnic and Racial Studies* 24: 845–65.

Mannheim, Karl (1893–1947)

Martin Ruef

Karl Mannheim was born in Budapest, Hungary, but developed his academic career in Germany (in Heidelberg and Frankfurt) and England (at the London School of Economics). He was the earliest proponent of the *sociology of knowledge*, a branch of theory concerned with the influence of social context on our way of perceiving, interpreting, and forming claims about the world. Although Mannheim began his career as a philosopher with an interest in epistemology, he became increasingly fascinated by the impact of society on thought processes, with particular emphasis on culture, intellectual competition, and intergenerational dynamics. In his most influential book, *Ideology and Utopia* (1936 [1929]), Mannheim distinguished between two forms of belief systems: *ideological* systems, which seek to ensure inertia in beliefs through an emphasis on the past; and *utopian* systems, which embrace change in beliefs through an emphasis on the future. After being forced from Germany in 1933, Mannheim's writings turned toward the contemporary crisis generated by fascism, examining the role of planning and the possibility of a democratic society.

Karl Mannheim spent his childhood in Hungary. Following several semesters at the University of Budapest, he moved to Germany to study philosophy at Freiburg and Heidelberg. During this early phase of his academic career, he was influenced by both Hungarian and German teachers, including Georg Lukács and Béla Zalay in the former camp, and Heinrich Rickert, Emil Lask, and Edmund Husserl in the latter. He was also influenced by Juliska Láng, a psychologist and fellow Hungarian student, whom he married shortly after graduation. In 1922, Mannheim published his doctoral dissertation on epistemology, under the title of *The Structural Analysis of Knowledge*.

Mannheim's interest in sociological theory developed in the early 1920s, through an intensive study of Max Weber, Alfred Weber, Max Scheler, and Karl Marx. These efforts came to fruition in 1925 with the publication of an article on "The Problem of a Sociology of Knowledge," which created a new subfield of the discipline. At the time, Mannheim accepted his first faculty position at the University of Heidelberg. His most widely read book, *Ideology and Utopia*, was published four years later and introduced the sociology of knowledge to a much broader audience. In the same year, Mannheim was offered a professorship at the University of Frankfurt, which he held until his dismissal by the Nazi regime in 1933.

Following his exile to England, Mannheim joined the London School of Economics and Political Science. In this third phase of his career, he became fascinated by the crisis of liberal democracy, as evidenced by the regime change in Germany. Mannheim expanded his existing scholarship on the role of the intelligentsia to address the problem of planning in a democratic society. This led to an interest in the sociology of education and an appointment to the chair in education at the University of London in 1945. In 1947, Mannheim was offered the job of directing the European division of UNESCO and appeared to have an opportunity to apply his theories on planning and education. Unfortunately, he died unexpectedly a few weeks later at the age of 53.

SOCIOLOGY OF KNOWLEDGE

Mannheim's pioneering efforts in the sociology of knowledge anticipated a number of recent developments, including a rapprochement between cognitive science and the sociology of culture (DiMaggio 1997), as well as the development of cognitive sociology in its own right (Zerubavel 1997). At the same time, he echoed intellectual concerns that were especially pronounced in early twentieth-century Europe, addressing the constraints imposed by conservatism and the question of whether humans can transcend irrational patterns of thought. Seen in this light, Mannheim's sociology of knowledge can be seen as both building on, and critiquing, the work of predecessors such as Karl Marx and Max Weber.

In his earliest writings, Mannheim began with a central question in interpretive sociology: How can philosophers or sociologists interpret the cognitive perspective of their subjects, especially if the life experiences and social context of the subjects are very different from those of the analyst? The problem is most acute when the analyst seeks to understand a worldview (*Weltanschauung*) holistically, including the large number of attitudes and beliefs that are tacit (pre-theoretical) and therefore resistant to scientific formalization (Mannheim 1993 [1921–2]). Mannheim identified three kinds of meaning that can be attached to a society's *Weltanschauung*, including its intrinsic meaning, elicited without reference to individuals' motives (*objective* meaning), its extrinsic or symbolic meaning, in light of individuals' motives (*expressive* meaning), and its meaning as reflected in textual and third-party perceptions (*documentary* meaning). From the standpoint of historical interpretation, documentary meaning is most amenable to systematic analysis, although it also tends to exclude pre-theoretical intuitions.

In his sociology of knowledge, Mannheim (1993 [1925]) analyzed different approaches to interpretation more systematically. A sociology of knowledge begins with the assumption that the thought of any individual is tied to that individual's social existence or *being*. How we specify the relationship between thought and being depends on our philosophical perspective. *Positivists* view this relationship as being relatively unproblematic, insofar as empirical evidence collected in an individual's daily existence can be used to adjudicate between conflicting thoughts. *Formal apriorism* argues that thought precedes being and, as a consequence, we ought to take steps to ensure the logical integrity of thought. *Material apriorism*, also known as phenomenology, questions the utility of formal logic. Instead, it seeks to understand the intrinsic ways in which individuals perceive the world and how, in turn, this influences their social existence. Finally, *historicism* agrees with many of the precepts of phenomenology, but emphasizes that distinctive modes of cognition tend to be characteristic of different historical eras. Mannheim showed clear favoritism toward the latter two positions, especially given his interest in the concept of a *Weltanschauung*.

These themes are continued in Mannheim's writings on specific types of worldviews, including conservatism, ideology, and utopianism. In analyzing these worldviews, Mannheim began to turn away from an abstract conception of the cognitive subject and toward an emphasis on *thought communities* (see also Zerubavel 1997). He noted that it is not individuals in isolation who do the thinking, but people in groups who develop distinctive styles of thought (Mannheim 1936 [1929]: 3). One style of thought that Mannheim studied was *conservatism*, a reaction against Enlightenment efforts toward rationalization. Following Weber's discussion of formal rationality, Mannheim (1986 [1927]) defined rationalization as an effort to impose abstract, quantitative laws on nature and society. Conservatism emerged as an intellectual backlash in the late eighteenth and early nineteenth centuries, highlighting concrete, qualitative, and religious features of western European culture. In contrast to *traditionalists*, who simply engage in habitual efforts to maintain older customs and institutions, conservatives actively reconstruct those customs and institutions for a modern audience. As a detailed exemplar, Mannheim analyzed the conservative Romantic movement in nineteenth-century Germany and its efforts to celebrate feudal institutions.

Mannheim's (1936 [1929]) *Ideology and Utopia* likewise can be seen as an effort to understand *Weltanschauungen* that diverge from modern rationalism. Ideological perspectives, which subsume conservatism, entail anti-rational thinking intended to retard social change. Utopianism, on the other hand, seeks social transformation, but also relies on strong anti-rational elements – in particular, an orientation toward goals which are not yet attainable in reality (p. 173). In advancing these conceptions, Mannheim sought to remove ideology from its then-dominant Marxist connotation, especially as reflected in the critique of "false consciousness." Mannheim suggested that all worldviews – including capitalism, socialism, and communism – might be classified as ideological or utopian thinking, depending on the context and interests with which they are advanced.

In pursuing his sociology of knowledge, Mannheim also attempted to clarify the impact of social structure on differences in *Weltanschauung*. One relevant structure in this respect involves *generations* – cohorts of individuals born around the same time. Mannheim stressed that generations, as demographic units, should be distinguished from "generations as actuality," which require that cohort members share a common culture. The second structural feature that interested Mannheim was *competition* among opposing worldviews. Extending basic economic terminology, Mannheim distinguished between prevailing worldviews achieved by virtue of consensus, by monopolistic interpretation, by atomistic competition, and by concentration among different thought communities. In many respects, he anticipated recent sociological developments concerning the competitive ecology of ideas (e.g., Barnett & Woywode 2004).

SOCIOLOGY OF INTELLECTUALS

In discussing his sociology of knowledge, Mannheim presented a distinctive perspective on intellectuals (Kurzman & Owens 2002). While other scholars of his day, such as the Italian communist Antonio Gramsci, characterized intellectuals as being tied to their social class of origin, Mannheim (1936 [1929]: 137) argued that the intelligentsia in modern society was a relatively autonomous and classless stratum. In the past, he suggested, intellectual activity had been monopolized by closed groups, such as the priesthood, defined along occupational or class lines. With the advent of the "modern bourgeoisie," however, the intelligentsia became largely detached from social class and, as a consequence, their worldviews are constantly in a state of change (p. 139). Members of the intelligentsia can therefore freely align themselves with a variety of social classes or political parties.

DEMOCRATIZATION OF CULTURE

Following the rise of fascism, Mannheim's writings increasingly turned toward social policy concerns. Considering his exile from Germany, Mannheim's perspective was often surprisingly optimistic. He stressed that trends toward democracy – not just in political life, but in intellectual life as a whole – were the destiny of modern society (1993 [1933]: 447). Democracy, in this sense, relied on three cultural principles. The first was the ontological *equality* of all individual members of society. By equality, Mannheim did not mean to imply a "mechanical leveling" of human beings, but simply that all members of society should pursue their goals with equal opportunity. The second principle was the *autonomy* (or "vital selfhood") of individuals, coupled with social responsibility. A third principle addressed the potential paradox of elites in a democratic society and appropriate methods of *elite selection*. Mannheim noted that democratic elite selection can proceed through bureaucratic advancement, unrestricted competition, or party politics.

Mannheim also identified pathologies that tend to be associated with processes of democratization. As evidenced in fascism, mass democratic movements could lead to anti-democratic outcomes. This was especially common when democracy became divorced from rationality and served as an instrument of emotional impulses and mob rule (1993 [1933]: 450). Mannheim's solution was to suggest ways in which rational planning could be combined with a democratic culture. A key aspect of planning that captured Mannheim's attention involved establishing a system of education that would prepare citizens for democracy. The discipline of sociology was viewed as an integral part of such educational reforms, particularly in helping average citizens understand the complex social institutions that can support a democratic civilization.

SEE ALSO: Ideology; Knowledge, Sociology of; Marx, Karl; Phenomenology; Rational Choice Theories; Utopia; Weber, Max

REFERENCES AND SUGGESTED READINGS

Barnett, W. & Woywode, M. (2004) From Red Vienna to the *Anschluss*: Ideological Competition among Viennese Newspapers during the Rise of National Socialism. *American Journal of Sociology* 109: 1452–99.

DiMaggio, P. (1997) Culture and Cognition. *Annual Review of Sociology* 23: 263–87.

Kurzman, C. & Owens, L. (2002) The Sociology of Intellectuals. *Annual Review of Sociology* 28: 63–90.

Mannheim, K. (1936 [1929]) *Ideology and Utopia: An Introduction to the Sociology of Knowledge.* Harcourt Brace, New York.

Mannheim, K. (1940) *Man and Society in an Age of Reconstruction.* Routledge & Kegan Paul, London.

Mannheim, K. (1986 [1927]) *Conservatism: A Contribution to the Sociology of Knowledge.* Routledge & Kegan Paul, London.

Mannheim, K. (1993 [1921–2]) On the Interpretation of *Weltanschauung.* In: Wolff, K. (Ed.), *From Karl Mannheim.* Transaction, London.

Mannheim, K. (1993 [1925]) The Problem of a Sociology of Knowledge. In: Wolff, K. (Ed.), *From Karl Mannheim.* Transaction, London.

Mannheim, K. (1993 [1933]) The Democratization of Culture. In: Wolff, K. (Ed.), *From Karl Mannheim.* Transaction, London.

Zerubavel, E. (1997) *Social Mindscapes: An Invitation to Cognitive Sociology.* Harvard University Press, Cambridge, MA.

Marcuse, Herbert (1898–1979)

Steven P. Dandaneau

Herbert Marcuse was a German philosopher and social theorist who immigrated to the US to escape Nazi persecution, becoming a naturalized US citizen in 1940. Marcuse is credited with having formulated a distinctive critical theory of society that combined a Hegelian reading of Marx with insights drawn from his masterful studies of modern and twentieth-century philosophy and social theory. As the only member of the famed Frankfurt School's inner circle at ease with partisanship, Marcuse's highly visible participation in 1960s revolutionary activism led to his celebration as a New Left intellectual hero on a par with Jean-Paul Sartre. His once-considerable presence and notoriety worldwide notwithstanding, Marcuse's scant influence on institutionalized sociology since is largely attributable to the fact that his lifelong commitment to dialectical forms of critical social analysis places his otherwise rich oeuvre at loggerheads with predominantly positivist sociology.

Marcuse's intellectual life may be divided into five periods. While a spiritual connection with Hegel and Marx is evident even in his earliest days, the facts of Marcuse's biography meant that he would be a material witness to the rise of Nazism as well as to the existentialist and phenomenological philosophies of Martin Heidegger and Edmund Husserl, with whom he studied between 1927 and 1932. Their intensive tutelage on conditions of radical subjective existence, experience, and perception during Germany's bitter interwar years enriched Marcuse's critical analysis of an emergent fascist society, and provided the basis for his first major scholarly synthesis, construed, characteristically, as a timely political intervention.

Marcuse's *Reason and Revolution: Hegel and the Rise of Social Theory* (1941), regarded by Marxists and non-Marxists alike as a classic study, sets out to rescue Hegelian philosophy from its Nazi-propagated association with totalitarian ideology. But Marcuse also demonstrates the radical implications of Hegelian philosophy for would-be ideologists of liberal-capitalist society by showing that the genesis of the dominant western positivist philosophy and social science lies in a series of self-conscious efforts to suppress the revolutionary implications of Hegel's dialectical method of sociohistorical analysis, the same method that Marx, of course, embraced rather than suppressed. Neither fodder for national socialism nor simply the long-vanquished foe of positivism, Hegel's historicizing phenomenology is viewed as the ideal expression of Reason's development through acts of radical negation, the material manifestation of which, for Marcuse as previously for Marx, is revolutionary praxis. Marcuse's distinctive vision of praxis would eventually, however, attend to elements of subjective existential experience – as suggested, for example, by his later demand for "new sensibilities" – that exceed even those evident in Marx's *Economic and Philosophic Manuscripts of 1844*.

During and after World War II, Marcuse worked for various pre-CIA US intelligence agencies in an effort to aid the defeat of the Nazi regime and its post-war remnants. The second major period of his intellectual life thus does not become widely evident until the publication of his perhaps most visionary book, *Eros and Civilization: A Philosophical Inquiry into Freud* (1955).

With McCarthy still calling witnesses, Marcuse decamped in 1952 to Columbia and Harvard before landing at Brandeis University in 1954, there joining Abraham Maslow and countless similarly luminous intellectuals in creating a veritable intellectual and cultural 1960s in the middle of the "Leave It to Beaver" 1950s. Much of Marcuse's study at this time was dedicated to demonstrating, as he had done for Hegel, the profoundly revolutionary character of Freud's psychoanalysis. Where in Freud there is analysis of repression, Marcuse, for example, distinguishes socially necessary forms of psychological repression from the "surplus repression" foisted upon the denizens of consumerist capitalist society. Freud's uncompromising emphases on sharply contradictory forces, such as elaborated in his famous *Civilization and Its Discontents*, is preferable, argued Marcuse, to the theoretical adjustments and inward-looking palliatives made popular by the leading neo-Freudians and ego-psychologists of the day, among them Karen Horney, Erik Erikson, and Marcuse's former Frankfurt School colleague, Erich Fromm. Frankfurt School critical theory is often characterized as having proffered a novel Marx–Freud synthesis, the foremost expression of which was given by Marcuse.

Marcuse's most straightforwardly sociological studies are the mainstay of his third period of intellectual work. *Soviet Marxism* (1958) and *One-Dimensional Man* (1964) advance highly critical analyses of what are depicted as essentially two competing forms of totalitarian society, the former evidently so and justified by the bastardization of a once-radical theory, the latter less evidently so and all the more threatening as a result. For Marcuse, advanced capitalist-industrial society systematically absorbs the sting of utopian criticism and papers over deep-seated contradictions via the diffusion of its extraordinary wealth and power through the mechanisms of mass society and culture. With basic needs largely met by the technologies of the Welfare/Warfare State and Reason impoverished via the seductive hegemony of diffuse technocratic thinking, Marcuse depicts an unsettling Cold War dystopia where choice of ice cream and candidates among competing flavors measures the extent of possible happiness and freedom. *One-Dimensional Man* tended to motivate, however, rather than discourage dissent, as it served as a surprising inspiration for radical social and cultural analysis as well as a call to redeem the promise of Reason via revolutionary praxis for many who took up the mantle of protest in the 1960s.

Marcuse's involvement in what he advocated as a "Great Refusal" constitutes his fourth major period of social and philosophical analysis and coincides with his move to the University of California at San Diego in 1965. In 1969 Marcuse published *An Essay on Liberation*; in 1972, *Counterrevolution and Revolt*. In these works and others, Marcuse peers unflinchingly into the abyss of war, assassination, and political repression, searching in the hope of finding reason to hope as much as for just cause for revolutionary action or for specific positions and strategies in the massive worldwide struggles then ongoing. Given his visibility and increasing stridency, it is perhaps not surprising that Marcuse was harassed by government officials, including California governor Ronald Reagan.

The final period of Marcuse's life and work is aesthetic in form and content and is summarized in his final book, *The Aesthetic Dimension*: *Towards a Critique of Marxist Aesthetics* (1978). With the new social movements of the 1960s lost in their long march through the institutions, Marcuse returned to the fundamental philosophical basis of his lifetime of advocacy for the inherent bond between Reason and Revolution. This book also suggests rapprochement with the more consistently aesthetic critical theory of Horkheimer and Adorno. As was the case with Adorno, Marcuse's last major study sought to wrest from the grips of an oppressive historical reality the almost unspeakable hope for the realization of utopian possibilities. Marcuse died in 1979, the same year as Margaret Thatcher was elected prime minister.

As the generation of the 1960s fades into their golden years, it is ever-more doubtful that Herbert Marcuse's intellectual legacy will again significantly influence sociological analysis. Major figures in social theory, from Anthony Giddens to critical theory's putative expositor, Jürgen Habermas, have defined their distance from Marcuse. Yet contemporary advanced capitalist society appears no less "one-dimensional" than when Marcuse first dubbed it such, no less incapable of imagining qualitative self-transformation. Nor do these societies appear

to thrive any less on what Marcuse called "repressive desublimation," the process whereby pseudo-gratifications translate into pseudo-freedoms, much as Prole Feed, Hate Week, and the up-scale satisfactions symbolized by Victory Gin were just about enough to ensure happiness in Oceania. "Either there will be a catastrophe or things will get worse," Marcuse sometimes prophesized to his students. The jury remains out on which it will be.

SEE ALSO: Adorno, Theodor W.; Dialectic; Critical Theory/Frankfurt School; Freud, Sigmund; Fromm, Erich; Horkheimer, Max; Positivism

REFERENCES AND SUGGESTED READINGS

Bokina, J. & Lukes, T. J. (Eds.) (1994) *Marcuse: From the New Left to the Next Left*. University Press of Kansas, Lawrence.

Breines, P. (Ed.) (1970) *Critical Interruptions: New Left Perspectives on Herbert Marcuse*. Herder & Herder, New York.

DeKoven, M. (2004) *Utopia Limited: The Sixties and the Emergence of the Postmodern*. Duke University Press, Durham, NC.

Jacoby, R. (1999) *The End of Utopia: Politics and Culture in an Age of Apathy*. Basic Books, New York.

Kellner, D. (1984) *Herbert Marcuse and the Crisis of Marxism*. University of California Press, Berkeley.

Wolff, K. H. & Moore, B., Jr. (Eds.) (1967) *The Critical Spirit: Essays in Honor of Herbert Marcuse*. Beacon Press, Boston.

marginal art

Yoshio Sugimoto

The term marginal art (*genkai geijutsu*) was coined by Shunsuke Tsurumi, an analyst of mass culture in Japan. Tsurumi classifies art forms into three analytical categories: pure, popular, and marginal. In what he terms pure art, both producers and their audience are art specialists, with the producers being professional artists and those who appreciate it being equipped with a degree of expert knowledge. For instance, paintings, symphonies, operas, *noh*, and formal tea ceremonies executed or performed by professionals fall into this category. Popular art is produced by professional artists in collaboration with mass media organizations, but is consumed by non-specialist masses and is therefore often regarded as vulgar art or pseudo-art. Its specific forms include television programs, popular songs, posters, detective stories, animations, and comic strips.

Marginal art differs from both pure and popular art in that both its producers and its consumers are laypeople that lack professional expertise. Marginal art emerges in the domain where everyday life and artistic expression intersect and includes such concrete forms as graffiti, house decoration, children's building blocks, everyday gestures, song variations, festivals, funerals, family videos, family albums, political demonstrations, calls to enliven physical labor, nicknaming, tongue twisters, and even gravesite decorations. These activities and their products are primarily devised and developed by amateurs who neither make a living through professional artistic practice nor claim specialist artistic know-how. Similarly, those who appreciate the work are also people untrained in artistic appreciation or do not possess specialist knowledge. To an extent, every person can be, and is, a marginal artist. By definition, marginal art lacks precision or rigor and contains ambiguities that constitute the seeds of more articulated forms of professionally produced art.

Tsurumi's perspective on art includes all kinds of symbols distilled from human aesthetic experiences. It also covers a wider range of human activities than is conventionally considered artistic and questions the narrow dichotomy between pure and popular art forms. He suggests that marginal art, as the most primordial art form, has existed since ancient times and thus preceded the other two forms of art. He contends that the development of the mass media and of modern economic and political institutions has removed marginal art from the sphere of legitimately recognized art.

According to Tsurumi, "playful activities" that go hand in hand with human labor constitute the core of marginal art. For example, most traditional, anonymously authored folk songs reflect agricultural work such as rice-planting, tea-picking, and log-carrying. Many artifacts of folk craft such as rice bowls, tea cups. and handcrafted furniture are produced by nameless craftspersons and are used every day by ordinary people who appreciate the beauty and utility of the object. Hence, central to the genre of marginal art is the "aesthetics of use," as opposed to the principle of art for art's sake, which operates in pure art, or art for commerce's sake, which animates popular art.

The various ways in which people and objects are named represents a verbal domain of marginal art. Riddles, anecdotes, funny little tales, and proverbs that have survived for centuries among the masses are the products of marginal art that have withstood the test of time. In the nonverbal sphere, the ways in which one smiles, cries, eats, and drinks often manifest themselves as marginal art. *Origami*, the Japanese marginal art of folding paper into figures and *bonsai*, the cultivation of dwarf trees in shallow pots, are now practiced internationally.

While large-scale festivals for tourists are, by and large, commercially organized expressions of popular culture in which the performers are separated from the audience, small local festivals, in which little distinction is made between the two, contain the widest range of marginal art and represent its most comprehensive manifestation. Centering on folk religious memories, small-scale, regional festivals bring together popular artistic skills, expressions, and products that have roots in community life. In the Japanese context, they may include portable shrines, summer Bon Festival songs and dances, goods sold at night stalls, and decorations in sacred places.

The notion of marginal art reflects and resonates with the perspectives of folklore studies. When studied collectively and systematically, marginal art provides a point of entry into the ways in which ordinary people have lived communally in various geographic locations and historical periods.

This perspective informed a variety of studies of Japan's grassroots culture that were conducted for a few decades after World War II by the *Shiso no kagaku* (Thought of Science) group, for which Tsurumi was the prime intellectual engine. Comprised of both academic researchers and non-professional observers, this popular-level, private research group had a number of branches around the country. Through its analysis of the lifestyles, aesthetics, conceptions, beliefs, and philosophies of common people it put marginal art and those that create and use it on the map of public discourse and debate.

SEE ALSO: Art Worlds; *Seikatsu/Seikatsusha*; Yanagita, Kunio

REFERENCES AND SUGGESTED READINGS

Tsurumi, S. (1967) *Genkai geijutsu-ron* (*On Marginal Art*). Chikuma Shobō, Tokyo.

marginality

Rutledge M. Dennis

The concept of marginality was first introduced by Robert Park (1928) and explained, almost as a minor theme, in Park's analysis of the causes and consequences of human migrations. In his article, Park referred to a "new type of personality" which was emerging out of rapid human migratory patterns during the end of the nineteenth century and the beginning of the twentieth, and how they would affect present and future relations between groups. The most interesting feature of this essay was Park's discussion of this new personality, which would be a "cultural hybrid, a man living and sharing intimately in the cultural life and traditions of two distinct peoples . . . a man on the margin of two cultures and two societies, which never completely interpenetrated and fused." Edwin Stonequist (1937) probed the marginality concept more extensively than Park, but he highlighted the personality features of marginality and focused his critique into an assessment of the mental state of those marginalized. So closely allied are the views of the two that we can without distortion discuss their views as the Park–Stonequist model of marginality. It became the predominant model and a reference point for studies of marginality (Dennis 1991: 4) until Dickie-Clark (1966) introduced the term "marginal situation"

and moved the discussion from the personality of the marginalized to a more pointedly sociological reference point. Dickie-Clark concluded that the Park–Stonequist model, largely Stonequist's extension of Park's early model, subverted and distorted the sociology of marginality by creating an exclusive model of the marginal who became permanently stereotyped as "irrational, moody, and temperamental."

Dickie-Clark's emphasis on the "marginal situation" is important in that he grounded the concept within sociology, not psychology, and made power and privilege precursors to its genesis. Likewise, the marginal situation evolved out of historical practices and policies which legitimized unequal status and opportunity structures. However, the heavy emphasis on demarcating marginal situations within largely unstructured temporary interactions and settings tended to deflate and underemphasize marginal situations within very structured institutional interactions (Dickie-Clark 1966: 28). The importance of Dickie-Clark's approach, however, gave credence to the argument that marginality was more nuanced, complex, and multidimensional than had been assumed.

The Park–Stonequist model of racial, ethnic, religious, or cultural groups caught between two contrasting worlds, neither of which accepted them, is no longer the model used today. The term has been expanded to include many groups that differ in a variety of ways from the dominant culture, who are viewed by that dominant society as the "other" and dwell on the fringes of their society. A current grouping of those who have made a case for themselves as being among the marginals would include women, the poor, homosexuals, and those with mental and physical illnesses. But central to the marginality query is the question of who wields power, who establishes policies, and the nature of the structural barriers created and the institutions most affected. The lack of access, however, does not translate into a non-societal role, because imposed marginality (see below) is designed to create emotional and social barriers as well as structural ones as it imposes specific though limited roles and positions to be acted and played out by marginals. Thus, marginals are both "of" and "in" the society but with limited access and prescribed positions, and with special roles.

There are two types of marginality: imposed marginality and marginality by choice. Powerful groups using an array of legal, social, economic, and political measures push less powerful groups to the edges of the society and generally attempt to utilize them in the labor market, but in other ways render them invisible (Dennis 2005). This pattern may be seen in the United States as well as throughout Africa, Europe, Asia, and Latin America (Dennis 1994). Usually, the group marginalizing another is numerically larger, but South Africa under apartheid was an example of how a numerically smaller population can marginalize and render momentarily powerless a much larger population. The Park–Stonequist model is of little help in defining or explaining marginality within the context of intergroup relations in the twenty-first century. Marginalization may often lead to anger and resentment, and to a situation in which the marginalized lay in wait for opportunities in anticipation of a time when scores might be settled. Contemporary battles and skirmishes in the Sudan, Spain, Kosovo, and Northern Ireland represent cases of formerly marginalized groups seeking redress for historical grievances. The histories of these cases depict situations in which an accommodation strategy had been the modus operandi, but quite often dominant groups assume that the accommodationist strategies used by powerless groups have been accepted by these groups as a way of life and as an acceptance of their marginal status. That is often far from true.

The second type of marginality is marginality by choice in which groups, usually for religious reasons or for artistic and scholarly reasons, desire to separate themselves and become marginal to the larger social, political, and economic community. Hasidic groups in New York City, the Amish, and the Nation of Islam during the 1950s, 1960s, and 1970s represent this focus. Unlike an imposed marginality in which the marginalized may desire more extensive political, cultural, or economic participation, groups which choose marginality are all too happy to be excluded and left alone, and only those among these groups who desire to leave the group might be said to experience this dual marginality as they seek to find a place in the formerly forbidden worlds beyond the group's enclaves. It is this dual marginality with its implied ambivalences, uncertainties, and choices which represents our present era and generation.

The concept continues to be useful in sociology because it describes structural linkages and relations, and permits us to chart, document, and locate who is a marginal and why, as well as probe the consequences of marginality for the larger society. This will require that we mine more extensively examples of marginality, especially in the areas of social class, ethnicity, and race.

Dual marginality has been suggested as a multidimensional approach to the marginality dilemma and as an approach which might rescue marginality from a theoretical cul-de-sac (Dennis 1991, 2003). A similar point had been made earlier by Peter Worsley (1984). In Dennis's 1991 study the dual marginality theme focused on black youth and their position and role in a medium-sized Midwestern city: they were caught between their role as youth under parental guidance and their role and position of soon-to-be independent young adults; caught between their role and position in a small and marginal black community and a larger, often hostile, white community; caught between their circumscribed role of black youth in a largely segregated city with its limited mobility and freedoms and the role of white youth and their greater freedom in the larger dominant community. The dualness of their marginality was described as the ambivalence of youth to their parents and the black community on the one hand, and their ambivalence toward both white youth and the white community on the other. What was clear in the definition of dual marginality was its structural framework and the fact that the youth were playing out specific roles and positions in segmented aspects of their dual marginal status: they had limited encounters with white youth in the white world, just as they had limited encounters with white adults in the dominant community. In each of these segmented worlds, black youth display both an acceptance and a rejection, mainly because their position is not clear to themselves and they believe that they are both accepted and rejected by parents, the black community, white youth, and the larger white community.

The youth are wedged between those segments presented above, but unlike the Park–Stonequist model, rather than the rejection by both and the personality problems which ultimately emerge, there are degrees of acceptance and rejection from the segmented structures, as well as degrees of acceptance and rejection by youth. The dualness of the marginality is seen more in the fact that the youth, though rejected by the "other," continue to seek an entrance into that world, but when opportunities arise which make possible their entrance or absorption into that world, they may well reject such opportunities. One might see parallel examples in an examination of racial and ethnic groups within large dominant group organizations. Individuals may reject aspects of the culture into which they were born, and may wish to experience and assimilate into another culture or group but may not be able or willing to shed many of the values and behavioral traits of that culture. The ambivalence centers around the tradeoffs seen as necessary to make the leap from one culture to another or from one group to another. So there is simultaneously a movement toward and away from the group to which entrance is sought, just as there is a movement toward and away from the group which has provided the primary socialization. In enlarging the scope of marginality beyond the Park–Stonequist model, it is apparent that today, individuals and groups must confront a world which reflects varying degrees of dual marginality (openness and closedness) as individuals and groups move in and out of group labels and identities and into a world of great certainties and uncertainties. It is this power and resource inequity and the blocked mobility experienced by those marginalized that warrant continued attention by both scholars and activist-scholars.

SEE ALSO: Accommodation; Acculturation; Assimilation; Biracialism; Caste: Inequalities Past and Present; Conflict (Racial/Ethnic); Culture; Marginalization, Outsiders; Plural Society; Social Integration and Inclusion; Solidarity

REFERENCES AND SUGGESTED READINGS

Dennis, R. (1991) Dual Marginality and Discontent Among Black Middletown Youth. In: Dennis, R. (Ed.), *Research in Race and Ethnic Relations*, Vol. 6. JAI Press, Greenwich, CT.

Dennis, R. (1994) Racial and Ethnic Politics. In: Dennis, R. (Ed.), *Research in Race and Ethnic Relations*, Vol. 7. JAI Press, Greenwich, CT.

Dennis, R. (2003) Towards a Theory of Dual Marginality: Dual Marginality and the Dispossessed. *Ideaz* 2(1): 21–31.

Dennis, R. (Ed.) (2005) *Marginality, Power, and Social Structure*. Elsevier, London.

Dickie-Clark, H. F. (1966) *The Marginal Situation*. Routledge & Kegan Paul.

Park, R. E. (1928) Human Migration and the Marginal Man. *American Journal of Sociology* 33: 881–93.

Stonequist, E. V. (1937) *The Marginal Man*. Russell & Russell, New York.

Worsley, P. (1984) *The Three Worlds*. University of Chicago Press, Chicago.

marginalization, outsiders

Hartley Dean

Marginalization is a metaphor that refers to processes by which individuals or groups are kept at or pushed beyond the edges of society. The term outsiders may be used to refer to those individuals or groups who are marginalized.

The expression marginalization appears to have originated with Robert Park's (1928) concept of "marginal man," a term he coined to characterize the lot of impoverished minority ethnic immigrants to a predominantly white Anglo-Saxon Protestant United States. It later became popular, particularly in Latin America (e.g., Germani 1980), as a term that captured the supposed "backwardness," not of immigrants in developed countries, but of people in developing countries who fail or are prevented from participating in the economic, political, and cultural transition to modernity. Modernity, it is argued, constitutes as anomalous the subordinate status and cultural differences of rural peoples and the urban poor who are not properly assimilated to the formal economy or the political or social mainstream. More recently, the term marginalization has been largely superseded by the term exclusion. Nonetheless, marginalization often appears as a synonym for extreme poverty or for social exclusion and it may sometimes be difficult to distinguish between the concepts other than in terms of who is choosing to use them. People may be marginalized from economic production; from consumption (including the consumption of public services); from political participation; and/or from social or cultural interaction. This can apply as much in the developed as in the developing world (e.g., Burchardt et al. 2002).

The nature of the capitalist process of production is such that not everybody will be employed within it, and Marx in his classic analysis referred to those who are rendered outsiders as the "reserve army of labor," who are pushed to the margins of the labor market. Those outside the formal economy may engage in marginalized forms of economic activity, for example in subsistence agriculture in the developing world, in informal or unregulated economic activity (e.g., Williams & Windebank 1998), or in street-level activities, such as hustling or begging (e.g., Dean 1999). Equally important, especially in the context of a society characterized by consumerism (Bauman 1998), is that those who cannot afford to obtain access to goods or services may be marginalized: not only can they remain or become outsiders or strangers to the kinds of shops and leisure facilities that others use, but also they may inhabit marginalized neighborhoods that are poorly served by public services or which may, for example, have been "redlined" by credit providers (e.g., Power 1999). Ultimately, they may exist outside the parameters that define a customary lifestyle, as happens, for example, when people become homeless. Democratic systems may marginalize or ignore the interests of minority groups, and those who are for whatever reason stigmatized or reviled may be marginalized from social networks and community life.

It is not only what people may be marginalized from, but also why they are marginalized. The poor may become outsiders, but so too can the rich when they choose to live separately in gated communities. Disabled people may quite literally be outsiders if, because their needs are marginal to the interests of architects, builders, and planners, they cannot obtain access to public buildings or housing accommodation. Minority and/or itinerant ethnic groups may be marginalized because of racism and so form outsider communities.

The most extreme form of marginalization is associated with criminalization, which occurs when individuals or groups are labeled as deviant (Becker 1963). This can occur when popular or media-inspired "moral panics" stigmatize particular kinds of behavior (which may or may not be technically criminal) and when the offenders assume a marginalized identity.

SEE ALSO: Deviance; Deviance, Criminalization of; Disability as a Social Problem; Ethnic/ Informed Economy; Homelessness; Marginality; Marx, Karl; Poverty; Race; Race (Racism); Social Exclusion

REFERENCES AND SUGGESTED READINGS

Bauman, Z. (1998) *Work, Consumerism and the New Poor*. Open University Press, Buckingham.

Becker, H. (1963) *Outsiders: Studies in the Sociology of Deviance*. Free Press, Glencoe, IL.

Burchardt, T., Le Grand, J., & Piachaud, D. (2002) Degrees of Exclusion: Developing a Dynamic, Multidimensional Picture. In: Hills, J., Le Grand, J., & Piachaud, D. (Eds.), *Understanding Social Exclusion*. Oxford University Press, Oxford.

Dean, H. (Ed.) (1999) *Begging Questions: Street-Level Economic Activity and Social Policy Failure*. Policy Press, Bristol.

Germani, G. (1980) *Marginality*. Transaction, New Brunswick, NJ.

Park, R. (1928) Human Migration and the Marginal Man. *American Journal of Sociology* 33: 881–93.

Power, A. (1999) *Estates on the Edge: The Social Consequences of Mass Housing in Northern Europe*. Macmillan, Basingstoke.

Williams, C. & Windebank, J. (1998) *Informal Employment in the Advanced Economies*. Routledge, London.

Marianne Weber on social change

Patricia Lengermann

Marianne Weber's work is being only slowly recovered and studied; her sociology in general and her analysis of social change in particular are informed by and respond to the ideas of Marx (Weber 1900), of her husband Max, of their mutual friend Georg Simmel, and of feminist activists and theorists like Charlotte Perkins Gilman and Ellen Key. Of these, her debate with Max is arguably the most important. Like him, she embraced a historical-comparative methodology. But her feminism led her to reject his stance in value neutrality, to offer a radically different interpretation of the significance of Protestantism and capitalism, and to use a three-part model of social change, in which ideas are only an equal player with materiality and human agency.

Marianne Weber's sociology emerges today as an almost archetypal representative of the practice of feminist sociology: it has as its central problematic the fundamental feminist principle of describing and explaining society from the standpoint of women and using those descriptions and explanations to analyze how to change society in the direction of greater justice. Her theories of social change are interwoven with the ongoing feminist commitment, common to critical sociologists generally, that the purpose of sociology is not just to know the world but to change it, and the corollary principle that in order to know the world one must try to change it. Marianne Weber was both a social theorist and an activist who built a career as an important player in a number of German feminist organizations, culminating in the period 1919–20, when she became the first German woman representative elected to a state assembly (Baden) and was elected president of the Federation of German Women's Organizations. For her, as for many sociologists speaking for oppressed groups, the sociological project is profoundly liberationist.

Weber's analysis of social change focuses on the description and explanation of the condition of women, a condition she viewed as equally complex and important to study and understand as that of men. She described the changes in women's condition from prehistory to the present (Weber 1907) as an uneven movement toward greater autonomy, and explained both the movement and its unevenness in terms of the dynamic interaction among three fundamental elements in social life – ideas, materiality, and agency. She saw this dynamic working at both the microsocial and macrosocial level and

producing both planned outcomes and unintended consequences.

Weber invoked this model of change at the microsocial level in her response to Simmel's thesis about gender and modernity. Simmel argued that while the massing of objective culture in the world has overwhelmed modern men to the point where they are in danger of losing their capacity for subjective culture (or an interior life), women, unsuited to and excluded from full participation in objective culture, retain a spirituality that men have lost. Weber responded in part by playing off Simmel's dichotomies between objective and subjective culture, arguing that modern women are fully capable of engaging in objective culture and that men must take responsibility for their subjective culture. Then, and using her tripartite model, she stated that all women occupy a particular place in the creation of culture, a third realm of cultural production that she named "women's special cultural task ... the shaping of immediate existence" (Weber 1998c [1918]: 225). She saw women, through acts of individual agency, taking the larger world of objective culture – both material and ideational – and translating it through work into the daily artifacts and atmosphere of the home. She argued that the human ability to create a meaningful subjective culture is largely determined by the efficacy and harmony of this middle ground in which people encounter – or miss or are denied – order, beauty, care, moral direction. Thus, the arrangements of the home – the aesthetic of its furnishings, the predictability of its routines, the tenor of its interactional style – lay the foundation in individual personality for the creation of the varieties of human relationships that bind individuals to each other; the very fabric of social life depends on women's cultural production in the home (Weber 1998c [1918]).

Where Simmel viewed cultural production being radically changed by modernity, Weber both accepted that claim and asserted a basic consistency in the role of women in this third realm of cultural production. She also held that new opportunities make it incumbent upon women – and especially women of the propertied classes who have more leisure – to acquire a deeper cultural content that they may actively shape the world of everyday life rather than merely maintain its customary routines. And she recognized that as women seize new opportunities, they must, like men, guard against the dangers of distorting their personalities under the pressure of the specialization of modern professional life. While Weber herself argued for changes in the marriage relationship and recognized that women working outside the home would impact the home, she never questioned the centrality of this middle ground of cultural production, nor that it was women's role through individual action to translate ideas into material arrangements and material arrangements into expressions of meaning. Her argument about the need for a public valuation of housework rests in part on the importance she assigned to this central female task of shaping the immediate experience of the daily world.

At the macrosocial level, Weber posited that materiality is most represented by the economy, ideas most manifested in religion, education, and law, and agency as expressing itself in collective action through social movements. Historically, a dynamic interaction among these structures has progressively changed to what is for women the central institution: marriage and family. Using this model, she took up two of the themes most known to sociologists through Max Weber – the "Protestant ethic" and the "spirit of capitalism." Marianne Weber argued that the significance of the Protestant ethic for women lies in the insistence in the most radical Protestant sects – most especially the Quakers – that every person, male or female, stands before God alone and accountable. Where Max found the seeds of capitalism, Marianne found the seeds of liberation: "Within the religious communities of the New World that were sustained by the Puritan spirit, the idea of the religious equality of woman first came to be taken seriously. ... Freedom of conscience, the mother of all personal rights of the individual, stood, across the ocean, at the cradle of women's rights as well" (1998a [1912]: 217). But Marianne also noted the limits of the power of ideas to produce social change. She criticized the German idealist philosophers, like Kant and Fichte, who refused to extend to women the primary duty they assigned to men, the duty of achieving moral agency or, in Weber's phrase, "autonomy"; she labeled as "self-serving" the patriarchal

argument that the married woman voluntarily gave over this right to the husband and argued instead that no one can yield that duty wholesale to another.

Indeed, within Weber's presentation, the idea systems of Protestantism and German idealism seem important chiefly in providing a legitimation for women's assertions of rights to autonomy; the rights themselves can only be won by a change in the material conditions which frame women's negotiations for agency. Specifically, women need access to and independent control of monetary resources in order to negotiate for autonomy within the structure of patriarchal marriage. While for Max Weber the growth of capitalism leads men into an iron cage of practical rationality, for Marianne Weber the growth of capitalism had liberated women from the strict confines of domestic life to which their gender had hitherto assigned them. Capitalism required women's participation in the paid workforce and thus gave women an independent economic base in the public sphere.

Marianne Weber perceived women – and men – in her time poised among at least three fundamentally conflicting assumptions: (1) the unintended but logical conclusion of Protestantism and German idealism that justifies woman as an independent moral agent; (2) the policies of the material world of the capitalist economy that require that women as workers and as consumers be able to act as independent contracting agents; and (3) the patriarchal ideas expressed in established religion, law, state, and philosophy that define woman, as wife, as dependent on and subservient to the husband.

It is at this historic moment of contradiction that women's agency in the form of mobilized feminist collective activism would become the force that would work to spell out the terms under which marriage would be reorganized and women's autonomy guaranteed. This reorganization would occur primarily by demanding that new laws, as the codification of collective ideas, be created to regulate the material relations of women's employment and status in marriage. Writing on the German women's movement, Marianne Weber stressed that while that movement represented a diversity of opinion, it was united in its understanding that women, in marriage and in the public sphere, must be empowered to stand as fully autonomous human beings equal to men. In marriage, Marianne Weber saw this leading toward "companionate marriage" rather than the old patriarchal marriage hierarchy.

In her most policy-oriented exploration of change, "On the Valuation of Housework" (1912), Weber focused on what she saw as one key piece in a total marriage reform – a method of compensating the housewife for the work she does in the home. She explored the possibility of writing a law that would guarantee women within marriage some right to personal income, recognizing both the worth of women's work and their need for financial independence. In considering how women could gain financial independence, Weber made a critical point for the development of feminist sociology: the recognition of differences among women. While acknowledging that perhaps an important fraction of women, chiefly from the professional classes, could find independence – in the way outlined by Charlotte Perkins Gilman – through employment outside the home, Weber argued that for many women the possibility of employment that paid an individual living wage was unlikely. She offered a range of empirical data about women's material condition, most especially their employment, to show that what Gilman dreamt of was not a possibility for the mass of women who had to work at low-paid jobs. Presenting a statistical overview of the employment of women, Marianne Weber argued that the typical woman worker in the new industrial order was recruited from the propertyless classes and had to continue to juggle the dual demands of wage-work and housework/motherhood. These women worked not out of some calling to a particular career nor with a hope of financial independence, but because they had to for the sake of survival. Weber, therefore, turned to the possibility that the economic value of housework could be calculated and that calculation codified into law.

In examining the possibility of wages for housework, Weber investigated the relationship between the macrosocial and microsocial in securing social change. She explored at some length whether compensation for housework should be paid by the government or by the individual husband, finally arguing for the latter, partly on the grounds of economic practicality (as the total sum would be staggering for the country) and partly on the grounds of the most effective mechanism for social change. Where in her discussion of "Authority and Autonomy in Marriage" (1912) she focused primarily on the macrosocial institutions of law and religion, in looking at the issue of the valuation of housework Weber turned to the microsocial. Arguing that on the basis of past performance the government could be expected to be slow to move in this area, she reasoned that women had to work out in their individual marriages the kind of egalitarian relationship they wished to see enacted in law. Custom (everyday ideas about material relations) developed out of individual agency (actions by women and men defining individual marriages) would pave the way for legal change, the macrosocial codification of ideas of right relations between women and men.

SEE ALSO: Cultural Feminism; Feminism; Gender, Social Movements and; Gender, Work, and Family; Gilman, Charlotte Perkins; Simmel, Georg; Stratification, Gender and; Weber, Max

REFERENCES AND SUGGESTED READINGS

Britton, A. C. (1979) The Life and Thought of Marianne Weber. Master's Thesis. San Francisco State University, San Francisco.

Lengermann, P. & Niebrugge-Brantley, J. (1998) *The Women Founders: Sociology and Social Theory, 1803–1930*. McGraw-Hill, New York.

Lengermann, P. & Niebrugge-Brantley, J. (2001) Classical Feminist Social Theory. In: Ritzer, G. & Smart, B. (Eds.), *A Handbook of Social Theory*. Sage, Thousand Oaks, CA.

Roth, G. (1990) Marianne Weber and Her Circle. *Society* 127: 63–70.

Van Vucht Tijssen, L. (1991). Women and Objective Culture: George Simmel and Marianne Weber. *Theory, Culture and Society* 8: 203–18.

Weber, M. (1900) *Fichte's Sozialismus und sein Verhältnis zur Marx'schen Doktrin*. J. C. B. Mohr, Tübingen.

Weber, M. (1907) *Ehefrau und Mutter in der Rechtsentwicklung*. J. C. B. Mohr, Tübingen.

Weber, M. (1998a [1912]) Authority and Autonomy in Marriage. Trans. E. Kirchen. In: Lengermann, P. & Niebrugge-Brantley, J., *The Women Founders:*

Sociology and Social Theory, 1803–1930. McGraw-Hill, New York, pp. 215–20. [Originally published in *Frauenfrage und Frauengedanke.* J. C. B. Mohr, Tübingen, pp. 67–79.]

Weber, M. (1998b [1912]) On the Valuation of Housework. Trans. E. Kirchen. In: Lengermann, P. & Niebrugge-Brantley, J., *The Women Founders: Sociology and Social Theory, 1803–1930.* McGraw-Hill, New York, pp. 220–4. [Originally published in *Frauenfrage und Frauengedanke.* J. C. B. Mohr, Tübingen, pp. 80–94.]

Weber, M. (1998c [1918]) Women's Special Cultural Tasks. Trans. E. Kirchen. In: Lengermann, P. & Niebrugge-Brantley, J., *The Women Founders: Sociology and Social Theory, 1803–1930.* McGraw-Hill, New York, pp. 224–8. [Originally published in *Frauenfrage und Frauengedanke.* J. C. B. Mohr, Tübingen, pp. 238–61.]

Wobbe, T. (1998) Marianne Weber (1870–1954). Ein anderes Labor der Moderne. In: Honegger, C. & Wobbe, T. (Eds.), *Frauen en der Soziologie. Neun Portraits.* Beck, Munich, pp. 153–77.

marital power/resource theory

Graham Allan

Questions about inequalities in marriage and the distribution of power within the relationship have long been a concern within family sociology. In particular, ideas about historic shifts in the dominance of husbands/fathers within families have vied with feminist-inspired views of the continuing significance of patriarchal control in both public and private spheres. The former perspective was captured well in Burgess's (Burgess & Locke 1945) influential idea of a shift from "marriage as an institution" to "marriage as a relationship," with some seeing the growth of "companionate" marriage as a sure indicator that marriage would increasingly become a relationship of equality (Clark 1991). (See Young & Willmott 1973 for a particularly optimistic analysis.) Others, however, argued that marriage continued to be a structurally unequal relationship as a consequence of both the differential opportunities open to men and women, especially in the workplace, and

the continuation of a highly gendered division of labor within the home (see, e.g., Delphy & Leonard 1992).

One of the earliest – and most cited – studies examining the distribution of power within marriage was conducted by Robert Blood and Donald Wolfe in *Husbands and Wives: The Dynamics of Married Living* (1960). In this, they report on a study in which over 900 wives were interviewed about the character of their marriage. More specifically, Blood and Wolfe were interested in finding out about who made decisions within the marriage, arguing that decision-making was a clear indicator of the exercise of power and authority within any relationship. In the study, each respondent was asked questions about eight different decisions that couples and families typically made. These included such decisions as: what job a husband should take; whether or not to buy life insurance; and how much money the family can afford to spend each week on food. As a result of their findings, Blood and Wolfe concluded that decision-making, and thus power, within marriage was based on the level of social and economic resource that each spouse brought to the marriage. Thus, the greater the differential in, for example, a spouse's earnings, education, and status, the greater power that spouse would have to make decisions over different aspects of family life.

Although highly influential, Blood and Wolfe's conclusions were questioned by many researchers concerned with marital power, on a combination of theoretical and methodological grounds. Overall though, the criticisms made of the study raised important questions about the nature of power in marriage and helped generate a far more sophisticated understanding of its exercise than had existed previously. Three levels of criticism were of particular moment. The first concerned the issues about which the respondents had been questioned. Seemingly simple, these criticisms of themselves raise important questions about what power is. As noted, Blood and Wolfe's strategy was to ask about different decisions that were made by the couple – some frequent, some rare, some highly significant, others less so. A key question raised by the study was whether each of these decisions was equally indicative of the exercise of power within the marriage. And if not, how should it be weighted, and who should decide on this? For example, is the choice of food purchase as consequential as decisions about what apartment/house to buy or rent, or a spouse's employment? If not, what is the value of asking about the less consequential decisions? How revealing of power are routine, everyday decisions? Moreover, within this model, how are "non-decisions" to be treated – that is, decisions over which there appears to be little disagreement or debate? As will be discussed below, this is a more theoretically significant question than it might at first appear to be.

The second criticism made of Blood and Wolfe's study concerned the constitution of the sample. The issue here was not its size or scope per se, but whether studies of marital power could ever be valid if only one party to the relationship was questioned. Implicit within Blood and Wolfe's methodology was the notion that decision-making was an objective feature of marriage which would be reported on similarly by either husbands or wives. There was, in other words, limited recognition that there might be competing understandings and experiences of a marriage – a "his" and "her" marriage, in Bernard's (1973) famous terms. Yet if husbands and wives were to have different understandings of decision-making within their marriage, which of these is "true"? Are either valid? And how is the researcher to decide between competing accounts? While, again, this seems like a methodological issue, it is actually more fundamental. It raises questions about the extent to which people's perceptions of decision-making are themselves constituted through an exercise of power rather than being, as Blood and Wolfe's model implies, "independent" of that power.

The third criticism, more radical than either of the above, calls into question the value of examining who it is who makes decisions as a means of measuring power. Instead of focusing on decision-making, it argues that the crucial question is who benefits most from the decisions that are made (Lukes 2005). Those with power are the ones who win out, irrespective of the process by which a decision is reached. There are a number of elements to this in the context of marital power. First, it recognizes the importance of social order, or, in the case of marriage, gender order. That is, conventional and normative agreements often disguise the distribution of benefits between actors. Thus, routine ways of organizing domestic and familial life often hide the ways in which one party – typically husbands – benefits from this mode of organization at the expense of the other – typically wives. It matters little who decides on a particular issue if the decision that is reached sustains an already unequal status quo. Indeed, as Lukes (2005) argues, the most powerful are those who can rely on the less powerful to make decisions which consistently operate in favor of the more powerful. Delegation of these decisions, as well as a social order that makes some decisions so "obvious" as to be non-contentious, can help legitimize the consequences of the decisions that are made.

In the light of this, analyzing who *makes* decisions in marriage is not of itself necessarily revealing of power. Moreover, open discussions and consultation are highly valued within contemporary ideologies of coupledom and partnership. Thus, as Edgell (1980) argued, joint, apparently democratic, participation within marital decision-making can help legitimize the relational basis of the marriage, while still operating to secure a structurally embedded and (largely) taken-for-granted gender order which prioritizes men's interests. Moreover, many routine decisions can also be "delegated" to wives because in practice the decisions they reach are liable to be ones which further, or at least do not harm, the interests of their husbands. For example, decisions about family meals may be left to wives as part of their domestic responsibilities with the outcome that wives choose food they know their husbands prefer.

If these arguments are accepted, then it becomes questionable whether decision-making can be used to reflect marital power in any simple fashion. Rather, what needs to be considered more is the distribution of material and non-material resources between the couple. Questions about who has access to more leisure time, who has more money for personal expenditure, whose needs are prioritized within the family, become more central than decision-making per se. One illustration of this alternative perspective on power can be found in the research literature on money management within families. What these studies repeatedly highlight is the extent to which wives and mothers in poorer households routinely sacrifice their own needs in order to provide better for their husbands and children. Although decisions about balancing household income and expenditure are clearly theirs to make, this does not reflect the exercise of power in a conventional sense so much as the (delegated) responsibility of managing inadequate household budgets.

No matter what the context, power remains a highly contested and complex concept (Lukes 2005). Within the study of marriage, it is further complicated by dominant ideologies of personal commitment that imbue behavior with motives of love and altruism rather more than power and self-interest. So too, within contemporary constructions of "partnership," divisions in domestic and paid labor tend to be viewed as negotiated familial and household organization rather than the operation of structural inequalities. The growth of cohabitation and what Cherlin (2004) refers to as the "deinstitutionalization of marriage" complicates further the interpretation of power within "marriage-like" relationships. With hindsight, decision-making approaches to the study of marital power are clearly subject to many questions and criticisms. Nonetheless, Blood and Wolfe's study was seminal in opening up debate about the ways in which power is exercised within marriage and helping family sociologists understand its inherent complexities.

SEE ALSO: Decision-Making; Divisions of Household Labor; Inequalities in Marriage; Marriage; Money Management in Families; Power, Theories of

REFERENCES AND SUGGESTED READINGS

Allan, G. & Crow, G. (2001) *Families, Households, and Society*. Palgrave, Basingstoke.

Bernard, J. (1973) *The Future of Marriage*. Bantam, New York.

Blood, R. & Wolfe, D. M. (1960) *Husbands and Wives: The Dynamics of Married Living*. Free Press, Glencoe, IL.

Blumstein, P. & Schwartz, P. (1983) *American Couples: Money, Work, Sex*. William Morrow, New York.

Burgess, E. & Locke, H. (1945) *The Family: From Institution to Companionship*. American Book, New York.

Cherlin, A. (2004) The Deinstitutionalization of American Marriage. *Journal of Marriage and Family* 66: 848–61.

Clark, D. (1991) *Marriage, Domestic Life, and Social Change*. Routledge, London.

Delphy, C. & Leonard, D. (1992) *Familiar Exploitation: A New Analysis of Marriage in Contemporary Western Societies*. Polity Press, Cambridge.

Edgell, S. (1980) *Middle-Class Couples*. Allen & Unwin, London.

Lukes, S. (2005) *Power: A Radical View*. Palgrave Macmillan, Basingstoke.

Young, M. & Willmott, P. (1973) *The Symmetrical Family*. Routledge & Kegan Paul, London.

marital quality

Lindsay Custer

Marital quality is a dynamic concept, as the nature and quality of people's relationships change over time. There have been two major approaches to conceptualizing and measuring marital quality: looking at the relationship itself (examining patterns of interaction, such as the amount and type of conflict) and looking at individual feelings of the people in the relationship (evaluative judgments of happiness or satisfaction). Marital quality and related concepts – adjustment, happiness, and satisfaction – are the most frequently studied variables in marital research. Despite the wealth of literature examining these constructs, there is a continuing lack of consensus among marital researchers on how to conceptualize and measure marital quality, as well as an absence of a unifying theoretical approach to studying this construct.

Some scholars view marital quality as an interpersonal characteristic. Proponents of this approach treat marital quality as a process, the outcome of which is determined by interaction patterns between spouses. Scholars who take this approach, which was dominant during the 1970s, favor the term "marital adjustment." These scholars also view marital quality as a multidimensional construct. Multidimensional measures of marital quality typically assess a number of specific types of interactions between spouses (e.g., spousal agreement about marital issues, time spent together/companionship, conflict, and communication). In addition to measuring reported behavioral characteristics of the dyad, some multidimensional measures also include global subjective evaluations of the relationship (such as happiness, satisfaction, or distress). The most frequently employed multidimensional measures of marital quality are: the Locke-Wallace Short Marital Adjustment Test (LWMAT), the Dyadic Adjustment Scale (DAS), and the Marital Satisfaction Inventory (MSI).

During the 1980s the interpersonal approach to the study of marital quality, and the multidimensional measures utilized by those who adhered to this approach, came under severe attack. First, many multidimensional measures, such as the LWMAT and the DAS, were criticized for combining scales assessing objective reports of interaction with subjective evaluations of the relationship. This combines both the unit of analysis (dyad and individual) and the type of report (objective and subjective). Second, critics pointed out that by including both evaluative judgments about marital quality and reports of specific behaviors and general interaction patterns, multidimensional measures inflate associations between marital quality and self-report measures of interpersonal processes in marriage. This is particularly problematic when dealing with cross-sectional data. Finally, multidimensional measures were criticized because the components that are frequently included in multidimensional measures of marital quality may, in fact, be determinants of marital quality. These factors, such as communication or couple interaction, also could be considered as independent variables that might influence marital quality. The criticisms of multidimensional measures raised in the 1970s led many researchers to conclude that scales assessing different dimensions of marital quality should not be summed.

In response to the criticisms of the interpersonal and multidimensional approach to marital quality, scholars began to take an intrapersonal and unidimensional approach to marital quality in the 1980s. This approach was also prompted by the fact that many of the large nationally representative data sets that were available in the 1980s contained only unidimensional measures of marital quality. According to the intrapersonal approach, marital quality should be conceived of as reflecting a person's evaluation of the marital relationship, not the interaction between two spouses. Scholars who take this approach frequently employ the terms "marital satisfaction" or "marital happiness." Evaluations of the marriage can be global (e.g., marital satisfaction) or specific (e.g., sexual satisfaction).

Scholars who take the intrapersonal approach to marital quality most often use unidimensional, global evaluative assessments of the relationship. Unidimensional measures take the individual (rather than the dyad) as the unit of analysis and are subjective reports of feelings (rather than objective reports of behaviors). The most frequently used unidimensional measures include: the Kansas Marital Satisfaction Scale (KMSS), the Marital Satisfaction Scale (MSS), and the Quality Marriage Index (QMI). Although unidimensional measures have not suffered the same degree of criticism as multidimensional measures of marital quality, two major shortcomings have been identified. Unidimensional measures may be subject to considerable social desirability response bias and global measures tend to be significantly skewed toward a positive evaluation.

During the 1990s the lack of consensus regarding how to conceptualize and measure marital quality persisted. In several studies, researchers included more than one assessment of marital quality (e.g., marital satisfaction and marital conflict), but treated them as separate measures. Other scholars have pointed out that marital quality may indeed contain more than one dimension, most likely a positive and negative dimension, but that these dimensions cannot necessarily be summed. Clearly, the debate regarding how to conceptualize and measure this important construct has not been resolved.

Disagreement regarding how to conceptualize and measure marital quality has contributed to the failure of marital researchers to develop a guiding theoretical perspective. Early theoretical attempts consisted primarily of drawing propositions from extant, general theories or of developing middle-range theories, such as Lewis and Spanier's Exchange Theory of Marital Quality.

In the 1980s marital quality research tended to be atheoretical, as scholars struggled to resolve the controversies surrounding how to measure and conceptualize marital quality. More recently, new theoretical approaches have been developed. For example, Fincham, Beach, and colleagues offered a new theoretical perspective of marital quality based on a two-dimensional structure of affect. It remains to be seen whether marital researchers will adopt this new theoretical approach.

The importance of understanding and measuring marital quality stems primarily from the assumption that it is a key determinant of marital stability. Early marital researchers assumed that marital quality and marital stability were directly correlated. However, it became clear that given a certain level of marital quality, some marriages would end in divorce and some would not. Spanier and Lewis identified four types of marriages: high quality/high stability, high quality/low stability, low quality/high stability, and low quality/low stability. A number of researchers have tried to identify factors that may moderate the relationship between marital quality and marital stability. External pressures and alternative attractions have been the focus of several studies.

Investigating the determinants of marital quality has occupied a central place in marital research. One topic that has received a great deal of attention is gender differences. Several studies have offered empirical support that gender shapes individual perceptions of many aspects of marriage. In general, men report slightly higher marital quality than women. Researchers have also investigated how race or ethnicity may shape marital quality. In general, African Americans report lower marital quality than whites, but few other groups have been studied.

Among the most intensely studied topics in marital quality research is the influence of family stage, presence of children, and duration of the marriage on marital quality. In their review of literature from the 1960s, Hicks and Platt (1970) reported that one of the most surprising findings of that decade was that children appear to detract from the marital quality of their parents. The transition to parenthood also was a popular topic of study during the 1970s. Several cross-sectional studies identified a curvilinear relationship between family stage and marital quality, whereby the average quality is higher in the preparental and postparental stages. The most common interpretation of this finding was that it reflected the addition of children to the family, their maturation, and their departure. However, more recent longitudinal studies have suggested that changes often attributed to the transition to parenthood are duration-of-marriage effects instead. Some of these studies suggested that rather than being curvilinear, marital quality declines sharply during the first few years of marriage and then tapers off more slowly.

The link between premarital cohabitation and marital quality also has been the subject of a great deal of investigation. A negative relationship between cohabitation and marital quality has been established, but it is unclear whether it is the fact of living together or the type of people who tend to live together before marriage that is responsible for this effect. Research on remarriage has also increased sharply in the past 20 years and much of it has focused on marital quality. This research indicates that average marital quality is slightly greater in first marriages than in remarriages after divorce. It also appears that the average quality in remarriages is somewhat higher for men than for women.

Wives' employment, spouses' gender role attitudes, and the division of household labor also have received some attention recently. It seems that congruency between spouses' attitudes toward gender roles, as well as congruency between attitudes and behaviors, are related to marital quality. A shared division of household labor and perceived fairness of the division of household labor also seem to enhance marital quality.

Marital quality is typically treated as a dependent variable. However, in the 1980s some studies used marital quality as an independent variable to predict the global well-being of married people. This research illustrated a strong link between marital quality and general well-being. The authors of these studies have suggested that marital quality influences well-being. However, the causal direction between these two variables is still unclear.

Bradbury et al. (2000) organized their review of recent marital quality research around two themes: interpersonal processes and sociocultural contexts within which marriages operate.

These authors stated that research conducted during the 1980s and 1990s supported the conclusion that spouses' attributions are linked to marital satisfaction. The 1990s also saw a dramatic surge in research on the affective dimension of marital interaction. Although it is clear that affect is linked to marital quality, the exact nature of the relationship is not clear yet. Interaction patterns (especially the demand/withdraw pattern), physiology, social support, and violence were also identified as factors that are linked to marital satisfaction. In the latter half of their review, Bradbury and colleagues focus on contextual factors (both microcontext and macrocontext) that may contribute to interpersonal processes of couples as well as moderate the relationship between processes and marital satisfaction. The effects of children, spouses' family background, life stressors and transitions, as well as broader social conditions are discussed.

SEE ALSO: Divorce; Family Conflict; Intimacy; Intimate Union Formation and Dissolution; Love and Commitment; Marriage

REFERENCES AND SUGGESTED READINGS

Bradbury, T. N., Fincham, F. D., & Beach, S. R. H. (2000) Research on the Nature and Determinants of Marital Satisfaction: A Decade in Review. *Journal of Marriage and the Family* 62: 964–80.

Fincham, F. D. & Bradbury, T. N. (1987) The Assessment of Marital Quality: A Reevaluation. *Journal of Marriage and the Family* 49: 797–809.

Fincham, F. D., Beach, S. R., & Kemp-Fincham, S. I. (1997) Marital Quality: A New Theoretical Perspective. In: Sternberg, R. J. & Hojjat, M. (Eds.), *Satisfaction in Close Relationships*. Guilford Press, New York, pp. 275–304.

Glenn, N. D. (1990) Quantitative Research on Marital Quality in the 1980s: A Critical Review. *Journal of Marriage and the Family* 52: 818–31.

Hicks, M. & Platt, M. (1970) Marital Happiness and Stability: A Review of the Research in the Sixties. *Journal of Marriage and the Family* 32: 553–74.

Johnson, D. R., White, L. K., Edwards, J. N., & Booth, A. (1986) Dimensions of Marital Quality: Toward Methodological and Conceptual Refinement. *Journal of Family Issues* 7: 31–49.

Karney, B. R. & Bradbury, T. N. (1995) The Longitudinal Course of Marital Quality and Stability: A Review of Theory, Method, and Research. *Psychological Bulletin* 18: 3–34.

Lewis, R. A. & Spanier, G. B. (1979) Theorizing about the Quality and Stability of Marriage. In: Burr, W. R., Hill, R., Nye, F. I., & Reiss, I. L. (Eds.), *Contemporary Theories about the Family*, Vol. 2. Free Press, New York, pp. 268–94.

Spanier, G. B. & Lewis, R. A. (1980) Marital Quality: A Review of the Seventies. *Journal of Marriage and the Family* 42: 825–39.

markets

Milan Zafirovski

Markets are a fundamental category of economic science often described as "market economics" (Schumpeter 1954a: 12). Economists place the analysis of markets at the "heart of economics" (Mises 1960: 3; Wieser 1956: 3) and view the evolution of economic theory as the history of their attempt to explain the "workings of an economy based on market transactions" (Blaug 1985: 6). As sociologists also note, a "central problem area" of conventional economic theory is the "structure of markets" (Parsons & Smelser 1965: 143). This emphasis often reaches the point of what critics from economic science and sociology alike call "market fundamentalism" (Stiglitz 2002) or "absolutization" of markets (Barber 1995) within orthodox economics.

Markets are also an important subject of economic sociology of which one of the main subfields is the "economic sociology of the market" (Boulding 1970: 153). However, economics, especially its orthodox version, and economic sociology usually differ in approaching the subject in that the first treats markets as purely economic phenomena or mechanisms, and the second conceives them as complex social structures or institutions. For instance, prominent economists like Joseph Schumpeter (1954b: 9–22) distinguish pure or theoretical economics as the "study of economic mechanisms," notably "market mechanisms," from economic sociology as the "analysis of social institutions" as societal forces shaping the economy, or of "economically relevant institutions." Consequently, Schumpeter regards markets as economic mechanisms from the stance of pure economics and as social institutions from that of economic sociology (or social economics). So do in their own ways other prominent economists-sociologists like Vilfredo Pareto and Friedrich Wieser. Generally, pure economists and economic sociologists (or socioeconomists) conceptualize markets differently, i.e., as mechanisms and institutions, respectively.

ECONOMIC DIMENSIONS: MARKETS–MECHANISMS

Both classical and especially neoclassical economics (or marginalism) treat markets as economic mechanisms, as does most of its contemporary economics. For instance, the idea of markets as economic mechanisms is already implicit in Adam Smith's concept of an "invisible hand" of the market as an assumed impersonal mechanism converting private gains into the "public good." So is it in Smith's description of the market as an "obvious and simple system of natural liberty" establishing and regulating itself on its "own accord," insofar as a defining trait of an economic (or any) mechanism is this self-establishment or self-regulation (as neoclassical economists like Leon Walras, Francis Edgeworth, and Irving Fisher later suggest). Developing Smith's insights, Jean-Baptiste Say provides a classical formulation or anticipation of the above idea by postulating what has come to be known as Say's "law of self-regulating markets." In this respect, the idea of markets as economic mechanisms represents economics' original and persisting trait to be adopted, made explicit, and reinforced in its subsequent developments, notably marginalism under the strong influence of physics and mechanics (Mirowski 1989) and its contemporary extensions and ramifications.

The general concept of markets as economic mechanisms involves a number of specific and interrelated notions. These notions are markets as (1) mechanisms or systems of supply and demand; (2) self-regulating and equilibrating mechanisms; (3) mechanisms (or realms) of free competition and economic freedom overall; (4) spontaneous mechanisms of economic coordination; (5) mechanisms of resource allocation; and (6) mechanisms of price determination.

First, conventional economics conceives markets as mechanisms, systems, and sets of relations and laws of supply and demand, or of economic exchange, which is probably the standard, best known, or most popular market conception. Moreover, some contemporary economists (e.g., Samuelson) suggest that the market mechanisms and laws of supply and demand are all that a (pure) economist needs to know. Within classical political economy, the above conception is implied in Smith's concept of the market as a "system of natural liberty," particularly Say's law of self-regulating markets positing some pseudomechanical adjustment between supply and demand. Their contemporary Thomas Malthus explicitly defines markets in terms of the system, mechanism, or principle of supply and demand (and competition). Also, Malthus argues that the market performs the "best adaptation" of supply to consumers' demand ("actual tastes and wants"), an argument also entailed in Smith's invisible hand and especially Say's law of self-regulating markets. Most neoclassical and contemporary economists adopt and further elaborate or reinforce this early argument for optimal market adaptation. For instance, Wieser (an Austrian marginalist economist) contends that markets perform an "ideal adaptation" of supply to demand, as does Lionel Robins (a contemporary economist influenced by Wieser and other Austrians), stating this adjustment in terms of relations of scarce resources or limited means to competing wants or multiple ends. Alfred Marshall also provides a definition of markets as systems, especially realms or sites of relations, of supply and demand by defining a (perfect) market as a geographical "district" that involves many economic agents with full knowledge of its conditions and features the same price for all (uniform) products. In retrospect, this represents or reflects the conventional definition (traced by Marshall and others to Augustine Cournot, an early French economist writing during the 1830s–1840s) of perfect or pure competition as a market form characterized by multiple economic units, uniform products and prices, full knowledge and foresight, free resource movements, and so on, in contrast to other forms like monopoly, oligopoly, and imperfect (or monopolistic) competition, having different or opposite properties. Also, Marshall's definition comes most closely to the common-sense understanding of markets as concrete sites of supply or selling and demand or buying, simply exchange or marketplaces, which most economists as well as sociologists find simplistic or superficial. Marshall's marginalist colleague Edgeworth injects a dose of mystery into markets, attributing to them what he calls the "mysteries of Supply and Demand" determining contracts (prices) in a "state of perfect competition," while another contemporary (Allyn Young) purports to define them in the "inclusive sense" as the "aggregate of productive activities, tied together by trade." Also, contemporary economists define markets as systems that tend to spontaneously "equate supply and demand" at an equilibrium price (Arrow 1994: 3), which evokes Say's law. A succinct contemporary formulation of the concept of markets as supply–demand or exchange systems is defining the market as the "system of multiple exchanges" (Hicks 1961: 73).

Second, traditional economics treats markets as economic mechanisms endowed with self-regulation or automatism and an inherent tendency to reach an equilibrium and optimum. Say's law of self-regulating markets contains an archetypical formulation or adumbration of this conception, stating that production "opens a demand for products" or "products created give rise to various degrees of demand" – i.e., simply, "supply creates its own demand" (reinforcing Smith's view that the "quantity of every commodity brought to the market naturally suits itself to the effectual demand"). Likely influenced by Say as well as physics (e.g., celestial mechanics), marginalist pioneer Leon Walras develops and reinforces this formulation, carrying it to its limiting consequences by equating or comparing markets with physical mechanisms, as do most other marginalists. Generally, Walras treats markets as primary economic mechanisms and the essence of "pure political economy" understood as a "theory of the determination of prices under a hypothetical regime of absolutely free competition." Notably, he describes a freely competitive market as a "self-regulatory and automatic mechanism" – for a transformation of productive services like capital and labor into commodities – that is almost identical or comparable to those of physics, including celestial mechanics (as Walras's model for pure mathematical economics). So does his marginalist follower Fisher, who also uses such terms as "self-regulative," "market mechanism," and "industrial machinery" or "hydraulics" to describe the nature and operation of markets. Similarly, Edgeworth follows Walras (including his celestial mechanics model for pure economics) by defining markets as "market-machine[s]" driven by the "law of motion" in physics and solving the "economical problem of exchange" made of "catallactic [exchanging] molecules" or the "maze" of contracting competing agents. In particular, Edgeworth emphasizes the "smooth machinery" of a free market or perfect competition. So does his marginalist contemporary Philip Wicksteed, who defines markets in terms of a "machinery" which resolves the excess of supply or demand through the "law" of market equilibrium presumed to implicate all economic laws. This law endows markets with the properties of quasi-automatic equilibrating "machineries" tending to reach equilibrium and so optimum as an assumed equivalent according to the equivalence theorem (Allais 1997) of neoclassical economics. Market equilibrium is, as Pareto states, the outcome of an "opposition" between effective demand ("tastes") and available supply ("obstacles"), and when established, especially under free competition, economic actors "enjoy maximum satisfaction." The latter, positing equivalence between equilibrium and optimal states in markets, implies what is known as the Pareto optimum defined as the market position of maximum utility so that "every small departure" from it increases the welfare of some individuals and reduces that of others.

Some contemporary economists adopt or revive the mechanistic conception of markets from marginalist economics (thus, openly or tacitly, Walras–Edgeworth's mechanics model for economic science). For example, Frank Knight describes markets as unconscious, automatic, and gradual orders resistant to external regulation, direction, and planning, a description following or resembling that in Austrian marginalism (from Carl Menger to Friedrich Hayek) and setting the tone for those by the Chicago School of economics (e.g., Milton Friedman). Also, influenced by Walras, Schumpeter in his pure economics treats markets as forms of "economic mechanisms" or simply "market mechanisms," while using terms like the "economic machine" and the "capitalist machine" with its "inner logic" for describing the economy, capitalism in particular. So does Schumpeter's student Paul Samuelson (1983: 203), who conceptualizes the market "simply as a mechanism" (yet with an "aesthetic content"), particularly an "equilibrium system," and comes closer to adopting and implementing Walras's mechanics model for pure economics by extolling the virtue of using simple concepts and methods from physics and mathematics over "literary" work in the analysis of markets. This holds true of some contemporary mathematical economists (Debreu 1969), who *à la* Walras describe the market as a self-sustaining economic system or mechanism that tends to reach a "valuation equilibrium" for a given "set of prices," so the Pareto optimum. Similarly, others define the market as a "perfectly competitive mechanism," with "optimality properties," "incentive compatibility," the high "scale of information efficiency" for the "narrow class of atomistic environments" (Hurwicz 1969), which apparently redefines in esoteric terms what Walras and Marshall call "absolutely free" or "perfect" competition. In turn, contemporary critical economists suggest that it is neither "perfectly competitive" nor completely efficient by pointing to "market failures – absent or imperfect markets" (Stiglitz 2002: 479).

Third, conventional economics regards markets as mechanisms, realms, or sources of free competition and economic freedom overall. A prototypical instance is Smith's concept of the market as a "system of natural liberty" that establishes itself on its own "accord," in particular a mechanism, domain, and source of universal "free and fair" competition. Most classical as well as neoclassical and contemporary economists adopt and elaborate on the concept of markets as mechanisms or systems of "natural liberty," notably of free competition. Thus, David Ricardo attributes to markets "fair and free competition" which, he suggests, should operate "without restraint" and "never" be regulated by external intervention (e.g., "interference of the legislature"). So does Thomas Malthus, who argues that markets (e.g., profits) operate in accordance with the law or principle of competition (and supply and demand), as well as William Senior suggesting that they function under "perfectly equal competition," which intimates the notion of a perfect market. John S. Mill probably codifies or condenses the classical position by stating that markets are regulated by the "principle of competition," particularly "perfectly free competition," which also anticipates the concept of a perfect market.

That neoclassical economics embraces and even reinforces this classical position is exemplified by Walras's conception of markets as mechanisms and domains of "absolutely free competition" and economic freedom (*laissez-faire*) as a whole. Similarly, Wicksell describes universal "free and unrestricted" competition as the "special" law of markets that function as the impersonal catalysts of individual agents' diverse attributes and orientations by generating a single equilibrium price. Also *à la* Walras, Edgeworth proposes that markets are mechanisms or fields that tend to reach the "perfect state of competition," thus amplifying or formalizing Mill Senior's ideas too, as does John B. Clark, stating that they are under the "perfect action of competitive law." Marshall generally defines the (perfect) market as the "system of economic freedom," apparently adopting and evoking Smith's notion of markets as systems of "natural liberty." Further, following Smith, Ricardo, and Mill, Marshall contends that this market system is the "best from both the moral and material point of view," which perhaps epitomizes what critics denote as the "absolutization" of markets in orthodox economics. Also, contemporary economists adopt Smith's idea of a "Simple System of Natural Liberty" to describe the character and operation of markets or the market economy (Buchanan 1991: 27).

Fourth, conventional economics defines markets as spontaneous and impersonal mechanisms or instruments for economic coordination, regulation, and control. The notion of markets as such coordinating mechanisms originates in Smith's idea of an invisible hand assumed to spontaneously coordinate the economy by converting individual interests into the common interest. Thus, Smith and other classical economists compare the workings of markets with an invisible hand that achieves economic coordination out of the "autonomous decisions of many separate units" (Lange 1946). In retrospect, Smith's invisible hand reformulates and reinstates in economic terms Mandeville's fable or paradox of "private vices, public virtues" and provides a classic *laissez-faire* argument, for arguably if markets spontaneously and efficiently perform economic coordination they should not be interfered with by the state. Smith restates and mitigates Mandeville's "shocking paradox" by replacing "vices" ("passions") and "virtues" with economic terms like "gain," "advantage," or "interest," notably by positing a "harmony of interests," private and public, and consequently argues in favor of the "minimal state doctrine" (Hirschman 1977). The invisible hand of markets has become a venerable axiom of classical political economy as well as neoclassical and contemporary economics. Thus, contemporary economists proclaim "hail that Smithian Invisible Hand" of market competition as the "grand solution of the social maximum position" (Samuelson 2001: 1206), which implies that markets are optimal coordinating mechanisms, another way to state their supposed tendency to optimum. Within classical political economy, Say's law of self-regulating markets is a particular ramification of Smith's invisible hand principle in postulating a spontaneous quasi-automatic coordination or equilibrium of aggregate supply and demand, so a sort of harmony between private and public interests (e.g., producers and consumers). Another, more general ramification is Ricardo's assertion that individual and community interests "are never at variance" in consequence of the impersonal operation and spontaneous coordination by market "free and fair competition" in the way of an "invisible hand," which evidently assumes such a harmony. Similarly, Mill argues that originally the "contrivance" of markets functions as the spontaneous mechanism or instrument for coordination (periodic meetings) between sellers and buyers, "without any intermediate agency." Also, most neoclassical economists, especially Austrian marginalists, emphasize the function of markets as mechanisms for spontaneous and efficient economic coordination. For instance, Menger invokes Smith's invisible hand to address the supposedly "most significant problem" of social science – i.e., how institutions promoting the common good have been created "without a common will

directed toward establishing them" – arguing that this is due to the impersonal coordination or harmonizing of individual interests by markets as spontaneous phenomena, thus implicitly in favor of *laissez-faire*. Menger's followers in Austrian economics adopt and reinforce this argument: thus, Mises contends that markets (including prices) achieve control or regulation of the economy with more rigor, justice, and precision than any other mechanism, including the "supervision by the State," which leads to an argument for *laissez-faire*. So does Hayek, emphasizing the "hard discipline" of markets. Notably, these and other Austrian economists embrace and elaborate on Menger's notion of markets as spontaneously coordinating mechanisms, as epitomized by Hayek's concept of the market as a kind of impersonal "spontaneous order" and "anonymous group." Also, Clark anticipates Hayek's latter concept by describing the market as a "group system" or an "expression of the totality of individual wants." Further, following Menger, Hayek claims that the unrestricted operation of markets, as spontaneous orders performing economic coordination via an invisible hand *à la* Smith (cited approvingly) or *laissez-faire*, is the "central problem" of social science. The notion of markets as coordinating mechanisms is summarized by Friedman, characterizing the market as the "technique of achieving coordination" as its "central characteristic."

Fifth, economics conventionally regards markets as mechanisms or instruments for objective, quasi-automatic, efficient, or optimal resource allocation, a view implied in or part of their definition as spontaneous systems of economic coordination. Thus, this view is germane to Smith's invisible hand principle as well as its ramifications in Say's law of self-regulating markets and Ricardo's impersonal operation of free market competition. In particular, Smith implies that markets perform a function of resource allocation in stating that the division of labor is "limited by the extent of the market" ("effectual demand"). So does Mill, who proposes that the wide "extent" of actual or potential markets permits a "considerable" division of labor, thus implicitly a substantial investment of productive factors, production, and productivity, in large business enterprises, and conversely. Further, some contemporary economists

(Debreu 1991) define the "core" of markets (or the market economy) as a set of competitive or final (i.e., Pareto-optimal) "allocations" of production factors and consumer goods. Overall, contemporary mainstream economics treats competitive markets as (decentralized) "allocative mechanisms" that attain a form of resource allocation as well as income distribution that is Pareto-optimal (Rosen 1997).

A sixth aspect of the idea of markets as economic mechanisms is their notion as factors in price determination or simply determinants of prices. For instance, echoing Smith's respective ideas, Ricardo proposes that all prices or contracts (including wages) must be governed by "fair and free" market competition and alternatively "never be controlled" by government interference. So does Mill, stating that (single or equilibrium) price represents the "natural effect of unimpeded competition" in markets. Neoclassical and contemporary economists elaborate on and reinforce the notion of markets as price-determining mechanisms. Thus, Walras considers markets mechanisms or realms for exchanging products and productive services, and consequently for determining their exchange values or prices. Moreover, he argues that exchange value or price "comes into being naturally in the market under the influence of free and unlimited competition." Adopting Walras's argument, Knut Wicksell contends that no economic value is more real than that determined by markets, and even that market prices are the sole factual exchange values in a modern economy.

Some other aspects of the idea of market mechanisms in orthodox economics, more or less implicit in the preceding, include: markets as mechanisms for natural selection ("survival of the fittest") in the economy, markets as mechanisms for optimal wealth and income distribution, markets as mechanisms or sources of economic growth, markets as factors of increased living standards or material welfare, and so on.

SOCIOLOGICAL DIMENSIONS: MARKETS–SOCIAL CONSTRUCTIONS

Markets are also a central concern for the "economic sociology of the market." However, in contrast to pure economics, economic sociology typically conceptualizes markets as social constructions, especially institutions, in contrast to their conceptualization as pseudo-automatic mechanisms in conventional economics. Economist-sociologist Schumpeter identifies and in a sense codifies this contrasting treatment by defining markets as institutions within the framework of economic sociology and as mechanisms in that of pure economics. In so doing, he seems influenced by Émile Durkheim (and Max Weber), who specifies, in contrast to orthodox economics, the subject matter of economic sociology as consisting of economic phenomena considered as institutional arrangements, including markets as "institutions relating to exchange." Another economist-sociologist, Talcott Parsons (1967: 4), remarks that orthodox economics has a "deep-rooted belief" in the market as an "automatic, self-regulating mechanism" presumably operating to transform the individual seeking of self-interest or private ends into the "greatest possible satisfaction of the wants of all," while economic sociology considers markets particular social systems or institutions. Contemporary economic sociologists object that mainstream economics empties markets from social relations and institutions or "elementary sociological concerns" like power, norms, and networks (Lie 1997: 342). Even some contemporary economists lament that orthodox economics (especially Austrian marginalism) lacks a "social concept" of markets described as an "obvious illustration of a social situation" (Arrow 1994: 2).

The social conception of markets conceptualizes them as (1) instances of social phenomena; (2) institutional arrangements; (3) social actions, relations, and networks; (4) social systems or structures; (5) power configurations and realms of conflict; and (6) cultural orders.

The most general, self-defining, and perhaps redundant dimension of the social conception of markets, implying to some degree all the others, including their definition as institutions, is treating them as societal phenomena. This treatment is common to classical and contemporary economic sociology and originates or is implicit in Auguste Comte's idea of the social economy whose functions, including that of exchange performed by markets, are "naturally implicated in relations of greater generality" or society. Durkheim adopts, elaborates, and makes Comte's ideas explicit by placing markets into the examples of social facts whose source or substratum "cannot be other than society." Since Durkheim views institutions as fundamental forms of social facts, he regards markets as special institutional arrangements. In retrospect, he provides a classical formulation of the concept of markets as social phenomena in general and as institutions in particular. So does Georg Simmel by arguing – counter pure economics as well as Marxism – that market exchanges are not "simply" economic facts but can be considered social phenomena, given their "preconditions in non-economic concepts and facts," including cultural and other institutions. Contemporary economic sociology fully embraces and further elaborates or specifies the classical social conception of markets as societal phenomena, including institutions.

The second dimension of the social conception of markets, entailed in their general idea as societal facts, is their definition as institutional arrangements or institutions. Like the general idea, the specific concept of markets as social institutions is germane to Comte's ideas of a social economy and is subsequently given an explicit classical formulation in Durkheim's economic sociology. Comte implies that society's "elementary" economy, including the market, has (like the family) the character or spirit of an institution in virtue of the principle or sentiment of cooperation being "preponderant." Also, he suggests that markets are influenced by political and other institutions by contending that government "shall intervene in the performance of all the various functions of the social economy, to keep up the idea of the whole, and the feeling of common interconnection." Building on and rendering Comte's rudimentary ideas methodical propositions, Durkheim provides an archetypical conception of markets as social institutions. First, Durkheim does so implicitly by placing markets or related economic categories (e.g., monetary or financial systems) in the examples of social facts and consequently institutions considered their essential (organized or crystallized) forms and defined as the "beliefs and modes of conduct instituted" by society. That Durkheim's "markets-as-social facts" idea specifically means "markets-as-institutions" is also suggested by his definition of sociology as

a science of the "genesis and functioning" of institutions, whose fundamental principle is the "objective reality" of social facts (which apparently equates "social facts" with "institutions"). Second, Durkheim explicitly conceives markets in institutional terms. Specifically, he defines markets as "institutions relating to exchange," which, alongside other classes of socioeconomic institutions – e.g., institutions related to the production and distribution of wealth – constitute the "subject matter of economic sociology." Durkheim therefore anticipates or leads to Schumpeter's alternative institutional definition of markets and his project of economic sociology as a branch of economics. Similarly, Durkheim considers markets, just as economic organizations, "public institutions" or instances of collective "beliefs and modes of conduct." Also, he suggests or hints at the institutional-normative bases of markets, emphasizing the social, including conventional, moral, and legal, elements of market contracts. Durkheim memorably argues that a commercial contract "is not sufficient unto itself, but is possible only thanks to a regulation of the contract which is essentially social," especially institutional, which includes legal or conventional norms. Simply, saying that in market contracts "not everything is contractual," Durkheim says that not all in markets is economic and mechanical, but also institutional and otherwise social. Akin to Durkheim, Ferdinand Tönnies points to the social dimensions of market contracts or transactions by noting that society is "involved in every contract or exchange."

Another prominent classical sociologist, Weber, basically converges (as Parsons implies in *The Structure of Social Action*) with Durkheim on an institutional-normative conception of markets as well as economy and society overall. Weber sociologically conceives markets as particular normative-institutional orders, arguing that group formation through market exchanges ("use of money") represents the "exact counterpart" to social institutions or rule systems, i.e., to associations formed via "rationally agreed or imposed norms." Also, in his early, more economic-oriented writings, Weber considers markets special cases of those social institutions – described as "purposive systems" – that are "not purposefully created by collective means, but which nevertheless function purposefully," apparently influenced by Menger's ideas of spontaneous market creation and evolution out of "individual interests." In particular, like Durkheim, Weber places markets among the "most advanced institutions" of (modern) capitalism, while suggesting that they historically predate this economic system. So does Thorstein Veblen, another early economic sociologist or social-institutional economist whose institutionalist conception of markets seems particularly influenced (in part) by or similar to that of Durkheim. Veblen considers markets the "prevailing institutions" of modern capitalism or the "price system." In general, he describes and analyzes markets in terms such as "institutions" or the "institutional scheme" of the price system, the "institutional basis" (e.g., monetary accounting and property rights) of economic enterprise, and the like. Notably, he regards modern markets and other "institutions of the price system" as products of social-cultural evolution, the "development of society" and the "growth of culture," thus subject to "developmental variation." The same can be said of such other early institutional economists as Commons and others who embrace and develop Veblen's (and indirectly Durkheim–Weber's) ideas. For illustration, Commons analyzes markets as social institutions by treating market transactions as institutional, including conventional and legal, relations.

Durkheim's and Weber's institutional conceptions of markets have not only proven influential and seminal in economic sociology, but also influenced some prominent neoclassical economists, alongside early economic institutionalists like Veblen and Commons. One (perhaps most) important case of such influences is Schumpeter, whose sociological concept of markets as social institutions is to a large measure inspired by or similar to those of Durkheim and Weber (Swedberg 1998). Schumpeter conceives markets as particular forms or effects of what he, apparently following Weber, denotes as "economically relevant institutions," a variation on or specification of the Weberian concept of "economically relevant phenomena." In particular, Schumpeter describes markets as essential institutions of the monetary, especially modern capitalist, economy, seemingly echoing Weber, and states (under the likely influence of Walras–Menger's *laissez-faire* ideas) that no

social institution is "more democratic" than a market. Notably, Schumpeter furnishes an underlying sociological rationale for the institutional or holistic conception of markets by declaring *à la* Durkheim and Comte that the "social process is really one indivisible whole" from which the analyst "artificially extracts" economic phenomena. Another pertinent instance of Durkheim's and Weber's (plus Marx's) sociological influences, via an institutional conception of markets, on economists involves Polanyi, a heterodox economist and economic anthropologist. Evoking Durkheim, Polanyi notices that markets have an "institutional history" and are complex social institutions, not simply or purely economic ones. Polanyi therefore points to or hints at what has come to be known in modern economic sociology as the institutional, or generally social, embeddedness of markets, though he usually, as critics object (Granovetter & Swedberg 1992), suggests that market economies are "dis-embedded" in this sense in contrast to their traditional non-market forms as "embedded and enmeshed in a variety of institutions." Specifically, at least the fact of having an "institutional history" allows or intimates that markets are also "embedded and enmeshed" in various social institutions, which solves Polanyi's market "dis-embeddedness" puzzle or weakens its criticism.

Within post-war economic sociology, Parsons adopts and elaborates on what he sees as Durkheim's and Weber's convergent institutional-normative conceptions of markets or market economies. Parsons and his collaborators analyze and emphasize the "institutional structure" of markets (Parsons & Smelser 1965: 143). In this view, the institutional structure of markets particularly involves or presupposes the "institutionalization of economic values" or an "institutionalized and internalized" value system of the economy, notably "institutionalized motivation" (e.g., the profit motive). Similarly, some heterodox economists (Myrdal 1953: 197) point to the "institutional factors" determining the structure of markets, even the entire economic system, thus adopting or echoing Durkheim–Weber's ideas.

Modern ("new") economic sociology has also embraced and further developed the classic Durkheimian-Weberian conception of markets as social institutions. Contemporary economic sociologists typically consider markets particular social institutions in deliberate contrast to their treatment as mechanisms in orthodox economics. In this view, markets constitute institutional arrangements in that they need social rules and structures, such as property rights, governance structures, rules of exchange, and conceptions of control (Fligstein 2001: 30–3), and are regulated by various formal and informal institutions (Carruthers & Babb 2000: 4). Also, the institutional conception of markets has received increasing acceptance or attention in some parts of modern economics, sometimes becoming a challenge or alternative to their orthodox and still prevailing concept as self-regulating economic mechanisms *à la* Walras. Moreover, the concept of markets as social institutions tends to become a major substantial point of convergence, affinity, or collaboration between contemporary, especially the new institutional, economics and economic sociology, just as it has been between their early or classic versions in Veblen et al. and Durkheim and Weber, respectively. Thus, some economists with otherwise different general theoretical positions redefine markets as "vigorous" social institutions with the "essential function" of registering consumer preferences (Robinson 1964), or as institutional arrangements for the "consummation" of exchange transactions (Stigler 1952). So do others by considering markets social institutions on which prices are "determined" (Arrow 1994: 118), as well as the "institutions of governance" or "governance structures" (Williamson 1998: 75–7). Particularly, some economists analyze labor markets as specific social institutions (Solow 1990). Others emphasize the operation of markets generally as institutional arrangements having "cultural consequences" for the "evolution of values, tastes, and personalities" (Bowles 1998). Other economists define markets as social institutions involving "practices, norms, rules" that contribute to economic and societal coordination, combined with "spontaneously organized complex phenomena" (Caldwell 1997: 1871). Notably, markets are admittedly embedded in (other) social institutions, including a legal-political "institutional infrastructure" (Tornell & Lane 1999), specifically democratic rules and values (Caldwell 1997: 1871). This suggests

that economists increasingly recognize or pay attention to some kind or degree of institutional, including political, embeddedness of markets, thus adopting or evoking a central idea of classical and modern economic sociology.

The third dimension of the social conception of markets is their definition as sets of social actions and relations or of networks, also implicit in their general sociological idea. If the institutional conception of markets is a macro-sociological specification of this idea, their definition as social actions, relations, or networks is the micro (Carruthers & Uzzi 2000). In classical economic sociology, Weber and Simmel furnish pertinent examples of the second treatment of markets. Weber treats the market as a "sociological category of economic action" and suggests that the study of markets as such categories constitutes "essentially" the subject of economic sociology (or social economics). Specifically, he defines markets as the "archetype" of rational social action or "consociation" via economic exchange, which exist when competition obtains "for opportunities of exchange among a plurality of potential parties." Weber stresses that by defining markets in terms of a "coexistence and sequence" of social relations or consociations he uses a "sociological point of view," as distinguished from the purely economic. In particular, he states that markets "constitute social action" to the effect that any market or money-mediated exchanges are such actions "simply because money derives its value from its relation to the potential action of others." Generally, what for Weber makes them sets or networks of social actions and relations is that in markets every action is directed by the "actions of all parties potentially interested in the exchange," not by individual action in mutual isolation. Finally, he implies some degree of embeddedness (while not using the term) of markets and the economy overall in social relations and their networks. Thus, Weber suggests that markets and other "forms of economic organization" are influenced by the "autonomous structure of social action" within which they exist and so are "embedded." In general, he posits what he famously describes as the "elective affinity" between "forms of economic organization," including markets, and "structures of social action," the best-known case being that between the "spirit and structure" of modern capitalism and the "ethic of ascetic Protestantism." Weber's contemporary Simmel provides another classical formulation of the notion of markets as sets or networks of social relations and interactions. Specifically, Simmel uses terms like an "incomparable sociological constellation," "sociological process," and "peculiarly interwoven form" of social interaction (e.g., conflict) to designate markets, especially market competition, thus hinting at their embeddedness in social relations and networks. Weber's and Simmel's contemporary Tönnies describes in particular the labor market as a "network of communication," thus of social interactions and relations, located in the "periphery" of the system of markets, including also the market for commodities. In addition, apparently reflecting Marx's view, Tönnies states that labor markets are not dependent on the "prior existence" of those for commodities (a statement contradicting neoclassical economics that argues the opposite by the principle of "derived demand" for labor and other production factors from that for products). Some leading contemporary economic sociologists essentially adopt and elaborate on Weber–Simmel's ideas by treating markets as representing or, more precisely, being embedded in networks of social relations and interactions among individuals. Hence, this reformulates or reinstates the conception of social embeddedness of markets (originating in Polanyi and implicit in Weber and Durkheim), which has become paradigmatic for the "new" economic sociology since the 1980s (Swedberg 1998). In this view, social relations are "fundamental" – even more so than are institutions and cultural norms ("generalized morality") downplayed as secondary – to markets in virtue of market behaviors and other economic actions being situated and embedded in micro-networks of interpersonal ("weak") ties (Granovetter 1985: 500).

The fourth dimension of the social conception of markets is defining them as social systems or structures, another definition derived from or part of their general sociological idea. The notion of markets and economies as social systems or structures can be deduced from Comte's "static study of sociology" as an "investigation of the laws of action and reaction of different parts of the social system." His sociological statics thus necessarily incorporates (as Durkheim also interprets it) markets and economies, alongside governments and politics, into "different parts of the social system." Notably, Comte suggests that the "scientific principle" of the relations between society and markets or economies (just as governments or politics) is a "spontaneous harmony between the whole and the parts of the social system." Developing Comte's insights, Durkheim defines markets in social system terms by stating that economies and other major social phenomena are "systems of values," a proposition embraced and developed by Parsons (e.g., "institutionalized and internalized" value economic system) and other functionalist sociologists. Also, like Comte, Durkheim suggests that markets as defined constitute systemic elements (or subsystems) of a larger societal system or macrosocial structure, a suggestion found in Pareto as well and carried further by Parsons and contemporary systems theorists. Pareto considers markets social systems and proposes that they and other "states of the economic system" represent just "particular cases" of the general state of the "sociological system." Further, *à la* Durkheim and Comte, he describes the social system (and so sociology) as "much more complicated" than the economic-market system (thus pure economics), due to the fact that the first involves not only rational actions and interests, as does the second, but also (and mostly) non-rational behaviors and sentiments ("residues"). Parsons and other contemporary systems theorists in sociology adopt and carry further Durkheim's and Pareto's ideas of markets as social systems. Thus, they suggest that in economic sociology the market and the economy overall be "considered as a social system" (Parsons & Smelser 1965: 174) or a "subsystem of the total society." Specifically, they consider the market/the economy a functional social subsystem that is differentiated from other subsystems on the basis of fulfilling the "adaptive function" of a society (i.e., "maximizing utility") within their AGIL (adaptation, goal-attainment, integration, latent-pattern maintenance) model. For example, they classify the market into labor markets, markets for consumer goods, capital markets, markets for entrepreneurship ("control of productivity"), all considered social subsystems. Building on Parsons, contemporary systems theorists in sociology define markets and economies as "self-referential" social systems whose operation "ultimately" refers to and depends on the larger societal environment (Luhmann 1995: 462). In this view, the "unavoidable coupling of self-and-other-referential meaning references" in markets and economies presupposes and functions within "special" social structural conditions (Luhmann 1995: 462) or the "wider macrostructure" of society (Munch 1994: 276). Similarly, other contemporary sociologists (Habermas 1971: 163) define the market (and the economy) in terms of a "behavioral system of instrumental action." Further, some prominent contemporary economists acknowledge that markets, just as economies overall, are part of the "social system in general" (Arrow 1994: 6), thus adopting or echoing Durkheim–Pareto–Parsons's macrosociological ideas.

Within contemporary economic sociology, an influential and perhaps prevailing (micro or network) variation on the (macro) theme of markets as systemic categories is their definition as social structures. In early formulations, contemporary economic sociologists define markets (especially their production or supply side) as "self-reproducing" social structures involving "cliques of firms" in reciprocal actions and reactions (White 1981: 518). Specifically, production markets are characterized as "induced role structures" that involve a "structure of roles with a differentiated niche" for each producer. This view also attributes to markets a historical or evolutionary trajectory that makes a market a "historically shaped" structure of specific roles for a "stable set" of producers as social actors (White 1981: 526). Other contemporary economic sociologists also adopt a structural or network approach to markets by treating them as "social rather than exclusively economic structures" (Baker 1984: 776). In particular, some identify the "social structure" of market competition as a "key ingredient" in the structures and processes of business organizations (Burt 1988: 356). Others analyze and compare the social structure of historical or precapitalist markets and that of modern or capitalist markets, both treated as Weberian ideal types (Swedberg 1994: 274). Generally, contemporary economic sociology emphasizes the societal constitution and construction of markets in the sense of constituting or being shaped by social structures (Fligstein 2001: 8). In this definition, markets constitute or involve

"complex and stable" social structures – resting on "repeated interactions" between market actors and their status or reputation – "types of social orders" or "forms of social organization" (Fligstein 2001: 7–32). Even prominent contemporary economists (Becker 1976: 3–8) implicitly conceive markets in sociostructural terms, stating that the market fulfills "most, if not all, of the functions assigned to 'structure' in sociological theories" (though this statement may lead to reducing all social structures to "market"). Notably, they recognize and analyze the "importance" of social structure for markets (Becker & Murphy 2000: 3).

The fifth dimension of the social conception of markets is considering them power configurations and realms of conflict, a consideration also specifying their general sociological idea. Such a consideration is particularly characteristic for Weber, who suggests that markets represent, involve, or are influenced by "power constellations" and "conflicts of interests." Thus, he holds that market prices are determined by "conflicts of interests and of compromises" and thus by "power constellations." Generally, Weber depicts markets or the "price system" in terms of "a struggle of man against man," with wealth as its "weapon" and prices as its "expressions." Notably, he identifies a special source of power and domination in a "formally free interplay" between economic actors in competitive markets, due to the fact that these, just as economic organizations, represent or exhibit a "structure of dominance." Some contemporary sociologists evoke Weber by observing that market economic exchanges are the "structural sources" of power and domination (Blau 1994: 166). So do some contemporary economists by describing markets as the "locus" of power (Bowles 1995) and as "populated by multiple powerful groups" (Tornell & Lane 1999). For Weber, the fact that dominance is often produced by free market relations is exemplified by what he calls domination "by virtue of a position of monopoly" or "monopolistic powers." Further, he adds that "indeed, because of the very absence of rules, domination which originates in [markets] may be felt to be much more oppressive than an authority in which the duties of obedience are set out clearly and expressly," an implicit counterargument to orthodox economics' view of the market as the supreme realm of freedom and democracy. Relatedly, Weber identifies and emphasizes what he denotes as the "non-monetary significance of political bodies" for markets or the "economic order" to indicate that the modern state influences them in various ways, including through the "structure" of authority and political power, beyond the simply monetary function of a *laissez-faire* government.

Akin to Weber, Simmel suggests that markets represent realms of power and social conflict by pointing to their "complete domination" by particular economic actors in the case of market monopolization or cartelization. So do some heterodox economists, who evoke Weber's ideas by arguing that those social groups with "enough" political power can, if they will, alter the institutional conditions that "determine" the structure of markets, thus indicating that market (and non-market) exchanges are "subject to the rules of those in power" (Myrdal 1953: 197). This is what contemporary economic sociologists also indicate by observing that markets show a history of the "repeated exercise of political power" in their operation as well as of establishing and defending property rights (Friedland & Robertson 1990: 6). Influenced by or reminiscent of Weber, other heterodox economists notice that historically political power "had precedence over profit" in the operation of "self-regulating" markets within capitalism to the point "ultimately" of war setting the "law to business," as during the late nineteenth and early twentieth centuries witnessing two world wars (Polanyi 1944: 12). Further, leading contemporary sociologists almost reproduce Weber's terms by describing contemporary markets as "factual constellations of power" (Habermas 1975: 68). In particular, this description is applied to labor markets diagnosed with a "quasi-political wage structure" primarily determined by "relations of political power" (i.e., negotiations between management and workers) rather than just by the market itself. In modern economic sociology, this dimension of their social conception is codified or summarized in treating "markets as politics" in the sense that they are (re)created by the "politics of the creation of market institutions" (Fligstein 2001: 46). This reaffirms and reformulates Weber's ideas, since treating "markets as politics" is another way to say that they

constitute power configurations and realms of conflict.

The sixth dimension of their social conception is defining markets as cultural orders or simply cultures, which, as another specification of their general sociological idea, is especially linked with their institutionalist-normative notion. This approach originates in and is particularly prominent for classical sociologists like Simmel, Weber, and Durkheim, who at this point converge on a culturalist conception of markets. Thus, Simmel proposes a culturalist explanation of markets by observing that historically market exchanges and money are particular results or expressions of "general economic culture." Moreover, he implicitly treats markets as a sort of climax in the evolution of culture by describing money and market exchange as the "pinnacle of a cultural historical series of developments" determining their emergence and direction. Some contemporary economic sociologists explicitly adopt, elaborate, and specify Simmel's ideas, particularly stressing the cultural underpinnings of money and related market phenomena (Zelizer 1989). A culturalist explanation of markets and the economy overall is also present or implicit in Weber's economic sociology, notably his concept of "economic cultures" exemplified by the work ethic of Protestantism and other world religions. In this sense, he implies that markets constitute instances of – or have an "ethical foundation" in – economic cultures that are mostly religiously based and consist of "constellations of norms, institutions, etc.," which illustrates the close link between culturalist and institutionalist market explanations. In particular, Weber's famous thesis of an "elective affinity" of the "spirit and structure" of modern capitalism with the work ethic of "ascetic Protestantism" entails an explanation of markets in terms of economic cultures (though he admonishes against a "one-sided spiritualistic" or culturalist conception). Like Simmel and Weber, Durkheim posits a cultural explanation of markets, as suggested by his assertion that, like other social phenomena, economies or markets are "nothing than systems of values and hence ideals." Consequently, he places markets and economies overall in the social "field of ideals" or cultural values. In a sense, Durkheim's sociological conception of markets and economies can

Table 1 Economic and sociological dimensions and conceptions of markets.

Economic dimensions and conceptions of markets: mechanisms
1 Mechanisms or systems of supply and demand (exchange).
2 Self-regulating and equilibrating mechanisms.
3 Mechanisms and realms of free competition and economic freedom.
4 Spontaneous mechanisms of economic coordination.
5 Mechanisms of resource allocation.
6 Mechanisms of price determination.

Sociological dimensions and conceptions of markets: social constructions
1 Instances of social phenomena.
2 Social institutions.
3 Social actions, relations, and networks.
4 Social systems or structures.
5 Power configurations and conflict fields.
6 Cultural orders.

be interpreted as, first and foremost, culturalist (or, relatedly, institutionalist), given that he essentially understands social facts as "immaterial" cultural phenomena (or institutions), with society described as a collective "moral entity." Some contemporary economic sociologists adopt and develop these classical culturalist conceptions of markets by arguing that market economic processes possess an "irreducible cultural component" (DiMaggio 1994: 27). So do others by treating markets and their reproduction as culture projects or social constructions reflecting a unique normative-cultural (and political) construction of economic organizations and national societies (Fligstein 2001: 70–97). This view is summarized in the proposition that markets involve or are embedded in "culture, or sets of meanings" (Carruthers & Babb 2000: 9), which suggests their cultural embeddedness. Lastly, even some contemporary economists (Becker & Murphy 2000: 3) acknowledge and explore the relevance of culture, including norms, for markets, thus subscribing or coming close to Simmel, Weber, and Durkheim's culturalist market explanations.

The above economic and sociological dimensions and conceptions of markets are summarized in Table 1.

SEE ALSO: Capitalism; Comte, Auguste; Culture, Economy and; Development: Political Economy; Durkheim, Émile; Economic Sociology: Neoclassical Economic Perspective; Economy (Sociological Approach); Economy, Culture and; Economy, Networks and; Mill, John Stuart; Parsons, Talcott; Polanyi, Karl; Rational Choice Theory (and Economic Sociology); Schumpeter, Joseph A.; Simmel, Georg; Smith, Adam; Social Embeddedness of Economic Action; Weber, Max

REFERENCES AND SUGGESTED READINGS

Allais, M. (1997) An Outline of My Main Contribution to Economic Science. *American Economic Review* 87 (Supplement): 3–12.

Arrow, K. (1994) Methodological Individualism and Social Knowledge. *American Economic Review* 84: 1–9.

Baker, W. (1984) The Social Structure of a National Securities Market. *American Journal of Sociology* 89: 775–811.

Barber, B. (1995) All Economies are "Embedded": The Career of a Concept, and Beyond. *Social Research* 62: 387–413.

Becker, G. (1976) *The Economic Approach to Human Behavior*. University of Chicago Press, Chicago.

Becker, G. & Murphy, K. (2000) *Social Economics*. Harvard University Press, Cambridge, MA.

Blau, P. (1994) *Structural Contexts of Opportunities*. University of Chicago Press, Chicago.

Blaug, M. (1985) *The Methodology of Economics*. Cambridge University Press, Cambridge.

Boulding, K. (1970) *Economics as a Science*. McGraw-Hill, New York.

Bowles, S. (1995) Review of *The Handbook of Economic Sociology*, edited by N. Smelser and R. Swedberg. *Contemporary Sociology* 24(3): 304–7.

Bowles, S. (1998) Endogenous Preferences: The Cultural Consequences of Markets and Other Economic Institutions. *Journal of Economic Literature* 36: 75–111.

Buchanan, J. (1991) *The Economics and the Ethics of Constitutional Order*. University of Michigan Press, Ann Arbor.

Burt, R. (1988) The Stability of American Markets. *American Journal of Sociology* 94: 356–95.

Caldwell, B. (1997) Hayek and Socialism. *Journal of Economic Literature* 35: 1856–90.

Carruthers, B. & Babb, S. (2000) *Economy/Society*. Pine Forge Press, Thousand Oaks, CA.

Carruthers, B. & Uzzi, B. (2000) Economic Sociology in the New Millennium. *Contemporary Sociology* 29: 486–94.

Debreu, G. (1969) Valuation Equilibrium and Pareto Optimum. In: Arrow, K. & Scitovsky, T. (Eds.), *Readings in Welfare Economics*. Allen & Unwin, London, pp. 39–45.

Debreu, G. (1991) The Mathematization of Economic Theory. *American Economic Review* 81: 1–7.

DiMaggio, P. (1994) Culture and Economy. In: Smelser, N. & Swedberg, R. (Eds.), *The Handbook of Economic Sociology*. Princeton University Press, Princeton, pp. 27–57.

Fligstein, N. (2001) *The Architecture of Markets*. Princeton University Press, Princeton.

Friedland, R. & Robertson, A. (1990) Beyond the Marketplace. In: Friedland, R. & Robertson, A. (Eds.), *Beyond the Marketplace*. Aldine de Gruyter, New York, pp. 3–49.

Granovetter, M. (1985) Economic Action and Social Structure: The Problem of Embeddedness. *American Journal of Sociology* 91: 481–510.

Granovetter, M. & Swedberg, R. (1992) Introduction. In: Granovetter, M. & Swedberg, R. (Eds.), *The Sociology of Economic Life*. Westview Press, Boulder, CO, pp. 1–26.

Habermas, J. (1971) *Knowledge and Human Interests*. Beacon Press, Boston.

Habermas, J. (1975) *Legitimation Crisis*. Beacon Press, Boston.

Hicks, J. (1961) *Value and Capital*. Oxford University Press, Oxford.

Hirschman, A. (1977) *The Passions and the Interests*. Princeton University Press, Princeton.

Hurwicz, L. (1969) Optimality and Informational Efficiency in Resource Allocation Processes. In: Arrow, K. & Scitovsky, T. (Eds.), *Readings in Welfare Economics*. Allen & Unwin, London, pp. 61–80.

Lange, O. (1946) The Scope and Method of Economics. *Review of Economic Studies* 13: 19–32.

Lie, J. (1997) Sociology of Markets: Heterogeneity, Power, and Macrosociological Foundations. *Annual Review of Sociology* 23: 341–60.

Luhmann, N. (1995) *Social Systems*. Stanford University Press, Stanford.

Mirowski, P. (1989) *More Heat than Light*. Cambridge University Press, Cambridge.

Mises, L. (1960) *Epistemological Problems of Economics*. Van Nostrand, Princeton.

Munch, R. (1994) *Sociological Theory*. Nelson-Hall, Chicago.

Myrdal, G. (1953) *The Political Element in the Development of Economic Theory*. Routledge & Kegan Paul, London.

Parsons, T. (1967) *The Structure of Social Action*. Free Press, New York.

Parsons, T. & Smelser, N. (1965) *Economy and Society*. Free Press, New York.

Polanyi, K. (1944) *The Great Transformation*. Farrar & Rinehart, New York.

Robinson, J. (1964) *Economic Philosophy*. Macmillan, London.

Rosen, S. (1997) Austrian and Neoclassical Economics: Any Gains from Trade? *Journal of Economic Perspectives* 11: 139–52.

Samuelson, P. (1983) *Foundations of Economic Analysis*. Harvard University Press, Cambridge, MA.

Samuelson, P. (2001) A Ricardo–Sraffa Paradigm Comparing Gains from Trade in Inputs and Finished Goods. *Journal of Economic Literature* 39: 1204–14.

Schumpeter, J. (1954a) *Economic Doctrine and Method*. Allen & Unwin, London.

Schumpeter, J. (1954b) *History of Economic Analysis*. Oxford University Press, New York.

Solow, R. (1990) *The Labor Market as a Social Institution*. Blackwell, Cambridge, MA.

Stigler, G. (1952) *The Theory of Price*. Macmillan, New York.

Stiglitz, J. (2002) Information and the Change in the Paradigm in Economics. *American Economic Review* 92: 460–501.

Swedberg, R. (1994) Markets as Social Structures. In: Smelser, N. & Swedberg, R. (Eds.), *The Handbook of Economic Sociology*. Princeton University Press, Princeton, pp. 255–82.

Swedberg, R. (1998) *Max Weber and the Idea of Economic Sociology*. Princeton University Press, Princeton.

Tornell, A. & Lane, P. (1999) The Voracity Effect. *American Economic Review* 89: 22–46.

White, H. (1981) Where Do Markets Come From? *American Journal of Sociology* 87: 517–47.

Wieser, F. (1956) *Natural Value*. Kelley & Millman, New York.

Williamson, O. (1998) The Institutions of Governance. *American Economic Review* 88: 75–9.

Zelizer, V. (1989) The Social Meaning of Money. *American Journal of Sociology* 95: 342–77.

marriage

David H. J. Morgan

Dictionary definitions of marriage usually begin with something like "the legal union of a man and a woman in order to live together and often to have children." Even in such a simple and limited definition, some key elements and some potential complexities are highlighted. First, we are dealing with a definition referring to legal criteria. However, since legal definitions differ, we can reasonably expect practices and understandings of marriage to differ. This dictionary definition is consequently a highly ethnocentric one, shaped by the cultural and historical conditions under which it is produced. Next, marriage is a way of identifying some particular kinds of ties between two, or sometimes more, people such that marriage is always something more than the characteristics of the individuals who compose it. There is also a suggestion of functionality; marriage exists in order to achieve something else.

Marriage is important to the individuals concerned, the others to whom they are connected, and to the society within which the marriage is recognized. Marriage will not necessarily be important in the same way across different societies or to the different individuals within these societies. Recognizing this qualification, the list here outlines some of the key ways in which sociologists have described the importance of marriage:

- Marriage is seen as a key element within a wider set of family relationships. It establishes links between different families and over different generations.
- Marriage is seen as a key element in the life course. It is seen as an important transition in the lives of individuals and of those to whom they are connected.
- Marriage is seen as a key element in the social ordering of gender and sexuality. This is the most widespread understanding of marriage (one man, one woman) and reaffirms distinctions between men and women and the dominant importance of heterosexuality.

- Marriage is seen as a key element in the wider social structure. This is because the parties involved in a marriage are not just gendered and sexualized individuals but have class, ethnic, religious, and other differently based identities.
- Marriage is important as an element in the mobilization of patterns of care and social support.
- Marriage is important in the formation of personal and social identity.

These are in addition to the key function which links marriage and parenthood and which sees marriage in terms of the production, legitimizing, and social placement of children.

Research into marriage may be classified under two headings: the comparative and historical, and the study of its internal dynamics. The first considers how marriage differs between different societies or different historical periods and how it has changed over time. Earlier comparative research into marriage explored different marriage systems and the ways in which these were linked to wider aspects of social structure such as the division of societies into classes or castes, or the distribution of property. The emphasis was often a strongly functional one considering the part that a particular marriage system (polygyny, polyandry, arranged, and so on) played within the wider social structure. Comparative research might also be linked to a wider theory of social evolution, speculating on the ways in which marriage patterns and the wider social order together change over time.

More recently, interests have become more theoretically focused. Goode's now classic study explored the ways in which, and the extent to which, family patterns throughout the world were converging into a single "conjugal" family model, one which focused on the unit created through marriage. This account, although influential at the time, suffered from being too closely tied to a functional mode of analysis and from smoothing over complexities and divergences. Other analyses have explored differences between premodern, modern, and postmodern patterns of marriage and family living, as well as the long-term decline of "patriarchalism" within family relationships (Cheal 1991; Castells 1997). These more recent accounts have been aware of differences in the pace of change between different parts of the globe and, increasingly, the possibilities of resistance to the forces of globalization. Thus, the reassertion of what might be described as "traditional" patterns of marriage might be seen as important in the construction of religious, ethnic, or national identities in the face of globalization and westernization.

More narrowly, attempts have been made to analyze changes in marriage in Britain, the United States, and other anglophone societies together with much of Western and Northern Europe. Sometimes this might be expressed simply as a "decline" of marriage, as increasing numbers of people do not go through a formal marriage ceremony, have children outside wedlock, or divorce. Further, with the partial recognition of cohabiting and non-heterosexual partnerships, the privileged status of heterosexual marriage seems to be less secure.

Notions of the decline of marriage may be countered by showing that marriage continues to be an important, if frequently delayed, transition in the life course and pointing to the increasing demands for the recognition of gay and lesbian marriages. The issue here is one of change rather than decline, with researchers often accounting for these changes in terms of a broad historical process of "individualization." The emphasis here is on the ways in which individuals are increasingly called upon to shape their own relational biographies with little reference to the expectations of others or previously established patterns of behavior. This may sometimes be seen as the extension of democratic ideals into intimate relationships.

Yet another formulation is in terms of a long-term shift in marriage from institution to relationship. Marriage may be seen as moving from a social context where it was clearly embedded in a wider network of familial and kinship ties and obligations and where it constituted the major legitimate adult identity. As marriage becomes more of a relationship, there is greater emphasis on individual choice and the needs and satisfactions of the participants. Choice here includes the possibility of choosing not to get married.

There are difficulties with this formulation which, as with other accounts, glosses over diversities in experiences and trends over time. A wholly "relationship marriage" would seem to be an oxymoron and it is probably better to think of different "mixes" of relational and institutional elements at different points of time and between individual marriages. Thus it can be argued that the very idea of "relationship" has itself developed some institutional features in that marital partners may be expected to share intimacies, enjoy sex, and monitor and evaluate the development of their marriages and, indeed, other less formally recognized relationships.

Turning to the more "internal" aspects of marriage, we can look at gender divisions and questions of identity. It is widely believed that marriages have become more equal in terms of gender; the very idea of a relationship suggests some degree of mutuality and equality between the partners. At the same time, there has been a considerable body of research exploring gendered inequalities and differences within marriage. These include unequal participation in household and parental tasks; differences in the management of money within the home; and differences in patterns of paid employment and leisure activities outside the home. The sources of these persisting differences include men's and women's differential labor market participation and earning power; the persistence of deeply held assumptions about the nature of men and women; and inequalities in power within the household, including physical power and the potential for violence. Some have argued that we should consider the different balances between "love" and "power" within marriage. There is a strong expectation that modern marriage should be based on love, but this expectation coexists with these continuing inequalities within this relationship (Dallos & Dallos 1997).

Evidence of change is uneven although generally pointing toward a greater degree of sharing. There has been an increasing acceptance of the idea of equality in marriage on the part of both men and women. Actual practices may fall behind ideals, although there is evidence of greater sharing, especially in childcare. Men and women still tend to do different kinds of tasks within the household and women are still more likely to take overall responsibility for parental or domestic planning. There is considerable variation, however, depending on factors such as patterns of paid employment, education, ethnicity, and social class. Despite some clear shifts, gender remains an important division within the institutionalized relationship of marriage.

In terms of identity, it is still the case that marriage represents an important life course transition and remains a significant adult relationship. Partly for this reason, marriage can still provide an important source of stability and security in an individual's life. Further, it can be a basis for identity and a key element in the development of a relational self. However, this self also exists in a world shaped by the changing labor market, globalization, individualization, and changes in the gender order. Sometimes, therefore, there may be a tension between the apparent stability provided by marriage and the possibilities within a marriage for shaping identity and personal development, especially where different gendered expectations develop within marriage.

Sociological research continues to find marriage an important social institution and a major area where the gender order, and changes within it, are manifested. While it has been affected by forces such as globalization and individualization, it has not been overwhelmed by these processes. Nevertheless, within western societies at least, it is increasingly clear that the boundaries between marriage and other adult intimate relationships have become blurred. The exclusively heterosexual character of marriage is being challenged and the distinction between marriage and cohabitation has become more blurred in terms of law and actual practices.

It is likely that future research will explore the whole spectrum of intimate relationships and the position of marriage within it. It may serve as a reminder of the limits of individualization through exploring the multiple interdependences that can develop over a life course. With an aging population, the significance of these relationships in later life will receive increasing attention. It is also hoped that there will be more systematic comparative research in order to provide a more rigorous exploration of the notions of globalization and individualization.

SEE ALSO: Cohabitation; Divisions of Household Labor; Inequalities in Marriage; Infidelity and Marital Affairs; Interracial Unions; Intimacy; Intimate Union Formation and Dissolution; Marital Power/Resource Theory; Marital Power/Resource Theory; Marital Quality; Marriage, Sex, and Childbirth; Money Management in Families; Same-Sex Marriage/Civil Unions

REFERENCES AND SUGGESTED READINGS

Beck, U. & Beck-Gernsheim, E. (1995) *The Normal Chaos of Love*. Polity Press, Cambridge.
Castells, M. (1997) *The Power of Identity*. Vol. 2 of *The Information Age: Economy, Society, and Culture*. Blackwell, Oxford.
Cheal, D. (1991) *Family and the State of Theory*. Harvester Wheatsheaf, London.
Dallos, S. & Dallos, R. (1997) *Couples, Sex, and Power: The Politics of Desire*. Open University Press, Buckingham.
Goode, W. J. (1970) *World Revolution and Family Patterns*. Free Press, New York.
Jamieson, L. (1998) *Intimacy*. Polity Press, Cambridge.
Therborn, G. (2004) *Between Sex and Power: Family in the World, 1900–2000*. Routledge, London.

marriage, sex, and childbirth

Graham Allan

As with ideas of community, public perceptions of family life highlight the extent to which change has been occurring. Usually the emphasis is on the "decline" of family values and family solidarities in comparison to some past, more stable and wholesome period. In most cases, these perceived changes are significantly exaggerated, with the past being idealized in a quite uncritical fashion. Under more rigorous examination, family relationships in the past can be recognized as somewhat less rosy than popular imagination usually supposes (Gillis 1997). However, there is one sphere of family life in which there has undoubtedly been real – and significant – change occurring. This concerns the patterning of partnership and household formation and dissolution, and more specifically the relationships between marriage, sex, and childbirth. Importantly, these changes have been occurring, albeit at different speeds, across a wide range of economically advanced societies especially in Europe and North America.

The changes there have been in these patterns have been radical, certainly in comparison to the trends that were dominant for much of the twentieth century. Each country is different; each has its distinct social and cultural influences; each develops its own legislative principles and welfare traditions which influence the dominant organization of sexual, domestic, and familial relations within the society. Nonetheless, for much of the twentieth century there was a very clear relationship in different European and North American societies between marriage, sex, and childbirth. In effect, they formed a strong trilogy, certainly ideologically, but also behaviorally. In other words, for the first two-thirds of the twentieth century, sex was only really considered legitimate within the relationship of marriage, as, both legally and socially, was childbirth.

Of course, sex occurred outside marriage, both before and during, and children were born outside wedlock. However, unmarried sex was typically furtive and covert, while illegitimate births brought shame and disapproval. Moreover, to live in a sexual relationship outside marriage was to "live in sin" – a powerful symbol of the moral significance of marriage. Indeed, marriage came to be seen as increasingly central within the individual's life course. For women especially, it was often the reason for leaving the parental home and thus symbolized independence and adulthood. Over this period of the twentieth century marriage rates steadily increased, while marriage age typically dropped. For example, in Britain women's rates of marriage by age 30 rose from 60 percent in 1900 to over 90 percent in 1970, while median age at first marriage fell for women from 25 in 1900 to 21 in 1970.

However, since the early 1970s the connections between marriage, sex, and childbirth have altered quite dramatically. The component elements are no longer linked as strongly as they were. Certainly there continues to be an overlap between the three, but they are not bound as tightly to each other in the ways they

were. Thus, counter to the trends dominant throughout most of the twentieth century, rates of marriage have fallen substantially, marriage age has increased, and many more people now cohabit outside marriage. Again drawing on Britain as an example, by 2002 fewer than 50 percent of women had married by age 30; median age at marriage for women had risen to 28, and nearly 30 percent of all non-married women aged 18–49 were cohabiting. At the same time, separation and divorce increased so that lifelong partnership became a less realistic expectation. Instead there has been a normalization of varied transitions over the life course in an individual's domestic and sexual arrangements. Indeed, especially where there are no young children involved, these issues are increasingly seen as matters of personal choice rather than ones requiring social sanction, control, or regulation.

This is evident in the rapid growth there has been in cohabitation over the last generation. From being a mode of partnership and domestic organization largely limited to those who were divorced, over the last 25 years it has become an entirely normal and acceptable practice throughout much of the western world. In the 1980s, cohabitation tended to occur for a period prior to marriage. It was, in other words, seen by many as a form of engagement through which the strength and suitability of the partnership could be tested. This trend has continued: cohabitation prior to marriage is increasingly normative. In addition, though, many couples cohabit without defining this as necessarily a prelude to marriage. Cohabitation has in this sense become simply another lifestyle option, through which couples come to choose how they pattern their sexual and domestic partnerships. There continue to be religious and ethnic differences in the social acceptability of cohabitation, but clearly the social and moral judgments made of this arrangement have changed significantly from the mid-part of the twentieth century.

Not surprisingly given these other changes, the link between marriage and childbirth is also now nowhere near as strong as it was in previous generations. For most of the twentieth century, births outside marriage were highly stigmatized. When women became pregnant outside wedlock, the most appropriate "solution" socially was for them to marry the father of the child. Often where this did not happen, the mother was sent away to give birth, with the child then being offered for adoption. Cultural reactions are quite different now, as the statistics on births in and out of marriage indicate. Once more drawing on Britain as an example, in the 1970s fewer than 10 percent of births were outside marriage, whereas by 2001, 40 percent were. Even more dramatically, the proportion of teenage births outside marriage rose to 90 percent by 2003 from less than 10 percent in 1976. Of course, changes in partnership behavior are also relevant here. Often births registered as outside marriage involve cohabitation – in Britain currently over 80 percent do. Not all of these will be "marriage-like" in terms of partnership commitment, but many are. However, even where there is no committed partner, it is evident that moral disapproval of births outside wedlock is far more limited than it was. In general, and again allowing for ethnic and religious differences, it seems largely to be restricted to concern over young mothers who, despite experiencing poverty, are perceived by some to be abusing the welfare system.

Behind these changes lies a fundamental shift in the ways in which sexual expression and behavior are culturally understood. As discussed above, the cultural "blueprint" governing legitimate sexual activities has been transformed over the last 30 years in most western societies. The limits that were placed around full sexual activity in the early and mid-twentieth century no longer carry weight with the majority of people. Instead, individuals now have far greater freedom to express their sexuality and engage in sexual relationships outside marriage than was the case in previous generations. Most noticeably, with the exception of some of those who hold strong religious beliefs, virginity is no longer something to be valued in the way it was. Instead, the cultural perception is that individuals – both male and female – should gain sexual experience prior to "settling down" in a marriage or a marriage-like relationship. Similarly, while infidelity within a committed relationship is rarely condoned (Duncombe et al. 2004), there is no moral disapproval of sexual relationships among the non-married, be they single, separated, divorced, or widowed. As above, these issues are seen as essentially a private matter of choice rather than a public issue requiring social sanction.

The reasons for this greater cultural acceptance of sexual activity outside marriage are numerous. Among the most important are cumulative changes in ideas of femininity and citizenship, and changes in the availability of effective contraception. Ideas about femininity and appropriate behavior for women have clearly altered since the 1970s. The rise of second-wave feminism in particular marked the development of different understandings of womanhood and changed representations of "feminine." Linked to this were changes in education and employment which enabled women to be less dependent on marriage and male patronage and thus less bound by domestic responsibility. These changes were also facilitated by developing ideas of citizenship. Over the last 30 years, women's citizenship rights in all western societies have been redefined and protected through legislation which attempts to outlaw discrimination, in public arenas at least, on the grounds of gender, sexuality, or partnership status. And quite crucial to these changes has been the ability of women – married and unmarried – to control their fertility. Symbolized by the development of the birth control pill, the reduction of the risk of pregnancy meant that women felt able to engage far more freely than previously in full sexual relationships outside marriage. In turn, for many, concerns about protecting and controlling daughters' sexuality became more muted as the moral climate changed.

These changes are in line with other transitions that social theorists have argued are having an impact on personal relationships in late modernity. In particular, the idea that sexual behavior and sexual identities are personal rather than public issues is clearly compatible with the growth of individualization in society as well as with changing expectations about the nature and permanency of committed relationships. The evidence of increasing divorce rates has played a symbolically important role in this. Not only were divorced couples at the forefront of changes in cohabitation, they also challenged traditional ideas about sexual abstinence outside marriage. Moreover, if marriage is no longer considered as necessarily a permanent union, then the idea of a single lifelong partner is undermined. If this is so, then so too the idea that individuals should "save" themselves sexually for that one partner also becomes questionable. In this context, gaining sexual experience prior to marriage comes to be valued rather than condemned.

Overall, there can be no doubt that the relationship between marriage, sex, and childbirth has altered quite dramatically over the last 30 years across different western societies. These shifts are having a clear impact on the nature of "family" and on our understandings of family solidarities. Yet while the patterns are clear, more detailed information is needed on how different people are making decisions about these matters and what influences them in these. Of course, it is also unclear what the longer-term implications of these trends are, especially with regard to parenting and the future of marriage as a regulatory institution. Already welfare systems are having to address the issue of non-custodial parents' responsibilities to children. In the coming years, governments will also have to consider more fully how issues of property division, including pensions, are resolved legally when the relationships in question are premised on informal rather than formal commitments.

SEE ALSO: Cohabitation; Divorce; Family Diversity; Feminism; Feminism, First, Second, and Third Waves; Intimacy; Lone-Parent Families; Marriage; Motherhood

REFERENCES AND SUGGESTED READINGS

Beck, U. & Beck-Gernstein, E. (1995) *The Normal Chaos of Love*. Sage, London.

Duncan, S. & Edwards, R. (Eds.) (1997) *Single Mothers in an International Context: Mothers or Workers?* UCL Press, London.

Duncombe, J., Harrison, K., Allan, G., & Marsden, D. (Eds.) (2004) *The State of Affairs: Explorations in Infidelity and Commitment*. Lawrence Erlbaum, Mahwah, NJ.

Giddens, A. (1992) *The Transformation of Intimacy*. Polity Press, Cambridge.

Gillis, J. (1997) *A World of Their Own Making*. Oxford University Press, Oxford.

Hawkes, G. (1996) *A Sociology of Sex and Sexuality*. Open University Press, Buckingham.

Heuveline, P. & Timberlake, J. (2004) The Role of Cohabitation in Family Formation: The United States in Comparative Perspective. *Journal of Marriage and the Family* 65: 1214–30.

Jamieson, L. (1998) *Intimacy*. Polity Press, Cambridge.

Lewis, J. (2001) *The End of Marriage? Individualism and Intimate Relations*. Edward Elgar, Cheltenham.

Rowlingson, K. & McKay, S. (2002) *Lone-Parent Families: Gender, Class, and State*. Pearson Education, Harlow.

Sassler, S. (2004) The Process of Entering into Cohabiting Unions. *Journal of Marriage and Family* 66: 491–505.

Marshall, Thomas Humphrey (1893–1981)

Jack Barbalet

Born in London, Tom Marshall was the fourth of six children in a prosperous and cultured middle-class family. His father was a successful architect, and his great-grandfather made a fortune in industry. He was educated at Rugby and Cambridge, where he read history. In 1914 he went to Germany to learn German and spent the next four years as a civilian prisoner of war at Ruhleben, near Berlin. Marshall described his period of imprisonment as "the most powerful formative experience" of his life up to that time. It was his first contact with working men, as the Ruhleben camp's inmates included merchant seamen and fishermen. Although Marshall's profession of sociology was a decade away, he wrote that from this time there was "a growing sociological curiosity about what was happening in me and around me."

On returning to England after the war, in 1919 Marshall won a six-year fellowship in history at Trinity College, Cambridge. During this time he wrote on seventeenth-century guilds, the life of James Watt, and revised and extended a popular textbook on English economic history. While a fellow at Trinity Marshall stood as a Labour candidate in the 1922 general election, through which his appreciation of working-class life and the depredations of class inequality were extended. He concluded that temperamentally he was not suited to political campaigning, and that it was not in his nature to spend his "working life poring over original documents to the extent demanded by reputable historical research." In 1925 he took a post at the London School of Economics to tutor social work students. In 1929 he moved to the sociology department, where he remained until his retirement in 1956, with the exception of the five years 1944–9 when he was head of the social work department. He was promoted to a readership in sociology in 1930. He was appointed Professor of Social Institutions in 1944 and Martin White Professor of Sociology in 1954.

Marshall had a successful public career as well as an academic one. During World War II he was in the British Foreign Office monitoring the foreign press, and immediately after the war served with the Control Commission in Germany. His involvement with German affairs continued in 1947–8 when he toured West German universities on behalf of the Association of University Teachers and during 1949–50 when he was Educational Adviser to the British High Commissioner in Germany. From 1956 to 1960 Marshall was director of UNESCO's Social Sciences Department, based in Paris. On his retirement Marshall returned to Cambridge, where he became involved in the introduction of sociology and taught part time in the university's economics faculty. He continued to live in Cambridge and in his eighty-eighth year died there, in 1981.

Marshall's reputation as a sociologist rests on *Citizenship and Social Class*, first given as the Marshall Lectures in Cambridge in 1949, in commemoration of the economist Alfred Marshall (no relative), and published in 1950. His other contributions remain part of a significant sociological legacy. The essays brought together in *Sociology at the Crossroads and Other Essays* (1963), published in America as *Class, Citizenship, and Social Development* (1964), and *The Right to Welfare and Other Essays* (1981) develop not only the themes of his chief sociological interests, namely social class inequality and social policy, but also the conceptualization of power, for instance, and also transformations of capitalism in the mid- to late twentieth century. Marshall also published a leading textbook, *Social Policy* (1965), that went through many revisions and editions.

Marshall's work has exercised much influence in British sociology and also had an impact on American sociology. Reinhard Bendix's's

Nation-Building and Citizenship (1964), for instance, owes much to Marshall and much of it reads like a commentary on Marshall's own treatment of that theme. It would not be unfair to say that the intellectual core of Talcott Parsons's discussion, "Full Citizenship for the Negro American?" (1965), draws enormously from Marshall. Marshall's influence on Gerhard Lenski, *Power and Privilege* (1966), is not insignificant and not unacknowledged. But the translation to American idiom of this very British thinker was not always successful, as one particular example demonstrates.

In his inaugural lecture, "Sociology at the Crossroads" (1946), Marshall sets out a methodological program in which "sociology can choose units of study of a manageable size – not society, progress, morals, and civilization, but specific social structures in which the basic processes and functions have determined meanings." He went on to describe these endeavors as "stepping-stones in the middle distance." Robert Merton, in his paper "On Sociological Theories of the Middle Range" (1968), refers to Marshall's discussion to support his own position on middle-range theorizing. What escaped Merton, and others who have referred to Merton's use of Marshall, such as Lipset, is that while Merton's approach arguably undermines the idea of a social system, as Alvin Gouldner's "Reciprocity and Autonomy in Functional Theory" (1959) shows, Marshall's presupposes it. Marshall had a very strong sense of the concrete historical reality of capitalism as a social system, and his "middle distance" theory of citizenship and social class was a historical-comparative theory about the development of the capitalistic class system and its attendant institutions.

Marshall's argument is that as capitalism develops as a social system and as the class structure develops within it, so modern citizenship changes from a system of rights that emerge out of and support market relations to one that bears an antagonistic relationship with the market system by placing rights in the political arena for electors without property and other market capacities, and also rights of access to social goods outside of market exchanges. This argument required Marshall to distinguish between elements or parts of citizenships, and to relate each interactively with a historically dynamic class system. Unlike most theorists of class structure, Marshall recognized the possible impact of citizenship on aspects of class inequality, including class loyalty and class resentment, which affect the nature and incidence of class antagonism. Marshall was able to develop this understanding because he conceptualized citizenship beyond its legal and political dimensions. This analysis was extended by Marshall into the late capitalist mixed economy in his discussion of "Value Problems of Welfare Capitalism" (1972).

SEE ALSO: Capitalism; Citizenship; Class; Nation-State; Welfare State

REFERENCES AND SUGGESTED READINGS

Barbalet, J. M. (1988) *Citizenship: Rights, Struggle, and Class Inequality*. University of Minnesota Press, Minneapolis.

Marshall, T. H. (1964) *Class, Citizenship, and Social Development*. Introduction by S. M. Lipset. Doubleday, New York.

Marshall, T. H. (1973) A British Sociological Career. *International Social Science Journal* 25(1/2): 88–100.

Marshall, T. H. (1981) *The Right to Welfare and Other Essays*. Heinemann, London.

Martineau, Harriet (1802–76)

Cynthia Siemsen

Harriet Martineau's 25 volumes of short novels illustrating the principles of political economy outsold the works of her contemporary, Charles Dickens; Martineau's travel chronicles of nineteenth-century American society and its cultural beliefs are comparative historical accounts that have been likened to Tocqueville's *Democracy in America*; she authored sociology's first systematic treatment of methodology six decades before Durkheim's *Rules of the Sociological Method*; and Martineau translated and condensed Auguste Comte's *Cours de philosophie positive*, and introduced his attempt to establish a sociological science within the English-speaking world. However, the story of sociology's emergence has been a history of men and their contributions to the formation of the discipline. Although Martineau achieved high intellectual success in applying scientific techniques borrowed from the natural sciences to theories of social observation, that status was limited to her lifetime alone (Harper 2001).

Martineau's works are usually found in the English literature section in most university libraries rather than on sociology's shelves (Hill 1991). Until the 1960s her pioneering sociological works appeared forgotten, suffering more than a century of neglect by the sociological community until "rediscovered" by Lipset (1962). Still, when her name appears in books dedicated to social theory, Martineau will at best be mentioned as "the first woman sociologist" (Rossi 1973), and will rarely be addressed in research methods texts. Most often, Martineau will remain in a last chapter devoted to the contributions of women to classical social theory, despite recent arguments that her work is on a par with the canonical masters (Terry 1983). As with those other original thinkers, Martineau's work cannot be separated from her historical moment or lived history. However, in her case the task is facilitated by Martineau's (1877) autobiography.

Martineau was born to a well-to-do textile manufacturer in Norwich, England, the sixth child in a family of eight. As was customary in the emerging middle-class English homes of the early nineteenth century, Martineau was sent to the care of a wet nurse for her first years, which has often been interpreted as an early indicator of the loneliness, self-doubt, and sense of abandonment she would experience throughout her youth. Martineau's isolation was compounded by her lack of taste and smell, and spans of childhood illness that resulted in an almost complete loss of hearing at age 12. Her family, rather than recognizing her disability, "considered her dull, awkward, and difficult, and clearly she thought so too" (Pichanick 1980: 7). Martineau fantasized that suicide would release her from a fearful world, and, if not, a good education resulting in "independence of action" would be necessary.

While not particularly attentive to her psychological needs, Martineau's parents were progressive when it came to her education, even though it was uneven in comparison with her brothers'. As Unitarians, the elder Martineaus emphasized education and social awareness for all their children. Martineau was home schooled in writing, math, Latin, and French by her older siblings. And then for two "delectable" years she attended a coeducational Unitarian school, receiving the same instruction given her brothers. Though the school unexpectedly closed, disrupting Martineau's formal education, she received two further years of master's instruction in French and Latin, and dedicated herself to further study in order to attain her longed-for independence.

Martineau's turn to scientific writing grew not only from a desire for self-sufficiency, but also from economic necessity. By the 1820s England was thrown into an economic crisis resulting from industrialization, sparing few, let alone textile manufacturers the likes of Thomas Martineau, who believed in profit sharing for hard-working employees. As the family fortune disappeared, Martineau became preoccupied with the emerging science of political economy. At a time when most middle-class Victorian women would use marriage as a way out of economic insecurity, Martineau experienced the breakup of two engagements, the second of which brought her great relief. After her Unitarian minister fiancé experienced a complete physical and mental breakdown, pragmatic Martineau declined any hospital visits. Recognizing her inability to form anything but intimate intellectual relationships, Martineau immersed herself in the life of the mind and concluded: "If I had had a husband dependent on me for his happiness, the responsibility would have made me wretched ... I am probably the happiest single woman in England ... I rejoice not to have been involved in a [marriage] for which I was, or believed myself unfit" (Martineau 1877 I: 133–4).

Early articles, essays, and commentaries in the Unitarian journal *Monthly Repository*, plus a novel and book-length religious history, helped establish Martineau's name for future publications (Lengermann & Niebrugge-Brantley 1998). The year 1832 signaled Martineau's entrance to secular writing. The first volumes of *Illustrations of Political Economy* became runaway bestsellers, explaining through fiction the new science of political economy as espoused by Adam Smith, David Ricardo, John Stuart Mill, and Thomas Malthus. Within two years she had published 25 volumes, outselling Charles Dickens at 10,000 copies per month. Though these volumes have been identified as an early example of the case method (Bosner 1929), their contents remain an untapped resource in sociology through literature (Hill 1991). Martineau's financial independence paralleled her entry into the intellectual circle of George Eliot, Florence Nightingale, Charles Dickens, Thomas Malthus, William Wordsworth, Charlotte Brontë, and Charles Darwin. With her name secure in London's literary society, Martineau turned her attention toward a science of society.

Martineau's initial move into what would become sociology began in 1834 with her two-year travels to the US. With *Society in America* (1836–7) and *Retrospect of Western Travel* (1838b) Martineau transformed travel writing into social scientific inquiry. In these works Martineau implemented the theories outlined in her yet-unpublished method's treatment, *How to Observe Morals and Manners* (1838a). She believed that any examination of society must take into account morals (i.e., cultural beliefs and values, and manners): social interaction. If a scientific observer of society seeks to understand the morals of a group, Martineau proposed that she examine the meanings of an activity for the social actor. Martineau did not propose value-neutrality on the part of the observer; however, she did propose that the researcher's biases be acknowledged. According to Martineau, sympathy toward the actor was a skill that separated the scientific study of society from the natural sciences. (The methodological approach is similar to Weber's *verstehen*.) *How to Observe Morals and Manners* is more than a methodological treatise; it sets social theoretical precedents. Before Marx, Weber, and Durkheim, "Martineau sociologically examined social class, forms of religion, types of suicide, national character, domestic relations and the status of women, delinquency and criminology, and the intricate interrelations between repressive social institutions and the individual" (Hill 1991: 292).

Martineau's approach to the study of American society dealt with the problem of ethnocentrism in comparative works written for a European male audience. She highlighted the importance of women's issues as an essential component to the study of a society. Although she presumed her readers to be male, Martineau directed their attention to the study of the household and the domestic role of women in culture as necessary for a sociological study. And instead of merely comparing the US to England, she divided her work into three volumes: political structure, economy, and a category she called "civilization" that dealt with social mores and values. Martineau (1836–7) identified the moral principles that Americans claimed to hold dear, and then contrasted them to the everyday reality of life in the US to see "how far the people of the United States lived up to or fell below their own theory."

Like Tocqueville (1835), Martineau distinguished between structural reality and the dominant American values of democracy, equality, freedom, and justice. However, rather than identifying the American tendency toward political conformity and the status quo through the tyranny of the majority, Martineau "analyze[d] the effect of values on structure and change" (Lipset 1962). In her trek through 20 of the then 24 United States, Martineau observed American society to be in transition, somewhere between feudal morals represented by the interwoven nature of slavery and democratic ideals embraced by the abolitionists; all the while she tackled a fundamental problem of sociology, how to study society as a whole.

Martineau's search for a scientific approach to the study of society where the old order was disappearing and a new order was coming to take its place eventually led her to observe Middle Eastern life. Martineau's move from her Unitarian upbringing occurred during her study tour of the Middle East. Through her observations of *Eastern Life: Past and Present* (1848) she grew to believe that truth and wisdom were not present in the knowledge of her day but rested in future history (Pichanick 1980). Moving in the direction of a theory of history, Martineau (1848) concluded: "The world and human life are . . . obviously very young. Human existence is, as yet, truly infantine . . . It can hardly be but that, in its advance to maturity, new

departments of strength will be developed" (vol. 3, p. 332). Much like Durkheim would hope for 40 years later, Martineau wished for a scientific study of society that would attract those like herself who needed an intellectual replacement for traditional religion.

Martineau's acquaintance with Comtean thought was largely secondhand until 1852 (Pichanick 1980). As interest in Comte grew in England, Martineau felt the need to translate and condense his masterpiece; in its original French form, *Cours de philosophie positive* was a difficult, rambling, repetitive, six-volume work taken on by only the most patient reader. She hoped to introduce Comte to those who would have been deterred from reading about his new scientific study of society because of the work's bulk. Martineau further hoped that this new science would be an ethical field that would move in the direction of social reform by pinpointing society's ills. Martineau accomplished more than translating Comte; through the clarification of his work she introduced sociology to the English-speaking world. Comte was not only pleased with the translation; he believed Martineau clarified his ideas. He wrote to her: "Looking at it from the point of view of future generations, I feel sure that your name will be linked with mine, for you have executed the only one of those works that will survive amongst all those which my fundamental treatise has called forth" (Comte, in Harrison 1913: xvii–xviii). The names of Comte and Martineau are indeed linked; however, he is recognized as coining the term sociology, and she as his translator. Martineau may also be rightly called the Mother of Sociology.

SEE ALSO: Comte, Auguste; Durkheim, Émile; Malthus, Thomas Robert; Mill, John Stuart; Smith, Adam

REFERENCES AND SUGGESTED READINGS

Bosner, H. A. (1929) Illustrations of Political Economy: An Early Example of the Case Method. *Social Service Review* 3 (June): 243–51.
Durkheim, É. (1938 [1895]) *The Rules of Sociological Method*. Free Press, New York.
Harper, L. M. (2001) *Solitary Travelers: Nineteenth-Century Women's Travel Narratives and the*

Scientific Vocation. Associated University Presses, Cranbury, NJ.

Harrison, F. (1913) Introduction. In: Martineau, H. (trans.), *The Positive Philosophy of Auguste Comte*, Vol. 1. G. Bell, London.

Hill, M. R. (1991) Harriet Martineau. In: Deegan, M. J. (Ed.), *Women in Sociology: A Bio-Bibliographical Sourcebook*. Greenwood Press, Westport.

Lengermann, P. M. & Niebrugge-Brantley, J. (1998) *The Women Founders*. McGraw Hill, Boston.

Lipset, S. M. (Ed.) (1962) Harriet Martineau's America. In: Martineau, H. *Society in America*. Doubleday, New York.

Martineau, H. (1832–4) *Illustrations of Political Economy*, 9 vols. Charles Fox, London.

Martineau, H. (1836–7) *Society in America*, 2 vols. Saunders & Otley, New York.

Martineau, H. (1838a) *How to Observe Morals and Manners*. Charles Knight, London.

Martineau, H. (1838b) *Retrospect of Western Travel*. Saunders & Otley, New York.

Martineau, H. (1844) *Life in the Sick Room: Essays by an Invalid*. Edward Moxon, London.

Martineau, H. (1848) *Eastern Life: Past and Present*, 3 vols. Edward Moxon, London.

Martineau, H. (1853) *The Positive Philosophy of Auguste Comte, Freely Translated and Condensed by Harriet Martineau*. John Chapman, London.

Martineau, H. (1877) *Harriet Martineau's Autobiography, with Memorials by Maria Westin Chapman*, 3 vols. Elder, London.

Pichanick, V. K. (1980) *Harriet Martineau: The Woman and Her Work, 1802–76*. University of Michigan Press, Ann Arbor.

Rossi, A. (1973) *The Feminist Papers*. Bantam Books, New York.

Terry, J. L. (1983) Bringing the Women ... In: A Modest Proposal. *Teaching Sociology* 10 (January): 251–61.

Tocqueville, A. de (1835) *Democracy in America*, 2 vols. Vintage Classics, New York.

martyrdom

Enzo Pace

If we use Durkheim's classic division of suicides into egoistic, altruistic, and anomic (*Le Suicide*, 1897), martyrdom is an altruistic suicide. According to Durkheim, those who consciously sacrifice their lives for a supreme ideal (religious, political, or moral) demonstrate not only a profound faith in the ideal, but also strong commitment to a group (be it micro or macro). In the martyr's hierarchy of values, the individual's life counts for less than the supreme and universal ideal he believes in (the Fatherland, the Nation, God, Religion). The *ego* places itself (i.e., the individual's whole life) under the *alter*, showing how far faith and trust enable the individual to transcend himself, to overcome the instinctive fear of violent death and to prove his supreme coherence with an ideal. Group solidarity pushes him to sacrifice his own life in an altered state of consciousness, a sort of mystical experience that allows him to go beyond human fears and anxieties. The heroic dimension of martyrdom means precisely the lucid awareness that, by acting in a particular way, death is a certainty. Martyrdom is a trial for the individual and for the group he belongs to. So the psychic system of a martyr tends to reduce the social complexity he lives in to a terrifyingly basic binary code, life/death (with the resulting give life/take life), which he believes is the fundamental moral code of every pure militant. After his death, he becomes the emblem of the group. This is why the martyr's body is so important in the social representation of the altruistic suicide: the members of the group are able to strengthen their conviction by exalting the blood of the martyr and worshipping his body. By commemorating his sacrifice, they transform the narrative of martyrdom into a narration of the cohesive strength of the group itself.

We can distinguish two types of martyrdom: passive and active. The former occurs when an individual is compelled to immolate his life to defend the ideal to which he adheres, because he refuses to repudiate his faith or the group's solidarity. This kind of martyrdom is frequent in both the religious and political fields. Everyday language distinguishes the political or civil hero from the religious martyr, but the formal profile of the martyr appears to be the same. The case of the Christian martyrs under the Roman Empire is a good example of passive martyrdom, as important as the other stories of various religious minorities persecuted by a dominant religion. Another interesting example is represented by the stories of the Buddhist monks who burned themselves in protest against the communist regime.

Active martyrdom, on the other hand, is a suicide attack where the act of self-destruction is designed to strike a perceived enemy. In passive martyrdom, the violence is suffered; in active martyrdom, it is used to kill both the martyr and the enemy. This second type of martyrdom has attracted much more attention in the social sciences because of its dramatic spread in contemporary society. The martyrdom of a suicide attack (Hassan 2004) has become a modern method of making war within a war context; in many cases, it covers both the religious and political aspects of modern conflicts (Iannaccone & Introvigne 2004; Pace 2004).

We should not forget the ancient roots of the present phenomenon. In the first century BCE, the Jewish Zealots directed a suicide attack against the Roman army occupying Judaea and Jerusalem, and tried to force the Jews to repudiate their faith. In the twelfth and thirteenth centuries, an extremist sect appeared in Islam – the Shiite Order of the Assassins (so called probably because they used to take hashish before attacking their enemies) – which came up with the practice of suicide attacks, seen as inner-world asceticism, as a desperate method of fighting against a much better-equipped and more numerous enemy. One of the best-known cases of this kind of suicide is the Japanese kamikaze. The kamikaze (from *kami*, God, and *kaze*, wind – the name of the typhoon which saved Japan from the invasion of the Mongol hordes in 1216) was, in fact, a soldier (an aviator, to be precise) willing to carry out an act of war, in the lucid awareness that he would die in the process, and exalting in the fact that one man alone, with a single airplane, would be able to inflict heavy losses on the enemy. As is well known, such attacks were widely used by the Japanese against the United States Navy in World War II. Not by chance, those willing to carry out these acts formed part of a special fighting force, the *ko-geki tai* (*divine storm special force units*) (Axell & Kase 2002). The story of the kamikaze illustrates the relationship between religion and politics, which was intensified by the war context; the more dramatic the political situation, the more the symbolic resources provided by religion to justify the resort to violent suicide attacks.

The issue disputed in the social sciences concerns the relations between the practice of martyrdom in the form of suicide attacks and the core message of a religion. Many references to the high value assigned to martyrdom may be found in the religious tradition. In the preaching of Jesus of Nazareth, for example, there are frequent references to the figure of a witness who should fear nothing because the Holy Spirit sustains those who cling to their faith even up to the ultimate sacrifice, up to "death on the cross." From the second century on, Christian martyrs are those who continue to publicly affirm, in the face of the power of the Roman Empire, their identity and membership of the Christian community even when it entails sacrificing their own lives. This idea of bloody martyrdom gradually tones down as Christianity becomes a majority religion; the figure of the martyr becomes more spiritual, apart from the modern throwback when Christians, and Catholics in particular, were persecuted by intolerant, totalitarian regimes (as occurred in many former eastern bloc countries, for example). Islam also exalts the figure of witness/martyr to the faith as he who, fighting on God's path, perishes in battle; the reward which awaits him is immediate entry to heaven. Moreover, the minority Muslim Shiite sect (nowadays concentrated mainly in Iran and Iraq) remembers the first two chiefs (*imam*), Ali and Husayn (the latter was killed in 680 CE in the battle of Karbala), as martyrs of the faith.

The continuity between the original religious doctrines of martyrdom and its modern use, removed from its historical context, has been disputed. Robert Papp has demonstrated, for instance, that the relationship between religious fundamentalism and radical religious traditions in general, on the one hand, and suicide attacks, on the other, is very weak. In support of his view, Papp quotes the case of the Tamil Tigers in Sri Lanka, the extremist faction of the Tamil ethnic minority, which claims independence for the northern part of the island. The Tamil Tigers have frequently made suicide attacks on Sinhalese-Buddhist political and religious targets, but they are not very sensitive toward religion despite their Hindu background. In this case, religion is simply a marker of ethnic identity, a symbolic resource among others to consolidate the collective identity. In contrast, the reference to a religious discourse is explicit in the case of the radical Palestinian movements

(Jihad, Martyrs of Al-Aqsa, 'Iz al-Din al Qasem Brigades), linked to the fundamentalist movement Hamas, because of the final goal of their strategy: first, to achieve independence for Palestine and, second, to build an Islamic republic. The same also applies to Lebanon and Kashmir (Martinez 2003). Analyzing all these cases, Papp argues that the martyrs follow a strategic logic for obtaining political and territorial concessions. In other words, the martyrdom/suicide attacks over the past two decades appear to be a means of shifting political power relations and gaining control of entire areas of the territory.

Some contemporary political scientists argue that martyrdom in a war context mobilizes people who are psychologically deprived, living in a permanent condition of social frustration, in poverty and ignorance. They argue that the socially marginalized are willing to be manipulated and indoctrinated by fanatical religious leaders. This explanation is contested by certain psychologists and sociologists who, having examined the evidence of the psychopathological origins of the phenomenon, found no empirical support for it. In particular, psychologist Scott Atran (2002) has pointed out that the active martyrdom/suicide attack is associated neither with mental or psychological ailments nor with the educational and economic deprivation of the individual who agrees to become a martyr-killer. According to Atran, most of those who undertook martyrdom training and then committed suicide, killing innocent victims, were not affected by particular pathologies. The choice they made depended more on political and social factors.

As Riaz Hassan (2004) has noted, in the Middle East, for instance, it is far more important to take into account the "collective sense of historical injustice and social humiliation in which the majority of people are living." Therefore, individuals may become martyrs and martyr-killers when, in their own consciousness and within that of the group to which they belong, martyrdom appears to be the sole means available for achieving several goals at the same time: empowerment versus powerlessness, salvation (in religious terms) versus damnation, and — very important in certain sociocultural contexts — honor versus a sense of humiliation (Hassan 1983, 1995). A United Nations relief worker in Gaza, Nasra Hassan (2001), has reported the findings of a survey carried out in the Gaza strip, involving 250 interviews with aspirant martyrs. The most interesting evidence to emerge from this empirical investigation is that none of the young Palestinians was uneducated, desperately poor, or psychologically depressed. The only explanation Nasra Hassan found was the desperate social disorder caused by the permanent state of war against Israel, a war that throws everyday life into turmoil, creating a pervasive sense of precariousness and impotence.

The followers' interiorization of the martyrdom model is the result of a sort of intra-world asceticism, a moral discipline (which only later becomes technical and military) based on the principle of sacrifice today for reward in heaven, as well as immediate benefits *on earth* (killing as many enemies as possible). It is, therefore, an act of symbolic violence on oneself to overcome the fear of death and of the horror of consciously putting to death the innocent and defenseless. However, the problem is to discover what religious suicide represents in an environment such as contemporary Islam. Khosrokhavar (2000) and Jürgensmeyer (2000) have shed light on this aspect. The body of the martyr becomes a sort of medium of communication to persuade other young boys and girls to lay down their lives for a supreme religious and political ideal. The contexts in which this occurs are those dominated by unresolved national issues (such as Palestine, Chechnya, Kashmir, and Iraq), others involving a crisis in a revolutionary project (such as Iran with Khomeini's regime in decline, at the time of the first Gulf War between Iraq and Iran, 1980–8), and lastly, the forms of transnational martyrdom used by the al-Qaida network. From this viewpoint, al-Qaida is a movement composed of defeated movements, veterans from groups that had lost their battles in their respective countries and who thus placed themselves at the service of an International of terror, in an international environment, that of the network of Bin Laden. By planning suicide actions, the leaders of al-Qaida thus reduced, with extreme symbolic as well as physical violence, the internal complexity of a system of beliefs such as Islam.

Martyrdom, in this sense, may be seen as a symptom of cognitive dissonance. Paraphrasing Festinger's well-known thesis outlined in

A Theory of Cognitive Dissonance (1957), people who perceive the collapse of the social and everyday life tend to come back to religion to compensate for the frustration arising from the acute crisis they are coping with.

SEE ALSO: Cognitive Dissonance Theory (Festinger); Durkheim, Émile; Fundamentalism; Sacrifice; Suicide; Violence

REFERENCES AND SUGGESTED READINGS

Atran, S. (2002) *In Gods We Trust: The Evolutionary Landscape of Religion*. Oxford University Press, Oxford.

Axell, A. & Kase, H. (2002) *Kamikaze: Japan's Suicide Gods*. Longman, New York.

Hassan, N. (2001) Letter from Gaza. An Arsenal of Believers. *New Yorker* (November): 36–41.

Hassan, R. (1983) *A Way of Dying: Suicide in Singapore*. Oxford University Press, Oxford.

Hassan, R. (1995) *Suicide Explained*. Melbourne University Press, Melbourne.

Hassan, R. (2004) Suicide Attacks, Life as a Weapon. *ISIM Newsletter* 14: 8–9.

Iannaccone, L. R. & Introvigne, M. (2004) *Il mercato dei martiri*. Lindau, Turin.

Khosrokhavar, F. (2000) *Les Nouveaux Martyrs d'Allah*. Fayard, Paris.

Jürgensmeyer, M. (2000) *Terror in the Mind of God*. Regents of the University of California Press, Berkeley.

Martinez, L. (Ed.) (2003) Violences islamistes. *Critique internationale* 20: 114–77.

Pace, E. (2004) *Perchè le religioni scendono in guerra?* Laterza, Rome-Bari.

Maruyama, Masao (1914–96)

Wolfgang Seifert

Masao Maruyama, historian of Japanese political thought and political scientist, was the son of the prominent political journalist Kanji Maruyama, who worked for the *Ôsaka Asahi* and *Ôsaka Mainichi* newspapers. After graduating from the First Higher School in Tokyo in 1934 he studied the history of western political thought at the Law Faculty of Tokyo Imperial University. In 1937 he became a graduate assistant, and in 1940 assistant professor at the same faculty. In the meantime he was persuaded by his teacher Nanbara Shigeru to delve into the texts of the Japanese tradition. Before he was drafted into the army in 1944 and posted to Pyongyang and later to Hiroshima, he had written three treatises on the development of political thought in premodern Japan for the academic *Kokka gakkai zasshi* (Journal of the Society of State Science). Appointed professor in 1950, he held the Chair in History of Political Thought of East Asia at Tokyo University. Compiled from the treatises mentioned above, *Studies in the Intellectual History of Tokugawa Japan* was published in 1952. When his essay "Theory and Psychology of Ultra-Nationalism" appeared in May 1946 in the opinion journal *Sekai*, it created a sensation. Maruyama decoded the emperor system (*tennôsei*) in an unprecedented way by focusing on the "magic power" its main ideas exerted on the thought and behavior of the Japanese. In 1956–7 he compiled this and several other scholarly works and essays on contemporary Japanese politics in *Thought and Behavior in Modern Japanese Politics*. In those years he frequently stated his opinions on major controversies of post-war Japanese politics. His *Japanese Thought* became a bestseller in 1961 and serves as a point of reference for ongoing debates on the intellectual development of modern Japan to date. In 1961–2 Maruyama delivered lectures as a visiting professor at Harvard and Oxford universities. Shortly after the student movement had reached its climax, he had to abandon lecturing for health reasons some years prior to retirement. In 1972 his analysis in "Ancient Substrata of Japanese Historical Consciousness" attracted attention, since it seemed to be a "return to Japan." In spring 1975 he once more left to lecture at Oxford and later at Princeton. He again immersed himself in the work of the Meiji enlightenment thinker Fukuzawa Yukichi (1834–1901) and published as his final major book a profound commentary of Fukuzawa's *Outline of a Theory of Civilization*. Another major project, "Seitô to itan" (orthodoxy and heresy), remained unfinished. In addition to his specialized field, his profound knowledge of western political philosophy and music (especially the operas of Richard Wagner) was well known. Maruyama was appointed a member of the Japan Academy. He died on 15 August 1996 in Tokyo.

Maruyama is one of the most outstanding and internationally best-known scholars of Japan. Though not a sociologist himself, sociology in Japan and sometimes abroad (e.g., that of Robert N. Bellah) was stimulated over decades by his work, in particular in the field of the ethos and values of the individual. Averse to all "grand theory," he can not be classed as belonging to a particular school, but was an original scholar. In recent years Maruyama has been paid attention to as a political philosopher as well, and it seems that debates about his works will continue. Shortly before his death, publication of his collected works began under the title *Maruyama Masao sh* (16 volumes): it was finished in 1997. Major works have been translated into western languages, as well as into Chinese, Korean, and Bahasa Indonesia.

Maruyama's work was written over more than half a century (1940–96). According to his own words, his approach to history and social science was very much shaped by: German idealism, especially Kant and the neo-Kantians, but by Hegel as well; Marxism, in particular the early works of Karl Marx; and later by "thinkers who take a middling position between German 'historicism' and English 'empiricism,' men like Max Weber, Hermann Heller, and Karl Mannheim."

Following a recent proposal by M. Kobayashi, in terms of its respective social context one may discern three periods in Maruyama's works corresponding to phases of political history and social change in Japan. However, in terms of his thought, there are no sharp turning points, and the different phases overlap in part. During the first period (1940–52) the main incentive for his work was the critique of ultra-nationalism or – in a broader sense – of "Japanese fascism," which he had experienced himself. Through what factors could ultra-nationalism succeed "in spreading a many-layered, though invisible, net over the Japanese people"? Closely connected to this issue was the question of the subject of democratic revolution after the collapse of the Empire of Greater Japan. Could democracy, conceived as the active participation of individual citizens in politics, take root in the

thought and behavior of the Japanese people, or would it simply be imported as a set of formal institutions under American occupation? Moreover, Maruyama's concern was the threat to democracy by the effects of the Cold War. The "reverse course" adopted by the occupation authorities as early as 1947, the "Red Purge" directed at the left, including liberal critics of the old elites like himself, and the emergence of McCarthyism in the US (which eventually drove his friend, the historian and diplomat E. H. Norman, to suicide) gave Maruyama cause to warn against "fascism in the name of democracy" even in the contemporary West. In view of the mass society emerging in Japan from the middle of the 1950s, he raised the question of how political participation could be achieved in a society whose members came closer and closer to the type of the atomized individual.

While Maruyama wrote during the years of oppression of Marxist and liberal thought, his treatises implied a covert critique of the fabrication of national myths. In "The Sorai School: Its Role in the Disintegration of Tokugawa Confucianism and Its Impact on National Learning" (1940) and in "Nature and Invention in Tokugawa Political Thought: Contrasting Institutional Views" (1941) he investigates how rational thinking replaced step by step metaphysical assumptions of a natural cosmic order. In particular, the second treatise works out how – in the thinking of the political philosopher Ogy Sorai (1666–1728) – social and political institutions were no longer considered "given" or "natural," but "invented." In the unfinished "The Premodern Formation of Nationalism" (1944) he examines early forms of Japanese nationalism that had emerged before the opening of the country in 1853 and its subsequent building of a "modern nation-state" after the Meiji restoration in 1868. These treatises became seminal for all later research on the political thought of the Tokugawa period (1603–1868).

With "Theory and Psychology of Ultra-Nationalism" Maruyama offered an anatomy of the emperor system, which sharply differed from the Marxist approach toward the analysis of the class structure. He focused instead on the legal structure of the state and the power structure in terms of political thought and social psychology. This essay, along with further works such as "The Ideology and Dynamics of Japanese Fascism" (1947), "Thought and Behavior Patterns of Japan's Wartime Leaders" (1949), and "Fascism – Some Problems: A Consideration of its Political Dynamics" (1952), served as a base for comparative research on fascism in Japan. Maruyama plainly distinguishes between phases of a movement and regime and brings out the peculiarities of the ideology of Japanese fascists. He coined the term "fascism from above" and thereupon described and explained the differences to "fascism from below," as he perceived National-Socialist Germany and Fascist Italy. This terminology became established internationally in research on fascism.

During the second or "middle" period (1952 to the late 1960s) Maruyama applied the results of his research on the historical background of Japanese nationalism and its extreme form to contemporary Japanese and international politics. These were the years when he addressed a wide audience with essays and statements in newspapers, mass media, and on public assemblies, without ever being a member of a political party. Especially during the conflict on the renewal of the US–Japan Security Treaty (Anpo) in 1958–60 he acted as a "public intellectual." However, his view of political developments was based on concrete experiences in Japan, and not on the adoption of imported western political concepts. As early as the late 1940s and prior to the outbreak of the Korean War, Maruyama argued – starting from his point of view, that war was "the worst evil of all" – against the "realists" in foreign policy. He supported a "general, comprehensive" peace treaty with all former enemies, including the communist countries. The public statements of the Peace Problems Symposium, a group of known intellectuals of different political views, were decisively influenced by him. In this middle period he published "Japanese Thought" (1957), "Loyalty and Rebellion" (1960), and "Patterns of Individuation and the Case of Japan: A Conceptual Scheme" (1965).

Maruyama argues in "Japanese Thought" that since no "axis"-like tradition such as Christianity in the West or Confucianism in China existed in Japan, tradition appeared to be "unstructured." In the political sphere, the founders of the Meiji state had to create a belief system centered on the emperor, who at the same time had to function as a modern monarch. From this, various unsolved contradictions resulted. In "Loyalty and Rebellion" Maruyama examined, by analyzing various texts, the inner tensions on the level of the individual produced by the Meiji reform of 1867–8 and the subsequent fundamental changes. Maruyama argues that traditional (feudal) loyalty by no means meant mere passive conformity or subjection, but in principle contained a dynamic element of influence of a vassal or servant on his master. This element was manifest in the rebellion of many samurai against Tokugawa rule. Moreover, when the Popular Rights Movement attacked the growing authoritarian tendencies of the newly established Meiji administration, its members, too, acted not only as adherents of western ideas of political participation, but were in many cases motivated by that "feudal spirit." These examples show that Maruyama did not consider the "progressives" to be the sole driving force of historical progress. Even less did he consider progress to develop linearly towards modernity in an affirmative sense or to consist in reaching it. In his treatise "Patterns of Individuation and the Case of Japan" Maruyama worked out the "disparity between what is expected of modern institutions – legal, political, and economic – and the interpersonal relations which in fact are at work." According to him, the discrepancies stretch from the individual level to the group level, reaching an exceptional extent in Japan. In contrast to "modernization theory" predominant in the 1950s and 1960s, Maruyama wanted "to lead the problem of modernization into areas related to 'ethos' or 'ideology' questions." Again, the compelling logic of his argument aroused sociological discussions.

After years of silence, Maruyama published in 1972 "Ancient Substrata of Historical Consciousness," which marks a significant change. From then on we may discern a third or late period of his work. He had returned to research on the history of political thought in Japan, yet his view of history had changed. The Hegelian notion of history progressing by stages of development was replaced by the theory that historical change is strongly influenced by contact between the different cultures of Japan and the outside world. Maruyama now focused more on continuities in political, historical, and ethical consciousness. Whereas he used to speak of "prototypes" of respective views, he replaced this term with "ancient substrata" or "deep structures," and in his late works by the musicological term *basso ostinato*. The basic views of the Japanese on politics and society showed a particularism hardly capable of being overcome. It appears as if these obstacles to forming universalistic ways of thinking drove Maruyama to despair, but still one would be mistaken in viewing his findings as a kind of "theory of Japaneseness" (*Nihonjin-ron*). Maruyama assumes that Japanese society is heterogeneous, and he is not offering comprehensive characteristics of Japanese society, nor applying a holistic approach. Instead, he kept searching for elements of ethical principles and for conditions of substantive democracy in the thought and behavior of the Japanese. In a way, he continued the task he had described as early as 1962: "to examine the nature of Japanese culture in a wider sense, and analyze the daily behavior of the Japanese people and the nature of their thought processes including not simply consciously held ideologies but more especially those unconscious assumptions and values which in a fragmentary way reveal themselves in the actions of daily life."

From today's perspective, Maruyama's works, albeit disputed, are still inspiring sociology and social sciences, even if he was not a sociologist himself. Not only for contemporary history, but also for political sociology and research of political culture, his essays on Japanese fascism offer important stimuli to comparative research, even though the historical data he used are out of date. The same is true of a number of self-coined terms and metaphors, for example for types of political personality during the rule of the "emperor system": the "portable shrine," the "official" and the "outlaw," represent respectively authority, power, and violence. With regard to the question of individual freedom and its relationship to society, Maruyama's insights will challenge not only non-western societies and East European societies, which are transforming themselves into more democratic societies, but also – again – western societies. His idea of subjectivity and his "scientifically imagined democracy" (Barshay 1992) might function as an antidote against adaptative tendencies of the social sciences in the contemporary world.

SEE ALSO: Democracy; Fascism; Historical and Comparative Methods; Modernity; Nation-State and Nationalism; Politics

REFERENCES AND SUGGESTED READINGS

Barshay, A. (1992) Imagining Democracy in Postwar Japan: Reflections on Maruyama Masao and Modernism. *Journal of Japanese Studies* 18(2).

Barshay, A. (2004) *The Social Sciences in Modern Japan: The Marxian and Modernist Traditions.* University of California Press, Berkeley.

Kersten, R. (1996) *Democracy in Postwar Japan: Maruyama Masao and the Search for Autonomy.* Routledge, London.

Koschmann, V. (1989) Maruyama Masao and the Incomplete Project of Modernity. In: Harootunian, H. D. & Miyoshi, M. (Eds.), *Postmodernism and Japan.* Duke University Press, Durham, NC.

Maruyama, M. (1969) *Thought and Behaviour in Modern Japanese Politics.* Ed. I. Morris. Oxford University Press, Oxford.

Maruyama, M. (1974) *Studies in the Intellectual History of Tokugawa Japan.* Trans. M. Hane. University of Tokyo Press, Tokyo-Princeton.

Maruyama, M. (1988) *Denken in Japan* [Japanese Thought]. Trans. W. Schamoni & W. Seifert. Suhrkamp, Frankfurt am Main.

Seifert, W. (1999) Politisches Denken bei Maruyama Masao und Max Weber. Aspekte eines Vergleichs. In: Mommsen, W. & Schwentker, W. (Eds.), *Max Weber und das moderne Japan.* Vandenhoek & Ruprecht, Göttingen.

Marx, Karl (1818–83)

Robert J. Antonio

Karl Marx's critique of economic inequality and appeals for social justice have inspired left-wing political parties, labor movements, and insurgencies across the world. His ideas often have been fused with local political cultures and employed in diverse ways. Marx's participation in the communist movement, call for worldwide revolution, and totemic status in communist regimes have made him a very controversial thinker. In wealthy capitalist countries he has been more of an oppositional reference point than an inspirational figure. For much of the twentieth century, western sociologists viewed him as an ideologue, on the margin of their discipline. During the later 1960s and early 1970s, however, sociological interest in Marx increased, spurred by anti-colonialist uprisings, student activism, and the New Left. In North American sociology, which previously had ignored or dismissed him, a new generation of theorists portrayed him as a founder of "conflict theory" or "critical sociology" and accorded him elevated status, along with Durkheim and Weber, as part of classical social theory's and sociology's founding troika. Later critics held that this canon was too narrow and Eurocentric and that the postmodern cultural shift and collapse of communism rendered Marx irrelevant. Others countered that globalization, deregulated capitalism, and increased economic inequality made him more relevant than ever. These divergent views aside, Marx's materialist perspective and concept of class have influenced much sociological work, including that claiming to disprove his theories. In the early twenty-first century, Marxist sociologists worked in many parts of the world, and they even had their own section of the American Sociological Association. Moreover, sociologists with diverse orientations have employed concepts and questions originating from Marx in well-established research and theory programs. Marx has had an enduring impact on sociology's development.

Marx built on ideas from Hegel, wider Enlightenment thought, and modern democratic ideology. Theorizing capitalist society as a whole, criticizing it historically, and calling for its fundamental transformation, Marx initiated the critical theory tradition of the broader practice of social theory. At least since Plato's *Republic*, social theorists have posed theories of society that address "what is" in arguments about "what should be." Arguably, Marx began modern social theory, which retains the normative thrust of the earlier tradition, but engages empirical-historical material in a much more comprehensive, systematic, and sociological manner. Marx wrote his masterwork, *Capital*, after many years of research in the British Museum, studying intensely social and economic theory, history,

and data. He foreshadowed a generation of late nineteenth and early twentieth-century social theorists who addressed social processes, structures, and ruptures, entwined with capitalist development. Expressing the era's scientific aspirations, they called for creation of social science and helped bring it forth. Later sociologists fashioned a more strictly empirical, theoretical practice, sociological theory, which is supposed to focus entirely on "what is" and exclude value questions. Social theory became an interdisciplinary enterprise, largely independent from sociological theory. However, borders between the practices are somewhat ambiguous or fluid. Marx made a major contribution to social theory and sociological theory, and his thought sheds light on the connections and tensions between these different practices.

HISTORICISM, ALIENATION, AND CRITICAL THEORY: MARX'S ENGAGEMENT WITH HEGEL

Marx was born into a middle-class household, the oldest male of six surviving children. His parents had Jewish origins, but converted to Protestantism in response to Prussian anti-Semitism. Marx was exposed to Enlightenment thought and socialist ideas in his teenage years. As a university student, he joined the Berlin Doctors Club, a group of left-wing intellectuals who embraced Hegel's philosophical vision of humanity, making itself historically through its own labor. They opposed right-wing Hegelians, who stressed his theory of the state and justified the Prussian regime. Left-Hegelians wanted to complete philosophy's break with religion and fashion an approach that favored progressive change. Marx finished his doctoral dissertation in 1841, but did not complete the second thesis required to enter German academe. After left-Hegelian Bruno Bauer lost his academic position for political reasons, Marx knew, especially given his Jewish roots, that this door was closed to him. He decided to try journalism.

In 1842 Marx wrote for the progressive *Rheinische Zeitung* and soon became its editor. Opposing laws that forbade peasants from gathering wood, he attacked the wealthy's monopoly of property and called the poor "the elemental class." He criticized Hegel's view of the state as a neutral arbiter and rational expression of the general will. By contrast, he held that bureaucratic officials cared little about the public, were grossly self-interested, and slavishly obeyed aristocratic and bourgeois demands. Marx attacked the Prussian state's press censorship and authoritarian approach to democratic civil society. He believed that average people were capable of grasping their own problems and self-governing. His early views about bureaucracy, free speech, and active citizens anticipated aspects of Dewey's and Habermas's ideas of radical or communicative democracy. The *Rheinische Zeitung* flourished under Marx's editorship, but, in 1843, Prussian officials shut it down because of its criticism of the monarchy and bureaucracy. That year Marx married Jenny von Westphalen and took an editorial position in Paris, where he would learn more about capitalism, the working class, and communism. A skilled journalist, he did part-time newspaper writing throughout much of his life.

Marx's "On the Jewish Question" (1843a) attacked Bruno Bauer's plea to deny Jews political rights. Marx's negative comments about Jews indicate that he had not come to terms with his own roots. However, he took a more radical position than before, decrying capitalism's emphasis on egoistic pursuit of self-interest. He argued that bourgeois "freedom" or "liberty" dissolved feudal ties and expanded legal rights, but it did not take account of the fact that most people in emergent capitalist societies were too poor to activate the new rights, especially given liberalism's stress on the inviolability of property rights and opposition to redistribution. In Marx's view, bourgeois "freedom" obscured capitalist unfreedom, undermined community, and precluded "human emancipation." He saw genuine freedom entailing access to the means of participation, which requires substantive, social justice as well as formal, legal equality. In another work, Marx (1843b) attacked Hegel for portraying the oppressive Prussian monarchy as if it mirrored its democratic constitution, and for attributing to it a transcendent, "Rational" logic. He held that Hegel's "idealist" idiom, stressing evolution of "spirit" or consciousness, easily mistakes normative justifications for sociopolitical realities.

Criticizing Hegel's philosophical idea of "estrangement," Marx's "Economic and Philosophical Manuscripts of 1844" formulated a historically specific idea of "alienated labor" manifesting the split between capital and labor. He held that the humanitarian possibilities of capitalism's unparalleled productive forces were undercut by its oppressive class hierarchy. Marx charged that Hegel failed to engage "corporeal" people in their social relations and to recognize that overcoming alienation and recovering human agency required a social transformation. Marx concurred with leading left-Hegelian Ludwig Feuerbach's "inversion" of Hegel, stressing historical, human subjectivity over transcendent spirit (e.g., humanity makes God) and holding that explanations of social life should start with material realities, rather than with ideas. However, Marx criticized Feuerbach for retaining too much Hegelian residue, over-emphasizing religion, treating the material realm too inertly, and speaking too generally about "Man."

Hegel still left a permanent, deep imprint on Marx. Hegel argued that we create our world and make ourselves in the process, but that our self-creation is "estranged" because we fail to recognize our agency and thus treat human creations as alien objects (e.g., human good or evil is seen as the product of God or heredity). Hegel contended that humanity eventually will overcome estrangement through heightened self-consciousness, struggle, and, especially, labor. His view of "lordship and bondage," a metaphorical discourse on domination, was crucial for Marx. Hegel held that masters seek self-recognition by dominating slaves, but languish in the contradiction that coerced recognition from unfree people is worthless. By contrast to the master's falsity and inactivity, he contended, slaves grow wiser and stronger through their striving, and ultimately triumph over the master. By this striving, he held, humanity will some day achieve a higher stage of development based on recognition of the equality of selves. Hegel saw this move as a major step toward the discovery of human authorship of the world and toward a terminus to preexisting history, after which "Absolute Spirit" or total freedom and rationality will reign; then we will make our world and ourselves deliberately and in a way that each person's particularity and worth is recognized by all others. Following Hegel, Marx rejected transcendental explanations and saw self-constitutive labor as the source of all culture. Substituting capitalists and wage workers, alienated labor, and communism for Hegel's masters and slaves, estranged objectification, and Absolute Spirit, he forged a historically specific, sociological version of Hegelian historicism.

Embracing Hegel's dialectical idea of "determinate negation," Marx aimed to overcome capitalism's class attributes, preserve its progressive facets (especially its heightened capacity to produce for human needs), and create a freer, more just society. He rooted his critique in liberal democratic claims about freedom and rationality, which he turned against bourgeois inequality and exploitation. He aimed to create a critical standpoint based on historical grounds, rather than on dogmatic claims about religious or metaphysical "Truth." Marx fashioned his critical theory to engage historical conditions, which could be analyzed sociologically and, hopefully, would inform emancipatory political practices. He intended to anchor normative critique in sociological claims about historical ideals, contradictions, developmental tendencies, and existent or possible social movements. However, tensions between the sociological and political sides of Marx's critical theory plagued his thought and later approaches that followed in its tracks.

FRAMING MATERIALISM: MARX'S COLLABORATION WITH ENGELS

Marx developed his materialist framework in the middle and later 1840s. Although motivated by political upheavals, accelerating capitalist development became his chief focus. He was influenced by left-Hegelians Moses Hess and Friedrich Engels's shift from philosophical criticism to a critique of political economy. Joining the communist movement, they criticized capitalist manufacture and its impoverished workers. Engels's (1845) study of the English working class was an especially important work. Becoming Marx's lifelong collaborator, Engels provided him constructive criticism, extensive editorial assistance, moral and intellectual comradeship, and even financial support. Engels understated his role in the partnership, but he contributed to the analytical basis and substance of Marx's thought.

Marx made his decisive move toward his materialist position in a collaborative effort with Engels, *The German Ideology* (1845–6). Claiming to turn Hegel's position "right-side up," they gave primacy to material needs and production over consciousness and ideas, and articulated a philosophical anthropology that portrayed language and symbolic culture as late arrivals in human development, shaped by productive practices. Marx and Engels established "mode of production" and "class" as their fundamental analytical categories. They argued that extractive social relationships between ruling classes and direct producers are the most decisive formative factors in a social formation and that they have variable historical forms, which must be analyzed on their own terms. Marx and Engels argued that capitalism had a unique "world historical" character; "large-scale industry" was enlisting natural science into production, supplanting labor with machinery, and creating a new type of global order. They saw capitalist factories, markets, and class relations evaporating traditional societies, destroying local particularity and autonomy, and creating global homogeneity and interdependence. Their ideas about large firms, scientific production, and globalization anticipated core aspects of Marx's later masterwork, *Capital*.

Marx and Engels's political pamphlet, "The Communist Manifesto" (1848: 487–9), expressed eloquently capitalism's radical modernizing force – "all that is solid melts into air, all that is holy is profaned" – and then humanity finally will "face with sober senses" their real social conditions and relations. Writing as revolutionary struggles for liberal institutions and rights swept across Europe, they thought that the capitalist class would soon smash the remains of feudal aristocracy and monarchy, attain full political power, create liberal democracy and global capitalism, and thus forge the material basis for a higher stage of social development. Marx and Engels expressed their materialism lucidly and succinctly, applied it to capitalism, and located it vis-à-vis competing anti-capitalist positions. They held that capitalism's "colossal" productive forces, which were already greater than those of all previous societies combined, were creating exceptionally extensive cooperative networks and "universal interdependence." Claiming to be giving voice to intensifying crises and mounting opposition to capitalism, they argued that cutthroat economic competition drives capitalists constantly to revolutionize productive forces, transform radically and untiringly society and culture, and create a mass of impoverished industrial workers destined to overthrow capitalism. Initially the platform for the Communist League, the Manifesto was circulated worldwide by left intellectuals, communist parties, revolutionary insurgencies, and labor movements. It became the political catechism for twentieth-century communism and the most widely read, politically important Marxist work. The Manifesto had a highly optimistic thrust: after the class war, a clear-eyed communist leadership will employ their materialist perspective to plan centrally, build on capitalism's progressive facets, reduce misery and, after their transitional dictatorship that eliminates reactionary opposition, create a participatory, democratic association of producers who will turn the state into a benign system of administration and facilitate "free development of all."

THEORIZING THE DETERMINANTS OF CAPITALISM'S DISTORTED SURFACE: MARX'S ROAD TO *CAPITAL*

In 1848 Marx went to Germany to edit the radical newspaper *Neue Rheinische Zeitung*. After the right defeated the recently ascendant, liberal-democratic forces there in 1849, he was expelled with a passport good only for Paris. The conservative French regime restricted him to Brittany. Marx fled to London, living the rest of his life in the bastion of liberal economic theory and liberal individualism, the first nation to develop large-scale capitalism. Great Britain was experiencing sweeping changes that did not come to other parts of Europe and North America until the late nineteenth and early twentieth centuries. Marx participated in radical working-class politics, leading the First International from 1864–72. However, when prospects for change dimmed, he reduced his political activity and gave fuller attention to his theoretical work. Although continuing journalism, he and his

family depended on Engels's generous financial help. Marx fathered eight children, four of them dying before reaching adolescence. He and the family maid had a son who was given to foster parents and kept secret. Overall, however, Marx was an attentive father, supportive of his three daughters' cultural and personal development. The Marx family apparently was closely knit and warm. First they lived in a poor neighborhood, then later moved to a middle-class area. Marx suffered from recurrent, painful, and probably work-related health problems. He was tormented by his inability to finish projects, especially *Capital*, and by his financial dependency and its impact on his family. In a letter to Engels he lamented that he was "still a pauper" at 50, recalling his mother's earlier admonition that he should have "made capital" instead of simply writing about it (Marx 1868: 25).

Although reactionary forces regained power in Europe, at first Marx and Engels believed that the bourgeois revolution would soon succeed. But they turned pessimistic in the face of counter-revolutionary paralysis and internecine class and subclass conflict. Marx's *Eighteenth Brumaire* (1852a) addressed the rise of France's second Napoleonic dictatorship. He reported how Louis Bonaparte attained total power, aided by the easily bribed Parisian underclass mob. In Marx's view, the new regime paralleled earlier absolutism, but concentrated power more fully and effectively, pushing aside bourgeoisie and proletariat. His opening paragraphs are among the most beautifully written and circumspect in his corpus. Marx (1852a: 103–4, 106) declared that people "make their own history, but they do not make it just as they please." Just when the old order appeared ready to be revolutionized, the state returned "to its oldest form," based on "the shamelessly simple domination of the sabre and the cowl." He lamented that "the tradition of dead generations weighs like a nightmare on the brain of the living."

Anticipating Weber's views, Marx held that the French parliamentary democracy's highly rationalized bureaucracy provided effective means for a *coup d'état* and usurpation of total power. He contended that the bourgeoisie created the conditions of their own demise, their pursuit of short-term, material interest paving the way for the total state. Marx held that the new regime appeared to be "completely independent" of the material base and bourgeoisie, but that state power could not really be "suspended in mid-air." He contended that the dictatorship manifested the class interests of the smallholding peasantry – a very large group in rural France that voted heavily for Louis Napoleon. Marx considered them to be the most backward stratum, living in "stupefied seclusion" on "isolated" family plots, unaffected by capitalism's extensive cooperative networks and interdependence, and alien to proletarian solidarity and revolutionary aims. He held that commodification of rural life and consequent proletarianization would eventually modernize the peasantry and undermine the dictatorship. Although clinging to class-based revolutionary theory by a thread, the *Brumaire* scuttled the Manifesto's optimistic vision of materially driven social progress and demonstrated dramatically that capitalist development might lead to unexpected reactionary fusions of modernity and tradition, rather than to freedom and rationality. The authoritarian regime blocked the type of capitalist development and class struggle that Marx promised would lead to proletarian revolution and communism. The *Brumaire* anticipated issues probed by the Frankfurt School, a major twentieth-century carrier of the critical theory tradition. Many of these thinkers moved toward post-Marxist positions while exploring Fascism, Nazism, and Stalinism, and capitalist democracies' depoliticized working classes, uninterested in revolution and vulnerable to seduction by demagogic chants.

Engels (1851–2) argued that the bourgeoisie were defeated more decisively in Germany than in other parts of Europe. Restoration of aristocratic power and dissolution of the provincial and national assemblies destroyed liberal democracy. He argued that the 1848 revolutions created new configurations of aristocratic and capitalist power, which undermined formation of a class-conscious, revolutionary proletariat. Moreover, Marx (1852b, 1852c) observed that Great Britain's prosperity was creating "political indifference," neutralizing the progressive possibilities of its liberal institutions and generating opposition to progressive democracy. The depoliticizing impact of affluence was a major factor in the decline of socialist and labor-centered left politics in later twentieth-century

European social democracies. Marx and Engels retained their materialist viewpoint, but abandoned the Manifesto's optimistic view that modernization would make capitalism transparent and emancipation imminent. In the *Brumaire* Marx spoke about the Napoleonic regime's "superficial appearance" as if it were a veil obscuring underlying capitalist realities. He raised the issue of ideological illusion in earlier work, but now he implied that one must dig much more deeply and theoretically to grasp the causal matrix of capitalism's highly distorted sociocultural and economic surface. Marx (1859: 275) asserted later that the "semblance of simplicity disappears in more advanced relations of production."

Marx started his intense study of capitalism in the early 1850s, but it was not until 1857 that he developed his theory (Marx 1857–8a; 1857–8b; 1859). He held that everyday experiences of the "economy" and "money" are profoundly "mystified." Capitalist exchange appears to be an independent realm of "things," rather than a "social relation." In his view, monetary exchange "shrouds" capitalism's contradictions, manifesting them in an indirect, distorted way. He claimed that dominant economic views ignore how capitalists attain the products of labor that they trade and from which they profit. Marx aimed to illuminate the hidden sociomaterial determinants of bourgeois political economy's hypostatized, or reified, economic categories. In particular, he argued that the mainstream view of the wage-labor relationship between capitalists and workers as a realm of "free" and "equal" individual exchange obscures its nature as an extractive class relation. In his view, this unequal exchange ultimately animates monetary circulation and accumulation.

In the *Brumaire* Marx suggested already that class structure and class conflict were becoming much more complicated than the linear scenario projected in the Manifesto. Modern industry's greatly expanded production and surpluses opened the way for a proliferation of intermediate classes and complex class and subclass splits. In *Capital*, however, Marx held that the social relationship between the historically specific ruling class and the class of direct producers – capitalists and wage workers – is still the key to grasping capitalism as a whole. Seeing the extractive, wage-labor process as the secret of capitalist accumulation, he made the labor theory of value the work's integrative analytical frame. He contended that the value of "commodities" manifests their common "social substance," or the "socially necessary labor time" that it takes to find, mine, refine, fashion, assemble, or otherwise make them (which presumes average efficiency relative to existing productive forces). Although acknowledging that supply and demand, monopoly, entrepreneurship, and certain other social conditions cause "exchange values" to fluctuate, Marx argued that they gravitate toward an average price determined by the "crystallized social labor" or the "labor time" contained in commodities. He saw the same contingent business factors to be vital for the success or failure of individual capitalists, but he believed that variations cancel each other out over the entire capitalist system and thus cannot explain accumulation as a whole. Most importantly, Marx argued that the worker's wage pays only for subsistence or the cost of his or her reproduction, which is only a fraction of the labor time that he or she transfers to the product during a pay period. Capitalists keep the unpaid portion and realize the "surplus value" when they sell the items. Holding that "labor power" is the only commodity to produce regularly and systematically more value than it commands in exchange, Marx identified the unequal wage relationship as the ultimate source of profit and growth. He contended that, under capitalism, as in earlier modes of production, ruling classes appropriate direct producer surplus. Like slaves and serfs, he held, wage workers cannot ordinarily choose positions that would allow them to retain their surplus product or to live off that of others. By contrast to slavery or serfdom, however, Marx claimed that capitalism's formally "voluntary" labor contract creates the illusion of freedom and commensurate exchange.

Marx held that a capitalist makes huge profits when he or she is the first to develop technical innovations that produce a commodity substantially below its socially necessary labor time (e.g., Henry Ford's assembly line). However, he contended that, eventually, other producers adopt the same innovation and socially necessary labor time is adjusted downward. Thus, he argued, in the long run, mechanization and automation, driven by capitalist competition, will reduce sharply the proportion of "living labor" (the only source of value) in the productive process, causing ever-increasing unemployment and falling profits. He thought that monopoly pricing, global expansion of capitalist production into low-wage countries, and other strategies would pump-up profits and slow the decline, but could not avert an eventual, terminal capitalist crisis and rise of communism. Marx claimed that automated production, highly rationalized and centralized productive organization, and applied science and technology, decoupled from capitalism and class by communist planners, would provide means to develop productive forces much more systematically, reduce their destructive impacts on people and nature, generate more surplus, reduce unnecessary labor, and create an equitable distribution of work and goods. However, Marx's vision of this transition presumed the prior spread of very advanced, knowledge-based capitalism and automated production to the entire globe, which at the millennium was still a far-off dream. Even Marx and Engels had doubts about this scenario.

The first volume of *Capital* (1867) was published about a decade after Marx began his effort to theorize systematically capitalist political economy. He planned to complete six volumes of his magnum opus. Although writing thousands of pages and filling numerous notebooks, Marx never completed the work. After his death, Engels edited and assembled the two unfinished core volumes (Marx 1885, 1894). Karl Kautsky edited the three volumes of *Theories of Surplus Value* (1905–10), Marx's critical history of economic theory.

MARX'S CORE MODEL: HEURISTIC MATERIALISM OR DOGMATIC MATERIALISM?

Like many other modern social theorists, Marx held that people are born into ready-made, hierarchical social worlds, which shape their ideas and actions in innumerable ways. However, he saw class to be the most pervasive source of systematic social constraint. It is an aggregate of people who share a common location in a mode of production and thus face similar material limits and possibilities. Marx and Engels (1845–6: 77–9) stated that class has an "independent existence as against individuals" that fixes conditions under which people make themselves, regardless of their identity, will, or effort. For example, feudal peasants were tied by law to their plots and endless toil, while the lord ruled by military means and appropriated their "surplus product," leaving them only the "necessary product" required for subsistence. This class relation shaped distinct types of superordinate and subordinate social beings, born into positions that were reproduced generation after generation. Marx was aware of individual divergences (e.g., some peasants fled to towns), but he thought that class position entails fundamental limits and opportunities and threats and possible costs for deviation from expected roles. Depending on historical circumstances, he argued, classes can be fragmented aggregates (i.e., composed of individuals, who are unaware of their common condition or who take a passive attitude toward it) or "class conscious" groups (i.e., in which individual and collective identities and actions are oriented to their shared position and common interests). In either case, Marx's "structural" idea of class stresses pervasive sociomaterial conditioning of individual and group development.

Marx's materialism holds that the historically specific way "in which unpaid surplus labor is pumped out of direct producers" is the "hidden basis of the entire social structure" (Marx 1894: 777–8). He argued that ruling classes and allied intermediate strata (e.g., priests, intellectuals, politicians) mystify this extraction, making it a reflection of God, nature, or reason and thus moral, inevitable, or legal. In his view, materialist analyses uncover systematically suppressed, "real bases" of society (e.g., social agents, structures, and processes). Marx argued that social formations are characterized by systematic interdependence and internal relations. He held that the mode of production, or base, is their primary, albeit nonexclusive, structuring factor. He saw it to be composed of an ensemble of "productive forces" (i.e., natural resources, tools, labor power, technology/science, modes of cooperation), or factors that contribute directly to creation of necessary and surplus product, and "property relations," or class-based social relationships that determine who

has effective control over productive forces and disposition of product and who must do productive labor. Although seeing this "material factor" to be the ultimate determinant, he conceived of it as a social construct with physical dimensions. Even simple productive forces, such as prehistoric stone tools, require rudimentary technical ideas, communication, and social cooperation. Stressing centrally class struggles over productive property, Marx usually focused more on social relationships oriented to material factors than on physical conditions per se.

Marx held that social formations also have a superstructure (i.e., "modes of intercourse" and "ideology") that reproduces the mode of production. For example, he saw the state's military, police, legal, and administrative arms to be primary means to perpetuate productive forces and property relations. He also argued that private associations and organizations (e.g., families or voluntary groups) control, socialize, or otherwise fashion people to fit the mode of production. Marx occasionally exaggerated the scope of such reproduction and other times left it vague, but he did not claim that all organizations, associations, and culture contribute equally to the process or necessarily do so at all. For example, he knew that, in liberal societies, labor organizations and political parties sometimes oppose capitalism, yet still participate in public life or operate at its borders. For Marx, ideology, or "ruling ideas," meant facets of culture that either play a direct role in, or make an indirect but clearly identifiable and determinate contribution to, justifying the mode of production (e.g., capitalist ideas of the state, economy, or possessive individualism). He was aware that certain individuals reject these ideas, or he could not have hoped to demystify the capitalist wage relationship or raise proletarian consciousness. Certain later twentieth-century, left-leaning "cultural studies" scholars applied the concept of ideology much more sweepingly than Marx, referring to culture as a whole (or else declaring it irrelevant), holding that the media's "floating signifiers" and "simulation" precluded distinguishing illusion from reality.

Marx spoke of relations of correspondence, which facilitate the reproduction of a mode of production, and relations of contradiction, which undermine the process. For example, feudal laws and customs, which bound serfs to lords and journeymen to masters and forbade unrestricted sale of property and market competition, "corresponded" to and reproduced the productive forces and property relations of the manor and guild, but they "contradicted" or "fettered" the nascent capitalist forms of labor organization and technology that were arising in feudalism's interstices. Increased capitalist development brought heightened contradictions and intensified class conflicts, which escalated sometimes into open political battles between the emergent bourgeoisie and the feudal aristocracy and guild masters. Capturing the state, victorious capitalists created administrative, legal, and sociocultural forms, which "corresponded" to and fostered development of the new productive forces and class structure. Marx saw class struggle to be the immediate "motor" of such transformations of modes of production and overall social formations, but he argued that fundamental shifts of productive forces are the ultimate causal agent. His view that epochal social transitions are rooted in qualitative transformations of production anticipated later, widely accepted arguments by non-Marxist anthropologists and comparative-historical sociologists (i.e., shifts between hunting and gathering, horticultural, agricultural, and industrial societies initiate fundamental sociocultural changes). However, Marx implied or asserted, at certain junctures, the normative claim that material progress leads to social progress. This "economism" has been expressed more emphatically and consistently by later "Orthodox Marxists" and has been attacked by "Critical Marxists" and non-Marxists. Durkheim, Weber, and various "institutionalists" have contested a parallel economism in the thought of Adam Smith, Herbert Spencer, and other liberals and neoliberals, as well as the Marxist version.

The claim that the material factor has "primacy," or is the ultimate determining force, has been an enduring, intense topic of Marxist debate and anti-Marxist criticism. Marx did not argue that all substantial sociocultural change originates from shifts in productive forces. His view of the relation of culture and nature is complex, because he saw the "material" realm to be social as well as natural. For example, he considered science and modes of cooperation to be part of determining productive forces. These

sociocultural elements depend on and are embedded in a social formation's overall culture. Thus, causality is a complicated matter for Marx. He often praised art and literature, and did not reduce them to a materialist reflux of class society. He did imply that entire social formations bear their mode of production's imprint, but he saw their parts to be, at variable levels, "relatively autonomous." Usually, Marx treated the mode of production as a social matrix that sets material limits and exerts variable, determinate influences on different parts of the social formation. This view implied heuristic materialism, a guide to historical-sociological inquiry. By contrast, however, he expressed occasionally a dogmatic materialism that reduced politics and culture to epiphenomenal "reflections" of material forces or stressed the "inevitability" of certain tendencies or "iron laws" of capitalism. Critical Marxists have charged that this overblown determinism is a chief flaw of Orthodox Marxism. Other post-Marxist, postmodernist, and anti-Marxist critics, asserting politics' or culture's sweeping autonomy, often have rejected Marx's ideas, branding him a dogmatic totalizer.

Regardless of the dogmatic passages, Marx stressed generally a complex, historically contingent, heuristic materialism, which is not reducible to "technological determinism" (i.e., social change arises only from technical change) or to "reflection theory" (i.e., ideas are mere emanations of physical reality). In substantive analyses he often pointed to diverse cultural and political conditions as well as to contingent material ones that heighten or deflect class struggles. He sometimes qualified theoretical arguments with the proviso that claims about analytical relationships must be grasped in light of different empirical circumstances, especially conditions under which they might not hold. Employed as a heuristic device, Marx's materialism provides the basis for a Marxist sociology with characteristic foci, problems, and hypotheses, which other approaches leave unexplored or address in different ways. By contrast, his dogmatic moments, which likely were meant to reassure the working class, his other supporters, and perhaps even himself that "history was on their side," suggest an absolutist ontology and irrefutable "Truths," which are beyond inquiry and which discourage it. These polar tendencies in Marx's thought have parallels in other types of social theory, manifesting tensions between their normative and empirical sides. Social theorists' effort to unify "theory and practice" has been a rocky road.

Even in the most complex premodern civilizations, productive forces usually have developed incrementally over many hundreds or even thousands of years, and major innovations have tended to diffuse very slowly between different regions, if at all. By contrast, as Marx argued, modern capitalism generated a greater variety of powerful productive forces than all preceding civilizations together. Bearing the marks of this peculiar historical moment, his materialism constituted an effort to come to terms with a new and unique capitalist world. The primacy that Marx gave to material factors arose from his experience of the radical changes wrought by an unparalleled socioeconomic revolution that altered everyday life profoundly across extremely extensive spaces in a few generations. By the late twentieth century, neoliberal capitalism made accumulation the measure of nearly everything, accelerated greatly the already intense pace and diversity of change, and fashioned a new global capitalism. Twenty-first century peoples still live in the wake of the world-historical transformation that Marx analyzed; the capitalist mode of production is still ongoing. Thus, his materialism still provides heuristic tools, which pose penetrating sociological questions about social inequality, wealth, growth, ideology, and overall social development. Finally, his social theory's ethical thrust, stressing just distribution of the sociomaterial means of participation, challenges us to rethink socioeconomic justice after twentieth-century communism and social democracy and to entertain fresh alternatives to unrestricted economic liberalism and its characteristic inequalities. Marx's specter hangs over sociology still.

SEE ALSO: Alienation; Anomie; Birmingham School; Bourgeoisie and Proletariat; Braverman, Harry; Capital, Secondary Circuit of; Capitalism; Communism; Conflict Theory; Crime, Radical/Marxist Theories of; Critical Theory/Frankfurt School; Cultural Studies, British; Dependency and World-Systems Theories; Dialectical Materialism; Exchange-Value; False Consciousness; Hegel G.W.F.; Hegemony; Ideology; Labor/Labor Power; Luxemburg, Rosa; Marxism and Sociology; Materialism; Materialist Feminisms; Neo-Marxism; New Left; Political Economy; Revolutions; Social Justice, Theories of; Socialism; Stratification and Inequality, Theories of; Structuralism; Structure and Agency; Use-Value

REFERENCES AND SUGGESTED READINGS

Unless otherwise indicated, references to works by Marx and/or Engels are from *Karl Marx and Frederick Engels: Collected Works* (50 volumes), published by International Publishers, New York, from 1975 on. The dates refer to the time that they were written or published.

Engels, F. (1845) *The Condition of the Working Class in England*. In *Collected Works*, Vol. 4, pp. 294–583.

Engels, F. (1851–2) Revolution and Counter-Revolution in Germany. In *Collected Works*, Vol. 11, pp. 3–96.

McLellan, D. (1973) *Karl Marx: His Life and Thought*. Harper & Row, New York.

Marx, K. (1843a) On the Jewish Question. In *Collected Works*, Vol. 3, pp. 146–74.

Marx, K. (1843b) *Contribution to the Critique of Hegel's Philosophy of Law*. In *Collected Works*, Vol. 3, pp. 3–129.

Marx, K. (1844) Economic and Philosophical Manuscripts of 1844. In *Collected Works*, Vol. 3, pp. 229–346.

Marx, K. (1852a) *The Eighteenth Brumaire of Louis Bonaparte*. In *Collected Works*, Vol. 11, pp. 99–197.

Marx, K. (1852b) Political Consequences of the Commercial Excitement. In *Collected Works*, Vol. 11, pp. 364–8.

Marx, K. (1852c) Political Parties and Prospects. In *Collected Works*, Vol. 11, pp. 369–72.

Marx, K. (1857–8a) *Outlines of the Critique of Political Economy* [First Installment]. In *Collected Works*, Vol. 28, pp. 3–561.

Marx, K. (1857–8b) *Outlines of the Critique of Political Economy* [Second Installment]. In *Collected Works*, Vol. 29, pp. 3–255.

Marx, K. (1859) *A Contribution to the Critique of Political Economy*. In *Collected Works*, Vol. 29, pp. 257–417.

Marx, K. (1867) *Capital: A Critique of Political Economy*, Vol. 1: *The Process of Capitalist Production*. Ed. F. Engels. In *Collected Works*, Vol. 35, pp. 43–807.

Marx, K. (1868) Letter from Marx to Engels: In Manchester. In *Collected Works*, Vol. 43, pp. 20–5.

Marx, K. (1885) *Capital: A Critique of Political Economy*, Vol. 2: *The Process of Circulation of Capital*. Ed. F. Engels. In *Collected Works*, Vol. 36, pp. 26–534.

Marx, K. (1894) *Capital: A Critique of Political Economy*, Vol. 3: *The Process of Capitalist Production as a Whole*. Ed. F. Engels. In *Collected Works*, Vol. 37, pp. 25–912.

Marx, K. (1963–71) *Theories of Surplus Value*, 3 vols. Ed. K. Kautsky. Progress Publishers, Moscow.

Marx, K. & Engels, F. (1845–6) *The German Ideology*. In *Collected Works*, Vol. 5, pp. 19–608.

Marx, K. & Engels, F. (1848) Manifesto of the Communist Party. In *Collected Works*, Vol. 6, pp. 477–519.

Seigel, J. (1993) *Marx's Fate: The Shape of a Life*. Pennsylvania State University Press, University Park.

Marxism and sociology

George Steinmetz

The twentieth century challenged some of Marxism's central theoretical concepts and empirical expectations. Contrary to the anticipation of capitalism's immanent downfall, capitalist societies reconfigured themselves repeatedly, overcoming economic and political crises and redirecting popular dissatisfaction toward less threatening aims. The links between people's social class locations and their political practices and subjectivities were weak or extremely variable across time and place (Burawoy & Wright 2000). During the 1930s and 1940s workers in some European countries were just as likely to support fascism as socialism. And finally, the self-designated socialist and communist societies turned out to be politically repressive and economically stagnant. Most of them collapsed under the weight of their internal weaknesses and oppositional movements. Although some Marxists continue to describe contemporary society as *late* capitalism (Fredric Jameson, Ernst Mandel), most agree with Theodor Adorno's early prognosis that capitalism's futures may not be socialist at all, nor even preferable to present-day conditions.

Marxism has also faced intensive theoretical and conceptual questioning. Critique has been directed against its claims to explain all of social life omnihistorically in terms of a uniform cluster of explanatory mechanisms such as class

or capital accumulation. Adorno's "negative dialectics" already opposed this totalizing with an "antisystem" that moved beyond the Hegelian "category of unity" (Adorno 1990 [1966]: 10). Writing around the same time, Louis Althusser (1990 [1965]) argued against essentialist, "Hegelian" Marxism that derives all practices from a unitary, core contradiction (e.g., bourgeoisie versus proletariat). Marxist orthodoxy had seen *ideology* and *the state* as "superstructures" that were derived from, and functionally reproductive of, the economic "base." In recent decades Marxists have acknowledged that culture is not simply derivative of the economic but is a determining force in its own right, and that modern states often pursue social order and other goals in ways that ignore or even run at odds with the needs of the capitalist economy (Steinmetz 1993). After a phase in which theorists proposed "dual systems theories" (e.g., gender and class, state and society), it gradually became evident that there is potentially an infinite number of different principles according to which social domination/exploitation can be socially organized. Laclau and Mouffe (1985) pushed this line of thinking to its logical conclusion, arguing that all social practices, including the economic ones that Marxism had long considered foundational, were the product of contingent discursive articulations. The unavoidable conclusion was that critical social science must accept the "rainforestlike profusion of different kinds of reality" (Collier 2005) – the complex variety of social structures and practices interacting in unexpected ways – that produce the flow of empirical events that we call history. Accepting the ontological pluralism of social structures does not negate the possibility that practices are *sometimes* he mechanisms intrinsic to Marxism.

Furthermore, traditional Marxism expected ideology and the state to wither away in post-capitalist societies. Against this, Althusser (1971) argued that ideology was an eternal feature of human existence. Cornelius Castoriadis, Claude Lefort, and other members of the group *Socialisme ou barbarie* (1949–65) argued that "actually existing" socialist societies had produced a hypertrophy rather than an evaporation of the state. Adorno criticized Marxists for elaborating particular, *affirmative* utopias and thereby reducing the "non-identical" to the familiar.

Despite these empirical and conceptual challenges, Marxism has continued to evolve and even flourish as a vital research program. Marxist sociology falls into differing methodological camps. These include ethnography, geography, historical sociology, cultural analysis, and survey research. At a deeper theoretical and epistemological level one can discern differing responses on the part of different groups to the challenges discussed above. (1) A *poststructuralist* version has reframed Marxism as a theory of *discursive* constructions or articulations (e.g., Laclau & Mouffe 1985). (2) *Critical theory*'s insistence that the substantive analysis of capitalism and the critique of (social) epistemology as inextricably linked has sparked renewed interest in the work of the Frankfurt School among sociologists of science. (3) *Regulation theory* focuses on the broadly "economic" social practices that were the main focus of Marx's own writing – on capitalism as a conflictual, crisis-ridden, and contradictory set of social relations. This approach rejects functionalism and economic reductionism, however, construing Marxism as a *regional theory* of the economic that no longer claims to explain the entirety of social life. Regulatory modes like "Fordism" are analyzed as social inventions that are fortuitous from the standpoint of capital but not inevitable resolutions of capitalist crisis. (4) Rational choice Marxism has responded to the problem of functionalism and supposed empirical conundra such as "false consciousness" by reframing the entire tradition in terms of methodological individualism (Wright 1985). (5) Marxian analysis of globalization (Arrighi 1994), empire (Harvey 2003), and the capitalist world-system (Wallerstein 2004) have continued to explain international dynamics in broadly economic terms while proposing various revisions of the inherited model of capitalism.

The question is, what ties all of this together as "Marxism"? It is still possible to identify a set of core Marxian assumptions underlying this work.

Capitalism is organized around social classes defined in terms of their unequal rights and powers over the means of production and capital and in terms of "unequal rights over the results" of using those resources (Burawoy & Wright 2000: 20). Class relations are relations of *exploitation*, meaning that the surplus created by the producing classes (those with few or no rights and powers over capital and productive resources) is appropriated by the owning classes. Marx's category of alienation (*Entfremdung*) refers above all to this estrangement of the product from the producers. To qualify as exploitative, furthermore, the material welfare of the exploiters must depend *causally* "upon the material deprivations of the exploited" (p. 21). Starting from this concept of exploitation, Erik Olin Wright (1985) has elaborated class categories that more adequately map the complexities of contemporary social structure.

Capitalism is intrinsically volatile and unstable because the exploiters and the exploited are locked in an intimate relationship with opposing interests. Of course the resulting explosiveness need not be directed toward the socialist forms that Marxists prefer. Class unrest in the overdeveloped capitalist countries has increasingly been channeled in the direction of religious fundamentalism and narratives of national humiliation and racist resentment (Steinmetz 1997).

Profit rates decline cyclically, leading to disinvestment, unemployment, the "creative destruction" of old infrastructure and productive spaces, and sometimes to the rescaling of space in a "spatial fix" that promises to undergird new rounds of accumulation. Marxist research on spatial transformations has been vibrant in recent years (see Brenner 2004).

There is also an almost inevitable decline in the functionality of the institutions that "defend and reproduce" capitalism (Burawoy & Wright 2000: 25). The neo-Marxist school known as "regulation theory" explores the stabilizing frameworks that are sometimes elaborated without assuming that one will be found. Regulationists insist that longer-term crises of capitalist profitability and "muddling through" are also possible since there is no omniscient agent or structural mechanism guaranteeing that solutions will be found.

Theories of Fordism and post-Fordism have proven extraordinarily useful in making sense of various empirical phenomena and historical transitions that had hitherto remained out of reach. The period between the late 1940s and 1973 now appears as a distinct formation in the advanced capitalist world, albeit with particular national emphases and different moments of consolidation and dissolution. Post-war social science can itself now be perceived as partly shaped by the spontaneous social epistemologies produced by the Fordist emphases on the mass consumption of standardized, uniform commodities (along with the imperatives of the Cold War and US empire; see Steinmetz 2005). Ironically, some critical theory and sociology from this period can also now be understood as mirroring the epistemic and substantive social premises that embedded within post-war Atlantic Fordism. Adorno's conviction that administered capitalism was annihilating the individual projected Fordist conditions into the infinite future. More recently, post-Fordist social forms seem to have stimulated a *heightened* emphasis on the individual and to have encouraged "promotional selfhood." At the core of the "post-Fordist" mode of regulation thought to have emerged in recent years is flexibilized and "just-in-time production," decentralized industry, and a remapping of economic practices in ways that no longer correspond closely to the boundaries of the nation-state. Individual and regional inequalities are exacerbated and the state becomes "hollowed out" (Jessop 1993). Even where the state is forced to take a leading role, as in foreign policy, the *form* of overseas military interventions increasingly mirrors the neoliberalism and privatization that dominate the "domestic" and economic sphere (Steinmetz 2003).

Marxists analyze capitalism as a system that is restlessly expansionist, constantly seeking to incorporate and encompass new external and internal regions and practices. Of course there are also moments of deliberate *decommodification*, in which specific zones are released into a non-capitalist state of being. According to theorists of the "articulation of modes of production" and colonial "indirect rule" (Mamdani 1996), for example, modern European colonialism preserved or produced non-capitalist zones in order to enhance political control and depress the costs of reproducing labor power. In the contemporary era US capitalism has found it preferable to abandon the urban populations that were central to mid-twentieth-century Fordist production, resulting in a partial reagrarianization and the emergence of a subsistence economy in the abandoned inner cities that is ever more distant from the central zones of capitalist vitality (Chanan & Steinmetz 2005). This abandoned population has also been shunted off into a booming prison-industrial complex.

Capitalism originated in Europe with the process that Marx called "primitive accumulation," consisting of concerted appropriations of land and property. David Harvey has proposed that primitive accumulation is not simply a chapter in the prehistory of capitalism but a practice that accompanies capitalism throughout its history, reappearing whenever there is a crisis of over-accumulation, that is, a "lack of opportunities for profitable investment" (2003: 139). Whereas Rosa Luxemburg, John Maynard Keynes, and others focused on strategies for increasing aggregate demand, Harvey notes that "it is also possible to accumulate in the face of stagnant effective demand if the costs of inputs (land, raw materials, intermediate inputs, labour power) decline significantly." Harvey calls the procedures used to accomplish this "accumulation by dispossession," arguing that they have become the principal strategy for capitalist accumulation since 1973.

SEE ALSO: Adorno, Theodor W.; Bourgeoisie and Proletariat; Capitalism; Commodities, Commodity Fetishism, and Commodification; Critical Theory/Frankfurt School; Dependency and World-Systems Theories; Fordism/Post-Fordism; Gramsci, Antonio; Lukács, Georg; Marx, Karl; Neo-Marxism; Regulation Theory

REFERENCES AND SUGGESTED READINGS

Adorno, T. W. (1990 [1966]) *Negative Dialectics*. Continuum, New York.

Althusser, L. (1971) Ideology and Ideological State Apparatuses. In: *Lenin and Philosophy*. NLB, London, pp. 121–72.

Althusser, L. (1990 [1965]) Contradiction and Overdetermination. In: *For Marx*. Allen Lane, London, pp. 87–128.

Amin, A. (Ed.) (1994) *Post-Fordism: A Reader*. Blackwell, Oxford.

Arrighi, G. (1994) *The Long Twentieth Century: Money, Power, and the Origins of Our Times*. Verso, London.

Brenner, N. (2004) *New State Spaces: Urban Governance and the Rescaling of Statehood*. Oxford University Press, Oxford.

Burawoy, M. & Wright, E. O. (2000) Sociological Marxism. Unpublished paper.

Chanan, M. & Steinmetz, G. (2005) *Detroit: Ruin of a City. A Documentary Road Movie about Detroit and the Automobile Industry.* Bristol Docs, Bristol.

Collier, A. (2005) Critical Realism. In: Steinmetz, G. (Ed.), *The Politics of Method in the Human Sciences: Positivism and its Epistemological Others.* Duke University Press, Durham, NC, pp. 327–45.

Harvey, D. (2003) *The New Imperialism.* Oxford University Press, Oxford.

Jessop, B. (1993) Towards a Schumpeterian Workfare State? Preliminary Remarks on Post-Fordist Political Economy. *Studies in Political Economy* 40: 7–40.

Laclau, E. & Mouffe, C. (1985) *Hegemony and Socialist Strategy: Towards a Radical Democratic Politics.* Verso, London.

Mamdani, M. (1996) *Citizen and Subject: Contemporary Africa and the Legacy of Late Colonialism.* Princeton University Press, Princeton.

Steinmetz, G. (1993) *Regulating the Social: The Welfare State and Local Politics in Imperial Germany.* Princeton University Press, Princeton.

Steinmetz, G. (1997) Social Class and the Reemergence of the Radical Right in Contemporary Germany. In: Hall, J. R. (Ed.), *Reworking Class: Cultures and Institutions of Economic Stratification and Agency.* Cornell University Press, Ithaca, NY, pp. 335–68.

Steinmetz, G. (2003) The State of Emergency and the New American Imperialism: Toward an Authoritarian Post-Fordism. *Public Culture* 15(2): 323–46.

Steinmetz, G. (2005) Scientific Authority and the Transition to Post-Fordism: The Plausibility of Positivism in American Sociology since 1945. In: Steinmetz, G. (Ed.), *The Politics of Method in the Human Sciences: Positivism and its Epistemological Others.* Duke University Press, Durham, NC, pp. 275–323.

Wallerstein, I. M. (2004) *World-Systems Analysis: An Introduction.* Duke University Press, Durham, NC.

Wright, E. O. (1985) *Classes.* Verso, London.

masculinities, crime and

James W. Messerschmidt

Gender consistently has been advanced by sociologists as the strongest predictor of criminal involvement: it explains more variance in crime cross-culturally than any other variable. As an explanatory variable, then, gender would seem to be critical. Yet early theoretical works in the sociology of crime were gender-blind. That is, although acknowledging that the vast majority of those who commit crime are men and boys, the gendered content of their legitimate and illegitimate behavior was virtually ignored (Messerschmidt 1993).

However, the rise of second-wave feminism – originating in the 1960s – challenged this masculinist nature of criminology by illuminating the patterns of gendered power that had been all but ignored. As a result of feminism, not only is the importance of gender to understanding crime more broadly acknowledged, but it has also led to the critical study of masculinity and crime. The three major contemporary theoretical perspectives in this endeavor are Hagan's (1989) power-control theory, Agnew's (1992, 2001) strain theory, and Messerschmidt's (2004) structured action theory.

Hagan (1989) argues that in industrialized societies an instrument–object relationship exists between parents and children. Parents are the instruments of control and their objects are children, and this relationship shapes the social reproduction of gender.

Hagan identifies two family structures based on women's participation in the paid labor market, "patriarchal" and "egalitarian." In patriarchal families, the husband/father works outside the home in an authority position and the wife/mother works at home. Patriarchal families, through sex-role socialization, "reproduce daughters who focus their futures around domestic labor and consumption, as contrasted with sons who are prepared for participation in direct production" (p. 156). In egalitarian families, the husband/father and wife/mother both work in authority positions outside the home. These families "socially reproduce daughters who are prepared along with sons to join the production sphere" (p. 157).

In both types of families daughters are less criminal than sons because daughters are more controlled by their mothers. Hagan argues, however, that daughters in patriarchal families are more often taught by parents to avoid risk-taking endeavors, whereas in egalitarian families, both daughters and sons are frequently taught to be more open to risk-taking. It is this combination of the instrument–object relationship and corresponding socialization of risk-taking that affects delinquency. As a result, egalitarian families maintain smaller gender differences in delinquency: "Daughters become more like sons in their involvement in such forms of risk-taking as delinquency" (p. 158). In this theory, sons are for the most part ignored and gender differences in crime are explained by a concentration on the characteristics of mothers and daughters.

Agnew (1992) identifies three forms of "strain" that may lead to delinquency: the failure to achieve positively valued goals (such as disjunctions between expectations and actual achievements), the removal of positively valued stimuli from the individual (such as a loss of a girlfriend/boyfriend or death of a parent), and the presence of negative stimuli (such as child abuse/neglect or negative relations with parents). In examining strain in relation to gender and crime, Agnew (2001) concentrates on the question: Why do males have a higher crime rate than females? Answer: This is *not* due to boys and men having higher levels of strain than girls and women. Instead, males experience different *types* of strain that are more likely to lead to crime. For example, Agnew argues that because of sex-role socialization, "males are more concerned with material success and extrinsic achievements, while females are more concerned with the establishment and maintenance of close relationships and with meaning and purpose in life" (p. 168). The resulting differences in strain, Agnew argues, explain the greater rate of property crime among males. Moreover, there are important additional differences in social control and sex-role socialization. For example, for females, forms of strain involve a restriction of criminal opportunities and excessive social control: "It is difficult to engage in serious violent and property crime when one spends little time in public, feels responsible for children and others, is burdened with the demands of others, and is under much pressure to avoid behaving in an aggressive manner" (p. 169). Because men are more likely to be in public, to experience conflict with others, and to suffer criminal victimization, they are more likely to be involved in violence. Thus, the different types of strain men and women experience result in higher rates of crime by the former.

Agnew does not stop there, however, but adds that males and females also differ in their emotional response to strain. Although both males and females may respond to strain with anger, they differ in their experience of anger: female anger is often accompanied by emotions like fear and depression, whereas male anger is often characterized by moral outrage. In explaining these differences, Agnew (p. 169), like Hagan, concentrates on sex-role theory, arguing that by reason of differences in "the socialization process," women learn to blame themselves for negative treatment by others and view their anger as inappropriate and a failure of self control; men blame others for their negative treatment and view their anger "as an affirmation of their masculinity." Consequently, men are more likely to commit violent and property crimes, whereas women are more likely to resort to self-destructive forms of deviance, such as drug use and eating disorders.

Power-control and strain theories acknowledge gender inequality and conditionally focus on the social dimensions of behavior. In addition, the theoretical conceptualizations of power-control and strain do present interesting insights on gender differences in crime, and these insights present an opportunity for a politics of reform.

By concentrating on gender *differences* in crime, however, power-control and strain theories ignore gender *similarities* in crime between men and women and disregard the differences *among* men and boys as well as *among* women and girls. Thus, these theories construct an essentialist criminology by collapsing gender into sex. They create an artificial polarization, thereby distorting actual variability in gender constructions and reducing all masculinities and femininities to one normative standard case for each: the "male sex role" and the "female sex role." Not only are there differences cross-culturally, but also within each particular society masculine and feminine practices by men and by women are constructed on the basis of class, race, age, sexuality, and particular social situation. These variations in the construction of masculinity and femininity are crucial to understanding the different types and amounts of crime. In addition, power-control and strain theories require that we examine masculinity exclusively by men and boys and femininity by women and girls, thus ignoring masculinities and femininities by people: the way individuals construct gender differently. Consequently, power-control and strain theories miss what must be acknowledged: women and girls also construct masculine practices that are related to crime.

Because of the above problems with power-control and strain theories, many sociologists of crime interested in masculinities have turned to structured action theory (Messerschmidt 1993, 1997, 2000, 2004). Following the work of feminist ethnomethodologists (West & Fenstermaker 1995), this perspective argues that gender is a situated social and interactional accomplishment that grows out of social practices in specific settings and serves to inform such practices in reciprocal relation: we coordinate our activities to "do" gender in situational ways. Crucial to this conceptualization of gender as situated accomplishment is West and Zimmerman's (1987) notion of accountability. Because individuals realize that their behavior may be held accountable to others, they configure their actions in relation to how these might be interpreted by others in the particular social context in which they occur. Within social interaction, then, we facilitate the ongoing task of accountability by demonstrating we are male or female through concocted behaviors that may be interpreted accordingly. Consequently, we do gender (and thereby crime) differently, depending upon the social situation and the social circumstances we encounter. "Doing gender" renders social action accountable in terms of normative conceptions, attitudes, and activities appropriate to one's sex in the specific social situation in which one acts (West & Zimmerman 1987).

"Doing gender" does not occur in a vacuum, but is influenced by the social structural constraints we experience. Social structures are regular and patterned forms of interaction over time that constrain and enable behavior in specific ways; therefore, social structures "exist as the reproduced conduct of situated actors" (Giddens 1976: 127). Following Connell (1987, 1995) and Giddens (1976), structured action theory argues these social structures are neither external to social actors nor simply and solely constraining; on the contrary, structure is realized only through social action, and social

action requires structure as its condition. Thus, as people "do" gender they reproduce and sometimes change social structures. Not only then are there many ways of "doing gender" – we must speak of masculinities and femininities – but also gender must be viewed as *structured action*, or what people do under specific social structural constraints.

In this way gender relations link each of us to others in a common relationship: we share structural space. Consequently, shared blocks of gendered knowledge evolve through interaction in which specific gender ideals and activities play a part. Through this interaction masculinity is institutionalized, permitting men (and sometimes women) to draw on such existing, but previously formed, masculine ways of thinking and acting to construct a masculinity for specific settings. The particular criteria of masculinity are embedded in the social situations and recurrent practices whereby social relations are structured (Giddens 1989).

Given that masculinities and femininities are not determined biologically, it makes sense to identify and examine possible masculinities by women and girls. Recent research has begun to move in this direction. For example, Jody Miller's important book *One of the Guys* (2001) shows that certain gang girls identify with the boys in their gangs and describe such gangs as "masculinist enterprises." Pointing out that unequal structured gender relations are rampant in the mixed-gender gangs of which these girls were members, certain girls differentiated themselves from other girls by embracing a "masculine identity." Similarly, recent life-history interviews of girls involved in assaultive violence indicate that some of these girls "do" masculinity by in part displaying themselves in a masculine way, by engaging primarily in what they and others in their milieu consider to be authentically masculine behavior, and by outright rejection of most aspects of femininity (Messerschmidt 2004). Nevertheless, like the girls in Miller's study, these girls found themselves embedded in unequal gender relations that disallowed them entrance into the same masculine place as the boys. Thus, their masculinity was constructed differently from, and subordinate to, that of the boys.

In short, structured action theory allows us to conceptualize masculinity and crime in new ways – ways that enable sociologists of crime to explore how and in what respect masculinity is constituted in certain settings at certain times, and how that construct relates to crime by men, women, boys, and girls.

SEE ALSO: Crime; Deviance, Crime and; Deviant Careers; Ethnomethodology; Femininities/Masculinities; Feminist Criminology; Gender, Deviance and; Hegemonic Masculinity

REFERENCES AND SUGGESTED READINGS

Agnew, R. (1992) Foundation for a General Strain Theory of Crime and Delinquency. *Criminology* 30: 47–87.
Agnew, R. (2001) An Overview of General Strain Theory. In: Paternoster, R. & Bachman, R. (Eds.), *Explaining Criminals and Crime: Essays in Contemporary Criminological Theory*. Roxbury, Los Angeles, pp. 161–74.
Connell, R. W. (1995) *Masculinities*. University of California Press, Berkeley.
Connell, R. W. (1987) *Gender and Power: Society, the Person, and Sexual Politics*. Stanford University Press, Stanford.
Giddens, A. (1976) *New Rules of Sociological Method: A Positive Critique of Interpretive Sociologies*. Basic Books, New York.
Giddens, A. (1989) A Reply to My Critics. In: Held, D. & Thompson, J. B. (Eds.), *Social Theories of Modern Societies: Anthony Giddens and His Critics*. Cambridge University Press, New York, pp. 249–301.
Hagan, J. (1989) *Structural Criminology*. Rutgers University Press, New Brunswick, NJ.
Messerschmidt, J. W. (1993) *Masculinities and Crime: Critique and Reconceptualization of Theory*. Rowman & Littlefield, Lanham, MD.
Messerschmidt, J. W. (1997) *Crime as Structured Action: Gender, Race, Class, and Crime in the Making*. Sage, Thousand Oaks, CA.
Messerschmidt, J. W. (2000) *Nine Lives: Adolescent Masculinities, the Body, and Violence*. Westview Press, Boulder.
Messerschmidt, J. W. (2004) *Flesh and Blood: Adolescent Gender Diversity and Violence*. Rowman & Littlefield, Lanham, MD.
Miller, J. (2001) *One of the Guys: Girls, Gangs, and Gender*. Oxford University Press, New York.
West, C. & Fenstermaker, S. (1995) Doing Difference. *Gender and Society* 9: 8–37.
West, C. & Zimmerman, D. H. (1987) Doing Gender. *Gender and Society* 1: 125–51.

mass culture and mass society

Nick Perry

"Mass culture" typically refers to that culture which emerges from the centralized production processes of the mass media. It should be noted, however, that the status of the term is the subject of ongoing challenges – as in Swingewood's (1977) identification of it as a myth. When it is linked to the notion of mass society, then it becomes a specific variant of a more general theme; namely, the relation between social meanings and the allocation of life chances and social resources. Considered as a repository of social meaning, mass culture is one of a group of terms that also includes high (or elite) culture, avant-garde culture, folk culture, popular culture, and (subsequently) postmodern culture. The interpretation and boundaries of each of these categories are routinely the subject of debate and dispute. This becomes particularly evident in attempts at ostensive definition (i.e., the citation of examples of each term and the reasoning employed to justify their allocation to the category in question). In combination, these concepts constitute a system of differences, such that a change in the meaning of any one of its terms is explicable through, and by, it's changing relation to the others. Those same terms frequently function as evaluative categories that – either tacitly or explicitly – incorporate judgments about the quality of that which they affect to describe.

In his introduction to Rosenberg and White's *Mass Culture Revisited* (1971) Paul Lazarsfeld suggested that in the US, controversy and debate with respect to mass culture had most clearly flourished between 1935 and 1955. It was a time when recognition of the mass media as a significant cultural force in democratic societies coincided with the development of totalitarian forms of control, associated with the regimes and media policies of Hitler and Stalin. The perceived affinities between these developments prompted concern about how best to defend the institutions of civil society, culture in general, and high culture in particular against the threats that they faced. Such preoccupations helped shape the pattern of the mass culture debate at that time. Certainly, what was evident among American social commentators and cultural critics was a widespread antipathy to mass culture that reached across the differences between conservative and critical thinkers. Even among the defenders of mass culture, the justifying tone was characteristically defensive and apologetic (Jacobs 1964).

For many of the critics, a typical strategy was to define mass culture negatively as high culture's "other" (Huyssen 1986). This convergence in defining and understanding mass culture as being everything that high culture is not, occurred under circumstances where the conception of high culture that was valorized might be either (1) generally conservative and traditional, or (2) specifically modernist and avant garde. For some conservatives, in a line of thought influenced by Ortega Y Gasset and T. S. Eliot, it took the form of an unabashed nostalgia for a more aristocratic and purportedly more orderly past. They therefore tended to see the threat posed by mass culture as generated from "below" (by "the masses" and their tastes). For critical theorists such as Theodor Adorno, mass culture served interests that derived from above (the owners of capital) and was an expression of the exploitative expansion of modes of rationality that had hitherto been associated with industrial organization. This critical group's understanding of the attributes of a high modernist culture is that it is – or rather aspires to be – autonomous, experimental, adversarial, highly reflexive with respect to the media through which it is produced, and the product of individual genius. The corresponding perspective on mass culture is that it is thoroughly commodified, employs conventional and formulaic aesthetic codes, is culturally and ideologically conformist, and is collectively produced but centrally controlled in accordance with the economic imperatives, organizational routines, and technological requirements of its media of transmission. The emergence of such a mass culture – a culture that is perforce made for the populace rather than made by them – serves both to close off the resistance associated with popular culture and folk art and that seriousness of purpose with which high culture is identified.

The debate around this opposition between the culture of high modern*ism* and mass culture

was, for the most part, carried forward by scholars in the humanities. What proved to be a point of contact with social scientists was the latter's related concern as to whether the development of modern*ity* (understood as a social process) was associated with the emergence of mass society. Insofar as the notion of such a society is grounded in the contrast between the (organized) few and the (disorganized) many, Giner (1976) suggests that its lengthy prehistory in social and political thought stretches back to classical Greece. In like fashion, Theodor Adorno had seen the foundation of mass culture as reaching as far back as Homer's account, in *The Odyssey*, of Odysseus's encounter with the Sirens and the latter's seductive, but deeply insidious, appeal.

A specifically sociological theory of mass society, however, with its antecedents in the writings of Alexis de Tocqueville, John Stuart Mill, and Karl Mannheim, is altogether more recent. As formulated by such writers as William Kornhauser and Arnold Rose that theory was concerned to highlight selected social tendencies rather than offering a totalizing conception of modern society. The theory does nevertheless advance a set of claims about the social consequences of modernity, claims that are typically conveyed by way of a stylized contrast with the purportedly orderly characteristics of "traditional" society or, less frequently, those forms of solidarity, collectivity, and organized struggles that exemplify "class" society. In brief, social relationships are interpreted as having been transformed by the growth of, and movement into, cities, by developments in both the means and the speed of transportation, the mechanization of production processes, the expansion of democracy, the rise of bureaucratic forms of organization, and the emergence of the mass media. It is argued that as a consequence of such changes there is a waning of the primordial ties of primary group membership, kinship, community, and locality. In the absence of effective secondary associations that might serve as agencies of pluralism and function as buffers between citizens and centralized power, what emerges are insecure and atomized individuals. They are seen as constituting, in an influential image of the time, what David Reisman and his associates called "the lonely crowd." The "other-directed" conduct of such individuals is neither sanctified by tradition nor the product of inner conviction, but rather is shaped by the mass media and contemporary social fashion.

In C. Wright Mills's (1956) version of the thesis the relevant (and media-centered) contrast was not so much between past and present, as between an imagined possibility and an accelerating social tendency. The most significant difference was between the characteristics of a "mass" and those of a "public," with these two (ideal type) terms distinguished from one another by their dominant modes of communication. A "public" is consistent with the normative standards of classic democratic theory, in that (1) virtually as many people express opinions as receive them; (2) public communications are so organized that there is the opportunity promptly and effectively to answer back any expressed opinion; (3) opinion thus formed finds an outlet for effective action; and (4) authoritative institutions do not penetrate the public, which is thus more or less autonomous. In a "mass," (1) far fewer people express opinions than receive them; (2) communications are so organized that it is difficult to answer back quickly or effectively; (3) authorities organize and control the channels through which opinion may be realized into action; and (4) the mass has no autonomy from institutions.

As these images imply, and as Stuart Hall was subsequently to suggest, what lay behind the debate about mass culture was the (not so) hidden subject of "the masses." Yet this was a social category of whose very existence Raymond Williams had famously expressed doubts, wryly noting that it seemed invariably to consist of people *other* than ourselves. Such skepticism was shared by Daniel Bell (1962), an otherwise very different thinker from Williams. In critiquing the notion of America as a mass society, he indicated the often contradictory meanings and associations that had gathered around the word "mass." It might be made to mean a heterogeneous and undifferentiated audience; or judgment by the incompetent; or the mechanized society; or the bureaucratized society; or the mob – or any combination of these. The term was simply being asked to do far too much explanatory work.

Moreover, during the 1960s, such a hollowing out of the formal, cognitive basis of the mass culture concept was increasingly complemented by altogether more direct empirical challenges. The emergence of a youth-based counterculture, the Civil Rights Movement, opposition to the Vietnam War, the emergence of second wave feminism, and the contradictions and ambiguities of the media's role in at once documenting and contributing to these developments, all served to bring the mass society thesis into question. In addition, both the control of the popular music industry by a handful of major companies (Peterson & Berger 1975) and of film production by the major studios were the subject of serious challenges from independent cultural producers with their own distinctive priorities (Biskind 1998). The result (for a decade at least, until the eventual reassertion of corporate control) was an altogether more diversified media culture. And in what was perhaps explicable as part reaction, part provocation vis-à-vis an earlier orthodoxy, what also emerged were instances of populist-style academic support for the very notion of mass culture – as, for example, in the *Journal of Popular Culture*. If this latter tendency sometimes displayed an unreflective enthusiasm for ephemera and a neglect of institutional analysis, it nevertheless presaged the more broadly based recognition of the diversity of mass culture that was evident during the 1970s (e.g., Gans 1974).

During the 1980s an emphasis on the cultural reception of popular cultural forms attracted innovative empirical work (Radway 1984; Morley 1986) at a time when the notion of the postmodern had become the subject of sustained critical attention. Postmodernism displayed none of high modernism's antagonism towards mass culture. On the contrary, as evidence of the blurring of cultural boundaries multiplied, practitioners of postmodernism either interrogated the very basis of such contrasts between "high" and "mass" and the hierarchical distinctions that sustained them (Huyssen 1986) or (somewhat matter-of-factly) proceeded to ignore them. For example, work on television soap operas subverted the convention of critical disdain for such texts by directing attention towards such structural complexities as multiple plot lines, absence of narrative closure, the problematizing of textual boundaries, and the genre's engagement with the cultural circumstances of its audiences (Geraghty 1991).

In its "classic" forms the mass culture/mass society thesis has thus lost much of its power to persuade. Contemporary permutations of its claims are nevertheless discernible in, for example, the post-Marxist writings of Guy Debord and Jean Baudrillard, and in the contention of the erudite conservative critic George Steiner that it is disingenuous to argue that it is possible to have both cultural quality and democracy. Steiner insists on the necessity of choice. It is, however, refinements to the closely related concept of "culture industry" which may prove to be the most enduring and most promising legacy of the thesis (Hesmondhalgh 2002). Culture industry had been identified by Adorno and his colleague Max Horkheimer as a more acceptable term than "mass culture," both because it foregrounded the process of commodification and because it identified the locus of determinacy as corporate power rather than the populace as a whole. As originally conceived, it presented altogether too gloomy and too totalizing a conception of cultural control. An emphasis on the polysemy of media texts or on the resourcefulness of media audiences offered an important methodological corrective. But these approaches could also be overplayed, and the globalization of media production and a resurgence of institutional analysis and political economy among media scholars during the last decade have revived interest in the culture industry concept.

SEE ALSO: Adorno, Theodor W.; Audiences; Critical Theory/Frankfurt School; Culture Industries; Hegemony and the Media; Mannheim, Karl; Mass Media and Socialization; Popular Culture; Public Opinion

REFERENCES AND SUGGESTED READINGS

Bell, D. (1962) America as a Mass Society: A Critique. In: *The End of Ideology*. Free Press, New York, pp. 21–38.

Biskind, P. (1998) *Easy Riders; Raging Bulls*. Simon & Schuster, New York.

Gans, H. (1974) *Popular Culture and High Culture*. Basic Books, New York.

Geraghty, C. (1991) *Women and Soap Opera*. Polity Press, Cambridge.

Giner, S. (1976) *Mass Society*. Martin Robertson, London.

Hesmondhalgh, D. (2002) *The Cultural Industries*. Sage, London.

Huyssen, A. (1986) *After the Great Divide*. Macmillan, London.

Jacobs, N. (Ed.) (1964) *Culture for the Millions?* Beacon Press, Boston.

Morley, D. (1986) *Family Television*. Comedia, London.

Peterson, R. & Berger, D. G. (1975) Cycles in Symbol Production: The Case of Popular Music. *American Sociological Review* 40(2): 158–73.

Radway, J. (1984) *Reading the Romance*. University of North Carolina Press, Chapel Hill.

Rosenberg, B. & White, D. M. (Eds.) (1971) *Mass Culture Revisited*. Van Nostrand, New York.

Swingewood, A (1977) *The Myth of Mass Culture*. Macmillan, London.

Wright Mills, C. (1956) *The Power Elite*. Oxford University Press, New York.

mass media and socialization

Stephen L. Muzzatti

Socialization is a lifelong process through which people learn the patterns of their culture, including behavioral expectations, values, and "truths." This process is facilitated by a host of groups and institutions such as the family unit, the educational system, peer groups, and the mass media. Debates in sociology and related social sciences over the relative importance and impact of these agents on individual behavior have raged for decades with little resolution. However, the mass media's increasing ubiquity and ever divergent forms leave little question as to their pervasiveness. While they are a more recently developed agent of socialization, the mass media strongly influence public opinion and our worldview. By imparting both approved and fugitive knowledges, media narratives shape the way we see ourselves and the world around us.

THE MASS MEDIA

While the mass media are often lumped into one homogeneous category, particularly by critics decrying a negative influence upon, for example, young people, it is important to recognize that there are many diverse media ranging from chart-topping CDs, best-selling novels, and Hollywood blockbusters through political affairs news magazines, amateur Internet pornography sites, and university textbooks. Hence, to suggest homogeneity of any sort is simplistic. While some media, such as newspapers, have been in existence for several centuries, most of the media we are daily exposed to have emerged much more recently. Advertisements, for example, undeniably the most ubiquitous of mass media's incarnations, only began to take on their current form in the 1920s, while television is largely a product of the post-World War II boom. Similarly, music videos and video games emerged in the 1980s, while commercial and personal websites are little over a decade old.

FOUR MODELS OF MEDIA INFLUENCE

While the "sociology of the media" and aligned areas of study – such as popular culture, communications studies, and cultural studies – are relatively recent developments, sociologists have studied and postulated media impacts for much of the last century. Early researchers theorized that the mass media destroy the individual's capacity to act autonomously. However, subsequent scholars posited a more complex interaction between the mass media and society. Elevating the role of human agency in the socialization process, this later work contended that individuals actively evaluate and interpret mass media narratives. Theories about media influence have evolved over the last half century from those which emphasized direct and immediate influence (a "hypodermic needle" model) and those which suggested relatively little influence (a "minimal effects" model) through those that maintained a select influence (an "agenda-setting" model) and long-term effects (a "cultivation" model). Recognizing the dynamic tension between human agency and social structure, most contemporary media scholars address both the media as a process and the relationships among the myriad elements of this process.

Theorists from the German Frankfurt School (such as Theodor Adorno, Walter Benjamin, Max Horkheimer, and Herbert Marcuse) provided some of the earliest and most systematic analyses of the mass media's influence, and best embody the "hypodermic needle" model. According to these scholars, the media, whether in the form of "news" or "entertainment," is a "culture industry" transmitting information to a passive audience. This model of a unified and powerful media further suggests that consumerist messages work together with political ideology to further the hegemonic designs of those in power. Absolutely docile, the general public hungrily consumes packaged media spectacles ranging from news magazines detailing the war on terrorism to primetime television dramas on the exploits of sex-crazed, upper-middle-class, suburban housewives.

Considerably less deterministic in its approach is the "minimal effects" model. American sociologists affiliated with Columbia University such as Paul Lazarsfeld and Robert Merton, working in the late 1940s and 1950s, contended that the mass media's influence was far less direct than was previously suggested. Focusing their work more on the media's news production than on their entertainment endeavors, these scholars found that interpersonal relations served to mitigate media messages. Furthermore, they found that media messages acted more to reinforce existing beliefs, values, and behaviors than to change them. This, they theorized, was a result of a multistage process wherein opinion leaders, who themselves were drawn to the mass media, incorporated media messages they were amenable to, and then worked to promulgate them among family, friends, and acquaintances.

The radicalization of American sociology in the 1960s and 1970s heralded the emergence of the "agenda-setting" model of the mass media. This model recognized the role of growing media monopolies to tell people not *what to think* but rather *what to think about*. According to this approach, the media organize public understanding in keeping with preferred social and cultural codes. By symbolically reflecting the structure of values and relationships of post-industrial capitalism which lie beneath the surface of our everyday/night worlds, the corporately owned mass media impart cultural, political, social, and economic statements of "truth," by which individuals fashion their identities and relate to one another.

Emerging in the mid-1990s, George Gerbner and his colleagues' "cultivation" model addresses the long-term cultural influence of the mass media on the people's beliefs and values. Focusing primarily on the impact of television, Gerbner et al. (1994) assert that lengthy exposure to messages from the corporately owned mass media have a mainstreaming or homogenizing effect on an otherwise heterogeneous population. Hence, rather than the direct causal effect posited by some, this model contends that continuous and sustained exposure will, over time, impact the audience's worldview. According to this model, the cultivation factor has moved the general population politically and ideologically to the right over the course of the last two decades. Not unlike the agenda-setting model, this model is particularly attentive to a shrinking media cosmos which, while on the surface appearing to offer more choices (more television channels, newspapers, etc.), actually offers a narrower perspective because of increasingly oligopolistic ownership patterns and the concomitant horizontal and vertical integration across media.

THE PUBLIC OUTCRY OVER THE MASS MEDIA

Contrary to much of the evidence provided by contemporary scholars in this area, public concern over the media's influence (perhaps itself in part a product of media influence) tends to center around the alleged deleterious influence of certain forms of popular culture on youth and unquestioningly embraces an overly simplistic cause–effect model. Many moral entrepreneurs, politicians, and action groups have long held that popular media contribute directly to a host of social problems ranging from truancy, vandalism, and teen pregnancy through gang activity, suicide, and mass murder. In the early twentieth century, comic books and dime-store novels were said to cause young readers to defy the authority of their teachers and the clergy, while jazz and, later, rock and roll were said to promote promiscuity and drug use among listeners. Today, many of these same arguments are directed against contemporary media forms. Over the past few years, some of the more high-profile targets of politicians and moral

entrepreneurs have included video games from the Grand Theft Auto series, the music of artists such as Marilyn Manson, Eminem, and most recently, 50 Cent, and Hollywood films such as those in the Matrix series. Ironically, the mass media themselves, particularly the corporately owned news media, have been a driving force behind much of this clamor over alleged antisocial media messages. Indeed, the news media are likely the single most influential actor in the orchestration and promulgation of moral panics involving young people, mass media, and popular culture. News coverage of certain kinds of popular media, particularly those catering to young people, is often quite sensationalistic and usually distorted. This coverage regularly couples mass media exposure to instances of youth crime, not only suggesting a direct causal link, but also inflating the seriousness of the incidents, making them appear more heinous and frequent than they truly are. Public anxiety is whipped up through the use of rhetorical journalistic devices. "Special cover story," "in-depth exposé," or "investigative report"-style coverage employs dramatic photos, video, and sound bites along with highly moralistic editorializing focusing on the corrupting influence of hip-hop, gaming, and Internet chat sites among others.

CRITICAL SCHOLARSHIP AND MEDIA LITERACY

While many politicians, religious leaders, and laypeople demonize the mass media and the youthful audiences that consume much of it, most sociologists of the media and aligned scholars approach the issue of mass media and socialization somewhat differently. To be certain, this is not to suggest that these researchers turn a blind eye to problems such as hedonism, misogyny, intolerance, and the glorification of violence present in some media targeted toward young people; rather, they recognize the audience's agency and the ability of its members to employ resistant and/or oppositional readings of mass media texts. Furthermore, many of the leading media scholars like Sut Jhally, Elizabeth and Stewart Ewen, and Henry Giroux contend that some of these allegedly destructive media messages embedded in youth-oriented media are more social justice-oriented than the mediated representations of them lead us to believe. According to these scholars, a far more prescient concern is the way in which the corporately owned mainstream (not the specialty or youth-oriented) mass media undermine the democratic public sphere by disseminating an ideology which, while serving the hegemonic imperatives of post-industrial capitalism, devalues human dignity, marginalizes difference, and reduces personal worth to commodity fetishism by pedaling unreflexive hyperconsumption and encouraging unquestioning deference to authority. For example, some like Barry Glassner (2000) and Mark Crispin Miller (2005) theorize that the American public's unrealistic fear of crime and terrorism is a result of a paucity of non-corporate, non-consumerist media messages. Similarly, some media scholars are more troubled by the destructive values of consumer capitalism and the rank dog-eat-dog individualism embedded in many "reality TV" programs such as *The Apprentice* or the latest incarnation of *Survivor*. Many too are concerned by the ubiquitous presentation of highly unrealistic female body types in all forms of visual media and the normalization of extreme body modification in programs such as *The Biggest Loser* and *The Swan*. As such, critical media scholars encourage all of us, as consumers of mass media, to engage in thoughtful and informed analyses of these texts in an effort to uncover and explore both the approved and oppositional meanings.

CONCLUSION

As indicated at the outset, the mass media are diverse, and clearly, so too is the range of opinion on the matter of their specific place in the broader process of socialization. As to the questions of how much, and in what direction, the media influence us, sociologists are still undecided. However, what is undeniable is that the mass media are vital sites of cultural and economic brokerage. Over the course of the last quarter century the mass media have expanded steadily, resulting in new forms of cultural pedagogy. As the mass media's omnipresence becomes more entrenched, traditional boundaries among news, entertainment, and advertising become increasingly fluid. Slick and

emotional, profound and poetic, rhythmic and insistent, and most of all, never fully shut out, mass media narratives serve as conduits through which society represents itself and ways by which social and personal identities are articulated and disseminated.

SEE ALSO: Audiences; Critical Theory/Frankfurt School; Fans and Fan Culture; Hegemony and the Media; Media and Consumer Culture; Socialization, Agents of; Socialization, Gender

REFERENCES AND SUGGESTED READINGS

Fiske, J. (1994) *Media Matters*. University of Minnesota Press, Minneapolis.

Gerbner, G. (2005) Who is Shooting Whom? The Content and Context of Media Violence. In: Pomerance, M. & Sakeris, J. (Eds.), *Popping Culture*, 3rd edn. Pearson Education, Boston, pp. 125–30.

Gerbner, G., Gross, L., Morgan, M., & Signorelli, N. (1994) Growing Up with Television: The Cultivation Effect. In: Bryant, J. & Zillman, D. (Eds.), *Media Effects Advances in Theory and Research*. Lawrence Erlbaum, Hilldale, NJ, pp. 17–41.

Glassner, B. (2000) *The Culture of Fear: Why Americans are Afraid of the Wrong Things*. Basic Books, New York.

Kellner, D. (1995) *Media Culture*. Routledge, London.

Lazarsfeld, P. F., Berelson, B., & Gaudet, H. (1949) *The People's Choice: How the Voter Makes Up His Mind in a Presidential Campaign*. Columbia University Press, New York.

Miller, M. C. (2005) Saddam and Osama in the Entertainment State. In: Pomerance, M. & Sakeris, J. (Eds.), *Popping Culture*, 3rd edn. Pearson Education, Boston, pp. 219–29.

Potter, W. J. (2005) *Media Literacy*, 3rd edn. Sage, Thousand Oaks, CA.

mass production

Dieter Bögenhold

Mass production was practiced in medieval times in places such as Venice, where pre-manufactured ships were produced along assembly lines. However, mass production is mostly concerned and identified with the rise of modern capitalism starting after the Industrial Revolution. In a narrow understanding, mass production is an industrial technique to organize the production of large amounts of consumer goods on production lines. The most popular entrepreneur who introduced industrial mass production was Henry Ford with his famous Ford Model T in the early twentieth century. The idea of mass production is the realization of economies of scale. Very high rates of production permit very inexpensive products for large consumer markets.

Mass production is often described by the existence of assembly lines where hundreds of people each do one simple specific job and run routine procedures. The worker's job uses the same tool to perform identical operations on a stream of products being produced. Formalization, differentiation, and specialization are key principles of the labor process.

A theoretical foundation for such industrial practices was found in the writings of Fredrick Winslow Taylor, an American engineer who became a pioneer of a new generation of writers on management. Taylor's book *Principles of Scientific Management* (1911) is a summary and extension of his well-known diverse presentations and working papers. Taylor combined existing pragmatically different ideas and concepts, and synthesized them for an audience of industrial managers who were open to new ideas and procedures to increase productivity. Terms such as labor studies, human resource management, or quality control did not exist prior to Taylor. Management conditions at the time of "scientific management" were (1) the development of a systematic science for each element of the industrial labor process, to overcome traditional procedures; (2) the controlled selection, training, and further education of employees in contrast to a practice in which everybody is doing and choosing his or her own task and job; (3) the establishment of an understanding of cooperation between blue-collar workers and management; and (4) the installment of hierarchy and of a corresponding system of formal rules and a rational system of authority lines within a company. Combined, this provides Taylor's framework for an organization theory, which includes ideas of a strict scheme of authority and responsibility, the separation of administrative and practical work elements, task specialization, and methods of motivation and gratification for blue-collar workers.

Taylor's ideas of "scientific management" were designed for industrial mass production within the context of rapidly developing capitalist economies, but they received enthusiastic attention from socialist observers. For example, W. I. Lenin admired and studied the works by Taylor because he identified within them a key to strengthen productivity.

Taylor's principles to organize the industrial production process were regarded as having an impact on the societal regime of production. People argued that mass production within an industrial regime of assembly lines and large factories goes hand in hand with fundamental changes in society and economy. In the view of many of Taylor's contemporaries, mass production would lead to a revolution of general lifestyles and cultural modes because the speed of the new production and the related organization of work would impact all other forms of life organization. The term Taylorism was coined to represent not only the single organization of the labor process, but also the wider context of a society based on industrial mass production. Taylorism acted as the face of a rationalized economy in which the society is sensitive to the needs of large manufacturing plants.

Another term for the same matter was Fordism, which stood for a similar societal philosophy to organize industrial production and social life. For several decades the terms Taylorism and Fordism were interchangeable. However, detailed discussion of Henry Ford's and Frederick Winslow Taylor's results underlined differences between both concepts. Where Taylor's concepts appear to be more static, Ford's were more dynamic, flexible, and open. Taylor never mentioned Ford and Ford never spoke about Taylor (Gottl-Ottlilienfeld 1926: 12). Despite this, Taylorism and Fordism were used synonymously as a trend of capitalist development toward a regime of mass production and related large industries. Mass production was regarded as the fate of the masses. Cultural interpretations in sociological and economic literature were almost always negative and assumed that people's living conditions would become visibly similar. Among many others, the Italian philosopher Antonio Gramsci

(1975) argued workers were going to lose their sovereignty and become degraded to a small wheel within a large machinery. Monogamy and the absense of alcohol and other drugs were prerequisites for the establishment and further development of Fordism.

In retrospect, although the bleak future prophesied in social and cultural terms was sociologically extremely plausible, not all developments headed purposely in one and the same direction. For example, debate on individualization and the plurality of lifestyles highlights that more than one "average existence" of human beings has emerged. And, of course, the twentieth century is also the century of the emergence of large enterprises, the so-called global players, but one has also to acknowledge the persistence of an astonishingly high ratio of small and medium sized enterprises in advanced capitalist economies. Among others, even authors at the beginning of the twentieth century stressed that a capitalist economy is not a "one-size firm" economy, as argued at that time by Gustav Schmoller and Werner Sombart. Sombart discussed very critical assumptions employed by theorems of Taylorism and Fordism (Bögenhold 2000). Much later, Piore and Sabel (1984) demonstrated the very high performance of small handicraft production for several economies after World War II. Changes in industries and markets are always more than just the automatic running for economies of scale (Fligstein 2001).

The (blue-collar) workers' movement and academic organization theory criticized concepts of Taylorism and Fordism for different reasons. Such criticism was explicit criticism of capitalism, but it was also a criticism of the perception of workers within the labor process. Ideas of mass production could not appropriately design work without referring to the needs and emotions of the human beings involved. For example, the beginning of the debate on human relations in the 1930s is not fully understandable without an appropriate awareness of the earlier rise of mass production and related academic reflection.

Nowadays, mass production must be regarded in combination with issues of globalization and social inequalities, and with the question of the development paths of modern economies and societies. While the beginning of reflection on mass production was extremely focused on the industrial production process, current discussion should try to turn further attention to the connections between mass production and mass consumer markets. The "McDonaldization thesis" – as introduced by Ritzer (2004 [1996]) – provides important hints to understand mass production in combination with the emergence of global mass markets by consumer demands (credit cards, colas, burgers, movies, music hits, etc.). Further discussion has to specify different scales in order to arrive at a better understanding of the topic.

SEE ALSO: Fordism/Post-Fordism; Industrial Revolution; Industrialization; Labor/Labor Power; Labor Movement; Labor Process; Laborism; McDonaldization; Mass Culture and Mass Society; Organization Theory; Taylorism

REFERENCES AND SUGGESTED READINGS

Bögenhold, D. (2000) Limits to Mass Production: Entrepreneurship and Industrial Organization in View of the Historical School of Schmoller and Sombart. *International Review of Sociology* 10(1): 57–71.

Fligstein, N. (2001) *The Architecture of Markets: An Economic Sociology of Twenty-First-Century Capitalist Societies.* Princeton University Press, Princeton.

Gottl-Ottlilienfeld, F. von (1926) *Fordismus? Von Frederick Winslow Taylor zur Henry Ford,* 3rd edn. Verlag von Gustav Fischer, Jena.

Gramsci, A. (1975 [1934]) Americanismo e fordismo. In: *Quaderni del Carcere,* Vol. 3. Giulio Einaudi Editore, Turin, pp. 2137–81.

Piore, M. J. & Sabel, C. F. (1984) *The Second Industrial Divide: Possibilities for Prosperity.* Basic Books, New York.

Ritzer, G. (2004 [1996]) *The McDonaldization of Society: Revised New Century Edition.* Pine Forge Press, Thousand Oaks, CA.

Taylor, F. W. (1911) *Principles of Scientific Management.* Harper & Brothers, New York.

massive resistance

Rutledge M. Dennis

American society has long resisted the idea of creating a truly egalitarian society. This was first noted in the early nineteenth century in one of the earliest comprehensive studies of the United States when Alexis de Tocqueville wrote that America's ability and willingness to confront its racial and color divide would determine its very survival. Toqueville's study took on added meaning later in the century as North and South engaged in a bloody civil war, largely over slavery. Closely connected were issues related to the industrialism of the North versus the agrarian economy of the South, the belief that all powers should be centralized in Washington versus the idea that the US Constitution sanctioned a federal system which guaranteed specific rights to the states (states' rights), and the jockeying by both the North and South for political power and supremacy which had plagued the United States since its very inception.

If there were moments evoking an optimism leading toward greater equity and egalitarianism in the decades following the Civil War (the Reconstruction, the 13th, 14th, and 15th Amendments designed to free the slaves, grant them citizenship, then give them the right to vote), this optimism would soon be shattered by the 1896 *Plessy* v. *Ferguson* decision (Cruse 1987; Bell 1992) which sanctioned and legalized racial inequality and would be the judicial framework for a national and comprehensive "separate but equal" view which undergirded a policy of racial segregation and exclusion. *Plessy* v. *Ferguson* would prevail until challenged and delegitimized by the 1954 *Brown* v. *Board of Education* decision which denounced the dual school system and ordered the desegregation of formerly segregated public schools.

Most white Southerners and politicians reacted with horror to the Brown decision and vowed to follow a policy of non-compliance. For this reason, between 1954 and 1965, 97.75 percent of black children continued to attend segregated all-black schools (Black & Black 1987). While average citizens and politicians simply sulked, denounced the court decision, declared themselves advocates for states' rights, and were content to play a waiting game, Virginia's US Senator Harry F. Byrd, the leader of the infamous and politically powerful "Byrd Machine," stepped into the limelight and became the leading opponent of the Brown decision under the banner of "massive resistance."

Prior to the call for massively resisting the Brown decision, Virginia proposed numerous measures to circumvent it. One was the Gray Plan (Sartain & Dennis 1981), named after Senator Garland Gray and made public in November 1955. This plan pleased very few, including some of the massive resisters. Under this plan, (1) tuition grants were to be given to white children to attend private schools if their schools were ordered to desegregate; (2) a pupil placement plan would allow local school boards to assign students to specific schools, thus slowing the pace of desegregation; and (3) the Virginia Constitution would be amended to eliminate compulsory education, thus no child would be forced to attend a desegregated school.

Senator Byrd sounded the call to arms which initiated the Massive Resistance Movement on February 24, 1956 (Moeser & Dennis 1982) when he contended: "If we can organize the Southern States for massive resistance to this order [Brown decision] I think that in time the rest of the country will realize that racial integration is not going to be accepted in the South." That Byrd and Virginia would lead the fight against the Brown decision, and thus become deeply involved in racial matters, was unusual in that historically Virginia generally sought to distance itself from the more rabidly racist states of the Deep South such as South Carolina, Georgia, Mississippi, and Alabama, though like the white public and politicians throughout the South, Virginia was ideologically committed to the myth of white supremacy. But as Sartain and Dennis (1981: 211) asserted, "geographically there are many states further South, but ideologically none is farther South in culture and tradition than Virginia. Richmond is a major focal point for the spirit of the Old South. Here are located the Museum of the Confederacy and other reminders of the days of Richmond's greatest era of fame, such as the Robert E. Lee House and the headquarters of the United Daughters of the Confederacy."

The Virginia General Assembly met for a special session in August 1956. The session was designed to address two issues: to apply political, social, and economic pressure on the local chapter of the NAACP and its members and to enact measures to thwart the school desegregation order (Sartain & Dennis 1981).

Regarding the former, pressures were brought on black parents to refrain from soliciting to have their children attend white schools, attempts were made to seize the records and membership of the local and state NAACP chapters, and individual NAACP members were fired from their jobs if they applied to enroll their children in white schools. The legal underpinnings of massive resistance were established by the General Assembly in three areas: (1) a State Pupil Placement Board was established which would be responsible for all pupil assignments and transfers; (2) the governor was given a mandate to close any school ordered to desegregate and reopen such schools only on a segregated basis; if this failed, state funds would be withdrawn from all schools operating as desegregated schools; (3) state-supported tuition grants would be awarded to white children whose schools were closed due to the desegregated order.

Though Harry F. Byrd had issued the "massive resistance" battle cry in February 1956, the legal battle for the movement began with the August 1956 special Virginia General Assembly session. The Assembly set the mood and tone for the opposition to the desegregation order, and even if many Southern politicians and white citizens sought to circumvent the decision, only Virginia would actually defiantly close its public schools in a show of massive resistance to desegregation. J. Harvie Wilkinson (1979: 83) indicts Senator Byrd for the social, educational, political, and economic pain inflicted upon Virginia and the South, and asserts that Byrd was determined, in his last years, to "reap the drama and glory of another Lost Cause." And it would be a lost cause (Wilkinson 1979: 83–101), though before the battle was over, Prince Edward County, a small rural and impoverished county, when ordered to desegregate, closed its schools from 1959 to 1964, deschooling more than 1,400 whites, the vast majority of whom were educated in churches, synagogues, homes, and other places. The 1,400 blacks were not so fortunate, and more than 800 would be denied any formal education. In Norfolk, Virginia six white high schools closed rather than desegregate, and more than 2,000 to 3,000 black students were without formal education. The legal rebellion came to a close in January 1959 (Sartain &

Dennis 1981), when a panel of federal judges declared Virginia's laws opposing desegregation to be illegal and unconstitutional. Two important movements and themes emerged out of the Massive Resistance Movement. One was the Committee to Save Public Schools, an interracial movement which would have an impact in the area of political alliances and coalitions for blacks and whites in the major cities in Virginia. The other was the creation, by young black professionals, of the Crusade for Voters, an organization designed to rally and develop black political power in urban areas. The Crusade (Dennis & Moeser 1982; Moeser & Dennis 1982: 34) would become the most important black political group in Richmond and the surrounding areas. It would change and reorder the political landscape in the city and state by "first increasing the political consciousness of blacks and then translating that consciousness into voting power."

SEE ALSO: *Brown* v. *Board of Education*; Civil Rights Movement; Discrimination; Hate Crimes; Human Rights; Integration; Majorities; Marginality; Paternalism; Race; Race and Ethnic Politics; Race (Racism); School Segregation, Desegregation; Slavery

REFERENCES AND SUGGESTED READINGS

Bell, D. (1992) *Race, Racism, and American Law*. Little, Brown, Boston.

Black, E. & Black, M. (1987) *Politics and Society in the South*. Harvard University Press, Cambridge, MA.

Cruse, H. (1987) *Plural But Equal*. William Morrow, New York.

Dennis, R. M. & Moeser, J. (1982) Metropolitan Reform and the Politics of Race in the Urban South, 1960–1980. *Western Journal of Black Studies* 6, 1 (Spring).

Moeser, J. & Dennis, R. M. (1982) *The Politics of Annexation*. Schenkman, Cambridge, MA.

Sartain, J. and Dennis, R. M. (1981) Richmond, Virginia: Massive Resistance Without Violence. In: Williw, C. V. & Greenblatt, S. (Eds.), *Community Politics and Educational Change*. Longman, New York.

Tocqueville, A. de (1966) *Democracy in America*. Harper & Row, New York.

Wilkinson, J. H. (1979) *From Brown to Bakke*. Oxford University Press, Oxford.

master status

Stephen Hunt

The term master status denotes a perceived social standing that has exceptional significance for individual identity, frequently shaping a person's entire social experience. The concept is at least implied within the theoretical framework of structural functionalism, especially the work of Talcott Parsons who was predisposed toward using the expression in a normative sense. Here, master status is attached to the prestige relating to the individual's primary social role (cf. Parsons 1951). However, in the disciplines of sociology and social psychology, master status is a concept used more specifically in the field of deviance.

The principal development of the notion of a master status is usually attributed to the theories of Howard Becker, especially through his work *Outsiders* (1963). For Becker, a master status usually implies a negative connotation. It is related to the potential effects upon an individual of being openly labeled as deviant. In Becker's analysis a deviant act only becomes deviant when social actors perceive and define it as such. It follows that deviants are those who are labeled as a result of these sociopsychological processes. A label is not neutral since it contains an evaluation of the person to whom it is attached. A major consequence of labeling is the formation of a master status surpassing and indeed contaminating all other statuses possessed by an individual. Other social actors subsequently appraise and respond to the labeled person in terms of the perceived attributes of the master status, thus assuming that he or she has the negative characteristics normally associated with such labels. Since individuals' self-concepts are largely derived from the response of others, they are inclined to see themselves in terms of the label, perhaps engendering a self-fulfilling prophecy whereby the deviant's identification with his or her master status becomes the controlling one.

The concept of master status has been further used in the area of deviance, including Jock Young's (1971) survey of the implications of labeling "hippie" marijuana users. However, it is probably in the seminal work of Erving Goffman where the concept has been used most effectively. The consequences of being labeled with a master status are analyzed by Goffman in terms of the effects of stigma upon self-conceptions. He focused, in particular, on the often vain struggle of the stigmatized to maintain self-respect and reputable public image by various coping strategies (Goffman 1968a). This is taken further in his volume *Asylums* (1968b), which explores the role of total institutions in the application of a stigmatized master status.

SEE ALSO: Goffman, Erving; Identity: The Management of Meaning; Identity: Social Psychological Aspects; Labeling; Labeling Theory; Organizations as Total Institutions; Self-Fulfilling Prophecy; Stigma

REFERENCES AND SUGGESTED READINGS

Becker, H. (1963) *Outsiders: Studies in the Sociology of Deviance*. Free Press, New York.

Goffman, E. (1968a) *Stigma: Notes on the Management of Spoiled Identity*. Prentice-Hall, Englewood Cliffs, NJ.

Goffman, E. (1968b) *Asylums: Essays on the Social Situation of Mental Patients and Other Inmates*. Penguin, Harmondsworth.

Parsons, T. (1951) *The Social System*. Free Press, New York.

Young, J. (1971) The Role of the Police as Amplifiers of Deviancy, Negotiators of Reality, and the Translators of Fantasy. In: Cohen, S. (Ed.), *Images of Deviance*. Harmondsworth, Penguin, pp. 27–61.

masturbation

Benjamin Shepard

The history of masturbation – self-pleasuring solitary sex – includes countless episodes of definition and redefinition. Intellectuals from Jean-Jacques Rousseau to Ludwig Wittgenstein agonized over masturbation. American social purists called for prohibitions against it. Sigmund Freud and his disciples debated it. By the early 1990s, an American surgeon general would be fired merely for suggesting that it was a worthy alternative to abstinence or unsafe sex.

From the thirteenth century until the mid-twentieth century, masturbation was viewed as a moral flaw. St. Thomas Aquinas noted that masturbation signaled the beginning of a slippery slope leading to sodomy, adultery, and bestiality; thus, in *Summa Theologica*, he categorized it with other "luxuria," signifying crimes against nature. Aquinas and others like him viewed masturbation as a gateway pleasure, much like marijuana is said to be a gateway to heroin: not very dangerous in and of itself, but capable of opening countless subversive possibilities. Like any sexual act other than reproductive missionary-position intercourse, masturbation was assumed to be a sin of irrational gratification – suspect because it emphasized pleasure over procreation. Medieval and early modern church leaders feared that the impure act of masturbation could overwhelm the sexual body of the laity. Thus, studies of masturbation grapple with core questions about social control and hierarchy.

For most historians of sex, the origin of masturbation as a moral issue can be located in the publication of an anonymous tract some time between 1708 and 1716 entitled *Onania; or, The Heinous Sin of Self Pollution*. Onan was a character in the biblical book of Genesis. Rather than deposit his seed inside the wife of his deceased brother, as required by law, Onan spilled it on the ground. For this transgression, Onan was struck down by God. The author of the tract, a doctor, thus suggested that ejaculating alone was "willful self abuse," and masturbation came to be known as "onanism." *Onania* became a publishing sensation as generations of readers were drawn to the lurid tales of harm produced by "self abuse." The publication of *Onania* provides a case study of the commodification of a social problem. The tract was sold in English public houses where people met socially. Not coincidently, relief for the new malady – a form of herbal snake oil – was also sold to the public.

Throughout the eighteenth century, onanism was considered outside the bounds of "normal" heterosexuality, much like sodomy and prostitution. Social purity advocates suggested the practice led to an excessive sex drive. By the

nineteenth century, the first steps toward adultery were thought to begin with self-pollution. The dilemma was how to stifle interest in this most available and democratic of sins. Talking about it stimulated further discussion of a brash new secular morality. Prohibitionist efforts backfired as discussions of sex led to the production of sexuality and the elaboration of fantasy where disciplinary regimes hoped to assert control.

Recognizing that masturbation offered a form of social and political transformation, reform-minded anti-vice crusaders Cotton Mather and Anthony Comstock sought to stop the practice. Well into the twentieth century, Alex Comfort notes masturbation was "encircled by a nearly unanimous form of vocal moralism." The moralist view was supported by advertising, preaching, and counseling, resulting in ever-increasing discourses propelling social anxiety. According to the nineteenth-century doctor Emma Drake, for example, the dangers posed by masturbation included "epilepsy, idiocy, catalepsy, and insanity." She explains: "It has been discovered that out of eight hundred and sixteen cases of insanity in New York State Insane Asylum, there were one hundred and six addicted to this practice." Thus, Drake advised mothers, "from their babyhood be watchful of your children's companions; allow no sensational books to be read" (Comfort 1967).

By the mid-twentieth century, however, prohibitions surrounding solitary sex began to relax. In contrast to Dr. Drake's advice, by 1953 a self-help book recommended that solitary sex should be viewed as "a normal and healthy act for a person of any age," rather than a practice in need of social control. "What happened?" Comfort (1967) ponders. "One is still at a loss for an explanation of the outburst – one of the most astonishing floods of psychologically damaging medical nonsense in history had somehow been unleashed." Yet, by the mid-twentieth century, this influence seemed to wane. Masturbation was redefined as a source of pleasure, joy, and social autonomy.

Kinsey's numbers only confirmed the trend. In 1948, Kinsey published *Sexual Behavior in the Human Male*, followed by *Sexual Behavior in the Human Female* in 1953. Kinsey's team found that 92 percent of males reported that they had masturbated. Among females, 62 percent reported that they had masturbated, with 45 percent reporting that they could reach orgasm within 3 minutes. Solitary sex was found to be the most important sexual outlet for single females and a close second for married females. A large majority of women (84 percent) reported clitoral stimulation, while 20 percent reported using artificial objects for vaginal insertion. Additionally, 2 percent reported that they simply used fantasy to reach orgasm.

Kinsey's research revealed a striking shift in social mores. After all, for many years, women had been told that the only way to find sexual pleasure was through vaginal orgasm. Freud suggested that women should reject anything else. Yet as the 1960s turned into the 1970s, the women's movement pointed out that clitoral orgasm offered new forms of pleasure and autonomy from patriarchy. For some, this included the rejection of men, as the penis lost its exclusivity as a phallus. For women's liberationists, embracing masturbation was a way to discover a better, less sexist society.

The practice of solitary sex gained new importance with the advent of AIDS, as gay men created "jack-off" (JO) clubs that functioned as safe alternatives to both disease and repressive heterosexual norms. Gay men across the US organized JO parties, where men could come together to build communities around pleasure. For many, masturbation offered nothing less than the realization of the essential human right to sexual happiness.

The cultural history of solitary sex is a story of the relation of the body to passion, desire, and selfhood. Masturbation is intimately bound up with the power to create, the process of self-making, and cultural combat against authoritarian control. This struggle is reflected in the works of a number of twentieth-century artists. For example, the work of Philip Roth, Egon Schiele, Vitto Acconci, and Lynda Benglis offer telling images of the relation between creativity, masturbation, selfhood, and the rejection of social control. Part of the reason for the ongoing debate surrounding masturbation is the insight that for many, the practice is a step toward self-discovery, part of the making of the modern, secular self. The release from the shackles of prohibition around solitary sex opened up a new chapter in the history of sexuality. Yet the

struggle was not without its emotional price. Throughout the twentieth century, guilt and other psychological costs replaced the mechanisms of religious and social control that had governed the practice in ages past. While not as terrifying as madness and death, anxiety and stigma remain vexing.

Historical research on masturbation has addressed questions concerning its legitimacy as a form of sexual exploration and expression. Future research might include questions about the relationship between masturbation fantasies, sexual activity, use of technology, gender, and sexual orientation. What is the relationship between masturbation, technology, and personal identity in the age of the Internet and Viagra? Donna Haraway suggests that the question "Who am I?" must be answered within the context of such technology-impacted environments. It is clear that technology has transformed the ways people practice, understand, and think about sexuality. The use of new technologies for sexual activity – including masturbation – must be reconciled with questions about the connections between real life, fantasy, and social identity (Waskul 2003).

SEE ALSO: Body and Sexuality; Cybersexualities and Virtual Sexuality; Freud, Sigmund; Kinsey, Alfred; Safer Sex; Sexual Practices; Sexuality Research: History

REFERENCES AND SUGGESTED READINGS

Comfort, A. (1967) *The Anxiety Makers: Some Curious Preoccupations of the Medical Profession*. Delta, New York.

Hall, D. E. (2003) *Queer Theories*. Palgrave Macmillan, New York.

Haraway, D. J. (1991) *Simians, Cyborgs, and Women: The Reinvention of Nature*. Routledge, New York.

Jackson, L. (2002) Jacks of Color: An Oral History. In: Shepard, B. & Hayduck, R. (Eds.), *From ACT UP to the WTO: Urban Protest and Community Building in the Era of Globalization*. Verso, New York.

Kinsey, A. C. et al. (1998 [1948]) *Sexual Behavior in the Human Male*. Indiana University Press, Bloomington; W. B. Saunders, Philadelphia.

Kinsey, A. C. et al. (1998 [1953]) *Sexual Behavior in the Human Female*. Indiana University Press, Bloomington; W. B. Saunders, Philadelphia.

Kinsey Institute (n.d.) Data from Alfred Kinsey's Studies. Masturbation. Online. www.indiana.edu/~kinsey/research/ak-data.html#masturbation.

Laqueur, T. W. (2003) *Solitary Sex: A Cultural History of Masturbation*. MIT Press/Zone Books, Cambridge, MA.

Waskul, D. (2003) *Self Games and Body Play: Personhood and Online Chat and Cybersex*. Peter Lang, New York.

material culture

Tim Dant

Material culture refers to the physical stuff that human beings surround themselves with and which has meaning for the members of a cultural group. Mostly this "stuff" is things that are made within a society, but sometimes it is gathered directly from the natural world or recovered from past or distant cultures. It can be contrasted with other cultural forms such as ideas, images, practices, beliefs, and language that can be treated as independent from any specific material substance. The clothes, tools, utensils, gadgets, ornaments, pictures, furniture, buildings, and equipment of a group of people are its material culture and for disciplines such as archeology and anthropology provide the raw data for understanding other societies. In recent years sociologists have begun to recognize that the ways that material things are incorporated into the culture shape the way that society works and communicates many of its features to individual members.

Jean Baudrillard's critique of Marx's analysis of production and exchange led him to explore how the "system of objects" circulates sign value within a society, articulating cultural distinctions and meanings. The uses of different materials such as wood or glass to create the atmosphere of interior spaces, the embedding of technology within "gadgets" and tools, how things extend the form and actions of the human body, and the relations between objects that are unique and those that are parts of series are all systems which shape the culture. The recent literature on the sociology of consumption has frequently recognized that material things are not only useful in themselves but can also be signs of social status and cultural location. A motorcar is much more than a functional transportation device because it encapsulates a set of cultural messages about the aesthetics, wealth, and technological values of a culture as well as the status of the individual who drives it.

The consumption of material stuff may locate individual identities within a culture (Csikszentmihalyi & Rochberg-Halton 1981), but it also threatens the environment and uses up scarce resources (Molotch 2003). The material stuff of a culture "co-evolves" not only with other stuff but also with human practices and systems of action (Shove 2003). Material objects are involved in interactions between human beings, providing a topic as well as a resource for constructing meaning (Hindmarsh & Heath 2003). But the embodied "material interaction" directly between individual humans and the stuff around them also releases the cultural meanings and practices embedded in the materiality of that stuff (Dant 2005).

SEE ALSO: Consumption; Materialism; Technology, Science, and Culture

REFERENCES AND SUGGESTED READINGS

Baudrillard, J. (1996) *The System of Objects*. Verso, London.

Csikszentmihalyi, M. & Rochberg-Halton, E. (1981) *The Meaning of Things*. Cambridge University Press, Cambridge.

Dant, T. (2005) *Materiality and Society*. Open University Press, Maidenhead.

Hindmarsh, J. & Heath, C. (2003) Transcending the Object in Embodied Interaction. In: Coupland, J. & Gwyn, R. (Eds.), *Discourse, the Body, and Identity*. Palgrave, Basingstoke.

Molotch, H. (2003) *Where Stuff Comes From*. Routledge, New York.

Shove, E. (2003) *Comfort, Cleanliness, and Convenience*. Berg, Oxford.

materialism

Walda Katz-Fishman, Ralph Gomes, and Jerome Scott

"It is not the consciousness of men [and women] that determines their being, but, on the contrary, their social being that determines their consciousness" (Marx & Engels 1986: 182).

Materialism is the philosophy that explains the nature of reality and the world – physical, social, cultural, etc. – in terms of matter. It asserts that reality and the universe are first and foremost material; they exist outside of human thought and ideas and are independent of the human mind. The human intellect can come to know the world of matter through experience and sense perception and can interact and shape the material world; but the world of material existence is primary. Philosophical materialism stands in opposition to the philosophy of idealism that states that ideas, thought, and mind are the essential nature of all reality and the world of matter is a reflection of mind, thought, and ideas.

Materialism, the philosophical outlook of science, has been an important philosophy in eras of scientific development in ancient times as early as the fourth century BCE among Greek philosophers (e.g., Epicurus and even Aristotle), and in modern times in the seventeenth and eighteenth centuries in Isaac Newton's scientific study of nature and the emerging social science of the Enlightenment *Philosophes*.

The economic, political, social, and intellectual ferment of the 1700s and 1800s gave rise to several streams of social thought informed by the materialist view of the world and the scientific method. The most important of these streams are the mechanical materialism of Feuerbach and especially the dialectical and historical materialism (i.e., historical materialism) of Marx and Engels. The empiricism and positivism of Saint-Simon, Comte, and Durkheim presented itself as science based in materialist methodology, but was actually rooted in philosophical idealism.

Mechanical materialism analyzes social life and even idea systems such as religion in terms of material conditions, but is static in its overall worldview and offers no theory of human agency or future beyond what was then emerging (i.e., industrial capitalism). Structures and processes of capitalism are examined – sometimes critically – and incremental quantitative changes of social reform may occur, but within mechanical materialist analysis qualitative transformation is not possible.

Historical materialism critically analyzes capitalism and its antecedents. But unlike other forms of materialism and social theory, it views the structures and processes of capitalism as a transient stage of human social development giving way to its negation through contradictions and antagonisms that give rise to socialism and communism. It embodies a dialectical image of the social world and a dialectical method in which theory and analysis are tested in experience and practice, including social and class struggle. Historical materialism contains a developed theory of political economy, the state, and ideology, as well as an analysis of agency and qualitative revolutionary social and historical transformation in which those classes, nations, peoples, and genders most oppressed and exploited organize themselves politically to reorganize society in their own interests through a process of consciousness, vision, and strategy.

Empiricism and positivism examine society and culture through the facts or data of sensory observation and perception. Only those data gathered through the senses exist as reality and as scientific truth. Belief in the existence of a material objective external world is suspended and the sense perceptions of that material reality in fact become the "reality." This limits the outlook of empiricism and positivism to the sense observations of social life, to those data immediately perceivable in the present moment of rising market capitalism or perhaps perceived and recorded in the past. Structures and processes of development and transformation not directly observable do not exist in empiricist and positivist analysis. There is no analysis of social change and the future beyond what is incremental and quantitative.

While many early philosophers and social thinkers grounded their understanding of social life in materialist philosophy, the centrality of materialism in shaping modern social theory arose in the eighteenth and nineteenth centuries. This was the age of rationality, science, and social transformation that gave rise to machine production, global markets, urban centers, and industrial capitalism, to Enlightenment thought and political revolutions overturning feudal monarchies and establishing constitutional, electoral, and representative political forms.

In this context, Enlightenment thinkers, who were challenging the pure rationality of Descartes and the hegemony of the Catholic Church in feudal society, rooted their scientific analysis, their theory and laws of social development in the materialist philosophy of the natural and physical sciences of the day – a mechanical materialism expressed in Newtonian laws of the natural universe. Montesquieu, Rousseau, and Wollstonecraft all presented their interpretation of past societies and the revolutionary process. This scientific and materialist understanding of the social world was quickly challenged by the romantic conservative reaction. It grounded its attack on science and the nascent social science of the day in the philosophical idealism of Hume, Kant, Burke, and Hegel, as well as the Catholic counter-revolution of Louis de Bonald and Joseph de Maistre.

It was a group of intellectuals – the Young Hegelians, including Feuerbach, Marx, and Engels – who studied Hegel's dialectical idealist philosophy of history and who broke with Hegel around the question of idealism versus materialism as the essential nature of reality and the driving force of social and historical development. Feuerbach offered an understanding of the social world in material terms, but with no dynamic process for social change. Marx and Engels embraced the dialectics of Hegel, but turned his analysis "on its head," locating reality and the forces of social transformation in the material conditions of the production and reproduction of social life and class struggle.

Together, Hegelian dialectics, Feuerbach's materialism, and the labor theory of value based on a critique of Adam Smith's and David Ricardo's understanding of labor, value, markets, and profit formed the basis of a new worldview. Historical materialism, often referred to as Marxism, is dialectical materialism applied to society, history, and the long struggle for the liberation of humanity from all forms of class exploitation and political and cultural oppression and war. It answers the question of how societies and their people produce and distribute the necessaries of life and reproduce themselves.

External material conditions are the primary forces of social life and history. The foundation of society are the forces of production (i.e., the tools and technology of production, communication, transport, etc.), the reproduction of human labor through various forms of kinship and family, and the relations of production – the emergence of private property, class relations, power relations and state forms, patriarchy, colonialism and imperialism, and white supremacy, etc. From this real foundation, the mode of production, the superstructure arises: ideas and culture, ideology, spiritual life, and various social institutions. Both the forces and relations of production are dynamic, with the forces being the most dynamic. Essential to historical materialism is human collective agency and struggle that creates the possibilities of quantitative change and qualitative or revolutionary transformation under certain objective and subjective conditions of technology, consciousness, and political organization.

From the time of Marx and Engels's critique of Hegel and Feuerbach and their development of historical materialism as a revolutionary theory, method, and practice, both forms of materialist social analysis have continued, as have empiricist and positivist theory and methods.

Social theory and research in the mechanical materialist tradition remains an important tendency in sociology. It examines materially based social problems, especially various forms of social inequality and domination. It may situate them within capitalist political economy and ideology and call for legal reforms, but systemic change to resolve these problems is not considered. This examination also often employs empiricist and positivist methods of research, further distancing this form of materialist social analysis from historical materialism. Analytic (non-Marxian) conflict theory focusing on gender, race, and class inequality is a key expression and includes, for example, Janet Chafetz's work on gender, Charles Willie's work on race, and Randall Collin's work on stratification.

Historical materialism as a revolutionary theory and practice in the twentieth century has been located primarily in political struggles and building socialist states outside the academy. Examples of political leaders who have done this intellectual and practical work include V. I. Lenin in Russia, Mao Zedong in China,

Ho Chi Minh in Vietnam, and Ernesto "Che" Guevara and Fidel Castro in Cuba.

Throughout the twentieth century scholars and scholar activists have conducted materialist analysis and engaged in practice along the continuum from a critical but non-revolutionary materialism to historical materialism. We know them in sociology as Marxists, neo-Marxists, radical and critical sociologists, underdevelopment and world-systems sociologists, materialist feminists, race-class-gender and intersectionality sociologists, globalization sociologists, and most recently public sociologists.

In the first half of the twentieth century some of the best-known of these sociologists included W. E. B. Du Bois, Oliver Cox, and E. Franklin Frazier on race and class; Anna Julia Cooper, Jane Addams, the Grimke sisters, and Ida Wells Barnett on gender, race, and class; Clara Zetkin and Alexandra Kollontai on patriarchy and class; Antonio Gramsci and Georg Lukács on ideology and class consciousness; the Frankfurt School on the critique of capitalist society, culture, and science; and C. Wright Mills on the power elite.

By mid-century, despite McCarthyism and anti-communism in the US, the rising social movements (e.g., black freedom struggle and modern civil rights, anti-Vietnam War, women's rights and sexual equality, and anti-colonial and national liberation struggles globally) created renewed interest in Marxism as theory and practice. In North America, graduate students and a few professor activists formed the sociology liberation movement in 1969 that gave birth to the Radical Caucus and publication of *The Insurgent Sociologist* that same year. In 1975 the American Sociological Association recognized and institutionalized radical and Marxist analysis with the formation of the Marxist Sociology Section; and in 1987 *The Insurgent* became *Critical Sociology*, suggesting a shift in ideology and practice.

During the next several decades many more scholars worked in the tradition along the critical materialist and historical materialist continuum. Among them were Louis Althusser, Nicos Poulantzas, Ralph Miliband, and William Domhoff on the state and the ruling class; Harry Braverman and Paul Baran and Paul Sweezy on the exploitation of service sector workers and monopoly capitalism; Frantz Fanon, Claude Ake, and Walter Rodney on colonialism, imperialism, and liberation struggles; Albert Szymanski and Goran Thernborn on class struggle and the state.

Over the last few decades of the twentieth and early twenty-first centuries, scholars and scholar activists have continued to work in the critical and historical materialist frameworks. They include Immanuel Wallerstein and Terence K. Hopkins on capitalist world systems; Erik Olin Wright and Edna Bonacich on labor and class analysis, especially empirical studies; Patricia Hill Collins on intersectionality of race-gender-class oppressions; Dorothy Smith, Maria Mies, Rose Brewer, and Martha Gimenez on a materialist analysis of race-gender-class; James Petras, Berch Berberoglu, and Samir Amin on imperialism and the state; Rod Bush on race and class struggles; Michael Burawoy on public sociology; and Anthony Giddens, Manuel Castells, Douglas Kellner, and William Robinson on technology, the information age, and twenty-first century globalization.

In the early twenty-first century materialist sociologists are especially looking at the new realities of globalization – capitalism in the age of electronics – and neoliberalism. This includes the technological revolution; deepening inequality, white supremacy, and sexism; growing polarization of wealth and poverty among classes, genders, peoples, races, and nations; the slashing of the social safety net for poor and oppressed peoples the world over; new forms of the state, ideology, social control, and militarism; ecological crises; emerging social movements for justice, equality, and popular democracy; and bottom-up movement processes of consciousness, vision, and strategy.

In identifying and conducting materialist sociology, it is not what is being examined, but the explanatory theory and its philosophical principles that are key. Thus, ideology, culture, the state, etc. can be analyzed from a materialist perspective. What makes it materialist is linking these phenomena to the material conditions of society and the material class interests of various groups and classes in maintaining the status quo, reforming it, or qualitatively transforming the whole system. In its historical materialist expression it asks and seeks to answer the question where in their historical development are society and the political process of human liberation led by those most marginalized, impoverished, and oppressed. Here human liberation means the abolition of all forms of private productive property, total reorganization of society, freedom from all forms of exploitation and oppression – class, gender, nationality, race, etc. – and building a cooperative, egalitarian, and peaceful global society.

Mechanical and critical to historical materialist forms of social analysis from analytic conflict sociology, Marxism, and neo-Marxism, various race–class–gender and public sociologies, to studies of today's globalization and its bottom-up anti-capitalist revolutionary movements, will continue to be developed. Throughout history historical materialists have lifted up as their mantra in response to mechanical materialists Marx's famous eleventh thesis on Feuerbach: "The philosophers have only *interpreted* the world, in various ways; the point however is to *change* it" (Marx & Engels 1986: 30). What the twenty-first century holds we will come to know through historical materialist analysis of and participation in the processes of political struggle and social transformation.

SEE ALSO: Globalization, Consumption and; Intersectionality; Marxism and Sociology; Materialist Feminisms

REFERENCES AND SUGGESTED READINGS

Berberoglu, B. (1998) *An Introduction to Classical and Contemporary Social Theory: A Critical Perspective*, 2nd edn. General Hall, Dix Hills, NY.

Bush, R. (1999) *We Are Not What We Seem: Black Nationalism and Class Struggle in the American Century*. New York University Press, New York.

Hennessy, R. & Ingraham, C. (Eds.) (1997) *Materialist Feminism: A Reader in Class, Difference, and Women's Lives*. Routledge, New York.

Katz-Fishman, W. & Scott, J. (2004) A Movement Rising. In: *An Invitation to Public Sociology*. American Sociological Association, Washington, DC, pp. 53–5.

Katz-Fishman, W. & Scott, J. (2005) Global Capitalism, Class Struggle, and Social Transformation. In: Berberoglu, B. (Ed.), *Globalization and Change: The Transformation of Global Capitalism*. Lexington Books, Lanham, MD, pp. 123–40.

Keat, R. & Urry, J. (1975) *Social Theory as Science*. Routledege & Kegan Paul, Boston.

Kivisto, P. (Ed.) (2001) *Social Theory: Roots and Branches (Readings)*. Roxbury, Los Angeles.

Marx, K. & Engels, F. (1986) *Selected Works*. International Publishers, New York.

Oppenheimer, M., Murray, M., & Levine, R. (Eds.) (1991) *Radical Sociologists and the Movement: Experiences, Lessons, and Legacies*. Temple University Press, Philadelphia.

Ritzer, G. & Goodman, D. (2004) *Modern Sociological Theory*, 6th edn. McGraw Hill, New York.

Zeitlin. I. (2001) *Ideology and the Development of Sociological Theory*, 7th edn. Prentice-Hall, Upper Saddle River, NJ.

materialist feminisms

Nilufer Isvan

A materialist feminist research program is one that places special emphasis on the material conditions underlying gender inequality. Scholars within this tradition may vary in their definition of the line of demarcation and conceptual relationships between material and ideological spheres, but most would agree that the organization of production is central to material reality. Although all feminist scholars acknowledge the importance of women's economic status, materialist feminist approaches are distinguished by the centrality and causal precedence ascribed to material forces over ideational ones in explaining women's oppression.

One consequence of this theoretical orientation is an emphasis on social class. The use of "women" and "men" as unified analytic categories is avoided, since individuals from different class backgrounds have differential access to power, autonomy, and other social resources. The specific mechanisms of gender oppression depend on women's class position, as do the conditions of their emancipation. Overlaps between the interests of some women and some oppressed men are acknowledged, resulting in political stances supportive of strategic alliances with some categories of men.

This brand of feminism is the outcome of engagements with the Marxist tradition. On one hand, it uses insights from feminist theory to challenge the gender-blind aspects of Marxist analysis. On the other, it uses Marxian methods to criticize liberal and radical feminisms for their lack of attention to differences *among* women and their failure to develop a systematic critique of capitalism. It is, in this sense, a doubly critical discourse.

Feminist scholarship that meets these criteria is characterized as "materialist," "Marxist," or "socialist," often interchangeably. Scholars who regard themselves as working within the Marxist tradition while revising some of its features within a feminist agenda usually characterize their work as Marxist-feminist. Those who consider their revisions to be so substantial as to alter the core elements of Marxism tend to shy away from this label. If they consider the critique of capitalism to be vital to their work or labor activism to be central to their political agenda, they may prefer the label socialist-feminist. On the whole, there is no consensus among sociologists on choice of label; whether a feminist's work is hyphenated as materialist, Marxist, or socialist is generally a function of personal or political preference rather than any formally definable theoretical criteria.

INTELLECTUAL ORIGINS

As noted by Hartmann (1981) and other contributors to the same volume, feminism's encounter with Marxism has been at once productive and problematic. Marx's analysis from the standpoint of the oppressed, his investigation of the mechanisms of exploitation, and his emancipatory political agenda provided fruitful models for feminists. Materialist feminisms are projects to reshape Marxist categories to better accommodate women's realities. Women's oppressed status, though acknowledged, appears in Marx's schema as a direct consequence of the asymmetrical relations of production. Thus, the emancipation of women is assumed to follow automatically from the emancipation of the worker. In subsuming kinship, marriage, and, at a more general level, the social relations of reproduction under the logic of production, this framework poses problems for feminist scholarship, for it leaves under-theorized precisely those areas of social reality that are the primary loci of women's lives. Consequently, much of

materialist feminist scholarship is concerned with bringing the sphere of reproduction into theoretical focus and highlighting its (partial) autonomy, while retaining Marx's insights into the vital role of production relations in shaping social reality.

Efforts to theorize reproduction within a materialist framework predate feminist interventions. During his later years, Marx himself grew increasingly dissatisfied with his theoretical neglect of family and kinship, as evidenced by his notes and marginalia on ethnographies such as Morgan's *Ancient Society*. Though he never published this research, his notes on Morgan constitute the core of Engels's *The Origin of the Family, Private Property and the State*, published in 1884 shortly after Marx's death.

In *Origin*, Engels develops a historical materialist analysis linking production, reproduction, and governance, conceptualizing reproduction as a determining force equal in importance to production. Although many of his conclusions have been severely challenged on both anthropological and feminist grounds, his definition of historical materialism is still widely embraced by materialist feminists: "The determining factor in history is, in the final instance, the production and reproduction of immediate life. This, again, is of a twofold character: on the one side, the production of the means of existence . . . and the tools necessary for that production; on the other side, the production of human beings themselves, the propagation of the species."

The production/reproduction link was further developed during the 1970s. In her classic work, *Women's Role in Economic Development* (1970), Ester Boserup demonstrated a historical correlation between types of farming and systems of family/gender. The British anthropologist Jack Goody (1976) further developed the theoretical implications of her theory.

Revisions to Marxism proposed by European "articulationists" are also significant in this context. This body of work asserts that at any given historical moment several modes of production coexist through articulations with each other and with the dominant mode, and identifies reproduction as the site of this articulation (Wolpe 1980; Meillassoux 1981). These revisions, combined with the notion of a domestic (or kin-based) mode of production developed by Marxist anthropologists, represent moves away from Marx's historicism, reductionism, and economic determinism. They helped set the stage for historical materialist analyses that problematized the articulation of capitalism and patriarchy.

THEORETICAL CONTRIBUTIONS

Marxist critiques of liberal feminism date back to the turn of the twentieth century. Socialist feminists of the era attacked bourgeois suffragists for their collusion with established political institutions, their support of property restrictions on voting rights, and their lack of attention to the double oppression of working-class women. Activists such as August Bebel and Clara Zetkin in Germany, Alexandra Kollontai and Nadezhda Krupskaya in Russia, Sylvia Pankhurst in England, and Emma Goldman and Margaret Sanger in the US, were leaders in both socialist and women's organizations. They are largely responsible for the inclusion of issues such as women's working conditions and labor organization, birth control, maternity insurance, and the socialization of childcare and domestic work in socialist platforms of this era. However, beliefs about the power of socialism to bring about the total emancipation of women were still widespread within these circles. Consequently, a feminist critique of Marxist doctrine did not emerge within the social movements of this era. In fact, most of the early socialist feminists were staunch anti-revisionists.

The first concerted efforts to revise Marxist theory from a feminist standpoint came from European feminists of the New Left during the 1960s and 1970s, when materialist feminism emerged as a doubly critical discourse. Having witnessed Stalinism, socialists of this era were more open to doctrinal revisions than their earlier counterparts. Likewise, the feminists among them were no longer as hopeful that socialism alone could offer a solution to women's oppression. Furthermore, the left's preoccupation with class to the exclusion of gender as a dimension of oppression was a source of disillusionment for these feminists.

Thus, the initial contributions to materialist feminism, such as Juliet Mitchell's (1966) seminal *New Left Review* essay and Christine Delphy's *Close to Home* (1984), were received with interest by feminists and Marxists alike. Mitchell's article attacked socialism for its failure to bring about women's emancipation, and argued that analyses of women's role in production were not sufficient for a truly materialist feminism. In addition, she maintained, Marxist feminists needed to problematize the psychosexual foundations of gender relations, which would require a fundamental revision of Marxist theory.

DOMESTIC LABOR

In an influential article, Benston (1979) proposed domestic production as the material base of women's oppression, initiating a debate about how best to insert housework and childcare into Marx's model of capitalism (for an overview of the debate, see Molyneux 1979). On the whole, these interventions are feminist corrections to Marx's schema using Marxist logic, without problematizing the psychosexual foundations of gender. Nonetheless, they made a major contribution to feminist and Marxist theories by bringing domestic labor under analytic scrutiny.

DUAL SYSTEMS

The dual systems approach is a product of efforts to integrate the psychosexual forces underlying gender relations and the cultural underpinnings of kinship into materialist analyses. Having its origins in Mitchell's *Psychoanalysis and Feminism* (1975), and best represented in the US by Zillah Eisenstein's (1979) early work, this line of theorizing regards women's oppression as a product of class (capitalism) and gender (patriarchy) simultaneously. Though patriarchy predates capitalism, it is argued, it has shaped capitalist development in important ways, reshaping itself in the process. Thus, women's emancipation requires two revolutions: an economic one to overthrow capitalism and a feminist one to end patriarchy. This approach has been criticized by some feminists for failing to specify sufficiently the mechanisms that link the two systems, and for treating patriarchy as a transhistorical entity.

The latter criticism is addressed by Rubin (1975). She defines a sex/gender system as the set of historically specific sociocultural mechanisms that transform biological sex into gendered subjectivities, and argues that historical analyses of gender need to use this general concept instead of patriarchy, which is one specific sex/gender system rather than an analytic concept. Similarly, in their *Feminism and Materialism: Women and Modes of Production* (1978), Kuhn and Wolpe outline a mode of analysis that relates modes of production to "the historically specific form of organization of procreation and sexuality."

Though the mechanisms that link capitalism and patriarchy have not been fully elaborated at the theoretical level, the dual systems approach inspired a number of valuable studies focusing on the interdependence between the two systems at specific empirical instances. Hartmann's *Signs* article "Capitalism, Patriarchy, and Job Segregation by Sex" (1976) and Seccombe's study of the historical construction of the male breadwinner norm published in *Social History* in 1986 are notable examples.

CLASS, RACE, AND SEXUALITY

The feminist challenge made important contributions to Marxist class analysis. By demonstrating the role of gender and kinship in reproducing class structures and mediating class outcomes, it cast serious doubt on the validity of economic determinism in predicting or explaining sociopolitical outcomes. The literature on class–gender interactions addresses issues such as gendered reinterpretations of Marxist class categories (Eisenstein 1979), the implications for women of living in class societies, gendered aspects of class formation, women's labor history, and class differences among women.

Especially in the US, where class discourse is intimately linked to race and ethnicity, it is by now customary to represent this interaction as a three-way relationship. Best exemplified by black feminist thought (Collins 1990), this "intersectionist" approach insists on the irreducibility of race to other dimensions of oppression. One of the most influential formulations of intersectionism is the Combahee River Collective's (2000) position statement, which included sexuality along with gender, class, and race as interacting sources of identity, power, and social status. This point was further developed by

queer materialists who combined insights from Marxism, materialist feminism, and queer theory to develop materially grounded analyses of heterosexism (D'Emilio 1983).

GLOBAL CAPITALISM

As first world deindustrialization and the consolidation of global capitalism accelerated during the 1980s, feminist scholarship focused on such phenomena as the relocation of manufacturing industries to the third world, the rise of free trade and export processing zones, and international labor migration. At the theoretical level, there were efforts to determine the impact of third world women's work on global capital accumulation. Building on the work of articulationist Marxists and the domestic labor debates of the 1970s, these studies argued that third world wage labor was rendered "inexpensive" through women's invisible and often unremunerated subsistence production. The value created by this domestic work, it was argued, met a large portion of wage workers' subsistence needs, reducing third world workers' need for cash income, and contributing to the profitability of manufacturing in the third world (Mies et al. 1988).

The 1980s also witnessed the publication of detailed empirical studies of the differential impact of global capitalism along the lines of class, race, gender, and world system location. *Women, Men, and the International Division of Labor* (1983) edited by Nash and Fernández-Kelly and Ong's *Spirits of Resistance and Capitalist Discipline: Factory Women in Malaysia* (1987) exemplify this literature.

THE POSTMODERN TURN

Materialist feminists responded along several lines to the rise to prominence of postmodern and poststructuralist approaches during the 1990s. First, there was a tendency to "take stock" of the entire materialist feminist project, resulting in several books, special journal issues, and anthologies critically reviewing past work and setting agendas for the future.

In line with the prevailing mistrust of determinist and totalizing explanations, there was a retreat from efforts to formulate a feminist version of Marxist theory. Relatedly, and partially in response to the conservatism of academic circles, fewer feminists self-identified as Marxist or socialist during this era, preferring instead to define their work as materialist. There was a reevaluation of the definition of "material," resulting in the inclusion of culture, representation, and meaning production within this sphere. Though written a decade earlier, Michèle Barrett's (1980) work was influential in these reformulations.

The role of discourse as mediator between material reality and individual subjectivity became a central focus of feminist analysis (Hennessy 1993). Growing awareness of the situated nature of knowledge brought the production of knowledge, including feminist knowledge, under critical scrutiny. Haraway's *Simians, Cyborgs, and Women* (1991) and the collection of essays edited by Mohanty, Russo, and Torres, *Third World Women and the Politics of Feminism* (1991), are notable examples of this mode of analysis.

The retrenchment of welfare capitalism and the decline of social services during the 1980s and 1990s drew feminists' attention to the political economy of privatized dependent care and its increased importance to survival (Folbre 2001). The uneasy fit between this category of work and prevailing definitions of production led some theorists to question the usefulness of the "productionist" paradigm for understanding women's relationship to material reality, and to advocate its replacement with a model more representative of the intersubjectivity that characterizes much of women's caregiving work in contemporary societies (Benhabib & Cornell 1987).

Feminist cultural materialism is a relatively new area of investigation that constitutes a productive source of new research. The theoretical connections among different dimensions of oppression are not yet fully explored, and materialist feminist work along intersectionist lines is likely to continue into the future. New reproductive technologies and advances in genetics pose important problems for women (not the least of which is a real danger of neo-eugenics), and abortion, gay marriage, and elderly care will also remain on political agendas for the foreseeable future, especially in the US. Newly emerging dimensions of globalization and especially those involving war, ethnic conflict, and terrorism are attracting increasing attention from feminist scholarship concerned with their gendered consequences. Establishing the material bases of these political struggles will challenge materialist feminists in the years to come.

SEE ALSO: Black Feminist Thought; Capitalism; Gender Oppression; Gender, Social Movements and; Marxism and Sociology; Materialism; Patriarchy

REFERENCES AND SUGGESTED READINGS

Barrett, M. (1980) *Women's Oppression Today: Problems in Marxist Feminist Analysis*. Verso, London.

Benhabib, S. & Cornell, D. (1987) Introduction: Beyond the Politics of Gender. In: Benhabib, S. & Cornell, D. (Eds.), *Feminism as Critique: On the Politics of Gender*. University of Minnesota, Minneapolis.

Benston, M. (1979) The Political Economy of Women's Liberation. *Monthly Review* 21(4): 13–27.

Collins, P. H. (1990) *Black Feminist Thought: Knowledge, Consciousness, and the Politics of Empowerment*. Unwin Hyman, Boston.

Combahee River Collective (2000 [1983]) The Combahee River Collective Statement. In: Smith, B. (Ed.), *Home Girls: A Black Feminist Anthology*. Rutgers University, New Brunswick, NJ, pp. 264–274.

D'Emilio, J. (1983) Capitalism and Gay Identity. In: Snitow, A., Stansell, C., & Thompson, S. (Eds.), *Powers of Desire: The Politics of Sexuality*. Monthly Review Press, New York, pp. 100–13.

Delphy, C. (1984 [1970]) *Close to Home: A Materialist Analysis of Women's Oppression*. Trans. D. Leonard. University of Massachusetts Press, Amherst.

Eisenstein, Z. (1979) Developing a Theory of Capitalist Patriarchy and Socialist Feminism. In: Eisenstein, Z. (Ed.), *Capitalist Patriarchy and the Case for Socialist Feminism*. Monthly Review Press, New York, pp. 5–40.

Folbre, N. (2001) *The Invisible Heart: Economics and Family Values*. New Press, New York.

Goody, J. (1976) *Production and Reproduction: A Comparative Study of the Domestic Domain*. Cambridge University Press, Cambridge.

Hansen, K. & Philipson, I. J. (Eds.) (1990) *Women, Class, and the Feminist Imagination: A Socialist-Feminist Reader*. Temple University Press, Philadelphia.

Hartmann, H. (1981) The Unhappy Marriage of Marxism and Feminism: Toward a More Progressive Union. In: Sargent, L. (Ed.), *Women and Revolution: A Discussion of the Unhappy Marriage of Marxism and Feminism*. South End Press, Boston.

Hennessy, R. (1993) *Materialist Feminism and the Politics of Discourse*. Routledge, New York.

Hennessy, R. & Ingraham, C. (Eds.) (1997) *Materialist Feminism: A Reader in Class, Difference, and Women's Lives*. Routledge, New York.

Landry, D. & MacLean, G. (1993) *Materialist Feminisms*. Blackwell, Oxford.

Meillassoux, C. (1981) *Maidens, Meal and Money: Capitalism and the Domestic Community*. Cambridge University Press, Cambridge.

Mies, M., Bennholdt-Thomsen, V., & von Werlhof, C. (1988) *Women: The Last Colony*. Zed Books, London.

Mitchell, J. (1966) Women: The Longest Revolution. *New Left Review* 40: 11–37.

Moi, T. & Radway, J. (Eds.) (1994) Materialist Feminism. Special issue *South Atlantic Quarterly* 93(4).

Molyneux, M. (1979) Beyond the Domestic Labour Debate. *New Left Review* 116: 3–27.

Rubin, G. (1975) The Traffic in Women: Notes on the "Political Economy" of Sex. In: Reiter, R. R. (Ed.), *Toward an Anthropology of Women*. Monthly Review Press, New York, pp. 157–210.

Sayers, J., Evans, M., & Redclift, N. (Eds.) (1987) *Engels Revisited: New Feminist Essays*. Tavistock, London.

Vogel, L. (1995) *Woman Questions: Essays for a Materialist Feminism*. Routledge, New York.

Wolpe, H. (Ed.) (1980) *The Articulation of Modes of Production: Essays from Economy and Society*. Routledge, London.

materiality and scientific practice

Ragna Zeiss

Studies of scientific practice were the first to investigate scientific practice and science-in-the-making empirically, something that had not been done by philosophers and historians of science. The outcomes of these studies opposed the standard view of science and instead showed how science and scientific knowledge are produced locally and scientists, instruments, computers, and other heterogeneous elements have to work together in order to co-construct science. They have stressed the importance of materiality in scientific practice and provided material for debate between different ways of studying materiality.

Science had long been considered as an activity that provides us with information about the world "out there." In other words, science tells us about how the world really is and delivers true explanations of inquiry-independent phenomena. In the 1960s the view of science as a rational and universal process that provides us with the "truth" began to change. Kuhn (1996) argued that "facts" were the outcomes of negotiations between scientists. These negotiations took place within a "paradigm" in which agreement existed about the methods that should be followed and the kinds of knowledge that were scientific. Innovative knowledge that would not fit in the contemporary paradigm could only be accepted if scientists were persuasive enough to convince others of their findings. Partly building on the work of Kuhn, some sociologists (but also, for example, anthropologists and historians) started to regard science as deeply embedded in society. This allowed them to investigate science as a social process.

Examples of studies of scientific practice are "laboratory studies." These occurred in the late 1970s. By inserting themselves into a laboratory, scholars of sociology (and others) participated and observed the practices inside laboratories – *the* place where scientific knowledge is produced. By writing ethnographies of science, they showed that knowledge construction is not a purely rational process. Instead, scientific practice can be rather "messy." Knowledge production is a process in which nonsolid and uncertain ingredients, day-to-day, and contingent factors play a role. An experiment is carried out at a particular time in a particular setting. It is performed by people who have certain interests and ideas about which parameters and materials are important and which are not. What experiments and how experiments are carried out thus depend on these aspects in addition to issues like the availability and costs of particular equipment. This also means that the outcome of these experiments, science, is not universal from the start. Latour (1988) illustrates this by analyzing the "fact" that microbes can cause disease.

Louis Pasteur was able to isolate microbes and show visible colonies of them in his laboratory, something that would have been impossible outside a laboratory. With the help of the instruments in the laboratory he was able to define what he regarded as a microbe and what was not. By giving public demonstrations he tried to convince others that microbes indeed cause disease. The public demonstrations were, in a sense, extended laboratories, since the same conditions as in the laboratory had to apply in order to obtain the same results. It was only when Pasteur convinced other scientists, doctors, and other groups that the existence of the microbe and it being the cause of disease became taken for granted and a "fact." Apart from illustrating that scientific outcomes are made into universal facts through hard work, this example has also shown that science can be regarded as a process of construction rather than description. In this process of construction, materiality plays an important role.

This is illustrated by Zeiss (2004). When the quality of our drinking water is tested, it is not the water "out there" that is brought into the laboratory to be tested. The water that is taken "out there" is put into sample bottles of various materials and with various preservatives to prevent the specific parameters for which the water has to be tested from changing. A bottle for a bacteriological sample contains a preservative that neutralizes the chlorine in the water. If this preservative were absent, the chlorine would decrease or extinguish the bacteria population and the bacteria population could no longer be analyzed when the sample arrived at the laboratory. In this process, however, other parameters – for which this specific sample will *not* be tested – will change or be eliminated. The water that was taken from a tap has thus in a certain sense been purified in order to be suitable for testing in a laboratory. The laboratory therefore does not study the water as it is "out there," just as other laboratories do not study nature as it is "out there."

The knowledge that science produces, whether this is inside or outside laboratories, is always mediated by perceptions and instruments. Scientists, instruments, and natural objects have to adjust to each other and take each other into account for scientific knowledge to be produced. In other words, they are all reconfigured in a specific practice to produce knowledge (e.g., water quality) together. The process of knowledge production is constitutive for what we know reality to be; scientists can therefore be said to construct rather than describe nature. This has (theoretical) consequences: it means that we cannot know nature as it is. However, this is not to say that scientific knowledge would therefore be less valuable. The specific knowledge about water quality that can be obtained through detailed analyses with technological instruments cannot be obtained in a different way. Scientists, the water, the sample bottles, and the measurement instruments together make knowledge production possible; they co-construct scientific knowledge.

Laboratory studies have been celebrated for being the first to explore scientific practice as it is and in real time. They did not focus on the context of scientific practice, but investigated how the content of scientific knowledge is produced. Constructivism and the widespread use of ethnographic studies in social studies of science and technology are important outcomes of laboratory studies. The stress on materiality in the production of scientific knowledge is another important result. How materiality can or should be analyzed theoretically has however been subject to debate. An example can clarify this.

It happens that experiments do not work, the scientist does not succeed in getting the material to work, the material does not do what it is supposed to do: the material resists. This has frequently been described in laboratory studies. Some would argue that it is not possible to grant material artifacts agency, since this would imply an essentialist – or technological determinist – assumption of a technological or material core in which the intrinsic properties of the material can be found. They do not deny that material (artifacts) can have constraining influences upon actors, but they contend that these constraints can be known as such: they are always subject to interpretation. In their eyes, materiality (and scientific practices) can only be studied through looking at accounts of these constraints and through exploring why some accounts are more convincing than others (for this approach to materiality, see Grint & Woolgar 1997). Scientists study purified and selected parts of nature or representations of nature in the form of diagrams, images, and graphs. Ethnographers entering the laboratory are not able to distinguish the same characteristics of, or patterns in, the material as the scientists distinguish. Scientists have learned to read the material in specific ways – they distinguish between what is relevant to see and what is irrelevant. They cannot deal with materiality as it is and neither can social scientists. According to Grint and Woolgar (1997), material resistances have to be interpreted and once they have been interpreted, the social world has been entered in which one's disciplinary background and the thoughts of previous scientists become important.

Others have argued that reducing materiality to accounts does not do justice to the role of materiality. They see work in laboratories as a process of active interaction with materiality. Actor-network theory (ANT) does not want to make a distinction between the technical and the social, since what counts as human and non-human is in itself a construction. ANT studies often follow an actor (or actant) in a network of social and technical elements with which the actor can make alliances and which are constitutive of science (e.g., Louis Pasteur, above). The mangle of practice approach (Pickering 1995) proposes to take material agency seriously in a different way. Pickering argues that the contours of material agency are never decisively known in advance. Instead, scientists have a continuous job to try "tuning" into the material agency. Material agency can then be *temporally emergent* in practice. Whereas ANT sees humans and non-humans as symmetric and interchangeable, Pickering argues that humans cannot be substituted for machines, especially since humans have intentions, goals, and plans that have to be taken into account. These intentions and possible futures are intertwined with existing ideas and scientific results and can also be changed by tuning. The process of tuning refers to a way of dealing with the resistance of the material by accommodating it and revising the goals, intentions, and/or material form of the machine. Terms similar to "tuning" are "tinkering" (Knorr Cetina 1981) and "bricolage" (Latour & Woolgar 1986), but these have less (explicit) connotations to theoretical ways of dealing with the issue of materiality.

SEE ALSO: Actor-Network Theory; Actor-Network Theory, Actants; Laboratory Studies and the World of the Scientific Lab; Realism and Relativism: Truth and Objectivity; Science, Ethnographic Studies of; Science, Social Construction of; Scientific Knowledge, Sociology of

REFERENCES AND SUGGESTED READINGS

Grint, K. & Woolgar, S. (1997) *The Machine at Work: Technology, Work and Organization.* Polity Press, Cambridge.

Knorr Cetina, K. (1981) *The Manufacture of Knowledge: An Essay in the Constructivist and Contextual Nature of Science.* Pergamon, Oxford.

Knorr Cetina, K. (1995) Laboratory Studies: The Cultural Approach to the Study of Science. In: Jasanoff, S., Markle, G. E., Petersen, J. C., & Pinch, T. (Eds.), *Handbook of Science and Technology Studies.* Sage, Thousand Oaks, CA, pp. 140–66.

Kuhn, T. S. (1996 [1962]) *The Structure of Scientific Revolutions.* University of Chicago Press, Chicago.

Latour, B. (1988) *The Pasteurization of France.* Harvard University Press, Cambridge, MA.

Latour, B. & Woolgar, S. (1986) *Laboratory Life: The Construction of Scientific Facts.* Princeton University Press, Princeton.

Pickering, A. (1995) *The Mangle of Practice: Time, Agency, and Science.* University of Chicago Press, Chicago.

Zeiss, R. (2004) Standardizing Materiality: Tracking Co-Constructed Relationships between Quality Standards and Materiality in the English Water Industry. Dissertation, University of York.

maternalism

Susan E. Chase

Maternalism has three meanings. First, it refers to social practices grounded in women's concern for children, especially when those practices extend beyond the home into community and/or political arenas. Maternalism has been used particularly to describe the activities of Progressive-era social reformers who shaped the emerging welfare states' policies concerning mothers and children. It has also been used to describe the activities of many women's clubs, associations, organizations, and social movements, from the nineteenth century to the present, that aim(ed) to improve the quality of children's lives. Second, maternalism refers to discourse that highlights women's connection to and responsibility for children and that emphasizes differences (which may be conceived either as biologically based or as socially conditioned) between men's and women's contributions to family and society. This discourse animates many of the social practices listed above, but it can also infuse institutions or systems, such as the welfare state itself. Maternal discourse often intersects with class, racial, national, or religious interests. Third, maternalism is sometimes used to describe feminist theory that critiques the cultural devaluation of mothering and that articulates the contributions of maternal practice to social and political life.

In the nineteenth and early twentieth centuries, feminists, women reformers, and women club members generally took for granted that women's responsibilities included mothering and other domestic tasks. By contrast, feminists of the 1960s, 1970s, and 1980s treated motherhood as a socially and historically specific institution requiring critical analysis. By the 1990s, feminist historians and social scientists had produced a substantial body of research on the (mostly) middle-class Progressive-era women whose work laid the foundation for welfare states in North America and Europe. In the United States, these reforms included the establishment of mothers' pensions, child labor laws, juvenile courts, protective legislation for women workers, public health nursing for mothers and infants, and the Children's Bureau.

Whether or not they had children of their own, these Progressive-era reformers viewed themselves as enacting maternal responsibilities in relation to and on behalf of other women and their children. Using maternalist discourse, they not only argued for reforms in other women's and children's interests, they also defended their incursion into occupational and political arenas from which women had been excluded. Before women won the right to vote, and thus the right to participate directly in the political process, maternalist discourse was a powerful tool for mobilizing women and a persuasive defense of women's political activity. The reformers' use of this discourse, however, sometimes embodied a paradox. On the one hand, by defining (middle-class) women's involvement in political arenas as municipal housekeeping, they challenged the ideological separation of private and public realms. On the other hand, the welfare policies they fought for tended to reinforce the ideology that mothers' primary responsibilities revolved around home and children. Although the intent was to help, the result was often intensified scrutiny of poor, working-class, and immigrant mothers' practices and employment (Skocpol 1992; Koven & Michel 1993; Gordon 1994; Ladd-Taylor 1994).

Historians and social scientists have paid particular attention to the ways in which maternalist reformers succeeded or failed in forging connections among women of different classes, races, and ethnicities. For example, white women's reform associations frequently (but not always) excluded African American women reformers or disregarded black communities' circumstances and needs. This treatment, along with government programs' racial discrimination, led African American women reformers to create private institutions in their communities, such as day nurseries, schools, and health clinics. Furthermore, while middle-class white women reformers tended to discourage working-class women's employment, middle-class African American women reformers were more accepting of working-class mothers' waged labor (Gordon 1994; Ladd-Taylor 1994).

Scholars have also studied how maternal practice and discourse have functioned in a wide range of grassroots organizations and social movements across time and place. Women have fought against environmental hazards such as toxic waste dumps near schools, against the state's use of their sons and daughters to fight wars they do not support, and against state-sponsored torture and disappearance of family members. They have fought for welfare reform, for decent, affordable health care, housing, childcare, and education, and for peaceful alliances across various borders. It is important to note, however, that maternal politics can pit mothers and children of different social groups against one another, that maternal activism can be found anywhere along the political spectrum from left to right, and that maternal discourse can be used not only to legitimate but also to disguise political aims (Jetter et al. 1997).

For instance, Tamara Neuman (2004) argues that, starting in the 1970s, Kiryat Arba women used maternal discourse to downplay the political nature of their efforts to expand Israeli settlement in Hebron. And Alexis Jetter et al.'s *The Politics of Motherhood* (1997) includes articles about how women have employed maternal rhetoric in the service of white supremacist and race-hate movements in the United States and Europe. Yet, an important theme in the literature on maternal activism is that what begins as a concern for one's own or one's communities' children sometimes develops into a broader struggle on behalf of other children (Jetter et al. 1997).

In the 1980s and 1990s, feminist scholars also theorized mothering as a particular form of social practice that has been unjustly devalued, both culturally and scientifically. Sara Ruddick's 1980 article, "Maternal Thinking," as well as her subsequent work, has been central in feminist revisioning of mothering. She coined the term *maternal thinking* to describe three values or intellectual capacities that may arise from the everyday work of caring for children, whether it is performed by men or women. First, she argues that children's demand for preservation and protection can produce the value of "holding," of trying to keep the child safe while knowing one can not always control the environment. Second, she suggests that children's demand for physical, emotional, and intellectual nurturance may lead to the intellectual capacity to understand complex and unpredictable change, both in children and in oneself. Third, children's demand for moral and social training, so that they may be accepted as members of their community, requires that the mother cultivate openness to the child's potential, including the child's potential difference from herself and from others in her community. Ruddick acknowledges that maternal thinking can lead mothers to defend their own children at others' expense. Nonetheless, she argues that maternal thinking can be mobilized beyond one's own children into a broader politics of resistance, including global peace politics (Ruddick 1995).

Other feminist theorists have resisted universalizing maternal practice. Patricia Hill Collins (1994) has been especially influential in theorizing mothers' practices from specific social historical locations. Starting from the perspective of poor and working-class women of color in the United States, Collins argues that these mothers, unlike their more privileged counterparts, must fight for their children's survival, struggle to teach their children about their racial/ethnic identities in a racist society, and fight for empowerment in a society that has controlled their bodies and reproduction as well as their relationship to their children.

A major issue in both empirical and theoretical explorations of maternalism as practice and discourse is the link between maternalism and feminism. In cases where maternalism focuses on children's needs while excluding mothers' needs, extols a limited sphere of influence for women, and/or seeks the well-being of some children while harming others, scholars have tended to view maternalism as non-feminist, if not anti-feminist. By contrast, when maternal practice, discourse, and activism include mothers' as well as children's needs, integrate women's rights and equality into the struggle, and build bridges across racial, ethnic, class, national, or other borders, scholars are more likely to define them as feminist (Gordon 1994; Ladd-Taylor 1994; Ruddick 1995; Chase & Rogers 2001).

Nonetheless, given the vast historical and geographical diversity among instances of maternalism (and of feminism), most scholars resist generalizations; consequently, study of particular manifestations of maternal practice, discourse, and activism has been crucial. In part because of the conflict and/or uneasy alliance between maternal and feminist practices, discourse, and activism, some scholars have chosen different terms than maternalism to describe instances where mothering and political activity intersect. Nancy Naples (1998), for example, uses *activist mothering* to describe the work of women community workers employed in Community Action Programs during the War on Poverty in the 1960s and 1970s. She uses this term to highlight the women's view of political activism as integral to their mothering, to emphasize their membership in the communities on whose behalf they work, and to underscore the cross-class, cross-racial nature of their work.

Some contemporary scholars argue for moving beyond maternalism as a paradigm for understanding women's relation to the family, the economy, and the state (Boris & Kleinberg 2003). In this context, some propose that a focus on *carework* offers a better analytical lens. Rather than highlighting women's connection to children, this term draws attention to women's caring as a form of *labor*, whether it is a labor of love or not, whether it is paid or not, whether it takes place in the home or in the workplace, and whether it is performed for children, adults, or one's own or others' family members. Research on carework explores how that work fits into the family–work nexus in workers' lives, attends to the ways that work is positioned in the economy and organized by the state, and investigates how that work embodies or resists gendered and racialized discourses. Teresa Swartz (2004) offers a good example of how these aspects of carework intersect. She explores the complexities of foster parenting as (minimally) paid carework, performed for and regulated by the state, and performed by mostly working-class women who use a gendered discourse of mothering. Research on carework covers many of the same issues as research on maternalism, but the latter emphasizes women's connection to and responsibility for children and how that concern can lead to political engagement.

Another new concept that builds on the scholarship on maternalism is *familialism*. Haney and Pollard (2003) suggest that familialism is especially useful for understanding cases where there is no welfare state, such as colonial regimes and state socialist and communist regimes. They argue that various regimes and states, in different historical periods and geographical locations, regulate not only mothers' but also fathers' family responsibilities, and that these gendered forms of regulation have wide-ranging consequences for family structures.

SEE ALSO: Carework; Ecofeminism; Ethic of Care; Feminism; Feminism, First, Second, and Third Waves; Gendered Organizations/Institutions; Motherhood; Women's Empowerment

REFERENCES AND SUGGESTED READINGS

Boris, E. & Kleinberg, S. J. (2003) Mothers and Other Workers: (Re)conceiving Labor, Maternalism, and the State. *Journal of Women's History* 15(3): 90–117.

Chase, S. E. & Rogers, M. F. (2001) *Mothers and Children: Feminist Analyses and Personal Narratives*. Rutgers University Press, New Brunswick, NJ.

Collins, P. H. (1994) Shifting the Center: Race, Class, and Feminist Theorizing about Motherhood. In: Glenn, E. N., Chang, G., & Forcey, L. R. (Eds.), *Mothering: Ideology, Experience, and Agency*. Routledge, New York, pp. 45–65.

Gordon, L. (1994) *Pitied But Not Entitled: Single Mothers and the History of Welfare, 1890–1935*. Free Press, New York.

Haney, L. & Pollard, L. (Eds.) (2003) *Families of a New World: Gender, Politics, and State Development in a Global Context*. Routledge, New York.

Jetter, A., Orleck, A., & Taylor, D. (Eds.) (1997) *The Politics of Motherhood: Activist Voices from Left to Right*. University Press of New England, Hanover, NH.

Koven, S. & Michel, S. (Eds.) (1993) *Mothers of a New World: Maternalist Politics and the Origins of Welfare States*. Routledge, New York.

Ladd-Taylor, M. (1994) *Mother-Work: Women, Child Welfare, and the State, 1890–1930*. University of Illinois Press, Urbana.

Naples, N. A. (1998) *Grassroots Warriors: Activist Mothering, Community Work, and the War on Poverty*. Routledge, New York.

Neuman, T. (2004) Maternal "Anti-Politics" in the Formation of Hebron's Jewish Enclave. *Journal of Palestine Studies* 33(2): 51–70.

Ruddick, S. (1995) *Maternal Thinking: Toward a Politics of Peace*, 2nd edn. Beacon Press, Boston.

Skocpol, T. (1992) *Protecting Soldiers and Mothers: The Political Origins of Social Policy in the United States*. Belknap Press of Harvard University Press, Cambridge, MA.

Swartz, T. T. (2004) Mothering for the State: Foster Parenting and the Challenges of Government-Contracted Carework. *Gender and Society* 18(5): 567–87.

math, science, and technology education

Larry E. Suter

The study of educational practices in mathematics, science, and technology considers the social, psychological, economic, and political forces that affect career choice and cognitive understanding of those subject areas. The field involves the development of theories and methods that explore how students learn complex topics in the sciences and engineering. Many products of research in technology apply theories and methods of psychology, education, political science, engineering, and all sciences as well as of sociology. The subject areas of mathematics, science, and technology are considered priority areas for study because the knowledge can affect economic production and invention. Moreover, these subjects are the domain of school learning rather than home learning in all countries.

The study of mathematics, science, and technology education has become an established body of research leading to greater efficiencies in the teaching, learning, and public understanding of those topics (Kilpatrick 1992). Researchers apply theoretical and methodological foundations of sociology (as well as insights from other behavioral disciplines such as education, anthropology, and psychology) to understand student performance, teaching practices, adult understanding, and behavior of large organizations. The study of a single set of "content areas" such as mathematics and science is not a common frame of reference for researchers from social sciences because it requires a specific knowledge of the disciplines as well as knowledge of the social forces that affect behavior. Thus, persons trained in the physical and mathematical sciences at some point in their careers dominate the study of mathematics, science, and technology education.

Sociologists participate in research on the content areas of mathematics and science by examining student career paths, teacher careers, cognitive learning, student motivation, school curriculum, international comparisons, college enrollment, technological applications, and demographic characteristics of enrollment. Thus expertise of sociologists in such areas as demography, community systems, organizational behavior, race relations, social stratification, interpersonal behavior, and educational institutions in particular is found throughout studies of mathematics and science education.

American elementary, secondary, and college student participation in mathematics, science, and technology education has been a concern of national policy since World War II, when it appeared as though US scientists might not be able to keep up with scientific developments in other parts of the world after the war. The launching of Sputnik in 1957 was especially troubling because it confirmed fears that the American educational system was behind the development of science and mathematics in other countries. It also spurred further Congressional funding of mathematics and science education.

Vannevar Bush (1945) urged Congress to establish the National Science Foundation in 1950 to increase domestic financial support for scientific research and scientific and technological education. Congressional committees have provided financial support for research in science, mathematics, and technology education through many federal agencies such as the National Science Foundation, the National Aeronautics and Space Administration, the National Institute for Standards in Technology, the Department of Energy, the Department of Defense, and the Department of Education (see National Science Board 2000). These agencies support basic research in the sciences as well as research and educational practices in science, mathematics, and technology (engineering).

The public (adult) understanding of science is also a matter of significant study and measurement (National Science Board 2000; Miller 2004). Studies of public understanding of scientific and mathematical principles have developed statistical surveys of popular understanding and have created theoretical frameworks for describing national and international trends in scientific understanding. These surveys have shown that the American public is not well informed about some areas of science. For example, only half of the US population correctly understood how long it takes for the earth to circle the sun.

The National Academy of Sciences (NAS) conducts many regular syntheses of research in many aspects of teaching and learning of science, mathematics, and technology through the National Research Council. Some recent major studies focus on how people learn, mathematics education, science education reform, children's health, and student motivation. The NAS conducts studies through a series of review committees of scholars in all fields that analyze the literature of a problem area. These analyses involve the work of sociologists who contribute background on the theory of social behavior as well as methodological experience with data for large social systems as well as smaller classrooms.

The study of mathematics, science, and technology education is conducted in every country of the world because the scientific manpower is considered a necessary asset to productivity. Comparative studies of the performance of elementary and secondary students in mathematics and science are conducted regularly by two international organizations. The International Association for the Evaluation of Educational Achievement (IEA) has produced detailed studies of student performance since 1966 and its databases are available to others for research (see the IEA website, www.iea.nl/). The Organization for Economic Cooperation and Development (OECD) regularly conducts studies of careers and student performance and publishes reports from its French office in Paris. Moreover, the UNESCO office in Paris regularly collects statistical summaries of the production of graduates for each field of study for secondary and tertiary institutions in all countries. These studies have identified differences in subject matter curriculum emphasis and aspects of teacher training as important factors in explaining large differences in student achievement in these subject areas across countries. The studies also have included analysis of basic student social conditions that accompany student performance such as time spent on entertainment, the use of computers and calculators, availability of books and supplies, the contribution of textbooks to learning, the educational level of parents, and income level.

International comparative studies of student achievement in mathematics, science, and technology have been conducted through surveys of students and teachers that include questions about student motivation, cognitive understanding, and social background. More recent methodological approaches have used video analysis of classroom behavior across a number of countries to establish classroom-level descriptions of differences in teacher and student performance (Stigler & Hiebert 1999). These studies have shown that no single aspect of teaching, student behavior, or extended use of computers in classrooms is associated with high average country performance in mathematics, science, or reading. Studies of technology in classrooms have

shown that the United States is not always the leading country in applying technology to classroom instruction. The IEA study of information in education found that technology innovations have limited impact on classrooms or schools. In the schools where innovations have been both disseminated and continued, continuation depended on the energy and commitment of individual teachers, student support, the perceived value for the innovation, availability of teacher professional development opportunities, and administrative support.

The field of mathematics and science education is largely composed of research by educational psychologists and educational practitioners attempting to solve practical problems about classroom presentation, curriculum organization, and teacher preparation. Many researchers begin their careers in one of the physical or mathematical sciences and then become interested in conducting formal research on student and teacher behavior. Committees of the National Academy of Sciences and funding programs of the National Science Foundation encourage collaboration between researchers in physical and mathematical science disciplines and those from social sciences disciplines.

Sociological theories of social behavior such as social stratification, gender relations, race and ethnicity, organizational behavior, family participation, rural sociology, and sociology of education are all present in significant studies on the conditions of mathematics and science education. The methods employed by sociologists for demographic analysis, survey research, statistical analysis, case studies, and interviews are the basic techniques used by all researchers of school practices. The development of particular methods that suit the needs of research areas has also occurred, such as in the application of multilevel models of statistical analysis to understanding the learning of mathematics by students in schools or classrooms. The field of sociology has also contributed to the development of methods for displaying statistical indicators of significant educational activities (Porter & Gamoran 2000). It has also contributed to understanding of the study of career development in mathematics, science, and technology (Mortimer & Shanahan 2003).

Kilpatrick examined the history of research on mathematics education and has found evidence that it has been a "disciplined inquiry" (Cronbach & Suppes 1969) that may not involve empirically tested hypotheses, but is scholarly, public, and open to critique and refutation. Mathematics education became a recognized area of study in the nineteenth century at Teachers College. More recent research efforts in mathematics education are likely to involve experimental designs about the uses of technology in the classroom.

Science educators have been concerned with the pipeline for science and engineering, arguing that the human resource pool is refined through a series of stages and that it is at a maximum level of popularity in the elementary grades. They noted that "leakage" of interest in science is especially visible in the middle school grades. They were also concerned with the cultural factors that condition the opportunity to learn science and the motivation to engage in doing science. The increase in the number of minorities who continued into higher classes of secondary school also needed special attention to continue engagement in science disciplines.

Since 1950, the US government has been concerned with appropriate production of scientists and engineers through the US educational system. Vannevar Bush's "Report to the President" emphasized the bipartisan nature of federal funding for science and established the principle that federal support of research in universities is necessary for the production of knowledge, innovation, and trained personnel for the nation's workforce.

The current emphasis area of research for funding agencies is to increase the integration of all sciences into the study of learning science and mathematics principles. The multidisciplinary study of educational practices includes researchers working together on the same projects from two or more different and diverse disciplines. Researchers may work together from neural sciences, cognitive science, computer science, engineering, behavioral psychology, social psychology, natural sciences, as well as sociology and anthropology.

New theories and research methods are needed that address the social construction of learning complex topics in mathematics and science. How do student interaction and cognitive knowledge of mathematics interact? Psychologists and psychometricians have developed theoretical frameworks of the science content areas (see National Assessment of Educational Progress), cognitive tests of the areas, and statistical models of individual differences. But few of these indicators include aspects of student interaction with other students and teachers or information about the contexts in which students learn and remember science and mathematics.

Research currently is developing a more sophisticated understanding of how group membership and social networks interact, affecting student careers choice and retention of cognitive knowledge in mathematics and science. The analysis of international comparisons on student achievement provides insights into cultural differences, but few of these studies have provided entirely new frameworks for understanding student motivation and cognitive learning as might be required to ultimately explain individual differences in achievement. Current research areas also include the relationship between individuals, disciplinary knowledge, and machines (computers) to better explain how modern technology alters the nature of science and mathematics and thus instructional requirements. Studies are under way to examine whether virtual experience with science studies substitutes for laboratory experience.

The study of mathematics, science, and technology education requires the collection of data from students and teachers as they are in the process of teaching and learning. New techniques for capturing and analyzing in-situation behavior, such as video analysis, are being developed and promise to provide new insights into student behavior and performance. Measures that capture the many dimensions of student achievement also need to be developed more fully. New statistical modeling and data collection techniques promise to provide many future opportunities for discovering new relationships between student and teacher behavior.

Measurement of student achievement in the United States has focused greatly on the development of paper and pencil tests of cognitive memory on mathematics and science topics. Cognitive learning, however, has social aspects that have yet to be captured in these models. Sociologists need to develop methods of capturing networks of interactions between students, families, peers, and teachers that help explain when and why students are able to retain and use mathematics and science knowledge in some settings but not in others. This will require the application and development of new data collection techniques and mathematical models of interpersonal behavior.

SEE ALSO: Educational Attainment; Educational Inequality; School Climate; School Segregation, Desegregation; Schooling and Economic Success; Technological Determinism; Technological Innovation; Technology, Science, and Culture

REFERENCES AND SUGGESTED READINGS

Bush, V. (1945) Report to the President on a Program for Postwar Scientific Research. *Science – The Endless Frontier* (July).

Cronbach, L. J. & Suppes, P. (1969) *Research for Tomorrow's Schools: Disciplined Inquiry for Education*. Macmillan, London.

Gamoran, A., Anderson, C. W., Quiroz, P. A., Secada, W. G., Williams, T., & Ashmann, S. (2003) *Transforming Teaching in Math and Science: How Schools and Districts Can Support Change*. Teachers College Press, New York.

Grouws, D. (Ed.) (1992) *Handbook of Research on Mathematics Teaching and Learning*. Macmillan, New York, pp. 3–38.

Hiebert, J., Gallimore, R., Garnier, H., Givvin, K. B., Hollingsworth, H., Jacobs, J., et al. (2003) *Teaching Mathematics in Seven Countries: Results from the TIMSS 1999 Video Study*. NCES 2003–013. US Department of Education, National Center for Education Statistics, Washington, DC.

Kilpatrick, J. (1992) A History of Research in Mathematics Education. In: Grouws, D. (Ed.), *Handbook of Research on Mathematics Teaching and Learning*. Macmillan, New York, pp. 3–38.

Miller, J. D. (2004) Public Understanding of, and Attitudes toward, Scientific Research: What We Know and What We Need to Know. *Public Understanding of Science* 13: 273–94.

Mortimer, J. & Shanahan, M. (Eds.) (2003) *Handbook of the Life Course*. Kluwer Academic/Plenum, New York.

National Science Board (2000) *Science and Technology Policy: Past and Prologue. A Companion to Science and Engineering Indicators – 2000*. National Science Foundation, NSB 0087. Online. www.nsf.gov/pubs/2000/nsb0087/start.htm.

Plomp, T., Anderson, R. E., Law, N., & Quale, A. (Eds.) (2003) *Cross-National Policies and Practices on Information and Communication Technology in Education*. Information Age Publishing, Greenwich, CT.

Porter, A. & Gamoran, A. (Eds.) (2000) *Methodological Advances in Cross-National Surveys of Educational Achievement*. National Research Council, Washington, DC.

Stigler, J. W. & Hiebert, J. (1999) *The Teaching Gap: Best Ideas from the World's Teachers for Improving Education in the Classroom*. Free Press, New York.

mathematical sociology

Thomas J. Fararo

After World War II, some sociologists began to employ mathematical models as part of a deepening and broadening of the interpenetration of mathematics and the social and behavioral sciences. These applications were quite different from traditional data analysis wherein statistical procedures are the main tools. The idea was to create more rigorous scientific theories than had hitherto existed in these fields. Traditionally, for instance, theories in fields such as psychology and sociology were strong in intuitive content, but weak from a formal point of view. That is, assumptions and definitions were not clearly stipulated and distinguished from factual descriptions and inferences. In particular, there was rarely a formal deduction of a conclusion from specified premises.

The phrase "constructing mathematical models" captured the new and preferred style. This means making explicit assumptions about some mathematical objects and providing an empirical interpretation for the ideas. It also means deducing properties of the model and comparing these with relevant empirical data. Mathematical sociology was part of this intellectual movement in the social and behavioral sciences.

INFLUENTIAL EARLY DEVELOPMENTS

The distinctive feature of sociology as a science is its focus on groups. But a group is not just a set of people. Rather, through processes of social interaction, a group is a set of people in social relationships with one another. How can the pattern of such relationships – a social network – be characterized in mathematical terms?

Two early and influential innovations in the use of mathematics in sociology emerged as answers to this question. Both developments were initiated by thinking of a pattern of relationships as a set of points connected by lines. The points (or "nodes") represent people or other actors and the lines (or "arcs") represent relations among those actors. A body of mathematics called the theory of graphs had been developed to deal with circuits and other such networks, but it could not be directly applied to social networks. Abstract concepts had to be developed that mirrored the special properties of social networks.

With this objective in mind, graph theorist Frank Harary and social psychologist Dorwin Cartwright collaborated in a discrete mathematical approach to social networks. They employed extensions of the mathematical theory of graphs, large parts of which were being created by Harary and his collaborators as they worked on social science problems. For instance, since the 1930s, social psychologists had been analyzing patterns of friendship and animosity between people in groups, such as schoolchildren. Starting from a representation of sentiment relations among persons in terms of lines with positive or negative signs, Harary and Cartwright went on to prove the important and non-obvious structure theorem (Cartwright & Harary 1956). The theorem says that if a structure of interrelated positive and negative ties is balanced – illustrated by the psychological consistency of "my friend's enemy is my enemy" – then it consists of two substructures, with positive ties within and negative ties between them. (There is a special case where one of the two substructures is empty.) Of course, this is an idealization because in the real world there may be more than two cliques. In fact, later work generalized this theory of structural balance so as to accommodate this and other facts about the world.

Graph theoretical concepts and theorems are difficult to apply to the complicated pattern of links among nodes that typically emerges in a large population. Beginning in the late 1940s, the mathematical biologist Anatol Rapoport developed a probabilistic approach to the characterization of large social networks. His insight was to start the analysis from a baseline model called a "random net," one in which ties are generated at random. It turns out that one can prove interesting results about random networks characterized by a parameter called the contact density – the average number of outgoing links from a typical node. For instance, by the "weak connectivity" of a network, we mean the expected proportion of the nodes in the network that will be reached by tracing links from an arbitrary small starting set of nodes. It can be shown that the weak connectivity of a random net depends only upon the contact density. In particular, for contact density 2, 3, and 4, the weak connectivity is 0.59, 0.80, and 0.94, respectively. By contrast, in empirical studies of large friendship networks we find that these numbers are much lower. For instance, not 80 percent but less than half that fraction is on average reached in tracings of "best three friends." How can we explain this departure from the derived predictions for a random net?

The model-building strategy to address this question employs the methodological principle of introducing social parameters. When the social parameters are equal to zero, the random net predictions are obtained. Parameter values greater than zero correspond to departures from randomness, or *biases*, that may occur in different kinds of networks in natural settings. The result is a theory applicable either to random or biased nets. For instance, if A has two friends B and C, then there is a greater than chance probability that B and C will be acquainted. This non-chance-level probability can be taken as a "bias" parameter that helps to account for the reduced reachability that we observe in empirical studies. In this way, using a probabilistic structural model, one can derive formulas that show how the contact density and bias parameters account for the global network feature of weak connectivity, which in turn has implications for studies of information diffusion in large networks (Rapoport 1957).

Structural balance theory and the theory of random and biased nets each pertain to the analysis of structure, but they differ formally in that one is deterministic and the other is probabilistic or stochastic. Two other early influential developments in mathematical sociology contrast in this way as well, but in the context of models of process.

Simon (1952) constructed a deterministic process model in his formalization of a theory set forth by George Homans in his book *The Human Group*, published in 1950. The classical mode of representation of dynamics employs a system of differential equations in which each equation combines certain mechanisms that contribute to the change of state of the system under analysis. Following Homans's lead of describing the group in terms of interaction, activity, and sentiment variables, Simon translated the hypotheses of Homans's theory into mechanisms that together generate the change of state of a group. The analysis of the system of differential equations obtained in this way leads to theorems pertaining to emergent equilibrium states as well as social change.

The other type of process model is probabilistic and involves the body of mathematics called stochastic processes. The influential early contribution here related to dynamic models of learning phenomena (Bush & Mosteller 1955). The typical application was to a single organism, human or not, adapting to a situation in which certain behaviors would lead to reward while alternative behaviors would not. In controlled experiments, analysts had recorded the proportion of organisms that respond in a particular way on each of a sequence of trials. Thus, for each trial there is a probability distribution over the possible responses and the complete set of data consists of a sequence of such trial-dependent distributions. The mathematical problem is to postulate a behavioral process in such a way as to be able to derive and thereby predict the over-time and equilibrium properties of such sequences. Thus, a stochastic model, which enables one to derive expected proportions over time, is a suitable form of model. The general probabilistic approach to behavior came to be known as stimulus sampling theory, in which human and other organisms are postulated to sample stimulus patterns and to connect these to responses as a function of situational contingencies, e.g., the relevance of particular responses to particular rewards. Later work in this program of research applied stimulus sampling theory to human social situations in which the outcome depends upon the acts of each of the actors, as in repeated game situations. In such cases, each actor is represented as a "stimulus sampler" and the data are trial-dependent distributions over the joint actions of the actors.

RESEARCH PROGRAMS AND MATHEMATICAL SOCIOLOGY

The four early developments sketched above have illustrated a pair of distinctions: models of structure versus models of process, and deterministic models versus stochastic models. This pair of distinctions was carried forward in subsequent work. To illustrate the sort of models and social phenomena studied, three important sociological research programs will be discussed.

The use of differential equations by Simon, as described earlier, raises a question: How can one connect a system of differential equations to the data of sociology? One clue is that empirical studies in sociology often report results in the form of proportions. This suggests the idea that the differential equations might refer to changes in proportions over time. In turn, this suggests a stochastic process model. Yet the proportion of people believing or doing something at a given time has to be correctly interpreted. Although each person in a population may hold a certain belief or be inclined to vote a certain way, the *processes* by which these individual orientations come about is socially mediated. Thus, we should understand the process by which states change over time as a social process in which persons influence one another to change their minds. This means that network ties loom large, and we have a linkage between social relations and social process.

These sorts of considerations animated the research program of James S. Coleman and led to his important book, *Introduction to Mathematical Sociology* (1964). The fundamental type of model discussed by Coleman is a continuous-time discrete-state stochastic process with "contagion" terms, i.e., terms that represent influence effects that emerge in social networks. With this type of model, a system of differential equations is derived and theoretical parameters of the postulated process can be estimated, leading to testable predictions about observable social phenomena (Fararo 1973: ch. 13). In later work, this sort of process analysis was linked to an approach to social theory that drew upon mathematical ideas about rational action. The use of rational choice models became more common in sociology but also somewhat controversial in that it seemed to depart from the structural emphasis that many sociologists favor (Coleman & Fararo 1992).

This concern for structural analysis dominates another research program with a strong focus on mathematical model building. The structural balance theory discussed above applied best to small interpersonal networks. Could a mathematics of social structures be developed that would apply to complex patterns of relations such as anthropologists had found in describing kinship systems? Sociologist Harrison White answered this question in the affirmative when he initiated a long-term research program on the mathematics of social structures that began with his 1963 monograph, *An Anatomy of Kinship*. This book illustrated how modern abstract algebraic ideas could be applied to the analysis of social structures. The immediate background was the analysis of kinship structures by anthropologists. White set out a set of axioms describing a certain type of prescribed marriage system where clans loom large in the structure. His analysis then consisted of a formal study of this class of systems using certain methods of abstract algebra. Subsequently, White embarked on an effort to generalize the algebraic approach by relaxing the axioms of mathematical group theory but preserving some of its methods. Most notably, the idea of homomorphism – a mapping that preserves structure while also simplifying it – was employed to map social relational data into simpler forms called block models. In turn, this work became part of an interdisciplinary social networks paradigm, home to a variety of research programs using both graph theory and algebraic methods coupled with statistical procedures for the analysis of social relational data (Wasserman & Faust 1994).

A third research program in which mathematical models became prominent originated in the collaborative work of three theoretical sociologists at Stanford University, Joseph Berger, Morris Zelditch, Jr., and Bernard P. Cohen. Classical sociological theorists had not made any important connections between theory and mathematics. The new developments that began to create such links called for work that would elucidate the nature of the efforts. The Stanford program began with the question: How does using mathematics advance theory in the social and behavioral sciences?

Their collaborative monograph, *Types of Formalization in Small Group Research* (1962), formulated a typology of models and selected three examples of model building in the literature to illustrate each type. In their approach, the key idea is that types of models are best understood in terms of the goal of the model builder. One goal is to explicate an important concept in a theory, as in the Cartwright–Harary graph-theoretic formalization of the concept of structural balance. A second goal is to represent a recurrent process, as in Coleman's process model building. A third goal is the formalization of a theory of a broad class of phenomena, illustrated by stimulus sampling theory. This third type was called a "theoretical construct model" because the mathematical theory postulates some underlying entity and processes associated with it that enables the derivation of various empirical findings.

In building their own research program, Berger and his colleagues aimed to develop a theoretical construct model for the domain of interpersonal processes (Berger & Zelditch 2002: ch. 3). The key explanatory processes deal with expectation states of people in social interaction. These states are not directly observable to the sociological analyst or to the interactants but, according to the theory, they account for such phenomena as social influence and the allocation of prestige in social interaction situations. Thus the concept of expectation state and the processes associated with it, when expressed in formal terms, constitute a theoretical construct model. The program associated with this "expectation states theory" is now one among a number of other programs in which mathematical models play a significant role, examples of which may be found in Berger and Zelditch (2002).

INSTITUTIONALIZATION OF MATHEMATICAL SOCIOLOGY

The institutionalization of a field is indicated by the appearance of such entities as textbooks, bibliographic surveys, journals, and graduate programs. Since 1971, the *Journal of Mathematical Sociology* has been open to papers covering a broad spectrum of topics employing a variety of types of mathematics, especially through frequent special issues. Three specialized publication outlets emerged for contributors to the three families of research programs originated out of the works reviewed above: *Rationality and Society*, *Social Networks*, and *Advances in Group Processes* (an annual publication). In addition, and this is important as an indicator of the penetration of mathematical model building into sociological research, the major comprehensive journals in sociology, especially the *American Journal of Sociology* and the *American Sociological Review*, regularly publish articles featuring mathematical formulations.

Thus, mathematical model building has become a recognized method in sociological theory and research. However, there are norms that are invoked in work with mathematics – such as idealization in constructing models, simplicity of framing assumptions, fertility of deductive consequences – that are often ignored or misunderstood by many sociologists despite efforts to communicate these standards to social scientists (see, for instance, Lave & March 1975). Thus, there is a continuing problem of absorbing the spirit and content of mathematical model building into general sociological theory.

SEE ALSO: Coleman, James; Expectation States Theory; Rational Choice Theory (and Economic Sociology); Theory Construction

REFERENCES AND SUGGESTED READINGS

Berger, J. & Zelditch, M., Jr. (Eds.) (2002) *New Directions in Contemporary Sociological Theory*. Rowman & Littlefield, Lanham, MD.

Berger, J., Cohen, B. P., Snell, J. L., & Zelditch, M., Jr. (1962) *Types of Formalization in Small Group Research*. Houghton Mifflin, Boston.

Bush, R. R. & Mosteller, F. (1955) *Stochastic Models of Learning*. Wiley, New York.

Cartwright, D. & Harary, F. (1956) Structural Balance: A Generalization of Heider's Theory. *Psychological Review* 63: 277–93.

Coleman, J. S. (1964) *An Introduction to Mathematical Sociology*. Free Press, New York.

Coleman, J. S. & Fararo, T. J. (Eds.) (1992) *Rational Choice Theory: Advocacy and Critique*. Sage, Newbury Park, CA.

Fararo, T. J. (1973) *Mathematical Sociology*. Wiley, New York.

Lave, C. & March, J. (1975) *An Introduction to Models in the Social Sciences*. Harper & Row, New York.

Rapoport, A. (1957) Contributions to the Theory of Random and Biased Nets. *Bulletin of Mathematical Biophysics* 19: 257–77.

Simon, H. A. (1952) A Formal Theory of Interaction in Social Groups. *American Sociological Review* 17: 202–12.

Wasserman, S. & Faust, K. (1994) *Social Network Analysis: Methods and Applications*. Cambridge University Press, New York.

White, H. C. (1963) *An Anatomy of Kinship*. Prentice-Hall, Englewood Cliffs, NJ.

matriarchy

J. I. (Hans) Bakker

The term matriarchy has a commonsense meaning today. It refers to a situation where a female becomes an important figure in a nuclear or extended household. Thus, for example, Rose Kennedy was a matriarch of the Kennedy clan. That current meaning has deep roots. At one time many thinkers believed that women had always been secondary to men. Early ideas concerning what Carl Linnaeus called "*homo sapiens*" (wise man) were biased in favor of "men's history." It was not clear to social scientists until the early twentieth century that male and female gender roles are social constructs and that biology is not always destiny. Comparative data on anthropologically indigenous, non-industrial societies makes it clear that the division of tasks in the household can be quite varied, with men often doing household tasks. Moreover, many cultures recognize a "third gender" in which biological men are treated in every outward respect as women.

Such micro-level phenomena in relatively less technological communities are only one part of the picture. Another aspect of matriarchy is the notion that some societies have been politically dominated by women. This is sometimes called Amazonism, based on the mythical

Greek "reverse gender" accounts of Scythian or independent female warriors. Bachhofen, a Swiss amateur classicist and judge, argued on the basis of the iconography of Roman tombs that the earliest stage of human culture was characterized by general promiscuity. He called his hypothetical stage *hetaerism*. When people became aware of maternity, the core of family life was the link between a mother and her children. Such matriarchy was a progressive evolutionary advance over promiscuity.

The theory of matriarchical civilization, first articulated by Bachhofen in 1861 (1992, 2003), was once very popular and indirectly influenced Morgan, Engels, and others (Bamberger 1974). Most scholars believe that while there is a grain of truth in Bachhofen's claims, he overgeneralized based on limited data. Some feminist writers took up the theme in the 1970s, which is ironic since Bachhofen also argued that the next evolutionary stage was patriarchy. But a number of semi-popular books (e.g., Gimbutas 1991) argue that matriarchy not only preceded patriarchy but was superior to it. With the advent of patriarchy the role of women, it was argued, was devalued. Many feminists still use the term patriarchy to describe male dominance. But the idea of patriarchy succeeding matriarchy is largely discredited. While the matrilineal clans may have preceded the Roman patrilineal *gens* and *curia*, that does not indicate matrilineal curia or a general, societal matriarchical power system in Rome, much less a more universal progression from one to the other.

There are *matrilineal* societies and there have been influential women rulers (e.g., Tang China), but there is no evidence of any civilization having been ruled exclusively by women. The Canadian novelist De Mille (1991 [1888]) wrote about a matriarchical society in the 1870s; but his fictional account is a Hegelian "negation" of nineteenth-century values. Gilman's (1979 [1915]) *Herland* is extremely important as an early feminist statement of utopia. Indeed, the feminist concept of patriarchy hinges on a polarization of male versus female-based institutionalized power. It is easier to conceptualize patriarchy if it replaced matriarchy, but it seems likely that that never took place (Sanday 1981). The literature contains studies of conflict between masculine and feminine gender identities in gathering and hunting societies.

Changes in kinship systems evoke rituals difficult to explain without reference to changes from matrilineal to patrilineal descent, as among the Iatmul of New Guinea (Bateson 1958 [1936]). Men from the female lineage (mother's brothers, *wau*) dress in women's clothes to signify their allegiance to older patterns of matrilineal descent, reinforcing the rights of the sister's children (*laua*).

Max Weber (1968 [1920]: 231–6) discusses "primary patriarchalism" as an elementary form of traditional "domination" or "legitimate authority" (*Herrschaft*). "Gerontocracy and patriarchalism," he states, "are frequently found side by side." Obedience is owed to the individual male leader. The extension and expansion of patriarchal authority, according to Weber, leads to patrimonialism (e.g., sultanism). The only mention of patriarchy in Weber's study of ancient civilizations is a brief reference to Deuteronomy, and Weber does not cite Bachhofen in his study of ancient Judaism.

SEE ALSO: Feminism; Kinship; Lesbianism; Myth; Patriarchy

REFERENCES AND SUGGESTED READINGS

Bachhofen, J. J. (1992) *Myth, Religion, and Mother Right: Selected Writings*. Trans. R. Mannheim. Introduction by J. Campbell. Princeton University Press, Princeton.

Bachhofen, J. J. (2003 [1861]) *Bachofen's Mutterrecht*. Trans. D. Partenheimer. Edwin Mellen, Lewiston, NY.

Bamberger, J. (1974) The Myth of Matriarchy: Why Men Rule in Primitive Society. In: Rosaldo, M. & Lamphere, L. (Eds.), *Women, Culture, and Society*. Stanford University Press, Stanford, pp. 263–80.

Bateson, G. (1958 [1936]) *Naven*, 2nd edn. Stanford University Press, Stanford.

De Mille, J. (1991 [1888]) *A Strange Manuscript Found in a Copper Cylinder*. Carleton University Press, Ottawa.

Engels, F. (1972 [1888]) *Origins of the Family, Private Property, and the State*. International Publishers, New York.

Gilman, C. P. (1979 [1915]) *Herland*. Pantheon, New York.

Gimbutas, M. (1991) *The Civilization of the Goddess: The World of Old Europe*. HarperSanFrancisco, San Francisco.

Morgan, L. H. (1871) *Systems of Consanguinity and Affinity*. Smithsonian Contributions to Knowledge 17. Smithsonian Institution, Washington, DC.

Morgan, L. H. (1877) *Ancient Society*. Henry Holt, New York.

Sanday, P. R. (1981) *Female Power and Male Dominance: On the Origins of Sexual Inequality*. Cambridge University Press, Cambridge.

Tooker, E. (1992) Lewis H. Morgan and His Contemporaries. *American Anthropologist* 94: 357–75.

Weber, M. (1968 [1920]) *Economy and Society: An Outline of Interpretive Sociology*. Ed. G. Roth & C. Wittich. University of California Press, Berkeley.

matrix of domination

Marjorie L. DeVault

The term matrix of domination is associated with the feminist thought of Patricia Hill Collins, who came to prominence in the academic movement that arose from women's activism in the 1960s and 1970s. Her project locates lived experiences of oppression within the social contexts that produce those experiences. Collins's term refers to the particular configurations of oppression and resistance (along varied lines of socially constructed difference) that shape life in specific communities and historical moments.

Collins indicates that her scholarship grew out of resistance to her experiences as a young African American student and then teacher, when she confronted a racist curriculum and schools that seemed to have no room for young people like her. Drawing from diverse texts produced by black women, she brought forward a body of subjugated knowledge in an influential article, "Learning from the Outsider Within" (1986), and then a book titled *Black Feminist Thought* (1991; revd. 2000). She emphasized the distinctiveness of black feminist thought in relation to undifferentiated feminist and race-based analyses, and she became a leader in the academic movement that began to challenge unitary gender or race analyses that did not account for the cross-cutting dynamics of these systems of oppression. Collins argued that these structures of inequality intersect, in any specific historical and community context,

in a matrix of domination that produces distinctive experiences of oppression and resistance. That idea has been taken up and extended, by Collins and others, under the rubrics of "intersectionality" (Collins 1998) and "race, class, and gender" (a phrase sometimes used as a shorthand meant to include other dimensions of difference related to sexuality, ability, etc.).

Collins (2000) locates a standpoint associated with the lived experiences and community lives of African American women. She deploys the idea of a matrix of domination as a heuristic device intended to stand for the various practices that constitute the particular pattern of domination and resistance that shapes these lives. Given a particular matrix, exploring the "standpoint" of this subjugated group allows her to sketch out their knowledge: a community-based "wisdom" that includes, for example, practices of resistance to dominant body ideals, and of "other mothering" or community care for African American children. While the first edition of the book emphasizes race, class, and gender, Collins's (2000) revision incorporates into her conceptualization of the matrix the dimensions of sexual orientation and nation, drawing from emergent social justice movements and scholarship focused on sexuality, citizenship, and transnationalism (see Collins 2004).

SEE ALSO: Black Feminist Thought; Consciousness Raising; Feminism and Science, Feminist Epistemology; Feminist Methodology; Feminist Standpoint Theory

REFERENCES AND SUGGESTED READINGS

Collins, P. H. (1986) Learning from the Outsider Within: The Sociological Significance of Black Feminist Thought. *Social Problems* 33: S14–32.

Collins, P. H. (1998) *Fighting Words: Black Women and the Search for Justice*. University of Minnesota Press, Minneapolis.

Collins, P. H. (2000 [1991]) *Black Feminist Thought: Knowledge, Consciousness, and the Politics of Empowerment*. Routledge, New York.

Collins, P. H. (2004) *Black Sexual Politics: African Americans, Gender, and the New Racism*. Routledge, New York.

Matthew effect

Yuri Jack Gómez Morales

When considering science as a social system, there is a continuous interplay between status and the class system which locates scientists at different positions within the opportunity structure of science. Social standing within science's opportunity structure is, then, a function of positive recognition by one's peers. All other extrinsic rewards, such as monetary income from science-connected activities, advancement within the scientific hierarchy, and enhanced access to human and material scientific capital, derive from this basic form of recognition.

In this sharply stratified and elitist social system of science, rewards tend to be concentrated among a few scientists, a few laboratories, and a few institutions. This uneven distribution results from differences in scientists' performance, from the scarcity of rewards, and most importantly, from processes of *cumulative advantage*. Within the social system of science, *cumulative advantage* refers to processes through which various kinds of opportunities for scientific inquiry, as well as the subsequent symbolic and material rewards for the results of that inquiry, tend to accumulate for individual practitioners, as they do for organizations engaged in scientific work.

Putting aside the problem of how to assess equivalence in quality among scientists' contributions, the Matthew effect (so-called by reference to St. Matthew's gospel) occurs when scientists receive differential recognition for particular scientific contributions depending on their location in the *stratification* system. Thus, if the accumulation of advantage shapes the distribution of rewards in science and leads to increasing disparities among scientists over the course of their careers, the Matthew effect refers to a special case in which cumulative advantage gets reinforced as a result of a complex pattern of credit misallocation for scientific performance. The social mechanism that leads to this misallocation operates through the accruing of large increments of peer recognition to scientists of considerable repute for their contributions, at the expense of less-known scientists of comparable performance. The Matthew effect therefore enlarges differences in reputation and rewards over and above those merely attributable to differences in quality of scientific performance and to processes of *accumulation of advantage*. Because the social mechanism at work is based on personal attributes of individuals rather than on assessment of their role performance, the Matthew effect introduces its own variety of *particularism* into the social system of science.

A functional analysis of the consequences of the Matthew effect, both for individuals and the social system, suggests that, as it involves misallocation of credit, it may become dysfunctional for the careers of some individuals who are penalized in the early stages of their development. In fact, deprived scientists see the Matthew effect in terms of a basic inequity in the reward system that affects their individual careers. On the other hand, this same misallocation is functional for science since evaluation and utilization of papers depend to an extent upon an author's reputation: discoveries made by eminent scientists or having eminent scientists as co-authors are more likely to be quickly incorporated into the body of scientific knowledge. Thus, the Matthew effect may heighten the visibility of new contributions, speed their diffusion, and increase the probability of recognition for it. Indeed, having learned the value of attending to the work of certain investigators in the past, and faced with a literature of unmanageable proportions, scientists tend to notice the work of well-known scientists, take it more seriously, and ultimately use it more intensively. Thus, contributions made by scientists of considerable standing are the most likely to enter promptly and widely into the communication networks of science accelerating its development. Looking at the Matthew effect from this perspective, it stands for the influence of all aspects of stratification on the reception of scientific ideas.

Empirical investigations on the Matthew effect – in which citations are taken as measurement of scientific quality – suggest that the Matthew effect has a greater influence on the extent of diffusion of a scientist's complete work than on any particular paper. Good papers have a high probability of being recognized regardless of who their authors are; but lesser papers written by high-ranking scientists are more likely to be widely diffused earlier than lesser papers by low-ranking authors. The Matthew effect also serves to focus attention on the work of little-known scientists who, by collaborating with high-repute scientists, might increase visibility for early contributions as he or she goes on to greater fame (Cole 1970).

Being an outcome of peer reviewing and communication processes in science, the effect was initially elaborated by looking at it in documented historical cases of multiple discovery and co-authorship. Merton considered that if two scientists independently make the same discovery, the considerably more eminent one will get the greater or perhaps all the credit. Likewise, if scientists of greatly differing status collaborate, the one who is most eminent will get the lion's share of the credit for the joint effort. Further empirical and theoretical investigations have advanced Merton's originally sociohistorical formulation of the Matthew effect from generalization of the effect over the entire range of scientific productivity (Cole 1970) to its deduction – on individualistic rather than functional premises – as a generalized principle at work in society at large (Goldstone 1979), from studies on the operation of the effect applied to gender differences (Rossiter 1993) to its application to the structure of the formal communication system of science (Bonitz & Scharnhorst 2001).

SEE ALSO: Intellectual Property; Peer Review and Quality Control in Science; Science/Non-Science and Boundary Work; Scientific Knowledge, Sociology of

REFERENCES AND SUGGESTED READINGS

Bonitz, M. & Scharnhorst, A. (2001) Competition in Science and the Matthew Core Journals. *Scientometrics* 51: 37–54.

Cole, S. (1970) Professional Standing and the Reception of Scientific Discoveries. *American Journal of Sociology* 76: 286–306.

Goldstone, J. A. (1979) A Deductive Explanation of the Matthew Effect in Science. *Social Studies of Science* 9: 385–91.

Merton, R. K. (1968) The Matthew Effect in Science. *Science* 159: 56–63.

Merton, R. K. (1988) The Matthew Effect in Science, II. *Isis* 79: 606–23.

Rossiter, M. (1993) The Matthew Matilda Effect in Science. *Social Studies of Science* 23: 325–41.

Zuckerman, H. A. (1988) The Sociology of Science. In: Smelser, N. J. (Ed.), *The Handbook of Sociology*. Sage, Newbury Park, CA, pp. 511–74.

Mead, George Herbert (1863–1931)

Lonnie Athens

Despite being a philosopher, George H. Mead became a titan in sociology. He was reared in a white, Protestant, middle-class family. Although not from a wealthy family, he did come from a culturally privileged background. His mother taught at prestigious New England preparatory schools and at Oberlin College. While later serving as president of Mount Holyoke, she oversaw its transition from a women's seminary to a general college. His father, a former pastor, held a special chair in Oberlin College's theological seminary for more than a decade. After graduating from Oberlin College in 1883 with an AB degree, Mead worked as a secondary school teacher, tutor, and surveyor. Unable to find satisfying work, Mead enrolled in 1887 at Harvard University, where he was most influenced by the romantic idealist Josiah Royce. After earning his MA in philosophy at Harvard in 1888, he went to Germany to obtain his PhD – enroling first at the University of Leipzig and later at the University of Berlin. Although Mead never finished his doctorate, he did study with several famous German scholars: Wundt, Ebbinghaus, and Dilthey.

While still in Germany, Mead applied for a job at the University of Michigan. In 1891 he became an instructor in the philosophy department, where John Dewey was the chairperson. The two quickly became friends. When Dewey was appointed chairman of the University of Chicago's philosophy department in 1894, he insisted that Mead accompany him as an assistant professor. Dewey was without doubt the person who exercised the greatest influence on Mead's intellectual development. Although Dewey later left the University of Chicago for

Columbia University, Mead stayed at Chicago, where he remained the rest of his academic life (Cook 1993: 1–38; Joas 1985: 15–20).

On the one hand, Mead is not generally considered to be one of America's major twentieth-century philosophers. His importance in philosophy is primarily limited to his contribution to the American philosophical school known as pragmatism. Most philosophers rate his contribution to the development of pragmatism as not only less than that of Dewey's, but also less than that of James and Pierce. Thus, Mead is considered to be a secondary rather than primary figure in this school. On the other hand, sociologists have come to appreciate his ideas far more than philosophers have. Today, he is recognized not only as one of the most important early sociological figures in America, but also in the entire world. In fact, most sociologists now place Mead on the same pedestal as Weber, Durkheim, and Marx.

Although all of Mead's major works were published before the outbreak of World War II, he did not enter the pantheon of classic figures in sociology until the last decade or two. Contrary to popular opinion, Mead achieved a significant record of publication. Despite publishing a hundred or so articles in academic journals, however, he never completed a single book. Whether considered individually or together, his journal articles do not provide a coherent statement of his mature philosophical thought. Although there are numerous books on which his name appears as the author, he never published any of them. In some cases, latter-day scholars (Mead 1964, 1968, 2001) have merely strung together a series of his previously published or unpublished articles to produce a book. In other cases, former students have created books (Mead 1936, 1938, 1982) from notes taken in various courses that he taught at Chicago. In the case of the only book that Mead actually intended for publication, *Philosophy of the Present* (1932), he died before finishing it. Arthur Murray, a colleague, completed the book for Mead by adding two previously published articles by Mead to his completed rough drafts of only three chapters, together with four previously unpublished manuscripts.

It is difficult to gauge how not finishing this book impacted Mead's intellectual legacy. If Mead had lived long enough to complete his apparent magnum opus, then he might have entered the pantheon of classic sociological figures much sooner, as well as significantly raised his standing in the school of pragmatism. Conversely, his failure to provide a well-rounded, systematic statement of his mature ideas does have some unrecognized benefits. It has not only created a permanent aura of mystery about the precise form or shape that his finished thought might have taken, but has also wrapped his completed work with a protective coating. Potential critics can never be sure whether what Mead said in his completed work was "right" but misunderstood, or whether what he said was wrong and they understood him "correctly."

Mead analyzes three ideas of significance to sociologists: (1) the social act, (2) the self, and (3) society. The starting point for understanding Mead's mature sociological views is not the self, as many sociologists have mistakenly thought, but the social act. Without engaging in social acts, people could never have developed selves, and without selves, societies as we know them could have never arisen. Thus, to be consistent with Mead's thinking, his most famous book, *Mind Self & Society* (1934), which was published posthumously, could have been more accurately titled *The Social Act, Self, and Society*.

Mead defines a social act as any activity that requires at least one other person to complete. According to him, social acts comprise five basic components: (1) roles, (2) attitudes, (3) significant speech, (4) attitudinal assumption, and (5) social objects. For Mead, roles are the basic building blocks from which all social acts are assembled. More specifically, they are the individual acts that each participant must carry out to ensure a social act's completion. Roles operate hand in hand with attitudes. Mead defines attitudes as the preparation or readiness to perform our specific roles within a larger unfolding social act. Because attitudes originate from vague bodily impulses, they unite our corporal and social existences. Mead uses his term "significant speech" as a synonym for language. It refers to our use of vocal or written gestures that have a similar meaning to us as they have to the other participants in a social act. For Mead, attitudinal assumption, which significant speech makes possible, refers to our assuming the attitudes of others so that we can anticipate the roles that they will perform in the social acts in which we are participants. Finally, according to Mead, a "social object" is the common attitude that participants assume toward the construction of a prospective social act. Thus, when participants form a social object of a social act, they simultaneously form what Mead called a "common plan of action" for its subsequent execution.

Mead speaks of the self, which for him inserts itself inside the social act, in two alternative ways. The most poetic way in which he speaks of it is as a conversation between an "I" and "me." The "I" represents the impulse that excites our attitudes or preparation to perform our roles in a social act, as well as the later expression of that attitude in the actual performance of our role. Conversely, the "me" represents the attitudes of the other participants or society at large that we assume during the performance of our particular role in a social act. The "me" affects the expression of our "I" and thereby how we perform our roles in a social act, but not always in the same way. It can outright endorse, veto, or make major or minor alterations in our "I's" expression. On rare occasions, the "I" can simply ignore the "me" altogether.

Mead also speaks of the self more mundanely as an attitudinal assumption process. People assume each other's attitudes by telling each other what they plan to do and how and when they plan to do it. To have a self, he argues, we must not only assume the attitudes of the other participants in a social act. Our assumption of their attitudes must also affect our attitude and, thereby, how we actually perform our role in the social act. Whether viewed as a conversation between "I" and "me," or as an "attitudinal assumption" process, Mead views the key ingredient of the self as "reflexivity" – the ability to adjust your attitude toward the performance of your role in a social act on the basis of your assumption of the other participants' attitudes toward the performance of their roles in it. Thus, for Mead, reflexivity and, in turn, selfhood, require more than our merely being conscious or aware of others' attitudes; it also requires that this awareness change, however slightly, our attitudes toward our roles and, thereby, the subsequent performance of them in a social act.

According to Mead, the self not only inserts itself into the social act but also, by its insertion, it makes society possible. Mead sees society as a community organized on the basis of institutions. Mead views an institution as only a special form of social action. Institutionalized social acts are launched to satisfy recurrent socio-physiological impulses, such as communication, sex, parenting, bartering, benevolence, and mentoring. The recurrent impulses that launch institutional social acts stir in us attitudes to perform complementary roles in these acts, such as speaker and hearer, mother and father, seller and buyer, minister and congregation member, and mentor and protégé.

Mead believed that during institutionalized social acts we always draw on common maxims to help us form a common social object of the unfolding social act and, in turn, construct a congruent plan of action for carrying out our particular roles in it. However, we cannot draw on common maxims to help us construct a congruent plan of action for carrying out an institutionalized social act without assuming the attitude of our society. Before we can assume the attitude of society, however, we must have selves. Institutionalized social acts are necessarily repetitive. Although our successful execution of a plan of action for the completion of an institutional social act satisfies the socio-physiological impulse that launched it, we will later need to satisfy this same impulse over and over again in future institutional social acts. Finally, for Mead, our social institutions are not immutable. Once made, they can be reinvented through individual ingenuity. The "I" can sometimes jump over the "me." We can invent new maxims to form novel social objects of our social acts and new congruent plans of action for their execution.

Without institutions, Mead believes that we would be still living in a disorganized mass. According to him, our institutions did not emerge simultaneously. Instead, they evolved at different times in society, depending on the level of "social participation" that they generated among the members of a community. By level of social participation, Mead only meant the width of the cross-section of the community members who regularly engage in the social action. According to him, the institutions with the widest social participation evolved the earliest and those with the narrowest social participation evolved the latest in society.

Mead (1936, 1964) identified only six basic societal institutions, which he believed evolved in the following order: (1) language, (2) family, (3) economy, (4) religion, (5) polity, and (6) science. Although Mead believes that all six of these institutions are of great importance not only to the development of human society, but also for its ongoing operation, he believes that language is the single most important one. According to him, language makes possible what he calls "human sociality" which, in turn, greases the wheels for the creation and subsequent operation of all the other institutions in society (Athens 2005).

For Mead, sociality is not limited to human societies or even the organic world, but operates throughout the universe. In the special case of human societies, it refers to the principle whereby different human beings who are participating together in some joint activity mutually adjust their separate activities to each other to complete the larger enterprise to which they are all contributing. In Mead's opinion, what distinguishes human sociality is the distinctive way that it operates. By consciously assuming each other's attitudes, human beings mutually affect the performances of each other's roles and the larger social acts in which these roles play parts. They can consciously assume each other's attitudes by informing each other what they plan to do, and when and how they plan to do it. Thus, because language makes it possible for human beings to engage consciously in the process of attitudinal assumption, it lies at the very root of human sociality.

Mead became more famous after his death than during his life. Since his death more than a half century ago, the interest shown in his work has not waned, but steadily increased. In fact, today the promotion and development of his ideas have created a veritable cottage industry. Both sociologists and philosophers are publishing more and more articles and books about how he developed his ideas, what their implications and meanings are, and how they deviate from and conform to the ideas of other intellectual giants. In an attempt to move beyond merely explaining or comparing Mead's ideas against the ideas of others, scholars are now embarking on their constructive criticism and improvement (Athens 1994). Shortly before Mead died, Columbia University invited him to join their faculty and offered double the salary he was earning at Chicago (Cook 1993: 191; Wallace 1967: 408). If his death had not prevented him from going to Columbia, then he would undoubtedly have not only had the opportunity to finish *Philosophy of the Present*, but also to finish it while interacting face to face again with Dewey. Since their early days together at Michigan, Dewey remained Mead's most important sounding board. Thus, as far as the development of Mead's mature thought is concerned, his death could not have come at a worse possible time.

SEE ALSO: Blumer, Herbert George; Dewey, John; Game Stage; Generalized Other; Language; Play Stage; Pragmatism; Self; Symbolic Interaction

REFERENCES AND SUGGESTED READINGS

Athens, L. (1994) The Self as a Soliloquy. *Sociological Quarterly* 35: 521–32.
Athens, L. (2005) Mead's Lost Conception of Society. *Symbolic Interaction* 28: 305–25.
Blumer, H. (2004) *George Herbert Mead and Human Conduct*. Altamira Press, Walnut Creek, CA.
Cook, G. (1993) *George Herbert Mead: The Making of a Social Pragmatist*. University of Illinois Press, Urbana.
Joas, H. (1985) *G. H. Mead: A Contemporary Re-Examination of his Thought*. MIT Press, Cambridge, MA.
Mead, G. (1936) *Movements of Thought in the Nineteenth Century*. Ed. M. Moore. University of Chicago Press, Chicago.
Mead, G. (1938) *The Philosophy of the Act*. Ed. C. Morris. University of Chicago Press, Chicago.
Mead, G. (1964) *Mead: Selected Writings*. Ed. A. Reck. Bobbs-Merrill, Indianapolis.
Mead, G. (1968) *George Herbert Mead: Essays on His Social Philosophy*. Ed. J. Petras. Columbia University Press, New York.
Mead, G. (1982) *The Individual and the Social Self: Unpublished Work of George Herbert Mead*. Ed. D. Miller. University of Chicago Press, Chicago.
Mead, G. (2001) *Essays in Social Psychology: George Herbert Mead*. Ed. M. Deegan. Transaction Publishers, New Brunswick, NJ.
Shalin, D. (2000) George Herbert Mead. In: Ritzer, G. (Ed.), *The Blackwell Companion to Major Social Theorists*. Blackwell, Oxford, pp. 302–44.
Wallace, D. (1967) Reflections on the Education of George Herbert Mead. *American Journal of Sociology* 72: 396–408.

Mead, Margaret (1901–78)

Joyce E. Williams

Margaret Mead was one of a very few academics to become known to the general public. Her discipline was anthropology but her contributions to knowledge were as critical to sociology and to psychology as to her own discipline. She pioneered fieldwork on women and children in various cultures; advanced ethnographic techniques; applied the social sciences to understanding everyday events and problems; and increased public awareness of culture as learned patterns of thought and behavior. Mead was ahead of her time as an anthropologist and as a woman when in 1925, at the age of 23, she went alone on her first field trip to study adolescents in Samoa.

Mead was born December 16, 1901 in Philadelphia, the first baby born at West Park Hospital and the first of four children born to parents Emily Fogg Mead and Edward Sherwood Mead. Thus began a life of firsts for America's best-known anthropologist. She was born into an academic family. Her father was a university professor of business and economics but with interest in the applied aspects of the business world, including coal mining. At the time of Margaret's birth, her mother was working on her doctorate. Although her father spent most of his professional life at the University of Pennsylvania, the family moved frequently. Some of the moves were regular and seasonal while another allowed her mother to do research for her doctorate. Mead once proclaimed that "few things are needed to make a home." The many moves of her childhood are recorded, along with the significance of home, in her autobiography, *Blackberry Winter* (1972). The title is reminiscent of childhood seasons spent on a five-acre "farm" in Hammonton, New Jersey. At the American Museum of Natural History in New York City, Mead identified her attic room, which grew in size and contents over the years, as "home" for all of her professional life. From 1928 until her death, she occupied the same space as Assistant Curator, Curator, and Curator Emeritus. It was the home to which she returned from numerous field trips, visiting professorships, and lecture junkets and became the repository of artifacts and mementos collected from far-flung corners of the globe. Only after Mead died at age 77 was the space cleared and the Mead collection removed to the Library of Congress.

Mead began her college work at her father's school, DePauw University, in Indiana. After one year she transferred to Barnard, where she majored in psychology but was introduced to anthropology in a class taught by Franz Boas. While she never lost her interest in psychology, and took her master's degree in that area, her doctorate was in anthropology, the field that became her life's work. Both of her graduate degrees were taken at Columbia. Although known as a university professor and educator as well as a researcher, Mead never held a full-time academic appointment. She taught as a visiting professor at New York University, the New School for Social Research, Emory University, and Vassar, among other schools. However, her most enduring academic affiliation was with Columbia University where she taught for more than 20 years as an adjunct professor. The primary benefit of this arrangement was that she was provided with graduate research assistants and freedom for long periods of time away from her faculty post. Mead was the second woman president of the American Anthropological Association (her mentor and friend Ruth Benedict was the first) and the first female anthropologist to become president of the American Association for the Advancement of Science. She was awarded the Presidential Medal of Freedom posthumously in 1979 by President Jimmy Carter. Mead's writings include 39 books, some of them co-authored, and more than a thousand articles and other writings spanning more than half a century (Howard 1984).

Any acknowledgment of contributions to the scientific and popular understanding of sex roles and male–female differences must include the work of Margaret Mead. Mead pioneered the ethnography of women and children. Prior to her fieldwork, most ethnographies were conducted by men and tended to focus on male roles. Not only did Mead focus on women and children in her studies of seven different South Sea Island groups, but she and husband Gregory Bateson also pioneered the use of still photography in ethnography. The end result was a recording of the everyday lives of the people studied, not only in words but also in the pictures brought back from the field. No doubt because of her early interest and training, Mead made anthropology more psychological. Throughout her life she maintained an interest in psychology and in psychoanalysis and often, to the chagrin of friends, suggested that they might be helped by psychoanalysis, although she herself never entered analysis (Howard 1984).

Mead did not identify herself as a feminist or feminist anthropologist, and even at times put down feminists – or more specifically, feminist rhetoric. She nevertheless made an indelible contribution to contemporary feminist thought. Although cross-cultural study and the preeminence of culture over biology are taken for granted in the study of gender roles today, this was not the case when Mead began her work. She documented female and male differences in diverse cultures, leaving little doubt that most of the differences attributed to sex in the United States were, in fact, culturally determined and learned through socialization rather than inherited with the male or female anatomy. Such knowledge contributed to moving women from the mentality of "I want to, but I'm a woman" to "I can do whatever I work at." Mead disliked the feminist critique of patriarchal society because she saw it as portraying women as the oppressed. Mead could not identify with the victim role even though the fact that she was a woman had initially made it difficult for her to do what she wanted. Teacher-mentor Edward Sapir objected to her field trip to Samoa based on her being a woman, and a very young one at that. Obviously, Mead did not allow Sapir's ideas to deter her and this experience may have increased her determination to succeed in her first field trip.

Throughout her life, Mead held to something of an old-fashioned idea of what it meant to be a "lady," when to wear gloves, for example. Some of her beliefs were inconsistent with those of the more radical behaviors and rhetoric of the second-wave feminists. She publicly disagreed with Betty Friedan's *The Feminine Mystique* (1963); she thought Friedan was assuming a victim role. Friedan included Mead in a chapter title and labeled Mead's *Male and*

Female (1949) as the "cornerstone of the feminine mystique." Even though Mead and Friedan were opponents, some would even say "public enemies," at Mead's death, Friedan attended her New York memorial service, explaining that she just felt a need to pay her respects (Howard 1984). Mead's life and work reflect contradictory views on feminism and women's equality. For example, she made the decision to retain her own name when she married for the first time in 1923, but once turned down a university presidency because "women make poor administrators." Yet in a 1975 conference she admonished women to stop pretending that they would live in a benevolent home where their husbands would never leave (Howard 1984).

Mead's work must be understood in historical context. In the early part of the twentieth century, the nature versus nurture argument was one of the major intellectual and philosophical issues of the day. Professor and mentor Franz Boas no doubt influenced Mead's work in his early rejection of the then dominant theory of racial superiority. Reconceptualized as heredity versus culture or learning, the argument was at the center in two of Mead's earliest and best-known works, *Coming of Age in Samoa* (1928) and *Growing Up in New Guinea* (1931). In the latter work she confronted the issue head on by posing the question in her Introduction: "How much of a child's equipment does it bring with it at birth?" While acknowledging that biological characteristics make all learning possible, Mead nevertheless concluded that human nature is malleable and responds to varying cultural conditions, including learning to be "male" or "female." Mead did recognize that restriction of either sex in exercising their abilities could leave them and the world the poorer, but argued that some restrictions are necessary to preserve a way of life. For example, in *Male and Female*, she questioned the value of bringing women into male-defined fields if it results in intimidating the men, "unsexes the women," and distorts the contributions each could otherwise make in their respective roles. As she saw it, the "cure" could be worse than the "disease."

Mead introduced the public to culture as more than the popular notion of music, art, and literature. She made it known that culture is all learned behavior, that it is patterned, and passed on from generation to generation through teaching and imitation but not by heredity. People in different places and at different times do things differently, including behaving as male or female. "We are our culture," she often said. During World War II, Mead popularized a concept borrowed from Ruth Benedict, of "national character," which she treated as the expression of American institutions and attitudes embodied to some degree in every American. Her book *And Keep Your Powder Dry* (1942) was published as a contribution to the war effort. She argued that the strengths and weaknesses of the American character were the psychological equipment with which the war could be won. Her work during World War II was indicative of her belief that science, anthropology specifically, should be useful. She spent time during the war in England and in Washington, DC, where she served as adviser to various governmental agencies and worked as a member of several wartime committees, most notably the Committee on Food and Nutrition and the Committee for National Morale.

Mead, unlike most intellectuals or academics, wrote for the public more often than for her colleagues. Mary Bateson (1984) described her mother's writings as always taking into account what would be helpful for people to know. Her field studies as well as other works were consistently cross-cultural; she compared unfamiliar customs with those of the everyday in the United States. It was unusual that an academic work such as *Coming of Age in Samoa* would become a bestseller, to be reissued in paperback, in several new editions and in several languages. Perhaps because of its popularity, Mead's Samoan work was questioned and challenged by other anthropologists for years to come.

Prior to World War II, Mead's career was defined by ethnographic fieldwork with seven different South Sea Island groups: the Samoans, the Manus of the Admiralty Islands, the Arapesh and the Tchambuli groups of New Guinea, the Mundugumor of the Yuat River, the Iatmul of the Great Sepik River, and the Balinese Islanders. During and after World War II, Mead became better known for her work on behalf of the war and her writings on domestic issues. These later works reflect both her interests in anthropology and in problems related to the family, communication, race, and the generation gap. Early in her career, Mead made a practice of educating the public about what anthropology is and what anthropologists do. *Sex and Temperament* (1935), for example, contains a chapter explaining in very accessible language and illustrations what anthropologists do and how they do it. At the end of a Mead work, readers were never left with the "so what?" syndrome. From her fieldwork, she always drew comparisons and "lessons" for her American readers.

While Mead was often controversial, she was always interesting. In her last years, she became an elderly statesperson or, as Howard (1984) described her, a "citizen philosopher" more than an anthropologist. She enjoyed public recognition and worked to make herself instantly recognizable. Because of a weak ankle, at age 60 Mead began using a hand-carved forked thumb stick which most people assumed to be the product of one of her field expeditions but which was, in fact, purchased from an umbrella shop in New York. She carried such a stick, which she called her pastoral rod, for the remainder of her life. She also took to wearing a long, flowing cape which she had made in several different colors, one being bright red. With her image, reputation, and identity buoyed by a monthly column in *Redbook* and by her frequent appearances on Johnny Carson's *Tonight* show, Mead became a kind of wise mother figure who never hesitated to express opinions or to dispense advice. In 1969, *Time* magazine named her "Mother of the World." Nor was Mead's public reputation lessened by the fact that she loved the acclaim and recognition. She is quoted by Howard (1984) as having made frequent statements in her youth that she would be famous – and indeed she was.

SEE ALSO: Bateson, Gregory; Culture, Gender and; Ethnography; Femininities/Masculinities; Feminism, First, Second, and Third Waves; Gender Ideology and Gender Role Ideology; Gender Oppression; Role; Sex and Gender; Socialization; Socialization, Gender

REFERENCES AND SUGGESTED READINGS

Bateson, M. C. (1984) *With a Daughter's Eye: A Memoir of Margaret Mead and Gregory Bateson.* William Morrow, New York.

Howard, J. (1984) *Margaret Mead: A Life*. Fawcett Crest, New York.

Mead, M. (1928, 1955, 1961) *Coming of Age in Samoa*. William Morrow, New York.

Mead, M. (1931, 1958, 1962) *Growing Up in New Guinea*. William Morrow, New York.

Mead, M. (1935, 1963, 1988, 2001) *Sex and Temperament in Three Primitive Societies*. William Morrow, New York.

Mead, M. (1949, 1967, 2001) *Male and Female*. HarperCollins, New York.

Mead, M. (1951) *The School in American Culture*. Harvard University Press, Cambridge, MA.

Mead, M. (1956, 1975) *New Lives for Old: Cultural Transformation – Manus, 1928–1953*. William Morrow, New York.

Mead, M. (1965) *Anthropologists and What They Do*. Franklin Watts, New York.

Mead, M. & Heyman, K. (1975) *World Enough: Rethinking the Future*. Little, Brown, Boston.

Mead, M. & Kaplan, F. B. (1965) *American Women*. Scribner, New York.

Mead, M. & Wolfenstein, M. (1955) *Childhood in Contemporary Cultures*. University of Chicago Press, Chicago.

measures of centrality

Ernest T. Goetz

Measures of centrality (or central tendency) are statistical indices of the "typical" or "average" score. They constitute one of three key characteristics of a set of scores: *center*, *shape*, and *spread*. Three measures of centrality are used in social science: mode, median, and mean.

The simplest measure of centrality is the *mode*, or most frequently occurring score. Since the mode is identified simply by counting the number of occurrences of each score, it can be found even for the categorical data of nominal scales, the lowest level of measurement. Nominal measurement sorts things into different types or categories, such as Republican, Democrat, or Libertarian. If more voters were registered as Republicans than any other party, then Republican would be the modal value for party membership. Note that Republicans need not represent a majority of voters in order to be the mode.

The *median* is the score that occurs in the middle of the set of scores when they are ranked from smallest to largest. It is the score at the fiftieth percentile, for which half of the scores are smaller and half larger. If half of the households in a community had incomes of less than $30,000, then that would constitute the median household income. Identification of the median requires at least ordinal data (i.e., data that can be ranked).

The most statistically sophisticated measure of centrality is the *mean*: the sum of the scores divided by the number of scores. Calculation of a mean is appropriate only for interval or ratio scales, which differ in whether they have an absolute zero (e.g., Fahrenheit or Celsius versus Kelvin temperatures, respectively). The mean is used to determine measures of variability such as the variance and standard deviation, and with them constitutes one of the key ingredients of all parametric statistics (e.g., analysis of variance (ANOVA), correlation, general linear modeling, hierarchical linear modeling, regression and regression analysis, structural equation modeling).

For interval and ratio data, the shape of the distribution of scores influences relationships among the three measures of centrality. For some distributions, such as the bell curve (i.e., normal distribution), the mean, median, and mode all have the same value. However, for skewed distributions, their values differ. For example, in positively skewed distributions, where the scores pile up at the lower end of the scale and tail off to the upper end, the mean will be largest, followed by the median and mode, respectively. In negatively skewed distributions, the order is reversed. Thus, for example, if most household incomes in a community were under $30,000 but a few were $100,000 or higher, the mean income would be highest, and the mode would be lowest.

Outliers, or scores that fall well outside the range of the rest of the distribution, also differentially affect measures of centrality. Since the mean is the only measure of centrality that reflects the exact value of every score, it is the only one affected by outliers. For example, it would not affect the modal or median income in a community if the highest income were $300,000 or $300,000,000, but it would affect the mean. The impact of outliers is greatest when the number of scores in the distribution (e.g., households in the community) is small.

Thus, despite its utility in inferential statistics, the mean can be a misleading indicator of central tendency. For this reason, the median typically is used to depict the "average" of scores in skewed distributions such as personal income and cost of houses in descriptive statistics. In addition, outliers sometimes are excluded to avoid distortion of the mean. When this is done, the researcher should report that fact, providing information about the number of outliers discarded and the reasons and rules for exclusion.

SEE ALSO: ANOVA (Analysis of Variance); Bell Curve; Descriptive Statistics; General Linear Model; Hierarchical Linear Model; Outliers; Regression and Regression Analysis; Statistical Significance Testing; Statistics; Structural Equation Modeling; Variance

REFERENCES AND SUGGESTED READINGS

Glass, G. V. & Hopkins, K. D. (1996) *Statistical Methods in Education and Psychology*, 3rd edn. Allyn & Bacon, Boston.
Shavelson, R. J. (1996) *Statistical Reasoning for the Behavioral Sciences*, 3rd edn. Allyn & Bacon, Boston.

measuring crime

Roland Chilton

All crime measures begin as attempts to count either incidents considered criminal or the people involved in such incidents. These basic counts may be combined, summarized, or modified in complex ways, but they are at the heart of all attempts to measure crime. Such counts can be generated by police departments or other public agencies or they can be created by anyone willing to design and use a questionnaire or interview schedule. Police measures include counts of offenses coming to their attention and counts of offenders based either on statements of victims and witnesses or direct police observation. Some police measures are counts of arrests or counts of the types of persons arrested. Other official agency measures are counts of prosecutions, convictions, persons in prison, or those under some kind of supervision imposed as a result of conviction for criminal conduct.

The numbers produced by these efforts are usually converted to crime rates because there has been a persistent interest in comparing the levels or amounts of crime occurring in specific places and in trends in crime over time. Since the size of the population limits the number of possible offenders and victims, comparing crime counts for places having very small populations with those for places having very large populations will result in misleading and inaccurate conclusions. Crime rates are usually computed by dividing a crime count by a specific population estimate. The police-based robbery offense rate for Chicago for 2003, for example, is the number of robberies coming to the attention of the Chicago police during 2003 divided by an estimate of Chicago's 2003 population. This fraction is usually multiplied by 100,000 and rounded to create the number of robberies per 100,000 residents (US Federal Bureau of Investigation 2004).

The major change in attempts to measure crime over the last 60 years was the development of survey approaches to produce victim counts and the use of a slightly different and less uniform set of surveys to produce offender counts for "self-report" measures of crime. These "self-report" surveys have been both national and local in scope. In such surveys, whether local or national, respondents are asked to report their own criminal activities over specified periods of time. They are usually asked if they have ever engaged in specific kinds of criminal or delinquent activity and sometimes how frequently they have done so.

This "self-report" approach was developed in the late 1940s and the early 1950s by social researchers dissatisfied with the limitations of police reports as crime measures (Nye et al. 1958). These efforts were initiated in part to measure the amount of crime that might not be reported to the police and to get more information on the backgrounds of offenders. Early self-reported crime studies usually asked questions of young people in school settings. They were often local in focus and their designers made no attempt to select national samples of respondents. This changed in the 1960s and 1970s and many criminologists now routinely rely on data from national samples. Some individuals in these national samples are questioned annually for several years (Elliott et al. 1985). In 1966, the President's Commission on Law Enforcement and Administration of Justice used a different procedure to assess the amount of crime that does not come to police attention. They asked a group of researchers to conduct a national victim survey. In contrast to the attempts to count all of the offenses reported to the police or public health agencies, this approach creates estimates of the number of victims of crime by asking carefully selected sets of ordinary people if they have been victims of a small set of crimes that closely parallel the list used in the Uniform Crime Reports program. The results of the initial survey were so interesting that the Commission recommended an annual victim survey. By 1973, the National Criminal Justice Information and Statistics Service (NCJISS), later to become the Bureau of Justice Statistics (BJS), created the National Crime Survey.

This approach, now called the National Crime Victimization Survey (NCVS), differs from the "self-report" surveys in its focus on victims rather than offenders. It was the most widely cited source of victim reports as measures of crime in the US for the last quarter of the twentieth century. Each year BJS has the Bureau of the Census carry out telephone interviews with adults in 40,000 randomly selected US households. Participants are asked a set of screening questions to see if they might have been victims of rape, robbery, assault, burglary, larceny, or vehicle theft. If the screening questions point to victimization, the participants are asked for more details. The counts made in this way are then "expanded" to estimate the number of offenses that occurred in the United States in the year under study. These surveys have had a consistent national focus and only provided victimization estimates for specific cities early in the program's history (NCJISS 1975; US Department of Justice and BJS 2003).

Historically, the earliest attempts to measure crime in the United States were efforts carried out by individual states to count and report prosecutions and convictions in criminal courts. But a groundbreaking measure of crime was created in 1929 when the International Association of Chiefs of Police (IACP) and the US Bureau of Investigation started the Uniform Crime Reports (UCR) program. Its founders developed a set of uniform descriptions of a small set of crimes – murder, rape, assault, robbery, burglary, and vehicle theft – and asked local police departments to submit counts of these offenses to the national program (IACP 1929).

In the early stages of its development, the UCR program used records of arrest and prosecution in the FBI's fingerprint file to produce arrest counts. The fingerprint file was compiled using information and fingerprints sent by local police agencies with requests for identification and the arrest history of the person whose prints were sent. This approach to arrest counts was later abandoned and police agencies were asked to submit separate summary reports of arrests and to indicate the age, race, and sex of persons arrested. During the 1930s and 1940s, UCR counts and rates were virtually the only national measures of crime in the United States. At the time, there were efforts to collect information from juvenile courts on the number of court referrals and the National Prisoner statistics program reported the number of prisoners received and released each year. But these specialized reporting programs made no effort to measure crime in the United States.

The three basic efforts to measure crime – police reports, self-reports, and victim reports – can be classified as attempts to estimate the extent of offending or the extent of victimization. Each of these approaches has specific strengths and weaknesses; each presents a different image of criminal activity and those involved in it. The basic strengths of police reports are their national scope and their provision of both national and local assessments of crime rates and crime trends. Another strength of police reports is the fact that they now provide information on far more than six types of crime. This has always been true for arrest counts but, in the new UCR program discussed below, it is also true for offense counts. The primary weakness of police reports is the fact that many crimes are never reported to the police and never come to police attention. In addition, since the UCR program is voluntary, some agencies do not provide reports and police departments have sometimes doctored the numbers reported in response to a variety of local pressures (President's Commission 1967: 26).

The great strength of victimization surveys is their lack of reliance on the police as sources of information. By going directly to a subset of ordinary citizens, they collect reports of crimes that may never have been reported to the police. In addition, the survey approach permits the collection of more information on the characteristics of victims and their households. In general, the NCVS is the only program that asks those victimized about their family income. The most important weakness of the NCVS is that it provides no local measures of crime, only a national estimate. Moreover, because some forms of crime are rare, the set of people surveyed must be large. This makes the NCVS expensive and limits the number of crimes that can be used in the survey. Finally, the basic focus of the survey on victims precludes the collection of any information on non-predatory or victimless crimes such as drug use.

Self-report studies, in contrast with victim surveys, are able to ask about victimless offenses. But their great strength is their ability to collect more detailed information about offenders than police reports or victim reports. Like victim surveys, self-report approaches do not rely on the police as a source of information. But the fact that the questions are asked anonymously limits the confidence we can have in the information collected. Most importantly, even though there have been several large-scale national surveys, there has always been a lack of uniformity in content and approach. Different questions are asked about different offenses and responses are classified and counted in different ways. There is no national uniform self-report program.

Although the Uniform Crime Reports and the National Crime Victimization Survey are very different in approach and have sometimes produced conflicting results, the two methods continue to provide widely accepted information on levels of offending and levels of victimization. All three approaches, police reports, self-reports, and victim reports, continue to provide some information about trends in crime and

responses to it. And all three provide information used to make assertions about the characteristics of offenders. With the development of the new UCR NIBRS program, discussed below, victim information is now available in two of the three basic approaches. Only the self-report surveys generally ignore victims.

Looking ahead, it appears that existing crime measures will be improved by a rapidly changing computer technology. Currently, the UCR program is being transformed from a summary statistics program to an incident-based program. The summary reporting approach requires local police agencies to classify and code all offenses and then to put summary counts on special forms designed by the FBI's UCR Section. The new approach, now called the National Incident-Based Reporting System (NIBRS), eliminates the need for local agencies to classify and summarize crimes coming to their attention every month. Instead, specially designed software collects information being keyed into computers as police officers report on the incidents to which they have been assigned. The primary purpose of the computer-generated reports is administrative. They create permanent records and help in the operation of the department. However, the NIBRS components of the computer programs collect and organize the incident information in a uniform format that is ready for transmission to a state UCR program, from where they are sent to the national UCR program. In some cases the information may be sent to the national UCR program directly (US Federal Bureau of Investigation 1992).

In 2003, the conversion to incident-based reporting was only partially complete. Police agencies representing about 20 percent of the US population were sending crime information in NIBRS format to the FBI. However, the percentage of the population represented by NIBRS agencies has increased every year since 1995. Unless there is a major policy change, this percentage will continue to increase until the UCR program has been completely converted from a summary statistics program to an incident-based program. When NIBRS information is processed it provides incident counts, offense counts, victim counts, offender counts, arrest counts, and information on the property involved in property crimes. The system permits police agencies to report multiple offenses, multiple victims, and multiple offenders in each incident. Since annual NIBRS data files are archived at the University of Michigan's Inter-University Consortium for Political and Social Research (ICPSR), there will be widespread use of the counts and this use will probably encourage improvements in the ways the UCR program presents the information to the public.

Another development that will probably have great impact on attempts to measure crime is primarily an extension of the NIBRS program. It requires the inclusion of street addresses in the NIBRS records, so the NIBRS records can be used to create computerized maps showing the local geographical distribution of specific offenses, offenders, and victims. This convergence of an improved crime measure with computerized mapping technology will not produce a new crime measure, but it will provide an informative and useful way to organize and view the information.

However, other computer technology may provide an improved crime measure through the statistical use of computerized criminal history (CCH) files. None of the approaches described above links a current criminal charge brought against an individual to that person's prior arrests and prosecutions. However, increased use of automatic fingerprint techniques and automated records of arrests and prosecution will make it possible to examine patterns of prior contact with the system of justice. Such a program could provide measures of the type and frequency of earlier charges brought against suspects at different points in their lives. It would provide indications of the existence or absence of patterns of involvement in specific types of crime. It would indicate the extent to which offenders specialize or engage in a variety of types of crime. It would permit extensive indications of the extent to which individuals persist or desist in criminal activities over the life course. Privacy concerns might impede the development of such a program. But concealing the identity of those in the file should not be an insurmountable problem. The Bureau of the Census creates public use files without providing identifying information and the incident numbers of archived NIBRS incidents are replaced with random characters in a way that retains the incident number as a unique

identifier without providing a link to any specific incident.

Nevertheless, experience with programs designed to measure crime in the past suggests that all of these new approaches to measuring crime may encounter resistance for a variety of reasons. One common objection to new crime measures is created by uncertainty about the impact of the new measure on local crime rates. This kind of uncertainty may be slowing the conversion of some traditional UCR programs to NIBRS. Although thousands of police departments in small and medium-sized cities have abandoned the summary statistics approach to crime reporting in favor of the new incident-based approach, many large city departments have resisted the conversion. This may reflect a concern by many large city mayors that conversion to NIBRS will create an appearance of rising crime rates. If the history of the UCR program is an indication of how long it takes to develop dependable crime measures, existing measures will continue to be used well into the twenty-first century.

SEE ALSO: Crime; Criminology: Research Methods; Index Crime

REFERENCES AND SUGGESTED READINGS

Elliott, D., Huizinga, D., & Ageton, S. (1985) *Explaining Delinquency and Drug Use*. Sage, Beverly Hills, CA.

International Association of Chiefs of Police (IACP) (1929) *Uniform Crime Reporting: A Complete Manual for Police*. J. J. Little & Ives, New York.

National Criminal Justice Information and Statistics Service (NCJISS) (1975) *Criminal Victimization Surveys in 13 American Cities*. US Government Printing Office, Washington, DC.

Nye, F. I., Short, J. F., & Olsen, V. J. (1958) Socioeconomic Status and Delinquent Behavior. *American Journal of Sociology* 63: 381–9.

President's Commission on Law Enforcement and Administration of Justice (1967) *The Challenge of Crime in a Free Society*. US Government Printing Office, Washington, DC.

US Department of Justice and Bureau of Justice Statistics (BJS) (2003) *Criminal Victimization, 2003*. US Government Printing Office, Washington, DC.

US Federal Bureau of Investigation (FBI) (1992) *Uniform Crime Reporting Handbook, NIBRS Edition*. US Government Printing Office, Washington, DC.

US Federal Bureau of Investigation (FBI) (2004) *Crime in the United States*. US Government Printing Office, Washington, DC.

media

Lyn Gorman

Discussions of media in a social context are generally concerned with mass media and, more recently, new media. Mass media are defined as communication systems by which centralized providers use industrialized technologies to reach large and geographically scattered audiences, distributing content broadly classified as information and entertainment. Media reaching mass populations emerged in the late nineteenth century – newspapers, magazines, the film industry – and expanded to include radio from the 1920s and television broadcasting from the 1950s. A range of "new media" developed from the 1980s, including video, cable and pay TV, CD-ROMs, mobile/cellular phones, and the Internet. In twenty-first-century societies media are pervasive and integral to modern life. Even in less developed societies they are widespread, although disparities in access remain. Economic profitability is also seen as a defining feature of modern media, reflecting the importance of commercial considerations to media institutions.

DEVELOPMENT OF MASS MEDIA

The newspaper press was the first "mass medium." In the late nineteenth century social and economic change (industrialization, growing urban populations, expanding education and rising literacy, changing patterns of work and leisure), technological developments (telegraph, telephone, printing technologies, the spread of railways), and policy changes such as the abolition of stamp duties that had restricted newspaper circulation, opened the way to development of newspapers attracting a mass readership. Changes in economic organization were crucial: the rise of

advertising made it possible to sustain a cheap popular press; and the development of newspaper (and magazine) chains achieved economies of scale. Powerful owners ("press barons") such as Lord Northcliffe in Britain and William Randolph Hearst and Joseph Pulitzer in the US built large-scale press enterprises and fostered journalistic styles that appealed to mass audiences, in turn attracting advertisers whose expenditure ensured profitability.

Throughout the twentieth century, wide-circulation, mass produced newspapers ("quality" newspapers/broadsheets and popular tabloids) remained significant. Advertising revenue sustained newspaper enterprises. Concentration of ownership, already apparent by the 1920s (Northcliffe and his family owned numerous newspapers and magazines in Britain), has persisted (Murdoch's global News Corporation is an outstanding contemporary example). Newspapers have overcome competition from emerging popular media (radio, television, the Internet), adapting to change. Some deplore the lowering of journalistic standards in the face of commercial pressures, but "quality" newspapers have survived (offering more sophisticated services via Internet websites); prestige dailies and tabloids continue to provide a cheap, easily distributed, and portable means of disseminating information and entertainment to a mass readership.

Film also emerged as a medium of mass entertainment in the late nineteenth century, drawing on inventions and technological developments in the US, Britain, France, and Germany (the application of electricity, developments in photography and celluloid film, invention of the motion picture camera, new projection techniques). Initially an urban, working-class entertainment, in the early twentieth century film became "respectable," appealing to middle-class audiences as film's potential to tell stories was exploited, permanent movie theaters were built, and more efficient distribution methods introduced. The luxurious picture palaces of the 1920s attracted growing audiences and increased film stars' popular attention. The Hollywood studio system developed: the "big five" – Paramount Pictures, 20th Century-Fox, Warner Brothers, Loew's (Metro-Goldwyn-Mayer was its production subsidiary), and RKO (Radio-Keith-Orpheum) – dominated the market, achieving vertical integration (controlling production, distribution, and exhibition), with Universal, Columbia, and United Artists also important. The appeal of cinema was enhanced when the introduction of sound ended the era of silent movies in 1927.

Hollywood enjoyed a golden age in the 1930s and 1940s: the film industry adjusted to changing circumstances (the Great Depression, another world war) and film was a major source of mass entertainment within the US and internationally. From the 1910s American companies came to dominate world cinema, due partly to their domestic success and ability to make substantial investment, partly to the diversity and high production values of American film. Success provoked criticism – of sex and violence on the screen, of depictions of national or racial groups, and of the use of cinema to promote consumer products and "Americanization." The industry succeeded in avoiding external censorship or regulation, adopting a Production Code in 1930 which influenced content over several decades. The industry faced its greatest challenge in the 1950s with the advent of television. In the US this came at a time when the Hollywood studios were weakened by a 1948 Supreme Court decision compelling them to cease involvement in exhibition and when the industry was affected by Cold War anticommunism that led to blacklisting of industry members after the investigations of the House Un-American Activities Committee.

By the 1960s the Hollywood studios had been absorbed into large conglomerates (Paramount purchased by Gulf and Western, Warner Brothers by Kinney National Services, United Artists by Trans America), and in later decades they became part of transnational concerns (20th Century-Fox part of Rupert Murdoch's News Corporation in 1985, Columbia taken over by the Japanese electronics firm Sony and MCA-Universal by Matsushita in 1990). Nonetheless, the film industry survived, developing mutually beneficial arrangements with television and increasingly involved in cross-media content provision and promotion. It remains a major source of mass entertainment in the twenty-first century. US cinema has remained dominant, even though film production has been internationalized (co-productions aimed at international audiences, investment in foreign

films). Other national and regional cinemas have also achieved a measure of international success (including film industries in the Indian subcontinent – "Bollywood" – and South America).

Radio developed as a mass medium in the 1920s. The US Navy was an early user of wireless telegraphy; technological developments contributed to the development of radio broadcasting, as did the pioneering work of individuals (Guglielmo Marconi from Italy, Lee De Forest in the US) and enthusiastic experimentation by amateurs with crystal sets. Building on technical developments during World War I, radio rapidly gained popularity in the 1920s, bringing information and entertainment into the home at a time when there was increasing emphasis on the private sphere in industrialized societies, and when other changes such as the spread of electricity made it possible to use radio sets.

Two contrasting institutional forms of radio broadcasting emerged in the US and Britain: commercial and public service broadcasting. These provided models for the development of sound broadcasting systems elsewhere, as well as the framework for the establishment of television as a mass medium in later decades.

The US model reflected the needs of commercial interests, with radio broadcasting seen as a source of profit (the companies General Electric, Westinghouse, and American Telephone and Telegraph formed the Radio Corporation of America/RCA). Networks were established and became enduring features of American radio and, later, television broadcasting: the National Broadcasting Company/NBC in 1926, Columbia Broadcasting System/CBS in 1927, the American Broadcasting Company/ABC in 1943. There was limited regulation of radio (and telephone and later television) by the Federal Radio Commission (the Federal Communications Commission/FCC from 1934). Financially, the US networks relied on selling time to advertisers who made or sponsored programs. The development of mass media and the growth of mass advertising and of consumer culture in the late nineteenth and early twentieth centuries were integrally connected. Radio (and newspapers and television) reached mass audiences; the advertising industry grew rapidly, developing techniques to persuade potential customers to acquire the expanding range of consumer products. Advertising has remained fundamental to commercial media. Its importance underlies the emphasis on entertainment programming appealing to mass audiences, and explains the importance of services such as audience ratings.

A different radio broadcasting model was adopted in Britain: a public service model, with the British Broadcasting Company licensed by the Post Office to begin transmissions in 1922. Rather than relying on advertising revenue, British radio relied on revenue from licence fees and royalties from the sale of wireless sets. In 1927 the Company became the British Broadcasting Corporation (BBC), established by royal charter as a national institution with a responsibility to "inform, educate, and entertain," with guaranteed income from licences and editorial independence. The contrasts with the US situation were marked: in Britain the BBC had a monopoly; it did not rely on advertising or sponsorship, but received public funding; and its charter set out public service responsibilities. The public service ethos was confirmed by Sir John Reith, who led the Company and Corporation until 1938. He stressed the BBC's educative role and importance as a leader of public taste and national culture.

The 1920s and 1930s are considered the golden years of radio, when a rich variety of program genres developed. Music was central to early radio, and this had an immense impact on the music industry. Broadcasters employed live bands and orchestras, then incorporated recorded music into programming as gramophone records became popular. A high level of dependence between radio and the music industry has continued, through technological change (tape recordings superseded records, which were superseded by compact discs) and changing patterns of audience consumption. In addition to music, other programs evolved: radio drama, comedy and variety shows, Westerns and detective programs, soap operas (soap-manufacturing companies were major sponsors), and quiz shows. The broadcasting of sporting events became an important component of radio programming. Radio was also used for political purposes (President Franklin D. Roosevelt broadcast "fireside chats" to national radio audiences in the US, Adolph Hitler used radio to deliver Nazi messages within and beyond German borders in the 1930s).

By the late 1930s radio had fundamentally changed home entertainment, offering mass audiences immediacy and a rich variety of programs. Arrangements for commercial broadcasting gave advertisers easy access to vast markets of listeners as consumers, a basis for expanding commercialism. Although radio declined as television gained in popular appeal, new forms were developed (portable transistors, car radios), and broadcasters successfully identified niche markets and particular "demographics" (continuing to attract relevant advertisers). By the late twentieth century radio, like other mass media, was subject to the effects of greater deregulation, economic concentration (with large corporations controlling many stations), and considerable emphasis on maximizing profits.

Limited television broadcasting began in the 1930s in Germany, Britain, and the US, but the outbreak of war in 1939 delayed its development, and it was not until the 1950s that television developed as a mass medium. It too drew on various developments (in electricity, telegraphy, photography, motion pictures, radio) and the work of inventors (including John Logie Baird in Britain and the Russian-born Vladimir Zworykin in the US on scanning devices).

In the US growth was rapid, with the radio broadcasting model adopted for the new medium (privately owned companies dependent on advertising revenue, with limited government regulation by the FCC). The existing networks – NBC, CBS, and ABC – dominated television, as they did radio broadcasting. The medium quickly became popular with advertisers. After initial competition, a profitable collaboration was established with Hollywood, films became a staple of programming, and the studios produced popular television series. By the 1970s the American networks were very profitable, paying attention to audience ratings in their quest for substantial advertising revenues; a fourth network, Fox (part of the Murdoch media empire), was added in 1986. A Public Broadcasting Service was established in 1967, but its role in commercially dominated US television has been minor.

In Britain, too, the radio broadcasting model was used as television developed. The BBC initially enjoyed a national monopoly, with no advertising and no direct government control, funded from the sale of radio and television licences. Programming conformed to public service values, emphasizing the cultural and educative role of television. In 1954 a commercial service was added, Independent Television (ITV), dependent on the sale of advertising spots but with higher levels of regulation and less scope for commercial pressure than in the US. With a second public service channel added in 1964 and the introduction of color in 1967, British television programming in the 1960s and 1970s was varied and of high quality. From 1982 Channel 4, a commercial channel regulated by the Independent Broadcasting Authority and catering to minority audiences, added diversity. By the turn of the century the BBC had survived as a significant public service broadcaster, despite two decades of deregulation and declining government support, alongside Britain's commercial but regulated channels.

Television development in other countries sometimes followed the US commercial model, sometimes adopted a hybrid of public service and commercial broadcasting, and in many cases was subject to high levels of state control. Television remains a powerful mass medium, although affected by changing contexts and patterns of ownership – the strength of free market ideologies, deregulation, and the quest for profits by the conglomerates that absorbed the networks. The influence of commercial interests has encouraged a blurring of the distinction between advertising and programs (product placement in entertainment programs is an example) and a proliferation of popular talk and "reality" shows with low production costs.

DEVELOPMENT OF NEW MEDIA

A range of new media developed from the 1980s. Again, technological innovation was essential, with the expansion of digital technologies allowing the convergence of previously separate media and more sophisticated links between traditional media and new information and communication technologies (ICTs). The expanding range of new media includes video recorders, home videotape players, pay TV delivered by cable and satellite, direct broadcasting by satellite, multimedia computers, CD-ROMs,

digital video discs (DVDs), the Internet and World Wide Web, mobile/cellular phones, and various handheld devices (the latest "generation" of these technologies offers not only telephone and messaging services but also commercial and personal video, photographs, and graphical information services). These have revolutionized communication, introduced opportunities for convergence of media content, and expanded audience choice and opportunities for interactivity.

Global take-up of the Internet is a noteworthy feature of new media development. Originating in US Cold War defense concerns to develop a distributed, indestructible communications system in the 1950s, the Internet was used by academic and research institutions in subsequent decades; commercial concerns became involved in the 1980s and 1990s through Internet service provision and growing use of the new medium for advertising and e-commerce; and development of the World Wide Web in the 1990s enabled use of the Internet as a public, global communications medium. Powerful corporations such as Bill Gates's Microsoft achieved prominence, and there was speculation, a rise and then fall in the profitability of "dotcom" ventures in the final years of the twentieth century. In the new millennium the Internet remains the most significant of new media, allowing for rapid information retrieval (through search engines such as Google) from ever-expanding resources, for interpersonal communication (through email) and for advertising and global commerce.

In a "media landscape" that has changed fundamentally through rapid global adoption of new media (as well as email, SMS and MMS, text and image messaging using mobile telephony, are proving immensely popular), traditional media have adapted to change. Newspapers, the film industry, radio, and television provide enhanced services and reach global audiences via websites. Commercial interests have been quick to exploit evolving media: the diversion of advertising business to the Internet is an example. For audiences, new media have provided greater choice and more control over how they receive information and entertainment. They have also introduced new problems such as piracy (the music industry has tried to curb free downloading of music via the Internet through litigation) and greater invasion of privacy; concerns about the relationship between media content and public morals have focused on the volume of, and easy access to, pornographic content on the Internet.

THEORETICAL APPROACHES

There has been debate about the relationship between media and society, especially since mass media developed in the late nineteenth century. Various theoretical approaches have been employed, drawing on different disciplines and areas of study. Fundamental to media research has been an understanding of human communication, with basic questions about who, says what, using which "channel," to whom, with what effect, underpinning different perspectives.

"Mass society" approaches have been influential in media studies. Early critics (T. S. Eliot, F. R. Leavis) deplored the effects of mass media, seeing "packaged" popular culture as inferior; their views reflected "critical anxiety" about the media, apprehension about mass society that grew as media industries developed. The Marxist Frankfurt School (Adorno, Horkheimer, Marcuse) saw the mass media as industries used to control the masses. The media contributed to the survival of capitalism by encouraging the working class to be passive recipients of the dominant ideology, allowing social control and maintenance of capitalist values. Other advocates of an "ideological control" approach (for example, Louis Althusser) saw media or their messages as supporting those in power (conveying a false view of reality, encouraging passivity and acceptance of the status quo). Theorists have pointed to the use of media in totalitarian societies to gain support for the ideology of those in power, and in democratic states to foster powerful consumer cultures. Mass society approaches became less influential in the late twentieth century as the concept of mass society lost ground and media institutions and patterns of ownership changed. Nonetheless, notions of media and the reproduction of ideology, linked to analysis of audience interpretations and reception of media messages, remained influential in late twentieth-century cultural studies.

"Effects research" (reflecting sociological and psychological interests) shifted attention from the impact of media on mass society to audiences and their "uses" of, and responses to, mass media. Some research derived from negative assumptions and fears (moral panics) about the impact of media (the effects of on-screen violence on children, or of sex and violence on public morals). There is growing consensus that it is difficult to reach firm conclusions about the effects of mass media. Such research has, however, introduced useful concepts. The idea of the "active audience," selective rather than passive, draws attention to ways in which audiences make sense of media communication, stressing pluralism and responsiveness, "uses and gratifications" (rather than a "hypodermic syringe model" whereby the media simply "inject" messages). Effects research also encouraged recognition of the many factors affecting audience reactions to mass media over the long term, encouraging research on cumulative and generalized effects (of forms of stereotyping, of omnipresent consumer culture images and values).

Approaches that concentrate on media content/messages have been influenced by disciplines such as literary and textual analysis and semiotics, as well as cultural studies. Here the emphasis is on what the media produce, leading to detailed analysis of images and meanings to determine how media represent or stereotype, particularly with respect to class, gender/sexuality, and race/ethnicity, but also raising more general questions of power. Cultural and social cultural approaches (drawing on the 1970s work of the Centre for Contemporary Cultural Studies in Birmingham) paid attention to both messages and audiences, examining the role of popular culture for particular social groups.

Growing interest in the political economy of the media stimulated late twentieth-century research that highlighted the importance of economics, institutional forms, and issues of ownership and power. This focus remains important in the context of globalization. Interest in the structure and dynamics of media organizations led to consideration of professional norms and expectations (of journalists and broadcasters) and their impact on media content (including "agenda-setting" and "gatekeeping"). In a broad sense, concern with the political economy of the mass media embraces issues such as media hegemony and cultural imperialism (building on 1970s concerns about media in the context of dependency approaches to third world development), the implications of highly concentrated ownership, the relative importance of market forces and public service values, and globalization and more standardized media products. Debates about media imperialism have gained new momentum with diffusion of the Internet and questions about its potential for local empowerment as opposed to globally homogenizing tendencies.

Specialized areas of study, such as various streams of feminism (liberal, radical, socialist, and postmodern), have used different theoretical perspectives to investigate aspects of media: effects research, content analysis, and political economy approaches to the impact of media representations on equality, the extent and power of gender stereotyping, the marginalization of women's activities such as sport, the role of media in creating a democratic public sphere in which women feel comfortable to participate, and so on.

There is growing appreciation of interdisciplinary perspectives that give due weight to the complexity of the issues relating to media, whether in modern nation-states or at the global level. These complexities include varying economic, cultural, and social contexts, the varieties of audiences and their interpretations of media products, recognition of the pervasiveness of media systems in contemporary societies, and the effects of convergence.

CURRENT EMPHASES

Contemporary media studies has vast scope, and many examples illustrate interest in the ways media influence or reflect social or individual experiences. Examples include the relationship between media and politics; the relationship between media and military during war and (a related issue) the use of media as propaganda tools; and the impact of media on sport.

It is generally accepted that mass media have had a profound impact on politics. They provided new means of communicating with national audiences. They assumed a significant role in agenda setting by selecting and interpreting information and helping to determine the issues that dominate public debate. Critics point out that television emphasizes image and "packaging" at the expense of issues and policies (the 1960 US presidential campaign television debate between John F. Kennedy and Richard Nixon was an early illustration of the importance of "image"). Contemporary media are seen as giving lower priority to traditional news values, with a decline in investigative journalism and "serious" current affairs programs; the lines between public affairs and entertainment have become blurred, with "infotainment" pervasive. Partly because of media involvement, political campaigns require enormous funds (the US is the prime example), thus limiting the range of political candidates. The advent of new media has provoked debate about their role in politics. On the one hand, new media afford greater access to information, with possibilities of enhancing individual empowerment, participatory democracy, and perhaps "civic reinvigoration." On the other hand, there is concern about high levels of image management (and "spin-doctoring") across traditional and new media by governments, politicians, and public relations agencies; about the continuing "digital divide," with great disparities in media access in industrialized and developing countries; and about the "reality" in political terms of "virtual communities."

Another area in which the role of media has been controversial is war. Relationships between mass media, the military, and governments during war have a long history, from the growing importance of war correspondents in the late nineteenth century through the Great War of 1914–18 and World War II in 1939–45. The relationship attracted increasing attention during the 1960s/1970s Vietnam War, when the media (particularly television) were blamed for the US defeat. Although historians argued that factors apart from television were important, in conflicts in the 1980s (the Falklands War, US invasions of Grenada and Panama) the British and US military exerted greater control over media during military operations. In the 1990s technological and institutional change (satellite broadcasting, global news services such as CNN) enabled media to provide "saturation" coverage of war to global audiences. To forestall adverse effects on public opinion, the military employed strategies of "media management." The US used a "pool" system during the Gulf War of 1991 and "embedded" journalists with military units during the Iraq War of 2003. Technological change challenges the extent to which media can be "managed" during war – it is difficult to control individual journalists' use of mobile and satellite communication and to regulate Internet communication. For western governments, the rise of new global broadcasters such as the Arabic television news channel al-Jazeera has also meant that global audiences have access to different perspectives. While global and national media are considered vitally important during both war and peace, there is continuing debate about the extent to which they shape or mirror public opinion.

A related issue is use of media for propaganda purposes. During war, media have been used to bolster patriotic and nationalist sentiment, to sustain morale at home, and to wage psychological warfare against the enemy (sometimes using blatant "demonization"). Totalitarian states' overt use of mass media for propaganda purposes is acknowledged (Hitler appointed Josef Goebbels as Minister for Public Enlightenment and Propaganda), although there is debate about the effectiveness of propaganda relative to methods of terror and repression. Democratic governments have also used media to persuade, "inform," and "educate." "Psychological warfare" using mass media has attempted to persuade populations to support particular causes. The Cold War (from the late 1940s to the 1980s) saw US and Soviet governments use media at home and abroad to disseminate their respective ideologies. In the US-led "war against terror" that followed the events of "9/11" (September 11, 2001) media largely reflected nationalist and patriotic values, but coverage of the war against Iraq has demonstrated that not all media images are likely to provoke sympathy for western policies. The role of media in war and the relationship between war reporting, public opinion, and support for government policy remain controversial.

With respect to sport, there is an integral relationship between media and sport. Sporting events are vital "commodities" for media, which in turn provide huge national and international audiences. Sport has responded to media requirements: it has become increasingly professionalized; there have been changes in game rules, sports attire, and the scheduling of events. The economics of sport has been transformed by mass media. The enormous amounts demanded by successful sportspersons, the sums paid for broadcasting rights to major international events such as the Olympic Games, and the relationships between international advertisers and sports personalities illustrate this point. Relationships of dependence link media organizations, sportspersons, sporting organizations, advertisers, and sponsors.

"Bigger questions" about media in the contemporary world also remain. They include the interrelationships of technological, cultural, economic, social, and political change. The technological determinist view was convincingly challenged by Raymond Williams in the 1970s, but debate continues on the extent to which economic conditions, social and cultural dynamics and preferences, and policy decisions affect the manner in which new media technologies are developed and adopted.

There is broad agreement that contemporary media give far greater weight to entertainment than to information and that traditional expectations have not stood the test of time. An example is the idea that media should fulfil a "watchdog" role in democratic societies, based on a perception of the newspaper press as the fourth estate. The development of giant media corporations in the late twentieth century (News Corporation, AOL-Time Warner, Disney) confirmed that media were big businesses driven by profit imperatives for whom old notions (such as investigative journalism or role in the nation-state) had little relevance.

Although media have expanded in type and reach, critics claim there has not been any corresponding expansion in media content or diversity – programming offers "more of the same," increasingly dominated by cheap formats (such as reality TV). Linked to this is debate about the extent to which both traditional and new media globally disseminate images of western consumer culture and influence audiences' attitudes, lifestyles, and values over the longer term. The history of traditional media in the twentieth century demonstrated the power of commercial interests, and the use of new media by advertisers in the twenty-first century indicates continuing commercialization. Linked with interest in the importance of consumer-society values are perennial questions about cultural hegemony and forms of "imperialism" in new guises ("Americanization" or the influence of global corporations). Recent research has pointed to the limits of US domination and the importance of local or regional cultural and social contexts (as well as individual reactions to media content), but the longer-term effects of control of media by profit-driven global corporations remain to be seen.

A notable feature of media history has been the adaptability and resilience of media forms. In an increasingly rich and diversified media world, traditional media – newspapers, the film industry, radio, television – remain important purveyors of entertainment and information despite rapid changes. However, it is noteworthy that Google, the Internet search engine, has, in a relatively short period, become the most used information source in the world.

Future research on media will build on existing areas (including work on established media – newspapers, cinema, radio, television) and expand into new realms. On particular topics such as media and politics, the impact of new media on public affairs, virtual communities, and citizens' participation is already attracting attention. Broader issues such as the relationship between media, consumption, and lifestyle continue to attract attention, now encompassing cyberspace and the multiple modes and means of delivery of advertisers' messages. The role of media in "digital lifestyles" and the implications of mobile, individualized access to a wide range of media products are areas for further research – work on the sociology of the mobile phone is already applying theories of social capital, networking, social atomism, and virtual walled communities. Research on other aspects of media and globalization will include political economy, content, and sociocultural impact. Continuing convergence (of services, products, and content) invites research on the implications for individuals, communities, societies, and globally of linkages between the media sector, ICTs, and telecommunications companies.

SEE ALSO: Audiences; Community and Media; Cyberculture; Film; Hegemony and the Media; Information Technology; Internet; Mass Culture and Mass Society; Mass Media and Socialization; Media and Consumer Culture; Media and Diaspora; Media and Globalization; Media Literacy; Media Monopoly; Media and Nationalism; Media, Network(s) and; Media and the Public Sphere; Media, Regulation of; Media and Sport; Multimedia; Music and Media; Photography; Politics and Media; Print Media; Propaganda; Public Broadcasting; Radio; Television

REFERENCES AND SUGGESTED READINGS

Axford, B. & Huggins, R. (Eds.) (2001) *New Media and Politics*. Sage, London.

Barker, C. (1999) *Television, Globalization and Cultural Identities*. Open University Press, Buckingham.

Baughman, J. L. (1992) *The Republic of Mass Culture: Journalism, Filmmaking, and Broadcasting in America since 1941*. Johns Hopkins University Press, Baltimore.

Briggs, A. & Burke, P. (2002) *A Social History of the Media: From Gutenberg to the Internet*. Polity Press, Cambridge.

Craig, G. (2004) *The Media, Politics and Public Life*. Allen & Unwin, Crows Nest.

Curran, J. & Gurevitch, M. (Eds.) (2000) *Mass Media and Society*, 3rd edn. Arnold, London.

Flew, T. (2005) *New Media: An Introduction*, 2nd edn. Oxford University Press, Melbourne.

Gorman, L. & McLean, D. (2003) *Media and Society in the Twentieth Century: A Historical Introduction*. Blackwell, Oxford.

Jones, M. & Jones, E. (1999) *Mass Media*. Macmillan, Basingstoke.

McQuail, D. (Ed.) (1972) *Sociology of Mass Communications: Selected Readings*. Penguin, London.

McQuail, D. (1987) *Mass Communication Theory: An Introduction*, 2nd edn. Sage, London.

Newbold, C. et al. (Eds.) (2002) *The Media Book*. Hodder, London.

O'Shaughnessy, M. & Stadler, J. (2002) *Media and Society: An Introduction*, 2nd edn. Oxford University Press, Melbourne.

Ward, K. (1989) *Mass Communications and the Modern World*. Macmillan Education, Basingstoke.

Wardrip-Frum, N. & Montfort, N. (Eds.) (2003) *The New Media Reader*. MIT Press, Cambridge, MA.

Williams, R. (1975) *Television: Technology and Cultural Form*. Schocken, New York.

Winston, B. (1998) *Media Technology and Society: A History from the Telegraph to the Internet*. Routledge, London.

media and consumer culture

Douglas Kellner and Clayton Pierce

"Media and consumer culture" is the transdisciplinary category used by theorists and social researchers to describe and understand the mediated experience of individuals and groups within consumer capitalist societies who are influenced and informed by a variety of different media, such as film, television, radio, newspaper, magazines, advertising, Internet, and other information and communication technologies. Implicit in the category of "media and consumer culture" is the connection drawn between the imperatives of capitalist consumer society and the harnessing of the methods of mass communication and culture that bolster the production/consumption paradigm.

By situating consumer society within the constellation of what is now being called a "media culture," theorists have attempted to explain how the relationship between media and consumer culture has developed into a qualitatively new social formation. This change in the relation between media and consumption illustrates the strengthening effect and influence this relationship retains on the politics, values, and ideals in contemporary society. Thus, it can be said that forms of media culture like television, film, popular music, magazines, and advertising provide role and gender models, fashion hints, lifestyle images, and icons of personality. This view also suggests that the narratives of media culture offer patterns of proper and improper behavior, moral messages, and ideological conditioning, sugar-coating social and political ideas with pleasurable and seductive forms of popular entertainment.

The expanding influence of media and consumer culture can be traced to its rise during the post World War II era and the emergence of theories that began to explore and examine the interconnectedness of advanced industrialized society and mass communication. After World War II, the consumer society emerged throughout the western world. Whereas the primary US corporations were developing systems of mass production and consumption in the 1920s (which saw the rise of media industries like broadcasting, advertising, and mass publications to promote consumer goods), the 1930s Depression and then World War II slowed the introduction of the consumer society. The Frankfurt School, living in exile in the US, was among the first to theorize this new configuration of society and culture in its critique of the culture industry, the integrative role of mass consumer society, and the new values and personality structures being developed.

Key Frankfurt School theorists included Theodor Adorno, Max Horkheimer, Leo Lowenthal, Walter Benjamin, and Herbert Marcuse. Horkheimer and Adorno's highly influential analysis of the culture industry published in their book *Dialectic of Enlightenment*, which first appeared in 1948 and was translated into English in 1972, provided a sharp critique of media and consumer culture. They argued that the system of cultural production dominated by film, radio broadcasting, newspapers, and magazines was controlled by advertising and commercial imperatives, and served to create subservience to the system of consumer capitalism. Horkheimer and Adorno combine analysis of the system of cultural production, distribution, and consumption with analysis of some of the sorts of texts of the culture industry and thus provide a model of a critical and multidimensional mode of cultural criticism.

Through the pioneering efforts of the Frankfurt School theorists, advanced industrialized society was shown to retain dynamic qualities that extended consumer culture through its domination of mass communications technologies into the sphere of private life. This view highlighted the fact that the advanced industrialized nations had increased the production paradigm to include the production of culture – deepening the understanding of the relationship between media and consumer culture to include theories on the transformations of subjectivities within the burgeoning media culture.

The Frankfurt School's theorists were joined by others from different parts of the industrialized western world who provided new interpretations and focused on the quickly evolving "media and consumer culture" of the mid-twentieth century. For example, in the US, marketing research for big corporations and advertising agencies took up broadcasting research and out of this process a dominant model of "mass communication" studies emerged. Paul Lazarsfeld and his colleagues at the Princeton Radio Research Institute, which included Frankfurt School member T. W. Adorno, began researching which programs audiences regularly tuned into, studied audience taste, and accordingly advised corporations concerning consumer demand for broadcasting product and what sort of programming was most popular (Kellner 1989). Hence, mass communications research emerged as an off-shoot of consumer research in the 1940s and 1950s, producing a tradition of empirical study of the established forms of culture and communications. Around the same time, new studies were beginning to take place in Europe that focused on another dimension of media and consumer culture. This expanded examination suggested that media and consumer culture's increasingly homogenizing and global quality could be viewed as a site of potential resistance to the dominant norms and values of advanced industrialized society's advancing consumer culture.

During the period between the early 1960s and the early 1980s, the University of Birmingham Centre for Contemporary Cultural Studies became one of the most important research centers for the study of society, culture, and media. The Birmingham group came to concentrate on the interplay of representations and ideologies of class, gender, race, ethnicity, and nationality in cultural texts, especially concentrating on media culture. They were among the first to study the effects on audiences of newspapers, radio, television, film, and other popular cultural forms. They also explored how assorted audiences interpreted and deployed media culture in varied ways and contexts, analyzing the factors that made audiences respond in contrasting manners to media artifacts. Stuart Hall's famous study "Encoding/decoding" (2002) highlighted the ability of audiences to produce their own readings and meanings, to decode texts in aberrant or oppositional ways, as well as the "preferred" ways in tune with the dominant ideology.

The Birmingham group offered new ways of understanding media and consumer culture, ones that looked to the proliferating hegemonic structure of media culture as a possible terrain for multiple readings and contestation. Indeed,

these innovative interpretations enlarged theorists' and social researchers' understandings of the increasingly complex dynamics of media and consumer culture as an active zone of engagement and social resistance. Congruently, it was during the same period in continental Europe and Canada that other interpretations of media and consumer culture were beginning to appear in French intellectual culture and North America.

Rapid modernization in France after World War II and the introduction of the consumer society in the 1950s provoked much debate and contributed to constructing a variety of discourses on the media and consumer society, inspiring Roland Barthes, Henri Lefebvre, Guy Debord, Jean Baudrillard, and their contemporaries to develop novel analyses of the emerging forms of society and culture. It was clear that the consumer society was multiplying images, spectacle, and new cultural forms and modes of everyday life. The leading French theorists of the period attempted to explain, make sense of, and in many cases criticize the novelties of the era.

Of these groundbreaking interpretations, Roland Barthes's *Mythologies* (1983), which drew upon earlier work in semiology and structuralism, analyzed codes and meanings embedded in artifacts of popular culture ranging from wrestling to soap ads, while dissecting their social functions. Other theorists, like Marshall McLuhan (1994), the most famous North American media theorist of this period, began to articulate the profound changes that media culture was beginning to have on everyday life and western civilization as a whole. The proliferating media culture, McLuhan argued, produced more fragmentary, non-rational, and aestheticized subjects, immersed in the sights, sounds, and spectacle of media such as film, radio, television, and advertising. It was in the sights and sounds of the emergent "global village" where McLuhan brought attention to the technological medium itself, claiming that in the new media age "the medium is the message."

Paralleling McLuhan, Guy Debord, in his masterful work *Society of the Spectacle* (1975), described the proliferation of commodities and the "immense accumulation of spectacles" that characterized the escalating consumer society. Grocery, drug, and department stores were exhibiting a dazzling profusion of commodities and things to purchase that in turn were celebrated in advertising campaigns that inscribed the novel consumer items with an aura of magic and divinity. Hence, the society of the spectacle refers to a media and consumer society, organized around the consumption of images, commodities, and spectacles.

Debord's society of the spectacle influenced Jean Baudrillard, another French theorist of the fetishization of media symbols and images in consumer culture. For Baudrillard, commodities form a system of hierarchically organized goods and services that serve as signs pointing to one's standing within the system. According to Baudrillard, consumers have a sense of the codes of consumption whereby certain cars, clothes, and other goods signify relative standing in the hierarchy of consumption. Thus luxury objects have more prestigious signification, are desired, and therefore provide seductive social gratifications. On this analysis, needs, use values, and consumer practices are all socially constructed and integrate individuals into consumer society. While Baudrillard's account lacks a critique of the political economy of media and consumer society, he nonetheless advances our understanding of the connection between media and consumer culture by stressing how uses, wants, needs, and sign values of commodities are all socially constructed, as part of a system of production and consumption.

These novel understandings of media and consumer culture also pointed to an emerging global character and the rapid movement of signs and cultural symbols through multinational corporate channels. Thus, in the post-World War II conjuncture, the spectacle became globalized as corporations such as Coca-Cola and Pepsi, sundry national automobile corporations, IBM and the nascent computer industry, and subsequently McDonald's, Nike, Microsoft, and a cornucopia of global products circulated throughout the world (Kellner 2003). With increasingly complex forms of media, a strikingly global quality was producing and disseminating the values, attitudes, and the rationality of consumer culture at unprecedented levels.

This globalizing quality of the consumption/production paradigm is captured by sociologist George Ritzer (2004) in his concept of "McDonaldization." Building on the work of German sociologist Max Weber, Ritzer argues that the phenomenon of McDonald's fast food restaurants now embodies and retools the principles of industrial rationality: efficiency, calculability, prediction, and control "particularly through the substitution of nonhuman for human technology." For Ritzer, the McDonaldization model has extended the "iron cage" of industrial society's rationalization process, moving beyond Weber's theory of bureaucratization as well as other production models such as Fordism and Taylorism. Moreover, Ritzer's model of McDonaldization suggests advancement in the rationality process by providing a template for social institutions and places of consumption such as hospitals, schools, and theme parks to emulate. For Ritzer, this new model of production accelerates the influence of instrumental reason by streamlining the production/consumption model, enabling the rationalization process to encroach into more sectors of society both within the US as well as the rest of the world.

Ritzer does note that the McDonaldization process is not a uniform one because it varies in degree depending upon context and setting. In doing so, Ritzer is able to take into account variances among consumer behaviors and production patterns that require flexibility from the McDonaldization process. Thus, for Ritzer, sociocultural context and differing consumer habits in fact generate multiple trajectories of the McDonaldization process, reflecting the malleable character of McDonaldization as opposed to a monolithic one.

As Ritzer provides new ways of understanding the transfer of consumer and production habits and methods with his McDonaldization model, in *Enchanting a Disenchanted World* (2005) he provides probing sociological analysis of the new forms and settings of consumer culture, ranging from hyperreal Disney worlds and virtual realities to the local mall and stadium. Engaging new "Cathedrals of Consumptions," Ritzer deploys modern and postmodern perspectives to explore how new means of consumption are providing a "reenchantment" of the world through the creation of spectacles via extravaganzas, simulation, and implosion of space and time in arenas such as malls and new modes of shopping, to Las Vegas and fantasy theme parks that implode shopping, travel, and entertainment. Although Ritzer recognizes "media and their ever present advertisements" are crucial "facilitators of consumption [that] are clearly of great increasing importance (p. 34), he chooses to focus on the new means of consumption themselves (compare Kellner (2003), who focuses on the role of the media in the reproduction of media spectacle and the consumer society).

Exploring similar themes as Ritzer, Mark Gottdiener (2000), another sociologist from the US, offers critical analysis of the new places in which people consume commodities and create identities deploying neo-Marxist, semiological, and other theoretical perspectives. Gottdiener has pointed to the strengthening influence of media and consumer culture and its effects on the formation of identity through "spaces of consumption," including malls, airports, entertainment parks, and the Internet. For him, spaces of consumption make up a material realm that is a conjuncture of many cultural influences that inform the construction of identity in contemporary society. According to Gottdiener, these new spaces of consumption are characterized by (as with Ritzer) their themed appearance, as is the case with such stores as Nike Town, Hard Rock Café, and Planet Hollywood. Gathered together in a spectacle of consumer delight, the shopping mall typifies the novel sites of consumption because it provides the individual with a multiplicity of value-laden commodities by which identities are influenced and formed.

Gottdiener's research charts emerging arenas of the media and consumer culture landscape by illuminating not only the workplace as a formative influence on the construction of identity, but also by delineating new spaces of consumption that constitutes a common experience in contemporary society. Indeed, these spaces of consumption are not limited to the material realm, as media spectacle provides entertainment fantasies through which individuals may create new identities, as well as experiencing the social and political dramas of the present age (Kellner 2003). Moreover, novel exciting spaces have opened up through the advent of the Internet, adding to the milieu of consumption the phenomenon of the virtual self. Consequently, online shopping, surfing, and interacting now plays a defining role in the construction of self and consumer habits, allowing people to sit comfortably at home and create one's identity through cyber shopping experiences, consuming and commenting on media culture, interacting with others in virtual space, and dabbling in politics.

Recent social theorists and researchers have argued that media and consumer culture's dialectic relationship offers potential for progressive and transformative meaning and identities while, at the same time, also acknowledging its assimilatory quality as a tool of the status quo. With the continued proliferation of media and information technologies coupled with the rise of the so-called "information age," the landscape of media and consumer culture has indeed entered a watershed era. The billions of dollars spent each year in the US on advertising and marketing indicate the amount of research and energy that goes into controlling the systems of mass communication by corporate interests. With massive government deregulations, the oligopoly of global media conglomerates, made up of multinational corporations such as AOL Time Warner, Disney, General Electric, News Corporation, Viacom, Vivendi, Sony, Bertelsman, AT&T, Liberty Media, Yahoo, and Google, signals an increasingly uniform and homogenized culture industry, one where politics, social values, information/disinformation, and images create a constellation of great complexity. Yet varying appropriations of these forms and active audiences and consumers are producing new hybrid forms of media and consumption, novel types of meanings and identities, and new modes of consumer technopolitics such as hacking, culture jamming, and organizing campaigns and boycotts against certain corporations like Nike or McDonald's. Hence, the complexity and contradictions of contemporary media and consumer culture requires transdisciplinary approaches whereby theorists and social researchers employ multiperspectival approaches that incorporate different theories and analyses in order to interpret and understand this highly fluid field that has now come to play a defining role in the lives of so many.

SEE ALSO: Consumption, Cathedrals of; Consumption and the Internet; Consumption, Mass Consumption, and Consumer Culture; Globalization, Consumption and; McDonaldization; Postmodern Consumption

REFERENCES AND SUGGESTED READINGS

Barthes, R. (1983) *Mythologies*. Trans. A. Lavers. Hill & Wang, New York.

Baudrillard, J. (1975) *For a Critique of the Political Economy of the Sign*. Telos Press, St. Louis.

Baudrillard, J. (1983) *Simulations*. Semiotext{e}, New York.

Castells, M. (2000) *The Rise of the Network Society*. Blackwell, Oxford.

Debord, G. (1975) *Society of the Spectacle*. Black & Red, Detroit.

Durham, M. & Kellner, D. (Eds.) (2002) *Media and Cultural Studies Keyworks*. Blackwell, Oxford.

Gottdiener, M. (Ed.) (2000) *New Forms of Consumption: Consumers, Culture, and Commodification*. Rowman & Littlefield, Lanham, MD.

Hall, S. (2002) Encoding/decoding. In: Durham, M. & Kellner, D. (Eds.), *Media and Cultural Studies Keyworks*. Blackwell, Oxford, pp. 166–76.

Horkheimer, M. & Adorno, T. W. (1972) *Dialectic of Enlightenment*. Herder & Herder, New York.

Kellner, D. (1989) *Critical Theory, Marxism, and Modernity*. Johns Hopkins University Press, Baltimore; Polity Press, Cambridge.

Kellner, D. (1995) *Media Culture: Cultural Studies, Identity, and Politics Between the Modern and the Postmodern*. Routledge, New York.

Kellner, D. (2003) *Media Spectacle*. Routledge, New York.

McLuhan, M. (1994) *Understanding Media: The Extensions of Man*. MIT Press, Cambridge, MA.

Ritzer, G. (2004) *The McDonaldization of Society: Revised New Century Edition*. Pine Forge Press, Thousand Oaks, CA.

Ritzer, G. (2005) *Enchanting a Disenchanted World: Revolutionizing the Means of Consumption*, 2nd edn. Pine Forge Press, Thousand Oaks, CA.

media and diaspora

John Sinclair

Since the late 1980s, the concept of diaspora has become ever more widely used to describe the movement of people away from their land of origin, such as migrants, exiles, refugees, expatriates, and "guestworkers." Literally, a diaspora is a dispersal of people from one country into many, such as the Jewish Diaspora of antiquity, or in modern times, the flow of people out of China and India and into the rest of the world. Strictly speaking, a diaspora is distinct from ordinary migration in that members of a diaspora are linked not only back to their compatriots in their land of origin, but also laterally, with each other, across the borders of however many countries they have moved into. In practice, the term is more often used in a loose way to refer to population movements across borders and "transnational communities" in general, but especially where cultural barriers also have to be crossed, and people are living in marginal situations within a dominant culture.

It is not just the flows of people that are of interest here, but the flows of media services and content that go along with them, both of which are part of what we mean by "globalization." Diasporic movement is both a cause and an effect of globalization, and this generates different classes of diasporic peoples. For example, while the expatriate capitalist groupings known as the "Overseas Chinese" and the "NRIs" (Non-Resident Indians) control substantial global investments, many other ordinary Chinese and Indians work in foreign countries as laborers. Correspondingly, there is a wide range of diasporic media in use. At one level, there are international satellite television services which relatively wealthy subscribers can enjoy in comfort, while more down-to-earth CDs and videos can be carried by people in diasporic movement in their luggage, or rented from the local grocery store. The Internet enables families and friends in different countries to send each other their news and photos via email, while organized groups maintain websites.

In this way, diasporic media reinforce ethnic identities, possibly at the expense of national cultural identities. Of most interest here are studies of how diasporic peoples are engaged in a productive construction of new hybrid identities and cultures through processes of cultural maintenance and negotiation.

Hamid Naficy's (1993) study of what he calls the "exilic" television produced by Iranians in Los Angeles in the 1980s is a model for how communication media can be used to negotiate the cultural politics of both "home" and "host." Drawing on political economy as well as cultural studies, he theorizes the Iranians' production and consumption of their own cable television as a dialectic between nostalgic longing for the lost homeland and an effort to achieve economic integration and develop a new sense of themselves.

Another classic study is Marie Gillespie's (1994) detailed ethnographic work with families of Punjabi origin in their homes in West London, which demonstrates the role of television watching, and family talk about television, in the construction of a British Asian identity among young people. Yet a darker side of diasporic media is revealed by Dana Kolar-Panov in her *Video, War, and the Diasporic Imagination* (1997), which explores the role played by video "letters" amongst overseas citizens of the former Yugoslavia as their country was breaking up during the early 1990s. Just as there are websites which still foster memories of the Sino-Japanese War decades ago, these "atrocity videos" played upon traditional ethnic divisions. Thus, the use of media in cultural maintenance and negotiation is not necessarily positive. Even nostalgia is not innocent if it locks émigrés into a time warp.

Taking communities of Chinese, Vietnamese, Indian, and Thai origin in Australia, Stuart Cunningham, John Sinclair, and colleagues (Cunningham & Sinclair 2001) studied the processes in which desires generated by diasporic experience, for example wanting to stay in touch with news and popular culture from the homeland, translate into demand for certain kinds of media services and products. This includes how diasporas, even when they are small and dispersed, can become formed as media markets through "global narrowcasting" technologies, notably international satellite television.

Most of these studies, as well as more recent work, have been brought together in *The Media of Diaspora* (2003), edited by Karim Karim. This covers not only case studies of the use of television and video amongst several deterritorialized peoples, but also the rise of computer-mediated communication – websites, e-magazines, chatlines – amongst diverse diasporas. Without downplaying the considerable capacity of diasporic groups to generate their own television and video content, the interactivity of the Internet can be seen to offer more inclusive, active, and accessible modes of communication than television and other "old" media.

As far as theory is concerned, the study of diasporas has tended to undermine the traditional concept of culture, that is, culture as a fixed, given essence, bounded by the territory of the nation-state, in favor of more hybrid notions of culture. For example, in *The Location of Culture* (1994), Homi Bhabha sees a process of "cultural translation," in which the diasporic individual actively opens up a "third space." Diasporic culture in such a perspective is thus the product of the constantly configuring process which occurs when immigrant or otherwise displaced cultures selectively adapt to host cultures, intermingling and evolving to form a regenerative "new" culture, a culture related to, but yet distinct from, both the original home and host cultures. Diasporic media are both an influence upon and an expression of this process of creative and adaptive fusion.

SEE ALSO: Community and Media; Diaspora; Media and Globalization; Media and Nationalism

REFERENCES AND SUGGESTED READINGS

Cohen, R. (1997) *Global Diasporas: An Introduction.* University College London Press, London.

Cunningham, S. & Sinclair, J. (Eds.) (2001) *Floating Lives: The Media and Asian Diasporas.* Rowman & Littlefield, Lanham, MD.

Gillespie, M. (1994) *Television, Ethnicity, and Social Change.* Routledge, London and New York.

Naficy, H. (1993) *The Making of Exile Cultures: Iranian Television in Los Angeles.* University of Minnesota Press, Minneapolis.

media and globalization

John Sinclair

While in everyday language "globalization" usually refers to economic and political integration on a world scale, it also has a crucial cultural dimension in which the media have a central role. Indeed, in sociology and other disciplines that focus on the media, the concept of globalization has had to be adopted so as to take account of a new reality in which global institutions, especially the media, impact upon the structures and processes of the nation-state, including its national culture. In that sense, media globalization is about how most national media systems have become more internationalized, becoming more open to outside influences, both in their content and in their ownership and control. This is a cultural phenomenon, one with implications for our contemporary sense of identity, but it is closely linked also to the economic and political factors driving globalization, notably the deregulation of national markets and the liberalization of trade and investment, which in turn facilitate the inroads of global corporations.

THE MEDIA AND GLOBAL CORPORATIONS

The corporations which characterize global capitalism today are privately owned institutions with their origins in large nationally based companies that were the "transnational corporations" of the 1960s and 1970s, and which since have globalized themselves. That is, they have become more complexly interpenetrated with other companies, and more decentralized in their operations. Of most relevance to the media are the long-established consumer goods companies whose products are made and marketed worldwide, such as Coca-Cola and Ford. They are predominantly of US origin, but not exclusively so: there are major British, Dutch, and French global companies, and more recently, Asian ones. These are the global advertisers from whom the media corporations, several of which are themselves global in scale, derive their income, and whose quest for markets is the motive force behind media globalization.

There are some global media corporations, such as Sony, which began as communications hardware industries and then branched into content production, in Sony's case, film and recordings. However, others have been built upon the basis of the media industries themselves. Their rapid growth over the closing decades of the twentieth century was due to the ideological and structural shift toward

privatization and economic liberalization of trade and investment which characterized this era, but also to a range of technological developments, particularly the trend to the convergence of media with telecommunications.

The new ideological climate greatly transformed the regulation of media industries. To take one significant example, widescale privatization of the television systems of most of the nations of Western Europe was brought about in the 1980s, including the advent of private ownership of international television satellites. News Corporation, under the chairmanship of Rupert Murdoch, can be regarded as an archetypical model of how the new regulatory mood and technological developments of the era became business opportunities that could be exploited, such as with its acquisition of BSkyB in Britain.

In a classification of global media corporations devised by Herman and McChesney (1997) toward the end of the 1990s, News Corporation ranked fifth amongst the companies that made up the first of the two tiers in their list. Even before its merger with America On Line, Time-Warner was at the top, followed by Disney, and the largest European-based media corporation, Bertelsmann. Notable others in the first tier were companies which had taken advantage of technological convergence, General Electric and Liberty Media. The second tier consisted mainly of US newspaper and information service companies, plus several European media groups, and the major media conglomerates that have developed in Latin America and Asia. However, the very largest media corporations are nearly all American, and this continues to be a major issue in media globalization.

As well as the horizontal integration of "new" media, such as Internet service provision and satellite television, with "old" media, such as the press and broadcast television, these corporations are characterized by vertical integration. This means that sequential layers of business activity are incorporated under the same conglomerate umbrella: for example, a corporation engaged in film production will have related companies to distribute the films, and the videos and DVDs made from them. It is worth noting that audiovisual media have proven to be more able to cross national frontiers than print.

FROM "CULTURAL IMPERIALISM" TO "GLOBALIZATION"

Much of the theoretical and critical debate over recent decades can be seen as a response to the rise of these various types of corporation, their influence upon national governments, and their social and cultural effects on populations. In particular, the whole discourse about "cultural imperialism" in the 1970s and 1980s now can be seen as the protest of nation-states as they adjusted to the globalization of the media and consumer industry corporations in an era in which international relations was dominated on one hand by the inequalities between the "West" and the "third world," and on the other by the pressures of the Cold War. Indeed, it was only since the collapse of the eastern bloc that the discourse of globalization began to supersede that of cultural imperialism.

The age of globalization has nevertheless adopted a number of notions from the past, the most persistent being that greater economic and political integration in the world also necessarily brings about a "global culture." This view assumes a decline in the power of the nation-state in the face of global forces, such that new forms of cultural identity, beyond the national, are seen to have growing significance, while national cultures are eclipsed by a universal popular culture of media and consumption. The cultural authority of the nation-state is believed to be under challenge in at least two ways. Firstly, globalization causes a massive increase in the movement of people across borders, resulting in much more culturally and linguistically diverse populations in each nation-state. That is, nation-states are much less culturally homogeneous than they believed themselves to be in the past, and furthermore, thanks to modern media, their diverse populations can maintain strong ties to the culture and language of their original homeland. This trend has important theoretical implications for the traditional sociological concept of culture itself, rooted as it has been in terms of the "organic" way of life of a certain people fixed in a certain place.

Secondly, the national cultures which cultural imperialism discourse once sought to defend against outside influence now stand revealed as ideological constructions through which the dominant social groups in each nation-state legitimize and perpetuate their domination, whether in terms of gender, ethnicity, or class. Thus, along with universal social movements based on gender and sexual preference, global migration has brought to the fore social differences which formerly were concealed by notions of national culture, so that nation-states are losing their cultural authority at the same time as their sovereignty is threatened by economic and political globalization.

THEORISTS OF GLOBALIZATION

The globalization of the media has enabled vast sections of humanity to gain access as never before to the enormous output of information and entertainment which flows around the world. On occasion, they also can become spectators to global media events, ranging from regularly scheduled ones such as the Olympics, to unique and totally unexpected ones like those of September 11, 2001 in the United States (Dayan & Katz 1992). Yet it is important to appreciate that contemporary globalization theorists do not necessarily fear global culture as an irresistible force of homogenization, as their predecessors did.

One of the most influential theorists has been Arjun Appadurai (1990), who identifies a series of "flows" – of people, media, technology, capital, and ideas – which constitute globalization. These flows are "disjunctive," that is, they operate independently of one another, unlike in theories derived from Marx which see cultural phenomena as being conditioned by economic processes. Marxist theories have emphasized what they see as a trend to cultural "homogenization," that is, the similarities in media content found throughout the world, particularly in the form of "Americanization." Appadurai acknowledges this trend but argues that it exists in tension with a countertrend to "heterogenization," which is the hybrid cultural differences that occur when global influences become absorbed and adapted in various local settings. Heterogenization happens now that people are presented by global media with a mélange of cultural and consumption choices that they never had when their cultural imagining was defined by a dominant national culture.

As well as the theoretical debate around cultural sameness and difference, there is another which is more concerned with "deterritorialization," or the social and cultural effects of media that can vanquish space as well as time. Media such as international satellite television and the Internet allow individuals to be free of the constraints of place, and instead act within a global context, regardless of where they are. Anthony Giddens (1990) believes that such "time-space distanciation" is one of the modes through which the institutional mechanisms of modernity have become global. Manuel Castells (1997) has drawn attention to the "space of flows" which underlies the global "network society." Location still matters, says Castells, but only in terms of its relation to other locations in the patterns of global flow (whether of capital, goods, people, information, and so on).

John Tomlinson, in his *Globalization and Culture* (1999), sees interconnectedness as the principal fact about globalization, calling it "complex connectivity," but also argues that complexity is a defining characteristic in itself. All these theorists agree that the control of space and time is the defining abstract principle behind globalization. The media are central to this control, not just because they transcend both space and time, but also because of their inherent interconnectedness, especially in their capacity to give individuals access to global networks, regardless of their location.

The idea that people can have more than one cultural identity at the same time, or rather, cultural affiliations existing at different levels, is the general contribution of postmodernist theory to understanding cultural globalization. Equally, there is the insight that the process of globalization is mediated by regionalization, and that the "regions" involved exist at both macro and micro levels, that is, both above and below the nation-state. Jan Nederveen Pieterse (1995) has shown how a number of criss-crossing levels of social organization can be seen to correspond to cultural identifications: transnational (or "global"), international, macroregional, national, microregional, municipal, and local.

Thinking of the production, circulation, and consumption of media and other cultural products as occurring at such an interlocking series of levels, with cultural identities corresponding to each level, puts the concept of global culture into a comprehensible perspective. Rather than a universal force for homogenization, global culture can be seen as just one more level at which particular kinds of cultural forms can circulate around the planet. For example, Oliver Boyd-Barrett (1997) refers to the "global popular," meaning a globally marketed cultural product of a certain kind, such as a Hollywood blockbuster movie. Such products receive maximum publicity and marketing support on a global scale, and are distributed through complex hierarchies of channels. Yet although this material might assert its own level of cultural influence, there is no reason to believe that it thereby drives out other media and consumption choices, and the identities they express, especially those based on ethnicity and religion.

GEOLINGUISTIC REGIONS AND THE CASE OF TELEVISION

Different media exhibit different patterns of globalization. The Hollywood blockbuster movie would most closely fit the notion in literal terms, being released and exhibited more or less simultaneously in the various national markets of the world, dubbed or subtitled as required. Television, arguably the most widely diffused and most influential of all the popular media, is different. In the 1960s and even the 1970s, the critics of cultural imperialism were alarmed to discover high levels of foreign content, mainly from the US, on the television screens of the world. However, as television markets have matured and developed the capacity for their own production, they have moved away from this initial dependence. The evidence now indicates that audiences prefer television programming from their own country, and in their own language, when that is available, or if not, from other countries which are culturally and linguistically similar (Straubhaar 1997).

Language is a fundamental factor in the globalization of media markets, and the main way in which the process is mediated by regional factors beyond the nation-state. The regions in this case can be thought of as "geolinguistic" in the sense that they are defined more by commonalities of culture and language than by geographical proximity. Historically, they have been formed by colonization and the world languages propagated in that process, notably English, Spanish, Portuguese, and French. As it is easily taken for granted in the English-speaking world, or what some now call the "Anglosphere," it is instructive to see how significant language is in other world regions. Thus, just as the huge size of the domestic market enables the US to hold sway over program exports in English, the major television corporations of Mexico and Brazil dominate the program export trade in the Spanish and Portuguese geolinguistic regions, since their home markets are the largest in those respective regions (Sinclair 1999).

Actually the world's largest geolinguistic region is "Greater China," in which programs are traded between the People's Republic of China (Mainland) and Republic of China (Taiwan) in spite of their political differences, while Hong Kong remains a major center for all kinds of audiovisual production and distribution. India provides a quite different case, where the liberalization of television has meant a boost for "local" languages. These are languages with tens of millions of speakers, such as Tamil and Bengali, forming commercially sustainable geolinguistic regions. Despite cries of "cultural invasion" that greeted the advent of STAR TV and CNN satellite-to-cable services at the beginning of the 1990s, by the end of the decade it was Indian channels that had won over the allegiance of audiences, most strikingly those broadcasting in the local languages. Also most significant in the Indian case is the fact that these channels undermine the traditional "nation-building" role of television in India, particularly the efforts of the nation-state to establish Hindi as a national language, and raise the question of just how much cultural and linguistic pluralism a large nation-state can bear.

In the age of transnational satellite television, geolinguistic regions have come to include users of particular languages dispersed on a global scale, however remote and isolated. This is most often where there have been great diasporic population flows out of their original countries, of which the Chinese and the Indian are classic cases. Just as English speakers can watch CNN or BBC World wherever they are, so too are their services distributed globally in other major world languages, and indeed, in a number of minor ones. In this way, far from eroding local cultural identities, as theorists of homogenization fear, global television contributes to their maintenance.

GLOBALIZATION, FREE TRADE, AND CULTURAL DIVERSITY

In 1995, the World Trade Organization (WTO) was set up, the culmination of years of international negotiations under the auspices of the United Nations General Agreement on Trade and Tariffs (GATT). The many nation-states that signed have thus committed themselves to the eventual removal of trade barriers across all sectors, which includes the media. Long before the establishment of the WTO, the United States had been putting direct pressure on the many nations of the world that have various policies – subsidies, screen quotas, import levies, and the like – aimed at bolstering their national cultural industries against market dominance by high-quality but low-cost media products and services from countries with comparative advantages in the media trade. In practice, this means the United States, since producers there can export films, television programs, and recorded music at low prices, because they have already recovered their costs and gone into profit in the large domestic market.

Thus, a global free trade regime in the media industries favors the United States, which refuses to accept that other countries might have their cultural trade policies as a means of protecting their forms of national cultural identity and expression. Such arguments are rejected as merely an excuse to maintain economic protection for uncompetitive national cultural industries. However, just as the United Nations Educational, Scientific, and Cultural Organization (UNESCO) became the forum for the international debate about cultural imperialism in the 1970s, in the new century it has taken up the cause of "cultural diversity." This concept embraces not only nation-states determined to foster their national cultures, but also minorities within them, including indigenous ones. UNESCO's proposed Convention on Cultural Diversity would at least provide an ethical if not a legislative basis for these cultures to resist pressures from those countries whose economic interests are served by free trade.

SEE ALSO: Globalization; Globalization, Culture and; Grobalization; Hegemony and the Media; Media and Diaspora; Media Monopoly; Media and Nationalism

REFERENCES AND SUGGESTED READINGS

Appadurai, A. (1990) Disjuncture and Difference in the Global Cultural Economy. In: Featherstone, M. (Ed.), *Global Culture*. Sage, London, pp. 295–310.

Boyd-Barrett, O. (1997) International Communication and Globalization: Contradictions and Directions. In: Mohammadi, A. (Ed.), *International Communication and Globalization: A Critical Introduction*. Sage, London, pp. 11–26.

Castells, M. (1997) *The Power of Identity*. Blackwell, Malden, MA.

Dayan, D. & Katz, E. (1992) *Media Events: The Live Broadcasting of History*. Harvard University Press, Cambridge, MA.

Giddens, A. (1990) *The Consequences of Modernity*. Polity Press, Cambridge.

Herman, E. & McChesney, R. (1997) *The Global Media: The New Missionaries of Corporate Capitalism*. Cassell, London and Washington, DC.

Nederveen Piertese, J. (1995) Globalization as Hybridization. In: Featherstone, M., Lash, S., & Robertson, R. (Eds.), *Global Modernities*. Sage, London, pp. 45–68.

Sinclair, J. (1999) *Latin American Television: A Global View*. Oxford University Press, Oxford and New York.

Straubhaar, J. (1997) Distinguishing the Global, Regional, and National Levels of World Television. In: Sreberny-Mohammadi, A., Winseck, D., McKenna, J., & Boyd-Barrett, O. (Eds.), *Media in Global Context: A Reader*. Edward Arnold, London, pp. 284–98.

media literacy

W. James Potter and William G. Christ

Media literacy is a term that has been used to refer to a great many ideas. It has been treated as a public policy health issue; a critical-cultural issue; as a set of pedagogical tools for school teachers or suggestions for parents; and as a topic of scholarly inquiry from a physiological, psychological, behavioral, sociological, and/or anthropological tradition. Some writers focus primarily on one culture, such as American culture, British culture, Canadian culture, or Chilean culture, while others concentrate on several countries and/or cultures. It is a term applied to the study of media industries, textual interpretation, context and ideology, production, and audience. The term is also used as synonymous with or as part of media education.

While the range of writing about media literacy is a positive characteristic that indicates widespread interest in the topic, it is difficult to make sense of all these ideas. For example, the media scholar Herb Zettl (1998) complained that the large amount of information on the Internet along with books, articles, and classroom materials does not help much in defining what media literacy is, because most of that material consists of recipes for how to prevent children from watching too much or unsuitable television programs.

It is possible, however, to group most of the writings on media literacy into two general categories. One of these categories includes conceptual concerns about what media literacy is. The writings in this category attempt to define media literacy, delineate its nature, and explain why it is so important. The other category includes implementation concerns about what to do about improving media literacy by working through existing institutions – particularly education and the family. The writings in this category provide suggestions about altering institutional structures and creating techniques that can be used to increase the general level of media literacy in the culture.

CONCEPTUAL CONCERNS

Many scholars have written about how "media" should be defined and how "literacy" should be defined. As for the first of these two terms, some writers emphasize certain media over others, such as oral and written language (Sinatra 1986), still and moving images (Messaris 1994), television (Zettl 1998), computers (Tyner 1998), or multimedia (Buckingham 1993), while others span across many different kinds of media (Silverblatt 1995; Potter 2005).

As for literacy, some definitions focus primarily on skills, others focus primarily on knowledge, and some focus on a combination of skills and knowledge. One trend in defining media literacy is to argue that there are multiple literacies, and this serves to expand the idea of media literacy beyond the ability to recognize printed symbols, that is, to read a printed language (Meyrowitz 1998). Adams and Hamm (2001) argue for multiple literacies. They say that being literate now implies having the ability to decode information from all types of media and by media they include technological literacy, visual literacy, information literacy, networking literacy, and more.

Scholars convened the National Leadership Conference on Media Literacy in 1992 to try to reach a consensus about what media literacy should be. After several days of discussions, they crafted a definition that media literacy is the ability to access, analyze, evaluate, and communicate messages in a variety of forms and that a media literate person needs to be able to decode, evaluate, analyze, and produce both print and electronic media (Aufderheide 1997). Furthermore, participants agreed that most conceptualizations include the following elements: media are constructed and construct reality; media have commercial implications; media have ideological and political implications; form and content are related in each medium, each of which has a unique aesthetic, codes, and conventions; and receivers negotiate meaning in media.

Another approach to making sense of all this thinking was undertaken by Potter (2004), who attempted to synthesize the major ideas in the various media literacy literatures and from that synthesis build a theory to explain how media literacy works. In his synthesis, he reports there are five major ideas that underlie almost all of the literatures. First, there is a growing consensus that media literacy is not limited to one medium. Media literacy is the ability to recognize symbols in visual, motion, and aural media as well as on the printed page. And furthermore, media literacy is more than recognizing symbols; it is also concerned with the construction of meaning by humans who are exposed to the messages from all media.

A second idea is that literacy requires skills. While there is a range of skills listed by different writers, the major skills that show up most often are those of critical thinking, analysis, and evaluation.

A third idea is that literacy requires certain types of knowledge. This knowledge is then used to evaluate the accuracy of media messages so that people can protect themselves from being influenced by false information or partial sets of information that distort reality.

A fourth idea is that the purpose of media literacy is focused on primarily improving individuals in some way. The assumption is that if enough individuals experience amelioration, then society at large will experience benefits. For example, if individuals become more conscious of their media choices and their own personal needs, they will change their media exposure patterns. If enough people do this, the demand for messages that are harmful to people will diminish, and the media industries will respond by altering the types of messages they present. Thus, lasting change in media content comes from educating people to change the market more so than regulating media industries.

A fifth idea is that media literacy must deal with values. There has been a shift away from criticizing the popular mass media as being harmful, while other kinds of messages (such as news, documentaries, great literature, symphonies, and the like) are automatically good for people. This elitist view sanctions particular kinds of content and ignores the role of individuals in valuing different forms of media messages. For example, Masterman (1997) argues that media education does not seek to impose specific cultural values. He takes the position that media education should not seek to impose ideas on what constitutes "good" or "bad" television, newspapers, or films. Instead, media literacy should try to produce well-informed citizens who can make their own judgments on the basis of the available evidence.

IMPLEMENTATION CONCERNS

Advocates of media literacy have moved beyond the conceptual debates and have tried to influence institutions (e.g., education and family) to develop practices to help people become more media literate and thus better protect themselves from the unwanted effects from exposure to the mass media.

Historically, media literacy efforts in the US can be traced at least as early as the 1920s if one includes the early persuasion and newspaper studies. Most scholars would agree that recent worldwide efforts to develop media literacy programs can be traced to the 1970s. These programs tended to be developed along one or more of three orientations: to protect children from media messages from other cultures, to inoculate children from media messages that promote specific "inappropriate" content (e.g., violence and/or sex), or to educate children to understand their culture and themselves through interpreting media content and their media use.

Critics have observed that the US lags behind Australia, Canada, Great Britain, South Africa, Scandinavia, Russia, and Israel. Also, many other countries in Europe, South America, and Asia are developing media literacy courses and curricula in public schools. These critics argue that the relative lack of attention to media education in the US is a serious problem because the US is the most media-saturated country in the world. However, in the US there are significant obstacles preventing media literacy advocates from getting their recommendations implemented in the public educational system. Perhaps the major obstacle is that decision-making about the public school curriculum is decentralized across 50 states and more than 10,000 school systems. Also, within each school system, administrators must consider curricular priorities, development and cost, teacher training, time, and demands, and parental interest (Kubey 1997).

The purpose or importance of media literacy education can also be inferred by where it resides in a curriculum. In different parts of the world, it has been positioned as (1) part of either K–12 and/or higher education, (2) elements within an interdisciplinary program that cuts across subject matter, (3) elements within other subject matter (e.g., history, English, or social studies), (4) a stand-alone course in secondary schools, (5) a course that is part of the general education or common curriculum of a college or university, (6) a course that is part of a larger media sequence or minor, (7) the media studies program or minor itself, and (8) part of a professional media program.

In the US, with all the other demands on teachers and curricula, there has been a move in K–12 education toward positioning media education as part of other core subjects (such as English or social studies) with one or two classes in high school that are either required or are electives (e.g., multimedia, video, or technology classes). In higher education, schools tend to see their general education Introduction to Mass Media class as a media literacy class.

Curriculum design rests on how people answer at least five questions. First, is production essential to media literacy? Second, what is the role of media practitioners in media literacy? Third, who is responsible for media literacy? Fourth, how should media literacy be taught? Fifth, how can we assess the effectiveness of media literacy education?

First, there are some scholars who feel that production is an essential part of understanding media. But other people take a counter position, arguing that students need not learn production of media messages before they can learn to understand those messages better. This argument has roots going back many years. It is similar to ones asked years ago about whether you can understand poetry if you have not tried to write it. Also, there are people who feel that teaching students to produce messages as they are produced by the mass media only reinforces the status quo, that is, it does not help students develop a wider perspective on messages beyond the typical formulas and values dominating the current media messages.

Second, there are media literacy advocates who argue that professionals who work in the media industries have a lot to offer students and should be invited into classrooms to help teach students and perhaps even fund media labs. In the US many media programs in higher education pride themselves on developing links with practitioners. There are those involved in the K–12 media literacy movement who suggest that practitioners, working closely with media educators, have much to offer media education. However, other people see a potential danger in this, arguing that media professionals may not be theoretically educated, will not be willing or able to criticize the media in which they work, or may simply tell "war stories" about how the media work without providing a broad context.

Third, who is responsible for media literacy: parents, schools, or both? If it is parents, who teaches them about the media, how it works, and its potential effects? Who gives them the skills to talk about media and the will to monitor what their children watch? If it is the schools, where does the money come from to buy equipment, train teachers, and develop coherent media literacy topics, courses, and/or curricula?

Fourth, how is media literacy taught? There are those who suggest a democratic approach to media literacy requires a paradigm shift in how media literacy classes should be taught. Instead of a hierarchical, top-down education, there are those who advocate an approach to media literacy where the teacher and students discover meaning together. It is an approach that changes the teacher role from preacher extolling the virtues and sins of media, to a guide who allows students to make up their own minds about media's meaning. By looking carefully at the teacher–student relationship, media literacy scholars also suggest the need to investigate not only teaching styles, but also student learning styles.

Fifth, in the US, assessment is being advocated by parents, legislative bodies, administrators, and accrediting associations, with faculty being called on to articulate what they are doing and provide evidence that they know their students are learning. Assessment is not only a pedagogical issue, but has also become politicized as funding and resources become allocated based on outcomes. Most media literacy scholars acknowledge the importance of evaluation in any media literacy program, but there are troublesome questions. How is it decided? Who decides that a student is becoming or has become media literate? What are the standards? What should be assessed: knowledge, skills, behaviors, attitudes, affect, and/or values?

In the US there are a number of state initiatives linking teaching objectives with assessment (e.g., New Mexico, North Carolina, Texas). However, these initiatives are hindered by a lack of a national standard. Some scholars have been arguing for the need of a national standard for media literacy and have suggested what that standard should be. The most visible example of this comes from the National Communication Association (NCA), which adopted a standard that says media literate communicators should be able to (1) demonstrate knowledge and understanding of the ways people use media in their personal and public lives; (2) demonstrate knowledge and understanding of the complex relationships among audiences and media content; (3) demonstrate knowledge and understanding that media content is produced within social and cultural contexts; (4) demonstrate knowledge and understanding of the commercial nature of media; (5) demonstrate ability to use media to communicate to specific audiences (National Communication Association 1998).

There are many consumer activist groups concerned with media literacy (e.g., Center for Media Education, Center for Media Literacy, Children Now, Citizens for Media Literacy, Children's Television Project). These groups are working to make parents more aware of the risks their children experience when they are exposed to the media, particularly video games, the Internet, and television. They create and distribute materials to help parents help their children.

Nathanson (2001) has found that there are primarily three strategies that parents use in dealing with their children's media education: active mediation, restrictive mediation, and co-viewing. Active mediation consists of conversations that parents or other adults have with children about television. This talk need not be evaluative. Restrictive mediation involves setting rules about how much, when, and which types of television can be viewed. Co-viewing involves parents and children watching TV together; no conversation is required and any guidance from the parents is very informal and unfocused. In her review of surveys of families, she concludes that most families do not have media usage rules, nor do most parents use active mediation. Furthermore, tools developed to help parents monitor and control their children's media use, such as the v-chip, are rarely used and not widely understood.

SEE ALSO: Literacy/Illiteracy; Orality; Mass Culture and Mass Society; Mass Media and Socialization; Media; Media and Consumer Culture; Public Broadcasting

REFERENCES AND SELECTED READINGS

Adams, D. & Hamm, M. (2001) *Literacy in a Multimedia Age*. Christopher-Gordon, Norwood, MA.

Aufderheide, P. (Ed.) (1993) *Media Literacy: A Report of the National Leadership Conference on Media Literacy*. Aspen Institute, Aspen.

Aufderheide, P. (1997) Media Literacy: From a Report of the National Leadership Conference on Media Literacy. In: Kubey, R. (Ed.), *Media Literacy in the Information Age*. Transaction Publishers, New Brunswick, NJ, pp. 79–86.

Bazalgette, C., Bevort, E., & Saviano, J. (Eds.) (1992) *New Directions: Media Education Worldwide*. British Film Institute, London.

Buckingham, D. (1993) *Children Talking Television: The Making of Television Literacy*. Falmer, London.

Christ, W. G. (Ed.) (1997) *Media Education Assessment Handbook*. Erlbaum, Hillsdale, NJ.

Galician, M. (Ed.) (2004) High Time for "Dis-Illusioning" Ourselves and Our Media: Media Literacy in the 21st Century, Part I and II. *American Behavioral Scientist* 48(1&2).

Hobbs, R. (1998) The Seven Great Debates in the Media Literacy Movement. *Journal of Communication* 48(1): 16–32.

Kubey, R. (Ed.) (1997) *Media Literacy in the Information Age: Current Perspectives, Information and Behavior*, Vol. 6. Transaction Publishers, New Brunswick, NJ.

Masterman, L. (1997) A Rationale for Media Education. In: Kubey, R. (Ed.), *Media Literacy in the Information Age*, Vol. 6. Transaction Publishers, New Brunswick, NJ, pp. 15–68.

Messaris, P. (1994) *Visual "Literacy": Image, Mind, and Reality*. Westview Press, Boulder.

Meyrowitz, J. (1998) Multiple Media Literacies. *Journal of Communication* 48(1): 96–108.

Nathanson, A. I. (2001) Mediation of Children's Television Viewing: Working Toward Conceptual Clarity and Common Understanding. In: Gudykunst, W. B. (Ed.), *Communication Yearbook 25*, pp. 115–51.

National Communication Association (1998) Speaking, Listening, and Media Literacy Standards for K through 12 Education. National Communication Association, Annandale, VA.

Potter, W. J. (2004) *Theory of Media Literacy: A Cognitive Approach*. Sage, Thousand Oaks, CA.

Potter, W. J. (2005) *Media Literacy*, 3rd edn. Sage, Thousand Oaks, CA.

Silverblatt, A. (1995) *Media Literacy: Keys to Interpreting Media Messages*. Praeger, Westport.

Sinatra, R. (1986) *Visual Literacy Connections to Thinking, Reading and Writing*. Charles C. Thomas, Springfield, IL.

Tyner, K. (1998) *Literacy in a Digital World*. Erlbaum, Mahwah, NJ.

Zettl, H. (1998) Contextual Media Aesthetics as the Basis of Media Literacy. *Journal of Communication* 48(1): 81–95.

media monopoly

Ben H. Bagdikian

The term media monopoly – concentrated control of major mass communications within a society – took on a new life in the second half of the twentieth century, thanks to global changes. These included new communications technology; growth of literacy in the population; demographics that increased the size of potential audiences; increasing democratization in the less developed world that heightened interest in politics and the media; and high profits and political influence that stimulated conglomerate ownership of all major means of mass communications. Since citizens increasingly depended on these media for political information and entertainment, the concentrated control by a small number of large business concerns inevitably produced public controversy.

Modern usage of the term mass media has its origins in the past. The word "mass," for example, in its ancient Greek origin meaning a shapeless dough, to the present, has carried a disparaging implication that it is designed for what the nineteenth-century British prime minister William Gladstone called the "lower orders" of society. Twentieth- and twenty-first-century usage commonly referred to the least elegant publications as "mass circulation magazines," implying Gladstone's "lower orders."

Its partner, "media," has been troublesome from the start because the word encompasses so many disparate meanings. The plural, "media," and its singular form ("medium"), have different meanings when used in mathematics, biology, logic, art, photography, and the theater. In modern political and commercial life it became used generically for the content and machinery of mass distribution of information and entertainment, as in newspapers, magazines, books, radio, television, and the cinema, forming the basis for discussion of media monopolies and oligopolies.

The term media monopoly has emerged only in recent decades. Neither *The Encyclopedia of the Social Sciences* (1934) nor *Webster's New International Dictionary of the English Language, Unabridged* (1955) have entries for "mass media" or "media" alone, as a body of information intended for wide public dissemination. In contrast, the 1998 edition of the *Oxford English Dictionary* has a substantial entry for "media" in the modern usage of "media monopoly."

In the distant past, there was little need for the term. Media monopolies were the unquestioned prerogative of high priests, shamans, and royal and religious rulers (Frazier 1922). In contrast, contemporary democratic societies require diverse information about public issues and candidates for political office in order to permit informed voting. The degree to which this information is arbitrarily controlled, and therefore vulnerable to self-serving censorship by governments or corporations, has become a significant public issue (Bagdikian 1983). Modern technology in the twenty-first century – high-speed printing, rapid and copious public distribution of information through devices like broad spectrum cable and satellite transmissions – permits near-unanimous reception within industrialized democracies. Commercially, global dimensions of these techniques represent profit-making possibilities of unprecedented magnitude and influence. These have intensified possible conflicts between corporate profit-making and public need for broad and diverse news and commentary (Bagdikian 1970).

Probably the first significant media monopoly of historic importance was the Alexandrian Library collection of 700,000 scrolls in the second century BCE, said to contain all learning in the known world. Media competition was introduced when Eumenes II, King of Pergamum (in what is now Turkey), challenged the Alexandrian monopoly, causing the Ptolemies in Egypt to forbid export of Nile River reeds, which could be split and pounded together when needed to form scrolls like those in the Alexandrian collection. The King of Pergamum was forced to use animal hides on which to write. In order to make the resulting multiple pages of the animal skins less unwieldy, the left edges were tied in a hinge, which is believed to be the origin of the modern book. The newly invented book had the unintended advantage of being a random access body of information. Scrolls had to be unrolled in order to read their content, while the book could be opened at any desired page (McShane 1964). Whether by scroll, book, or official documents, rulers controlled the media. During the last days of the Roman Empire, posting of various *Acta* – official documents in public places – was permitted only to the authorities. From the beginnings of Gutenberg's fifteenth-century printing press, the published sheets created by handset type were almost exclusively the documents of the Roman Church, or sanctioned by it (Stephens 1988).

For centuries in Western Europe, media monopoly took the form of the exclusive use of Latin by the church, officialdom, and scholars in letters, literature, and ritual. Since Latin was not used by the masses, it was the language of the educated classes and served to prevent wide dispersion of new ideas among the populace. In the seventeeth century, for example, one of the charges that sent Galileo to the Roman Church Inquisition was his failure to use Latin in writing about his discovery that the sun, not the earth, was the center of the solar system – at the time a heresy in dogma. Because he wrote in vernacular Italian, authorities saw this as engendering religious doubt among the population at large (Licklider 1966; Drake 1999).

Until Gutenberg's creation of the printing press (ca. 1436), writing was done laboriously by hand. Mechanical reproduction of documents permitted relatively rapid and broad distribution of official and religious edicts and, eventually, unofficial ideas and information. Over time, the use of wine presses (origin of "the press" as news carriers) converted to make multiple imprints was improved by the rotary press, and new techniques for manufacturing large rolls of paper to feed presses continuously made possible large quantities of printed matter in hours rather than days (*Johns Hopkins Magazine* 1967). The ability to produce and sell large numbers of newspapers in a few hours led to both political influence and opportunities for successful publishers to gain unprecedented profits and mass influence. Inevitably, as each publisher fought to gain a larger share of the profits from sales and advertising in the newspapers, some gained dominance in the competition. In the UK, great power accrued to publishers like Viscount Northcliffe (1865–1922); in the US, William Randolph Hearst (1863–1951), Joseph Pulitzer (1847–1911), and Edward Wyllis Scripps (1835–1906) created competing chains of newspapers. The competition paralleled the growth of literacy and centrality of the press in imperial and national politics. Ultimately, economies of scale produced dominating papers, monopolies, and near-monopolies (Bagdikian 1970). Magazines arose as distinct from newspapers as early as 1165 in France, followed quickly by others, including *Philosophical Transactions of the Royal Society* in the UK in 1665 and in the early eighteenth century, *Tatler, Spectator,* and *Guardian.* Checked only momentarily by the Crown's costly Stamp Act, by the nineteenth century, magazines were once more a growing medium.

In the US, women's magazines became a substantial presence in national distribution and remained a major category well into the twenty-first century. *Godey's Lady Book* (1830) employed 150 women to hand-paint illustrations in every copy of the magazine. The 1879 Postal Act lowered magazine rates and quadrupled circulation of the genre. Among the most common were *Ladies Home Journal* and *Saturday Evening Post,* which by 1922 reached 2 million circulation. The 1930s were characterized by the emergence of three popular general circulation magazines – *Life, Look,* and *The Saturday Evening Post* – that thrived because they were the only national distribution of quality four-color printing widely seen by the national population, and therefore highly desired by advertisers. Yet all three magazines died in the late 1960s, by which time color television had become a near-universal household appliance and the dominant vehicle for full-color advertising (Peterson 1975).

The term press enjoyed universal usage until radio became a popular medium in the 1920s. The addition of television in the late 1930s created more complex competition, eventually with major newspaper chains also operating radio and then television broadcasting chains. Thus, the obsolete generic use of "the press" was replaced by "mass media," and "press lords" by "media monopolies."

The US experience in commercial broadcasting was not typical. The UK and most other nations had long initial periods of governmental systems, like the BBC in the UK and CBC in Canada.

Radio in the US began in the 1920s as an officially approved monopoly. Called the National Broadcasting (NBC) system, the government assigned differing functions (manufacture of sets, creation of programs, and wire transmissions to carry broadcasts to cities) to three firms. The tripartite division of functions fell apart when the first commercials showed how much more money could be made from sponsors of programs. The NBC divided into a Red and a Blue network. In the 1930s, William Paley (1901–90) established the Columbia Broadcasting System (CBS). A 1943 court decision forced divestiture of NBC's Blue network to form the American Broadcasting System (ABC), operated by the Chicago Tribune (Barnouw 1975).

After World War II, television quickly grew from a storefront demonstration novelty to a common household appliance. The three networks (ABC, NBC, and CBS) dominated all radio and television until Rupert Murdoch entered the US media scene. From his start as publisher of an inherited daily paper in Adelaide, Australia, Murdoch rose with skill and, some said, guile, to a powerful international presence in the mass media. His satellite broadcasting covered much of Europe and Asia. In London he owned a Sunday sex-and-sensation newspaper *News of the World* and the *Sun,* and despite objections by the country's Monopoly Commission, added the influential *London Times,* a morning daily, and the *Sunday Times,* thanks to his friendship with Prime Minister Margaret Thatcher.

Emigrating to the United States, Murdoch became a major operator in American broadcasting. American law forbade any foreign-based company to own more than 24.9 percent of any US broadcast station. Nevertheless, though he kept his basic firm in Australia, the US government momentarily waived that law in his case. Murdoch eventually changed his citizenship to US and created the Fox network. Fox became dominant in sports, and his radio and television featured highly conservative commentators with a reputation for corrosive, conservative, and frequently questioned assertions. His network expanded to become a leading conglomerate with holdings in all the major media: radio, TV, magazines, books, cinema, and satellite broadcast channels (Shawcross 1997).

Media conglomerates, most prominent in the US, became the norm in the late twentieth and early twenty-first centuries. Five or six large firms dominated all the major media, each firm with strong positions in newspapers, magazines, books, radio, television, recordings, and cinema, with both partnerships and, at times, competition, involving Western European and Japanese communications industries. The major corporations dominating the mass media in the US were Time Warner (the largest media firm in the world); the News Corporation of Rupert Murdoch's Fox network; Viacom, the former CBS network; Disney Company; Bertelsmann, of Germany, the world's largest publisher of English-language books as well as a leading producer of recordings; and General Electric, one of the largest corporations in the world, that, while traditionally a producer of nuclear reactors, electric generators, and home appliances, entered the media field through the NBC network because of its high profit levels. Sony of Japan also held major media worldwide (Bagdikian 1983).

Scholarly study of the subject has centered on various aspects of conglomerate control of the media. Chief among them is copyright, which is important for exclusive rights and licensing fees for texts and images in the mass media. Disney's Mickey Mouse became a worldwide popular film figure augmented by billions of dollars earned by the rodent's image on toys, clothing, and trinkets. When the Mickey Mouse image copyright was due to expire in 2003, Disney became a leader in convincing the US Congress to extend copyright terms (Bagdikian 1983).

Scholars and much of the public feared that the periodic lengthening of copyright would soon place too much information under corporate control. Of intense concern to scholars was a trio of publishing conglomerates, two in the Netherlands and one in the US, that controlled most of the scholarly and scientific journals used in research and teaching. The three-firm oligopoly had raised prices to such high levels that even the largest universities were forced to limit purchases of scientific and academic journals. In reaction, hundreds of universities in North America, Europe, and Australia joined in the Scholarly Publishing and Academic Resources Coalition to apportion purchase of commercial journals and share requests for specific articles with their fellow academic member libraries. The concern also led to the Commons Movement, which urged scholars and authors to produce more works in the public domain or with only moderate copyrights (Bagdikian 2004). Controversy over modern mass communications in the twenty-first century covered a broad spectrum of disputes. One side, enunciated by commercial broadcasters and promoters of free-market philosophies, insisted that there was no monopoly danger because of multiple new channels and new visual and audio techniques. They expressed fear that inhibitions on conglomerates would hamper future inventions. Contrary opinions asserted that the size and multiple holdings of dominant firms had given existing conglomerates formidable lobbying power on governments that served industrial power and profit over public needs. They noted that despite growing numbers of channels, control by conglomerates produced routine duplication of the least expensive programs and replaced public interest information with narrow, self-serving commentary. It was seen as evasion of US law that establishes airwave frequencies as public property.

The broad differences of opinion have stimulated a variety of methods of calculating what defines a media monopoly or oligopoly in modern society. Methods vary from complex mathematical formulae with which to calculate degrees of concentration, to social analysis based on case studies and anecdotal histories, the differing techniques often reflecting opposing opinions on media concentration. Global media communication techniques have created conflicting responses. Because powerful transmissions ignore national boundaries, the phenomenon caused some less developed nations and large ethnic populations to feel victimized by giant media conglomerates that reflect content suitable mainly for industrialized countries. In contrast, others have expressed a sense of liberation from local parochialism. The future of media monopolies became further complicated by growth of the Internet and a rapid succession of similar new techniques that have increased the unpredictability of media monopoly issues (Bagdikian 2004).

SEE ALSO: Culture, Economy and; Culture Industries; Media; Media and Consumer Culture; Media and Globalization; Media Network(s) and; Media and the Public Sphere; Media, Regulation of; Public Broadcasting

REFERENCES AND SUGGESTED READINGS

Bagdikian, B. H. (1970) *The Information Machines.* Harper & Row, New York.

Bagdikian, B. H. (1983) *The Media Monopoly.* Beacon Press, Boston.

Bagdikian, B. H. (2004) *The New Media Monopoly.* Beacon Press, Boston.

Barnouw, E. (1975) *Tube of Plenty.* Oxford University Press, Oxford.

Drake, S. (1999) *Essays on Galileo*, Vol. 1. University of Toronto Press, Toronto.

Frazier, J. G. (1922) *The Golden Bough.* Macmillan, New York.

Johns Hopkins Magazine (1967) Special Issue: The Information Explosion. Johns Hopkins University Press, Baltimore.

Licklider, J. C. R. (1966) A Crisis in Scientific and Technical Communications. *American Psychologist* (November).

McShane, R. B. (1964) *Foreign Policy of the Attalids of Pergamum.* University of Illinois Press, Chicago.

Peterson, T. (1975) *Magazines in the Twentieth Century.* University of Illinois Press, Urbana.

Shawcross, W. (1997) *Murdoch.* Simon & Schuster, New York.

Stephens, M. (1988) *History of the News: From the Drum to the Satellite.* Viking, New York.

media and nationalism

Sabina Mihelj

Over the past few decades the relationship between media and nationalism has rapidly developed from a rather marginal topic to one of the most prominent issues in the field of media and communication studies. Developments in communication technology, especially the introduction of satellite television and the World Wide Web, have fueled hopes about the gradual weakening of nation-states and national attachments and the creation of an interconnected worldwide community. Yet nation-states, nations, and nationalisms are alive and well despite – and perhaps because of – the dense communication flows circumventing national borders and challenging the national order of things both from above and from below.

As with many other social scientists, media and communication scholars have proved to be ill-equipped to account for the proliferation of overt nationalist sentiments after the end of the Cold War, and more specifically for the role of media and communications in these changes. Tacitly accepting the main assumptions of the modernist vision of the world, they have long been accustomed to an understanding of modern society inside which nations and nationalisms were only marginal phenomena, bound to dissipate with the advancement of modernization and globalization. By and large, communication was seen as a crucial means of attaining higher levels of development and social integration, rather than an instrument for enhancing differences and fostering conflicts. The work of Deutsch (1953), and even more explicitly that of Lerner (1958), two of the most influential authors dealing with the relationship between nationalism and communication before the 1980s, has been driven by such a set of assumptions and ideals. Deutsch's widely quoted *Nationalism and Social Communication* (1953) was essentially an attempt to identify the main factors fostering the assimilation of various nations into a worldwide community of mankind. An increase in the skills and facilities of communication was, he believed, vital for the attainment of this goal. Since a nation was, according to his definition, primarily "a larger group of persons linked by … complementary habits and facilities of communication" (p. 70), the creation of a global community would therefore require the establishment of habits and facilities of communication on a global basis.

Although the main drive behind Deutsch's work – the ideal of a homogeneous worldwide community – soon came into disrepute, his understanding of the relationship between nation-formation and communication remained unchallenged for several decades. Within communication and media studies this was largely due to the fact that in the Cold War period the issues of nationalism, nation, and national identity did not command much attention, and if they were addressed at all they were often explained away as mere epiphenomena of some more fundamental reality, usually that of economy and the class struggle. Admittedly, within international communication studies, especially among the proponents of the cultural imperialism thesis, the relationship between cultural identity and the emerging global communications was an intensely discussed topic (Schiller 1976). Yet, as a rule, the debate started from a notion of culture as a bounded unit and communication as a kind of "hypodermic needle," an external force which can either protect a specific culture or destroy it by injecting foreign cultural values. However, as was demonstrated by several studies of reception developed from the 1980s onwards (e.g., Liebes & Katz 1990), the very same cultural product may be interpreted and used in a variety of different ways, depending on the cultural framework of reception. But while the turn towards reception has provided an important corrective to the cultural imperialism thesis, it has also led researchers to focus on micro-processes and away from the broader question of how media might succeed in creating a certain level of cultural homogeneity and arousing nationalist sentiments despite the variegated decodings occurring in the process of reception.

If most media and communication scholars have tended to overemphasize the effects of media and communication on culture and identity, nationalism scholars were prone to overlook the role of media and communication altogether. At best, the improvements in communication in the nineteenth century were mentioned as one among many factors laying the grounds for the proliferation of nationalism, alongside the development of transport, a standardized system of education, the army system, the modern state, etc., usually without any specification of the particular role of communication vis-à-vis other factors. Gellner's (1987) theory of nationalism is a classic formulation of such an understanding of the relationship between nationalism and communication. Nationalism scholars did however offer some

persuasive criticisms of Deutsch's theory considerably earlier than media and communication researchers. Connor (1972), and subsequently Breuilly (1993), pointed out that far from automatically inducing cohesion and agreement, an increase in the intensity of communication can in fact enhance differences and foster internal conflicts. Moreover, Deutsch himself expressed doubts about the cohesive potential of communication in states whose populations are already divided into several groups with different languages, cultures, or basic ways of life. But since these doubts appeared in a more explicit form only in some of his more recent texts, rather than in his usually quoted *Nationalism and Social Communication*, they were largely overlooked by his followers. Connor also emphasized that Deutsch, just like other early modernization theorists, generalized from experiences with the largely immigrant American society, overlooking the fact that these generalizations may not apply to societies with territorially based, indigenous minorities. A similar argument was developed by Smith (1971), who argued that one of the crucial defects of approaches such as Deutsch's is their omission of the particular context of beliefs and interests within which the mass media operate; usually, the effects of western-type mass media outside the West were held to be identical to the effects within the West itself.

In placing communication as the focus of attention, Anderson's (1983) theory of imagined communities was a notable departure from the prevailing pattern of thinking about communication among nationalism scholars. According to Anderson, it was a particular form of communication, associated with print technology and the capitalist system of production and productive relations, that made nations imaginable and was thus central to the formation and spread of nationalism. This theory has a considerable influence among communication and media scholars. Although Anderson's analysis was limited to newspapers and fiction books, his notion of imagined communities was quickly implemented in research dealing with modern electronic media, including the use of these media among diasporas (Karim 2003). This was partly a consequence of the fact that many of Anderson's followers adopted a very partial reading of his theory, taking the role of imagination, rather than print capitalism, as the principal inspiration. Such a reading led them to focus almost exclusively on textual analysis and abandon any sociological investigation or historical causal explanation of the origins, spread, and effects of nationalism. Another theory that aroused substantial interest among media and communication scholars and received a similarly one-sided reading was Hobsbawm and Ranger's (1983) theory of invented traditions. Together with the concept of imagined communities, the notion of invented traditions has become a standard phrase in explorations of nationalism in the field of media and communication studies in the past two decades.

While the shortcomings of recent works on nationalism and communication can in part be blamed on the one-sided reading of Anderson's and Hobsbawm and Ranger's theory, they are also a direct consequence of a blind-spot inherent in these theories themselves. Although he never explicitly refers to Deutsch, Anderson actually perpetuates some of the questionable assumptions characteristic of his theory. First and foremost, his theory is still modeled on the cultural geography of the nation-state in a world of sovereign states (Schlesinger 2000), which makes it entirely unsuited for tackling the contemporary complexities of relations between media and nationalism. Historically, the coincidence of nation, state, and communication is an exception rather than a rule. Even in the period when the nation-state monopoly over collective identity and the communication space was strongest, at least some circuits of exchange of information and some collective attachments were established both at international as well as subnational levels. With the advent of satellite television and the Internet, border-circumventing flows of cultural products became particularly dense, making a close fit between the nation-state, nation, and communication virtually impossible (Morley & Robins 1995). Finally, a model assuming a close fit between nation, state, and communication is entirely inapplicable to landscapes of media and identity arising within political formations such as Canada or the European Union (Collins 2002). Yet while it is clear that the actual complexity of the relationships between nationalism and communication is far beyond the grasp of Deutsch's model, persuasive alternative

theoretical frameworks are still lacking. Castells's (1996, 1997) theory of the network society, which manages to capture all the multifarious levels of intersection between communication and collective identity, including those below and above the level of nation-state, still remains largely centered on the role of communication in inducing cohesion rather than disassociation or conflict, and does not resolve the question of how contradictory interests, identities, and loyalties are dealt with in the context of a network-like communicative space (Schlesinger 2000).

Another shortcoming of most theories dealing with the relationship between nationalism and communication or media is the fact that they cannot satisfactorily explain what, if anything, makes modern media and communication particularly suitable for spreading and perpetuating national attachments rather than, for example, regional or global ones. While one could easily agree, argue the critics, that communication is an indispensable means of achieving and maintaining a set of commonalities that transcend the differences within a certain group, it is far less clear why these commonalities should be national rather than of some other kind (Schlesinger 1991; Breuilly 1993: 421). Arguably, this shortcoming is closely related to the tendency to focus on the relationship between nationalism and the form or structure of communication rather than its content. Both Anderson and Gellner, for example, paid attention almost exclusively to the way media address their audiences and categorize reality, and not to the exact content of their messages (Schlesinger 2000). However, the structure of communications does not directly indicate what types of conflict or solidarity exist within a particular society, and therefore cannot in itself provide us with much idea about what kinds of nationalism will develop (Breuilly 1993: 406–7).

Finally, most existing theories fail to define how the role of media and communication in the rise and spread of nationalism differs from the role of other vital factors, such as the development of modern armies, nation-states, education systems, etc. While some of these factors might have been crucial for the initial formulation of nationalism and national identity, others may have played the leading role in their spread, yet others in their continual reproduction, and yet others may have been involved in the development of competing versions of nationalism and national identity (Schlesinger 1991: 160). A promising version of this approach has been developed by Rubert de Ventos (1994), who regards the development of communications as one of the "generative factors" contributing to the emergence of a national identity, and distinguishes it from "primary," "induced," and "reactive" factors. Another fruitful avenue to explore is the one opened by Billig's (1995) theory of banal nationalism, which draws attention to the fact that in well-established nations the contribution of media to the perpetuation of nationalism may be far less visible and more "banal" than in the case of recently established nations.

SEE ALSO: Community and Media; Media and Diaspora; Media and Globalization; Media and the Public Sphere; Nation-State and Nationalism; Politics and Media; Postnationalism

REFERENCES AND SUGGESTED READINGS

Anderson, B. (1983) *Imagined Communities: Reflections on the Origins and Spread of Nationalism.* Verso, London.
Billig, M. (1995) *Banal Nationalism.* Sage, Thousand Oaks, CA.
Breuilly, J. (1993) *Nationalism and the State,* 2nd edn. University of Chicago Press, Chicago.
Castells. M. (1996) *The Rise of the Network Society.* Blackwell, Oxford.
Castells. M. (1997) *The Power of Identity.* Blackwell, Oxford.
Collins, R. (2002) *Media and Identity in Contemporary Europe: Consequences of Global Convergence.* Intellect Books, Bristol.
Connor, W. (1972) Nation-Building or Nation-Destroying. *World Politics* 24: 319–55.
Deutsch, K. W. (1953) *Nationalism and Social Communication: An Inquiry into the Foundations of Nationality.* MIT Press, Boston.
Gellner, E. (1987) *Nations and Nationalism.* Blackwell, Oxford.
Hobsbawm, E. & Ranger, T. (Eds.) (1983) *The Invention of Tradition.* Cambridge University Press, Cambridge.
Karim, K. H. (Ed.) (2003) *The Media of Disapora.* Routledge, London.
Lerner, D. (1958) *The Passing of Traditional Society: Modernizing the Middle East.* Free Press, Glencoe, IL.
Liebes, T. & Katz, E. (1990) *The Export of Meaning: Cross-Cultural Readings of Dallas.* Oxford University Press, Oxford.
Morley, D. & Robins, K. (1995) *Spaces of Identity: Global Media, Electronic Landscapes and Cultural Boundaries.* Routledge, London.
Rubert de Ventos, X. (1994) *Nacionalismos: el laberinto de la identidad* (Nationalism: The Labyrinth of Identity). Espasa Calpe, Madrid.
Schiller, H. (1976) *Communication and Cultural Domination.* International Arts and Sciences Press, White Plains.
Schlesinger, P. (1991) *Media, State and Nation.* Sage, New York.
Schlesinger, P. (2000) Nation and Communicative Space. In: Tumber, H. (Ed.), *Media Power, Professionals and Policy.* Routledge, London.
Smith, A. D. (1971) *Theories of Nationalism.* Duckworth, London.

media, network(s) and

Terry Austrin and John Farnsworth

Networks have been described as one of the most significant features of the modern world. So central and pervasive are they that Manuel Castells (2000), for instance, has dubbed contemporary society the "network society." More than that, a network society is one in which the media play a preeminent role because of their capacity to distribute and disperse information, and their facility in traversing, and even reconfiguring, space and time zones. Media networks can be regarded, then, as becoming foundational to the way modern societies function.

Yet the very idea of a network involves a paradox. Despite their pervasive global presence networks commonly appear to be largely invisible entities. Broadcasting networks are generally experienced only through television schedules or individual programs. Cellular networks are known to most users only through phone calls and text messaging. The Internet is mostly represented through individual web pages or links that lead like worm holes off into the unknown. Even those most human of networks, social networks, are often only experienced when they are actively mobilized in the interests of either politics or a good party.

If networks are both so central and yet so elusive, how can they best be understood, let alone studied? One answer is to look at how accounts of what constitutes a network have changed over time, as networks themselves have evolved. Within a huge literature in the field, there are four approaches which are worth identifying. Each of these works within and across the whole domain of the media and mobilizes an image of the network in different ways. To some extent, they articulate different areas of social science research or theory that sometimes have their origins far from the media. For this reason, too, they are not a tidy set of categories, but are derived from a multiplicity of sources and debates. Nonetheless, it is possible to distinguish four: (1) a political economy perspective that highlights mass media network forms; (2) an everyday life perspective that takes up interactive usage, mobility, and domestic locales as key themes; (3) a social networks perspective which emphasizes the social linkages and connections both for different communities and for civil society as a whole; and (4) an actor network perspective which follows network formation and the key significance of sociotechnical assemblages to understanding how a complex, mobile modern society emerges or changes.

The first approach, drawing on thinking in political economy, divines how firms and markets are first organized and then stabilized through networks of corporate ownership and transactional relationships. In the broadcasting world this includes the way major broadcasting networks, so called, create ties to stable suppliers, distributors, and markets so that they can routinely produce and disseminate programming material. In the process, also of concern is how they attempt to shape regular patterns of audience consumption. It also involves networks of media industries and alliances of media occupations – whether producers, journalists, or craft groups – struggling to secure favorable regulatory protection, state patronage, monopoly control, or other forms of market advantage. Together, these activities have created the mass media landscape familiar, in most parts of the world, for most of the twentieth century.

A second approach that examines the impact of media on everyday life has emerged particularly from the development of new media technologies. Such technologies, many of them digital, include everything from the Internet to the mobile phone, from GPS handsets to MP3 players; in all, a vast, constantly changing range of hybrid devices, many with multiple, miniaturized functions. Together, these have reconfigured every aspect of media activity, and created new forms of networks, many of them interactive, at all levels of production, distribution, and consumption, in the process. John Urry (2000) describes this as "the mediatized nature of contemporary civil society." On this view, new media networks and forms help to produce new societies or social arrangements. One important academic response to these developments, particularly through the European Media Technology and Everyday Life Network (EMTEL), has been to study how such networks infiltrate and rework the routines of domestic and everyday life. Researchers have examined how the complexes of new communication technologies shape patterns of mobility, inclusion, and exclusion, or how they enable new, interactive arrangements for ordinary individual users, as the mobile phone has for teenagers. Yet such technologies also create possibilities for a mobile, globalized world of flows – a constantly proliferating outflow of goods, services, and information that ceaselessly reshapes the relationships between producers and consumers. This raises the question for some commentators (e.g., Thompson 2003) as to whether the whole world is increasingly becoming an undiscriminated complex network.

This concern points to a third approach to networks. Political economy theorists, such as Thompson, distinguish markets (horizontal networks), hierarchies (vertical, often corporate networks of command and control), and social networks (including civil society, informal relationships, or ties of clan, kin, or friendship). While this approach attempts to impose some order on an otherwise undifferentiated network world, it also highlights the role of social networks in media worlds. A focus on the social ranges from Granovetter's (1983) work on how strong and weak ties impact on the formation of communities – whether or not this is through media technologies – to how civil society itself can be reworked or re-represented, and then governed through the development of new "political technologies of the social," as Patrick Joyce (2002: 8–9) puts it. Such technologies encompass diverse ways of constructing images of social networks, from maps and statistics to polling or social analysis, and then distributing them through media forms such as journalism, advertising, or promotional activities. This suggests how social networks struggle over the process of representation in ways which rework not only the sociopolitical terrain with which they are engaged, but also the technologies of representation. A recent example is the complex, shifting battle over P2P Internet file-sharing of audio and visual materials, and whether this is defined as either legitimate free distribution or illegitimate piracy. At stake are moral, organizational, technological, and community boundaries that have not only persistently rearranged the networks engaged in the struggle, but also the file-sharing technologies and regulatory restraints designed to gain a decisive advantage in a global dispute that defines notions of civil and commercial activity.

The fourth approach to networks implicitly undoes the assumptions of the other three. Beginning from the work of Bruno Latour, and incorporating actor-network theory (ANT) and, more recently, science and technology studies (STS), it points to a major gap in the social account. This is the lack of attention paid in much recent social science literature to the centrality of objects and technologies in the formation of any network. The "social" is social on this account, precisely because it overlooks the importance of the technological. Yet, ANT researchers argue, the entire formation of contemporary society is only possible through the existence of the sea of technologies that enable social networks to take the form they do. The very invisibility of cellphone towers, microwave links, the precise segmentation of the frequency spectrum, the complex miniaturization of mobile technologies, the sophisticated digitization of analogue devices from clocks to X Boxes – provides just some of the foundations on which current communities, corporate fortunes, and contemporary market arrangements are increasingly built.

ANT researchers go a step further. It is not enough to point to how assemblages of humans and technologies create networks (for example, the cuddly image of "me and my mobile phone" in Lasen's (2004) phrase). Certainly, highlighting how human networks assemble around particular objects or technologies is important – Latour (1983, 2002) argues that such assemblages have been intrinsic to human societies since their beginning. ANT researchers go on to point to how unanticipated combinations of actors and technologies have themselves produced new assemblages that reshape central features of modern society. Pickering (1995) describes this as "the mangle of practice" which has produced, for instance, the institutions of television and radio that were the unanticipated assemblage of individual photographic, military, or sound experiments. No one, in this case, was attempting to "invent" television. Such outcomes were no more anticipated in their day than the emergence of the assemblage called the Internet was in ours. And this is the actor network point. The implications of this perspective are not only to do with how networks are understood, but also how they might be studied. It is helpful to contrast this with other approaches.

Where mass print and electronic forms are concerned, political economy approaches typically focus on how stable industrial and market arrangements are created or managed. In one version of mass media study, technologies dominate or determine how such networks are shaped (the technological determinism argument, now heavily challenged). In another version, corporate actors and key occupations deploy their expertise or power to control both specific technologies and the production of media products, as well as understandings of what audiences are, or what they are presumed to want. From this flows the huge volume of largely quantitative research that has looked not only at how production, distribution, and consumption patterns are organized, but also at the relationship between audiences and media institutions. It also involves, in both the reception and the uses and gratifications literature, what influences and shapes this relationship.

In contrast, everyday life approaches reconfigure the image of a relatively passive, variably receptive audience into one that depicts interactive, often mobile users engaged in fluid arrangements where they produce, rework, or consume reversioned media materials. Crudely speaking, couch potatoes are transformed into smart, multi-tasking, multi-locational transacters reworking both domestic and public spaces. Such active, mobile subjects increasingly point to the use of qualitative or ethnographic study in order to track and engage them.

Of course, such approaches are far from distinct. There are overlaps, such as the accounts of Marvin (1988) or Boddy (2004) that describe the historical reconfiguration of private and public worlds brought about by new media forms. Both, for instance, discuss how the early telephone, a seminal network device, was used in different ways as both a private (one-to-one) and a public (one-to-many) technology, depending on its setting. Other researchers have indicated how these alternatives have been reproduced once again, after a long period of telephone use as a private technology, with the emergence of the mobile a century later (Grint & Woolgar 1997: 21). In each case, attention is paid to historical processes, institutional practices, and everyday engagements to highlight how networks of production and consumption are formed and reformed.

The same can be said of social network approaches where research shifts between the occupational adoption and employment of technologies, as well as the resistance and reworking of technological forms around class, gender, or ethnicity. Community radio, the alternative and radical press, blogging and bulletin boards are all typical examples where groups attempt to organize and shape the construction of civic spaces. Study here often emphasizes, for example, the social use of the Internet (Wellman & Haythornthwaite 2002), or how public media spaces or an information commons are constructed.

Yet, from the perspective of ANT, each of these three approaches privileges, and assumes, exactly the issue that requires problematizing: how the new sociotechnical arrangements called networks come into being in the first place (Latour 1997). How, actor-network researchers ask, does the array of constituents for a potentially new assemblage come into conjunction? How are they aligned; how are supporters enrolled for them; how are political transactions mediated that may produce either the success or failure of the new configuration? And so on. The solution for actor-network research is to trace the active work required to produce particular, local networks, and the risks and struggles this necessitates, rather than settling on generalized or global descriptions.

As an example, Hennion (1989) pays "systematic attention to the role of the intermediary" in the formation of particular media networks, such as pop music. Intermediaries can be either humans or artifacts: interpreters, instruments, producers, recording devices, programmers – even documents that people these collective worlds. Intermediaries can be found, as Hennion and others show, in recording studios, in advertising, art worlds, or radio, where they assemble the work of others by negotiating and brokering the complex sociotechnical constituents that go into any media output. Within all media industries there are chains of such intermediaries: networks that together assemble products that may, or may not, find a public at their conclusion. And assemblages organized around different technologies produce, in different times and places, different genres and ideas of what constitutes authentic music. As Zolberg (1994) puts it: "In classical music, it is the score that has primacy; the instrument in ethnic or folk music; and media and the disc in rock music." Compare this mode of research to one founded more in a political economy perspective, such as Petersen and Berger's (1975) work on US pop music hits, which set out to identify, through quantitative methods, and in hindsight, patterns of innovation across a mass industry.

Each of these four approaches assumes a different image of the network but, whether this image is a mass, interactive, social, or sociotechnical one, it also serves to represent the network in different ways. Inevitably, this has implications for how study and research on networks is carried out. Ironically, where each approach is concerned, both the importance of networks to contemporary mobile societies and their elusiveness as actual objects of inquiry – the place we began – becomes figural to how each approach argues media networks can be studied or understood.

SEE ALSO: Actor-Network Theory; Internet; Media; Media and Globalization; Media and the Public Sphere; Mediated Interaction; Networks; Telephone

REFERENCES AND SUGGESTED READINGS

Boddy, W. (2004) *New Media and Popular Imagination: Launching Radio, Television, and Digital Media in the United States.* Oxford University Press, Oxford.

Castells, M. (2000) *The Rise of the Network Society, The Information Age: Economy, Society and Culture*, Vol. 1, 2nd edn. Blackwell, Oxford.

Granovetter, M. (1983) The Strength of Weak Ties: A Network Theory Revisited. *Sociological Theory* 1: 203–33.

Grint, K. & Woolgar, S. (1997) *The Machine at Work: Technology, Work and Society.* Polity Press, Cambridge.

Hennion, A. (1989) An Intermediary between Production and Consumption: The Producer of Pop Music. *Science, Technology and Human Values* 14(4): 400–24.

Hesmondhalgh, D. (2002) *The Culture Industries.* Sage, Thousand Oaks, CA.

Joyce, P. (2002) *The Social in the Question: New Bearings in History and the Social Sciences.* Routledge, London.

Lasen, A. (2004) Affective Technologies – Emotions and Mobile Phones. *Receiver* 11. Online. www.receiver.vodafone.com.

Latour, B. (1983) *We Have Never Been Modern.* Harvard University Press, Cambridge, MA.

Latour, B. (1997) The Trouble with Actor Network Theory. Online. www.ensmp.fr/~latour/poparticles/poparticle/p067.html.

Latour, B. (2002) Morality and Technology: The End of the Means. *Theory Culture Society* 19: 247–60.

Marvin, C. (1988) *When Old Technologies were New: Thinking About Communications in the Late Nineteenth Century.* Oxford University Press, New York.

Peterson, R. & Berger, D. (1975) Cycles in Symbol Production: The Case of Popular Music. *American Sociological Review* 40: 158–73.

Pickering, A. (1995) *The Mangle of Practice: Time, Agency, and Science.* University of Chicago Press, Chicago.

Thompson, G. F. (2003) *Between Hierarchies and Markets: The Logic and Limits of Network Forms of Organization.* Oxford University Press, Oxford.

Urry, J. (2000) *Sociology Beyond Societies.* Routledge, London.

Wellman, B. & Haythornthwaite, C. (Eds.) (2002) *The Internet in Everyday Life.* Blackwell, Oxford.

Zolberg, V. (1994) Sociology of Culture – La passion musicale: Une sociologie de la mediation by Antoine Hennion. *Contemporary Sociology* 23(4): 605–6.

media and the public sphere

Peter Dahlgren

Increasingly, discussions on issues of democracy and the media are framed within the concept of the public sphere. In schematic terms, a functioning public sphere is understood as a constellation of communicative spaces in society that permit the circulation of information, ideas, debates – ideally in an unfettered manner – and also the formation of political will, i.e., public opinion. In the normative vision of the public sphere, these spaces, in which the mass media and now, more recently, the newer interactive media figure prominently, serve to permit the development and expression of political views among citizens. These spaces also facilitate communicative links between citizens and the power holders of society. While in the modern world the institutions of the media are the institutional core of the public sphere, we must recall that it is the face-to-face interaction, the ongoing talk between citizens, where the public sphere comes alive, so to speak, and where we find the actual bedrock of democracy.

While versions of the concept of the public sphere appear in the writings of a number of authors during the twentieth century, such as Walter Lippman (1922), Hannah Arendt (1998), and John Dewey (1954 [1923]), most people today associate the concept with Jürgen Habermas's version that was first published in 1962. Though the full text was not translated into English until 1989 (Habermas 1989), his concept had by the 1970s come to play an important role in the critical analysis of the media and democracy in the English-speaking world. Since the translation, both the use of the concept and critical interventions in relation to it have grown considerably (see Calhoun 1992 for an excellent collection, including a reply by Habermas). Habermas has not attempted a full-scale reformulation of the public sphere; it is clear that his view of the concept is evolving as his work in other areas develops (Habermas 1996).

In its original formulation, the public sphere is seen by Habermas to consist of two basic domains. The first, and conceptually most developed, is the political public sphere. Yet Habermas also addresses the cultural public sphere, a domain constituted by the circulation – and discussion – of literary and artistic works. Certainly in today's mediated world, the cultural public sphere is of enormous import. All media output cannot be reduced to politics, and though Habermas did not develop this notion as much as he did the political public sphere, it still can be enormously fruitful to approach the mediation of culture from this conceptual angle. This is not least because the boundary line between the political and the cultural is not something that we can take for granted. This is especially the case today when there are new forms of public engagement emerging in the extra-parliamentarian domain that challenge traditional conceptions of what constitutes politics.

After an extensive historical overview, Habermas (1989) surmises that a public sphere began to emerge within the bourgeois classes of Western Europe in the late eighteenth and early nineteenth centuries. The institutional basis for this public sphere consisted of an array of milieux and media, such as clubs, salons, coffeehouses, newspapers, books, and pamphlets, all of which in various (though incomplete) ways manifested Enlightenment ideals of the human pursuit of knowledge and freedom. For Habermas, the key here was not only the institutional basis, but also the manner in which communication took place in this burgeoning public sphere. However imperfectly, he saw that interaction in this social arena embodied the ideals of reason, i.e., the Enlightenment goals of rational thinking, argument, and discussion. In his notion of the public as a rational, dialogic process, Habermas's account of communication and democracy bears similarities with that of John Dewey. We can note that Habermas's work from the 1980s on communicative rationality (Habermas 1984, 1987) further developed normative perspectives on how communication should take place in order to enhance intersubjectivity and the democratic character of society.

Habermas sees the public sphere growing and deepening in the first few decades of the nineteenth century with the spread of mass literacy and the press. Gradually the decay sets in. Journalism increasingly loses its claim to reason; public discourse degenerates into public relations. As the logic of commercialism increasingly shapes the operations of the media, the domain of rationality diminishes. Moving into the twentieth century, Habermas observes with pessimism the trivialization of politics, not least in the electronic media, the industrialization of public opinion, and the transformation of publics from discursive to consuming collectivities. These and other ills serve to constrict society's potential for democratic development, though, as noted, he has seemingly become somewhat less pessimistic and categorical in recent years. Offering horizons and entry points for empirical and critical analysis, the concept has inspired many studies of the media and their role in democracy.

THREE DIMENSIONS OF THE PUBLIC SPHERE

To render the notion of the public sphere into an analytic tool, it can be useful to conceptualize it as comprising three constitutive dimensions: the structural, the representational, and the interactional (Dahlgren 1995).

The structural dimension has to do with the formal institutional features of the public sphere. At bottom, the public sphere rests upon the idea of universality, the norm that it must be accessible to all citizens of society. This puts key structural aspects of the media into the limelight. If the media are a dominant feature of the public sphere, they must be technically, economically, culturally, and linguistically within reach of society's members; any a priori exclusions of any segment of the population collides with democracy's claim to universalism. Seen from this angle, the vision of a public sphere raises questions about media policy and economics, ownership and control, the role of market forces and regulation, issues of the privatization of information, procedures for licensing, rules for access, and so forth. The practical tasks of shaping media policy are often conceptually complicated and politically difficult, given the array of competing interests at stake.

The representational dimension refers to the forms and contents of mass media output (the newer interactive media are taken up below). This includes all the traditional questions and criteria about media output – e.g., fairness, accuracy, pluralism of views, sensationalism, infotainment, diversity of cultural expression. Today, the media have become the language of our public culture, and the grammars of this language impact on the way we experience and think about the world and about ourselves. Yet, while the media are central to the public sphere, they also generate a semiotic milieu that far exceeds the boundaries of the public sphere. More specifically, we should recall that most media output does not address politics, but deals with entertainment, popular culture, sports, advertising, and so on. The mediated public sphere is competing for attention in a semiotic environment overwhelmingly oriented toward consumerist, rather than civic, matters.

The dimension of interaction reminds us that democracy resides, ultimately, with citizens who engage in talk with each other. The public sphere as a process does not "end" with the publication of a newspaper or the transmission of a radio or TV program; these media phenomena are but one step in a larger communication chain which includes how the media output is received, made sense of, and utilized by citizens in their interaction with each other. Here it is useful to recall that Habermas as well as other writers, such as Dewey (1954 [1923]), argue that a "public" should be conceptualized as something other than just a media audience. A public, according to Habermas and Dewey, exists as discursive interactional processes; atomized individuals, consuming media in their homes, do not comprise a public. To point to the interaction among citizens is to take a step into the sociocultural contexts of everyday life. Interaction has its sites and spaces, its discursive practices, its contextual aspects; politics, in a sense, emerges through talk (cf. Benhabib 1996).

CONCEPTUAL ISSUES AND DEBATES

Habermas's work on the public sphere had a major impact on thinking about media, publics, democracy, and the nature of political communication. Observers have noted that Habermas's historical account bears many of the markings of the original Frankfurt School of critical theory. With T. W. Adorno as his academic mentor, it is not surprising that Habermas shares many of the attributes of the leftist high cultural critique of "mass society," advanced capitalism, and the cultural industries. There is also a decidedly nostalgic quality to the analysis, the sense that there once was a historical opening, which then became closed off. Habermas certainly sees the limits of this bourgeois public sphere, not least in class terms; an early counterpoint to Habermas's model even argued for a proletarian public sphere (Negt & Kluge 1993). Feminists have been quick to point out the gender limitations of the bourgeois public sphere – as well as in Habermas's own thinking (cf. Fraser 1992). He has responded generously to his critics (cf. Calhoun 1992) and made constructive use of their interventions.

There is ambiguity with the concept: it is not fully clear whether what Habermas describes is the empirical reality of a historical situation, or whether he is fundamentally presenting a normative vision. Most readers conclude that it is both. He describes the structural mechanisms that erode the public sphere, yet at the same time he – and many of his readers – continue to be inspired by the vision of a robust public sphere serving a well-functioning democracy. Indeed, as the use of the concept spreads, the idea of the public sphere has tended to gravitate away from its neo-Marxian origins and joined mainstream discussions about media performance, journalistic quality, political communication, and the conditions of democracy. In practical terms, the normative horizons from the liberal or progressive traditions that promote "good journalism" or "information in the public interest" are not so different from ideals about the media inspired by the framework of the public sphere.

Another key theme of debate has centered on the tension between a unified, national public sphere versus a pluralistic or even fragmented one. The argument that each nation-state should strive for a large, encompassing public sphere is based in part on the criteria for governability – with too many forums and too many voices, democracy ends up with an ineffective cacophony. This position also derives from concern that isolated islands of public discourse will become politically ineffectual. This view of the public sphere – as providing a unified political culture – was utilized (albeit indirectly) in, for example, defining the mission of European public service broadcasting. Today, the importance of the public sphere concept is being reiterated in the context of the European Union (EU); there is a need to achieve some such semblance of a transnational public sphere, as well as the profound difficulty in attaining anything other than a collection of national mediated spheres in which EU matters are aired and discussed.

The arguments that see the public sphere in essentially plural terms base their claims in part on the complex and heterogeneous sociocultural realities of late modern society, including its increasingly globalized character. To even think of a unified communicative space for all citizens seems simply sociologically out of touch with the real world. Habermas seems to be moving in this direction in a more recent reformulation of the concept (Habermas 1996). Yet there is another, more assertive argument, namely that in a democracy, various groups, movements, interests, and other collectivities need a semi-sheltered space to work out their own positions, promote collective identity, and foster empowerment. In some ways, the tension here reflects two basic perspectives on the public sphere: on the one hand, that it should provide a forum where opinion processes can feed into political decision-making, and on the other hand, that it should offer a communicative space for horizontal civic communication that can have other important democratic functions beyond impacting on decisions. Obviously a democracy needs both, yet the heterogeneous quality of late modern life certainly raises problematic issues about shared political cultures.

One way to go beyond the either–or deadend is to conceptualize the public sphere as consisting of many communicative spaces structured in a tiered fashion. The major mass media of a society can be seen as creating the dominant public sphere, while smaller media outlets can generate a cluster of smaller spheres defined by interests, gender, ethnicity, and so on. Smaller spheres "feed into" larger ones, ideally resulting in interfaces that allow collective views to "travel" from the outer reaches toward the dominant center. This tendency is arguably beginning to grow with increased use of the Internet, where some interfaces between micro, meso, and macro levels might be observed (see below).

A further point of contestation has been the normative view of the kind of communication that should take place in the public sphere. There is in Habermas a strong leaning toward the rational; communication is theorized in a rigorous manner that emphasizes formalized deliberation. Among the common criticisms leveled against his approach is that he seemingly reduces democracy's communication in a manner that excludes affective, rhetorical, symbolic, mythic, bodily, humorous, and other dimensions (cf. Dahlgren 1995). Furthermore, it could be argued that the criteria of traditional notions of rational speech may exclude other, specific communicative registers prevalent among particular groups, thereby undercutting their communicative legitimacy in the public sphere – a line of argument that readily links up with the theme above of a unified versus pluralistic public spheres.

PUBLIC AND PRIVATE

Certainly, one of the central quandaries of public sphere theory is that social and cultural evolution continues to scramble the distinction between public and private. This is a development that is abundantly visible in the late modern media milieu. The traditionalist stance is to define politics in a narrow way, focusing on the formal political arena in the mainstream media. In the process it thereby shuts its eyes, so to speak, to a lot of reality. The concepts of public and private encompass an ensemble of notions that readily align themselves into sets of polarities. The idea of "public" in traditions like the Habermasian is implacably associated with reason, rationality, objectivity, argument, work, text, information, and knowledge. One might also add, historically: the discursively dominant, the authoritative, the masculine, the Caucasian. The private resonates with the personal, with emotion, intimacy, subjectivity, aesthetics, style, image, and pleasure. (There is a large literature on these themes as they pertain to the media; for some recent treatments, see the collection by Corner & Pels 2003; Weintraub & Kumar 1997 offer some more overarching perspectives.) In the media context, the private is also closely related to consumption, entertainment, and popular culture.

At a fundamental level, what is at stake in the modern use of the public sphere perspective is the question of where the political resides, and how it is positioned against that which is deemed non-political. There has been a flood of discussion and debate around this issue. Depending on circumstances, the seemingly private can often harbor the political, a point that has been forcefully made not least by feminist political theorists (Meehan 1995; Lister 1997; Voet 1998). And certainly cultural studies since its inception solidly affirms the always potentially political character of popular culture, a view that has also entered into some corners of political science. The possibilities for topics to become politicized are key elements of the open, democratic society. In the final instance, it can be said that politics has to do with decision-making, but the realm of "political relevance" is larger, always shifting – and can never be fully specified.

INTERNET AND THE PUBLIC SPHERE

It is generally understood that the dramatic changes in the media landscape are having complex and long-term impacts on the political system of western democracies (Bennett & Entman 2001). In recent years, considerable research attention has been devoted particularly to the Internet's role in the public sphere. The past 15 years or so have given rise to an international consensus that western liberal democracy is facing deep difficulties, and it did not take long before many enthusiasts were promoting the Internet as a means for enhancing democracy, precisely by offering the technology for a revitalized public sphere. Much of the enthusiasm soon began to wane, and a very modest view emerged, suggesting that while there have been some interesting changes for the way democracy works, on the whole, the import of the Internet is unexceptional; the Net is not deemed yet to be a factor of transformation. Margolis and Resnick (2000: 14) conclude that: "There is an extensive political life on the Net, but it is mostly an extension of political life off the Net." So while the major political actors may engage in online campaigning, lobbying, policy advocacy, organizing, and so forth, this perspective underscores that there does not seem to be any major change in sight for the public sphere.

Other scholars challenge this view, arguing that the Internet has become particularly salient for the public sphere, but in the domain of informal, extra-parliamentarian politics. There has been a massive growth in what is called advocacy or issue politics, often in the form of ongoing campaigns. Some of the advocates are large and powerful interest groups, others take the form of social movements or activist networks; some operate on the global level, while others have a more grassroots character. Many represent versions of "new" politics (called "life politics" by Giddens 1991); such politics can materialize all over the social terrain, and manifest itself in many contexts.

Especially among young citizens, many have refocused their political attention outside the parliamentary system. Or they are in the process of redefining just what constitutes the political. Among such groups, the boundaries between politics, cultural values, identity processes, and local self-reliance measures become fluid (Beck 1997). Politics becomes not only an instrumental activity for achieving specific goals, but also an expressive activity, a way of asserting, within the public sphere, group values, ideals, and belonging. These new politics are characterized by personalized rather than collective engagement, and by a stronger emphasis on single issues than on overarching platforms or ideologies (Bennett 2003).

It is precisely in the arena of new politics that the new interactive media become not only relevant, but also crucial: their capacity to facilitate "horizontal communication" is decisive. Access to the Net has helped promote the growth of massive, coordinated digital networks of citizens engaged in a vast array of issues, not least in global contexts. Single-issue campaigns against specific corporations, movements for alter-globalization, women's groups, environmental activists, human rights organizations, and many others – including, unfortunately, even neo-nazi, racists, and various hate-groups – can be found on the Internet. Many such groups and movements are in fact generating their own "counterpublic spheres" (cf. Warner 2002), where discussions, debates, and the exchange of information and experience take place.

Yet, for all its compelling qualities, the perspective of the public sphere thus still leaves unclear a number of important issues. Perhaps most significantly, it does not have much to say about *why* people actually participate in the public sphere. This points to the need to link up public sphere theory with more empirical sociocultural perspectives, including such themes as agency, practices, and identity.

SEE ALSO: Internet; Media; Media and Globalization; Media, Network(s) and; Politics and Media; Public Broadcasting; Public Opinion; Public and Private; Public Sphere

REFERENCES AND SUGGESTED READINGS

Arendt, H. (1998) *The Human Condition*. University of Chicago Press, Chicago.
Beck, U. (1997) *The Reinvention of Politics*. Polity Press, Cambridge.
Benhabib, S. (Ed.) (1996) *Democracy and Difference*. Princeton University Press, Princeton.
Bennett, L. & Entman, R. (Eds.) (2001) *Mediated Politics: Communication in the Future of Democracy*. Cambridge University Press, New York.
Bennett, W. L. (2003) Lifestyle Politics and Citizen-Consumers: Identity, Communication, and Political Action in Late Modern Society. In: Corner, J. & Pels, D. (Eds.), *Media and Political Style: Essays on Representation and Civic Culture*. Sage, London, pp. 137–50.
Calhoun, C. (Ed.) (1992) *Habermas and the Public Sphere*. MIT Press, Cambridge, MA.
Corner, J. & Pels, D. (Eds.) (2003) *Media and Political Style: Essays on Representation and Civic Culture*. Sage, London.
Dahlgren, P. (1995) *Television and the Public Sphere*. Sage, London.
Dewey, J. (1954 [1923]) *The Public and its Problems*. Swallow Press, Chicago.
Fraser, N. (1992) Rethinking the Public Sphere: A Contribution to the Critique of Actually Existing Democracy. In: Calhoun, C. (Ed.), *Habermas and the Public Sphere*. MIT Press, Cambridge, MA, pp. 109–42.
Garnham, N. (1992) The Media and the Public Sphere. In: Calhoun, C. (Ed.), *Habermas and the Public Sphere*. MIT Press, Cambridge, MA.
Giddens, A. (1991) *The Consequences of Modernity*. Polity Press, Cambridge.
Habermas, J. (1984, 1987) *The Theory of Communicative Action*, 2 vols. Polity Press, Cambridge.
Habermas, J. (1989) *The Structural Transformation of the Public Sphere*. Polity Press, Cambridge.
Habermas, J. (1996) *Between Facts and Norms*. MIT Press, Cambridge, MA.
Lippman, W. (1922) *Public Opinion*. Macmillan, New York.
Lister, R. (1997) *Citizenship: Feminist Perspectives*. Macmillan, London.
Margolis, M. & Resnick, D. (2000) *Politics as Usual: The Cyberspace "Revolution."* Sage, London.
Meehan, J. (Ed.) (1995) *Feminists Read Habermas*. Routledge, London.
Negt, O. & Kluge, A. (1993) *The Public Sphere and Experience*. University of Minnesota Press, Minneapolis.
Voet, R. (1998) *Feminism and Citizenship*. Sage, London.
Warner, M. (2002) *Publics and Counterpublics*. Zone Books, New York.
Weintraub, J. & Kumar, K. (Eds.) (1997) *Public and Private in Thought and Practice*. University of Chicago Press, Chicago.

media, regulation of

Denis McQuail

Media regulation refers to all means by which media organizations are formally restrained or directed in their activities. In this context, the reference is primarily to external control by way of public policy, law, and regulation, although it also includes some forms of self-regulation, especially when these are intended to meet public concerns. The term media refers to publicly available means of communication, in particular the mass media of print, film, television, and radio, however distributed. Media regulation may also apply to the distribution infrastructure, including cable, wireless, satellite, etc. New means of communication, especially the Internet, may be an object of regulation, especially where they are used as pubic means of communication. The emphasis in this entry is on the external regulation "in the public interest" and with attention to matters of organization and content rather than economic and technical matters. Internal regulation is only considered where it has public causes or consequences. However, new forms of interactive communication are blurring the distinction between public and private communication and the forms and purposes of regulation are changing. Media regulation has always responded to changes in communication technology and successive "regimes" of media regulation can be identified, largely matching the dominant technology of the time.

Media regulation had its beginnings in the restraints placed by church and state authorities on printers and authors in order to protect the established order. The first forms of regulation involved the licensing of printers, advance censorship of particular works, and control of importation, plus laws by which authors and printers could be punished after the event of publication. Regulation in the form of censorship and licensing did not cease until democratic reform movements gained freedom of the press as a basic right guaranteed by the state itself. The first statutory right to freedom of the press was gained in Sweden in 1769, ahead of the more famous First Amendment to the US Constitution in 1791 that outlawed any federal lawmaking in respect of the press. In many societies freedom of the press came very late and it has often been intermittent or not respected in fact. Other restrictions, especially in the form of taxation of newspapers, were applied with a view to restricting circulation to the higher orders of society. Some regulations affecting media, including the self-regulation by printers of their trade and later copyright laws, were designed to protect authors and the public.

These remarks are intended as a reminder that regulation is very mixed in its forms, aims, and effects, but there is always an intention to control publication on behalf of various beneficiaries, ranging from the state to the individual citizen or consumer. For this reason the regulation of media in democratic societies is always a sensitive social and political issue and any claims to benefit the public by way of regulation have to be viewed with caution. Resistance to regulation may also be suspect for other reasons. Nevertheless we can agree that an inescapable tension exists between media regulation, however well intentioned, and the freedom of publication that is a core value of democratic societies. There has to be a clear balance of advantage to the society for governmental regulation to be accepted as legitimate.

Regulation can be applied at four main levels of media operation. Firstly, to the infrastructure of distribution (cable, wireless, satellite, transport, cinemas, etc). Secondly, it can apply to the organization and structure of the organs of production (mainly but not only commercial firms). Thirdly, it can apply to production itself. Fourthly, it can apply to the content of what is published or disseminated. At the first level, regulation mainly relates to technical matters of standards, connectivity, and pricing, ostensibly in the interests of the industry itself and consumers. At the second level, issues of ownership, concentration, and diversity are most prominent. Regulation of production is not extensive, but there are sometimes controls on the amount of production and use of raw materials and other resources, plus various labor and industry-related laws. The conduct of media organizations in collecting information may also be subject to regulation or self-regulation. Content regulation is hard to reconcile with media freedom, but it is nevertheless quite extensive, justified by fears of public and private harm, especially where large-scale audiovisual media are involved. In many broadcasting systems there is still effectively a form of censorship, largely with public approval. In general, the more distant regulation stands from the point of production and the actual content, then the more compatible it is deemed to be with press freedom.

ISSUES OF MEDIA REGULATION

The issues leading to demands for regulation can be classified as either of public or private concern. They can also be differentiated as either negative (the prevention of harm) or positive (securing some public benefit). In respect of public issues, the main headings of potential regulatory activity are as follows:

- *Safeguarding public order and the security of the state.* Most relevant are the possible stimulation of unrest, encouragement of criminal activities, subverting the justice system, publishing state or defense secrets, and assisting (wittingly or not) terrorist actions.
- *Respecting public mores.* This relates to matters of public taste and decency, portrayal

of sex and violence, bad language, blasphemy, and disrespect for national or patriotic symbols.

- *Securing public sphere benefits.* The reference is mainly to the encouragement of positive media contributions to the working of the democratic political system and other social and cultural institutions. The heading covers issues of access and diversity arising out of media concentration. Similar remarks apply to expected cultural benefits from the media.
- *Respecting human rights.* Questions of discrimination, prejudice, and encouragement of violence in relation to various kinds of minorities arise here.

In the private sphere, the following issues are prominent:

- *The protection of individual rights* to reputation, privacy, respect, and dignity.
- *Preventing offense to individuals* by way of shock, alarm, fear, disgust, distress, insult, etc.
- *Preventing harm to individuals.* Harm to publication can take several forms, including material loss as a result of defamation, moral corruption, instigation to suicide or violence, and incitement to violence on the part of others.
- *Protection of property rights* in communication and information. New media have extended the forms of intellectual property beyond those covered by original copyright laws.

There are other matters on which media may be regulated, especially in relation to infrastructure and structural and economic matters. In the latter respect, media are generally subject to regulations that apply to other firms and organizations.

MEDIA POLICY AND REGULATION

Although there are many ad hoc regulations to deal with specific issues arising from the operation of mass media, we can also identify some general principles underlying public policy for media that provide some degree of consistency

and also justifications for intervention in what should be free activities. The principles vary in salience and form of expression in policy according to place and circumstances, but there is widely shared agreement that mass media have a considerable potential for good or ill that may require some limitation or supervision. The main purposes of public policy can be summarized as follows:

- To guarantee freedom of publication.
- To protect individuals and society from possible harm.
- To promote a diversity of provision in terms of sources and content.
- To ensure wide or even universal access to communication facilities for private use and to participation in the mass-media audience.
- To promote a number of social and cultural goals, including local, national, and sectional identification.
- To maintain open and effective markets in media services.

These goals are not always consistent with each other, especially when market operation conflicts with social and cultural objectives or where intervention to secure social and cultural goals interferes with market operation. The most basic potential contradiction is between guaranteeing freedom and also willing ends that freedom may not deliver.

PHASES AND MODELS OF REGULATION

The main phases of development of media technology had given rise to successive and corresponding models of media regulation that have coexisted with each other and to some extent still do so. The main models are as follows.

Print media, having escaped from early forms of control, have also avoided re-regulation, especially any applying to content or involving advance censorship. Even so, print media can be held accountable for certain forms of private harm to individuals and limits can be placed on ownership and control. The general model of (non) regulation of print can be described as a "free press model." By default, music and film have a similar regulatory position, although often without any constitutional protection.

Regulation of telegraph, wireless, telephony, and postal services accompanied the introduction of these new technologies in the late nineteenth century, with particular reference to ownership and control, connectivity, security, and technical standards. These media were not used for mass distribution, but mainly for internal use by businesses, bureaucracies, governments, transport services, and the military. The main aims of regulation were to ensure rapid development, technical efficiency and, where relevant, universality of service; to serve the strategic and military interests of the state; and to comply with international agreements for cross-border communication and use of airwaves. A common instrument of regulation was the state monopoly (although not in the US) – the traditional national PTT that has only recently largely disappeared. The model of regulation covering these media has been called that of a "common carrier" because they offer open access to all persons and content. For the most part, new online media have been developed under this model.

The new audiovisual media, starting with the cinema and extending to include radio and television broadcasting by mid-twentieth century, attracted stringent forms of control. The aims of regulation of these "new" mass media were mixed and not always openly stated. The more ostensible reasons were the allocation of limited access to the channels; to protect health and safety (e.g., cinema regulation and rules affecting advertising of alcohol and tobacco); to safeguard morals and uphold public decency; to prevent harm to vulnerable individuals and to society (by the possible stimulation of violence, crime, or public disorder); allocation of limited access; to provide various educational, cultural, and informational public benefits. Less open motives were to maintain political and social control of a potentially destabilizing or disruptive influence; to protect the security and sovereignty of the state; to serve the national interest, commercially and politically; to protect existing media from excessive competition. This type of regulation has generally been described as a "broadcasting model." Despite varied aims, this model is characterized by a strong focus on content and potential (harmful) effects.

Since the late twentieth century, regulatory models have gradually been adapted in order to take account of new communication technologies and other changes. Firstly, "broadcasting" is no longer limited in its distribution capacity (end of scarcity), nor restricted to the national space, thus removing the motive of allocating the scarce resource of access. In practice, allocation has been increasingly left to the market. Secondly, digital technology has abolished the clear boundary between print, broadcasting, and telecommunications, and along with it the rationale for the separate regimes (convergence of modes of communication). An additional factor has been a strong deregulatory trend, driven by liberal ideology, forces of globalization, and the widespread wish to maximize the economic benefits from new information technology. Between them, these changes have led to expansion, convergence, and the development of new media. This phase of media (de)regulation has also seen a further withdrawal from control of content, not least for reasons of practicality, given the impossibility of systematic monitoring and the lack of international forms of jurisdiction.

The most significant new medium – the Internet – has a somewhat ambiguous position in this account. It is the quintessential new medium, with immense capability, overlapping with all previous media. It is still almost entirely free from direct regulation of any kind. It began as a system for the exchange of scientific information by way of connected computers, but open for other uses and users, and it expanded rapidly after the invention of the web capability in the early 1990s, using international telephone connections. It has no formal central organization or national location, although there is a limited amount of direction by international, non-profit bodies, especially the International Committee for Assigned Names and Numbers (ICANN). However, there are now many commercial Internet service providers with national locations that organize many activities and have in practice often come to be held liable in more than one national jurisdiction for uses of the Internet that contravene general laws affecting communication (e.g., libel). There is no international legal control for a medium whose activities often cross frontiers. As far as it can be placed within one of the regimes, it belongs to the "common carrier" model applying to point–to–point communication. However, the Internet is increasingly being developed, as a result of broadband, as an alternative means of mass distribution (e.g., the downloading of music and film). There are also new issues of social concern that have arisen in relation to the Internet, especially to do with new types of "cybercrime," national security, and threats to the integrity of the Internet system itself, on which so much business and other activity now depends. There are also new threats arising from the access that the Internet gives to young or vulnerable people in matters such as pornography and pedophilia. Despite its origins and some of its uses, the Internet is not beyond the scope of control and regulation (Lessig 1999) and increased regulation is more rather than less likely.

The factors mentioned have presented dilemmas for regulatory policy that have not been resolved, partly because they require international agreements. There has been international regulation of postal and telecommunications media from the early days of the telegraph, but traditionally mass media have been treated as matters for sovereign states and there is still only limited potential for cross-national control, not least because of the need to safeguard communication freedom. The European Union has succeeded in agreeing some regulatory measures relating to cross-border television transmission, but it is up to national governments to implement the rules.

THE MEANS OF REGULATION

When regulation is broadly defined to cover all forms of governance and all varieties of media, the range of forms is very wide. However, we can summarize the possibilities in terms of two dimensions, one of degree of formality (and thus of compulsion), the other according to whether the regulation is predominantly external or internal. This gives rise to four main categories. *Formal, external* regulation refers to laws and other public regulations to which media are obliged to conform. This includes the specific laws for press, broadcasting, and communication that some countries have, as well as general laws applying to all citizens that also apply to media (e.g., concerning defamation, respect for property rights or privacy, incitement to hatred, crime, or violence). The largest body of media law is directed at broadcasting, both in respect of the constitution of public broadcasting systems that are still an important feature of many systems and dealing with the external regulation of private broadcasting. *Formal, internal* regulation covers the management and financial control exerted by a media firm in the pursuit of its objectives and with reference to obligations to clients, audiences, and society generally. The term *self-regulation* applies to this category, where responsibility for meeting certain public standards is delegated to the media themselves. *Informal and external* regulation is a somewhat elastic category that covers the constraints exerted by market forces, lobby and pressure groups, and public opinion. *Informal, internal* regulation covers the control exerted by professionalism, organizational and work cultures, and sometimes embodied in voluntary codes of norms and practices that media claim to adhere to.

In the case of broadcast media, a near-universal circumstance is that operators are licensed by the state or a regulatory body for a limited period and the licenses carry some conditions and requirements that form part of the regulatory framework. The reasons for licensing broadcasting, a practice inconsistent with true press freedom, lay originally in the scarcity of wavelengths and the need to allocate fairly and according to some principle of public benefit. Another reason lay (and still lies) in the fear of potentially harmful effects from what are believed to be powerful means of influence. There is great variability in the degree to which performance according to licenses is assessed.

A significant feature of change is the gradual shift from the direct regulation of the "broadcasting model" to a greater degree of self-regulation by the various branches of the media themselves, by professional bodies such as associations of journalism, and by various external pressure groups and voluntary agencies concerned with media standards and transgressions. In a number of countries this has involved setting up a new (government appointed) regulatory authority between government and media with a wide-ranging jurisdiction over economic, technical and accountability issues concerned with content.

Broadcasting aside, the means for regulating media are not considered very effective in practice or are uncertain in their efficacy. There are several reasons for this general state of affairs. One lies in the attachment to freedom of expression and publication which inhibits any drastic interference in what the media do. A second reason lies in the fact that most media operate in the free market and market disciplines are expected to take care of many external expectations or requirements of performance. The very fact of media operating under market conditions inhibits regulation, except where there is clear evidence of market failure, since this involves interfering in the working of the market and disturbing its operation. Where the market principle dominates there is a strong presumption that regulation should not require any aspect of performance that cannot be supported in economic terms. Despite these obstacles, one of the more effective instruments of regulation is action to limit concentration of ownership or cross-ownership, since this is widely accepted in general as in the public (and market) interest.

THE FUTURE

The main trends in regulation that have been described involve a continuing process of deregulation, especially by increasing distance of government from media and increased reliance on market disciplines; a greater emphasis on economic and technological than content issues; the encouragement of self-regulation by media industries; an attempt to increase the coherence of regulatory measures across different media; and small steps towards international regulation (accelerated somewhat by the wish to combat international crime and terrorism). A limiting condition for regulatory policy stems from the continuing expansion and change of all forms of media activity, making effective regulation more difficult or even impossible.

These issues are also influencing topics for research and theory. There is a good deal of international comparative inquiry, with a search for newer and more useful models of regulation. The emphasis has shifted somewhat from sociological approaches to legal, administrative, economic, and policy perspectives. Philosophical, ethical, and normative matters are also receiving more attention in this area. The problems posed are evidently multidisciplinary as well as international in character. Even so, the basic tension referred to at the outset between freedom and regulation persists, although in changed forms. There is a real fear that digitalization can increase the powers of central control by way of electronic surveillance and monitoring, with an international reach. The apparent decline of regulatory power may be an illusion, although it will not be used, as in the past, to try and improve "communication welfare" in terms of equality, fairness, and quality of content, but for reasons of security.

SEE ALSO: Media; Media and Consumer Culture; Media and Globalization; Media Monopoly; Media, Network(s) and; Media and the Public Sphere; Politics and Media; Surveillance

REFERENCES AND SUGGESTED READINGS

Bertrand, J.-C. (2003) *An Arsenal for Democracy: Media Accountability Systems*. Hampton Press, Creskill, NJ.

Feintuck, M. (1999) *Media Regulation, Public Interest and the Law*. Edinburgh University Press, Edinburgh.

Lessig, L. (1999) *Code and Other Laws of Cyberspace*. Basic Books, New York.

McQuail, D. (2003) *Media Accountability and Freedom of Publication*. Oxford University Press, Oxford.

Napoli, P. M. (2001) *Foundations of Communication Policy*. Hampton Press, Creskill, NJ.

Ó Siochrú, S. & Girard, B. (2003) *Global Media Governance*. Rowman & Littlefield, Lanham, MD.

media and sport

Toni Bruce

In the twenty-first century, it is almost impossible to escape the sports media. Mediated versions of sports events saturate the popular landscape via television, newspapers, magazines, video games, and the Internet. Billions of television viewers watch global events such as the soccer and rugby world cups and the Olympics. Television has helped to transform sport to the point where broadcasters often dictate the constitution of specific competitions, rules and game times are regularly shifted to fit broadcast schedules, and advertisers pay huge sums to associate themselves with televised sports events. However, despite a long history of interdependence between sport and the media, the sociological analysis of the sports media has a relatively short history, and several significant areas remain underresearched.

Sociologists of sport initially paid little interest to the sports media as a research area. Intent on establishing the emerging subfield of sociology of sport within more traditional social scientific approaches grounded in structural functionalist theorizing, few of the early North American anthologies of sport in the late 1960s and early 1970s included a chapter on the sports media, and those that did relied upon historical research or the opinions of sports journalists rather than sociological analysis. However, by the 1980s, in concert with the burgeoning economic impacts of media investment in sports, the sociological analysis of the sports media appeared as a topic in its own right. By the 1990s, a diverse array of anthologies dedicated to the sports media began to appear.

Three major sport sociology publications, the *Sociology of Sport Journal*, the *Journal of Sport and Social Issues*, and the *International Review for the Sociology of Sport*, have regularly published analyses of the sports media, and special issues devoted to the topic have appeared in a variety of other journals including the *Gannett Center Journal*, *Media Information Australia*, *Arena Review*, and the *Journal of Communication*. More recently, the widespread and accelerating interlinking of sport and the media which has led to the unprecedented visibility of sport in popular culture has resulted in an explosion of interest from many fields of study, including the humanities, media studies, communication, leisure studies, and history.

However, sociologists of sport – operating at the intersection of mainstream sociology which showed little interest in the media, and mass communication and media studies which have rarely focused on sport – have been at the forefront of mapping the importance of the sports media in reinforcing dominant cultural ideologies. They have demonstrated that the sports media, and particularly television, operate as a powerful conservative force. Rather than merely reflecting culture, the sports media play a constitutive role in a culture's understandings of itself. The popularity of sport and its apparent separation from political interference, reinforced by seemingly objective visual evidence, mean that sports media stories and narratives are potent sites for essentializing and naturalizing difference, particularly in regard to gender and race.

Early research was conducted in one of two theoretical traditions, both of which continue to inform the field, albeit unevenly. The "uses and gratifications" approach, based in social psychology, emerged from the North American mass communications field and was prominent in early United States research. Its continuing focus is on how the media, and television in particular, meets individuals' internal psychological and biological needs. Research drawing on British cultural studies and feminist theorizing has focused on issues of cultural power and ideology. Much of this work explains how media texts and production techniques ideologically construct cultural understandings of race, gender, sexuality, national identity, disability, class, and consumption in ways that maintain current power relations. Thus, at the same time that researchers in the United States were conducting experimental manipulations of television commentary to assess the effects of violence and conflict on television viewers, British researchers were drawing upon the ideas of Louis Althusser, Antonio Gramsci, and Raymond Williams to identify the structural and ideological effects of the mediation of sport through analyses of media coverage.

Current research is interdisciplinary and reflects a wide variety of theoretical positions, ranging from positivist and liberal feminist to figurational, phenomenological, and postmodern. The bulk of research engages at some level with the key concepts of power and ideology, and much of it is either directly or implicitly influenced by cultural studies, semiotics, critical theory, and various feminisms. The openness to a variety of theoretical perspectives that marks this field of research is reflected in the multiplicity of methods that have been employed by sports media scholars, including experimental and quasi-experimental designs, random sample telephone surveys, in-depth interviews, fieldwork with media workers, personal narratives, collective stories, case studies, and content analysis and textual readings of sports media texts.

The focus of most research has been on media coverage of highly visible professional sports and athletes competing in global competitions such as the Olympic Games and tennis grand slams, international men's world cups in soccer and rugby, and major men's within-nation sports such as basketball, football, baseball, and hockey in North America. Other sports that have attracted attention include handball, skydiving, women's basketball, windsurfing, skateboarding, women's rugby, professional wrestling, boxing, hammer throwing, and women's soccer.

Sports media scholars understand the sports media nexus as consisting of three interrelated areas. The first is the encoding or production of media texts, including the broader social, economic, and political contexts within which media organizations operate. The second is the texts and the "preferred" messages that are encoded in them, and the third is the decoding or interpretation of the texts by audiences. Although sport scholars acknowledge the importance of all three areas, empirical and theoretical research into production and audience interpretations has lagged behind an overwhelming focus on sports media texts.

Most sports media research involves content analysis and textual readings of sports media texts with a focus on how the media representation of sports reproduces, legitimates, and sometimes challenges relations of domination. Much of this research has been influenced by Stuart Hall's (1980) encoding/decoding model of communication and, in particular, his proposition that "preferred" messages supporting dominant ideologies are encoded through production techniques such as visual images and commentary. Thus, much attention has been devoted to identifying the "preferred" or "dominant" messages that are encoded into sports media texts. Textual readings have encompassed a wide range of topics, including gender, race, national identity, sexuality, drug use, violence, illness, disability, football hooliganism, and celebrity. The range of content analyses has remained more limited, focusing primarily on gender, race, and disability.

Despite being underpinned by a wide variety of theoretical and methodological approaches, textual readings and content analyses clearly indicate that sport is overwhelmingly constructed in the mass media as a male arena, with professional male sports represented as the pinnacle of sporting value and achievement. The media representation of sport as the natural domain of men has ensured an ongoing concern with issues of gender in sports media texts. The analysis of gender has expanded from an early and continuing liberal feminist focus on documenting the absence and trivialization of sportswomen to include a variety of critical feminist positions focused on the role of the sports media in the social construction of masculinities, femininities, and sexualities. More than 25 years of textual and content analyses have identified a variety of techniques that operate to trivialize and sexualize female athletes and celebrate violent and instrumental masculinity. Independent of their level of success, females who reflect western ideals of attractiveness and heterosexuality and males who demonstrate willingness to risk pain and injury in full-contact or physically dangerous sports receive the most coverage. Analysis of everyday media coverage of female athletes has revealed that most coverage reflects ambivalence, where positive descriptions and images of women athletes are juxtaposed with descriptions and images that undermine and trivialize their efforts and successes. Even during international sporting events, when coverage of women increases markedly as nationalism overrides gender as the key marker of identity, examples of ambivalent coverage abound.

Analyses of race strongly suggest an ongoing commonsense acceptance of black athleticism that works to naturalize the categories of "black" and "white" as distinct and biologically based. More specifically, despite research with male television commentators showing an awareness of racial stereotyping and a desire to avoid it, the texts of mediated sport appear to regularly draw upon racial stereotypes of black men as "athletes" and white men as leaders and hard workers. In its visual and narrative representations, televised sport naturalizes the fascination with black athleticism and recaptures the mind–body dualism that has dominated popular racial discourses.

In the face of theoretical arguments about the death of the nation-state, sports media scholars point to the importance of the sports media in actively recreating and constructing the nation. Although sport itself is marked by the transnational flow of athletes, media coverage of international sport is imbued with ideologies of nationalism. Through visuals of national flags and athletes in national uniforms, the music of national anthems, and narratives and headlines emphasizing national unity, the sports media function as a potent site at which the nation is symbolically reconstructed.

Some research has focused on specific production techniques, such as image choice and length, music, commentary and narrative, headlines, and the use of slow motion and instant replay, that are intended to appeal to audiences and generate the intense involvement and identification demonstrated by sports fans.

A continuing drawback of textual and content analysis is an implicit assumption that analyses of texts reveal something about how audiences might interpret or be influenced by them. Many analyses of sports media texts imply that audiences may internalize and accept sports media messages as truth. For example, underlying much of the research on mediated images of women's sport is the assumption that trivializing, stereotypical, or ambivalent messages must necessarily disempower females. This assumption may partly explain the absence of empirical research into audiences for sport. Thus, despite the billions of people who regularly watch, listen to, and read about sports, sport sociologists know little about the ways that audiences actually make sense of the media representations they consume.

Although research on sports media audiences continues to reflect the existing division in theoretical traditions between uses and gratifications and cultural studies approaches, researchers using both perspectives reject the notion that audiences passively and uncritically absorb media content. Research points to a variety of responses by audiences who engage with sports media texts for a range of reasons. A number of studies have drawn upon Hall's theory that although preferred messages construct the boundaries within which audiences can interpret media texts, there are a variety of positions – ranging from dominant to negotiated to oppositional – within which decodings can occur.

The importance of commentary in structuring audience understandings emerged from some early research from a uses and gratifications perspective. Using experimental methods to manipulate commentary to highlight or downplay violence or conflict, the researchers concluded that commentary was more important than images in influencing audience understandings of what they were viewing. Researchers working in the critical cultural studies traditions have drawn upon in-depth interviews and observations of small groups of television viewers to suggest that making sense of the sports media is an active, interpretive process involving texts and audience members in specific personal, cultural, and historical locations that cannot be predicted from analysis of texts alone. Research on sports media audiences points to gender differences in consumption, with the undeniable masculine bias of sports coverage making it more difficult for many females to identify as fans and experience pleasure in their viewing.

Research on media production falls into two key areas. The first explores the broad cultural, political, and economic contexts within which media and sports organizations collaborate to produce mediated sport, and the second focuses on the processes of producing media texts. Researchers focused on the broader context have drawn attention to the ways in which the increasing linkages between sports and global media organizations have affected the structure and global circulation of popular professional sports. Grounding their analysis in theories of political economy, sports scholars have identified a global sports media nexus that is increasingly marked by vertical and horizontal integration in which global communications companies simultaneously own interests in sports teams, television rights, and media outlets such as newspapers, magazines, Internet sites, and radio and television stations. Research into the sports media nexus identifies the importance of sport to global corporations for whom it offers relatively inexpensive television programming that is highly desired by a key target audience of males aged 18–49 with disposable income. Thus, sport becomes *the* spectacle through which these corporations generate viewers, corporate sponsorship, advertising, and profits.

The small but growing research into the processes of producing televised sport has identified a wide range of beliefs and practices that media workers use to translate "what happened" into a program that makes "good" television. Field-based observations and interviews form the core methodologies as sports media scholars have explored the production of televised downhill skiing, golf, track and field, soccer, ice hockey, and basketball. With few exceptions, the television research focuses on the production of men's sports. It has identified taken-for-granted professional beliefs that generally reflect dominant ideologies of masculinity and femininity, race, capitalism, and the importance of success.

The practices and ideologies that underpin the production of print media have been captured primarily by interviewing, field observation, and survey methods. Research concerns include how sports writers understand their position in the broader field of journalism, interactions between sports writers and sports personnel such as athletes, coaches, and support staff, and how specific professional ideologies embraced by sports writers contribute to the stories and images that are published. This research reveals that sports media personnel tend to draw upon and generally reflect widely circulating ideologies as they attempt to construct coherent narratives and images about sports events. A small body of phenomenological and feminist work investigating the experiences of women sports writers covering major men's sports in North America has pointed to the importance of gender in determining interactions within the men's locker rooms that the sports designate as the official interview areas.

Although the conservative role of the media in reinforcing and producing dominant ideologies has been well researched, studies of sites in the sports media nexus, such as during production or audience consumption, at which relations of domination might be challenged or subverted, are rare. Few full-scale projects incorporating all three levels – production, texts, and audiences – have been undertaken and there remains a need for more studies of production and audience interpretation.

The first anthology devoted to sports advertising appeared in 2005, and it may encourage research into a broader range of sports media production and consumption contexts such as talkback radio, non-commercial media, video games, the Internet, specialist magazines, and non-live sports television shows which have received only limited attention. Sociologists of sport are expected to expand their research into these and other emerging forms of sports media as they continue to develop sophisticated explanations of the media in contemporary society.

SEE ALSO: Disability Sport; Gender, Sport and; Media; Media and Consumer Culture; Sport and Culture; Sport and Ethnicity; Sport and Race; Sport as Spectacle

REFERENCES AND SUGGESTED READINGS

Andrews, D. L. & Jackson, S. J. (Eds.) (2001) *Sport Stars: The Cultural Politics of Sporting Celebrity.* Routledge, London.

Baker, A. & Boyd, T. (Eds.) (1997) *Out of Bounds: Sports, Media, and the Politics of Identity.* Indiana University Press, Bloomington.

Barnett, S. (1990) *Games and Sets: The Changing Face of Sport on Television.* British Film Institute, London.

Bernstein, A. & Blain, N. (Eds.) (2003) *Sport, Media, Culture: Global and Local Dimensions.* Frank Cass, London.

Blain, N., Boyle, R., & O'Donnell, H. (1993) *Sport and National Identity in the European Media.* Leicester University Press, Leicester.

Boyle, R. & Haynes, R. (2000) *Power Play: Sport, the Media, and Popular Culture.* Pearson Education, Harlow.

Brookes, R. (2002) *Representing Sport.* Arnold, London.

Buscombe, E. (Ed.) (1975) *Football on Television.* British Film Institute, London.

Chandler, J. M. (1988) *Television and National Sport: The United States and Britain.* University of Illinois Press, Urbana.

Creedon, P. J. (1994) *Women, Media, and Sport: Challenging Gender Values.* Sage, Thousand Oaks, CA.

Davis, L. (1997) *The Swimsuit Issue and Sport: Hegemonic Masculinity in Sports Illustrated.* State University of New York Press, Albany.

Hall, S. (1980) Encoding/Decoding. In: Hall, S., Hobson, D., Lowe, A., & Willis, P. (Eds.), *Culture,*

Media, Language. Hutchinson, London, pp. 128–39.

Horne, J., Tomlinson, A., & Whannel, G. (1999) *Understanding Sport: An Introduction to the Sociological and Cultural Analysis of Sport*. E. & F. N. Spon, London.

Jackson, S. J. & Andrews, D. L. (Eds.) (2005) *Sport, Culture, and Advertising: Identities, Commodities, and the Politics of Representation*. Routledge, London.

Kinkema, K. M. & Harris, J. C. (1992) Sport and the Mass Media. In: Holloszy, J. O. (Ed.), *Exercise and Sport Sciences Reviews*, Vol. 20. Williams & Wilkins, Baltimore, pp. 127–59.

Lowes, M. D. (1999) *Inside the Sports Pages: Work Routines, Professional Ideologies, and the Manufacture of Sports News*. University of Toronto Press, Toronto.

Morse, M. (1983) Sport on Television: Replay and Display. In: Kaplan, E. A. (Ed.), *Regarding Television*. American Film Institute, Los Angeles, pp. 44–66.

Rowe, D. (Ed.) (2004a) *Critical Readings: Sport, Culture, and the Media*. Open University Press, Milton Keynes.

Rowe, D. (2004b) *Sport, Culture, and the Media: The Unruly Trinity*, 2nd edn. Open University Press, Milton Keynes.

Wenner, L. A. (Ed.) (1989) *Media, Sports, and Society*. Sage, Newbury Park, CA.

Wenner, L. A. (Ed.) (1998) *MediaSport*. Routledge, London and New York.

Whannel, G. (1992) *Fields in Vision: Television, Sport, and Cultural Transformation*. Routledge, London.

Whannel, G. (2002) *Media Sport Stars: Masculinities and Moralities*. Routledge, London.

mediated interaction

Helen Wood

The phrase mediated interaction is now more popularly associated with the speed and ease of Internet connections which facilitate new ways of creating electronic interpersonal relationships and community-building through facilities like web forums, SMS messaging, and ICQ. But that is to ignore the involvement of much of the "mass media" – and that phrase itself is problematic – interceding in forms of human life and relationships. Psychiatrists

Horton and Wohl (1956) wrote of the ways in which the mass media, radio, television, and film, give an illusion of face-to-face relationships between spectator and performer which they describe as "*para*-social." More recently, John Caughie has talked about the potential for *pseudo*-involvements with media figures as "mediated social relationships." The focus here is on continuities produced through different media over time in their various involvements in the human business of "interaction."

Take television as a case in point. When talking about some forms of television like talk shows, there is discussion about how the elevation of the audience to the stage is part of a breaking down of the distinction between spectacle and spectator in modern public life. This has an important impact on the communicative strategies of the media, since Carpignano et al. (1990) suggest that the phenomenon is bringing about "new social relationships of communication embodied in the television medium which have progressively undermined the structural dichotomy between performance and audience." How then can we think of these "new social relationships" built by the media's forms? Traditional semiotic tools from media studies, which illuminate symbolic meanings, do not help us here. More useful is a perspective generated by authors such as Meyrowitz (1985) and Thompson (1994, 1995), who are concerned with the media's communicative impact on daily life.

These authors locate such phenomena within wider conceptual themes presented by late modernity. They begin to represent a *social theory* of the media which reaches beyond traditional schools of thought descended from structuralism and semiotics. Thompson (1994) suggests that there is a poverty of resources in thinking about the way in which the media are embedded within the social world and are part of daily communicative action: "One is left with the impression that, for most social theorists, the media are like the air that we breathe: pervasive, taken-for-granted, yet rarely thought about as such." Refusing some of the dominant paradigms which have overly concentrated on the determining effect of the media as a form of social control, he attempts to describe the way in which the media have had an impact on the nature of social interaction whereby "mediated *quasi*-interaction" supplements face-to-face communication in the modern world.

Television has often been thought about as a domestic medium whereby the home, the domestic, and suburbia are embedded within television's history and form, which necessitates research into television's place within family relationships and domestic politics. In turn, the space of the home as a site of the reconstruction of patriarchal relations has made gender central to thinking about television and the home. Hobson's (1980) pioneering essay exactly intervened in this debate when she described the importance of the radio in providing companionship in the lonely space of the home in the daytime, as well as the way in which the scheduling of radio programs helped order the otherwise structureless day-to-day of the housewife. Notions of companionship and the everyday are suggestive of a type of familiar and even intimate relationship that women might have with broadcasting that is not directly related to the semiotic encoding of meaning. It is possible that this relationship is partly experienced as a type of mediated interaction (Wood 2005).

The media clearly play a determining role in generating new forms of interaction and new kinds of social relationships between individuals which have emerged from the changing phenomenological conditions of the contemporary era. Although not directly addressing the media per se, Giddens (1990) highlights the characteristics of modernity as partly due to the changes that have occurred in the social arrangements of space and time, whereby people inhabiting the premodern world would experience time as inextricably bound to a sense of place, whereas the modern era is characterized by "empty time" as an increasingly globalized sense of temporal arrangements. He refers to this as "time-space distanciation," whereby time and space have become increasingly dislocated in a modern world through the ongoing process of the disembedding of social systems: "by disembedding I mean the 'lifting out' of social relations from local contexts of interaction and their restructuring across indefinite spans of time-space" (p. 21).

What then does this mean in terms of the media? Put simply, technological mechanisms have "lifted" social relations out of face-to-face contexts and "stretched" them across vast distances. Therefore, we experience events happening at a distance, possibly even at a different moment in time, as though they are "live," whereby "media events" are increasingly choreographed for the cameras as much as for the co-present spectators (Dayan & Katz 1992). Social relationships therefore are no longer confined to the local. Modern communications systems mean that we can engage in interaction with distanced and absent speakers where co-present and co-spatial arrangements are no longer required. While at the same time consumption of media takes place in locations distant from each other, the moments of reception are simultaneous, which may have a huge impact on human relationships and the shaping of individual and collective identities (Moores 1997).

The process of "reembedding" provides a key to understanding the formation of new social relationships through the mediation of experience. Reembedding is "the reappropriation or recasting of disembedded social relations so as to pin them down ... to local conditions of time and place" (Giddens 1990: 79–80). Moores (1997, 2000) articulates the way in which one can take this concept and apply it to mediated encounters. For instance, in the modern age we rely upon the trust we place in the institutional representatives of "expert systems," such as that we place in architects as we sit in our homes, or in the aircrew as we board a plane. As we, lay individuals, come into contact with representatives of these expert systems, they engage in "facework commitments" where we are encouraged to place our trust in them – such as the rehearsed pleasantries of flight attendants as they allay our fears in the air. According to Moores (2000:112): "Without pushing Gidden's notion of reembedding too far ... we can fruitfully extend his notes on trust in co-present encounters so as to take account of the facework commitments made by media figures in their regular interactions with absent viewers and listeners." In taking his lead, we are not drawing upon concepts such as "simulacrum" and "hyperreality," as put forward by Baudrillard and other postmodern theorists, which are suggestive of a "fake" or "substitute" world in which the media have duped the masses into an "unreal" set of relationships. Rather, we are focusing on how the media, and our use of them (despite the reticent use qualifiers such *pseudo* and *para* in describing mediated social forms), can reconfigure parts of everyday communication through a mediated reality.

It is not too difficult to apply these sentiments to the ever-changing space of new media forms. Obviously, the Internet and its encroaching impact upon other media technologies, gaming, broadcasting, cinema, etc., produces a context in which, increasingly, "connectivity" and not just "reception" defines our modes of engagement with different aspects of the media. While at present "interactivity" remains a marketing buzzword in the push to establish and maintain new kinds of relationships with niche audiences, it is clear that there is a continuum in which "mediated interaction" is taking on new forms of more explicitly two-way communication which open out the electronic/lived space of everyday interaction. That is not to say that there is a finite economy of interaction where there exists a deficit model in which forms of mediated interaction encroach upon "real" interaction. Rather, we need to account for the spaces in which newly negotiated identities, "virtual communities," etc. take shape in the contemporary context, and begin to redraw the lines and barriers of/to communication. All of which of course require charting in terms of their relationship with the very real, and not "quasi," inequalities of the social world.

SEE ALSO: Audiences; Community and Media; Consumption and the Internet; Cyberculture; Information Technology; Interaction Order; Internet; Media; Mediation; Reception Studies; Television

REFERENCES AND SUGGESTED READINGS

Carpignano, P. et. al. (1990). Chatter in the Age of Electronic Reproduction: Talk Television and the Public Mind. *Social Text* 25(6): 33–55.

Dayan, D. & Katz, E. (1992) *Media Events: The Live Broadcasting of History*. Harvard University Press, Cambridge, MA.

Giddens, A. (1990) *Modernity and Self Identity*. Polity Press, Cambridge.

Hobson, D. (1980) Housewives and the Mass Media. In: Hall, S. et. al. (Eds.), *Culture, Media, Language*. Hutchinson, London, pp. 105–14.

Horton, D. & Wohl, R. (1956) Mass Communication and Para-Social Interaction: Observations on Intimacy at a Distance. *Psychiatry* 19(3): 215–29.

Meyrowitz, J. (1985) *No Sense of Place: The Impact of Electronic Media on Social Behaviour*. Oxford University Press, Oxford.

Moores, S. (1997) The Mediated Interaction Order. Paper presented at British Sociological Association Conference, Edinburgh.

Moores, S. (2000) *Media and Everyday Life in Modern Society*. Edinburgh University Press, Edinburgh.

Thompson, J. (1994) Social Theory and the Media. In: Crowley, D. & Mitchell, D. (Eds.), *Communication Theory Today*. Polity Press, Cambridge, pp. 27–47.

Thompson, J. (1995) *The Media and Modernity*. Polity Press, Cambridge.

Wood, H. (2005) Texting the Subject: Women, Television and Modern Self-Reflexivity. *Communication Review* 8(2): 115–35.

mediation

Brett Nicholls

The term mediation has historically functioned in four distinct ways. First of all, the concept has been employed as a third term in a triadic structure, mediating between one state of reality and another. Secondly, the concept refers to the technical transmission of messages, such as mass media. In this case, the sense of reality that the transmission conveys is under scrutiny. Thirdly, the concept refers to the dominance of media in contemporary constructions of knowledge. In this case the concept is analogous to mediatization. And fourthly, mediation refers to the process of linking nodal points in a network or an assembled structure, where reality is produced or performed. The first understanding has been the main focus of critical thought. The second developed in the context of industrial forms of mass media. And the third and fourth emerged recently as a consequence of post-industrial or postmodern processes and the subsequent transformation of society.

Conventionally, the verb "mediate" has the meaning of interposing something as a medium between two things that are not connected.

This implies a separation of the things and the necessity of mediation, as in the human soul and God, the subject and the object, the individual and society. To mediate is to connect or reconcile separate things. Mediation is thus a third term between two things. It can function as a technological form in the case of media, the structure of consciousness in philosophy, or in the form of a third person in Christian theology or law. "Mediation" is also the contrary of immediacy, a direct connection or relation without the necessity of a third term. We could, for instance, distinguish between immediate experience, which would be to experience and understand an object directly as it is, and mediated experience, which would be to experience and understand an object via an intermediary. For the most part, the view that experience and understanding are mediated prevails. As social beings, our knowledge of the world is not received first hand but is mediated through specific structures such as mass media and institutions, language, the body, and consciousness itself.

The concept of mediation thus marks the tension between the "real" world as it is and the world as it is perceived and understood. This tension has been a philosophical problem since the ancients. It stands at the center of Plato's well-known "Allegory of the Cave," in which Plato describes knowledge that fails to achieve the condition of philosophy. Occupying "a sort of underground den," the inhabitants are cut off from the outside, apart from the light that passes through an entrance that remains unseen. The world outside appears in the form of shadows and reflections on the wall of the cave, and even though these images are merely the mediation of the actual world, the people in the cave, who know no other reality, think that they are reality. For Plato, the perceived reality of the cave dwellers is incomplete, and they themselves are in many senses duped.

As the "Allegory of the Cave" reveals, Plato viewed mediated knowledge with suspicion. This suspicion continues to prevail in contemporary thinking and serves as a basis for critiques of social institutions and mass media. The tension between the actual world and our knowledge of it, between the material object and its mediation, has been central for philosophy and sociology. The possibility of direct knowledge was a crucial issue for the idealist philosopher Immanuel Kant. Kant famously established the view that we cannot know the thing in itself. What we do know are the appearances of things as they are presented to consciousness through the senses. The demarcation of appearances and things was crucial to Kant, who aimed to outline the validity of reason free from the object, and guarantee the condition of freedom, the necessary condition for morality.

The prevailing sense of "mediation," in German *Vermittlung*, that emerges within idealism is that of reconciling opposites or establishing the harmony of opposites within the totality. After Kant's insistence upon appearances, mediation was celebrated as the basis for a stable sense of selfhood. Fichte would champion mediation dialectically as the unity of "the I," in which subject and object become one. Mediation is the third space of reflection, the arbitration of a dispute between opposites, with the result that in the middle everything is unified and connected, but the extremes remain opposed. Schelling likewise uses the term to describe the philosophical task of designating a point in which the object and its concept originally and without any mediation become one. Following Fichte and Schelling, Hegel refined the term via its relation to immediacy. To shore up the harmony of absolute knowledge with the structure of the known object, the core of Hegel's idealism, he introduces a triadic structure: the immediate, the mediated, and mediated immediacy. The immediate, the intrinsic nature of the object, is situated in an opposite relation to the "mediated," the object as it has been formed in a field of relations. This opposition is itself mediated, since both immediate and mediated processes structure things, knowledge, and logic for Hegel. Descartes, for instance, is mediated by his education, but through the process of sublation is able to rise above this education to be immediately aware of his own existence. The condition of doubt, famously outlined by Descartes, is a mediated immediacy (Hegel 1991: 113). Similarly, Hegel (1942) draws mediation into his theory of the state. Focusing on the immediacy of life and the will, Hegel charts how the minds of individuals are in conflict with other individuals in the marketplace and within civil society. These conflicts, however, are ultimately mediated by the state. The state, Hegel argues, is an actuality with a history that is the materialization of the Absolute Spirit, God. It "is the actuality of the ethical Idea," existing "immediately in custom, mediately in individual self-consciousness, knowledge, and activity, while self-consciousness in virtue of its sentiment towards the state, finds in the state, as its essence and the end-product of its activity, its substantive freedom" (Hegel 1942: 155).

If idealism championed mediation as reflection and harmony, Marx focused upon contradiction and disharmony and opened the way for critical thought. A suspicion of the processes of mediation is central in this endeavor. Questioning the emphasis upon harmony in idealism, Marx (1975) contended that Hegel's theory of the state is merely an "abstraction" that fails to grasp the life of individuals "in their specific character" (p. 12). With this emphasis on the material conditions of life, Marx went on to demonstrate how the movement of Spirit in Hegel's philosophy is materially produced. Hegel's state is not the actual realization of the ethical idea and freedom; it is the effect of the actual relations of bourgeois civil society.

Emphasizing the inequality of the material conditions of life between workers and the owners of capital, Marx argued that bourgeois civil society is violent rather than harmonious. Within the capitalist mode of production the self-mediating labor of natural being, the uncoerced labor that mediates between the subject and nature, is perverted by the second-order mediations – money, exchange, and private property – that are imposed upon productive activity. The mature Marx developed his suspicion of second-order mediations in his examination of the relationship between production and consumption (1986: 28–9), and the "mystical character of the commodity" (1996: 81–94). Production provides the material and structure for consumption, while consumption provides a subject for commodities. Consumption thus mediates production by reproducing the need for commodities, but production mediates consumption by "producing a definite object which must be consumed in a particular way" (Marx 1986: 29). Moreover, commodities themselves are mystical in the sense that they possess the material power to mediate social relations.

In this account, mediation functions surreptitiously, or ideologically, producing social harmony on the surface while injustice and possible conflict remain hidden underneath.

In the study of media the concept of mediation has taken a slightly different form. With the same suspicion that marks Plato's account of the cave, media studies has focused on the media as a system of transmitting messages between parties. In this approach, media serve the function of mediating the relationship between the state and the citizen, and the market and the consumer. In this process the media represent and mediate the differences between social categories such as race, class, gender, sexuality, ethnicity, and age. Metaphors such as mirror, reflection, window, and frame (McQuail 1994: 64–6) have been employed to critically describe this mediating function of mass media. Issues of media power (Lazarsfeld & Merton 1948), consensus (Wirth 1948), bias (Innis 1951; Glasgow University Media Group 1976), distortion (Lang & Lang 1968), ideology (Hall 1977), media hegemony (Gitlin 1994), and the social agency of the media audience (Ang 1985) have emerged to critically engage with this mediating function. In each of these, the referential capacities of media texts and the social power of the media industries and media audiences are, in varying degrees, in question.

If understandings of mass media are produced in terms of mediation as the transmission of messages between unequal parties, in the context of the digitalization of media, the increased proliferation of information and images, and the rise of immaterial commodities, the conventional concept of mediation has been transformed. A new set of issues and problems for critical approaches to the media have begun to emerge. At the forefront of this emergence, the French sociologist Jean Baudrillard contends that the relationship between representation and reality has been fundamentally transformed. Conventionally, the media have been understood as a transmission technology representing reality, mediating social differences and mediating the individual and the actual world. But now instead of standing in for something other than itself, that is to transmit messages about the social world, the media are producing a (hyper)reality, a media reality that is "more real than the real world" (2001: 14–15). In other words, the representation of reality produced by media texts has become privileged over, or is now more believable than, actual reality. Moreover, Baudrillard (1983) argues pessimistically that the increasing proliferation of signs and information in the media destroys conventional meaning and leads to the breakdown of the division of representation and reality. In this way of thinking, the media are reality and reality is the media. Mediation, for Baudrillard, is thus no longer possible. To put this another way, media in the conventional sense – a force mediating between reality and the individual and between individuals – disappear. What we have today are media that function as a black hole of signs, information, and images that produce and reproduce meanings as effects of simulation rather than political and economic reality.

Baudrillard's extreme position is highly contentious. Giddens, for instance, holds the view that media continue to serve an important existential function. A mediated experience, for Giddens, is detached from experiences that "raise disturbing existential questions" in everyday life. This is a process that he calls "sequestration" (1991: 168). The media's preoccupation with death and love, and so on, serves the purpose of furthering the process of sequestration. The media enable the audience to enrich existential sensibilities at a distance and shore up the ontological security necessary for everyday life. There is, of course, no ontological security in Baudrillard, but he does open up the question of mediation in ways that have been important for contemporary media studies. Giddens seems to have mass media in mind in his outline of the process of sequestration. Baudrillard, on the other hand, has a different view of media. Rather than mass media, which are associated with the rise of industrial capital, Baudrillard's work addresses post-industrial capital and the increasing centrality of information in everyday life. As the critical differences between Giddens and Baudrillard reveal, the contemporary employment of the concept of mediation tends to be shaped by assumptions about the validity of post-industrial capital and the information economy. If no radical transformation is assumed, critical approaches tend to discuss media as transmission. If the contemporary moment is considered as a newly formed informational order, critical approaches

reject the possibility of mediation or employ it in order to mark the process of assemblage.

Following the trajectory of post-industrial capital, it is possible to push Baudrillard's insights in affirmative directions, while paying heed to his strong reservations about contemporary media culture. Through new media studies and work on networks, mediation has come to stand in for the processes of assemblage. This is the approach that sees social categories and identities as being produced in the process of connection and interaction. Media are an integral part of this process, along with other social institutions and social practices. What counts here are the connections themselves and the sorts of social realities that they produce. Baudrillard's pessimism is undermined by this view, since the process of mediation produces social interactions and possibilities. And Plato's suspicion no longer holds any ground. The focus is not on the harmonious or ideological intersection of two fixed entities but on the linkage of disparate entities, whereby these entities (human or institutional) gain power and identity only through the quantity, solidity, and strength of the linkages.

Stuart Hall's (1986a, b) concept of articulations, built on an engagement with Gramsci, anticipates this idea of mediation. Hall's idea of "articulated traditions" as a constructed and contingent collective voice is an assemblage of sorts. Articulations are concrete linkages that produce social realities. Hall uses the example of an "articulated lorry" – with the cab and trailer hooked together – to explain the term. Something that is hooked together, such as an articulated lorry, can be unhooked and recombined to produce a new permutation. As social and cultural arrangements, articulations are a kind of sorting process, organizing and linking disparate elements to produce social and cultural relationships. Importantly, these relationships and the political reality that they produce are flexible and contingent. The relationships do not prefigure the arrangement, as if produced by a social agent, they are produced by the linkages themselves. Articulated arrangements thus produce social and political identities, and are more like cyborgs than organic bodies that have evolved through time.

As the new form of mediation, articulated arrangements rely upon communicative networks that enable real-time connections. Articulations can be quickly formed as a response to shifting conditions and then deformed and reformed in new arrangements. Articulations thus produce new political and critical possibilities but they also open up new problems. The first is the problem of access to networks. As communicative infrastructures, such as the Internet, become more central in everyday life, the issue of who controls the infrastructure and our access to it becomes crucial. Moreover, access points can be easily commodified – as in Internet service providers and telephone services – and social and cultural arrangements can become dependent upon the commercial imperatives of the owners of communicative infrastructures. The second problem is the impact of speed on critical thought. The mediating possibilities of information processing technologies operating at absolute speed, in real time, close down the temporal delay that enables a critical relation to media and to the production of knowledge.

As information processing technologies increasingly take on the role of organizing social life – through databases that store information about social subjects, along with devices for storing and organizing cultural memories such as photographs and movie files, profiling software for managing the vast media choices that are available, and search engines for packaging information in digestible chunks – social life is increasingly impacted by processes external to human thought that are operating with a machinic speed and precision. Rather than a reflective relationship to this knowledge – there is no third space of reflection in this structure as in idealism's celebration of mediation as arbitrating the dispute between opposites – the subject is caught up in the flow of information exchange. The task for the subject is to access the already organized information and set it to work as quickly and efficiently as possible (Deleuze 1992).

The question of mediation today is thus inseparably linked to philosophical and sociological understandings of technology, which engage with the function and the impact of technologies upon human consciousness, and with the production, distribution, and social use of knowledge. Along with the possibility of flexible arrangements, mediation is a term that now marks the problem of critical reflection, so

central for critical theory, and perhaps reveals the necessity for critical interventions that operate at speed. As Scott Lash (2002: 65), acutely aware of the problem of speed, writes, "sociocultural theory … at the turn of the twenty-first century increasingly must take on the form of information, increasingly take on the form of media." The issue here is whether or not critical thought should speed up or slow down (Virilio 1986; Latour 2004). Clearly, the question of mediation today demands a form of critical thinking that is adequate to its speeding object.

SEE ALSO: Hyperreality; Information Technology; Internet; Media; Media, Network(s) and; Mediated Interaction; Representation; Stereotyping and Stereotypes; Technological Innovation; Technology, Science, and Culture

REFERENCES AND SUGGESTED READINGS

Ang, I. (1985) *Watching Dallas: Soap Opera and the Melodramatic Imagination*. Routledge, London.

Baudrillard, J. (1983) *In the Shadow of the Silent Majorities*. Trans. P. Foss, J. Johnston, & P. Patton. Semiotext(e), New York.

Baudrillard, J. (2001) *Impossible Exchange*. Trans. C. Turner. Verso, London.

Deleuze, G. (1992) Postscript on Societies of Control. *October* 59: 3–7.

Giddens, A. (1991) *Modernity and Self-Identity: Self and Society in the Late Modern Age*. Polity Press, Cambridge.

Gitlin, T. (1994) *Inside Primetime*. Routledge, London and New York.

Glasgow University Media Group (1976) *Bad News*. Routledge & Kegan Paul, London.

Hall, S. (1977) Culture, the Media, and the Ideological Effect. In: Curran, J., Gurevitch, M., & Woollacott, J. (Eds.), *Mass Communication and Society*. Edward Arnold, London, pp. 315–48.

Hall, S. (1986a) Gramsci's Relevance for the Study of Race and Ethnicity. *Journal of Communication Inquiry* 10(2): 5–27.

Hall, S. (1986b) On Postmodernism and Articulation: An Interview with Stuart Hall. *Journal of Communication Inquiry* 10(2): 45–60.

Hegel, G. W. F. (1942) *Hegel's Philosophy of Right*. Trans. T. M. Knox. Clarendon Press, Oxford.

Hegel, G. W. F. (1991) *The Encyclopaedia Logic*. Trans. T. F. Geraets, W. A. Suchting, & H. S. Harris. Hackett, Indianapolis.

Innis, H. A. (1951) *The Bias of Communication*. University of Toronto Press, Toronto.

Lang, K. & Lang, G. E. (1968) *Politics and Television*. Quadrangle, Chicago.

Lash, S. (2002) *Critique of Information*. Sage, London.

Latour, B. (2004) *Politics of Nature: How to Bring the Sciences into Democracy*. Trans. C. Porter. Harvard University Press, Cambridge, MA.

Lazarsfeld, P. F. & Merton, R. K. (1948) Mass Communication, Popular Taste, and Organized Social Action. In: Bryson, L. (Ed.), *The Communication of Ideas*. Harper, New York, pp. 95–118.

McQuail, D. (1994) *Mass Communication Theory: An Introduction*. Sage, London.

Marx, K. (1975) *Karl Marx, Frederick Engels, Collected Works*, Vol. 3. Lawrence & Wishart, London.

Marx, K. (1986) *Karl Marx, Frederick Engels, Collected Works*, Vol. 28. Lawrence & Wishart, London.

Marx, K. (1996) *Karl Marx, Frederick Engels, Collected Works*, Vol. 35. Lawrence & Wishart, London.

Virilio, P. (1986) *Speed and Politics: An Essay on Dromology*. Trans. M. Polizzotti. Semiotext(e), New York.

Wirth, L. (1948) Consensus and Mass Communication. *American Sociological Review* 13: 1–15.

medical malpractice

Ferris J. Ritchey

Medical malpractice is "an instance in which a physician or other medical practitioner causes injury or death to a patient through negligent behavior," involving actions that fail to follow acceptable standards of practice (Cockerham & Ritchey 1997: 81). Uncertain medical conditions, however, make establishing negligence very difficult. Less than 20 percent of claims involve *res ipsa loquitur* cases, those that "speak for themselves," such as amputation of a healthy limb. Some claims for injury and/or negligence are questionable, while out-of-court settlements occur to avoid litigation costs. After 1970, malpractice claims increased dramatically with crisis periods of greatly inflated liability insurance costs. Liability reform legislation has been introduced in every state.

Obtaining reliable data on claims rates, settlement/jury awards, efficacy of capping awards, and insurance company profits is hampered by accounting complexities, decentralized records systems, and the politics of stakeholders, including physicians, patient consumers, hospitals, trial lawyers, and the liability insurance industry. Nonetheless, enough physicians have incurred claims that it is no longer a surprising event, especially for obstetricians and surgeons. Many historical and structural changes in medicine, law, and society are posited to explain increasing litigation. Whether it is due to more injuries or to changes in tort law is unclear; however, the rapid increase of all types of litigation suggests the latter.

Increasing litigation is consequential for health care access. Premium increases result from claim losses, anticipated losses, and periodic downturns in investment markets and insurance carrier profits. These costs ultimately are covered by consumers and third-party payers. Fears of litigation and risk-reduction strategies incur additional costs, including defensive medicine – physicians ordering extra tests, second opinions, and referrals to high-cost specialists for fear that records may be scrutinized in court. Surgeons and obstetricians avoid rural areas where hospitals are ill equipped to handle problems. Liability insurance industry competition forces carriers to restrict underwriting of liability policies to less risky segments of the health care industry.

Malpractice issues are reflected in sociological theories such as "medical deprofessionalization" and "countervailing powers," concepts that challenge notions of professional dominance (Hartley 2002). A key feature of risk management is that institutional forces outside of medicine impinge on a physician's interactions with patients and other practitioners. Greater peer review, involvement of lawyers and risk-avoidance consultants, and skepticism of patients greatly reduce practitioner work satisfaction and autonomy. Jurisdictional disputes and cultural conflict between the values and interests of lawyers and medicine are another theoretical perspective on the dynamics of litigation (Peeples et al. 2000).

Increased litigation is an instance of Max Weber's rationalization theory and George Ritzer's McDonaldization thesis. At the organizational level, rationalization increases specialization and reorders role-task boundaries. When actuating premium charges, liability insurance carriers restrict procedures according to medical specialty and require certification, resulting in clearer delineations among specialists (Ritchey 1981). Fear of litigation and mandated risk management tasks make physicians more willing to relinquish tasks to assisting health practitioners, such as clinical pharmacists and physical therapists. At the interpersonal level, fear of litigation influences patient–practitioner interaction. Early research on increasing litigation focused on patient attributes and "suit-prone" patients. Later research focused on institutional and practitioner characteristics (years in practice, medical specialty) and circumstances (practice setting) (Ritchey 1993).

A specific aspect of rationalization theory as it applies to medical liability is the development of an "audit culture" (Strathern 2000) that calls for greater accountability: "external regulatory mechanisms transform the conduct of organizations and individuals in their capacity as 'self-actualizing agents'" (Shore & Wright 2000: 61). After the 1980s, regulatory trends in business and government were reflected in "new managerialism," which fashioned strategies such as continuous quality management, discipline, cost-benefit analysis, best practices, external verification, accountability, and total quality management (Pollitt 1993). These trends coincided with increases in litigation as well as shifts to managed care. Underlying these management strategies are the assumptions that all behavior can be made efficient and certain, but that judgments to these effects cannot be entrusted to those who are behaving. Peers, superiors, and external agents oversee performance audits. "[A]udit procedures present themselves as rational, objective and neutral, based on sound principles of efficient management – as unopposable as virtue itself" (Shore & Wright 2000: 61; Pollitt 1993: 49). Resistance to accountability procedures implies unethical incompetence and even immorality. An untoward treatment outcome perhaps unrelated to physician behavior, such as an infant born with congenital defects, may nonetheless be perceived as a moral failure. In an accountability-oriented society, medical uncertainty must coexist with the highly valued ideal of calculated certainty. Practice standards are defined within legal and moral as well as medical contexts. Although very few malpractice suits make it to court, the potential for a trial or deposition hearing can be perceived as a "Day of Judgment" (Shore & Wright 2000: 59). Extra-professional regulatory mechanisms, the means by which accountability is purported to be achieved, often become ends in themselves. Even where indicators of quality are of suspect validity and reliability, measuring it becomes a "ritual of verification" (Power 1997). This shift to asserting legitimacy in form rather than substance is a classic case of formal rationalization and it clashes head on with the ideal of professional autonomy.

SEE ALSO: Health Care Delivery Systems; Health Professions and Occupations; McDonaldization; Managed Care; Media Sociology; Professional Dominance in Medicine; Rational Choice Theories; Weber, Max

REFERENCES AND SUGGESTED READINGS

Cockerham, W. C. & Ritchey, F. J. (1997) *Dictionary of Medical Sociology*. Greenwood Press, Westport, CT.

Hartley, H. (2002) The System of Alignments Challenging Physician Professional Dominance: An Elaborated Theory of Countervailing Powers. *Sociology of Health and Illness* 24: 178–207.

Peeples, R., Harris, C. T., & Metzloff, T. (2000) Settlement Has Many Faces: Physicians, Attorneys, and Medical Malpractice. *Journal of Health and Social Behavior* 41: 333–46.

Pollitt, C. (1993) *Managerialism and the Public Services: Cuts or Cultural Change in the 1990s?* Blackwell, Oxford.

Power, M. (1997) *The Audit Society: Rituals of Verification*. Oxford University Press, Oxford.

Ritchey, F. J. (1981) Medical Rationalization, Cultural Lag, and the Malpractice Crisis. *Human Organization* 40: 97–112.

Ritchey, F. J. (1993) Fear of Malpractice Litigation, the Risk-Management Industry, and the Clinical Encounter. In: Clair, J. M. & Allman, R. M. (Eds.), *Sociomedical Perspectives on Patient Care*. University Press of Kentucky, Lexington, pp. 114–38.

Shore, C. & Wright, S. (2000) Coercive Accountability. In: Strathern, M. (Ed.), *Audit Cultures: Anthropological Studies in Accountability, Ethics, and the Academy*. Routledge, New York, pp. 57–89.

Strathern, M. (Ed.) (2000) *Audit Cultures: Anthropological Studies in Accountability, Ethics, and the Academy*. Routledge, New York.

medical school socialization

Frederic Hafferty

The study of medical education as a process of professional socialization is at best a dormant and at worse a dying object of academic inquiry. What once helped to legitimate an emerging academic field (medical sociology) in the 1950s and 1960s has since fallen on hard conceptual and analytic times. Today, cutting edge work on socialization appears not in sociology journals (where many of the earlier studies were published), but in journals such as *Academy of Management Journal*, *Administrative Science Quarterly*, and the *Journal of Organizational Behavior*. Within sociology, current work on socialization appears in subfields such as political sociology, the sociology of family (including parenting, child, adolescent, and spousal roles), mass media, and organizational sociology. Even when we restrict our focus to the "medicine," studies of training and socialization are more apt to highlight other professions (or "quasi-professions") such as nursing, pharmacy, dentistry, physical therapy, mortuary science, and athletic training.

LEGACY

Forty years ago, the two most frequently cited studies on medical student training and socialization were Robert Merton and colleagues' *The Student Physician* (1957) and Howard Becker and colleagues' *Boys in White* (1961). The same is true today – a glaring commentary on the current paucity of well-designed and comprehensive research in this field.

Both the Merton and Becker studies were large-scale and well-funded efforts to study the normative impact of undergraduate medical education. What sometimes is overlooked is that both were less about medical school training than they were opportunities to advance competing theoretical perspectives. The Merton team operated from a structural functional perspective, while Becker and company approached their study from a symbolic interactionist perspective.

Neither Becker nor Merton would return to the study of medical education in any substantive way, and while neither study provided the hoped-for empirical knockout punch, both studies played a highly important role in advancing the subfield of medical sociology, along with the study of socialization (at least for a while), primarily in the field of nursing.

The legacy of these studies is multifaceted. Prior to the 1950s, the prevailing view of medical education was grounded in a "traits" perspective (Bloom 1989). Medical school admissions committees selected students who possessed "good" traits for a medical-professional career and screened out students with "bad" traits. In turn, the education process would transmit the requisite knowledge and skills. "Core" personality traits were seen as fixed, unalterable by medical education. At best, students might internalize, via physician role models, what might be termed "clinical refinements." Important work on adult ("secondary") traits was still a decade into the future (Brim & Wheeler 1966). State-of-the-times work on socialization is illustrated by Parsons and Platt (1970), who studied the widespread unrest taking place during the late 1960s on college campuses (including the particulars of student demonstrations at Harvard College, of which this author was a participant) and concluded that they had identified a new (and "important") type of socialization: "studenty." Merton and Becker, in comparison, represented a bolt of lightning across a field primarily lit by fireflies.

The flurry ignited by Becker and Merton would be short lived. In 1970, Eliot Freidson published his groundbreaking "Profession of Medicine" and "Professional Dominance." Freidson argued, among a great many other things, that the current work environment was more predictive of work attitudes and efforts than prior socialization – and the sociological study of medicine began to shift from a more micro focus on professionalism and identity transformation to a more macro focus on organizational dynamics and structural change. Articles on medical school training continued to be published, but with a focus on student attitude change and the relationship of personality traits to specialty choice. The age of large-scale investigations of education on identity and professionalism appeared to be over.

Nursing, reflecting a concern with its own professional status, continued to direct energies to the study of socialization and the internalization of a professional identity. Over time, however, even this commitment began to fade, finding some final respite within British sociology and studies of British medical and nursing training.

DEFINITIONS AND DIMENSIONS

The theoretical clashes between the Merton and Becker studies and the subsequent preference of sociologists for a symbolic interactionist approach to the study of medical student socialization notwithstanding, socialization is a process (sometimes involving rituals, ceremonies, and/or rights of passage) by which initiates/neophytes/"outsiders" acquire or internalize the norms (and normative behaviors), value systems (and related rationales supporting that value system), skills, and language (e.g., the culture) of a desired society, organization, or group. More colloquially, socialization involves "learning the ropes" or the "rules of the game." A commonly used metaphor, particularly within organization studies, is socialization as the "glue" that links the individual to social groups, as those groups wrestle with the dual problems of adapting to external forces and internal differentiation (Schein 1968). These definitional framings highlight (but do not exhaust) a number of important distinctions with respect to socialization. Specifically, socialization (1) involves the transmission of knowledge, skills, and values, with values sometimes assuming primacy; (2) involves the transmission of group or organizational "culture;" and (3) is (for some theoretical orientations) a special form of learning that involves internalization and identity formation.

EVOLVING FRAMEWORKS

Currently, medicine is being intersected by a number of social movements, all of which have implications for the way medicine is practiced – and with the potential for impact on medical student socialization. The three most prominent movements are professionalism, patient safety, and evidence-based medicine (EBM).

Beginning in the mid-1980s, and driven by fears that medicine's "identity" and "soul" were being corrupted by the advent of managed care and the rise of "corporate medicine," organized medicine began to "rediscover" its professional core. A variety of medical groups, led by the American Board of Internal Medicine, the Accreditation Council of Graduate Medical Education, and the Association of American Medical Colleges, began to establish "core competencies" for medical students and residents, including "professionalism." Other groups (e.g., National Board of Medical Examiners) and private organizations (e.g., Arnold P. Gold Foundation) began to underwrite efforts to establish valid and reliable measures of professionalism. All of these (and related) efforts have direct implications for professional socialization, since there is still the issue of whether organized medicine will approach professionalism as something to be internalized (e.g., as a "core professional value") or as a "surface" attribute. Such distinctions will have a fundamental impact on how medical education is structured and delivered.

Similarly, issues of patient safety and EBM can be approached at the level of "knowledge" and/or "skill," or as an issue of "professional identity" and thus as something that would be grounded in socialization rather than "teaching." Organized medicine insists that it seeks change at the level of identity, but it remains to be seen whether the education and assessment processes will be structured to reflect this claim or whether things will play out at the level of social rhetoric – and thus outside the realm of socialization.

SEE ALSO: Emotion Work; Health Professions and Occupations; Hospitals; Mass Media and Socialization; Medical Sociology; Professional Dominance in Medicine; Resocialization; Socialization; Socialization, Agents of; Socialization, Anticipatory; Socialization, Gender; Socialization and Sport

REFERENCES AND SUGGESTED READINGS

Becker, H., Geer, B., Hughes, E., & Strauss, A. (1961) *Boys in White: Student Culture in Medical School.* University of Chicago Press, Chicago.

Bloom, S. (1989) The Medical School as a Social Organization: The Sources of Resistance to Change. *Medical Education* 23: 228–41.

Brim, Jr., O. & Wheeler, S. (1966) *Socialization After Childhood: Two Essays*. Wiley, New York.

Hafferty, F. & Franks, R. (1994) The Hidden Curriculum, Ethics Teaching, and the Structure of Medical Education. *Academic Medicine* 69: 861–71.

Merton, R., Reeder, L., & Kendall, P. (1957) *The Student Physician: Introductory Studies in the Sociology of Medical Education*. Harvard University Press, Cambridge, MA.

Parsons, T. & Platt, G. (1970) Age, Social Structure, and Socialization in Higher Education. *Sociology of Education* 43: 1–37.

Schein, E. (1968) Organizational Socialization and the Profession of Management. *Industrial Management Review* 9: 1–15.

Wear, D. & Castellani, B. (2000) The Development of Professionalism: Curriculum Matters. *Academic Medicine* 75: 602–11.

medical sociology

William C. Cockerham

Medical sociology is a subdiscipline of sociology that studies the social causes and consequences of health and illness (Cockerham 2004). Major areas of investigation include the social aspects of health and disease, the social behavior of health care workers and the people who utilize their services, the social functions of health organizations and institutions, the social patterns of health services, the relationship of health care delivery systems to other social systems, and health policy. What makes medical sociology important is the significant role social factors play in determining the health of individuals, groups, and the larger society. Social conditions and situations not only cause illness, but they also help prevent it.

In recognition of the broad impact of social factors on health, medical sociology is sometimes referred to as "health sociology" or the "sociology of health." However, the traditional name "medical sociology" persists because it is preferred by many of its practitioners. Medical sociologists comprise one of the largest groups of sociologists in the world. They have employment opportunities both within and outside of academia. Medical sociologists work not only in university sociology departments, medical, nursing, and public health schools and various other health-related professional schools, but also in research organizations and government agencies.

Medical sociology is a relatively new sociological specialty. It came of age in the late 1940s and early 1950s in an intellectual climate far different from sociology's traditional specialties. Specialties like theory, social stratification, urbanization, social change, and religion had direct roots to nineteenth-century European social thought. These specialties were grounded in classical theory with major works by the subdiscipline's founding figures. However, sociology's early theorists ignored medicine because it was not an institution shaping society. An exception is Émile Durkheim's *Suicide* (1951 [1897]), which is sometimes claimed as the first major work in the field. Medical sociology appeared in strength only in the mid-twentieth century as an applied field in which sociologists could produce knowledge useful in medical practice and developing public policy in health matters.

Moreover, physicians, not sociologists, produced much of the earliest literature in medical sociology. In the United States, John Shaw Billings, organizer of the National Library of Medicine and compiler of the *Index Medicus*, wrote about hygiene and sociology in 1879; Charles McIntire defined medical sociology in 1894; Elizabeth Blackwell, the first woman to graduate from an American medical school, published a collection of essays on medical sociology in 1902, as did James Warbasse in 1909 (Bloom 2002). The most important contribution came from Lawrence Henderson, a physician who taught a sociology course at Harvard in the 1930s. Henderson espoused structural functionalist theory and published a 1935 work on the patient–physician relationship as a social system. Henderson's most direct influence on medical sociology was through Talcott Parsons, one of his students who became a leading figure in sociology (Bloom 2002). The first sociologist to publish extensively on medical sociology was Bernhard Stern, who wrote historical accounts of the role of medicine in society from the late 1920s until the early 1940s.

Medical sociology evolved as a specialty in sociology in response to funding agencies and policymakers after World War II who viewed it as an applied field that could produce knowledge for use in medical practice, public health campaigns, and health policy formulation. Ample funding for research to help solve the health problems of industrial society and the welfare state in the West during the post-World War II era stimulated its growth. In 1949, for example, the Russell Sage Foundation in the United States funded a program to improve the utilization of social science in medical practice that resulted in books on social science and medicine and the role of sociology in public health. Particularly important was the establishment of the National Institute of Mental Health (NIMH) in the United States that funded and promoted cooperative projects between sociologists and physicians. A significant result of such cooperation was the publication in 1958 of *Social Class and Mental Illness: A Community Study* by August Hollingshead (a sociologist) and Frederick Redlich (a psychiatrist). This landmark study produced important evidence that social factors were correlated with different types of mental disorders and the manner in which people received psychiatric care. The book remains the seminal study of the relationship between mental disorder and social class. This study also played a key role in the debate during the 1960s leading to the establishment of community mental health centers in the United States.

At the beginning of medical sociology's expansion, many people in the field had tenuous roots in mainstream sociology and an orientation toward applied rather than theoretical work. Some had no training in medical sociology whatsoever. Many had been attracted to the subdiscipline because of the availability of jobs and funding for research. This situation led Robert Straus (1957) to suggest that medical sociology had become divided into two areas: sociology in medicine and sociology of medicine. The sociologist in medicine performed applied research and analysis primarily motivated by a medical problem rather than a sociological problem. Sociologists in medicine typically worked in medical, nursing, public health or similar professional schools, public health agencies, or health organizations like CDC and WHO.

Sociologists of medicine primarily worked in academic sociology departments and engaged in research and analysis of health from a sociological perspective.

The division in orientation created problems in the United States. Medical sociologists in universities were in a stronger position to produce work that satisfied sociologists as good sociology. Sociologists in medical institutions had the advantage of participation in medicine as well as research opportunities unavailable to those outside clinical settings. Disagreement developed between the two groups over whose work was the most important. What resolved this situation over time was a general evolution in medical sociology that saw both applied and theoretical work emerge on the part of medical sociologists in all settings. Medical sociologists in universities responded to funding requests for applied research, while some of their counterparts in medical institutions, like Anselm Strauss, produced important theoretical work.

A related problem in the early development of medical sociology was its potential to become dependent on medicine for its direction and research orientation. However, this did not happen, as medical sociologists adopted an independent course and made the practice of medicine one of its major subjects of inquiry, including its core relationships with patients and the organizational structure of health care delivery systems (Bloom 2002). Medical sociologists, in turn, brought their own topics to the study of health such as social stress, health lifestyles, and the social determinants of disease.

TALCOTT PARSONS

A decisive event took place in medical sociology in 1951 that provided a theoretical direction to a formerly applied field. This was the appearance of Parsons's *The Social System*. This book, written to explain a complex structural functionalist model of society, contained Parsons's concept of the sick role. Parsons had become the best-known sociologist in the world and having a theorist of his stature provide the first major theory in medical sociology called attention to the young subdiscipline – particularly among academic sociologists. Anything he published attracted interest. Not only was Parsons's concept of the sick role a distinctly sociological analysis of sickness, but it was widely believed by many sociologists at the time that Parsons was charting a future course for all of sociology through his theoretical approach. This did not happen. Nevertheless, Parsons brought medical sociology intellectual recognition that it needed in its early development by endowing it with theory. Moreover, following Parsons, other leading sociologists of the time such as Robert Merton and Erving Goffman published work in medical sociology that further promoted the academic legitimacy of the field.

THE POST-PARSONS ERA

The next major area of research after Parsons developed his sick role concept was medical education. Merton and his colleagues (1957) extended the structural functionalist mode of analysis to the socialization of medical students, with Renée Fox's paper on training for uncertainty ranking as a major contribution. Four years later, Howard Becker and his associates published *Boys in White* (1961), a study of medical school socialization conducted from a symbolic interactionist perspective. This study became a sociological classic and was important for both its theoretical and methodological content. The techniques in participant observation provided a basis for the seminal work on death and dying and subsequent innovations in theory and methods by Barney Glaser and Anselm Strauss (1965, 1967).

With the introduction of symbolic interaction into a field that had previously been dominated by structural functionalism, medical sociology became a significant arena of debate between two of sociology's major theoretical schools. This debate helped stimulate a virtual flood of publications in medical sociology in the 1960s. Moreover, the Medical Sociology Section of the American Sociological Association (ASA) was formed in 1959 and grew to become one of the largest and most active ASA sections. American influence was also important in founding Research Committee 15 (Health Sociology) of the International Sociological Association in 1967 (Bloom 2002). The Medical Sociology Group of the British Sociological Association (BSA) was organized in 1964 and

became the largest specialty group in the BSA, with its own annual conference.

In 1966 the *Journal of Health and Social Behavior*, founded in 1960, became an official ASA publication, making medical sociology one of the few sociological subdisciplines publishing its own journal under ASA auspices. In the meantime, in Great Britain, a new journal, *Social Science and Medicine*, was founded in 1967 and became an especially important journal for medical sociologists throughout the world. The growing literature in medical sociology also led to the publication of textbooks. The first textbook was Norman Hawkins's *Medical Sociology* (1958), but the early leaders were the first editions of books by David Mechanic (1968) and Rodney Coe (1970). Howard Freeman, Sol Levine, and Leo Reeder likewise made an important contribution by publishing the *Handbook of Medical Sociology*, which contained summary essays on major topics by leading medical sociologists. The first edition appeared in 1963 and the fifth edition in 2000, edited by Chloe Bird, Peter Conrad, and Allen Fremont.

During the 1960s, the symbolic interactionist perspective temporarily dominated a significant portion of the literature. One feature of this domination was the numerous studies conducted with reference to labeling theory and the mental patient experience. Sociologists expanded their work on mental health to include studies of stigma, stress, families coping with mental disorder, and other areas of practical and theoretical relevance. For example, Goffman's *Asylums* (1961), a study of life in a mental hospital, presented his concept of "total institutions" that stands as a significant sociological statement about social life in an externally controlled environment. An abundant literature emerged at this time that established the sociology of mental disorder as a major subfield within medical sociology (Cockerham 2006).

PERIOD OF MATURITY: 1970–2000

Between 1970 and 2000 medical sociology emerged as a mature sociological subdiscipline. This period was marked by the publication of two especially important books, Eliot Friedson's *Professional Dominance* (1970) and Paul Starr's *The Social Transformation of American Medicine*

(1982). Friedson formulated his influential "professional dominance" theory to account for an unprecedented level of professional control by physicians over health care delivery that was true at the time but no longer exists. Starr's book won the Pulitzer Prize and countered Friedson's thesis by examining the decline in status and professional power of the medical profession as large corporate health care delivery systems oriented toward profit effectively entered an unregulated medical market. Donald Light (1993) subsequently used the term "countervailing power" to show how the medical profession was but one of many powerful groups in society – the state, employers, health insurance companies, patients, pharmaceutical and other companies providing medical products – maneuvering to fulfill its interests in health care.

Another major work was Bryan Turner's *Body and Society* (1984), which initiated the sociological debate on this topic. Theoretical developments concerning the sociological understanding of the control, use, and phenomenological experience of the body, including emotions, followed. Much of this work has been carried out in Great Britain and features social constructionism as its theoretical foundation. Social constructionism has its origins in the work of the French social theorist Michel Foucault and takes the view that knowledge about the body, health, and illness reflects subjective, historically specific human concerns and is subject to change and reinterpretation. Other areas in which British medical sociologists have excelled include studies of medical practice, emotions, and the experience of illness. Medical sociology also became a major sociological specialty in Finland, the Netherlands, Germany, Italy, Spain, and Israel, and began to emerge in Russia and Eastern Europe in the 1990s after the collapse of communism. In the meantime, the European Society for Health and Medical Sociology was formed in 1983 and hosts a biannual conference for European medical sociologists. In Japan, the Japanese Society for Medical Sociology was established in 1974 and, since 1990, has published an annual review of work in the field. Elsewhere in Asia, medical sociology is especially active in Singapore, Thailand, and India, and is beginning to appear in China. In Africa, medical sociology is strongest in South Africa. Medical sociology is also an important field in Latin America, and because of its special Latin character, many practitioners prefer to publish their work in books and journals in Mexico, Brazil, Argentina, and Chile (Castro 2000).

From the 1970s through the 1990s, medical sociology flourished as it attracted large numbers of practitioners in both academic and applied settings and sponsored an explosion of publications based upon empirical research. Major areas of investigation included stress, the medicalization of deviance, mental health, inequality and class differences in health, health care utilization, managed care and other organizational changes, AIDS, and women's health and gender. Several books, edited collections of readings, and textbooks appeared. The leading reader was edited by Peter Conrad and Rochelle Kern in 1981 and is now in a seventh edition (2005), with Conrad the sole editor. The leading textbook was William Cockerham's *Medical Sociology*, first published in 1978 and due to appear in a tenth edition in 2007. Another major medical sociology journal, the *Sociology of Health and Illness*, was started in Britain in 1978, as was a new journal, *Health*, in 1999.

However, the success of medical sociology also brought problems in the 1980s. Research funding opportunities lessened and the field faced serious competition for existing resources with health economics, health psychology, medical anthropology, health services research, and public health. Not only did these fields adopt sociological research methods in the forms of social surveys, participation observation, and focus groups, some also employed medical sociologists in large numbers. While these developments were positive in many ways, the distinctiveness of medical sociology as a unique subdiscipline was nevertheless challenged as other fields moved into similar areas of research. Furthermore, some of the medical sociology programs at leading American universities had declined or disappeared over time as practitioners retired or were hired away. Yet the overall situation for medical sociology was positive as the job market remained good, almost all graduate programs in sociology offered a specialization in medical sociology, and sociologists were on the faculties of most medical schools in the United States, Canada, and Western Europe (Bloom 2002).

The 1990s saw medical sociology move closer to its parent discipline of sociology. This was seen in a number of areas, with medical sociological work appearing more frequently in general sociology journals and the increasing application of sociological theory to the analysis of health problems. The *American Journal of Sociology* published a special issue on medical sociology in 1992, and papers on health-related topics are not unusual in the *American Sociological Review*. While medical sociology drew closer to sociology, sociology in turn moved closer to medical sociology as the field remains one of the largest and most robust sociological specialties.

THE PRESENT

Ultimately, what allows medical sociology to retain its unique character is (1) its utilization and mastery of sociological theory in the study of health and (2) the sociological perspective that accounts for collective causes and outcomes of health problems and issues. No other field is able to bring these skills to health-related research and analysis. Today it can be said that medical sociology produces literature intended to inform medicine and policymakers, but research in the field is also grounded in examining health-related situations that inform sociology as well. Medical sociology no longer functions as a field whose ties to the mother discipline are tenuous, nor has it evolved as an enterprise subject to medical control. It now works most often with medicine in the form of a partner and, in some cases, an objective critic. Moreover, medical sociology owes more to medicine than to sociology for its origin and initial financial support, so the relationship that has evolved is essentially supportive. As medical sociology continues on its present course, it is likely to emerge as one of sociology's core specialties as the pursuit of health increasingly becomes important in everyday social life.

SEE ALSO: Goffman, Erving; Health and Medicine; Medical School Socialization; Medical Sociology and Genetics; Medicine, Sociology of; Merton, Robert K.; Parsons, Talcott; Sociology in Medicine

REFERENCES AND SUGGESTED READINGS

Becker, H., Greer, B., Hughes, E., & Strauss, A. (1961) *Boys in White: Student Culture in Medical School*. University of Chicago Press, Chicago.

Bird, C., Conrad, P., & Fremont, A. (2000) *Handbook of Medical Sociology*, 5th edn. Prentice-Hall, Upper Saddle River, NJ.

Bloom, S. (2002) *The Word as Scalpel: A History of Medical Sociology*. Oxford University Press, New York.

Castro, R. (2000) Medical Sociology in Mexico. In: Cockerham, W. (Ed.), *The Blackwell Companion to Medical Sociology*. Blackwell, Oxford, pp. 214–32.

Cockerham, W. (2004) *Medical Sociology*, 9th edn. Prentice-Hall, Upper Saddle River, NJ.

Cockerham, W. (2006) *Sociology of Mental Disorder*, 7th edn. Prentice-Hall, Upper Saddle River, NJ.

Coe, R. (1970) *Sociology of Medicine*. McGraw-Hill, New York.

Conrad, P. (Ed.) (2005) *The Sociology of Health and Illness*, 7th edn. Worth, New York.

Durkheim, E. (1951 [1897]) *Suicide*. Free Press, New York.

Friedson, E. (1970) *Professional Dominance*. Aldine, Chicago.

Glaser, B. & Strauss, A. (1965) *Awareness of Dying*. Aldine, Chicago.

Glaser, B. & Strauss, A. (1967) *The Discovery of Grounded Theory*. Aldine, Chicago.

Goffman, E. (1961) *Asylums*. Doubleday Anchor, Garden City, NY.

Hawkins, N. (1958) *Medical Sociology*. Thomas, Springfield, IL.

Hollingshead, A. & Redlich, F. (1958) *Social Class and Mental Illness: A Community Study*. Wiley, New York.

Light, D. (1993) Countervailing Power: The Changing Character of the Medical Profession in the United States. In: Hafferty, F. & McKinlay, J. (Eds.), *The Changing Medical Profession*. Oxford University Press, New York, pp. 69–79.

Mechanic, D. (1968) *Medical Sociology*. Free Press, New York.

Merton, R., Reader, G., & Kendall, P. (1957) *The Student Physician*. Harvard University Press, Cambridge, MA.

Parsons, T. (1951) *The Social System*. Free Press, Glencoe, IL.

Starr, P. (1982) *The Social Transformation of American Medicine*. Basic Books, New York.

Straus, R. (1957) The Nature and Status of Medical Sociology. *American Sociological Review* 22: 200–4.

Turner, B. (1984) *Body and Society*. Blackwell, Oxford.

medical sociology and genetics

Robert Dingwall

The rapid progress in genetic science associated with the Human Genome Project has attracted considerable interest among medical sociologists (Conrad & Gabe 1999; Pilnick 2002a). The basis of genetics is the observation that the biological constitution of all living things – plants, animals, fish, insects, bacteria, humans, etc. – is shaped by a chemical called DNA (deoxyribonucleic acid) found in the nuclear material of the cells from which they are all made. The various ways in which this chemical can be made up carry the instructions for the construction, articulation, and operation of cells. A gene is a segment of DNA that carries a particular set of instructions to perform a particular task in relation to cell assembly or functioning. The totality of genes found in an organism is called its genome. The human genome is made up of about 30,000 genes, whose instructions combine to produce the varied bodies recognizable as members of our species, *Homo sapiens*.

There is a considerable element of indeterminacy in these processes. The expression of genes is significantly influenced by their environment. This begins at the point of conception. During reproduction, a new combination of genes is assembled out of the set contributed by each parent, resulting in an organism that derives some features from each. The offspring is not identical to either parent and the novel combination may result in features that are not apparent in the parents. A first point of indeterminacy, then, is the combination of parents that actually occurs, which, in turn, reflects environmental opportunities to meet and fertilize. A second may be the conditions under which fertilization actually occurs: there are, for example, suggestions that the sex ratio in humans is influenced by climate and possibly by vaginal acidity. A third is the availability of nutrients and other chemicals, both *in utero* and after, affecting the resources on which gene products can operate. A fourth is the interaction between genes and the way in which one gene constitutes an environment for others that contribute to a particular process or structure. A fifth is in the mutability of DNA itself, which can, rarely, lead to spontaneous and unpredictable changes, both at the level of an organism and at the cellular level. Finally, there is the overall interaction between the combined expression of a genome and the environment within which an organism is located: a gene that favors body fat, for example, may be advantageous during an Ice Age and disadvantageous under conditions of global warming.

The interest of medical sociology in genetics lies in the social attempts to manage the consequences of this indeterminacy. This is particularly apparent in three areas:

- The pressures that favor or disfavor the reproduction of organisms with particular traits.
- The possible identification of traits, derived from the absence or presence of particular genes, that affect the structure and/or functioning of individual organisms, making them more or less susceptible to particular environmental hazards.
- The possible identification of genes that make individuals more or less likely to behave in particular ways in particular environments.

SELECTIVE REPRODUCTION

All human reproduction is selective and socially structured. We can only reproduce with people that we actually encounter, either directly or indirectly as sperm or egg donors. None of these is a random subset of the population: medical sociologists have long established that our reproductive partners are most likely to be people like ourselves in terms of age, ethnicity, social status, and so on (Kalmijn 1994). Some groups are more likely to be invited, and to agree, to act as gamete donors: traditionally, medical students have been a major source of sperm. Selection also has a cultural dimension, the ideals of "fitness" that we use to choose among potential partners. These ideals – body aesthetics, moral character, intellect, practical skills, etc. – reflect the thinking in a social group about what contributes to its members' adaptation to both the material and the cultural environment in which they live. If any of these have a genetic basis, reproductive selection will increase their prevalence within that group. Even if they do not have a genetic basis, though, their prevalence may still increase, if they are seen to be necessary for successful reproduction, by group members copying behaviors that seem to attract more, or more valuable, partners.

As the basic mechanisms of genetics and evolution were understood, in the late nineteenth century, some people thought that the direction of humanity's development could be consciously controlled (Kevles 1995). Eugenicists believed that characteristics such as intellect or moral character were strongly determined by biology. Existing societies showed the results of undirected but selective breeding, which had led to some individuals establishing themselves as respectable people with secure lifestyles while others drifted to the bottom – drunks, vagabonds, and delinquents, with little intelligence and low morals. The eugenics movement planned to build a better world by encouraging the "best" humans to reproduce more and discouraging the "worst" from reproducing at all. The limited success of their early voluntary strategies led many eugenicists to advocate compulsion. Laws facilitating the sterilization of people who were considered to be physically, mentally, or morally unfit were passed in many Northern European countries, Canada, and some US states during the early twentieth century. The excesses of the Nazi period in Germany discredited eugenics as a social movement, although many countries retained sterilization laws until the 1970s.

Contemporary geneticists have tried to escape the stigma of Nazi eugenics by emphasizing the role of individual choice in acting on genetic information. Currently, the only options are negative, in the form of terminating pregnancies or not implanting embryos where undesired characteristics are identified. Medical sociologists have questioned this in two ways. The first derives from studies of genetic counseling that have shown how the difficulties of giving information in a neutral and non–directive fashion often result in the manipulation or encouragement of the recipients toward particular choices (Kolker & Burke 1998; Pilnick 2002b). The second looks at the aggregate consequences

of those decisions and argues that the result is still a form of "soft eugenics" (Shakespeare 1998). Judgments have been made about the value of human lives that are insensitive to the rights of people with disabilities and the extent to which disabilities are the result of disabling environments rather than essential properties of individuals.

In theory, positive choices could be made available by cloning, leading to the creation of embryos with preferred characteristics (Nussbaum & Sunstein 1998; McGee 2000). Although this technology has been used on animals, that experience raises serious safety concerns about its use in humans. Sociologists would also question the extent to which a cloned human would actually resemble its original because an infant born into a different generation would inevitably have different environmental experiences.

LIVING WITH OUR GENOTYPE

A major area of development has been in attempts to predict individuals' future health from knowledge of their genotype. This is well established in disorders caused by a single gene, like Huntington's disease, a neurological condition that only becomes evident in adult life and leads to serious disability and early death. More recently, it has become possible to identify genes or combinations of genes that influence susceptibility: carriers do not necessarily develop the condition but have a greater risk of doing so. The presence of BRCA1 or BRCA2 genes, for example, increases the probability that a woman will develop breast cancer in early adulthood. Medical sociologists are interested in the consequences of these developments in two ways.

One is the impact of being identified as the carrier of genes that increase the risk of ill health. There are currently few therapeutic options, which provokes concern over the ethics of testing for risks where no effective remedy is available: BRCA carriers can only be offered a prophylactic mastectomy, which may still leave some residual breast tissue in which cancers can develop, while those with Huntington's can only be advised to refrain from reproduction to avoid passing on their genes. Medical sociologists are examining the communication issues involved in giving people information about their genetic status, especially as this will include indications about that of their close kin. This raises new problems of patient confidentiality, because relatives may have chosen not to receive or share that information. It underlines the extent to which all medicine is ultimately family or community medicine rather than being concerned with individuals outside their social and cultural environment. To the extent that risks can be managed, medical sociologists have examined the choices made, like decisions to undergo disfiguring surgery or to adopt long-term changes in diet or exercise regimes (Hallowell & Lawton 2002). The latter links to other work by medical sociologists on the relationship between medical advice or health education and behavior, variously known as the problem of compliance, of adherence, or of concordance.

Knowledge of a person's genotype also has implications for other institutions. It creates particular problems for welfare provision based on personal insurance products – health insurance, disability insurance, or pensions – which raise issues for medical sociology (McGleenan et al. 1999). Insurance requires uncertainty, that we do not know when we are going to fall ill, become disabled, or die. People who stay fit or die young share the costs of those who fall ill or live longer. However, if we knew our fate in advance, low-risk people would not buy insurance and subsidize high-risk people. Conversely, high-risk people might cheat by buying more coverage than their current premium warrants. Genetic knowledge reduces people's uncertainty about their fate and makes such behavior more likely. However, if people are required to share their knowledge with insurers, high-risk people may find that coverage is unavailable or unaffordable. This is not a serious problem in many European countries, where personal insurance products are luxury goods and the whole population can be required to share risks through taxation or social insurance payments. However, it is a major issue for the US. The genetically disadvantaged may be excluded from personal insurance. They could also encounter job discrimination, either to minimize employer-linked insurance costs or because their genotype affects their susceptibility to chemical or biological materials used in production processes.

THE GENETIC CONTROL OF BEHAVIOR

Early eugenicists were convinced that both intelligence and behavior were under strong genetic influences. Although this view was discredited by the early 1960s, it has never been extinguished and has been revived alongside the other new developments in genetics. The publication of *The Bell Curve* in 1994, claiming a biological basis for the association between intelligence and social class in the US, provoked a wide international debate among social scientists (Herrnstein & Murray 1994; Duster 1995; Taylor 1995). The authors derived this claim indirectly, by seeking to eliminate other explanations, rather than by identifying specific genetic markers. However, others have claimed the discovery of particular genes for aggression, crime, and sexual orientation. This has led to proposals for the pharmacological control of these behaviors. Medical sociologists have critically examined these claims. They have noted that the bioscientists' understanding of social action is often very crude: aggression may simply be assertiveness that offends bourgeois gentility; crime is not a universal but defined by the laws, rules, or other conventions established in a society; homosexuality is a very different phenomenon in environments where there is a free choice of sexual partners compared with those where there is not, like prisons. The complexity and plasticity of human social behavior makes it implausible to suppose that there is a simple genetic foundation (Dingwall et al. 2003). Medical sociology, then, is more interested in what these claims, and the credulity with which they are widely received, tell us about our society. Why is there a demand for knowledge of this kind? Whose interests are served by it? However, medical sociologists have also been reminded of the importance of the body as a material base for action or cultural interpretation, and of the need to acknowledge that it may be a constraint on the possibilities for social construction.

THE GENE INDUSTRY

The scale of investment needed to map the human genome required a strong marketing effort by research scientists to governments, industry, and venture capitalists. This involved the projection of a future of molecular medicine, where knowledge of a person's genotype would allow physicians to use more precise therapies and where an understanding of the genetic basis of life would unlock new avenues for therapy, either by modifying defective genes or by introducing alternative means of achieving the structures or functions that they were not generating. In practice, this vision has been hard to deliver. The modern pharmaceutical industry exemplifies Fordism, with standardized products and huge economies of scale: highly individualized therapies seem unlikely to pass any reasonable cost-benefit test. Gene therapy has proved technically difficult and risky. Some of the most promising areas, like cystic fibrosis, have seen considerable resistance from potential consumers, who have refused to participate in trials that may compromise their current health status for uncertain benefits, except to investigators who, they consider, are more interested in Nobel Prizes or corporate profit from selling new therapies back to them at high prices (Stockdale 1999). There has been a significant convergence between medical sociology and the sociology of science and technology to examine these issues with work on the present impact of different imagined futures, on the balance between science, commerce, and regulation in research and development, and on the organization and ethics of trials (Hedgecoe & Martin 2003).

GENETICIZATION AND GENETIC EXCEPTIONALISM

When genetic issues first reemerged into popular and scientific discourse, they were associated with claims that they represented revolutionary challenges to established institutions, practices, professional interests, and so on. The term "geneticization" was coined, by analogy with medicalization, to describe the way in which differences between humans were being reduced to differences in their DNA (Lippman 1992). It has been loosely associated with the idea of "genetic exceptionalism," the idea that genetic information is so radically different from other types that it requires an entirely new body of

thought about the ways in which it should be managed institutionally. In retrospect, however, these claims have come to look like medical sociologists buying into the marketing effort for gene research rather than critically assessing it. As further empirical work has been conducted, many of the supposedly unique features of genetic medicine have proved to be reincarnations of well-established topics within medical sociology like professional–patient communication, the nature of disease and its relation to other forms of deviance, the structuring of health services and the choice between public and private systems of funding, and so on. The immediate challenge for medical sociologists, as genetically informed elements begin to creep slowly into health care, will be to avoid reinventing wheels.

SEE ALSO: *Bell Curve, The* (Herrnstein and Murray); Eugenics; Genetic Engineering as a Social Problem; Human Genome and the Science of Life; Medical Sociology

REFERENCES AND SUGGESTED READINGS

Conrad, P. & Gabe, J. (Eds.) (1999) *Sociological Perspectives on the New Genetics.* Blackwell, Oxford.

Dingwall, R., Nerlich, B., & Hillyard, S. (2003) Biological Determinism and Symbolic Interaction: Hereditary Streams and Cultural Roads. *Symbolic Interaction* 26: 631–44.

Duster, T. (1995) Review of *The Bell Curve. Contemporary Sociology* 24: 158–61.

Hallowell, N. & Lawton, J. (2002) Negotiating Present and Future Selves: Managing the Risk of Hereditary Cancer by Prophylactic Surgery. *Health* 6: 423–44.

Hedgecoe, A. & Martin, P. (2003) The Drugs Don't Work: Expectations and the Shaping of Pharmacogenetics. *Social Studies of Science* 33: 327–64.

Herrnstein, R. J. & Murray, C. (1994) *The Bell Curve: Intelligence and Class Structure in American Life.* Free Press, New York.

Kalmijn, M. (1994) Assortative Mating by Cultural and Economic Occupational Status. *American Journal of Sociology* 100: 422–52.

Kevles, D. (1995) *In the Name of Eugenics: Genetics and the Uses of Human Heredity.* University of California Press, Berkeley.

Kolker, A. & Burke, B. M. (1998) *Prenatal Testing: A Sociological Perspective.* Bergin & Garvey, Westport, CT.

Lippman, A. (1992) Led (Astray) by Genetic Maps: The Cartography of the Human Genome and Health Care. *Social Science and Medicine* 35: 1469–76.

McGee, G. (2000) *The Perfect Baby: Parenthood in the New World of Cloning and Genetics*. Rowman & Littlefield, Lanham, MD.

McGleenan, T., Wiesing, U., & Ewald, F. (Eds.) (1999) *Genetics and Insurance*. BIOS Scientific, Oxford.

Nussbaum, M. C. & Sunstein, C. R. (Eds.) (1998) *Clones and Clones: Facts and Fantasies about Human Cloning*. Norton, New York.

Pilnick, A. (2002a) *Genetics and Society: An Introduction*. Open University Press, Buckingham.

Pilnick, A. (2002b) "There Are No Rights and Wrongs in These Situations": Identifying Interactional Difficulties in Genetic Counselling. *Sociology of Health and Illness* 25: 66–88.

Shakespeare, T. (1998) Choices and Rights: Eugenics, Genetics and Disability Equality. *Disability and Society* 13: 655–81.

Stockdale, A. (1999) Waiting for *the* Cure: Mapping the Social Relations of Human Gene Therapy Research. *Sociology of Health and Illness* 21: 579–96.

Taylor, H. F. (1995) Review of *The Bell Curve*. *Contemporary Sociology* 24: 153–8.

medicine, sociology of

Carey L. Usher

Sociology of medicine is the sociological investigation of medicine as a subsystem of society. This label is given to the traditional study within medical sociology of the influences social forces have on the sciences, practices, and teachings of medicine, and how these components of medicine, in turn, affect society. Thus, the sociologist of medicine aspires to contribute to the development of sociological knowledge using medicine as a social institution worthy of study in itself. In the pure versus applied dichotomy of the social sciences, the work of the sociologist of medicine represents the academic or pure pursuit of knowledge. The sociologist of medicine is most often positioned outside the medical setting, in contrast to the position of the medical sociologist working in collaboration with medical or health organizations. The dichotomy of sociology of medicine and sociology in medicine was formalized by Robert Straus in 1957, in an effort to identify the affiliations and activities of medical sociologists in the United States for creation of a communication network among this newly institutionalized professional group. The distinction is in part based on the structural position of the scholar, on where the basic professional affiliation of the scholar is held. Sociologists of medicine are likely to hold academic appointments in sociology departments.

Early in the institutionalization process of medical sociology, examination of the methodologies, organization, and structure of the medical institution was an obvious avenue of study, due to medicine's influence over as well as dependence on social forces. Organizational structure, role relationships, value systems, rituals, functions of medicine as a system of behavior, and social components of health and illness have been and still are predominant areas of study for the sociologist of medicine. During the 1950s and 1960s, however, sociology of medicine took a backseat to sociology in medicine. A majority of medical sociologists were involved in the applied side of the new discipline due to increases in research funding and expansion of medical schools, and well over half of the medical sociologists in the United States were positioned within medical or health organizations. Inadequate access to quality resources was a tremendous difficulty faced by sociologists of medicine who were operating from outside medicine rather than within medicine. Sociology of medicine recovered substantially during the Cold War as sociology in medicine's influence declined dramatically and medical sociologists moved into sociology departments in large numbers.

The sociologist of medicine uses the basic research methods of sociology to generate insights into the properties and patterns of social relationships and social organization of health and medicine. Potential hazards in this pure pursuit of knowledge have, however, been thoroughly documented. Similar to any sociologist involved in scrutiny of organizational systems, a danger faced by sociologists of medicine is a loss of objectivity through identification with the medical organization. Retention of a sociological perspective to serve the basic interests of the discipline while studying health and medicine has proven difficult. This danger has been combated by the positioning of the sociologist of medicine outside of the medical organization. In a response to this positioning, it is argued that medicine's failure to respond to the sociological critique may be caused in large part by the failure of sociologists of medicine in becoming more actively involved in the social organization and culture of medicine. Thus, maintaining allegiance to the objective pursuit of knowledge for the sake of sociology has often restricted the voice of sociologists of medicine in potential influences of the medical system. This restriction, however, is experiencing change.

From the 1990s onward, sociologists of medicine have had increasing access to research opportunities within the field of medicine, and emphasis in the parent discipline on applied sociological work has led to some convergence of sociology of and sociology in medicine. Sociology of medicine retains its focus on the organizational and professional structures, roles, values, rituals, and functions of medicine as a subsystem of the social structure, and on the social psychology of health and illness. The acceptance and pursuit of applicable studies in sociology departments is increasingly pushing medical sociology to deliver a sociology with medicine rather than the dichotomous sociologies of and in medicine. A sociology with medicine contributes to a sociological understanding of medicine as a reflection of social life in general, as well as the opportunity to influence medical and health systems with applicable knowledge.

SEE ALSO: Health and Medicine; Medical Sociology; Sociology in Medicine

REFERENCES AND SUGGESTED READINGS

Blackwell, G. W. (1953) Behavioral Science and Health. *Social Forces* 32: 211–15.
Bloom, S. (1986) Institutional Trends in Medical Sociology. *Journal of Health and Social Behavior* 27: 265–76.
Cockerham, W. C. (2004) *Medical Sociology*, 9th edn. Prentice-Hall, Upper Saddle River, NJ.
Hirsh, J. (1941) A New Course in the Social-Studies Curriculum for Colleges and Universities. *Journal of Educational Sociology* 14: 561–6.
Levine, S. (1987) The Changing Terrains in Medical Sociology: Emergent Concern with Quality of Life. *Journal of Health and Social Behavior* 28: 1–6.
Straus, R. (1957) The Nature and Status of Medical Sociology. *American Sociological Review* 22: 200–4.
Straus, R. (1999) Medical Sociology: A Personal Fifty Year Perspective. *Journal of Health and Social Behavior* 40: 103–10.
Twaddle, A. (1982) From Medical Sociology to the Sociology of Health: Some Changing Concerns in the Sociological Study of Sickness and Treatment. In: Bottomore, T., Nowak, S., & Sokolowska, M. (Eds.), *Sociology: The State of the Art*. Sage, Beverly Hills, pp. 323–58.

megalopolis

Kevin Fox Gotham

Megalopolis refers to a cluster of densely populated cities stretching over a large region. The late geographer Jean Gottmann (1915–94) popularized the term in the early 1960s to classify the region from Washington to Boston, including New York, Philadelphia, and Baltimore. Gottmann urged researchers to view the megalopolis as a novel urban form that is multinucleated and multifunctional. Population growth fueled suburbanization and suburbs later became their own independent and autonomous regions that merged with the central city to form an extensive metropolitan region on the United States East Coast. In 1950, the megalopolis had a population of 32 million inhabitants. Today, the megalopolis includes more than 44 million people, 16 percent of the entire US population. Four of the largest CMSAs (Consolidated Metropolitan Statistical Areas) in the United States overlap with the megalopolis and account for over 38 million of the megalopolis's population. The four CMSAs are New York–Northern New Jersey–Long Island, Washington–Baltimore, Philadelphia–Wilmington–Atlantic City, and Boston–Worcester–Lawrence. The implication of Gottmann's study of the megalopolis was that "[w]e must abandon the idea of the city as a

tightly settled and organized unit in which people, activities, and riches are crowded into a
very small area clearly separated from its non-
urban surroundings. Every city in this region
spreads out far and wide around its original
nucleus; it grows amidst an irregularly colloidal
mixture of rural and suburban landscapes; it
melts on broad fronts with other mixtures, of
somewhat similar though different texture,
belonging to the suburban neighborhoods of
other cities" (Gottmann 1961: 5).

Over the years, different scholars have
defined the megalopolis in several ways, and
used the term to refer to different types of
metropolitan growth patterns. Most studies seek
to challenge ecological models that view metropolitan areas as comprising an economically
dominant central city surrounded by bedroom
suburban communities. Some researchers categorize a megalopolis as a complex urban region
that has a density of 500 inhabitants per square
mile. Others use the term to refer to an urban
region made of several large cities, including
suburbs and surrounding areas, that are economically and socially interconnected with a
single urban agglomeration. More recently,
scholars have defined a megalopolis as consisting of large core cities that are connected by
an industrial or commercial belt of activities,
including office parks, shopping centers, factories, refineries, warehouses, green areas, and
residential areas. In particular, scholars draw
attention to the process of megalopolitanization
in which complex economic activities spread to
small rural towns and assimilate into large core
cities to establish a distinct continuum of cities.
In addition to the US East Coast, megalopolises
can be found, for example, in California, via the
metropolitan areas of San Diego, Los Angeles,
and San Francisco; in the United Kingdom
in the Silicon Glen between Glasgow and
Edinburgh; and on Japan's Pacific coast from
Tokyo to Osaka. More recently, scholars have
noted that megalopolises are also developing
across national borders, forming cross-border
or multinational megalopolises. Notable examples include the Brussels to Zurich region, the
Munich–Frankfurt–Stuttgart region, and the
United States–Mexico border between San
Diego and Tijuana.

Several methodological issues and unresolved questions currently define scholarly

understanding of the megalopolis and will guide
future research on megalopolis growth and
development. Research is not clear about the
mechanisms that foster megalopolis growth.
For example, why do megalopolises arise in some
areas and not others? While some researchers
contend that megalopolises are a natural result
of central city and suburban population growth,
others are skeptical and maintain that megalopolitanization is the outcome of the growth of new
small cities between large cities, irrespective of
large city growth. In the latter case, megalopolis formation may occur as central cities lose
population and suburban areas grow and prosper economically. Other scholars suggest that
geographical clustering of similar economic
industries discourages megalopolis growth. Still
others maintain that megalopolis growth contributes to spatial fragmentation which, in turn,
feeds back to promote megalopolitanization
through processes of functional interdependence and differentiation. What explains the
uneven growth of megalopolises? Does megalopolis growth reinforce inequalities between
cities and/or within cities? What role does networking among and between the government
sector, the non-profit sector (especially universities), and private business play in the development of different megalopolises? Such questions
will remain central to urban research as technological advances, globalization, and the changing
nature of work and residential life transform
cities and regions into what might be called
"network megalopolises."

SEE ALSO: Cities in Europe; Ecological Mod-
els of Urban Form: Concentric Zone Model,
the Sector Model, and the Multiple Nuclei
Model; Exurbia; Inequality and the City;
Metropolis; Metropolitan Statistical Area;
Multinucleated Metropolitan Region

REFERENCES AND SUGGESTED
READINGS

Fishman, R. (1990) Megalopolis Unbound. In:
Kasinitz, P. (Ed.), *Metropolis: Center and Symbol
of Our Time*. New York University Press, New
York, pp. 395–417.
Gottmann, J. (1961) *Megalopolis: The Urbanized
Northeastern Seaboard of the United States*. Twen-
tieth Century Fund, New York.

Gottmann, J. & Harper, R. A. (Eds.) (1989) *Since Megalopolis: The Urban Writings of Jean Gottmann*. Johns Hopkins University Press, Baltimore.

Olalquiaga, C. (1992) *Megalopolis: Contemporary Cultural Sensibilities*. University of Minnesota Press, Minneapolis.

Patten, J. (Ed.) (1983) *The Expanding City: Essays in Honour of Professor Jean Gottmann*. Academic Press, London and New York.

Warner, S. B., Jr. (1972) The Megalopolis: 1920–. In: LeGates, R. T. & Stout, F. (Eds.), *The City Reader*. Routledge, London and New York, pp. 69–76.

melting pot

Juan Battle and Antonio Pastrana, Jr.

Mainly used as a metaphor to evoke the experiences of assimilation for immigrants in the United States, the *melting pot* is a term that has been used by scholars in the field of race/ethnicity, immigration, and inequality. One strand of this concept rests on the belief that immigrant groups eventually shed beliefs, linguistic styles, and other cultural practices from their country of origin and meld with other people in order to form a new US-based culture. However, another strand says that a melting of previous identities occurs but that what is newly created is a reflection of the dominant culture that exists in the US. The melting pot encompasses both of these ideas and has contributed to the growing literature on assimilation.

More broadly, this term has been used to identify areas of settlement where many different immigrant groups live in close proximity to one another. Still, the melting pot is usually used to reference immigrant settlement processes in the US, especially about the experiences of those in the late nineteenth and early twentieth centuries. Other metaphors used to describe similar assimilation processes include *mosaic* and *salad bowl*. Similar to the mythologized rags-to-riches stories of Horatio Alger, the melting pot leaves individual- and group-level dynamics untouched, further perpetuating the status quo and leaving inequality unquestioned. Critics of the melting pot often point to the fact

that many racial/ethnic groups in the US have yet to be represented by political, economic, and cultural centers of power. Scholars have documented the various ways in which the melting process does not apply equally to all immigrant and racial/ethnic groups.

The actual term melting pot has its origin in a paper written by historian Frederick Jackson Turner in 1893. He was challenging the proposition that America's culture and institutions were formed solely by the original Anglo-Saxon settlers. He argued that, instead, it was immigrants and their descendants from various places within Europe who were settling on the western frontier who had more influence: "in the crucible of the frontier the immigrants were Americanized, liberated, and fused into a mixed race" (1920 [1893]: 22–3). Turner's "crucible" became known as the melting pot – a phrase taken from a play written by Russian immigrant Israel Zangwell: "America is God's crucible, the great Melting Pot where all races of Europe are melting and reforming" (1909: 37).

An early study of the melting pot process was conducted in 1944 by Ruby Jo Reeves Kennedy. She was particularly interested in interethnic marriage rates. Reeves found that between 1870 and 1940 interethnic marriage soared; however, people did not tend to marry outside of their religious groups. This led her to coin the term *triple melting pot* – the theory that assimilation occurs first within religious groups and then later across religious groups.

Eventually, the melting process became (erroneously) synonymous with the assimilation process. In *Assimilation in American Life* (1964), Milton Gordon delineates at least seven stages or levels of assimilation, which influenced future race/ethnicity and immigration scholars. Central to the development of classical assimilation theory, Gordon's work is based on the experiences of early white immigrants to the US. This work was influential and important because it argued that assimilation occurs at various levels and at varying rates for different groups, starting with what Gordon called "cultural or behavioral assimilation" – when immigrant groups willfully change their cultural habits to reflect those of the host country. However, as some critics have noted, this type of assimilation does not always occur for some groups. Additionally, Gordon identified three consequences of assimilation: (1) Anglo-conformity, which occurs when immigrants are taught to adopt the dominant culture's normative behaviors and institutions; (2) melting pot, which, according to Gordon, occurs when something new and different is created when various cultures mix; and (3) cultural pluralism, which is when immigrants retain their native identities while still interacting within the host environment. All of these features helped to identify the various stages that immigrants and racial/ethnic groups go through in the assimilation process and contributed to the ever-expanding notion of the melting pot.

Almost in direct contrast to the melting pot's ideas of cohesion, Nathan Glazer and Daniel Patrick Moynihan's *Beyond the Melting Pot* (1970) underscored how some immigrants and racial/ethnic groups often rely on the power of distinction in order to succeed. In fact, for Glazer and Moynihan, the melting pot did not happen. The important observation in this work was that the melting pot metaphor needed further expansion in order to include such things as individual choices and agency. Later, in *We Are All Multiculturalists Now* (1997), Glazer suggests that the melting pot metaphor should not be used anymore. Because US blacks have not melted, the promise of assimilation has turned into a myth. Instead, difference is viewed as a form of multiculturalism that highlights distinctions without really examining the types of cultures that continue to dominate and continue to form unjust policies.

The historical trajectory of research on assimilation suggests, then, that early white immigrant groups in the US were capable of melting and assimilating but that later immigrant groups, especially the non-white-identified ones, do not melt as easily. Instead, these groups often retain their native culture and function accordingly. Such a development coincides with the growth of identity politics in the US, which often rests on aspects of difference rather than on how well one assimilates to the dominant society. Researchers have found, for instance, that some black immigrants from the Caribbean consciously reject notions of the melting pot in order to differentiate themselves from US blacks, many of whom remain unassimilated and are disempowered by dominant cultures and institutions.

Social scientists make distinctions among three terms that are all too often used interchangeably: accommodation, acculturation, and assimilation. Sociologist William Kornblum (2005: 641) offers some clear definitions for these terms. Accommodation is the process by which a smaller, less powerful society is able to preserve the major features of its culture even after prolonged contact with a larger, stronger culture. Acculturation is the process by which members of a civilization incorporate norms and values from other cultures into their own. Assimilation is the process by which culturally distinct groups in a larger civilization adopt the norms, values, and language of the host civilization and are able to gain equal statuses in its group and institutions. The melting pot is, in theory, the new product that results from the assimilation process.

Throughout, the melting pot has been evoked to both support and challenge various government-sponsored policies such as affirmative action, bilingual education, and numerous immigration limitation statutes.

SEE ALSO: Accommodation; Acculturation; Anglo-Conformity; Assimilation; Immigration; Race; Race (Racism)

REFERENCES AND SUGGESTED READINGS

Alba, R. (1990) *Ethnic Identity: The Transformation of White America*. Yale University Press, New Haven.

Gans, H. (1979) Symbolic Ethnicity: The Future of Ethnic Groups and Cultures in America. *Ethnic and Racial Studies* 2: 1–20.

Glazer, N. (1997) *We Are All Multiculturalists Now*. Harvard University Press, Cambridge, MA.

Glazer, N. & Moynihan, D. P. (1970) *Beyond the Melting Pot: The Negroes, Puerto Ricans, Jews, Italians, and Irish of New York City*, 2nd edn. MIT Press, Cambridge, MA.

Gordon, M. M. (1964) *Assimilation in American Life: The Role of Race, Religion, and National Origins*. Oxford University Press, Oxford.

Kennedy, R. (1944) Single or Triple Melting Pot? *American Journal of Sociology* 49: 331–9.

Kornblum, W. (2005) *Sociology in a Changing World*, 7th edn. Wadsworth, Belmont, CA.

Turner, F. (1920 [1893]) *The Frontier in American History*. Holt, Rinehart, & Winston, Fort Worth, TX.

Waters, M. C. (2001) *Black Identities: West Indian Immigrant Dreams and American Realities*. Harvard University Press, Cambridge, MA.

Zangwell, I. (1909) *The Melting Pot*. Macmillan, New York.

Mendieta y Núñez, Lucio (1895–1988)

Margarita Olvera Serrano

Lucio Mendieta y Núñez graduated in law in 1920 and was awarded a doctorate in the discipline in 1950. He is unanimously considered the founder of the first sociological institutions to exist in Mexico. Although the Institute for Social Research (*Instituto de Investigaciones Sociales*, IIS) of the National Autonomous University of Mexico (*Universidad Nacional Autónoma de México*, UNAM) was created in 1930, it was not until Mendieta assumed the position of IIS director nine years later that the first institutionalized sociological research began in Mexico, along with steps to form Mexico's first communities of practitioners of this discipline. That moment also marks the beginning of the generation of a specific literature on the subject, around the *Mexican Sociology Journal* (*Revista Mexicana de Sociología*, *RMS*), founded by Mendieta in 1939. Mendieta's directorship marked the beginning of sociology's separation from law, ethnography, and anthropology, to gradually acquire its own identity. Lucio Mendieta y Núñez was also the primary promoter of the opening of the first school dedicated to training professional social scientists in Mexico, the National School of Political and Social Sciences (*Escuela Nacional de Ciencias Políticas y Sociales*, ENCPyS), which opened its doors in 1951, thereby marking the end of the phase of initial institutionalization of sociology and the formation of its first communities of knowledge.

The fact that he directed the IIS and the *RMS* for more than 25 years – in a period in which these were practically the only institutions dedicated to sociology in Mexico – and the fact that he authored the project upon whose base the ENCPyS was created are sufficient reasons to explain why Lucio Mendieta is recognized by historians of sociology in Mexico as the intellectual leader of the institutionalization of the discipline. In addition to his contribution as creator of institutions, Mendieta also authored more than 50 articles, most of them published in the *RMS*, approximately 40 books (some translated into English, German, and French), and a long list of presentations and notes published in the minutes of the 16 national sociological congresses that he organized between 1950 and 1965. Parallel to this work, he promoted two important collections: the *Sociological Notebooks Library of Sociological Essays* (*Cuadernos de Sociología* and *Biblioteca de Ensayos Sociológicos*). the publication of more than 100 titles by the most prestigious sociologists of the time from Latin America, Europe, and the United States, with the intention of making available to the sociological community relevant professional literature in Spanish. The practical and textual work of Lucio Mendieta y Núñez defines the institutional horizon and the representations of the knowledge that oriented sociology in Mexico for almost 30 years. Mexico's current institutions and communities are therefore in one way or another the heirs of the pioneering generation headed by Mendieta.

Lucio Mendieta y Núñez was born in the city of Oaxaca in January of 1895. Mendieta was a member, chronologically as well as physically, politically, and existentially, of the so-called Generation of 1915, which constituted the guiding minority of the constructivist era that followed the 1910 Mexican Revolution, and whose outstanding and relevant members numbered no more than 300. He completed his basic education at the school associated with the Normal School of Oaxaca, and studied his first year of middle- to upper-level studies at the Institute of Sciences, also in Oaxaca. He completed his high school-level studies at the ENP associated with the National University, which conclusively suggests that the majority of his intellectually formative years took place within the politically effervescent climate of a Mexico immersed in an armed struggle that would last more than ten years and would radically modify the country's political, economic, and social structures. Furthermore, this movement produced significantly politicized students of the time, in particular among ENP and ENJ students.

In those years the National University of Mexico was not simply the oldest but in fact the only upper-level education institution in the country. After a relatively calm existence in the colonial era, the university became the center of fierce disputes between liberals and conservatives in the conflictive independent Mexico of the nineteenth century. In May 1910, the Constitutive Law of the National University of Mexico was published, through which the university reopened – in a way as a sign of the country's attempt to join the ranks of the select group of modern nations – to integrate the national high schools, the law, medical, and engineering schools, the fine arts school, and the upper-level studies schools. The importance of these schools is explained by the fact that, from the nineteenth century, the privileged routes of social mobility were the military, the priesthood, law, and, to a lesser degree, the fields of medicine and engineering. It is relevant to note that on the eve of the 1910 Revolution, students at the National University numbered barely a thousand.

At the ENP Lucio Mendieta was influenced by the French positivist tradition, which had completely permeated this institution's intellectual atmosphere since its origins in the latter third of the nineteenth century. In the years of the Porfirio Díaz dictatorship, the intellectuals aligned with the regime took from Comte in particular his ideas on order and progress, which they considered highly pertinent in a society that had endured more than half a century of profound political and military disputes, as was the case of nineteenth-century Mexico. The Porfirian intellectuals reinterpreted the assumptions contained in the discourse of Auguste Comte and accorded them a privileged position in the ENP curriculum, founded in 1867. During Lucio Mendieta's formative years, the established purpose of the ENP was to create an upper-level elite capable of establishing an order based on a common foundation of truths. The expectation was that society's evolution would imply, at a determined moment, that scientific reason would displace commonsense judgments and would provide an objective basis for political decisions. Middle- to upper-level education spanned six years and was broad and scholarly,

including the study of foreign languages. This would turn out to be very important in the 1930s – when the first sociological institutions were built in Mexico – given that the country's intellectual environment was poor and sociological knowledge reached Mexico through works published primarily in France and the United States.

It would have been difficult for an author with the intellectual profile and social background of Lucio Mendieta y Núñez to step outside the boundaries of the legal field and pursue the incipient empirical research that would begin to open the way for sociology in Mexico as a discipline independent of law, ethnography, and anthropology. The event that radically modified the horizon of possibilities that lay before the generation of Lucio Mendieta was the Revolution of 1910, given that it opened lively new fields of participation, critique, discussion, and debate. While this generation was rooted in book learning and a scholarly and erudite environment, those roots branched out toward a social field in which the future appeared, and in fact was, open to action and unprecedented forms of intellectual sociability. The 1910 Revolution cracked the representation of the positivist world peculiar to the dictatorial years in which society appeared to be gradually evolving toward increasingly rational stages, confronting young university students with the political reality and the violence this could imply.

From this intellectual and political horizon was born Lucio Mendieta's concern for the indigenous situation and for the role of scientific knowledge in the reconstruction of postrevolutionary society, a context in which emerged the possibility of the existence of the social sciences in Mexico. Sociology germinated in Mexico as a disciplinary field precisely during those years, in which a minimum development of sociological reflection converged; an external situation in which society was reconstructing itself; a conception of science according to which its legitimacy in society would depend on the production of rational knowledge capable of illuminating action; and, finally, a group of individuals thoroughly convinced of the importance and pertinence of efforts to open and consolidate spaces designated to research the social reality. Lucio Mendieta y Núñez possessed the political and intellectual sensitivity to understand that sociology did not fit within the boundaries of the legal field, and became convinced that a specific and solid niche was required to generate a sociological understanding of Mexican reality, nonexistent until then, but considered indispensable for the future of the nation.

In play in the 1930s were not only the institutional spaces for a new discipline in Mexico, but also the formation of a group of institutions capable of legitimizing the new governing elites, producing authorized empirical knowledge about the country, and attempting to orient lines of political action tending to resolve the gravest problems of a nation encumbered by a ten-year civil war. In this scenario, in 1939 Lucio Mendieta y Núñez was named director of the IIS of the National University, and only then did this institution effectively begin to function as a research space, despite its foundation dating back to 1930.

As part of a reorganization process he initiated from his arrival at the IIS, Lucio Mendieta proposed the creation of new bodies of knowledge capable of justifying the existence of sociology in Mexico as an independent discipline. One of his first decisions was the foundation of the *RMS* as an instrument for the establishment of new forms of intellectual communication and social interaction. The purposes of this publication were to stimulate sociological research, disseminate the most recent studies by sociologists from Europe and the United States, and foment relations and promote exchanges with the primary intellectual institutions dedicated to social science studies. This editorial pursuit was based not only on naturalist-type cognitive assumptions, but also on shared values and beliefs in regard to the reality derived from those assumptions, which functioned as a potent symbolic facet that oriented the practice of the communities of social scholars integrated by Lucio Mendieta within the IIS.

Lucio Mendieta conceived the relations between knowledge and power as collaborative rather than critical or oppositional. He proposed a collaborative link under the unfulfilled assumption that those in governing positions should guide their action in accordance with the results of the research that the IIS was soon to carry out, and thanks to that proposal he was able to secure the necessary material resources

and public support for the institutionalization of sociology in Mexico. For that purpose he put together a group primarily of lawyers, but also, in particular to support his editorial pursuits, a Latin American community of sociologists that included the likes of Ricardo Levene of the University of Buenos Aires; Raúl Orgaz of the University of Córdova; Manuel Dieguez, Brazilian historian and sociologist; Roberto Agramonte of the University of Havana; Oscar Alvarez Andrews of the University of Chile; the Brazilian Mario Lins; Pitirim Sorokin of Harvard University; and Robert Redfield of the University of Chicago. These scholars, together with the Mexicans Francisco Rojas González Bonilla, Emilio Uribe Ramos, Roberto de la Cerda, and René Barragán, were Mendieta's most constant interlocutors and collaborators, forming a type of "invisible college" that put into play formal and informal links which, over time, defined what was understood as sociology and established what could and should be ascribed to this discipline between the 1940s and 1950s in Mexico. Through the *RMS*, Mendieta also maintained contacts with authors outside of his own naturalist intellectual tradition, as was the case of the exiled Spaniards in Mexico, among whom stand out José Medina Echavarría and Luis Recaséns, scholars of the German culturalist tradition linked to Max Weber, Ferdinand Tönnies, and Georg Simmel.

During the 1940s, the axis of Mendieta's work was the study of diverse ethnic groups that existed in Mexico, which led to the first empirical sociological research to take place in the country, relying primarily on the cognitive tools of the positivist methods as well as the intellectual contributions of anthropology and ethnography. The questions he attempted to answer were: Who are the indigenous peoples? How and where do they live? How should they be organized for their integration into national development? The study of indigenous peoples had strong political pertinence at the time; there was generalized agreement among university and political circles as to the need to integrate the empirically unknown indigenous population as quickly as possible within the whole of national society. This objective was animated by a concept of modernity particular to the positivist tradition. Integration of indigenous peoples was therefore envisioned as a homogenization process that would necessarily imply the dissolution of the backwardness of the past and the indigenous tradition to make way for a developed and modern nation.

This body of research led to various publications, the most important of which was the *Ethnographic Atlas of the Mexican Republic* (*Atlas etnográfico de la República Mexicana*). Mendieta's analysis in these works remained within the boundaries of anthropological and ethnographic conceptions, as suggested by the use of the notion of "race," which was mixed with elements from a current of North American functionalist anthropology. Lucio Mendieta identified the indigenous as part of a traditional world that was dissolving in the face of the modern and rational world. According to this logic, the indigenous were different from the rest of the nation, therefore requiring specific governmental policies oriented to facilitate their access to the modern world that was opening to Mexico in the 1940s and 1950s. In other writings, such as *The Indigenous Room* (*La habitación indígena*, 1939) and *Sociological Essay on the Zapotecos* (*Ensayo sociológico sobre los zapotecos*, 1949), Mendieta reiterated this conception of the status of the indigenous. Sociology's task in this scenario consisted of empirically researching the indigenous to promote their integration around an imagined modern and homogeneous national culture. According to Lucio Mendieta, achievement of these objectives depended on a community of expert sociologists separated from them. These studies had a constituent rather than analytical character, given that sociology in Mexico at the time lacked an autonomous development differentiating it from neighboring fields of knowledge. Nevertheless, these first empirical research pursuits were the axis around which was consummated the creation of a distinct institutional space for sociology in Mexico, despite the absence of a solid profile of the discipline.

The opening of distinct institutional spaces for sociology in a country that lacked a well-established intellectual community, a strong sociological tradition, and precise and clear cognitive boundaries vis-à-vis other fields of knowledge was made possible in particular by the close relations existing during those years between knowledge and public power. Institutionalized sociology emerged in Mexico, unlike in Europe and the United States, to respond to an external demand for expert knowledge that could be applied to political-social modernization programs that were just beginning to appear in Mexico.

Between the 1950s and 1960s, Lucio Mendieta delved into the terrain of concepts with speculative and essay-type books that implied a gradual separation from the cores of law, anthropology, and ethnography. He addressed unprecedented topics in the Mexican intellectual sphere, such as experimental methods in sociology, sociological statistics, bureaucracy, social classes, the concept of revolution, planning and development, political parties, and methodological problems of definition in sociology. The most important publications of this period were: *Theory of Social Groupings*, *Theory of Revolution*, *Three Political Sociology Essays*, *Sociology of Development*, and *Essays on Planning, Journalism, the Legal Profession* (*Teoría de los agrupamientos sociales*, 1951; *Teoría de la revolución*, 1960; *Tres ensayos de sociología política*, 1961; *Sociología del desarrollo*, 1962; and *Ensayos sobre planificación, periodismo, abogacía*, 1963). The objective of these publications was to provide Mexican sociology with its own conceptual coordinates, as well as to define the type of processes and structures implied in the economic-social modernization being experimented in by the country. The sociological tradition to which he had recourse was deeply linked with positivism and North American structural functionalism. Mendieta therefore assigned great importance to the adoption of a set of concepts that could unify sociological language.

Parallel to that work, Lucio Mendieta undertook intense public promotion of sociology, achieving two very important results for development of this discipline in Mexico: the foundation of ENCPyS in 1951, and the organization of annual national sociological congresses between 1950 and 1965 that brought together not only the incipient Mexican sociological community, but also, importantly, functionaries, politicians, government figures, and diverse professionals. The external scenario was favorable to these initiatives. International institutions with close ties with the majority of Latin American governments, such as the United Nations (UN), the UN Educational, Scientific, and Cultural Organization (UNESCO), and the

Latin American Economic Commission (CEPAL), among others, constituted the political and economic framework that demanded from the social sciences technical knowledge applicable to the development of the region's countries. This demand was seized upon by social scientists with shared optimism, providing important public promotion for these disciplines in Mexico, thereby consummating their definitive insertion in the institutional panorama of science in the country.

Lucio Mendieta y Núñez was the author of both the founding project of the ENCPyS and its first curriculum. Upon returning from a trip to Europe in 1949, where he had been invited by UNESCO to participate in the foundation of the International Sociological Association and the International Political Science Association, Mendieta proposed the creation of a school within UNAM dedicated to the professional formation of social scientists. His project included undergraduate degree programs in social sciences, diplomatic sciences, journalism, and political sciences. Years later, the first of these would change its denomination to sociology. The University Board approved this initiative in May 1951 and the novel ENCPyS opened its doors in July of that year, with 136 students distributed among the distinct programs. In this first stage, classes were taught primarily by lawyers, along with some legal philosophers, historians, anthropologists, physicists, physicians, and, to a lesser degree, economists. A well-established teaching staff was lacking, so many courses were taught in the departments of philosophy and law. This was indicative of the nonexistence of a sufficiently broad sociological community in Mexico, which meant that the formation of the first generations of professional social scientists was left in the hands of lawyers. Nevertheless, thanks to this new space, by the mid-1950s Mexico would have its own nationally formed sociologists, such as Emma Salgado, María Luisa Rodríguez Sala, and Raúl Benítez Zenteno, who were systematically dedicated to empirical research of the Mexican reality.

Lucio Mendieta y Núñez left the direction of the IIS and the *RMS* in 1965. Through his work and organizational labor, in the almost 30 years in which he directed these spaces, Mendieta achieved the insertion of sociology in Mexico, the creation of a distinct disciplinary profile, and the consolidation of its first community of practitioners. The contemporary significance that can be found in his work resides in the first-order role he fulfilled in the institutionalization of this discipline in Mexico, the opening to the reception of the primary sociological traditions of his time through the *RMS* and his editorial work, and the winning of public recognition and of resources for development of this discipline. His work was of course not exempt from limitations, the most notable of which were the corporative and centralized character of his leadership, his close alliance with public power, and the absence of a critical approach to the sociological traditions that oriented him. Nevertheless, the professionalized and specialized sociology that was gradually constructed in Mexico starting in the 1970s would have been very difficult to develop without Mendieta's legacy and the pioneering generation he led.

SEE ALSO: *Caudillismo*; Indigenous Peoples; Modernization; Positivism; Structural Functional Theory

REFERENCES AND SUGGESTED READINGS

Agramonte, R. (1961) *Mendieta y su magisterio sociológico*. Eds. Cultura, Mexico.

Aguilar Villanueva, L., Andrade Carreño, A., et al. (1995) *Estudios de teoría e historia de la sociología en México*. UNAM/UAM-A, Mexico.

Andrade Carreño, A. (1998) Teoría sociológica en México: temas, campos científicos y tradiciones disciplinarias, FCPyS/UNAM, Mexico.

Castañeda, F. (1990) La constitución de la sociología en México. In: Paoli Bolio, J., *Origen y desarrollo de las ciencias sociales en México*. Porrúa/UNAM, Mexico.

Leal y Fernández, J. F. (1994) *La sociología contemporánea en México*. FCPyS/UNAM, Mexico.

Mendieta y Núñez, L. (1939) Balance, perspectivas y propósitos. *Revista Mexicana de Sociología* 1, 4/5 (September/December). IIS/UNAM, Mexico.

Mendieta y Núñez, L. (1943) Programa para la integración de la investigación social en las Américas. *Revista Mexicana de Sociología* 4, 1 (September/December). IIS/UNAM, Mexico.

Mendieta y Núñez, L. (1950) Estudios Sociológicos. Primer Congreso Nacional de Sociología. IIS/UNAM, Mexico.

Mendieta y Núñez, L. (1955) Origen, organización, finalidades y perspectivas de la ENCPyS. *Revista de Ciencias Políticas y Sociales* 1, 2 (October/December). ENCPyS/UNAM, Mexico.

Olvera Serrano, M. (2004) *Lucio Mendieta y la institucionalización de la sociología en México, 1939–1965*. Porrúa, Mexico.

mental disorder

Mark Tausig

Sociologists who study mental disorder work from a number of assumptions that define and distinguish their approach from other ways of understanding mental disorder. First, sociologists may view mental disorder as a normal consequence of social life caused by structured inequality rather than as a form of individual dysfunction. Second, they may regard mental disorder as the outcome of social processes that include the labeling of deviant behavior and stigmatic societal reactions to those labels. Third, they may define the object of study as psychological distress rather than as specific psychiatric disorders. Fourth, they may view the mental health treatment system as an institution for the social control of deviant behavior. Finally, the sociological perspective is concerned with properties of groups and populations and it is less informative regarding individual and clinical concerns. Although not all sociologists employ all of these assumptions in their research and some of these assumptions have generated considerable debate, collectively they represent what is distinctive about the sociological study of mental disorder.

The psychiatric medical model accounts for mental disorder as a function of individual biological reactions to environmental (including social) hazard and/or individual biochemical or genetic dysfunction – the broken brain. Biological psychiatry now dominates the way psychiatrists explain the origins of mental disorder and the way disorder is treated. The *social causation model* by contrast accounts for psychological distress as a function of the effects of positions in social structures of inequality.

Sociologists argue that disorder or distress arises from a *stress process* in which eventful, chronic, and traumatic stressors represent risks to well-being. In turn, individuals can mobilize resources to offset the effects of stressors and, broadly speaking, the balance between risk and protective resources determines the psychological consequences of stressors.

Exposure to risk and the ability to mobilize protective resources are a function of social status. Although some risks are serendipitous, many are related to socioeconomic status, gender, or race. Also, protective resources such as access to information and effective instrumental and expressive social networks are related to social status. Over the life course individuals are exposed to stressors and have access to resources that consistently affect well-being as a direct function of socially structured access to resources and exposure to risk factors. Hence, both risk and protective resources arise in the normal day-to-day lives of persons as a function of social status.

The strongest evidence for social structural effects on mental health is found in the relationship between socioeconomic status (SES) and psychological distress. SES affects income, work conditions, housing conditions, and neighborhood context in such a way that persons in lower SES positions are exposed to considerably more stressors and they have considerably fewer resources to deal with those stressors. Hence higher rates of distress are observed among persons of lower SES that are a direct function of what life is like for people who have low education and low income. As a group, young, single working mothers are found to have very high rates of depressive symptoms. They are also exposed to many stressors that are a function of social position. These young mothers are often solely responsible for childcare. Because they are young, their wages are lower and because they are women their wages will also be lower. The temporal, emotional, and financial strains they experience are clearly a function of social position and role expectations. Similarly, and beyond differences in education and occupational levels, recent research shows that racial and ethnic minorities in the United States are significantly affected psychologically by perceived discrimination in their daily lives.

Sociologists also view mental disorder as the outcome of a social process in which others evaluate and label deviant behavior. The labeling perspective represents an external causal explanation for disorder in which others confer a label on certain forms of deviant behavior. When an individual behaves in ways that others find deviant and unexplainable, that individual can be diagnosed (labeled) as having a mental illness as a way of explaining the deviant behavior. The label has powerful effects for both those who encounter the labeled individual and the labeled individual. The mental illness label is stigmatic and it is associated among the general public with negative attributes of dangerousness, unpredictability, and lack of personal responsibility. The public avoid and condemn persons with these labels. The unpopularity of neighborhood-based housing for persons with mental disorders is a direct reflection of the negative attributes accorded to persons who have been given psychiatric diagnoses. Stigma may also explain why coverage for the treatment of mental disorders in medical insurance plans is not nearly as generous as for the treatment of physical illness.

The effects of labeling extend to the labeled person as well. The label of mental illness is deeply discrediting so that an individual's entire identity is *spoiled* by the label and the individual loses status, "drifting" into a lower SES, for example. Persons who have been labeled feel estranged from *normals* and often withdraw from or circumscribe their behavior in public as a result. Labeled persons are well aware of the negative reactions of others to psychiatric labels and to them. Anticipation of rejection by others can lead to demoralization, it can affect work performance, and it can strain interpersonal relationships. The label leads to isolation and secrecy and reinforces the notion that labeled individuals are *different*. Even persons who have been successfully treated for mental disorders report feelings of exclusion and hostility based on the continuing stigma of the label. They may be barred from some forms of employment, and access to other opportunities may be restricted as well.

Finally, labeling is a form of social control because it can be used to constrain behavior and because it reflects power relations in social systems. It takes power to confer a label and to make it stick. Family members may refer to a member as crazy but there are few notable social consequences from such a label. When psychiatrists diagnose individuals, by contrast, the stigmatic consequences of the label are much more apparent.

Sociologists are not sure that psychiatric labels refer to real entities or diseases. There are strong theoretical and empirical grounds for believing that diagnostic categories of disorder such as those making up the *Diagnostic and Statistical Manual of Mental Disorders* (DSM) of the American Psychiatric Association can be arbitrary, value-laden, and normative. Diagnostic categories can change based on changing social attitudes and political influence processes that seem unrelated to disease. In addition, empirical studies show that symptoms for different mental illness diagnoses often overlap so that similar symptoms can lead to different diagnoses. Neither the stress perspective nor the labeling perspective used by sociologists requires a formal nosology of disorder. The stress perspective accounts for *distress* as a generalized form of demoralization and unhappiness that may appear in forms that are consistent with symptoms of depression, alcohol or substance use, anxiety, antisocial behavior, or dysphoric mood. Similarly, although there are some variations in public reactions to psychiatric labels depending on the label, the more general observation is that any psychiatric label results in rejection, avoidance, and condemnation. For sociologists, the specific diagnostic category is secondary to observing a psychological response to consequences of structured inequality or to labels imposed on individuals to account for and control deviant behavior. It should be noted that not all sociologists agree that diagnostic categories are unimportant or arbitrary.

Sociologists have observed that some deviant, *bad* behavior has been redefined as biological deviance and hence it becomes amenable to medical/psychiatric treatment. The medicalization of deviance argument describes a social process that turns deviant behavior into illness symptoms. In turn, this leads to medical treatment of mental disorder rather than punishment of a crime or delinquency, for example. The behavior is the same but it is categorized in terms of illness. Medicalization highlights the notion of the social control of deviant behavior by showing, for example, how disruption of a school classroom can be controlled by treating attention deficit disorder. Although a medical explanation for disorder is claimed, the discovery of such a medical explanation is often preceded by recognition of the need to control deviant behavior. A review of diagnostic categories in the DSM suggests that many of the disorders described could also easily be labeled simply as non-normative behavior. Also, the process whereby disorders are added to the DSM also suggests that social norms of behavior are a measuring stick for identification of illness symptoms.

If people in lower-status positions in social structures are more apt to experience distress/disorder and those with less power are more likely to have mental illness labels attached to their behaviors, then the treatment of mental disorders takes on the appearance of social control. In this regard, sociologists view the mental health treatment system as a social control institution and they are interested in patterns of the use of mental health treatments, differences between public and private treatment modalities, the goals of treatment, and differential access to mental health services.

Large-scale representative studies of the prevalence of mental illness in the community confirm that those in lower socioeconomic levels, especially, are more likely to have diagnosable mental disorders. Those same studies indicate that less than half of all those with a diagnosable mental disorder are so labeled and receive treatment. Persons in low SES positions and racial and ethnic minorities are less likely to receive treatment for those symptoms/disorders than high SES persons and whites. Higher-status individuals are more likely to be treated in the private mental health system as a function of insurance availability and higher levels of trust in psychiatric care, while low SES individuals use the public mental health system, receive no mental health care, or are channeled into the criminal justice system to deal with drug- and alcohol-related disorders.

The evidence to support the notion that mental health treatment is a form of the social control of deviance is only partially supported by these data. However, when these data are combined with critiques of the possible over-diagnosis of attention deficit disorder and the widespread use of drugs such as Prozac, for example, a substantial case can be made that deviant behavior (if not mental disorder) is the object of medical control.

The study of mental disorder from the sociological perspective must be seen as complementary to biological and psychological perspectives on mental disorder because it focuses on the mental health status of social groups and populations. Sociologists do not attempt to explain why a particular individual feels depressed but why persons with low socioeconomic status, for example, are more likely to feel depressed compared to persons with high socioeconomic status. The perspective has limited application to clinical concerns and is not especially useful for explaining individual cases of disorder. By contrast, biological and psychological perspectives rarely recognize patterns of disorder prevalence or variations in treatment modalities.

It should be noted that many sociologists study mental disorder without making any of the assumptions described above. There are valuable studies of the impact of family structure and process on mental health, in-depth studies of mental health treatment systems, and numerous studies of the consequences of mental illness for individual functioning over the life course.

SEE ALSO: Aging, Mental Health, and Well-Being; Deviance, Medicalization of; Disease, Social Causation; Labeling; Madness; Social Epidemiology; Stigma; Stress, Stress Theories; Stressful Life Events

REFERENCES AND SUGGESTED READINGS

Aneshensel, C. S. & Phelan, J. C. (Eds.) (1999) *Handbook of the Sociology of Mental Health.* Kluwer Academic/Plenum, New York.

Conrad, P. & Schneider, J. W. (1992) *Deviance and Medicalization: From Badness to Sickness.* Temple University Press, Philadelphia.

Kessler, R. C., McGonagle, K. A., Zhao, S., et al. (1994) Lifetime and 12-Month Prevalence of DSM-III-R Psychiatric Disorders Among Persons Aged 15–54 in the United States: Results from the National Comorbidity Survey. *Archives of General Psychiatry* 51: 8–19.

Kutchins, H. & Kirk, S. A. (1997) *Making Us Crazy: DSM: The Psychiatric Bible and the Creation of Mental Disorders.* Free Press, New York.

Link, B. G. & Phelan, J. C. (2001) Conceptualizing Stigma. *Annual Review of Sociology* 27: 363–85.

Pearlin, L. I. (1989) The Sociological Study of Stress. *Journal of Health and Social Behavior* 30: 241–56.

Scheff, T. J. (1984) *Being Mentally Ill.* Aldine, New York.

Turner, R. J., Wheaton, B., & Lloyd, D. A. (1995) The Epidemiology of Social Stress. *American Sociological Review* 60: 104–25.

meritocracy

Gad Yair

The term "meritocracy" has three interrelated meanings. First, it refers to the type of social order where rewards are distributed to individuals in accordance with criteria of personal merit. Put differently, it denotes the "rule of the talented," a system of governance wherein the brightest and most conscientious individuals are accurately and efficiently assigned to occupy the most important positions, based on their talent and achievements. Second, the concept pertains to an elite social class, a definite group of people that enjoys high prestige because its select members proved to have merit based on their unique abilities and attainments (i.e., the aristocracy of merit as coined by Thomas Jefferson). Third, the term touches upon the criteria of allocation of positions, roles, prestige, power, and economic reward, whereby excellent individuals are over-benefited in relation to others. These criteria are based on achieved rather than ascribed characteristics, and reflect the assumption that while achievements of merit are rare and difficult to attain, they are culturally valued.

In its elementary form, meritocracy is based on the allocation of rewards in congruence with human excellence, defined by Young (1958) as the sum of intelligence and effort ($M = I + E$, where M is merit, I is IQ, and E is effort). Practically, however, merit is usually equated with the achievement of educational qualifications, commonly measured by cognitive achievements and educational attainments. Meritocracy is also contrasted with systems that are based on selection by ascribed characteristics such as inherited wealth, social class, ethnicity, race,

and, more generally, with any system of nepotism (Daniels 1978).

In essence, a meritocracy is based on inequality of outcome. Paradoxically, however, it refers to the prior arrangement of equal opportunities that – when operated fairly in free markets and open societies – should result in unequal but morally deserving outcomes. Like the *Theory of Justice* proposed by John Rawls (1971), the meritocracy justifies social inequality under conditions of antecedent equality. Based on a principle of equity (rather than equality or need), it states that individuals should be provided with equal opportunities to make the most of their intellectual potential and moral character. But since there are inherent inequalities in human potential (e.g., the bell curve of IQ distribution), and since individuals exhibit variable levels of motivation to excel, the social order should reflect the hierarchy of attained merit.

The meritocratic ideal states that – given that equality of opportunity is in place – the distribution of outcomes should be decided by open competition between individuals. Furthermore, the behavior of individuals during the preparatory stages of this competition is to rank them according to their merits. Intelligent individuals who invest effort in the competition (i.e., education) deserve to benefit. Others of lesser merit should be ranked lower. The resulting hierarchical rank order in the educational competition should then be transferred to the distribution of rewards in adult society.

Based on these definitions and orienting remarks, the following discussion focuses on three interrelated themes. The first analyzes the modernist intellectual traditions of meritocratic ideas. The second and major theme focuses on the centrality of education in meritocratic systems. The final theme comments on the relationship between meritocracy and sociology.

INTELLECTUAL TRADITIONS: STATE AND MARKET

There were early precursors to the idea of a meritocracy (e.g., discussions of "philosophers as kings" and distributive justice in Greek philosophy). However, the meritocracy is largely a modern idea. The moral and legal basis for the meritocracy rests on a twofold edifice. First, it is inscribed in modern precepts of democracy and the "just society" which refer to universal human and citizenship rights. Second, it is based on a Darwinian rationale of social and economic selection which states that individual capital and social utility are maximized in competitive free markets.

The modern nation–state and its universal principles of citizenship and human rights constituted the preconditions for the appearance of meritocratic principles and social orders. Modern national constitutions were first to define citizenship by universal criteria and to outlaw unequal treatment of citizens based on ascribed characteristics, such as gender, race, ethnicity, or immigration. Based on the universal spirit of equality of opportunity expressed by the constitutions, court rulings have continually expanded the realms of meritocratic principles. By gradually expanding the rights of equal opportunity for women, minorities, and ethnic and racial groups, the courts have reestablished the basic principle of true meritocracy, namely, that rewards are to be allocated according to rational criteria of achievement in realms which are, in principle, open for all (Dworkin 1996).

The second edifice of the meritocracy rests on capitalist economic principles of the free market. The capitalist worldview assumes that by expanding universal access to the market and by withholding state interference, products will improve and prices will decrease. The model assumes that the ensuing competition among suppliers will necessitate innovation and decrease prices. On the demand side, it is assumed that availability of alternatives in the free market will benefit the more resourceful and motivated clients who can cleverly negotiate with different suppliers for their benefit. This theory assumes that economic efficiency and personal utility will be maximized when the market is left unregulated, making intelligence and effort the prime drivers for success, or in other words, for economic merit.

THE CENTRALITY OF EDUCATION

Education plays a prominent role in meritocratic systems. Educational credentials are often used as the equivalents of merit. They also constitute the yardstick for assessing the extent to which other institutions are meritocratic. In that sense, education is both the gatekeeper for the meritocracy and its standard.

Individual merit is a latent trait. As with other latent traits, techniques of educational and psychological measurement are used to arrive at reliable and valid estimates of achievement. Haunted by a fear of inefficiency and litigation, the state deploys an industry of merit (e.g., Educational Testing Service) which uses sophisticated estimation and equating techniques (e.g., item response theory models) so as to verify that equal opportunities are supplied and that students are correctly detected and selected across tracks, classrooms, schools, and states. The boom of mandatory testing and the adoption of national standards are signs that – from the state's legal standpoint – meritocracy cannot be left to be decided at a local level. If equal opportunity is the business of the state, so is meritocracy. There is no surprise, then, that the modern nation–state and schooling go hand in hand.

The creation and expansion of the modern school system – in its ideal, egalitarian, and meritocratic form – was to provide the functional arrangement for a true meritocracy. Realizing the resistance of traditional separatist arrangements, governments and courts have increasingly imposed school integration policies in order to bring diverse populations together and provide equal opportunities for all. The expansion of citizenship and human rights required schools to become more inclusive, thereby fulfilling the promise of the "common school": to provide equal opportunity for all to compete for merit, irrespective of gender, race, or ethnicity. Affirmative action and social promotion procedures are pursued to provide minority and failing students with opportunities for improvement. The inclusion of students with special needs is undertaken to allow all students to fully develop their potential merit. Furthermore, selectivity into ability groups, tracks, and streams is criticized as the censorship of equal opportunities to compete over merit (Oakes 1985).

In rising to the challenge of the meritocracy, the modern school provides intellectual preparation and moral socialization, thereby developing the two components of merit: intelligence and effort. The main task of schooling is to impart knowledge and develop the intellectual abilities of students. Schools are also expected to inculcate the will to learn, either by setting high expectations or by constructing interesting and challenging learning environments. In this sense, schooling provides opportunities to learn, and schools are expected, at least during the early years of childhood, to distribute these opportunities on an equal basis.

While they are required to develop students' ability and aspirations, schools are also chartered as systems of organized competitions and examinations. Notwithstanding their compassionate mission of nurturing students' merit, schools have to assess merit and therefore produce inequality of outcome. In their capacity as arbiters of merit, schools construct open competitive arenas and repeatedly provide challenges and examinations in order to accurately decide student merit. In this capacity, schooling comprises the sorting machine that ranks students according to their cumulative merit in a lock-step series of examinations in different intellectual disciplines. Schools supply opportunities to learn, and an open and free arena for exhibiting intellectual excellence. But it is students who have to perform at their best and prove their merit.

Schools are required to record and publicize this merit (Hanson 1993). Actually, school-achievement-as-merit is repeatedly screened by tests, quizzes, book reports, and individual research papers, thereby producing a cumulative grade that is used as a proxy for student merit (intelligence tests and their equivalents aim for the same goal: predicting students' future merit). The highly achieving students (those who have proved their merit) are then selected by Ivy League universities, while their peers are funneled to lesser-ranking institutions or directly to manual occupations in the labor market. In this way, the meritocratic order of the school is reproduced in the labor market. When these ranks match, the order is defined as efficient and morally deserving. This is the ideal way a meritocracy should work.

However, an overwhelming body of scholarship has repeatedly shown that schools and the schooling process betray the ideals of meritocracy. Often referred to as "social reproduction" approaches to schooling, these studies have deciphered how ethnic, racial, and gender inequalities are perpetuated and exacerbated by education. Studies of tracking and ability grouping, like those of teacher expectations and school effectiveness, have repeatedly pointed at social biases in student selection, instruction, and assessment. They have shown that rather than serving as a mechanism for identifying and selecting intelligent students, education in fact tracks them by race and ethnicity (Bowles & Gintis 1976). Also driven by meritocratic ideals, these studies show that schools are yet to face the challenges of equal opportunities and real meritocracy.

Furthermore, the realization of meritocratic ideals in education is continually debated in political arenas, at times inviting intervention by the Supreme Court. Most conspicuous, perhaps, is the debate which proponents of meritocracy hold with advocates of affirmative action and anti-discrimination lobbyists in higher education. Since the number of prestigious positions is limited (e.g., number of students accepted to medical school), and as there are more candidates than there are openings, the question of "who shall be educated" becomes a truly political one. The answers to this question are volatile and change with time. Leaders of the Civil Rights Movement argued that selection criteria into higher education should be partly based on ascribed characteristics in order to guarantee social representation in the student body, and as a consequence in elite positions in the labor market. Their political success has indeed opened new opportunities for minorities and diversified the student body. However, critics have recently countered this by showing that many deserved applicants are rejected while candidates of lesser merit are accepted, simply because the latter are from minority groups.

The last decade indeed witnessed winds of change. By the end of the 1990s, California's legislature decided to retract policies of affirmative action and adopt achievement criteria of admission into higher education institutes (a policy which promises the top 4 percent of each class an automatic place in California State universities). In 2003, however, the United States Supreme Court – seeking to protect a diverse student body – reaffirmed the legitimacy of race and ethnicity as just criteria for selection to universities (*Gratz* v. *Bollinger* and *Grutter* v. *Bollinger*). The argument is that a true meritocracy will be served by diverse and socially representative student bodies. These changing sensibilities are likely to continue fluctuating as long as real equal opportunities for all are lacking. Therefore, the political and ethical debates over meritocratic principles in education are likely to continue.

SOCIOLOGY AND DEVIATIONS FROM CONSTITUTIONAL MERITOCRACY

The ideals of meritocracy and equal opportunity are, indeed, ideals. In practice, however, the project of modernity has yet to put merito-cratic arrangements in their appropriate place. Families still reproduce social hierarchies. Schools are only partially effective in supplying equal opportunities. And the labor market is only loosely coupled to education. As a result, to paraphrase Young (1958: 14), the upper classes still have their fair share of geniuses and morons, and so do the workers. This implies that many individuals do not maximize their human capital and do not completely fulfill their potential. It also means that different social arrangements cause waste and economic inefficiency. Progress, although not halted, is slowed down.

Sociological studies of *stratification* monitor these deviations from the meritocratic ideal. Studies of social reproduction in families, schools, and universities are motivated by the Constitution and its ideals of equal opportu-nities and meritocracy. Such studies focus on mechanisms that make it difficult for individuals and social categories to realize their potential. Some of these studies focus on different organi-zational strategies which either expand partici-pation and fair competition or actually decrease opportunities (e.g., studies of tracking, streams, ability groups, and private schools). Compara-tive studies of stratification share a similar bent. In measuring different facets of social inequality in different countries, scholars seek to assess progress toward the meritocratic and egalitarian ideals of western democratic countries, and to understand the features that withhold opportu-nities and hinder meritocracy. In this respect, the sociological science of stratification springs from modern conceptions of citizenship, equal opportunities, and meritocracy, but is also bound by these political ideals.

CONCLUSION

Meritocracy is a modern capitalistic ideal. It promised to maximize efficiency and ensure a just distribution of rewards. Sociologists – from Durkheim in *The Division of Labor in Society* to these very early days of the twenty-first century – have pledged allegiance to the ideals of meritocracy and equal opportunity (see Coleman 1974). Since a meritocratic order is implicitly set as their ideal standard for com-parison, sociologists of stratification are preoc-cupied with issues of inequality of opportunity. Implicitly, they wish for a just, meritocratic yet deservedly hierarchical social order. As true modernists of state and market, they seek jus-tice and join governments in battling the causes of undeserved inequality. Unwittingly, they call for deserved, or merited, social stratification. A kingdom yet to come.

However, the accomplishment of a working meritocracy is not likely to finalize the mod-ern project of an open meritocracy. The open competitive basis of the social order is likely to produce new aristocracies of merit which will challenge this very basis. Highly educated and merited families are likely to guard their advan-tages, even though some offspring may be intel-lectually undeserving of their ascribed status. This tendency toward filial perpetuation is likely to challenge the openness of the merito-cratic order. This means that tendencies for closure and bias are likely to continue challen-ging meritocratic social orders and the science of society. After all, sociology and meritocracy are children of similar intellectual traditions.

SEE ALSO: *Brown* v. *Board of Education*; Edu-cational and Occupational Attainment; Oppor-tunities for Learning; School Segregation, Desegregation; State; Stratification and Inequality, Theories of

REFERENCES AND SUGGESTED READINGS

Bowles, S. & Gintis, H. (1976) *Schooling in Capitalist America*. Basic Books, New York.

Coleman, J. S. (1974) Inequality, Sociology, and Moral Philosophy. *American Journal of Sociology* 80(3): 739–64.

Daniels, N. (1978) Merit and Meritocracy. *Philosophy and Public Affairs* 7(3): 206–23.

Dworkin, R. (1996) *Freedom's Law: The Moral Reading of the American Constitution*. Harvard University Press, Cambridge, MA.

Hanson, A. F. (1993) *Testing, Testing: Social Consequences of the Examined Life*. University of California Press, Berkeley.

McNamee, S. J. & Miller, R. K. (2004) *The Meritocracy Myth*. Rowman & Littlefield, Lanham, MD.

Oakes, J. (1985) *Keeping Track: How Schools Structure Inequality*. Yale University Press, New Haven.

Rawls, J. (1971) *A Theory of Justice*. Belknap Press of Harvard University Press, Cambridge, MA.

Young, M. (1958) *The Rise of the Meritocracy, 1870–2033*. Thames & Hudson, London.

Merton, Robert K. (1910–2003)

Barry V. Johnston

Robert K. Merton is among the last of the pansophic scholars in American sociology. His works have opened or deepened new fields of study in the sociology of science, studies of social time, the development and analysis of social theory, and the exploration of the dynamic relationship between sociological theory and empirical research. To this brief list of intellectual contributions should also be added a highly improbable journey from working-class origins in South Philadelphia to Harvard, a 62-year association with Columbia University, and a journey to the White House in 1994 as the first sociologist to receive the National Medal of Science. The last distinction was one of many acknowledgments for a renowned and distinguished life of scholarship and contributions to sociology and society.

According to Morton Hunt's (1961) profile of Merton the sociologist was born in a South Philadelphia slum, where rows of dingy, decrepit houses sheltered first generation immigrants from Italy, Ireland, and (Merton's parents among them) Eastern Europe. However,

Merton (1994) contested Hunt's assertion about his parents, the poverty of his early life, and the slum-like qualities of his neighborhood. There he recalls that he felt no sense of deprivation, but instead a rich environment that stimulated discovery and learning. Among the avenues to this wider world was a large Carnegie Library, where he started reading biographies, literature, autobiographies, and the histories of science and literature with the help of the staff of then all-lady librarians. It was also through the library that he came across the works of James Gibbons Huneker, the drama and literary critic that introduced him to new and unexpected dimensions of European culture. These included the French symbolists and the works of Ibsen, Bernard Shaw, and Flaubert among others. Merton was provided the opportunities for a stimulating and engaging introduction to the sciences and mathematics, as well as schooling in four years of Latin and two years of French. Clearly, it was an environment in which the young scholar thrived. These experiences demonstrate enrichment activities that led to an early engagement with a rich body of ideas and emersion in science, culture, and the arts.

Merton was clearly on his way to becoming one of sociology's most literate citizens and possessed a distinctive ability to see the unique in the ordinary. It was this keen intellectual capability that brought him to the attention of his first university mentor, George E. Simpson at Temple University. Through Simpson he learned that an objective science of sociology was possible, and this was later reinforced when, on his own, he read Sorokin's *Contemporary Sociological Theories* (1928). Simpson quickly identified Merton's intellectual promise, and as a mentor led Merton deeper into the works of the versatile and prolific Sorokin. When Merton later saw Sorokin in action at the meetings of the American Sociological Association in Washington DC, he firmly decided that it was with Sorokin that he wanted to do his graduate studies and it did not matter where he might be.

Once at Harvard Merton developed a style of life made up of hard work, long hours, creative adaptations to student poverty, fox-trotting with the ladies, and a competitive tennis game. It was there too that he developed a close and professional relationship with George Sarton, who was even then considered a founding force in the history of science. Sarton and Sorokin were the initiating stimuli that led to Merton's development and lifelong engagement with the history and sociology of science. While busy with these activities Merton also explored and published with Sorokin in 1937 the article "Social Time: Methodological and Functional Analysis" in the *American Journal of Sociology*. This early publication was later followed by such works as "Socially Expected Durations: A Case Study of Concept Formation in Sociology" (1984) and "On Becoming an Hororand at Jagiellonian University: Social Time and Socio-Cognitive Networks" (1990). On his Harvard mentors Merton would later acknowledge that Sarton and Sorokin were quite different and these differences separated them widely from each other. While the contrast was palpable, little effort was required to work well with either of them. Discipleship was not necessary and independent thought was appreciated and acknowledged by each, though to different degrees. Merton later used these acquired skills to navigate the very stormy waters separating Sorokin and Talcott Parsons. Merton completed his degree in 1936. His dissertation's focus and title was "Science, Technology and Society in Seventeenth Century England." Sarton thought so highly of it that it was published in its entirety in his journal *Osiris*. This early work has often been considered one of the most widely read and reproduced dissertations in the discipline.

After Harvard, Merton taught and then chaired the sociology department at Tulane. Two years later he moved to Columbia University and there spent the next 62 years of his career. When he arrived, Harvard, Columbia, and the University of Chicago were the major institutions vying for preeminence in sociology. For some time, Robert McIver had provided leadership in theory at Columbia, while Robert Lynn did the same in methodology and empirical research. By 1941 these men were seeking their replacements. Lynn obtained a permanent position for Paul Lazarsfeld as a professor of sociology who would serve simultaneously as the director of the Bureau of Applied Social Research. Merton became the new theoretical voice in the department. The choices by Lynn and McIver resulted in one of the most synergistic and creative collaborations in the history

of the discipline. In the process the mathematician and the theorist added depth and luster to the practice of their respective and common crafts. By so doing they also kept Columbia in the trinity of competitors for disciplinary hegemony.

Such intertwining of theory and methods was a result of two critical, yet open-minded scholars challenging the implicit and explicit assumptions of their different specializations. In the process of explaining to each other their methods of theory building and doing research they constantly engaged in explications of how they came to know what they knew. In the process Merton became more attuned to empirical and statistical methods, while Lazarsfeld gained new insights into construction and the explanatory power of theory. Their complementarities were visible in their seminars, where they often demonstrated for their students the blending of their sociological orientations as well as their distinctive personalities (Heeren 1975).

By the age of 40 Merton was a very important sociologist, a member of the National Academy of Sciences, and working with Lazarsfeld to establish a program of theoretically informed and empirically rigorous research at Columbia. Both of these scholars had great influence on many graduate students. Lazarsfeld inspired them to engage in rigorous empirical analysis, and many students considered him brilliant. They admired his commitment and that of Merton to reliable empirical evidence, and their image of sociological research as combining theory, testable hypotheses, and high-quality data.

Students were also deeply drawn to Merton. Indeed, very few students did not consider him among their reasons for coming to Columbia. He was a major influence on their intellectual development. The power of Merton's lectures, the clarity and elegance of his ideas, and the promise they demonstrated for sociology's development as a theoretical and applied discipline confirmed students' beliefs that they were onto something important. Indeed, the ideas and research methods that they were learning had great promise of yielding a deeper theoretical understanding of society that could be applied to social problems and the improvement of the human condition. Many students found in the teaching of Merton and Lazarsfeld the elements necessary for a genuine science of society (Heeren 1975).

The relationship between these two great scholars resulted in not only more powerful, substantive, and empirical contributions that furthered theoretical sociology, but also bought to center stage what Merton called theories of the middle range. These theories existed between what their colleague C. Wright Mills called abstracted empiricism, which was gathering data for their own sake, without any connection to a body of theory, and grand theory, which had little or no connection to the real world and was only significant to the originating theorist and his followers. For Merton and Lazarsfeld, the most productive theoretical forms were those grounded in empirical data, and used to guide further research and theoretical development.

The influence of Merton and Lazarsfeld reached a broad audience at Columbia and the Russell Sage Foundation. Indeed, Merton would be a mentor to several generations of promising sociologists toiling at the boundaries and increasing the scientific rigor of contemporary sociology. Included among them were Peter Blau, James Coleman, Lewis and Rose Coser, Alvin Gouldner, Seymor Martin Lipset, Alice Rossi, and Arthur Stinchcomb. To these one could add Stephen and Jonathan Cole, Harriet Zuckerman, and Tom Gieryn, who Merton mentored in the social studies of science.

Merton was an unreconstructed pioneer working at the outer boundaries of his wide range of interests. He had a mind that constantly found the unique in the ordinary. Behind the incredible intellect was a loyal and exceptionally principled man committed to fairness and the highest professional standards. A case in point was his participation in a spontaneously organized, grassroots write-in campaign to get his old friend and mentor Pitirim Sorokin on the ballot for presidency of the American Sociological Association. The idea emerged from a conversation among O. D. Duncan, Beverly Duncan, and Albert J. Reiss, Jr. They recalled that Sorokin had yet to receive the traditional renomination for the office after his earlier defeat by Florian Znaniecki in 1952. In order to right the perceived wrong they formed a committee for his presidential renomination. Among those first contacted was Merton, who

not only accepted membership, but suggested that they begin by forming a committee of correspondence, followed by a mass mailing of postcards to solicit support for Sorokin. This committee of 8 reached 677 others with its initial letter. Among them were those who also chose to participate and in the process contacted 1,026 voting members of the ASA in their first mailings. By February 1963 almost all voting members of the ASA were aware of the campaign. In the end Sorokin received 1,344 votes out of the 2,073 votes cast. The strategy suggested by Merton, and implemented by the committee and the converts, had attained its goal and purpose. In the process it also righted a historical wrong (Johnston 1987).

On February 23, 2003 Merton died of terminal cancer in New York City. As many at his memorial service that May proclaimed, he had opened new areas of study, crafted many new and important ideas, and was a role model for the practice of the craft. He had lived an incredibly active and productive life characterized by engagement, brilliance, broad learning, endurance, and integrity. He was an exemplar of the classical scholar in an age of specialization.

SEE ALSO: American Sociological Association; Anomie; Lazarsfeld, Paul; Mills, C. Wright; Sorokin, Pitirim A.; Theory and Methods; Znaniecki, Florian

REFERENCES AND SUGGESTED READINGS

Heeren, J. (1975) Functional and Critical Sociology: A Study of Two Groups of Contemporary Sociologists. PhD dissertation, Duke University.

Hunt, M. M. (1961) How Does It Come To Be So? Profile of Robert K. Merton. *New Yorker* 5(36): 39–63.

Johnston, B. V. (1987) Pitirim A. Sorokin and the American Sociological Association: The Politics of a Professional Society. *Journal of the History of the Behavioral Sciences* 23 (April): 103–22.

Merton, R. K. (1970) *Science, Technology and Society in Seventeenth-Century England*. Harper & Row, New York.

Merton, R. K. (1984) Socially Expected Durations: A Case Study of Concept Formations in Sociology. In Wallace, W. P. & Robins, R. (Eds.), *Conflict and Consensus: A Festschrift for Lewis A. Coser*. Free Press, New York, pp. 262–83.

Merton, R. K. (1990) On Becoming an Honorand at Jagiellonian University: Social Time and Socio-Cognitive Networks. *International Sociology* 5: 5–10.

Merton, R. K. (1994) A Life of Learning. American Council of Learned Societies, Charles Homer Haskins Lecture. Occasional Paper 25.

Merton, R. K. (1996) Robert K. Merton On Social Structure and Science. Ed. P. Sztompka. University of Chicago Press, Chicago, pp. 339–59.

Merton, R. K. & Sorokin, P. A. (1937) Social Time: A Methodological and Functional Analysis. *American Journal of Sociology* 42: 615–29.

Sorokin, P. A. (1928) *Contemporary Sociological Theories: Through the First Quarter of the Twentieth Century*. Harper & Row, New York.

mesostructure

Jeffery T. Ulmer

As the name suggests, mesostructure refers to the social processes and ordering that occur between the macro and micro levels of social organization. Mesostructure is the level of social analysis within which more macrostructural or cultural arrangements shape and condition situations of interaction between individuals or groups, and within which the latter in turn maintain, modify, or change the former. Mesostructure also provides a perspective from which to study social organization and structure without compromising an emphasis on the importance of interaction process and human agency. Mesostructure therefore extends Herbert Blumer's insight that people collectively and individually act in situations, and situations are conditioned (though not determined) by larger social structures and processes, but the latter are produced and potentially changed by the former.

The term was coined in print by David R. Maines in a 1979 essay in *Contemporary Sociology* titled "Mesostructure and Social Process." Maines further fleshed out the mesostructural perspective in a 1982 essay in *Urban Life*. Peter M. Hall (1987) then more explicitly formalized the notion of mesostructure and how it could guide empirical inquiry. More recently, Hall (1997) has expanded his treatment of mesostructure into an analytical framework for studying the exercise of power at the mesostructural level.

Maines's and Hall's explication of the notion of mesostructure was animated by debate in sociological theory, especially in the 1970s and 1980s, about "the micro–macro problem," and how to link together micro and macro in sociological analysis. They argued that conventional treatments of the micro–macro issue tended to reify a false separation or dualism between the levels of face-to-face interaction processes on one hand, and large-scale social organization and structure on the other.

Drawing on pragmatist ontological assumptions about human social life, they argued that micro and macro levels are not opposed dualisms, and certainly do not require different ontological assumptions and epistemologies. Rather, micro and macro are dialectically linked by social processes and the orders that emerge from them. Both Maines's essays and Hall's address pointed to Anselm Strauss's theory of negotiated order (which Strauss later renamed processual order) and his conceptualization of social worlds as prime exemplars of mesostructural thinking. Maines also argued that the idea was implicit in the work of earlier symbolic interactionists such as Herbert Blumer, Everett Hughes, Tomatsu Shibutani, and Gregory Stone.

Hall's (1987) formalization of mesostructure as an analytical perspective identifies six analytical categories focusing on the interrelationship between macro and micro:

1 *Process and temporality* focus attention on the ways in which past actions condition and constrain decisions and activities in the present, and the ways in which actors project future scenarios and strategies.
2 *Conventions and practices* focus attention on the generally shared, habitual, taken-for-granted ground rules for action and interaction. Conventions and practices facilitate cooperation and coordination, but also constrain participants' alternatives and choices.
3 *Collective activity* draws attention to chains of joint actions by two or more individuals with regard to some social object. Parenting, business enterprise, social movements,

and war are examples of such collective activity.

4 *Networks* are the sets of linkages, representing transactions or relationships, between actors. To study social networks is therefore to study mesostructure.

5 *Resources and power* are essential to mesostructural analysis. Resources represent "any attribute, possession, or circumstance" at the disposal of collective or individual actors to achieve desired goals. Power is seen as the capacity to achieve goals, gain compliance, overcome resistance, or limit others' alternatives.

6 *Grounding* lodges micro-level interaction and decisions in historical, cultural, and structural contexts. Grounding interaction processes in such contexts is essential for understanding the conditions, constraints, and opportunities that shape situations of interaction.

More recently, Hall (1997) has elaborated on the fifth analytical category above (resources and power) and pushed the idea of mesostructure toward a theory of what he calls "metapower." Key mechanisms for wielding metapower are: (1) the ability to exercise strategic agency; (2) the ability to construct and routinize rules, regulations, and conventions that govern others; (3) the ability to structure situational contexts and establish relational control of others; (4) the ability to shape group culture and the socialization of group members; and (5) the ability to enroll subordinates as delegates. These analytical categories thus enable sociologists to analyze the exercise of power at the mesostructural level.

Mesostructural analysis, in principle, could be done with either quantitative or qualitative methods, so long as there is an emphasis on agency, interaction process, and situational embeddedness. Hall's (Hall & McGinty 1997) empirical work on national and state education policy and local schools is a particularly good methodological exemplar. On the other hand, quantitative data could be potentially useful for assessing the distribution and variation of mesostructural processes across large numbers of empirical cases, or for documenting the quantifiable characteristics of situations or local contexts and how they relate to the outcomes of interaction.

Several explicit empirical applications of mesostructure exist across a variety of substantive topics, in addition to Hall's research on education noted above. Maines and Morrione (1990) interpret Blumer's analysis of industrialization and social change in mesostructural terms. Clarke's (1991) and Fine's (1984) applications of negotiated order and social worlds perspectives to organizational theory are very mesostructural. In addition, research has analyzed mesostructure in criminal courts and sentencing (Ulmer 1997), prisons (Thomas 1984), the accounting profession (Fischer & Dirsmith 1995), marriage and the family (Pestello & Voydanoff 1991), and other topics.

Anthony Giddens's theory of structuration and Pierre Bourdieu's theory of field and habitus are very parallel and compatible concepts with mesostructure, though there appears to have been little recognition of their common ground in the sociological literature. As Maines and Hall point out, however, the notion of mesostructural analysis in symbolic interactionism thinking considerably predates the work of Giddens and Bourdieu.

SEE ALSO: Habitus/Field; Micro-Macro Links; Social Worlds; Symbolic Interaction

REFERENCES AND SUGGESTED READINGS

Clarke, A. (1991) Social Worlds/Arenas Theory as Organizational Theory. In: Maines, D. R. (Ed.), *Social Organization and Social Process: Essays in Honor of Anselm Strauss.* Aldine de Gruyter, New York, pp. 119–58.

Fine, G. A. (1984) Negotiated Orders and Organizational Cultures. *Annual Review of Sociology* 10: 239–62.

Fischer, M. & Dirsmith, M. (1995) Strategy, Technology, and Social Processes within Professional Cultures: A Negotiated Order, Ethnographic Perspective. *Symbolic Interaction* 18: 381–412.

Hall, P. M. (1987) Interactionism and the Study of Social Organization. *Sociological Quarterly* 28: 1–22.

Hall, P. M. (1997) Meta-Power, Social Organization, and the Shaping of Social Action. *Symbolic Interaction* 20: 397–418.

Hall, P. M. & McGinty, P. (1997) Policy as the Transformation of Intentions: Producing Program from Statute. *Sociological Quarterly* 38: 439–67.

Maines, D. R. (1979) Mesostructure and Social Process. *Contemporary Sociology* 8: 524–7.

Maines, D. R. (1982) In Search of Mesostructure: Studies in the Negotiated Order. *Urban Life* 11: 267–79.

Maines, D. R. & Morrione, T. (1990) On the Breadth and Relevance of Blumer's Perspective: Introduction to his Analysis of Industrialization. In: Blumer, H., *Industrialization as an Agent of Social Change.* Aldine de Gruyter, New York, pp. xi–xxiv.

Pestello, F. & Voydanoff, P. (1991) In Search of Mesostructure in the Family: An Interactionist Approach to the Division of Labor. *Symbolic Interaction* 14: 105–28.

Thomas, J. (1984) Some Aspects of Negotiated Order, Loose Coupling, and Mesostructure in Maximum Security Prisons. *Symbolic Interaction* 7: 213–31.

Ulmer, J. (1997) *Social Worlds of Sentencing: Court Communities Under Sentencing Guidelines.* State University of New York Press, Albany.

meta-analysis

J. I. (Hans) Bakker

There are at least three distinct meanings of the term "meta-analysis" in social science. It can be used to indicate (1) a literature review of a body of empirical findings, especially in psychology; (2) a summary of replication research on a specific topic; or (3) a theoretical or methodological analysis of the complex philosophical problems associated with commonalities in scientific approaches. The first usage is common in psychology while the second is often used in physical science. Such reflexivity is predicated on an inductive approach. Involved in the third usage is, for example, Ritzer's (1975a, b) emphasis on the importance of *paradigmatic* "metatheory." His schema for analyzing sociological theory involves a "meta-meta-analysis" of three kinds of metatheory: (1) a means for deeper *understanding*; (2) a *prelude* to theory construction; and (3) a source of *overarching perspectives* (Ritzer & Goodman 2004: A-1 to A-22).

All calls for "reflexive sociology" (e.g., Bourdieu & Wacquant 1992) could be considered meta-analyses. A meta-analysis of methodological exemplars for different paradigms is often viewed as part and parcel of a metatheory, although there is a meta-method, as well. The second-order analysis of any theoretical formulation involves an attempt to clarify the relationship between that theory and other theories. Therefore, it is important to examine epistemological, ontological, axiological, and other philosophical aspects of the theory and its attendant methodology. For example, a discussion of "methodological individualism" requires sorting out the ontological assumption that only individual human beings are real versus the methodological assumption that real collectivities can be empirically studied through analysis of data which have been gathered through interviews of people who are members of such collectivities (e.g., organizations, neighborhoods). If the two assumptions are conflated, then a meta-analysis that assumes all studies that are based on individual-level interviews are representative of the category "methodological individualism" would be incorrect (Lukes 1994). A certain amount of "boundary work" is necessary in science (Gieryn 1983), and that is also true in social science. Merton (1976) argues that there may be conflicting norms in science. The ambiguous content of social scientific theories may create a certain degree of ambivalence concerning the degree to which certain criteria should be foregrounded. For example, there may be disputes in metatheory as to whether there should be theoretical or empirical commonalities that are emphasized. Theories can be similar to one another and yet have widely different applications to substantive topics. A theory developed in the study of deviance may be relevant to the study of social conflict but may also pertain to a meta-analysis of topics such as socialization and collective behavior. Meta-analysis is difficult to carry out. To take a bird's-eye view of a substantive field and decide on commonalities requires an intimate knowledge of that field as well as a philosophical grasp of fundamental assumptions.

SEE ALSO: Economic Determinism; Metatheory; Methods; Paradigms; Science/Non-Science and Boundary Work

REFERENCES AND SUGGESTED READINGS

Bourdieu, P. & Wacquant, L. J. D. (1992) *An Invitation to Reflexive Sociology*. University of Chicago Press, Chicago.

Gieryn, T. F. (1983) Boundary-Work and the Demarcation of Science from Non-Science. *American Sociological Review* 48(6): 781–95.

Lukes, S. (1994) Methodological Individualism Reconsidered. In: Martin, M. & McIntyre, L. C. (Eds.), *Readings in the Philosophy of Social Science*. MIT Press, Cambridge, MA, pp. 451–8.

Merton, R. K. (1976) *Sociological Ambivalence and Other Essays*. Free Press, New York.

Ritzer, G. (1975a) *Sociology: A Multiple Paradigm Science*. Allyn & Bacon, Boston.

Ritzer, G. (1975b) Sociology: A Multiple Paradigm Science. *American Sociologist* 10: 156–67.

Ritzer, G. & Goodman, D. J. (2004) *Sociological Theory*, 6th edn. McGraw-Hill, Boston.

metatheory

George Ritzer

A metatheory is a broad perspective that overarches two, or more, theories. There are many metatheories – positivism, postpositivism, hermeneutics, and so on – of importance in sociology and other social sciences. Two of the best known and most important are methodological holism and methodological individualism. Methodological holism takes as its basic unit of analysis, and focuses most of its attention on, "social wholes" such as social structures, social institutions, imperatively coordinated associations, and capitalism. It overarches such large-scale, macro-level theories as structural functionalism, conflict theory, and some varieties of neo-Marxian theory. Methodological individualism takes as its unit of analysis and focal concern individual-level phenomena such as the mind, self, action, accounts, behavior, rational action, and so on. It overarches a series of micro-level theories such as symbolic interactionism, ethnomethodology, exchange theory, and rational choice theory. There is a third, methodological relationism, that concerns itself with the relationship between social wholes and social individuals and overarches a series of theories that arose mainly in the 1980s to compensate for the micro- and macro-extremism of the two extant metatheories. Methodological relationism encompasses a number of largely American micro–macro theories and more European agency–structure theories.

A particularly useful term to use in thinking about metatheories is Thomas Kuhn's famous, albeit highly ambiguous and controversial, notion of a paradigm. In fact, a paradigm is broader than a metatheory because it encompasses not only theories, but also methods, images of the subject matter of sociology, and a body of work that serves as an exemplar for those who work within the paradigm (Ritzer 1975).

The social facts paradigm derives its name and orientation from the work of Émile Durkheim and his contention that sociology should involve the study of social facts that are external to and coercive over individuals. He distinguished between two broad types of social facts – material (now most commonly called social structures) and non-material (now usually called social institutions). The two major theories subsumed under this heading are structural functionalism and conflict theory, and to a lesser extent systems theory. The social definition paradigm derives its name from W. I. Thomas's "definition of the situation" (if people define situations as real, they are real in their consequences). Symbolic interactionism is a theoretical component of the social definition paradigm, as is ethnomethodology. Finally, there is the social behavior paradigm, adopting a focus on behavior from the psychological behaviorists, especially B. F. Skinner. Exchange theory and rational choice would be included in this paradigm.

The relatively narrow macro (social facts) and micro (social definition and social behavior) foci of extant paradigms led to the delineation of a more integrated sociological paradigm. Marx and his dialectical approach, especially to the relationship between the capitalists and proletariat on one side and the structures of capitalism on the other, are taken as the exemplar of this approach and this paradigm can be seen as encompassing the micro–macro and agency–structure theories mentioned above.

Metatheorizing can be seen as a specific form of metasociology that examines sociological theory. While sociological theorizing attempts to make sense of the social world, metatheorizing attempts to make sense of sociological theorizing. As with other forms of metastudy, reflexivity is a crucial component of sociological metatheorizing. All metatheorizing involves a high level of reflexivity, although the highest level of reflexivity is found among metatheorists.

Metasociology encompasses not only metatheorizing, but also meta-methods and meta-data-analysis. Meta-methods involves the reflexive study of the discipline's various methods, while meta-data-analysis takes as its subject a range of studies of a given phenomenon and seeks to gain an overall sense of them and to aggregate the data in order to come to a more general conclusion about a particular issue.

A wide variety of work can be included under the heading of sociological metatheorizing. What distinguishes this work is not so much the process of metatheorizing (it may vary greatly in a variety of ways), but rather the nature of the end products. There are three varieties of metatheorizing, largely defined by differences in their end products.

The first type, "metatheorizing as a means of attaining a deeper understanding of theory (Mu)," involves the study of theory in order to produce a better, more profound understanding of extant theory. Mu is concerned, more specifically, with the study of theories, theorists, and communities of theorists, as well as with the larger intellectual and social contexts of theories and theorists.

The second type, "metatheorizing as a prelude to theory development (Mp)," entails the study of extant theory in order to produce new sociological theory. Thus Marx's intensive (and critical) study of the theoretical work of economists like Adam Smith and David Ricardo, philosophers such as Georg Hegel and the Young Hegelians, utopian socialists such as Charles Fourier and Pierre-Joseph Proudhon, and many others provided the basis for his own theory. More contemporaneously, the McDonaldization thesis is derived, at least in part, from a study of the theories of Max Weber, especially his theory of rationalization.

The third type, "metatheorizing as a source of overarching theoretical perspectives (Mo)," is oriented to the goal of producing a perspective, a metatheory, that overarches some part or all of sociological theory. Alexander's attempts to develop a "general theoretical logic for sociology," as well as his later effort to develop a postpositivist approach, would both be examples of this third type of metatheorizing.

Although metatheorizing takes place in other fields, it is particularly characteristic of sociology. The prevalence of metatheorizing in sociology is rooted in the fact that sociologists deal with culturally diverse and historically specific subjects. This makes universal truth claims difficult or impossible. The failure to discover universal truths and invariant laws of the social world has informed many metatheoretical efforts. The clashes of multiple paradigms competing in the realm of sociological theorizing create a perfect condition for the emergence of metatheoretical discourse.

Social theory is embedded not only in academia but also in the larger society. As a result, there are a series of larger forces that impinge on, even control, it. Metatheorizing serves to alert theorists to the existence of these forces as well as to the need to resist them.

The coming of age of metatheorizing in American sociology can be traced to the collapse of the dominant social facts paradigm during the 1960s. That paradigm, especially its major theoretical component, Parsonsian functionalism, had dominated American sociology for more than two decades before it was seriously challenged by rival paradigms, as well as critics from a wide range of other perspectives. The emergence of a multiparadigmatic structure in sociology in the late 1960s reflected the growing disunity of the discipline and increasingly fragmented sociological research. There emerged a widespread feeling that sociology was facing a profound crisis. It was this sense of imminent disciplinary crisis that helped to invigorate meta-analyses of all types. At first, this took the form of what was, at the time, called the sociology of sociology. Later, metasociology had to overcome strongly negative views of the sociology of sociology as being dominated by minor studies of trivial aspects of the discipline. However, metasociology, especially metatheorizing, has survived, even prospered, as the sociology of sociology and its weaknesses have receded into history.

A more recent challenge and spur to metatheorizing is the rise of postmodern social theory. Since the latter involves an assault on rationality and the modern orientation and metatheorizing is both modern and rational, it has come to be questioned by postmodernists. On the other hand, postmodernism has provided metatheorists with a whole series of new tools and approaches with which to study theory.

One example is deconstruction, a form of textual criticism that scrutinizes the ways in which texts, including theoretical texts, are constructed. A deconstructionist takes a finished text and analyzes the ways in which various literary devices and strategies of argumentation are used to give the impression of a coherent whole.

One important deconstructionist technique is decentering. This can mean several things to metatheorists. First, it might mean moving away from according primacy to the author (especially one associated with the discipline's canon) and giving up on the objective of attempting to discern what an author "really" means.

Second, it can mean the end of the effort to get to the heart, or central meaning, of a theory. Rather, the objective might be to focus on more promising peripheral aspects of that theory. Certain passages of specific works often are presented in such a way that they are made to seem of central importance. Over the years, metatheorists have tended to emphasize those passages or to enshrine other passages as being of key importance. In this context, deconstructionism leads one away from the familiar passages and into ignored aspects of the theory or perhaps rarely read footnotes.

Third, it might be advisable to focus on an undecidable moment in the history of social theory and an analysis of some of the courses taken and, more importantly from the point of view of deconstructionism, not taken by social theory.

Fourth, an effort might be made to reverse the resident hierarchy, only to displace it. There is, for example, a clear hierarchy of schools of sociological theory and there is a tendency to devote most attention to the leading schools. This suggests that what metatheorists need to do is focus more attention on the most marginal of schools (this is another version of decentering) for their marginality may tell us a great deal about the theoretical system

in which they exist. Furthermore, their very marginality may make them far easier to study than high-ranking theoretical perspectives. This is traceable to the fact that those associated with lower-ranking perspectives have little to hide, while thinkers linked with the premier schools have a vested interest in concealing things that may adversely affect their exalted status. Similarly, specific ideas have come to be seen as of central importance in every theoretical perspective. These ideas tend to come to the fore any time a given theory is examined or discussed. However, it is entirely possible that important ideas have been lost and a search for those marginal ideas could pay huge dividends.

However, the search for marginal schools, theorists, or ideas should not be turned into a routine or into a new, albeit reversed, hierarchy. Deconstructionism leads to the idea that all such routines, or hierarchies, need to be continually displaced. This prevents metatheoretical work from settling into any comfortable routines; any new construction immediately must be deconstructed.

It is this last aspect of deconstructionism that has the most important implications for metatheorizing. As modernists, most metatheorists have implicitly engaged in deconstruction, but almost always with the objective that they and/or those influenced by their work would engage in a process of reconstruction. This could involve the rebuilding of the theory they have just deconstructed or the use of the lessons learned to create an entirely new theoretical perspective. As modernists, most metatheorists would reject the idea of deconstruction in order to further deconstruct. Rather, they would be oriented to the modern view of progress toward the goal of the ultimate theoretical perspective, or truth about it. However, as with all modern notions, this seeks an end or closure of the theoretical "conversation" in the creation of that ultimate theory. The postmodern view is that the goal is not to end the conversation in some ultimate truth, but rather to continually deconstruct in order to keep the conversation going. Such an objective makes sense for metatheoretical work; in fact, it may be *the* raison d'être for such work. A round of metatheoretical work may be seen as merely the basis for the next one and not as aimed at some ultimate and conclusive objective. In these terms, metatheorizing may be seen as the exercise par excellence in keeping the theoretical conversation going.

While it is possible to look at postmodern theory as a threat to modern forms of metatheorizing, it also is possible to see it as offering an array of provocative new ideas that could be of great use to it and point it in a variety of new directions.

SEE ALSO: Deconstruction; Durkheim, Émile; Hermeneutics; Meta-Analysis; Positivism; Postmodernism; Postpositivisim; Theory Construction

REFERENCES AND SUGGESTED READINGS

Furfey, P. H. (1965) *The Scope and Method of Sociology: A Meta-Sociological Treatise.* Cooper Square, New York.
Kuhn, T. (1970) *The Structure of Scientific Revolutions,* 2nd edn. University of Chicago Press, Chicago.
Ritzer, G. (1975) *Sociology: A Multiple Paradigm Science.* Allyn & Bacon, Boston.
Ritzer, G. (1981) *Toward an Integrated Sociological Paradigm: The Search for an Exemplar and an Image of the Subject Matter.* Allyn & Bacon, Boston.
Ritzer, G. (1991) *Metatheorizing in Sociology.* Lexington Books, Lexington, MA.
Ritzer, G., Zhao, S., & Murphy, J. (2001) Metatheorizing in Sociology: The Basic Parameters and the Potential Contributions of Postmodernism. In: Turner, J. (Ed.), *Handbook of Sociological Theory.* Kluwer, New York, pp. 113–31.
Zhao, S. (2001) Metatheorizing in Sociology. In: Ritzer, G. & Smart, B. (Eds.), *Handbook of Social Theory.* Sage, London, pp. 386–94.

methods

J. I. (Hans) Bakker

In sociology the term methods can encompass different aspects of a methodical approach to empirical research. We can distinguish between "methodology" as the theoretical understanding of basic principles, and "method" as research techniques (Abbot 2001a). The topics discussed under methods often include both. A classical experimental design (CED), with random assignment to an experimental group and a control group, is a basic aspect of methodology, while the importance of the specific statistical techniques that attempt to emulate aspects of a CED (without actually carrying out an experiment) is a topic in statistical methods. In most sociological research there is a multivariant approach. It would be very difficult to actually carry out an experiment on such multivariable models, hence we rely on "path analysis" (Land 1969) to simulate the logic of CED. The term methods is often used to represent specific techniques of research, both quantitative and qualitative, with the underlying logic of utilizing such techniques often left implicit in "normal science" (Kuhn 1970) approaches. But different individuals may be more knowledgeable about one or the other. Thus, for example, all of the inferential statistics, parametric and non-parametric, may be studied as aspects of quantitative methods. Similarly, all aspects of ethnographic fieldwork, open-ended interviewing, and observation may be considered in the context of qualitative methods. We do not consider a person who has specialized in certain techniques a "methodist." We use the term methodologist to cover expertise in either techniques of research (e.g., Manton et al. 1994) or the underlying logic or methodology (e.g., Popper 1969).

There has been considerable work done on specific aspects of both quantitative (Raftery 2005) and qualitative (Atkinson & Delamont 2005) techniques, although there is also an interest in moving beyond the quantitative–qualitative distinction (Ragin 1987). There is a very vibrant literature on statistical techniques. For example, Karl Pearson's "product moment correlation coefficient" (rho, ρ) is based on a set of assumptions, including having data with a ratio or at least an interval "level of measurement." But much sociological data are categorical, numerically ordinal, or even nominal. So many researchers have attempted to use Pearson's ρ with ordinal- or even nominal-level data (Lyons 1971). Similarly, in qualitative data analysis there has been a move away from intuitive scanning of a complex body of material to the use of computer software packages which allow for summaries of aspects of the information gathered, especially blocks of text files. There is an ongoing industry devoted to further refinement of specific techniques used in sociological research.

However, it is important to also consider the ways in which specific techniques relate to general problems in the logic of method. But the logic of method tends to overlap with the philosophy of science. That, in turn, has been influenced by science and technology studies (STS). Work on what actually happens in a laboratory (Latour 1999) provides a window on methodology in the broader sense. In the philosophical discussion of methodology there have been many efforts to discuss types of approaches or frameworks. For example, one widely discussed typology differentiates among positivism, interpretivism, and criticalism (Habermas 1971; Neuman 2006). Those "meta-paradigms" can be seen as requiring quite different ways of collecting and evaluating evidence.

For the positivist social scientist, it is important to stress the epistemological questions related to conducting research in such a way that a truly scientific body of data will be collected. But there is considerable disagreement concerning the precise nature of science in the social sciences (Adorno et al. 1976). The term positivism has many different definitions. Halfpenny (1982) lists 12. Most important today are: (1) an epistemology stressing observation and empirical inquiry; (2) a natural science "social physics" approach to the study of sociological topics; (3) a program for unifying science (Wilson 1998); (4) stress on the hypothetico-deductive method (Hempel 1965; Zetterberg 1965; Wallace 1971); (5) belief in the possibility of causal laws which are transhistorical and transcultural; (6) Popper's (1965 [1934], 1969) "falsificationism." Those who hold rigidly to one or more of those principles can be said to be positivistic.

Many conceive of methods in terms of "positivism and its epistemological others" (Steinmetz 2005). Until the late 1960s there was a strong trend within sociology to try to make the discipline "scientific." Sociology hit a "crisis" and a host of non-positivist methods were reiterated or invented. That crisis was predicted by Gouldner (1970), although he did not foresee the great variety of methodologies that would ensue. A great variety of methods became more acceptable. Pathbreaking was

an inductive "grounded theory" approach (Glaser & Strauss 1967). But the epistemological stress on grounded theory eventually led to a wider discussion reminiscent of the *Methodenstreit* (Nagel 1961: 535–606; Adorno et al. 1976).

The interpretive approach (Alford 1998: 72–85) downplays epistemological concerns and takes distance from physical sciences. Interpretive sociologists accept that the study of human beings is likely to produce different methodologies. One strain can be traced to Wilhelm Dilthey (1989). Another important root source for the interpretive meta-paradigm is Georg Simmel, whose work directly influenced the Chicago School. For the interpretive social scientist it is the question of "philosophical anthropology" that should be highlighted. How are human beings different? Are people different from rocks and stars? Are humans cognitively and emotionally different from other animals, even the higher apes? This sometimes leads to the conclusion that the best methodological approach is to study individual social actors and to regard all "functional" arguments about collective "structures" as ontologically suspect. The Chicago School of Sociology (Bulmer 1984) stresses the interpretive approach, as in the famous study of *The Polish Peasant in Europe and America* (1918–20) by Thomas and Znaniecki, which utilizes the kinds of documents that Dilthey thought highly of (Bulmer 1984: 53).

Where both the positive and the interpretive meta-paradigms tend to agree is that questions of axiology (morals and ethics) as well as long-term, historical teleology (future end goals) are better left out. As Max Weber (1949), following Heinrich Rickert, argued persuasively with regard to his own interpretive sociology (*verstehende Soziologie*), it is important to distinguish between the reasons we carry out research studies and the way in which we examine the evidence. A topic may have "value relevance" but the actual study, positive or interpretive, should strive to be as "value neutral" as possible.

The strong dissenting voice on this question of axiology and teleology is critical theory. The term is derived from the Frankfurt School but has gained wider coinage. Criticalists feel that some specific value or future end goal is of such importance that considerations of epistemology and ontology are less important. Those who hold to this position tend to emphasize the ways in which notions of value-free objectivity can be used to justify certain kinds of policy. The neo-Marxian version of the critical approach is summarized by Gouldner (1962) in his critique of Weberian value freedom. Feminists (Harding 1986) also emphasize axiology and teleology, a society that has eliminated "patriarchy." Other forms of criticalism are environmentalism and Gandhianism.

Considerable debate continues to mark sociological research studies. The topic of triangulation has led to many different ways of conceiving a multimethod approach. The idea that it would be possible in principle to combine insights from positive, interpretive, and critical meta-paradigms is a key to Habermas's general theory. Bourdieu (1984) has utilized multiple correspondence analysis (MCA), a form of data reduction based on dual scaling.

This has led to acceptance by some of a fourth attitude toward methods which can be called the postmodernist meta-paradigm in sociology. The social science version of postmodernism is a rejection of all "foundationalisms." That lack of any methodological foundations does not, however, restrict postmodernist thinkers like Foucault, Baudrillard, Barthes, Lyotard, and Derrida from holding positions. A distinction needs to be made between postmodern epistemology and empirical study of the phenomena of late modernism (Mirchandani 2005). There have been modernist approaches to the study of postmodern societies (Ritzer 2004).

The confusion caused by the existence of many paradigms within sociology (Ritzer 1980) has led to a lack of agreement on methods. There is some question as to whether the "incommensurability" of paradigms may be overstated (Freidheim 1979). Nevertheless, those who adhere to a specific approach tend to continue to refine and adjust their own methods and invent new techniques. The ways in which specific approaches have been promoted have sometimes led to distortions of the historical record. Marx is often perceived as a contributor to scientific Marxist theory, but his Marxism is often interpretive and his scientific arguments are frequently clouded by his teleological goal: a future communist ideal society.

Durkheim is frequently still viewed as a follower of Comte who established a "scientific" approach to sociological research by using the logic of statistical argument. Durkheim's *Rules* and his *Suicide* are introduced to many students as adequate representations of Durkheim's œuvre, but that ignores his interest in social change and the division of labor. Max Weber is usually seen as a comparative-historical researcher, but he also carried out empirical work on farm labor and on factory workers (Lazarsfeld & Oberschall 1964). Platt (1996) has applied historical, archival methods to the study of the history of sociological research methods and has corrected many fallacious interpretations.

The move from cross-tabulation to regression and path analysis in sociology in the 1970s (Heise 1969; Land 1969) led to speculation concerning the possibility of a mathematical and statistical approach to sociology (Kemeny & Snell 1962; Beauchamp 1970), but to date the discipline as a whole has not embraced mathematical sociology.

Ragin (2000) has criticized the conventional approach to quantitative methods. He points out that researchers are often insensitive to the difficulty of determining a population. He also points out that we need to distinguish between necessary and sufficient conditions when making causal claims. He introduces a qualitative comparative analysis (QCA) that emphasizes the comparison of diverse cases. Ragin also indicates the usefulness of fuzzy sets versus crisp sets (Laio 2001). There has been significant rethinking of fundamental assumptions once taken as axiomatic (Abbot 2001b).

In the future it is likely that techniques such as partial least squares (PLS), singular value decomposition (SVD), penalized logistic regression (PLR), and recursive feature elimination (RFE) will lead to more sophisticated techniques for the study of complex sociological systems. Secondary data sets generate a large volume of sociological data. Bioinformatics (Chen & Wong 2005) will probably be extended to human social structures. Bayesian statistics will also be important (Iverson 1969).

SEE ALSO: Chicago School; Critical Qualitative Research; Critical Theory/Frankfurt School; Durkheim, Émile; Epistemology; Experimental Design; Experimental Methods;

Falsification; Grounded Theory; Mathematical Sociology; Methods, Arts-Based; Methods, Bootstrap; Methods, Case Study; Methods, Mixed; Methods, Postcolonial; Methods, Visual; Positivism; Quantitative Methods; Simmel, Georg; Statistical Significance Testing; Theory and Methods; Validity, Qualitative; Validity, Quantitative; Weber, Max

REFERENCES AND SUGGESTED READINGS

Abbott, A. (2001a) *Chaos of Disciplines*. University of Chicago Press, Chicago.

Abbott, A. (2001b) *Time Matters*. University of Chicago Press, Chicago.

Adorno, T. W., Albert, H., Dahrendorf, R., Habermas, J., Pilot, H., & Popper, K. R. (1976) *The Positivist Dispute in German Sociology*. Introduction by D. Frisby. Trans. G. Adey & D. Frisby. Heinemann, London.

Alford, R. R. (1998) *The Craft of Inquiry: Theories, Methods, Evidence*. Oxford University Press, New York.

Atkinson, P. & Delamont, S. (2005) Qualitative Research Traditions. In: Calhoun, C., Rojek, C., & Turner, B. (Eds.), *The Sage Handbook of Sociology*. Sage, London, pp. 40–60.

Beauchamp, M. A. (1970) *Elements of Mathematical Sociology*. Random House, New York.

Bourdieu, P. (1984) *Distinction: A Social Critique of the Judgment of Taste*. Trans. R. Nice. Harvard University Press, Cambridge, MA.

Bulmer, M. (1984) *The Chicago School of Sociology: Institutionalization, Diversity, and the Rise of Sociological Research*. University of Chicago Press, Chicago.

Chen, Y.-P. P. & Wong, L. (Eds.) (2005) *Proceedings of the Third Asia-Pacific Bioinformatics Conference*. Imperial College Press, London.

Dilthey, W. (1989) *Introduction to the Human Sciences: Selected Works*, Vol. 1. Trans. and Ed. R. A. Makkreel & F. Rodi. Princeton University Press, Princeton.

Freidheim, E. (1979) An Empirical Comparison of Ritzer's Paradigms and Similar Metatheories: A Research Note. *Social Forces* 58(1): 59–66.

Glaser, B. G. & Strauss, A. L. (1967) *The Discovery of Grounded Theory: Strategies for Qualitative Research*. Aldine de Gruyter, New York.

Gouldner, A. (1962) Anti-Minotaur: The Myth of Value-Free Sociology. *Social Problems* 9: 199–213.

Gouldner, A. (1970) *The Coming Crisis in Western Sociology*. Heinemann, London.

Habermas, J. (1971) *Knowledge and Human Interests*. Trans. J. J. Shapiro. Beacon Press, Boston.

Halfpenny, P. (1982) *Positivism and Sociology: Explaining Social Life*. George Allen & Unwin, London.

Harding, S. (1986) *The Science Question in Feminism*. Cornell University Press, Ithaca, NY.

Heise, D. R. (1969) Problems in Path Analysis and Causal Inferences. In: Borgatta, E. F. & Bohrsted, G. W. (Eds.), *Sociological Methodology*. Jossey Bass, San Francisco, pp. 38–73.

Iverson, G. R. (1969) Statistics According to Bayes. In: Borgatta, E. F. & Bohrsted, G. W. (Eds.), *Sociological Methodology*. Jossey Bass, San Francisco, pp. 185–99.

Kemeny, J. G. & Snell, J. L. (1962) *Mathematical Models in the Social Sciences*. Ginn, Blaisdell, New York.

Kuhn, T. S. (1970) *The Structure of Scientific Revolutions*, 2nd edn, enlarged. University of Chicago Press, Chicago.

Land, K. C. (1969) Principles of Path Analysis. In: Borgatta, E. F. & Bohrsted, G. W. (Eds.), *Sociological Methodology*. Jossey Bass, San Francisco, pp. 3–37.

Latour, B. (1999) *Pandora's Hope: Essays on the Reality of Science Studies*. Harvard University Press, Cambridge, MA.

Lazarsfeld, P. F. & Oberschall, A. R. (1964) Max Weber and Empirical Social Research. *American Sociological Review* 30(1): 185–99.

Liao, T. F. (2001) Fuzzy-Set Social Science. *Social Forces* 80(1): 354–6.

Lyons, M. (1971) Techniques for Using Ordinal Measures in Regression and Path Analysis. In: Costner, H. L. (Ed.), *Sociological Methodology*. Jossey Bass, San Francisco, pp. 147–71.

Manton, K. G., Woodbury, M. A., & Tolley, H. D. (1994) *Statistical Applications Using Fuzzy Sets*. Wiley, New York.

Mirchandani, R. (2005) Postmodernism and Sociology: From the Epistemological to the Empirical. *Sociological Theory* 23(1): 86–115.

Nagel, E. (1961) *The Structure of Science: Problems in the Logic of Scientific Explanation*. Harcourt, Brace, & World, New York.

Neuman, W. L. (2006) *Social Research Methods: Qualitative and Quantitative Approaches*, 6th edn. Pearson Education, Allyn & Bacon, Boston.

Platt, J. (1996) *A History of Sociological Research Methods in America: 1920–1960*. Cambridge University Press, Cambridge.

Popper, K. (1965 [1934]) *The Logic of Scientific Discovery*. Harper & Row, New York.

Popper, K. (1969) *Conjectures and Refutations: The Growth of Scientific Knowledge*, 3rd edn. Routledge & Kegan Paul, London.

Raftery, A. E. (2005) Quantitative Research Methods. In: Calhoun, C., Rojek, C., & Turner, B. (Eds.), *The Sage Handbook of Sociology*. Sage, London, pp. 15–39.

Ragin, C. (1987) *The Comparative Method: Moving Beyond Qualitative and Quantitative Strategies*. University of California Press, Berkeley.

Ragin, C. (2000) *Fuzzy-Set Social Science*. University of Chicago Press, Chicago.

Ritzer, G. (1980) *Sociology: A Multiple Paradigm Science*, rev. edn. Allyn & Bacon, Boston.

Ritzer, G. (2004) *The McDonaldization of Society*, rev. edn. Pine Forge Press, Thousand Oaks, CA.

Steinmetz, G. (Ed.) (2005) *The Politics of Method in the Human Sciences: Positivism and Its Epistemological Others*. Duke University Press, Durham, NC.

Wallace, W. (1971) *The Logic of Science in Sociology*. Aldine Atherton, Chicago.

Weber, M. (1949) *The Methodology of the Social Sciences*. Trans. and Ed. E. A. Shils & H. A. Finch. Free Press, New York.

Wilson, E. O. (1998) The Social Sciences. In: *Consilience: The Unity of Knowledge*. Alfred A. Knopf, New York, pp. 181–209.

Zetterberg, H. L. (1965) *On Theory and Verification in Sociology*, 3rd enlarged edn. Bedminster Press, New York.

methods, arts-based

Tom Barone

The arts and sciences have exhibited fundamental similarities since their beginnings. Each has always been an inherently aesthetic activity. There has always been artistry in science (including the social sciences) as there is inevitably an empirical basis to good art. Other commonalities include the imaginative process that inhabits the work of both the artist and the scientist, the drive of each to illuminate and interpret facets of the physical and social worlds, and the personal nature of these inevitably human enterprises. Indeed, historians of western thought have noted that before the nineteenth century no substantial differences were recognized between the arts and sciences.

Still, following the period of the Enlightenment, the arts and sciences were forced to occupy separate methodological chambers, as within western culture distinctive techniques and modes of representation of each were emphasized. This strict segregation within an art/science dichotomy was most famously described in C. P. Snow's *The Two Cultures* (1959). This dualism, reaching its crescendo during the reign of the logical positivists, led to a widespread assumption among social scientists that any trafficking in artistic premises, principles, or procedures serves to sully and discredit their work.

Nevertheless, within the twentieth century certain developments began challenging the clear distinction drawn between the two cultures by social scientists referred to as *traditionalists* or *modernists*. Within the newly legitimated qualitative approaches to social science research, a heightened use of arts-based methods became evident. Qualitative researchers in the human studies were increasingly employing approaches to inquiry and representation that had, since the nineteenth century, been associated primarily with the literary arts.

This spate of methodological experimentation became obvious in the 1970s, during a phase of qualitative research called the moment of blurred genres (Denzin & Lincoln 1998). Against that intellectual backdrop, Robert Nisbet, in his 1976 book *Sociology as an Art Form*, declared boldly that the science of sociology is "also one of the arts – nourished . . . by precisely the same kinds of creative imagination which are to be found in such areas as music, painting, poetry, the novel, and drama" (p. 9).

During this period, only a few commentators could be found insisting that art and science are identical. Nevertheless, the anthropologist/storyteller Clifford Geertz (1973) famously observed that within the human studies the boundary between Snow's cultures was indeed becoming increasingly "blurred." In social criticism, journalism, ethnography, educational studies, and elsewhere, experimentations with arts-based methods and representational forms yielded literary-style ethnographic essays, New Journalistic reportage, sociological portraits, and so on.

This experimentation with, and recognition of, aesthetic design elements in social research texts gained momentum through subsequent decades. Increasing attention was paid to the "poetics" of social texts. Visual images and other modes of disclosure could be found accompanying the written word in multimedia texts. The idea of performing study findings was recommended as a means of enhancing their impact on the research audience. Some methodologists questioned the value of, and some researchers defied, the established boundary between fact and fiction in textual representations.

Most of these researcher-pioneers in the human studies continued to identify themselves as social scientists rather than as artists, no doubt because of their academic training and professional socialization. Most were sociologists and ethnographers who nevertheless came to appreciate the potential power and utility of literary elements in disclosing their research findings. But this aestheticization of the social sciences was matched by a parallel movement in which social researchers who identified themselves as *artists* began to emphasize the empirical basis of art-making.

This emphasis accompanied the intellectual overthrow of the formalists within the field of art criticism. The formalists had characterized art as the creation of an inevitably elaborate construction of illusion. The work of art, in this view, is designed to transport the viewer to an aesthetic remove, bracketed off from the nearby world of experience. Pragmatist and postmodernist critics, however, successfully argued against this radically subjectivist rationale, noting that the roots of the arts, like those of all human endeavors, are planted in the mundane, "real" world of social commerce. The artist was now revealed as "searching" (and "re-searching") for empirical evidence to be shaped into aesthetic content in the ongoing stream of everyday life. Honoring this new emphasis, an innovative group of scholars began to imagine a new form of social research.

The term arts-based research was first used by qualitative researchers within the field of education. Elliot Eisner, an arts educator and painter, is credited with coining the term (1979). Eisner was initially interested in the application of arts criticism to phenomena within the fields of educational evaluation. What, he asked, might be learned from critics of theater, painting, literature, architecture, etc., for better appreciating and disclosing dimensions of schooling? Later, Eisner and others began to advocate for (and experiment with) renderings that were not pieces of art criticism, but texts that themselves resembled works of literary art (e.g., the poem, novel, novella, short story, life story, autobiography, memoir) and, more iconoclastically, works of plastic or performing art (e.g., film, ethnodrama, readers theater, collage, painting, multimedia installations, and digital hypertext).

However, while most arts-based researchers refused to label themselves as social scientists, many of the research methods and writing strategies employed (especially by those working in literary genres) were comparable and even identical to those used by qualitative researchers in sociology and cultural anthropology. These included interviewing, participant observation, gaining rapport with informants, the use of "thick description," and so on.

Still more overlap could be found in a prominent list of methodological features of arts-based research (Barone & Eisner 1997). These features included (1) the creation of *virtual textual realities*, literary, storied recreations of lived worlds through the use of language that is (2) *expressive* rather than declarative, and (3) *vernacular/contextual* rather than technical/abstract. The use of contextualized and expressive language promotes vicarious participation in the lives of informants/story characters and thereby (4) *empathic understanding* of their worldviews. Within the same text, several perspectives may be represented. Some may stand in contrast to others.

The researcher's perspective is also included as the text is shaped into an expressive (5) *aesthetic form*. This form exists within a dialectical relationship with aesthetic content, or empirical observations, embodied within the work. The resulting work bears the researcher's (6) *personal signature*, one crafted to reflect his or her perspective on the phenomena under study. But the researcher's perspective is meant to stand, without special privilege, alongside that of the others, within an open, or indeterminate, text that creates in the reader a sense of (7) *ambiguity*. This "writerly" text, with multiple perspectives enhanced, signals a refusal to supply the reader with a final, single, correct meaning of events. Moreover, it demands his or her active reconstruction (or "rewriting") of textual meaning and significance.

The overlap between the arts and social sciences is evident in this list in at least three ways. First, it honors the reality stemming from traditional social science that, for most arts-based researchers, words rather than non-verbal symbols and images have continued to be the preferred mode of expression. Second, several of these supposedly "arts-based" textual characteristics can be found in aesthetically sensitive social science texts. The emphasis on empathic understanding, for example, is reminiscent of Weber's formulation of *Verstehen* as a goal of a sociological text that moves beyond cognition into the realms of feeling and motivation.

Finally, since not all of these seven formal design elements can be located in every arts-based text, a research text may be characterized as arts-based to the *degree* that these features are present. This implies a continuum (rather than a clean division) of research texts, with art and (traditional) social science representing the poles.

Still, most current arts-based researchers are unwilling to conflate arts-based and social science research. Insofar as design is associated with function, these seven elements are meant to serve, like the design elements in traditional texts, as means to an end. For many arts-based researchers what most distinguishes their work is indeed the end, or purpose, that its design elements enable it to serve.

In his book *Philosophy and the Mirror of Nature* (1979), Richard Rorty posited two fundamental purposes of human inquiry: the discovery of truth and the enhancement of meaning. Social science has traditionally been primarily aimed toward the first of these – toward an enhancement of certainty; Barone (2000) has suggested that arts-based research usually honors the second.

Within a work of art, meaning – aesthetic substance – is enhanced through an expressive form. Instead of merely stating or declaring, the work of art reconfigures observed and experienced phenomena into a semblance, a composed and shaped apparition. But the purpose of arts-based research texts has also been expressed in other, perhaps more fundamental, ways. What, after all, is the ultimate point of enticing a reader to empathically understand, to "deeply feel," dimensions of lives lived by others, or to appreciate the social world from an array of enhanced perspectives?

Eisner (1991) has argued that the point is to offer considerations to be shared and discussed, reflected on, and debated. The findings of arts-based research are therefore not so much located in Truth as in their ability to refine perception and deepen conversation, or as Geertz (1983) put it, to "increase the precision with which we vex each other."

More fundamentally, the aim of arts-based research may be likened to that of postmodern art, as one of *critical persuasion*. Arts-based projects may be valued according to the degree that they effectively persuade readers to interrogate commonly accepted norms, beliefs, and values. Good arts-based texts will do this through artful redescriptions of social practices and viewpoints that have come to be taken as givens, uncritically accepted as useful and virtuous.

Active reconstructions of the art-based text by readers are invited as the author-researcher relinquishes control of the text – a generous but sometimes anxiety-ridden act that signifies a shift of power in the politics of textual representation and interpretation. As readers from within different experiential and cultural spaces approach the text, its perceived meaning and import will vary. Nevertheless, the text itself maintains a presence, luring its audience into a (re)consideration of the social phenomena portrayed within, into a conversation about perspectives previously unavailable or unrecognized.

As suggested, the purpose of raising questions in the minds of readers stands in contrast to the rationale of traditional, modernist social science, the aim of which may be to enhance certainty about the phenomena under study through the production of valid and reliable knowledge. Many arts-based researchers see the tendency of traditionalist critics to dismiss arts-based research as inappropriate and even dangerous as a failure to grasp this shift in fundamental research purpose. Proponents argue that, because their research honors a historically disregarded but crucial purpose of social inquiry, traditional "goodness" criteria, such as objectivity, validity, and reliability, are inappropriate for judging arts-based research. More appropriate would be an assessment of the degree to which arts-based design elements

2974 *methods, bootstrap*

have been crafted into a form that enhances multiple meanings and so creates doubts and disturbances in the minds of readers of the research text.

For those proponents, arts-based research should be judged in the same manner that works of arts are judged: within open, public reviews and critiques of the value of the work. Judgments about each piece may vary among reviewers; but as with social science-based manuscripts, peer review of arts-based studies is viewed as important for good decision-making regarding suitability for dissemination and publication.

Some critics are willing to accept arts-based studies as useful forms of scholarship or inquiry, but would deny them the label of "social research." Reponses to this denial have varied. While some are content to label their work as "arts-inspired inquiry," other arts-based research proponents emphasize issues of language and power. The term "research" generally carries greater professional prestige than "scholarship" or "inquiry." Others add that the *research* done by dramaturgs, filmmakers, painters, poets, and novelists in preparation for the production of their work is precisely that – even if its features are not identical to those honored by social inquirers with a different research purpose in mind.

SEE ALSO: Epistemology; Ethnography; Investigative Poetics; Methods; Naturalistic Inquiry; Objectivity; Paradigms; Poetics, Social Science; Representation; Subjectivity; Trustworthiness; Validity, Qualitative

REFERENCES AND SUGGESTED READINGS

Banks, A. & Banks, S. (Eds.) (1998) *Fiction and Social Research: By Ice or Fire.* AltaMira Press, Walnut Creek, CA.

Barone, T. (2000) *Aesthetics, Politics, and Educational Inquiry.* Peter Lang, New York.

Barone, T. (2001) *Touching Eternity.* Teachers College Press, New York.

Barone, T. & Eisner, E. (1997) Arts-Based Educational Research. In: Jaeger, R. M. (Ed.), *Complementary Methods for Research in Education.*

American Educational Research Association, Washington, DC, pp. 75–116.

Denzin, N. & Lincoln, Y. (1998) Introduction. In: Denzin, N. & Lincoln, Y. (Eds.), *The Landscape of Qualitative Research: Theories and Issues.* Sage, Thousand Oaks, CA, pp. 1–34.

Eisner, E. W. (1979) *The Educational Imagination.* Macmillan, New York.

Eisner, E. W. (1991) *The Enlightened Eye.* Macmillan, New York.

Ellis, C. & Bochner, B. (Eds.) (1996) *Composing Ethnography.* AltaMira Press, Walnut Creek, CA.

Geertz, C. (1973) *The Interpretation of Cultures.* Basic Books, New York.

Geertz, C. (1983) *Local Knowledge: Further Essays in Interpretive Anthropology.* Basic Books, New York.

Nisbet, R. (1976) *Sociology as an Art Form.* Oxford University Press, New York.

Rorty, R. (1979) *Philosophy and the Mirror of Nature.* Princeton University Press, Princeton.

methods, bootstrap

Xitao Fan

Quantitative researchers in social and behavioral sciences rely heavily on statistical inference. The validity of parametric statistical inference, however, can be in question when the theoretical assumptions are violated. In addition, there may be situations where the theoretical sampling distribution (e.g., function coefficient in discriminant analysis) is not yet known. In these situations, an empirical resampling procedure may be considered as an analytic alternative.

Resampling procedures date back to the permutation test by R. A. Fisher in the 1930s. Quenouille's work on bias estimation by deleting "one observation at a time" and Tukey's "jackknife" approach for standard error estimation made resampling procedures popular. As generally recognized now, Efron (1979) extended the "jackknife" approach to what is now known as the "bootstrap" method.

The basic idea of the bootstrap method is to approximate *empirically* the sampling distribution of an estimator (e.g., regression slope) by repeatedly drawing "bootstrapped" samples from the original sample, using *sampling with replacement* method. From these "bootstrapped" samples, the estimator is obtained and accumulated. With a reasonable number of bootstrapped samples (e.g., from hundreds to thousands, depending on the desired precision), the sampling distribution of the estimator can be approximated empirically. Because *sampling with replacement* method is used in bootstrap resampling, in a given "bootstrapped" sample, a particular observation may appear multiple times. The sample size for each "bootstrapped" sample is the same, and it is generally equal to the original sample size.

Once this sampling distribution is *empirically* approximated via bootstrap resampling, statistical estimation/inference (e.g., bias estimation, confidence interval construction) can be made based on this sampling distribution. For example, in the bootstrap method, a confidence interval for a population parameter can be constructed based on one of several approaches: normal approximation method, percentile method, bias-corrected percentile method, and percentile-*t* method (Stine 1989; Mooney & Duval 1993).

Conventional parametric statistical inference is based on a *theoretical* sampling distribution that typically has some assumptions. For the theoretical sampling distribution (e.g., sampling distribution of regression slope) to work well, the data must satisfy these assumptions (e.g., normality, homoscedasticity). However, because bootstrapped sampling distribution is approximated *empirically* from the data at hand, rather than derived theoretically under certain assumptions, the bootstrap method has few theoretical assumptions; as a result, the bootstrap method is considered a non-parametric approach. As discussed by Lunnenborg (2000), statistical inference typically relies on ideal data/model assumptions, even though such assumptions may not be appropriate for the data being analyzed. The availability of inexpensive computing power makes resampling technique practical, which, in turn, makes it possible for us to draw analytical inferences based on our actual data conditions, instead of relying on inappropriate theoretical assumptions.

Bootstrap method has been applauded as one of the recent breakthroughs in statistics (Kotz & Johnson 1992). Because of its simplicity and versatility as a non-parametric analytic approach for statistical inference, the significance of bootstrap method has been widely recognized by quantitative researchers in different disciplines. Quantitative researchers in social sciences have applied the bootstrap method in a variety of situations, such as in structural equation modeling (Bollen & Stine 1993; Yung & Bentler 1996), in factor analysis and discriminant analysis (Lambert, Wildt, & Durand 1991; Dalgleish 1994), and in correlation analysis (Mendoza, Hart, & Powell 1991).

The bootstrap method is a computing-intensive data resampling strategy that requires considerable computing power. Current computing technology makes bootstrapping an attractive and viable analytic choice. Unfortunately, although the logic of bootstrapping is conceptually straightforward, bootstrapping has yet to enjoy widespread use in substantive research in social sciences. The major obstacle to its application appears to be the lack of automated options in major statistical software packages (e.g., SAS, SPSS). Consequently, researchers who desire to use this approach usually have to deal with programming for performing bootstrap resampling, a daunting task for many social science researchers.

This situation, however, appears to be changing. Some customized programs have been published for performing bootstrapping for different statistical techniques (e.g., for regression analysis, Fan & Jacoby 1995; for factor analysis, Thompson 1988). More recently, some commercial software programs have incorporated the bootstrap method as an analytic option, making bootstrapping widely available to many. For example, AMOS, a software program for structural equation modeling (SEM), has an automated option for performing bootstrapping (Arbuckle & Wothke 1999). Because SEM is a general analytic approach that subsumes many other techniques (e.g., *t*-test, ANOVA, correlation, regression), this means that, using AMOS's automated bootstrap option, a researcher can perform bootstrapping for many statistical techniques (Fan 2003). It is very likely that, in the not so distant future, bootstrapping will be more widely available from major statistical analysis software.

SEE ALSO: Factor Analysis; Quantitative Methods; Statistical Significance Testing; Structural Equation Modeling; Theory and Methods

REFERENCES AND SUGGESTED READINGS

Arbuckle, J. L. & Wothke, W. (1999) *Amos 4.0 User's Guide*. SmallWaters Corporation, Chicago.

Bollen, K. A. & Stine, R. (1993) Bootstrapping Goodness-of-Fit Measures in Structural Equation Models. In: Bollen, K. A. & Long, J. S. (Eds.), *Testing Structural Equation Models*. Sage, Newbury Park, CA, pp. 111–35.

Dalgleish, L. I. (1994) Discriminant Analysis: Statistical Inference Using the Jackknife and Bootstrap Procedures. *Psychological Bulletin* 116: 498–508.

Efron, B. (1979) Bootstrap Methods: Another Look at the Jackknife. *Annals of Statistics*, 7: 1–26.

Fan, X. (2003) Using Commonly Available Software for Bootstrapping in Both Substantive and Measurement Analyses. *Educational and Psychological Measurement* 63: 24–50.

Fan, X. & Jacoby, W. R. (1995) BOOTSREG: A SAS Matrix Language Program for Bootstrapping Linear Regression Models. *Educational and Psychological Measurement* 55: 764–8.

Kotz, S. & Johnson, N. L. (1992) *Breakthroughs in Statistics*, vols. 1 and 2. Springer-Verlag, New York.

Lambert, Z. V., Wildt, A. R., & Durand, R. M. (1991) Approximating Confidence Interval for Factor Loadings. *Multivariate Behavioral Research* 26: 421–34.

Lunnenborg, C. E. (2000) *Data Analysis by Resampling: Concepts and Applications*. Duxbury Thompson Learning, Pacific Grove, CA.

Mendoza, J. L., Hart, D. E., & Powell, A. (1991) A Bootstrap Confidence Interval Based on a Correlation Corrected for Range Restriction. *Multivariate Behavioral Research* 26: 255–69.

Mooney, C. Z. & Duval, R. D. (1993) *Bootstrapping: A Nonparametric Approach to Statistical Inference*. Sage, Newbury Park, CA.

Stine, R. A. (1989) An Introduction to Bootstrap Methods: Examples and Ideas. *Sociological Methods and Research* 8: 243–91.

Thompson, B. (1988) Program FACSTRAP: A Program that Computes Bootstrap Estimates of Factor Structure. *Educational and Psychological Measurement* 48: 681–6.

Yung, Y. & Bentler, P. M. (1996) Bootstrapping Techniques in Analysis of Mean and Covariance Structures. In: Marcoulides, G. A. & Schumacker, R. E. (Eds.), *Advanced Structural Equation Modeling: Issues and Techniques*. Lawrence Erlbaum, Mahwah, NJ, pp. 195–226.

methods, case study

Kristina Wolff

Case study methods encompass a range of research techniques that are used to examine social phenomena. Researchers primarily focus their study on the micro level, concentrating on individuals, groups, organizations, institutions, and/or events. The analysis is aimed at investigating contemporary issues or events within their real-life setting. A case study is considered a specific approach or strategy that can be used as a unit of analysis and also the means by which data have been gathered, organized, and presented.

A variety of disciplines utilize this mode of research, including medicine, law, political science, history, public administration, and policy studies as well as sociology. In sociology, case studies examine society to understand a variant of a specific social phenomenon such as the progression of an event, changes that may occur due to something like the implementation of a policy, program, or specific event, and/or as a means to understand a specific segment or group in society. This method is often used as a pilot study or as foundational research to support a larger study. Case studies are also a common method of research for thesis and dissertation projects.

One of the primary goals of conducting a case study is to generate thick, rich, detailed explanations of the phenomenon that is being investigated. This research is largely descriptive and/or exploratory in nature. Many cases focus on the "how" or "why" something is occurring in society. Researchers seek to document the complexities of a situation. For sociologists, case studies have historically been used as a means to develop an understanding of marginalized groups. For example, Liebow's (1967) study of "streetcorner men" and Becker's (1962) examination of marijuana users provide insight into groups that are considered subcultures in mainstream US society. Both conducted ethnographic case studies, utilizing a variety of qualitative techniques to gather rich data.

Becker and Liebow's studies are considered single case design case studies. These studies were conducted holistically, there were no subunits involved, and the material was gathered using multiple methods, which adds to the depth of the data. Most case studies focus on a specific group or event, often as a means to observe or analyze something that has previously been inaccessible to researchers. By studying these subcultures, Liebow and Becker were able to provide insights in the complexities of these men's lives while also dispelling myths and stereotypes. While their results are not generalizable to the whole of society, this exploratory research illustrated the effects of macro-level social problems such as racism and classism on these groups.

Case studies can also provide data that support or refute existing social theory. For example, Becker's work expanded as well as solidified theories about deviance in society. These studies also provide the foundation for the development of new theory. Grounded theory is formed out of the process of in-depth, far-reaching observation of society (Glaser & Strauss 1967). This group of theorists posits that sociological theory must be constructed in reference to real life. A series of case studies or multiple case studies enable scholars to build complex theories of society.

One of the critiques of case study methods within sociology as well as other disciplines is that while this type of research has brought into focus populations that are traditionally ignored within social science, many studies continue to overlook the experiences of a variety of groups. Feminist case studies purposefully concentrate on the lives of women in society. This approach has widened to include explorations of the complexities of the ways in which social factors such as race, ethnicity, gender, class, sexuality, ability, and age operate in relationship to one another in society. Research by Simonds (1996) and Diamond (1992) represents this expansion in case study methods. Simonds's examination of a feminist women's clinic and Diamond's analysis of nursing home caregivers place women's experiences and the relationships of gender/race/class at the center of their research.

These studies are considered embedded design case studies as they focus on one organization and the various groups and individuals within the organization. Often this approach is used when examining changes in policies or practices. Investigators will conduct research that follows the progression of change from before the policy was adopted through to the implementation process and then to the outcomes of the policy. Both Diamond and Simonds utilize multiple methods in their research and they place their findings in the context of larger issues in society, particularly in relationship to health care policy and practices. They also provide recommendations for policy change.

One of the main critiques of the case study method is that it can result in biased accounts and narrow understandings of a specific event or group. Rigorous case studies utilize triangulation or multiple methods as a means of gathering their data. The examples provided here have primarily consisted of qualitative approaches, involving one-on-one interviews and participant observation. Case studies utilize an array of both qualitative and quantitative approaches including historical analysis, content analysis, discourse analysis, policy analysis, surveys, and secondary data analysis. These techniques of investigation are used to reduce bias, increase validity and reliability, and to provide the "rich" data required of case studies and to allow for flexibility in conducting the research. Data are analyzed for common themes and patterns with the purpose of providing new insights into a specific social phenomenon.

SEE ALSO: Grounded Theory; Methods; Quantitative Methods; Theory and Methods

REFERENCES AND SUGGESTED READINGS

Becker, H. (1962) *Outsiders: Studies in the Sociology of Deviance*. Free Press, New York.

Berg, B. (2004) *Qualitative Research Methods for the Social Sciences*, 5th edn. Pearson, Allyn, & Bacon, Boston.

Burawoy, M. (1998) The Extended Case Method. *Sociological Theory* 16: 4–33.

Diamond, T. (1992) *Making Gray Gold: Narrative of Nursing Home Care*. University of Chicago Press, Chicago.

Glaser, B. & Strauss, A. (1967) *The Discovery of Grounded Theory*. Aldine, Chicago.

Liebow, E. (1967) *Tally's Corner: A Study of Negro Streetcorner Men*. Little, Brown, Boston.

Ragin, C. & Becker, H. (1992) *What Is a Case: Exploring the Foundations of Social Inquiry*. Cambridge University Press, New York.

Reinharz, S. (1992) *Feminist Methods in Social Research*. Oxford University Press, New York.

Simonds, W. (1996) *Abortion at Work: Ideology and Practice in a Feminist Clinic*. Rutgers University Press, New Brunswick, NJ.

Snow, D. & Trom, D. (2002) The Case Study and the Study of Social Movements. In: Klandermans, B. & Staggenborg, S. (Eds.), *Methods of Social Movement Research*. University of Minnesota Press, Minneapolis.

Stake, R. (2005) Qualitative Case Studies. In: Denzin, N. & Lincoln, Y. (Eds.), *The Sage Handbook of Qualitative Research*. Sage, Newbury Park, CA, pp. 443–66.

Yin, R. (1984) *Case Study Research: Design and Methods*. Sage, Beverly Hills.

methods, mixed

Anthony J. Onwuegbuzie

Over the last several decades, numerous fields from the social and behavioral sciences, including the field of sociology, have undergone three methodological waves in research. In many disciplines, the quantitative research paradigm, which has its roots in (logical) positivism, marked the first methodological wave (circa the nineteenth century), inasmuch as it was characterized by a comprehensive and formal set of assumptions and principles surrounding epistemology (e.g., objectivism, independence of knower and known, real causes determining outcomes reliably and validly, time-free and context-free generalizations), ontology (e.g., single reality), axiology (e.g., value-free), methodology (e.g., deductive logic, testing or confirming hypotheses/theory), and rhetoric (e.g., rhetorical neutrality, formal writing style, impersonal passive voice, technical terminology).

The years 1900 to 1950 marked the second methodological wave, in which many researchers who rejected positivism embraced the qualitative research paradigm. Denzin and Lincoln (2005) refer to this era as the first historical moment or the Traditional Period for qualitative research. Vidich and Lyman (2000)

describe earlier forms of ethnography that took place prior to the seventeenth century. However, Denzin and Lincoln's (2005) Traditional Period represents the first organized qualitative research movement. Although this moment was characterized by qualitative researchers attempting to write reliable, valid, and objective accounts of their field experiences, it paved the way for the subsequent qualitative moments that have incorporated paradigms that are extremely far removed from positivism. For example, in stark contrast to positivism, constructivism has been characterized by a different set of epistemological (e.g., subjectivist, knower and known are inseparable), ontological (e.g., relativism), axiological (e.g., value-bound), methodological (e.g., dialectical, hermeneutical), and rhetorical (e.g., informal writing style using personal voice and limited definitions) assumptions.

Shortly after the end of the Traditional Period for qualitative research came the third methodological movement, which, during the 1960s, saw an increase in the number of researchers combining quantitative and qualitative approaches. (Combining qualitative and quantitative methods had taken place well before the 1960s. However, the mixing occurred unsystematically and often unconsciously, and these studies were not labeled as representing mixed methods research.) This movement was led by classical pragmatists (e.g., Pierce, Dewey, James) and later by neopragmatists (e.g., Davidson, Rescher, Rorty, Putnam). However, Campbell and Fiske's (1959) seminal article is credited as formalizing the idea of using multiple research methods. Campbell and Fiske introduced the idea of triangulation. This third methodological movement has been given many names, such as blended methods, integrative research, multimethod research, multiple methods, triangulated studies, pragmatist research, and mixed research. However, mixed methods research is the most popular term used to describe this wave. As noted by Johnson and Onwuegbuzie (2004), mixed methods research involves collecting, analyzing, and interpreting quantitative and qualitative data in a single study or in a series of studies that investigate the same underlying phenomenon.

Mixed methods research has been distinguished by an integrated and interactive set of epistemological (e.g., adopting both subjective and objective points of view), ontological (e.g., accepting external reality; choose explanations that best produce desired outcomes), axiological (e.g., value-bound), methodological (e.g., research influenced by theory/hypothesis and by text and observations), and rhetorical (e.g., formal and informal writing style using both impersonal and personal voice) assumptions that promote the compatibility thesis, which posited that quantitative and qualitative approaches were neither mutually exclusive nor interchangeable. Rather, the actual relationship between the two paradigms is one of isolated events lying on a continuum of scientific inquiry (Reichardt & Rallis 1994). Moreover, pragmatists contend that the logic of justification does not prevent researchers from combining quantitative and qualitative approaches within the same study or series of studies. Thus, researchers from the social and behavioral science fields can strive to attain the fundamental principle of mixed research, in which they collect multiple data using different strategies, approaches, and methods in such a way that the resulting mixture or combination is likely to result in "complementary strengths and nonoverlapping weaknesses" (Johnson & Turner 2003).

In recent years, mixed methods research has received increased recognition in the social and behavioral science fields and has become popular in many disciplines. In addition to sociology (Hunter & Brewer 2003), mixed methods research has been promoted by researchers representing the health sciences, education, psychology, nursing, management and organizational research, library and information science research, and program evaluation. These disciplines are represented in Tashakkori and Teddlie's (2003) seminal book.

To date, the third methodological movement has undergone three phases. The first phase (1960–ca. 1990) saw the emergence of a myriad of mixed methods research designs in which "qualitative and quantitative approaches are used in the type of questions, research methods, data collection and analysis procedures, and/or inferences" (Tashakkori & Teddlie 2003: 711). The second phase (ca. 1990–8) saw the birth of mixed model designs, in which qualitative and quantitative approaches are combined in all stages of the research process or across stages of the study (Tashakkori & Teddlie 1998). The publication of Tashakkori and Teddlie's (1998)

book gave rise to a period of eclecticism (from 1998), representing the third phase of the mixed methods movement. This third phase has seen a proliferation in the number of research designs, which have been based on an array of dimensions, such as time ordering (e.g., concurrent vs. sequential), type of mixing involved (e.g., within vs. across), degree of mixing, paradigm emphasis (i.e., equal status vs. dominant status), stage where mixing occurred (e.g., data collection vs. data analysis), goal of the study (e.g., understand complex phenomena vs. test new ideas), and type of mixed methods stance (e.g., dialectic vs. pragmatist). Indeed, in Tashakkori and Teddlie's (2003) book alone, at least 35 mixed methods research designs are presented (for a review of mixed methods research designs, see Teddlie & Tashakkori 2003).

The present era of eclecticism has identified what Teddlie and Tashakkori (2003: 4) refer to as "six major unresolved issues and controversies in the use of mixed methods in the social and behavioral sciences," namely: (1) the terminology used in mixed methods research; (2) the utility of mixed methods research; (3) the epistemological foundations for mixed methods research; (4) issues associated with designing mixed methods research; (5) issues associated with drawing inferences in mixed methods research; and (6) the logistics associated with conducting mixed methods research. Onwuegbuzie and Collins (2004) added a seventh unresolved concern: the issue of sampling. Specifically, these authors outlined the problems associated with combining samples from the qualitative and quantitative phases of a study.

The period of eclecticism has brought with it the following four challenges or crises that researchers face when undertaking mixed methods research: representation, legitimation, integration, and politics. The challenge of representation refers to the fact that sampling problems characterize both quantitative and qualitative research. With respect to quantitative research, the majority of studies utilize sample sizes that are too small to detect statistically significant differences or relationships (i.e., average statistical power of .5) and utilize non-random samples that prevent effect-size estimates from being generalized to the underlying population (Onwuegbuzie et al. 2004). In qualitative research the challenge of representation refers to the difficulties researchers encounter in capturing lived experiences via their social texts. As noted by Denzin and Lincoln (2005), the challenge of representation asks whether qualitative researchers can use text to represent authentically the experience of the Other.

The second challenge pertains to legitimation or validity. The importance of legitimation or what is more commonly referred to as validity has long been acknowledged by quantitative researchers. For example, extending the work of Campbell and Stanley (1963), Onwuegbuzie (2003) presented 50 threats to internal validity and external validity that occur at the research design/data collection, data analysis, and/or data interpretation stages of the quantitative research process.

With respect to the qualitative research paradigm, Denzin and Lincoln (2005: 17) argue for "a serious rethinking of such terms as *validity*, *generalizability*, and *reliability*, terms already retheorized in postpositivist ..., constructivist-naturalistic, feminist ..., interpretive ..., poststructural ..., and critical ... discourses. This problem asks, 'How are qualitative studies to be evaluated in the contemporary, poststructural moment?'" Part of their solution has been to reconceptualize traditional validity concepts and to use new labels. For example, Lincoln and Guba (1985) presented the following types: credibility (replacement for quantitative concept of internal validity), transferability (replacement for quantitative concept of external validity), dependability (replacement for quantitative concept of reliability), and confirmability (replacement for quantitative concept of objectivity).

In mixed methods research the crises of representation and legitimation often are exacerbated because both the quantitative and qualitative components of studies bring to the fore their own unique crises. In mixed methods studies the challenge of representation refers to the difficulty in capturing (i.e., representing) the lived experience using text in general and words and numbers in particular. The problem of legitimation refers to the difficulty in obtaining findings and/or making inferences that are credible, trustworthy, dependable, transferable, and/or confirmable.

The third challenge pertains to integration. This challenge compels mixed methods researchers to ask questions such as the following: Is it appropriate to triangulate, consolidate, or compare quantitative data originating from a large random sample on equal grounds with qualitative data arising from a small purposive sample? How much weight should be placed on qualitative data compared to quantitative data? Are quantitatively confirmed findings more important than findings that emerge during a qualitative study component? When quantitative and qualitative findings contradict themselves, what should the researcher conclude?

The fourth challenge is the challenge of politics. This refers to the tensions that arise as a result of combining quantitative and qualitative approaches. These tensions include any conflicts that occur when different investigators are used for the quantitative and qualitative components of a study, as well as the contradictions and paradoxes that come to the fore when the quantitative and qualitative data are compared and contrasted. The challenge of politics also pertains to the difficulty in persuading the consumers of mixed methods research, including stakeholders and policymakers, to value the results stemming from *both* itative components of a study. Additionally, the challenge of politics refers to tensions ensuing when ethical standards are not addressed within the research design.

In the last half century the field of mixed methods research has advanced far. However, as can be seen by the number of challenges and unresolved issues and concerns, it has a long way to go. As noted by Teddlie and Tashakkori (2003: 3), "the [mixed methods] field is just entering its 'adolescence' and ... there are many unresolved issues to address before a more matured mixed methods research area can emerge." Yet this means that the door is wide open for an array of exciting possibilities for mixed methods research in sociology and beyond.

SEE ALSO: Methods; Naturalistic Inquiry; Quantitative Methods; Validity, Qualitative; Validity, Quantitative

REFERENCES AND SUGGESTED READINGS

Campbell, D. T. & Fiske, D. W. (1959) Convergent and Discriminant Validation by the

Multitrait-Multimethod Matrix. *Psychological Bulletin* 56: 81–105.

Campbell, D. T. & Stanley, J. C. (1963) *Experimental and Quasi-Experimental Designs for Research*. Rand McNally, Chicago.

Denzin, N. K. & Lincoln, Y. S. (2005) The Discipline and Practice of Qualitative Research. In: Denzin, N. K. & Lincoln, Y. S. (Eds.), *Handbook of Qualitative Research*, 3rd edn. Sage, Thousand Oaks, CA, pp. 1–32.

Hunter, A. & Brewer, J. (2003) Multimethod Research in Sociology. In: Tashakkori, A. & Teddlie, C. (Eds.), *Handbook of Mixed Methods in Social and Behavioral Research*. Sage, Thousand Oaks, CA, pp. 577–94.

Johnson, R. B. & Onwuegbuzie, A. J. (2004) Mixed Methods Research: A Research Paradigm Whose Time Has Come. *Educational Researcher* 33 (7): 14–26.

Johnson, R. B. & Turner, L. A. (2003) Data Collection Strategies in Mixed Methods Research. In: Tashakkori, A. & Teddlie, C. (Eds.), *Handbook of Mixed Methods in Social and Behavioral Research*. Sage, Thousand Oaks, CA, pp. 297–319.

Lincoln, Y. S. & Guba, E. G. (1985) *Naturalistic Inquiry*. Sage, Beverly Hills.

Onwuegbuzie, A. J. (2003) Expanding the Framework of Internal and External Validity in Quantitative Research. *Research in the Schools* 10(1): 71–90.

Onwuegbuzie, A. J. & Collins, K. M. T. (2004) Mixed Methods Sampling Considerations and Designs in Social Science Research. Paper presented at the RC33 Sixth International Conference on Social Science Methodology, Amsterdam.

Onwuegbuzie, A. J., Jiao, Q. G., & Bostick, S. L. (2004) *Library Anxiety: Theory, Research, and Applications*. Scarecrow Press, Lanham, MD.

Reichardt, S. S. & Rallis, S. F. (1994) Qualitative and Quantitative Inquiries Are Not Incompatible: A Call for a New Partnership. In: Reichardt, C. S. & Rallis, S. F. (Eds.), *The Qualitative–Quantitative Debate: New Perspectives*. Jossey-Bass, San Francisco, pp. 85–91.

Tashakkori, A. & Teddlie, C. (1998) *Mixed Methodology: Combining Qualitative and Quantitative Approaches*. Applied Social Research Methods Series Vol. 46. Sage, Thousand Oaks, CA.

Tashakkori, A. & Teddlie, C. (Eds.) (2003) *Handbook of Mixed Methods in Social and Behavioral Research*. Sage, Thousand Oaks, CA.

Teddlie, C. & Tashakkori, A. (2003) Major Issues and Controversies in the Use of Mixed Methods in the Social and Behavioral Sciences. In: Tashakkori, A. & Teddlie, C. (Eds.), *Handbook of Mixed Methods in Social and Behavioral Research*. Sage, Thousand Oaks, CA, pp. 3–50.

Vidich, A. J. & Lyman, S. M. (2000) The History in Sociology and Anthropology. In: Denzin, N. K. & Lincoln, Y. S. (Eds.), *Handbook of Qualitative Research*, 2nd edn. Sage, Thousand Oaks, CA, pp. 37–84.

methods, postcolonial

Wenda K. Bauchspies

Postcolonial methods utilize social, cultural, and political analysis to engage with the colonial discourse. Postcolonialism has been defined as both a social movement and a research approach whose main agenda addresses racism and oppression. Postcolonial research names the cultural, political, and linguistic experiences of former colonized societies by including voices, stories, histories, and images from people traditionally excluded from European/western descriptions of the world. It is through the shared experience of colonialism that postcolonial scholars and writers are articulating how colonialism has worked "through" and "upon" individuals, societies, and material culture.

Postcolonial theory started as a subversive literary phenomenon in the 1960s entitled New Literatures in English or Commonwealth Literatures that critiqued British imperialism by discussing and naming issues of identity, nationalism, colonialism, and otherness (for examples, see the journals *World Literature Written in English* and *Journal of Commonwealth Literature*). The early postcolonial writers/scholars were from former British colonies. These early authors were producing English literature that disrupted the European canon because they addressed migration, slavery, suppression, resistance, representation, difference, race, gender, place, and master narratives. In the late 1970s colonial discourse became popular through Edward Said's application in *Orientalism* (1978) of Michael Foucault's "discourse." Colonial discourse theory focuses on the ways in which cultural practices, metaphors, and signs organize and reproduce social life within colonial relationships. Commonwealth literature intersected with colonial discourse to become what is thought of as postcolonialism today. The label has shifted, but the focus has remained on understanding the cultural and political identities and experiences of colonialized subjects as object and subject, authority and subaltern, and self and other.

Postcolonial critics aim to address the absences, omissions, and forgotten tales of colonial history. In the process of recovering lost or silent knowledges, postcolonial researchers have helped the colonized to develop strategies for traversing the chasms of their experiences, to create greater self-understanding both within and outside of the postcolonial moment, and to understand the complexity of the dance of oppression maintained and perpetuated through dependency and desire. Postcolonialism as an interdisciplinary critique is committed to cultural pluralism that analyzes domination and resistance by acknowledging that colonialism is always present as a practice, not only as a metaphor or sign.

Post typically defines "after" and European colonialism was not the first time a nation/region dominated its neighbors. However, "postcolonialism" became such a strong label because European colonialism covered approximately three-fourths of the world, making it truly a global event that significantly impacted a large percentage of the world population and their land usage. The term postcolonialism acknowledges that the impact, definitions, control, and experiences of colonialism linger long after "decolonization" has happened and continues in part as neocolonialism, the continuation of colonialism through economic and political means.

Postcolonialism occurs at the juncture of Marxism, poststructuralism, and postmodernism. The major divide between postcolonialism and postmodernism as defined by Simon During in *Postmodernism or Postcolonialism?* (1985) occurs over the role of the master narratives that postcolonialism uses and postmodernism denounces. Postcolonial theory uses the master narrative to make sense of the colonial encounter through epistemology, theory, and politics. Postcolonial theory "attempts to reform the intellectual and epistemological exclusions of [the western] academy, and enables non-western critics located in the West to present their cultural inheritance as knowledge" (Gandhi 1998: ix).

From one perspective, postcolonialism predates the other "post-isms" while in practice postcolonialism is the youngest of the theories. Defining postcolonialism as beginning in opposition to colonialism rather than at the end of colonialism situates postcolonialism as older than postmodernism and poststructuralism. However, it is through the prominence of postmodernism and poststructuralism that postcolonialism has gained wider acceptance and validity in the academy. The "post-isms" share a focus on decentering the center, employing subversive tactics and theories, and understanding experience through language and writing. However, postcolonial studies of imperialism, colonialism, and neocolonialism define its perimeters within strategies of resistance, subversion, appropriation, and rejection. Postcolonialism draws upon poststructuralism, postmodernism, feminism, critical race theory, and queer theory to study postcolonial discourse and culture.

Postcolonial methodology is being built upon feminist methods and shares much the same agenda, where instead of women or gender, postcolonialism is studying the third world, subaltern, other, oppressed, or colonized. Postcolonialism and feminism are clearly siblings and perhaps twins, as they both seek to include the marginalized, address inequities, and resist and critique the center. By sharing theories and methods they are challenging the other, while simultaneously stimulating themselves to explore new avenues of study within gender/colonialism. Similar overlaps occur between critical race theory, queer theory, and postcolonialism in the domains of difference, race, ethnicity, and sexuality. Critical race theory makes race and its intersection with other inequities the focus of research to challenge mainstream knowledge claims while including issues of social justice. Postcolonial, critical race theory and feminism utilize and value experiential knowledge within an interdisciplinary and transdisciplinary context.

The postmodern, poststructural, postcolonial lens has shown that qualitative research grounded in the disciplines of anthropology and sociology has been historically complicit with imperialism. This has redefined ethnography from a "timeless truth" to a situated story that includes the researcher in the history and analysis. Thus, anthropology and postcolonialism share interests in developing a postcolonial ethnography that reflects and articulates cultures through a reflective (and perhaps experimental) voice of researcher and informants, as R. P. Clair illustrates in *Expressions of Ethnography* (2003). For example, part of the postcolonial discussion is about the production and meaning of postcolonial texts and how they communicate culture both within and outside their cultures. Postcolonialism is helping qualitative research to address questions of voice, language, resistance, subversion, and difference to the extent that researchers are beginning to write in opposition to the western research canon. Linda T. Smith in *Decolonizing Methodologies* (1999) offers an alternative research method by arguing that researchers need to be more responsible/responsive to the community they are studying by giving it agency in the research process, through direct involvement in knowledge production.

Theoretically and methodologically postcolonialism is an avenue to address the duality found in lived realities. It is not simply that postcolonialism gives voice to the other, but it recognizes the difficulties of doing so. It acknowledges the globalizing power of European colonialism while attempting to resist the universalizing power of that acknowledgment. However, as with feminism, it was not until attention was given to the category of women that the multiplicity of women's experiences could be valued. A similar move is occurring in postcolonialism: by working under the shared umbrella of colonialism the diversity, difference, hybridity, resistance, alterity, mimicry, and marginality of colonized peoples is finding voice.

There is the question of what is postcolonial: is it a historical moment that began at the end of colonialism and the moment of independence? Or is it grounded in the resistance that began with colonialism? Those that argue it began at the beginning of colonialism and in opposition to colonialism write post-colonial with a hyphen. Those who use postcolonial without the hyphen are not necessarily making that same distinction. Postcolonialism is a story about power and oppression designed to shift the discussion to the "third world" perspective and experience. Some postcolonial critics do not use the terms first world and third world in order to avoid entering into the oversimplification and generalizations attached to such labels.

Many cultures and societies share the title of being postcolonial; however, different communities experienced colonialism differently, even under the same European power. Postcolonial theory acknowledges and addresses that the postcolonial condition is not universal, but a shared condition. Thus, postcoloniality is unified in addressing colonialism and its impact while exploring difference from various spaces and places. Postcolonialism is a social process that signifies "linkages and articulations" and is not static, monolithic, or universal. Postcolonial discourse "provides a methodology for considering the dialogue of similarity and difference; the similarity of colonialism's political and historical pressure upon non-European societies, alongside the plurality of specific cultural effects and responses those societies have produced" (Ashcroft et al. 1995: 56).

Postcolonialism acknowledges how hybridization has been both a strength and weakness of postcolonial cultures that are continually transforming themselves at the boundary of colonial/indigenous culture. Through hybridity postcolonial scholars challenge typical binary categories with the hope of creating, finding, and naming new models of cultural expression, national identity, and celebrations of difference to address the silencing and subordination of imperialistic processes. Hybridization stresses continual, continuous, and mutual co-creation, not the disappearance of difference, cultures, or knowledge. It is this focus on hybridization that is traditionally at odds with traditional anthropology and sociology, whose study of indigenous groups has often defined them as marginalized, endangered, static, and old-fashioned. By maintaining and continuing to inscribe the binary distinction of "other" in traditional social sciences, postcolonial critics are excluded from engagement with the "non-other." In other words postcolonial theory incorporates the dynamics of the borderland between colonized and colonizer, self and other, and dominator/dominated through hybridization.

The goal of postcolonial research is to highlight dichotomies and illustrate multiplicities. One method is through the study of place, as it symbolizes the confluence of language, environment, and history while capturing the displacement of the colonizer, colonized, settler, native elite, or other individual created in the colonial encounter. Another method that addresses the multiplicities and inequalities of postcolonialism is the study of educational institutions and materials. Education was and still is a major imperial/colonizing force that is produced by a powerful (colonial) authority and is consumed by (colonized) locals. It is a rich site of postcolonial theory because education is simultaneously a technology of subjectification and a technology of resistance and subversion. Education and postcolonialism both embody "the possibility of thinking our way through, and therefore, out of the historical imbalances and cultural inequalities produced by the colonial encounter" (Gandhi 1998: 176).

Language is a discourse of power. The colonizer used language and education to control and subject the colonized. The colonized employed language as a tool of resistance and counter-attack. Aime Cesaire, Albert Memmi, Frantz Fanon, and Leopold Senghor all wrote at the time of independence for many of the former European colonies. They articulated and captured the ideas that were emerging as these new nation-states were creating national identities and new literary spaces in the aftermath of colonialism. They began the postcolonial discourse by analyzing the colonial discourse (that today has come to mean orientalism, primitivism, or tropicalization) and looking for ways to dismantle it, replace it, or diminish it through a anti-hegemonic discourse.

Cesaire, with *Discourse on Colonialism* (1955), argued that colonialism and imperialism were obstacles to economic and cultural development. Memmi, with *The Colonizer and the Colonized* (1957), described the colonial enterprise as racist, contradictory, and detrimental to both colonizer and colonized. Fanon, with *Wretched of the Earth* (1963), identified three stages of development for colonial literature that would ultimately lead writers to an active political stage that would further the nation's culture and consciousness. Senghor, with *Négritude* (1970), compared African ontology to European philosophy to conclude that négritude embraces and affirms the self-realization of the African self through values based upon reciprocity, dialogue, equity, and equilibrium of communities and social organizations. J. M. Dash objected to the view of history espoused by négritude in an article in *Caribbean Studies* (1973) because he

perceived it to be destructive rather than creative for new theories and identities. Needless to say, among the early writers in the "Commonwealth Literatures" (that later became known as postcolonial literature) there was a lively debate and discussion about colonialism, colonizer, colonized, identity, nationalism, racism, and political activism that still continues in postcolonialism today.

The three major theorists in colonial discourse are Edward Said, Gayatri Spivak, and Homi Bhabha. Said's discursive analysis of colonialism showed how the administrative, scholarly, and cultural colonial institutions imagined and represented the Middle East as an "other" that was a composite of European fears and desires. Said's *Orientalism* (1978) decenters and dismantles the institutions of the West to illustrate the colonial and imperialist underpinnings of western intellectual authority and how this authority created the Orient as an oppositional other that enhanced the stature and status of Europe. Spivak's *In Other Worlds* iving voice to the subaltern is multifaceted, complex, and should not be oversimplified. (*Subaltern* was used by Gramsci to denote an oppressed person.) For Spivak, it is impossible to give voice to the subaltern. Therefore, part of the role of the postcolonial critic is to make the marginal visible. Bhabha's *The Location of Culture* (1994) identified the use of mimicry by colonial subjects to destablize knowledge production and was read to signify "insurgent counter-appeals." Bhabha established the notion of hybridization within postcolonial theory with the story of how the Bible was transformed in India and its authority diminished when merged and appropriated by local knowledge communities.

Since the 1970s, postcolonial theory has moved beyond literature and English departments into other areas of the academy that include sociology, anthropology, economy, business, and architecture, to name a few. This outward expansion has made postcolonial theory both highly contested and an engaging field of research that has developed more nuanced and sophisticated analyses, particularly in the fields of neocolonial domination. For example, Chicano theory may not have been embraced by early postcolonial theory, but it is clearly included in postcolonial theory today, with its unique placement between two (or more) cultures.

Often interdisciplinary and multicultural, postcolonial writings do not appear to be "academic" in voice, focus, or presentation. Minh-ha's *Woman, Native, Other* (1989) was one of the early postcolonial/feminist texts that highlighted the colonializing process of publishing, being a woman, doing anthropology, and being a third world other. She decentered the center of academic writing through a text written as a story that flows and tumbles upon itself, juxtaposed with images, quotes, and poetry. Anzaldúa's *Borderlands/La Frontera* (1987) (another early postcolonial work) challenges the male, white hegemony through a text woven in Spanish and English. Through the rich poetry of the text, Anzaldúa provided a vivid sense of the contested ground, bodies, experiences, and memories in the borderland between two cultures. Both Anzaldúa and Minh-ha utilized postcolonial method to help make space for and validate other voices in the academy.

During the 1990s postcolonialism expanded its own hybridization into historical and anthropological theories, concepts, and ideas. This increased the interactions and cross-pollination within the social sciences (e.g., James Clifford's *Routes*, 1997). Postcolonial theorist looked to sociology and anthropology for richer understanding of culture and society. One such scholar is Anne McClintock, who analyzed the contradictions of colonial discourse in a sociocultural historical framework in her work *Imperial Leather* (1995). She illustrated how institutions of power in addition to narratives contributed to the creation of "father and families, labor and gold, and mothers and maids." Through the dangerous and contradictory bonds of imperial/anti-imperial, money/sexuality, violence/desire, and labor/resistance, McClintock contributed to the postcolonial discussion of the interconnectivity of race, gender, and class.

Thus, by applying postcolonial methods to the context of study and to postcoloniality itself, postcolonialism has become a rich source of descriptions, knowledge, and understanding of social worlds. It started in the margins from the alienation of colonialism and has grown into a perspective, method, and theory that provides space and readings of "marginal" experiences in such a way to celebrate the pluralistic, multifarious, and marginal nature of all experiences and knowledges.

Postcolonialism does not propose to be a grand theory of everything. Rather, it wishes to be a useful tool that can highlight the dominant discourse and the unspoken discourse in order to discuss questions, issues, and dilemmas of resistance, nationality, language, power, ethnicity, culture, and community. Its goal is to transform the dominant discourses in order to provide alternative models for understanding the place and role of the local in a global world.

As postcolonialism continues to affirm the dynamic potentiality in cultures colliding through resistance, hybridization, appropriation, and subversion to create new forms, alongside the dominant and indigenous narratives it will continue to articulate and comprehend knowledge and power production in order to apply it to new situations such as globalization, transnationalism, and the "rapidly mutating present" (Loomba et al. 2005). If traditional social sciences have served the nation-state, then a postcolonial social science will address the global interests and more seriously question the nation-state. Postcolonial methods are modifying the existing methods of the social sciences in order to remember who has been silenced, erased, and oppressed within colonial/postcolonial contexts and to rethink the predominant stories in order to include multiplicity and reflectivity.

SEE ALSO: Class, Status, and Power; Colonialism (Neocolonialism); Ethnography; Feminism; Globalization; Globalization, Values and; Hybridity; Nation-State and Nationalism; Nationalism; Orientalism; Postmodernism; Poststructuralism; Power, Theories of; Queer Theory; Race; Stratification, Race/Ethnicity and; Third World and Postcolonial Feminisms/Subaltern; Transnationalism

REFERENCES AND SUGGESTED READINGS

Altbach, P. G. & Kelly, G. P. (Eds.) (1984) *Education and the Colonial Experience*. Transaction Books, New Brunswick, NJ.

Asad, T. (Ed.) (1973) *Anthropology and the Colonial Encounter*. Humanities Press, Atlantic Highlands, NJ.

Ashcroft, B., Griffiths, G., & Tiffin, H. (1995) *The Post-Colonial Studies Reader*. Routledge, London.

Ashcroft, B., Griffiths, G., & Tiffin, H. (2000) *Post-Colonial Studies: The Key Concepts*. Routledge, London.

Ashcroft, B., Griffiths, G., & Tiffin, H. (2002 [1989]) *The Empire Writes Back: Theory and Practice in Post-Colonial Literatures*. Routledge, London.

Desai, G. & Nair, S. (Eds.) (2005) *Postcolonialisms: An Anthology of Cultural Theory and Criticism*. Rutgers University Press, New Brunswick, NJ.

Gandhi, L. (1998) *Postcolonial Theory: A Critical Introduction*. Columbia University Press, New York.

Loomba, A. (1998) *Colonialism/Postcolonialism*. Routledge, London.

Loomba, A., Kaul, S., Bunzl, M., Burton, A., & Esty, J. (Eds.) (2005) *Postcolonial Studies and Beyond*. Duke University Press, Durham, NC.

Mongia, P. (Ed.) (1996) *Contemporary Postcolonial Theory: A Reader*. Arnold, London.

Nandy, A. (Ed.) (1988) *Science, Hegemony and Violence: A Requiem for Modernity*. United Nations University, Tokyo.

Narayan, U. & Harding, S. (Eds.) (2000) *Decentering the Center: Philosophy for a Multicultural, Postcolonial and Feminist World*. Indiana University Press, Bloomington.

Young, R. (1990) *White Mythologies: Writing History and the West*. Routledge, London.

Young, R. (2001) *Postcolonialism: A Historical Introduction*. Blackwell, Oxford.

methods, visual

John Grady

Concern with visible evidence has been a part of sociology since the beginning with mostly still photographs, maps, and charts being deployed for various illustrative and emotive purposes. Rarely, however, did authors concern themselves with what made these images useful as data. Thus, while many social scientists acknowledged that visuals could make an argument clearer and more memorable, few considered how they might make an argument sounder. Only in the last three decades have researchers interested in a more visual sociology or anthropology responded to this challenge.

Visual methods refer to any research or analytic technique that produces or interprets visually perceptible representations as data in a social scientific argument. Still photographs constitute the most commonly utilized form of imagery, but increasingly visual methods include film, video, and non-figurative ways of displaying data for various analytic purposes.

Concern with developing protocols for research with visual materials first emerged in cultural anthropology where photography and film were used to document (if not salvage) the material culture, rituals, and other aspects of life in tribal societies. Gregory Bateson and Margaret Mead's ethnographic collaboration in Bali represents the first use of visual data that was methodologically rigorous and influenced by formal theory. Their work, however, did not have any significant influence on subsequent anthropological research (Bateson & Mead 1942). Applied anthropologists, however, continued to use visual methods, which led to the publication of Collier and Collier's *Visual Anthropology* (1986), an inventory of various techniques for studying culture and behavior photographically.

Howard Becker and Erving Goffman first developed an explicit concern with using images in sociological research. Becker (1974) contended that a major obstacle to using images in sociology was the widely held view that images spoke for themselves and were worth a thousand words. In contrast, Becker argued that images were only as informative as the questions that were addressed to them. Goffman (1976) demonstrated that analysis of print advertisements in popular magazines revealed a pattern of gender norms regulating how men and women should be displayed. He suggested that such typifications were idealized representations of social mores, and no less real than those mores themselves. Furthermore, Jon Wagner's collection, *Images of Information* (1979), established that images could be used for very diverse research agendas. Since then sociologists continue to explore using images to study pattern and variation in social life, social change, and the ways in which people create meaning in their lives (Grady 1996; Harper 2000; Wagner 2002).

There are many ways in which investigations are enriched by visual methods:

- Environments and events in a field study may be documented on a regular basis.

Visual documents of this sort provide information that supplements field observations and can be reviewed and reanalyzed much as field notes are. Ceremonial displays of one kind or another contain rich information about values and relationships (Collier & Collier 1986).

- *Rephotographing* the same situations and places at different times and over long periods provides invaluable information about variation and social change, although the framing of earlier images must be replicated as closely as possible (Rieger 1996, 2003).
- Images may be used to draw meaning from informants about the world depicted in the image. *Photo-elicitation* can be carried out with photographs and other images produced or collected by the researcher or by the subjects themselves (e.g., family photo albums, home movies, and various kinds of yearbooks and other informal and official documents). The elicitation interview is conducted in a "closed-ended" fashion – where the subject explains the function or operation of something displayed in a photograph – or in an "open-ended" manner – where the image is used to jog a subject's memory about the events displayed in the photograph. Photo-elicitation has been used with both individuals and small groups (Gold 1991; Suchar 1992; Stiebling 1999; Harper 2002).
- Subjects have been provided with cameras and asked to record events in their lives that are of interest to themselves or the investigator. While *Subject image-making* requires that subjects undergo training in composition and lighting, this technique illuminates a subject's world and preoccupations (Rich & Chalfen 1999).
- Finally, all of these techniques and approaches can be combined in full-blown *ethnographies* of different social worlds. Apart from their value as a supplement to memory and note-taking, images that are taken sensitively and empathetically capture the emotions and feel of a situation or a moment in a way that few other sources of data can (Bateson & Mead 1942; Harper 1987). This is especially true if the medium is film or video. Notable examples include James Ault's *Born Again: Life in a*

Fundamentalist Baptist Church (1987) and Robin Anderson and Bob Connolly's trilogy about social change in the highlands of Papua New Guinea: *First Contact* (1982), *Joe Leahy's Neighbors* (1988), and *Black Harvest* (1992).

All images share certain characteristics that affect their analytic use:

- An image *documents* something other than itself.
- What an image represents is invariably *framed* within boundaries established by the physical medium of representation.
- Most images are *composed*. Even photographic novices know to point the camera toward the picture to be taken and put what is of interest in the frame.
- Most images are *reproducible*. They can be copied.
- All images are *artifacts* that can be reused for purposes different from that for which they may have been intended.
- Most images, and certainly their reproductions, are *portable*. They can be carried from one place to another, the manner of their display often being little more than an accident of history.

Thus, an image always represents an event that interested the image-maker and how the whos and the whats in the photograph were oriented to each other and the event. An image is also, however, a repository of diverse meanings, many of which are imputed to it after the fact of its creation. An image, therefore, can serve as data for a wide range of questions, many of which might not have occurred to either the photographer or those being photographed. Visual researchers are exploring the boundaries of what can be studied visually as well as developing standards for how research might most usefully be conducted.

Most researchers begin their investigations by determining who produced the image, as well as where and when – and for what purposes, and in what organizational context – it was both produced and preserved. This information establishes how various factors may have shaped the relationship between the representation and the empirical world it represents.

These include the contingencies of technology and technique; temporality (time of day; season and chronological date); the beliefs and ideological commitments of the photographer and/or collector; display conventions (whether professional or vernacular); and how the photographer and subjects were influenced by the social and cultural milieu within which the photographs were taken.

Most investigators using images look for specific information in the image as an answer to a theoretically informed question. But, whatever the purpose, all researchers attend to any information an image might contain. First, an image is carefully examined to identify everything that might provide information. Researchers make mental notes of their observations, very often by actually verbalizing them as a memory aid. Researchers then look at the image in its entirety to ascertain how specific elements relate to the entire picture. Second, researchers identify variables by comparing the images in their sample. Looking for patterns and how they may vary in all images usually reveals information that is not immediately apparent in a single image. Careful scrutiny encourages the development of more robust explanatory models.

Moving images, in particular, are especially useful for studying social processes and interactions, although posing challenges for coding and analysis. Moving images cannot be simply inspected like photographs are but must be "viewed" and reviewed many times to discover and retrieve the information in the clip.

Visual investigators require a clear research design to guide the production and collection of images. This is true whether the investigation is behavioral, ethnographic, or a content analysis of preexisting images. The research design must identify sites to be filmed or explored, events to be sampled, and relevant variables. To successfully conduct visual research in the field, however, requires that investigators balance the demands of the research design with two conflicting imperatives: the need for a comprehensive representation of the scene and its doings versus a more micro-level coverage of social interaction and how people respond to the situations they find themselves in. Assigning different roles to two or more camera operators can resolve this dilemma. Investigators with only one camera, however, will construct a shooting script for making images of the physical and institutional settings and events that establish a visual context for the investigation (Suchar 1997). In addition, more experienced investigators will build on the eye's natural propensity to frame action. Learning how to conduct research rigorously yet imaginatively while avoiding the pitfalls and temptations of impressionistic image-making is an essential component of visual methods.

The photographer Robert Capa is quoted as saying, "If your pictures aren't good enough, you're not close enough." The same is true for visual methods generally. Visual research requires immersion in the subjects' worlds and developing a rapport where subjects take the camera for granted. For the researcher, immersion is surrender to the moment, following subjects on a journey deeper into their world and its meanings.

Developing a rewarding relationship with subjects is a complex process that raises many ethical and personal issues that have to be addressed in a professional manner. Because subjects can be readily identified in an image, it is necessary that they sign legally binding releases granting researchers the right to their image for various professional purposes. Additionally, because images can be taken out of context for various purposes, it is necessary that researchers be aware of the consequences that displaying an image might have for the subject and assume responsibility for those consequences that the subject might not be aware of. This is especially true for minors and other dependents. This might require the researcher to disguise a subject's identity or not use the image at all. Balancing the interests of the subject with the intellectual needs of the researcher's peers and the wider public is an abiding challenge.

Innovations in information technology have had a revolutionary impact on the making, archiving, and analysis of images. These developments include digital cameras and desktop software programs for altering, editing, storing, analyzing, and publishing images. It is now possible to create enormous amounts of high-quality visual data for very little cost. Images are produced in the field and shared with subjects, enhancing their participation in the research process. The Internet also makes it possible to integrate visual data into research reports. Prior to the digital revolution, social scientists only shared their visual data as illustrations. Now, entire databases can be put on CDs and DVDs, stimulating the research community to discuss the quality of evidence that images can provide.

Making visual data accessible, for example, promises to transform the social scientific study of popular culture. The content analysis of advertisements, cartoons, news photographs, feature films, and the like has often been hampered by researchers' inability to make and store legible copies of data. In the past, analysis depended on coders making accurate judgments on the spot. As a result, there was a tendency to restrict studies to those variables that coders could be trained to recognize reliably. The study of imagery in popular culture often became little more than establishing obvious correlations between status markers and social values and interests. Constructing large digital databases, however, makes for more flexible and sensitive analytic approaches to data analysis – like grounded theory – that invite replication. Nevertheless, it must be noted that images of readily identifiable individuals exacerbate the ethical issues that are raised in social research.

SEE ALSO: Barthes, Roland; Content Analysis; Grounded Theory; Methods; Photography; Representation; Semiotics

REFERENCES AND SUGGESTED READINGS

Anderson, R. & Connolly, B. (1982) *First Contact*. Filmmaker's Library, New York.
Anderson, R. & Connolly, B. (1988) *Joe Leahy's Neighbors*. Filmmaker's Library, New York.
Anderson, R. & Connolly, B. (1992) *Black Harvest*. Direct Cinema, Santa Monica, CA.
Ault, J. (1987) *Born Again: Life in a Fundamentalist Baptist Church*. James Ault Films, New York.
Bateson, G. & Mead, M. (1942) *Balinese Character: A Photographic Analysis*. New York Academy of Sciences, New York.
Becker, H. S. (1974) Photography and Sociology. *Studies in the Anthropology of Visual Communication* 1: 3–26.
Collier, J. & Collier, M. (1986) *Visual Anthropology*. University of New Mexico Press, Albuquerque.
Goffman, E. (1976) *Gender Advertisements*. Harper & Row, New York.
Gold, S. J. (1991) Ethnic Boundaries and Ethnic Entrepreneurship: A Photo-Elicitation Study. *Visual Sociology* 6(2): 9–22.
Grady, J. (1996) The Scope of Visual Sociology. *Visual Sociology* 11(2): 10–24.
Harper, D. (1987) *Working Knowledge: Skill and Community in a Small Shop*. University of Chicago Press, Chicago.
Harper, D. (2000) Reimagining Visual Methods: Galileo to Necromancer. In: Denzin, N. & Lincoln, Y. (Eds.), *Handbook of Qualitative Research*, 2nd edn. Sage, Thousand Oaks, CA, pp. 717–32.
Harper, D. (2002) Talking About Pictures: A Case for Photo-Elicitation. *Visual Studies* 17(1): 13–26.
Rich, M. & Chalfen, R. (1999) Showing and Telling Asthma: Children Teaching Physicians with Visual Narrative. *Visual Sociology* 14(1/2): 51–71.
Rieger, J. (1996) Photographing Social Change. *Visual Sociology* 11(1): 5–49.
Rieger, J. (2003) A Retrospective Visual Study of Social Change: The Pulp-Logging Industry in an Upper Peninsula Michigan County. *Visual Studies* 18(2): 157–78.
Stiebling, M. (1999) Practicing Gender in Youth Sports. *Visual Sociology* 14(1/2): 127–44.
Suchar, C. (1992) Icons and Images of Gentrification: The Changed Material Culture of an Urban Community. *Research in Urban Sociology* 2: 165–92.
Suchar, C. (1997) Grounding Visual Sociology Research in Shooting Scripts. *Qualitative Sociology* 20(1): 33–55.
Wagner, J. (Ed.) (1979) *Images of Information: Still Photography in the Social Sciences*. Sage, Beverly Hills.
Wagner, J. (2002) Contrasting Images, Contemporary Trajectories: Sociology, Visual Sociology, and Visual Research. *Sociological Imagination* 38(1/2): 7–27.

metropolis

James Dickinson

Metropolis broadly refers to the largest, most powerful and culturally influential city of an epoch or region. Historically, the metropolis is a city which is relatively open, attracts commercial and other forms of exchange, and offers opportunities for sophisticated living.

A succession of great metropolitan cities charts the course of western urban history. In this history, three forms of the metropolis can be identified. In Antiquity, cities such as Athens and Rome developed the political and cultural potentialities of the polis, in part laying foundations for the later emergence of western urban democracies. With the revival of urban life in the Middle Ages, a strong symbiotic relationship between the form of the metropolis and economic growth was revealed, leading to the rebirth of the metropolis as the great mercantile, commercial, and later industrial center of modern capitalism. More recently, globalization and decentralization, vastly aided by new communication and transportation technologies, have transformed the metropolis from a single-centered, bounded urban entity into a multi-centered urbanized region extending over a vast geographic area. Within the rise, fall, and transformation of the metropolis are shards of a cultural continuity stretching over millennia.

METROPOLIS IN ANTIQUITY

Two features of the metropolis are revealed in the etymology of its Greek origins (*meter/* mother + *polis/*city). As population pressure forced some city-states to found colonies, they became the "mother city" of those colonies. Within a region, one city might exploit its strategic location, dominate trade or control resources, accumulating wealth and attracting population as a result. Apex of a chain of lesser settlements, the metropolis was continually enriched by its control and exploitation of distant colonies, hinterland, or commercial empire (Mumford 1938). As polis, however, ancient metropolis is distinguished from other historical forms of the imperial city, for example, city-states arising in pre-Hellenic Mesopotamia, Egypt, and the Indus Valley, or the great urban centers of pre-Columbian Aztec and Mayan civilizations. These cities were typically rigid, closed, and hierarchical. Residents had no independent rights and were ruled by totalitarian god-kings and priests (LeGates & Stout 1996). In particular, they lacked any public space or realm which is central to life within a metropolis.

In its cultural and political moments, the metropolis was an extension of the Greek ideal of the polis: a political community where strangers could gather as equals to forge a new identity around ideals of citizenship transcending the limited ties of family and tribe (Kitto 1964). Citizens had independent worth as well as rights and duties. The city consequently became an attractive place offering residents security, prosperity, and intellectual stimulation. For Aristotle, it constituted the natural home of mankind; forming the "point of maximum concentration for the power and culture of a community," it was where "the goods of civilization are multiplied and manifolded" (Mumford 1938).

Ancient Athens is often considered the epitome of the Greek polis, its contributions to democracy, humanism, free and open inquiry, literature and the arts without parallel in shaping western values and civilization. By the fifth century BCE, Athens was in actuality a great metropolis, many times the size of the ideal polis as envisioned by Plato or Aristotle. Despite the magnificence of its public buildings most of the city's residents lived in poverty and squalor. Its great wealth derived from confederation of the states Athens dominated, control of a vast trading empire, and exploitation of non-citizens including metics (resident aliens who organized trade), and a huge population of slaves (Hall 1998).

Imperial Rome also developed the metropolitan urban form. Here politics was understood more as public authority than self-ruling democracy. Citizens were passive bearers of rights granted by a sovereign power. The public domain thus centered on issues of rulership, including the nature, modes, and limits of power. Fostering compliance and combating resistance to legitimate authority were key political concerns (Weintraub 1995). Yet management of empire also emphasized practical arts such as military organization, civil engineering, and city planning. Roman power established many cities which shared features such as a *defined center* (a *forum* where the most important civic buildings and institutions were concentrated); *a clear boundary or perimeter* marked ritually (the *pomerium*, or sacred belt) as well as physically (walls or fortifications); and an overall spatial distribution of groups and activities in which the core was typically valued over more distant parts (Mumford 1961).

METROPOLIS AS GREAT CITY OF MODERNITY

Antiquity bequeathed to modernity a form of the metropolis which was conducive to economic growth. The modern metropolis is the foremost expression of the centralizing and accumulating tendencies of first mercantile, then industrial, now global capitalism. While accumulated wealth in Antiquity was generally consumed unproductively (extravagant lifestyles, public monuments), in the new metropolis wealth extracted from dependent satellites was more systematically invested in its own development (Braudel 1981). During its mercantile and industrial stages, capital accumulation found the inherited forms of the city useful, adapting existing ones (London, Paris), or creating new ones (Manchester, Chicago).

Growth of the market economy initially amplified the importance of the urban core in minimizing costs and maximizing the speed of communication. The modern metropolis grew up around a single center or business district; here opportunities multiplied for face-to-face interaction, exchanges of vital information, and access to capital and other business services. Comparatively, locations at a distance from the hub were at a disadvantage (Mumford 1938). Thus city growth produced the distinctive concentric ring pattern of development described by Ernest Burgess (Park et al. 1925). Urban populations continued to swell, confounding all notions that there was a natural upper limit to the size of even the richest cities.

METROPOLIS IN THE THIRD WORLD

Structural distortions inherited from colonial pasts have produced a severely unbalanced pattern of urbanism in the third world. Many developing countries are dominated by a single gigantic metropolis, or primate city, which as the main center of investment and growth is the principal destination of rural migrants. While cities such as Mexico City, Jakarta, and Bangkok have grown recently to rival or exceed those in the developed world, interior regions remain relatively under-urbanized (Gottdiener 1994). As a result of rapid growth, many such cities face formidable economic, social, and ecological problems. São Paulo has been described as a "colossus" (its population approaches 20 million) where "every notion about planning and architecture evaporates" and "every municipal organization is powerless against the proliferation of the city" (Nijenhuis & De Vriers 2000). As overpowering, chaotic, and violent as these third world cities may be, they continue to act as magnets.

THE CONTEMPORARY METROPOLIS

Relentless growth has transformed the metropolis from a bounded city with a single center into a vast urbanized region stretching over multiple jurisdictions. Early evidence of this shift is found in Victorian London, where the term "metropolitan" first appears in legislative and administrative language to describe services extending over the "whole city." This new usage coincided with a movement towards consolidation; the city annexed adjacent areas or adjusted boundaries to retain control over the increasingly large area that now made up the social and economic relations of the city. Elsewhere, New York and Philadelphia likewise responded to growth by annexing peripheral zones of population and economic resources. However, economic and technological forces have continually pushed development beyond the city. As a result, the metropolis has become redefined as a geographic or statistical area composed of one or more established urban nuclei with neighboring areas linked to it by continually built-up sections and commuting links.

In the US, federal government agencies have been at the forefront of such redefinition. In 1910 the Census Bureau devised the *metropolitan district*, a central city with a population of at least 200,000 plus adjacent townships, to describe and measure growth occurring beyond the city proper. In 1949 this measure was replaced by the *standard metropolitan area*, consisting of the whole county containing a city of at least 50,000, plus surrounding counties which had a high degree of economic and social integration with the nucleus.

Rules now defining metropolitan areas are exceedingly complex. However, three principal types of metropolitan area are currently recognized. *Metropolitan Statistical Areas* (MSAs) are metropolitan areas with populations of less than 1 million, regardless of the number of counties they may contain. If the metropolitan area exceeds 1 million, it is designated a *Consolidated Metropolitan Statistical Area* (CMSA). *Primary Metropolitan Statistical Areas* (PMSAs) are metropolitan areas in their own right, but are integrated with other adjacent PMSAs, forming multi-centered CMSAs. These ever-changing statistical constructions are part of the necessary "counting and mapping" the state does in order to "know the governed" (Joyce 2003).

Such designations describe a fundamental transformation of the metropolis from dense, bounded, single-core city to extended urban region containing many centers of work, residence, and shopping which cross multiple administrative boundaries. These multi-nucleated urban regions are perhaps the "first really new way people have organized their living and working arrangements in ten thousand years" (Gottdiener 1994). Similar developments have also appeared in Japan and Germany.

New metropolitan regions are typically sharply bifurcated into areas experiencing either rapid growth or severe decline. In recent decades, globalization of economic activity, emergence of a new international division of labor, and revolutions in communication and transportation technology have reduced the importance of fixed urban aggregations of labor, skills, and resources in shaping regional and national economies. Downtown business districts steadily erode as corporations shift management operations to the suburbs and beyond; manufacturing jobs have likewise disappeared from cities as corporations seek cheaper labor in rural and suburban areas as well as in the third world (Fogelson 2003).

Growth beyond the city proper, however, has been unprecedented. In the US, undeveloped land adjacent to cities and a multiplicity of weak, competing jurisdictions have facilitated suburban hypergrowth. Subsidized highway construction, reform of mortgage lending, and tax breaks for homeowners have contributed to the spatial reorganization of the urban periphery. Traditional residential suburbs are now surrounded by or absorbed into multifunctional "technoburbs" or "edge cities" (Fishman 1987; Garreau 1992). Antiquated zoning laws, weak or divided local governments, and powerful developer interests have combined to produce a miasma of centerless sprawl (Duany et al. 2000).

FUTURE OF METROPOLIS

For Mumford (1938), metropolis inevitably gave way to megalopolis, a "sprawling gigantism" destined to expire as nekropolis. In the 1950s, Gottman used the term megalopolis more positively to describe continuous zones of urbanization appearing in the US. More radical was the anticipation of "ecumenopolis," a single global settlement Doxiadis saw emerging from expansion of megalopolis over entire continents (LeGates & Stout 1996). Others still see a continuing role for the traditional metropolis with a few "global cities" providing the necessary specialized and shifting infrastructure on which globalization depends (Sassen 2001). As creative destruction, capitalism also continually reinvents older cities, transforming landscapes of production into new landscapes of consumption (Zukin 1991).

SEE ALSO: Central Business District; Cities in Europe; Exurbia; Global/World Cities; Megalopolis; Metropolitan Statistical Area; Multinucleated Metropolitan Region; Mumford, Lewis; Primate Cities

REFERENCES AND SUGGESTED READINGS

Braudel, F. (1981) *Civilization and Capitalism 15th–18th Century*. Vol. 1: *The Structures of Everyday Life*. Harper & Row, New York.

Bridge, G. & Watson, S. (Eds.) (2002) *The Blackwell City Reader*. Blackwell, Oxford.

Duany, A., Playter-Zyberk, E., & Speck, J. (2000) *Suburban Nation: The Rise of Sprawl and the Decline of the American Dream*. North Point Press, New York.

Fishman, R. (1987) *Bourgeois Utopias: The Rise and Fall of Suburbia*. Basic Books, New York.

Fogelson, R. M. (2003) *Downtown: Its Rise and Fall, 1880–1950*. Yale University Press, New Haven.

Garreau, J. (1992) *Edge City: Life on the New Frontier*. Anchor Books, New York.

Gottdiener, M. (1994) *The New Urban Sociology*. McGraw-Hill, New York.

Hall, P. (1998) *Cities in Civilization*. Weidenfeld & Nicolson, London.

Joyce, P. (2003) *The Rule of Freedom: Liberalism and the Modern City*. Verso, London.

Kitto, H. D. F. (1964) *The Greeks*. Aldine, Chicago.

Kotkin, J. (2005) *The City: A Global History*. Modern Library, New York.

LeGates, R. T. & Stout, F. (Eds.) (1996) *The City Reader*. Routledge, New York.

Mumford, L. (1938) *The Culture of Cities*. Harcourt, Brace, New York.

Mumford, L. (1961) *The City in History: Its Origins, Its Transformations and Its Prospects*. Harcourt, Brace, & World, New York.

Nijenhuis, W. & De Vriers, N. (2000) *Eating Brazil*. 010 Publishers, Rotterdam.

Park, R. E., Burgess, E. W., & McKenzie, R. D. (1925) *The City*. University of Chicago Press, Chicago.

Sassen, S. (2001) *The Global City: New York, London, Tokyo*. Princeton University Press, Princeton.

Weintraub, J. (1995) Varieties and Vicissitudes of Public Space. In: Kasinitz, P. (Ed.), *Metropolis: Center and Symbol of Our Times*. New York University Press, New York, pp. 280–319.

Zukin, S. (1991) *Landscapes of Power: From Detroit to Disney World*. University of California Press, Berkeley.

Metropolitan Statistical Area

John E. Farley

A Metropolitan Statistical Area (MSA) is a geographical entity, defined by the Office of Management and the Budget (OMB) and used by the Census Bureau and other agencies, to represent a city or group of cities and its surrounding built-up and/or economically integrated region. Counties form the building blocks of MSAs and are used because they allow for comparison between censuses, are widely recognized, and are geographical areas for which a wide variety of data are available. The basic concept of the MSA has existed, under various terminology, since the 1950 census, and various modifications in the definition have been made by OMB just prior to each census since. The number of MSAs has increased significantly over time, as smaller urban areas have grown large enough to become recognized as MSAs.

There is no limit to the number of counties that may be included in an MSA, and MSAs can cross state lines, with some including parts of as many as three states. The reason for having MSAs is that city boundaries are arbitrary political boundaries, and the true area in which a metropolitan region's residents live and work is always larger than the incorporated area of any given city. By having a metropolitan area defined on the basis of county boundaries, it is possible to have an entity that (1) captures the entire metropolitan region, not just an area arbitrarily defined by political decisions about incorporated area boundaries, annexations, etc., and (2) is based on county boundaries that remain relatively constant, thus permitting geographical comparisons of data over time.

The latest set of rules for defining and naming MSAs was announced by OMB in December 2000 and became effective in late 2003. Currently, an area is defined as an MSA if it contains a core urbanized area (i.e., a city, group of cities, and/or densely built-up area, all contingent) with a population of at least 50,000. Any county containing a core urbanized area will automatically be part of an MSA, and is designated as a "central county." If the core urbanized area includes parts of more than one county, and if at least 10,000 of its residents live in an adjoining county that has at least half of its population in urban areas, that county will also be designated as a central county of that MSA. Additional counties will be added to the MSA as "outlying counties" if either (1) at least 25 percent of their residents work in the central county or counties of the MSA or (2) at least 25 percent of the workers employed in that county commute from the central county or counties. Thus, the criteria for defining MSAs and determining what counties are included in them are the presence of a large urban core and commuting patterns.

Within metropolitan areas, certain cities are identified as "principal cities," a new term in the definitions that went into effect in 2003. This replaces the widely recognized "central city" terminology used from 1950 until 2003. Formerly, it was possible for a metropolitan area to have up to three "central cities," which were typically the main city or group of cities around which the metropolitan area developed. Beginning in 2003, there is no longer a limit on the number of "principal cities" that may be contained in a metropolitan area, although it remains the convention in most cases to name the metropolitan area on the basis of no more than its three largest principal cities. A city is designated as a principal city if *any* of the following conditions are true:

1 It is the largest city in the metropolitan area and has a population of at least 10,000.
2 It has a population of at least 250,000, with at least 100,000 persons employed in the city.
3 It has a population of at least 50,000 but less than 250,000, and the number of people employed in the city is at least as great as the city's population.
4 It has a population of at least 10,000 but less than 50,000, is at least one-third the population of the largest city, and the number of people employed in the city is at least as great as the city's population.

Historically, it has been common practice to divide metropolitan areas into the portions of the MSA inside and outside the central city or cities (as was the terminology until 2003) and to examine aggregated statistics for those two parts of the metropolitan area. The part outside the central city or cities was considered to be an approximation of the aggregated suburban population of the metropolitan area. This view, regarding the part of the MSA outside the central city or cities as representing the suburban part of the metropolitan area, was common among census data users, and at one time this part of a metropolitan area was commonly referred to as the "suburban ring." This was never precisely correct, however, because portions of the metropolitan area outside the central city are rural, since even counties with large suburban areas also include rural areas. However, analyses comparing the parts of the metropolitan area inside and outside the central city or cities were common, because the MSA offered the most readily available representation of central city and suburban areas that was geographically comparable between censuses. Given the removal of the three-city limit on principal cities, and the new criteria for defining them, researchers using data for MSAs as defined in 2003 should use caution in this type of analysis,

and in particular need to recognize that the new "principal cities" and the old "central cities" are not comparable because they are defined according to different criteria, and the old limit of three such cities no longer exists. This has led to an increase in the portion of *some* metropolitan areas that falls within principal cities as compared to the old central city definition. For example, under the old definition, the only central city in the St. Louis, MO-IL MSA was St. Louis, MO, but under the new definition, St. Charles, MO, an area widely regarded as suburban in character, is also recognized as a principal city. And in what is now designated the Minneapolis-St. Paul-Bloomington, MN-WI MSA, there are now seven principal cities, in contrast to two central cities under the old definition. While the number of cities that may be recognized as principal cities is now unlimited so long as they meet the criteria, it remains the practice to name MSAs for no more than three cities, normally the three largest.

Another important change effective in 2003 is the creation of Micropolitan Statistical Areas. These are similar in concept to Metropolitan Statistical Areas, but are areas that develop around smaller urban cores, with urban core populations of at least 10,000 but less than 50,000. Like Metropolitan Statistical Areas, Micropolitan Statistical Areas are based on counties. Both Metropolitan Statistical Areas and Micropolitan Statistical Areas are subsumed under a broad category created for the 2003 definitions: Core-Based Statistical Areas (CBSAs). Every CBSA is either a Metropolitan Statistical Area or a Micropolitan Statistical Area. At the end of 2003, there were 922 CBSAs in the United States, including 362 Metropolitan Statistical Areas and 560 Micropolitan Statistical Areas. There were an additional 13 CBSAs in Puerto Rico, including eight Metropolitan Statistical Areas and five Micropolitan Statistical Areas. In the United States, 82.6 percent of the 2000 population lived in Metropolitan Statistical Areas, 10.3 percent lived in Micropolitan Statistical Areas, and 7.1 percent lived outside CBSAs.

In 2000, Metropolitan Statistical Area populations ranged from a maximum of 18,323,002 in the New York-Northern New Jersey-Long Island, NY-NJ-PA MSA down to a minimum of 52,457 in the Carson City, NV MSA.

Forty-nine MSAs had populations of at least 1 million, the five largest being New York-Northern New Jersey-Long Island, NY-NJ-PA, Los Angeles-Long Beach-Santa Anna, CA, Chicago-Napierville-Joliet, IL-IN-WI, Philadelphia-Camden-Wilmington, PA-NJ-DE, and Dallas-Fort Worth-Arlington, TX. Each of these MSAs, along with the Miami-Fort Lauderdale-Miami Beach, FL MSA, has total populations above 5 million. The 2000 populations of Micropolitan Statistical Areas range from a maximum of 182,193 in the Torrington, CT Micropolitan Statistical Area to a minimum of 13,004 in the Andrews, TX area.

Another change effective in 2003 is the system for defining MSAs in New England. Prior to 2003, MSAs in the six New England states were defined on the basis of towns rather than counties, reflecting the relatively unimportant basis of counties in that part of the country. However, beginning in 2003, Metropolitan and Micropolitan Statistical Areas in New England are defined on the basis of counties, as in the rest of the country. This makes MSA definitions in New England consistent with the rest of the country, and simplifies what was a very complex and laborious process of identifying the geographical area of MSAs in New England. However, to permit consistency with earlier MSA definitions, a new concept, the New England City and Town Area (NECTA), has been created that is similar in nature to the way MSAs were previously defined in New England. Thus, in New England, data may be obtained either for Metropolitan and Micropolitan Statistical Areas, or for NECTAs.

A final important change in metropolitan area definitions effective in 2003 is the elimination of Consolidated and Primary Metropolitan Statistical Areas. These entities were the product of one of several attempts by OMB to address the situation of the megalopolis, in which two or more adjoining metropolitan areas grow together into one very large urban agglomeration. The concept was replaced by a new area, the Combined Statistical Area (CSA), which is simply a combination of two or more nearby Metropolitan or Micropolitan Statistical Areas. This is done only when justified by commuting patterns between the two adjacent areas and/or local opinion (as represented by the area's Congressional delegation) that the areas are closely related. In many cases, the total population of the CSA is not greatly larger than that of its largest constituent MSA, because they often are the combination of one or more small Micropolitan Statistical Areas with one very large Metropolitan Statistical Area. In a handful of cases, though, the population difference is quite large. For example, the Los Angeles-Long Beach Riverside CSA, consisting of three Metropolitan Statistical Areas, has a population of 16,373,645 – about 4 million more than its largest constituent MSA. There were 113 CSAs in 2003. These can range widely in size, because some are combinations of very large Metropolitan Statistical Areas, while others are combinations of two small Micropolitan Statistical Areas. The largest is the New York-Newark-Bridgeport, NY-NJ-CT-PA CSA, with a population of 21,361,797; on the other hand, the Clovis-Portales, NM CSA had a population in 2000 of just 63,062.

A related but different situation is that in which one very large metropolitan area has multiple centers, such as Miami, Fort Lauderdale, and West Palm Beach in the Miami-Fort Lauderdale-Miami Beach, FL metropolitan area. In this case, which applies only when the urban core of the metropolitan area exceeds 2.5 million, the area may be subdivided into groupings of counties known as "Metropolitan Divisions." Note from this example that the divisions do not necessarily correspond to the name of the MSA. The divisions represent groupings of counties around separate nodes or centers of the MSA, whereas the MSA is named for the three largest cities.

SEE ALSO: Exurbia; Megalopolis; Metropolis; Multinucleated Metropolitan Region; Urban

REFERENCES AND SUGGESTED READINGS

Office of Management and Budget (OMB) (2000) Standards for Defining Metropolitan and Micropolitan Statistical Areas. Online. www.census.gov/population/www/estimates/00–32997.txt. Downloaded July 12, 2004.

US Census Bureau (2003a) About Metropolitan and Micropolitan Statistical Areas. Online. www.census.gov/population/www/estimates/aboutmetro.html. Downloaded July 12, 2004.

US Census Bureau (2003b) Historical Metropolitan Area Definitions. Online. www.census.gov/population/www/estimates/pastmetro.html. Downloaded July 12, 2004.

US Census Bureau (2004) Ranking Tables for Population of Metropolitan Statistical Areas, Micropolitan Statistical Areas, Combined Statistical Areas, New England City and Town Areas, and Combined New England City and Town Areas: 1990 and 2000 (Areas defined by the Office of Management and Budget as of June 6, 2003) (PHC-T-29). Online. www.census.gov/population/www/cen2000/phc-t29.html. Downloaded July 13, 2004.

Michels, Robert (1876–1936)

Dieter Rucht

Robert Michels is one of the founding fathers of modern political sociology. His writings focus on mass democracy, fascism, political leadership, political parties, and social movements. He has become famous for his widely cited "iron law of oligarchy," which continues to be an important reference point for both social scientists and political activists.

Michels, born in Cologne in 1876, grew up in a liberal bourgeois merchant family. He studied in France, Germany, and Italy. After having joined the German Social Democratic Party, he also became a member of the Italian Socialist Party. In the early years of the twentieth century, he embraced the ideas of revolutionary syndicalism and socialist internationalism. However, when his academic career was blocked in part due to his political engagement, Michels discontinued his membership in both political parties. In 1907, he left Germany to teach economics, sociology, and political science in Turin. He became Professor of National Economics in Basel (Switzerland) in 1914. In 1923, he joined the Italian Fascist Party. His shift to the far right helped him obtain an appointment as chair of economics and the history of doctrines in Perugia (Italy) in 1928. This position had been deliberately created to provide academic support to the fascist regime. Michels died in Rome in 1936.

Among his many writings, his monograph *Political Parties* (first published in German in 1911) stands out as his most widely read work. Based on his observation that modern democracy needs organization, Michels argues: "It is organization which gives birth to the domination of the elected over the electors, of the mandatories over the mandators, of the delegates over the delegators. Who says organization says oligarchy" (1962 [1911]: 365). Michels supports this view with a threefold set of what he calls technical-administrative, psychological, and intellectual causes of oligarchy. The prototypical case for his general argument is the German Social Democratic Party which, according to Michels, transformed itself from a vibrant social movement to a rigidly controlled bureaucratic apparatus, whose basic concern was an interest in its own maintenance at the cost of the former movement's revolutionary aims. Gradual oligarchization cannot be reversed, but can only be mitigated by raising public awareness. When oligarchy reaches an extreme state, it triggers resistance. However, after a period of glorious fights and a subsequent period of inglorious participation in power, the initial challengers are themselves subject to the iron law of oligarchy. Hence, the "cruel game" between the "incurable idealism of the youth and the incurable thirst for power of the old people" will never end. It is particularly this view that prompted J. D. May to characterize Michels as a "pessimistic romantic revolutionary."

SEE ALSO: Authority and Legitimacy; Democracy; Democracy and Organizations; Fascism; Mosca, Gaetano; Oligarchy and Organization; Pareto, Vilfredo; Political Leadership; Political Parties; Political Sociology; Social Movements

REFERENCES AND SUGGESTED READINGS

May, J. D. (1965) Democracy, Organization, Michels. *American Political Science Review* 59(2): 417–29.

Michels, R. (1962 [1911]) *Political Parties: A Sociological Study of the Oligarchical Tendencies of Modern Democracies*. Free Press, New York.

Michels, R. (1987 [1908]) Die oligarchischen Tendenzen der Gesellschaft. In: *Robert Michels, Masse, Führer, Intellektuelle. Politisch-soziologische Aufsätze 1906–1933.* Campus, Frankfurt am Main.

Nye, R. A. (1977) *The Anti-Democratic Origins of Elite Theory: Pareto, Mosca, Michels.* Sage, Beverly Hills.

Röhrich, W. (1972) *Robert Michels. Vom sozialistisch-syndikalistischen zum faschistischen Credo.* Duncker & Humblot, Berlin.

micro–macro links

Jonathan Turner and Barry Markovsky

Macrosociology addresses large-scale phenomena such as institutional systems, whereas microsociology deals with smaller-scale phenomena such as interpersonal behavior. Over the years, the theoretical agendas of macrosociology and microsociology have developed almost independently of one another. For some time, the issue of how to link these disparate levels of analysis – or how to close what is often termed the "micro–macro gap" – has been debated within theoretical sociology.

Empirically, it is relatively easy to link micro and macro levels. For example, a researcher may observe that individual political opinions and voting behavior are affected by social class membership, thus indicating an empirical linkage between micro variables (opinions and voting behavior) and a macro variable (social class). In most attempts to develop theories that link micro to macro (or macro to micro), however, conceptual gaps appear in the exposition. These gaps typically involve an inability to specify conceptually the processes by which micro- and macro-level forces influence each other. For example, Max Weber's (1958 [1905]) famous analysis of how the psychological motivations of Protestants at "the level of meaning" led to the inception of capitalism is vague on the exact processes by which individual-level motivations generate societal-level outcomes. Similarly, it is often implicit in macro theories that large-scale processes and phenomena have direct effects on individual behaviors, but again, the conceptual linkage between macro- and micro-level processes is typically not specified.

To speak of a micro–macro "gap" may imply that there is a chasm that must be traversed, but that is not necessarily true. It is true that, for some purposes, linking micro and macro levels may generate insights that otherwise could not have been achieved. For other purposes, however, linking to other levels may provide no explanatory benefits whatsoever. In the social realm, as in any other realm of empirical investigation, some micro and macro phenomena are naturally interrelated, others are not. Still, mature sciences do make systematic efforts to link conceptualizations of micro and macro processes, although the sciences vary considerably in just how well their cross-level theoretical connections are made. Even physics, certainly the most advanced science theoretically, has yet to complete its task of fully unifying theories of the micro and macro domains of the physical universe. Therefore, it should not be surprising that the younger social sciences have not achieved this goal. We can gain an appreciation for the problems in achieving theoretical integration by reviewing the various strategies that sociologists have employed to connect different levels of the social universe.

STRATEGIES FOR MICRO–MACRO LINKAGE

One of the most extreme approaches to linking micro and macro levels is simply to proclaim that the micro-level takes precedence, and that intermediate ("meso") and macro structures ultimately are "built from" or "emerge out of" behavioral and interpersonal processes (Schelling 1978). For example, Herbert Blumer (1969) asserted that society is no more than "symbolic interaction." Randall Collins (1981, 2004) has argued that macro reality ultimately consists of "chains of interaction rituals" among individuals. In making such assertions, there is a presumption, rarely developed theoretically, that individual-level behaviors somehow aggregate over time and space in ways that generate meso- and macro-level structures. Even rational choice approaches that tend to employ rigorous theoretical models become vague when trying to explain how macrostructures, in all their complexity, emerge from individuals who are seeking to maximize their payoffs and minimize their costs (e.g., Coleman 1990). However, within the rational choice genre, some game-theoretic models and computer simulations do successfully demonstrate mechanisms through which certain kinds of individual decisions produce certain macro-level outcomes (see Carley 2001 for a review of simulation approaches to theorizing). Even here, however, the computer programs generating the outcomes do not necessarily incorporate sociological assumptions concerning the processes involved.

At the other extreme are macro theorists who assert that individual behaviors and interactions are inconsequential for the study of society (Blau 1977), or that they are so highly constrained by macrostructural forces that micro phenomena can be understood only through macro-level theories. For example, a feminist theory of social power might contend that all male–female interactions at the micro household level are affected by the macro-level distribution of political and economic power (e.g., Chafetz 1990). Each of the extreme positions, or what we might call *chauvinisms*, embodies a kernel of truth: structure and culture are not possible without being energized by human behavior and interaction, and behavior or interaction that is free of any influence by the larger social context is virtually inconceivable. Still, neither approach offers a strong case for how the linkages between the micro and macro levels are to be conceptualized.

Between the above positions is a range of alternatives. One strategy is to build a conceptual staircase from the micro to macro. Here, a conceptualization of individual action is first delineated, and then successively more structure is added. For example, Talcott Parsons (1937, 1951) began with unit acts and moved stepwise up to a social system and, eventually, to an overall action system (Parsons et al. 1953) and on to a general conception of the universe (Parsons 1978). But in moving up the conceptual staircase, large gaps appear in Parsons's argument. For example, Parsons argued that actions become "institutionalized" into social systems, but he never specified exactly how this occurs. In essence, Parsons jumped a number of steps at just the points where micro and macro levels should have been connected. An alternative

approach is to move down the staircase. For instance, in Anthony Giddens's (1984) *structuration theory*, structure provides "rules and resources" guided by "structural principles" leading to properties of "institutions" directed by "modalities" that, in turn, structure "social systems of interaction" driven by "unconscious motives" and by "discursive consciousness." Much like Parsons's ascent of the staircase, Giddens's descent appears to jump several steps, without specifying the processes through which macro and micro levels connect.

Another approach simply bypasses the micro–macro link by examining relational forms rather than the properties of actors. For example, Georg Simmel's (1950) call for a formal sociology has been heeded in network theories that attempt to explain the dynamics of resource flows based on the shapes of networks, regardless of whether these are networks composed of micro-level units like individuals in interaction, or collective actors such as nation-states (e.g., Emerson 1962; Willer 1981). By positing that there are isomorphisms between micro and macro processes, the theoretical gap presumably disappears because the same theoretical principles and models are used to explain the form of social relations at different levels of social reality. Although this approach provides an elegant macro-to-micro linkage, it fails to address an important issue: sometimes the nature of the unit does make a difference in the nature of social processes that ensue. There are, no doubt, isomorphic processes that cut across all types of social units, but it is also the case that some processes are unique to a particular level of reality. Thus, Simmel's formal sociology offers one way to bypass the problem of micro–macro linkage, but it does not obviate the problem of connecting theoretically diverse social forces operating at different levels of social reality. Moreover, even if person-to-person behaviors reveal properties similar to relations among collective units, the problem of how the collective units are generated by interpersonal behaviors, and vice versa, is not resolved. Rather, the problem is simply bypassed.

Another strategy for linking micro and macro is what we might call deductive reductionism. George C. Homans (1974) was perhaps the most prominent advocate of the view that the laws of sociology pertaining to social structure can be deduced from the laws of psychology. Thus, the linkages between the micro and macro are to be found in the calculus of deductive logic whereby laws about macro- and meso-level phenomena are "derived" from those about micro-level phenomena. Like formal sociology, this solution to the problem would be elegant, but Homans never completed the job.

Still another strategy for linking the micro and macro levels of reality can be found in recent lines of argument about "embeddedness" (Granovetter 1985). By this view, structures are conceptualized as residing inside of more inclusive structures and their associated cultures. The approach recognizes that, despite the constraints imposed by their broader contexts, micro processes have a life of their own and need to be addressed through concepts and principles appropriate to their level – just as the macro level requires conceptualization in its own terms. Most arguments about embedding tend to be empirical, however, and merely describe how a given behavior or microstructure is constrained by what transpires in the macrostructure and the particular culture that contain it. As such, descriptions of embedded social processes do not provide general *theoretical* insights into micro–macro relationships.

One final strategy for dealing with micro–macro connections is to focus attention on phenomena at one level, and to attach an "all else being equal" or ceteris paribus clause to theoretical assertions. Presumably, one may then safely ignore the impact of other levels. The approach does not deny potential cross-level effects, but rather treats them as constants, at least provisionally. This approach can be a useful short-run strategy because it allows the theorist to focus on a particular set of processes without introducing complexities that may confound them. The strategy breaks down, however, when – as is most often the case – there is no theoretical follow-up that relaxes the ceteris paribus constraint. Indeed, if this approach is not fully implemented in unpacking what has been bracketed out by the ceteris paribus, it becomes yet another end-run around theoretically connecting the micro and macro.

The failure of each of the above strategies to resolve the micro–macro linkage problem does not mean that these strategies are unviable. On the contrary, they all have generated useful theoretical insights. As noted earlier, the macro–micro problem is inherent in all sciences, not just sociology. It may be that sociologists worry about the issue more than other scientists, but the problem is not unique to the study of social reality.

Before leaving this review of various strategies for closing the micro–macro "gap," we should note that this question is often conflated with another debate in sociology – the issue of "agency vs. structure" (see Ritzer 1990 for a review). Those who argue on the agency side generally are anti-science and want humans to have free will, while those on the structure side are interested in generating theoretical principles about generic patterns of action and interaction, or structure. As a result, those who push for agency often emphasize microsocial processes in which individuals are seen as creative actors, whereas those who argue for the power of structure are often more macro in focus and see structure as highly constraining on individual actions. Still, collectively organized units can reveal agency (as when a society goes to war) and encounters almost always reveal structure. Thus, the agency–structure debate is a different kind of controversy in sociology than the micro–macro questions that concern us here.

A COMPREHENSIVE APPROACH

If current theoretical strategies do not fully resolve the problem of integrating conceptually the micro and macro, we can reasonably ask: is there an approach that might better address the problem? One way to get a better purchase on the theoretical problem of linking the micro, meso, and macro levels of reality is to begin with a controversial assertion: social reality actually unfolds at these three levels (Turner 2002, 2003). That is, while the micro, meso, and macro distinctions are analytical distinctions, they may be more than mere conceptual conveniences: they may denote just how social reality is organized. The following approach suggests a more comprehensive metatheoretical account of the kinds of cross-level connections we have discussed thus far.

Assume that social reality exists at three levels: face-to-face encounters at the micro level, embedded within corporate or categoric units at the meso level, embedded within institutional systems at the macro level. Corporate units include organizations and communities, as well as larger social groups that extend beyond a micro-level encounter. Categoric units include social categories, such as social class, ethnicity, gender, and age, that are differentially evaluated and that arouse differential responses from people. Often social categories become a basis for corporate unit organization, as when an ethnic minority organizes to pursue its interests. Conversely, positions within corporate units can become broader social categories, such as mother, father, student, worker, and the like. Corporate and categoric units almost always are lodged within macro-level *institutional systems*, such as economy, polity, law, kinship, religion, sport, medicine, and education.

Cultural systems direct action at each level. Looking from the bottom up, social reality is ultimately constructed from encounters of face-to-face interaction that become elaborated into corporate and categoric units that, in turn, generate institutional systems from which societies and inter-society systems are built. A macro chauvinist would proclaim that encounters are so embedded in macro and meso units that what transpires at the interpersonal, face-to-face level can only be understood by the culture and structure of meso and macro units, whereas a micro chauvinist would argue just the opposite and proclaim that institutional systems are, at their core, strung-together encounters that are organized across time and in space. They would both be right, but this conclusion does not get us past a good shouting match. We need, instead, a way to conceptualize how these levels of reality are *interconnected*.

One way to conceptualize the process of embedding is to visualize the three levels – micro, meso, and macro – as driven by sets of forces or processes uniquely associated with each level (Turner 2002, 2003; Turner & Boyns 2001). If this assertion is correct, then theories should be about the forces that drive the formation and reformation of structural units of each level. Theories are not about the units of each level, but about the forces that drive their organization and culture. Once this conceptual step is taken, the argument about which level is primary disappears. Instead, each level manifests its *own set of forces* driving the

formation and operation of its own sociocultural units.

The next question is how the levels are connected to each other, and here is where embedding enters as one conceptual "solution" to the micro–macro problem. The values or loadings of forces at one level are very much determined by the values of the forces operating at the next higher level and the sociocultural units in which the more micro units are embedded. For example, if an encounter is embedded within a formal organization and a couple of categoric units – say gender and ethnicity – the dynamics of the encounter will be greatly constrained by this particular pattern of embedding. To take another example, if a corporate unit, such as the nuclear family and the categoric units that also flow from this unit (e.g., mother, father, children), are embedded within a larger kinship system, then the culture of the kinship system will load the values of the variable for the corporate unit (nuclear family) and categoric units that become salient (mother, father, child). Notice that there is no effort to reduce one unit to another but, instead, the goal is to see how the loadings of the forces driving the formation of units at one level are related to the forces and units of the next higher. For example, an encounter (micro level) in a workplace (meso) may be embedded in an economy that is part of a world economic system (macro); and because of this embedding, the values for the forces driving the encounter will be directly influenced by the structure and culture of the workplace (and by categoric units, if any are salient). Because the workplace is part of an organization that is embedded in an economy which is also part of a system of economies, the culture and structure of the ever-more macro systems also influence the loadings for the forces driving the encounter.

With this relatively simple conceptual edifice, it becomes possible to develop principles about the dynamics of the forces operating at each level and, at the same time, to incorporate the effect of the units at the next higher level in loading the values of the variables expressed in the principle. For example, if an encounter is embedded in an organization with an authority structure and a culture supporting this structure, and if those high in authority are of one gender or disproportionately so while those in low-authority positions are of another gender, the dynamics of the encounter – say, status, roles, expectation states, emotions, frames, exchanges, and other processes driving the formation of encounters – will all be loaded by this pattern of embeddedness. Moreover, it becomes possible to develop abstract principles about these loadings that are more than empirical summaries. For instance, we might assume that, if there is a high correlation between rank and categoric unit membership at the meso level, then encounters will reveal particular patterns of expectations states, rituals, framing, emotional arousal, and other forces operating at the micro level. Such an approach bridges the "gap" by seeking patterns at one level as they are conditioned by laws operating at higher levels.

One could argue that this solution to micro–macro linkage biases inquiry toward the macro chauvinist side of the debate. After all, it takes many more events at a given level to influence higher levels. For example, what transpires in one encounter is not likely to affect the division of labor of a corporate unit, whereas virtually every encounter will be influenced by each individual's position in a corporate unit and membership in a categoric unit. Or, the behavior of one organization in an economy rarely impacts institutional systems to a significant degree. Thus, the fact of embedding biases theories toward a top-down perspective. It is true, no doubt, that an economy is, in some ultimate sense, built from micro-level encounters. However, the dynamics of these encounters are not likely to change the dynamics of the economy as much as the embedding of the encounter in the economy, via corporate and categoric units, will influence what transpires in the encounter. Hence, most bridging laws developed from this perspective will be of a top-down character. We should not forget that sometimes what occurs in encounters in corporate units or in categoric units does influence the values of the variables in laws about macro-level structures and cultures. It is possible to make bridging statements that are bottom up, such as when one has a special interest in the initial emergence of macrostructures. Thus, whether the principles one develops from this perspective appear to favor micro-to-macro or macro-to-micro bridges will likely depend on

the interests of the theorists utilizing the approach, e.g., whether they focus on the emergence of social structures or on the impacts of extant structures.

Note that these efforts to link levels of reality revolve around seeing how one level loads the values of variables in propositions governing the operating of another level. The debate is not about which level is primary but about whether or not the propositions can explain the operation of forces at any given level. As bridging propositions are developed, forces at one level will be increasingly linked to forces operating at another level. Thus, so long as the goal of theory is to develop laws that explain the operation of dynamics at one level of social reality and, then, to supplement these laws with bridging propositions across levels, the micro–macro problem becomes solvable in theoretical rather than philosophical terms.

CRITERIA FOR MULTILEVEL THEORIES

A multilevel theory has one or more bridges across levels of analysis. These may include micro-to-macro bridges, macro-to-micro bridges, or both. To aid in the production of multilevel theories – whether via the approach just described or some alternative orientation – we need to specify some provisional criteria that should promote explicit and concise micro–macro linkages, apply to any substantive units of sociological interest, and establish points of contact for linkages to theories that may address phenomena at even more macro or more micro levels (Markovsky 1997). Arguably, the greatest impediments to building micro–macro linkages are ambiguities in the language used to express theories and in the logic used to derive their conclusions and predictions. These issues are not mere formalities: first, ambiguity in the terms referring to micro units or macro units will transfer to any cross-level linkages involving those terms, leaving different readers with varying impressions of the author's intended meanings. Second, logical gaps rob theoretical conclusions of their force by disconnecting them from the very justifications offered to support them.

Theory Units

Among the terms that do not have a consistent meaning in sociology is "theory." Because it would be futile to discuss multilevel theory without a clear picture of what a theory is, it will help to provide an explicit definition. First, however, we will define a useful building block called a *theory unit*. A theory unit includes logical operators, a minimal set of terms, a theoretical statement, and a scope statement. Logical operators are used in the construction of theoretical statements and might include words such as: "If. . ., then. . ., therefore. . ." or mathematical symbols. Their precise meanings are provided by a system outside of the theory unit, such as symbolic logic or algebra. The terms of a theory are the words used to carry meanings from theorist to readers. To accomplish this, meanings must be shared and so it is important that theorists define any terms that may not be understood the same way by all readers. To enhance communication, the theory unit should use as few terms as possible. Also, if the theory is to generalize beyond specific cases, the terms should be defined abstractly so that they can subsume specific cases without being limited by them. The theoretical statement within the theory unit uses logical operators to express an assumed relationship between theoretical terms, such as: "If an official has high status, then the official will have high power." (Presumably, "official," "status," and "power" would be defined clearly for readers.) Finally, scope statements express conditions under which the theorist claims the theoretical statement applies, e.g.: "The statement applies in primitive economies," or "The statement applies in face-to-face groups."

Theories

Although a useful building block, theory units have limited value on their own. With only one theoretical statement to work with, it is not possible to use some statements to justify others, or to use multiple statements to generate new conclusions. Theories provide these services. A theory contains two or more theory units that are linked by their logical operators and terms such that they create logical arguments – chains of reasoning whose conclusions are logically derived from prior statements. To be more precise, two or more theory units can form a theory only if (i) the set of terms of each theory unit overlaps with the terms of at least one other theory unit; (ii) their scope statements overlap; and (iii) the theoretical statement of each theory unit connects logically to at least one other. If (i) does not hold, then the theory units are talking about different things. If (ii) is not satisfied, then the theory units apply to different domains of phenomena. To illustrate (iii), the earlier statement "If an official has high status, then the official will have high power" could be combined with the statement "If an official has high power, then the official will have high autonomy" because the "then. . ." part of the first statement overlaps with the "If. . ." part of the second. In this manner, a new statement appearing in neither theory unit may be derived: "If an official has high status, then the official will have high autonomy." Although this is only a simple example, it manifests an important quality of well-formed theories: their capacity to capitalize on prior knowledge to generate new insights.

Multilevel Theories

Having thus defined theories, it is a relatively simple matter to provide criteria for multilevel theories. The micro–macro link requires two further conditions: *containment* and *bridging*. Conditions for containment ensure that the theory incorporates two or more distinct levels, defined in such a way that one is completely contained within the other. Examples could be members within groups, or organizations contained by industries. Bridging conditions are designed so that a statement that refers to terms existing at one level is explicitly connected to terms referring to another level.

Two rather different kinds of bridges may be built. First, there may be a theoretical statement, "If *x* then *y*," in which the level of *x* differs from that of *y*. For example, "If each member of a group feels powerless, then the group will revolt." Note that while a group revolt contains multiple group members, it cannot exist at the level of the individual person.

It would be defined as a collective phenomenon, the same way that a "beach" cannot exist at the level of the grain of sand.

The second type of bridge is definitional: the macro unit of one of the theory's statements (e.g., the x in "If x...") is defined in terms of a micro unit that is the subject of another theoretical statement, or vice versa. For example, "A group exists if and only if a set of interacting individuals define themselves as a distinct unit." Here, the relationship between "individuals" and "group" is established by definition. Thus, in this example, if there is a theoretical statement that asserts something about groups (macro), then by definition it also implies something about individuals (micro) because the former is explicitly defined in terms of the latter.

Multilevel theories abound in other scientific disciplines. In physics one may trace a chain of micro-to-macro theoretical linkages that span from the smallest "micro" particles at the subatomic level to the "macro" structure of the cosmos, via a host of meso-level structures and processes. At each level, macro properties such as energy fields, states of matter, or nuclear forces also exert influences in macro-to-micro directions. Although sociology does not yet approach the breadth and precision of physics, nevertheless it has some exemplary multilevel theories, one of which is examined below.

Network exchange theory (NET) provides a good illustration of a multilevel sociological theory (Willer 1999). It was developed to explain and predict the role that social structures play in producing power differences that result in resource differentials among members. The theory operates on three levels: the behavior of individual *actors* whose exchanges of resources are guided by rules applying to their social ties or *relations*, which in turn apply within larger, relatively fixed *networks* of potential exchange relationships. The scope conditions of the theory specify constraints on actors' negotiation strategies and their responses to being included or excluded in exchanges, along with rules for how resources are infused into relations and distributed to actors. Definitions are provided for key terms such as actor, network, power, and others used in its theoretical statements or *axioms*.

The theory has expanded over the years to accommodate a broadening range of phenomena and to generate more exact predictions, but the four basic axioms in the core part of the theory will serve to illustrate its capabilities. The axioms are abstract and general, and so they apply to networks of any size and shape, and to any kind of actors and resources. These theoretical statements allow the derivation of predictions for the quantities of resources that will end up at each network position after negotiations and exchanges play out. NET's Axiom 1 is a mathematical model for translating each position's location within a network structure into a numerical index of its potential power. The second axiom uses the power indices to determine which actors will seek exchange with each other by assuming that no actor will seek exchange with another actor in a higher-power position if there is an available exchange partner in an equal- or lower-power position. The third axiom indicates that no exchange occurs between two actors unless they seek exchange from each other, and the fourth axiom asserts that profits from exchange will correspond to differences in power indices: more power results in more profit.

Not only is it possible to derive individual profits from information on the exchange network structure (a macro-to-micro link) but the theory also has been used successfully to predict (i) structural changes based on exchange-seeking assumptions (micro to macro), and how changing exchange rules causes changes in (ii) profits (meso to micro) and (iii) network structure (meso to macro).

CONCLUSION

The issue of how to link micro, meso, and macro levels of reality theoretically is not easily resolved in sociology and, for that matter, any other science. We have reviewed the various approaches and proposed substantive and logical pathways to dealing with the problem of closing the conceptual gap between levels. The most important conclusion, we feel, is to recognize that social reality operates at different levels and that chauvinistic proclamations about one level being more primary simply do not resolve the problem of conceptual linkages. Another key conclusion is that levels of reality are embedded in each other and, hence, have effects on the operation of processes at other levels. Embedding does not mean that one level is reduced to another but, instead, that processes operating at one level are influenced by those at another level. This fact suggests that theories seeking to bridge across levels need to develop concepts, propositions, and models that capture the key dynamics of each level and, then, to develop bridging propositions connecting the concepts across levels.

There are many ways to formulate such bridging propositions. Network exchange theory proposes viewing the macro level as an exchange network that, through the workings of meso-level relations, influences and is influenced by the actions of individuals located at various places in the network. Other theories reveal this same potential. For example, the large theoretical literature on social movements presents ample opportunities to explore how the emotions and actions of individuals lead to the formation of meso-level organizational units that push for change in macro-level institutional structures and culture. Conversely, these approaches can develop bridging propositions on how macro- and meso-level conditions, such as a stratification system embedded in the institutionalization of power and production, generate micro-level responses of individuals that can explain, under conditions specified by bridging propositions, how micro encounters coalesce into change-oriented social movements. The key point is that many theories illustrate what we advocate – moving across levels with a variety of bridging propositions – but most often they are ad hoc in character. Needed is more attention to the criteria, enumerated earlier, for developing multilevel theory. The key is to locate the level of reality to which most of the concepts and propositions of a particular theory pertain. Then, the next step should be to determine how the values for these concepts are loaded by other processes at other levels of reality. Finally, bridging propositions can be developed that denote generic relationships among concepts denoting properties of different levels of reality. If sociological theorists consistently followed these three guidelines, the cross-level linkages would be more consistently made and, over time, broader theoretical (as opposed to

specific empirical) insights into the generic forms of linkage across levels of reality would become ever more evident.

SEE ALSO: Exchange Network Theory; Mathematical Sociology; Mesostructure; Microsociology; Structuration Theory; Theory; Theory Construction

REFERENCES AND SUGGESTED READINGS

Alexander, J., Munch, R., & Smelser, N. J. (Eds.) (1986) *The Micro–Macro Link*. University of California Press, Berkeley.

Blau, P. (1977) *Inequality and Heterogeneity*. Wiley, New York.

Blumer, H. (1969) *Symbolic Interactionsim*. Prentice-Hall, Englewood Cliffs, NJ.

Carley, K. M. (2001) Computational Approaches to Sociological Theorizing. In: Turner, J. H. (Ed.), *Handbook of Sociological Theory*. Kluwer/Plenum, New York, pp. 69–84.

Chafetz, J. S. (1990) *Gender Equity: An Integrated Theory of Stability and Change*. Sage, Newbury Park, CA.

Coleman, J. S. (1990) *Foundations of Social Theory*. Harvard University Press, Cambridge.

Collins, R. (1975) *Conflict Sociology*. Academic Press, New York.

Collins, R. (1981) The Microfoundations of Macrosociology. *American Journal of Sociology* 86: 984–1014.

Collins, R. (2004) *Interaction Ritual*. Princeton University Press, Princeton.

Emerson, R. (1962) Power–Dependence Relations. *American Sociological Review* 17: 31–41.

Giddens, A. (1984) *The Constitution of Society*. University of California Press, Berkeley.

Granovetter, M. (1985) Economic Action and Social Structure: The Problem of Embeddedness. *American Journal of Sociology* 90: 481–510.

Homans, G. C. (1974) *Social Behavior: Its Elementary Forms*, 2nd edn. Harcourt Brace Jovanovich, New York.

Huber, J. (Ed.) (1991) *Macro–Micro Linkages in Sociology*. Sage, Newbury Park, CA.

Markovsky, B. (1997) Building and Testing Micro–Macro Theories. In: Szmatka, J., Skvoretz, J., & Berger, J. (Eds.), *Status, Network, and Structure: Theory Development in Group Processes*. Stanford University Press, Stanford, pp. 13–28.

Mayhew, B. (1981a) Structuralism vs. Individualism, Part I. *Social Forces* 59: 335–75.

Mayhew, B. (1981b) Structuralism vs. Individualism, Part II. *Social Forces* 59: 627–48.

Parsons, T. (1937) *The Structure of Social Action.* McGraw-Hill, New York.

Parsons, T. (1951) *The Social System.* Free Press, New York.

Parsons, T. (1978) *Action Theory and the Human Condition.* Free Press, New York.

Parsons, T., Bales, F. R., & Shils, E. (1953) *Working Papers in the Theory of Action.* Free Press, New York.

Ritzer, G. (1990) Micro–Macro Linkage in Sociological Theory. In: Ritzer, G. (Ed.), *Frontiers of Sociological Theory.* Columbia University Press, New York, pp. 1–30.

Schelling, T. (1978) *Micromotives and Macrobehaviors.* New York: Norton.

Simmel, G. (1950) *The Sociology of Georg Simmel.* Trans. K. Wolf. Free Press, New York.

Turner, J. H. (1983) Theoretical Strategies of Linking Micro and Macro Processes: An Evaluation of Seven Approaches. *Western Sociological Review* 14: 4–16.

Turner, J. H. (2002) *Face to Face: Toward a Sociological Theory of Interpersonal Behavior.* Stanford University Press, Stanford.

Turner, J. H. (2003) *Human Institutions: A Theory of Societal Evolution.* Roman & Littlefield, Lanham, MD.

Turner, J. H. & Boyns, D. E. (2001) The Return of Grand Theory. In: Turner, J. H. (Ed.), *Handbook of Sociological Theory.* Kluwer/Plenum, New York, pp. 353–78.

Weber, M. (1958 [1905]) *The Protestant Ethic and the Spirit of Capitalism.* Trans. T. Parsons. Charles Scribner, New York.

Willer, D. (1981) The Basic Concepts of the Elementary Theory. In: Willer, D. & Anderson, B., *Networks, Exchange, and Coercion.* Elsevier, New York.

Willer, D. (1999) *Network Exchange Theory.* Greenwood, New York.

microsociology

Thomas J. Scheff

The basic idea of microsociology is to fill in the human detail missing from abstract representations of human beings and their societies. The endeavor begins by describing, second by second, the structure/process of social life. The goal is to show the reciprocal relationship between these events and the nature of the society in which they occur, how each causes the other. There have been three main approaches: ethnographic, experimental, and linguistic.

Ethnography fills in some of the details by close observations and reportage of behavior in context. One example is the study by Edwin Lemert of paranoia among executives in business organizations. By interviewing and observing several subjects, Lemert was able to make a signal contribution to the development of labeling theory.

Experimental studies by Asch and others provide an important example of the use of the quantitative approach to show fine-grained aspects of context that influence conformity and non-conformity. Perhaps the most surprising result of these studies was that a large minority of subjects are easily but inappropriately influenced by their blatant conformity to the behavior of the majority.

Finally, discourse and conversation analysis of social interaction has demonstrated lawful regularities in linguistic sequences (such as questions and responses) that usually go unnoticed. Unlike the first two approaches, close reading of verbal texts reveals the otherwise invisible filigree that makes up a vital core of human relationships.

However, each of the three approaches is specialized to the point that important aspects are omitted or obscured. Ethnography is usually reported at the level of ordinary language, missing systematic observation and analysis of fine details. Quantitative studies are systematized, but leave out the details of context, sequence, and, for the most part, nonverbal components. Conversation analysis emphasizes system and sequence, but omits the link to the larger social context in which dialogue takes place. These difficulties pose a crucial problem for sociology. How can we represent human reality if there are no actual persons anywhere in our studies?

In one of Milan Kundera's essays on the history of the novel he addresses the problem of accessing human reality:

> Try to reconstruct a dialogue from your own life, the dialogue of a quarrel or a dialogue of love. The most precious, the most important situations are utterly gone. Their abstract sense remains (I took this point of view, he took that one. I was aggressive, he was defensive), perhaps a detail or two, but the acoustic-visual concreteness of the situation in all its continuity is lost. (Kundera 1995: 128–9)

And not only is it lost, but we do not even wonder at this loss. We are resigned to losing the concreteness of the present. We immediately transform the present moment into its abstraction. We need only recount an episode we experienced a few hours ago: the dialogue contracts to a brief summary, the setting to a few general features. This applies to even the strongest memories which affect the mind deeply like a trauma: we are so dazzled by their potency that we do not realize how schematic and meager their content is.

When we study, discuss, analyze a reality, we analyze it as it appears in our mind, in our memory. We know reality only in the past tense. We do not know it as it is in the present in the moment when it is happening, when it *is*. The present moment is unlike the memory of it. Remembering is not the negative of forgetting. Remembering is a form of forgetting.

We can assiduously keep a diary and note every event. Rereading the entries one day we will see that they cannot evoke a single concrete image. And still worse: the imagination is unable to help our memory along and reconstruct what has been forgotten. The present – the concreteness of the present – as a phenomenon to consider, as a *structure*, is for us an unknown planet: so we can neither hold on to it in our memory nor reconstruct it through imagination. We die without knowing what we have lived.

How can a scientist or scholar capture reality, when we and the people whom we study usually cannot? As Kundera suggests, only the greatest of novelists, giants such as Tolstoy and Proust, have even come close, by reporting the evocative details of sight, sound, and context that we usually ignore or immediately forget.

Kundera's comments clarify and extend the Proustian quest, not only for the lost past, but for the lost present. Although most of Proust's commentary concerns the recovery of the distant past, a few passages concern a past so immediate that it edges upon the present. For example, in the section called Within a Budding Grove, there is an incident in which the narrator, Marcel, finally meets Albertine, the girl he has been yearning for (and who later becomes the love of his life). At first he is deeply disappointed with the meeting; the whole episode seems banal and empty; he and she both conventional and distant. However, that evening, as

he reconsiders the meeting, he begins to remember the fine details of her gestures, facial expression, and inflections. She comes to life for him, in his "darkroom," as he says, where he is able to develop the "negatives" of his impressions of her earlier in the day. By focusing on the details, he is able to regain a past so immediate that it points toward the possibility of recovering the present.

Proust is still ridiculed for his seeming preoccupation with minutiae. A favorite joke is that it takes him 15 pages to describe turning over in bed. This joke is a defensive maneuver, serving to protect the status quo described by Kundera. Proust implies that the ability to recover even fleeting moments of the past and present are the sine qua non of the great artist: it is these recovered moments that breathe life into art.

But why do we need the living present in the human sciences? Because it is needed to breathe life into our enterprise, also. Linking the minutia to larger wholes can restore human reality to the social sciences. This approach is a way of filling in the details of Proust's method of "developing our negatives in our darkroom." Using transcripts or verbatim texts as data, one interprets the meaning of the smallest parts (words and gestures) of expressions within the context of the ever greater *wholes* within which they occur: sentences, paragraphs, the whole dialogue, the whole relationship, the whole culture and social structure. A central theme in the work of Spinoza was that understanding human beings requires relating the "least parts to the greatest wholes." Microsociology proposes that this method may be carried out in a disciplined program of inquiry.

Social relationships can be represented by two main dimensions: power and integration. Marx's early work gave these dimensions equal attention, social class and rank representing power, alienation/solidarity, integration. But in his later work he focused almost entirely on the power dimension, leading to a huge gap in our understanding of social relationships.

The idea of the social bond can be seen as a way of representing integration in terms of alienation and its opposite, solidarity. The structure/process of actual social relationships involves mixtures of alienation and solidarity, and the exact proportion can be determined through the analysis of verbatim discourse. The difficulty is that in order to carry out this program, one must enter a world that is all but forbidden in western societies: the world of specific emotions and actual relationships.

Charles Horton Cooley provided an important step toward understanding social integration: the looking-glass self "seems to have three principal elements: the imagination of our appearance to the other person; the imagination of his judgment of that appearance, and some sort of self-feeling, such as pride or mortification." Cooley's elements point to the basic components of social integration. The first two involve the imagination of the other's view of self. The two elements combined can be called *degree of attunement*. The other component is made up of the emotional reactions that are real, not imagined, either pride or shame.

The first component, attunement, of "living in the minds of others, without realizing it," as Cooley put it, is directly contrary to the very foundation of western culture, violating the canon of individualism. Living in the minds of others implies that individuals, as well as being separate units, may also be united, at least momentarily, as a pair or member of a larger group. Although the idea of unity between two or more persons (collective consciousness) instead of separation is a staple in eastern cultures, it is unacceptable to the extent of being taboo in western thought.

Cooley's focus on pride and shame is also a deviation. Western culture has at its center the embedded idea of the isolated, self-contained individual. The pride/shame component of social integration implies that our self-feelings are dependent on other people. For this reason, discussions of shame and its relatives are usually avoided, both in lay and social science discourse.

Goffman did not acknowledge a debt to Cooley, but his analysis of concrete examples led him to a deep exploration of the looking-glass self (Scheff 2006). Indeed, Goffman's treatment of a large number of examples implies a fourth element. Cooley stopped at the third, with the experience of pride or shame. Goffman's analyses, especially of impression management, imply a fourth step: the management of emotion. Goffman had nothing to say about the pride option, but his examples suggest that actors usually do not accept shame/embarrassment passively. Instead, they try to manage it, by avoidance, if possible. Most of the embarrassment/shame possibilities in Goffman's examples are not about the actual occurrence of emotions, but anticipations, and management based on these anticipations. (In European languages other than English, the anticipation of shame/embarrassment is taken to be a shame variant, such as the French *pudeur* – modesty.) This idea is expressible in English as "a sense of shame." Goffman's examples further imply that if shame/embarrassment cannot be avoided, then his actors actively deny it, attempting to save face, on the one hand, and/or to avoid pain, on the other. It is Goffman's fourth step that brings his examples to life, because it touches on the dynamics of impression and emotion management that underlie most moments of everyday life.

The Cooley/Goffman looking-glass self provides an underlying model of structure/process of social integration. Alienation/solidarity can be understood in terms of degree of attunement (Goffman called it mutual awareness), on the one hand, and the emotional responses that follow from it, on the other. Pride signals and generates solidarity. Shame signals and generates alienation. Shame is a normal part of the process of social control; it becomes disruptive only when hidden or denied. Denial of shame, especially when it takes the form of false pride (egoism), generates self-perpetuating cycles of alienation.

Threats to a secure bond can come in two different formats: either the bond is too loose or too tight. Relationships in which the bond is too loose are *isolated*: there is mutual misunderstanding or failure to understand, or mutual rejection. Relationships in which the bond is too tight are *engulfed*: at least one of the parties in the relationship, say the subordinate, understands and embraces the standpoint of the other at the expense of the subordinate's own beliefs, values, or feelings. The other is accepted by rejecting parts of one's self. In engulfed families, a child can only be "good" by blind obedience and conformity, by relinquishing its curiosity, intuition, or feelings.

This view of alienation is congruent with, and further develops, Durkheim's theory of social integration, which he derived from his study of the causes of suicide (Durkheim 1952). He argued that suicidal inclinations were generated by bonds that were too loose (egoism) or too tight (altruism). This theory extends Durkheim's by describing the microscopic components of this system, and also the structure of a secure bond, which Durkheim only implies – one that is neither too loose nor too tight. In this scheme, a secure bond involves a balance between the viewpoint of self and other. Although each party understands and accepts the viewpoint of the other, this acceptance does not go to either extreme: neither giving up major parts of one's own viewpoint out of loyalty (engulfment), nor discounting the other's viewpoint (isolation).

The idea of balance leads to a crucial distinction between a secure bond (genuine solidarity) and an engulfed bond (blind loyalty). These two states are usually confounded in social science. Instead of seeing blind loyalty as a type of alienation (from self), it is seen as closeness. But the individual who is not attuned to self cannot be close (attuned) with anyone else either.

A second advantage is that this model of integration is grounded at both the interpersonal and the intergroup levels. The Kunderarian idea of the concrete reality of relationships can be implemented by close study of verbatim recordings at the interpersonal level, and by the close analysis of the texts of exchanges between leaders of groups at the collective level. An example of dialogue between leaders of groups can be found in an analysis of the letters exchanged immediately before the beginning of World War I by the Kaiser of Germany and the Tsar of Russia, and between the Kaiser and the prime minister of England (Scheff 1994: 82–4). Their letters betray some of the emotional bases of what turned out to be an unnecessary and ruinously destructive war.

The version of microsociology proposed here can be applied both to interpersonal and societal interaction in a way that may afford a path to linking the least parts (words and gestures) to greatest wholes (abstract theories and social structures).

SEE ALSO: Conversation Analysis; Cooley, Charles Horton; Ethnography; Goffman, Erving; Looking-Glass Self; Mead, George Herbert; Micro–Macro Links; Social Psychology

REFERENCES AND SUGGESTED READINGS

Durkheim, É. (1952 [1905]) *Suicide*. Routledge, London.

Kundera, M. (1995) *Testaments Betrayed*. Harper Collins, New York.

Scheff, T. J. (1994) *Bloody Revenge: Emotions, Nationalism, War*. Westview Press, Boulder.

Scheff, T. J. (2006) *Goffman Unbound: Toward a New Paradigm*. Paradigm Publishers, Boulder.

middleman minorities

Pyong Gap Min

Before the 1960s, social scientists usually used the dichotomous concepts of majority–minority groups or dominant–subordinate groups to discuss ethnic and race relations in the United States and other multi-ethnic societies. However, they found they needed a new concept to refer to those minority groups that stood between these two poles in social status and economic role. Thus, they created the concept of middleman minorities to refer to these intermediate groups since the 1960s (Blalock 1967: 79–84; Eitzen 1971; Bonacich 1972; Bonacich & Modell 1980; Turner & Bonacich 1980; Zenner 1991; Min 1996).

The most important characteristic of middleman minorities is their intermediary economic role between the producers of the dominant group and the consuming masses (minority customers). Middleman minority members bridge a huge status gap existent in the host society by distributing products made by members of the ruling group to minority customers. Thus, their businesses are heavily concentrated in trade in low-income minority neighborhoods. Middleman minorities are also characterized by their subjection to "host hostility." On the one hand, middleman merchants encounter boycotts and arson of their stores, and other forms of rejection, by minority customers they serve. On the other hand, in time of political crisis, they can be scapegoated by the ruling group that controls the economy. Finally, another important characteristic of middleman minorities is their strong ethnic ties/solidarity. Middleman minorities tend to maintain ethnic traditions and solidarity over generations. Although their lack of assimilation and ethnic solidarity may be partly caused by their group characteristics, it is largely the result of their economic segregation and reactions to their experiences with host hostility.

Social scientists consider Jews in medieval Europe and in pre-war Poland, Asian Indians in South and West Africa, and Chinese in various Asian countries (Thailand, the Philippines, and Vietnam) as typical middleman minorities (Eitzen 1971; Bonacich 1972; Zenner 1991). These groups concentrated in small retail businesses (moneylending in the case of Jews in medieval Europe). They also experienced boycotts and other forms of rejection by minority customers. In addition, they maintained strong ethnic ties and solidarity. Bonacich and Modell (1980) consider Japanese truck farmers and Japanese wholesalers and retailers of farm products in the first half of the twentieth century as middleman merchants. Min (1996) has examined contemporary Korean immigrant merchants in black neighborhoods as middlemen that distribute white corporate products to low-income minority customers.

Bonacich and other scholars (Bonacich 1972; Bonacich & Modell 1980; Light 1980; Light & Bonacich 1988: 17–18) have used the term "middleman minority" to refer to immigrant and ethnic groups with high concentrations in commercial occupations. In this definition, the group characteristics of middleman minorities, such as the proclivity to "take risks," "sojourning orientation," and the "separatist mentality," mainly contributed to their middleman role. However, it is better to use the term "trading minorities" to refer to these immigrant and minority groups that are or were merely concentrated in commercial occupations. As noted above, classical theorists have reserved "middleman minorities" for the immigrant and minority groups that played the economic intermediary role between the ruling group of producers and the consuming masses. Since middleman minorities were needed to bridge the two socially stratified groups, the social structure of the host society in the form of a "status gap," rather than the characteristics of middleman minorities, was the main cause of the development of a middleman minority in a particular society.

The middleman literature shows that middleman minorities existed in two forms of societies with extreme types of social stratification. First, middleman minorities existed in pre-industrial, aristocratic societies such as those found in medieval Europe or pre-war Poland (Eitzen 1971; Zenner 1991). Jews played the role of the economic intermediaries as moneylenders or merchants in these pre-industrial societies because there was no intermediate class that could have bridged the gap between the ruling group and the consuming masses. Second, middleman minorities developed in colonial societies, such as the Philippines or South Africa. The colonial ruling groups, Spaniards in the Philippines and whites in South Africa and other African countries, did not allow, or at least discouraged, the indigenous populations from developing economic power, which they feared might have been used to overthrow the colonial governments (Palmer 1957; Eitzen 1971). Thus, they brought in or encouraged the alien groups, Chinese in the Philippines and other Asian countries, and Asian Indians in South Africa and other African countries, to specialize in minority-oriented businesses.

As noted above, middleman minorities existed in pre-industrial or colonized societies where social strata were more or less polarized and fixed, and which had no significant middle class. The twentieth-century United States, with the middle class accounting for a significant or a majority of the population, was not a society favorable for the development of a middleman minority. However, Rinder (1959: 257) pointed out that "although strata boundaries are continuous and flexible in American society, a status gap is apparent in the margins of white–Negro relations." In the early twentieth century, Jews in New York, Los Angeles, Chicago, and other cities dominated retail businesses in black neighborhoods, playing a middleman minority role bridging white manufacturers and suppliers on the one hand and poor black residents on the other (Cohen 1970).

Compared to the number of Jewish merchants, the number of Chinese merchants in black neighborhoods was insignificant. Yet, the middleman role of the earlier Chinese immigrants in black neighborhoods, too, received scholarly attention. For example, Loewen (1971) emphasized the white–black status gap in explaining the concentration of Chinese immigrant families in the Mississippi Delta in the black-oriented grocery business. Loewen argued that the social structure of the Delta, characterized by rigid segregation, a large racial status gap, and a sizable social distance between blacks and whites, was mainly responsible for the Chinese immigrants' concentration and success in black-oriented grocery retailing.

Compared to a small number of Chinese immigrants running grocery stores in black neighborhoods in the pre-1965 era, an exceptionally large number of post-1965 Korean immigrants engage in grocery, liquor, produce, and other types of retail businesses in black neighborhoods in Los Angeles, New York, and other major cities. The similar structural forces relating to the white–black racial stratification system that contributed to the Jewish-owned businesses in black neighborhoods in the earlier period have helped Korean immigrants establish these retail stores in black neighborhoods (Min 1996).

Blacks in inner-city neighborhoods, even in contemporary America, have some resemblance to indigenous colonized minorities in the Philippines and South Africa. They still live in an "internal colony" controlled by an outside white society (Blauner 1972). Thus, the internal colonial model seems to be useful to understanding the middleman minority role of Korean immigrants in low-income black neighborhoods in the United States. Like middleman minorities in other colonized societies, these Korean merchants have encountered boycotts, arson, and riots. However, unlike in colonized societies, in American society various immigrant groups have usually achieved intergenerational social mobility. Fluent in English, second-generation Koreans have moved into the mainstream economy (Min 2005). Thus, in the United States, a series of new immigrant groups plays the role of middleman minorities, without transmitting it over generations.

SEE ALSO: Assimilation; Boundaries (Racial/Ethnic); Colonialism (Neocolonialism); Division of Labor; Majorities; Scapegoating

REFERENCES AND SUGGESTED READINGS

Blalock, H. (1967) *Toward a Theory of Minority Group Relations*. Wiley, New York.

Blauner, R. (1972) *Racial Oppression in America*. Harper & Row, New York.

Bonacich, E. (1972) A Theory of Middleman Minorities. *American Sociological Review* 37: 583–94.

Bonacich, E. & Modell, J. (1980) *The Economic Basis of Ethnic Solidarity: Small Business in the Japanese American Community*. University of California Press, Berkeley.

Cohen, N. (1970) *The Los Angeles Riots: A Sociological Study*. Praeger, New York.

Eitzen, D. S. (1971) Two Minorities: The Jews of Poland and the Chinese of the Philippines. In: Yetman, N. R. & Steele, C. H. (Eds.), *Majority and Minority: The Dynamics of Racial and Ethnic Relations*. Allyn & Bacon, Boston.

Light, I. (1980) Asian Enterprise in America: Chinese, Japanese, and Koreans in Small Business. In: Cummings, S. (Ed.), *Self-Help in Urban America*. Kenikart, Port Washington, NY.

Light, I. & Bonacich, E. (1988) *Immigrant Entrepreneurs: Koreans in Los Angeles*. University of California Press, Berkeley and Los Angeles.

Loewen, J. (1971) *The Mississippi Chinese: Between Blacks and White*. Harvard University Press, Cambridge, MA.

Min, P. G. (1996) *Caught in the Middle: Korean Communities in New York and Los Angeles*. University of California Press, Los Angeles.

Min, P. G. (2005) Korean Americans. In: Min, P. G. (Ed.), *Asian Americans: Contemporary Trends and Issues*, 2nd, expanded edn. Sage, Newbury Park, CA.

Palmer, M. (1957) *The History of Indians in Natal*. Natal Regional Survey, Vol. 10. Oxford University Press, Cape Town.

Rinder, I. (1959) Strangers in the Land: Social Relations in the Status Gap. *Social Problems* 6: 253–60.

Turner, J. and Bonacich, E. (1980) Toward a Composite Theory of Middleman Minorities. *Ethnicity* 7: 144–58.

Zenner, W. (1991) *Minorities in the Middle: A Cross-Cultural Analysis*. State University of New York Press, Albany.

migration, ethnic conflicts, and racism

Karin Scherschel

Migration refers to a process of people shifting across borders. Recently, sociology has discussed migration as a core element of globalization. Some theorists, like Stephen Castles and Mark J. Miller (1993), have gone so far as to label the last decade of the twentieth century and the first decade of the twenty-first as the "Age of Migration." A currently discussed topic has been classified as "new migration," which is founded on the following reasons: the number of countries and the amount of people that are nowadays involved in migratory processes is distinct from earlier movements. Contemporary migration flows have become globally significant because of the improvement of travel and communication facilities. This crucial effect of globalization has overcome further distances than before. Furthermore, one important aspect is diversity. Scholars distinguish between a wide range of migration types such as asylum seekers, refugees, undocumented migrants, and labor migrants (highly skilled, unskilled). Finally, since the 1990s the increasingly restrictive measures to control migratory process, particularly the flow of asylum seekers, has been qualified as a remarkable feature.

However, migration is an old phenomenon with people migrating from the beginning of humankind. Well-known historical types of migration were caused by colonialism and capitalism. As the Industrial Revolution began, after the decline of feudalism, national awakening provoked a great labor migration. Theorists emphasize the important rule of labor and forced migration (slavery) for the dynamics of colonialism, capitalist expansion, and the process of nation building. Contemporary migration and postcolonial ethnic conflicts are often seen as a result of former relationships between receiving and sending countries.

Migration study became a research area of sociology at the beginning of the twentieth century. The most influential work in this area was initiated by the Chicago School of Sociology. The important tendency in the first period of migration study was to examine the process of assimilation and integration. Concepts such as generational, ecological, and economic cycle models, which focused upon different stages of assimilation, represented the broad body of scholarship during this time. One of the best-known key concepts of this type of thinking was the "race relation cycle" developed by Robert Ezra Park (1950). According to Park, the process of assimilation has the following five stages: contact, competition, conflict, accommodation, and assimilation. All these concepts had an affinity to modernization theory because they were based on the assumption that assimilation is a gradual, progressive, and inevitable process. Racism against immigrants and ethnic inequality were treated as temporary periods and transitory tensions between groups in the process of incorporation into a modern society.

In contrast, ethnic groups and racist-motivated actions did not disappear but rather became a prominent marker of multi-ethnic societies over time. Considering the socioeconomic position of minorities, studies in this area have shown that these groups are systematically disadvantaged relative to the "life chances" of the majority group. A great amount of ethnic groups occupy structurally subordinate positions in some areas such as unemployment, housing, education, and health.

Later approaches became more sophisticated in two important ways. First, theorists took into consideration that race and ethnic relations must be seen as a reciprocal or dialectical process between social groups. Second, assimilation should be conceptualized as one possible result of others in dealing with interethnic relations. The consequence of this theoretical shift was that the assimilation approach relinquished its teleological bias.

The international migration process became an influential topic in sociology and subsequently led to a wide variety of works. One of the best-known concepts of international migratory processes is the "laws of migration" developed by Ernest G. Ravenstein (1885, 1889). He was interested in examining empirical regularities of migration flows such as the relationship between distance and migration frequency. He also stressed the importance of migrants' economic patterns in migration process.

The international migratory process is based on interplay between various factors and it is impossible to identify one main movement pattern. The migratory process could be caused by economic, political, cultural, or environmental factors. Scholars differentiate between push and pull factors. Migration process on a micro level is seen as the result of decision processes made by individuals. Some theorists emphasize that individuals calculate risks, interests, and aims to maximize and improve their living conditions. Proponents of this assumption highlight that migrants act as rational choice decision-makers. Other theorists focus upon subjective mind maps; they also take into consideration the important role that social networks such as kinship and family play for individual decisions (chain migration).

Migration flows on a macro level are often seen as a result of economic conditions and historical relationships between receiving and sending countries. Past and contemporary policies on immigration also play an important role in explaining migration flows. Recent debates stress the relationship between increasing transnational flows of capital, goods, information, and people. Migration should not be treated as an isolated phenomenon but rather should be seen as an interlaced relationship of the above factors. From an economic view, globalization has provoked a restructuring of capitalism which has led to a great demand for immigrant labor.

Of course, economic conditions play an important role in interpreting the conditions that initiate migratory process, but they are not capable of providing an explanation for the unfolding and the continuation of international migration across time and space.

Considering the above, the transnationalism approach offers a new scope of the perpetuation of the migratory process, thus providing a new framework for the study of international migration. Here the sociological focus is on social network building. A growing number of scholars identify the social networks of immigrants as a fundamental key in understanding contemporary migration. The reconsideration of the migratory process is based on the assumption that many migrants nowadays manage to live in two or more societies, their homeland and their host countries. Transnational migrants create through exchange, reciprocity, and social support a common space or field of symbolic and collective representations beyond the nation-state.

While the boundaries of nation-states are more permeable than earlier times, we are simultaneously witnessing a resurgence of nationalist movements and politics of differentiation. As a topic of migration study, ethnic conflict became a prominent feature. Today, theorists observe minority groups and identity movements worldwide that struggle to have their culture, territories, and sometimes even sovereign states of their own. Such movements are, in most cases, accompanied by activities such as racist attacks, violence, expulsion, and extreme ethnic cleansing.

Ethnic conflict refers to a struggle between groups constructing themselves or constructed by others through some features such as traditions, a similar geographical origin, values, language, symbols, and artifacts. Ethnic conflict is a contested category and there is not a common scientific agreement of how the term should be defined. Ethnic conflict addresses migration and ethnicity studies in various ways.

Such conflicts are often seen as a push factor regarding the migratory process, especially for refugees who escape violence or persecution. After the collapse of the communist system, the proliferation of nationalism in successor states of the former East was treated as one fundamental factor for creating migration flows toward Western Europe. Theorists also label attacks on and violence against migrants in their host societies as ethnic conflicts.

Most of the work on ethnic conflicts deals with the meanings, origins, causes, extent, and persistence of ethnic conflicts. Some explanations stress economic conditions to approach ethnic conflicts. An early influential framework was the split labor market theory developed by Bonacich (1972), which focuses on conflicting resource interests of different ethnic groups. Working with two different ethnic groups at different wages for the same job, such a labor market will be created. Some theories argued that ethnic conflicts should be seen as a consequence of competition for scarce resources. Inequality among majority and subordinate groups is often seen as rooted in former relationships between the colonizer and the colonized.

Other theorists have emphasized the notion of mobilization, collective actions, and solidarity for articulating common group interest and achieving aims such as political, cultural, or material gains. In this respect, ethnic struggle should be conceptualized as an important resource and a powerful instrument to actualize group interests. Thus, ethnicity helps people to create a self-understanding, thereby forming a distinct identity in relation to other groups, and furthermore helps them to define and struggle for their own place and identity in a globalized world.

Despite theoretical disagreements, most scholars consider the notion of ethnic conflicts to be treated as a complex phenomenon. A framework should take into consideration the interplay between economic, historical, and cultural dimensions. The majority of theories have overcome the modernistic view on ethnic conflicts as a transitory occurrence. The recent debate is influenced by anti-essentialist thinking. In this respect, ethnic conflicts must be conceptualized as a relational concept including self-identifications and social ascription. The analysis also should reflect how discourses such as academic, media, everyday, or political discourses emerge and heighten ethnic topics.

Ethnic conflicts mostly use images of blood, kinship, homeland, and common ancestry. In this respect, the concept of ethnic conflict is connected to the understanding of racism.

While racism on a micro level refers to a set of practices, beliefs, and attitudes of everyday cultures, the phenomenon is often treated on a macro level as an ideology, discourse, or marker of social stratification. Sociological interest in racism has developed over time into a broad body of studies, especially related to migration issues. Similar to ethnic conflicts, racism is a highly debated and also contested topic. There are a great number of accounts in which racist practices and ideologies have been conceptualized. Some theorists emphasize that the way scholars should theorize and define racism should take into consideration its empirical appearance in specific historical settings. Stuart Hall (1989: 917) suggested referring not to one single racism but to empirical racisms.

The word racism was first used in a book written by Magnus Hirschfeld (1938). The term racism was applied to criticize and refute scientific racism during the eighteenth and nineteenth centuries. In this respect, racism is related to the category of race. During this period, race was used as a category to classify human beings into unchanging, natural, and distinct groups. The historical scientific concept of race claimed a strict relationship between biological, moral, and intellectual characteristics of human groups. The use of the category race led to a hierarchical classification of human types that made it possible to distinguish them into "superior" and "inferior" racial groups. After World War II and the experience of German fascism, during the 1950s and 1960s UNESCO initiated four meetings where reputable theorists discussed the explanatory value of the category race. The result was the rejection of scientific racism. Since then, a growing number of theories of racism have dealt with race as a social construction.

The modern sociology of racism offers a broad range of topics regarding the persistence of racial categories, their influence on stratification, and institutional practices as well as the process of racialization, which describes how groups became naturalized. Sociologists also deal with the question of how the relationship and interplay between racism and related issues such as race, class, gender, ethnicity, and nation can be theorized.

Early Marxist approaches maintained that racism and ethnic identities could be explained by the dynamics of capitalism. Race was treated comparatively to class as a subordinated category, and furthermore as a transitory occurrence. The capitalist class used racism firstly as an ideological strategy to avoid class solidarity between working-class blacks and whites. Distracting working-class attention from the reality of class exploitation, racism leads secondly to a delusion of class consciousness. Critics of the above emphasize the reductionist tendency and its affinity to modernization theory because of its teleological imagination from a classless society.

Recent decades have witnessed new forms of racism and new extreme right primordialism. With the collapse of communism there emerged nationalist movements, which were accompanied by racist attacks and violence.

Some theorists highlight the role of migration policies and public debates that created "fears" about the likelihood of mass migration.

A more recent debate questions how contemporary racism differs from older concepts. Influential proponents like Barker (1981) and Balibar (1990) argue that the growing public debate about immigration in western countries and the foundation of such groups calling themselves, and being called, the new right have given rise to a new racism. The key issue of this racism is to claim the uniqueness of every culture and the necessity to preserve difference. From this position, thinkers of the new right derive the right of cultural difference and the argument that the presence of other cultures in their country will be threatening. Culture became a prominent marker and has justified unequal treatment of immigrants. The term has taken the place of biological arguments. According to Balibar and other proponents of the new racism or "cultural racism," the term culture substitutes the older concept of race.

From a postmodern view, the relationship of racism to other modes of discourse, such as gender, nation, and class, should be centered on the question of the overlapping and multiplying of the above modes. Cultural study theorists view the notion of race as a contingent and unstable cultural category. Representatives of this field also raise the question of how people construct their identities along various lines in an increasingly migratory and globalized world. An anti-essentialist understanding of racism highlights that racist discourses are always woven together with other divisions such as class, gender, and ethnicity.

Migration, ethnic conflicts, and racism are multidimensional social phenomena. There is no simple model to explain their relationship in all its complexity. More research is needed to clarify their interplay on different levels such as everyday ideology production, modern institutions, nation-state, and global change. While several studies deal with labor migrants, the living conditions of other groups, such as asylum seekers and undocumented migrants, are undertheorized. Further, future research should ask in which ways racism and ethnic conflicts emerge from global change. Racism and ethnic conflicts should not only be interpreted as a reaction to a deterritorialized and globalized world; it is essential to see also how such phenomena will be fostered by opportunities such as worldwide communication and traveling created by the process of globalization.

SEE ALSO: Ethnic Cleansing; Ethnic Enclaves; Ethnic Groups; Ethnicity; Globalization; Hate Crimes; Migration: Internal; Migration: International; Nation-State; Race; Race and Ethnic Politics; Race (Racism); Scientific Racism; Social Integration and Inclusion; Transnationalism; Violence

REFERENCES AND SUGGESTED READINGS

Balibar, E. (1990) Gibt es einen Neorassismus? In: Balibar, E. & Wallerstein, I. (Eds.) *Rasse, Klasse, Nation.* Ambivalente Identitäten, Hamburg/Berlin.

Barker, M. (1981) *The New Racism: Conservatives and the Ideology of the Tribe.* Junctions Books, London.

Bonacich, E. (1972) A Theory of Ethnic Antagonism: The Split Labor Market. *American Sociological Review* 37: 547–59.

Castles, S. & Miller, M. J. (1993) *The Age of Migration: International Population Movements in the Modern World.* Macmillan, London.

Hall, S. (1989) Rassismus als ideologischer Diskurs. *Das Argument* 178: S913–21.

Hirschfeld, M. (1938) *Racism.* Victor Gollancz, London.

Park, R. E. (1950) *Race and Culture: Essays in the Sociology of Contemporary Man.* Free Press, Glencoe, IL.

Ravenstein, E. G. (1885) The Laws of Migration. *Journal of the Royal Statistical Society* 48: 167–227.

Ravenstein, E. G. (1889) The Laws of Migration. *Journal of the Royal Statistical Society* 52: 241–301.

migration: internal

Kyle Crowder and Matthew Hall

In general, internal migration refers to the movement of individuals or populations within a social system. More specifically, following the United Nations definition, internal migration is a permanent change in residence from one geographical unit to another within a particular country. For example, internal migration may involve a change in residence from a rural area to a city, from one city to another, or from one region of a country to another. From the perspective of the destination or receiving area, an individual making such a move is an in-migrant, while that same individual is an out-migrant from the sending area. Because internal migration has profound individual-level and collective repercussions, research on the topic remains a popular endeavor for economists, geographers, and demographers, despite the absence of ideal data or definitional consensus.

THE IMPORTANCE OF INTERNAL MIGRATION

The importance of migration derives primarily from its position as one of the central demographic processes that shape the size, distribution, and composition of populations. Changes in the size of a population can be thought of as a function of two forces, natural increase (the relative numbers of births and deaths) and net migration (the relative number of in-migrants and out-migrants). Whereas overall rates of mortality and fertility tend to change fairly slowly over time, the size of a population may increase or decrease substantially over a short period as a result of a sudden change in the number of in-migrants or out-migrants. Thus, internal migration tends to be the most volatile component of population change for geographical units within a country. Since internal migration represents a redistribution of the existing population of a country, internal migration flows simultaneously affect the size of the sending and receiving populations, affecting competition for food, housing, and other resources in both locations. Economists have long viewed internal migration as the primary mechanism through which the equilibrium between the distribution of economic opportunities and the distribution of labor across areas of a country is maintained.

Because migrants are rarely representative of the populations in either the sending or receiving areas, often differing from non-migrants in terms of average age, education, race or ethnicity, and other sociodemographic characteristics, patterns of migration have the potential to dramatically alter the composition of both sending and receiving areas. In fact, large numbers of in-migrants to an area may be balanced by a similar number of out-migrants leaving the area, producing a relatively low level of net migration, but a high level of total migration (in-migration + out-migration). While such a pattern may have little effect on the size of the population, it could, depending on the relative characteristics of in- and out-migrants, profoundly affect the composition of the population. Typically, high levels of internal migration affect both the size and the composition of a population, often with profound impacts for social and economic conditions in both sending and receiving areas.

The importance of migration extends well beyond the effects on sending and receiving populations; the effect on migrants themselves is at least as profound. Conceptually, a migration event not only involves a change in residence, but also represents a change in social environment and reorientation of the context of daily activities. In many cases, internal migration necessitates a search for new housing, competition for employment, and the loss of social contacts developed in the place of origin. The extent of these disruptions depends largely on the type of move undertaken and the relative social context of the place of origin and destination; a move from a city to a neighboring city may be less socially and economically disruptive than a move from a rural area to an urban center.

DEFINING AND MEASURING INTERNAL MIGRATION

Unlike fertility and mortality, migration has no biological basis and cannot be measured unequivocally. The definitional ambiguity of the term is reflected in two aspects of the UN guidelines. First, efforts to consistently define internal migration are complicated by the dubious permanence of many moves. The UN guidelines suggest that a permanent relocation is indicated by an absence from the place of origin that lasts for at least one year. Following this convention, internal migration is differentiated from daily commutes, vacations, and the mobility of students and migrant workers who plan to return to their original place of residence within a few months. However, this temporal standard is somewhat arbitrary and has not been universally adopted, nor does it unambiguously distinguish migrants who have no intention to return to their place of origin from those making a longer but essentially impermanent sojourn to another city, state, or region for educational or employment purposes. Second, and perhaps more problematic, is the fact that the standard definition of internal migration does not specify the scale of geographical units or the distance across which a move must occur in order to be considered true internal migration. This lack of specificity creates the potential for tremendous variation in the operational definitions used in research on the topic.

Data on internal migration generally come from three sources, each of which is characterized by unique strengths and weaknesses. First, population registry systems, essentially continuous records of citizens' vital statistics, typically require individuals to register with the local administrative office upon moving to a new area of the country, creating a record of each internal migration event. Unfortunately, few countries maintain a population registry and many of those that do exist contain limited social and economic characteristics with which to assess the determinants or consequences of migration.

In lieu of data from population registries, migration researchers often rely on data from periodic population censuses. Based on these data, the magnitude of net migration (in-migrants minus out-migrants) can be assessed using an indirect method in which the estimated natural increase of the population (births minus deaths) is subtracted from the total population change in an area, leaving the component of change attributable to the net addition of migrants. While these estimates are simple and widely utilized, their reliability depends greatly on the quality of mortality and fertility data and they provide little information about the factors affecting migration or the influence of migration on the composition of the population. In most countries, census records document individuals' place of birth, place of current residence, and perhaps the place of residence at some intermediate point

of time. Comparing the place of residence at different points in time provides the basis for inferring internal migration events and for estimating population flows between specific origins and destinations. However, this basic method fails to capture migration events experienced by an individual between the two reference points and the potential for effective cross-national comparisons is undermined by differences in the mobility intervals and levels of geography utilized in census items.

Surveys represent a final, somewhat rarer, source of data on internal migration behavior. In the US, surveys such as the Current Population Survey provide regular snapshots of annual migration behavior and afford the opportunity to assess the basic association between various types of migration and a variety of micro-level characteristics. Even more powerful are panel studies that collect detailed information on the set of panel members at regular intervals across an extended period of time. These data make it possible to trace, prospectively, multiple occurrences of various types of migration behavior by individual panel members and offer the opportunity to rigorously test theoretical arguments about the determinants of migration. However, these surveys are of limited utility for assessing the overall magnitude of internal migration between areas or its impact on aggregate population change.

In combination with the definitional ambiguity of the phenomenon, the inadequacies associated with available data sources undermine the ability to make reliable cross-national comparisons of the magnitude and dynamics of internal migration or to compare the results of research that may employ different operational definitions. Nevertheless, the combination of various sources has enabled the development of a rich and varied literature on the patterns, determinants, and consequences of internal migration.

EXPLAINING INTERNAL MIGRATION

Although a wide range of theoretical models has been employed in migration research, the push–pull theory remains the most widely used explanatory framework in the study of internal migration. While this model has been criticized for its lack of predictive power, it provides a parsimonious framework for examining both aggregate flows of population between two locations and individual-level variations in the propensity to migrate. In short, the model argues that migration events result from the combined influence of three types of factors. Push factors include undesirable characteristics in the place of origin that compel population members to consider leaving the area. Pull factors, in contrast, are those characteristics of a potential destination that attract migrants to the area. Following a rational choice framework, the likelihood of migration is high when the potential destination offers individuals more advantages than does the place of origin. However, responses to these relative push and pull factors are shaped by a third set of factors referred to as intervening obstacles. In essence, these intervening obstacles are conditions that increase the social or economic costs of migration and intervene between the desire to move and the actual act of migrating. Some intervening obstacles, such as a great physical distance or a high cost of transportation between the origin and potential destination, may increase the cost of migration for all potential migrants, thereby limiting the overall magnitude of population flow between two locations. Other intervening factors, such as the strength of social ties in the community of origin or destination, the availability of financial resources, health, and risk aversion, vary across individuals.

Economic opportunities available in the area of destination have long been treated as the primary push and pull factors in migration decisions and considerations such as relative employment levels in, and wage differentials between, the origin and destination areas continue to dominate explanations of many migration flows. However, the push–pull model also accommodates non-economic factors as potential pushes and pulls, including the availability of housing and other resources, the relative political or sociodemographic conditions in the origin and destination, or the location of family and friends. For many individuals, internal migration accompanies major life transitions and represents a tool for attaining higher levels of education, a better job, or more attractive social surroundings.

Individual-level variations in the response to various push and pull factors and the strength of intervening obstacles help to produce migrant populations that are highly selective of certain characteristics. For example, internal migration (especially longer-distance migration) is positively associated with education because, in comparison to those with less education, highly educated population members are often in the best position to take advantage of economic opportunities in the place of destination and tend to have access to both information about potential destinations and financial resources to carry out a move. The likelihood of migrating also varies by age, peaking in young adulthood when the long-term, cumulative benefits of economic opportunities in another location are greatest and the obstacles associated with poor health, social obligations, and economic investment in the community of origin are least restrictive. A gender imbalance also characterizes many migration streams, and individuals who are married and/or have children are less likely to make a move because the cost of disrupting the social and economic ties maintained by family members often outweighs the pull of another geographical area. These selectivity factors depend on the type of internal migration considered and the amenities in the origin and destination that potential migrants must weigh, but all have important repercussions for the composition of both sending and receiving populations.

PATTERNS OF INTERNAL MIGRATION AND RECENT RESEARCH

Although data inconsistencies make cross-national comparisons difficult, there is fairly strong evidence that the magnitude of internal migration varies across countries and regions of the world. Rates of migration are thought to increase with economic development, but the percentage of the population relocating each year varies even among highly industrialized countries; populations in Japan and European countries exhibit internal migration rates that are only one-half to two-thirds as high as those in the US, Canada, New Zealand, and Australia. Perhaps even more pronounced are international variations in the types of moves that affect various populations. While moves between rural areas, from urban areas to rural areas, and within urban areas are common in many countries, internal migration patterns in developing nations are generally dominated by high rates of migration from rural to urban areas. As a result of this migration, combined with rapid population growth, the number of people living in urban areas has increased sixfold in Asia, Latin America, and the Caribbean, and by over nine times in Africa in the second half of the twentieth century. Thus, despite the countervailing force of rapid natural increase in rural areas, the percentage of the population residing in urban areas is expected to surpass the 50 percent mark in virtually every region of the world by 2025. Reflecting the importance of this urban transition, much of the research on internal migration in developing countries has focused on cross-national variations in the pace of rural-to-urban migration, the uneven pattern of urban development, and the consequences of rapid urbanization for future economic development, the provision of city services, and environmental conditions in developing nations.

Consistent with Wilbur Zelinsky's (1971) migration transition thesis, patterns of internal migration tend to be somewhat more diverse in economically developed parts of the world where levels of urbanization are already high. In the United States, for example, researchers have focused on a wide range of major internal migration processes, including both historical and contemporary shifts in patterns of interregional migration, ongoing metropolitan decentralization, and migration between demographically and economically differentiated neighborhoods. Research on migration between states and regions within the US documented the westward expansion of the population during the early decades of the country's history, the concentration of population in the urban centers of the Midwest and Northeast as migrants from surrounding rural areas and other regions of the country were attracted to the economic opportunities available during industrialization, and then the reversal of these migration flows after World War II, with the original industrial core of the Northeast and Midwest losing both economic prominence and migrants to southern and western states. In addition to tracking these basic migration patterns and documenting their efficiency in redistributing the population, social scientists have investigated the causes of these population shifts, giving rise to debates about the relative effects of aggregate adjustments to changing ecological conditions and the political and economic manipulation by corporate interests to spur competition between regions and cities for increasingly mobile capital. Common to most theoretical arguments is the acknowledgment that patterns of internal migration continue to respond to the distribution of economic opportunities. However, in the context of a post-industrial, electronic economy, many researchers have also argued that non-economic conditions are increasingly important in determining migration patterns. According to these arguments, the push and pull factors that shape patterns of internal migration in the US have become increasingly complex in recent decades, producing migration flows to various regions and states that differ sharply in terms of their sociodemographic composition.

Recent patterns of internal migration within regions of the US have been characterized by cycles of decentralization. As in most nations, American cities represented the central nodes of economic activity during the initial stages of industrialization and experienced explosive growth as a result of in-migration. In the US, however, the process of population decentralization away from the urban core began almost immediately after the birth of US cities. After World War II, a combination of consumer preferences, demographic forces, and federal policy accelerated the pace of migration from central cities into suburban counties of metropolitan areas and set into motion a process of decentralization that continues today with the perpetual expansion of low-density suburban fringes, the extension of metropolitan areas into surrounding counties, and residential development of non-metropolitan counties. While suburban growth is largely the product of internal migration flows that cover fairly short distances – from central cities to suburban counties of metropolitan areas – the purported impacts have been dramatic, including economic disinvestment and the concentration of poverty in central cities, the entrenchment of residential segregation by race, metropolitan political fragmentation, the erosion of civic engagement, the loss of land available for agriculture, and environmental degradation.

Given continual shifts in the patterns of internal migration in both developing and more developed parts of the world, and the importance of these processes for social, political, and demographic conditions, mobility between geographical areas within countries will continue to garner a good deal of research interest. Ideally, data from censuses and surveys will be supplemented by new sources that provide the basis for more effective cross-national comparisons of migration behaviors, the direct assessment of multifaceted motivations for migration, and the opportunity to explore how the composition of social networks, social structural conditions, and other factors alter internal migration behaviors.

SEE ALSO: Demographic Data: Censuses, Registers, Surveys; Environment and Urbanization; Metropolis; Migration: International; Migration and the Labor Force; Residential Segregation; Suburbs; Sunbelt; Uneven Development; Urban–Rural Population Movements

REFERENCES AND SUGGESTED READINGS

Bilsboro, R. E. (Ed.) (1998) *Migration, Urbanization, and Development: New Directions and Issues.* UNFPA/Kluwer, Norwell, MA.
DeJong, G. & Gardner, R. (Eds.) (1981) *Migration Decision Making.* Pergamon, New York.
Frey, W. H. (1995) The New Geography of Population Shifts. In: Farley, R. (Ed.), *State of the Union: America in the 1990s.* Vol. 2: *Social Trends.* Russell Sage Foundation, New York.
Jackson, K. (1985) *Crabgrass Frontiers: The Suburbanization of the United States.* Oxford University Press, New York.
Kasarda, J. & Crenshaw, E. M. (1991) Third World Urbanization. *Annual Review of Sociology* 17: 467–501.
Lee, E. S. (1966) A Theory of Migration. *Demography* 1: 47–57.
Long, L. H. (1988) *Migration and Residential Mobility in the United States.* Russell Sage Foundation, New York.
Schachter, J. (2001) Why People Move: Exploring the March 2000 Current Population Survey. *Current Population Reports* (P23–204). US Census Bureau, Washington, DC.
Squires, G. D. (Ed.) (2002) *Urban Sprawl: Causes, Consequences, and Policy Responses.* Urban Institute Press, Washington, DC.
Tolnay, S. E. (2003) The African American "Great Migration" and Beyond. *Annual Review of Sociology* 29: 209–32.
United Nations (1970) *Methods of Measuring Internal Migration, Manual VI.* United Nations, New York.
Zelinsky, W. (1971) The Hypothesis of the Mobility Transition. *Geographical Review* 61: 219–49.

migration: international

Mary M. Kritz

International migration is generally defined as the change of a person's usual place of residence from one country to another. The United Nations recommends that a time element of at least one year be added to this definition in order to differentiate international migrants from international visitors. Because international migration is a dyadic process, this definition applies both to moves into and out of a given country and the process can be examined from the standpoint of the sending or receiving country. Arrivals and departures of citizens and foreigners are part of the international migration process, which has four components: (1) the in-migration of persons to a country other than that of their place of birth or citizenship; (2) the return migration of nationals to their home country after residing abroad; (3) the out-migration of nationals from their home country; and (4) the out-migration of foreigners from the foreign country to which they migrated. The first component, commonly referred to as immigration, has received the most research and policy attention.

MIGRATION AND THE NATION-STATE

International migration is an appendage of the nation-state era. Throughout history, people have migrated or left their communities and homelands and established residence elsewhere. Only after the world's territory became organized into states with internationally recognized boundaries did the distinction between internal and international migrants emerge.

The movement to divide the entire globe into states with territorially defined borders accelerated in Western Europe during the Middle Ages and spread rapidly to other world regions in the nineteenth and twentieth centuries as former European colonies in North and South America, Asia, and Africa declared their independence. By the beginning of the twenty-first century, all of the globe's territory was part of some nation-state but boundary disputes between states and civil conflicts between ethnic groups within states continue to reshape the global state system and, in turn, the global migration system.

State boundary changes lead to changes in the volume and pool of persons who get classified as international migrants in today's world. After the USSR disintegrated in 1991, emigration from the former Soviet Union was transformed into emigration from 13 new sovereign countries, and in-migrations from neighboring republics became either return migration of nationals from other Soviet Republics or in-migrations of foreigners. In the Soviet case, migrations that used to be considered internal to the USSR became international migrations after state partition. The splitting up of the former Yugoslavia into Bosnia-Herzegovina, Croatia, Macedonia, Slovenia, and Serbia and Montenegro in the 1990s led to similar changes in the designation of international and internal migrants by those states. The partitioning of the Indian subcontinent into Pakistan and India in 1947, the subsequent partition of Pakistan into Pakistan and Bangladesh in 1971, and Eritrea's declaration of independence from Ethiopia in 1993 are other cases where states subdivided, leading to changes in who was classified and counted as an international migrant.

Cooperation as well as conflict between states can lead to changes in state definitions of who is an international versus an internal migrant and thus to changes in the volume of migration between states. In the second half of the twentieth century, many states in different world regions entered into reciprocal economic and political treaties that have clauses that specify conditions under which their citizens and commercial goods can move across neighboring borders. Many of those treaties also specify the conditions under which nationals of the signatory countries can move to one of the other signatories for work or residency purposes. Typically, these regional treaties place no restrictions on the migration of business people and highly skilled professionals but do restrict the migration of unskilled workers in order to protect native workers from low-wage competition.

An example of such a treaty is the North American Free Trade Agreement (NAFTA) signed by Canada, Mexico, and the United States in 1994. NAFTA permits business people and highly skilled professionals who are citizens of any one of the three signatories to migrate to one of the other countries to engage in professional or business activities. While migrations within the NAFTA region are still considered international migrations by the sending and receiving countries, by easing travel and residency conditions, the overall volume of migrants increased sharply after NAFTA was signed. For instance, 2000 US Census data show that immigration in the 1990s from Canada and Mexico increased by 98 percent and 84 percent, respectively, over levels from those two countries in the 1980s. In comparison, recent immigration from all other countries to the United States in the 1990s increased by only 19 percent.

Europe is another region where cooperation between states in recent decades led to changes in the international migration system. In 1985, five countries (Belgium, France, Germany, Luxembourg, and the Netherlands) signed the Schengen Agreement in which they set the goal of removing border controls for people and commerce between their countries. By 2001, those five countries and nine other Western European countries had implemented the Schengen Agreement. Eastern European countries admitted to the European Union (EU) in the early 2000s will be allowed to implement the open-border system in the near future. Among countries where Schengen is already operative, nationals of participating states are no longer subjected to internal border controls. Although intra-European migrations can still be considered international migration, several EU countries no longer compile migration statistics on these flows because they consider them to be internal migrations. Increasingly, migration management in the EU focuses on monitoring entries and exits of foreigners from non-EU countries. As a result, flows within the region are in reality no longer international migrations.

In 2000, the United Nations estimated that there were 175 million persons worldwide currently living outside their country of birth, 14 percent more than did so in 1990. While this is a crude estimate of the total number of international migrants in the world, other evidence indicates that international migration is on the increase. The *Cambridge Survey of World Migration* (1995) documents the growth in international migrations that has occurred since 1945 in North America, Western Europe, Asia and Oceania, the Middle East, Latin America, and Africa. In contrast to previous historical eras when international migrations consisted of relatively small flows of settlers moving from Europe to overseas colonies or to former European colonies following their independence, today's flows are much larger and involve persons of all nations and creeds migrating along pathways that crisscross the globe. At the beginning of the twenty-first century, virtually every country in the world was a sender or receiver of international migrants. While the United Nations estimated that only 3 percent of the world's people were international migrants in 2000, the trend was upward and believed likely to continue increasing in the decades ahead. In 1970, for instance, only 2 percent of the world's people were international migrants.

TYPES OF INTERNATIONAL MIGRANTS

While some of today's migrants are moving for the same reasons that propelled migration in earlier epochs, new types of migrants have emerged in recent decades or what may be called the globalization era. Today most international migrants can be classified as refugees, labor migrants, institutional migrants, family reunification migrants, and lifestyle migrants. Refugee migrations have existed for centuries and are propelled when persons are forced to flee their homeland in fear of their lives. Given their forced and involuntary character, these population movements are generally measured and managed differently than other international migrations. Most of the world's refugees are located in Asia and Africa but some are

admitted for resettlement in North America and Europe. In addition, growing numbers of foreigners from Africa, Asia, Eastern Europe, and Latin America come to Western European countries annually seeking asylum.

Labor migrations are driven by economic inequalities between countries as workers seek to improve their incomes and economic security by moving to countries where economic conditions are better than in their homelands. Workers participating in labor migrations are generally of low skill and typically moving from a poorer country to a richer neighboring country. While some labor migrations historically and today were started by labor recruitment and demand for labor in receiving countries, increasingly today those flows are driven by an oversupply of workers in sending countries and migrant networks that link sending and receiving countries. Large numbers of labor migrants do not have residence and work authorization from receiving countries, which raises concerns regarding whether the rights of these migrants are being adequately protected.

Institutional migrations include highly skilled migrants who are hired or transferred by corporations, governments, and other entities to another country for work purposes. In contrast to labor migrations, which are propelled mainly by migrants themselves and their households but often facilitated by labor recruiters, smugglers, and other intermediaries, institutional migrations are sponsored and organized by formal institutions that operate transnationally in the globalization era. Institutional migrations include a number of migrant flows that have increased during the globalization era. While these flows occur mainly from southern to northern countries, a significant volume of institutional migrations occurs from northern to southern countries as well as among countries in the North or South that have comparable economic levels. Included in this category would be: employees transferred by multinational corporations from one country to another; government officials; employees of international and regional institutions; foreigners who move to another country for graduate study; aid workers moving from northern to southern countries to work with bilateral and multilateral assistance agencies or non-governmental organizations; religious workers proselytizing for their faith;

and a wide array of other foreigners who move to other countries for a few years to carry forward the work of the institution that sponsors them. Most receiving countries welcome institutional migrants and place few restrictions on their entry.

Whereas political factors are the underlying cause of refugee migrations and economic factors drive labor and most institutional migrations, social factors stimulate family reunification and lifestyle migrations. Foreigners who move to another country for refuge or work want their family members to join them. While most receiving countries in North America and Europe allow some family reunification, they also have established rules that limit which immigrants can bring their family members. For instance, countries differ in whom they consider an immediate family member and in the conditions that have to be met by immigrants before their family members can rejoin them. Family reunification also includes international migrations that result from the marriage of nationals of two different countries. Typically, one partner moves to the other partner's homeland. While statistics on international intermarriage are scarce, census data on spousal origins indicate that such marriages are increasing.

Of the five migrant types, lifestyle migrants are the smallest category and occur when people move to another country because they prefer its climate, cost of living, investment system, cultural milieu, or other factors. This category includes retirees who move to another country seasonally or permanently, migrants returning to their homelands after living abroad for decades, and wealthy investors who move to countries that are tax havens or that offer amenities not available in their homeland. Lifestyle migrations are enabled by the increased volume of international mobility in the globalization era, the lack of restrictions on the international mobility of people of means, and the general recognition by countries that relatively rich individuals such as retirees and investors bring capital that can stimulate their economies.

In order to keep international migration inflows at acceptable levels to their populaces, since the early 1900s governments of receiving countries have increasingly taken steps to control the volume of immigration and types of migrants. However, the management of immigration is complicated in the globalization era because of increasing flows of capital, raw materials, goods, and information among countries. In general, countries view short-term travel for business and tourism as in their national interest and adopt policy measures that encourage or accommodate institutional migrants, lifestyle migrants, and foreigners migrating for family reunification. Some countries also resettle modest numbers of refugees. While some countries allow large numbers of labor migrants to enter and work, as demand for admission by labor migrants has risen, debates have started in many receiving countries about the costs and benefits of labor migration and the numbers and means under which labor migrants should be admitted. Receiving countries face a dilemma, namely, how to control unauthorized labor migration while maintaining ready access for other types of migrants. Concerns over national security and unauthorized labor migration have led governments to increase vigilance over their borders in recent decades.

Countries use different policy modes to regulate the in-migration of foreigners. A handful of countries – Australia, Canada, New Zealand, and the United States – grant foreigners the right to permanent immigration prior to entry. All other countries, and increasingly the permanent immigration countries too, issue foreigners temporary residence and work visas that permit them to reside and work for a fixed time period in order to carry out an activity considered to be in the receiving country's political, economic, or social interests. While the length of the residence period granted by countries to foreigners admitted on temporary visas varies, countries generally are willing to renew these temporary visas and some do so multiple times or indefinitely. Thus temporary migration becomes permanent settlement as social and economic networks between nationals and foreigners expand, leading to the growth of a group of persons who might be called "transnationalists." These transnationalists tend to be frequent international travelers, carry two passports and maintain dual citizenship, spend parts of the year in both of their homelands, and are comfortable living in multinational settings.

THEORIES OF INTERNATIONAL MIGRATION

Why international migrations occur is a question asked by scholars of migration. Several partial theories have been advanced by social scientists to explain international migration but there is no general theory of international migration. Theories that have been offered to explain international migration tend to stem from disciplinary paradigms. Political scientists focus on the role of the state and the importance of state policies in channeling and limiting immigration while economists direct their attention to economic differentials between countries, particularly wage gaps and supply and demand for labor in sending and receiving countries, and look at how migration and development interact. Sociologists continue to be influenced by the Chicago School of Sociology which developed theories of immigrant incorporation and assimilation based on the experiences of European immigrants to US urban areas in the early 1900s. While immigrant assimilation remains a central study issue for sociologists, a number of sociologists have started to examine the origins of contemporary international migration and the global forces driving it.

Under the auspices of the International Union for the Scientific Study of Population (IUSSP), Douglas Massey and colleagues (1993a, b) undertook an evaluation of migration flows into North America, Western Europe, the Gulf States, the Asia Pacific region, and South America and concluded that those flows have their origins in the social, economic, and political transformations now occurring in sending and receiving countries. The IUSSP group also advanced the argument that international migrations are not driven by a lack of development, as is commonly argued, but by development itself (Taylor & Massey 2004) and are likely to grow in the years ahead. In other research, Massey (1990) offered the theory of cumulative causation to explain why international migrations continue after the precipitating economic or political factors that initiated the migration flow changes. According to cumulative causation theory, "new conditions that arise in the course of migration come to function as independent causes themselves:

migrant networks spread, institutions supporting transnational movement develop, and the social meaning of work changes in receiving societies" (Massey et al. 1993a).

New theories of international migration have been advanced by social scientists because earlier theories were considered inadequate to account for the changing direction, volume, and types of migration that have emerged during the globalization era of international migration. The earlier theories, including Lee's (1966) push–pull, Stouffer's (1940) intervening opportunities, and Zelinsky's (1971) mobility transition, were judged as too static to explain the directions of contemporary international migration or why some people migrate while most do not. Neoliberal theories advanced by economists that posited that individuals will migrate to destinations where they expect to receive the greatest net benefit were also criticized by sociologists for assuming both that labor market differentials alone determine international migration and that potential migrants can calculate those risks.

Criticisms have also been directed at the new theories. For instance, the theories advanced by the IUSSP group focus on explaining why labor migrations occur but ignore other types of migration. Alejandro Portes (1999) argues that the dimensions that are part of contemporary international migration are too disparate to be explained by a single theory. Portes (1999: 28) argues further that rather than focusing on a "grand theory" of international migration, scholars should direct their attention to four separate processes, including: the origins of immigration, the directionality and continuity of migrant flows, the utilization of immigration labor in receiving countries, and the integration and assimilation of immigrants in receiving countries.

Some scholars have begun the process of advancing theories on parts of the international migration process. Zolberg et al. (1989) elaborated a theory of refugee migrations that held that those flows have been transformed in recent decades by globalization forces that affect the scale of civil and political conflict within and between nations. Others situate the new international migrations in the changing transnational networks and systems of countries that forge ties between particular sets of countries that stem from the sharing of historical relations or geographical location in a common region (Kritz et al. 1992). France, for instance, has received large influxes of migrants from North Africa and its former Francophone colonies in Sub-Saharan Africa in the globalization era. Similarly, the United Kingdom has received most of its migrants from former British overseas colonies. Spain has received many migrants from Spanish-speaking countries in the Americas.

METHODOLOGICAL ISSUES

Despite the growing importance of international migration for population growth in more developed countries and for economic and social structures and change in both sending and receiving countries, the statistics needed to monitor changes in migration volume and directions are poor. Available statistics tend to be gathered by receiving countries and determined by policy approaches toward immigration. Because policy approaches vary across countries, there is "lack of comparability between the statistics produced by different countries or even between those produced by different sources within a single country" (United Nations 1998). While scholars of international migration have lamented the lack of adequate data to study international migration, and the United Nations has issued recommendations to countries on the form that international migration statistics should take, the situation has not improved. As a result, compared to study and knowledge of other demographic processes, scholars know relatively little about the magnitude of international migration, or its determinants and consequences.

SEE ALSO: Chicago School; Citizenship; Consumption, Tourism and; Family Migration; Immigrant Families; Immigration; Immigration and Language; Immigration Policy; Migration, Ethnic Conflicts, and Racism; Migration: Internal; Migration and the Labor Force; Migration: Undocumented/Illegal; Networks; Refugee Movements; Transnational Movements

REFERENCES AND SUGGESTED READINGS

Brettell, C. B. & Hollifield, J. F. (Eds.) (2000) *Migration Theory: Talking Across Disciplines.* Routledge, New York.
Cohen, R. (Ed.) (1995) *The Cambridge Survey of World Migration.* Cambridge University Press, Cambridge.
Kritz, M. M. & Gurak, D. T. (2004) *Immigration and a Changing America.* Russell Sage Foundation and Population Reference Bureau, Washington, DC.
Kritz, M. M., Lim, L. L., & Zlotnik, H. (1992) *International Migration Systems: A Global Approach.* Oxford University Press, Oxford.
Lee, E. (1966) A Theory of Migration. *Demography* 3: 47–57.
Massey, D. S. (1990) The Social and Economic Origins of Migration. *Annals of the American Academy of Political and Social Science* 510: 60–72.
Massey, D. S., Arango, J., Hugo, G., Kouaouci, A., Pellegrino, A., & Taylor, J. E. (1993a) Theories of International Migration: A Review and Appraisal. *Population and Development Review* 19: 431–66.
Massey, D. S., Arango, J., Hugo, G., Kouaouci, A., Pellegrino, A., & Taylor, J. E. (Eds.) (1993b) *Worlds in Motion: Understanding International Migration at the End of the Millennium.* Oxford University Press, New York.
Portes, A. (1999) Immigration Theory for a New Century: Some Problems and Opportunities. In: Hirchman, C., Kasinitz, P., & DeWind, J. (Eds.), *Handbook of International Migration: The American Experience.* Russell Sage Foundation, New York, pp. 21–33.
Poulain, M. & Perrin, N. (2003) Can UN Recommendations Be Met in Europe? In: *Migration Information Source.* Migration Policy Institute, Washington, DC. Online. www.migrationinformation.org/feature/display.cfm?ID=139).
Stouffer, S. A. (1940) Intervening Opportunities: A Theory Relating Mobility and Distance. *American Sociological Review* 5: 845–67.
Taylor, J. E. & Massey, D. S. (Eds.) (2004) *International Migration: Prospects and Policies.* Oxford University Press, New York.
United Nations (1998) *Recommendations on Statistics of International Migration, Revision 1.* Department of Economic and Social Affairs, Statistics Division, United Nations, New York.
United Nations (2004) *Trends in Total Migrant Stock: The 2003 Revision.* United Nations Population Division, New York.
Zelinsky, W. (1971) The Hypothesis of the Mobility Transition. *Geographical Review* 61: 219–49.

Zolberg, A. R., Suhrke, A., & Aguayo, S. (1989) *Escape from Violence: Conflict and the Refugee Crisis in the Developing World*. Oxford University Press, New York.

migration and the labor force

Harriet Orcutt Duleep and Regan Main

The labor force includes those who work and those who are unemployed but wish to work. It is typically defined for a nation as a whole, or for a demographic or geographic subgroup within a nation. Migration is the movement of people across borders. If the borders are within a country, the migration is called internal or domestic migration, or simply migration. If the borders divide countries, it is international migration, with "immigration" denoting people entering a country and "emigration" denoting their exit. Social scientists' interest in internal versus international migration has waxed and waned with the ebbs and flows of immigration. When US immigration was severely restricted in the 1920s, the study of immigration lost its luster; after the restrictions were lifted in the 1960s, it reemerged as a hot topic.

Two focal points unite research on domestic or international migration and the labor force: how do migrants fare in the new labor market and what effect does migration have on "natives" of the host labor market? Similar methodological hurdles also shape research on the labor force and (internal or international) migration. These include how to discern migrant earnings and employment trajectories from cross-sectional and cohort data, whether to use the individual, the family, or the group as the unit of analysis, and how to disentangle migration effects on a host region's labor market from the effect of the host region's labor market on migration.

MIGRANTS' LABOR FORCE OUTCOMES IN THE HOST REGION

The dominant model in the study of immigration and the labor market was an assimilation model spawned in the 1920s University of Chicago sociology department and associated with the works of Robert E. Park. This model portrayed immigrants' trajectories in the host country as a single process relevant to all immigrants that eventually led to their cultural and economic assimilation.

Echoing Park's assimilation thesis, but focusing on labor market outcomes, Chiswick theorized that migrants often lack specific skills that would permit their home country human capital to be fully valued in the host country labor market. Assimilation in this context is acquiring host country-specific skills that restore the market value of the immigrant's homeland human capital. For the US labor market, an obvious example is English fluency. Empirical research, based on cross-sectional data, suggested that following an initial period of adjustment, immigrant earnings grew and generally approached the earnings of natives with similar years of schooling and experience after about 15 years in the US. Analogous findings surfaced in other immigrant host countries. A review of British immigration research, for instance, concluded that labor market conditions improve for immigrants the longer they live in the host country (Hatton & Price 1999).

This optimistic picture was shattered in a series of articles by Borjas. He showed that recent immigrants started at much lower earnings than their predecessors, a decline caused by changes in the country-of-origin composition of US immigration. A decline in immigrant entry earnings also occurred in other immigrant host countries (see, for instance, Winkelmann's 1999 study of New Zealand immigration). Tracing the earnings of earlier immigrant cohorts across censuses revealed only modest earnings growth, substantially lower than the cross-sectional prediction. Borjas showed that where immigrant initial earnings are falling over time, as in the US and other economically developed countries, pairing the initial earnings of more recent immigrants with the earnings achieved by earlier cohorts after 10-15 years in the host country overstates the earnings growth of the earlier immigrants: his research invalidates the cross-sectional approach. It does not follow, however, that the earnings growth of earlier cohorts is a good predictor of the earnings growth of more recent cohorts.

A third stream of papers by Duleep and Regets highlighted two overlooked aspects of immigrant skill transferability. (1) Immigrants whose home country skills transfer poorly to the new labor market will, by virtue of their lower wages, have a lower opportunity cost of human capital investment than natives or immigrants with high skill transferability. (2) Home country skills that are not fully valued in the host country labor market are still useful for learning new skills. Combined, these factors imply that low-skill-transferability immigrants will invest more in human capital and will do so over a longer period than high-skill-transferability immigrants or natives with similar levels of education and experience. A crucial prediction from the immigrant human capital investment (IHCI) model is that the higher incentive to invest in human capital pertains not only to human capital that restores the value of specific source-country human capital, but also to new human capital investment in general. Empirical observations bolster this perspective. For instance, a Canadian study by Green (1999) finds higher rates of occupational change, and at older ages, for immigrants than for natives.

Because immigrants will invest more in human capital than natives, and low-skill-transferability immigrants will invest more than high-skill-transferability immigrants (holding initial human capital levels constant), immigrants will experience higher earnings growth than natives, and among immigrants there will be an inverse relationship between entry earnings and earnings growth. These expectations emerge in empirical analyses that follow cohorts and individuals: across groups, the lower the entry earnings, the higher the earnings growth; over time, as entry earnings have fallen, earnings growth has increased. Studies that use longitudinal data on individuals show high earnings or occupational mobility of recent immigrants, in the US (Duleep & Dowhan 2002), in Australia (Chiswick et al. 2002), and in Denmark (Husted et al. 2000). Further confirmation of the IHCI model comes from the earnings convergence that occurs among immigrant groups characterized by low and high skill transferability, as for instance immigrants who enter the US via family admissions versus employer-based requests for specific employment skills. Immigrant entry earnings are thus poor predictors

of immigrant economic success. Methodologically, the inverse relationship invalidates the popular approach of controlling for cohort effects by including a zero-one variable for each cohort in analyses that pool more than one cross-section to measure immigrant earnings growth.

EARNINGS AND EMPLOYMENT WITHIN A CONTEXT

While much sociological research has followed in the footsteps of the Chicago School assimilation model and emphasizes the importance of human capital in determining labor market outcomes, sociologists also explore how predictors of immigrant economic assimilation and success are affected by a variety of contexts not necessarily captured by individual traits. Sociological studies highlight heterogeneity across immigrant groups in assimilation, unique social capital and networking patterns of various immigrant groups, geographic dispersion and concentration patterns, the importance of local labor market structures, and differences in the treatment of specific immigrant groups based on societal perception and government policy.

The structure of the host country's labor market is of course a key context that affects immigrant earnings and earnings growth. One conceptualization of the labor market stems from human capital theory. Another postulates that two types of demand determine the characteristics of jobs. Jobs in the primary sector (responding to the stable component of demand) are "good jobs" with security, responsibility, and career lines; jobs in the secondary sector (responding to highly variable demand) are dead-end jobs. A third sector is the "enclave economy," which may help immigrants lacking access to primary sector jobs escape the confines of the secondary sector.

Case studies of the enclave economy document an immigrant sector in various industries characterized by mutually beneficial arrangements between recent and longer-term immigrants in which recent immigrants working as unskilled laborers at low wages (or even no wages) in immigrant-run businesses are provided training and other forms of support eventually leading to more skilled positions or self-employment. Close-knit communities, nurtured by kinship ties, ease the economic assimilation of new immigrants providing both economic and social support, facilitating investment in human capital, and promoting immigrant entrepreneurial activities. Indeed, from a survey of various immigrant groups, an Australian Bureau of Immigration Research report by Morrissey et al. (1991) concluded that family and informal networks provide the most important and frequently utilized services for immigrants.

LABOR MARKET OUTCOMES FOR IMMIGRANT WOMEN

Paralleling the earnings and employment findings for men, several studies have found the decision of immigrant women to work and their earnings to be positively associated with years since migration, perhaps reflecting the learning of skills relevant to the host country's labor market. Yet, the labor force behavior of immigrant women differs from that of immigrant men and there are distinct differences in women's labor force behavior among immigrant groups. Monica Boyd's research reveals considerable stratification among groups of Canadian immigrant women in the extent to which they have lower occupational statuses than natives.

Underlying the differences in labor force behavior between immigrant men and women may be the same factors that contribute to differences in labor force behavior between native men and women. Analyses of immigrant women find that, like native women, their labor force participation is affected by children and by personal characteristics that affect labor market productivity such as level of schooling. Yet controlling for variables traditionally included in female labor force models, and controlling for variables that measure skill transferability such as host country language proficiency and years since immigration typically included in immigrant men models, large differences exist across immigrant groups in female labor force behavior. To understand these persistent differences, researchers are pursuing a family perspective. There has also been a growing consensus that men's labor market outcomes, typically the focus of earlier economic studies, cannot be fully understood without also considering the activities of their wives.

The family investment model, developed by Canadian, Australian, and US researchers, posits that family members can increase the future labor income of the family either directly by pursuing activities that increase their own skill levels, or indirectly by engaging in activities that finance or support the human capital investment activities of other family members. The expected return to a husband's or wife's investment in US-specific human capital affects the spouse's decision about whether to work, how much to work, the timing of work decisions, and the kind of work that is pursued. Immigrant families may also temporarily postpone fertility to facilitate an initial period of heavy human capital investment.

Finally, a nascent body of research focuses on the role that immigrant women play within the household concerning decisions about work and how work affects the relationship between wives and husbands. This research finds that households become less patriarchal and more egalitarian as women gain access to social and economic resources previously beyond their reach.

EARNINGS AND EMPLOYMENT: INTERNAL MIGRATION

Several similarities unite international and domestic migration analyses of earnings and employment. In both arenas, the role of social networks is prominent. In both, a key variable is age. The younger migrants are, the longer the payoff time from migration. Opportunity costs also increase with age; as one works in a particular locality and firm, it becomes increasingly difficult to transfer the accumulated work experience.

Also common to studies of the labor force and internal or international migration is the problem that not all those who migrate stay in their new destination. Who leaves will affect the measurement of migrant earnings and employment profiles and underscores the importance of following the same individuals over time.

Another oft-noted phenomenon in both internal and international migration is that once a group of persons begins to migrate to a particular area, the process persists. A shared unanswered question is: why does migration start when it does? What scholars sometimes suggest as the pivotal factors often were in place years before the migration began. A case in point is the US black migration out of the South. Given that the higher incomes of the North from industrialization predate 1940, why did the pace of the black Southern exodus quicken so much after 1940? Perhaps a certain threshold must be passed in terms of the characteristics of the group in the original location and the fortitude of the network in the new location before a sizable group of potential migrants is ready to migrate. In both internal and international migration, it is not the poorest poor who migrate.

LABOR MARKET REPERCUSSIONS OF MIGRATION ON THE HOST REGION'S NATIVES

The second focal point in studies of migration and the labor force is how migration affects the labor force of the host region or country. Social scientists are far from resolving whether immigrants hurt, help, or have no significant effect on native-born employment and wages. Angrist and Kugler (2002) find a negative immigration effect on employment in countries with restrictive institutions. Hartog and Zorlu (2002) find very small immigration effects on natives' wages in their analysis of the Netherlands, Britain, and Norway. Using aggregate time series data for Australia, Pope and Withers (1994) find increases in immigrant labor positively affect natives' wages. Hercowitz and Yashiv (2002) estimate negative employment effects in a study of immigration from the former Soviet Union to Israel, while an Italian study (Venturini & Villosio 2002) finds no negative effect on natives' employment.

Several interrelated problems contribute to this diversity of results. These include difficulties with measuring immigration, disentangling immigration's effect on natives from the effect of economic conditions on immigration, the clustering of immigrants within a country, the migration of natives in response to immigration, reconciling statistical evidence with anecdotal evidence and theoretical expectations, and failure to consider how industries may change their production practices or develop in response to immigration.

Immigrants may move to areas with better than average wages and employment opportunities, thereby obfuscating any potential adverse immigration effect on the economic status of the native-born in cross-area analyses. Even if immigrants do not locate in response to the economic conditions of areas, their presence may still correlate with economic conditions. Natives' wages in areas of high immigration may be lower than they would have been in the absence of immigration, even though the across-area snapshot reveals a positive association between percent immigrant and native-born wages and employment. This problem also afflicts time series; historical analyses have consistently shown an inverse relationship between immigration and the host country's unemployment rate. Natural experiments may help elucidate migrants' impacts on natives (see, for instance, Hunt 1992).

Another problem that may contribute to the variety of estimated effects is that immigrants tend to cluster in a few places. In the US, immigrants are concentrated in six states. Within those states, they are concentrated in the largest cities or SMSAs. One-time cross-state estimates of the effect of immigration on native-born employment and wages (or the effect of changes in immigration) may be sensitive to economic circumstances (or changes in economic circumstances) in any of the principal immigration states. The problem of isolating the effect of immigration on native-born economic status from the effect of perturbations in these states' economies can only be overcome by using time series information in combination with cross-sectional information.

In gauging the effect of immigration on natives' economic outcomes, domestic and international migration research intertwine. Several scholars argue that analysts find little or no immigration effect on native-born wages and employment in cross-area comparisons because natives move in response to immigrant inflows: immigrants reduce the wages and employment opportunities of the native-born and, in response, natives leave. No wage or employment effect is observed in analyses comparing areas of high and low immigration since the native-born labor supply in high immigration areas has decreased with the out-migration of natives from these areas. This migration response obscures the measurement of potentially adverse immigration effects on natives' wages and employment.

A connection between native migration flows and immigration has been noted in historical periods such as the relationship between the South–North migration of blacks and the imposition and relaxation of immigration controls (Muller & Espenshade 1985). More recently, scholars have found that low-educated natives move out and high-educated natives move in to areas with large increases in immigrants. The differential response provides circumstantial evidence that immigrants, in particular recently arrived immigrants, are substitutes for low-educated natives and complements for high-educated natives. According to this interpretation, the migration response of natives is evidence of a negative wage and employment effect of immigrants on low-educated natives and a positive wage and employment effect on high-educated natives. There are, however, alternative explanations for this particular migration pattern and causality is difficult to determine.

Anecdotal and theoretical considerations suggest that an influx of unskilled immigrant labor will adversely affect unskilled native labor. One problem with reconciling anecdotal evidence of native job displacement with statistical estimates of no negative wage or employment effects stems from a tendency of researchers to conclude that an estimated negative relationship between percent immigrant and native-born wages and employment in cross-area analyses means that immigrants and natives are substitutes, and a positive relationship indicates that they are complements. In fact, there is no direct evidence in these studies on the nature of the relationship in production between immigrants and natives. A positive or negative estimated wage or employment effect of immigration only suggests that to the extent this relationship is causal there is on balance a positive or negative immigration effect on native-born employment and wages. This is not inconsistent with the existence of specific cases of displacement and immigration-induced wage declines. Furthermore, turnovers from native labor to immigrant labor do not necessarily constitute evidence that displacement has taken place. Where jobs traditionally filled by natives become dominated by

immigrants, case-study evidence could elucidate how this occurred and what happened to the native workers who were formerly employed in these jobs.

The theoretical expectation that an increase in unskilled immigrant labor must necessarily harm the employment and wages of native unskilled labor comes from a tendency to think only in terms of two types of labor – skilled and unskilled. Yet immigrants and natives are differentiated by the nature of their work and the process by which they become employed, trained, and promoted even within specific unskilled occupations within specific industries. These distinctions need to be brought into discussions of the economic impacts of immigrants.

Beyond the relationship between native and immigrant labor in the production process, the economic effect immigration has on native labor will depend on how immigrants affect the demand for products produced by natives. Immigrant consumption patterns have only rarely been studied. Beyond the simple fact that immigrants themselves spend money and buy native-produced products, natives' incomes will be affected by the extent to which the products produced by immigrant and native labor are substitutes or complements. If the presence of immigrants makes one product cheaper, the demand for complementary products will increase. There is also interplay between immigrant/native relationships in production and consumption effects: the availability of immigrants to tend children and clean homes allows middle-class women to work and spend money on goods and services that may be produced by low-educated natives. These types of relationships involving consumption and others have yet to be theoretically developed or empirically analyzed, even though they could affect whether and how immigrant inflows affect the wages and employment of native labor. Finally, businesses may develop or persist in response to the availability of certain types of labor that immigrant groups provide. Industries may change their production practices in response to immigration. This too is an area that merits further exploration.

SEE ALSO: Family Migration; Feminization of Labor Migration; Immigration; Immigration Policy; Labor/Labor Power; Labor Markets;

Migration: Internal; Migration: International; Migration: Undocumented/Illegal

REFERENCES AND SUGGESTED READINGS

Angrist, J. & Kugler, A. (2002) Protective or Counter-Productive? Labor Market Institutions and the Effect of Immigration on EU Natives. *Discussion Paper No. 433, IZA*.

Bailey, T. R. & Waldinger, R. (1991) Primary, Secondary, and Enclave Labor Markets: A Training Systems Approach. *American Sociological Review* 56 (August): 432–45.

Bean, F. D. & Stevens, G. (2003) *America's Newcomers and the Dynamics of Diversity*. Russell Sage Foundation, New York.

Chiswick, B. R. (1991) Review of International Differences in the Labor Market Performance of Immigrants. *Industrial Labor Relations Review* 44(3): 570–1.

Chiswick, B. R., Lee, Y. L., & Miller, P. W. (2002) Longitudinal Analysis of Immigrant Occupational Mobility: A Test of the Immigrant Assimilation Hypothesis. *Discussion Paper No. 452, IZA*.

Duleep, H. O. & Dowhan, D. (2002) Insights from Longitudinal Data on the Earnings Growth of US Foreign-Born Men. *Demography* 39: 485–506.

Duleep, H. O. & Regets, M. (1999) Immigrants and Human Capital Investment. *American Economic Review* 89: 186–91.

Duleep, H. O. & Wunnava, P. V. (Eds.) (1996) *Immigrants and Immigration Policy: Individual Skills, Family Ties, and Group Identities*. JAI Press, Greenwich, CT.

Enchautegui, M. E. (1995) Immigrants and the Low-Skilled Market. *Discussion Paper*. Urban Institute, Washington, DC.

Filer, R. K. (1992) The Effect of Immigrant Arrivals on Migratory Patterns of Native Workers. In: Borjas, G. J. & Freeman, R. B. (Eds.), *Immigration and the Work Force*. University of Chicago Press, National Bureau of Economic Research, Chicago, pp. 245–70.

Gang, I. N. & Rivera-Batiz, F. L. (1994) Labor Market Effects of Immigration in the United States and Europe: Substitution vs. Complementarity. *Journal of Population Economics* 7(2): 157–75.

Green, D. A. (1999) Immigrant Occupational Attainment: Assimilation and Mobility Over Time. *Journal of Labor Economics* 17, 1 (January): 49–79.

Haines, M. R. (1989) Consumer Behavior and Immigrant Assimilation: A Comparison of the United States, Britain, and Germany, 1889/1890. *Working Paper No. 6*. Historical Factors and Long Run Growth, National Bureau of Economic Research.

Hartog, J. & Zorlu, A. (2002) The Effect of Immigration on Wages in Three European Countries. *Discussion Paper No. 642, IZA*.

Hatton, T. J. & Price, S. W. (1999) Migration, Migrants, and Policy in the United Kingdom. *Discussion Paper No. 81, IZA*.

Hercowitz, Z. & Yashiv, E. (2002) A Macroeconomic Experiment in Mass Immigration. *Discussion Paper No. 475, IZA*.

Hirschman, C., Kasinitz, P., & DeWind, J. (Eds.) (1999) *The Handbook of International Migration*. Russell Sage Foundation, New York.

Hunt, J. (1992) The Impact of the 1962 Repatriates from Algeria on the French Labor Market. *Industrial and Labor Relations Review* 45(3): 556–72.

Husted, L., Nielsen, H. S., Rosholm, M., et al. (2000) Employment and Wage Assimilation of Male First-Generation Immigrants in Denmark. *Discussion Paper No. 101, IZA*.

Jasso, G. & Rosenzweig, M. R. (1990) *The New Chosen People: Immigrants in the United States*. Russell Sage Foundation, New York.

Manson, D. M., Espenshade, T. J., & Muller, T. (1985) Mexican Immigration to Southern California: Issues of Job Competition and Labor Mobility. *Review of Regional Studies* 15: 21–33.

Massey, D. S. (1990) The Social and Economic Origins of Immigration. *Annals* 510: 60–72.

Morrissey, M., Mitchell, C., & Rutherford, A. (1991) *The Family in the Settlement Process*. Australian Government Publishing Service, Bureau of Immigration Research, Canberra.

Muller, T. & Espenshade, T. J. (1985) *The Fourth Wave: California's Newest Immigrants*. Urban Institute Press, Washington, DC.

Pope, D. & Withers, G. (1994) Wage Effects of Immigration in Late Nineteenth-Century Australia. In: Hatton, T. J. & Williamson, J. G. (Eds.), *Migration and the International Labor Market, 1850–1939*. Routledge, London.

Portes, A. (1995) Economic Sociology and the Sociology of Immigration: A Conceptual Overview. In: Portes, A. (Ed.), *The Economic Sociology of Immigration: Essays on Networks, Ethnicity, and Entrepreneurship*. Russell Sage Foundation, New York.

Venturini, A. & Villosio, C. (2002) Are Immigrants Competing with Natives in the Italian Labour Market? The Employment Effect. *Discussion Paper No. 467, IZA*.

White, M. J. & Liang, Z. (1994) The Effect of Immigration on the Internal Migration of the Native-Born Population, 1981–1990. *Population Research and Policy Review*, 17 (April): 141–66.

Winkelmann, R. (1999) Immigration: The New Zealand Experience. *Discussion Paper No. 61, IZA.*

Zhou, M. (1997) Segmented Assimilation: Issues, Controversies, and Recent Research on the New Second Generation. *International Migration Review* 31(4): 975–1008.

migration: undocumented/illegal

Joanna Hadjicostandi

Illegal migration involves people moving away from a country of origin to another country in which they reside in violation of local citizenship laws. Entry into the receiving country can be legal (student, temporary work, or tourist visas) or illegal (crossing the border from places other than the legal entry ports). Illegal immigration has been studied widely and systematically only in the past two decades, partly because of the difficulties involved in obtaining information. The literature shows that illegal immigrants in most countries share certain characteristics closely related to their position of insecurity, fear, and precarious existence. Multiple reasons lead to people's movement from their country of origin to another illegally. Typically, illegal immigrants seek better livelihoods for themselves and their families, or seek to avoid persecution. Lack of and/or poor statistical recording systems and the illegal status and high spatial mobility of migrants make the measurement of numbers extremely unreliable. Nonetheless, examples from Southern Europe, the US, and Canada here will illustrate a few commonalities as well as differences.

Southern Europe has played a major role in shaping the global map of migration during the last few centuries. In the early 1980s it witnessed a remarkable migration turnaround from emigration to immigration – both return migration in the 1970s and early 1980s and the great influx of Eastern European, African, and Asian nationals. Reasons for the rapid change are multiple. They include the changes that happened in Eastern Europe and the effects of globalization on people in third world countries. Another is local changes, which include some economic growth, characterized by increasing tertiarization and prevalence of small-scale family enterprise, along with the development of segmented labor markets with large informal sectors. Further, the seasonal nature of intensive agriculture and construction, and the need for technologically backward areas of the economies to survive global competitiveness, have increased the demand for a flexible non-unionized, cheap labor force able to move from place to place on short notice. Migrant workers typically operate within the informal labor market. Migrants find it easier to enter Southern European countries, either settling or using them as a step towards moving northwards. Southern Europe has become an alternative to traditional "more desirable" destination countries with strict frontier controls. Another reason is the proximity of Southern Europe to the countries of migrants (North Africa, the Balkans, Eastern Mediterranean) and the long coastlines, numerous islands, and mountainous border regions which are almost impossible to "seal" (King 2000). Cross-border smuggling has become important in relation to the massive flow of Albanians into Italy and Greece. Ease of entry is also related to inadequate immigration policies, weak mechanisms for controlling migration flows, and national bureaucracies.

According to Lazaridis and Poyago-Theotoky (1999) migrants from Eastern Europe are employed in six segments or niches of the Southern European labor market, some of which are monopolized by one gender. We find males working as seasonal agricultural workers in periods when demand is high, as well as in construction. Many nationalities are involved, including nationals of the former Yugoslavia in Madrid, and Ukrainians, Albanians, and Poles in Athens. Some are employed in small manufacturing and artisan workshops, others in tourism and catering (males and females). Street-hawkers are all males, but females dominate domestic service, some as live-in servants, others on a live-out basis (Lazaridis 2000). Other females are involved in the sex industry. Each of these occupations involves some interaction with local people, but because they operate through the informal sector, with no contracts or welfare provisions, and with wages below the legal minimum, they embody marginality and social exclusion.

With regard to policymaking no Southern European country has adequate immigration infrastructure or legislative enactments, although framework immigration laws were introduced at different stages in the four countries: 1985 in Spain, 1986 and 1990 in Italy, 1991 in Greece, and 1993 in Portugal. For example, the participation of migrant women with work permits in the collectivity of the modern Greek state is restricted in terms of legal, political, economic, civil, and social rights, depending on the color of their skin and ethnic origin. Undocumented migrant female workers without permits are the most restricted and therefore the most vulnerable of all workers, living a precarious existence, often institutionalized in legal, social, cultural, and economic apartheids. These patterns are not unlike patterns in informal labor markets globally, especially for undocumented workers. Discrimination in the provincial towns and villages is an area that is hugely under-investigated.

In another part of the world, Hobbs and Sauer (2005) argue that the non-status residents of Canada constitute a vast and highly exploited workforce, often working for very low wages and no benefits in unsafe conditions with no job security, although they contribute to the economy through paying taxes such as GST and PST, property tax, and gas tax. The Canadian economy benefits from and depends on this marginal, non-citizen labor force, even as it denies non-status individuals access to services to which they contribute. In addition to their paid work, non-status persons also perform socially essential unpaid labor within the "private" spheres of home and family, often without the support of social assistance. Far from being a "drain on the economy," non-status immigrants and refugees are crucial to economic well-being. From a purely economic perspective, it is highly unreasonable to deny people without status the right to adequate social services.

In the US a number of immigration laws have been passed to implement a policy of restricting illegal immigration. Mexican immigrants – including those without documentation – have long provided a crucial labor force supporting, and at times rescuing, US agribusiness enterprises. Particularly in regions of the American

West, where labor-intensive, hand-harvested fruits and vegetables are the predominant farm crops, agribusiness development has encouraged a mobile, transient labor force. This has contributed to a migrant flow from Mexico that is deeply rooted temporally, and broadly enmeshed socially, in communities in the US. US immigration policies aimed at curtailing undocumented immigration appear, at best, to be generally ineffective. At worst, they may prove counterproductive, creating "an undocumented population that is markedly poor, less healthy, less educated, and more tenuously connected to the rest of society" (Massey & Espinosa 1997). Neither the US political economy nor its immigration policies provide reason to anticipate much, if any, reduction in the undocumented immigrant Mexican population. Despite significant associated human costs, including both traumas of the border-crossing experience and the difficult "lived experience" that follows for most in the US, the steady flow of undocumented immigrants continues. Demographic estimates indicate that undocumented Mexican women, and particularly those accompanied by children, are migrating to the US in increasing numbers.

Theoretical frameworks (such as classical migration theory based on push–pull factors and Marxist labor-market theory based on social class within capitalist expansionism) that have historically dominated international migration analyses have focused on men. Where mentioned, women are incorporated as a component of the male study respondents' "social capital," or network of social ties that influence potential costs, risks, and benefits associated with the men's migration (Massey & Espinosa 1997).

The growing selection of explicitly gendered field studies that took off during the 1980s reveals the great complexity of issues migrant women face, particularly as they intersect with the fate of children. Studies initially were concerned with how to "add" women to the migration field, where their presence was either peripheral or simply invisible. They often appeared when issues of employment or reproductive rights were discussed. Numerous studies in the 1990s, however, placed women at the center of analysis as proper agents of structural and social change, thus reconceptualizing tools central to conventional models of migration, such as regulating the patterns of skill transfer, household decision-making, labor market segmentation dynamics, networking, and residential location choice. These studies debunk some of the myths on migration in general and illegal migration in particular by addressing issues pertinent to female migration, kinship relations, and the interconnections among gender, class, and race. The issues addressed in these studies, usually grounded in feminist theoretical analysis, vary from general gender migration theory, international labor migration, transnationalism, construction of national identity, participation in immigrant politics, citizenship, refugees, and gendered work, to emigration and household reproduction. The analytical frameworks, although unique to each study, address several dimensions: (1) the implications on policymaking and networking at the international and national levels, taking into account specific ideological, political, and socioeconomic constraints; (2) the importance of women at the center of economic production as well as social reproduction, not only in research but also in policymaking; (3) the analytic model of reconciling structure and agency with the importance of gender (Giddens's structuration model); (4) recognizing that families are important actors in the migration process and – most important for the analysis of female migration – whether this involves migration of the whole family, reunification, improvement of the family economic status, or reliance on the family for support; (5) the concept of "mothering" and "motherhood" as a central issue for mothers, who migrate often in search of better conditions for their children whom they leave behind with extended family members; (6) the role of kinship support, and of gendered aspects of household survival in shaping "migration work," which varies by class (Willis & Yeoh 2000). For example, the limited data available on undocumented Mexican immigrant women follows the bulk of migration studies in focusing on the US–Mexico borderlands of the Southwest and California. Broadening the scope of inquiry beyond the borderlands poses significant questions about extrapolating from existent data, and may identify emerging second-stage migration patterns that should be incorporated into immigration analyses (Andrews et al. 2002).

Thousands of people living without status in different parts of the world face the fear and very real threat of deportation or imprisonment. This situation prevents many people of low social status not only from obtaining decent employment, but also from using services such as social housing, education, health care, social assistance, and emergency services, including police protection. An example is the 1994 Proposition 187 in California, barring illegal immigrants from non-emergency health care and public schooling (the proposition was later found to be unconstitutional) and the various reports presented by undocumented women (Tastsoglou & Hadjicostandi 2003).

The DADT (Don't Ask Don't Tell) Toronto Campaign is a policy which presents a local solution to the problem by preventing city employees from inquiring about the immigration status of people accessing city services. Also, it prohibits city employees from sharing information with federal and provincial enforcement agencies, including the Department of Citizenship and Immigration Canada (CIC), on the immigration status of anyone accessing city services (Hobbs & Sauer 2005) This policy represents a recognition of some of the most pressing theoretical and practical concerns of transnational anti-racist feminist solidarity, which would provide all workers, including illegal workers, with a structure of dignity and societal inclusion. Transnational feminist solidarity work must be attentive to the different ways that "nations" are imagined and constructed by sexist and racist immigration policies, within a national landscape that is experienced very differently according to a person's identity.

SEE ALSO: Class, Status, and Power; Discrimination; Diversity; Family Migration; Inequality/Stratification, Gender; Migration: International; Migration and the Labor Force; Race; Race and Ethnic Consciousness; Race (Racism); Uneven Development

REFERENCES AND SUGGESTED READINGS

Andrews, T. J., Ybarra, V. D., & Miramontes, T. (2002) Negotiating Survival: Undocumented Mexican Immigrant Women in the Pacific Northwest. *Social Science Journal* 39(3): 431–49.

Hobbs, S. & Sauer, A. (2005) Women and Environments. *International Magazine* 68/69: 41–3.

Kimer, J. T. (2005) A Generation of Migrants. *NACLA Report on the Americas* 39(1): 31–7.

King, R. (2000) Southern Europe in the Changing Global Map of Migration. In King, R., Lazaridis, G., & Tsardanidis, C. (Eds.), *Eldorado or Fortress? Migration in Southern Europe.* Macmillan, New York, pp. 3–26.

Lazaridis, G. (2000) Filipino and Albanian Women Migrant Workers in Greece: Multiple Layers of Oppression. In: Anthias, F. & Lazaridis, G. (Eds.), *Gender and Migration in Southern Europe.* Berg, Oxford, pp. 49–79.

Lazaridis, G. & Poyago-Theotoky, J. (1999). Undocumented Migrants in Greece: Issues of Regularization. *International Migration* 37: 715–40.

Massey, D. & Espinosa, K. (1997) What's Driving Mexico–US Migration? A Theoretical Empirical and Policy Analysis. *American Journal of Sociology* 102: 939–99.

Massey, D., Durand, J., & Malone, N. (2002) *Beyond Smoke and Mirrors: Mexican Immigration in an Era of Economic Integration.* Russell Sage Foundation, New York.

Tastsoglou, E. & Hadjicostandi, J. (2003) Never Outside the Labour Market, But Always Outsiders: Female Migrant Workers in Greece. *Greek Review of Social Research:* 189–220.

Willis, K. & Yeoh, B. (Eds.) (2000) *Gender and Migration.* Edward Elgar, Northampton, MA.

Milgram, Stanley (experiments)

Markus Kemmelmeier

Stanley Milgram was one of the most influential social psychologists of the twentieth century. Born in 1933 in New York, he obtained a BA from Queen's College, and went on to receive a PhD in psychology from Harvard. Subsequently, Milgram held faculty positions in psychology at Yale University and the City University of New York until his untimely death in 1984. Although Milgram never held a formal appointment in sociology, his work was centrally focused on the social psychological aspects of social structure.

Milgram is mostly recognized for his research on obedience to authority. As many social scientists of his time and as a Jew himself, Milgram was deeply influenced by the experience of the Holocaust. Based on earlier work of his mentor Solomon Asch (1907–96), Milgram suspected that notions of an aggressive personality or authoritarian cultural traits were not sufficient to explain the mass murder of the Holocaust. Rather, he suspected that the hierarchical structure of bureaucratic organizations and the willingness of people to submit to legitimate authority provided a more plausible explanation of why so many educated and civilized people contributed to barbaric torture and mass killings.

In a historic coincidence, in 1961, just as Milgram was about to begin work on his famous obedience experiments, the world witnessed the trial of Adolf Otto Eichmann, a high-ranking Nazi official who was in charge of organizing the transport of millions of Jews to the death camps. To many, Eichmann appeared not at all to be the fervent anti-Semite that many had suspected him to be; rather, his main defense was that he was only "following orders" as an administrator. To the political theorist Hannah Arendt, Eichmann's case illustrated the "banality of evil," in which personal malice appeared to matter less than the desire of individuals to fulfill their roles in the larger context of a bureaucracy. Milgram's research is arguably the most striking example to illustrate this dynamic.

Milgram planned and conducted his obedience experiments between 1960 and 1963 at Yale University. In order to be able to study obedience to authority, he put unsuspecting research participants in a novel situation, which he staged in the laboratory. With the help of actors and props, Milgram set up an experimental ruse that was so real that hardly any of his research participants suspected that, in reality, nothing was what it pretended to be.

For this initial study, using newspaper ads promising $4.50 for participation in a psychological study, Milgram recruited men aged 20 to 50, ranging from elementary school dropouts to PhDs. Each research participant arrived in the lab along with another man, white and roughly 30 years of age, whom they thought to be another research participant. In reality, this person was a confederate, that is, an actor in cahoots with the experimenter. The experimenter explained that both men were about to take part in a study that explored the effect of punishment on memory. One man would assume the role of a "teacher" who would read a series of word pairings (e.g., *nice day*, *blue box*), which the other ("the learner") was supposed to memorize. Subsequently, the teacher would read the first word of the pair with the learner having to select the correct second word from a list. Every mistake by the learner would be punished with an electric shock. It was further made clear that, although the shocks would be painful, they would not do any permanent harm.

Following this explanation, the experimenter assigned both men to the roles. Because the procedure was rigged, the unsuspecting research participant always was assigned to the role of teacher. As first order of business, the learner was seated in an armchair in an adjoining room such that he would be separated by a wall from the teacher, but would otherwise be able to hear him from the main room. Electrodes were affixed to the learner's arms, who was subsequently strapped to the chair apparently to make sure that improper movements would not endanger the success of the experiment.

In the main room, the teacher was told that he would have to apply electric shocks every time the learner made a mistake. For this purpose, the learner was seated in front of an electric generator with various dials. The experimenter instructed the teacher to steadily increase the voltage of the shock each time the learner made a new mistake. The shock generator showed a row of levers ranging from 15 volts on the left to 450 volts on the right, with each lever in between delivering a shock 15 volts higher than its neighbor on the left. Milgram labeled the voltage level, left to right, from "Slight Shock" to "Danger: Severe Shock," with the last two switches being marked "XXX." The teacher was told that he simply should work his way from the left to the right without using any lever twice. To give the teacher an idea of the electric current he would deliver to the learner, he received a sample shock of 45 volts, which most research participants found surprisingly painful. However, despite its appearance, in reality the generator never emitted any electric shocks. It was merely a device that allowed Milgram to examine how far the teacher would go in harming another person based on the experimenter's say-so.

As learning trials started, the teacher applied electric shocks to the learner. The learner's responses were scripted such that he apparently made many mistakes, requiring the teacher to increase shock levels by 15 volts with every new mistake. As the strength of electric shocks increased, occasional grunts and moans of pain were heard from the learner. At 120 volts the learner started complaining about the pain. At 150 volts, the learner demanded to be released on account of a heart condition, and the protest continued until the shocks reached 300 volts and the learner started pounding on the wall. At 315 volts the learner stopped responding altogether.

As the complaints by the learner started, the teacher would often turn to the experimenter, who was seated at a nearby desk, wondering whether and how to proceed. The experimenter, instead of terminating the experiment, replied with a scripted succession of prods:

Prod 1: "Please continue."
Prod 2: "The experiment requires that you continue."
Prod 3: "It is absolutely necessary to continue."
Prod 4: "You have no other choice: you must go on."

These prods were successful in coaxing many teachers into continuing to apply electric shocks even when the learner no longer responded to the word memory questions. Indeed, in the first of Milgram's experiments, a stunning 65 percent of all participants continued all the way to 450 volts, and not a single participant refused to continue the shocks before they reached the 300 volt level! The high levels of compliance illustrate the powerful effect of the social structure that participants had entered. By accepting the role of teacher in the experiment in exchange for the payment of a nominal fee, participants had agreed to accept the authority of the experimenter and carry out his instructions. In other words, just as Milgram suspected, the social forces of hierarchy and obedience could push normal and well-adjusted individuals into harming others.

The overall level of obedience, however, does not reveal the tremendous amount of stress that all teachers experienced. Because the situation was extremely realistic, teachers were agonizing over whether or not to continue the electric shocks. Should they care for the well-being of the obviously imperiled learners and even put their life in danger? Or should they abide by a legitimate authority figure, who presented his instructions crisply and confidently? Participants typically sought to resolve this conflict by seeking assurances that the experimenter, and not themselves, would accept full responsibility for their actions. Once they felt assured, they typically continued to apply shocks that would have likely electrocuted the learner.

Milgram expanded his initial research into a series of 19 experiments in which he carefully examined the conditions under which obedience would occur. For instance, the teacher's proximity to the learner was an important factor in lowering obedience, that is, the proportion of people willing to deliver the full 450 volts. When the teacher was in the same room with the learner, obedience dropped to 40 percent, and when the teacher was required to touch the learner and apply physical force to deliver the electric shock, obedience dropped to 30 percent.

Milgram further suspected that the social status of the experimenter, presumably a serious Yale University researcher in a white lab coat, would have important implications for obedience. Indeed, when there was no obvious connection with Yale, and the above experiment was repeated in a run-down office building in Bridgeport, Connecticut, obedience dropped to 48 percent. Indeed, when not the white-coated experimenter but another confederate encouraged the teacher to continue the shocks, all participants terminated the experiment as soon as the confederate complained. Milgram concluded that "a substantial proportion of people do what they are told to do, irrespective of the content of the act and without limitations of conscience, *so long as they perceive that the command comes from a legitimate authority*" (1965). However, additional studies highlighted that obedience is in part contingent on surveillance. When the experimenter transmitted his orders not in person but via telephone, obedience levels dropped to 20 percent, with many participants only pretending to apply higher and higher electric shocks.

Since its initial publication in 1963, Milgram's research has drawn a lot of criticism, mainly on ethical grounds. First, it was alleged that it was unethical to deceive participants to the extent that occurred in these studies. It is important to note that all participants were fully debriefed on the deception, and most did not seem to mind and were relieved to find out that they had not shocked the learner. The second ethical criticism is, however, much more serious. As alluded to earlier, Milgram exposed his participants to tremendous levels of stress. Milgram, anticipating this criticism, interviewed participants after the experiment and followed up several weeks later. The overwhelming majority of his participants commented that they enjoyed being in the experiment, and only a small minority experienced regret. Even though personally Milgram rejected allegations of having mistreated his participants, his own work suggests that he may have gone too far: "Subjects were observed to sweat, tremble, bite their lips, groan, and dig their fingernails into their flesh . . . A mature and initially poised businessman entered the laboratory smiling and confident. Within 20 minutes, he was reduced to a twitching, stuttering wreck who was rapidly approaching a point of nervous collapse" (1963: 375). Today, Milgram's obedience studies are generally considered unethical and would not pass muster with regard to contemporary regulations protecting the well-being of research participants. Ironically, partly *because* Milgram's studies illustrated the power of hierarchical social relationships, contemporary researchers are at great pains to avoid coercion and allow participants to terminate their participation in any research study at any time without penalty.

Another type of criticism of the obedience studies has questioned their generality and charged that their usefulness in explaining real-world events is limited. Indeed, Milgram conducted his research when trust in authorities was higher than it is nowadays. However, Milgram's studies have withstood this criticism. Reviews of research conducted using Milgram's paradigm have generally found obedience levels to be at roughly 60 percent (see, e.g., Blass 2000). In one of his studies Milgram further documented that there was no apparent difference in the responses of women and men. More recent research using more ethically acceptable methods further testifies to the power of obedience in shaping human action (Blass 2000).

Milgram offers an important approach to explaining the Holocaust by emphasizing the bureaucratic nature of evil, which relegated individuals to executioners of orders issued by a legitimate authority. Sociologists have extended this analysis and provided compelling accounts of obedience as root causes of many horrific crimes, ranging from the My Lai massacre to Watergate (Hamilton & Kelman 1989). However, it is arguably somewhat unclear to what extent Milgram's findings can help explain the occurrence of the Holocaust itself. Whereas obedience kept the machinery of death running with frightening efficiency, historians often caution against ignoring the malice and sadism that many of Hitler's executioners brought to the task (see Blass 2004).

Milgram's dramatic experiments have left a lasting impression beyond the social sciences. They are the topic of various movies, including the 1975 TV film *The Tenth Level* starring William Shatner. Further, the 37 percent of participants who did not obey were memorialized in a 1986 song by the rock musician Peter Gabriel titled "We Do What We're Told (Milgram's 37)."

SEE ALSO: Aggression; Asch Experiments; Authority and Conformity; Experimental Methods; Holocaust; Organizations; Social Networks; Social Psychology; Zimbardo Prison Experiment

REFERENCES AND SUGGESTED READINGS

Blass, T. (Ed.) (2000) *Obedience to Authority: Current Perspectives on the Milgram Paradigm.* Erlbaum, Mahwah, NJ.

Blass, T. (2004) *The Man Who Shocked the World: The Life and Legacy of Stanley Milgram.* Basic Books, New York.

Hamilton, V. L. & Kelman, H. (1989) *Crimes of Obedience: Toward a Social Psychology of Authority and Responsibility.* Yale University Press, New Haven.

Milgram, S. (1963) Behavioral Study of Obedience. *Journal of Abnormal and Social Psychology* 69: 371–8.

Milgram, S. (1965) Some Conditions of Obedience and Disobedience to Authority. *Human Relations* 18: 57–76.

Milgram, S. (1974) *Obedience to Authority: An Experimental View.* Harper & Row, New York.

military research and science and war

Brian Woods

The relationship between science, technology, and war has a long history. Studies of catapults, for example, have highlighted the important role of science and technology in ancient society and in ancient warfare. The rise of advanced catapults not only attracted the interest and financial support of "governments," but also combined early studies of geometry, physics, and technology, and led to the rise in the visibility and status of the engineers that worked on them. The medieval period also saw advancements in arms and armor, artillery, fortifications, and warships. Unlike the Roman Empire, which had centralized its arms manufacture, producing standardized weapons, it seems that the medieval arms industry was made up of a diverse array of artisans forging personalized weapons.

A challenge to the independent artisans came in eighteenth-century France when state military engineers introduced technical drawings and the tools of manufacturing tolerance to affect standardization and the production of interchangeable parts for weapons and other military artifacts. Notwithstanding, science and engineering in France remained a relatively disorganized activity up until the Franco-Prussian war (1870–1). The French defeat and the siege of Paris in 1870 had both an immediate and a long-term effect on science in France. During the siege, a range of science and engineering societies came up with ideas for both defense and survival. The Society of Civil Engineers, for example, developed mobile ramparts and the Paris Chemical Society was involved in improvements to the manufacture of explosives and cannon, developments in synthetic foods and artificial milk (though with limited success), and the development of microphotography, which enabled a single pigeon to carry up to 30,000 telegrams. After the war, French scientists argued that their lack of success necessitated an increase in state funding and a rethinking of both science and scientific education. The Third Republic thus saw both the centralization of science and the increasing involvement of scientists in politics.

The American Civil War (1861–5) was the first war to witness the full impact of the industrial revolution. Although the institutionalization of science and the American preoccupation with its practical applications were stimulated in part during the American War of Independence (1775–83), which among other things saw the first use of a submarine in warfare and the establishment of West Point. The expansion of the American frontier during the nineteenth century brought with it among other things the mechanization of agriculture, the development of the railroads, steamships, telegraph, and advancements in both rifles and small arms, most notably the Colt revolver. While military requirements were not the primary driver of this build up of the industrial and technological base, they provided a powerful added stimulus. There was a strong interaction between military and civilian needs and between the engineers, inventors, entrepreneurs, and factory owners, who responded to both. While science and technology shaped warfare, again the Civil War shaped the institutions of science. The Union government established the National Academy of Science in 1863 to advise on the application of science and technology in warfare and, while it contributed little to the war effort, it eventually become one of the most important scientific institutions in the US.

The branch of the armed services with the longest history of sustained, organized scientific research in both Europe and the US has been the navy. For example, during the period of relative global peace from the end of the Napoleonic Wars (1799–1815) to World War I (1914–18), the British Navy substantially increased its investment in scientific research across a range of activities, including the establishment of specialized institutions dealing with matters such as the scientific design of ships' hulls using models and towing tanks. World War I also brought with it further increases in the size and commitment to scientific naval research and development (R&D) and moves toward improving its organization to make it more responsive to navy needs.

Command technology (as William McNeill termed the deliberate attempt to create new weapon systems that surpass existing capabilities) was also a navy invention. Warships were the most expensive and complex weapon systems of their day and in the build up to World War I played a major role in the arms race between Britain and Germany. It was with World War I, however, that command technology came ashore. Faced with dependence on Germany for essential items such as optical glass, magnetos, and even khaki dye for uniforms, Britain established the Department of Scientific and Industrial Research and began the systematic incorporation of science and technology into government.

For many observers, however, the watershed of military science came with the outbreak of World War II (1939–45). Not only were radical new technologies developed during the war, but the very scale of effort and complexity of the science/military organization was also revolutionized. During the interwar years any large armaments company could count itself the equal of any government in terms of the resources and organizational input into weapons-related R&D. By 1945, government science had grown enormously and shifted the balance toward scientists and government research laboratories. During World War II scientists came to play a new role: as advisers at the highest level of government.

Probably the most renowned collaboration between science and the military is the Manhattan Project, which brought together resources and scientific labor power on an unprecedented scale to produce the first atomic bombs, which the US dropped on the cities of Hiroshima and Nagasaki in 1945, ending the war with Japan. Soon after World War II the Soviet Union successfully exploded its first atomic bomb (1949), closely followed by Britain (1952), then France (1960), China (1964), India (1974), and Pakistan (1998). Other nuclear powers included Israel and South Africa, although only suspicion surrounds a possible test program by both countries, which collaborated closely during the

1970s and 1980s. In the early 1990s the Republic of South Africa became the first nuclear state to disarm, followed by Belarus, Kazakhstan, and the Ukraine after the breakup of the Soviet Union. The proliferation of nuclear weapons led many scientists to take a political stance against further development. The most recognized forum of this politics is the *Bulletin of the Atomic Scientists*, founded in 1945 by scientists who worked on the Manhattan Project at the University of Chicago.

In the US, the Manhattan Project affected post-war science in three distinctive ways. First, it created a number of R&D facilities that survived the project and continued to play a critical role in the development of US science. Second, it created an operating philosophy – a set of operating procedures – that various agencies adopted on a range of scientific endeavors, including space and weapon-systems development. Third, it influenced the post-war US science policy of locating large government-sponsored research projects in the private sector, the rationale for which was that it would be the best way to assemble quickly the labor power necessary to accomplish goals of national importance and then (in theory) disperse them when the goals were achieved.

Internationally, the effect of the nuclear arms race along with the collapse in US–Soviet relations was the Cold War (1949–89). For many observers, the Cold War was an R&D war. The intense rivalry between the Soviet Union and the US motivated government investment in R&D that was sustained, massive, and gave rise to projects that may have not been possible otherwise. In countries like the US and the UK, more than half of government-funded research in the last half of the twentieth century, and close to a quarter of the national total, was funded out of defense budgets. By international standards, the UK remained a high-spender on military R&D (although an order of magnitude behind the two superpowers, the US and the USSR) at least until the 1980s. In part, this pattern arose from Prime Minister Clement Attlee's decision after World War II to leap a generation and begin major R&D programs in atomic weapons, new aircraft, guided missiles, etc. In contrast, Germany, Italy, and Japan were limited by treaty from engaging in certain defense activities and the French recovery in military R&D did not begin until the 1960s.

Increased government/state spending on evermore sophisticated, evermore destructive weapon systems was part of what Paul Baran and Paul Sweezy termed the permanent arms economy. In her seminal work *The Baroque Arsenal*, Mary Kaldor echoed many of Baran and Sweezy's concerns when she reflected on a runaway military-technological machine that absorbed increasing amounts of public money on gross, elaborate, and very expensive hardware, but which produced little in the way of benefit, even for the military itself. For Kaldor, the emphasis on evermore costly and complex weapons systems could only be explained in terms of the structure of the military-industrial institutions: the competitive dynamic of the armorers combined with the conservatism of the armed forces. To keep the whole system going new systems are continually dreamt up.

Within this environment, science, especially state-sponsored science, often took on Cold War aims as its own. Military or quasi-military R&D frequently received the highest priority, which, along with massive projects like the space program, diminished the difference between civilian and military science by encouraging scientists who were looking for funding to suggest that even so-called pure or basic research had potential practical applications. As such, many observers have noted that it is difficult to make a distinction between military and civil R&D and that it is probably better to describe a spectrum with the extremes at either end rather than make any clear division.

Perhaps one of the most renowned sociological texts on military science and technology is Donald MacKenzie's *Inventing Accuracy* (1993). Tracing the development of nuclear missile accuracy, MacKenzie revealed the inner dynamics of military research and development, showing how individuals and group interests drive institutional patterns of organizational and technical change. Questioning ideas of both technological and political determinism, *Inventing Accuracy* illustrates how the missile revolution involved not only transformations in science and technology, but also the reworking of national defense strategies as well as military organization. Against the interests of the US Air Force, who were committed to long-range bombers, the Draper Laboratory and other powerful actors created an interest in guided missile technology. Importantly, the construction of the strategic need for guided nuclear missiles was simultaneous with (not prior to) their technical development. The technology was neither above politics nor beneath it. Guided missiles were not inherently better than long-range bombers and so ordained to replace them, and Draper was not "ordered" from above to find alternative weapons of nuclear war. Instead, there was a creation of an interest in a particular technological form in order to institutionalize it – to make it appear a logical and natural progression.

More recently, Mary Kaldor has argued that increased weapon accuracy combined with information technology (IT) has revolutionized warfare in that it has enabled what she terms "the spectacle war" to take place: warfare that the aggressor can fight at a distance, with minimal casualties and beam home live for its citizens to watch on their televisions. For Kaldor, the cruise missile is the paradigmatic weapon of the spectacle war, but she also highlights computer gaming as an example of defense transformation because it enabled the military to image future wars through IT simulations from which they derived new ways of thinking and new ways of fighting. More notable, however, is Kaldor's paradox: modern military technology has led to a decline in military power. The increasing destructiveness of modern weapon systems means that superior technology rarely affords control of a territory or outright military victory. In the "new wars" battles between armed opponents are rare, with almost all the violence inflicted on civilian populations.

SEE ALSO: Big Science and Collective Research; Gendered Aspects of War and International Violence; Military Sociology; Political Economy of Science; Technological Determinism; Technological Innovation; War

REFERENCES AND SUGGESTED READINGS

Bud, R. & Gummett, P. (Eds.) (1999) *Cold War, Hot Science: Applied Research in Britain's Defence Laboratories 1945–1990*. Science Museum, London.

De Vries, K. (1992) *Medieval Military Technology*. Broadview, Peterborough.
Kaldor, M. (2003) American Power: From Compliance to Cosmopolitanism. *International Affairs* 79: 1–22.
Mac Kenzie, D. (1993) *Inventing Accuracy: A Historical Sociology of Nuclear Missile Guidance*. MIT Press, Cambridge, MA.
Roland, A. (1985) Science and War. *Osiris* (2nd series) 1: 247–72.
Solovey, M. (Ed.) (2001) Science and the Cold War. *Social Studies of Science* (special issue) 31.

military sociology

Irving Smith

Military sociology is an interdisciplinary subfield of sociology that employs sociological concepts, theories, and methods to analyze the internal organization, practices, and perceptions of the armed forces as well as the relationships between the military and other social institutions. Some of the topics generally covered in military sociology include small group processes related to race/ethnicity, gender, and sexual orientation, leadership, policy, veterans, historical cases, United States and foreign military organization, international affairs, manpower models, the transition from conscription to all-volunteer forces, the social legitimacy of military organization, the military as a form of industrial organization, and civil–military relations.

The military institution and members of the armed forces have been an abundant source of information to address a broad range of sociological subfields including demography, stratification, social psychology, comparative sociology, and theory. Military sociologists often use both the differences and similarities between the military and society in conducting their analysis. The differences often spring from the unique cluster of duties and sacrifices asked of service members and the technology they use to perform their jobs. The similarities examined often assume that the military is a microcosm of society. This assumption stems from the fact that military service members represent every part of their host society including its culture, values, attitudes, and demographic makeup. As such, military sociology has been used to understand not only the military and its relationship to other social institutions, but also social institutions in and of themselves. For example, research conducted on the relationship between the military and labor markets has increased our understanding of both military labor markets and labor markets in general.

Military sociology can roughly be divided into three distinct time periods corresponding roughly to the World War II (1941–50), Cold War (1950–89), and post-Cold War (1989–present) eras. During each of these periods there have been general topics of study which have driven analysis, debate, and study within the field.

Although some of the earliest known sociological theorists, including Karl Marx (1848), Émile Durkheim (1897), Herbert Spencer (1902), and Max Weber (1927), used the military as a unit of analysis, the field of military sociology did not begin in earnest until the World War II period. During that period several sociologists and psychologists were mobilized by the US armed forces. Their research and observations both during and after the war were the foundations of the field of military sociology. This early period of military sociology focused on applying sociological knowledge to gain an understanding of the social dynamics involved in mobilizing and fighting a war. Some of the questions they sought to answer were: What motivated the rapidly mobilized US forces to fight? How did personnel policies affect motivation? What happens to veterans when they return to society?

Early military sociology was dominated by Americans. In 1941 the US Army's Information and Education Division conducted over 200 experiments and surveys to better understand the effects of military personnel policies on morale and motivation. These studies, conducted between 1941 and 1945, produced four volumes collectively known as *Studies in Social Psychology in World War II*. Stouffer et al. (1949) also used a great deal of this research to produce the American Soldier Studies, which included a wide range of topics including cohesion, small group dynamics, race relations,

morale, motivation, communication, and leadership. Stouffer et al.'s effort was the defining work of the period in that it set the agenda for work in military sociology and served as a model for the nascent field of survey methodology for several decades to come.

Another notable work of the period was Shils and Janowitz's "Cohesion and Disintegration in the Wehrmacht in World War II" (1948), which studied Wehrmacht prisoners and found that Wehrmacht soldiers fought because of interpersonal relationships within the primary group. Additionally, S. L. A. Marshall's *Men Against Fire: The Problem of Battle Command in Future Wars* (1947) found that infantry soldiers fought because of the presence or the presumed presence of a comrade. Marshall's work has for the most part been discounted because of allegations that he invented the data; however, his work is still significant in that he was one of the pioneers in bringing a sociological perspective to the study of the combat soldier.

The Korean War produced an increase in the volume of research on group processes and cohesion. During this period Roger Little conducted a study in which he observed a rifle company in combat for several months and found that "buddy relations" between men were critical to combat performance. As a result of President Harry S. Truman's 1948 Executive Order 9981 and manpower shortages, the United States Armed Forces were integrated and race relations studies were initiated by the Special Operations Research Office at Johns Hopkins. They found that integrated units did not suffer a decrease in performance in combat; however, the results were not released until the 1960s.

In general, the studies of this period used an applied research approach, applicable at the individual level of analysis, to gain a better understanding of soldier adjustment, motivation, and small group processes.

As the Cold War began to take shape, the field of military sociology rapidly expanded. The number of military sociologists, topics of inquiry, organizations dedicated to the study of military sociology, and literature increased during this period.

The Cold War broke a longstanding pattern of nations conducting mass mobilizations, fighting wars, and then rapidly demobilizing.

Several nations, including the United States, moved from mass mobilization models to large standing forces. This phenomenon caused many to think about how best to control these large standing forces and ensure that they remained subservient to civil authority. This is often referred to as the civil–military relations debate. The progenitors of this debate were Samuel Huntington and Morris Janowitz. Huntington (1957) expressed the view that a professional military could best be controlled by physically separating it from society and using objective control. Janowitz (1960) believed that isolating the military from its host society was dangerous and that a professional military could best be controlled by integrating it into society and using more informal controls.

In 1960 Janowitz founded the Inter-University Seminar on Armed Forces and Society (IUS), which is still thriving today. His goal was to create an organization that facilitated the analysis of military organizations and collaboration across university, organizational, disciplinary, theoretical, and national lines. The IUS began publishing its own journal, *Armed Forces and Society*, in 1972.

In 1965 Charles C. Coates and Roland J. Pellegrin published the first major military sociology textbook titled *Military Sociology: A Study of American Military Institutions and Military Life*. In general, the topics that Coates and Pellegrin presented are still generally regarded as the focal points of military sociology.

In the late 1960s and early 1970s the research focus of military sociology moved from civil–military relations and the military profession to issues revolving around US involvement in the unpopular conflict in Vietnam and the perception of inequitable conscription in the US force. Simultaneously, America was engulfed in social tension created by strained racial relations, affirmative action, changing definitions of gender roles, changing definitions of the obligations and rights of citizenship, rising oil prices, and fear of nuclear destruction. These issues were manifest in the US military in the form of increased use of illicit drugs, fragging incidents, absenteeism, draft evasion, and race riots within the ranks of the United States Armed Forces.

The ensuing debates over the causes, remedies, and future issues associated with these problems fueled research and discussion within

both the field of military sociology and society at large and ultimately contributed to the end of military conscription in the United States. The end of conscription in the United States led to the establishment of the All-Volunteer Force in 1973. The result of the strife within the American armed forces and the associated literature compelled other nations to focus on their armed forces as well; however, the field was still dominated by Americans. The *Journal of Political and Military Science*, founded in 1973 at Northern Illinois University, and *Armed Forces and Society* were the two major journals that provided a forum for these debates.

In the early 1970s Charles C. Moskos developed his institutional/occupational (I/O) model. He envisioned the military evolving from an institution being primarily oriented by tradition, patriotic values, and a sense of calling to an institution primarily oriented by economics, general business principles, and the self-interest of individual service members. In essence, he believed that the military was moving from a calling to a job. This theoretical model was the impetus for much of the debate within the field throughout the 1970s and early 1980s. Many used this model as a springboard to examine military families, recruiting, veteran status, changing military missions (e.g., peacekeeping versus traditional war fighting), demographic changes, racial composition, and gender issues to understand how the armed forces and its relationship to society were changing.

During the 1980s the field continued to grow and became more internationally focused. The number of international governments, sociologists, and students studying within the field increased substantially during this decade.

The fall of the Berlin Wall in 1989 and the subsequent end of the Cold War in Europe opened a new chapter in the field of military sociology. These events essentially changed the nature of war and how states viewed the use of their militaries. Militaries around the world were confronted with new challenges, tasks, and missions that included responses to regional threats, peacekeeping operations, and military operations other than war.

These changes applied not only to American armed forces but to European armed forces as well. In the post-Cold War period European armed forces became smaller, more mobile/

agile, and more professional. Several moved away from conscription and, like their American counterparts, their missions changed from traditional internal and territorial defense to international military peacekeeping and crisis management. Many of the eastern bloc nations transformed or are in the midst of transformation in their quest to gain admission to supranational organizations (e.g., the North Atlantic Treaty Organization, the European Union). Additionally, the post-Cold War era has witnessed an increase in tribal conflict in Africa, ethnic strife in the Balkans, and increased hostility in both the Middle East and the Korean Peninsula. China, a major arms producer and a nuclear power, is booming economically and represents an imposing threat to the balance of power. Military sociology has attempted to understand how these changes have impacted the relationship between the military and society.

These post-Cold War changes led some notable military sociologists to characterize the changes as evidence of a move from late modern to postmodern militaries. Charles Moskos, the architect of this thesis, developed it as an extension to the I/O model. Moskos and colleagues envisioned militaries with fewer differences based on rank, service, and combat versus support roles; increased interdependence between the military and civilian spheres; changing missions (wars to operations other than war); more international missions (loosening ties with the nation-state); movement toward smaller volunteer forces; and increasingly more androgynous in composition. However, not all military sociologists subscribed to the postmodern military theory. In fact, some have argued that Moskos et al.'s conceptualization of a postmodern military was simply a post-Cold War evolution of modern militaries (Booth et al. 2001).

Throughout this period there was also great concern that a culture gap existed between civil society and the military. Many believed that the United States military and its civilian leadership had very disparate political and social beliefs. As evidence of the civil–military gap, some argued that the military was becoming increasingly conservative and Republican in nature and that the vast majority of civilian leaders had little or no military experience. The ensuing debate over the civil–military

gap, originated by Peter Feaver and Richard Kohn, produced large volumes of work within the field.

The events of September 11, 2001 added a new chapter to military sociology. Several of the accepted norms about who, how, and why nations fight, including the boundaries between military and civilian, combat and support, ally and adversary, and even war and peace, have been obscured. The changes that are currently occurring are not confined to war fighting or even to military forces and their roles. These changes are part of a bigger movement concerning the spread of technology and globalization, and the threat of organized, ideologically motivated coercive violence experienced by the general citizenry of nations via terrorism. Military sociology has taken up the study of understanding the extent of this change and its effects on the military and civil–military relations.

SEE ALSO: Elites; Gendered Aspects of War and International Violence; Leadership; Life Course Perspective; Military Research and Science and War; Mobilization; War

REFERENCES AND SUGGESTED READINGS

Booth, B., Kestnbaum, M., & Segal, D. R. (2001) Are Post-Cold War Militaries Postmodern? *Armed Forces and Society* 27: 319.

Huntington, S. P. (1957) *The Soldier and the State: The Theory and Politics of Civil–Military Relations.* Harvard University Press, Cambridge, MA.

Janowitz, M. (1960) *The Professional Soldier: A Social and Political Portrait.* Free Press, Glencoe, IL.

Moskos, C. C., Jr. & Wood, F. R. (Eds.) (1988) *The Military: More Than Just a Job?* Pergamon-Brassey's International Defense Publishers, McLean, VA.

Segal, D. R. (1989) *Recruiting for Uncle Sam: Citizenship and Military Manpower Policy.* University Press of Kansas, Lawrence.

Siebold, G. L. (2001) Core Issues and Theory in Military Sociology. *Journal of Political and Military Sociology* 29 (Summer): 140–59.

Stouffer, S. A., Suchman, E. A., DeVinney, L. C., Star, S. A., & Williams, R. M. (1949) *The American Soldier: Adjustment During Army Life*, Vol. 1. Princeton University Press, Princeton.

Mill, John Stuart (1806–73)

Sandra J. Peart

In the nineteenth century, social scientists such as John Stuart Mill struggled with the problem of the individual in society: how to achieve the "improvement of mankind" (Robson 1968) when society consists of free and responsible individuals. As he speculated about how behavior is conditioned by culture, habit, and institutions, and new habits form in the context of institutional change, Mill stepped into the burgeoning field of "speculative politics" or what we know of today as sociology. Social scientists, who now sometimes neglect questions relating to the acquisition of tastes or "character," may fail to appreciate how much of Mill's writing was designed to deal with problems of human development and interaction in the context of social change. Examples in what follows include the Irish land question, emancipation, the laboring poor, and women's rights.

Mill was also, of course, at the forefront of explicating methodological principles for social science. He followed the method of Auguste Comte to the extent that he urged practitioners to adopt the positive approach for the investigation of social and political phenomena (Mill 1969 [1865]). Economic analysis treats "man's nature as modified by the social state" (Mill 1967 [1836]: 321). Since the treatment of man in a social state runs into the problem of multiple causation, Mill urged that the study of different types of social facts might be "studied apart." This supposition enabled him to develop a method for the science of society in which exchange was essentially a social activity. Towards the end of the century, social sentiments disappeared from economic analysis and material concerns become singularly important (see Peart & Levy 2005). At about the same time, political economists separated their study from that of sociology.

ABSTRACTING FROM DIFFERENCE

For analytical purposes, Mill presumed that people were essentially the same and circumstances (society) differed. Observed behavior varied widely due to "custom" and "institutions," but humans were humans whether black, American, Irish, or English. Mill's 1836 *Essay on the Definition of Political Economy* urged the social scientist to abstract from differences to focus on the common. The "assumed" hypotheses of political economy include a set of behavioral assumptions relating to wealth maximization (Mill 1967 [1836]: 321, 323; see Blaug 1980). For reasons of practicality in the face of multiple causation, Mill called for specialization in the social sciences (Hollander & Peart 1999). In this, he departed respectfully from Comte. In his 1865 review of Comte's *Positivism*, Mill insisted, contra Comte, on the scientific legitimacy of the specialized science of political economy (Mill 1969 [1865]: 305). In his 1848 *Principles*, Mill outlined the implication of such a method: it implied a rejection of racial (or gender) "explanations" of outcomes, which he condemned:

> Is it not, then, a bitter satire on the mode in which opinions are formed on the most important problems of human nature and life, to find public instructors of the greatest pretensions, imputing the backwardness of Irish industry, and the want of energy of the Irish people in improving their condition, to a peculiar indolence and *insouciance* in the Celtic race? Of all vulgar modes of escaping from the consideration of the effect of social and moral influences on the human mind, the most vulgar is that of attributing the diversities of conduct and character to inherent natural differences. (Mill 1965 [1848]: 319)

Mill's abstraction from race and his focus instead on property rights and incentives were sharply disputed in the decades that followed. Early critiques of abstract economic man held that important "inherent" differences characterized the Irish, former slaves, and women. The political economist and co-founder (with Francis Galton) of the eugenics movement, W. R. Greg, attacked classical political economy for its assumption that the Irishman is an "average human being," rather than one prone to "idleness," "ignorance," "jollity," and "drink" (Greg 1869; see Peart & Levy 2005).

The Irish question raised the issue of whether the conclusions of political economy were universally relevant or of limited applicability (Bagehot 1876). In the latter half of the century, attacks on economics focused in part on the legitimacy of studying economic phenomena separately from society as a whole (Peart 2001). Mill's proposal for land reform in Ireland, and his 1870 review essay *Leslie on the Land Question*, argued, in line with the historicists such as T. E. C. Leslie (1873) and J. K. Ingram (1878), that institutional – but not "inherent" – differences in Ireland rendered the conclusions of political economy invalid there.

SOCIAL IMPROVEMENT, HIGHER AND LOWER PLEASURES

So the conclusions of political economy are of limited applicability because man functions in a social world whose institutions vary across time and space. One is led to wonder, how do societies progress? First and foremost, Mill held, progress in nineteenth-century Britain required the acquisition of improved habits of self-reliance among the laboring poor. Experience and discussion reveal to individuals that, for instance, their welfare depends on their decision to marry and have children. Mill's statement regarding the role of experience in revealing the difference between higher and lower pleasures provides a case in point. The same idea appears in the 1848 *Principles*, where Mill tackles the problems of emancipation. Emancipation is justified by the increase in human happiness and not by any increase in material output. Progress, however, will come as former slaves are first immersed in material desires, "provided that their gratification can be a motive to steady and regular bodily and mental exertion" (Mill 1965 [1848]: 104). While Mill might not approve of these material desires in *his* society, they are critical to the development of a capacity for self-reliance.

PUNCH, OR THE LONDON CHARIVARI.—March 30, 1867.

MILL'S LOGIC; OR, FRANCHISE FOR FEMALES.
"PRAY CLEAR THE WAY, THERE, FOR THESE—A—PERSONS."

Similar logic underscores Mill's assessment of the relative merits of schemes for improving the lot of the laboring poor: socialist proposals by Charles Fourier and the Saint-Simonians compared to the capitalist exchange system in place at the time (Mill 1965 [1848]: 210–14). Whatever institutional system is in place, Mill argued, it must preserve the incentives for workers to habits of self-reliance, including adequate foresight to control family size.

Yet how was concern for the self related to concern for others and how might the latter develop over time? Again, Mill's answer lies in experience and discussion, the mechanisms by which people increasingly come to sympathize with others around them (Peart & Levy 2005). In *Utilitarianism* Mill claimed that, with progress, education and "a complete web of corroborative association" serve to make us increasingly concerned with others: "[The individual] comes, as though instinctively, to be conscious of himself as a being who *of course* pays regard to others. The good of others becomes to him a thing naturally and necessarily to be attended to, like any of the physical conditions of our existence" (Mill 1969 [1861]: 232) Ideally, we count others equally *with ourselves* as we move from our own desires to those of all others: "the happiness which forms the utilitarian standard of what is right in conduct, is not the agent's own happiness, but that of all concerned. As between his own happiness and that of others, utilitarianism requires him to be as strictly impartial as a disinterested and benevolent spectator (Mill 1969 [1861]: 218).

Whether Mill succeeds or fails in his explanation is a subject on which authorities are divided (Schumpeter 1954; McPherson 1982). He points to a continuing difficulty for social scientists considering the transition between social states: habits that evolve for sensible reasons in one society, might be counterproductive in another.

CONCLUSION

Mill paid dearly for his agitation in support of people of color, the laboring poor, and women. A glance at the Victorian magazine *Punch* for the first half of 1867 (when the Reform Bill agitation centered on the inclusion of women) reveals a large number of articles with titles such as "Shall Lovely Woman Vote" (May 4, 1867) and "A Certain Person to Mr. Mill" (June 1, 1867). A "Letter to Mr. Punch" of June 8, 1867, entitled "Female Suffrage," ends: "One can hardly fancy a Woman in Opposition!" and is signed "An Old and Ugly M. P." In a *Punch* cartoon, Mill is mocked for using the degendered "persons."

As noted at the outset, Mill was also on the losing methodological side of debates over the nature of social science. Late in the century, the political economist William Stanley Jevons urged economists to specialize in the analysis of strictly economic phenomena (Peart 2001). As the profession came to do so, it moved away from the broad set of social concerns and analyses that so preoccupied Mill. Economics came to focus more narrowly on the individual, independently of custom, institutions, or society. Concern for self versus others then became a "normative" question outside the purview of economic analysis.

SEE ALSO: Comte, Auguste; Economic Sociology: Neoclassical Economic Perspective; Economy (Sociological Approach); Jevons, William; Political Economy; Race; Race (Racism)

REFERENCES AND SUGGESTED READINGS

Bagehot, W. (1876) The Postulates of Political Economy. *Fortnightly Review* 21 o.s. (15 n.s.) (1): 215–42.

Blaug, M. (1980) *The Methodology of Economics, or How Economists Explain.* Cambridge University Press, Cambridge.

Greg, W. R. (1869) Realities of Irish Life. *Quarterly Review* 126: 61–80.

Hollander, S. & Peart, S. J. (1999) John Stuart Mill's Method in Principle and in Practice. *Journal of the History of Economic Thought* 21(4): 369–97.

Ingram, J. K. (1878) Address of the President of Section F of the British Association. *Journal of the Royal Statistical Society* 41 (August): 602–29.

Leslie, T. E. C. (1873) Economic Science and Statistics. *Athenaeum* (September 27).

McPherson, M. S. (1982) Mill's Moral Theory and the Problem of Preference Change. *Ethics* 92: 252–73.

Mill, J. S. (1965 [1848]) *The Principles of Political Economy with Some of Their Applications to Social*

Philosophy. Volumes 2 & 3 of *Collected Works of John Stuart Mill*. Ed. J. M. Robson. University of Toronto Press, Toronto.

Mill, J. S. (1967 [1836]) On the Definition of Political Economy; and on the Method of Investigation Proper to It. *Essays on Economics and Society*. Volume 4 of *Collected Works of John Stuart Mill*. Ed. J. M. Robson. University of Toronto Press, Toronto.

Mill, J. S. (1967 [1870]) Leslie on the Land Question. Volume 5 of *Collected Works of John Stuart Mill*. Ed. J. M. Robson. University of Toronto Press, Toronto, pp. 671–85.

Mill, J. S. (1969 [1861]) Utilitarianism. Volume 10 of *Collected Works of John Stuart Mill*. Ed. J. M. Robson. University of Toronto Press, Toronto, pp. 203–59.

Mill, J. S. (1969 [1865]) August Comte and Positivism. Volume 10 of *Collected Works of John Stuart Mill*. Ed. J. M. Robson. University of Toronto Press, Toronto, pp. 261–368.

Peart, S. J. (2001) Theory, Application and the Canon: The Case of Mill and Jevons. In: Forget, E. & Peart, S. (Eds.), *Reflections on the Classical Canon in Economics: Essays in Honor of Samuel Hollander*. Routledge, London, pp. 356–77.

Peart, S. J. & Levy, D. M. (2005) The *"Vanity of the Philosopher": From Equality to Hierarchy in Post-Classical Economics*. University of Michigan Press, Ann Arbor.

Robson, J. M. (1968) *The Improvement of Mankind: The Social and Political Thought of John Stuart Mill*. University of Toronto Press, Toronto.

Schumpeter, J. A. (1954) *History of Economic Analysis*. Oxford University Press, New York.

millenarianism

John Fulton

The term millenarianism, and its alternatives millennialism and chiliasm, are derived from the last book of the Christian Bible, Apocalypse (or Revelation), in which the prophet John recounts his vision of a thousand-year godly kingdom, the return of Christ, and the end of time itself (20:1–7). In the social sciences, the term is applied to all movements and organizations that hold as a central belief the imminent arrival of a divinely inspired and this-worldly society, whether a religious golden age, messianic kingdom, return to paradise, or egalitarian order. Such movements can take on an active or passive, violent or peaceful, even revolutionary role. They are found the world over and throughout recorded history. Some writers extend the term to deep-seated beliefs in secular utopias such as revolutionary communism, certain environmental and scientistic-technological movements such as eugenics and cryonics (Bozeman in Robbins & Palmer 1997), and racist movements such as white supremacy. Jewett and Lawrence (2003) argue for the existence of a contemporary form of millenarianism in the United States that reunites the secular and religious, calling it "millennial civil religion." They find it in popular culture, the politics of the New Right, Reaganism, Bushism, and the "war on terror."

The most documented cases occur within cultures significantly affected by Judaism, Christianity, and Islam, though there is a mainly historical and theological literature on millenarianism in Hinduism (the coming of Kalki), and most of the Buddhist and some Daoist traditions, e.g., the coming of Maitreya, the Bodhisattva, and the future messiah of the secret "White Lotus" sects. From the 1950s, there was an accelerated interest in the subject, beginning with Worsley's (1957) study of cargo cults, Cohn's (1957) classic on medieval movements, and, later, Wilson's (1973) reappraisal of tribal and third world millenarianism. These better-known studies were accompanied by the work of many other sociologists, anthropologists, and historians on African, Asian, and Native and Latin American millenarianism. The approach of the second Christian millennium led to an increasing number of studies on US millenarianism (e.g., Robbins & Palmer 1997) and contemporary millenarian sects worldwide (e.g., Barkun 1996; Hunt 2001). Contemporary mass media have focused on Doomsday Cult massacres: the Jim Jones's People's Temple at Jonestown, Guyana (1978), Aum Shinrikyo's sarin gas attack in the Tokyo metro (1993), David Koresh's Branch Davidian sect at Waco, Texas (1993), and the Order of the Solar Temple in Canada and Switzerland (1994).

Millenarianism has its roots in the religion founded by Zarathustra, Zoroastrianism (900 BCE). From around 600 BCE, its believers subscribed to a future this-worldly savior, the Saoshyant, as well as to their founder prophet.

In Judaism, movements date back to the period 200 BCE–100 CE with the sects of the monastic-style Essenes, the peasant-driven and violent Zealots, and the very early Jewish Christians: all fervent believers in the imminent coming of a political-religious messiah. Since then, millenarianism has appeared at varying times within Judaism, and especially in the Sabbatian movement of the 1660s (followers of messiah Sabbatai Zevi) that affected most Jews of the period, surviving today as an underground movement in both Judaism and Islam.

In Christianity, the millenarian biblical reference in Apocalypse is partnered by earlier ones in Paul's two letters to the Thessalonians. High millennial points in Christian history were the late medieval Taborites, who set up millennial and egalitarian communities outside the Czech city of Prague (1420–30). With the Protestant Reformation (from 1517), and freedom of access to the Bible, a spate of millenarian movements developed in the northern half of Europe, many from the Anabaptist sects. While followers of Menno Simons and Jakob Hutter were passive millenarians, those inspired by the anti-Lutheran Thomas Münzer (d. 1524) took up arms to set up the "Kingdom of God" in the city of Münster, Germany (1534–5). In Britain, the Civil War (1641–9) between Crown and Parliament, particularly the execution of the monarch, led to a general state of millennial expectation among Puritans and to the appearance of the Diggers, Levelers, and, above all, the Fifth Monarchy Men, who vowed to install the millennial kingdom and came very close to doing so (St. Clair 1992).

The patterns of millenarianism were different in Islam. It is true that Christ appears in Qur'anic commentary as future slayer of the Antichrist and ruler of the Islamic community. However, Islamic chiliasm has developed mainly from the post-Qur'anic *hadith* ("tradition") writings concerned with the period of war and intrigue over Muhammad's succession. The Shia movement (Iraq and Iran) has looked for its political-religious messiah or Mahdi to the transfer of Muhammad's divine charisma through the line of descent of Ali, Muhammad's grandson-in-law. It believes that this person will be the self-same descendant of Ali, Ibn al-Hanafiyya, who disappeared in 700 CE without ever becoming ruler and who has been

"in concealment" ever since. But while Sunni and Shia share the belief in a Mahdi, Sunnis hold that its exact identity is still to be revealed, thus leaving the possibilities of millenarian movements among them more likely. Millenarianism played a significant role in the shaping of modern Iraq and Iran and, in particular, the Safavid movement (early seventeenth century – the Muslim followers of Sabbatai Zevi, above).

The explosive spread of millenarianism in the nineteenth and twentieth centuries was truly global. It grew out of clashes between modernity and imperialism on the one hand, and the more traditional beliefs of both western and non-western societies on the other. Christian millenarianism even reached China in the T'aiping Rebellion (1851–64). In Islam, the millenarian movement of Baba'u'llah led to the founding of the Baha'i religion, and the most politically successful millenarian movement of Islam was the Sudanese Mahdi rebellion and the setting up of a Mahdi Caliphate (1882–98). In Judaism Chabad Lubavitch, a millenarian movement from Belarus, settled in the US after World War II and its seventh leader, Rebbe Schneerson (d. 1994), became the messiah for many of its members.

Because of the large number of European protest sects that settled there, the US experienced millennial movements since its inception. Their numbers grew in the nineteenth century, particular additions being the Mormons, the Millerites (the future Seventh Day Adventists), and Jehovah's Witnesses, each of whom would develop into worldwide churches. Then in the twentieth century, the number of millennial Pentecostal churches grew significantly, many to merge into the Assemblies of God in the 1920s. Their missionaries and those of the Seventh Day Adventists were main sources for the spread of Christian-derived millenarianism to Africa, Southeast Asia, and Latin America, where they are now numbered in their millions and where local populations have incorporated local beliefs and values into their worship, such as spirit possession.

At the same time as white millenarianism was growing in the US, millenarianism arose first among the West Coast Native Americans in the 1870 Ghost Dance movement, and then in 1890 among the far more important Plains Indians, whose Ghost Dance offered them solidarity, however briefly, and the hope of a return to the old ways of plenty. Elsewhere in the world similar movements were being formed. These were the cargo cults of Southeast Asia and Oceania. Numbered in hundreds and spread over the other half of the globe, they too took place where tribes were disintegrating, as status and power through the ownership or access to animals or lands and the rituals of their cultural and religious heritage collapsed in front of western technology, capital, and military resources. Often combining tribal and Christian religious elements, prophets and messiahs arose almost spontaneously across this vast region to form both passive and aggressive movements, expecting to receive from above the wealth, knowledge, and technology typical of their white imperialists and, sometimes, a return to the ways of the past. In one such movement, the Maori Hau-Hau (New Zealand 1864–6), the prophet Te Ua revealed that men from heaven would come down to teach them all the arts and sciences of the Europeans; all dead Maoris would rise again and share in their earthly paradise and a chant would protect them from the bullets of the local colonial regiment (Wilson 1973). The movement was shattered like others in the subsequent conflicts. Some of the more peaceful movements survived longer in the form of indigenous sects.

THEORIZING MILLENARIANISM

Generally speaking, millenarian movements and groups are socially significant primarily because such beliefs become active during periods of social uncertainty or unrest. They challenge oppressors and the current social and moral order of society or the religious establishment, promising reform – at least for the believers – or revolution. They are protest movements often ending in breakaway sects from parent bodies. Believers have expectations that divine intervention will favor them against their enemies. Marx and Engels integrated the movements into their general theory of social conflict and revolution. While they may be faulted for reducing the religious and cultural causes of the movements to a smokescreen hiding underlying class warfare, they were the first to recognize the dominant role of oppression in many of them.

Since then, other researchers have pointed to other elements affecting or constituting these movements. Imminent expectation of millennial events is as important to the movements as the millennial beliefs themselves. Key strategists are often required to maintain momentum. Also, such expectation requires states of high alertness accompanied with either great enthusiasm or deep depression. These elements are hard to sustain in the long term, leading to a loss of their vital potency. In fact, most active movements do not last and either implode or are suppressed. If believers retain their beliefs in the long run, it is because they have become institutionalized or more peaceful. Weber's notion of charisma has considerable relevance here: millenarianism is unstable and prophecy may be intermittent or disappear. To retain some of the charisma, organization supported by rituals is necessary, particularly where the prophet has little organization of his own, lost his charisma, or died.

Millenarian movements may foster violence when certain conditions prevail: believers view the rest of society as evil, corrupt, and irredeemable; the movement is relatively small and isolated; the leader of the movement is messianic and has tight control of people's minds and actions; believers are provoked by exploitation, dispossession, and sacrilege committed by outsiders. Of course, the violence may come instead from outside: non-believers may fear the movement and suppress it.

Many movements have the additional belief of apocalypticism or *catastrophic millenarianism*: the conviction that cataclysmic events and the violent end of an evil world are imminent and precede the divine millennium. For the many Christians that believed this in the early nineteenth century, it was a dreadful thought. Hence the appearance in the 1830s of the doctrine of the Rapture: Jesus is going to take his faithful off to heaven before the "tribulation" begins. An alternative belief to apocalypticism is *progressive millenarianism*. Believers have a role to play in building the millennial society, whether it is preparation for a messiah or not (see Wessinger in Robbins & Palmer 1997). Some authors still use the terms premillenarianism (the messiah and the "tribulation" come at the beginning of the millennium) and postmillenarianism (the messiah comes at the end) as earlier alternatives to the above; but such terms are less inclusive, referring principally to Christian millenarianism.

SEE ALSO: Charisma; Charismatic Movement; Christianity; Conflict Theory; Engels, Friedrich; Islam; Jehovah's Witnesses; Judaism; Religious Cults; Revolutions

REFERENCES AND SUGGESTED READINGS

Barkun, M. (Ed.) (1996) *Millennialism and Violence*. Frank Cass, Portland, OR.

Cohn, N. (1957) *The Pursuit of the Millennium: Revolutionary Millenarians and Mystical Anarchists of the Middle Ages*. Oxford University Press, New York.

Hunt, S. (Ed.) (2001) *Christian Millenarianism*. Hurst, London.

Jewett, R. & Lawrence, J. S. (2003) *Captain America and the Crusade against Evil: The Dilemma of Zealous Nationalism*. William B. Eerdmans, Grand Rapids.

Landes, R. (2000) *Encyclopedia of Millennialism and Millennial Movements*. Routledge, New York.

Marx, K. & Engels, F. (1981) *Marx and Engels on Religion*. Progress Publishers, Moscow.

Robbins, T. & Palmer, S. J. (Eds.) (1997) *Millennium, Messiahs, and Mayhem: Contemporary Apocalyptic Movements*. Routledge, New York.

St. Clair, M. J. (1992) *Millenarian Movements in Historical Context*. Garland, New York.

Wilson, B. R. (1973) *Magic and the Millennium: A Sociological Study of Movements of Protest among Tribal and Third World Peoples*. Heinemann, London.

Worsley, P. (1957) *The Trumpet Shall Sound: A Study of Cargo Cults in Melanesia*. McGibbon & Kee, London.

Mills, C. Wright (1916–62)

Steven P. Dandaneau

C. Wright Mills is the most recognized figure in the history of American sociology. Mills is to American sociology as Margaret Mead is to American anthropology. He was prolific, provocative, and prescient. The author of, not one, but three of American sociology's most influential and debated books – *White Collar* (1954), *The Power Elite* (1956), and *The Sociological Imagination* (1959) – Mills's scholarly oeuvre is a veritable microcosm of American sociology's distinctive character. Likewise, Mills's political writings remain partisan touchstones for social critics and citizens grappling with the baleful consequences of the postmodern society that Mills was among the first to glimpse at its inception, but did not live to fully decipher. A hero to some, a villain to others, the name C. Wright Mills evokes passion, for no one before or since has more fully embodied, nor more courageously battled, American sociology and its self-imposed gods and demons.

C. Wright Mills was born Charles Wright Mills in Waco, Texas, on August 28, 1916. On March 20, 1962, he suffered a fatal heart attack in the West Nyack, New York, house that he had helped design and build. An obituary appeared in the *Washington Post and Times Herald*. Fidel Castro sent a wreath to mark Mills's grave.

Forty-five years previous, Mills came of age as the only child of Charles Grover and Frances Wright Mills. Leavened by his mother's Catholicism, Mills was raised in an otherwise typical Texas middle-class milieu. "Charleswright," as he was known to his mother, graduated from Dallas Technical High School in 1934 and endured an unhappy year at Texas Agricultural & Mechanical College (Texas A&M) before transferring to the University of Texas at Austin, where he earned a BA in sociology and an MA in philosophy. Married at 21, Mills was but 23 years old when his first scholarly paper was published, notably, in sociology's leading journal.

In that same year, 1939, Mills began graduate work in sociology at the University of Wisconsin at Madison, where he established a productive collaboration with the brilliant émigré German sociologist, Hans H. Gerth. Together, they produced the edited volume *From Max Weber: Essays in Sociology* (1946), which is perhaps the most influential single volume of Weber's work rendered in English, as well as the co-authored *Character and Social Structure* (1953), a work in social psychology. Mills received his doctorate in sociology in 1942 on the strength of a dissertation that advanced a sociological account of American pragmatist philosophy via study of its leading originators, namely, Charles Sanders Pierce, William James, and John Dewey. Originally "A Sociological Account of Pragmatism: An Essay on the Sociology of Knowledge," Mills's first book-length study was published posthumously as *Sociology and Pragmatism: The Higher Learning in America* (1964), a title that captures the Alpha and Omega of Mills's sociology – European sociology and American philosophy – as well as suggests how the confluence of Weberian sociology and Deweyian pragmatism in his own intellectual origins facilitated his development as a latter-day Thorstein Veblen.

Mills spent World War II as a professor of sociology at the University of Maryland at College Park. He also worked briefly for the Smaller War Plants Corporation, preparing a report for the US Senate entitled *Small Business and Civic Welfare* (with Melville J. Ulmer, 1946). At the conclusion of the war, Mills accepted a post at Columbia University's Bureau of Applied Social Research, which was directed by the eminent sociologist Paul F. Lazarsfeld, and an affiliation with the department of sociology, with the support of luminaries Daniel Bell, Robert K. Merton, and Robert S. Lynd. At the Bureau, Mills served as Director of the Labor Research Division, which resulted in the important study of American labor leaders, *The New Men of Power* (with the assistance of Helen Schneider, 1948), and he supervised the Bureau's field research that led to *The Puerto Rican Journey* (1950). Mills left the Bureau in 1949 for a full-time appointment in the department of sociology. In that same year he undertook a prestigious semester-long visiting professorship at the University of Chicago. In 1951, *White Collar* was published and Mills was awarded tenure and promotion.

At the age of 35, Mills was as a member of the discipline's premiere faculty and was well on his way to being a publicly recognized intellectual, yet controversy and discord continued to characterize much of his personal and professional life, just as it had since his first year in college. Many of the collegial relationships that facilitated Mills's movement from Texas to Wisconsin, and from Wisconsin to Maryland and then to Columbia, for example, soon frayed

or were sundered altogether. Mills was also in these years twice divorced and remarried, with daughters Pamela and Kathryn children of Dorothy Helen Smith (known as Freya Mills) and Ruth Harper Mills, respectively, and son Nikolas the child of Mills's third spouse, Yaroslava Surmach Mills. Nor did Mills benefit from stable relationships with graduate students (Maryland's William Form was his only doctoral advisee), although Mills did on occasion befriend the exceptional undergraduate, such as Columbia's Dan Wakefield.

Recognizing his restless nature, Mills sought creative avenues for self-expression far beyond typically effete forms of academic recreation and amusement. He tried subsistence farming and photography, baked bread, built houses, and experimented with motorcycle engines. (Mills's first trip to Europe was a sojourn to the BMW factory in Munich!) These distractions did not, however, provide sufficient respite from the stresses concomitant with Mills's own raison d'être, thorough-going sociological criticism that goes full-bore at the given and its existing justifications, and that is, therefore, always tilting toward unflinching self-criticism, warts and all. More to the point perhaps, the irascible manner and prose style that brought Mills notoriety also left him repeatedly estranged from former sources of stability and support, as though having adopted the persona of Veblen, Mills's own life, private and public alike, was fated to mirror Veblen's tragic example.

Mills seems to have followed Veblen in another respect as well, as a harsh critic of wealth and power and an even harsher critic of the hypocrisies these generate in manifestly pious America. This is no more true than in *The Power Elite*, Mills's critical study of the concentration of power in mid-century America, a study which may have been on President Eisenhower's mind when he later warned of the anti-democratic consequences likely to result from an emergent "military-industrial complex." Mills came to think of this book as the last in an emergent "trilogy" on the subject of power in advanced industrial society. *The New Men of Power* is thus construed as volume one, in which Mills analyzed the increasingly anti-communist and, for the most part, anti-socialist leadership of the newly legitimate American industrial unions. By virtue of their unions' strategic position in the US economy and their own command over substantial political mobilization, post-war labor leaders wielded power sufficient, if used wisely, to expand the scope of democratic freedom within the sanctum sanctorum of western modernity. Volume two is *White Collar*, Mills's searing portrait of the new middle classes, the armies of pencil-pushing managerial, technical, clerical, and sales functionaries who worked for the proverbial gray flannel suits, and who strode toward an abundant if also ticky-tacky suburban version of the American Dream. Goodbye farm and factory, hello Levittown.

In both earlier works, the structural antecedent to the power of labor leaders and various and sundry managers, technicians, and professionals is the advent of what Weber called legal-rational or, simply, bureaucratic social organization. *The Power Elite* is consistent in its attention to the analysis of the command positions at the apex of post-war US military, capitalist, and state bureaucracies. Mills also analyzes expansion of mass society, which mirrors the bureaucratization of everyday life. Only upon the basis of an analysis of this type and scope does Mills then analyze the nearly interchangeable types of men (and they were all men) who, by virtue of their position in society, were called upon to fill these increasingly integrated positions of national and global power. The former general and Columbia University president, Dwight D. Eisenhower, not only echoed Mills's analysis as he left the White House in 1961, he embodied it.

If *The Power Elite* is the third in a trilogy, it is also the first in a series of publications and life events in which Mills followed the logic of his own sociology toward a direct and at times startling participation in worldwide political crises. Between 1956 and 1962 Mills lectured and traveled widely in Western Europe, less frequently venturing to Mexico, Eastern Europe, the Soviet Union, and Cuba. Mills befriended young left intellectuals such as England's Ralph Miliband and E. P. Thompson, and he also made personal contact with those his senior, such as Jean-Paul Sartre and Simone de Beauvoir. Having received a prestigious Guggenheim Fellowship in 1946, Mills was appointed a Fulbright lecturer in Denmark in 1956 at about the same time that several of his earlier books were deemed worthy of translation

into German, Russian, French, Italian, Japanese, and Polish.

In 1960 Mills became an adviser to Fidel Castro, who identified *The Power Elite* as a valued influence. Mills also issued his own political manifesto, the influential "Letter to the New Left" (1960). As an increasingly full-time political writer, Mills focused his energies on influencing the politics of the day. He sought means to produce accessible and affordable mass circulation polemics. As capable of self-criticism and irony as, at times, bravado and spite, Mills called these often-strident pamphlets and articles his "preachings."

Among Mills's explicitly political writings are three major books. *The Causes of World War Three* (1958), which sold over 100,000 copies, addresses the bureaucratically rational, although obviously insane, preparation for nuclear holocaust promulgated as unavoidable by rival Soviet and American elites alike. This volume is replete with Mills's penchant for colorful neologisms such as Crackpot Realism and the Science Machine, and includes Mills's incendiary "A Pagan Sermon," an actual sermon twice delivered before church groups in which he reproaches Christians for their hypocritical submission to, if not overt support for, national defense by means of thermonuclear weapons.

As if his rebuke of Cold War Christians and his equation of US and Soviet elites as joint partners in the prevailing "higher immorality" were not enough, Mills also joined the Fair Play for Cuba Committee, known to history for Lee Harvey Oswald's membership more than for Mills's. Not surprisingly, Mills came under FBI surveillance, which only intensified with the publication of *Listen, Yankee! The Revolution in Cuba* (1960). Adopting the point of view of a fictional Cuban revolutionary (a composite of the revolutionary leaders Mills interviewed for the book), Mills argued passionately for the merit and glory of the Cuban revolution. A staggering 400,000 copies later, *Listen, Yankee!* was apparently even on President Kennedy's mind when, in a moment of apparent exasperation, he told a visiting French journalist critical of the US policy toward Cuba: "I'm not some sociologist, I'm the President of the United States."

The Marxists (1962) would not have further endeared Mills to Kennedy or J. Edgar Hoover, but, alas, it appeared in print a few weeks after Mills's death. Not viewed as among his most discerning works, Mills's study of Marx's corpus and selected Marxian theoreticians and revolutionaries contains his declaration of allegiance to "plain Marxism," his own neologism that marks in theory the distance from his roots in American pragmatism and Weberian sociology evident in the praxis of his last years.

It would be incorrect, however, to regard Mills as having gone to his grave a Marxist. There is no question that Mills had come to share Marx's view that sociologists and their academic kin had long-interpreted the world whereas the greater need was to change it. This commitment to a radical attitude toward history-making did not, however, cause Mills to abandon academic self-criticism.

Appearing in 1959, *The Sociological Imagination* is Mills's most complex and enduring book. Mills toyed with using "autopsy" in the title, but thought better of implying a discipline irretrievably expired when what he sought above all was to restate sociology's compelling original promise. *The Sociological Imagination* may be profitably viewed as an immanent critique of the professional ideology of American sociology. Ironically, portions of its first chapter commonly appear in introductory texts, as though either American sociology had long ago welcomed and favorably absorbed the essence of Mills's critique or, conversely, could stomach only a thimble's worth of his tonic.

In Mills's reading, American sociology had instituted a set of ideas and practices that functioned to suppress the implicit radicalism of sociology's mainly European founders, but which was also present in the Deweys and Veblens on his side of the Atlantic. This ideology included, not surprisingly, sociology's own professionalization and nearly wholesale adoption of a bureaucratic ethos. Mills also criticized the unacknowledged and untenable infusion of American traditions of moralistic reformism into sociological analysis, which threatened to render American sociology little more than the academic arm of the Salvation Army and increasingly punitive post-war welfare state. Mills's greatest venom was reserved, however, for his celebrated contemporaries, Harvard's Talcott Parsons, who he charged with having created and then sanctified as unassailable a

historically irrelevant "grand theory," and his former boss at the Bureau of Applied Social Research at Columbia, Paul Lazarsfeld, who he charged with having sold his soul to an equally irrelevant "abstract empiricism."

For Mills, Parsons's and Lazarsfeld's versions of sociology – one too philosophical, the other too empirical – pointed to an alarming lapse in sociology's institutional memory, a systematic loss of contact with the animating purpose and promise that is evident in the work of those who knowingly and, more often than not, unknowingly, founded the new discipline of sociology. Mills identifies this spirit in what he calls "the classic tradition" (selections of which he collected and analyzed in an edited volume, *Images of Man*, 1960), which includes most prominently Marx and Weber, but also Durkheim, Simmel, Spencer, and Mannheim, among many others. Borrowing from each, Mills describes a shared desire to inculcate in modernity's democratic citizenry the quality of mind and type of self-knowledge needed to make history in modern times; that is, make history without recourse to illusions ready at hand, under conditions, as it were, of no one's choosing.

Mills's argument that sociology should maintain fidelity to this posited founding raison d'être is tantamount to equating sociology and "critical theory." Critical theory is social and cultural analysis with emancipatory intent. Critical theory aims to unmask the true nature of prevailing institutions and cultural patterns – those which, when functioning even normally, produce forms of unnecessary unfreedom and distorted self-understandings – and to do this by critically analyzing ideologies, the systems of ideas and patterns of life that inhibit such recognition. The hope and expectation is that sociological knowledge of this type would be used to guide practical forms of democratic self-emancipation. *The Sociological Imagination* depicts American sociology as dominated by wordsmiths, number-crunchers, the historically uninformed, and knee-jerk liberal professors indistinguishable from the middle classes of *White Collar*. Fairly or unfairly, Mills perceived that something like a "sociological imagination" was becoming publicly recognized as the most needed and potentially most fruitful form of self-consciousness available to make sense of the "traps" of postmodern life, the "issues" and "troubles" that tormented the denizens of advanced industrial society, and also the "magnificent" new types of knowledge and understanding resulting from radical self-awareness. Mills therefore held sociology to the highest possible expectations, the most lofty of purposes.

Since Mills was an inveterate writer, it is not surprising that he bequeathed to the archives not only the content of his own research file-system, the general method for creating an assured beneficence which he promoted somewhat incongruously in an appendix to *The Sociological Imagination*, but also numerous significant works-in-progress, among them full-length books on the "cultural apparatus," a critical study of elites in Soviet society, and preliminary data for a massive multi-volume world-historical "comparative sociology." Mills also began to elaborate on his previously published views on a much-needed "new left," which only furthers the impression that Mills had set out in his last days to create a full-blown critical theory of postmodern society. Critique of the propaganda and the public sphere gives way to an emphasis on the critique of an emergent culture industry or apparatus, and critique of oppressive bureaucratic organization in post-revolutionary societies is subordinated to an immanent critique directed, not to the working class, but to intellectuals and would-be intellectuals strategically positioned in the post-industrial mode of production, capitalist or communist in character.

Most importantly, however, Mills recognized the need for a critical alternative to modernization theory in the "third world," which implicitly assumed that most of the earth's inhabitants would want to, and would eventually, live as Americans or Soviets did. Mills understood that "the hungry-nation bloc," as he called them, faced massive obstacles to the full realization of reason and freedom, not the least of which was their obvious material and political impoverishment at the hands of a neocolonial world-system. As *Listen, Yankee!* makes abundantly clear, Mills was inclined to give revolution a chance. So strongly was he committed to this struggle that he sacrificed his academic reputation and, later, his health, in efforts to support social change worldwide.

Evaluating Mills's intellectual legacy in full is impossible for the simple reason that it continues to be debated and reformulated. This fact notwithstanding, serious studies of Mills's oeuvre are few. Mills-the-critical-theorist is often overshadowed by circulating images of his riding his motorcycle at high speed and the not always apocryphal stories of his hulking 6' 2" frame, insatiable appetite, and square-jawed bravado. It is as though the new generation of academics in postmodern society crave little else beyond the titillation of endless tales of Mills's wanton transgression of the new middle-class habits of the heart. It is also easy to imagine a discipline in which neophyte instructors read only the same few pages from *The Sociological Imagination* that they assign neophyte students, or a discipline resigned to the illusion that professional societies doling out C. Wright Mills Awards is not the very sort of hypocrisy that Mills opposed. Mainstream sociology would appear mostly untroubled by Mills's legacy framed in terms of 1960s student movement nostalgia and the simple-minded question, who rules America?

Serious study of Mills would need to address his biography, which has yet to be treated in a fair and thorough manner, and would analyze the numerous theoretical mediations of vexing actual and conceptual polarities in his vast published and unpublished work that Mills sought, proposed, achieved, and failed to achieve. Among these are Mills's synthesis of European and American social thought, including his translation of pragmatist philosophical insight into empirical sociological research programs. Mills is also a keen interpreter of Marx and Weber, which he undertook mindful of, but largely independent from, the Frankfurt School's more familiar and influential efforts in this vein. Mills's relatively early identification of postmodern society, what he also called the "fourth epoch," deserves sustained analysis, and while he did not live long enough to more than experiment with the new styles of thinking and communicating called for by the emergence of postmodernity (e.g., his composite Cuban revolutionary in *Listen, Yankee!*, the dialogue format of the proposed "Soviet Journal," his newfound concern for publicity over and against mere publication), any history of postmodern theory and presentation should account for Mills's pioneering efforts to effect a form of ideology-critique in an age where mass society had first reproduced itself via mass media, and where as a result daily reality seemed eerily to confirm that all that is solid really had melted into air: polluted, ozone-depleted air.

Academic appraisal aside, remembrance of C. Wright Mills-the-person should acknowledge that his supreme desire – to play a part in making history veer in the direction of human liberation – cruelly eluded him. A biographical vignette, then, as finality.

In December, 1960 – that is, 5 months prior to the Bay of Pigs invasion, 14 months prior to Mills's death, and 22 months prior to the Cuban Missile Crisis – C. Wright Mills was asked to debate A. A. Berle, Jr. on NBC Television. The subject was US policy toward Cuba and the expected audience numbered 5 million. Just prior to the scheduled broadcast, Mills suffered a severe heart attack and was hospitalized. He had known of a heart condition since being rejected as fit for conscription at the outset of World War II. With Mills in a coma, Congressman Charles O. Porter of Oregon filled in and the broadcast went ahead otherwise as planned. A few weeks after checking himself out of hospital, Mills learned that he had been named in a $25 million lawsuit and that he was the target of an assassination plot, the former initiated by a Cuban libel claimant and the latter purportedly threatened by anti-Castro sympathizers. Mills bought a gun. He traveled to Europe, Eastern Europe, and to the Soviet Union, in search of therapy for his heart, R&R, to visit a few of his remaining friends, and to consider immigration to England. Mills, however, returned to the US in January of 1962 and continued to work on various manuscripts, and Soviet freighters traversed their way to and from Cuba as Mills's estranged academic colleagues gathered at his Columbia University memorial service to confabulate on *his* having gone over the edge.

SEE ALSO: Critical Theory/Frankfurt School; New Left; Power Elite; Pragmatism; Sociological Imagination

REFERENCES AND SUGGESTED READINGS

Aronowitz, S. (Ed.) (2004) *C. Wright Mills*, 3 vols. Sage, Thousand Oaks, CA.

Form, W. (1995) Mills at Maryland. *American Sociologist* 26(3): 40–67.

Horowitz, I. L. (Ed.) (1963) *Power, Politics and People: The Collected Essays of C. Wright Mills*. Oxford University Press, Oxford.

Horowitz, I. L. (1983) *C. Wright Mills: An American Utopian*. Free Press, New York.

Mills, C. Wright (2000a) *The Power Elite: New Edition*. Oxford University Press, Oxford.

Mills, C. Wright (2000b) *The Sociological Imagination: 40th Anniversary Edition*. Oxford University Press, Oxford.

Mills, C. Wright (2001) *The New Men of Power: America's Labor Leaders*. University of Illinois Press, Urbana.

Mills, C. Wright (2002) *White Collar: Fiftieth Anniversary Edition*. Oxford University Press, Oxford.

Mills, K. (Ed.) (2000) *C. Wright Mills: Letters and Autobiographical Writings*. University of California Press, Berkeley.

mind

David D. Franks

In common parlance, mind means cognitive intelligence, self-consciousness, mentality, or reason, all of which were once considered unique to humans. While some animal forms exhibit these capacities to some extent, only in humans are they developed as primary adaptive mechanisms. In more academic circles, the use of the term mind rather than its other synonyms recalls its place in broader debates in western theories of knowledge. This is especially true in social psychology since the philosophically trained George Herbert Mead demonstrated the dependency of individual mind on society and behavior. Mind had been previously understood purely mentally, as a self-enclosed, enduring entity in the head rather than an episodic biosocial, behavior-dependent process. The broad outline of Mead's theory of mind remains important for a thoroughly social rendition of human mentality. Mead's theory and some current continuities and refinements from neuroscience are presented below.

Through his school of social behaviorism Mead transcended the futile debates between the idealists, rationalists, and empirical realists of the Enlightenment era. Rather than viewing the primary link between mind and world as the rationalist's *reason* or the realist's *senses*, Mead saw the primary link as *behavior*. The world became known actively through the way it responded to our actions upon it, rather than by mere reflection or by passive registration through the senses. This view made mind dependent on behavioral *process* rather than some substantial tabula rasa on which experience could write "carbon copies," as contended by empiricists. Nor was mind solely a "projector" imposing its inherent forms on the experienced world, as some rationalists and idealists argued. For Mead, human knowledge was as much a result of the knower's contribution as what the impartial world contributed.

Behavior was defined through Mead's theory of the social act, which in turn provided the context for his theory of mind. Four phases comprised the act – impulse, perception, manipulation, and consummation. Thought, consciousness, and thus "minded behavior" arose in the manipulative phase of the act. Action was prior to, and necessary for, reflection since consciousness typically occurred when behavior was blocked. Otherwise one acted unreflectively and thus mindlessly. It was the "obdurate character" of the world of resistance that caused action to stop as individuals considered two things: hypothetical alternatives around the resistance and their own capacities for alternative conduct. Such processes assumed the capacity for *self-consciousness* which relied on the capacity for *taking the role of the other* – seeing one's own behavior from others' standpoints. Minded behavior incorporates both capacities, fostering flexible and coordinated social action.

In role-taking, actors respond to their own oncoming behavior *as would the other* and then use the anticipated response to guide their lines of conduct. The cognitive demands on such a process guarantee that role-taking will be episodic and situated. For example, it may be triggered when the person is confronting those whose responses matter or who have some capacity to constrain spontaneous behavior. Much of Mead's work centered on how self-awareness, and thus minded behavior, arose through the process of role-taking.

Accuracy in role-taking also implies a pre-existing social world of shared linguistic meanings that enable actors to respond to their own oncoming behavior in the same way as the other. Mead referred to words with shared meanings as *significant symbols*. Without them, role-taking and coordinated behavior could not proceed.

Role-taking, then, is a process of *voluntary self-control of behavior*. Rather than behavior being passively pushed by external past conditioning, behavior was pulled along by one's own future anticipation of its consummation. Lines of minded human behavior then were teleologically constructed wherein the termination of the act was implicit in its beginnings. Social behaviorism and Mead's theory of mind were born in opposition to the psychological and individualistic behaviorism of Watson and Skinner and offered the only available alternative as a voluntaristic theory of behavioral and self-control.

The extrasensory character of symbols meant that humans could think beyond the immediately sensed actuality, considering the hypothetical or possible, i.e., how two originally unrelated objects could be joined together in a new way to produce tools. It also enabled cognition transcending particular time or space. Rather than thinking only of particular red objects, the symbol allowed one to think of abstract redness itself. This gave a great efficiency to human mentality.

A final feature of minded behavior consisted of the capacity for internal dialogues with oneself using significant symbols. This involves the self-reflexive, conscious process of being both speaker and spoken to as actors make indications to themselves in the flexible weighing of alternative behaviors before acting.

Giving balanced weight to the role of the organism and environment in forming the individual's perceptual experience made Mead's basic framework amenable to findings from contemporary neuroscience. Any individual *working* brain owes its functioning to interactions with other brains operating within symbolic cultural systems. But current findings are mounting that the brain itself adds significantly to our sociality with propensities for rudimentary prelinguistic thought, concepts, and innate sensitivities to facial expressions and gazes (Brothers 2001). Independently of Mead's notion of role-taking, neuroscientists currently talk of the infant's early capacities to create "theories of minds." This is the prelinguistic disposition to construct other's thoughts and to develop the notion of self and others' selves beyond observable bodies (Bloom 2000; Brothers 2001). According to Brothers, "it is by virtue of social participation that the practices constituting mind emerge." For example, the inability to invest other bodies with intentions and feelings is now thought to be a major deficit in autism. A theory of mind is also necessary for learning languages, which is often problematic for autistics. They have pronounced difficulty with pronouns, the understanding of which Mead attributed to the ability to role-take.

Mead's theory of mind recognized the importance of the central nervous system long before the field of neuroscience had advanced enough to be useful to him (Mead 1934: 236n). Mind presupposes a highly developed brain, but the brain alone is not sufficient for mind. Current findings from neuroscience will no doubt further refine and change Mead's original theory.

SEE ALSO: Behaviorism; Complexity and Emergence; Identity: The Management of Meaning; Mead, George Herbert; Reflexivity; Role-Taking; Self; Semiotics

REFERENCES AND SUGGESTED READINGS

Bloom, P. (2000) *How Children Learn the Meaning of Words*. MIT Press, Cambridge, MA.

Brothers, L. (2001) *Mistaken Identity: The Mind–Brain Problem Reconsidered*. SUNY Press, Albany, NY.

Mead, G. H. (1934) *Mind, Self, and Society*. University of Chicago Press, Chicago.

Mead, G. H. (1938) *Theory of the Act*. University of Chicago Press, Chicago.

Meltzer, B. N. (2003) Mind. In: Reynolds, L. T. & Herman-Kennedy, N. J. (Eds.), *Handbook of Symbolic Interaction*. AltaMira Press, New York, pp. 253–6.

minzoku

Kosaku Yoshino

Minzoku is a Japanese word meaning an ethnic group, a nation, a race, or even a combination of all these. A Japanese dictionary defines *minzoku* as "(1) a social group sharing many common characteristics in race, language, culture, religion, etc.; (2) a social group sharing a territory, an economy and a fate and forming a state. A nation" (Umesao et al. 1989). *Minzoku* Japanese words coined in the westernizing Meiji era (1868–1911) on the basis of original western concepts.

The multivocal nature of the word reflects the fact that ethnic, national, and racial categories rather vaguely overlap in the Japanese perception of themselves. The Japanese view of nation is very much an ethnic one. Japan's national identity has centered around the notion of the uniqueness of Japanese ethnicity shared by its members, a uniqueness which is a function of culture, religion, and race.

Although *minzoku* is commonly used in everyday language as well as in political discourses in Japan, conceptual ambiguities surrounding this concept render it unsuitable as an analytical tool in social sciences. In an effort to ensure greater analytical clarity as well as to deconstruct the notion of *minzoku* itself, social scientists generally make use of English social scientific terms such as nation, ethnicity, and race in examining *minzoku*-related phenomena in Japan.

JAPANESE *MINZOKU* AS AN ETHNIC/RACIAL NATION

Traditionally, use of the term "ethnic" in English was restricted to minorities and immigrant groups. Many social scientists now extend the use of the word to connote a broader historical prototype or substratum of national community. For example, Anthony D. Smith understands nation – in the case of the first nations of Western Europe and several other leading states including Japan – as being based on ties of ethnicity, arguing that a nation arises upon an ethnic community, which he calls *ethnie*. In the Japanese context, this can be taken to refer to a community or a group of communities that existed in what is now called the Japanese Archipelago in the period prior to the Meiji era, which was characterized by ethnic sentiment and an ethnic state but was not fully conscious of itself as a nation. In the Japanese language, however, there is no need to distinguish between premodern *ethnie* and modern nation. In fact, use of the notion of *minzoku* accentuates a sense of continuity between premodern developments in the formation of Japanese identity and the building of the modern Japanese nation.

The concept of "ethnic" can also refer to a substratal sense of identity among the contemporary Japanese based on culture and descent – though ambiguities surround the boundaries between ethnic and national sentiment. Again, it appears more realistic to use the Japanese notion of *minzoku* in depicting issues of Japanese identity, since ethnic and racial elements are fused with one another to form Japanese national identity.

The making of the Japanese *minzoku* (nation) had very much to do with the formulation in the late nineteenth century of the nationalist ideology that conceived Japan as a "family-nation" of divine origin. Members of the family-nation were perceived to be related "by kin" to one another and ultimately to the emperor. Kinship, religion, and race were fused with one another to produce an intensely felt collective sense of "oneness." This nationalist ideology went into eclipse following Japan's defeat in World War II.

More recently, the myth of Japan as a distinctive ethnic/racial nation resurfaced in a more subtle form as part of a resurgence of cultural nationalism in the 1970s and 1980s. Cultural nationalism of this period was closely associated with the dominant discourses, commonly referred to as *nihonjinron*, which defined and redefined the distinctiveness of the Japanese. It was widely held that Japanese patterns of behavior and thought are so unique that one cannot understand and acquire them unless one is born Japanese. It may be said that Japanese culture is here perceived to be the exclusive property of the "Japanese race." It must be stressed that in reality there is no such thing

as a "Japanese race" and that "race" itself is a socially constructed notion. If ethnicity is a collectivity of people defined by virtue of belief in shared culture and history, race focuses upon, and exaggerates, a particular aspect of ethnicity, that is, kinship and kin lineage. Here, race is a marker that strengthens ethnic and, therefore, national identity. Subconsciously, the Japanese have perceived themselves as a distinct "racial" community, and this perception is characteristically expressed by the fictitious notion of "Japanese blood." Although most Japanese may doubt that such an entity exists in reality, this rhetorical symbol facilitates the sentiment that "we," members of the "imagined kinship," are the product of our own special formative experience in history and that, because of this, "we" possess unique qualities.

This type of thinking, which closely associates culture with "race," is, again, reflected in conceptual ambiguities surrounding race, ethnicity, and nation in the Japanese word *minzoku*. In addition, there is a myth of Japan as a homogeneous, uniracial/ethnic nation (*tan'itsu minzoku*), that is, a strong emphasis on the homogeneity of Japanese society and a corresponding lack of adequate scholarly attention given to ethnic minorities in Japan such as Koreans, Chinese, Ainu, and Okinawans.

CHANGING PERCEPTIONS OF JAPANESE *MINZOKU*

Due to developments in studies of nationalism and national identity as well as to changes in Japan itself and its external relations, discourses emphasizing the ethnic and racial qualities of the Japanese *minzoku* (nation) now tend to be identified as problematic among concerned scholars. In particular, use of the cliche *tan'itsu minzoku* (uniracial/ethnic nation) increasingly provokes controversy and criticism, given the now dominant trend toward demythologization of the uniracial/ethnic nation of Japan. Some of the changes that have been occurring in the discourse on Japanese ethnic/racial/national identity may be mentioned here.

First, an increasingly large influx of migrant workers from Southeast Asia, the Middle East, and other developing regions in the 1980s and 1990s served as a catalyst for the Japanese to reconsider the myth of homogeneous Japan. A growing number of newspaper articles, books, and television programs have featured race and ethnic relations involving these migrant laborers. The undeniable presence of visible foreigners living as neighbors in the community and working side by side with Japanese at construction sites and in factories and other workplaces has made it more and more unrealistic to refer to Japan (at least, urban Japan) as being homogeneous.

Second, in a wider context, the development of studies of ethnicity and nationalism has also provided stimulus for a critique of the *tan'itsu minzoku* myth. Recent years have seen a steady increase in the number of scholars who apply insights provided by theorists such as Anthony Smith and Benedict Anderson to explore some of the interesting issues of *ethnie* and nation that had hitherto been neglected. For example, it was long assumed that Japan was without a regionally based ethnic community comparable to the Basques in Spain or Bretons in France. With the development of the sociological debate on ethnicity, Japan's own prefecture of Okinawa has increasingly drawn the attention of scholars. Indeed, Okinawans' strong sense of possessing their own distinctive culture and history may well entitle them to be regarded as a distinct ethnic community.

A group of historians is now calling into question the very concept of the Japanese *minzoku* (*ethnie*) itself. A leading example is Amino, who is a long-time critic of the notion of Japan as a uniracial/ethnic nation and whose writings have attracted increasing attention as the deconstruction of the *tan'itsu minzoku* myth has become part of the popular scholarly agenda. Amino maintains that, despite popular belief, the Japanese did not constitute an *ethnie* in the early medieval period or in the Kamakura period (1185–1333 CE). On the contrary, he argues that early medieval Japan consisted of an "East Country" and a "West Country" with two distinct types of social structures, political systems, and religious beliefs, and that the differences between the two "countries" were as large as or even larger than those between Portugal, Spain, Italy, and France or between the Netherlands and Germany before they became nations as we know them today. Even though different regions of Japan had objective conditions for

and the potential to develop into distinct *minzoku* (nations), Amino maintains that history did not take such a course due to various historical coincidences. His new interpretations of Japanese history are regarded as a prominent challenge to the *tan'itsu minzoku* ideology.

The notion that Japanese culture is the exclusive property of the "Japanese race" is also being challenged by the growing presence in Japan of "obvious" foreigners who speak Japanese just as naturally as the native Japanese, on the one hand, and those Japanese returnees from abroad (*kikokushijo*) whose behavior and use of the Japanese language appear "foreign," on the other. One result of these cases of Japanese-like foreigners and un-Japanese Japanese is a lack of fit between cultural and "racial" boundaries of difference, which in turn causes an inconsistency in and inefficacy of the symbolic boundary system that defines Japanese identity. The increasing occurrence of such "boundary dissonance," one byproduct of globalization, is posing a challenge to the assumption that those who speak and behave like the Japanese should be "racially" Japanese, and vice versa.

Still, the racial and cultural overtones in the notion of Japanese *minzoku* have deep roots. Ironically, these roots often reveal themselves in the process of the so-called internationalization of Japan. Just to give one noteworthy example, Japan's immigration law prohibits the entry of unskilled workers partly because of fear that such an influx might endanger the racial homogeneity and harmony of Japanese society. While there is a real need for migrant workers in the labor market, the state is unwilling to change the immigration law. One measure the business community took to cope with this dilemma was to recruit South Americans of Japanese ancestry, as the law allows second- and third-generation Japanese South Americans to work legally in Japan provided that proof is submitted that one parent is of Japanese nationality. This case shows the continued relevance and changing arenas of the racial and ethnic nature of Japanese national identity amidst the phenomenon of globalization in the world economy and labor markets.

SEE ALSO: Ethnicity; Nation-State; Nationalism; *Nihonjinron*

REFERENCES AND SUGGESTED READINGS

Amino, Y. (1992) Togoku to Saigoku, Kahoku to Kanan (East Country and West Country, North China and South China). In: Arano, Y. et al. (Eds.), *Ajia no Naka no Nihonshi IV: Chiiki to Etonosu (The History of Japan in Asia IV: Regions and Ethnos)*. University of Tokyo Press, Tokyo.

Anderson, B. (1991) *Imagined Communities: Reflections on the Origins and Spread of Nationalism*, rev. edn. Verso, London.

Gluck, C. (1985) *Japan's Modern Myths: Ideology in the Late Meiji Period*. Princeton University Press, Princeton.

Oguma, E. (2002) *A Genealogy of "Japanese" Self-Images*. Trans. D. Askew. TransPacific Press, Melbourne.

Smith, A. D. (1986) *The Ethnic Origins of Nations*. Blackwell, Oxford.

Umesao, T. et al. (Eds.) (1989) *Nihongo Daijiten (The Great Japanese Dictionary)*. Kodansha, Tokyo.

Yoshino, K. (1992) *Cultural Nationalism in Contemporary Japan: A Sociological Enquiry*. Routledge, London and New York.

mobility, horizontal and vertical

Wout Ultee

The notion that in contemporary highly industrialized societies persons may climb up or slide down the social ladder presupposed some scale with an upper end and a lower end and the possibility of ranking people on it. Individual income can be taken as such a scale, and if this is used it is possible to speak of upward and downward mobility and to quantify the extent to which a person is upwardly or downwardly mobile. Occupational status, as indicated by the prestige accorded to occupations in surveys involving representative samples from a country's population, also makes it possible to ascertain mobility. In these cases a sociologist speaks of *vertical* mobility.

Sometimes sociologists also speak of *horizontal* mobility. In that case, they do not avail themselves of a scale allowing a full ranking of persons. A case in point are class schemas, for instance the one developed first by Goldthorpe (1980) for Britain and later by Erikson and Goldthorpe (1992) for research on social mobility involving a comparison of countries. This schema has a "top": the persons belonging to what they call the service class. It has a "bottom," too: the unskilled and semi-skilled manual workers in industry, together with agricultural workers. However, the schema does not rank the intermediate categories, such as those for skilled manual workers, routine non-manual workers, farmers, and small proprietors. Movement from these categories to the service class is upward mobility, and movement to the class of unskilled manual workers is downward mobility, but movement from one of these intermediate categories to another of these intermediate categories is horizontal mobility.

Of course, it is possible to rank the various intermediate categories according to the average income of their members, but class schemas are not about income. They refer to the work relations of persons (and the hypothesis for further research is that work relations affect income). Persons in some jobs follow commands, persons in other jobs give commands, and some persons have a business all their own that involves neither supervision nor being commanded. The labor contract of some persons stipulates that they can be laid off immediately in slack periods, while other contracts do not allow for this. The output of some persons is easily monitored and of others not at all. This multiplicity of work relations makes for classes that can be ranked below other classes and above yet other classes, but not among each other.

According to Goldthorpe, horizontal mobility is as interesting to study as vertical mobility. A case in point is the contraction of the agricultural sector in industrial societies. Farm laborers left their jobs, mainly going to unskilled manual jobs in the industrial sector, and farmers often became self-employed in small businesses connected to the agrarian sector. Thus, this sectorial transformation of a country's economy did not lead to upward mobility, as some theories of modernization have held, but only to horizontal mobility.

SEE ALSO: Income Inequality and Income Mobility; Mobility, Measuring the Effects of; Occupational Mobility

REFERENCES AND SUGGESTED READINGS

Goldthorpe, J. H. (1980) *Class Structure and Social Mobility in Britain*. Oxford University Press, Oxford.

Erikson, R. & Goldthorpe, J. H. (1992) *The Constant Flux*. Oxford University Press, Oxford.

mobility, intergenerational and intragenerational

Wout Ultee

In *Social Mobility* (1927) Sorokin attempted to ascertain for early twentieth-century western societies like England, France, Germany, Italy, and the US the extent to which "the occupational status of a father determines that of his children," as well as "the intensiveness of inter-occupational shifting within the life of one generation." Later, these two phenomena were called intergenerational mobility and intragenerational mobility. Behind this distinction lurks the casual observation or conventional wisdom that, whereas in agrarian societies with autocratic or oligarchic rule the transmission of occupation from father to son along the whole range of occupations is strong, in democratic industrial societies people may work their way up the social ladder during the course of their lives. Because of issues concerning the comparability of data, Sorokin could do no more than suggest that intergenerational inheritance was never fully complete nor fully absent, leaving questions about differences between countries in intergenerational mobility and intragenerational mobility to future generations of sociologists.

The first comparison of father–son mobility across the line between blue-collar and white-collar jobs was that of Lipset and Bendix (1959).

It pertained to Denmark, France, Germany, Great Britain, Italy, Japan, Sweden, Switzerland, and the US in the first decade after World War II and involved the percentage of manual sons who were upwardly mobile, the percentage of nonmanual sons who were downwardly mobility, and the total mobility rate. Total mobility rates – the percent of sons in a job (manual, nonmanual) differing from that of their father (manual, nonmanual) – were around 30, which, according to the authors, was not only surprisingly high, but also surprisingly similar. The authors pointed to differences between countries in upward and downward mobility and maintained that similarity in the percentage of the population that is socially mobile does not mean that "equal opportunity" prevails to the same extent in these countries. However, they did not indicate how equal chances should be measured given tables cross-classifying father's and son's occupation according to a schema grouping occupational titles into a limited number of categories.

Around 1980, primarily through the research of John Goldthorpe on Britain, it became clear that the degree to which the results of competitions between persons from two different origins for two different destinations amount to unequal chances is to be measured by odds ratios. First, make a table in which the occupation of a sample of persons, divided into manual and nonmanual occupations, is related to the occupation of the fathers of these persons, again divided into manual and nonmanual occupations. Then, compute the odds that sons from nonmanual fathers wind up in a nonmanual rather than a manual job. After that, compute the odds that sons of manual occupation fathers attain a nonmanual rather than a manual job. Divide the odds of downward mobility by the odds of upward mobility. Now, if the resulting odds ratio is unity, then competitions have equal outcomes. The more it goes beyond unity, the more loaded are the dice. Odds ratios below unity are logically possible, but societies in which high origins go together with low destinations have rarely been observed. Heath (1981) compared odds ratios for manual/nonmanual father–son mobility in some 20 highly developed industrial countries in the 1970s. The conclusion was that they indicated more equal outcomes in countries with long periods of social democratic government, and the highest inequalities for countries with persistent conservative government. Erikson and Goldthorpe (1992), in a comparison involving a dozen highly industrial countries in the 1970s, used a more elaborate schema to classify the occupations of fathers and sons. They found that in some countries what they call "social fluidity" was more widespread than in others. However, when it came to specific combinations of pairs of origins and destinations, they found several historical particularities.

Blau and Duncan's (1967) model for the socioeconomic life cycle for the US in 1962 pertains to both intergenerational and intragenerational mobility. There are statistically significant "paths" from father's occupational status to son's first occupation after leaving school, and from father's occupational status to son's 1962 occupational status. The stronger these effects, the less intergenerational mobility. Son's 1962 occupation also is affected by his first job and his education. The stronger the effect of person's first job, the less intragenerational mobility. The path from first to present occupation indicates that persons who start out higher in occupational status, independent of their level of education, get even higher in later life.

As some reviewers pointed out, in Blau and Duncan's model for the socioeconomic life cycle the path from first to present occupation, depending upon the age of the person, covers a shorter or longer period in this person's life. In addition, when comparing models for several countries, the path stands for periods that perhaps do not differ much in average length, but may differ strongly in what happened in these periods, such as the number of years with or without double-digit unemployment and the involvement or non-involvement of a country in a war fought by a large part of the young population. To study effects of these factors on intragenerational mobility, sample surveys on some national populations need to include not only information on a person's first and present job, but also full job histories.

The prime collection of full job histories took place in Germany under Karl-Ulrich Mayer in the early 1980s. The data were analyzed by event-history techniques. Results, as reported by Mayer and Blossfeld (Blossfeld 1986), indicate the presence of effects of the business cycle, both at time of entry into the labor markets as well as during later years of a person's job history. War effects were present, too. Persons born in 1930, who went through such matters as the shutting down of their schools due to allied bombing, evacuation from the cities to the countryside, forced relocation from the parts of Germany that became Polish, and finding a job in a time when industry was still in a shambles, despite the later German "economic miracle" in the wake of US Marshall Aid, never fully caught up in their career trajectory compared with persons born 10 years earlier, and were quickly overtaken in this respect by persons born 10 years later. An important study comparing job histories for four countries was published in 1997 by an international group headed by Thomas DiPrete.

SEE ALSO: Income Inequality and Income Mobility; Intergenerational Mobility: Methods of Analysis; Mobility, Measuring the Effects of; Occupational Mobility; Sorokin, Pitirim A.

REFERENCES AND SUGGESTED READINGS

Blau, P. & Duncan, O. D. (1967) *The American Occupational Structure*. Wiley, New York.

Blossfeld, H.-P. (1986). Career Opportunities in the Federal Republic of Germany: A Dynamic Approach to the Study of Life-Course, Cohort and Period Effects. *European Sociological Review* 2: 208–27.

DiPrete, T., de Graaf, P. M., Luijkx, R., Tahlin, M., & Blossfeld, H. P. (1997) Collectivist versus Individualist Mobility Regimes? Structural Change and Job Mobility in Four Countries. *American Journal of Sociology* 103: 318–58.

Erikson, R. & Goldthorpe, J. H. (1992) *The Constant Flux*. Oxford University Press, Oxford.

Goldthorpe, J. H. (1980) *Class Structure and Social Mobility in Britain*. Oxford University Press, Oxford.

Heath, A. (1981) *Social Mobility*. Fontana, Glasgow.

Lipset, S. M. & Bendix, R. (1959) *Social Mobility in Industrial Society*. University of California Press, Berkeley.

Sorokin, P. (1927) *Social Mobility*. Harper, New York.

mobility, measuring the effects of

David L. Weakliem

Social mobility has always been a central concern of sociology, and theorists have offered a wide range of hypotheses concerning the social, political, and cultural consequences of mobility. For example, mobility has been claimed to reduce class solidarity, to produce tension or strain that finds an outlet in extremist politics, and to produce tolerance and breadth of outlook. Some of the claims about the effects of mobility apply primarily at the societal level, others at the individual level, and still others refer to both levels. Claims about the societal level effects can be evaluated only by comparing societies with different amounts or patterns of mobility. Such studies are difficult, since the number of units is necessarily small and obtaining reliable information on mobility patterns requires representative samples using comparable measures of social position. Hence, most empirical research on the effects of social mobility focuses on individuals.

The general approach of early studies was to compare the average attitudes or behaviors of "stayers" to those of people who had experienced upward or downward mobility. In an important article, Duncan (1966) pointed to a difficulty with studies of this kind. Suppose that position of origin and destination (designated x and z) are measured on the same interval scale, and y is some outcome of interest, also measured on an interval scale. The natural measure of mobility is $z - x$, the difference between destination and origin positions. If this difference is called v, a regression of y on v gives an estimate of mobility effects. However, an investigator would also have to consider the possibility that origin and destination have some effects in their own right, apart from mobility. Considering origin, destination, and mobility leads to the regression:

$$y = a + b_1 x + b_2 z + b_3 v + e$$

Because each independent variable is an exact linear function of the other independent variable, the parameters cannot be estimated. That is, any variation in the dependent variable can be interpreted as a consequence of origin and mobility, destination and mobility, or origin and destination. There is no statistical basis for preferring one of these interpretations over the others. Duncan's point applies not only to measures of social mobility, but also to all discrepancy measures, such as differences between spouses, geographical mobility, or "status inconsistency" (Lenski 1954).

Duncan recommended that investigators begin with the model:

$$y = a + b_1 x + b_2 z + e \qquad (1.1)$$

and invoke mobility effects only if there were systematic departures from the predictions of the model. This approach means that mobility effects are equivalent to effects of non-linear combinations of these variables. Some hypotheses about mobility effects can easily be expressed in these terms. For example, the idea that any discrepancy in status produces strain implies that the absolute value $|x - w|$ will affect relevant dependent variables even when controls of origin and destination are included. However, some hypotheses about mobility effects are more difficult to translate into this framework, and detecting departures from linearity generally requires large data sets and high-quality measurement. Hence, studies that adopted Duncan's framework generally failed to find evidence of mobility effects, and the volume of research on mobility effects declined even as research on other aspects of social mobility flourished.

When categorical measures of social position are used, Duncan's approach involves fitting the main effects of origin and destination class. Sobel (1981) argued that theoretical conceptions of class effects were better represented by an alternative model:

$$y = w s_i + (1 - w)s_j + e \qquad (1.2)$$

where i and j are indexes for the origin and destination classes, and s is a set of scores representing class effects. The parameter w can then be thought of as the weight or relative influence of the class of origin. In principle, w could have any value, although in practice it usually falls between 0 and 1. Values outside of this range could be interpreted as representing "overconformity" (Blau 1956).

The w parameters give the predicted values for the diagonal of the mobility table – that is, for people whose class of origin and destination are the same. Hence, (1.2) is generally known as the "diagonal" or "diagonal reference" model. However, when the parameters are estimated by maximum likelihood, the cases on the diagonal do not have any special importance in producing the estimates of class effects. The feature that distinguishes the diagonal model from the standard model of main effects is that the relative positions of the classes are the same for origins and destinations. For example, a class cannot be "moderate" as an origin and "extreme" as a destination. Thus, the diagonal model is a special case of the standard model, and the implied restriction can be tested using standard methods. Like the standard model, the diagonal model can be extended to include controls for other independent variables that might affect the outcome.

Sobel originally proposed (1.2) as an analogue to (1.1): a baseline model to which terms representing mobility effects could be added. However, the framework of diagonal models has also suggested a new way of understanding mobility effects – as variations in the weight of origin and destination. That is, rather than the single value of w in (1.2), there may be multiple values depending on the values of origin or destination classes or other variables. For example, it has been suggested that people with ties to multiple classes tend to adopt the norms of the higher class. This hypothesis can be tested by specifying the combinations of classes representing upward and downward mobility and estimating the weight parameters separately for the groups. It is also possible that some classes have more weight as an origin or destination. For example, a class that required extensive training might put a strong stamp on new recruits and largely eliminate the effect of social origins. This possibility could be examined by estimating a separate p for each destination class. The weights of origin and destination class may also differ depending on other variables, such as gender, age, or marital status.

The development of diagonal models led to a modest revival of research on mobility effects.

Most of these studies fail to support classical hypotheses about mobility effects such as differential effects of upward and downward mobility. However, weights often vary depending on other characteristics – for example, the influence of origin declines with age (Nieuwbeerta et al. 2000). The majority of these studies examine political views or behavior, so it is not clear whether their conclusions would apply to other areas. However, since many discussions of mobility effects focused on politics, these findings are of considerable importance.

Although the study of mobility effects is not as prominent as it once was, there is still considerable theoretical interest in the effects of combinations of statuses, notably in recent discussions of the "intersection" of race, class, and gender (McCall 2006). The general principles and models developed for the analyses of mobility effects therefore remain significant for sociological research.

SEE ALSO: Income Inequality and Income Mobility; Intersectionality; Mobility, Horizontal and Vertical; Mobility, Intergenerational and Intragenerational; Regression and Regression Analysis

REFERENCES AND SUGGESTED READINGS

Blau, P. M. (1956) Social Mobility and Interpersonal Relations. *American Sociological Review* 21: 290–5.

Duncan, O. D. (1966) Methodological Issues in the Analysis of Social Mobility. In: Smelser, N. J. & Lipset, S. M. (Eds.), *Social Structure and Mobility in Economic Development*. Routledge, London.

Clifford, P. & Heath, A. (1993) The Political Consequences of Social Mobility. *Journal of the Royal Statistical Society A* 156: 51–61.

Lenski, G. (1954) Status Crystallization: A Non-Vertical Dimension of Social Status. *American Sociological Review* 19: 405–13.

McCall, L. (2006). The Complexity of Intersectionality. *Signs: Journal of Women in Culture and Society*.

Nieuwbeerta, P., de Graaf, N. D., & Ultee, W. (2000) The Effects of Class Mobility on Class Voting in Post-War Western Industrialized Countries. *European Sociological Review* 16: 327–48.

Sobel, M. E. (1981) Diagonal Mobility Models. *American Sociological Review* 46: 893–906.

Sobel, M. E. (1985) Social Mobility and Fertility Revisited. *American Sociological Review* 50: 699–712.

mobilization

Hank Johnston

Mobilization is a basic concept in the study of social change, protest, and social movements. It captures the processes by which groups and resources are transformed from a state of quiescence, non-involvement, and inconsequence to availability, application, and influence in the social, political, and economic life of the broader community. In current practice the term most commonly refers to activating, marshaling, and putting to use groups and material resources – and often cultural resources – to achieve the success of a collective effort or campaign. So basic and general is the concept of mobilization that it has remained central in the study of protest and social movements despite major theoretical shifts in the field. These shifts have changed the concept's emphasis and application, but not the fundamental principle that in order for disparate and previously uncoordinated individuals and groups successfully to work together to achieve a goal or a collective good, mobilization is necessary. Thus, it is worth noting that *Mobilization* is also the title of the major peer-reviewed research journal in the field of protest and social movement studies.

Theoretical perspectives current during the 1960s and 1970s, grouped under the rubric of collective behavior approaches, emphasized spontaneous and individual-level mobilization. Later, resource mobilization and political-process approaches focused the meaning of mobilization on social groups, material resources, organizational strategy, and rational decisions to commit to collective action. Also, in a different sense, the terms social mobilization, political mobilization, and electoral mobilization have been used widely by political scientists and sociologists (most notably Karl Deutsch, Amitai Etzioni, and David Apter) to refer to broad social changes whereby previously unintegrated segments of society are brought into political, economic, and social participation as part of modernization and political development.

Spontaneous processes of individual mobilization were emphasized as the subfield of collective behavior gained prominence in sociology beginning in the 1960s. At this time, social disorganization was theorized to be the primary cause of the various ways that individuals were mobilized into action: panics, riots, crazes, and fads, as well as social movements and protest campaigns. The grouping together of these distinct social phenomena was justified because they all shared the characteristics of being (1) relatively uncommon and (2) uninstitutionalized responses to (3) the breakdown of various levels of social integration. Additionally, mobilization to action occurs in response to (4) the social and psychological strain caused by social breakdown and social isolation. This collective behavior approach to mobilization would include, for example, a financial panic in which depositors converge upon banks to demand return of their money as confidence in the banking system breaks down. A macro-level example of mobilization to action would be when the breakdown of traditional social relations during periods of rapid social change leads to riots or protest. For example, in England between 1811 and 1816 craft workers destroyed looms and spinning machines during Luddite riots. In this example, individual workers were said to respond to strains produced by changing employment relations, low wages, and increasing unemployment caused by new technologies and the reorganization of textile production. They coalesced into protesting groups as a result of these pressures and in order to effect restoration of traditional ways of organizing production.

These spontaneous approaches to mobilization have been grouped under the rubric of breakdown theories, even though the label embraces two distinct perspectives. On the one hand, Neil Smelser stressed the centrality of mobilization for action in his *Theory of Collective Behavior* (1962), which was a structural analysis of panics, crazes, hostile outbursts, and social movements. Also, one might include in this category Kornhauser's mass society thesis, whereby groups that are socially isolated from authority and community structures are most prone to mass mobilization. On the other hand, Turner and Killian (1987) stressed emerging definitions of the situation and new normative guidelines – drawing on symbolic interactionist traditions – to explain why people behave as they do in fads, crowds, publics, and social movements.

More recent usages of the mobilization concept stress the ability to lay claim upon and extend control over political, social, and economic resources. This is accomplished by intentional, goal-directed, planning and implementation of strategized courses of action by organizations, networks, and their leaders. These activities have the immediate objective of bringing to bear broader organizational and material resources for the sake of a collective cause. This usage draws upon images of broadly based and coordinated social mobilization for war; namely, putting social, cultural, organizational, economic, and psychological resources to work to ensure victory – dimensions that are widely recognized as crucial factors in the mobilization of social movements, protest, and organizing for or against social change.

The history of this definition can be traced to two seminal works in social movements and protest studies: Oberschall's *Social Conflict and Social Movements* (1973) and Tilly's *From Mobilization to Revolution* (1978). Oberschall challenged the social-breakdown thesis – in particular its mass-society elaboration – by showing that prior organization was the key to the mobilization of conflict groups. He stressed the communal nature of protest by demonstrating that participation is usually the result of group membership via bloc recruitment. Rather than the mobilization of isolated individuals from structural changes or pressures, Oberschall emphasized that groups are more correctly considered the unit of analysis for mobilization, and that it is through the existing structure of groups – their internal and external social linkages – that the probabilities of mobilization can be analyzed. For example, strong internal group ties reduce the costs of mobilization and increase the probability that the group can be mobilized to action.

By effectively shifting the focus of mobilization from individual participation to group participation, Oberschall ushered in a sea-change in the analysis of mobilization processes that was extended and elaborated by Tilly. In contrast to earlier usage of the term that conflated the action and the mobilization, Tilly defined mobilization processes as the way that contending groups lay claim and activate control over resources necessary to act – not the action itself. Mobilization, according to his model, is but one

of five necessary components for a social movement or protest campaign to occur: common interest, organization, mobilization, opportunity, and then the collective action, which is defined as communal pursuit of shared goals and interests. Tilly concurred with Oberschall by (1) emphasizing that mobilization capacity is a function of organization, and (2) introducing other organizations into the equation – most notably the state and contending groups – via the category "opportunity to act together." Specifically, the state and opposing groups find their way into Tilly's analysis through the way their actions affect the perception of costs for mobilizing actors. If costs are too high (say, if contending groups accord the state a strong propensity to repress), collective action will not occur.

These were the building blocks of the resource mobilization perspective, which provided the paradigmatic model for the analysis of social movements and protest during the 1970s and 1980s. It is arguable that because the resource mobilization perspective provided a focus on variables that were more easily measurable, the study of mobilization processes grew rapidly as a subdiscipline in sociology during this period. It is a fair characterization that as the field expanded, scholars often blurred the original distinction between mobilization of resources and collective action, that the independent variable – laying hold of resources – became synonymous with the dependent variable – collective action. The implicit assumption was that if groups can effectively mobilize resources, most of the collective-action task was already accomplished, and the leap from resource mobilization to street protest would be automatic – a leap, incidentally, that often ignored considerations of opportunity factors such as opposing groups, state agencies, and institutional political structures. This oversight was later corrected by political process models of mobilization elaborated by McAdam and Tarrow in the 1990s.

Following the lead of John McCarthy and Mayer Zald, the resource mobilization perspective emphasized new variables: organizational capacity, material resources, cost reduction and mobilizing strategies, and the professionalization of movement activists, especially a cadre of upper-level strategists in movement organizations called social movement entrepreneurs. This approach accurately captured a trend in social movement development; namely, mobilization tasks were becoming increasingly rationalized and strategized, and in some cases, undertaken by large, bureaucratized social movement organizations. In the extreme, some organizations take on the characteristics of for-profit corporations seeking to maximize income as a means to pursue their cause – such as Greenpeace, Amnesty International, or Transcendental Meditation. For example, Johnston showed that TM started out as a small religious cult and grew to a multinational organization through mobilization efforts that mirrored multinational marketing campaigns rather than fitting the pattern of religious proselytization. In the case of Greenpeace, the concept of resource mobilization takes on new meaning as the resources it commits to ensure cash flow via solicited contributions parallel the resources applied to its various ecological campaigns.

Apart from this kind of highly professionalized organization, research has shown that preexisting groups and networks are the primary vehicles by which individuals are brought into participation in a protest campaign or social movement. Central to the emphasis on *mobilizing structures* was Morris's (1984) path-breaking study of the origins of the Civil Rights Movement. He showed that Southern black churches were the basis of group recruitment into the early Civil Rights Movement. Similarly, McAdam (1982) demonstrated how social networks among students were the basis of participation in the 1964 Freedom Summer campaign. These preexisting mobilizing structures and networks influence how other mobilization processes are performed: they shape perceptions of opportunity, framing processes, and repertoires of contention.

Finally, consensus mobilization is a term that was introduced by Klandermans in reaction to the overemphasis on material and organizational resources characteristic of resource mobilization and the corresponding deemphasis of social psychological influences. Consensus mobilization refers to the ways that new attitudes, beliefs, and frames of interpretation are activated and spread among a previously quiescent group – or the *mobilization potential* of a movement. It is now widely recognized that mobilization of participant consensus to act must occur alongside mobilization of resources in order for social movements and protest campaigns to occur. Consensus mobilization is most clearly treated by the recent literature on collective action frames, developed most notably by William Gamson, David Snow, Robert Benford, Hank Johnston, and others. A frame is a cognitive concept that represents a schema of interpretation that reorients participants' perception of events to make collective action more likely. Snow and Benford tended to emphasize the organizational activities of framing in order to achieve a consensus to act, thereby providing a social psychological link to resource mobilization perspectives. Gamson studied the social processes by which framing of consensus is achieved, especially the role of media in consensus mobilization. Johnston has emphasized broader cultural currents in his concept of frame mobilization.

SEE ALSO: Contention, Tactical Repertoires of; Crowd Behavior; Frame; Framing and Social Movements; Resource Mobilization Theory; Social Change; Social Movements; Social Movements, Recruitment to; Social Movements, Strain and Breakdown Theories of

REFERENCES AND SUGGESTED READINGS

Apter, D. (1965) *The Politics of Modernization.* University of Chicago Press, Chicago.

Chazel, F. (2003) Mobilization. In: *Du pouvoir à la contestation.* Librairie Générale de Droit et de Jurisprudence, Paris pp. 77–135.

Deutsch, K. (1966) *Nationalism and Social Communication,* 2nd edn. MIT Press, Cambridge, MA.

Etzioni, A. (1968) *The Active Society.* Free Press, New York.

Gamson, W. A. (1992) *Talking Politics.* Cambridge University Press, Cambridge.

Gamson, W. A., Fireman, B., & Rytina, S. (1982) *Encounters With Unjust Authority.* Dorsey, Homewood, IL.

Johnston, H. (1980) The Marketed Social Movement: A Case Study of the Rapid Growth of TM. *Pacific Sociological Review.*

Johnston, H. (1991) *Tales of Nationalism.* Rutgers University Press, New Brunswick, NJ.

Johnston, H. & Noakes, J. A. (2004) *Frames of Protest.* Rowman & Littlefield, Lanham, MD.

Klandermans, B. (1984) Mobilization and Participation: Social-Psychological Expansions of Resource Mobilization Theory. *American Sociological Review* 49: 583–600.

Kornhauser, W. (1959) *The Politics of Mass Society.* Free Press, Glencoe, IL.

McAdam, D. (1982) *Political Process and the Development of Black Insurgency 1930–1970.* University of Chicago Press, Chicago.

Morris, A. (1984) *The Origins of the Civil Rights Movement: Black Communities Organizing for Change.* Free Press, New York.

Oberschall, A. (1973) *Social Conflict and Social Movements.* Prentice-Hall, Englewood Cliffs, NJ.

Smelser, N. J. (1962) *Theory of Collective Behavior.* Free Press, New York.

Snow, D. A. & Benford, R. (1988) Ideology, Frame Resonance and Participant Mobilization. In: *International Social Movement Research: From Structure to Action.* JAI Press, Greenwich, CT.

Snow, D. A. et al. (1986) Frame Alignment Processes, Micromobilization and Movement Participation. *American Sociological Review* 51: 464–82.

Tilly, C. (1978) *From Mobilization to Revolution.* Addison-Wesley, Reading, MA.

Turner, R. & Killian, L. (1987) *Collective Behavior,* 3rd edn. Prentice-Hall, Englewood Cliffs, NJ.

modernity

Gerard Delanty

The idea of modernity concerns the interpretation of the present time in light of historical reinterpretation. It refers too to the confluence of the cultural, social, and political currents in modern society. The term signals a tension within modern society between its various dynamics and suggests a process by which society constantly renews itself.

The word "modern" comes from the Latin word *modus*, meaning now, but the term "modernity" has a stronger meaning, suggesting the possibility of a new beginning based on human autonomy and the consciousness of the legitimacy of the present time (Blumenberg 1983). In Agnes Heller's words, modernity means: "Everything is open to query and to testing; everything is subject to rational scrutiny and refuted by argument" (Heller 1999: 41).

The first use of the term modern goes back to the early Christian Church in the fifth century when it was used to distinguish the Christian era from the pagan age. Arising from this was an association of modernity with the renunciation of the recent past, which was rejected in favor of a new beginning and a reinterpretation of historical origins. However, the term did not gain widespread currency until the seventeenth-century French "Quarrel of the Ancients and the Moderns" on whether modern culture is superior to classical culture. The term modernity as opposed to modern did not arise until the nineteenth century. One of the most famous uses of the term was in 1864, when the French poet Baudelaire gave it the most well-known definition: "By modernity I mean the transitory, the fugitive, the contingent" (Baudelaire 1964: 13).

Baudelaire's definition of modernity was reflected in part in modernism to indicate a particular cultural current in modern society that captured the sense of renewal and cosmopolitanism of modern life. It signaled a spirit of creativity and renewal that was most radically expressed in the avant-garde movement. But the term had a wider social and political resonance in the spirit of revolution and social reconstruction that was a feature of the nineteenth century. Marx and Engels in the *Communist Manifesto* invoked the spirit of modernity with their description of modern society and capitalism as the condition "all that is solid melts into air." The writings of Walter Benjamin have been a point of reference for many of the recent debates on modernity. In his work, the cultural movement of modernism was blended with a social theory of modern society. Benjamin was interested in the ways modern society is experienced, in particular the highly mediated modes of experience that are a feature of modern life. He was struck by the momentary nature of such experiences.

Within classical sociology, Georg Simmel is generally regarded as the figure who first gave a more rigorous sociological interpretation of modernity, with his account of social life in the modern city. For Simmel, as for Benjamin, modernity is expressed in diverse "momentary images" or "snapshots" (see Frisby 1986). The fragmentation of modern society, on the one side, and on the other new technologies such as the camera and the cinema led to more and more such moments and the feeling that there is nothing durable and solid.

Modernity may thus be described simply as the loss of certainty and the realization that certainty can never be established once and for all. It is a term that also can simply refer to reflection on the age and in particular to movements within modern society that lead to the emergence of new modes of thought and consciousness.

The concept of modernity was for long associated with the work of culturally oriented thinkers such as Baudelaire, Benjamin, and Simmel and was overshadowed by other terms, such as capitalism, within mainstream sociology and social theory as far as the conceptualization of modern society is concerned. Since the so-called cultural turn in the social sciences and the rise of post-disciplinary developments, new interpretations of history have led to a wider application of the idea of modernity. The turn to modernity since the late 1980s can be in part explained by a dissatisfaction with the older ideas of modernization, on the one hand, and on the other capitalism as the key features of modern society. The idea of modernity indicated a concern with issues and dimensions of modern society that were largely ignored by some of the main currents in sociology.

As both modernization theory and Marxist theory lost their influence, modernity suggested a more fruitful theoretical approach to interpret modern society. The debate about postmodernism was central to this. Habermas's attack on postmodernism and his defense of modernity as "an incomplete project" was hugely influential in reopening the debate on modernity is a way that linked it into a systematic reappraisal of sociological theory.

In Habermas's social theory, the project of modernity concerns the extension of a potentially emancipatory communicative rationality to all parts of society. The implication of this is the permanent condition of a fundamental tension at the heart of modern society between communicative rationality and instrumental rationality. For Habermas this tension gives to modernity its basic normative orientation and the defining feature that it is an open horizon of possibilities as a result of this tension. It is for

this reason that modernity cannot be reduced to one particular structure, but is a societal condition formed out of the ongoing contestation of power. The modernity of modern societies is thus to be found in the ways societies find communicative solutions to problems created by instrumental rationality, such as capitalism.

Johann Arnason (1991) explains modernity as a "field of tensions." One major example of this is Castoriadis's (1987) characterization of modernity in terms of a radical imaginary confronting the institutional imaginary, which tries to domesticate it. His conception of modernity has become increasingly influential. The very condition of the possibility of society is made possible by the radical imaginary which projects an image of an alternative society. For Castoriadis, this is a constitutive feature of all societies and it is one that even the tendency toward domination and instrumental mastery does not eliminate. This approach has been developed into a more elaborated theory of modernity by Agnes Heller (1999) and has been taken up by Arnason. These approaches give prominence to the creative dynamics and tensions in modernity which result from the pursuit of the goal of autonomy, on the one side, and on the other the pursuit of power and material accumulation. Emerging out of these dynamics are self-transformative tendencies and a self-conscious reflexivity.

Developments within postmodern thought gave additional weight to modernity as containing autonomous logics of development and unfulfilled potential. Several theorists argued that the postmodern moment should be seen to be merely modernity in a new key (Bauman 1987). What has emerged out of these developments is a new interest in "cultural modernity" as a countermovement in modern society, but also what Koselleck has called a historical semantics. So modernity is now not just seen as an "incomplete project," to use Habermas's formulation, but it is also one that is on "endless trial," to cite Kolakowski (1990). For Koselleck (1985), modernity is characterized by the constantly changing interpretation of the present by reference to its past and to the open horizon of its future.

So what is emerging out of this way of theorizing modernity is an approach that stresses the ambivalence of modernity, which cannot be reduced to a single dimension, as in the work of Weber, the Frankfurt School, or Foucault, for whom modernity is a matter of a disciplinary apparatus of power. Many theorists of modernity look instead to a double logic, which Peter Wagner (1994) has described as a relation of liberty and discipline, or in Alain Touraine's (1995) terms can be seen as a struggle of reason and the subject. This tension within modernity can also be illustrated by reference to Adam Seligman's characterization of modernity in terms of a "wager" over the nature of authority: modernity staked everything on reason and the individual as opposed to the sacred. There is some evidence to suggest this bet has not been won, given the return of ethnic and religious identities (Seligman 2003: 32–3). Whether or not this bet has been won or lost, this is one way of seeing modernity in terms of a tension that put risk at the center of its consciousness.

Anthony Giddens and Ulrich Beck, in different but related ways, have highlighted the reflexivity of modernity. The notion of reflexive modernization, or reflexive modernity, is aimed to capture the ways in which much of the movement of modernity acts upon itself. Beck has introduced the notion of late modernity as a "second modernity," while Giddens characterized modernity in terms of "disembedding" processes such as the separation of time and space. Such approaches to the question of modernity have been principally responding to the challenge of globalization. Globalization can be seen as a process that intensifies connections between many parts of the world, and as such it is one of the primary mechanisms of modernity today. This has led some theorists to refer to global modernity, for modernity today is global.

It is obvious from this outline of modernity that it does not refer to a historical era. Rather, the term refers to processual aspects, especially tensions and dynamics. Modernity is thus a particular kind of time consciousness which defines the present in its relation to the past, which must be continuously recreated; it is not a historical epoch that can be periodized. However, this issue has become more complicated as a result of new developments in the theory of modernity. Much of these developments follow from the relation of globalization to modernity. On the one side, modernity is indeed global,

but on the other there is a diversity of routes to modernity. The problem thus becomes one of how to reconcile the diversity of societal forms with a conception of modernity that acknowledges the consequences of globalization.

It is in this context that the term multiple modernities can be introduced. Originally advocated by S. N. Eisenstadt (2003), this has grown out of the debate on globalization, comparative civilizational analysis, and the postcolonial concern with "alternative modernities" (Gaonkar 2001). Central to this approach is a conceptualization of modernity as plural condition. Associated with this turn in the theory of modernity is a gradual movement away from the exclusive concern with western modernity to a more cosmopolitan perspective. Modernity is not westernization and its key processes and dynamics can be found in all societies.

Rather than dispensing with modernity, postmodernism and postcolonialism have given a new significance to the idea of modernity which now lies at the center of many debates in sociology and other related disciplines in the social and human sciences.

SEE ALSO: Benjamin, Walter; Capitalism; Civilizations; Globalization; Globalization, Culture and; Modernization; Postmodern Social Theory; Postmodernism; Secularization; Simmel, Georg; Social Change

REFERENCES AND SUGGESTED READINGS

Arnason, J. (1991) Modernity as a Project and as a Field of Tension. In: Honneth, A. & Joas, H. (Eds.), *Communicative Action*. Polity Press, Cambridge.

Baudelaire, C. (1964) The Painter of Modern Life. In: *The Painter of Modern Life and Other Essays*. Phaidon Press, London.

Bauman, Z. (1987) *Legislators and Interpreters: On Modernity, Postmodernity, and Intellectuals*. Polity Press, Cambridge.

Beck, U., Giddens, A., & Lash, S. (1994) *Reflexive Modernization*. Polity Press, Cambridge.

Blumenberg, H. (1983) *The Legitimacy of the Modern Age*. MIT Press, Cambridge, MA.

Castoriadis, C. (1987) *The Imaginary Institution of Society*. Polity Press, Cambridge.

Eisenstadt, S. N. (2003) *Comparative Civilizations and Multiple Modernities*, Vols. 1 and 2. Brill, Leiden.

Frisby, D. (1986) *Fragments of Modernity: Theories of Modernity in the Work of Simmel, Kracuer, and Benjamin*. MIT Press, Cambridge, MA.

Gaonkar, D. P. (Ed.) (2001) *Alternative Modernities*. Duke University Press, Durham, NC.

Heller, A. (1999) *A Theory of History*. Blackwell, Oxford.

Kolakowski, L. (1990) Modernity on Endless Trial. In: *Modernity on Endless Trial*. Chicago University Press, Chicago.

Koselleck, R. (1985) *Futures Past: On the Semantics of Historical Time*. MIT Press, Cambridge, MA.

Seligman, A. (2003) *Modernity's Wager: Authority, the Self, and Transcendence*. Princeton University Press, Princeton.

Touraine, A. (1995) *Critique of Modernity*. Blackwell, Oxford.

Wagner, P. (1994) *A Sociology of Modernity: Liberty and Discipline*. Routledge, London.

modernization

Ronald Inglehart and Christian Welzel

Modernization is an encompassing process of massive social changes that, once set in motion, tends to penetrate all domains of life, from economic activities to social life to political institutions, in a self-reinforcing process. Modernization brings an intense awareness of change and innovation, linked with the idea that human societies are progressing.

Historically, the idea of human progress is relatively new. As long as societies did not exert significant control over their environment and were helplessly exposed to the vagaries of natural forces, and as long as agrarian economies were trapped in a steady-state equilibrium where no growth in mass living standards took place, the idea of human progress seemed unrealistic (Jones 1985; McNeill 1990). The situation began to change only when sustained economic growth began to occur (North 1981; Lal 1998).

After 8,000 years of agrarian history, economic growth began to outpace population growth in a sustained way only with the rise of pre-industrial capitalism in sixteenth-century Northwestern Europe (North 1981; Hall 1989; Lal 1998; Landes 1998). As this happened, the philosophies of humanism and Enlightenment

emerged. The idea that technological innovations based on human intellectual achievement would enable societies to overcome the limitations nature imposes on them gained credibility – contesting the established view that human freedom and fulfillment can come only in the after-life. Science began to provide a source of insight that competed with divine revelation, challenging the intellectual monopoly of the church (Weber 1958 [1904]; Landes 1998). The idea of human progress was born and with it theories of modernization began to emerge.

However, the idea of human progress was contested from the beginning by opposing ideas that considered ongoing societal changes as a sign of human decay. Thus, modernization theory was doomed to make a career swinging between wholehearted appreciation and fierce rejection, depending on whether the dominant mood of the time was rather optimistic or pessimistic. The history of modernization theory is thus the history of anti-modernization theory. Both are ideological reflections of far-ranging dynamics that continue to accelerate the pace of social change since the rise of pre-industrial capitalism.

THE ORIGIN AND CAREER OF MODERNIZATION THEORY

Modernization theory emerged in the Enlightenment era with the belief that technological progress would give humanity increasing control over nature. Antoine de Condorcet (1979 [1795]) was among the first to explicitly link technological innovation and cultural development, arguing that technological advances and economic growth would inevitably bring changes in people's moral values. This idea of human progress was opposed by notions that considered the changes they observed as indications of moral decay. Edmund Burke (1999 [1790]) formulated such an anti-modern view in his *Reflections on the Revolution in France*, while Thomas R. Malthus (1970 [1798]) developed a scientific theory of demographic disasters.

Adam Smith (1976 [1776]) and Karl Marx (1973 [1858]) propagated competing versions of modernization, with Smith advocating a capitalist vision, and Marx advocating communism. Competing versions of modernization theory enjoyed a new resurgence after World War II when the capitalist and communist superpowers espoused opposing ideologies as guidelines for the best route to modernity. Although they competed fiercely, both ideologies were committed to economic growth, social progress, and modernization, and they both brought broader mass participation in politics (Moore 1966). Furthermore, both sides believed that the developing nations of the third world would follow either the communist path or the capitalist path to modernization, and the two superpowers struggled to win them over.

Modernization theory's career is closely linked with theories of underdevelopment. In the post-war US, a version of modernization theory emerged that viewed underdevelopment as a direct consequence of a country's internal characteristics, especially its traditional psychological and cultural traits (Lerner 1958; Pye & Verba 1963; Inkeles & Smith 1974). This perspective was strongly influenced by Max Weber's theory of the cultural origins of capitalism, which viewed underdevelopment as a function of traditionally irrational, spiritual, and communal values – values that discourage human achievement motivation. From this perspective, traditional values were not only mutable but could – and should – also be replaced by modern values, enabling these societies to follow the path of capitalist development. The causal agents in this developmental process were seen as the rich developed nations that stimulated the modernization of "backward" nations through economic, cultural, and military assistance.

This version of modernization theory was not merely criticized as patronizing, it was pronounced dead (Wallerstein 1976). Neo-Marxist and world-systems theorists argued that rich countries exploit poor countries, locking them in positions of powerlessness and structural dependence (e.g., Frank 1966; Wallerstein 1974; Chirot 1977, 1994; Chase-Dunn 1989). Underdevelopment, Frank claimed, is *developed*. nveys the message to poor countries that poverty has nothing to do with their traditional values: it is the fault of global capitalism. In the 1970s and 1980s, modernization theory seemed discredited; dependency theory came into vogue (Cardoso & Faletto 1979). Adherents of dependency theory claimed that the third world nations could only escape from

global exploitation if they withdrew from the world market and adopted import substitution policies.

In recent years, it became apparent that import substitution strategies had failed. The countries that were least involved in global capitalism were not the most successful – they actually showed the *least* economic growth (Firebaugh 1992). Export-oriented strategies were more effective in bringing sustained economic growth and even, eventually, democracy (Barro 1997; Randall & Theobald 1998). The pendulum swung back. Dependency theory fell out of favor and the western capitalist version of modernization regained credibility. The rapid development of East Asia, and the subsequent democratization of Taiwan and South Korea, seemed to confirm its basic claims: producing low-cost goods for the world market initiates economic growth; reinvesting the returns into human capital qualifies the workforce to produce high-tech goods; exporting these more expensive goods brings higher returns and enlarges the educated urban middle class; and once the middle class becomes large enough and confident about its strength, it presses for liberal democracy – the natural political system of middle-class societies (Diamond 1993; Lipset et al. 1993). Evidence for this sequence discredited world-systems theory.

However, one should be aware that the dispute between modernization and dependency/ world-systems theory was not a dispute about whether modernization takes place or not. It was a dispute about its causes and the repeatability of the Anglo-Saxon model in other parts of the world. Dependency theorists and world-systems theorists did not deny modernization took place, nor did they reject modernization as a goal for societies in the third world. They only claimed that the global power structure does not allow peripheral countries to modernize by integrating themselves into the international division of labor. They recommended dissociation from the world market and "autocentric development." Despite the dominant rhetoric of neoliberalism, it is not clear that this strategy is entirely wrong. Actually, it seems that both autocentric development and world market integration work, if they are applied sequentially. The industrial histories of Germany, Japan, and South Korea illustrate that creating competitive domestic industries requires an initial phase of protection of the domestic market from cheaper imports. In any case, the contradiction between liberal modernization theory and Marxist dependency theory shows that some of the most fundamental debates in the social sciences centered on the dazzling phenomenon of modernization.

DIMENSIONS OF MODERNIZATION

Consciously or not, even capitalist notions of modernization have adopted the Marxist idea that modernization starts with changes at the "socioeconomic basis," from which it moves on to changes in the institutional and cultural "superstructure." Modernization theorists usually avoid using these Marxist terms. Nevertheless, most descriptions of modernization start with technological and economic changes, tending to portray related changes in social structures, cultural values, and political institutions as reflections of technological progress. Most explicit in this respect is the ecological-evolutionary approach of Nolan and Lenski (1999), which argues that, since economic production is the most basic sphere of human activities, changes in production technology are the most basic changes, instigating changes in all other domains of social life.

Hence, the term modernization connotes first of all changes in production technology inducing major economic transitions from pre-industrial to industrial societies and from industrial to post-industrial societies. If one tries to extract a standard model of how these transitions proceed, it can be portrayed in the following way. The whole sequence starts with labor-saving innovations in production technology, which increase labor productivity in a certain field of human activities. As this happens, the same material output can be produced by fewer and fewer people. This process sets part of the workforce free for productive activities in new areas. This happened first in the agrarian sector, which set people free for industrial production activities. Then labor productivity in the industrial sector grew to such an extent that people were set free for new activities in the service sector (Bell 1973). Nowadays, we observe a shift within the service sector toward intellectually creative activities, giving rise to a "creative

class" in the fields of marketing, consulting, communication, education, research and development, engineering and design, as well as art and entertainment (Florida 2002). These transformations have various consequences.

All these changes originate in humans' intellectual achievements in the sciences, which manifest themselves in an ever-increasing technological control over various mechanical, chemical, electronic, and biological processes. The social transformations initiated by these technological changes have various massive consequences on the societies' outlook, as the following selection indicates.

(1) *Growth of mass-based human resources.* As humans gain technological control over natural processes and increase their productivity, material standards of living rise. Thus, financial resources, technological equipment, and information become available in growing amounts to widening parts of the public, partly closing the gap between elites and the masses.

(2) *Occupational diversification.* With each technological breakthrough in productivity, a new type of economic activity is added to the scope of productive human activities. This leads to growing occupational diversification, professional specialization, division of labor, interdependence, and thus increasing social complexity.

(3) *Organizational differentiation.* Growing social complexity proliferates an ever-increasing diversity of economic, social, cultural, and political entities, such as corporations, congregations, agencies, departments, bureaus, associations, parties, committees, loose informal groups, and social movements, increasing the variety and interdependence of organized social life. Modern society is a highly organized society, consisting of a multiplex network of interwoven entities. All human activities in modern societies are channeled through the web of organized life.

(4) *State capacity growth and state activity extension.* Compared to modern welfare states (even the more limited Anglo-Saxon version), premodern states were rudimentary. To be sure, premodern states could be utterly despotic. But their despotism

was restricted to what came into the reach of a despot, which was severely limited in premodern times, for the "nerves of government" (Deutsch 1968) were rudimentary in pre-industrial times. Industrialization changes this situation drastically, since it enlarges mass-based human resources. This broadens the state's tax basis, enabling it to extract more resources. States have invariantly invested these resources in the creation of a more elaborate administrative infrastructure and the extension of performed tasks. Thus, the widening of state capacities as well as the diversification of state services and regulations is another concomitant of modernization.

(5) *Mass political involvement.* Through the extension of state activities, each individual comes into the reach of the state and is affected by what the state is doing and deciding. This creates a need to legitimize state activities by mass approval, leading to universal suffrage and other forms of mass participation. Thus, mobilizing the masses into politics, whether in authoritarian or democratic ways, is a core political aspect of modernization.

(6) *Rationalization and secularization.* New kinds of human activities bring different existential experiences. Thus, each social transformation changes people's life perspectives, interests, psychological orientation, and values, fueling cultural changes. Many authors argue that the most fundamental value change emerging with modernization is a transition from spiritual-religious values to secular-rational values, implying that the belief in rational forces and scientific human capabilities replaces the belief in supernatural forces and divine fate. Thus, everything from the production system to the political order comes to be considered objects of human creation, not divine creation.

THREE PERSPECTIVES ON MODERNIZATION

The common denominator of all these aspects of modernization is the growing complexity, knowledge intensity, and sophistication of performed human activities. This overarching feature manifests itself on three levels: the system of organized entities, the mass of individuals, and connections between the individuals.

(1) *The system of organized entities.* On the system level, growing complexity is reflected in the increasing functional differentiation of organized processes and entities. This makes organized entities increasingly interdependent but at the same time increases the autonomy of their internal operations. Division of labor and specialization in modern societies have reached such a degree that no entity can survive without the contributions of the others. But each entity is so specialized in performing its own task within the social system that no other entity can intervene in its internal operations (at least not without lowering the performance of the respective entity).

(2) *The mass of individuals.* On the individual level, growing complexity is reflected in an increasing differentiation of social roles and a growing diversification of role models. Role differentiation means that people perform their social roles in different social circles. In pre-industrial society, the family is the core unit in which all social roles, from biological reproduction to economic subsistence, are performed. In modern societies, family roles and economic roles fall apart and are performed in different social circles. Role diversification means that the role models used as devices to perform a social role multiply. This multiplication gives people a choice of which role model they want to follow or how they like to combine elements of different models. Role differentiation and role diversification increase individual autonomy, fueling "individualization."

(3) *Connections between the individuals.* On the level of social relations, growing complexity manifests itself in a transformation in the nature of social ties. Durkheim (1988 [1893]) noticed a transformation from "mechanical solidarity" to "organic solidarity," meaning that people are no longer automatically interconnected on the basis of family or common lineage. Inherited

communal attributes, such as one's ethnicity, religion, and language, no longer suffice to bond communities into which people invest their entire personality. Instead, people cooperate voluntarily on the basis of mutually agreed interests. Such cooperation is partial, not holistic: it does not involve an individual's entire personality but only his or her interests. Tönnies (1955 [1887]) depicted this development as a transition from holistic "communities" to specific "associations." Simmel (1984 [1908]) introduced the concept of "cross-cutting social circles" to illuminate that these associations bring together people from various social circles, replacing the bonding ties of communities with the bridging ties of associations. The crucial point here is the change in the nature of social cohesion: from clientelist relationships based on *inherited* loyalties to contractual relationships based on *negotiated* ties. The emerging bargaining character of social ties reflects the logic of a social contract, making social relationships a matter of giving and taking and voluntary mutual exchange. Beck describes this as a transition from "communities of necessity" to "elective affinities." This contractual transformation of social ties does not reduce people's dependence on social interactions, but it makes them less dependent on bonds to specific persons.

MODERNIZATION AND CULTURAL CHANGE

Modernization theories have been criticized for their tendency toward technological and socioeconomic determinism. Usually these critiques cite Max Weber (1958 [1904]), who reversed the Marxian notion that technologically induced socioeconomic development determines cultural change. Indeed, in his explanation of the rise of capitalism, Weber turns causality in the opposite direction, arguing that the Calvinist variant of Protestantism (along with other factors) led to the rise of a capitalist economy rather than the other way round. Revised versions of modernization theory (Inglehart & Baker 2000) emphasize that both Marx and Weber were

partly correct: on one hand, socioeconomic development brings predictable cultural changes in people's moral values; but on the other hand, these changes are path dependent, so that a society's initial starting position remains visible in its relative position to other societies, reflecting its cultural heritage. Nevertheless, recent evidence indicates that – even though the relationship between socioeconomic development and cultural change is reciprocal – the stronger causal arrow seems to run from socioeconomic development to cultural change (Inglehart & Welzel 2005).

While partly confirming Weber, Inglehart and Welzel (2005) correct him and his followers in still another respect. The rise of secular-rational values is not the ultimate cultural aspect of modernization, nor is it the aspect that is most conducive to democracy. Instead, they argue, secular-rational values arise in one specific phase of modernization – the industrialization phase – when increasing technological control over the forces of nature conveys the impression that everything is subject to human engineering and that all problems can be solved by human rationality. However, with the transition to post-industrial society, all ideological dogmas, including the dogma of rational science, become subject to criticism. Moreover, an awareness of the risks of technological progress emerges, giving rise to new spiritual concerns about the meaning of life and the dignity of creation. Hence, the processes of secularization and rationalization are not permanent aspects of modernization.

MODERNIZATION AND DEMOCRACY

Another important debate involves the question of whether modernization necessarily leads to democratization, or whether authoritarian forms of mass politics are also compatible with modernization. The first position has been argued most explicitly by Talcott Parsons (1967), who saw the principle of "voluntary association" as the only political way to cope with modernity. He argued that social systems that do not give room to the principle of voluntary association are unable to produce legitimacy and unable to harness people's intrinsic motivation for the goals of the political system. Such a system has access only to support that it can win by force and by bribes. Other things being equal, systems that are unable to mobilize people's intrinsic support will be unable to compete effectively with those that can. Hence, Parsons concluded that the Soviet system will either adopt the principle of association (i.e., democracy) or fail. Luhmann's (1995 [1984]) systems theory also predicted the failure of communist systems, arguing that totalitarian systems deny the subsystem autonomy that is needed to run complex modern systems in an effective way. According to these theories, modernization inevitably leads to democracy, for only democracies are able to generate legitimacy and to provide sufficient subsystem autonomy for a highly complex society to function effectively.

Moore (1966), by contrast, argued that the western path to liberal democracy was historically unique. Industrialization led to stable mass democracies only where limited versions of democracy already were in place in pre-industrial times. This was only the case in commercial freeholder societies that sustained a capitalist urban middle class, the bourgeoisie. Examples are Switzerland, the Lowlands, England, Scandinavia, or the British settler colonies in America and Australia. By contrast, when industrialization emerged in traditionally absolutist societies (Germany) or despotic societies (Russia), where the pre-industrial economies were largely "labor repressive," fascist or communist forms of mass polities have been the consequence. These totalitarian polities, too, employ universal suffrage to involve the masses, but they use it simply to enforce public expressions of mass loyalty.

Ironically, again, both Parsons and Moore are partly right – but they apply to different phases of modernization. Moore's insights are valid in that not all forms of economic development are necessarily conducive to democracy. If this were the case, the oil-exporting countries should be model democracies. Today, it is evident that revenue from natural resources can make a country rich but not democratic. Industrialization is not the phase of modernization that is most conducive to democracy. As Moore pointed out, it can lead to fascism or communism as readily as to democracy, but the post-industrial phase of modernization makes democracy become increasingly likely.

MODERNIZATION AS HUMAN DEVELOPMENT

In a recent revised version of modernization theory, Inglehart and Welzel (2005) argue that the distinctive implications that industrialization and post-industrialization have for democracy reflect distinctive types of values that emerge in these two phases of modernization. Industrialization vastly expands technological human control over the natural environment. Humans spend most of their activities in an entirely man-made environment and are no longer helplessly exposed to the vicissitudes of natural forces. Everything, even the political order, seems to be a question of human engineering and all problems can be solved by science: everything, from economic growth to space exploration, is subject to human rationality. These perceptions in the industrial world favor the emergence of secular-rational values.

The industrial phase of modernization links secular-rational values with conformist values that emphasize group discipline over individual liberty. The reason for this is the standardization of life in the industrial world. This is particularly true for the working class whose members experience little personal autonomy, spending most of their lives at the assembly line or in their apartment buildings, in homogeneous groups, living under strong social controls and group pressures. These experiences support conformist values that do not give top priority to individual freedom. As a consequence, liberal democracy does not necessarily emerge in industrial societies. The mass mobilization of industrial societies requires mass involvement in politics, which leads to universal suffrage. But universal suffrage has more often been organized in authoritarian ways than in democratic ones. Even traditional democracies showed a relatively authoritarian outlook in the industrial age, operating an elite-led model in which party bosses commanded loyal troops of voters.

The emergence of a service-based economy in post-industrial societies destandardizes economic activities and social life, and in the knowledge society individual judgment and innovation take on central importance. Increasingly, people experience themselves as individuals who are autonomous in their judgments, activities, and life choices. This gives rise to emancipative values that place individual liberty over group conformity. These values are closely linked with the core ideal of liberal democracy – human freedom. The emergence of these values has contributed to the emergence of new democracies in much of the world – and it also leads to a humanistic transformation of established democracies. Post-industrial democracies lose their authoritarian aspects as rising emphasis on emancipative values transforms modernization into a process of human development. This type of society unfolds the emancipative potential inherent in democracy. This process can be described as human development because it features the most specifically human quality: the ability to base decisions and activities on autonomous judgments and choices.

MODERNIZATION, HUMAN DEVELOPMENT, AND SOCIAL CAPITAL

Another important debate is whether modernization erodes or creates social capital – an important debate because it is widely believed that any erosion of social capital undermines democracy. Putnam (2000) argues that some inherent aspect of post-industrial society, such as the growing amount of time spent watching television, erodes social ties between people and diminishes their communal engagement. In line with this reasoning, many authors claim that, even if communal engagement does not entirely vanish, remaining forms of communal engagement are of a lower civic quality because they are based on egocentric cost calculations of people who become excessively self-assertive.

Florida (2002), Inglehart and Welzel (2005), and others advance an opposite interpretation. Rising self-expression values, they argue, have brought a decline of participation in elite-controlled communal activities. The bureaucratic organizations that once controlled the masses, such as political machines, labor unions, and churches, are losing their grip – but more spontaneous, expressive, and issue-oriented forms of actions, such as participation in petitions and demonstrations, are becoming more widespread. As Inglehart and Welzel (2005) argue, the rise of self-expression values is linked with higher

levels of elite-challenging collective action, focused on making elites more responsive to popular demands. The rise of elite-challenging mass action is one more aspect of the humanistic transformation of democracies, making them increasingly people-centered.

SEE ALSO: Bureaucracy and Public Sector Governmentality; Democracy; Dependency and World-Systems Theories; Developmental Stages; Economic Development; Industrialization; Knowledge Societies; Legitimacy; Mobilization; Political Economy; Post-Industrial Society; Postmodern Culture; Secularization; Social Capital; Social Change; Solidarity, Mechanical and Organic

REFERENCES AND SUGGESTED READINGS

Barro, R. J. (1997) *Determinants of Economic Growth: A Cross-Country Empirical Study*. MIT Press, Cambridge, MA.

Bell, D. (1973) *The Coming of Postindustrial Society*. Basic Books, New York.

Burke, E. (1999 [1790]) *Reflections on the Revolution in France*. Oxford University Press, Oxford.

Cardoso, F. H. & Faletto, E. (1979) *Dependency and Development in Latin America*. University of California Press, Berkeley.

Chase-Dunn, C. (1989) *Global Formations: Structures of the World-Economy*. Blackwell, Cambridge, MA.

Chirot, D. (1977) *Social Change in the Twentieth Century*. Harcourt Brace Jovanovich, New York.

Chirot, D. (1994) *How Societies Change*. Pine Forge Press, Thousand Oaks, CA.

Condorcet, J.-A.-N. de Caritat (1979 [1795]) *Sketch for a Historical Picture of the Progress of Human Mind*. Hyperion Press, Westport, CT.

Deutsch, K. (1963) *The Nerves of Government*. Free Press, New York.

Diamond, L. (1993) The Globalization of Democracy. In: Slater, R. O., Schutz, B. M., & Dorr, S. R. (Eds.), *Global Transformation and the Third World*. Lynne Rienner, Boulder, CO, pp. 31–69.

Durkheim, É. (1988 [1893]) *Über soziale Arbeitsteilung (On Social Division of Labor)*. Suhrkamp, Frankfurt am Main.

Firebaugh, G. (1992) Growth Effects of Foreign and Domestic Investment. *American Journal of Sociology* 98: 105–30.

Florida, R. (2002) *The Rise of the Creative Class*. Basic Books, New York.

Frank, A. G. (1966) The Development of Underdevelopment. *Monthly Review* (September): 17–30.

Hall, J. A. (1989) States and Societies: The Miracle in Comparative Perspective. In: Baechler, J., Hall, J., & Mann, M. (Eds.), *Europe and the Rise of Capitalism*. Blackwell, Oxford, pp. 20–38.

Inglehart, R. & Baker, W. E. (2000) Modernization, Cultural Change, and the Persistence of Traditional Values. *American Sociological Review* 65 (February): 19–51.

Inglehart, R. & Welzel, C. (2005) *Modernization, Cultural Change, and Democracy*. Cambridge University Press, New York.

Inkeles, A. & Smith, D. (1974) *Becoming Modern: Individual Changes in Six Developing Societies*. Harvard University Press, Cambridge, MA.

Jones, E. L. (1985) *The European Miracle: Environments, Economies, and Geopolities in the History of Europe and Asia*, 3rd edn. Cambridge University Press, Cambridge.

Lal, D. (1998) *Unintended Consequences: The Impact of Factor Endowments, Culture, and Politics on Long Run Economic Performance*. MIT Press, Cambridge, MA.

Landes, D. S. (1998) *The Wealth and Poverty of Nations: Why Some Are So Rich and Some So Poor*. W. W. Norton, New York.

Lerner, D. (1958) *The Passing of Traditional Society: Modernizing the Middle East*. Free Press, New York.

Lipset, S. M., Seong, K.-R., & Torres, J. C. (1993) A Comparative Analysis of the Social Requisites of Democracy. *International Social Science Journal* 45 (May): 155–75.

Luhmann, N. (1995 [1984]) *Social Systems*. Stanford University Press, Stanford.

McNeill, W. (1990) *The Rise of the West: A History of the Human Community*. University of Chicago Press, Chicago.

Malthus, T. R. (1970 [1798]) *An Essay on the Principle of Population*. Penguin, Harmondsworth.

Marx, K. (1973 [1858]) *Grundrisse*. Penguin, Harmondsworth.

Moore, B. (1966) *The Social Origins of Democracy and Dictatorship: Lord and Peasant in the Making of the Modern World*. Beacon Press, Boston.

Nolan, P. & Lenski, G. (1999) *Human Societies: An Introduction to Macrosociology*, 8th edn. McGraw-Hill, New York.

North, D. C. (1981) *Structure and Change in Economic History*. W. W. Norton, New York.

Parsons, T. (1967) *The Structure of Social Action*, 2nd edn. Free Press, New York.

Putnam, R. D. (2000) *Bowling Alone: The Collapse and Revival of American Community*. Simon & Schuster, New York.

Pye, L. & Verba, S. (Eds.) (1963) *Political Culture and Political Development*. Princeton University Press, Princeton.

Randall, V. & Theobald, R. (1998) *Political Change and Underdevelopment*, 2nd edn. Duke University Press, Durham, NC.

Simmel, G. (1984 [1908]) *Das Individuum und die Freiheit: Essays (The Individual and Freedom)*. Duncker & Humboldt, Berlin.

Smith, A. (1976 [1776]) *An Inquiry into the Nature and Causes of the Wealth of Nations*. Chicago University Press, Chicago.

Tönnies, F. (1955 [1887]) *Community and Association*. Routledge & Kegan Paul, London.

Wallerstein, I. (1974) *The Modern World System I*. Academic Press, New York.

Wallerstein, I. (1976) Modernization: Requiescat in Pace. In: Coser, L. A. & Larsen, O. N. (Eds.), *The Uses of Controversy in Sociology*. Free Press, New York, pp. 131–5.

Weber, M. (1958 [1904]) *The Protestant Ethic and the Spirit of Capitalism*. Charles Scribner's Sons, New York.

money

Nigel Dodd

The sociology of money is a new and thriving field. Significant theoretical contributions to a sociological understanding of money were made by Marx, Simmel, and Weber, among others. While Weber focused primarily on the legal status of money – he broadly agreed with Knapp's characterization of money as a "creature of the state" – Marx and Simmel undertook extensive investigations into the nature of money as a medium. According to Marx, money is a commodity, and its quantitative relationship to other commodities – its function as a "universal measure of value" – is made possible by the amount of labor-time that it contains. This is true not only of precious metals but also of other forms of "credit" money, such as banknotes, which derive their value from a commodity such as gold. Thus, to view exchange relations merely as "monetary" relations or as a series of prices determined by supply and demand is to overlook the social relations of production – and, of course, exploitation – on which they fundamentally depend. Simmel took a quite different view of the value of money. By his reckoning, money represents an abstract idea of value that is underwritten by "society": its value, in other words, ultimately depends on a form of trust in society that Simmel likened to "quasi-religious faith." On the basis of the characterization, Simmel explored the roots and consequences of the development of the "mature money economy," whereby an increasing number of social relationships are mediated by money.

Although the work of Marx and Simmel threw up some rich questions for debate, subsequent sociological theorists who contemplated money – for example, Parsons, Habermas, Luhmann, and Giddens – used it mainly to illustrate elements of their work without seriously investigating the nature of money itself. Those instances of a more explicit sociological examination of money that one finds scattered in the twentieth-century literature were usually quite narrow in focus and too unrelated to constitute a "field" of inquiry in its own right.

Recently, however, a number of sociologists have produced major publications in which they sought to develop a systematic sociological treatment of money. Zelizer (1994) argued against an image of money as "neutral" and "impersonal" through a historical analysis that examined money in relation to the social context of its use. Dodd (1994) sought to elaborate Simmel's concept of money as a "pure instrument" by relating it to consumerism and the globalization of finance. More recently, Ingham (2004) has brought sociological arguments to bear on theories of money in orthodox and heterodox economics.

Besides these programmatic efforts to develop a sociological interpretation of money, an increasing number of specialist studies have focused on particular lines of research. For example, they have looked at the role of money in the domestic economy, the emergence of monetary forms such as LETS (Local Exchange Trading Scheme) tokens and other "complementary currencies," and the growth of Internet currencies and electronic money (or e-money). But for all the empirical richness that these recent contributions bring to our understanding of money, there is no common view of what money is. There has never been a consensus

about this. The extant literature on money, not only in sociology but also in neighboring disciplines such as geography and anthropology, is replete with debates over competing definitions.

In economics, money is usually defined in terms of three main functions: money is a medium of exchange, a store of value, a unit of account. Classical sociologists were mainly concerned with money's role as a store of value. Marx explored the relationship between money and gold, for example, while Weber discussed the distinctiveness and viability of state-issued "paper" money. Even Simmel, who used money as a means for a much wider philosophical investigation into the role of exchange in modern culture, began his study with the question of value.

At the beginning of the twenty-first century, sociologists are addressing a rather different set of concerns than their classical forebears. The central question no longer concerns the "value" of money once its connection with gold has been severed. Instead, sociologists, together with scholars in related disciplines (see Hart 2000; Helleiner 2003; Cohen 2004), have been exploring an apparent decline in the relationship between money and the state. This development is not a straightforward process, and its implications remain contested.

The work of Ingham revolves around the assertion that the social production of money is integral to a broader struggle for power. On one side of the struggle, monetary agencies (banks and so forth) compete to preserve and store value in money, to control its supply, and to extract interest. Against the monetary agencies, industrialists attempt to "monetize their market power" through rising prices or by borrowing. Problems such as inflation arise whenever this struggle becomes unstable. Although money's *value* is determined by these competing interests, the definition of what *counts* as money is declared by a political authority that transcends such interests. In the modern era, this authority consists of the state, which defines the unit of account – or what Keynes called *money-of-account* – for the money which circulates within its territory (e.g., US dollar). It follows that any form of "money" that is not denominated in the official unit of account will be deficient. Unofficial money is too specialized in terms of its possible uses, and too restricted in its potential sphere of circulation, to rival official currency. E-money is likely to have an extremely limited capacity for success unless it is denominated in the official money-of-account. And local alternatives to currency are merely media of exchange which facilitate bartering. According to Ingham, then, states are likely to continue as the major suppliers and regulators of money.

Zelizer's work presents an intriguing contrast to that of Ingham. She conveys money as "multiple," i.e., as *monies*, not *money*. According to Zelizer, the multiplicity of money derives from the differentiated ways in which we impute meanings to it whenever it is in our possession. She calls this process "earmarking." Earmarking works in a number of interrelated ways: by restricting the use, regulating the allocation, modifying the appearance, and attaching special meanings to a particular quantity of money. For instance, by allocating specific quantities of our income to manage a domestic budget, or by setting aside currency received as a gift for a specific purchase, we impute a specific meaning to money which undermines its supposedly impersonal character. Zelizer (2004) has recently developed her analysis of the multiplicity of money with the concept of "circuits of commerce." Each circuit incorporates its own medium, for example "localized tokens." Zelizer's approach suggests that we need to take a micro as well as a macro approach to the analysis of money. In contrast to the argument that is advanced by Ingham, she suggests that we need to look at money from the perspective of its users, not its producers. By adopting this perspective, one can glean many insights from the fluid meanings of money – not the least of which is that the future of state-issued currency is by no means assured.

Zelizer works with a broad and inclusive definition of money, while that of Ingham is narrow and exclusive. But their perspectives are by no means incompatible. The present-day world of money is characterized by two countervailing trends. To some degree, these reflect the contrasting approaches of Ingham and Zelizer to the sociology of money. On the one hand, large-scale currencies such as the US dollar are increasingly circulating outside the borders of their issuing states, and in some cases are actually replacing smaller currencies. This process constitutes a trend toward increasing

homogeneity. On the other hand, the range of monetary forms in circulation that are not stated-issued currency is increasing, primarily through the development of e-money and complementary currencies. This constitutes a trend toward increasing *diversity*.

For sociologists, these developments offer some exciting research opportunities. One such opportunity is offered by the euro (see Dodd 2005). On the face of it, the single currency is consistent with the phenomenon of currency homogenization. Having replaced 12 separate national currencies, the euro is an internationalized currency in its own right, and already circulates beyond the borders of the euro zone. The euro represents a quantum leap in the homogenization of currency. Its emergence was due not to the dynamics of currency competition but to political fiat. As such, it was introduced into an unusually uneven – and sometimes hostile – socioeconomic terrain. It is possible that the operation of a single monetary policy in the euro zone might even foster conditions under which alternative forms of money could thrive. The euro has not been the unmitigated failure that many commentators were predicting, nor the spectacular success that its architects might have hoped for, economically, politically, and even culturally. As the euro zone expands, it will provide especially fertile ground on which competing sociological accounts of money can be put to the test.

SEE ALSO: Economy (Sociological Approach); Globalization; Markets; Money Management in Families; Simmel, Georg; Marx, Karl

REFERENCES AND SUGGESTED READINGS

Cohen, B. (2004) *The Future of Money*. Princeton University Press, Princeton.

Dodd, N. (1994) *The Sociology of Money*. Polity Press, Cambridge.

Dodd, N. (2005) Reinventing Monies in Europe. *Economy and Society* 34(4): 558–83.

Hart, K. (2000) *Money in an Unequal World*. Texere, London and New York.

Helleiner, E. (2003) *The Making of National Money*. Cornell University Press, Ithaca, NY.

Ingham, G. (2004) *The Nature of Money*. Polity Press, Cambridge.

Marx, K. (1976) *Capital*, Vol. 1. Penguin, Harmondsworth.

Simmel, G. (1907) *The Philosophy of Money*. Routledge, London.

Zelizer, V. (1994) *The Social Meaning of Money*. Princeton University Press, Princeton.

Zelizer, V. (2004) Circuits of Commerce. In: Williams, C. (Ed.), *Self, Social Structure, and Beliefs: Explorations in Sociology*. University of California Press, Berkeley, pp. 122–44.

money management in families

Vivienne Elizabeth

The equal sharing of financial resources and, hence, material well-being has become an assumed norm of contemporary heterosexual families. Of course, this is not to say that heterosexual couples actually enjoy financial equality or that they share a similar standard of living. In fact, as Pahl (1989) pointed out over 15 years ago, the failure to open up the black box of familial economies to sociological scrutiny has operated to disguise intrafamilial inequalities: amongst married couples these inequalities, as numerous studies have consistently demonstrated, possess a strongly gendered character. It is women and children who tend to be poor even when the households to which they belong are in receipt of adequate incomes.

Sociologists, in taking heed of Pahl's call to investigate the money management practices of families, have paid attention to a number of different dimensions of domestic economies. Firstly, they have sought to discover the practices through which families combine, distribute, spend, and save their financial resources. Secondly, they have examined the effects of these practices on different family members in both financial and social terms. Thirdly, they have pointed out that variations in the use of particular financial systems are associated with differences of class, ethnicity, and family structure. Fourthly, they have recently begun to consider the role remittances play in the choice of money management systems within ethnic minority families.

In pursuing this line of inquiry, largely with respect to married and, to a lesser extent, remarried and unmarried heterosexual couples and families, sociologists have consolidated and refined Pahl's original insight into the gendered inequalities produced through contemporary money management practices. Disparities in personal spending money are a particularly sensitive marker of the ways in which different financial systems operate to reduce or enlarge gendered inequalities. Other widely recognized sites of gendered disparity within the economies of heterosexual families include: differences in the power of each partner to influence decision-making, especially over extraordinary expenditure; differences in who is accountable to whom for how they manage their financial affairs; and differences in the value attributed to each person's monetary contributions to the household. As Pahl (2000) aptly points out, these inequalities may well be aggravated by the emergence and increased usage of electronic banking practices that enable "credit-rich" individuals to pursue their own financial goals without consulting other family members.

Four money management systems are now widely recognized to reflect the ways in which heterosexual couples and families organize their finances; the little we know about the money management practices of same-sex couples and families suggests that two of these financial systems – the pooling and independent systems – are also in use within these households. The other two money management systems discussed below – the whole wage system and the housekeeping system – are clearly connected to a traditional gendered division of labor that allocates responsibilities for paid work to a male breadwinner and for unpaid domestic work to a female housewife and mother. Because a traditional gender division of labor, and the ideologies that have given it legitimacy, is in decline, both the whole wage and housekeeping systems are also decreasing in popularity. Furthermore, their strong connection to the practices of heterogender means that these systems are rarely, if ever, used by same-sex couples.

The whole wage system consists of two variations. In the more common female whole wage system (in use by approximately 25 percent of households in the UK), men retain a portion of their earnings for their own personal use before passing over the remainder to their female partners who, after adding in their own earnings if any, are charged with the responsibility of meeting the household's expenses. In effect, the female whole wage system enshrines earner entitlement by guaranteeing men's access to personal spending money, while making women's access to personal spending money contingent upon the presence of a monetary surplus. Given the preponderance of the use of this system in low-wage households, combined with a now well-recognized tendency for women to prioritize expenditure that meets the needs of their children, the typical outcome of the female whole wage system is large differences in the personal spending capacities of men and women. In the second variant, the male whole wage system (used by approximately 10 percent of households in the UK), men retain and manage the income they bring into the household. Under this system men are positioned as financial gatekeepers and women as supplicants who, to the extent that they have no or limited incomes of their own, must ask their male partners for access to money in order to make autonomous purchases. Thus, women's capacity to influence financial decisions or engage in personal spending is even more highly constrained than within the female whole wage system.

In the housekeeping system (also used by approximately 10 percent of heterosexual families within the UK), men pass over a set amount of money at fixed intervals to their partners, whilst "husbanding" the remainder of their income in a separate account to cover both their personal spending needs and extraordinary household expenses. Typically, the housekeeping allowance is used to cover day-to-day household expenses and in many cases it is also expected to provide women with their personal spending money. Once again this system limits women's access to the combined financial resources of the household, their ability to influence major spending decisions, and their capacity to spend on themselves.

Unsurprisingly, given the emphasis on equal sharing within contemporary marital discourse and the growth in women's financial contributions to households through their increased labor market participation, pooling has become the most common system in use amongst heterosexual couples (with around 50 percent of

heterosexual households using it in the UK and upwards of 65 percent of couples in the US). Although research on the money management practices of non-traditional couples and families, especially same-sex families, is sparse, it appears that pooling also enjoys reasonable uptake amongst cohabiting heterosexual and homosexual couples (Blumstein & Schwartz 1983; Elizabeth 2001; Vogler 2005). Arguably, the use of pooling by these couples reflects their level of commitment to each other and hence their beliefs in the longevity of their relationships. However, the choice to use the pooling system may simply be a practical response to a partner's loss of income through childbearing, unemployment, or full-time study.

In the pooling system, all (or nearly all) of the couple's income is placed in a joint bank account, permitting each partner to enjoy direct and, in principle, equal access to their combined financial resources. Despite the rhetoric that surrounds pooling, widespread inequalities in access to the family's joint income persist. These disparities are clearly evident in differences in the personal spending practices of major and minor (or non-) earners. To a considerable extent, the discrepancy in personal spending money amongst pooling couples (both heterosexual and homosexual) reflects the difficulty many couples experience in completely setting aside ideas about "your" or "my" money in favor of "our" money, particularly with respect to discretionary expenditure. In other words, despite adhering to the principle of equal sharing, many pooling couples continue to hold onto a vestigial belief in the rights of income earners to determine how this money is allocated. The effects of an ongoing belief in earner entitlement amongst couples who pool are several. Firstly, it boosts the decision-making power of the major earner even as it diminishes the influence of the minor (or non-) earner. Secondly, it undercuts the capacity of lower- or non-earning partners to spend on personal items: this occurs as much, if not more, through self-imposed restrictions as it does through restrictions imposed by the major earning partner.

Amongst heterosexual couples who pool, these inequalities of money and power are reinforced by the performance of heterogender in a context of ongoing gender-related income differentials and the continued gendered division of labor within many heterosexual families. Paradoxically, even in couples where the woman is the main earner, her superior income often fails to translate into greater decision-making power or higher levels of personal spending money. Rather, women in this situation tend to divest themselves of this form of power in an attempt to minimize the discomfort that arises for many men when they find themselves in positions of dependency. This raises the question: to what extent are the well-known inequalities in the domestic economy ameliorated in families that are formed around non-heterosexual couples? Available research suggests an affirmative reply: both lesbian and gay couples report achieving high levels of egalitarianism in their relationships, a finding that is partly a result of maintaining high levels of workforce involvement, and hence financial independence.

Finally, the independent system is reliant upon each partner being in receipt of his or her own income: for this reason, the use of this system is associated with higher-income, often childless, households. Its uptake is also connected to newer forms of family life: in the small number of studies on the financial practices of remarried and cohabiting (heterosexual and homosexual) couples, findings point to their higher rates of usage of this system: around 50 percent of these couples appear to use an independent system compared with less than 10 percent of the married population. However, the findings of several recent studies suggest that, although subject to geographical variability, the use of an independent system amongst married couples may well be on the rise: in Heimdal and Houseknecht's (2003) study, just under 20 percent of married couples from the US organized their money separately. Interestingly, the independent system is also in higher use in New Zealand, especially amongst Pacifica families where its use may facilitate the payment of remittances to extended family members (Fleming 1997).

In the independent system, each partner holds his or her earnings separately whilst making an agreed-upon contribution to nominated joint expenses. Typically, this contribution is defined in terms of a 50:50 split of their joint household expenses; amongst some couples this contribution is placed in a joint purse (or kitty) or bank account to avoid the complicated accounting processes that are often a feature of this system. Having made the appropriate contribution, the remainder of a person's income is defined as an individually owned and controlled resource. In other words, couples using an independent system place emphasis on the equality of their financial contributions to the family and, in exchange for making equal contributions, each partner enjoys equal control over his or her disposable income.

The attractions for women of this system are clear: the need to ask and seek approval for money to cover personal purchases, a key hallmark of financial dependency, is circumvented. Indeed, where women earn more than their male partners, the independent system, in affirming the principle of earner entitlement, makes it possible for women to wield more influence over spending decisions – both ordinary and extraordinary – than is often the case amongst heterosexual couples. But how frequently women are in receipt of an income that would enable them to exercise greater power, and secondly, how often they actually take advantage of this capacity, is a matter for further research. Early indications amongst lesbian couples who use this system, however, suggest that they avoid income differentials and downplay the significance of such differences in an attempt to maintain egalitarian relationships; amongst heterosexual couples the chances that women will earn more than their male partners, although on the rise, remains low. On the contrary, disparities in income levels tend to be skewed in men's favor. In this more common scenario, the failure of the independent system to address equality of access issues, at the same time as it entrenches earner control, may well disadvantage heterosexual women. Where incomes are disparate the principle of equal contributions will result in one partner paying a much higher proportion of his or her income toward the couple's joint expenses, thereby leaving that person with comparatively lower levels of spending power.

The independent and pooling systems each represent promising possibilities for the achievement of financial equality within contemporary heterosexual families. Yet attempts to eliminate inequalities between family members through the use of these systems have proved to be flawed, at least under some circumstances. The continued emergence of financial disparities within families can be largely attributed to the ongoing salience of earner entitlements in contexts of income inequalities. As argued herein, both earner entitlements and income disparities are strongly inflected by the structures and norms associated with the operation of gender within heterosexual relationships. To understand more about the effects of earner entitlements and income disparities, it is time that sociologists turned their attention to the financial practices of same-sex couples and families. It is entirely conceivable that through such research new ways of resolving the tensions between equality and autonomy will be brought to light.

SEE ALSO: Divisions of Household Labor; Family Poverty; Households; Inequalities in Marriage; Marital Power/Resource Theory; Money

REFERENCES AND SUGGESTED READINGS

Blumstein, P. & Schwartz, P. (1983) *American Couples*. William Morrow, New York.
Burgoyne, C. (2004) Heart-Strings and Purse-Strings: Money in Heterosexual Marriage. *Feminism and Psychology* 14: 165–72.
Elizabeth, V. (2001) Managing Money, Managing Coupledom: A Critical Examination of Cohabitants' Money Management Practices. *Sociological Review* 49: 389–411.
Fleming, R. (1997) *The Common Purse*. Auckland University Press and Bridget Williams Books, Auckland.
Heimdal, K. & Houseknecht, S. (2003) Cohabiting and Married Couples' Income Organization: Approaches in Sweden and the United States. *Journal of Marriage and the Family* 65: 525–38.
Pahl, J. (1989) *Money and Marriage*. Macmillan, London.
Pahl, J. (2000) Couples and their Money: Patterns of Accounting and Accountability in the Domestic Economy. *Accounting, Auditing, and Accountability Journal* 13: 502–17.
Vogler, C. (2005) Cohabiting Couples: Rethinking Money in the Household at the Beginning of the Twenty-First Century. *Sociological Review* 53: 1–29.

moral economy

Steffen Mau

Moral economy can be defined as a common notion of the just distribution of resources and social exchange. The concept has been developed and is used in the context of political and social analysis to understand, for example, various systems of social exchange or instances of rebellion. It is claimed that social communities tend to invoke a moral repertoire for all kinds of social exchanges and transfers that leads them to distinguish between legitimate and illegitimate social practices. The transition from traditional to market economies is emphasized by many authors, in particular, because this transition challenged traditional communal norms and values and can lead to social and political unrest. In more recent accounts, moral economy contends that economic activities are insufficiently understood in narrow economic terms. Rather, they need a broader understanding of how economic and normative motives are blended and how markets are permeated by social norms and values. The centerpiece of the moral economy argument claims that human action is embedded within the wider social environment and institutions and is therefore deeply colored by non-economic considerations.

E. P. Thompson's (1971) study on the eighteenth-century food riots first popularized the term moral economy. He observes how the emergence of the market order seriously challenges traditional normative standards, and thereby evoked popular resistance and protest. According to his account, it was not "objective" forms of hardship that engendered social protest, but rather the violation of well-entrenched communal values. Since there is a traditional and widespread consensus about legitimate and illegitimate social practices, and since the cash nexus of the market tends to threaten deep-rooted moral precepts of a fair price or the right to subsistence, people are ready to engage in a moral protest. Thompson's contribution has inspired a whole branch of anthropological and ethnographic studies dealing with diverse peasant societies (e.g., Scott 1976, 1985). Their findings show that the marketization of traditional societies tends to violate well-entrenched norms and reciprocities and thereby triggers social and political unrest. In most of the scholarship, the peasantry appears to be a group especially vulnerable to the disruptive impact of the emerging market order because norms of reciprocity and subsistence prevail. Their social rather than economic way of reasoning and their lack of rational calculation can be explained by the intersection between economic and social functions of production, the close relation between production and consumption, and their risk-proneness. According to moral economists these types of agrarian communities do not allocate resources so as to maximize total output, but to fulfill their subsistence needs (Bates & Curry 1992).

One of the key concepts of the moral economy approach is the idea of embeddedness, which highlights the notion that economic behavior in traditional societies takes place within the context of religious, social, and political institutions. Karl Polanyi's book *The Great Transformation* (1957) investigates the conditions and rationales of economic exchanges and distinguishes the embedded and the disembedded or autonomous economies. Polanyi argues that traditional societies are characterized by the fact that economic relationships are submerged in social relationships. In traditional societies there is no clear boundary line separating the economic sphere from society's institutions and values (e.g., religion, politics). Economic activities are also governed by non-market institutions, traditions, and a set of normative expectations so that means and ends cannot be considered as autonomous. Following the Aristotelian notion of the good life and the distinct characteristics of "householding" in contrast to money-making, he suggests that traditional economic forms of production and distribution were subordinated to the pursuit of the good life.

However, it is often remarked that this contrast between traditional and modern societies is largely overestimated. In the light of more recent evidence it has been suggested that the concept of the moral economy rests too heavily on the distinction between market and non-market-based societies (Booth 1994). Also, modern societies are not devoid of forms of moral regulation. Thus, beyond the accounts that deal with the trajectory from traditional to modern societies, the moral economy framework has inspired a larger part of economic sociology challenging some of the propositions of economic and rational choice theory. Moral economists argue that the economic approach focuses too narrowly on the self-interested and utility-maximizing individual and it cannot be fruitfully applied to the many instances in which economic behavior is guided by and embedded in non-economic institutions and values. Rather than conceiving the profit-seeking individual as *the* pivot of economic behavior, a closer understanding of the sociocultural components and determinants of behavior is needed. By the same token, the idea of autonomous, self-regulating markets needs critical revision in favor of revealing the institutional and political, but also normative prerequisites of how the market functions. Critics of the moral economy approach suggest that it "moralizes" and "over-socializes" individual actions. Hence, it fails not only to conceive that morality can be a bearer of self-interest, but also that economic considerations can generate non-market institutions (Arnold 2001). For some, the moral economic framework sticks to a rather generalized understanding of morality that is not prepared to construe and to identify the role of specific social relations (Granovetter 1985). Recent renewals of the moral economy concept have sharpened the analytical perspective by focusing on concrete social exchanges, highlighting the impact of institutional contexts and promoting the idea of social goods.

SEE ALSO: Community and Economy; Distributive Justice; Norm of Reciprocity; Polanyi, Karl

REFERENCES AND SUGGESTED READINGS

Arnold, T. C. (2001) Rethinking Moral Economy. *American Political Science Review* 95: 85–95.

Bates, R. H. & Curry, A. F. (1992) Community versus Market: A Note on Corporate Villages. *American Political Science Review* 86: 457–63.

Booth, W. J. (1994) On the Idea of the Moral Economy. *American Political Science Review* 88 (3): 653–67.

Granovetter, M. (1985) Economic Action and Social Structure: The Problem of Embeddedness. *American Journal of Sociology* 91: 481–500.

Polanyi, K. (1957 [1944]) *The Great Transformation: The Political and Economic Origins of Our Time.* Beacon Press, Boston.

Scott, J. C. (1976) *The Moral Economy of the Peasant: Rebellion and Subsistence in Southeast Asia.* Yale University Press, New Haven.

Scott, J. C. (1985) *Weapons of the Weak: Everyday Forms of Peasant Resistance.* Yale University Press, New Haven.

Thompson, E. P. (1971) The Moral Economy of the English Crowd in the Eighteenth Century. *Past and Present: A Journal of Historical Studies* 50: 79–136.

moral entrepreneur

Mary de Young

A moral entrepreneur is an individual, group, or formal organization that takes on the responsibility of persuading society to develop or to enforce rules that are consistent with its own ardently held moral beliefs. Moral entrepreneurs may act as rule creators by crusading for the passage of rules, laws, and policies against behaviors they find abhorrent, or as rule enforcers by administering and implementing them. Although these are different and distinct roles, the effect of moral entrepreneurship, according to Howard Becker who coined the term, is the formation of a new class of outsiders whose behavior now violates these newly minted regulations and therefore is subject to the opprobrious label of "deviant."

In *Outsiders: Studies in the Sociology of Deviance* (1963), Becker elaborates on the concept of moral entrepreneurs through a case study of US marijuana laws. He identifies the Federal Bureau of Narcotics as the rule creator that mobilized its considerable resources to initiate an unrelenting moral crusade against marijuana use. Using rhetoric that resonated with hegemonic moral standards, the Bureau saturated the news media and popular culture with horror stories about the moral and social threats posed by those who violated these imperatives by smoking marijuana. As a rule creator, the Bureau provided the enterprise that culminated in the passage of the 1937 Marijuana Tax Act, a new bill that created a new class of outsiders – marijuana users.

Rules, however, must be enforced. This obligation provides another, albeit different, opportunity for moral entrepreneurship. Becker presents the police as the quintessential example of rule enforcers. More objective and detached than the morally fervent rule creators, the police are armed with a great deal of discretion. They may or may not enforce a rule, depending on institutional priorities for doing so, the deference shown by the rule violators, and the insinuation of "the fix," that is, the political and social connections and savvy of the rule violators, into the encounter. The influence of these variables illustrates Becker's contention that rule enforcement is always socially structured.

Although Becker cautions against the simple dismissal of rule creators as "meddling busybodies," if only because history reveals that many moral crusades, as exemplified by Abolition and Prohibition, are humanitarian in intent and consequence, he describes them as self-righteous ideologues who often are quite willing to use whatever means possible to accomplish their stated mission. Rule enforcers, in contrast, are carrying out professional roles and are motivated to do the job well not so much by moral passion as by the institutionally created needs to win the respect of those they deal with and, more importantly, to justify their rule-enforcing jobs.

Each of these needs creates a conundrum. Rule enforcers' sense of security and of efficacy is, in part, dependent upon the respect of others, therefore a good deal of their professional activity is devoted to coercing that respect from those they tend to view with pessimism and even acrimony. If those alleged rule breakers respond with deference, if not respect, rule enforcers may exercise their discretion and drop the matter entirely; if not, they may use their power to label the alleged rule breakers as deviant. In exercising that choice, rule enforcers are subject to criticism by those in positions of authority and by the rule creators whose dogmatic expectation is that rules will be enforced without exception. A conundrum also is created by the rule enforcers' need to justify their positions. They must successfully convince the larger society that the evil and threatening behavior of rule violators is an exigent problem, while at the same time they must assure the larger society that the enterprise of rule enforcement is actually successful. The failure to skillfully negotiate these conflicting demands may put them at odds with authorities or with the larger society and, once again, with the rule creators whose righteous wrath may fuel yet another moral crusade to create even more or better rules.

Becker's concept of moral entrepreneurs is predicated upon the premise that deviance is inherent neither to a particular behavior nor to a particular rule breaker, but that it is nothing more than a label successfully applied by more powerful moral entrepreneurs to rule violators. This theory of deviance resonated with the American sociological imagination of the early 1960s. Becker's labeling theory, or interactionist theory as he preferred to term it, provided an alternative to the functionalist paradigm that had predominated since the turn of the century. By setting aside the functionalist tenet that deviance is a functional requisite of civil and moral society because it defines moral boundaries and strengthens social solidarity, interactionist theory could focus on how deviance is signified by the claims and activities of moral entrepreneurs as rule creators, why, and with what consequences. By rejecting the functionalist assertion that what constitutes deviance is consensually agreed upon, it could concentrate on the political enterprise of moral entrepreneurs as rule enforcers in deciding what rules are to be enforced, why, and with what consequences.

By theoretically positioning moral entrepreneurs as the initiators and executors of the enterprise of labeling deviants, and as the orchestrators of the social reaction to them, Becker vested interactionist theory with a specificity absent from the theories of his intellectual forebears. In doing so, he inspired generations of sociologists to examine the role of moral entrepreneurs as rule creators in both historical and contemporary international contexts. Among those falling under sociological scrutiny are individuals such as the nineteenth-century American anti-vice campaigner Anthony Comstock and British MP David Alton who spearheaded the campaign against "video nasties" a

century later; organized pressure groups like People for the Ethical Treatment of Animals, the Club to Protect Children from Comic Books in Japan, the Snowdrop Petition that crusaded for gun control laws in the wake of the massacre of schoolchildren in Dunblane, Scotland, and anti-globalization groups around the world; and bureaucratic agencies such as the nineteenth-century Societies for the Prevention of Cruelty to Children, the Legion of Decency that for three decades campaigned against morally objectionable films, the internationally organized Coalition Against Trafficking in Women, and the mass media.

Moral entrepreneurs as rule enforcers also came under sociological scrutiny. Becker's interactionist theory resonated well with the sociopolitical milieu of the early 1960s and its liberal critique of agencies of social control. With its thesis that rules and their enforcement are relative, persons already marginalized as outsiders – the poor, the powerless, the disenfranchised – increasingly were treated by sociologists as romantic, if not heroic, victims of rule enforcers. Thus, agencies of social control like the police and the courts, as well as professions that have a stake in social control, such as social workers, medical doctors, and psychologists, also became the subjects of critical sociological analysis.

In the years following the publication of *Outsiders*, the concept of moral entrepreneurs achieved an iconic status that has outlived the popularity of the interactionist or labeling theory of deviance to which it is central. The concept was not only exemplified in case studies, but also used to account for the claims and activities that generated the social construction of such diverse social problems as road rage, the HIV/AIDS epidemic, and "crack babies," and fueled such social movements as the anti-nuclear movement in the United States and the boycott movement in South Africa. Yet, despite its contribution to sociological analysis, only a few refinements of the concept, let alone criticisms of it, have been ventured.

Jenkins (1992), as an example, extends the concept of moral entrepreneurs beyond the traditional examples of it. He identifies a loosely organized coalition of feminists, sexual abuse survivors, fundamentalist Christians, social workers, and conservative politicians who fomented a moral crusade against satanic ritual abuse in Great Britain. This spin on moral entrepreneurs provides an entrée for the analysis of how such "strange bedfellows" come together in the first place, stay together, and act together to create and enforce the rules that label outsiders. In a multimediated, globally connected world, this notion of moral entrepreneur coalition building among grassroots, special interest, professional, and elite representatives remains a subject for further sociological analysis. O'Sullivan (1994), as another example, refines the concept. He criticizes Becker for underestimating the structural limitations on the power of most moral entrepreneurs to create and enforce rules. By contextualizing moral entrepreneurship within an arena of "local morality," or limited social power, he reveals the theoretical necessity for another role of moral entrepreneurs – that of rule interpreters. This role describes professionals, such as judges, who are obligated to evaluate rules of evidence, procedure, and testimony before passing judgment and officially labeling a rule breaker as deviant. Since this role also is played in settings other than the legal arena that O'Sullivan describes, the moral entrepreneur as rule interpreter emerges as a subject for further sociological analysis.

The strongest challenges to the concept of moral entrepreneurs are embedded in critiques of Becker's case study of the Marijuana Tax Act. Galliher and Walker (1978), for example, conclude that Becker's focus on the role of moral entrepreneurs as rule creators and enforcers so resounded with the zeitgeist of the early 1960s that it created a synthetic history of the Act. Their review of newspaper articles and the Congressional Record found no evidence of the moral crusade that Becker alleges was orchestrated by the Federal Bureau of Narcotics. They conclude that the Bureau envisaged the Act not in moral terms at all, but as a means, more symbolic than real, of tightening social control of the economic and racial minorities who already were designated as outsiders. The Bureau, in their assessment, played an insignificant role, if any, in the creation of outsiders, or in the enterprise of labeling them as such.

The interactionist or labeling theory, to which the concept of moral entrepreneurs is central, has been the subject of criticism over

the last several decades and has lost much of its cachet. As it is, the concept has fallen prey to appropriation by the mass media that tend to use it as a sobriquet for virtually any person, group, or organization that makes any kind of moral claim, as well as by the corporate world to describe the captains of industry who fund initiatives to solve the world's social problems, and by political analysts to describe the moral agendas of world leaders. Without a distinct tie to the interactionist or labeling theory of deviance, however, these appropriated descriptions are devoid of sociological meaning.

Over recent years, however, the concept of moral entrepreneurs is being reclaimed by sociologists who are turning a critical eye to moral panics and, in doing so, are restoring the term's sociological relevance. While there are critical differences between the concept of moral *crusades*, such as the Federal Bureau of Narcotic's campaign against marijuana use that Becker describes, and moral *panics*, such as the American drug panic of the 1980s that Goode and Ben-Yehuda (1994) describe, moral entrepreneurs play a central role in each. Whether as representatives of grassroots, professional, or elite interests or whether as initiators, organizers, propagandists, ideologues, or enforcers, moral entrepreneurs endeavor to influence the content and the enforcement of rules. Some of their moral crusades will fail to achieve their mission, but those that do succeed will designate those who will become society's "outsiders."

SEE ALSO: Deviance; Deviance, Moral Boundaries and; Labeling Theory; Moral Panics; Social Control

REFERENCES AND SUGGESTED READINGS

Becker, H. S. (1963) *Outsiders: Studies in the Sociology of Deviance*. Free Press, New York.
Galliher, J. F. & Walker, A. (1978) The Politics of Systematic Research Error: The Case of the Federal Bureau of Narcotics as a Moral Entrepreneur. *Crime and Social Justice* 10: 29–33.
Goode, E. & Ben-Yehuda, M. (1994) *Moral Panics*. Blackwell, Oxford.
Jenkins, P. (1992) *Intimate Enemies: Moral Panics in Contemporary Great Britain*. Aldine de Gruyter, Hawthorne, NY.

McCrea, F. B. & Markle, G. E. (1989) *Minutes to Midnight*. Sage, Newbury Park, CA.

McGarry, M. (2000) Spectral Sexualities: 19th-Century Spiritualism, Moral Panics, and the Making of US Obscenity Laws. *Journal of Women's History* 12: 8–29.

Ortiz, A. T. & Briggs, L. (2003) The Culture of Poverty, Crack Babies, and Welfare Cheats: The Making of the "Healthy White Baby Crisis." *Social Text* 21: 39–57.

O' Sullivan, R. G. (1994) Moral Entrepreneurs, Local Morality, and Labeling Processes. *Free Inquiry in Creative Sociology* 22: 73–7.

moral panics

David G. Bromley

Moral panic is an analytic concept that refers to a distinctive type of social deviance characterized by a heightened sense of threat in some segment of the population, sudden in emergence and subsidence, attribution of the troubled condition to a "folk devil," and a disproportionate response relative to an objectively assessed threat level. The concept is particularly useful in focusing analytic attention on the socially constructed nature of deviance through the interaction of claimsmakers, folk devils, and audiences.

The term moral panic was initially coined by Jock Young in an essay in Stanley Cohen's *Images of Deviance* (1971) and subsequently developed theoretically and applied empirically in Cohen's *Folk Devils and Moral Panics* (1972). Cohen studied two British youth movements of the 1960s, the Mods and Rockers, whose feuding in 1964 triggered what he analyzed as a moral panic. According to Cohen, the episode he studied was not unique; indeed, he proposed that societies are likely to experience moral panics periodically through their histories. He defined a moral panic as a group or condition that is a response to a threat to established values or interests. The group or condition is analyzed and diagnosed by various spokespersons and experts who make moral pronouncements and becomes the focus of sensationalized media coverage. Societal responses may lead either to a subsidence or exacerbation of the situation.

Cohen identified the central actors that conveyed and expressed the moral panic as the media (which dispensed hyperbolic, stereotypical coverage), the public (which had to possess some level of concern that served as the foundation for the episode), law enforcement agencies (which broadened and intensified concerns as well as justified new methods of control and punitive counter-measures), political officials (who symbolically aligned themselves against the condition or group at issue), and action groups (which coordinated the response to the problematic condition or group). In addition, he asserted that moral panics are characterized by the creation of "folk devils" (individuals or groups who personify evil by engaging in harmful behavior that must be halted) and a disaster orientation (in which warnings of impending catastrophe, rumors and speculations, and coping responses resemble behavior in natural disaster situations).

The most systematic theoretical formulation of the moral panics concept was developed by Goode and Ben-Yehuda (1994). As they conceptualize the dynamics of moral panics, there is popular but exaggerated concern about a perceived threat; remedial action is undertaken but popular interest ultimately declines and turns to other issues. In their view, moral panic constitutes a significant, distinctive category of sociological analysis because it combines elements of deviance, social problems, collective behavior, and social movements, but is analytically distinguishable from each of these important analytic concepts. For example, while moral panics involve the social construction of deviance and social problems, neither of the latter concepts necessarily entails public concern that does not correspond to a demonstrable level of objective threat or the creation of folk devils. Similarly, moral panics share certain features with collective behavior. They involve rumor-mongering that generates fears and an exaggerated sense of threat. They also involve certain features of natural disasters: an impact phase, damage assessment, survivor rescue, remedy proposals, and a recovery period. However, in disasters, causal agents and their consequences are usually more clearly defined, phases are more sharply demarcated, and folk devils may not be created.

Goode and Ben-Yehuda enumerate a number of indicators of the existence of a moral panic episode: (1) heightened concern (which may or may not overlap with fear) about the conduct of a group or category, as indicated by public opinion polls, media reports, social movement activity, or legislative proposals; (2) an increased degree of hostility toward the group or category resulting from a threat to the values or interests of a substantial segment of the society; (3) a consensus (agreement among a substantial segment of the population) that the threat is significant and attributable to the group or category; (4) disproportionality – an assessment that the number of individuals engaged in the behavior and the threat posed by the behavior are far greater than an independent, empirical evaluation would conclude; and (5) volatility – a pattern of sudden eruption followed by quiescence, even if the issue becomes institutionalized through legislation, control mechanisms, or social movement organization. Disproportionality is a key dimension of moral panics in the Goode and Ben-Yehuda formulation. Indices of disproportionality include fabrication of evidence on the issue, inflation of indices of the issue, and public attention to the condition that appreciably exceeds attention paid to conditions that pose a comparable hazard or during previous times when the hazard was no greater.

A variety of theoretical explanations and approaches have been offered for interpreting moral panics. Hall et al. (1978) proceed from a Marxist perspective, treating the moral panics over mugging in England as the product of crises in the historical development of capitalism. In their formulation, the targets of moral panics are constructed to serve the interests of the ruling elite and deflect attention away from a crisis in the capitalist system. The ruling elite orchestrates moral panic episodes with support from the media and social control agencies. In the case of mugging, they argue, the law-and-order campaign against street crime was designed to deflect attention away from the real problem of the day – declining corporate profitability and growing economic recession. The exercise of repressive power by the state against street crime thus served to buttress the position of the ruling elite during a historical moment of vulnerability.

Jenkins (1998) traces the social construction of child molestation over the last century. During this period there have been ebbs and flows in perceived child endangerment and shifts in the perceived sources of that threat. By contrast with Hall et al.'s Marxist explanation for moral panics, Jenkins explains the occurrence of the moral panic over child molestation by linking structural changes in the social order with the activities of a constellation of interest groups. For example, in the two decades beginning in the late 1950s child endangerment concerns increased. Jenkins explains this shift by delineating a number of socio-demographic changes in contemporary America and Britain (e.g., age distribution of the population, percent of women in the labor force, percent of young children in daycare) and connecting them to a set of interest groups (therapists, child welfare agencies, law enforcement agencies, mass media organizations) that both shaped and responded to those changes.

Goode and Ben-Yehuda also focus on the structural source of moral panic episodes by offering three alternative explanatory models for moral panics: grassroots, elite-engineered, and interest group. They eliminate the elite model as useful for interpreting most moral panic episodes and propose a combination of the grassroots and interest-group models. They conclude that active or latent stress at the grassroots level is a prerequisite for moral panics that provides the "raw material" for an episode. However, the way that stress or fear is directed is shaped by organizational activists who provide the focus and direction for moral panics. They illustrate this model using the cases of the Renaissance with craze, the American drug panic of the 1980s, and the 1982 drug panic in Israel to demonstrate the applicability of moral panics analysis across time and cultures.

Theorizing from a social constructionist perspective, the concept of moral panic offers a useful critique of naturalistic theories that presume a correspondence between problematic social conditions and the social control response. The emphasis on sudden emergence and decline without apparent changes in the environment, and attribution of troubling conditions to folk devils, invites a constructionist perspective.

Further, an analysis that focuses on the structural conditions that foster claimsmaking, the social processes through which claims achieve plausibility, and the success or failure of attempts to demonize certain individuals or groups sets the stage for an analysis that hinges on the location, resources, and interaction of claimsmakers, folk devils, and audiences. The concept of moral panics has been profitably applied to a number of episodes over the last several decades involving controversy over issues such as illicit drug use, the existence of religious and satanic cults, the vulnerability of young children, predatory crime, troublesome youth, and sexual exploitation and deviance.

As with many sociological concepts and theories, there is continuing debate over the conceptualization, measurement, and utility of moral panic. The most fundamental debate is whether moral panic constitutes a discrete, meaningful category of sociological analysis. Critics assert that case studies often proceed with the objective of demonstrating that the episode under study conforms to the moral panics profile rather than problematizing those relationships. Put simply, the problem is asserted to be presuming what should be empirically demonstrated. In the case of the characteristic of broad consensus on a high degree of threat, critics observe that a variety of measures (public opinion, media coverage) may be employed without stipulated thresholds or evidence that these measures are related in a specific case. With respect to the pivotal concept of disproportionality, it is typically asserted without supporting evidence that third-party observers are more objective than involved parties and assumes that pre- and post-episode responses were proportional. Finally, while structural characteristics often are linked to the activation of interest groups in the emergence of moral panics, identifying decline is more problematic, particularly if structural characteristics remain unchanged. For example, decreased media coverage may or may not be indicative of a decline in concern; and since the impact of moral panics can vary considerably, it can be difficult to determine when a watershed point has been reached. Critics thus propose treating putative characteristics of moral panics as variables whose interrelationships should be determined empirically. These

various critiques suggest a number of theoretical and methodological issues that have yet to be resolved.

Such debates notwithstanding, there are some intriguing potential lines of exploration in moral panics analysis. One involves a sociology of knowledge investigation of the incorporation of the concept of moral panics into popular culture. As McRobbie and Thornton (1995) have observed, the succession of moral panics in recent decades has created a conscious awareness of the phenomenon and some understanding of its dynamics by both interest groups and control agencies. As a result, certain commercial interests and countercultural groups have strategically sought to precipitate moral panics in order to profit financially or promote group solidarity through the social reaction that is generated. At the same time, equally aware social control agents and media have developed a corresponding interest in discounting claims and discouraging strong reactions in episodes designated as moral panics as part of their organizational mandates. Obviously, the dynamics of moral panics emergence and development would be altered by such culturally savvy actors. It might also transpire that such manipulation would generate public cynicism about moral panics that would constrain their emergence and development. Should such developments occur, the dynamics of some moral panics, as well as the sociological analysis of them, may be transformed.

A second important issue that merits further exploration is the relative utility of consensus and conflict theoretical approaches for interpreting moral panics. A central idea in the analysis of moral panics is that at least some actors in the episode do not respond objectively or proportionately to the perceived threat. The nature of the response presumably could be the result of broadly based anxiety attendant to disruptive social change and/or manipulative tactics by interest or elite groups. Various mechanisms for creating a disproportionate response have been suggested, such as creating a mythic past that increases discontent and displacing tensions on to folk devils who serve as scapegoats. Since moral panics are such dramatic events, they offer a unique window on how public crises occur and hence a particularly productive social venue for assessing the role of consensus and conflict in the social construction of deviance.

SEE ALSO: Child Abuse; Deviance; Deviance, the Media and; Deviance, Moral Boundaries and; Moral Entrepreneur; Satanism; Sex Panics

REFERENCES AND SUGGESTED READINGS

Ben-Yehuda, N. (1990) *The Politics and Morality of Deviance: Moral Panics, Drug Abuse, and Reversed Stigmatization.* State University of New York Press, Albany.

Bromley, D. & Shupe, A. (1979) *Strange Gods: The Great American Cult Scare.* Beacon Press, Boston.

Cornwell, B. & Linders, A. (2002) The Myth of "Moral Panic": An Alternative Account of LSD Prohibition. *Deviant Behavior* 23: 307–30.

Goode, E. (1990) The American Drug Panic of the 1980s: Social Construction or Objective Threat? *International Journal of the Addictions* 25(9): 1083–98.

Goode, E. & Ben-Yehuda, N. (1994) *Moral Panics: The Social Construction of Deviance.* Blackwell, Oxford.

Hall, S. et al. (1978) *Policing the Crisis: Mugging, the State, and Law and Order.* Macmillan, London.

Jenkins, P. (1998) *Moral Panics: Changing Concepts of the Child Molester in Modern America.* Yale University Press, New Haven.

McRobbie, A. & Thornton, S. (1995) Rethinking "Moral Panic" for Multi-Mediated Social Worlds. *British Journal of Sociology* 46(4): 559–74.

Reinarman, C. & Levine, H. (1997) *Crack in America: Demon Drugs and Social Justice.* University of California Press, Berkeley.

Richardson, J., Best, J., & Bromley, D. (Eds.) (1991) *The Satanism Scare.* Aldine de Gruyter, New York.

moral shocks and self-recruitment

Mikaila Mariel Lemonik Arthur

Many analysts of social movements are interested in how it is that people come to participate in social movement activity. The decision to participate is not a simple one – social movement participants may face significant risks and personal costs, such as arrest or violence, if they become involved. In addition, individuals often perceive social movements as being able to obtain desired goals without their own personal action, a dilemma that has come to be known as the "free-rider" problem. Some popular explanations for individuals' decisions to join social movements have included biographical availability (McAdam 1986) and mobilization through preexisting social networks. However, there are individuals who participate in social movements without being connected to any existing networks or being in any significant way biographically available. The moral shocks perspective shows how these individuals, often ignored in research about participation in social movements, can recruit themselves into social movement activity due to their experience of a moral shock.

The term "moral shock" refers to the experience of a sudden and deeply emotional stimulus that causes an individual to come to terms with a reality that is quite opposed to the values and morals already held by that individual. Moral shocks can take a variety of forms. They often emerge as suddenly imposed grievances, but can also arise as a result of rhetorical appeals on the part of movement leaders or through shocking personal experiences (Jasper & Poulsen 1995). Some research on moral shocks and self-recruitment looks at the framing strategies that movement leaders use to create a sense of shock in potential recruits, in particular the use of extreme graphics in public or through direct-mail campaigns. Those moral shocks which are related to powerful and well-known symbols are most influential in generating self-recruitment on the part of potential social movement participants. Research using the moral shocks perspective has focused on social movements around environmental or nuclear hazards, abortion, animal rights, religious values, and other matters where individuals have strong personal and moral reactions to the issues at hand while not necessarily being part of networks which have a preexisting commitment to these issues.

Once potential recruits have experienced a moral shock, they are galvanized to participate in social movement activity. The "self-recruitment" portion of the moral shocks and self-recruitment model then suggests that rather than waiting for an appropriate social movement organization to seek them out, potential recruits who have experienced a moral shock are likely to seek out social movement participation on their own. These individuals will search for a social movement organization that shares their personal, moral, and value-based commitments to the issue that they believe in, and they will then join without much prompting from the social movement organization. As noted above, social movement organizations can take advantage of the self-recruitment process by designing recruitment campaigns relying on moral shocks which cause individuals to believe that they are joining the social movement organization on their own out of a sense of moral duty.

Criticisms of the moral shock and self-recruitment model of mobilization have tended to be rooted in the hypothesis that the majority of social movement participants are recruited through preexisting social networks like friendship groups or church memberships, and that therefore even if moral shock sometimes drives potential social movement participants to seek out and join social movement organizations, moral shocks are not very significant overall in explaining why people participate in social movements. In particular, those who study recruitment to high-risk activism highlight the necessity of networks to fulfill the function of convincing people to participate (McAdam 1986), since merely coming to care deeply about an issue will not make an individual willing to take significant risks of arrest or physical harm in pursuit of social movement goals.

One of the most well-known works that uses the moral shocks and self-recruitment perspective to explain why people join social movements is Kristen Luker's *Abortion and the Politics of Motherhood* (1984). Luker explains how women who had never previously been active in social movements or in any kind of politics became mobilized as part of the anti-abortion movement because of a variety of moral shocks. In particular, Luker outlines two main varieties of moral shocks that these potential recruits experienced: those surrounding their own reproductive decisions or options and those concerning the ways in which they first heard about the *Roe* v. *Wade* court decision.

SEE ALSO: Emotions and Social Movements; Framing and Social Movements; Mobilization; Moral Panics; Pro-Choice and Pro-Life Movements; Social Movements; Social Movements, Biographical Consequences of; Social Movements, Recruitment to; Values

REFERENCES AND SUGGESTED READINGS

Jasper, J. M. (1999) *The Art of Moral Protest: Cultural Dimensions of Social Movements*. University of Chicago Press, Chicago.
Jasper, J. M. & Poulsen, J. D. (1995) Recruiting Strangers and Friends: Moral Shocks and Social Networks in Animal Rights and Anti-Nuclear Protests. *Social Problems* 42(4): 493–512.
Luker, K. (1984) *Abortion and the Politics of Motherhood*. University of California Press, Berkeley.
McAdam, D. (1986) Recruitment to High-Risk Activism: The Case of Freedom Summer. *American Journal of Sociology* 92: 64–90.
Piven, F. F. & Cloward, R. A. (1992) Normalizing Collective Protest. In: Morris, A. D. & Mueller, C. M. (Eds.), *Frontiers in Social Movement Theory*. Free Press, New York.

moralpolitik (Confucian)

SangJun Kim

Moralpolitik means politics based on moral-ethical concerns. That politics and morals are closely related is a familiar idea. As Rousseau once stated, "those who want to treat politics and morals separately will never understand anything of either of them" (Rousseau 1980: 235). In this regard, *realpolitik*, which means politics excluding moral-ethical concerns, signifies a rather exceptional mode of politics, mainly applicable to a certain aspect of international politics, and is a residual concept of *moralpolitik*,

In *moralpolitik*, the relationship between morals and politics is double-faceted: morals and politics are collaboratively intertwined on the one hand, and in antagonistic tension on the other. This double-faceted relationship originates from the worldview of ethical religions.

From the viewpoint of ethical religions, the world has a double meaning: one sinful (morally wrong), the other blessed (God-made). Moral discontent with the world marks the ethical character of "ethical religions" in the Weberian sense. This moral discontent causes the sharp tension between religious morals and worldly politics. The sharp tension between morals and politics leads to moral interventions in politics. These interventions constitute *moralpolitik*.

In the premodern era, *moralpolitik* took the form of religious politics, in which religious moral commands and politics were indivisibly fused. To take some prominent historical examples: the papal-ecclesiastical politics of medieval Europe, the sage politics of Confucianism, the *purohita* politics of Hinduism, the *sangha-cakravatin* politics of Buddhism, and the *imam-ulamma* politics of Islam. These all took the form of theocracy, in which the sacred encompasses the secular.

In modern times, the relationship between the sacred and the secular is reversed: now, the secular encompasses the sacred (Kim 2003; see Fig. 1). The well-known "secularization thesis" points to this relationship. The thesis, however, contains some flaws, because it has been often misunderstood as the claim that the sacred has withered away in the modern era. The sacred, however, has not withered away in modern times; it has become internalized. The internalization of the sacred is the core of the secular encompassment of the sacred. Internalized sacredness, or, in other words, individualized sacredness, cannot any longer be theocratic in modernity. Modern *moralpolitik* stands on the moral base of internalized, individualized sacredness. In premodern *moralpolitik*, religious commands and their representative church

dominated over politics. In modern *moralpolitik*, alized reflection mediates moral values and politics.

In the premodern era, the priests of ethical religions, armed with moral discontent about the world, made themselves the practitioners of *moralpolitik*. Thus premodern *moralpolitik* was also a priestly politics. However, by making themselves the politicians of the world, the priests of premodern *moralpolitik* were criticized on moral grounds by the theologically more radical wings, usually classified as heterodoxies in the history of religions. These challengers usually made themselves into another, usually more fanatic, brand of priestly politicians.

The Reformation in sixteenth- and seventeenth-century Europe is the most famous and dramatic example of this. Protestants challenged Catholic *moralpolitik*, criticizing Catholic priests' involvement in worldly political affairs. Protestants themselves, however, became deeply and even fanatically involved in political affairs, including wars. The "politics of the saints" of Calvinism represents one of the most fanatic forms of theocracy in human history. Historians have called the warring period of Reformation and Counter-Reformation "the early modern era." This early modern era was the time when religious fanaticism or "religious tyranny" rose at an unprecedented rate and intensity (Weber 1958).

Here originates the modern worry about extreme forms of *moralpolitik*. Immanuel Kant, who is one of the most important conceivers of the concept of modern *moralpolitik*, was well aware of this danger, and attempted to distinguish between the "moral politician" and "despotic moralists." The former, according to Kant, is "someone who conceives of the principles of political expediency in such a way that they can co-exist with morality"; the latter, on the other hand, are "those who err in practice, frequently act contrary to political prudence by adopting or recommending premature measures" (Kant 1991: 118, 119). For Kant, both types could be *moralpolitik*, but only the former is desirable. One must note, however, that for Kant the worst type of *moralpolitik* is that of the "political moralist" who "fashions his morality to suit his own advantage as a statesman."

It is ironic that modernity, the process of the "internalization of the sacred," was conceived

Premodern   Modern

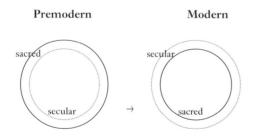

Figure 1 The changing relationship (reversion of encompassment) of the sacred and the secular.

during the rampant wars of religious fanaticisms and intolerance when priestly *moralpolitik* he terrible experience of fanaticism and religious wars, the sacred moved inward. Through theological or philosophical reflections and also through political compromises for survival, the idea of religious individualism and the value of religious tolerance grew. Modern liberal ideas and the modern way of life grew out of religious individualism and religious tolerance. In sum, the unprecedented fanaticism of *moralpolitik* conceived and introduced modernity.

The general pattern of *moralpolitik* can be summed up as follows: the distinction of moral and political values; institutionalization of religious politics that attempts to realize religious moral principles in politics; the consequential tensions between religious-moral authorities and mundane powers; the conflict between the two distinctive powers which eventually conceives and introduces modernity. This is also the case with Confucian *moralpolitik*.

According to Kim (2000, 2002), in the Confucian political history (of Korea and China), there existed double powers: one royal-military, the other quasi-priestly. In Confucian terms, the former is the royal-dynastic lineage (*jeongtong* in Korean, *zhengtong* in Chinese), the latter the lineage of the Confucian Way (*dotong, daotong*). The power of the former was based on worldly dominance of the ruler, the latter on meticulous practice of Confucian moral principles.

Confucian doctrines were established by Confucian founders who engaged in moral struggle against the hegemony of the warlords of the pre-Qin era. The prime founder of Confucian doctrine, Confucius, strove to persuade warlords of his time to stop waging wars and instead to govern their people in accordance with moral principles of humaneness, benevolence, compassion, and harmony. Later Confucians put Confucius at the head of the Confucian lineage, calling him "the king without the throne" (*sowang, suwang*). "The king without the throne" symbolized the moral and thus sacred kingship of Confucianism. "The king within the throne" could be legitimized only if he obeyed the moral teachings of "the king without," Confucius and his disciples. Some prominent disciples of Confucius, like Mencius, earned the title of Confucian sage and were

deemed qualified to continue the sacred Confucian Way originated by Confucius.

The contrast between the material interests of the worldly rulers and the ideal interests of Confucian moralists produced sharp tension between the two. Nevertheless, this tension did not exclude the occasional cooptation of each other: the rulers' need for moral justification of the throne and the Confucians' need to expand their worldly influence frequently met. Therefore, the royal-dynastic and Confucian sacred lineages were partly in tension and partly in collaboration, as were religious authorities and worldly power in the civilizations where ethical religions prevailed.

Confucians invented sage politics and consistently attempted to check the worldly power of the throne. Their weapons were Confucian morals and manners. In the famous opening chapter of *Mencius*, Mencius criticizes King Hui of Liang for pursuing "profits" instead of "benevolence" and "rightness." In this argument, "profits" represent military, economic, and logistic empowerment, while "benevolence" and "rightness" indicate moral principles according to which peaceful harmony of a state (and the world as well) is to be achieved. These two principles of action – one military, economic, and logistic; the other moral – were in sharp tension in Confucian doctrine. Confucian manners or rituals (*ye, li*) were means through which Confucian moral principles were realized and practiced.

Confucians believed that the ruler's pursuit of "profits" instead of moral principles would eventually result in continual usurpations of the throne by those seeking power. Historically, these usurpations were frequently accompanied by regicide and patricide – according to Confucianism, the most terrible signs of moral degradation. Confucians believed that only moral codes consolidating family values (or kinship orders) could prevent such moral failures. Therefore, Confucian morals and manners upheld family values like deference to elders and the earlier generations. The unique fusion of political and familial moral codes in Confucianism was thus created.

The "Confucian sage" (*seongin, shengren*) was the Confucian paragon who perfected the moral demands of political-familial obligations in his person and fulfilled these obligations most meticulously in his daily actions. Confucian *moralpolitik* was thus Confucian sage politics carried out in public action. Moral remonstration and recurrent ritual disputes to correct the throne characterized Confucian *moralpolitik*. Confucians considered moral remonstration even to death as their sacred obligation, and they attempted to regulate their king through recurrent moral critiques and ritual disputes. Many Confucian martyrs sacrificed their lives in order to confront their rulers who went against Confucian moral doctrine. Confucian *moralpolitik* represents Confucian moral discontent with worldly power.

In the western image of Confucianism, the concept of Confucian *moralpolitik* described above does not exist. For example, Max Weber fails to find the existence of the double powers in the Confucian world and to acknowledge the tension between them. His failure to recognize the moral discontent with worldly power in Confucianism results in his well-known denial of the inner motivation and momentum toward modernity in Confucianism.

Confucian *moralpolitik* was on many occasions fanatic, waging moral wars not only against the ruler with moral defects but also against non-orthodox Confucians who were usually labeled as "heretics" or, more literally, "rebel enemies against our doctrine" (*samunnanjeok, siwenluanzei*). The fanatic Confucian *moralpolitik* in late Ming China (sixteenth to seventeenth centuries) and late Joseon Korea (seventeenth to eighteenth centuries) in particular opened the door to "Confucian modernity" in both societies (Kim 2003). The specific historical paths through which Confucian modernity has unfolded cannot be the same as those of the West. Rather, it is more commonsensical to suppose that the paths of different civilizations toward modernity must have been different from each other.

SEE ALSO: Confucianism; Moral Economy; Religion; Secularization

REFERENCES AND SUGGESTED READINGS

Kant, I. (1991) *Kant: Political Writings*. Ed. H. Reiss. Cambridge University Press, Cambridge.

Kim, S. (2000) Inventing Moralpolitik: A Sociological Interpretation of Confucian Ideology, Ritual, and Politics. PhD dissertation, Columbia University.

Kim, S. (2002) The Genealogy of Confucian Moralpolitik and Its Implications for Modern Civil Society. In: Armstrong, C. (Ed.), *Korean Society: Civil Society, Democracy, and the State*. Routledge, New York and London.

Kim, S. (2003) Interpreting Confucian Modernity in Late Joseon Korea. *Daedong Munhwa Yeongu* 42: 59–91.

Rousseau, J.-J. (1980) *Emile*. Ed. A. Bloom. University of Chicago Press, Chicago.

Weber, M. (1958) *The Protestant Ethic and the Spirit of Capitalism*. Scribner, New York.

mortality: transitions and measures

Irma T. Elo

In the course of human history, life expectancy at birth has increased from around 20–30 years during prehistoric times to 75–80 years in many low-mortality countries today. Nearly half of this decline has taken place during the twentieth century. In the middle of the 1500s, at the start of the first available continuous series of national mortality estimates, life expectancy in England was still in the mid-30s and showed little sustained improvement until the nineteenth century. By the end of the 1800s, however, steady mortality decline had begun in all European countries for which reliable data series are available, and by the end of the twentieth century, life expectancy had reached the mid- to upper 70s in many industrialized countries. Although national-level mortality data did not become available for the United States until 1933, existing evidence suggests that mortality decline in the US was similar to that in England. The highest life expectancy has been recorded in Japan, a developed country where health improvements in the early part of the twentieth century lagged behind those of European countries, but where mortality declines have been particularly impressive since the

1950s. Life expectancy at birth in Japan reached 84.6 years for women and 77.6 years for men by the year 2000. Moreover, the United Nations' estimates show an average life expectancy of 74.8 years in the more developed regions of the world, with 56 percent of industrialized countries having life expectancies of over 75 years in 1995–2000 (Table 1). The lowest life expectancies in industrialized countries are found in Eastern Europe and the former Soviet Union, where health conditions stagnated during the late twentieth century, particularly for adult men.

Historical mortality estimates for developing countries are scarce. The few estimates that do exist show life expectancies in the early twentieth century to be similar to those estimated for prehistoric populations – 24 years in India in 1901–11, 24 years in China around 1930, 27.9 years in Taiwan in 1920, and 30.6 years in Chile in 1909. By the middle of the twentieth century, however, life expectancy in the less developed regions of the world had reached 40.9 years and it had further increased to 62.5 years by the end of the century according to the United Nations' estimates. These gains are impressive and suggest that life expectancy more than doubled between 1900 and 2000 in most parts of the developing world. As a result, the gap in average life expectancy between more and less developed regions has narrowed over time – from about 26 years in 1950–5 to about 11 years in 1995–2000.

The mortality decline in developing countries, however, has not been uniform, and the slower pace of improvement in the least developed regions relative to others has led to a greater disparity among developing countries over time. This inequality is clearly evident in Table 1, which displays United Nations' estimates of life expectancies at birth and the distribution of countries by life expectancy for major regions of the world in 1995–2000. These estimates show an average life expectancy of only about 50 years in Africa, with only 21 percent of African countries having estimated life expectancies of 60 years or more. In contrast, the average life expectancy was estimated to be around 69 years in Latin America, with 64 percent of Latin American countries having life expectancies of 70 years or more (Table 1).

EPIDEMIOLOGIC TRANSITION

The epidemiologic transition, a shift from infectious diseases to chronic degenerative diseases as leading causes of death, has been instrumental in shaping trends in human mortality and the age pattern of mortality decline. The fall in death rates from infectious diseases led to significant improvements in the survival chances of infants and young children and was largely responsible for the rise in life expectancy in the late nineteenth and early twentieth centuries in industrialized countries, and during the second half of the twentieth century in less developed regions of the world. These reductions in infant and child mortality, together with a decline in fertility, have contributed to a shift in the population age distribution toward an older population in both developed and developing countries. As a result, chronic degenerative diseases have become more common and today represent an ever-increasing percentage of all deaths even as adult mortality has continued to decline in most places. These transitions were already well under way in the middle of the twentieth century in industrialized countries and today well over 80 percent of all deaths in developed countries are due to chronic diseases. Future gains in life expectancy in industrialized nations will thus largely depend on trends in mortality from such leading chronic diseases as heart disease and cancer at older ages. Many observers are optimistic in this regard. Recent empirical evidence has revealed persistent declines in death rates at older ages in developed countries where reliable old-age mortality estimates are available.

The epidemiologic transition is not as far along in less developed regions where the pace of change has varied considerably. According to the Global Burden of Disease Study, in 1990 communicable diseases continued to make up about 50 percent of all deaths in India and close to 65 percent in Sub-Saharan Africa, where all five leading causes of death were communicable diseases. It has been further estimated that in 1990, 59 percent of the deaths in the poorest 20 percent of the countries in the world were due to infectious and parasitic diseases compared to only about 8 percent in the world's richest quintile. In contrast, non-communicable diseases accounted for over 70 percent of all deaths

Table 1 Expectation of life at birth and distribution of countries according to life expectancy at birth for the world and the major regions of the world, 1995–2000.

	Life expectancy at birth	Percentage of countries with life expectancy at birth of:				Number of countries
		>75 years	70–75 years	60–70 years	<60 years	
World	64.6	21	24	27	28	184
More developed regions	74.8	56	26	19	0	43
Less developed regions	62.5	10	24	30	36	141
Africa	50.0	2	2	17	79	53
Asia and Oceanic		12	33	40	14	57
Asia	65.7					
Oceania	73.2					
Latin America and the Caribbean	69.4	19	45	32	3	31

Source: United Nations 1998.

in China and around 55 percent of all deaths in the Caribbean and Latin America, with other developing regions falling somewhere in between the estimates discussed above. These differences are reflected in the estimates of life expectancy shown in Table 1 and in regional variation in infant and child mortality. In 1995–2000, 56 percent of the least developed countries in the world had child mortality rates in excess of 140 per 1,000, with 45 percent of all African countries falling into this category. In contrast, none of the Latin American countries experienced child mortality this high and in over half of Latin American countries child mortality was estimated to be less than 45 per 1,000 in 1995–2000.

In its original formulation, Abdel Omran's (1971) theory of the epidemiologic transition predicted a unidirectional movement from the predominance of infectious diseases to chronic degenerative diseases as leading causes of death with variation only in the pace and timing of the transition. Different explanatory models were proposed for western countries, Japan, and the developing world. In subsequent decades, however, it has become increasingly evident that infectious diseases continue to play an important role in mortality transitions, a fact that is most apparent in less developed regions although also manifest in industrialized countries where infectious diseases take their highest toll among disadvantaged population subgroups.

Many less developed countries have experienced an epidemiologic transition characterized by overlapping eras whereby chronic diseases of middle and older ages have become more common as populations have aged, at the time that childhood infectious diseases have continued to create a major health burden among the poor. The emergence of HIV/AIDS and drug-resistant varieties of tuberculosis and malaria is perhaps the best example of the continued impact of infectious diseases on mortality. HIV/AIDS has been responsible for increasing child and adult mortality in countries with high HIV prevalence and HIV/AIDS has become the most important public health concern in much of Sub-Saharan Africa. In its 2002 revision of the world population prospects, the United Nations estimated that in 2000–5 there would be nearly 15 million excess deaths in

Africa due to AIDS – 36 percent more deaths than in its absence. The impact of HIV/AIDS will be felt in less developed regions for some time to come and the course of the epidemic will depend on many factors including behavioral responses of individuals to the epidemic, public health measures to reduce transmission, and development of new medical technologies. In most developed countries, HIV/AIDS has had a less devastating, although not a trivial, impact on mortality. In the United States, for example, HIV/AIDS has emerged as one of the leading causes of death among African American men and women in young adulthood and HIV/AIDS contributed to the widening of the black–white difference in adult mortality in the 1980s.

EXPLANATIONS OF MORTALITY DECLINE

Many factors have influenced the mortality trends discussed above, including improvements in living standards, public health measures, cultural and behavioral factors, modern medical technologies, and the actions of governments and international agencies and organizations. Although there is general agreement that each factor has played some role, there is far less consensus about their relative importance. Thomas McKeown (1976) underscored improved nutrition due to a rise in standards of living as the key cause of mortality decline in England and Wales between 1848 and 1971. He dismissed alternative competing hypotheses such as the role of public health interventions and medical technologies. Although research on individual's height points to the importance of improved nutritional status as a factor in mortality decline, it is important to remember that nutritional status is determined not only by the amount of food consumed but also by the disease environment that in turn is shaped by public health and sanitary measures and personal hygiene practices. The contribution of these causes has been emphasized among others by Simon Szreter (1988), who has made an empathetic case for the importance of public health measures in the mortality decline in England, and by Samuel Preston and colleagues, who have pointed to the importance of public health and personal hygiene practices in the United States after the turn of the twentieth century as the germ theory of disease became widely accepted. Based on data from 43 countries, Preston (1976) further concluded that between the 1930s and the 1960s factors other than a country's current income level most likely were responsible for somewhere between 75 percent to 90 percent of the increase in life expectancy. He reached a broadly similar conclusion in subsequent analyses for a somewhat later period that incorporated calorie consumption and literacy level as independent explanatory variables, results that pointed to the importance of factors other than income and nutrition in mortality decline during the twentieth century (Preston 1980).

By the middle of the twentieth century, drugs to treat infectious diseases, such as sulfa drugs and penicillin, made further contributions to the decline of mortality from infectious diseases, and chronic diseases emerged as leading causes of death in developed countries. In subsequent decades, medical interventions for treatment of chronic diseases have played an increasingly important role in mortality reductions, particularly from heart disease. New drugs to dissolve blood clots and reduce high blood pressure and cholesterol, and surgical procedures such as heart bypass surgery and angioplasty, have been credited for saving thousands of lives from early death. In fact, much of the mortality reduction at older ages in the latter decades of the twentieth century was due to decline in death rates from cardiovascular diseases. In addition, behavioral changes, most importantly reductions in smoking, have contributed to mortality decline, especially among men.

Medical technologies played a more important role in the early phases of mortality transition in developing countries than was the case in developed countries, although other factors have also been important. For example, effectiveness of governmental interventions in the form of public health measures, such as the influential role of malaria control programs in mortality decline in Sri Lanka and Mauritius, has been well established. Others have emphasized the role of cultural, social, and behavioral factors, and public investments in

health and education, especially in female education, egalitarian social policies, and widespread access to health care services as being important for achievement of low mortality. That the right combination of the above characteristics can lead to low mortality even in relatively poor countries has been demonstrated by the experiences of China, Costa Rica, Sri Lanka, and the state of Kerala in India among others, where life expectancies are close to those of many industrialized countries. A challenge these countries now face is how to manage the growing burden of chronic diseases and the relatively high cost of medical measures to treat such diseases. At the same time, many poor countries continue to face a high burden of infectious diseases, including HIV/AIDS.

DATA AND MEASURES

Accurate assessment of the levels and trends in mortality is greatly hampered by the absence of good quality data for much of the world's population. Only industrialized countries and a few Latin American, Caribbean, and East Asian countries have vital registration systems that are complete enough for accurate mortality estimates. Sample registration systems for selected areas are also available for China and India, but for the rest of the world registration systems are wholly inadequate for estimating mortality. In the absence of vital registration data, demographers have developed methods to estimate mortality from alternative data sources, including surveys and censuses. For example, the World Fertility Surveys (WFS) and Demographic Health Surveys (DHS) have been used to produce infant and child mortality estimates for a large number of developing countries. In addition, indirect demographic estimation techniques can be used to estimate child mortality from questions included in many population censuses asking women about the number of children they have ever had and the number of those children who are still alive. The above data sources have enabled demographers to map levels and trends in child mortality in many countries lacking vital registration systems, although these estimates are not always available for the most recent past.

Adult mortality is more difficult to estimate accurately than child mortality in the absence of death registration. A number of indirect estimation techniques have, however, been developed that are useful in this regard. These methods utilize information obtained from surveys or censuses on survival of siblings and parents, or census questions about deaths in the household in some defined period prior to the census. In addition, two consecutive censuses have been used to infer mortality conditions between two census dates. In the absence of any data on adult deaths, mortality is estimated with the aid of model life tables that combine empirical estimates of child mortality with model-based estimates of adult mortality. Using a combination of the above techniques, both the United Nations population division and the World Bank publish mortality estimates for most countries in the world. Because of the considerable uncertainty in these estimates for countries with few data points, it is possible that the estimates prepared by the two agencies will differ.

Accurate estimates of cause-specific mortality are even more limited than estimates of overall mortality. Cause-specific estimates require both complete data on deaths and reliably recorded causes of death. In the absence of vital statistics data on causes of death, cause-specific mortality estimates have been obtained from sample registration systems in a small number of countries, population centers and surveillance sites, and epidemiologic studies of special populations. In addition, model-based estimates of cause-specific mortality have also been developed in which the cause of death structure is modeled as a function of overall level of mortality. The most ambitious effort ever undertaken to estimate cause-specific mortality worldwide using a combination of techniques is an effort to estimate the global burden of disease.

SEE ALSO: Biodemography; Demographic Data: Censuses, Registers, Surveys; Demographic Techniques: Gender, Health, and Mortality; Life-Table Methods; Demographic Techniques: Population Projections and Estimates; Demographic Transition Theory; Healthy Life Expectancy; HIV/AIDS and Population; Infant, Child, and Maternal Health and Mortality; Socioeconomic Status; Health and Mortality

REFERENCES AND SUGGESTED READINGS

Acsadi, G. & Nemeskeri, J. (1970) *History of Human Life Span and Mortality.* Akademiai Kiado, Budapest.

Bongaarts, J. (1996) Global Trends in AIDS Mortality. *Population and Development Review* 22(1): 21–45.

Caldwell, J. C. (1986) Routes to Low Mortality in Poor Countries. *Population and Development Review* 12: 171–220.

Heuveline, P., Guillot, M., & Gwatkin, D. R. (2003) The Uneven Tides of the Health Transition. *Social Science and Medicine* 55: 313–22.

Kannisto, V., Lauritsen, J., Thatcher, A. R., & Vaupel, J. W. (1994) Reduction in Mortality at Advanced Ages. *Population and Development Review* 20: 793–810.

McKeown, T. (1976) *The Modern Rise of Population.* Academic Press, New York.

Murray, C. J. L. & Lopez, A. D. (1996) *The Global Burden of Disease.* Harvard University Press, Cambridge, MA.

Omran, A. R. (1971) The Epidemiologic Transition: A Theory of the Epidemiology of Population Change. *Milbank Memorial Fund Quarterly* 49(4): 509–37.

Preston, S. H. (1976) *Mortality Patterns in National Populations.* Academic Press, New York.

Preston, S. H. (1980) Causes and Consequences of Mortality Declines in Less Developed Countries during the Twentieth Century. In: Easterlin, R. A. (Ed.), *Population and Economic Change in Developing Countries.* University of Chicago Press, Chicago, pp. 289–327.

Preston, S. H. (1995) Human Mortality throughout History and Prehistory. In: Simon, J. L. (Ed.), *The State of Humanity.* Blackwell, Cambridge, MA.

Preston, S. H. & Haines, M. R. (1995) *Fatal Years: Child Mortality in Late Nineteenth-Century America.* Princeton University Press, Princeton.

Schofield, R., Reher, D., & Bideau, A. (Eds.) (1991) *The Decline of Mortality in Europe.* Clarendon Press, Oxford.

Szreter, S. (1988) The Importance of Social Intervention in Britain's Mortality Decline ca. 1850–1914: A Reinterpretation of the Role of Public Health. *Social History of Medicine* 1: 1–38.

United Nations (1998) *World Population Prospects: The (1996) Revision.* United Nations, New York.

United Nations (1999) *Health and Mortality Issues of Global Concern.* United Nations, New York.

Vaupel, J. W., Carey, J. R., Christensen, K., Johnson, T. E., et al. (1998) Biodemographic Trajectories of Longevity. *Science* 280: 855–60.

Wrigley, E. A. & Schofield, R. S. (1981) *The Population History of England, 1541–1871.* Harvard University Press, Cambridge, MA.

Mosca, Gaetano (1858–1941)

Bernd Weiler

Along with Vilfredo Pareto (1848–1923) and Robert Michels (1876–1936), Gaetano Mosca is commonly regarded as the main representative of the so-called Italian School of Elitists. After graduating in law from the university of his hometown, Palermo, Mosca combined the life of a scholar, teaching constitutional law, administrative law, political economy, and political theory at the universities of Turin (1896–1923), Milan (1902–23), and Rome (1924–33), with a political career as editor of the proceedings of the Chamber of Deputies (1887–96), as deputy (1909–19), as Under-Secretary for the Colonies (1914–16), and, from 1919, as senator. In December 1925, the 67-year-old Mosca, who had been a staunch conservative, fierce critic of the parliamentary system, and moralistic pessimist throughout his life, delivered a famous speech to the Senate opposing the bill that was designed to strengthen the "prerogatives of the head of the government" and that actually granted dictatorial powers to Benito Mussolini. Shortly afterwards, Mosca retired from active politics to concentrate on his academic work.

Influenced by positivist philosophy, Mosca argued that the field of the social sciences was still in its infancy, irreducible to racial or environmental factors, and, like the natural sciences, in need of general principles which could be discovered by thorough and objective historical analysis. Imbued with the spirit of disillusioned, anti-romantic realism, Mosca discarded the idea of societal progress and the Kantian notion of "man's emergence from his self-imposed immaturity." Following Saint-Simon's and Comte's ideas concerning the role of the new scientific elite in modern society, Taine's interpretation of the French Revolution as the replacement of an old ruling class by a new one, and Gumplowicz's reflections upon the eternal conflict between social groups, Mosca forcefully argued that in every society an organized minority (*classe politica, minoranza organizzata*) ruled over an unorganized majority. The idea that power was always in the hands of the few, which implied a rejection of the classifications of the forms of government by Aristotle and Montesquieu, was based upon his belief that it was impossible for the masses to get organized, and upon his deep-seated conviction that some people always stood out from the masses because of their physical, material, intellectual, or even moral qualities. While the characteristics of its members changed, the ruling class remained. Furthermore, Mosca stated that the ruling class always sought to legitimate its power by appealing to an abstract principle or "political formula" (*formula politica*), held in high esteem in a particular historical situation, such as the popular or divine will, the ancient tradition of a king, and so on. Mosca first formulated his central ideas in the early work *Sulla teorica dei governi e sul governo parlamentare* (*On the Theory of Governments and the Parliamentary System*) (1884), published when he was 26. With some minor changes of emphasis he elaborated his theories in his best-known book, *Elementi di scienza politica* (*The Ruling Class*) (1896), which went through three editions during his lifetime. Far from being a detached observer, Mosca was quite explicit in his writings that the "good" ruling class should be composed of rational, cultured, and honest public servants who were committed to the common good, knew that all reform had to proceed slowly, and were aware of the faults of the masses.

Critics have pointed out that, compared with Michels's analysis of the oligarchical tendencies in society, Mosca's strict dichotomy of an organized minority versus an unorganized majority is simplistic, non-operationalizable, and too rigid when dealing with modern societies. Compared with Pareto's more general conception of the elite, on the other hand, Mosca's conception of the ruling class appears narrower, being more closely tied and applicable to the specific judicial and political sphere of late nineteenth-century

Italy (cf. Albertoni 1987: 109–13). This might at least partially explain why Mosca's work, a large part of which has not yet been translated, has not gained a larger audience in the English-speaking world.

SEE ALSO: Elites; Gumplowicz, Ludwig; Michels, Robert; Pareto, Vilfredo; Political Sociology

REFERENCES AND SUGGESTED READINGS

Albertoni, E. A. (Ed.) (1982) *Studies on the Political Thought of Gaetano Mosca: The Theory of the Ruling Class and its Development Abroad.* Giuffrè, Milan.

Albertoni, E. A. (1987) *Mosca and the Theory of Elitism.* Blackwell, Oxford.

Bobbio, N. (1972) *On Mosca and Pareto.* Librairie Droz, Geneva.

Delle Piane, M. (1949) *Bibliografia di Gaetano Mosca.* Circolo giuridico dell'Università, Siena.

Ghiringhelli, R. (Ed.) (1992) *Elitism and Democracy: Mosca, Pareto, and Michels.* Cisalpino, Milan.

Meisel, J. H. (Ed.) (1962 [1958]) *The Myth of the Ruling Class: Gaetano Mosca and the "Elite."* University of Michigan Press, Ann Arbor. [With the first English translation of the final version of "The Theory of the Ruling Class."]

Meisel, J. H. (Ed.) (1965) *Pareto and Mosca.* Prentice-Hall, Englewood Cliffs, NJ.

Mosca, G. (1939) *The Ruling Class (Elementi di scienza politica).* Trans. H. D. Kahn. Ed., rev. and with an Introduction by A. Livingston. McGraw-Hill, New York and London.

Sereno, R. (1938) The Anti-Aristotelianism of Gaetano Mosca and Its Fate. *Ethics* 58(4): 509–18.

Sola, G. (Ed.) (1982) *Scritti politici di Gaetano Mosca (The Political Writings of Gaetano Mosca)*, 2 vols. Utet, Turin.

motherhood

Susan Walzer

Motherhood is the word that sociologists tend to use to refer to the social expectations, experiences, and structures associated with being a mother. The use of the term motherhood differentiates the biological fact of producing a baby (becoming a mother) and the practices involved in taking care of children (mothering) from the public and cultural norms linked to the creation and care of children. Motherhood, in other words, is a social institution – one that contributes to the reproduction of gender differentiation and hierarchy in family and work.

Scholarship about motherhood shares the challenge of much sociology to represent a general social experience while at the same time acknowledging the diversity of social actors. Spanning disciplines beyond sociology, research about motherhood also exists outside of conventional academic contexts. One general body of work emphasizes social expectations for mothers and the processes through which mothers negotiate these norms. This literature tends to be more qualitative, interpretive, and directed at generating theoretical perspectives on mothering as a practice and motherhood as a social institution. Another body of work about mothers represents more positivistic attempts to document the determinants and effects of individual mothers' behavior through the use of surveys and other statistical methodologies (Arendell 2000).

The study of motherhood parallels and was shaped by changes in behavior and beliefs related to gender that emerged in the late 1960s and early 1970s. Increases during this time in the labor force participation of married women and mothers generated a vast amount of academic work – in part because the employment of mothers of very young children seemed to conflict with a particular image of mothers as always present and ultimately responsible for the well-being of their children. Some researchers tested empirically for negative effects of maternal employment. Others criticized the question, suggesting that the "stay-at-home" mother image associated with institutionalized motherhood was historically specific to the splitting of productive and reproductive labor that occurred during nineteenth-century industrialization.

The social construction of mothering as ideologically separate from material provision, most visible in the United States during the post-war 1950s, has been identified as anomalous across cultures, races, and classes (Bernard 1974). Paradoxically, the expectation of constant maternal presence to children remains a standard to which many mothers hold themselves, including scholars of motherhood. Some sociologists, such as Maushart (1999), write openly about being motivated to study motherhood by their own experiences of becoming mothers, their observations of contradictory expectations for mothers, and their identification with feminism as a conceptual framework with which to understand and change these experiences and expectations.

Theorists of motherhood treat its institutionalization as a social arrangement to explain, rather than as a biological given. Intensive social norms for mothers exceed biological necessity, Hays (1996) notes, and many mothers nurture children to whom they are not biologically linked. One of the approaches taken to explaining more sociologically why mothers mother the way that they do is the view, grounded in psychoanalytic theory, that mothering behavior is transmitted intergenerationally. In Chodorow's (1978) influential work on the "reproduction of mothering," she argues that daughters internalize their mothers' identities, which tend to include an overinvestment in motherhood as a primary source of self-esteem and accomplishment. Sons, on the other hand, develop their gender identities by disidentifying with their mothers, resulting, according to Chodorow, in a devaluing of the caretaking behavior that they associate with femaleness.

Another theoretical strand that surfaced in the 1980s suggests that maternal practice is not simply an outcome of gender hierarchy and women's disempowerment in a sexual division of labor, but represents an alternative to more self-centered and competitive approaches to social life. McMahon (1995) notes, for example, that women change as a result of becoming mothers in ways that produce in them a moral transformation. In this view, first argued by Ruddick (1983), the behaviors of mothers contain the potential to be morally redemptive of society. "Maternal thinking" develops in mothers' responses to children's needs, which, at their best, reflect a desire to preserve and foster life. Maternal thinking offers the possibility of increasing human caring and peace beyond the private relationships of mothers and children.

Along with the interactions they have with their children, other social influences affect how mothers think about their children's needs and arrange their lives as parents. Some sociology of motherhood examines dominant ideologies about appropriate maternal behavior as they are reinforced in expert advice literature, sustained in interactions between women and men, and internalized and owned by women as their identities. In these approaches, mothers are perceived as active agents in constructing motherhood, but they do so while encountering already existing prescriptions for mothers – perhaps most notably about whether and where labor force participation should fit into maternal identity.

Although some scholars suggest that employment is being integrated into dominant social conceptions of motherhood, others argue that mothers continue to be perceived as either more oriented to family or to work. Financial need is apparently the number one (though not only) impetus for maternal employment, yet what Garey (1999) refers to as an "opposition model" of motherhood and paid work is reflected in research that seeks to identify why mothers do or do not work. This question is not asked of fathers, and assumes that mothers are in a nuclear family context and generally have a choice about whether to earn money. More research is emerging, however, that looks at mothering from particular social locations, examining differences in ideology related to work as well as potentially negative outcomes, including poverty, of becoming a mother outside of marriage or in other ways that are not socially sanctioned (Arendell 2000).

Another twist on social definitions of motherhood appears in scholarship exploring implications of reproductive technology and situations in which maternity may be contested, such as when a surrogate mother does not want to give up custody of the baby to whom she has given birth. These types of circumstances resurface the question of how biology enters into definitions of motherhood, but with some new answers. While scholars in the 1970s dismissed biological arguments as justifications for maternal responsibility, some more recent work, such as Rothman's (1989), invokes the physical connection mothers have to babies as a way to empower them with decision-making power for the fetuses they grow. Hrdy (1999) draws on an evolutionary perspective to argue for the "naturalness" of women combining work and mothering.

There is a circular process to scholarship about motherhood – certain questions being asked, answered, and asked again about how motherhood is socially defined, the implications of its institutionalization for individual mothers and children, and its intersections and conflicts with other social institutions (Walzer 2004). Although some scholarly work about motherhood combines theoretical examination with empirical grounding, there remain gaps between what scholars think about motherhood and what they actually know through examination of mothers' experiences. Future research should seek to close these gaps – testing theoretical contentions emerging from qualitative studies with larger, diverse samples that in turn generate new theory-generating studies. Future researchers will also continue to struggle with the difficulty of recognizing mothers' diversity without positioning them as entirely the same or different by virtue of their social locations, relationship statuses, family arrangements, and life courses.

Finally, future scholarship about motherhood is likely to benefit from less exclusive attention to mothers and greater exploration of the relationships and institutions in which they live. Mothers enact mothering with other people: their children certainly, and often, other adult partners. We will increase our understanding of motherhood by studying these interactions as well as the complementary and constraining assumptions underlying other institutions that intersect with motherhood: fatherhood, work, marriage, heterosexuality, and gender.

SEE ALSO: Childhood; Fatherhood; Gender, Work, and Family; Marriage, Sex, and Childbirth; Role

REFERENCES AND SUGGESTED READINGS

Arendell, T. (2000) Conceiving and Investigating Motherhood: The Decade's Scholarship. *Journal of Marriage and the Family* 62: 1192–1207.

Bernard, J. (1974) *The Future of Motherhood*. Dial Press, New York.

Chodorow, N. (1978) *The Reproduction of Mothering: Psychoanalysis and the Sociology of Gender*. University of California Press, Berkeley.

Garey, A. I. (1999) *Weaving Work and Motherhood*. Temple University Press, Philadelphia.

Hays, S. (1996) *The Cultural Contradictions of Motherhood*. Yale University Press, New Haven.

Hrdy, S. B. (1999) *Mother Nature: A History of Mothers, Infants, and Natural Selection*. Pantheon, New York.

McMahon, M. (1995) *Engendering Motherhood: Identity and Self-Transformation in Women's Lives*. Guilford Press, New York.

Maushart, S. (1999) *The Mask of Motherhood: How Becoming a Mother Changes Everything and Why We Pretend It Doesn't*. Penguin, New York.

Rothman, B. K. (1989) *Recreating Motherhood*. Norton, New York.

Ruddick, S. (1983) Maternal Thinking. In: Trebilcot, J. (Ed.), *Mothering: Essays in Feminist Theory*. Rowman & Littlefield, Savage, MD, pp. 213–30.

Walzer, S. (2004) Encountering Oppositions: A Review of Scholarship about Motherhood. In: Coleman, M. & Ganong, L. H. (Eds.), *Handbook of Contemporary Families: Considering the Past, Contemplating the Future*. Sage, Thousand Oaks, CA, pp. 209–23.

multiculturalism

Tariq Modood

Multiculturalism or the political accommodation of minorities became a major demand in the last quarter of the twentieth century, filling some of the space that accommodation of the working classes occupied for a century or more earlier. It thus constitutes powerful, if diverse, intellectual challenges in several parts of the humanities and social sciences, with profound political ramifications. Nevertheless, by the early years of the twenty-first century it was in theoretical and practical disarray over the accommodation of Muslims in the West.

The term "multiculturalism" emerged in the 1960s and 1970s in countries like Canada and Australia, and to a lesser extent in Britain and the United States. The policy focus was often initially on schooling and the children of Asian/black/Hispanic post-/neocolonial immigrants, and multiculturalism meant the extension of the school, both in terms of curriculum and as an institution, to include features such as "mother-tongue" teaching, non-Christian religions and holidays, halal food, Asian dress, and so on. From such a starting point, the perspective can develop to meeting such cultural requirements in other or even all social spheres and the empowering of marginalized groups. In Canada and Australia, however, the focus was much wider from the start and included, for example, constitutional and land issues and has been about the definition of the nation. This was partly because these countries had a continuous and recent history of ethnic communities created by migration, usually from different parts of Europe; and because there were unresolved legal questions to do with the entitlements and status of indigenous people in those countries; and, in the case of Canada, there was the further issue of the rise of a nationalist and secessionist movement in French-speaking Quebec. Hence, the term "multiculturalism" in these countries came to mean, and now means throughout the English-speaking world and beyond, the political accommodation by the state and/or a dominant group of all minority cultures defined first and foremost by reference to race or ethnicity, and, additionally but more controversially, by reference to other group-defining characteristics such as nationality, aboriginality, or religion. The latter is more controversial not only because it extends the range of the groups that have to be accommodated, but also because it tends to make larger political claims and so tends to resist having these claims reduced to those of immigrants.

Hence, even today, in both theoretical and policy discourses, multiculturalism means different things in different places. In North America, for example, multiculturalism encompasses discrete groups with territorial claims, such as the Native Peoples and the Québécois, even though these groups want to be treated as "nations" within a multinational state, rather than merely as ethnocultural groups in a mononational state (Kymlicka 1995). Indeed, in Europe, groups with such claims, like the Slovaks and the Scots, are thought of as nations, and multiculturalism has a more limited meaning, referring to a post-immigration urban mélange and the politics it gives rise to. While in North America, language-based ethnicity is seen as the

major political challenge, in Western Europe, the conjunction of the terms "immigration" and "culture" now nearly always invokes the large, newly settled Muslim populations. Sometimes, usually in America, political terms such as multiculturalism and "rainbow coalition" are meant to include all groups marked by "difference" and historic exclusion such as women and gays (Young 1990).

The latter meaning derives from the fact that the ethnic assertiveness associated with multiculturalism has been part of a wider political current of "identity politics" which first germinated in the 1960s and which transformed the idea of equality as sameness to equality as difference (Young 1990); or, in a related conceptualization, adding the concept of respect or "recognition" to the older concept of equality as the equal dignity of individuals (Taylor 1994). Black power and feminist and gay pride movements challenged the ideal of equality as assimilation and contended that a liberatory politics required allowing groups to assert their difference and to not have to conform to dominant cultural norms. Indeed, the attack on colorblind, culture-neutral political concepts such as equality and citizenship, with the critique that ethnicity and culture cannot be confined to some so-called private sphere but shape political and opportunity structures in all societies, is one of the most fundamental claims made by multiculturalism and the politics of difference. It is the theoretical basis for the conclusion that allegedly "neutral" liberal democracies are part of a hegemonic culture that systematically de-ethnicizes or marginalizes minorities. Hence, the claim that minority cultures, norms, and symbols have as much right as their hegemonic counterparts to state provision and to be in the public space, to be recognized as groups and not just as culturally neutered individuals.

The African American search for dignity has contributed much to this politics which has shifted attention from socioeconomic disadvantage, arguably where their need is greatest. It has inadvertently promoted identities based on indigenous claims, language, religion, and suppressed nationhood, none of which properly addresses the identity concerns of African Americans. Nathan Glazer has indeed argued that there is no prospect of multiculturalism in the US; the processes of assimilation are doing their work with non-European immigrants, as they have done with their European predecessors (although Spanish has emerged as a major second language in parts of the US). Insofar as there is a group that will not melt in, it is African Americans; not because of cultural difference, but because American society lacks the determination to combat the racism and severe disadvantage to make it happen (Glazer 1997). In Glazer's view, the rise of multiculturalism in the US is a reflection of the lack of will to overcome the black–white divide.

On this reading it is of no surprise that the multiculturalist debate in the US is primarily in the field of education and, uniquely, higher education, where passion has been expended on arguments about the curriculum in the humanities ("the canon"), punctilious avoidance of disrespect ("political correctness"), and anxiety about the ethnicization of student dorms ("balkanization"). Academic argument has, however, no less than popular feeling, been important in the formulation of multiculturalism, with the study of colonial societies and political theory at the forefront. The ideas of cultural difference and cultural group have historically been central to anthropology and other related disciplines focused on "primitive" and non-European societies. The arrival in the metropolitan centers of peoples studied by scholars from these disciplines has made the latter experts on migrants and their cultural needs. They also enabled critics from previously colonized societies, often themselves immigrants to the "North," to challenge the expert and other representations of the culturally subordinated. These intellectual developments have been as influenced by the collapse of Marxism as by postcolonial migrations. The failure of the economic "material base" explanations of the cultural "superstructure," as the social sciences took what has been described as "the cultural turn," shifting from the study of economic to cultural structures, has contributed to highlighting cultural identities and discursive analyses of cross-cultural power relations (Said 1978).

The prominence of political theory in multiculturalism is also to be partly understood in terms of the internal dynamic within the discipline. Rawls's *Theory of Justice* (1971) is the founding text in the modern revival of normative Anglo-American political theory. It promised a philosophically grounded, systematic answer to questions of distributive justice in societies, such as the contemporary United States, which were assumed to be characterized by a value pluralism. Subsequent debate, including Rawls's reformulation of his own position, focused not on Rawls's conclusions about distribution but his assumptions about rationality and value pluralism. The generation of political theorists following Rawls thus has come to define their questions more in terms of the nature of community and minority rights than in terms of distributive justice, no less than their social theory peers defined it in terms of difference and identity rather than class conflict, and in each case the intellectual framework lent itself to multiculturalism, even when the term itself was not favored. While for most political theorists academic liberalism has been the primary reference point, Bhikhu Parekh has offered a philosophical multiculturalism grounded in an analysis of human nature and culture and which elaborates the intrinsic value of diversity as more fundamental than the accommodation of minorities (Parekh 2000).

One of the most fundamental divisions amongst scholars concerns the validity of "cultural groups" as a point of reference for multiculturalism. The dominant view in sociocultural studies has become that groups always have internal differences, including hierarchies, gender inequality, and dissent, and culture is always fluid and subject to varied influences, mixtures, and change. To think otherwise is to "essentialize" groups such as blacks, Muslims, Asians, and so on. Political theorists, on the other hand, continue to think of cultural groups as sociopolitical actors who may bear rights and have needs that should be institutionally accommodated. This approach challenges the view of culture as radically unstable and primarily expressive by putting moral communities at the center of a definition of "culture" (Parekh 2000). Empirical studies, however, suggest that both these views have some substance. For while many young people, from majority and minority backgrounds, do not wish to be defined by a singular ethnicity but wish to actively mix and share several heritages, there is simultaneously a development of distinct communities, usually ethnoreligious, and sometimes seeking corporate representation.

Multiculturalism has had a much less popu-lar reception in mainland Europe. Its prospect has sometimes led to extreme nationalist par-ties winning control of some towns and cities, a significant share of the national poll, and some-times even a share in the national government, as in the case of the Freedom Party in Austria. Anti-multiculturalism is, however, not confined to extremist parties, nor even to those of the right. In France, where intellectual objections to multiculturalism have been most developed, multiculturalism is opposed across the political spectrum, for it is thought to be incompa-tible with a conception of a "transcendent" or "universal" citizenship which demands that all "particular" identities, such as those of race, ethnicity, and gender, which promote part of the republic against the good of the whole, be confined to private life. The implosion of Yugo-slavia, with its "ethnic cleansing," marks the most extreme reaction to multinational state-hood and plural societies, and the political status of historic minorities, including the Roma (Gyp-sies), is conflicted throughout the territories of the former Austro-Hungarian, Ottoman, and Russian empires. Many postcolonial states in Asia and Africa are experiencing ethnonationalist and secessionist movements and some, such as India, Malaysia, and Indonesia, are also strug-gling with non-territorial multiculturalism.

Since "9/11" and its aftermath, it is Mus-lims that have become the focus of discourse about minorities in the West. This is partly an issue of security, but more generally is accom-panied by a "multiculturalism is dead" rhetoric. This has led to, or reinforced, policy reversals in many countries, even pioneering ones such as the Netherlands, and is most marked by the fact that a new assimilationism is espoused not just on the political right, but also on the center-left and by erstwhile supporters of multiculturalism. Muslims in Western Europe, it is argued, are disloyal to European states and prefer segrega-tion and sociocultural separatism to integration; they are illiberal on a range of issues, most notably on the personal freedom of women and on homosexuality; and they are challenging the secular character of European political culture by thrusting religious identities and communal-ism into the public space. The last charge marks the most serious theoretical reversal of multiculturalism as the non-privatization of

minority identities is one of the core ideas of multiculturalism (Modood 2005). Yet the emer-gence of Muslim political mobilization has led some multiculturalists to argue that religion is a feature of plural societies that is uniquely legitimate to confine to the private sphere. This prohibiting of Muslim identity in public space has so far been taken furthest in France, where in 2004 Parliament passed, with little debate but an overwhelming majority, a ban on the wearing of "ostentatious" religious symbols, primarily the *hijab* (headscarf), in public schools.

SEE ALSO: Assimilation; Balkanization; Bilin-gual, Multicultural Education; Colonialism (Neocolonialism); Immigration; Melting Pot; Race and Ethnic Politics

REFERENCES AND SUGGESTED READINGS

Glazer, N. (1997) *We Are All Multiculturalists Now.* Harvard University Press, Cambridge, MA.
Kymlicka, W. (1995) *Multicultural Citizenship: A Liberal Theory of Minority Rights.* Oxford Univer-sity Press, Oxford.
Modood, T. (2005) *Multicultural Politics: Racism, Ethnicity, and Muslims in Britain.* Minnesota and Edinburgh University Presses, Edinburgh.
Parekh, B. (2000) *Rethinking Multiculturalism: Cul-tural Diversity and Political Theory.* Macmillan, London and Harvard University Press, Cambridge, MA.
Said, E. (1978) *Orientalism.* Routledge, London.
Taylor, C. (1994) Multiculturalism and "The Poli-tics of Recognition." In: Gutmann, A. (Ed.), *Mul-ticulturalism and "The Politics of Recognition."* Princeton University Press, Princeton.
Young, I. M. (1990) *Justice and the Politics of Differ-ence.* Princeton University Press, Princeton.

multimedia

Chris Chesher

Multimedia is the integrated use of more than one medium of communication, usually mediated through digital computing technolo-gies. "Multimedia" is a term with a complex and ambivalent history that risks being either too narrow or too broad in its meaning. In its narrower sense, it was closely associated with the dead-end that was CD-ROM interactive multimedia in the mid-1990s. In its broad sense, multimedia can refer to any text, technology, or event that combines more than one medium of communication: a meaning so broad that it fails to denote any distinctive cultural form. Any definition of multimedia therefore needs to operate between these limits. Multimedia has specific meanings in different contexts, including performance, libraries, social semiotics, and computer science. In spite of these complications, recent attention on multimedia has raised some significant wider questions about media and communication.

Before multimedia was computer-based and interactive, the term sometimes referred to presentations using multiple slide projectors with dissolve systems and synchronized music to deliver carefully choreographed linear sequence of images with a soundtrack accompaniment. Such systems were commonly used in museum exhibits, educational presentations, and popular culture happenings in the 1960s and 1970s. Another earlier use of the term was for multimedia resources and teaching machines marketed for schools and parents in the 1960s. In a fine arts context the term "multimedia" is sometimes used to refer to mixed media works that do not fit into conventional categories of oil painting, watercolors, sculpture, and so on. Librarians have long used the term "multimedia" to refer to collections of materials other than print publications. Such artifacts require libraries to maintain not only collections of work, but also specialized equipment for viewing such material: from video players and slide viewers to computer systems. In the context of constantly changing technical standards, demanding requirements for configuring and operating equipment, and the deterioration of physical media, maintaining a multimedia collection can be an expensive and complex task. A wider definition of multimedia puts it under the same umbrella as many cultural forms: opera, cinema, educational resources, computer games, performance art, consumer electronic devices, and more.

COMPUTER-BASED INTERACTIVE MULTIMEDIA

The most common contemporary understanding of the term "multimedia" is in the paradigm of interactive computer-based multimedia introduced in the 1990s. Research into sound synthesis, music, and computer graphics was conducted as early as the 1950s, but most business and scientific computers had very limited capabilities in image and sound. Exceptions included machines designed to support computer games, including 1980s microcomputers such as the popular Commodore 64, which had relatively advanced sound and graphics. Games have always been the main driver for more powerful sound and graphics hardware and software, but manufacturers and publishers began to advocate a more respectable and expansive promise of multimedia.

Multimedia achieved a high public profile in the early 1990s as a pretender to transform or even replace conventional forms of publishing. This more restricted conception of multimedia was often qualified by the prefix "interactive," in which users have some capacity to influence the flow of multimedia events, usually by browsing menus, submitting queries through search fields, direct manipulation control, or gameplay. The term was closely associated with commoditized titles published on compact disk read-only memory (CD-ROM). Driven largely by extravagant claims from hardware manufacturers and start-up companies, "multimedia" quickly became a marketing cliché more than an actual technology or cultural form.

Advocates of interactive multimedia in the 1990s discovered a history that allowed them to place it in a context. This history typically credits Vannevar Bush, the wartime director of the Office of Scientific Research and Development in the US, with anticipating the future form for multimedia computing. His article, "As We May Think," was published in the July 1945 edition of *Atlantic Monthly*, proposing an electromechanical machine called the "Memex," which individuals could use to store all their documents as an "enlarged supplement to memory." He envisioned that the documents would not be categorized by conventional library classification, but rather would be connected by association, in the same ways that he understood the mind to work.

Another key figure in this history is Ted Nelson, who is credited with coining the term "hypertext" to refer to electronic text that includes "hyperlinks" that allow users to jump from one textual unit to another. Hypertext becomes "hypermedia" when multiple media, such as images, video, animations, and sound, are incorporated in the works.

The multimedia paradigm emerged as an actual consumer technology with computers featuring graphical user interfaces (GUIs), largely superseding "command line" text-only interaction. This style of interface is traced from the 1960s US Defense Department's Augmentation Research Center, headed by Doug Engelbart (Bardini 2000) through to the Xerox Palo Alto Research Center (PARC), which developed a GUI interface for the "Alto," but never commercialized it. The GUI was finally popularized by the Apple Macintosh, released in 1984, which used bitmapped graphics, a Windows, Icons, Menus, and the mouse Pointing device (WIMP) interface, and built-in sound (Levy 1994). The GUI style of interface was also adopted by Microsoft, with Windows, which became the dominant personal computer operating system by the mid-1990s.

Multimedia over the Internet became viable with the 1993 release of the NCSA Mosaic browser. The World Wide Web standards that became HTML (HyperText Markup Language) and http (HyperText Transfer Protocol) had been developed by Tim Berners Lee at CERN by 1990. Mosaic added a GUI interface, and supported embedded images and, soon, plug-ins that allowed animations, panoramas, sound, video, 3D, and other types of content to be included on a web page. Although websites could not compare in audiovisual terms even with CD-ROMs, they were mainly accessible for free, and supported more complex transactions between users and site owners. Electronic mail attachments and real-time chat also supported transfer of multimedia files.

Multimedia developers and theorists identified and extended a range of functional and aesthetic conventions distinctive to this media form. Some early theory was largely either speculative or descriptive, extending on early experiments with new aesthetics and capabilities (e.g., Benedikt 1992). Later work became more concerned with emerging aesthetics apparent in actual multimedia works and applications. Janet Murray (1997) identifies immersion, agency, and transformation as key aesthetics of the medium. Lev Manovich (2001) nominates the database and navigable space as forms distinctive to new media. He argues that databases displace narrative as key organizing form by presenting the world as a list without any necessary ordering: they remain open to unending search, navigation, and viewing. Navigable space also organizes elements in virtual space, rather than presenting them with the linearity of narration characteristic of most cinema.

While some conventions did emerge, actual multimedia applications established a diverse range of styles and genres. For example, there are many different ways of producing and presenting immersive and navigable spaces. Some applications (e.g., Cyan Worlds' 1993 game *Myst*) present single images with hotspots that take users from one space to another. Another model is found in the immersive panoramas created by stitching together multiple still images, introduced with Apple's QuickTime VR (Virtual Reality) in 1994, which retains a close connection with photography. On the other hand, navigable 3D virtual reality spaces such as those featured in the first person-shooter games genre popularized by id Software's *Doom* in 1993 generate moving images in real time by rendering the perspective of a moving virtual camera position within a mathematically described environment modeled with polygon primitives. While each creates a sense of immersion (and there are many other variations of applications that operate with this aesthetic), no general purpose or universal system emerged.

By the end of the 1990s, CD-ROMs had not established themselves as a mainstream format for publishing authored content titles. The crash in high technology stocks in 2000 deflated any remaining optimism about this form, ironically just at the time that multimedia applications were being taken up, particularly on the Internet. The CD-ROM was a critical but flawed component of this generation of multimedia. It was a storage medium that could hold 650 MB of data – at the time a very substantial capacity. However, as the drives were based on a standard developed for audio, the early CD-ROM drives were initially frustratingly slow. The audiovisual impact of multimedia did not compare well with television, cinema, or even games. Most importantly, CD-ROM content titles had no clearly defined market, never sitting comfortably in computer shops, bookshops, or video rental outlets.

Within less than a decade, the mid-1990s paradigm of multimedia had clearly failed. A new range of digital communications and media technologies grew dramatically, most notably the Internet, computer games, digital stills cameras and video cameras, DVDs, and mobile telephones. Each of these had advantages over CD-ROMs: more direct cultural progenitors, stronger affective resonances, better economic models, and better defined locations within increasingly complex technical and social networks.

The conception of multimedia that emerged in the 2000s moved away from the emphasis on packaged, integrated, and commoditized CD-ROM titles toward communications products and campaigns that employ multiple media (Lévy 2001). For example, advertising and entertainment increasingly produced media events that integrated television programs with mobile data (SMS: short message service), iMode multimedia phones (particularly in Japan), 3G phones, interactive television, and websites. Media industries such as cinema became increasingly dependent on cross-media tie-ins such as games and soundtrack rights, product placement, and DVD releases.

In the early 2000s, the increasing accessibility of broadband Internet connections, as well as advances in rich media and data compression standards, made it increasingly possible to distribute multimedia content online. The Internet also became infamous for its informal and even illegal use for distributing multimedia files: copyrighted music, pornographic images, pirated software, and even entire new release movies.

LOGOCENTRISM, MULTIMEDIA, AND MULTIMODALITY

If multimedia is the marked term for any communication that involves more than one medium, this implies that communication using a single and discrete medium is the normal state of affairs in western culture. Canadian media theorist Marshall McLuhan is most prominent among those who have argued that writing is the dominant medium. He argues that the West inordinately privileges the visual sense, encouraging excessively linear thought and diminishing the immediacy, involvement, and the immersiveness of sound (McLuhan 1962). He sees some promise in electric media to challenge the dominance of print, to rebalance sense-ratios. McLuhan's work has recently been taken up enthusiastically by multimedia advocates (Packer & Jordan 2001).

Another perspective is offered by Jacques Derrida (1976), who argues in *Of Grammatology* m in western culture is actually speech. Writing is most often (wrongly) seen as a diminished record of the speech that supposedly calls on the presence of the speaker for its authority. Derrida claims that western rationality is based on a logocentrism that privileges language over non-verbal communication, and reduces all communication to language (and the implied presence of a speaker).

Some advocates of multimedia (and hypertext, in particular), notably George Landow, invoke Derrida's critiques of the logic of presence in written texts, but reach an almost opposite conclusion: that the technology of hypermedia actually overcomes the metaphysical limitations of previous media (Landow 1992). While such claims might be too strongly technologically deterministic, the development and adoption of new communication technologies does have significant implications for cultural and social practices.

The emergence of multimedia has foregrounded an important distinction between "multimedia" and "multimodality" – the materiality of a mode of communication, and the codes and conventions in operation. The term "media" (which is already complex and plural) refers to an interval between two entities, the intervening substrate, which is crossed using some mode of transportation or communication. The modality refers to the qualitative properties of the mechanisms by which this interval between entities is crossed. The modality of human communication includes the senses involved (sight, hearing, touch), and the conventions that make the contact between entities significant or meaningful.

Multimodality has recently become a significant question for linguistics, which has traditionally privileged the structural features of written and spoken language. Image, gesture, and action have usually been seen as only supplements to the communication carried by language. Recent work by Gunther Kress and Theo van Leeuwen (1996), among others, insists that cultural shifts have displaced writing on paper as the dominant mode of communication in favor of images on screens. All communicational events mobilize more than language. In this light, all meaning-making practices need to be reexamined.

Multimedia production also requires changes in work practices of media producers (Woolgar 2002). Production often combines the work of professionals from very different worlds. Larger projects require designers (interface, visual, and instructional), programmers, writers, artists (computer and traditional), and others to collaborate closely.

The term "multimedia" remains a problematic but important term. While multimedia has not become a discrete and well-defined cultural form, many applications of computers can be described as multimedia. Media production for traditional media including print, sound, photography, video, and cinema now almost universally involves computers. Many of the aesthetics developed in CD-ROM interactive multimedia have been adapted to DVD videos, interactive television, broadband Internet, computer games, and mobile audiovisual and data applications.

SEE ALSO: Cyberculture; Digital; Information Technology; Internet; Text/Hypertext

REFERENCES AND SUGGESTED READINGS

Bardini, T. (2000) *Bootstrapping: Douglas Engelbart, Coevolution, and the Origins of Personal Computing.* Stanford University Press, Stanford.

Benedikt, M. (1992) *Cyberspace: First Steps.* MIT Press, Cambridge, MA.

Derrida, J. (1976) *Of Grammatology.* Johns Hopkins University Press, Baltimore.

Kress, G. & van Leeuwen, T. (1996) *Reading Images.* Routledge, London.

Landow, G. P. (1992) *Hypertext: The Convergence of Contemporary Critical Theory and Technology.* Johns Hopkins University Press, Baltimore.

Lévy, P. (2001) *Cyberculture.* University of Minnesota Press, Minneapolis.

Levy, S. (1994) *Insanely Great: The Life and Times of Macintosh, the Computer that Changed Everything.* Viking, New York.

McLuhan, M. (1962) *The Gutenberg Galaxy.* University of Toronto Press, Toronto.

Manovich, L. (2001) *The Language of New Media.* MIT Press, Cambridge, MA.

Murray, J. H. (1997) *Hamlet on the Holodeck: The Future of Narrative in Cyberspace.* Free Press, New York.

Packer, R. & Jordan, K. (2001) *Multimedia: From Wagner to Virtual Reality.* Norton, New York.

Woolgar, S. (Ed.) (2002) *Virtual Society? Technology, Cyberbole, Reality.* Oxford University Press, New York.

multinucleated metropolitan region

Chigon Kim

The multinucleated metropolitan region is an emerging spatial configuration characterized by massive regional sprawl and the presence of multiple specialized activity centers outside of the downtown central business district (CBD). This concept is useful for understanding both changes in metropolitan spatial structure and the dynamics of metropolitan life. It underlines the interactive character of the metropolitan region tied together by the complex webs of communications and traffic flows. As a pattern of settlement space, it suggests that urban life is organized into multiple centers spreading across an extensive metropolitan region.

The idea of the multinucleated metropolitan region can be traced to the early Chicago School of urban ecology. Roderick D. McKenzie, among others, was a pioneer who extended the ecological approach to the study of the metropolitan region. In 1933 McKenzie published a seminal book, *The Metropolitan Community*, in which he investigated structural and historical changes in urban settlement space. Unlike advocates of other ecological models focusing on the internal structure of the city as a container, McKenzie called attention to the metropolitan region as an appropriate unit of analysis and explicitly highlighted metropolitanization and multinucleation as dominant social trends. As McKenzie pointed out, the pattern of metropolitan development has deviated significantly from the monocentric urban form (epitomized in the Burgess's concentric zone model) since the early 1930s.

The sprawling, polynucleated nature of metropolitan growth has been of particular concern among scholars, practitioners, policymakers, and journalists since the early 1960s. They have coined a number of neologisms to describe this phenomenon, focusing primarily on changes in the urban fringes and peripheries. Examples include edge cities, exopoles, network cities, postsuburbia, outer cities, suburban downtowns, suburban employment centers, suburban growth corridors, technoburbs, and urban villages. Many of these labels underscore a particular aspect of polycentric metropolitan spatial structure, such as the regional scale of metropolitan growth, the suburban location of specialized centers, the spatial array of clustering, and the socioeconomic function of multiple nuclei.

In the early 1970s the suburbanization of employment came to the attention of the public. Beginning in the mid-1970s, various types of specialized clusters, such as high-technology corridors and office parks, emerged and increased in number and kind. By the mid-1970s, urban spatial structure shifted from the monocentric to the polycentric form with a multitude of specialized centers mushrooming in the suburban ring. Since the 1980s the trend toward economic decentralization has been increasingly dominated by highly specialized business functions. These functions include headquarters, FIRE (finance, insurance, and real estate), and advanced business services. In the 1990s, many suburban downtowns matured into full-fledged regional centers.

Although the spatial layout of suburban employment centers may vary from place to place, clustering and scattering remain two of the most salient forms. Clustering is a geographic concentration of economic activities in the nodal point in which industrial parks or campus-like office complexes are located. Benefits of clustering include easy access to the specialized labor force, the creation of innovation networks, the exchange of tacit knowledge, and the development of business infrastructure. The concentrated activity centers become highly diversified and functionally specialized as the deconcentration of business functions and services continues.

Clustering is characterized by concentrated and mixed land use. By contrast, scattering is characterized by widely dispersed, somewhat random, and usually single land use. As shown in high-technology corridors or commercial strips along highways, accessibility is the key to a scattered pattern of nucleation. In many metropolitan regions, suburban employment centers share less than half of total metropolitan employment due to the scattering of business functions and services without any distinct land-use patterns. This unorganized, scattered, and sprawling pattern of suburban economic nodes is congruent with the postmodern conception of urban spatial structure.

There are various ways in which polycentric spatial structure can emerge. Some metropolitan areas have developed with multiple nuclei from the beginning; others have transformed into polycentric structures through migration and functional specialization; and still others have undertaken polycentric development through incorporating or merging several previously independent centers. The origin and growth dynamics of suburban activity centers may differ from place to place, but these new centers are beginning to rival the traditional CBD.

To explain the dynamics of this spatial formation, the ecological perspective tends to delineate a general evolutionary path of metropolitanization such as urbanization, suburbanization, and the urbanization of the suburbs. In this perspective, the development of multicentered metropolitan structure is attributed to advances in transportation and communication technology, agglomeration economies and diseconomies, or a tradeoff between housing and commuting costs. The relocation decision of business and industry, for example, is accounted for by a tradeoff between agglomeration economies (e.g., reduced transaction costs, face-to-face information flows, and innovation capacities) and congestion costs (e.g., traffic congestion, pollution, higher land values, and higher labor costs). From this perspective, the relocation decision is made when congestion costs far exceed the benefits from agglomeration economies. While an increase in congestion costs in dense locations pushes business and industry to decentralize their economic activities, the benefits from agglomeration economies provide a strong incentive for recentralization.

Although the ecological perspective highlights the spatial process of metropolitanization, it tends to ignore how emerging urban spatial structure is linked to underlying structural transformations. The sociospatial perspective provides a more comprehensive framework for understanding the newly emerging metropolitan form, its underlying processes, and its social consequences. The benchmark is Mark Gottdiener's *The Social Production of Urban Space* (1985). Contrary to ecologists, Gottdiener defines the multinucleated metropolitan region in terms of macro-level structural changes which may be conceptualized as the transition from Fordism or monopoly capitalism to the regime of flexible accumulation or global capitalism. Such structural transformations were coupled with the spatial process of deconcentration.

Deconcentration comprises two movements of people and activities within and between metropolitan regions: decentralization and recentralization. Decentralization means the movements of people and activities away from the urban core. It includes the shift of industries, jobs, and workers from the older central cities toward the suburbs, Sunbelt regions, and overseas. Recentralization refers to the process whereby those movements tend to concentrate into functionally specialized areas. This tendency toward concentrated decentralization in conjunction with recurrent socioeconomic restructuring generates multiple nodes around which interconnected activities and functions cluster.

The sociospatial perspective posits that the sprawling, multinucleated metropolitan region is a product of the dialectical articulation between structural forces and agency. The rise of the multinucleated metropolitan region involves a complex but contingent articulation of political, economic, and social factors operating at local, regional, national, and global levels. In addition, the distribution of people and activities within and across metropolitan regions is not amorphous; rather, it is driven by powerful actors and channeled by institutional mechanisms.

First of all, the rise of global capitalism has altered the landscape of metropolitan areas. Under the pressure of intensified international competition over fragmented consumer markets, the structure of industrial organization has been transformed into a flatter, leaner, and more flexible one. In search of greater flexibility in production, flexible firms put a premium on strategic alliances and subcontracting relations. They sell off their divisions in pursuit of lean and mean organizational structures, focusing on core competencies. This widespread tendency toward vertical disintegration, along with the mobility of capital, has contributed to the spatial dispersal of production. This decentralization of production has increased the need for centralizing the coordination and control functions in corporate headquarters. Coupled with the concentration of administrative and control functions is the explosion of advanced business services supporting business operation on a global scale. These administrative functions and advanced business services, which used to locate in large CBDs, are burgeoning in the suburban centers.

Government intervention also played a significant role in the restructuring of urban space after World War II. Governments at the local, regional, and national levels have facilitated private profit making not only indirectly in the form of housing and transportation policies, but also directly through government expenditures and subsidization. For example, strategic industries located in the Sunbelt, such as energy and high-technology industries, have been heavily subsidized by governments. Together with defense-related spending, these industries are pillars of Sunbelt growth. Additionally, in an effort to attract global investment, local governments often offer tax breaks, loans, grants, or other subsidies. The mobility of capital and the competition among different places for their share of investment have much to do with the geographic differentiation and functional specialization of concentrated economic centers.

In addition to economic and political forces, cultural representations and practices play a role in shaping multicentered metropolitan regions. The production of urban space is a contentious process involving many contending interests of the stakeholders, who justify their actions by appropriating cultural representations. The real estate industry incorporates images and symbols into themed environments as a marketing strategy to attract clients. Local government uses place representations as a source of legitimacy for urban development and redevelopment policies. Local residents produce, circulate, and consume a set of images and symbols that signify a particular place identity. In the struggle over social space, they reaffirm these place representations. In addition, locational choices are affected by cultural values and lifestyle preferences.

The major agent of urban change is the real estate sector. Under late capitalism, competition between capitalists results in overaccumulation. A temporary solution to this chronic problem is a switch of capital flow into the secondary circuit of capital, which involves investment in the built environment for profit. The flow of investment in the built environment is usually induced by government intervention. Whereas real estate development is a separate source of acquiring wealth, returns on investment in the built environment are uncertain because of the long investment cycle. For this reason, local governments, interested in increased tax revenues, usually provide incentives to make real estate an attractive investment. Thus, land-based interest groups, aligning themselves with local governments, carve out growth networks which are active in making profit from the turnover in land use.

Growth networks are coalitions of individuals and groups that channel spatial transformations into specific places and directions. They are composed of land developers, government officials, financial institutions, speculators, construction companies, and real estate agents. These coalitions usually cut across rigid class boundaries. Growth coalitions produce and disseminate boosterism and pro-growth ideology to legitimate real estate development. Their land-based interests are powerful enough to produce the unique features of the built environment. However, opponents of pro-growth interests

counter development with the idea of "community control," which emphasizes the social costs imputed to local residents, including pollution, traffic congestion, and higher crime rates. The restructuring of urban space, in sum, represents a deep-rooted ideological battle over the use of space.

The polycentric spatial formation has become the focus of urban studies in North America, Europe, and Japan. Recent studies have explored various issues relevant to the development of multinucleated metropolitan regions. Some studies empirically examined how these centers emerge, grow, and change over time. Others explained their competitive advantages, functional specialization, location, and interdependence. Still others explicated their effects on the quality of urban life. Now, the fear of terrorism is added to a list of structural forces behind the decentralization of key business activities and services.

A major methodological issue associated with polycentric spatial structure is how to specify its boundaries. At the inter-metropolitan level, the multinucleated metropolitan region is a functionally integrated area encompassing a constellation of politically independent cities. Proximity and interaction are two criteria generally used to specify boundaries. The level of interaction, usually measured by commuting flows, is an indicator of functional interdependence of separate cities, whereas proximity, measured by traveling time, is an indicator of spatial integration. Yet there is little consensus about what minimum thresholds should be applied before a place can be considered part of a single, functionally integrated metropolitan region.

Operationalization is another methodological issue related to the concept of polycentricity. Operationalization and measurement differ from study to study, depending on the available data used. The units of analysis vary greatly, ranging from counties, incorporated municipalities, ZIP codes, and census tracks, to transportation analysis zones (TAZs).

Polycentric spatial structure is first measured by comparing the growth of jobs in the suburbs and in the central city. The degree of economic deconcentration is the key to this measure. If a metropolitan region has more jobs in the outlying suburban areas than in the central city, then it is considered to be an indicator of polycentricity. Although this indicator is easy to measure, it fails to capture a tendency toward the concentrated decentralization of economic activities and the functional specialization of a place.

The employment-to-residence (ER) ratio is a measure that takes into account the functional specialization of a place. An employment center is characterized by a high ER ratio. If the ER ratio is greater than 1, then it is classified as an employment subcenter; by contrast, if the ER ratio is less than 0.5, then it is considered as a residential community. Many studies show that the suburban share of employment within metropolitan areas has dramatically increased and many suburban areas contain jobs that outstrip the number of resident workers.

Polycentric spatial structure is also measured by commuting patterns based on census journey-to-work data. Most OECD member countries, including the US, use the intensity of commuting patterns to identify the functional integration of contiguous urban areas. Changes in commuting patterns reflect changes in the distribution of employment within a metropolitan area. As a result of economic deconcentration, commuting flows to and from urban peripheries increase, whereas commuting trips to the urban center decrease. By 1980 the volume of suburban-to-suburban commuting flows doubled that of suburban-to-central city work trips. Along with the dominant suburban-to-suburban commuting flows, reverse commuting from the central city to the suburbs has become quite significant.

The disadvantage of the above three measures is that they are unable to identify the number and location of suburban employment centers. An alternative measure that overcomes this limitation is the employment density gradient. The popular unit of analysis in the employment density gradient is the TAZ. Employment growth outside the downtown CBD is often concentrated in a relatively small number of zones. If changes in employment density are drawn on a graph along the distance from the downtown CBD, then the gradient tends to decrease with multiple peaks. These peaks will rise in the areas around outlying employment centers.

The identification of employment centers may vary depending on the threshold employment density (e.g., 5,000 employees per square mile instead of 7,000) and the threshold total employment (e.g., 10,000 total employees instead of 20,000). The density of suburban employment centers could be low relative to the density in the downtown CBD, but the number of outlying employment centers and their share of the total metropolitan employment tend to increase. In addition, these employment centers become economically more diversified and specialized. The functional specialization of an employment center can be assessed by examining its composition of industries, jobs, or business functions and their relative shares in the entire metropolitan area. More recent studies use remote sensing, GIS, or other mapping techniques to identify an employment center and its functional specialization.

Multinucleated metropolitan regions share some defining features, although they may have followed different trajectories of development with unique spatial configurations. The size of a metropolitan area is highly associated with its number of suburban employment centers. In general, larger metropolitan areas exhibit more suburban employment centers. However, there are regional differences and geographical variations in multinucleation. For example, the dispersed, leapfrogging development of economic nodes in the urban fringe is more prevalent in rapidly expanding metropolitan areas of the Sunbelt region.

Some urban scholars and practitioners highlight the benefits of polycentric metropolitan development, including improved regional economic competitiveness and greater choices of urban services. For others, however, uneven development is the end product of the rapid, uncoordinated spatial transformations under late capitalism. Both spatial dispersal and agglomeration result in geographical splits and disparities, as represented by the vivid contrast between well-off and impoverished areas across and within metropolitan regions. The pattern of uneven development is reinforced by spatial competition that makes capital resources bypass impoverished areas. Spatial transformations generate, rather than solve, a host of urban problems. Those problems include residential segregation, social polarization, fiscal crisis, crime, pollution, and traffic congestion. The scope of these urban problems is beyond the reach of fragmented political jurisdictions and calls for regional cooperation and interdisciplinary research.

SEE ALSO: Growth Machine; Uneven Development; Urban Ecology; Urban Political Economy; Urban Space

REFERENCES AND SUGGESTED READINGS

Anas, A., Arnott, R., & Small, K. A. (1998) Urban Spatial Structure. *Journal of Economic Literature* 36: 1426–64.

Commission of the European, Communities (CEC) (1999) *European Spatial Development Perspective: Towards Balanced and Sustainable Development of the Territory of the European Union.* Office for the Official Publications of the European Communities, Luxembourg.

Dear, M. (2002) Los Angeles and the Chicago School: Invitation to a Debate. *City and Community* 1: 5–32.

Dieleman, F. M. & Faludi, A. (1998) Polynucleated Metropolitan Regions in Northwest Europe: Theme of the Special Issue. *European Planning Studies* 6: 365–78.

Gottdiener, M. (1985) *The Social Production of Urban Space*, 2nd edn. University of Texas Press, Austin.

Gottdiener, M. & Kephart, G. (1991) The Multinucleated Metropolitan Region: A Comparative Analysis. In: Kling, R., Olin, S., & Poster, M. (Eds.), *Posturban California: The Transformation of Orange County since World War II.* University of California Press, Berkeley, pp. 31–54.

Hughes, H. L. (1993) Metropolitan Structure and the Suburban Hierarchy. *American Sociological Review* 58: 417–33.

Irwin, M. D. & Hughes, H. L. (1992) Centrality and the Structure of Urban Interaction: Measures, Concepts, and Applications. *Social Forces* 71: 17–51.

Kloosterman, R. C. & Musterd, S. (2001) The Polycentric Urban Region: Towards a Research Agenda. *Urban Studies* 38: 623–33.

multiracial feminism

Michele Berger and Silvia Bettez

Women of color have always actively participated in women's issues. However, their experience with feminist work has often been overlooked and largely undocumented (Hurtado 1996). Multiracial feminism refers to the activist and scholarly work conducted by women of color and anti-racist white allies to promote race, class, and gender equality. In comparison to the highly documented second-wave white, middle-class feminism, which centered on abolishing patriarchy and privileged patriarchy as an oppression over all others, women of color feminism resists separating oppression and insists on recognizing the intersectionality of race, class, and gender oppression.

A metaphor increasingly used to identify the various stages of feminism in the United States has been that of "waves." The first wave denotes the period when white abolitionist women and free black women organized for the right to vote and won passage of the 19th Amendment. The second wave is identified as 1970s feminism, which challenged women's exclusion from the public sphere of employment and politics. The third wave is ongoing and marks the ways in which young women manage some of the social and political freedoms gained from the previous generations. Multiracial feminist organizing and theory building can be identified throughout every historical period of these waves.

Multiracial feminism refers most often to the feminisms of Black/African American, Latina/Chicana, Native American, and Asian American women; however, it includes the voices of anti-racist white women and of all women of color including East Indian women, Arab women, mixed-race women, and women of color not from the United States. Multiracial feminists have often identified themselves under the rubric of "women of color." The identification of women of color as a political, strategic, and subjective identity category is a relatively recent phenomenon. The term "women of color" connotes both affinity and similarity of experience.

To demonstrate an alliance with women of color across the globe and a commitment to postcolonial struggles, in the early 1970s some feminist women of color in the US began claiming the term "third world women" (Sandoval 1990; Mohanty et al. 1991). Third world feminists used the term to deliberately mark a connection with global women's issues foregrounding colonization, immigration, racism, and imperialism – concerns that many white feminists did not address.

This identification with other women across the globe also encouraged US women of color to acknowledge long traditions of anti-racist collective organizing that was often ignored, suppressed, or obscured during second-wave feminist activism. These conditions helped to solidify the strategic use of the term women of color and have supported over the last two decades global organizing in Brazil, England, Africa, Australia, and New Zealand. Aída Hurtado (1996) argues that there are four over-arching principles that connect almost all feminists of color: (1) an insistence on recognizing the simultaneity of race, class, and gender oppressions; (2) a claim to their racial group's history as part of their activist legacy, including struggles in their native lands; (3) an understanding that theorizing can emerge from political organizing, everyday interactions, and artistic production as well as the academy; and (4) an opposition to heterosexism in their communities.

Although there are commonalities between multiracial feminists, there are also concentrations on specific topics that distinguish over 30 years of scholarship and activism. Asian American women have documented pervasive and debilitating stereotypes that promote passivity and exoticization, domestic violence, and the US military's role in sex tourism. African American multiracial feminists have consistently called attention to "controlling images" of black female bodies (especially regarding sexuality) that seek to justify disenfranchisement through law, ideology, and social policy. Chicanas and Latinas have often concentrated on immigration, challenging patriarchal definitions of family, the sexual double standard, and critiquing the black/white conceptualization of US racial politics. Sovereignty and land rights, environmental justice, spirituality, and experiences of cultural appropriation and genocide have been primary concerns of Native women who espouse multiracial feminism.

Multiracial feminism is often viewed in contrast and reaction to white, middle-class feminism; however, it is important to recognize that there have often been women of color working within white-dominated feminist groups pushing for a multiracial feminist politic. For example,

two African American women, Margaret Sloan and Pauli Murray, helped found the National Organization for Women (NOW) in 1966, and black feminist Doris Wright was a founding member of *Ms. Magazine* in 1972 (Thompson 2001).

Women of color feminists organized around a wide range of public issues historically ignored by white, middle-class feminists. Multiracial feminism addressed: reproductive rights, sterilization abuse, welfare rights, police brutality, labor organizing, environmental justice issues, rape, domestic violence, childcare access, school desegregation, prison reform, and affirmative action. To address these public issues, in addition to working in white-dominated groups, women of color also developed their own autonomous feminist organizations and caucuses. These organizations grew out of both civil rights groups and white women's groups. Black women organized in 1973 to create the New York-based National Black Feminist Organization (NBFO) and launched a conference attended by 400 women representing a variety of class backgrounds (Thompson 2001). Additionally, the NBFO inspired the formation of another black feminist group in 1974, the Combahee River Collective, who wrote a now famous statement describing the genesis and politics of black feminism. Other women of color groups that grew out of race-based political organizations include the Third World Women's Alliance, which emerged from the Student Non-Violent Coordinating Committee; the Chicana group Hijas de Cuauhtemoc, founded as an offshoot of the United Mexican American Student Organization; Asian Sisters, which grew out of the Asian American Political Alliance; and Women of All Red Nations (WARN), initiated by members of the American Indian Movement (Thompson 2001). These feminist multiracial groups addressed a multitude of issues related to racism, classism, and sexism that were affecting women of color.

Multiracial feminism came to the fore with the 1981 publication of *This Bridge Called My Back: Writings by Radical Women of Color*, an anthology representing black, Latina/Chicana, Native American, and Asian American women grappling with issues of racism, sexism, homophobia, and classism. The writings reflect women of color activism in previous years.

Although there were activist women of color texts preceding *Bridge*, such as the anthology *The Black Woman* by Bambara (1970), the 1980s marked a burgeoning of feminist texts by women of color. In 1983, Barbara Smith published *Home Girls: A Black Feminist Anthology* featuring writings by black feminist activists, and in 1984 Beth Brant published *A Gathering of Spirit: A Collection by North American Indian Women*. All of these texts included the voices of lesbian and feminist women of color, and the second edition of *Bridge*, printed in 1983, provided a largely international perspective expanding the concept of intersectionality from race, class, and gender oppressions to include sexuality and nation.

Simultaneously, there was an explosion of creative work by multiracial feminists that contributed to the vibrancy of the activism of the late 1970s and early 1980s and that expanded the theory building that was taking place in multiple locations (e.g., community centers, conferences, women's centers, educational institutions). Writers of both fiction and non-fiction created academic and popular interest in exploring the multidimensional lives of women of color in ways that had not been previously attempted.

Alice Walker advanced the articulation of multiracial feminism as distinctive, culturally specific, and part of a legacy of social justice. Her groundbreaking book *In Search of My Mother's Gardens* (1983), a collection of essays, introduced the term "womanism." Walker does not reject the term feminism but offers a parallel affirmative expression for the multiple and complex ways that women of color view their communities and commitments in those communities. It also explores many facets of life important to women of color that a radical strand of 1970s feminism often eschewed, including spirituality, the suffering of men of color due to racist oppression, and the relationship between art and activism.

Multiracial feminism has been critical in identifying new metaphorical spaces for theory, praxis, healing, and organizing, highlighting the intersection of experience including the concept of "borderlands," "sister outsiders," "new mestizas," and "Woman Warriors" (Sandoval 2000). Transformation of the self is considered important to counteract the reductive and homogenizing tendencies of the uncritical idea of "sisterhood" espoused by white feminists; it can include renaming, recasting, and reclaiming buried components of one's identity. Women of color feminists organizing in early second-wave feminism, whose needs were often marginalized or ignored in both white women organizations and race-based organizations led by men, also emphasized the importance of creating exclusive women of color spaces, as evidenced by *This Bridge Called My Back* and the various women of color caucuses.

Women of color entered into the academy in greater numbers during the 1980s. Many were from activist backgrounds and espoused multiracial feminist viewpoints; they began documenting their experiences challenging prevailing theoretical frameworks. Some scholars revisited the historic tensions of the mainstream feminist movement, arguing for a more relevant analysis applicable to diverse communities. Beginning with her landmark book *Ain't I A Woman? Black Women and Feminism* (1981), bell hooks blended personal narrative, theory, and praxis in a distinctive style. hooks is one of the most prolific and widely read multiracial feminists. Multiracial feminism has changed the landscape of both theory and methods in the social sciences and humanities.

Multiracial feminists have argued that multiple oppressions can combine and create new and often unrecognized forms of encounters in daily life. The concept of "multiple oppressions" and the "intersection of experience" approach have been primarily used to help understand non-dominant groups' experiences navigating the social world. In the last 20 years, activists and theorists located outside the US have developed these insights to support a global analysis of power and difference.

The call to redefine work through a race, gender, and class analysis has had a significant impact, beginning in women's studies and spiraling out across other fields and disciplines, especially in the field of sociology. Patricia Hill Collins introduced the concept of the "matrix of domination." She argues for viewing race, class, and gender as a central organizing principle that allows scholars to investigate how individuals and groups can simultaneously occupy areas of privilege and domination. Sarah Mann and Michael Grimes note the influence of "intersectional work" in the academy and suggest that its scope is pandisciplinary. Scholars have used the concept of "race, class, and gender" as an interlocking site of oppression, in multiple ways, to create theory as an analytical tool or as a methodological practice (Berger 2004). Research explicitly utilizing intersectional analysis tends to cluster in pockets in a few traditional social science disciplines (sociology, psychology, education) and in multidisciplinary programs including women's studies, ethnic studies, criminology, and environmental studies. Several sociologists have compiled anthologies that examine the intersections of race, class, and gender. Two key texts that provide a conceptual framework for understanding the complex intersections of oppressions have been written by sociologists: *Privilege, Power, and Difference* (2001) by Allan Johnson and *Understanding Race, Class, Gender, and Sexuality: A Conceptual Framework* (2001) by Lynn Weber.

Multiracial feminism is a burgeoning field that centers on the voices of women of color but includes writings by anti-racist white women, women outside the US, and feminist men of color. Comprehending the intersections of oppressions in order to promote equity across lines of race, class, and gender and nation differences is a key component of multiracial feminism.

Sociologists have contributed greatly to this endeavor. Multiracial feminism offers new formulations about organizing, coalition building, and critical theory production. The field has reached a maturity and sophistication in both activist and scholarly communities, enriching the conceptualization of power, identity, and inequality.

SEE ALSO: Black Feminist Thought; Feminism; Feminism, First, Second, and Third Waves; Intersectionality; Matrix of Domination; Race; Race (Racism); Third World and Postcolonial Feminisms/Subaltern; Transnational and Global Feminisms

REFERENCES AND SUGGESTED READINGS

Anzaldúa, G. (1987) *Borderlands/ La Frontera: The New Mestiza*. Aunt Lute Foundation Books, San Francisco.

Anzaldúa, G. (Ed.) (1990) *Making Face, Making Soul/ Haciendo Caras: Creative and Critical Perspectives by Feminists of Color*, 1st edn. Aunt Lute Foundation Books, San Francisco.

Bambara, T. C. (Ed.) (1970) *The Black Woman: An Anthology*. Washington Square Press, New York.

Berger, M. (2004) *Workable Sisterhood: The Political Journey of Stigmatized Women with HIV/AIDS*. Princeton University Press, Princeton.

Brant, B. (Ed.) (1984) *A Gathering of Spirit: A Collection by North American Indian Women*. Firebrand Books, Ithaca, NY.

Hurtado, A. (1996) *The Color of Privilege: Three Blasphemies on Race and Feminism*. University of Michigan Press, Ann Arbor.

Mohanty, C. T., Russo, A., & Torres, L. (Eds.) (1991) *Third World Women and the Politics of Feminism*. Indiana University Press, Bloomington.

Moraga, C. & Anzaldúa, G. (Eds.) (1983) *This Bridge Called My Back: Writings by Radical Women of Color*, 2nd edn. Kitchen Table Women of Color Press, New York.

Sandoval, C. (1990) Feminism and Racism: A Report on the 1981 National Women's Studies Association Conference. In: Anzaldúa, G. (Ed.), *Making Face, Making Soul/ Haciendo Caras: Creative and Critical Perspectives by Feminists of Color*, 1st edn. Aunt Lute Foundation Books, San Francisco, pp. 55–71.

Sandoval, C. (2000) *Methodology of the Oppressed*. University of Minnesota Press, Minneapolis.

Smith, B. (Ed.) (1983) *Home Girls: A Black Feminist Anthology*. Kitchen Table Women of Color Press, New York.

Thompson, B. (2001) *A Promise and a Way of Life: White Antiracist Activism*. University of Minnesota Press, Minneapolis.

Wong, D. & Cachapero, E. (Eds.) (1989) *Making Waves: An Anthology of Writings By and About Asian American Women*. Beacon Press, Boston.

multivariate analysis

Nina Baur and Siegfried Lamnek

One way to classify quantitative methods of social research is by the number of variables involved in statistical data analysis procedures. In univariate statistics, just one variable is of interest, while in bivariate statistics the relation between two variables is analyzed. Multivariate analysis involves, in the loose sense of the term, more than two variables and, in its strict sense, at least two dependent and two independent variables. With increasing numbers of variables, statistical modeling becomes necessary and more complex. At the same time, these models are more appropriate for social sciences, since in social reality many variables are intertwined and there is rarely one central determination.

Once data are collected and read into a database processable by statistical software, the typical steps in a multivariate data analysis are the following.

1 *Framing the research question* in such a way that it can be modeled mathematically.
2 *Selecting the right statistical model*, since many kinds of multivariate methods exist and researchers continually develop new multivariate methods. Every multivariate model searches for certain patterns in data. It might miss other patterns. Using different multivariate methods therefore may lead to different results. Thus selecting the right theoretical model at the beginning of data analysis is essential. For example, a statistical correlation may point to a "causal" relation or a latent variable. If one applies regression analysis, one usually only investigates the possibility of a causal relation. However, experienced researchers can use the same statistical method for different theoretical goals, e.g., regression analysis could also be used in other ways than causal analysis.
3 *Verifying that assumptions and prerequisites* for the chosen statistical procedure are met. Most multivariate procedures require at least (a) valid, standardized data; (b) a minimum number of cases; (c) a random sample; (d) a specified variable scale type; (e) a certain (very often, a normal) distribution of variables and residuals; (f) a minimum variance of variables; (g) in causal analysis usually independence of independent variables. If any of these assumptions are not met, a different multivariate procedure should be chosen as results may be erroneous. Again, profound research experience and statistical knowledge are needed to assess when violated assumptions lead to invalid results and when they lead only to less stable results.

4 *Preparing data for the specific analysis.* A special case of data preparation is data mining, which specializes in extracting variables from complex data banks for statistical analysis.
5 *Computing the model* using a special statistical computer package such as SAS, SPSS, or Stata.
6 *The results of data analysis always have to be interpreted.* Statistics may help in interpreting data, but they never prove theories.

Multivariate analysis procedures can be classified in different ways, and no classification is exhaustive, especially due to the dynamics of the field. Two common ways are (1) on what scale variables have to be measured in order to apply the model and (2) what kind of theoretical model underlies the analytic procedure. Among the theoretical questions multivariate analysis can address are (a) identifying latent classes; (b) causal analysis; (c) identifying patterns in time; (d) network analysis; and (e) multilevel analysis. Most multivariate procedures can be viewed as a special case of general linear models (GLM).

Identifying latent classes. Associated variables can be interpreted measuring a background variable that was not or cannot be measured, such as typologies, classes, or dimensions. For example, the correct number of answers in a test can be seen as a sign of greater or lesser intelligence. Esping-Andersen identified welfare regimes by classifying countries according to socioeconomic and political similarities. Multivariate analysis procedures that identify latent classes include cluster analysis, correspondence analysis, factor analysis, principal component analysis, and multidimensional scaling (MDS).

Causal analysis. Correlation can also mean that one or more variables induce one or more other variables. For example, education and country of origin both have a strong influence on income. Note the specific underlying concept of causality: "cause" in the sense of statistical techniques usually means the relationship between variables, while, as Abbott (2001) points out, only persons (not the variables used to describe them) can act – and thus "cause" anything. Most statistical techniques

Table 1 Types of cases and groups.

		Independent variables	
		Nominal	*Metric*
Dependent variables	Nominal	Correspondence analysis Log-linear models Tree analysis, e.g. CHAID	Discriminant analysis Logistic regression
	Metric	Analysis of variance (ANOVA; MANOVA)	Canonical regression Partial correlation Multiple regression Multivariate regression Path analysis (LISREL)

of causal analysis try to assess existence, kind, and strength of causal relationships between variables. One distinguishes, for example, non-recursive relationships (i.e., one-way causal relationships); recursive relationships (variable A influences variable B and vice versa); additive multicausality (many causes independently affect the dependent variable); interaction (a cause only impacts if the case belongs to a certain category in a third – control – variable); common causes (one dependent variable influences several distinct independent variables); intervention (a causal chain exists, i.e., variable A influences variable B, which in turn influences variable C, etc.); circularity (variable A influences variable B; variable B causes variable C; variable C affects variable A). Causal links between variables can be much more complex, especially if variable number increases. Most social scientists focus on establishing the kind of causal relationship between many variables and on distinguishing causally relevant variables from irrelevant variables. Table 1 gives an (incomplete) overview of multivariate procedures for establishing causal relations, classified by the minimum variable scale required. If few relevant variables (preferably on a metric scale) exist, one can try to estimate the exact effect size using econometric techniques.

Identifying patterns in time. Many methods exist to analyze the change of (typical) human action. Most of them originally stem from demography, economic sociology, and life course research. Examples are cohort analysis, times series, event-history analysis (survival analysis), latent growth curve models, and sequential analysis (optimal matching techniques). These methods usually either require a variable measuring time (such as age) or research designs with several measuring points (such as trend design, panel design, continuous measuring).

Network analysis. An individual case (such as a person, a word, situation) can interact with other individuals but is often part of higher-level cases forming a collective (= aggregate), e.g., a person can be part of an organization or a country; a word can be an element of a sentence or a book; a situation can be part of an interaction system. Network analysis procedures investigate the relation between individuals forming a collective on a higher level, for example the intensity of social contacts between members of a non-governmental organization.

Multilevel analysis. Sometimes, the relationship between different analysis levels is of interest, e.g., the influence of regional unemployment rate (analysis level: region) on voting behavior (analysis level: persons) or the effect of youth violence (analysis level: persons) on legislation (analysis level: countries). In this case, multilevel analysis procedures are applicable.

SEE ALSO: ANOVA (Analysis of Variance); Computer-Aided/Mediated Analysis; Experimental Methods; Factor Analysis; General Linear Model; Hypotheses; Latent Growth Curve Models; Log-Linear Models; Mathematical Sociology; Path Analysis; Quantitative Methods; Regression and Regression Analysis; Social Network Analysis; Statistics; Structural Equation Modeling; Time Series; Variables

REFERENCES AND SUGGESTED READINGS

Abbott, A. (2001) *Time Matters: On Theory and Method*. Chicago University Press, Chicago.

Abbott, A. & Tsay, A. (2000) Sequence Analysis and Optimal Matching Methods in Sociology: Review and Prospect. *Sociological Methods and Research* 29: 3–33.

Blasius, J. & Greenacre, M. (2004) *Correspondence Analysis in the Social Sciences: Recent Developments and Applications*. Academic Press, London.

Blossfeld, H.-P. & Rohwer, G. (2002) *Techniques of Event History Modeling: New Approaches to Causal Analysis*. Erlbaum, Mahwah, NJ.

Han, J. & Kamber, M. (2006) *Data Mining: Concepts and Techniques*. Morgan Kaufmann, San Francisco.

Kennedy, P. (2003) *A Guide to Econometrics*. MIT Press, Cambridge, MA.

Scott, J. & Xie, Y. (Eds.) (2005) *Quantitative Social Science*, 4 vols. Sage, London.

Snijders, T. A. B. & Bosker, R. J. (1999) *Multilevel Analysis: An Introduction to Basic and Advanced Multilevel Modeling*. Sage, London.

StatSoft Inc. (1984–2005) *Electronic Textbook StatSoft*. Online. www.statsoft.com/textbook/stathome.html.

Mumford, Lewis (1895–1990)

Mark Luccarelli

Lewis Mumford was born in New York City. He is best known as an architectural critic and urban historian, and author of *The City in History* (1961), undoubtedly his greatest work. Of mixed German and German-Jewish heritage, Mumford grew up with his mother and maternal grandfather – an immigrant and head waiter who took the boy for long walks, initiating Mumford's lifelong interest in cities. With the publication of *The Culture of Cities* (1938) Mumford achieved widespread recognition that grew when the *New Yorker* magazine hired him to write its *Skyline* column. A journalist by profession, he had wide-ranging intellectual interests and wrote convincingly on a variety of topics, including technology and culture, literary criticism, social ethics, and politics.

Mumford was a "public intellectual" who addressed the educated public rather than a specific academic community. Despite or perhaps because of his audience, he undertook an ambitious intellectual project: the reexamination of modernity in the light of growing scientific and imaginative understandings of evolutionary processes. Mumford thought that in respect to developments in technology, architecture, and urban form, culture could be likened to the workings of nature, and like the philosopher John Dewey he held that creative innovation holds the key to evolving designs appropriate to the task of reconciling human values and natural processes.

The barbarism of World War I and the subsequent collapse of Progressive Era reform politics in the US set the stage for Mumford's intellectual journey. A polymath, he naturally took to Emerson's maxim that all education is essentially autobiographical. Aside from diverse courses he took at the City College of New York that failed to add up to a Bachelor's degree, his most important training came from contacts he developed himself, particularly during a formative trip to Britain undertaken in the 1920s. These contacts included the botanist and urbanist Patrick Geddes and the sociologist Victor Branford. From Geddes, Mumford learned the technique of the "regional survey" of the city and its environs. Through Branford, he was introduced to sociological theory and in particular the ideas of the nineteenth-century French regionalist, Frederick Le Play. Regionalism became a philosophy of living and an expression of Mumford's concern for the dynamics of place. As visiting editor of Branford's journal *Sociological Review*, Mumford published a series of articles on regionalism in which he argued that an empirical understanding of both the natural and man-made environment is fundamental to the assessment of culture. Natural geographic patterns contribute to fundamental ecologies that shape culture, regardless of the level of sophistication (technological and economic) achieved. Mumford was primarily interested in *regional ecologies*; that is, in the technological and aesthetic principles that underlie a built environment and structure its relation to the surrounding natural region. At the same time, he reasoned along the lines of the Chicago School of sociology, that the emphasis on place opens the need for social scientists, city officials, and planners to understand and support the *social ecologies* of neighborhoods.

In one sense, Mumford's project was defined by a paradox: a modernist cosmopolitan who turned to the past for inspiration. His inclination toward landscape and community was in line with nineteenth-century sociological observations of modernity as productive of anomie (Durkheim) and loss of organic community (Tönnies). But unlike cultural conservatives' attempt to locate an authoritative cultural voice based on memory and tradition, Mumford's interest in landscape and community was linked to a strong faith in technological modernization and modernity. Reexamining nineteenth-century American intellectual and cultural life in books on architecture (*Sticks and Stones*, 1924) and literature (*The Golden Day*, 1926 and *Herman Melville*, 1929) inspired a number of successors in the soon-to-be-created academic field of American studies and piqued interest in the antebellum New England writers. But his purpose was to find a "usable past" that could serve to remind the reader that history should not be seen as an inevitable progression to the present moment. It was meant, furthermore, to demonstrate that liberal capitalism had undermined an earlier America that Mumford now held up as a mirror to the faults of the liberal capitalist order: environmental rapacity, lack of social solidarity, dismissal of the intellectual and cultural life, and lack of creativity.

Mumford was not particularly interested in socialism or social democracy as an alternative, though he certainly accepted the idea of the positive state and, during the 1930s, even flirted with notions of centralized economic planning. He advocated the use of state power in the late 1930s, arguing forcefully for early American entry into World War II, even though it certainly contributed to the build-up of the American military power which he later denounced. His imagined syntheses between community and innovative technology, natural landscape and modernist architecture, were along the lines of Henri Bergson's notion of a technically inspired unity with nature. To the contemporary reader, Mumford's images of gleaming machines in verdant settings in *Technics and Civilization* (1934) can feel flat and

overdetermined. Yet Mumford was also practical, pragmatic, democratic, and tough-minded, and the naïveté implied in his treatment of technology in the 1930s was clearly corrected in his two-volume work *The Myth of the Machine* (1966, 1970). His thesis is the detachment of technology from human purpose. Both the "megamachine" – great and terrible technologies of production and destruction – and the "pentagon," the symbol of the "fortress of power," began in the quest for predictability, order, and control, but quickly descended into a pursuit of the one human value capable of subverting all others: power. What is frightening about certain machines is not the mechanism itself. At root, Mumford argues, the machine is human. Its origin is bureaucratic and organizational: the "mechanisms" of "organized work" (forced labor) and "organized destruction" (war). Alternatively, machines can be designed to preserve and extend human values – technologies compatible with humanistic objectives: the full development of the human personality and the establishment of a satisfying community life.

Early on Mumford decided that reworking urbanization was the key to change. The ongoing transportation and communication revolution was transforming the city from the inside out, placing a premium on mobility and access, and calling central place theory into question. In part, Mumford saw this as an encouraging development: it undermined the centralized and hierarchical order that had structured western urban life. In addition, society had become more fluid as the consequence of the multiplication of social networks. It was in this combination of fluidity and spatial diffusion that Mumford saw the promise of a new democratic regional order. Working with a small group of visionaries who dubbed themselves the Regional Planning Association of America, Mumford launched a verbal assault on conurbation while arguing that the movement of population, industry, and commerce out of the metropolitan centers (what we now call the edge city or more simply, sprawl) might still find an appropriate form: a decentralized multi-modal urban pattern. Careful attention to the natural ecology of the region became a key component in the planning and development of what might be called a regional metropolis. Town planning should develop a principled program of decentralization that could permit the amorphous strivings of post-metropolitan society to find its own characteristic form and purpose. The resulting landscape would preserve significant natural features and functions and shape healthy urban centers – of varying sizes – within the urban region as a whole.

By the 1960s the real-world effects of urban diffusion looked positively sinister to Mumford. He had always complained about overdevelopment of the urban core. High densities brought over-crowding that made the preservation or creation of adequate public spaces difficult. Inhuman housing projects that warehoused people in massive towers were symptomatic of an architecture that had forgotten about the importance of human scale. Mumford was not against tall buildings per se, but he argued that they should not be permitted to form a dense and relentless mass of concrete and steel. The construction of a massive network of superhighways had added other problems. The highways tore up the fabric of urban life as they encouraged abandonment of the city. Yet overdevelopment of the metropolitan core had not ceased. Instead, the historic urban core continued its march toward overspecialization of function, becoming a "city" of office buildings – a tendency now conjoined with the abandonment of significant historic buildings and spaces. In the rush to accommodate a society moving steadily toward the goal of an automobile for every resident of driving age, a "parking lot city" was being created. It is a city given over to the habit of "space-eating" and it marked, Mumford feared, the beginning of the end of urbanity – of pedestrian-orientation, mixed-use spaces, and human scale.

Democratization of the workings of the civil society was a theme of the 1960s and 1970s, and it was one that Mumford had long endorsed. But when the rising urban critic Jane Jacobs argued that ordinary people living in urban neighborhoods should be the sovereign planners of their own future, Mumford rebuked her. He refused to repudiate the traditional spheres of professional design and technical expertise that comprise what he meant by town planning, and he argued that neither neighborhood planning nor historic preservation alone or in combination could possibly address the coming ecological crisis of the edge city.

Mumford died in 1990 in Amenia, New York, at the beginning of a decade that saw a massive revival of interest in his work.

SEE ALSO: Built Environment; Chicago School; Ecological Models of Urban Form: Concentric Zone Model, the Sector Model, and the Multiple Nuclei Model; Environment and Urbanization; Evolution; Exurbia; Urban Ecology; Urban Renewal and Redevelopment

REFERENCES AND SUGGESTED READINGS

Blake, C. (1990) *Beloved Community: The Cultural Criticism of Randolph Bourne, Van Wyck Brooks, Waldo Frank, and Lewis Mumford*. University of North Carolina Press, Chapel Hill.

Hughes, T. P. & Hughes, A. C. (Eds.) (1990) *Lewis Mumford: Public Intellectual*. Oxford University Press, New York.

Luccarelli, M. (1995) *Lewis Mumford and the Ecological Region: The Politics of Planning*. Guilford Press, New York.

Miller, D. L. (1989) *Lewis Mumford, A Life*. Weidenfeld & Nicolson, New York.

Mumford, L. (1934) *Technics and Civilization*. Harcourt, Brace, New York.

Mumford, L. (Ed.) (1959) *Roots of Contemporary Architecture: 37 Essays from the Mid-Nineteenth Century to the Present*, 2nd edn. Grove Press, New York.

Mumford, L. (1961) *The City in History: Its Origins, Its Transformations, and Its Prospects*. Harcourt, Brace, New York.

Mumford, L. (1966, 1970) *The Myth of the Machine*, 2 vols. Harcourt, Brace, New York.

Novak, F. G., Jr. (Ed.) (1995) *Lewis Mumford and Patrick Geddes: The Correspondence*. Routledge, London.

Wojtowicz, R. (1996) *Lewis Mumford and American Modernism: Utopian Theories for Architecture and Urban Planning*. Cambridge University Press, New York.

museums

John Dorst

In its modern application, the term "museum" has become the umbrella for a bewildering array of institutions. At a minimum, these institutions share the functions of preserving and putting on display cultural goods deemed by some social group to be especially valuable, noteworthy, representative, unique, or otherwise deserving of public attention. Beyond this basic commonality, it is difficult to generalize about cultural institutions that range from comprehensive, flagship organizations addressing the arts, the sciences, and history (e.g., the Metropolitan Museum of Art, the Smithsonian museums) to local collections of memorabilia and oddities from nature that, in some cases, closely resemble the premodern cabinets of curiosity frequently cited as one point of departure for what we think of today as museums. Between these extremes lies a seemingly endless array of general or specialized, meagerly or opulently supported, fully or barely professionalized, well-known or obscure institutions devoted to collecting and displaying cultural goods.

The American Association of Museums, the field's principal professional organization in the United States, estimates there are over 16,000 museums in the US alone, a number that includes zoos, aquariums, and botanical gardens. Taken together, these institutions account for more than 850 million individual museum visits per year. An Association survey conducted between 2000 and 2002 revealed that more than a billion dollars are expended annually, solely to care for the estimated 750 million objects and living specimens in the varied collections of American museums. Comparable statistics from Europe confirm that great density of museums and widespread museum-going may fairly be taken as signature features of the industrialized first world. The level of a country's or a region's museum "saturation" provides a meaningful index to its degree of integration into global economic and cultural systems.

In broadest conception, museums have affinity with other cultural institutions devoted mainly to non-commercial, intellectual enterprises, notably libraries, archives, and universities. For many museums, education and research are as important as collection and display. Indeed "museum," in its literal meaning of "seat of the muses" (*mouseion*), was the name of a particular university building in ancient Alexandria. According to the Oxford English Dictionary, by the seventeenth century the word's generalized application in English was to buildings or apartments "dedicated to the pursuit of learning or the arts." The British Museum continues to exemplify the close historical connection between the collection and display of artifacts and the production of texts and ideas.

Although one may point to some eighteenth- and early nineteenth-century precursors, such as the Peale Museum in Philadelphia, the basic principles and structures of modern museology took shape mainly over the last third of the nineteenth century. Above all, the spirit of scientific rationality, with its emphasis on taxonomic and sequential ordering, informed the public museums established in this period, no less so those focused on art than on the sciences. The emergence of the discipline-based comprehensive university is an analogous and closely related cultural development. Unlike the university or the archive, however, the museum makes visual experience, or more specifically, the sequential, transitory perusal of objects, images, and designed displays, the primary vehicle for educating and edifying the public. Thus the modern museum, despite its elite associations and scientific foundations, also has affinity with popular forms of display and spectacle – fairs, arcades, circus sideshows and theme parks, to name a few.

It has also been widely observed that the appearance of the modern museum is roughly contemporary with, and in various ways connected to, the creation of the department store. Though the latter is explicitly commercial and the former non-profit, these institutions offer very similar kinds of experience, notably, feelings of wonder and enticement generated through visual encounter with compelling objects and attractive displays. That the refinement of public taste and the cultivation of bourgeois sensibility were among the avowed goals of early museums places them squarely in the context of emerging consumer capitalism in the nineteenth century (Leach 1993).

Recent developments in the museum world seem especially explicit reflections of consumer culture's pervasive presence. For example, the "blockbuster" exhibition and the explosion of museum merchandising through greatly expanded museum shops, catalogue sales, and online marketing bespeak a well-established trend toward commodification of museum artifacts, images, and experiences. The many forms of revenue-generating reproduction deployed by museums make them virtual laboratories of the advanced consumer social order. Walter Benjamin's famous essay, "The Work of Art in the Age of Mechanical Reproduction" (1936), is the *locus classicus* for theoretical reflection on these issues.

If processes of reproduction make museum goods available as a class of commodity, an even more complex and subtle commodification may be seen in the increasingly pervasive *museumization* of mundane social experience. The trend in recent years toward more "interactive" interpretive strategies – hands-on exhibits in science museums and personal encounters with historical figures at living history museums, for example – strives to break down the boundary between the institutional space of display and the personal space of the visitor. Less self-conscious but more subtly revealing of modern social life is the complementary process through which many people transform private spaces into museum-like environments. The more or less formal display in homes of personal collections, often accompanied by highly developed connoisseurship, is the most obvious example here. One also increasingly finds such things as the domestic display of animal trophies not as heads on the wall but as diorama-like natural history exhibits and the reproduction of historical periods in the form of room decor and furnishings (Dorst 1989). Such museumizing of the private sphere, while especially intense and socially dispersed in advanced capitalism, is hardly a creation of the present age. The Victorian era already saw such processes at work, at least among elites. Whatever their other functions, museums, past and present, have educated the public in the protocols of such consumer culture display.

There has emerged recently a branch of cultural studies devoted to the critical examination of museums as components of the culture industry, having important agency in the reproduction of ideologies and the construction of social identities. The "museum studies" movement addresses such issues as the politics of exhibitions, the formation of audiences, and the discursive patterns of museum display. Attention to historical contexts also characterizes this scholarly trend, which views museums in relation to the other "disciplinary" institutions of modernity. Among the many promising future directions in this field is the analysis of global flows in goods, images, and people, as mass tourism, movements to repatriate artifacts and human remains, and proliferation of online "virtual museums" contribute to an unprecedented expansion of museum-related experience around the world.

The museum and art worlds are currently engaged in reflexive self-examination analogous to that found in academe. Often marked by a tone of playful irony, a growing number of individual works and whole exhibitions self-consciously call attention to the nature of museum objects, displays, and implicit gallery "narratives." One of the most complete examples of this trend, the wry Museum of Jurassic Technology in Culver City, California, presents in the sober guise of authoritative museum discourse exhibits on subjects that play along the edges of plausibility, passing in some cases into the blatantly fantastic. The museum-going experience is purposely defamiliarized, and the whole institution takes on the quality of a reflexive work of art (Weschler 1995).

SEE ALSO: Consumption, Tourism and; Cultural Studies; Department Store; Popular Culture Forms

REFERENCES AND SUGGESTED READINGS

Bennett, T. (1995) *The Birth of the Museum: History, Theory, Politics*. Routledge, London and New York.

Dorst, J. D. (1989) *The Written Suburb: An American Site, An Ethnographic Dilemma*. University of Pennsylvania Press, Philadelphia.

Hein, H. S. (2000) *The Museum in Transition: A Philosophical Perspective*. Smithsonian Institution Press, Washington, DC.

Hooper-Greenhill, E. (1992) *Museums and the Shaping of Knowledge*. Routledge, London and New York.

Karp, I. & Lavine, S. D. (Eds.) (1991) *Exhibiting Cultures: The Poetics and Politics of Museum Display*. Smithsonian Institution Press, Washington, DC.

Karp, I., Kreamer, C. M., & Lavine, S. D. (Eds.) (1992) *Museums and Communities: The Politics of Public Culture*. Smithsonian Institution Press, Washington, DC.

Leach, W. (1993) *Land of Desire: Merchants, Power, and the Rise of a New American Culture*. Vintage, New York, pp. 164–73.

Weschler, L. (1995) *Mr. Wilson's Cabinet of Wonders: Pronged Ants, Horned Humans, Mice on Toast, and Other Marvels of Jurassic Technology*. Vintage, New York.

music

Richard A. Peterson

Music has been a focus of sociological inquiry since the earliest days of the discipline. Max Weber, for example, used the development of the system of musical notation as a prime illustration of the increasing rationalization of European society. Nevertheless, music has not become the locus of a distinctive fundamental approach in sociology as have topics like socialization, deviance, and the like. While no musical sociology has developed, and there is no comprehensive text on the sociology of music, numerous aspects of music making and appreciation have been the substantive research site for addressing central questions in sociology. Five ongoing research concerns can be identified.

First, sociologists have been concerned with the relationship between *society and culture*. What began as an attempt to link distinct types of societies with distinct kinds of music has become an effort to identify specific links (e.g., the circumstances of a nation's founding and its national anthem, or the construction of "Englishness" in contemporary British pop music). Other contemporary studies exploring the society–music link focus on the globalization of music culture. They show the resilience of local forms of musical expression in spite of media globalization.

Second, there have been many studies of specific *art worlds* or *scenes* where music makers, managers, devoted fans, and tourists congregate around a kind of music and its subculture. The perspective focuses on the interaction of individuals and groups in making and appreciating music. There have been studies of hip hop scenes as well as scenes built around jazz, blues, goth, classical music, women's music, punk, dance music, and music recording in places like Los Angeles, Bombay, and Nashville.

Recent studies have explored the role of the Internet in shaping music scenes.

Third, studies have focused on the *organizations and infrastructure* that support distinctive music fields. This is of special interest because the process of music production influences the content of the music created. Three general sorts of practices can be identified. The forms of *popular music* are shaped by the commercial nexus that dictates an oligopoly of a few multinational companies, a rapid succession of hits, and attempts to shape mass consumer tastes. This structure is under threat from the effects of digital technology in music production and distribution. In sharp contrast with the mass market pop field, diverse *niche markets* foster a vast array of kinds of musics. Due largely to digitalization and their do-it-yourself mode of organization, they can thrive outside the realm of the oligopolies. Finally, *art music* forms the third way of organizing music fields. Here the criterion of success is critical acclaim, service to dedicated patrons, and the ability to garner private, government, and corporate patronage sufficient to make possible training, composition, and performance. Classical music, opera, and increasingly jazz fit this model.

Fourth, music is used in all known societies as a means of expressing *identity* and *marking boundaries between groups*, and a number of authors have shown the place of music in social class and status displays. Also, music is gendered in many ways. Men are more likely to be producers. Women are often demeaned in the lyrics of rock, rap, and heavy metal, but they are characterized as strong in country music lyrics. Numerous studies since the "jazz age" of the 1920s have explored issues of racism in the meanings ascribed to music and its creators. And music has been one of the primary ways that generations are defined and define themselves. In the 1990s, for example, one slogan of the young was "If it's 'too loud,' you're too old."

Fifth, there are studies on *how music affects people*. Adults have tended to equate the music of young people with deviant behavior. Jazz, swing, rock, punk, disco, heavy metal, and rap, in turn, have been seen as the cause of juvenile delinquency, drug-taking, and overt sexuality. Researchers have made analyses of song lyrics on the often unwarranted assumption that one can tell the meaning a song has for its fans by simply interrogating lyrics (Frith 1996). Music has also been an integral part of most social movements, as has been shown by studies such as that of Eyerman and Jamison (1998).

SEE ALSO: Art Worlds; Consumption of Music; Content Analysis; Culture, Production of; Deviance; Institution; Music and Media; Music and Social Movements; Race; Race (Racism); Social Movements

REFERENCES AND SUGGESTED READINGS

Bennett, A. & Peterson, R. A. (2004) *Music Scenes: Local, Translocal, and Virtual.* Vanderbilt University Press, Nashville.
Cerulo, K. (1999) *Identity Designs: The Sights and Sounds of a Nation.* University Press of New England, New Brunswick, NH.
DeNora, T. (1995) *Beethoven and the Construction of Genius.* University of Chicago Press, Chicago.
DiMaggio, P. J. (1982) Cultural Entrepreneurship in Nineteenth Century Boston: The Creation of an Organizational Base for High Culture in America. *Media, Culture and Society* 4: 33–50.
Eyerman, R. & Jamison, A. (1998) *Music and Social Movements.* Cambridge University Press, Cambridge.
Frith, S. (1996) *Performing Rites.* Harvard University Press, Cambridge, MA.
Jones, S. (1992) *Rock Formation: Music, Technology, and Mass Communication.* Sage, Newbury Park, CA.
Lopes, P. (2002) *The Rise of a Jazz Art World.* Cambridge University Press, Cambridge.
Manuel, P. L. (1993) *Cassette Culture: Popular Music and Technology in North India.* University of Chicago Press, Chicago.
Peterson, R. A. & Kern, R. (1996) Changing Highbrow Taste: From Snob to Omnivore. *American Sociological Review* 61: 900–7.
Peterson, R. A. & Ryan, J. (2003) The Disembodied Muse: Music in the Internet Age. In: Howard, P. N. & Jones, S. (Eds.), *The Internet and American Life.* Sage, Newbury Park, CA, pp. 223–36.

music and media

Christopher J. Schneider

Popular music is a basic part of culture in the United States and much of the world. Music in the broadest sense is not clearly definable.

When considering the significance and impact of the media in the modern world, developing a concrete definition becomes more problematic. Definitional concerns are most apparent when music is discussed or thought of in a "universal sense" (music as the universal language). Nevertheless, music can be generally understood as the human temporal organization of sounds that differentiates such sounds from noise, speech, and so on. Modern developments that accompany changes in the ways in which music is produced and consumed can be attributed directly to the media. Generally, use of the term media refers to the ability to disseminate information to a wide variety of people. For centuries this process was accomplished exclusively through the circulation of printed materials, most notably newspapers; however, more recently this also includes radio, television, and the Internet.

Music has been studied under the auspices of musicology (the historical and scientific study of music), ethnomusicology (the study of music as culture), and the general social sciences. The sociological study of music has been a subject of inquiry for the better part of a century. Sociological work that addresses some of the ways meaning is conveyed through music has yielded key insights into the ways in which we understand music production and consumption as an important social activity. Max Weber's classic work, *The Rational and Social Foundations of Music* (1958), remains among the most prolific and largely overlooked sociological pieces concerning music. Other sociological works by Alfred Schütz (1951), Theodor Adorno (1973, 1976), and Howard Becker (1951, 1974) are equally noteworthy.

In general, these works operate on the basic assumption that music acts not only as a form of expression, but also as an important and socially significant realm of symbolic communication. When considering the ways in which meaning is produced and reproduced through music, it then becomes imperative to consider the subtle contextual and more blatant ways the logic employed by the media contributes to this process (Altheide & Snow 1979). The media have taken on a role in the twenty-first century unseen in any previous historical epoch. Understanding then the dominant, if not hegemonic, role of contemporary media, the association of music with these media, how this process might change or alter existent music, and how music is now produced, consumed, and subsequently interpreted remains for the most part an area of emerging scholarship.

There are very few places in industrialized nations that have not been affected by prerecorded (recorded) music. Initially, the ability to disseminate music to large audiences can be directly attributed to the advent of the radio. In the western world, recorded music has quickly developed into an integral component of both our personal and public lives. It is present in our homes, cars, workplaces, shopping malls, movie theaters, and even in prisons. The pervasiveness of recorded music in our everyday lives cannot be overstated. It is not uncommon, for instance, that we make a conscious effort in seeking out (absent of music or sound) a place of peace and quiet. The most significant historical developments to establish the current inextricable linkage between music and media concern the invention of recorded sound and the development of radio technology.

MUSIC AND THE DEVELOPMENT OF MODERN MEDIA (RECORDED SOUND AND THE RADIO)

Prior to the development of recorded sound, music was enjoyed live and always transmitted through human agency. The history of the development of recorded sound can be traced to the 1850s. However, it was not until the invention of the phonograph (a device for recording and replaying sound) by Thomas Edison in 1877 that a noticeable market ensued. The invention of the phonograph paved the way for the development of the modern era of recorded music media and remained a market stronghold for nearly 100 years. In the United States, early recordings were played on a phonographic cylinder, but were soon phased out with the introduction of disc records. Phonographic discs (records) were easier and less expensive to market and mass produce. Although, there was little if any fidelity distinction between the two recorded media, market forces can nonetheless be attributed to the subsequent rise and fall of the phonographic cylinder. With the development of the radio, recorded sound (one of the

great marvels of the early twentieth century) expanded well beyond the phonograph.

The social impact of the radio and the technology to broadcast recorded music to the masses is simply immeasurable. The first radio waves were created in Germany just before the turn of the twentieth century and the first transatlantic tests were conducted in 1901 and 1902 (Hillard 1970). The ability to disseminate information (and later music) to larger audiences and the resultant excitement that ensued were bolstered in the early twentieth century by the advent of the radio, which thrust the emerging possibilities of broadcast media to insatiable heights. In 1907, Lee DeForest (considered by many as the founding father of radio) patented the vacuum tube, which would later be developed and used in early tube amplifiers. The first applications of this technology in the United States can be traced back to the American military. Use of the term "radio" is thought to have derived from US naval use of the term "radiotelegraph" rather than "wireless," whereby naval orders were then "broadcast" to the fleet (Hillard 1970).

According to the *Oxford English Dictionary*, people began to speak of "the media" in the United States in the 1920s, and around this time Dr. Frank Conrad (a Westinghouse engineer) is credited as the first person to broadcast music over the radio airwaves. Conrad, who operated an experimental radio station in Pittsburgh, caused a fury of excitement in 1919 when he used music rather than spoken words to test reception of his radio broadcast. In addition to receiving hundreds of letters of fan mail, a local department store began advertising Westinghouse crystal sets for sale to hear "Dr. Conrad's popular broadcasts" (Emery & Emery 1978: 394). Shortly thereafter, the first American radio stations that sought to gain a consistent listenership began emerging.

In the 1930s it was unusual to hear records on the radio because many radio stations had their own in-house musicians and also because records were widely regarded as a sign of poverty (Gronow & Saunio 1998). Nevertheless, the popularity of the phonograph was booming and in 1929 (shortly before the stock market crash) the recording industry had sold nearly 150 million records in the United States. Just four years later in 1933, in the midst of the

Depression, sales had plummeted to 10 million (Gronow & Saunio 1998). Around this time, a copyright infringement movement forged by the American Society of Composers, authors, and various corporations publishing musical compositions emerged to outright ban the play of records on the radio based on rights conferred by the Copyright Act, which among other things granted the exclusive right to perform copyrighted musical compositions in public for profit. Imperative to the future of broadcasted music, the United States Supreme Court ruled on behalf of the stations (see *Gibbs* v. *Buck*, 307 US 66 (1939)).

Many credit Martin Block as the first radio disc jockey to regularly play records on the radio during his popular program "Make-Believe Ballroom," where Block created the illusion that he was broadcasting from a live ballroom. The widespread popularity of the program prompted the station, WNEW in New York, to construct a simulated ballroom for his broadcasts. Block was among the most popular, imitated, and highest-paid radio personalities on the air. The booming popularity of the radio and the introduction of the jukebox resulted in an increase of record sales (from the Depression-era slump) and also characterized the initial shift of recorded music slowly working its way into the context of everyday life.

During the period of World War II (1941–5), widespread radio broadcasts had reached near epic proportions. However, the ways in which Americans listened to the radio would be fundamentally changed with the introduction and development of the FM (frequency modulation) radio. The FM frequency sought to draw listeners away from the standard AM (amplitude modulation) radio format. FM radio was capable of providing smaller towns with thousands of radio stations and thus a greater variety (FM radio frequency covers smaller areas, often with improved or better reception). The FM radio was slow to catch on and lagged in popularity during the 1950s. In 1960, there were 688 FM stations and this number had almost doubled to 1,270 in 1965. Just 12 years later, the number of FM radio stations would nearly triple to 3,743 (Emery & Emery 1978).

The dramatic increase in the popularity of the radio was met with an increase of the development of home audio systems marketed generally as high-fidelity (hi-fi) as a broad reference to available audio equipment, most notably a record player or turntable, tube amplifiers, and loudspeakers. As a direct result of the war, recording technology was vastly improved and the introduction of tape recording and the LP (long-play) record fueled the popularity of the hi-fi industry. Until the late 1950s, however, the standard for hi-fi consisted only of monophonic (mono) recordings that limited sound reproduction to one line of sound over a single channel. The introduction of stereophonic (stereo) records in 1958 expanded sound reproduction to dual-channel, which reproduced sound more consistent with a natural listening experience. The record, although by contemporary standards obsolete, continues to remain popular among audiophiles and music enthusiasts alike and has enjoyed a recent resurgence with the ever-increasing popularity of rap and hip-hop music, which make extended use of this media (see Rose 1994).

MUSIC AND TELEVISION (THE SHIFT FROM AURAL TO VISUAL)

With the introduction of televisions into the consumer market in the 1950s, providing popular and attractive entertainment was imperative to the television networks' ability to attract the largest audience, and so to increase revenues through advertisements. Broadcast music had been widely successful on the radio and thus the format was maintained (in part) for television. The most notable and successful program to utilize an equivalent format was the Ed Sullivan Show. The Ed Sullivan Show ran on the Columbia Broadcasting System (CBS) (one of the three dominant networks at the time) every Sunday night from 1948 to 1971. All types of entertainment were featured on the show, including musical acts. As its popularity increased, watching the show soon became a staple of American life. The Ed Sullivan Show rose in popularity in the 1950s with the then controversial Elvis Presley performance in 1956, and its popularity culminated in the 1960s, highlighted by the four performances given by the Beatles and the controversy surrounding the Doors' performance in 1967. Many attribute to the Beatles performances on the Ed Sullivan

Show the start of what has been described in the US as the "British Invasion," but more importantly credit these performances as the genesis of American modern popular culture.

In the 1970s, the music industry stagnated. The breakup of the Beatles in 1970 and the cancellation of the Ed Sullivan Show in 1971 surely contributed to this. Moreover, conventional radio programming, although still largely popular, was beginning to be eclipsed by other forms of entertainment. Popular television sitcoms, technological advances in television quality, and the affordability of color television sets partially accounted for this. The music industry needed resurgence. The development of cable television in the late 1970s and the introduction of Music Television (MTV) in the early 1980s would not only resurrect the depressed music industry, but also catapult it to unimaginable heights.

MTV was created in August of 1981 with financial support of the Warner Amex Satellite Entertainment Company (WASEC). In 1981, MTV was first broadcast locally and sparsely in the New York City area. With the introduction of cable television, MTV expanded nationally and broke into the two major music markets (New York City and Los Angeles) in January of 1983. The creators of MTV relied heavily upon radio as their model. The early MTV format consisted merely of a reflection of Top 40 music (with a particular allegiance to rock music) and was marketed toward the generation of post-war baby boomers. Oddly enough, the Top 40 radio format (referring to the list of the 40 best-selling singles), many suggest, was initially created to draw back listeners from the subsequent audience shifts from radio to television. Music videos that initially aired on MTV often consisted of sparse concert footage mixed with promotional music video clips. However, as the popularity of MTV soared, the recording industry soon realized the commercial potential and funded the production of more elaborate music clips by hiring well-known directors for the purpose of producing and creating music videos.

With newfound popularity, MTV soon became the leading commissioner (trumping the traditional radio outlet) of forthcoming talent. Aside from a few shortcomings in the mid-1980s, the popularity of the MTV format grew steadily throughout the duration of the decade. Several artists such as Madonna saw what could have otherwise been lackluster careers skyrocket due to the exposure MTV accorded. MTV spinoffs soon followed, one of the more popular of these being Video Hits 1 (VH1), which was marketed toward an older age cohort. The 1990s saw a different MTV, one with much less music and more programming. In an effort to recapture their initial demographic, MTV2 was introduced on MTV's fifteenth anniversary as an all-music channel (much like the MTV of old). Various format changes have accompanied MTV2 throughout its tenure (including the elimination of strictly music videos) and currently MTV2 much resembles its parent station, MTV. Although MTV no longer dedicates itself to the exclusive format of music videos, the indelible earmark that MTV continues to leave on popular culture, and the way music is marketed, produced, and consumed, is simply astounding.

MUSIC AND CONTEMPORARY MEDIA: THE DIGITAL ERA (COMPACT DISC AND MP3)

In between the record and the compact disc (CD) there were two basic forms of music media available to the public, and both were relatively short-lived: the 8-track and audiocassette (both magnetic audio storage cartridges). The 8-track, initially introduced in the 1950s, sold moderately, remained largely unpopular, and by the 1970s had been swept into the dustbin of history. The audiocassette (the first media capable of recording and rerecording music) was introduced nearly a decade after the initial introduction of the 8-track and was a popular alternative to records. The popularity of the audiocassette grew steadily during the late 1970s and culminated in the 1980s with the introduction of the Sony Walkman, the first and widely marketed personal and portable music-playing device. With the introduction of the CD, these two formats have been nearly erased from existence in popular culture.

The CD was first marketed in the United States in 1984. The following year CD players were readily available. Compact discs were the first available music media to store their contents digitally (rather than in analog format as previous music media had). The difference between the two media rests with high-fidelity reproduction. Over time, and through prolonged use, analog recordings drastically wear down, thus compromising the quality of the music. Digital recordings, on the other hand, sound exactly the same every single time, no matter how many times the recording is played. As a selling point, this distinction was crucial during the transition from records and cassettes (both analog) to compact discs (digital). Overall, growth in the music industry slowed during the early 1990s; however, profit margins increased because CDs were on the average $4 to $6 more expensive than records. Moreover, with great success, the recording industry repackaged and aggressively marketed digitally "cleaned" versions of records (wear and tear on records caused them to produce "pop" and "scratch" noises).

The next and most recent phase in digital music media rests with the introduction and development of the MPEG-1 Audio Layer 3 (MP3). The MP3 was designed to reduce the amount of data needed to reproduce audio. The MP3 is a digitally compressed music file and was first developed in Germany in the early 1990s. The technical process by which the digital data file is minimized, when compared to CD, compromises the quality of the music (to reduce the file size certain elements of the composition must be eliminated, most of which are not distinguishable by the human ear). Because of its size and potential for accessibility via Internet technology, the MP3 invigorated the possibility for expansion toward unprecedented consumer access of recorded music, although due to regulation issues this was initially vehemently opposed by the recording industry.

In the United States, the arrival of the Internet occurred sometime between 1993 and 1995. The media popularized the Internet by promoting its ability to foster economic opportunities for both entrepreneurs and corporations. Storage of MP3s on home computers coupled with the rise of the Internet made it very simple to "share" music with others through such media as email, but most notably through "peer-to-peer" networks. In 1999, Shawn Fanning introduced Napster, a peer-to-peer file-sharing network that facilitated the capability to share music files (copyrighted or otherwise) globally, with little if any restraint. Napster was subsequently sued by the recording industry for copyright infringement leading to its eventual restructuring (see *A&M Records, Inc.* v. *Napster, Inc.*, 239 F .3d 1004 (9th Cir., 2001)). This injunction, however, spawned a multitude of unauthorized peer-to-peer file-sharing networks.

Resultant technological advancements coupled in part with the Internet's ability to quickly deliver these media heralded the development of digital audio (MP3) players. The world's first mass-produced MP3 players were introduced in 1998. These early devices were quickly met with litigation from the Recording Industry Association of America (RIAA) (see *Recording Industry Association of America* v. *Diamond Multimedia Systems, Inc.*, 180 F. 3d 1072 (9th Cir., 1999)). Due to rapid advancements in technology these older devices, now primitive by today's standards, were noticeably larger and heavier and, although portable, were often too large to even fit into one's pocket (they were usually clipped to a belt).

Currently the most popular and dominant portable digital audio player is the iPod. Developed and marketed by Apple Computers, the first-generation iPod model (originally only compatible with Apple Macintosh computers with a capacity to hold approximately 1,000 MP3 files) was introduced late in 2001. The interface of the iPod is designed around a user-friendly scroll wheel that provides easy access to the data stored on the device. The iPod is designed to work with Apple's iTunes software, which allows users to store and "manage" their music libraries on their home computers.

The iPod continues to dominate the market share of portable MP3 players through subsequent release of new multimedia "generations" of iPods, with each model significantly upgraded. These updated versions of the iPod can now hold vast amounts of data (some models allow the capacity to hold as many as 15,000 MP3 files), digital photographs, and digital videos, and can store other data such as word processing documents (serving as a portable hard drive) and in some instances even act as a personal digital assistant (PDA) device.

The music industry is currently struggling to cope with these emergent technologies because it cannot yet regulate with any fixed authority the copying and unauthorized distribution of copyrighted music. It seems certain that the recording industries' adjustment to these emerging technologies will certainly direct the future of music media.

SEE ALSO: Consumption of Music; Hegemony and the Media; Media; Music; Music and Social Movements; Popular Culture Forms (Hip-Hop; Jazz; Rock 'n' Roll)

REFERENCES AND SUGGESTED READINGS

Adorno, T. (1973) *The Philosophy of Modern Music*. Seabury Press, New York.
Adorno, T. (1976) *Introduction to the Sociology of Music*. Seabury Press, New York.
Altheide, D. (2002) *Creating Fear: News and the Construction of Crisis*. Walter de Gruyter, New York.
Altheide, D. & Snow, R. (1979) *Media Logic*. Sage, Thousand Oaks, CA.
Becker, H. (1951) The Professional Dance Musician and His Audience. *American Journal of Sociology* 57(2): 136–44.
Becker, H. (1974) Art as Collective Action. *American Sociological Review* 39(6): 767–76.
Becker, H. (1982) *Art Worlds*. University of California Press, Berkeley.
Benjamin, W. (1968) The Work of Art in the Age of Mechanical Reproduction. In: *Illuminations*. Harcourt Brace, New York.
Emery, E. & Emery, M. (1978) *The Press and America*. Prentice-Hall, Englewood Cliffs, NJ.
Gronow, P. & Saunio, I. (1998) *An International History of the Recording Industry*. Cassell, New York.
Hillard, R. (1970) *Radio Broadcasting*. Hastings House, New York.
Malhotra, V. A. (1979) Weber's Concept of Rationalization and the Electronic Revolution in Western Classical Music. *Qualitative Sociology* 1(3): 100–20.
Rose, T. (1994) *Black Noise: Rap Music and Black Culture in Contemporary America*. Wesleyan University Press, Middletown, CT.
Schütz, A. (1951) Making Music Together: A Study in Social Relationships. *Social Research* 18 (1): 76–97.
Weber, M. (1958) *The Rational and Social Foundations of Music*. Southern Illinois University Press, Illinois.

music and social movements

Ron Eyerman

In academic discussions, social movements and music have rarely been conceptualized together, while in actual practice the two have always been linked. Music has been important to social movements as an organizing tool: drawing individuals to participate in movement-related activities, it has served as a source of courage and strength in trying situations, and has helped create the sense of collectivity, of moving together, that is so vital to any form of collective action.

Social movements are more than organizations and it takes more than effective leadership to gather, motivate, and move collections of individuals in what is often risky activity. Music has provided an important resource in this process of mobilizing individuals to collective action. It has been central to the building of collective identities and a powerful resource in building and maintaining group awareness and solidarity. Music has been used as a recruiting tool to help draw sympathizers among the curious into the fold and has been a source of strength in trying situations or of solace in defeat. Collective singing has helped striking peasants stand up to armed cavalry, helped create "workers" out of working individuals, and helped students withstand the blows of police batons. Beyond organization and mobilization, social movements create spaces not only for collective action, but also provide alternative social spaces, arenas in which to raise consciousness, promote critical reflection; they are in other words incubators of social and cultural creativity. The interplay between social movement and music can help alter aesthetic values, as well as political values. Social movements have inspired musicians and other artists to creative acts and to political action. One can make a case that social movements often challenge and change aesthetic, as much as political, values in a society.

With an emphasis on mobilizing resources, Denisoff (1971) and Pratt (1990) provide insight into the roles of singers and songs in social movements, giving to each social functions and roles. Music as a resource for social action is also a central part of Bourdieu's social theory. Bourdieu (1984) discusses music and art as resources, forms of symbolic capital, useful in attaining social position in the realm of production and social distinction in the realm of consumption. Within British cultural studies, Hebdige (1979) and Gilroy (1993) have shown how subcultures have used music as central resources in resisting societal demands for conformity and integration. Eyerman and Jamison (1998) have explored how songs can act as a cultural resource for collective action, identity, and memory, a device to learn values and goals of a movement, or as an expression of protest. Roscigno and Danaher (2004) explore how music and local radio served to unify striking textile workers in the American South.

If we ask how social movements move individuals to collective action, we understand the significance of music and of expressive and representative culture to social movements. As part of a specific movement culture, music helps shape the structures of feeling that are part of what being in movement means. Music is often used as a resource in recruitment, in shaping a sense of collective identity and mission, and as a source of strength and courage in threatening situations. Music is also a form of communication and knowledge, providing an alternative to established mass media. It can unite a local community and help link an imagined one.

At another level, social movements, like music, can also be usefully studied as performances. While it is common to view movements as events, organizations, and even as texts, social movements can be viewed as forms of acting in public – political performances which involve representation in dramatic form. As political performance, social movements engage the emotions of those inside and outside their bounds, expressing and communicating a message of protest. They are meant to evoke as well as provoke. Music is often part of this performance, and thus expressive of the movement itself, a form of exemplary action rather than an instrument or resource for something else.

Professional musicians have offered their creative performances to support social movements. During the American Civil Rights Movement of the 1950s and 1960s performing

artists offered their services to promote movement aims, lending their prestige through public appearances and giving benefit concerts (e.g., the gospel singer Mahalia Jackson and more popular singers like Harry Belafonte and Ray Charles) (Ward 1998). Singing groups emerged from the ranks of movements, like the Freedom Singers, some of whom went on to professional careers. At the same time, social movements have offered amateurs and professionals new sources of inspiration and new audiences. Musical genres have survived and been revitalized through social movements, like folk singing and song in the US. By mobilizing and recombining musical traditions, the movements of the 1950s and 1960s made important contributions to fundamental processes of cultural transformation. Traditional as well as newly written topical songs were performed at political demonstrations and festivals that helped provide a collective identity which was at the core of social movements. Topical songs and so-called freedom songs were central to these movements.

The relation between social movements and music can also be seen to have altered the popular culture of American society, as well as the careers of the performers. Music and popular culture generally may also have influenced participation in or affected sympathy for social movements. Ward (1998) argues that white youths listening to black radio stations may have predisposed them for a more sympathetic attitude toward the aspirations of the Civil Rights Movement. It may also have helped move them toward more active participation.

Nationalist movements have used traditional musical forms to raise emotions and to ground claims of national origin and identification. These need not necessarily be indigenous forms of traditional music. Ramos-Zayas (2003) has shown how urban Puerto Rican youth in Chicago draw on hip hop and rap music in their attempts to raise a nationalist consciousness. Music embodies tradition through the ritual of performance. It can empower and help create collective identity and a sense of movement in an emotional and almost physical sense. This is a force which is central to the idea and practice of a social movement. Singing a song like "We Shall Overcome" at a political demonstration is a ritual event, as is singing "Solidarity Forever" or the

"International" at trade union meetings or the singing of a national anthem or other patriotic songs at a nationalist rally. Such preordained ceremonies serve to reunite and to remind participants of their place in a collective and also to locate them within a longstanding tradition of struggle and protest, or, as in the case of a national anthem, a tradition of national identity. Such songs can also have a wider and more multidimensional appeal. Songs from the Irish Rebellion in the early part of the twentieth century still resonate with audiences today, both as forms of collective memory and, more generally, as powerful musical performance.

SEE ALSO: Bourdieu, Pierre; Music; Music and Media; Popular Culture Forms (Hip-Hop); Social Movements

REFERENCES AND SUGGESTED READINGS

Bourdieu, P. (1984) *Distinction*. Harvard University Press, Cambridge, MA.
Denisoff, R. S. (1971) *Great Day Coming*. Penguin, Baltimore.
Eyerman, R. & Jamison, A. (1998) *Music and Social Movements*. Cambridge University Press, Cambridge.
Gilroy, P. (1993) *The Black Atlantic*. Verso, London.
Hebdige, D. (1979) *Subculture*. Routlege, New York.
Pratt, R. (1990) *Rhythm and Resistance*. Smithsonian Institution, Washington, DC.
Ramos-Zayas, A. (2003) *National Performances*. University of Chicago Press, Chicago.
Roscigno, V. & Danaher, W. (2004) *The Voice of Southern Labor*. University of Minnesota Press, Minneapolis.
Ward, B. (1998) *Just My Soul Responding*. University of California Press, Berkeley.

myth

Leslie Wasson

A myth is a story that has a parallel structure linking the past to the present and suggesting directions for the future. A myth may be a cautionary tale, as in the urban myths that teenagers tell about the dangers inherent in parking on dark side roads. A myth may also be a moral tale, as in morality plays and bedtime stories. Myths also may be about idealized behavioral standards, as in hero myths. As a sociological term, however, the primary use of the word myth has been rather casual. Sociological writers are likely to refer to the "myth" of masculinity (Pleck 1981), the "myth" of self-esteem (Hewitt 1998) or the "myth" of the mommy role (Douglas & Michaels 2006). This use of the term imputes a less-than-factual status to the topic of reference and calls into question the veracity of others' accounts and theories. However, sociology currently lacks a clear concept of myth such as is found in anthropology or cultural studies.

Comparative evolutionary anthropology, of which Frazer's *The Golden Bough* (1890) is perhaps the most recognized example, links contemporary myths to primitive rituals in the search for meaning through mystical experiences. This set of comparative principles was developed by T. S. Eliot in both his poetic work and in his 1923 article "*Ulysses*, Order, and Myth." Later, in 1966, Vickery suggested that an interdisciplinary examination of the larger patterns of myth-making was more effective than analyses of single texts. This "myth criticism" enjoyed great academic and popular success, propelled in part by Campbell's 1949 work, *Hero with a Thousand Faces*.

A more modern structural approach to the anthropology of myth derives primarily from the work of Lévi-Strauss (1995), in which he reexamines the dismissive attitude of western cultures toward the myths (cultural narratives) of non-industrial societies and suggests the valuable purpose of myth in human culture and history. Myth, according to Lévi-Strauss, allows anthropology to understand the underlying structure of a culture by examining linguistic elements and their relations to one another. Lévi-Strauss locates the modern use of the term myth in the seventeenth and eighteenth centuries with the development of science as a category of logical endeavor separate from the messy everyday world of the making of common sense from our perceptions of reality. He also suggests that science will progressively broaden its purview to incorporate many problems previously considered outside its territory, such as myths, which appear the world over, yet in different forms in each culture.

Myth is a form of meaning-making that seems ideal for sociologists, yet few have risen to the challenge of studying its processes. Durkheim (2001) begins to develop a sociological concept of myth. However, its energetic pursuit by anthropologists may have resulted in its being abandoned as a boundary-setting maneuver by sociologists. One direction for contemporary sociologists seeking to investigate a sociological construct of myth might be the work of Barthes (1972), in which he uses the narrative of myth-making to explain sense-making of everyday lives and experiences. Also, although they do not employ the term myth, Holstein and Gubrium (2000) describe a narrative self that relies on its reflexive yet socially embedded story for temporal structure and continuity. Readers seeking an empirical use of the term myth might seek out the literature on rape myths reviewed by Lonsway (1995).

SEE ALSO: Critical Theory/Frankfurt School; Culture; Durkheim, Émile; Mythogenesis; Narrative; Postmodernism

REFERENCES AND SUGGESTED READINGS

Barthes, R. (1972) *Mythologies*. Hill & Wang, New York.
Campbell, J. (1993 [1949]) *The Hero with a Thousand Faces*. Harper Collins, New York.
Clifford, J. & Marcus, G. E. (Eds.) (1986) *Writing Culture: The Poetics and Politics of Ethnography*. University of California Press, Berkeley.
Douglas, S. J. & Michaels, M. W. (2006) The Mommy Myth: The Idealization of Motherhood and How It Has Undermined All Women. *Journal of Marriage and Family* 68(1): 255–6.
Durkheim, É. (2001 [1912]) *The Elementary Forms of the Religious Life*. Oxford University Press, Oxford.
Hewitt, J. (1998) *The Myth of Self-Esteem*. St. Martin's Press, New York.
Holstein, J. A. & Gubrium, J. F. (2000) *The Self We Live By: Narrative Identity in a Postmodern World*. Oxford University Press, Oxford.
Lévi-Strauss, C. (1995) *Myth and Meaning: Cracking the Code of Culture*. Shocken, New York.
Lonsway, K. A. (1995) Attitudinal Antecedents of Rape Myth Acceptance: A Theoretical and Empirical Reexamination. *Journal of Personality and Social Psychology* 68(4): 704–11.
Manganaro, M. (1992) *Myth, Rhetoric, and the Voice of Authority: A Critique of Frazer, Eliot, Frye, and Campbell*. Yale University Press, New Haven.
Marcus, G. & Fischer, M. M. J. (1999) *Anthropology as Cultural Critique: An Experimental Moment in the Human Sciences*, 2nd edn. University of Chicago Press, Chicago.
Pleck, J. (1981) *The Myth of Masculinity*. MIT Press, Cambridge, MA.
Vickery, J. (Ed.) (1966) *Myth and Literature: Contemporary Theory and Practice*. University of Nebraska Press, Lincoln.

mythogenesis

Richard Slotkin

Myths are stories drawn from a society's history, which have acquired through persistent usage the power of symbolizing that society's ideology, and explicating the meaning and direction of its history. A society's mythology is, in effect, its memory system. Myths usually develop around cultural crises or moments of collective shock or trauma, when events challenge the belief system on which the society has hitherto operated. The most durable myths develop around issues or problems that are fundamental to the society's organization and persistent in its history: for example, the problem of kingship and succession in premodern societies, and the tensions between individual rights and social authority in modern nation-states.

As a society experiences the stress of events, its cultural leadership recalls and deploys mythologized "memories" of the past as precedents for understanding and responding to contemporary crises. Over time, through frequent retellings and deployments as a source of interpretive metaphors, the original mythic story is increasingly conventionalized and abstracted, until it is reduced to a deeply encoded and resonant set of symbols, "icons," "keywords," or historical clichés. In this form, myth becomes a basic constituent of linguistic meaning and of the processes of both personal and social "remembering." Each of these mythic icons is in effect a poetic construction of tremendous economy and compression, and a mnemonic device capable of evoking a complex system of historical associations by a single image or phrase. For an American, allusions to "the Frontier," or to events like "Pearl Harbor," "The Alamo," or "Custer's Last Stand," evoke our implicit understanding of the entire historical scenario that belongs to the event, and of the complex interpretive tradition that has developed around it.

This kind of mythology is of a different order from the cosmogonic mythologies that inform the religious worldview of tribal cultures and religions; different too from the archetypal mythologies linked to psychological development in Jungian theory – although social myths necessarily draw on religious mythology, and resonate with personal and group psychology. The myths being discussed here are historical fables that have a special function in human societies, and especially in modern nation-states. As such they are an important source for the study of cultural history, and an analysis of the form and content of political rhetoric.

Myth expresses a society's ideology in the form of a symbolic narrative, rather than in a discursive or argumentative form. Its language is metaphorical and suggestive rather than logical and analytical. The movement of a mythic narrative, like that of any story, implies a theory of cause and effect, and therefore a theory of history (or even of cosmology); but these ideas are offered in a form that disarms critical analysis by its appeal to the structures and traditions of storytelling and the clichés of historical memory. Although myths are the product of human thought and labor, their identification with venerable tradition makes them appear to be products of "nature" rather than history – expressions of a transhistorical consciousness or of some form of "Natural Law."

Myths are formulated as ways of explaining problems that arise in the course of historical experience. The most important and longest-lived of these formulations develop around areas of concern that persist over long periods of time. But no myth/ideological system, however internally consistent and harmonious, is proof against all historical contingencies. Sooner or later the bad harvest, the plague, defeat in war, changes in modes of production,

internal imbalances in the distribution of wealth and power produce a crisis which cannot be fully explained or controlled by invoking the received wisdom embodied in myth. At such moments of cognitive dissonance or "discontent," the identification of ideological principles with the narratives of myth may be disrupted; a more or less deliberate and systematic attempt may be made to analyze and revise the intellectual/moral content of the underlying ideology. But in the end, as the historical experience of crisis is memorialized and abstracted, the revised ideology acquires its own mythology, typically blending old formulas with new ideas or concerns.

This approach to the formation and evolution of social myth emphasizes the role of historical and social contingency, and the activity of human culture producers or "authors" in creating and modifying the various forms of cultural expression that serve as vehicles of myth. It is distinctly different from theories which treat significant cultural expressions as the products of an autonomous (or semi-autonomous) mental activity, in which a linguistic or psychological program of some sort – a "collective unconscious" or "grammar" of tropes or archetypes – determines the structure of all myth/ideological expression.

Myths are cultural clichés, stories whose patterns we recognize instantly. They function socially through a more or less spontaneous process of pattern recognition, which leads people to deploy a myth in response to a crisis. It is this recognition factor that makes mythic associations effective. They offer a reading of a crisis that is familiar, and therefore wins a credulous rather than a skeptical response. If the analogy between mythic pattern and real-world event proves apt, we will be inclined to treat the new phenomenon as a recurrence of the old; to the extent that the new phenomenon differs from the remembered one, our sense of the possibilities of experience will be extended. If symbol and experience match closely enough, our belief in the validity and usefulness of the symbol will be confirmed; if the match is disappointing, we will be forced to choose between denying the importance of the new experience, or revising our symbolic vocabulary. As the course of experience confirms or discredits its symbolism, the structure of mythology is continuously confirmed or subjected to revision.

The mythologization of history is common to all cultures, but is of critical importance to the development and maintenance of the modern nation-state. Versions of this idea have been a commonplace in American studies at least since 1950; the recent work of Anthony Smith, Benedict Anderson, Étienne Balibar, and Immanuel Wallerstein (among others) on the cultural origins and development of modern nations has given this idea a more rigorously theoretical formulation, and a broader comparative application. The nation-state was a distinct innovation in human politics. It had no history, as such. The cultural and political elites who were the founders of most modern nations invented or reinvented their peoples' histories, revising the traditional chronicles of tribes, empires, and dynasties so that they would explain (and justify) the development of the nation.

Hence, nationalities are to a large extent "imagined communities" (as the anthropologist Benedict Anderson has called them) – or, in Balibar's phrase, "fictive ethnicities." No one is really "born American." People are born into the "organic" communities of family, clan, and tribe; they have to be taught to "imagine" themselves as American nationals. The teaching is done through organized public rituals, in schools provided (mostly) by the state, and by mass media organized to address a national public. That public is divided by differences of class, culture, provincial loyalties, religion, and interest. They are able to function as a national public because they have been taught to share certain basic values and beliefs – call these the "national ideology" or "consensus." But the base of this consensus is the belief that all elements of the public share a common "American" or other history; that we belong to a single society, continuous in time; that we, collectively, are heirs to a common past and so bear responsibility for a common future. As the term is used here, myths are the stories – true, untrue, half-true – that effectively evoke that sense of nationality.

The mythology produced by mass or commercial media has a special role in the US cultural system: it is the form of cultural production that addresses most directly the concerns of Americans as citizens of a nation-state. The history of the development of the forms and institutions of commercial or "mass" popular culture is directly related to the development of a political ideology of American nationality, and to the creation of nationwide networks of production and distribution. The basic structures of this commercialized national culture were developed between the Revolution and the Civil War: the emergence of national parties; the development of a nationwide trade in books, magazines, and newspapers utilizing an ever-expanding transportation network. Between the Civil War and the Great War the nascent "culture industries" took advantage of new technologies to meet the demands of an ever-growing and increasingly polyglot culture, with varied and complex needs and tastes. By the 1920s this form of cultural production was fully industrialized, and had become so ubiquitous that it is fair to characterize it as the clearest expression of American "national culture": when one looks beyond the family, ethnic community, or workplace for symbols expressive of "American" identity, one finds the mythologies of the popular culture industry.

Since the concern of commercial media is to exploit as wide an audience as possible, their repertoire of genres in any period tends to be broad and various, covering a wide (though not all-inclusive) range of themes, subjects, and public concerns. Within this structured marketplace of myths, the continuity and persistence of particular genres may be seen as keys to identifying the culture's deepest and most persistent concerns. Likewise, major breaks in the development of important genres may signal the presence of a significant crisis of cultural values and organization. The development of new genres, or the substantial modification of existing ones, can be read as a signal of active ideological concern, in which both the producers and consumers of mass media participate – producers as exploitative promulgators and "proprietors" of their mythic formulations, consumers as respondents capable of dismissing a given mythic formulation, or affiliating with it.

But one should not assume that the mythologies of mass media are a kind of modern "folklore," or that they constitute the totality of "American culture." The productions of the cultural industries are indeed varied and ubiquitous – from the newspapers and mass entertainment to the textbooks that teach our children the authorized versions of American history and literature – but the authority of these "mass culture" productions has been and is offset by the influence of other forms of culture and expression that are genuinely "popular": produced by and for specific cultural communities like the ethnic group, the family clan, a town, neighborhood or region, the workplace or the street corner. Although few of these subcultural entities are now isolated from the influence of mass media, they are still capable of generating their own myths, and their own unique ways of interpreting the productions of the media. A Harlem or Little Italy, an Appalachian or Mississippi Delta county, a Hasidic or Mennonite community, a Rustbelt mill or mining town, to take US examples, have been and in many cases continue to be centers of exception or resistance to the formulations of the commercial culture industries; and their productions (particularly in music) affect the development of mass culture. Nonetheless, the symbols and values generated by mass culture have steadily infiltrated, transformed, and compromised the autonomy of "local" cultures. For that reason, it is useful to speak not only of "mass culture," but also of the development of an "industrial popular culture," whose artifacts are produced primarily by a commercial culture industry, but whose symbols become active constituents of a *popular* culture: i.e., the belief and value structures of a national audience or public.

SEE ALSO: Culture Industries; Culture, Production of; Ideology; Myth; Narrative; Popular Culture Icons (Myth of the American Frontier)

REFERENCES AND SUGGESTED READINGS

Anderson, B. (1983) *Imagined Communities: Reflections on the Origin and Spread of Nationalism*. Verso, London.

Apter, D. E. (Ed.) (1964) *Ideology and Discontent*. Free Press, New York.

Balibar, E. & Wallerstein, I. (1991) *Race, Nation, Class: Ambiguous Identities*. Trans. C. Turner. Verso, London.

Frye, N. (1973) *The Critical Path: An Essay on the Social Context of Literary Criticism*. University of Indiana Press, Bloomington.

Hosking, G. & Schopflin, G. (Eds.) (1997) *Myths and Nationhood*. Routledge, New York.

Huggins, N. I. (1995) *Revelations: American History, American Myths*. Ed. B. S. Huggins. Oxford University Press, New York.

McNeill, W. (1982) The Care and Repair of Public Myth. *Foreign Affairs* 61(1): 1–13.

Mali, J. (2003) *Mythistory: The Making of a Modern Historiography*. University of Chicago Press, Chicago.

Sahlins, M. (1981) *Historical Metaphors and Mythical Realities: Structure in the Early History of the Sandwich Island Kingdom*. University of Minnesota Press, Minneapolis.

Slotkin, R. (1998 [1985]) *The Fatal Environment: The Myth of the Frontier in the Age of Industrialization, 1800–1890*, 3rd edn, corrected. University of Oklahoma Press, Norman.

Slotkin, R. (1998 [1992]) *Gunfighter Nation: The Myth of the Frontier in Twentieth-Century America*, 2nd edn, corrected. University of Oklahoma Press, Norman.

Slotkin, R. (2000 [1973]) *Regeneration Through Violence: The Mythology of the American Frontier, 1600–1860*, 3rd edn, corrected. University of Oklahoma Press, Norman.

Smith, A. D. (1981) *The Ethnic Revival*. Cambridge University Press, Cambridge.

Smith, A. D. (1987) *The Ethnic Origin of Nations*. Oxford University Press, New York.

Smith, A. D. (1999) *Myths and Memories of the Nation*. Oxford University Press, Oxford.